THE OXFORD HA

# EARLY MODERN

# THEOLOGY,

# 1600–1800

*Edited by*

ULRICH L. LEHNER, RICHARD A. MULLER

*and*

A. G. ROEBER

OXFORD

UNIVERSITY PRESS

## OXFORD
### UNIVERSITY PRESS

Oxford University Press is a department of the University of Oxford. It furthers
the University's objective of excellence in research, scholarship, and education
by publishing worldwide. Oxford is a registered trade mark of Oxford University
Press in the UK and certain other countries.

Published in the United States of America by Oxford University Press
198 Madison Avenue, New York, NY 10016, United States of America.

© Oxford University Press 2016

First issued as an Oxford University Press paperback, 2020

Library of Congress Cataloging-in-Publication Data
Names: Lehner, Ulrich L., 1976– editor.
Title: The Oxford handbook of early modern theology, 1600–1800 /
edited by Ulrich L. Lehner, Richard A. Muller, and A.G. Roeber.
Description: New York City : Oxford University Press, 2016. | Includes index.
Identifiers: LCCN 2016010008 (print) | LCCN 2016029560 (ebook) |
ISBN 9780199937943 (cloth : alk. paper) | ISBN 9780190082864 (paper : alk. paper) |
ISBN 9780199937950 (updf) | ISBN 9780190632489 (epub)
Subjects: LCSH: Theology—History—17th century. | Theology—History—18th century.
Classification: LCC BR118 .O94 2016 (print) | LCC BR118 (ebook) | DDC 230.09/032—dc23
LC record available at https://lccn.loc.gov/2016010008

# CONTENTS

*Other Christian Theologies and Awakening Movements*

# PART III  THEOLOGY AND THE OTHERS

*Western Christian Theologies and Other
Religions or Churches*

# ACKNOWLEDGMENTS

...................................................................................

We are indebted to the meticulous work of those who aided us in the completion of this volume. We especially thank David Bodin for his work both as a research assistant and for preparing the index. We wish to thank Theo Calderara, Marcela Maxfield, Alison Britton, Kathrin Immanuel, and Janish Ashwin and the entire staff at Oxford University Press who responded to our questions and suggestions for the volume. We also wish to thank our spouses, Angela Lehner, Gloria A. Muller and Patricia A. Stutzman-Roeber for their support and encouragement.

# Contributors

**Carolina Armenteros** is an intellectual historian specializing in eighteenth- and nineteenth-century Europe. She has published a monograph and three coedited collections on Joseph de Maistre, as well as articles and chapters on Rousseau and counter-revolutionary thought.

**Willem J. van Asselt** († 2014) was Professor of Historical Theology at the Evangelical Theological Faculty in Louvain, Belgium, and Emeritus Associate Professor of Church History at the Faculty of Humanities (Department of Religious Studies and Theology), Utrecht University, the Netherlands. He wrote numerous articles and edited several volumes on Reformed theology, including *Reformation and Scholasticism: An Ecumenical Enterprise* (2001), *The Federal Theology of Johannes Cocceius (1603–1669)* (2001), *Reformed Thought on Freedom: The Concept of Free Choice in Early Modern Reformed Theology* (2010), and *Introduction to Reformed Scholasticism* (2011).

**Craig D. Atwood** holds the Charles D. Couch Chair in Moravian Theology and Ministry at the Moravian Theological Seminary in Bethlehem, Pennsylvania. He is also Director of the Center for Moravian Studies at Moravian College and Theological Seminary. He is the author of *Theology of the Czech Brethren from Hus to Comenius* (2009), *Community of the Cross: Moravian Piety in Colonial Bethlehem* (2005), and is on the editorial board of the *Journal of Moravian History* and the series *Pietist, Moravian, and Anabaptist Studies*.

**Jeff Bach** is the Director of the Young Center for Anabaptist and Pietist Studies at Elizabethtown College, Pennsylvania, where he teaches courses on the history of Anabaptist and Pietist groups.

**Andreas J. Beck** is Professor of Historical Theology and Academic Dean at the Evangelical Theological Faculty in Leuven, Belgium, and the Director of the Institute of Post-Reformation Studies at the same institution. His research focuses on late medieval and early modern theology and philosophy.

**Stephen G. Burnett** is Professor of Classics and Religious Studies at the University of Nebraska–Lincoln. His research focuses on Christian Hebraism, Jewish printing, and Jewish–Christian relations in early modern Europe.

**Eric Carlsson** is Lecturer in the Department of History and the Religious Studies Program at the University of Wisconsin–Madison. His research focuses on the theological Enlightenment and the intellectual history of Christianity in the seventeenth and eighteenth centuries.

**Emanuele Colombo** is Associate Professor of Catholic Studies in the College of Liberal Arts and Social Sciences at DePaul University.

**Robert von Friedeburg** is Professor of History at Erasmus University, Rotterdam. His work combines social and political history with the history of political thought, without denying the indigenous dynamics of each of these approaches. His most recent book is *Luther's Legacy: The Thirty Years' War and the Modern Notion of "State" in the Empire, 1530s–1790s* (2015).

**Stephen Gaukroger** is Professor of History of Philosophy and History of Science at the University of Sydney. Since 1995, he has been working on a long-term project on the emergence of a scientific culture in the West. To date, two volumes (of a projected five) have appeared: *The Emergence of a Scientific Culture: Science and the Shaping of Modernity, 1210–1685* (2006) and *The Collapse of Mechanism and the Rise of Sensibility: Science and the Shaping of Modernity, 1680–1760* (2010). He is presently at work on a third volume, *The Naturalization of the Human and the Humanization of Nature: Science and the Shaping of Modernity, 1750–1830*.

**Ursula Goldenbaum** has served as Associate Professor in the Department of Philosophy at Emory University since 2004. Professor Goldenbaum has published a monograph on the philosophy of Baruch Spinoza (1995), two volumes on the public debates of the German Enlightenment (2004), and coedited (with Douglas Jesseph) *Infinitesimal Differences: Controversies between Leibniz and his Contemporaries* (2008).

**Aza Goudriaan** is Associate Professor of Historical Theology at the University of Amsterdam.

**Crawford Gribben** is Professor of Early Modern British History at Queen's University Belfast, and is the author of several recent studies of the history of Reformed and Evangelical eschatology.

**Stephen Hampton** is a priest of the Church of England. He served as Chaplain of Exeter College, Oxford, where he also studied for his doctorate under Professor Diarmaid MacCulloch. He then served as Senior Tutor at St. John's College, Durham. In 2007, he became Dean of Peterhouse, Cambridge.

**Ian Hazlett** is Honorary Professorial Research Fellow at the University of Glasgow, where he had been Professor of Ecclesiastical History and Principal of Trinity College. His research interests focus on Reformation history, especially Bucer studies and the Reformation in Scotland. He is editor of *Renaissance & Reformation Review*.

**John Henry** is Professor of History of Science, and Director of the Science Studies Unit at the University of Edinburgh. He has published widely on the history of science from the sixteenth to the nineteenth century, and has a special interest in the historical relations between science and religion. He has recently published a collection of his essays: *Religion, Magic, and the Origins of Science in Early Modern England* (2012).

**Ronnie Po-chia Hsia** is Edwin Erle Sparks Professor of History at Pennsylvania State University. His research has focused on the history of the Protestant Reformation, Catholic renewal, anti-Semitism, and the encounter between Europe and Asia.

**Jonathan I. Israel** is Andrew Mellon Professor of Modern History at the Princeton Institute for Advanced Study and author of many books on early modern history, including his trilogy on the Enlightenment: *Radical Enlightenment* (2001), *Enlightenment Contested* (2006), and *Democratic Enlightenment* (2011).

**Robert Kolb** is Professor Emeritus of Systematic Theology at Concordia Seminary, St. Louis, Missouri; coeditor of the English translation of *The Book of Concord* (2000) and author of, among other works, *Luther and the Stories of God* (2012) and *Martin Luther, Confessor of the Faith* (2009).

**Hartmut Lehmann** became full Professor of Modern History at the University of Kiel in 1969. From 1987 to 1993, he was the founding director of the German Historical Institute in Washington, DC, and from 1993 to 2004 he served as Director of the Max-Planck-Institut für Geschichte in Göttingen. He has published widely on topics ranging from Luther and the Reformation, Pietism, Max Weber, and the globalization of Christianity. Among his current research interests are commemorations of Luther in the last two centuries.

**Ulrich L. Lehner** is Professor of Religious History and Historical Theology at Marquette University. He is the author and editor of several books about early modern religious history, including *The Catholic Enlightenment: The Forgotten History of a Global Movement* (2016).

**Ulrich G. Leinsle** is Professor Emeritus of Philosophy in the Theology Department of the University of Regensburg in Germany. His work focuses on early modern philosophy and theology.

**Thomas Marschler** is Professor of Dogmatic Theology in the Faculty of Catholic Theology at the University of Augsburg in Germany. His main research interests focus on the history of Catholic theology (especially medieval and early modern scholasticism), Christology, and eschatology.

**Benjamin T. G. Mayes** is an editor at Concordia Publishing House, St. Louis, Missouri, where he serves as the general editor for *Johann Gerhard's Theological Commonplaces* and as managing editor for the extension of *Luther's Works: American Edition*.

**Sarah Mortimer** is University Lecturer and Official Student and Tutor in Modern History at Christ Church, Oxford. Her research focuses on the relationship between political thought and religion in the early modern period.

**Dimitrios Moschos** is Assistant Professor of Church History in the Faculty of Theology at the National and Kapodistrian University of Athens, and private lecturer (Privatdozent) at the Theological Faculty of Rostock University in Germany. His research interests focus on the interrelation between broader religious and cultural currents, like asceticism or Greek philosophy and institutional and social transformations within the Christian church (especially the Orthodox Church).

**Richard A. Muller** is P. J. Zondervan Professor of Historical Theology at Calvin Theological Seminary.

**William P. O'Brien, SJ** is Assistant Professor of Modern Christianity in the Department of Theological Studies at St. Louis University.

**Trent Pomplun** is the author of *Jesuit on the Roof of the World: Ippolito Desideri's Mission to Tibet* (2010) and coeditor of *The Blackwell Companion to Catholicism* (2007). His articles have appeared in *The Journal of Religion, Modern Theology,* and *History of Religions* (among others), and his interests include baroque theology, missions history, and Indo-Tibetan religion and culture.

**Jean-Louis Quantin** is Professor of the History of Early Modern Scholarship at the École pratique des Hautes Etudes (Sorbonne, Paris). He has published extensively on Jansenism and rigorism in the seventeenth and eighteenth centuries. He is currently researching the relationship between Gallican culture and the papacy, in the light of the archives of the Roman Inquisition and Index.

**Ephraim Radner** is Professor of Historical Theology at Wycliffe College, Toronto, an evangelical seminary of the Anglican tradition at the University of Toronto. He is the author and editor of several books on ecclesiology and the Bible, including *The End of the Church, Spirit and Nature, Hope Among the Fragments, Leviticus,* and *The World in the Shadow of God.* A former church worker in Burundi, he has been active in the affairs of the global Anglican Communion.

**Marius Reiser** was from 1991 to 2009 Professor for New Testament Exegesis at the University of Mainz, Germany. He then surrendered his chair in protest against the Bologna Process, an educational reform of the European Union. Since then he has been a private scholar specializing in philology, the Hellenistic world of the New Testament, and the history of exegesis.

**A. G. Roeber** is Professor of History and Religious Studies at The Pennsylvania State University and Co-Director of the Max Kade German-American Research Institute. His main area of interest is the history of the law and Christianity. He is the author of (among others) *Palatines, Liberty and Property: German Lutherans in Colonial British America* (1993); *Changing Churches: An Orthodox, Catholic and Lutheran Theological Conversation* (with Mickey L. Mattox) (2012); and *Hopes for Better Spouses: Marriage and Protestant Church Renewal in Early Modern Europe, India and North America* (2013).

**Risto Saarinen** is Professor of Ecumenics at the University of Helsinki and Guest Professor at the Catholic University of Leuven. He is the author of *Weakness of Will in Renaissance and Reformation Thought* (2011).

**Paul Shore** is Adjunct Professor of Religious Studies at the University of Regina. His publications include *Narratives of Adversity: Jesuits on the Eastern Periphery of the Habsburg Realms (1640–1773)* and *The Eagle and the Cross: Jesuits in Late Baroque Prague.*

**Keith D. Stanglin** is Associate Professor of Historical Theology at Austin Graduate School of Theology in Austin, Texas. His research focuses on Reformation and post-Reformation theology, the history of biblical interpretation, and Arminianism.

**John R. Stephenson** is an ordained pastor of Lutheran Church–Canada, Professor of Historical Theology at Concordia Lutheran Theological Seminary, and author of *The Lord's Supper and Eschatology* in the series *Confessional Lutheran Dogmatics.*

**Jonathan Strom** has taught at Emory University since 1997, and is currently Associate Professor of Church History and Director of International Initiatives. His work focuses on Christianity in Germany, especially the late Reformation and Pietism. His current research focuses on conversion in German Pietism.

**Ola Tjørhom** has served as Professor of Dogmatics and Ecumenical Theology at the School of Mission and Theology in Stavanger; Research Professor at the Institute of Ecumenical Research in Strasbourg; Director of the Nordic Ecumenical Institute in Uppsala; and as of January 1, 2016, Professor at the Norwegian University of Science and Technology. The chief topics of his research are ecumenical theology and ecclesial diversity, ecclesiology, and sacramentality.

**Carl R. Trueman** is Paul Woolley Professor of Church History at Westminster Theological Seminary, Pennsylvania. He is the author of a number of books and articles, including *John Owen: Reformed Catholic, Renaissance Man* (2007).

**Stefania Tutino** is Professor of History at the University of California, Los Angeles. Her research focuses on the cultural, intellectual, and political aspects of post-Reformation Catholicism.

**Eric Watkins** is Professor of Philosophy at the University of California, San Diego. He has published widely on Kant's philosophy, including *Kant and the Metaphysics of Causality* (2005) and "Kant on the Hiddenness of God" (2009).

**Peter Yong** is a PhD candidate at the University of California, San Diego. His dissertation investigates the role of givenness in Hegel's philosophical system. He also researches and writes on Kant, German idealism, phenomenology, and the philosophy of mind.

THE OXFORD HANDBOOK OF

# EARLY MODERN THEOLOGY, 1600–1800

# INTRODUCTION

### ULRICH L. LEHNER, RICHARD A. MULLER, AND A. G. ROEBER

## 1 INTENTION AND SCOPE

THE *Oxford Handbook of Early Modern Theology, 1600–1800*, comprising essays by a wide array of European and North American scholars, offers a comprehensive introduction to Christian theological literature originating in Western Europe, from roughly the end of the French Wars of Religion (1598) to the Congress of Vienna (1815). The time between 1600 and 1800 has been undeservedly neglected, despite the fact that important and ingenious theological work was done in these centuries. This was the time in which the ideas of the Reformation and the Catholic Counter-Reformation were synthesized, systematized, and widely disseminated. Generations of Protestants after Luther (1483–1546) and Calvin (1509–64) created a new technical and terminologically precise theology. Likewise, Catholics took up the ideas of the Council of Trent and implemented them in their systems of thought. Spiritual theologies—whether of Catholic mystics, Quietists, or Protestant Pietists—took on new forms, and theologies of all confessionalities encountered the challenge of the Enlightenment. Philosophies from empiricism, to Descartes (1596–1650), to Kant (1724–1804), influenced theology or were themselves shaped by theological reflection. Despite such colorful diversity, until now no one has taken up the challenge of bringing scholars together to give readers an insightful introduction to this world of ideas.

The essays in this volume review major forms of early modern theology (including scholasticism, Cartesian scholasticism, various schools of the Enlightenment, early Romanticism, and so forth); present main theological topics and their development; introduce the principal practitioners of each kind of theology and delineate their contributions, both positive and polemical, as well as problems they confronted. Taken together, the essays present a comprehensive, accessible survey of the main features of early modern theology and serve as the basis for more specialized research.

## 2 Boundaries of the Volume

The practice of examining history by century, pioneered in the sixteenth century by the *Magdeburg Centuries* and maintained into the beginnings of critical historiography by Johann Lorenz von Mosheim (1693–1755), has long since given way to attempts to begin and end "periods" with epochal events—more recently the attempt to define clear periods has also been ruled out as ultimately unsatisfactory, given the large-scale continuities of history and the unlikelihood of any particular seemingly epochal event having consequences for each and every aspect of the historical narrative. Strict periodization has given way to a retention of traditional terms for historical eras—Middle Ages, Renaissance, Reformation, post-Reformation, Enlightenment—that at the same time recognize vagueness of transitions, ongoing conversation and debate, continuities as well as discontinuities. Beyond this approach, there have been scholarly calls to abandon even the terms referencing eras or periods, either using them only for pedagogical purposes (Hamm 2004 and 2014) or jettisoning them entirely (Schorn-Schütte 2006); in both cases, largely because of the implications resident in the terms of direction, purpose, and meaning in history as such. One might respond to these last objections by pointing out that the changes in historiographical approaches from centuries to strict periods or epochs, to vaguely identified eras, to the denial of all periodization itself indicates periods, eras, and epochs: the objection to all periodization itself implies a teleology based on the assumption that finally, a proper view of history has been offered. One might also respond that a measured or generalized identification of eras that recognizes the vagueness of transitions is not merely a useful pedagogical device, and that without any implied teleology, actually does more justice to the materials and provides a better understanding of the past than the removal of a sense of eras or periods.

Still, the problem of periodization is particularly acute for what might be called post-Reformation or early modern intellectual history. It would not be utterly outlandish to declare that nothing significant has ever happened in years that end in two zeros. More to the issue of early modernity, just as there was no sudden passage from the Middle Ages and Renaissance into the era of Reformation, there is also no abrupt transition from Reformation to post-Reformation, from post-Reformation to Enlightenment, from Enlightenment to the modernity of the nineteenth century. The element of legitimacy in the call for removal of all periodization is that, on a day-to-day, week-to-week, or even month-to-month basis, neither living persons nor the evidences that they leave behind indicate a great sense of transition from one era to another.

Even the terms Reformation and Enlightenment have been subjected to critique and subdivision: we now recognize various "Reformations" and several patterns of "Enlightenment" (Israel 2001; Sorkin 2009; Lindberg 2010). Nor is it particularly useful, in this context, to follow one presently stylish approach to the problem and speak of "long centuries"—where one "century" expands to include several extra decades, presumably at the expense of a preceding or following "short century." We retain the somewhat impractical rubric of a two-century span, while recognizing that the chronological boundaries of the essays that follow are not precisely 1600 and 1800: some necessarily examine issues and materials from before 1600, and all extend into the eighteenth century, but seldom past 1800.

Nonetheless, there is something to be said for such vaguely stated boundaries. A person living in the late sixteenth century might never register anything like epochal change between, say, 1570 and 1590—but such a person transplanted suddenly into 1770 or 1790 would be shocked by a world of change. Various upheavals—theological, philosophical, scientific, social, or political; the interrelated alterations of thought and method brought about by economic and political changes in the fifteenth and sixteenth centuries—identify an era of Reformation, whether Protestant, Catholic, or Radical. So too do debates over scholastic and humanistic methods and the reception of a wide array of ancient philosophical alternatives to Aristotle, as well as the increasing recognition of differences between the original Aristotelian corpus and medieval interpretations, taken together with the ecclesial unrest that brought on the Reformation. These developments also serve to identify a subsequent era, somewhat vaguely or broadly defined, in which many of the issues related to the diverse but interrelated phenomena of the institutionalized Reformation—the defining of distinct confessionalities, the shifts in society, trade, and nationhood, and significant alterations in philosophical and scientific understanding—coalesced into a very different intellectual milieu than that of the early sixteenth century. Specifically, after the establishment and confessional solidification of the various religious and theological trajectories of Protestantism, the parallel solidification of post-Tridentine Catholicism, and the rise of theological, intellectual, and sociopolitical confessionalization in the latter half of the sixteenth century, a fairly distinct era in intellectual history can be identified (Holzem 2015).

Even so, many of the more inherited patterns of thought characteristic of the beginning of the era either were diminished or utterly disappeared by its end. By way of example, in the wake of the Lutheran, Calvinist, and Catholic Reformations, early modernity evidences an initial solidification of confessionalities and an institutionalization of Lutheranism and Calvinism in political, social, and cultural as well as theological patterns. At the same time, there was both considerable cross-fertilization and, in many states and localities, a plurality of confessional positions represented (Safley 2011). These patterns were altered in the course of the seventeenth and eighteenth centuries; yielding, particularly among the Reformed or Calvinist groups but also in the other confessionalities, a deconfessionalization that marks the beginnings of modern religious pluralism and secularism. In short, this broadly defined era that includes late sixteenth-, seventeenth-, and various eighteenth-century developments, evidences the alterations of thought and culture that led to what we today (somewhat redolent of attitudes of the fifteenth century!) have called "modernity."

## 3  Why "Early Modern"?

One of the decisions made by the editors in designing the present volume was to identify it as a handbook of "early modern theology" rather than "post-Reformation theology" or "post-Reformation and Enlightenment Theology." There are several reasons for this choice, which relate to the issues broached in the initial section of this introduction. The term post-Reformation, although quite functional for the late sixteenth and much of the seventeenth century, does have a tendency to yield a sense of the seventeenth and eighteenth centuries as an aftermath, and to give the impression like that once held of the later Middle Ages, that there was both a discontinuity and a significant decline in the vitality of thought. That view of the later Middle Ages is no longer accepted by a majority of the scholarly community—and the parallel view of seventeenth-century thought should also be set aside. Post-Reformation would also tend to limit the study to the seventeenth century or part of it, not recognizing either the ongoing debate or conversation that did not cease circa 1660 or 1700, and thereby artificially severing seventeenth-century developments from the Enlightenment. A similar problem arises when characterizing the era from an eighteenth-century perspective and attempting to distinguish "early Enlightenment" from "post-Reformation" on one side and "Enlightenment" on the other. The term "early modern" offers a broader and more generalized meaning, as well as providing a salutary chronological vagueness and a less value-charged identification of the era or period.

## 4  Approaching Theology in the Early Modern Context: Patterns of Analysis

Analysis of theological developments in the early modern era has itself become a more complicated exercise than it was even half a century ago. The same scholarship that disabused us of neat periodizations has also pressed the issues of continuities, if not in the precise repetition of ideas and issues, certainly in ongoing debates and conversations. Parallel developments in late medieval and Renaissance thought not only are recognized as continuing into the era of the Reformation, but also past it into early modernity. For example, even as Catholicism was experiencing its "second scholasticism," the institutional theologies of the magisterial Reformation were experiencing what can be called their "first scholasticism," with both of these scholasticisms being developments in a long tradition of academic discourse. Similarly, the Renaissance revivals of a series of non- or even anti-Aristotelian philosophies, perhaps most notably Epicureanism, were instrumental in creating the intellectual foment of early modernity that both stimulated the scientific revolution and radically altered the philosophical underpinnings of theology.

Intellectual historians of the era have also learned from social history to move the discipline past what has been identified as "confessional historiography." Specifically, the history of theology in the Reformation and post-Reformation eras, although it continues (quite necessarily) to observe the confessional boundaries of the era, no longer takes as its primary motive the justification of the teachings of particular confessional groups. Even so, "orthodoxy" in the present volume indicates the intention of writers belonging to various confessionalities to teach "right doctrine" and to define the means, whether biblical, traditionary, or philosophical, by which to arrive at that right teaching. The orthodoxies, moreover, not only are recognized as holding much in common, whether theological or philosophical, but as each contending for possession not only of doctrinal truth and right religion but also of what each took to be the better part of the tradition. Much of the analysis of the thought of the era, therefore, also includes both reception history and observation of ongoing conversation and debate that often crossed over the confessional boundaries. Inclusion of the churches of the East in the discussion raises the issues of the contributions of Eastern thought in the West after 1453, of developments in the Eastern church brought on by confessional divisions in the West, and of Western use of Eastern thought, whether positive or polemical.

The movement away from confessional historiography has also led to broader recognition among scholars of the significance of dissident and "radical" groups to the development of theology in the early modern era: notably, the Arminian or Remonstrant, Anabaptist, and Socinian-Unitarian theologies; and in England, the variant theologies of the Baptist and other dissenting groups. In the cases of Remonstrant and Socinian-Unitarian theologies in particular, we have evidence—clearer than among the orthodox confessionalities—not only of the impact of the new rational philosophies and the critical reading of scripture, but also of active contribution to those developments and their theological impact.

# 5 ORGANIZATION OF THE VOLUME

The handbook divides into three main parts: "I. Theology—Content and Form"; "II. Theological Topics"; and "III. Theology and Others." Part I is foundational and sets the stage for what follows. In this and subsequent sections, the authors understand "theology" as a principled reflection on the revelation conveyed in scripture, which also engages issues current in philosophy, society, church, and state. Individual chapters dealing with theological developments beyond Europe; sources, methods, and forms of early modern theology in general; and the relationship of early modern theology to the confessional state will introduce the main kinds of theologizing found in these centuries and give an overview of the ecclesial and societal contexts.

Part II addresses theological issues and topics such as the Trinity, Christ, grace, moral theology, the theological virtues, the Eucharist and other sacraments, and the church. Principal developments on these topics are outlined, as well as the main disagreements among the confessional groups. Between 1600 and 1800, theological reflection was exercised in great variety, and across a spectrum of religious denominations. In order to categorize this immense variety, the coverage of theological topics is divided into four sections that indicate the main lines of theological direction. The first three sections deal, respectively, with Catholic, Reformed, and Lutheran theology. Anglican theology in the line of the Thirty-Nine Articles is included under the broad rubric of "Reformed," albeit allowing for Arminian and latitudinarian developments (Atkinson 1997; Hampton 2008). A fourth section deals with other Christian theologies that cannot be subsumed under these categories, such as Socinianism and Unitarianism, and Anabaptist, Arminian, Moravian, Jansenist, and Pietist theologies. These dissenting or dissident groups had significant impact both on the character of early modern thought as it emerged into the Enlightenment and on the orthodoxies of the day. Beyond the broadly confessional categorization, the essays therefore also emphasize common characteristics of main forms and themes of theological work and the tensions among theologians of various groups.

Part III is divided into two sections. The first section examines Western early modern theology and its practitioners in engagement with various others, especially the churches of the East, but also Islam and Judaism. The Eastern-rite Catholic and Orthodox churches are examined particularly in terms of their interaction with Western Christendom. A chapter on Islam focuses on Western engagement, both positive and negative, while a chapter on Judaism examines the interrelationships of various early modern Christian theologies with Jewish thought. The second section offers a series of perspectives on the engagement of theology with trends in early modern philosophy, with chapters that focus on the rise of Cartesian philosophy, natural law theory, the impact of empiricism, early modern science, and Spinoza (1632–77); and also look to the somewhat later impact of Rousseau (1712–78), Kant, and the rise of neology. This final section serves to round out the volume by describing the intellectual forces—ranging chronologically from Bacon (1561–1626) and Descartes to Kant—that so radically altered the substance of early modern theology and prepared the way for the further alteration of theological thought in the nineteenth century.

Our definition of theology as a principled reflection on the revelation conveyed in scripture also explains what is excluded from this volume, namely authors and groups with nontheological aims. It desires to provide a multilayered orientation to Christian theological literature of the post-Reformation era; and accordingly, Islam and Judaism, as well as those who placed themselves outside the ecclesial groups, and developments of Christian thought in non-European countries, are referenced in terms of Christian theologians' use of their works and ideas, and to mention possible interactions and influences in their contributions. The handbook offers, then, an approach to early modern theology that is both transconfessional and transnational.

# BIBLIOGRAPHY

Atkinson, Nigel. 1997. *Richard Hooker and the Authority of Scripture, Tradition, and Reason: Reformed Theologian of the Church of England?* Carlisle: Paternoster.

Hamm, Berndt. 2004. "Farewell to Epochs in Reformation History: A Plea." *Reformation & Renaissance Review* 16 (3): 211–245.

Hamm, Berndt. 2014. *The Reformation of Faith in the Context of Late Medieval Theology and Piety: Essays by Berndt Hamm*. Edited by Robert J. Bast. Leiden: Brill.

Hampton, Stephen. 2008. *Anti-Arminians: The Anglican Reformed Tradition from Charles II to George I*. Oxford: Oxford University Press.

Holzem, Andreas. 2015. *Christentum in Deutschland 1550–1850: Konfessionalisierung—Aufklärung—Pluralisierung*. Paderborn: Ferdinand Schöningh.

Israel, Jonathan. 2001. *Radical Enlightenment: Philosophy and the Making of Modernity, 1650–1750*. Oxford: Oxford University Press.

Lindberg, Carter. 2010. *The European Reformations*. 2nd ed. Oxford: Blackwell.

Safley, Thomas Max, ed. 2011. *A Companion to Multiconfessionalism in the Early Modern World*. Leiden: Brill.

Schorn-Schütte, Luise. 2006. "Reformationsgeschichtsschreibung—wozu? Eine Standortbestimmung." In *Historie und Leben: Der Historiker als Wissenschaftler und Zeitgenosse*, edited by Dieter Hein, et al. Munich: Oldenbourg.

Sorkin, David. 2009. *The Religious Enlightenment: Protestants, Jews, and Catholics from London to Vienna*. Princeton, NJ: University of Princeton.

# PART I

## THEOLOGY—CONTEXT AND FORM

CHAPTER 1

....................................................................................................

# THEOLOGICAL DEVELOPMENTS IN THE NON-EUROPEAN WORLD, 1500–1800

....................................................................................................

## RONNIE PO-CHIA HSIA

IN the age of European expansion, the first Christian missions were undertaken during the late fifteenth century by the Portuguese in West Africa. Despite reports of a massive number of baptisms in the Kingdom of Kongo, these early conversions resulted more from political alliances between African chieftains and Portuguese traders, and reflected only superficial efforts at evangelization. The Spanish conquest of the Americas in the sixteenth century brought about a much deeper engagement between Christianity and the native peoples; but despite native voices, there was little impact on theological developments in Christianity itself. In the major Mesoamerican civilizations (Aztec, Maya, and Inca), Spaniards encountered human sacrifice, which provoked a profound sense of disgust and rejection. The result was repression, due to the Catholic clergy's wholesale rejection of native American religious practices and beliefs. The term "spiritual conquest," coined by Robert Ricard in 1933 to describe the evangelization of sixteenth-century Mexico by the mendicant orders, is thus an accurate description of the coercive and colonial nature of the conversion effort (Ricard 1974). Even if Catholic theology remained unchallenged, evangelization among native Americans necessitated the examination of cultural approaches: should Christianity be conveyed in Spanish or in Mesoamerican languages; and if in the latter, how would divine names and key theological terms be rendered? To what extent can indigenous cultural practices be incorporated into Christian worship and converts recruited and trained for the clergy? To what degree, therefore, was the Mesoamerican church an extension of European civilization—or alternatively, in what ways did Christianity undergo a process of indigenization with the success of conversion? All these questions would also be raised when Catholic missionaries encountered the civilizations of India, Japan, and

China. Before turning to this aspect, we need to examine the theological controversy surrounding the very idea of the mission itself as a result of the Protestant Reformation.

# 1 PROTESTANT SKEPTICISM CONCERNING OVERSEAS MISSIONS

In the decades following 1517, when the Protestant Reformation snatched the allegiance of a great part of Christian Europe away from Rome, one of the few bright spots for Catholicism shone from the distant horizon. Writing from Cologne in 1534, the Carthusian monk Theodor Loher (n.d.–1554) lamented the damage to the Catholic Church inflicted by followers of various heretical teachings, the most recent being the Anabaptists who had taken over the nearby city of Münster in Westphalia and proclaimed it the apocalyptical site of the Second Coming of Christ. His only consolation was the knowledge that various peoples called by God had fallen away by disobedience in the past—the Jews, the Greeks, and now his own people—but the true church has always flourished. That consolation came in the voyages of discovery by Spain and Portugal, and the conversions made among peoples hitherto ignorant of the Gospels. These new converts to Roman Catholicism would eventually more than match the souls lost to the heretical teachings of Luther (1483–1546), Zwingli (1484–1531), and other heresiarchs; so the monk reasoned.

This confidence was not misplaced. After the Council of Trent, Catholic overseas mission assumed a clear polemical and confessional tone. In 1585, Johann Mayer, publisher for the Jesuit College in Dillingen, brought out a German translation of selected Jesuit missionary letters from Japan covering the years between 1577 and 1581. Mayer dedicated the book, *Historischer Bericht . . . in Beköhrung der gewaltigen landschafft und insel Jappon*, to Bishop Marquardt of Augsburg (1528–91), a staunch enemy of the Protestants in his diocese, with these words:

> the Almighty God, in the place of so many thousands of souls in Upper and Lower Germany, who have been miserably seduced by those stubborn persons inspired by the Evil Enemy, and through countless new and inconstant teachings, particularly by the Lutheran, Calvinist, and Zwinglian heretical preachers, has chosen another people in another part of the world, who has hitherto known nothing about Christ and his holy faith. (Hsia 1995, 158)

Religious polemic was not far from the minds of some missionaries, even as they labored in faraway lands. One example was that of Gabriel de Magalhães (1610–77), a Portuguese Jesuit missionary in China, whose discourse on Buddhist converts to Christianity led unexpectedly to a fierce denunciation of Jewish conversos in his native Portugal. Nor was anti-Judaism confined to the Portuguese; Magalhães's colleague, the French Jesuit André Grelon (1618–96), also advocated a restrictive policy on admitting Buddhist converts to Christianity: they had to break their vegetarian fast before admission to baptism. Turning to Jewish converts in comparison, Grelon asked rhetorically: would any Jewish converso dare to ask the Inquisition to be exempted from eating pork? (Hsia 2009, 272–73). A third example is provided by the Belgian Jesuit Ferdinand Verbiest (1623–88), who wrote to his confreres in Europe in 1678 to ask for donations and missionary recruits. In this famous letter, Verbiest recounts an event that took place in 1658, when the ship carrying him and his fellow missionaries encountered an English vessel at the Bay of Gibraltar. A Protestant chaplain engaged him in conversation. Learning they were missionaries to China who were receiving no salary from the pope, the Englishman scoffed at their foolishness. From this, Verbiest quipped, "one knows that the heretic was inspired not by missionary but by mercenary zeal" (Verbiest 1938, 238–39).

How did Protestants react to this Jesuit polemic? Orthodox Lutherans tended to hold a negative view on the dispatch of missionaries overseas. Many regarded Catholic missions as motivated by economic greed and political ambition. The fact that the Society of Jesus was a driving force both in Catholic overseas missions and anti-Protestant polemic hardened this stance, and missions retained a negative connotation in Lutheran orthodoxy. Typical of this attitude is that of Jesper Brochmand (1585–1652), Bishop of Zealand and Professor of Theology at Copenhagen. "Brochmand claimed that the apostolic call only applied to the first apostles, that they had preached to all the world, and that the 'heathens' themselves had rejected salvation, even though it had been preached to them three times. 'We Lutherans do not,' Brochmand writes, 'as does the Pope, arrogate any right towards all the people of the world. Therefore, it is not up to Lutherans, but to papists "ex officio" to convert heathens to the Gospel'" (Glebe-Møller 2006, 98–99).

With the rise of Pietism in the late seventeenth century, the theological debate concerning overseas missions flared up once more in the Lutheran Church. The spiritual renewal that animated Phillip Jakob Spener (1635–1705) and other Pietists nourished a clear millenarian vision, and with it a strong sense of mission among Jews and "heathens" in eschatological preparation.

Pietism influenced King Frederik IV of Denmark (1671–1730) to call two German students from Halle, Bartholomäus Ziegenbalg (1682–1719) and Heinrich Plütschau (1679–1752), who became in 1706 the first missionaries of the Danish-Halle mission at Tranquebar in India, despite strong opposition from the orthodox establishment. Bishop Henrik Bornemann failed the two Halle students in their first ordination examination, until royal pressure changed his stance. The anti-Pietist theologian Johann Georg Neumann (1661–1709) denigrated the motive behind the mission as purely making money; Morten Caspar Wolfburg (1686–1729), professor of theology and bishop of Viborg, dismissed the two Pietists' first reports from India as "a pack of lies"—and these words came from one of the supporters of the royal India mission!

Arguments against overseas missions within Lutheran orthodoxy were more sustained and vehement. One of the most articulate opponents was the theologian Hans Bartholin (1665–1738). In his controversial pamphlet, *Sententia de hodierna indorum conversione*, Bartholin shared eleven "weighty observations" with his readers:

First, the Jews represent a natural branch of the Christian tree but the heathens are not. Even if St. Paul was teacher and apostle to the heathen, we do not read that he has accompanied the heathen as willingly and devotedly as with the Jews.

Second, the Gospel has been preached to the whole world by the apostles and we are not obliged to proclaim the law again.

Third, the proclamation of the Gospel was more solemn than that of the law.

Fourth, we are no more under an obligation to send out missionaries to convert the heathen.

Fifth, nowhere in the Old Testament does one read that the prophets attempted to make proselytes by sea and by land.

Sixth, there is no trace in the Scriptures of the apostles having given their successors instruction to go out into the whole world but rather the opposite. It is not the duty for the ministers of the Church to preach everywhere outside their own stalls; neither are they entitled to preach the Gospel in lands that are under the control of another sovereign.

Seven, Catholic missionaries mix up invented worship with that of Christ's pure teachings. All who are sent out ought to be orthodox.

Eighth, if papists criticize that Lutherans are not true Christians because they do not convert heathens, then, the conversion of heathens is not our duty but theirs.

Ninth, Pietists draw the conclusion that the millennium is drawing near because the Gospel is now finally being proclaimed to the whole world.

Tenth, should special prayers also be said for the conversion of the heathen without any particularly pressing necessity?

Eleventh, skepticism as to the possibility of doing missionary work in the Finnmark.

Despite the objections of Bartholin and other orthodox theologians, the Danish-Halle mission continued thanks to princely support. Secular authority, in fact, provided a major impetus for Protestant missions, its interests in foreign lands inspired by mercantilist interests. Such was the case with the Dutch West and East India Companies as well, which furnished some support for missionary work. Calvin himself had written that "God desires all men to be saved"; consequently, the obligation to preach the Gospel to "foreign peoples" (Glebe-Møller 2006, 91). We will have occasion now to see how the Christian missions of the different churches performed in the actual mission fields of Asia and the Americas.

# 2 THE NAMES OF GOD: LANGUAGE AND CONVERSION

According to the Oxford English Dictionary, the word "conversion" was used interchangeably with "conversation" in Middle English. Indeed, words—conversations, speech-acts, and texts—were the indispensible tools of the missionary. Christianity itself can be understood as a speech-act: the Gospels as the Word of God, *Verbum Dei*, Christ as the sign made flesh. Words indeed, but in what language(s)? Must one preach the faith using the languages of the scriptures (Protestants) or that of the church (Catholics), or should one resort to the European common languages—Spanish in the New World and Portuguese in Asia? Or must one learn the languages of the nonbelievers and bring Christianity to them in their own idiom and metaphors? And if so, which non-European languages? Should one use Mandarin (written and spoken) in China versus the many regional and mutually incomprehensible dialects? In China, the Jesuits mostly resorted to the first, while the mendicant orders, especially the Dominicans, preferred the second; an approach also favored by Protestant missionaries in the early nineteenth century. Should one employ the imperial languages of the Mesoamerican empires even after their destruction by Spanish conquest to spread the faith of the Spaniards, using Nahuatl, Quechua, and Guarini as *linguae francae* in the complex multiethnic and multilingual societies of colonial America; or would it be more expedient to reduce native converts to Spanish speakers and Spanish subjects? The question of language in the missionary enterprise was simultaneously a destructive, deconstructive, and constructive act: thus Spanish friars destroyed Nahua and Mayan codices in Mesoamerica, while a French Jesuit created the modern Vietnamese written language using the Latin alphabet, and Dutch Calvinist preachers in Taiwan recorded the first traces of aboriginal culture by giving textual form in catechisms to the Austronesian languages spoken by the aborigines in mid-seventeenth century Taiwan.

Whatever language is chosen in the propagation of Christianity, there is the problem of translating the name of God: the question of whether to adopt a native term, thereby risking misidentification, or to use a strange-sounding and alien term of transliteration. Upon arriving in Japan in 1542, Francis Xavier (1506–52) naively used the name *Dainichi* (Great Sun) to denote the Christian God, ignorant of the fact that *Dainichi*, a Buddhist term, was itself translated from the Sanskrit denoting *Mahavairocana*, the all-encompassing cosmic Buddha. Discovering his mistake, the Jesuit missionary resorted to reproducing the sound of the Christian term, *Deus*, in Japanese and came up with the neologism *Daiusu*. Avoiding any more embarrassments, other terms borrowed from Buddhism were retranslated according to the principle of representing Latin terms by the Japanese alphabets of Hiragana and Katakana.

The same principle of nomenclature applied in Spanish colonial America: the Spanish term for God, *Dios*, was imposed on native American converts, although terms for supreme deities were not lacking in Quechua, Aymara, and other Andean languages. While conceding that pre-conquest Andeans acknowledged a supreme deity, the Jesuit José da Acosta (1540–1615) argued that native appellations, divine names such as *Viracocha* and *Pachacamac*, were improper. In his *Natural and Moral History of the Indies*, Acosta writes: "If we shall seek into the Indian tongue for a word to answer to this name of God, as in Latin, *Deus*, in Greek, *Theos*, in Hebrew, *El*, in Arabic, *Alla*; but we shall not find any in the Cuzcan [i.e. Inca] or Mexican tongues. So as such as preach or write to the Indians use our Spanish name Dios, fitting it to the accent or pronunciation of the Indian tongues" (Kim 2004, 92).

This reasoning, however, was strongly opposed by native American converts. A Quechua speaker and one of the first Christian Peruvian writers, Felipe Guaman Poma de Ayala (ca. 1535–1616) argued that Quechua speakers had an equivalent term to Dios, namely Runa Camac, whom they acknowledged as the supreme deity. It was counter-productive to impose a foreign loan word on Peruvian converts, Ayala continued, whose ancestors already believed in an omnipotent single God, whose name should continue to inspire the piety of Christian neophytes.

This sentiment was entirely shared by the Inca writer Garcilaso de la Vega (1539–1616), who explains that the Quechuan term *Pachacamac* is a composite term meaning *pacha*, the whole world, and *camac*, the present participle of the verb *cama*, to animate. A well-educated Christian convert of the Inca elite, Garcilaso was proud of his cultural heritage, and wrote "The Inca kings and their *amautas*, who were the philosophers, perceived by the light of nature the true supreme God our Lord, the maker of heaven and earth, as we shall see from the arguments and phrases some of them applied to the Divine Majesty, whom they called *Pachacamac*" (Kim 2004, 96–97).

What philology provided, in the arguments of Ayala and Garcilaso, was a cultural antidote to Spanish colonialism: Christianity, although brought to the Americas by Spanish missionaries, was not necessarily a Spanish religion, for the Christian Divinity had revealed itself in different historical epochs to many peoples of the world.

Adapting Christian evangelizing to non-European ways, indeed, was the key to success in the early Jesuit mission to late sixteenth-century China. Here, we see the opposite process in the naming of the Christian God. Instead of using Portuguese, Spanish, or Latin loan words, Jesuit missionaries chose equivalent terms from ancient Chinese texts or used neologisms. A spirit of experimentation animated the early Jesuits: the term *Shangdi* (God-on-High), which appeared in the oracle bones inscriptions of the Shang dynasty (ca. 1600–1046 BC) and the ancient Confucian Classics (notably in the *Book of History*), was used until the 1630s before it was discarded, although the term still appeared in the writings of Chinese Christians; the name *Tianzhu* (Lord of Heaven), a neologism, was adopted by Michele Ruggieri (1543–1607) and Matteo Ricci (1552–1610), the first Jesuit missionaries, from an invented term by one of their first converts, and to this day this appellation denotes Roman Catholicism. Interestingly, the discarded term *Shangdi*, God-on-High, came to be adopted by Protestant missionaries in nineteenth-century China as the major appellation for the Christian God (Lai 2010, 311).

# 3 PROTESTANT MISSIONS AND NATIVE LANGUAGES

Problems of translation aside, theological concepts and ecclesiastical terms needed to be rendered into non-European languages for the use of the new Christian communities. Facing common problems of translation, Catholic and Protestant missionaries produced catechisms, prayer books, and liturgical texts; but they differed in one major question: translating the Bible. Three case studies illustrate the differences and similarities in the question of language and conversion: the Calvinist mission in Taiwan, the Lutheran mission in India, and the Catholic mission in China.

Between 1624 and 1662, the Dutch East India Company (VOC) made Port Hollandia (today part of Tainan) in southern Taiwan its entrepôt in East Asia. Building fortifications, draining channels, and attracting Chinese settlers from the mainland, the VOC also pursued a policy of pacifying the aboriginal populations. Conversion to Christianity was very much part of that strategy. In 1627, the predikant Georg Candidius (1597–1647) was sent from Batavia, followed two years later by a second missionary, Robert Junius (1606–55). By 1636, the VOC had sent four predikants; a school was set up for the Sinckan tribe who lived closest to the Dutch settlement, and by the end of this year 106 Sinckan households agreed to abandon their ancestral rituals and join the Reformed Church. In Janaury 1637, the first reformed service was performed. By 1638, the VOC estimated the total number of aboriginal converts to be between four and five thousand. The year 1641 represented a turning point: aboriginal converts were admitted to the Eucharist and the decision was made to train native religious personnel. By 1643, Dutch preachers had trained nearly fifty native catechists, who were crucial in compiling catechetical material in native languages.

In the short time of evangelization in Taiwan, the Dutch Reformed Church produced an impressive number of religious texts in different Austronesian languages. While texts in Sirayan and other aboriginal languages are lost, there is still a substantial extant corpus of texts in Sinckan and Favorlang. Candidius was the pioneer in compiling a grammar for Sinckan, while his successor Junius translated into Sinckan three catechisms, two collections of prayers, three sermons, and seven hymns. The 1640s saw the greatest effort in further translations, also into Sirayan and Favorlang. In addition to prayers and catechisms, the Lord's Prayer, the Credo, the Ten Commandments, the *Heidelberg Catechism*, as well as two Gospels (Mark and John) were translated into aboriginal languages (Hsin 2011, 72–73, 82, 177–79, 203–5).

In all probability, Ziegenbalg (1682–1719) in India benefited from the Christian vocabulary the Jesuit missionary Roberto de Nobili (1577–1656) had created in an earlier attempt to convert the Hindu upper castes (Zupanov 1999). For example, Ziegenbalg frequently used the word *Caruvecuran* (in Sanskrit, *Sarvesvara*, the Almighty) as a term for the revealed biblical God. There are also striking resemblances to other words, such as "angel," "devil," "world," "human being," and the like, that de Nobili had used in his own works. Nobili and his Madurai Mission allowed converts to retain native attributes such as the sacred string, the tuft of hair at the back of the head (*sikha*), as well as other emblems. Despite criticisms, Nobili attached great importance to the so-called Malabar Rites and tried to defend those characteristic features as an indivisible part of the social order that had nothing to do with faith or devotion, although those features undoubtedly have soteriological implications. He thus laid stress on the purely social character of the Malabar Rites in order to manage the "pagan customs" by restricting them exclusively to the devotion of Hindu gods and goddesses. The Danish-Halle mission and the later English-Halle mission were inspired or influenced by the writings of the early Jesuit mission in India.

An important area of work started initially by Ziegenbalg and then later taken up by Fabricius was Tamil Christian hymnody. Johann Phillip Fabricius published a collection of 335 Tamil hymns, most of them translated from German. The initial compositions by Ziegenbalg were not very well done, and when Fabricius came to Madras he had this field of work entirely to himself and gained quite a mastery over this art. Even today hymns by Fabricius are sung by Christians in South India.

# 4  BIBLE TRANSLATION

In bringing Christianity to historically non-Christian peoples, Bible translation assumed a particular importance with Protestant missionaries. Bible translation represented a collective and cumulative undertaking. Ziegenbalg was the first to work on a Tamil translation, but he read Tamil books written by Jesuit missionaries in order to familiarize himself with religious terminologies and style. Collaboration was indispensable. For his translation of the Old Testament, the Protestant missionary Benjamin Schultze in Madras relied on the native informant and convert Peter Malieappan and other Tamil scholars, even occasionally consulting a Brahmin for particularly difficult linguistic problems.

With concurrent translation efforts in Tranquebar, Cuddalore, and Madras, it was ultimately Fabricius who brought out the first printed Bible translation in an Indian language, Tamil. This work was based on the previous translation by Ziegenbalg during his stay in Madras. As Fabricius read through the translation along with his native catechist, he realized the translated text lacked clarity and style. In 1750 he began work on the New Testament, publishing first some of the Pauline letters. The New Testament that emerged from the press in 1758 was a peculiar combination; the first seven books had no sign of the influence of Fabricius, while the rest of the work was entirely his translation. At last in 1766, Fabricius could print the entire New Testament from a press that the British government made available to him. Work on the Old Testament was vastly more difficult. In 1756 a Tamil translation of the Psalms was printed. However, the final translation of the Old Testament was only published in 1798.

In China, where Catholics dominated the Christian mission until 1800, no attempts were made to translate the Bible into Chinese, in accordance with the Tridentine prohibition of vernacular editions. Stories from the Bible were transmitted in fragments—the life of the patriarchs and prophets, the work and death of Jesus—through reworkings of late medieval and sixteenth-century Catholic works. An eminent example was a book published by the Italian Jesuit Giulio Aleni (1582–1649), entitled *Tianzhu jiangsheng chuxiang jingjie* (Illustrated Explanation of the Lord of Heaven's Incarnation), published in 1637 in Quanzhou, with fifty-five woodcut pictures copied from a work by the sixteenth-century Spanish Jesuit Jeronimo Nadal (1507–80), *Evangelicae Historiae*

*Imagines*, a collection of 153 folio-size copper engravings of biblical scenes published in Antwerp in 1593. Aleni supplied short explanations in Chinese to these scenes, and this book represented the first and most important example in the visual propagation of Christianity in Chinese art.

The publishing center of Antwerp also produced the famous polyglot Plantin Bible (1568–73), which was first imported into China in 1604. Matteo Ricci, pioneer of the Jesuit mission and its superior, proudly displayed it in the Catholic Church in Beijing, in order to showcase the superiority of western book production and by extension its religious message. So impressed were his congregation that some converts asked Ricci to undertake its translation, to which the Jesuit demurred, citing the prodigious work involved and that the essence of its story has already been transmitted.

True to Tridentine injunctions, Catholic missionaries in China did not attempt any biblical translations until the eighteenth century. Jean Basset (1662–1707) of the Paris Foreign Missions (Missions Etrangères de Paris) translated most books of the New Testament from the Latin Vulgate Bible around 1700. His Jesuit colleague, Louis de Poirot (1735–1813), who reached China at the time of the Society's suppression in Europe, made a complete translation of the New Testament and a partial translation of the Old Testament. This massive work, *Guxin shengjing*, also based on the Latin Vulgate, never saw print—like Basset's earlier work, lacking ecclesiastical license. Of Basset's work only one manuscript copy has survived, and Poirot's manuscript has disappeared. However, both works served as drafts for the first Protestant translations of the Bible into Chinese during the early nineteenth century, an indebtedness that was not acknowledged for most of the period of the Protestant Chinese mission.

# 5 SACRAMENTS

In Christianity's global missions, one of the main obstacles to conversion was the practice of polygamy. Established as a mark of Christian civilization in Europe during the conversion of the early Middle Ages, monogamy ran counter to deeply rooted social practices that prevailed from the native Americans to Africans, Indians, and Chinese. In some societies, polygamy ensured demographic survival; as with the Mapuche of Chile, a semi-nomadic people who struggled for survival in a harsh environment. In other societies, it reflected the status of elite men, as in the Congo or India. In China it signified the imperative of patriarchal lineage descent: the securing of sufficient male heirs for lineage survival was the most powerful rationale behind concubinage, and sanctioned in the *Code of the Great Ming*.

For Christian missionaries, polygamy was a grave challenge: it represented the nadir of sexual sin; it opposed a cornerstone of Christian civilization; it negated the authority of the Christian clergy; and it put the baptized partner in such a union in a pastorally untenable position. This last problem extended even to monogamous marriages between a convert and a non-Christian. If the wife was a Christian, her husband and in-laws could forbid or restrict her religious exercises, and her children might be denied baptism. Letters by Catholic missionaries in seventeenth- and eighteenth-century China report many such examples. Even ideal Christian marriages—between two converts— could infringe on Catholic prohibitions of marital consanguinity, reflecting the reality that conversions, especially in the countryside, occurred very frequently in the same extended family groups and the wide geographical dispersion of converts in the rural areas made marital consanguinity a hard thing to avoid.

Social relations posed a particular challenge to Christian missions where different gender norms called into question established sacramental practices. In addition to the problems associated with Christian marriages, Catholic missionaries in China refrained from overt contact with women converts in order to avoid scandal. This pertained especially to baptism and confession. Given the segregation of the sexes and the mores of female modesty, Jesuit missionaries debated the propriety of anointing the faces of female neophytes during baptism. They advocated hearing confessions from women in private, but with older male relatives standing at a distance to demonstrate proper behavior. For the celebration of the Mass, missionaries constructed separate chapels for men and women where possible, or held alternate services for their male and female congregations. The different relations between the sexes in the Paris of Louis XV in fact scandalized the Catholic convert John Hu, assistant to the French Jesuit Jean-François Foucquet (1665–1741), who ranted against the mixed congregations in the churches. Unjustly committed to an insane asylum by Foucquet, Hu was eventually sent home to China in 1725 to a Christianity he was more comfortable with.

In other missionary areas, a model of Christian sexuality was successfully established. Dominican missionaries from the Spanish Philippines seemed to have less scruples respecting Chinese gender rules. In their devotion to Mary and the cult of virginity, the Dominicans inspired fervent female converts to embrace life-long virginity, sometimes against the express wishes of their families, Christian or nonbelievers, to live the life of the *beata* within a traditional Chinese kinship setting.

The encounter between Christian theology and social customs in missionary countries accentuated the question of *adiaphora*: the indifferent things that pertain to aspects of Christian beliefs and practices that are not essential to soteriology and could be adapted to non-Christian rituals and practices. In the Reformation, disagreements over *adiaphora* tore deep divisions within the evangelical church, as followers of Philipp Melanchthon (1497–1560) and his opponents fought over Luther's legacy and the degree to which concessions could be made to the Roman church in the context of a general church council. Outside of Europe, the practical reality of the missions convinced most missionaries to adopt some flexibility. In the celebration of Catholic Mass, Mesoamerican congregations were allowed to sing hymns in their own languages, accompanied by traditional musical instruments; in seventeenth-century China, the men were allowed to keep their hats on during Mass, for baring one's head was considered a sign of disrespect, in contrast to the custom in Europe. In Protestant services, the use of native languages was universal and the liturgy simplified to its essential elements in order to accommodate local usage and avoid a Eurocentric appearance.

Amidst this cultural accommodation, which was particularly prominent in the first two centuries of Christian missions in the early modern period (sixteenth and seventeenth centuries), there were nonetheless signs of cultural intransigence that cropped up in the Catholic missions. French Jesuit and Capuchin missionaries to the Levant targeted members of Eastern Christianity for their conversion effort, and insisted on the superiority and exclusivity of Roman Latin rites over Armenian, Greek, and Syrian ones. In seventeenth-century Ethiopia, instead of ecumenism, Portuguese Jesuits pushed for the replacement of Coptic Christianity by Roman Catholicism, eventually provoking an ecclesiastical and political backlash that destroyed the Catholic mission. The early success of converting Syriac St. Thomas Christians on the Fishery coast in South India during the sixteenth century gave way to an eventual schism in the new convert community, as resentment against Portuguese domination and Roman Catholic superiority led many to revert back to their ancestral rituals and allegiances.

Symptoms of a new inflexibility appeared in the first phases of the so-called Chinese Rites controversy during the seventeenth century. This controversy originated with a critique by Spanish Franciscans and Dominicans of the Jesuit accommodation to Chinese rituals in their mission; namely, the dispensation for Chinese converts to attend the annual ceremonies in honor of Confucius, the great philosopher of antiquity and the patron of all aspiring scholars, and to participate in rituals of filial piety in honor of departed parents and ancestors. Essentially, the mendicant friars accused their Chinese converts of making sacrifices to Confucius and ancestors, and condemned these practices as superstitions incompatible with Christian faith. In opposition, the Jesuits defended these practices as civic rituals, inherent and central to Chinese culture and sensibilities, things *adiaphora*, the prohibition of which would severely jeopardize the Christian mission. Pitting religion against culture, the Chinese Rites controversy provoked similar controversies in India—the eighteenth-century Malabar Rites controversy and to a lesser extent, controversy between missionaries of the Paris Foreign Mission and the Jesuits in Vietnam.

The friars and the Jesuits filed appeals to Rome in the seventeenth century; the ambiguous and contradictory rulings at the Congregation for the Propagation for the Faith reflected indecision rooted in ignorance of Chinese culture and local conditions. A war of words raged on, with the tide gradually turning against the Chinese Rites, due to a strong alliance between anti-Jesuit Catholics and Protestants in European public opinion. In 1705, the papacy sided with the opponents of Chinese Rites, and demanded obedience from all missionary orders in China. Despite several appeals from Chinese converts to Rome, the prohibition was repeated, resulting in the diplomatic break between the Qing government and the papacy and the outlawing of Christian evangelization in the Qing empire. The resulting catastrophe was manifest in the sharp decline of elite conversions, sporadic persecutions, and a mission that stagnated until the legal repeal after 1860, when China was defeated in the Second Opium War.

# 6 ECCLESIOLOGY

The conflict between culture and religion increasingly assumed a character of European superiority, as Christianity was equated with European civilization. Racial superiority, of course, was present at the moment of Spanish conquest and Portuguese explorations. This was clearly expressed in colonial and missionary policies over the admission of non-Europeans into the clergy. At the heart of this question was ecclesiology: if the new missionary territories were to be organized eventually into dioceses and incorporated into the universal body of the Roman Church, then the ecclesiastical hierarchy must provide for adequate pastoral care to guide the neophytes and prevent any relapses into "paganism." This imperative, therefore, ensured the domination of Europeans in the mission churches into the mid-twentieth century. Despite various attempts at incorporating native rites into global Christianity, the reluctance to admit non-European converts into the clergy (and the ecclesiastical hierarchy) formed an insurmountable barrier to indigenization.

The first two Mexican provincial church councils in 1555 and 1565 prohibited Indians, mestizos, and mulattos, together with descendants of Moors, Jews, and others sentenced by the Inquisition, from entering the clergy. The 1585, the third Mexican church council allowed for the ordination of clergy of mixed blood (mestizos and mulattos), although racial prejudice kept the numbers low and assigned the candidates to mostly rural and poorer parishes. In Peru, while the first Spanish settlers succeeded in having the crown accept their mestizo offspring for ordination, the Spanish Jesuit José de Acosta wrote against the ordination of Native Americans in his 1577 work, *De procuranda Indorum salute*.

In 1650, Archbishop Juan Palafox y Mendoza (1600–59) reported he personally knew of only one full-blooded Indian Catholic priest in Mexico City. Despite occasional voices championing an indigenous clergy, the religious orders in the Americas only admitted Europeans and Creoles, yielding to prejudice in colonial society. Jesuit colleges in Spanish America and Portuguese Brazil were closed to Indians, mestizos, mulattos, and Africans. Only in 1769 did the Spanish monarchy order all prelates in their overseas dominions to establish quotas in seminaries for indigenous students.

The debate over the ordination of non-European clergy in Portuguese colonies mirrored the discussion in the Spanish Americas. A minority, far-minded and outspoken, advocated the training of African and Asian priests; the majority of colonists and clerics adamantly opposed racial equality, with the Portuguese crown showing little will to enforce any policy at all until the mid-eighteenth century reforms of the Marquis de Pombal. Where the indigenous were admitted to the priesthood, they were still excluded from the more elitist religious orders. In São Tomé and Angola, the Portuguese trained a small number of Africans and mulattos, but only for the secular clergy. Likewise, the Jesuit College in Goa, India, one of the largest Jesuit colleges outside of Europe, trained many Indians as auxiliaries to European priests, but excluded them from the more advanced courses in theology with the justification that with superior education, the

Indians would become too proud to accept the poorer benefices and posts reserved for them in a two-tier clerical system. One ostensible reason for this barrier was that proper clerical training was only to be had in Europe. But even when Mattheus de Castro (ca. 1594–1677), a Goa from the Brahmin caste, received ordination and consecration as bishop in Rome in 1625, Portuguese authorities in India still refused to recognize his credentials upon his return.

The situation was somewhat better in Japan and China, the only two countries acknowledged by sixteenth-century missionaries as equal in civilization to Europe. In Japan, Jesuit and Franciscan missionaries recruited catechists mainly among former Buddhist monks. A Jesuit college was established in Funai for the training of Japanese priests, and a small number of Japanese were admitted into the Society of Jesus before the storm of persecution in early seventeenth-century Tokugawa Japan all but destroyed Christianity.

In China, initially the Jesuits relied on "the sons of Macao" in their missionary work. Either Chinese converts or mestizos, sons of Portuguese fathers and Chinese mothers, these men, accepted as brothers (spiritual *adjutores*) into the Society, had the advantage of physical appearance and linguistic ability in missionary work, which were not available to missionaries newly arrived from Europe. Nonetheless, these men were not admitted into the priestly rank. The breakthrough came only after the mid-seventeenth century, when a coalition of Italian, Belgian, and Portuguese Jesuits supported the ordination of mature Chinese scholars in the Society. During the eighteenth century, the two Jesuit missions in China (one operating under Portuguese patronage and the other under the French) both trained and admitted Chinese into priesthood of the Society. Except for a privileged few, trained in Paris or Rome, the others were educated in Macao or in the mission by experienced European missionaries.

The eighteenth century also witnessed the establishment of seminaries for the secular clergy. A college for Chinese priests, under the sponsorship of the Congregation for the Propagation of the Faith, was opened in Naples in 1732 and trained several dozen Chinese secular priests. The Paris Foreign Missions educated their own Chinese students at a seminary in Siam. Together with the small number of Chinese Jesuits, these Chinese secular priests increasingly assumed an ever more important role in pastoral work, especially during the two waves of persecutions in 1748–52 and 1785–86, which made it more dangerous and difficult for European missionaries to enter into and operate in the Qing Empire.

## 7 CONCLUSION

Reluctant to engage in global missions in the early seventeenth century, Protestants were rapidly surpassing Catholic missionaries after 1800. Suffering a reversal of fortunes in the French Revolution, Roman Catholicism, even after its revival in 1814, would never regain its earlier energy in the global missions. The entrance of Protestant missionaries from northern Europe and North America changed dramatically the character of the missionary fields. The emphasis on the Bible and on native liturgies gave a major push to the translation of Christian texts into non-European languages; an achievement that was partly based (and little acknowledged) on the earlier work of the Jesuit missions. In the shift away from sacerdotalism, Protestant global missions injected a new emphasis on Christian education and the formation of a native clergy. This new vision of a non-European ecclesiology would eventually challenge the Eurocentric and sacerdotal visions of global Catholicism as well.

## BIBLIOGRAPHY

Acosta, José de. 1596. *Natural and Moral History of the Indies.* Venice.

Acosta, José de. [1577] 1984–1987. *De procuranda Indorum salute.* Madrid.

Aleni, Giulio. 1637. *Tianzhu jiangsheng chuxiang jingjie (Illustrated Explanation of the Lord of Heaven's Incarnation).* Quanzhou.

Glebe-Møller, Jens. 2006. "The Realm of Grace Presupposes the Realm of Power: The Danish Debate about the Theological Legitimacy of Mission." In *Halle and the Beginning of Protestant Christianity in India,* edited by Andreas Gross, Y. V. Kumaradoss, and Heike Liebau, 89–106. Halle: Franckesche Stiftungen.

Hsia, R. Po-chia. 1995. "Mission und Konfessionalisierung in Übersee." In *Die Katholische Konfessionalisierung. Wissenschaftliches Symposion der Gesellschaft zur Herausgabe des Corpus Catholicorum und des Vereins für Reformationsgeschichte,* edited by Wolfgang Reinhard and Heinz Schilling, 158–165. Münster: Aschendorff.

Hsia, R. Po-chia. 2009. "Religion and Race: Protestant and Catholic Discourses on Jewish Conversions in the Sixteenth and Seventeenth Centuries." In *The Origins of Racism in the West,* edited by Miriam Eliav-Feldon, Benjamin Isaac, and Joseph Ziegler, 265–275. Cambridge: Cambridge University Press.

Hsin, Cha. 2011. "Helan gaige zongjiaohui zai shiqishiji Taiwan de fazhan (The Dutch Reformed Church in seventeenth-century Formosa)." PhD diss., National University of Taiwan.

Kim, Sangkeun. 2004. *Strange Names of God. The Missionary Translation of the Divine Name and the Chinese Responses to Matteo Ricci's Shangti in Late Ming China, 1583–1644.* New York: Peter Lang.

Lai, John T.P. 2010. "Doctrinal Dispute within Interdenominational Missions: The Shanghai Tract Committee in the 1840s." *Journal of the Royal Asiatic Society* 20 (3): 307–317.

Mayer, Johann. 1585. *Historischer Bericht . . . in Beköhrung der gewaltigen landschafft und insel Jappon.* Dillingen.

Nadal, Jeronimo. 1593. *Evangelicae Historiae Imagines.* Antwerp.

Ricard, Robert. 1974. *The Spiritual Conquest of Mexico: An Essay on the Apostolate and the Evangelizing Methods of the Mendicant Orders in New Spain, 1523–1572.* Berkeley: University of California Press.

Verbiest, Ferdinand. 1938. *Correspondance de Ferdinand Verbiest de la Compagnie de Jésus (1623–1688). Directeur de l'Observatoire de Pékin.* Edited by H. Josson and L. Willaert. Brussels: Palais des Académies.

Zupanov, Ines G. 1999. *Disputed Mission. Jesuit Experiments and Brahmanical Knowledge in Seventeenth-Century India.* New Delhi: Oxford University Press.

CHAPTER 2

..................................................................................................................

# SOURCES, METHODS, AND FORMS OF EARLY MODERN THEOLOGY

..................................................................................................................

## ULRICH G. LEINSLE

# 1 SOURCES

..................................................................................................................

WITH all its confessional differences, the theology of the early modern period largely draws, at least outwardly, on the same sources: above all, the Bible and the church fathers. However, significant differences appear in approach, inventory, and the weighting of these sources. In Catholic theology a system of *loci theologici* was developed, which is in itself flexible and in which the weighting of the individual authorities (scripture, fathers, magisterium, philosophical arguments, etc.) is explained (see, e.g., Melchior Cano, Dionysius Petavius).

## 1.1 Holy Scripture

Although Holy Scripture is the common source of all Christian theology, opinions already differed, up until the Council of Trent, on the question of the canon of the Old Testament (Hebrew canon or Septuagint), and the "canon in the canon" which decides the theological worth of the individual books of the Bible (e.g., for Luther, the writings of Paul have the highest worth), and the choice of permitted or prohibited Latin and vernacular translations (Ehses 1916, 22–37). The first steps toward humanistic textual criticism by Lorenzo Valla (ca. 1407–57), Erasmus of Rotterdam (1466–1536), and others, were obscured by confessional disputes. It was not until the end of the seventeenth century that the historical biblical criticism developed in 1680 by the Catholic priest Richard Simon (1638–1712) gained an influence on theology, initially on the Protestant side (*Fragmentenstreit*). The theory of the verbal inspiration of scripture, represented in

Lutheran and Reformed orthodoxy, was superseded by the theory of accommodation (Benin 1993); namely, that in its use of language, scripture conforms itself to the audience's powers of understanding and is then amenable to historical criticism (Johann Salomo Semler [1725–91]) (Hornig 1961). In the neology influenced by Christian Wolff (1679–1754), biblical events were interpreted in the light of general human reason and natural moral law. Of interest within theology, however, is the hermeneutical approach to scripture. Is it, as in Luther's rigorous principle of *sola scriptura* and the scriptural principles of Lutheran orthodoxy the sole, clear, sufficient, and salvific source of theology, to which the development of all theological theories must be traced back? Is it, as the later Protestant orthodoxies contended, an issue of maintaining the scriptural principle while also drawing selectively on trajectories of patristic and medieval theology? Or is it, as assumed by post-Tridentine Catholic theology, just one source of revelation, albeit a preeminent one, which is to be supplemented with other *loci*, above all tradition (Schmidt-Biggemann 2002)? Is it to be interpreted by its own means because it is, thanks to divine inspiration, clear in itself (*scriptura sui ipsius interpres*), or does it need the tools of secular science and philosophy in order to unlock its secrets—if need be also borrowing from a Christianized Kabbala (Schmidt-Biggemann 2012)? What was called for in the seventeenth century was no longer the medieval fourfold sense of scripture, but rather a dogmatic, ontological, or moral interpretation that goes beyond the *sensus historicus*, to be fitted into confessional theology or scholastic Aristotelianism, including the natural sciences.

## 1.2  Sources of the early church

Orientation towards scripture and the initially humanistic-philological approach also determine the evaluation of the church fathers, among whom the exegetes are especially highly esteemed, above all Jerome and Origen (Fürst and Hengstermann 2012). Anglican theology develops a decidedly close connection with the fathers, particularly among the Caroline Divines—including Archbishop William Laud (1573–1645), Jeremy Taylor (1613–67), and Herbert Thorndike (1598–1672)—in their defense against Puritanism with its appeal to scripture alone (Gaßmann 1980, 383–86). As far as the creation of a system of theology and the inclusion of Aristotelian philosophy is concerned, of major significance on the Catholic side is John of Damascus, whose work *De fide orthodoxa* one Jesuit suggested should replace Aquinas's *Summa* as the basis of theological teaching (Lukács 1992, 121–27). Among the Lutherans and the Reformed, handbooks of patristic theology arose (by Abraham Scultetus [1566–1625], Amandus Polanus [1561–1610], and Johann Gerhard [1582–1637]), both for the sake positively of identifying the catholicity of the Reformation, and polemically of refuting Catholic appeals to tradition.

Of inestimable importance for all confessionalities, however, is Augustine. His significance is less as an exegete than in his doctrine of grace, which initially had a strong influence on the Reformers in their *sola gratia* teaching, and then in the post-Tridentine argument about the help of God's grace, and in Jansenism sparked off a controversy that ran through all confessionalities (Leinsle 2010, 232–346). It was not without good reason that Jansen's *Augustinus*, as interpreted by Antoine Arnauld (1612–94), was placed alongside Descartes's *Discours de la méthode* as the new theological methodology (Lettieri 2000; Sokolovski 2012).

In addition to the church fathers, the early councils—in which, after all, the essential definitions regarding the doctrine of God and Christology were formulated—are especially important sources for the early modern theology of all confessionalities, precisely in their ongoing controversies, too. For the polemicizing theologians they are the foundation from which the respective opposing side has deviated and revived ancient heresies, or lapsed into "syncretism." For Irenicists like Georg Calixtus (1586–1656) and for the Caroline Divines, the consensus in questions of faith in the first five centuries constitutes the basis for seeking ways of reaching an understanding, even across the confessionalities (Merkt 2001). The question remains, however, of how to evaluate the further development of dogmas up to the split into confessionalities and the hardening in individual "Confessions" or Concords. Here the emphasis on the *consensus quinquesaecularis* itself in turn had the effect of creating confessionalities in that efforts were made to work out what was specific to the particular confessionality in contradistinction to the others (Merkt 2001, 176). The eighteenth century is characterized by a new turning to the church fathers, starting in France and employing the tools of historical-literary criticism. Groundbreaking here within the Catholic Church was the dispute between the Benedictine Jean Mabillon (1632–1707) and the founder of La Trappe, Armand-Jean Le Bouthilier de Rancé (1626–1700), over the justification and nature of monastic studies (Quinto 2001, 255–71). However, the Gallican theologians, too, appealed to the *auctoritas Patrum* in defending themselves against the claims of the Apostolic See and the Jesuits (Merkt 2001, 206–16).

## 1.3  Medieval authors

The medieval scholastics are rated in different ways in the early modern period. Humanistic theology distances itself from scholastic "barbarism" as much as the Reformation does. On the other hand, the Anglican tradition of a middle way does indeed, for example in Richard Hooker (1554–1600), draw on Thomas Aquinas, above all in questions of practical theology (Shirley 1949). Catholic theology has a different approach to the medieval authors, whose teachings it further develops in the post-Tridentine "Second Scholasticism," or in the unbroken school traditions of the religious orders in disputes with contemporaries. Here the transition from commenting Peter Lombard's *Sentences* to reading Thomas Aquinas's *Summa Theologiae* is significant. The individual orders cultivated their own traditions: for the Dominicans it was a reinvigorated Thomism, for the Discalced Carmelites likewise; for the Franciscans it was Scotism; whereas for the Capuchins, Bonaventure became an important point of reference; for the Augustinian Hermits it was Aegidius Romanus; for the Servites, Henry of Ghent; and for the Carmelites of the Ancient Observance, John Bacon. They then developed their own theology *ad mentem* of the great master and defended his *incon-cussa dogmata* in shields (*clypeus theologiae thomisticae* or *scotisticae*) or in full armor (*panoplia*) against all other opinions (Leinsle 2010, 290–94).

The most influential post-Tridentine Catholic order, the Jesuits, did not possess its own theological tradition dating from the Middle Ages. Consequently they were able to create their theology, programmatically following Thomas Aquinas, by selecting ten-able opinions (*delectus opinionum*), a procedure that led to fierce disputes within the order on specifics (Leinsle 1997). Thus Jesuit theologians like Francisco Suárez, Gabriel Vázquez, and others incorporate numerous Scotist elements alongside Thomistic think-ing, while others like Rodrigo de Arriaga also absorb nominalist ideas, combining them into independent syntheses or critically examining what has, in their view, been pre-maturely synthesized. On the Protestant side, particularly following the encounter of Lutheran and Reformed writers with Bellarmine, there was a significant, albeit eclectic reception and use notably of Thomist and Scotist patterns of argumentation.

## 1.4 Contemporaries

Controversy with contemporaries takes up a great deal of space in the theological discussions of the early modern period. A tradition was created, so it turned out, by the stipulation of the Jesuit Order that in discussing theological opinions the rejected opinion, too, must always be accorded the probability befitting it—that is, it must not be rejected outright, let alone made to appear absurd (Lukács 1974, 500). This is why most large theological works include for every question a more or less comprehen-sive presentation of the opinions of contemporary authors, so that from studying one theological writer you can find out about the views of that writer's contemporaries as well, even though these are not always named but often cited as *quidam*. When hereti-cal authors are mentioned, they are never to be praised with epithets that honor them (Reusch 1961, 523). Such epithets are then quite often blacked out or made unreadable by the censors (Leinsle 2009, 259). It is not only in controversial theology and preach-ing that one has to distance oneself clearly from heretical opinions; this goes for sys-tematic theology, too.

So early modern theology also lived on disputes with contemporaries: on the one hand, with other confessionalities; on the other hand, with the other schools within confessionalities, whose sources are for the most part studied and annotated in detail. Of significance within confessionalities are the conflicts about double truth (Daniel Hofmann [1540–1611]) in Lutheranism (Frank 2003, 44–52), and the battle of the Wittenberg and Leipzig theologians, Abraham Calov (1612–86) and Johann Adam Scherzer (1628–83), against Georg Calixtus's syncretism in Helmstedt (Merkt 2001, 146–53); among the Reformed, the dispute with the Remonstrants and the Covenant theology (*Föderaltheologie*) of Johannes Cocceius (1603–69), and over the inclusion of Cartesianism in theology (by, e.g., Gisbertus Voetius [1589–1676] and Samuel Maresius [1599–1673]) (Goudriaan 1999); among the Anglicans, the resistance to Puritan doctrines and customs and the justification of a "middle way" of the Reformation since John Jewel's *Apologia Ecclesiae Anglicanae* (1562) and Richard Hooker's *Laws of Ecclesiastical Polity* (1593–1662, in 7 books). Contemporaries take on a particular significance in the eighteenth century, when confessional controversial theology and apologetics directed against rationalist and historical criticism change into a defense of Christianity against the claims of modern science, including philosophy (Gaßmann 1980, 390–95).

## 1.5 Philosophy

Philosophy in the form cultivated at the universities is not only a source of early modern theology, but also both a tool and a challenge; for without philosophy there would be no systematic, speculative theology. In the higher-learning curriculum, philosophy had to be taken as a propaedeutic before studying theology, and thus provided the methodological equipment for approaching theological problems. Here there are also striking differences to be noted in the development of the individual confessionalities. The humanists and Reformers were in general not well disposed towards medieval Aristotelianism as a foundation for theology. So as to serve the study of the Bible and the church fathers, scholastic schooling was to be replaced by a program of teaching languages and literature (Leinsle 2010, 243–50). The fewest problems with philosophy were encountered by those institutes of higher learning that lay outside the area of application of the Formula of Concord, and those Reformed Protestants who returned relatively quickly to employing a version of philosophy that was compatible with theology; this covered a spectrum reaching from Aristotle (via Plato) and a Christianized Neoplatonism, down to the encyclopedic projects of followers of Peter Ramus (Schmidt-Biggemann 2001, 392–97). Even the metaphysics so vehemently rejected by Luther found a home within the framework of Reformed theology. Around 1600, however, it also experienced a significant resurgence even in orthodox Lutheranism (Sparn 1976), which led to a clear change in the formulation of theological questions. In Lutheranism, philosophy is nevertheless always seen at a distance from theology, not within its framework: "The heterogeneousness of natural and supernatural epistemological principles did not need and was not meant to be derived from a superordinate unified science" (Sparn 2001, 477). As a discipline separate from theology, philosophy at the Lutheran universities was able to adopt a great deal from Catholic philosophy, especially from the Jesuits, since it was with them that the fiercest disputes had to be waged on questions of theology. Under the influence of Enlightenment philosophy and historical biblical criticism, Lutheran theology in the eighteenth century developed in part into "Neology," which advocated an accommodation in principle between revelation and a pristine religion of reason, and in some cases completely dispensed with the assumption of there being any revelation that went beyond this (see, e.g., Wilhelm Abraham Teller [1734–1804]).

In the Anglican tradition, the engagement with philosophy early on displayed a very high profile, especially among the Cambridge Platonists (Henry Moore [1614–87], Ralph

Cudworth [1617–88], etc.) and the Latitudinarians (Edward Stillingfleet [1635–99], John Wilkins [1614–72], etc.), both of which largely changed positive dogmatic theology into philosophy of religion. The latter was then able in the eighteenth century to grapple in depth with the Enlightenment ideas of reason and tolerance (see, e.g., John Locke [1632–1704], and Matthew Tindal [1657–1733]), in which the questions of the binding foundation of revelation, the fundamental articles of dogma, and the sufficiency of natural reason became dominant (see, e.g., Samuel Clarke [1675–1729]) (Gaßmann 1980, 386–90).

In Catholic theology, a close connection was maintained in everything with Aristotelian philosophy, as it was taught at the universities and other places of higher learning in a two- or three-year course of logic, natural philosophy, and metaphysics. Since philosophy had a merely propaedeutic character in the *facultas artium* and was basically incomplete, many questions relating to philosophy and natural science were not dealt with until the theological course (e.g., within the framework of the dogmatic or exegetical doctrine of creation, of action theory, of the doctrine of the Eucharist) (Knebel 2000, 15–29; Roling 2008; Roling 2010). The result of this was, as a 1649 report criticizes, that among the Jesuits theology was taught philosophically, whereas philosophy was taught theologically (Hellyer 2003; Seifert 1984). A positive engagement with the new philosophies like Cartesianism and corpuscular theories, is not to be found in Catholic theology until the late seventeenth century—first in France, for example in Robert Desgabets (1610–78) (Armogathe 1977), then, under the influence of the Enlightenment (see, e.g., Christian Wolff), and in association with various attempts at academic reform, also in the German-speaking countries (Leinsle 2010, 348–53; Lehner 2011, 204–25).

## 2  Methods and Forms of Presentation

As in the Middle Ages, methods and forms of presentation of theology in the early modern period are so closely connected with one another that they cannot be discussed separately. For the employment of a method gives rise to a particular system of arrangement and this in turn determines the form of presentation. However, method and form of presentation in theology depend crucially on the aim and type of teaching. For post-Tridentine Catholic theology, this results in a significant change in the separation (including the institutional separation) between scholastic and positive theology (Quinto 2001, 238–95). In the Jesuits' *Ratio Studiorum*, scholastic theology is bound to the *doctrina scholastica Divi Thomae*; nevertheless, the *Sentences* of Peter Lombard are still to be read until such time as the order's own textbook should be made compulsory. This was, however, never to come about. According to the *Ratio Studiorum* of 1599, the business of the scholastic theologian is explicitly to comment on Thomas. The method follows the thirteenth-century commentaries on the *Sentences*: explication of the text, stating its *ratio*, and after every article giving, if necessary, a more detailed explanation of the matter through *quaestiones*. On no account was it permitted simply to list various Sentences; instead, Aquinas's teaching was, where appropriate, to be defended (Pachtler 1968, 1:25; Lukács 1986, 380). Positive theology as pastoral training, on the other hand, comprises "Council decisions, works by ecclesiastical authors, parts of Canon Law—excluding procedural law—and writings or topics with a moral content" (Theiner 1970, 106–7). Right up to the academic reforms of the eighteenth century, the historical-positive method of Dionysius Petavius was considered exemplary (Karrer 1970; Leinsle 2000, 76).

## 2.1 *Methodus* as a key to sacred scripture

If theology is, as was the case for the humanists, above all an explanation of sacred scripture, teachers and students must be offered a hermeneutical key with which they can read scripture correctly (including as it served their confessionality). In the Middle Ages, this task was initially fulfilled by reading the *Sentences* (Leinsle 2010, 126–31); from the humanist point of view, a *methodus* or short *summa* of the whole of systematic theology was to be given as well, such as that offered, for example, by Erasmus in his "Introductions" to the New Testament (Winkler 1974), and as was also demanded at the Council of Trent, but then not put into practice (Ehses 1916, 79–123). For such systematic presentations, what first suggests itself is an arrangement according to topics in which the most important elements (*loci*) are presented either according to familiar patterns like the Creed, Decalogue, Our Father, and the sacraments; or in a new systematization (Wiedenhofer 1976). Since, however, in the eyes of the humanists any interpretation of scripture requires the whole *orbis doctrinae* of the secular sciences, including philosophy, this encyclopedic education must be acquired from appropriate encyclopedias in which theology is then also included (e.g., the work of Johann Heinrich Alsted [1588–1638]), or at least from manuals such as those produced by Melanchthon's school.

## 2.2 Catechisms

It is significant that although the drawing up of a humanistic *methodus* was discussed at the Council of Trent—some council fathers even daring to suggest Erasmus's work—(Ehses 1916, 117–19), its place was then taken by the *Catechismus Romanus*. This met the desire to have a handy systematic presentation of doctrine for imparting it to the faithful, such as Luther had produced in the Large and Small Catechisms (1529) and the Reformed had in the Heidelberg Catechism (1563). On the Catholic side, above all the catechisms of Peter Canisius (1521–97) were very influential. Thus, from the point of view of the respective confessionality, the catechism also provides the hermeneutical key for understanding scripture. Interpreting the catechism is also part of the study of theology.

## 2.3 Bible commentaries

Like its medieval forerunner, early modern theology is also a text-based discipline that is expressed first and foremost in the form of commentaries. Here commentaries on individual books of the Bible or on the scriptures as a whole are found considerably more frequently in the Protestant tradition than in the Catholic. But scripture commentaries, too, are mostly also subject to systematic considerations; in Lutheranism, for example, in an orientation toward the doctrine of justification. In their rejection or repression of spiritual interpretations of scripture in favor of literalism there is, under the influence of humanism, broad agreement among confessionalities; this is not, however, the case with the scriptural principles then formulated by Lutheran orthodoxy (perspicuity, sufficiency, efficacy, and so forth) (Rothen 1990). The spiritual interpretation, in part with a new allegorization or updating of biblical situations (e.g., in Bartholomew Holzhauser's [1613–58] commentary on the Apocalypse), is separated from academic exegesis, which in the Catholic sphere is, however, mostly regarded as a merely auxiliary discipline. Thus, for example, the first large-scale post-Tridentine commentary on the New Testament by Alfonso Salmerón, SJ (1515–85), in 16 volumes (1597–1602), works only in the *Historia evangelica* as a literal commentary with occasional systematic excurses, whereas the commentary on the Pauline epistles takes the form of a disputation, consistently setting forth the falsehood and inconsistency of Protestant positions (Leinsle 2003a). Historical-positive exegesis does not come to prominence until the Benedictine Antoine Augustin Calmet (1672–1757).

## 2.4 From *Sentences* to *Summa* commentaries

On the Catholic side, scholastic (i.e., speculative) theology is bound to the methods of *lectio* and *disputatio* as laid down in an exemplary fashion in the Jesuit order. The reading of the *Sentences* continued in the early modern period (mostly in the form of a commentary on *quaestiones*), above all at the non-Thomist schools; the Jesuits, on the other hand, very soon went over to commentating Thomas's *Summa Theologiae*. We distinguish between complete commentaries on the entire *Summa* and the more frequent works on individual parts, especially on the *Secunda* (with *de actibus humanis* of fundamental importance for speculative moral theology) (Mitschelich 1981). In accordance with the order's instructions for the method of teaching, the mostly extensive Jesuit commentaries on the *Summa* are often of a mixed nature. Francisco Suárez (1548–1617), for example, offers a fairly short commentary on Aquinas's individual articles in order then to follow the *quaestio* with an extremely broad discussion of the contentious matters in the form of a *disputatio*. This is divided into several *sectiones*. The commentary and 25 disputations on the first nine questions of Aquinas's *Tertia* make up one whole volume of the Vivès edition (vol. 17).

## 2.5  Cursus theologici

The systematic arrangement of the *Sentences* or *Summa* commentaries led to a system-atic manner of presentation in the *cursus theologici*, which were organized according to treatises. Some of these were the collective works of a local school, and even codify the theology of a school in their title. To be mentioned are, for example, the *Theologia Universitatis Coloniensis* (1638), the Thomist *Theologia scholastia Salisburgensis* (1695) by Fr Paulus Metzger (1637–1702), the *Cursus theologicus S. Galli* (1670), down to the *Theologia Wirceburgensis* (1766–71). What was undoubtedly to become the most impor-tant course of a religious community was the *Cursus theologicus Salmanticensis* of the Discalced Carmelites from San Elia in Salamanca, which took almost a hundred years to complete. In the Paris edition of 1879/80 alone it comprises twenty volumes. The decision to print it (without naming its authors) was made in 1616/17; the first volume appeared in 1631; the last volume of the course, which like Thomas's *Summa* remained incomplete, was published in 1712 (Merl 1947). In the process of publication there was a tendency for the twenty-four individual treatises to take on a separate existence. Furthermore, in moral and sacramental theology the twin track of *theologia scholastica* and *theologia positiva* becomes noticeable. Fr Johannes ab Annuntiatione asks himself whether it still makes any sense at all to dispute on the sacraments in the scholastic man-ner, since they are in any case dealt with in the *Cursus moralis* in the way necessary for the practical formation of the confreres (Merl 1947, 49).

In the second half of the eighteenth century, a change came about in the systemati-zation and method of the theological course. The treatises on fundamental theology dealing with the *demonstratio religiosa, christiana* and *catholica* in the debate with con-temporary philosophy and the "heresies" were now given markedly greater prominence (see, e.g., Benedict Stattler [1728–97]) compared to the doctrines of dogmatics, which were generally presented in a scholastic or positive manner. At the same time, the *his-toria litteraria* was widely included for the individual treatises (e.g., Stephan Wiest, *Institutiones theologicae* 1782–89) and a precise distinction was made between dogmatic teachings and *opiniones privatae* (including the scholastic *quaestiones*) (Leinsle 2012, 663–70).

## 2.6  Disputation

While the major *cursus* are intended primarily for the hand of teachers, alongside them we find a large number of smaller compendia (often in octavo) and individual dogmatic treatises that are not infrequently the immediate object of disputations. If a professor's individual treatises were defended several times a year or in several years, a more or less complete *cursus* could develop from this as well (examples at Leinsle 2010, 297). Often a treatise was also given to several respondents or defendants, who had to publish it, each with a different title page, at the expense of the person to whom it was dedicated. One requirement for obtaining a licentiate in theology was a disputation *ex universa theolo-gia*, the theses selected often providing an overview of the professor's complete teaching. On the other hand, in sacramental theology the influence of a positive-theological treat-ment is often noticeable: the *quaestiones* style is largely abandoned and instead a positive presentation of the theological doctrine is given. Particularly in the case of the theses *ex universa theologia* for the licentiate, a special literary form developed in the Catholic sphere: the graphically designed thesis page (Appuhn-Radtke 1988). The theological content of the theses, which can be omitted completely in the presentation copy, was frequently reduced to a list of propositions which were printed, often in tiny typeface, in a box or at the bottom of the page. It was not until the beginning of the Enlightenment that the disparity between the baroque packaging and the meager content of the thesis pages troubled anyone, and there was a return to the lengthier thesis or dissertation with a changed method of disputation and an independent role for the respondents (Marti 2010; Leinsle 2012).

## 2.7  Positive theology

The course of positive theology, often abbreviated as *theologia moralis*, dispenses with the scholastic disputation and instead teaches the *casus conscientiae*. The students were therefore referred to as *casistae* (also *casuistae*) or *positivistae*. Whereas in the *cursus maior* moral theology is developed speculatively according to the *Secunda pars* of Thomas Aquinas's *Summa*, the practical course is concerned with solving cases of conscience on the basis of general principles and their application to the individual case. Here, too, in addition to the lectures, practical exercises are offered in solving often difficult hypothetical "cases." With future pastoral work in mind, the subjects studied are: sacraments; ecclesiastical punishments; the duties of the different estates; and the Decalogue, with contracts also having to be treated under the seventh com-mandment. Expressly forbidden is the *apparatus scholasticus*, i.e., the usual method of disputation with its citing, if possible, of all opinions and arguments. Moral the-ology works with *dubitationes* and *conclusiones* are used instead. Authorities are to be employed sparingly; general laws or rules are to be exemplified with a number of individual cases (about three). Casuistic conferences as practical exercises are to be clearly distinguished from scholastic disputations. The "proof" of one's own solution takes place according to the principle of probability; even the rejected *sententia* is to be accorded a certain probability depending on the reasons and authorities adduced (Pachtler 1968, 2:322–29).

As a result of excluding the speculative parts of theology, all that remains is a the-ory of principles of human action as the basis for the practical treatment of the virtues, commandments, sins, sacraments, and ecclesiastical punishments. Whereas the great textbooks of Enrique Henriquez (*Summa theologiae moralis* 1591) down to Paul Layman (*Theologia moralis* 1625) or the idiosyncratic *Theologia moralis* of the Cistercian Juan Caramuel Lobkowitz (1606–82) (Armogathe 2008) do indeed display some theological depth, theological thought withers to a commandment morality and a casuistry for confessors in individual *dubia* which can be used as a pastoral manual. One example of this is the *Medulla theologiae moralis* of Hermann Busenbaum, SJ (1600–68), which had run to more than 200 editions by 1776. Yet it was precisely this work that became the standard equipment of the pastoral clergy, who were often educated exclusively in moral theology and who then also had practical pastoral guides like Johannes Opstraet's *Pastor bonus* (1689) at their disposal (Schuchart 1972); until, as a result of the 1777 reform of theological studies in the Hapsburg territories, pastoral theology was for the first time established at the university as a subject in its own right. Not to be underestimated as far as formation in the religious orders was concerned is the influence of the *Theologia regularis* by Juan Caramuel Lobkowitz (1646), which took the form of commentaries on the rules of the orders (Leinsle 2008).

Above all, in the courses of study of religious orders attempts were also made to combine the two types of theology so as to impart both the necessary theoretical knowledge and the skills in moral theology and canon law required for practical pastoral work (Leinsle 2000, 97). Thus, for example, Eusebius Amort in his *Theologia eclectica moralis et scholastica* (1752) clearly builds on the humanistic way of teaching theology with reference to the church fathers (Leinsle 2010, 351–53). Methodologically, Amort commits himself to a refined scholastic method, contending that its advantage lies in precise terminology and brevity of presentation. It can inculcate the individual controversies clearly and distinctly by means of definition, division, axioms, postulates, conclusions, and proofs, and offers the reader the greatest possible assurance since it draws the individual conclusions directly from a small number of premises. Thus the individual questions then also have a very clear structure: *notanda* (presuppositions)—*dico* (conclusion)—*probatur* (proof through authority and reason)—*solvuntur objectiones* (objections and their solution).

## 2.8 Protestant systematic theology

Among the Protestants in so-called orthodoxy, a new systematic theology develops whose methods and forms of presentation nevertheless remain more clearly indebted to the humanistic heritage than those of the Catholics. The Formula of Concord and the more recent creedal documents of the Reformed confessionalities already display strong systematic tendencies. Nonetheless, they still require a systematic theological interpretation. Unlike Catholic scholasticism, Protestant orthodoxy cannot fall back on a well-established method but has to derive one—with a greater or lesser degree of reflection—from contemporary philosophizing, in which treatises *De methodo* are highly popular (Leinsle 2010, 299–300). The following lend themselves to this:

1. The relatively simple topics of Philipp Melanchthon (1497–1560) and his school, which restricted their understanding of philosophy to logic, ethics, and physics, and were thus easily assimilated into theology. This resulted in

collections of *loci* or *propositiones* (axiomatics) arranged systematically according to Melanchthon's model.

2. The dialectic of Peter Ramus (1515–72), which was adopted particularly by the Reformed. Originally rigorously antimetaphysical, in the 1572 edition Ramus places methodology at the center and develops a universal method of definition and arrangement based on conceptual logic. This often results in tabular representations of theology or of the sciences (e.g., Johann Heinrich Alsted, Johannes Scharff [1595–1660]). The reception of Ramism in the Melanchthon school led to the development of the Philippo-Ramism that was typical of the German schools before 1600, then combined with Aristotelian elements in the *methodus definitiva* of a Johannes Hülsemann (1602–61) and Johann Adam Scherzer.

3. The Aristotelian methodology and theory of science in the *Posterior Analytics*, revived most notably by Paduan Aristotelianism. Unlike the Ramist disposition, the *methodus* here is essentially deduction, argumentation, and syllogistic proof according to the rules of the *Posterior Analytics*. All theoretical sciences are bound to the synthetic-deductive method, all practical ones to the analytical (goal—means of attaining it).

The methodological and metaphysical thinking of orthodoxy is expressed in a theology that was forced by its abandonment of medieval scholasticism and by a new start as Reformers to discover its own systematic form of presentation. "*Methodus*," "*Syntagma*," or "*Systema*" are therefore frequently chosen as titles for the textbook presentation of theology in the compendia designed for students (sometimes with practical and edifying applications). For this reason—and thanks also to the Philippist or Ramist logic that had prevailed for over half a century instead of metaphysics—an awareness of methodology has an incomparably greater effect in theology, too, among the Protestants than it does in the *cursus* and the commentaries of Catholic scholasticism. The choice of method, however, depends on whether the theology is of a theoretical or practical nature. Across the confessional boundaries between Lutherans and Reformed, both synthetic and analytical ways of presentation can be observed, often also hybrid forms corresponding to the theoretical and practical nature of theology.

Methodological reflection is already displayed in the equally influential and monumental principal work of the father of Lutheran orthodoxy, Johann Gerhard, in his *Loci theologici* (1610–25). Gerhard takes his method from humanistic Aristotelianism. It combines philology and synthetic procedure with a strongly topical element, in that a nominal definition is first sought in the *Onomatologia* while the real definition is not given until the conclusion of the whole discussion of the *locus*, the *Pragmatologia*. The onomatology is treated stereotypically according to etymology, homonyms, and synonyms; the pragmatology is ordered according to patterns of topical questions: *an sit, quid sit, principia, causae, opposita*. Subdivisions are often given for teaching purposes; in between, however, a syllogistic treatment is also to be found, above all when arguing against opponents and heretics (Leinsle 2010, 302–6; Wallmann 1961).

Systematic thinking also characterizes the trained mathematician, philosopher, and theologian Abraham Calov in Wittenberg (Leinsle 2010, 306–11). The topical structure of the *Loci* is now no longer adequate, so a system of *loci* is to be devised instead. This becomes clear in the *Theologia positiva* (1682), which he created for his son Abraham. In the Protestant tradition "*theologia positiva*" denotes the simple presentation of theology in the form of theses with short proofs, dispensing with questions and controversies. It serves, completely in accordance with the humanistic *methodus*, above all as an Ariadne's thread to guide its user through the labyrinth of scriptural exegesis. Here, for example, an outline of the *Systema locorum theologicorum* (1655) is offered in 1135 paragraphs on 610 octavo pages. In principle, the structure follows the analytical method obligatory for practical sciences: the goal and the means of attaining it. In fact, though, this schema is mixed with an epistemological model that desires to explain the whole structure of theology from its purpose (goal—subject—means). After the prolegomena on theology, religion, revelation, sacred scripture, and the articles of faith, the goal of theology is introduced: God and the blessed enjoyment of God (the latter is admittedly not treated, whereas creation and providence are). The subject of theology is divided into indirect subject (angels) and direct subject (mankind), so that now *angelognosia* and *anthropologia* (including sin, works, Law, and Gospel) follow. Part 3 then deals with the causes and means of salvation—namely, the divine economy (Christology, soteriology), the church (*ecclesiometria*), the means of salvation on God's side (word and sacrament) and man's (*soteropoiia*), divine legislation (*divina nomosthesia* in the Decalogue), and eschatology. This structure shows clearly the intention to proceed reflectively and systematically—which, however, occasionally stumbles against the theological material (Leinsle 2010, 309–11). The *Theologia positiva* also shows the tendency of Protestant theology towards smaller and smaller mnemonically structured textbooks to be used for memorization and reference in school; for example, Johann Adam Scherzer's *Brevilicus theologicus* (1675), in which the whole of theology is summarized according to the *modus definitiva* in one sentence extending over 11 pages (Leinsle 2010, 312–15). In the eighteenth century these methods are largely superseded by the mathematically oriented "demonstrative-deductive" method of proof of Christian Wolff and his school.

In the English-speaking world, which took leave of Latin at an early date, interest is focused less on systematic theology than on the practical implementation of the Reformation and securing it through the state, combined with apologetic debate with the other confessionalities. Hence it is significant that the principal work of Anglican theology by Richard Hooker is titled *The Laws of Ecclesiastical Polity*. In the *Laws* Hooker offers a system of governance (polity) not only for the church, but also a theologically based system of ordering the whole of ecclesiastical and public life in a hierarchy of legal systems of divine and human law, with reason accorded an important role as insight into natural and human law (Gaßmann 1980, 379–83). This refutes the rigorous scriptural principle of the Puritans. In addition, as a result of the attachment to the church fathers, there is an increase in the value accorded to theological tradition and natural reason as elements of theological method and parts of the one "theological instrument" (McAdoo 1965, V).

## 2.9 Controversial theology

For disputes with other confessionalities, early modern theology develops a special discipline: controversial theology (*theologia polemica*); which, on the Catholic side, is soon
institutionally established in the universities, above all those run by the Jesuits, by being
given its own chairs. Controversial theology understands itself as a dispute with the heretics on those points of doctrine that they attack. Here, too, the method is no longer the
scholastic commentary but rather the positive presentation of the true doctrine and the
apologetic refutation of false doctrines, among the Jesuits often combined with an explanation of the catechism. For the controversial disputation, the individual confessionalities develop their own methods and strategies (Paintner 2012). Quite frequently the
professor of sacred scripture or a professor of scholastic theology will share supervision
of the debates (Mancia 1985). The following became standard works of Catholic controversial theology: Johannes Eck's *Enchiridion locorum communium adversus Lutherum
et alios hostes ecclesiae* (1525) (Minnich 1988), Robert Bellarmine's *Disputationes de controversiis* (1586–93) (Dietrich 1999, 62–70) and Martin Becanus's *Manuale controversiarum huius temporis* (1625).

On the Protestant side, the *theologia polemica* became a weapon not just against the
Catholics but also against any teachings that deviated from the confession in question. In
the first stages of confessional polemics, Martin Chemnitz's *Examen Concilii Tridentini*
(1565–73) served primarily the first purpose, and his 1578 *De Duabus Naturis in Christo*
the second, becoming the basis for the eighth article of the Formula of Concord (see
ch. 19 in this volume). This approach was then developed on a large scale by, above all,
Abraham Calov and Johann Adam Scherzer in their polemical works. To be mentioned
in particular are Scherzer's *Bibliotheca Pontificia* (1677), *Collegium Anti-Socinianum*
(1672), *Anti-Bellarminus* (1681), and *Disputationes Anti-Calvinianae* (1681). On the other
hand, in his *Encyclopaedia*, the influence of which reaches as far as Harvard College, the
Reformed theologian Johann Heinrich Alsted stresses that controversial theology ought
rightly to be termed *theologica irenica*, as its aim is church unity. He gives independent
methods for pursuing this goal, which was admittedly more hindered than attained
by controversial theology, and holds fast to the goal of a consensus being achievable at
least on fundamentals. The guiding principles (*canones*) necessary for this are those of
faith (*sola scriptura canonica*), love (edification of the weak, equity in judgment), and
judiciousness (discretion in social intercourse and in teaching). For controversial theology, Alsted proposes a weaving together of historical, biblical, comparative (*parallela*),
catechetical, and systematic methodology (a reduction to the *loci communes*). The easi-
est way is to list the deviant doctrines synoptically, adding the reasons to every page
and then prescribing the appropriate antidote in each case; this results in the following
sequence: *Thesis, Antithesis, Confirmatio theseos, Confirmatio antitheseos, & Antidorum*
(Alsted 1992, 5:1639–60; Clouse 1963; Klein and Kramer 1988).

The Anglican tradition of controversial theology also dates back to the mid-
sixteenth century (see, e.g., John Jewel [1522–71]) and was for decades to remain a

main field of activity for theologians in the later disputes with the Puritans on the one hand and the Deists, who denied positive revelation, and Enlightenment philosophers on the other. The preferred literary format here is the tract or dialogue in the vernacular. The formulation of Reformed content in the Articles of Religion (the Forty-Two Articles of 1554; the Thirty-Nine Articles of 1563) gave rise to the question of "fundamental articles" common to all confessionalities, which proved insoluble due to what was in effect a failure to derive them from scripture alone (Puritans) or from scripture and the consensus of the church fathers (Caroline Divines) (Gaßmann 1980, 390–95).

## BIBLIOGRAPHY

Alsted, Johann Heinrich. 1992. *Encyclopaedia (1630)*. Stuttgart-Bad Cannstatt: Frommann–Holzboog.

Appuhn-Radtke, Sibylle. 1988. *Das Thesenblatt im Hochbarock: Studien zu einer graphischen Gattung am Beispiel der Werke Bartholomäus Kilians*. Weißenhorn: Konrad.

Armogathe, Jean Robert. 2008. "Caramuel, a Cistercian Casuist." In *Juan Caramuel Lobkowitz: The Last Scholastic Polymath*, edited by Petr Dvořák and Jacob Schmutz, 117–127. Prague: Filosofia.

Armogathe, Jean Robert. 1977. *Theologia Cartesiana: L'explication physique de l'Eucharistie chez Descartes et dom Desgabets*. Archives internationales d'histoire des idées 84. La Haye: Nijhoff.

Benin, Stephen D. 1993. *The Footprints of God: Divine Accommodation in Jewish and Christian Thought*. Albany, NY: State University of New York Press.

Clouse, Robert Gordon. 1963. *The Influence of John Henry Alsted on English Millenarian Thought in the Seventeenth Century*. Ann Arbor, MI: UMI Dissertation Services.

Dietrich, Thomas. 1999. *Die Theologie der Kirche bei Robert Bellarmin (1542–1621): Systematische Voraussetzungen des Kontroverstheologen*. Konfessionskundliche und kontroverstheologische Studien, 69. Paderborn: Bonifatius-Verlag.

Ehses, Stephan, ed. 1916. *Concilium Tridentinum: Diariorum, Actorum, Epistularum, Tractatuum nova collectio*. Vol. 5. Freiburg im Breisgau: Herder.

Frank, Günther. 2003. *Die Vernunft des Gottesgedankens: Religionsphilosophische Studien zur frühen Neuzeit*. Stuttgart-Bad Cannstatt: Frommann–Holzboog.

Fürst, Alfons and Hengstermann, Christian, eds. 2012. *Autonomie und Menschenwürde: Origenes in der Philosophie der Neuzeit* (Münster: Aschendorff).

Ganoczy, Alexandre, and Stefan Scheld. 1983. *Die Hermeneutik Calvins: Geistesgeschichtliche Voraussetzungen und Grundzüge*. Wiesbaden: Steiner.

Gaßmann, Günther. 1980. "Die Lehrentwicklung im Anglikanismus: Von Heinrich VIII. bis zu William Temple." In *Handbuch der Dogmen- und Theologiegeschichte*, edited by Carl Andresen, vol. 2, 353–409. Göttingen: Vandenhoeck & Ruprecht.

Goudriaan, Aza. 1999. *Philosophische Gotteserkenntnis bei Suárez und Descartes im Zusammenhang mit der niederländischen reformierten Theologie und Philosophie des 17. Jahrhunderts*. Brill's Studies in Intellectual History 98. Leiden: Brill.

Hellyer, Marcus. 2003. "The Construction of the Ordinatio pro studiis superioribus of 1651." *Archivum Historicum Societatis Iesu*, 72: 3–43.

Hornig, Gottfried. 1961. *Die Anfänge der historisch-kritischen Theologie: Johann Salomo Semlers Schriftverständnis und seine Stellung zu Luther*. Göttingen: Vandenhoeck & Ruprecht.

Karrer, Leo. 1970. *Die historisch-positive Methode des Theologen Dionysius Petavius*. Munich: Max Hueber.

Klein, Jürgen and Johannes Kramer, eds. 1988. *J. H. Alsted, Herborns calvinistische Theologie und Wissenschaft im Spiegel der englischen Kulturreform des frühen 17. Jahrhunderts: Studien zu englisch-deutschen Geistesbeziehungen in der frühen Neuzeit*. Aspekte der englischen Geistes- und Kulturgeschichte 16. Frankfurt am Main: Lang.

Knebel, Sven K. 2000. *Wille, Würfel und Wahrscheinlichkeit: Das System der moralischen Notwendigkeit in der Jesuitenscholastik, 1550–1700*. Paradeigmata 21. Hamburg: Meiner.

Lehner, Ulrich L. 2011. *Enlightened Monks: The German Benedictines, 1740–1803*. Oxford: Oxford University Press.

Leinsle, Ulrich Gottfried. 2003a. "Commentarii in evangelicam Historiam et in Acta Apostolorum. Disputationes in Epistulas Divi Pauli, Alfonso Salmerón SJ." In *Lexikon der theologischen Werke*, edited by Michael Eckert, 112–113. Stuttgart: Kröner.

Leinsle, Ulrich Gottfried. 1997. "Delectus opinionum: Traditionsbildung durch Auswahl in der frühen Jesuitentheologie." In *Im Spannungsfeld von Tradition und Innovation: Festschrift für Joseph Kardinal Ratzinger*, edited by Georg Schmuttermayer, 159–175. Regensburg: Pustet.

Leinsle, Ulrich Gottfried. 2012. "Impune disceptant theologi: Der Wandel der Disputation in der Spätzeit des Hausstudiums der Prämonstratenserabtei Speinshart." In *Dichtung–Gelehrsamkeit–Disputationskultur: Festschrift für Hanspeter Marti zum 65. Geburtstag*, edited by Reimund Szduj et al., 650–671. Vienna: Böhlau.

Leinsle, Ulrich Gottfried. 2010. *Introduction to Scholastic Theology*. Translated by Michael J. Müller. Washington, DC: The Catholic University of America Press.

Leinsle, Ulrich Gottfried. 2003b. "Medulla theologiae moralis, Hermann Busenbaum SJ." In *Lexikon der theologischen Werke*, edited by Michael Eckert, 494. Stuttgart: Kröner.

Leinsle, Ulrich Gottfried. 2008. "Probabilismus im Kloster: Caramuels Theologia regularis." In *Juan Caramuel Lobkowitz: The Last Scholastic Polymath*, edited by Petr Dvořák and Jacob Schmutz, 99–116. Prague: Filosofia.

Leinsle, Ulrich Gottfried. 2000. *Studium im Kloster: Das philosophisch-theologische Hausstudium des Stiftes Schlägl, 1633–1783*. Bibliotheca Analectorum Praemonstratensium 20. Averbode: Praemonstratensia.

Leinsle, Ulrich Gottfried. 2009. "Wie treibt man Cardano mit Scaliger aus? Die (Nicht-) Rezeption Cardanos an der Jesuitenuniversität Dillingen." In *Spätrenaissance-Philosophie in Deutschland, 1570–1650: Entwürfe zwischen Humanismus und Konfessionalisierung, okkulten Traditionen und Schulmetaphysik*, edited by Martin Mulsow, 253–277. Tübingen: Max Niemeyer Verlag.

Lettieri, Gaetano. 2000. *Metodo della grazia*. Rome: EDB.

Lukács, László, ed. 1974. *Monumenta Paedagogica Societatis Iesu*. 2, Monumenta Historica Societatis Iesu 107. Rome: Institutum Historicum Societatis Iesu.

Lukács, László, ed. 1986. *Monumenta Paedagogica Societatis Iesu*. 5, Monumenta Historica Societatis Iesu 129. Rome: Institutum Historicum Societatis Iesu.

Lukács, László, ed. 1992. *Monumenta Paedagogica Societatis Iesu*. 6, Monumenta Historica Societatis Iesu 140. Rome: Institutum Historicum Societatis Iesu.

Mancia, Anita. 1985. "La controversia con i protestanti e i programmi degli studi teologici nella Compagnia di Gesù, 1547–1599." *Archivum Historicum Societatis Iesu*, 54: 3–43; 209–266.

Marti, Hanspeter. 2010. "Disputation und Dissertation: Kontinuität und Wandel im 18. Jahrhundert." In *Disputatio 1200–1800: Form, Funktion und Wirkung eines Leitmediums universitärer Wissenskultur*, edited by Marion Gindhart and Ursula Kundert, 63–85. Berlin: de Gruyter.

McAdoo, Henry R. 1965. *The Spirit of Anglicanism: A Survey of Anglican Theological Method in the Seventeenth Century*. London: Black.

Merkt, Andreas. 2001. *Das patristische Prinzip: Eine Studie zur theologischen Bedeutung der Kirchenväter*. Suplements to Vigiliae Christianae 58. Leiden: Brill.

Merl, Otho. 1947. *Theologia Salmanticensis: Untersuchung über Entstehung, Lehrrichtung und Quellen des theologischen Kurses der spanischen Karmeliten*. Regensburg: Pustet.

Minnich, Nelson H. 1988. "On the Origins of Eck's Enchiridion." In *Johannes Eck (1486–1543) im Streit der Jahrhunderte*, edited by Erwin Iserloh, 37–73. Reformationsgeschichtliche Studien und Texte 127. Münster: Aschendorff.

Mitschelich, Anton. 1981. *Kommentatoren zur Summa Theologiae des hl. Thomas von Aquin*. Hildesheim–New York: Georg Olms.

Pachtler, Georg Michael. 1968. *Ratio Studiorum et Institutiones Scholasticae Societatis Jesu per Germaniam olim vigentes*. 4 vols. Osnabrück: Biblio-Verlag.

Paintner, Ursula. 2012. "Zum Nutzen der akademischen Jugend. Zwei antijesuitische Gymnasialdisputationen von Johann Matthäus Meyfart." In *Dichtung–Gelehrsamkeit–Disputationskultur: Festschrift für Hanspeter Marti zum 65. Geburtstag*, edited by Reimund Szduj et al., 430–447. Vienna: Böhlau.

Quinto, Riccardo. 2001. *Scholastica: Storia di un concetto*. Subidia Mediaevalia Patavina 2. Padua: Il Poligrafo.

Reusch, Franz Heinrich, ed. 1961. *Die Indices librorum prohibitorum des sechzehnten Jahrhunderts*. Nieuwkoop: de Graaf.

Roling, Bernd. 2010. *Drachen und Sirenen. Die Rationalisierung und Abwicklung der Mythologie an den europäischen Universitäten*. Mittellateinische Studien und Texte 42. Leiden: Brill.

Roling, Bernd. 2008. *Locutio angelica. Die Diskussion der Engelsprache als Antizipation einer Sprechakttheorie in Mittelalter und Früher Neuzeit*. Studien und Texte zur Geistesgeschichte des Mittelalters 97. Leiden: Brill.

Rothen, Bernhard. 1990. *Die Klarheit der Schrift*. Göttingen: Vandenhoeck & Ruprecht.

Schmidt-Biggemann, Wilhelm. 2002. "Exegese und Tradition. Bellarmins biblische Hermeneutik." In *Bene scripsisti ... Filosofie od středověku k novověku. Sborník k sedmdesátinám Stanislava Sousedíka*, edited by Jiří et al., 109–140. Prague: Filosofia.

Schmidt-Biggemann, Wilhelm. 2012. *Geschichte der christlichen Kabbala*. Clavis Pansophiae 10/1. Stuttgart-Bad Cannstadt: Frommann–Holzboog.

Schmidt-Biggemann, Wilhelm. 2001. "Die Schulphilosophie in den reformierten Territorien." In *Das Heilige Römische Reich deutscher Nation, Nord- und Mitteleuropa*. Vol. 4 of *Die Philosophie des 17. Jahrhunderts*, edited by Helmut Holzhey and Wilhelm Schmidt-Biggemann, 393–474. Basel: Schwabe.

Schuchart, Alfred. 1972. *Der "Pastor bonus" des Johannes Opstraet. Zur Geschichte eines pastoraltheologischen Werkes aus der Geisteswelt des Jansenismus*. Trierer theologische Studien 26. Trier: Paulinus-Verlag.

Seifert, Arno. 1984. "Der jesuitische Bildungskanon im Lichte der zeitgenössischen Kritik." *Zeitschrift für bayerische Landesgeschichte*, 47: 43–75.

Shirley, Frederick J. 1949. *Richard Hooker and Contemporary Political Ideas* London: SPCK.

Sokolovski, Richard Augustin. 2012. *Matrix omnium conclusionum: Den "Augustinus" des Jansenius lessen*. Fribourg: Reinhardt Verlag.

Sparn, Walter. 2001. "Die Schulphilosophie in den lutherischen Territorien," In *Das Heilige Römische Reich deutscher Nation, Nord- und Mitteleuropa*. Vol. 4 of *Die Philosophie des 17. Jahrhunderts*, edited by Helmut Holzhey and Wilhelm Schmidt-Biggemann, 475–587. Basel: Schwabe.

Sparn, Walter. 1976. *Wiederkehr der Metaphysik: Die ontologische Frage in der lutherischen Metaphysik des frühen 17. Jahrhunderts*. Calwer Theologische Monographien 4. Stuttgart: Calwer Verlag.

Theiner, Johannes. 1970. *Die Entwicklung der Moraltheologie zur eigenständigen Disziplin*. Studien zur Geschichte der katholischen Moraltheologie 17. Regensburg: Pustet.

Wallmann, Johannes. 1961. *Der Theologiebegriff bei Johann Gerhard und Georg Calixt*. Beiträge zur Historischen Theologie 30. Tübingen: Mohr.

Wiedenhofer, Stephan. 1976. *Formalstrukturen humanistischer und reformatorischer Theologie bei Philipp Melanchthon*. Regensburger Studien zur Theologie 2. Bern: Lang.

Winkler, Gerhard. 1974. *Erasmus von Rotterdam und die Einleitungsschriften zum Neuen Testament: Formale Strukturen und theologischer Sinn*. Reformationsgeschichtliche und Texte 108. Münster: Aschendorff.

CHAPTER 3

....................................................................................................

# THEOLOGY AND THE DEVELOPMENT OF THE EUROPEAN CONFESSIONAL STATE

....................................................................................................

## PAUL SHORE

THE story of the role of theology in the formation of confessional states is in part a story of the subjective perceptions of men (and a few women) who held vast political power: how they understood the function of formal religious thinking during the period of the creation of modern European states. It is also the story of social forces driven by religious experience, emotion, and reason, which once unleashed often became more powerful than many of the temporal or ecclesiastical rulers who sought to control them. In addition, the role of confessional identities that extended across the borders of these states is an important aspect of this story. The evolution of the state in the sixteenth and seventeenth centuries, and the development of national languages both influenced the dissemination of theological concepts, while these concepts themselves became reference points in the shaping of such states.

## 1 THEORETICAL MODELS

....................................................................................................

The term *confessionalization* was first applied by Heinz Schilling and Wolfgang Reinhard, in a series of essays that started to appear in the 1980s, to processes during the sixteenth and seventeenth centuries in several continental European settings in which Catholic, Lutheran, and Calvinist "confesssions" became churches supported by and at times integrated into the civil governments of states. The term and the model have since been applied, with modifications, to a wide range of European and even extra-European polities (Schilling 1981; Reinhard 1981). Our understanding of the role of theology in the creation of confessional states has therefore been shaped by the documentation left behind by both of these collections of events, and especially by the way this evidence has been employed to interpret religious experience in the early modern period. The reappraisal of documentation prompted by this and other new approaches eventually impacted historiography with a challenge to the definition of confessionalization itself. Critics now point out that the initial focus on the nation state neglected other political outcomes and the complexities of relations between civil and ecclesiastical authorities. Regina Pörtner suggests that the debates regarding the nature of confessionalization have resulted in loss of conceptual precession (Pörtner 2001). Retention of the word "confession," which in its original German context was usually restricted to European Catholicism, Lutheranism, and Calvinism, creates a challenge when considering the development of states such as Anglican or even Cromwellian England or of more ephemeral polities, such as those founded by Anabaptists.

Phenomenological questions persist. The claim that Lutheran baptism, for example, was "a 'sociological' sacrament that identified the newly baptized person as a member of the local political community" may hinge on the contemporaneous understanding of "local" and also on our willingness to accept the records of literate and institutionally vested church employees as representative of what the broader community was experiencing. Robert Scribner's scholarship points to the possibility that what people were taught they should believe was not necessarily always what they actually believed (Scribner 1994). Scribner's solution to this problem, to study religious practices and ways of thought, is a step forward but not a complete solution: the former are no sure guide to the latter. Authorities coerced and subjects outwardly obeyed, but how the latter understood the theological implications of their modified behavior, and how this behavior came to shape belief, is not always easily discerned. Moreover, the very fact that the concept of confessionalization has called attention to how closely linked the religious and the secular were during this period, reminds us how different the a priori assumptions regarding the state and the functions of recordkeeping were during this period.

The confessionalization model is not the only one that may be applied to the European state emerging in the early modern period. A polarity of "magisterial" and "radical" models of confessional evolution has been proposed by George Williams (Williams 1995). In both of these models, the tools of theology were employed both to articulate positions and to draw upon the emotions of laypersons and clergy alike to build commitment to social organizations. The magisterial reformers received support from or collaborated with temporal authorities, with the result that their theological vocabulary quickly achieved high visibility and acceptance, sometimes entering the legal documents of the realm. The radical reformers often became proscribed outcasts, but their theology still influenced the shaping of the emerging state. In Bohemia, crypto-Protestants occupied the attention of the civil and ecclesiastical authorities for more than a century following the battle of White Mountain, arguably delaying the development of state-supported general education and adding to a climate in which great efforts were applied to the eradication of heresy. Occasionally, radical reformers would gain access to political power at critical moments: two Fifth Monarchy Men, Thomas Harrison (1606–60) and John Carew (1622–60), were commissioners at the trial of Charles I, thus becoming arguably more "magisterial" than radical. More often the influence of radicals on the new nation state was indirect and sometimes through a literary legacy, as when Diggers such as Gerrard Winstanley (ca. 1609–77) formulated a communist creed of the earth as a "common treasury" which was cited by communitarian and pantheistic movements in later centuries (Sutherland 1990).

Within the various early modern polities affected by the power of theology in civil life were several common threads. These include the effects of increased literacy and engagement with religious texts, and a backdrop of more external factors such as poor harvests (as well as the causes for these crises that were rooted in climate change, war, etc.), which exacerbated a mood of dissatisfaction, fear, and anxiety and in turn helped shape an understanding of theology. In addition, regional variations shaped by geography, climate, urbanization, population density, and dynastic history each played important roles, with the result that the process of confessionalization and its relation to the development of the modern European state is likely to be debated by historians for some time. The unquestioned assumption of the day that civil government would take a decisive part in the religious life of the individual is another important commonality in the relationship between theology and these emerging nation states. The familiarity among laypersons with stories from the Old Testament that detailed relations between prophets and kings, and the capacity of these laypersons to identify with such characters, serve as yet another recurring link through which ideas about the relations between theology and the state were conveyed to the masses. Lastly, art, literature, and music not only reflected the drive towards confessionalization but provided the vocabulary, imagery, and emotional states through which this process was understood by ruler and subject alike.

## 2  THEOLOGY, STATES, AND REGIONS

An overview of some of the states and regions affected by these events can shed light on the complex relationship of theology to nation building.

The final expulsion of the Moors from the Iberian Peninsula in 1492 presented King Ferdinand (1452–1516) and Queen Isabella (1451–1504) with an opportunity to forge a confessionally and dynastically unified Spain; this process advanced with the military and bureaucratic support of the now united kingdoms of Aragon and Castile (and which between 1580 and 1640 also included Portugal). The long process of expulsion and subsequent coercion applied to Muslims and Jews both intensified the sense of connection between the civil and military elements of government on the one hand, and the Catholic Church on the other. These trends also provided a clearly identifiable "enemy within" on whom secular and religious leaders could focus. The result was the earliest instance of religious territorialization in early modern Europe, accomplished through a process that may be denominated ethno-religious cleansing overlaid with passionate commitment to theological positions. In this, the Spanish state had the support of some of the leading writers on theology of the day. While Erasmus (1466–1536) (a subject of Charles V, but not of the Spanish crown) sought a religious consensus that was not coerced, and even experienced the disapproval of the Spanish Inquisition, both he and the Habsburg rulers of Spain agreed on the importance of eschewing discord in matters theological (Estes 2007, 64). As the sixteenth century wore on and the notion of a cohesive Christendom collapsed completely, the dangers of discord seemed to grow more acute, and appeals for order were embraced by secular leaders of the Spanish state. Meanwhile the conversion of the inhabitants of Spain's vast overseas empire was another project that combined national identity and articulation of religious beliefs, with implications in both cases for the mother country. From 1568 onward, Spain's loss of the increasingly Calvinist Netherlands, and the iconoclasm associated with the earliest phase of this transition placed Spanish identity and devotion to Catholic practices in bolder opposition to the actions of Spain's enemies, intensifying the former.

Scotland exemplifies the intertwining of articulated confessional polemic and raw emotion, frequently manipulated by secular and religious leaders. The mobs that sacked the Dominican priory in Perth and the Cathedral of St. Andrews felt genuine grievances against these material symbols of Catholic authority and wealth, as well as unhappiness with what were seen as idle men and women living surrounded by others who had to struggle in a harsh environment. Simultaneously, grave doubts had been raised regarding the doctrine of transubstantiation and surviving documents make clear that this and other controversies were of real importance to many laypeople. These controversies were seen both as spiritual concerns and as matters to be resolved through action by the community, or at least within the context of Scotland, as opposed to the actions of a supranational power. The identification of Scots with the children of Israel of the Old Testament, an analogy repeated in many non-Catholic European lands, provided vocabulary and a narrative through which the local and national aspects of these debates were understood, as well as a way to envision divine covenants, punishment, and redemption. Between 1560 and 1689, church government in Scotland and its relationship to political power underwent successive radical shifts, culminating in a compromise among several Protestant positions (Murdoch, 2006, 85), while small independent confessional groups such as Quakers went their own way. Meanwhile, Catholicism survived among the clans of the Highlands, even when the Mass was outlawed; a factor that would play a role in the eighteenth-century Stuart challenges to the Hanoverian state that by then was known as the United Kingdom.

By contrast, Olaf Mörke sees confessionalization in the Dutch Republic as something experienced within diverse individual communities rather than codified through compromise at the state level (Mörke 1996). Here the state remained de facto multi-confessional while the dominant dynasty, the House of Orange, adhered to the Reformed Church and conducted its diplomacy accordingly. Catholic clergy, without state support, had to justify the survival of their lay communities on theological grounds, thereby perpetuating a gulf between confessional commitment and identification of confession with the state. State building proceeded with an ideology tacitly supportive of toleration (within strictly understood limits), while many Dutch continued to be committed to their own confession, even while the outwardly perceived strength and cohesion of the United Provinces increased.

The principal "other" for the Dutch Republic was external: the exclusively and militantly Catholic Spanish Monarchy, from which the Netherlands had won independence. The externalization of this "other," who was defined in both national and theological terms, while it encouraged the oligarchization of urban centers, also fostered a climate in which communities of devout Calvinists resisted efforts of the civil government to provide, for example, poor relief (Parker 1998, 5). Scholars have interpreted these developments as a consequence of communal discipline, since according to Reformed teaching no amount of individual effort could increase the chances of an individual being admitted to the Elect, and most tellingly, the presence of a single unrepentant sinner could sully an entire community (Gorski 2003, 124). Awareness of these facts shaped attitudes of theologians throughout Protestant Europe who advised princes, as when Johann Bugenhagen (1485–1558) warned Christian III of Denmark (1503–59) to hire only "our scholars" as preachers and teachers at Copenhagen University (Rummel 2000, 48).

Sweden progressed relatively smoothly from a late medieval feudal state to an early modern sovereign state in which, despite the spectacular conversion of Queen Christina (1626–89, reigned 1632–54) to Catholicism in 1654, Lutheranism became strongly identified with the centralizing monarchy. The experience of theologians in Sweden has been described as twofold, with an active if discreet scholarly culture existing as a "parallel world" alongside the more pragmatic context of struggles between court and gown. The Swedish example is instructive because it suggests the compartmentalization of theological versus more concrete and worldly concerns that existed elsewhere. We are reminded that confessionalization could have an interior component, and that definitions of orthodoxy that were refined during this process sometimes touched on occult practices such as astrology and on the experience of personal piety. Related to this point is the tendency of many theologians to keep their views to themselves, even when these views might not draw immediate censure. The social and especially the professional position of theologians, and the desire of theologians to preserve these positions, thus influenced the dissemination of new ideas and indirectly the impact of these ideas on the understanding of how theology might shape the state and vice versa. Simultaneously, there persisted a strain of passionately and widely held theological thought that had a negative impact on the building of any state; for example, the millennial teachings of mostly non-university trained preachers. And while legions of parish priests, even after the Council of Trent, had a practical and only faintly theological understanding of their duties, theology continued to be a high-prestige undertaking in places as varied as Paris and Prussia, with the result that the framing of theological debate was undertaken by elites who wove an understanding of their own status and relation to city and state into their discourses.

Ireland experienced a process of simultaneous dual confessionalization: the arrival of Protestant settlers and pressure from the English crown produced a "confessionalization from above," while a Catholic "confessionalization from below" continued, often supported by traditional landed elites (Lotz-Heumann, 2005). The role of theology per se in the intense rivalry that followed is opaque. Differences between Catholic and Anglican understandings of sin and salvation were often less important to laypersons than allegiances to ritual, community, and powerful families; home-grown Catholic professional theologians were in short supply, while priests trained on the Continent filled the void created by the closing of Catholic convents and monasteries. Efforts to develop an influential native-born Anglican clerical class that could shape the populace to the new dominant models of religious thinking (and promote loyalty to the government in London) were a disappointment. The forms of religion became rallying points for sectarian quarrels that would last centuries. Yet deeply held religious belief would remain an important part of the cultural landscape far longer than in many other parts of Europe.

The continuing debate among scholars as to the progress of the Reformation in England points to the challenges inherent in interpreting the evidence of the emergence of the confessional state. Eamon Duffy has argued that earlier historiography had an anti-Catholic bias and that reform was gradual and even haphazard (Duffy 1992). Alec Ryrie proposes an even more radical idea—that scholarship has made the British Reformations look more important than (and thus quite different from) what they really were (Ryrie 2006). The prominence of the United Kingdom and its language, English, in subsequent centuries thus not only unduly magnified the importance of its early religious reformations but has also caused them on occasion to be viewed from a perspective not as theologically oriented as the points of view of the reformers. Complicating this picture further was the underdeveloped nature of the early Tudor English state, which has been described as a series of mobile concentric circles centered upon the monarch, wherein confessionalization might be enlisted to get these circles all moving in the same direction.

A coherent approach to theology undoubtedly was very important to Thomas Cranmer (1489–1556), Mary Tudor (1516–58, reigned 1553–58), John Colet (1467–1519) and other key players, but it is not possible to speak of a coherent English theology during much of the sixteenth century. Among the flashpoints was purgatory, an idea denounced by many as false, downplayed by others as less worthy of attention than were clerical abuses, and defended by others, including Mary and her ecclesiastical allies, as sound—if now to be more subtly emphasized—doctrine. Related to purgatory, devotion to the saints may have declined during the latter part of Henry VIII's (1491–1547, reigned 1509–47) reign, although this surmise is based on evidence from middle-class wills and thus excludes a large segment of the population. Since many of the most often venerated late medieval saints were not English, this decline could also be interpreted as a symptom of increasing identification with Englishness, although other explanations are also possible. Later documents more readily express a national vision: the *Book of Common Prayer* (1549) and the *Thirty-Nine Articles* (1563) articulated a confessional identity that was distinctly English and which sought a *via media* between Catholicism and some Protestant sects. The linking of confessional and national identities was short-lived.

The Restoration of 1660 saw the endurance of visible, organized, and ultimately tolerated religious dissent that left its mark on British colonies, as well as on literature (e.g., *Pilgrim's Progress*, published in 1678).

France presents a different picture from its neighbors. The most populous of the regions evolving into nation states, it was also geographically sprawling and made up of highly disparate components. Theology as taught in universities, most notably Paris, retained a strongly scholastic character, as suggested in the writings of Calvin (1509–64), and also in the articles drafted by the Sorbonne between 1542 and 1563, which were taken by law to define Catholic orthodoxy. The monarchy, like those of many other polities, was sacral; but Francis I (1494–1547, reigned 1515–47) was spared the worst of the religious controversies of his age and seemed uninterested in theological debates. At the end of the sixteenth century, Henri IV (1553–1610, reigned 1589–1610) had to deal with pressures from many directions as he realigned his public confessional identity, and functioned somewhat as a bridge between the eras of sacral kingship and the rationalized politics of the mid-seventeenth century and later. Catholic devotional practices in France after the Edict of Nantes (1598) suggest not a growing spirit of toleration but the mood of a dominant confessional group in a state where a stopgap measure had been undertaken to prevent further civil discord. According to the "weak theory of confessionalization," rivalry and emulation among religious groups in France fostered solidarity within these groups; again academic theology provided the vocabulary with which the experience of solidarity might be described and remembered. By the reign of Louis XIII (1601–43, reigned 1610–43), the personal piety of the monarch, as represented in the visual and performing arts, was being linked with the confessional identity of the state (Monod 1999, 113) and with the sacral basis of royal sovereignty. These connections were continued during the reign of Louis XIV (1638–1715, reigned 1643–1715), when France was engaged in a struggle with the Habsburgs, who also made claims for the sacral basis of their sovereignty, but who neither ruled over a confessionally conformed territory, nor were able to build a cohesive state. But by this point the "Most Christian" monarch, having been raised to near-deification by poets, artists, and homilists, was merely using the confessional idea to advance the centralized power of a French state that, aside from seeking the suppression of Jansenism, cared little about theology.

Ian Hunter notes "serial waves of confessionalisation" (Hunter 2007, 32) washing over Central Europe during the sixteenth and seventeenth centuries, resulting in a predominantly Lutheran Brandenburg ruled by Calvinist princes and in smaller territories where the principle of *cuius regio eius religio* functioned awkwardly, unlike Scotland where the royal government (personally linked to that of England after 1603) exercised some central authority. In Brandenburg, the struggles that ensued took on a distinctly theological character, with Lutheran congregations experiencing a shared rite of salvation that forged the identity of a group prepared to resist even minor changes in the liturgy imposed by Calvinist officials. Hunter's use of the phrase "confessionalizing states" highlights this ongoing tension, and also hints at why it is hard to point to a successful "confessional state" in the region during this period.

In the part of Hungary not controlled by Turkey, as in so many other polities, sincerely held theological convictions were at times impossible to separate from the desire to take a stand against what was seen as a foreign and unwelcome dynasty, in this case the Catholic Habsburgs. Ultimately, this dynasty achieved victory over the Ottomans not through a program of what Charles Ingrao calls "confessional absolutism" (Ingrao 2000, 1664) but by drawing consensus from its corporate estates, which included Protestants, while simultaneously relying on external (Catholic) allies. Dotted with new Catholic churches and foundations, Hungary in the early eighteenth century nevertheless saw confessionalizing forces stalled by local Protestant resistance and a loss of momentum by the order spearheading the project, the Jesuits.

A recently identified and more broadly construed "confessionalization" of the Ottoman, Safavid, and Mughal empires during the same period as confessionalization was underway in Christian Europe has also been noted (Krstić 2011), in which a "learned hierarchy" of Sunni muftis had access to the Ottoman civil authorities. Within Europe itself, Jewish communities experienced confessionalization externally, when pressed by the authorities driven by their own confessionalization programs.

The solidifying of nation states possessing a confessional identity had a secondary impact on other confessional communities. Exiles, both Protestant and Catholic, who had fled their homes because of their commitment to their confession, intensified the confessional quality of the communities into which they immigrated. They simultaneously made these communities more cosmopolitan, at times producing highly visible new theological spokesmen such as John Knox (ca. 1514–72), who was briefly a prominent figure in Geneva. Conversely, the presence of conspicuous heretics, such as Michael Servetus (ca. 1511–53) in Calvinist Geneva, threw the spotlight on theology from another, "levitical" direction, where the alien functioned as the Other, against whose beliefs the faithful must rally to preserve the purity and integrity of the state.

The framing of national identity through adherence to confessional positions was often understood more through opposition to another confession or hierarchy than through adhesion to a static set of doctrines. Political and ecclesiastical leaders became at various times participants, objects, and subjects in this process. Where theology took a moral turn, judicial practice and social control both enforced application of theological standards and shaped public perceptions of what constituted orthodox beliefs. Formal schooling and lay reading were powerful shapers of belief and identity; local and Biblical heroes were celebrated while confessional doctrine was set forth (Russell 1986). The printing of books in the vernacular by both Catholic and Protestant publishers fostered local and national identities even as they promoted transnational theologies. Both groups trained political elites with the aid of emblems that expressed moral and theological ideas graphically, at times employing images of national "types." School dramas could allude more vividly to national themes expounded in books, while presenting role models of leadership and piety. Even such public rituals as executions for crimes against the official religion reinforced the connection between theology and the increasing authority of the confessionally conformed state.

# 3  POLITICS, THEOLOGY, AND WRITING

The personalities, programs, and prospects of specific political figures also loomed large in the shaping of this dynamic. The much-dissected career of Henry VIII is that of a monarch who, whatever other factors drove him to make decisions, believed himself to be an expert regarding theology. Likewise John Calvin, a very different man in charge of a very different polity, was equally assured that his understanding of theology was true and absolute. Calvin's at times legalistic approach to theological exposition encouraged imitators, who in turn honed the terminology and categories with which the laity expressed and understood their own beliefs. England's Elizabeth I (1533–1603) desired her church to promote obedience, but her personal view was that preaching should not play a major role, a decision that invited endless theological debates and a diversion of energy to struggles over ritual and liturgy. Louis XIII and Leopold I (1640–1705) were both genuinely pious Catholics, but their differing circumstances resulted in varying results for the confessional evolution of their realms. As Voivode of Transylvania, Stephen Báthory (1533–86) ruled a polity already committed to a significant degree to the Reformed Church. Yet he also possessed intellectual curiosity and a desire to improve the literary culture of his realm, factors that prompted him to encourage Jesuit education (Pop 2014, 172).

Emperor Ferdinand II (1578–1637, reigned 1619–37) was a passionate, if not fanatical Catholic, and his own approach to confessional conformity in the Austrias reflected his determination to root out Calvinism, which from his perspective was pernicious and sinful, even if the costs to his realm were significant. For their part, the radical and inflexible policies of Calvinist leaders in the estates of Upper and Lower Austria drove Ferdinand to even more extreme measures. When these bodies refused homage to the emperor, publicly expressed heresy was seen as combined with an affront to the majesty of the ruler and even to his person, so that Ferdinand's theological convictions were inextricably connected to his wounded dynastic and personal pride. For their part, Calvinist leaders saw their resistance to Ferdinand's authority as a virtuous act. It was not, however, a successful one: Protestantism was rooted out of the Habsburg crown lands through confiscation and emigration, and although Catholic confessionalization got a late start, its ultimate impact was lasting. However, owing to the organization of the Holy Roman Empire the lands it affected did not grow into a recognizable nation state.

The very fact that Holy Roman Emperor Maximilian II (1527–76, reigned 1564–76) seemed to vacillate in his private religious convictions had consequences for several confessional groups within his German speaking territories. On the other hand, Rudolf II (1552–1612, reigned 1576–1612), a highly idiosyncratic Catholic, lacked the energy or interest to promote vigorously either religious conformity or a state with a national identity. Nor was the impact of such personalities found only in the early years of the confessionalization process. Queen Ulrica Eleonora of Sweden (1688–1741, reigned 1718–20) intervened personally not only in the appointment of preachers but also in the topics of sermons and scriptural passages forming part of services at court. Influenced by Protestant models, Peter the Great (1672–1725, reigned 1694–1725) altered relations between Russian secular and ecclesiastical powers in ways reminiscent of confessional-ization processes elsewhere (Steindorff 2010).

Being a theologian in early modern Europe was a profession still requiring academic credentials, something quite different from the more descriptive designation of human-ist. This professional status of theology had been confirmed in the Late Middle Ages within the context of a transnational collection of universities training and certifying theologians who often had wide-ranging authority. Thus the pronouncements of theo-logians, while they could always reflect the communities to which they were addressed, often had little that could be called a restrictively national point of view. Even Jan Hus (1369–1415), whose life and death became a rallying point for Czechs, had not framed his critiques of the church in exclusively nationalist terms. The creation of non-Catholic churches supported by secular rulers after 1523 changed this arrangement, although the new order still preserved the notion that theology was a specialized discipline address-ing universals and requiring rigorous training. This did not prevent radical innovators lacking this training, from John of Leiden (1509–36) to Jakob Hutter (ca. 1500–36), from charting their own courses. But even such innovators had to deal with the enduring presence of professional theologians who frequently had the ear of the local ruler, mas-tery of Latin (still the international language), and access to printing presses and pulpits. The process of confessionalization was therefore often mediated by the presence of these career theologians whose widely broadcast ideas were a feature of the intellectual and cultural landscape.

In general rulers expected predictability, if not supine obedience from theologians of their territories (Appold 2008, 82–83). Yet at the same time, some rulers saw them-selves as both legitimate leaders and Christian brethren of their theologians: Luther's (1483–1546) correspondence with the Elector Friedrich the Wise (1463–1525, reigned 1486–1525) displays a melding of these two roles. The dynamics of any specific situation were inevitably affected by the personalities of the individuals involved, yet we can say that the common thread was the perception that theologians were experts trained in a content area whose points of view might not be ignored. Lutheranism, like Calvinism, rapidly became a transnational phenomenon, which gave the pronouncements of its theologians potentially more power.

It must be recalled that numerous religious movements, from the Pietists and Mennonites to the followers of Shabbetai Zvi (1626–76), combined fervent confessional commitment and desire for community with a lack of focus on (or realistic prospect of) the establishment of a state. Others, like the New England Puritans, sought to create a theocracy that retained strong ties to existing states with different confessional identi-ties. And a few attempts to create new political units based on a commonly held and rad-ically defined confession were failures; the Münster Anabaptist theocracy led by John of Leiden being a spectacular example.

Diarmaid MacCulloch has described the lay population of Elizabethan England as "probably punch-drunk on religious change" (MacCulloch 2001, 135): the same applies to many of the regions of Europe. While the coalescence of confessionally defined states continued, weariness, anxiety, and doubt also thrived; forces that could be mobilized in support of a top-down approach to confessional conformity. Yet these same factors might contribute to the creation of a different kind of polity: the Edict of Torda, which recognized four "received" religions—Lutheranism, Calvinism, Catholicism, and Unitarianism—and "tolerated" several others, was proclaimed in 1568 after decades of strife in Transylvania (Keul, 2009, 245), another region that had been engulfed by "waves of confessionalisation." Reports of strife were sometimes enough to prompt guarantees of toleration: less than a year after the Bartholomew's Day Massacre (1572), Polish nobles and freemen gained a large degree of religious liberty in the Warsaw Confederation. In each case, in an atmosphere of religious pluralism the certainty with which individuals regarded theological propositions may have been undermined, although determining this with certainty is difficult. Yet the desire and need to achieve theological consensus among lay and clergy alike might remain strong, as Michael J. Halvorson has demonstrated in his study of Lutheran Hildesheim (Halvorson 2008).

Confessional historiography was driven by theological concerns and read through theological lenses. The Lutheran *Magdeburg Centuries* (1559–74) and Caesar Baronius' (1638–1707) Catholic response, *Annales Ecclesiastici* (1588–1607) provided new dimensions to confessional identity, which might be exploited by state-building leaders and absorbed by lay believers. History provided archetypes and role models that could be fit to a confessional mold, while setting a forth a pattern of providentially produced events that reinforced confessional commitment and justified political action, often within the context of a political unit. Even antique pagan regimes might be enlisted as models for Christian rulers to follow. *Foxe's Book of Martyrs* (1563) documented an Elizabethan faith that was both national and theologically rooted. Yet these trends did not assure the development of a historiography that was both national and confessional. Jesuits writing the history of their order created a transnational narrative, combining the deeds of men from competing nation states (*Imago* 1640), while the *Centuries* themselves were, in the words of Irena Dorota Backus, "consciously anti-nationalist in their view of ecclesiastical history" (Backus 2003, 374).

We may also consider the intersection of the theology of suffering, confessionalization, and the expression of the power of the emerging state through violence. The Wittenberg doctrine of sin and suffering as beneficial and even necessary began to be enforced by Lutheran pastors and theologians almost as soon as it appeared (Rittgers 2012, 210). Simultaneously, those territories whose princes had embraced Lutheranism continued to use rituals of public violence to reinforce the connection between behavior that violated the laws of the state and suffering. Elsewhere, rebellion against Catholic sovereigns was frequently associated with Protestant or other "heretical" confessions. The 1678 rebellion of Imre Thököly (1657–1705) against Habsburg rule in Hungary was suppressed with the public torture and execution of Thököly's supporters, with Catholic priests at hand to hear confessions. The disruption of the fragile state was thereby correlated with deviant confessional allegiance and subsequent and deserved suffering. From a somewhat different perspective, the torture and execution of the accused in the

Shimon Abeles (ca. 1682–94) case in Prague in 1694 provided an occasion both to extol the supposed piety of the victim and thereby glorify Catholicism, and to call attention to the suffering inflicted on those who transgressed the laws of state and church in a kingdom where confessional conformity was still being imposed. Stories of martyrs to the Catholic faith were employed to emphasize the universality of Catholicism, a point that could also be played to the advantage of a Catholic nation state against Protestant ones. Mass suffering inflicted by an outsider might also be enlisted in theological arguments about the destiny of a people or state: Hungarian Catholic preachers explained the invasion of the kingdom by the Ottomans as God's just punishment for those who deserted Catholicism for Protestantism, and New England Puritan divines made similar points about misfortunes in their own communities.

Theological "proximity" to the religious positions of other polities combined with pragmatic statecraft contributed to the survival of some confessional states. Elizabeth I's push towards a Protestant alliance after 1585 led her to establish contacts with Lutheran princes in Germany and Calvinists in the Low Countries, thereby strengthening the position of her own state and church and leaving her prospective allies less exposed.

# 4 CONCLUSION

What has usually been called the Age of Confessionalization ended by the middle of the seventeenth century (Fitzpatrick 2000, 31), but the echoes of the widespread engagement of both the mighty and less powerful alike with theological questions lasted through the revocation of the Edict of Nantes (1685) and the Glorious Revolution (1689). Even Maria Theresia's (1717–80, reigned 1740–80) efforts in the middle of the following century to create *Ein Totum* with a common element of dominant Catholicism out of her motley and scattered territories suggests the lingering power of the idea of what would later be called confessionalization. The conspiracies imagined by Titus Oates and the organization of communities in early Puritan New England are further reverberations of the storms unleashed by the engagement of theology with matters of state that became the central preoccupation of ruler and subject alike. In these last instances fear, the increasing role of mass communications such as broadsides, and a vulnerability to rumors of conspiracies are virtually impossible to separate from popular commitment to theological positions. One of the three "paradigm shifts" proposed by Stefan Ehrenpreis for recent German research in confessionalization is a growing emphasis on identities and cultures (Ehrenpreis 2012); this model likewise has value for the study of British, Habsburg and other states.

The power of the ideas of confessionalization and of the magisterial and radical models has been that they enable us to look at the ongoing process of political reorganization of Western and Central Europe through new lenses that devote more attention to the interplay of secular and religious forces. The more subjective religious experience of individuals remains harder to identify, but is key to understanding both the forces that drove change and the ways in which theological concepts were understood and acted upon. Most striking to the modern reader is how the powers of an unseen world drove the energies of many who sought to build political entities in this world.

Thorny questions remain: was Theresian Hungary, where Catholicism enjoyed a privileged legal position but significant non-Catholic populations endured and Hungarian speakers were at best a bare majority (Shore 2012), ever "confessional" or a "state"? Can what Richard Butterwick has called the "confessional noble republic" (Butterwick 2010, 297) of eighteenth-century Poland-Lithuania with its aristocratic understanding of "Polishness" be made to fit the mold of the confessional nation state? What light do the Calvinist Republic of Geneva or the widely scattered territories ruled by the House of Savoy—which claimed sanctity for its members—shed on our understanding of confessional polities that are not nations in the modern sense (Vester 2013, 10)? How to proceed when, as in the case of Scotland, different confessional traditions perpetuate conflicting versions of a state's confessional past?

Modifications proposed for the theory of confessionalization do not exclude the importance of theology: the self-discipline perceived by Heinrich Richard Schmidt in rural districts of Switzerland that drove confessionalization forward could have included many components, among them the desire to maintain a pure and righteous local community (Schmidt 1995). The process by which nation states, formed around theological constructs, evolved into entities largely indifferent to religious experience suggests a fragility embedded in these formerly deeply held beliefs. Yet the success of the acknowledged confessions of colonial powers in the colonies themselves—as well as after their independence—reveals the complexity of this process. Further research may shed additional light on the relationship between religious convictions of the day and the *Realpolitik* of leaders both secular and ecclesiastical, as well as on the impact of the "crisis of the seventeenth century" on the internal religious experiences of laypersons throughout the Continent.

## Bibliography

Ahdar, Rex, and Leigh, Ian. 2013. *Religious Freedom in the Liberal State*. 2nd ed. Oxford: Oxford University Press.

Appold, Kenneth G. 2008. "Academic Life and Teaching in Post-Reformation Lutheranism." In *Lutheran Ecclesiastical Culture: 1550–1675*, edited by Robert Kolb, 65–115. Leiden: Brill.

Backus, Irena Dorota. 2003. *Historical Method and Confessional Identity in the Era of the Reformation (1378–1615)*. Leiden: Brill.

Betteridge, Tom. 2005. *Literature and Politics in the English Reformation*. Manchester, UK: Manchester University Press.

Estes, James Martin, 2007. *Christian Magistrate and Territorial Church: Johannes Brenz and the German Reformation*. Toronto: University of Toronto Press.

Burak, Guy. 2013. "Faith, Law and Empire in the Ottoman 'Age of Confessionalization' (Fifteenth–Seventeenth Centuries): The Case of 'Renewal of Faith.'" *Mediterranean Historical Review* 28 (1): 1–23.

Butterwick, Richard. 2010. "Catholicism and Enlightenment in Poland-Lithuania." In *A Companion to Catholic Enlightenment in Europe*, edited by Ulrich Lehner and Michael Printy, 297–359. Leiden: Brill.

Casanova, José. 2008. "Public Religions Revisited." In *Religion: Beyond a Concept*, edited by Hent de Vries, 101–119. New York: Fordham University Press.

Collinson, Patrick. 1998. "Comment on Eamon Duffy's Neale Lecture and the Colloquium." In *England's Long Reformation 1500–1800*, edited by Nicholas Tyacke, 71–86. London: UCL Press.

Duffy, Eamon. 1992. *The Stripping of the Altars*. New Haven, CT: Yale University Press.

Ehrenpreis, Stefan. 2012. "Deutsche Forschung zur urbanen Konfessionalisierung 2000–2011." Paper presented at the conference *Město v převratech konfesionalizace v 15. až 18. století*. Archive of the Capital City Prague, in collaboration with the Historical Institute of the Czech Academy of Sciences and the Institute for International Studies, Charles University, Prague.

Estes, James Martin. 2005. *Peace, Order and the Glory of God: Secular Authority and the Church in the Thought of Luther and Melanchthon, 1518–1559*. Leiden: Brill.

Fitzpatrick, Martin. 2000. "Toleration and the Enlightenment Movement." In *Toleration in Enlightenment Europe*, edited by Ole Peter Grell and Roy Porter, 23–58. Cambridge: Cambridge University Press.

Gillespie, Michael Allen. 2008. *The Theological Origins of Modernity*. Chicago: University of Chicago Press.

Gorski, Philip S. 2003. *The Disciplinary Revolution: Calvinism and the Rise of the State in Early Modern Europe*. Chicago: University of Chicago Press.

Halvorson, Michael J. 2008. "Jews and Jesuits in a Confessional Age: Heinrich Heshusius and the Boundaries of Community in Hildesheim." *The Sixteenth-Century Journal* 39 (3): 639–655.

Hunter, Ian. 2007. *The Secularisation of the Confessional State: The Political Thought of Christian Thomasius*. Cambridge: Cambridge University Press.

*Imago Primi Sæculi*. 1640. Antwerp: Plantiniana.

Ingrao, Charles. 2000. *The Habsburg Monarchy, 1618–1815*. Cambridge: Cambridge University Press.

Keul, István. 2009. *Early Modern Religious Communities in East-Central Europe*. Leiden: Brill.

Krstić, Tijana. 2011. *Contested Conversions to Islam: Narratives of Religious Change in the Early Modern Ottoman Empire*. Stanford: Stanford University Press.

Lotz-Heumann, Uta. 2005. "Confessionalization in Ireland: Periodization and Character, 1534–1649." In *The Origins of Sectarianism in Early Modern Ireland*, edited by Alan Ford and John McCafferty, 24–53. Cambridge: Cambridge University Press.

Marshall, Peter. 2012. "Confessionalization, Confessionalism and Confusion in the English Reformation." In *Reforming Reformation*, edited by Thomas F. Mayer, 43–64. Farnham, UK: Ashgate.

MacCulloch, Diarmaid. 2001. *The Later Reformation in England, 1547–1603*. New York: Palgrave.

MacCulloch, Diarmaid. 2004. *Reformation: Europe's House Divided, 1490–1703*. London: Penguin.

Monod, Paul Kléber. 1999. *The Power of Kings: Monarchy and Religion in Europe, 1589–1715*. New Haven: Yale University Press.

Mörke, Olaf. 1996. "Die politische Bedeutung des Konfessionellen im Deutschen Reich und in der Republik der Vereinigten Niederlande. Oder: War die Konfessionalisierung ein 'Fundamentalvorgang'?" In *Der Absolutismus—ein Mythos? Strukturwandel monarchischer*

*Herrrschaft in West- und Mitteleuropa (ca. 1550–1700) (Münstersche historische Forschungen 9)*, edited by Ronald G. Asch and Heinz Duchhardt, 125–164. Köln: Böhlau.

Murdoch, Steve. 2006. *Network North: Scottish Kin, Commercial and Covert Associations in Northern Europe, 1603–1746*. Leiden: Brill.

Parker, Charles H. 1998. *The Reformation of Community: Social Welfare and Calvinist Charity in Holland, 1572–1620*. Cambridge: Cambridge University Press.

Pop, Ioan-Aurel. 2014. *Cultural Diffusion and Religious Reformation in Sixteenth-Century Transylvania: How the Jesuits Dealt with Orthodox and Catholic Ideas*. Lewiston, NY: Edwin Mellen Press.

Pörtner, Regina. 2001. *The Counter-Reformation in Central Europe: Styria 1580–1630*. Oxford: Oxford University Press.

Reinhard, Wolfgang. 1981. "Konfession und Konfessionalisierung in Europa." In *Bekenntnis und Geschichte: Die Confessio Augustana im historischen Zusammenhang*, edited by Wolfgang Reinhard, 165–189. München: Vögel.

Rittgers, Ronald K. 2012. *The Reformation of Suffering: Pastoral Theology and Lay Piety in Late Medieval and Early Modern Germany*. Oxford: Oxford University Press.

Rodén, Marie-Louise. 2005. "The Crisis of the Seventeenth Century: The Nordic Perspective." In *Early Modern Europe: From Crisis to Stability*, edited by Philip Benedict and Myron P. Gutmann, 100–119. Newark, DE: University of Delaware Press.

Rummel, Erika. 2000. *The Confessionalization of Humanism in Reformation Germany*. Oxford: Oxford University Press.

Russell, Paul. A. 1986. *Lay Theology in the Reformation: Popular Pamphleteers in Southwest Germany, 1521–1525*. Cambridge: Cambridge University Press.

Ryrie, Alec. 2013. *Being Protestant in Reformation Britain*. Oxford: Oxford University Press.

Ryrie, Alec. 2006. "Britain and Ireland." In *Palgrave Advances in the European Reformations*, edited by Alec Ryrie, 124–146. Basingstoke, UK: Palgrave, 2006.

Schilling, Heinz. 1981. *Konfessionskonflikt und Staatsbildung*. Gütersloh: Quellen und Forschungen der Reformationsgesch i chte.

Schmidt, Heinrich Richard. 1995. *Dorf und Religion: Reformierte Sittenzucht in Berner Landgemeinden der frühen Neuzeit*. New York: G. Fischer.

Scribner, Robert. 1994. "Elements of Popular Belief." In *Handbook of European History 1400–1600*, edited by Thomas Brady, vol. 1, 231–262. Leiden: Brill.

Shore, Paul. 2012. *Narratives of Adversity: Jesuits on the Eastern Peripheries of the Habsburg Realms*. Budapest: Central European University Press.

Steindorff, Ludwig. 2010. "Donations and Commemoration in the Muscovite Realm—A Medieval or Early Modern Phenomenon?" In *Religion und Integration im Moskauer Russland*, edited by Ludwig Steindorff, 477–498. Wiesbaden: Otto Harrassowitz.

Sutherland, Donald R. 1990–1991. "The Religion of Gerrard Winstanley and Digger Communism." *Essays in History* 33 (2): 18–42.

Tazbir, Janusz. 1994. "Poland." In *The Reformation in National Context*, edited by Robert Scribner, Roy Porter, and Mikuláš Teich, 168–180. Cambridge: Cambridge University Press.

Vester, Matthew. 2013. "Introduction." In *Sabaudian Studies: Political Culture, Dynasty, and Territory (1400–1700)*, edited by Matthew Vester, 1–13. Kirksville, MO: Truman State University Press.

Williams, George. 1995. *The Radical Reformation*. 3rd ed. Kirksville, MO: Truman State University Press.

# PART II

# THEOLOGICAL TOPICS

# Catholic Theologies

CHAPTER 4

....................................................................................

# MYSTICISM AND REFORM IN CATHOLIC THEOLOGY BETWEEN 1600 AND 1800

....................................................................................

ULRICH L. LEHNER AND WILLIAM P. O'BRIEN, SJ

THIS section deals with the variety within Roman Catholic theology between the Council of Trent, which opened in 1545 and closed in 1563, and the period of the Enlightenment, which ended roughly in the late eighteenth century. Our concentration on a few theological discourses within each ecclesial tradition naturally leaves out a great deal of material. We therefore decided in this introduction not to summarize the other chapters on Catholic theology, but rather to indicate a number of additional themes. These include Trent's focus on a universal call to holiness, the effect of parish missions on popular faith, and practical reforms such as the founding of seminaries and improving the moral life of the clergy. We also will consider Trent's support for positive theology, which made extensive use of both scripture and sacred Tradition. And, since Protestant early modern theology developed in a strongly anti-Trinitarian context, we will take note too of Catholic attempts to defend traditional Trinitarian theology. Finally, we will consider the rise of Catholic mysticism, especially with regard to its contra-authoritarian character.

## 1 THE COUNCIL'S INFLUENCE

....................................................................................

The Council of Trent (1545–63) profoundly shaped early modern Catholic theology. The Council's agenda involved confirming such Catholic teachings as purgatory and transubstantiation, and rejecting central doctrines of the churches of the Reformation, such as sola scriptura and justification by faith alone. Note, however, that the council refrained from reformulating Christological or Trinitarian doctrines. At least as important as the canons were the reform decrees of Trent, which centered on the proper behavior of the clergy. While these latter documents constituted in some sense a theory of Tridentine Catholicism, much of the spirit of Tridentine reform derives from the actions of the council's most prominent activists, including Charles Borromeo. Reform-minded bishops disseminated widely the decrees of the provincial councils of his archdiocese of Milan. Those decrees and their implementation became throughout the seventeenth and early eighteenth centuries a "how-to" book of church reform (O'Malley 2013; Ditchfield 2013). Likewise, the founding of the Congregation for the Propagation of the Faith (1622), the Congregation of the Missions (1633), and a number of religious orders, including the Society of St. Sulpice (1641), came about in the context of this Tridentine activism. In this sense the Congregation of the Missions aspired not only to disseminate the Catholic faith in overseas colonies, but also to reignite religious zeal through parochial missions in the heartlands of Catholicism (Chatellier 1997; Gray 2012).

Trent thus intended pastors to make practical reforms on the local level and to this end commissioned the Roman Catechism, which appeared in 1566. This and other pedagogical works, from Canisius (1556) to La Salle (1713), "probably had in the long run more considerable effects than any other innovation of the sixteenth century" (Bossy 1985, 119; Bireley 1999; Mullett 1999). Capuchin and Jesuit missionaries made extensive use of these tools—along with preaching, spiritual counsel, and the celebration of the sacraments—to evangelize rural Europe, converting lingering folk religion sensibilities and transforming well into the eighteenth century the attitude and practice of average Catholics regarding Communion and confession (Châtellier 1997; Delumeau 1977; Frijhoff 2006). The responsibility for tending and reaping the fruit of the fields that the missionaries sowed then fell to the pastors, whose bishops charged them with the instruction of children (Delumeau 1977). By the late seventeenth century, rates of infant baptism had begun to rise, pastoral visits of the bishop normalized confirmation, and regular attendance at Mass and observance of Easter duties increased, although because of the retention of Latin as the language of worship, congregations remained largely unengaged in the liturgy apart from congregational prayers and parish notices (Delumeau 1977). Indeed, because the clergy controlled the sacraments so as to ensure their proper celebration, the laity increasingly favored pious devotions and sacramentals, including litanies, Eucharistic adoration, and the way of the cross, all of which allowed them to engage more actively in the practice of their faith (Bireley 1999; Cooke 1976; Dehne 1975; Evennett 1968; Martos 2001).

Another stimulus of Trent included a new understanding of holiness. In 1588, Pope Urban VIII passed new regulations on saint making. While in earlier causes for sainthood the promoter had to demonstrate that the candidate either possessed mystical gifts or brought about miracles during her or his lifetime, the canonization process now centered on the character of the person in question. A good example for this changed view of sainthood appears in the case of Ignatius of Loyola (1491–1556), canonized in 1622 without having performed any authenticated miracles during his lifetime. Jesuit theologian Pedro de Ribadeneira (1527–1611) stated that the true miracle in Ignatius's life consisted in his spiritual transformation from a worldly soldier seeking vainglory to a soldier of Christ working for the greater glory of God (*ad maiorem Dei gloriam*). From this perspective, although early modern saints might not perform miracles, their virtuous lives themselves represented the miraculous. This shift thus enabled Catholic thought "to absorb the idea of an individual and autonomous religious self" and present it to the faithful as a role model worthy of imitation (Leone 2010). As such, the heroic lives of canonized saints might motivate the faithful to answer the universal call to holiness by "responding to the realistic demands of everyday life through humility, gentleness and simplicity" (McDonnell 2009, 219). In consequence, there developed a popular spiritual theology that provided Catholics with inexpensive pocket editions of spiritual bestsellers, notably the *Introduction to the Devout Life* (1609) of Francis de Sales (1567–1622), which focused less on theological subtlety than on the main tenets of the faith.

## 2  Positive and Historical Theology

Already by the late fourteenth century, Renaissance humanists had pointed to scripture and history as important sources for theology, but only after Trent did "positive" theology, understood as reflection on the revealed God of scripture and tradition, move along with polemical theology to the center of theological discussion (Delumeau 1977, 41–43). One of the greatest achievements of positive theology appeared in the development of historical theology. In order to defend Catholic tradition against the Reformers and critics, theologians began to research the history of their discipline. In this regard, Cardinal Cesar Baronius (1538–1607) saw theology as key to placing historical mosaics into a coherent vision of ecclesiastical history that would support the truth of Catholicism. For Baronius, Agostino Mascardi (1590–1640), and many others, serious historical scholarship thus could counter skepticism and demonstrate theological claims (Tutino 2014). The French Maurists continued this tradition by developing methodological approaches to diplomacy, and the Bollandists edited sources dealing with the lives of the saints (Wallnig 2012). In the context of this approach that used historical considerations for apologetic ends stood also Jacques-Benigne Bossuet (1627–1704), arguably the most influential theologian of the second half of the seventeenth century (Lehner 2014). Note too the widely read *Apparatus ad Positivam Theologiam Methodicus* (1756) of Petrus Annatus (1638–1715), which offers a late example of positive baroque theology.

## 3  Trinitarian Theology

Since the Council of Trent emphasized the long overdue reforms that had been demanded for generations, it overlooked possible challenges to the most basic of Christian teachings. Disagreements about the Trinity were on nobody's horizon because they were predominantly thought of as disputes with the Orthodox, and thus with the past. Thus it should not surprise us that a proactive engagement with the challenges of the anti-Trinitarian movement and other Western attacks on basic Christian beliefs was absent.

The *De theologicis dogmatibus* (1644–50) of French Jesuit Denis Pétau (Dionysius Petavius, 1583–1652) was one of the first creative Catholic defenses of the Trinity against anti-Trinitarians, arguing that the foundation of the Trinitarian dogma rests upon the Bible and the post-Nicene fathers. However, he also stated that Platonism had fermented Christian theology through the pre-Nicene fathers. He even thought that many of these early fathers contradicted the Nicene Creed and held to Arianism or Tritheism. This gave critics new ammunition: if early Christians had held other doctrines, then the faith had changed fundamentally and perhaps thus deviated from the truth. In response, French Oratorian Louis Thomassin (1619–95) and his Jesuit compatriot Jean-François Baltus (1667–1743) set out to defend the pre-Nicene fathers against Pétau's charges (Werner 1867, 27). From now on, Catholic theologians carefully established in their textbooks the orthodox faith of the pre-Nicene fathers so as to prove the continuity of Trinitarian faith throughout the early church (Berti 1770, 457–86).

In contrast, the Spanish Jesuit Francisco Suarez (1548–1617) maintained that only positive—that is, revealed—theology can serve as the basis for Trinitarian theology. According to Suarez, God inserted Trinitarian wisdom into the Old Testament in order to prepare the chosen people for the Incarnation of Christ. However, only after the explicit revelation of the Trinity through Jesus Christ did belief in the dogma appear necessary for obtaining salvation. In *On the Mysteries of Christ's Life* (1592) Suarez reflected on Mary's knowledge of the Godhead: in contrast to her son, she did not have an earthly vision of the Trinity but did have perfect faith, which included an equally perfect belief in the Trinitarian mystery—a proposition Luther vehemently denied. Furthermore, Suarez considered heretical the opinion of Erasmus that Mary, still unaware of her son's divinity, did not adore Jesus as divine immediately after his birth (Marschler 2007, 81–115). Regarding the immanent Trinity, Suarez maintained that the acts of the divine persons are necessary but also free—which is to say that there exists no difference between necessity and freedom in the Trinitarian act of love. This has consequences for the theological anthropology of Suarez, since he uses his doctrine of the Trinity to argue that necessary actions of a personal will accord with the freedom of that will, such that freedom involves more than choice (Marschler 2007, 712). By affirming that all three divine persons act *ad extra* through their common nature, Suarez thus avoided the modalist trap; moreover, by separating strictly the necessary processes within the Trinity from the contingent dynamics of Creation, he maintained God's absolute freedom with regard to the world (Marschler 2007, 684). As for the divine persons, Suarez argued for a virtual distinction between person and nature, thus avoiding an "absolute person" in God (Marschler 2007, 719).

A Jesuit innovation in Trinitarian theology was the so-called figurist theology of the missionaries to China, which stated that the Chinese religion contained important elements of Christian wisdom. In his highly influential *General History of China* (1735), French Jesuit Jean-Baptiste Du Halde (1674–1743) went so far as to claim that the pre-Christian Dao-de-jing anticipated the Trinity. The papal rejection of the Jesuit attempts to reconcile Chinese religion and Christian faith in the so-called rites controversy also meant an end to this experiment in interreligious Trinitarian metaphysics (Rowbotham 1956). Figurist theology, however, influenced Leibniz, Wolff, Scots-Catholic Wolffian Andrew Ramsay (1686–1743), and even Jonathan Edwards, who himself came to see signs of Trinitarian belief among the Chinese (McDermott 2000, 207–16).

Despite a great variety of approaches, scholastic Trinitarian theology met criticism early on within the church, as from the French Oratorian Pierre Faydit (1644–1709), who accused scholasticism of modalism and the early fathers of Tritheism (Faydit 1696/ 1702). Unorthodox reinterpretations of Trinitarian theology, however, did not arise until the eighteenth century, when the Catholic Enlightenment began to take hold; for example, in the work of Anton Oehms (1735–1809), who proposed that each divine person corresponds to one substance (Lehner 2011).

# 4 Catholic Theology
# in the Enlightenment

A remarkable open-minded engagement with modern philosophy and science shaped seventeenth-century Catholic thought. After all, it was in 1613 the Jesuit Cardinal Bellarmine who demanded from Galileo Galilei (1564–1642) scientific proof for his defense of heliocentrism (Mayer 2012). The most important example of using empirically demonstrable knowledge to make Catholic beliefs intelligible, however, are the works of Niels Steno (1636–86), who not only discovered the ovarian follicles but also laid the groundwork for the science of geology (Sobiech 2013). The situation began to change over the course of the eighteenth century. While even in the first half, many attempts were made to merge traditional Catholic philosophy with empiricism—for example, by the Jesuits of the Sorbonne (Burson 2010)—this positive attitude changed in the 1750s as progressive Enlighteners increased their anticlerical attacks and polemics against the Catholic faith.

Moreover, Enlightenment source criticism and historiography seemed to undermine the trustworthiness of revelation and Catholic tradition. More importantly, it appeared to marginalize the truth of the faith by placing reason in judgment over it. Yet without a doubt, a great number of Catholic thinkers continued to believe that elements of Enlightenment could help to update theological vocabulary, initiate reforms in church and state, and disseminate the Tridentine reforms. In this vein, as early as 1714 the Italian theologian and historian Ludovico Muratori (1672–1750) called for a reform of Catholic theology by rediscovering the riches of the patristic era and integrating the knowledge of modern academic disciplines such as history, geography, and anthropology. For Muratori, Catholic thought thus could enjoy a fruitful dialogue with modern culture as long as Catholicism respected certain clear doctrinal boundaries. Due to his friendship with Pope Benedict XIV (1740–58), Muratori's views enjoyed for a short time almost canonical status in progressive Catholic circles. A generation later, Nicolas-Sylvestre Bergier (1715–90) established himself among the best contemporary critic of Rousseau, Voltaire, Diderot, and d'Holbach. Carefully analyzing the arguments of Catholicism's critics, imitating their terminology and vivid literary style, Bergier conceded that the Enlighteners had insights valuable to theologians. Due to Bergier's fair and irenic stance, his apparent breadth of knowledge, and the sharpness of his arguments, his peers and critics alike soon regarded him as the most important Catholic theologian of the eighteenth century (Burson 2014).

The engagement of Catholicism with the Enlightenment thus showed a tremendous diversity regarding both method and result. While many theologians wanted to use modern thought to update Catholic theology in order to make the latter intellectually attractive and intelligible, some desired to restructure the faith by excising essential elements. At best, the Catholic Enlightenment reinterpreted the Tridentine reform along modern lines; at worst, it subjugated Catholic theology to the objectives of princes and theoreticians of the state and in so doing accepted heretical compromises. Recognizing the trend of Catholic Enlighteners working with the state against the papacy helps to explain the latter's resistance toward state interventions in the nineteenth century, and its increasing distrust of the Enlightenment after the French Revolution. By the end of the eighteenth century, the papacy had come to understand the power of public opinion—in particular of popular devotion—better than the Catholic Enlighteners. With an enormous gain of moral authority during and after the Napoleonic exile, the popes could use popular Catholic sentiment to strengthen their own position against nationalist tendencies (Burson and Lehner 2014; Palmer 1961).

# 5 Mysticism after Trent

The encounters of Margaret Mary Alacoque (1647–90), famous for her visions of the Sacred Heart of Jesus, with her Jesuit confessors Claude La Colombière and Jean Croiset typify the dialectical movement, apparent in the late medieval period and continuing into the modern era, which characterized the relationship between many holy women and their authoritative male advisers (Coakley 2006; Hsia 2005). This education of a cleric by an "enlightened illiterate" reflects the way in which those formally excluded from religious authority instructed the institutional church (de Certeau 1992). The central challenge posed by mysticism involved "a dissent of the individual in relation to the group; an irreducibility of desire within the society that represses or masks it without eliminating it; a 'discontent within civilization'" (de Certeau 1992, 12). According to de Certeau, the development in the first half of the seventeenth century of the noun la mystique, understood as domain or place, delineated this peculiar sector at the edge of the space that religion had come to occupy within an increasingly secularized world (de Certeau 1996, 101–8; 1992, 13–14). Unable to articulate their psychosomatic experiences in theological terms, the mystics took recourse to the corporeal language of emotion and sensation (de Certeau, 1992, 15), from which issued forth a whole literature expressing knowledge of what remains essentially secret (*mystikos*). The corresponding development of the term *mysticism* in English would not appear until much later, in Henry Coventry's mid-eighteenth-century critique of religious fanaticism (Schmidt 2003).

In the sixteenth century, the center of Roman Catholic mysticism shifted from the Rhineland, the Low Countries, Italy, and England to Spain (McGinn 2013), although the Oratory of Cardinal Berulle and Philipp Neri continued to be of importance for the formation of Catholic spirituality (Thompson-Uberuaga 1989). The intimate personal experiences that Teresa of Avila and John of the Cross expressed in their writings represent the center common to Spanish mysticism—namely, God's love of humanity and humanity's disposition to collaborate with God (Andrés Martín 1994, 5). Although Ignatius of Loyola did not publish directly on his own prayer life, perhaps for fear that the religious authorities would associate him with the theologically suspect *alumbrados* (Hamilton 2010; Sluhovsky 2007), both his spiritual diary and what he dictated to Portuguese Jesuit Gonçalves da Câmara in 1555 by way of autobiography show clear signs of mystical experience, which would have influenced his composition of both the *Spiritual Exercises* (1548) and the *Constitutions* of the Society of Jesus (1559). Over a century later, Spanish theologian and spiritual director Miguel de Molinos would publish in Rome his influential *Spiritual Guide* (1675), in which he presented the idea that the devout life ought to lead from meditation, vocal prayer, and pious action to quiet, passive contemplation. While church authorities initially judged his doctrine sound, however, the tide later shifted and Pope Innocent XI anathematized Molinos in the constitution *Coelestis pastor* (1687).

Scholars have argued that the condemnation of Molinos had to do not so much with the contents of the *Guide* as with his oral teaching, which seemed to embrace quietism and antinomianism (McGinn 2010). The first section of the *Guide* contains the more controversial material, which deals with the role of diabolical action in leading people to commit objectively evil acts without having consented to committing them. But while *Coelestis pastor* condemns the idea that the soul ought not resist such attacks, the *Guide* makes a more modest suggestion: "when dealing with impertinent, importunate, and lewd thoughts in the time of recollection, know that God values the peace and resignation of your soul more than good propositions and grand sentiments. The very force that you use to resist these thoughts is an impediment and will leave your soul more unquiet" (I.11.68) (McGinn 2010, 31–32). Furthermore, *Coelestis pastor*'s denunciation of the view that one initial act or intention directed toward God can also direct subsequent acts may stem not from problems with the view itself, but rather from the concern that the "one act" doctrine could lead the faithful to neglect the renewal of that act in daily life. The document also condemns the notion, not stated explicitly in the *Guide*, that prayer should not use images and ideas but rather rest in quiet. In fact, Molinos affirms that souls should neither "altogether abandon the remembrance of the passion and death of the Savior," nor "wholly separate the most holy humanity from the highest elevation of mind at which the soul has arrived" (I.16.118) (McGinn 2010, 96). Finally, the document censured the idea that pure love desires for itself neither the reward of heaven nor the punishment of hell—the "impossible supposition" (Le Brun 2002, 10) not actually so formulated in the *Guide*—that one would love God as much in anticipation of damnation as one would love God expecting salvation.

By the time of the Spanish director's condemnation, mysticism already had had its day in France. Less austere than Spanish mysticism and less philosophical than the German variety, mysticism in France was marked by a strong affective character along with a tendency toward the quietism of Molinos (Smith 1973). Regarding affect, Francis de Sales presents in his preaching, correspondence, and publications the theme of a heart-centered love of God. His *Introduction to the Devout Life* and *Treatise on the Love of God* (1616) developed these themes and set the tone for French spirituality during the Grand Siècle. At the same time, the principles and attitudes of Spanish mysticism would continue to develop in the experiences and writings of Bérulle, Marie de Valence, Jean-Joseph Surin, Blaise Pascal, Marie Guyart, and Jeanne-Marie Guyon. Guyart, widowed in 1619 at age nineteen, left her eleven-year-old son in 1631 to enter the Ursuline convent and, as Marie de l'Incarnation, helped to establish Christianity in New France, earning for herself from Bossuet the title of "the Teresa of Avila of the New World" (Choquette 1992, 169; Pourrat 1955, vol. 4; Mali 1996). Guyart illustrates well Henri Bremond's comment that "in the majority of the great religious undertakings of the seventeenth century, one discovers the inspiration of a woman" (Bremond 2006, 1: 462)—a phenomenon apparent since the eleventh century in Hildegard of Bingen and other women religious, and later in the Beguines (Borchert 1994, 206–19). On the far end of that history, the influence of Madame Guyon would precipitate what Louis Cognet (1991) calls the "twilight of the mystics." Her *Spiritual Torrents* (1682) and *Short and Easy Method of Prayer* (1685), both of which focus on the prayer of quiet, "irritated Bossuet and seduced Fénelon," leading to the Quietist controversy that ended in the condemnation of her teachings (Miquel 1999, 252).

As for Molinos, the question came to bear once again on whether and to what extent passivity before God exempts one from the sacramental and moral life, brings one to a state of indifference regarding reward or punishment, and renders unnecessary the contemplation of the humanity of Jesus. Regarding distractions and temptations, however, the *Short and Easy Method* offers counsel resembling that which appears in the *Spiritual Guide*: "instead of fighting them directly, which will only augment the problem and draw the soul away from its adherence to God's will, which must be our main concern, the soul must simply turn its gaze and move closer and closer to God, like a child who, seeing a monster, tries neither to fight it nor to look at it, but only turns to its mother's bosom where he finds comfort" (XIX) (Guyon 2012, 78). Moreover, in his *Maxims of the Saints* (1697), Fénelon transposed the problematic from the "one act" of Molinos to the question of pure love (Le Brun 2002). The debate reached a crisis point with the intervention of Pope Innocent XII (1699), who took the side of Bossuet against Fénelon and effectively brought both the Quietism affair and the golden age of European mysticism to a close.

Despite this closure, many of the principles and practices associated with mysticism would continue through the eighteenth century. In a letter dated 1711, French

Jesuit Claude-François Milley wrote to the Visitandine Mère de Siry about a state of abandon wherein "one seems less to act than to suffer the action and the operation of God" (Milley 1943, 314). More influentially, French Jesuit Henri Ramière (1821–84) published in 1861, under the title *Abandonment to Divine Providence*, a remarkable manuscript that he attributed to his compatriot and confrere Jean-Pierre de Caussade (1675–1751). While in all likelihood Caussade did not compose the treatise (see Olphe-Galliard 1984), it epitomizes the spirituality of abandonment already evident in Milley, de Sales, Brother Lawrence, Guyon and Fénelon, and Angelus Silesius, which later would appear in Pierre-Joseph de Clorivière, Jean Grou, and Thérèse of Lisieux: "a vision of all time submitted to providence's ordering" (Salin 2007, 28; Oury 1993). Apparently written in the period after the condemnation of Fénelon, the *Abandonment*, while not using the images and vocabulary of mysticism, nevertheless continues the same theme of God's hiddenness found in Denys and the Spanish Carmelites—a "mysticism for a time of crisis: a crisis which began with the dawn of modernity" (Salin 2007, 34).

## BIBLIOGRAPHY

Andrés Martín. 1994. Melquíades. *Historia de la mística de la Edad de Oro en España y América*. Madrid: Biblioteca de Autores Cristianos.

Bireley, Robert. 1999. *The Refashioning of Catholicism, 1450–1700: A Reassessment of the Counter Reformation*. Washington, DC: Catholic University of America Press.

Berti, Laurentius. 1770. De Theologicis Disciplinis Accurata Synopsis. Vol. 1. Bamberg.

Borchert, Bruno. 1994. *Mysticism: Its History and Challenge*. York Beach, ME: Samuel Weiser.

Bossy, John. 1985. *Christianity in the West: 1400–1700*. Oxford: Oxford University Press.

Bremond, Henri. 2006. *Histoire littéraire du sentiment religieux en France: Depuis la fin des guerres de religion jusqu'à nos jours*. Rev. ed. Edited by François Trémolières. Grenoble: Jérôme Millon.

Brockey, Liam Matthew. 2007. *Journey to the East: The Jesuit Mission to China, 1579–1724*. Cambridge, MA: Belknap Press of Harvard University Press.

Burson, Jeffrey D. 2014. "Nicolas Bergier: An Enlightened Anti-*Philosophe*." In *Catholicism and Enlightenment in Europe: A Transnational History*, edited by Jeffrey D. Burson and Ulrich L. Lehner, 65–91. Notre Dame, IN: University of Notre Dame Press.

Burson, Jeffrey D. 2010. *The Rise and Fall of Theological Enlightenment: Jean-Martin De Prades and Ideological Polarization in Eighteenth-Century France*. Notre Dame, IN: University of Notre Dame Press.

Burson, Jeffrey D., and Ulrich L. Lehner, eds. 2014. *Catholicism and Enlightenment in Europe: A Transnational History*. Notre Dame, IN: University of Notre Dame Press.

Certeau, Michel de. 1996. *The Mystic Fable*. Translated by Michael B. Smith. Chicago: University of Chicago Press. First published by Éditions Gallimard, 1982.

Certeau, Michel de. 1992. "Mysticism." Translated by M. Brammer. *Diacritics* 22: 11–25. First published in the *Encyclopaedia Universalis*, 1971.

Châtellier, Louis. 1997. *The Religion of The Poor: Rural Missions in Europe and the Formation of Modern Catholicism, c.1500–c.1800*. Translated by Brian Pearce. Cambridge: Cambridge University Press; Paris: Maison des Sciences de l'Homme.

Choquette, Robert. 1992. "An Age of Missionaries, Mystics, and Martyrs." In *Christianity Comes to the Americas, 1492–1776*, edited by Charles H. Lippy, Robert Choquette, and Stafford Poole, 148–175. New York: Paragon House.

Coakley, John W. 2006. *Women, Men and Spiritual Power: Female Saints and Their Male Collaborators*. New York: Columbia University Press.

Cognet, Louis. 1991. *Crépuscule des mystiques: Bossuet–Fénelon*. Edited by J. R. Armogathe. Paris: Desclée De Brouwer.

Connolly, Thomas K., and Robert L. Fastiggi. 2010. "Quietism." In *New Catholic Encyclopedia Supplement 2010*. Vol. 2, edited by Robert L. Fastiggi, 923–925. Detroit, MI: Gale.

Cooke, Bernard. 1976. *Ministry to Word and Sacraments: History and Theology*. Philadelphia, PA: Fortress Press.

Dehne, Carl. 1975. "Roman Catholic Popular Devotions." *Worship* 49: 446–460.

Delumeau, Jean. 1977. *Catholicism between Luther and Voltaire: A New View of the Counter-Reformation*. Translated by Jeremy Moiser. London: Burns and Oates; Philadelphia, PA: Westminster Press. Original French text published by Presses Universitaires de France, 1971.

Ditchfield, Simon. 2013. "Tridentine Catholicism." In *The Ashgate Research Companion to the Counter-Reformation*, edited by Alexandra Bamji, et al., 15–32. Aldershot, UK: Ashgate.

Evennett, H. Outram. 1968. *The Spirit of the Counter-Reformation*. Edited by John Bossy. Cambridge: Cambridge University Press.

Faydit, P. 1702. *Apologie du sistême des saints pères sur la Trinité*. Nancy, France.

Faydit, P. 1696. *Eclaireissements sur la doctrine et histoire ecclésiastiqes des deux premiers siècles*. Paris.

Frijhoff, Willem. 2006. "Popular Religion." In *Enlightenment, Reawakening and Revolution 1660–1815*. Vol. 7 of *The Cambridge History of Christianity*, edited by Stewart J. Brown and Timothy Tackett, 185–207. Cambridge: Cambridge University Press.

Gray, Richard. 2012. *Christianity, the Papacy, and Mission in Africa*. Edited by Lamin Sanneh. Maryknoll, NY: Orbis Books.

Gregory, Brad S. 1999. *Salvation at Stake: Christian Martyrdom in Early Modern Europe*. Cambridge, MA: Harvard University Press.

Guyon, Jeanne. 2012. *Jeanne Guyon: Selected Writings*. Translated and edited by Dianne Guenin-Lelle and Ronney Mourad. New York: Paulist Press.

Haliczer, Stephen. 1996. *Sexuality in the Confessional: A Sacrament Profaned*. New York: Oxford University Press.

Hamilton, Alastair. 2010. "The *Alumbrados: Dejamiento* and Its Practitioners." In *A New Companion to Hispanic Mysticism*, 103–124. Edited by Hilaire Kallendorf. Brill's Companion to the Christian Tradition. Leiden: Brill.

Hecht, Christian. 2012. *Katholische Bildertheologie im Zeitalter von Gegenreformation und Barock: Studien zu Traktaten von Johannes Molanus, Gabriele Paleotti und anderen Autoren*. 2nd ed. Berlin: Gebr. Mann Verlag.

Hsia, R. Po-chia. 2005. *The World of Catholic Renewal, 1540–1770*. 2nd ed. New York: Cambridge University Press.

Lehner, Ulrich L. 2011. "Trinitarian Thought in the Early Modern Era." In *The Oxford Handbook of Trinitarian Theology*, edited by Gilles Emery and Matthew Levering, 240–253. Oxford: Oxford University Press.

Lehner, Ulrich L. 2014. "Apocalypse 2014? Alphonsus Frey's Futurist Commentary on Revelation (1762)." *Journal of Baroque Studies* 2: 25–53.

Le Brun, Jacques. 2002. *Le Pur Amour de Platon à Lacan*. Paris: Éditions du Seuil.

Leone, Massimo. 2010. *Saints and Signs A Semiotic Reading of Conversion in Early Modern Catholicism*. Berlin: De Gruyter.

Maher, Michael, SJ. 2000. "Confession and Consolation: The Society of Jesus and Its Promotion of the General Confession." In *Penitence in the Age of Reformations*, edited by Katharine Jackson Lualdi and Anne T. Thayer, 184–200. Aldershot, UK: Ashgate Publishers.

Mali, A. 1996. *Mystic in the New World: Marie De L'Incarnation (1599–1672)*. Leiden: Brill.

Martos, Joseph. 2001. *Doors of the Sacred*. Rev. ed. Liguori, MO: Liguori/Triumph.

Mayer, Thomas F. 2012. *The Trial of Galileo, 1612–1633*. North York, ON: University of Toronto Press.

Marschler, Thomas. 2007. *Die speculative Trinitätslehre des Francisco Suarez in ihrem philosophisch-theologischen Kontext*. Münster: Aschendorff.

McDermott, G. R. 2000. *Jonathan Edwards Confronts the Gods: Christian Theology, Enlightenment Religion, and Non-Christian Faiths*. New York: Oxford University Press.

McDonnell, Euan. 2009. *The Concept of Freedom in the Writings of St. Francis de Sales*. Bern: Peter Lang.

McGinn, Bernard J. 2013. "Christianity–History of Christian Mysticism." In *Encyclopaedia Britannica Online, Academic Edition*. Article updated March 5, 2013. http://www.britannica.com/EBchecked/topic/115240/Christianity/67548/History-of-Christian-mysticism#toc67551.

McGinn, Bernard J. 2010. "Miguel de Molinos and the *Spiritual Guide*: A Theological Reappraisal." In *Miguel de Molinos: The Spiritual Guide*, translated by Robert P. Baird, edited by Robert P. Baird and Bernard McGinn, 21–39. Mahwah, NJ: Paulist Press.

Menegon, Eugenio. 2009. "Ritual Agency and Interpretive Paradigms of Rituality in the Japanese and Chinese Missions." In *Christianity and Cultures: Japan and China in Comparison, 1543–1644*, edited by M. Antoni J. Üçerler, 142–147. Rome: Institutum Historicum Societatis Iesu.

Milley, Claude-François. 1943. *Le courant mystique au XVIIIe siècle: L'Abandon dans les lettres du P. Milley*. Edited by Jean Bremond. Paris: Pierre Lethielleux.

Miquel, Pierre. 1999. *L'Expérience spirituelle dans la tradition chrétienne*. Paris: Beauchesne.

Mullett, Michael A. 1999. *The Catholic Reformation*. New York: Routledge.

Olphe-Galliard, Michel. 1984. *La Théologie mystique en France au XVIIIe Siècle: Le Pére de Caussade*. Paris: Beauchesne.

O'Malley, John W. 2000. *Trent and All That: Renaming Catholicism in the Early Modern Era*. Cambridge, MA: Harvard University Press.

O'Malley, John W. 2013. *Trent: What Happened at the Council*. Cambridge, MA: Harvard University Press.

Osborne, Kenan B. 2006. "Priestly Formation." In *From Trent to Vatican II: Historical and Theological Investigations*, edited by Raymond F. Bulman and Frederick J. Parrella, 117–135. New York: Oxford University Press.

Oury, Guy Marie. 1993. *Histoire de la spiritualité catholique*. Chambray-lès-Tours: Éditions C.L.D.

Palmer, Robert R. 1961. *Catholics and Unbelievers in Eighteenth-Century France*. 2nd ed. New York: Cooper Square Publishers.

Pourrat, Pierre. *Christian Spirituality*. 1953–55. Translated by W. H. Mitchell, S. P. Jacques, and Donald Attwater. Vols. 1–4. Westminster, MD: Newman Press. Vols. 1–3 first printed 1927.

Rowbotham, A. H. 1956. "The Jesuit Figurists and Eighteenth-Century Religious Thought." *Journal of the History of Ideas* 17: 471–485.

Salin, Dominique. 2007. "The Treatise on Abandonment to Divine Providence." *The Way* 46: 21–36.

Schmidt, Leigh Eric. 2003. "The Making of Modern 'Mysticism.'" *Journal of the American Academy of Religion* 71: 273–302.

Sluhovsky, Moshe. 2007. *Believe Not Every Spirit: Possession, Mysticism, and Discernment in Early Modern Catholicism.* Chicago: University of Chicago Press.

Smith, Margaret. 1973. *An Introduction to the History of Mysticism.* Amsterdam: Philo Press. Reprint of the London 1930 edition.

Sobiech, Frank. 2013. *Radius in manu Dei: Ethos und Bioethik in Werk und Rezeption des Anatomen Niels Stensen (1638–1686).* Münster: Aschendorff.

Thompson-Uberuaga, William. 1989. *Bérulle and the French School: Selected Writings.* New York: Paulist Press.

Tutino, Stefania. 2014. *Shadows of Doubt: Language and Truth in Post-Reformation Catholic Culture.* Oxford: Oxford University Press.

Viller, Marcel, S.J., F. Cavallera, and J. de Guibert, S.J., eds. 1932–1995. *Dictionnaire de spiritualité ascétique et mystique: Doctrine et histoire.* Paris: G. Beauchesne et ses fils.

Wallnig, Thomas. 2012. *Europäische Geschichtskulturen um 1700 zwischen Gelehrsamkeit, Politik und Konfession.* Berlin: De Gruyter.

Werner, Karl. 1867. *Geschichte der apologetischen und polemischen Literatur.* Vol. 5. Schaffausen.

.....................................................................................................

# CHAPTER 5

# THE HISTORY OF CATHOLIC EXEGESIS, 1600–1800

.....................................................................................................

MARIUS REISER

## 1 THE HERITAGE OF THE SIXTEENTH CENTURY

.....................................................................................................

THE history of modern Christian exegesis, Catholic and Protestant, begins with two humanists: Erasmus of Rotterdam (1469–1536) and Johannes Reuchlin (1455–1522). Both remained Catholic all their lives. Reuchlin's Hebrew grammar of 1506 marked the beginning of a renaissance of Central European studies in Hebrew, and a new esteem for Jewish exegesis. In 1516, Erasmus' Greek-Latin edition of the New Testament gave prominence to the Greek source texts over the Latin Vulgate, which had been the standard translation up to that time. He wanted to show that the Vulgate translation needed to be corrected in many places according to the Greek original. He justified with philological explanations (*annotationes*) the areas of his translation that differed from the Vulgate, and the number of *annotationes* increased from edition to edition. Such *annotationes* would become a characteristic of erudite, critical exegesis. The six-volume *Complutensian Polyglot Bible*, which was scientifically much broader, consisted of both Old and New Testaments and the first New Testament dictionary. However, it was not published until 1520 and was too expensive to have an impact on a wider audience. This project had been supervised by the Franciscan theologian and grand inquisitor, Cardinal Ximénes de Cisneros, who in 1508 had opened a *Collegium trilingue* in Alcalá (*Universitas Complutensis*), a college specializing in the three sacred languages of Latin, Greek, and Hebrew. Publication of his *Complutensian Polyglot Bible* marked the first time that Christian printers had dared to use Hebrew letters (Schenker 2008a). Among the contributors to this project were three Jewish converts. Overall, Jewish converts played a major role during this "golden era" of Spanish exegesis (Domínguez Reboiras 1998). The later *Biblia Regia* was an improved and amended edition of the *Complutensian Polyglot*, consisting of eight volumes in folio format, of which 1,200 copies were printed in Antwerp by Plantin between 1568 and 1673. King Philip II of Spain had given scientific oversight of this project to his court chaplain, Benito Arias Montano (1527–98), a gifted Orientalist (Arias Montano 2006). The edition also contained a volume that was similar to a biblical encyclopedia. Montano was its sole author and it was reprinted as late as 1693 in Leiden; this time, however, under the title *Antiquitates Judaicae*. In order to receive a papal endorsement for the *Biblia Regia*, Montano had travelled twice to Rome. The nine-volume *Polyglot Bible of Paris* (1628–45) was, in its first four volumes, a reprint of the Spanish *Biblia Regia*, but lacked the Spanish edition's critical apparatus and exegetical tools (Schenker 2008b).

The new exegesis was first carried out by private scholars and only gradually gained a footing in universities. Its main characteristic was the attempt to better understand the literal meaning of the biblical texts with the help of philological and historical explanations. From the second half of the sixteenth century, this became known as "criticism." To scholastic theologians who worked at universities, such an approach was lacking an essential component—namely, a proper theological explanation of the texts. Martin Luther and Calvin agreed with this critique. Wherever the humanists picked up theological themes, scholastic theologians viewed this as an invasion into their own theological realm.

In 1546, the Council of Trent responded to Protestant questioning by defining the extension of the canon of Holy Scripture. Another conciliar decree, which became even more important, defined the "authenticity" of the Vulgate. "Authentic" meant, in this regard, only that the Vulgate must be considered the official biblical text for use in the liturgy and as the basis for biblical translations and theological explanations. According to Jesuit Cardinal Robert Bellarmine (1542–1621), the Vulgate's infallibility concerned only questions of faith and morals (Horst 2008). Nevertheless, the decree was widely misunderstood to mean that the Vulgate must be regarded as infallible text, thus rendering critical investigation with the help of Hebrew and Greek philology irrelevant. Such a discouragement from studying the original texts never existed, and Catholic academic exegesis has never followed such a path (Wicks 2008, 624–36). Rather, the Council wished the Vulgate to be corrected according to the findings of contemporary exegesis. The desired revision of the text was only published in 1592, as the so-called *Sixto-Clementina*. While Bellarmine was responsible for the principles and methodology of this edition, the erudite Jesuit Francisco de Toledo (Toletus) (1532–96), who also published a well-known commentary on the gospel of John, was responsible for the critical apparatus (Stummer 1928). This edition was in use until the 1979 revision, published as *Nova Vulgata*.

## 2  THE JESUITS AND THE GOLDEN AGE OF CATHOLIC EXEGESIS

The second half of the sixteenth and the first half of the seventeenth centuries were considered the "golden age of Catholic exegesis." Catholic scholars were the predominant leaders in the field of critical exegesis. It is noteworthy that Protestant scholar Louis Cappel's *Critica sacra* of 1650, which was a milestone in Old Testament textual criticism, could be printed only with the help of the Catholic Oratorian priest Jean Morin in a Catholic publishing house in Paris. The reason for this was that among Protestants in general, but also among some Catholics, scholarly work on variant readings of scripture was unpopular because it brought the doctrine of verbal inspiration into difficult travails and revealed the "*obscuritas*" or unclarity of many of its textual passages. This was seen as a diminution of biblical authority.

Jesuits were among the most notable exponents of humanistic exegesis. Their scholarship soon achieved an academic quality that was mostly unmatched by their Protestants peers. Most of these Jesuit Bible scholars were Spanish. They did not limit themselves to philological comments (*annotationes*), but integrated these into fullfledged and detailed theological commentaries. Like their Protestant peers, they focused on the literal meaning of scripture but included the entire tradition of exegesis since the fathers. With the promulgation of the Jesuit rules for study, the *Ratio Studiorum* of 1599, the Jesuits began establishing chairs for biblical exegesis—long before they existed in the Protestant world (Reiser 2007, 236f). The most important among these early Jesuit exegetes were Benito Perera (Pereira; Pererius) (1535–1610), Juan Maldonado (1533–83), and Luis de Alcázar (1554–1613). Perera taught in Rome and wrote a commentary on Genesis comprising 1400 folio pages. It is an amazing and still breathtaking monument of thoroughness and diligence, down to the exact bibliographic information this tome provides. In the preface to Genesis 1, Perera states the principle that no explanation of a text could be allowed to contradict "true reasoning and experimental knowledge" (*veris rationibus et experimentis contraria*). Later, Galileo would appeal to this principle for his Copernican interpretation of the cosmos. Perera not only summarized the opinions of previous scholars for each exegetical question, but also discussed their value, made substantiated decisions in favor or against certain opinions, and left highly ambiguous accounts open to interpretation. More than most of his contemporary commentators, he included—without polemic—a large number of Jewish and rabbinic explanations. He did not even shy away from comparisons with pagan literature. For questions regarding geography, he made use of travel accounts from the time of the Crusades. Arnold Williams fittingly describes his enterprise as such: "One can hardly see how Elizabethan drama could do anything but decline after Shakespeare; for the same reason it is hardly possible that anyone should outdo Pererius. Protestants could redo his work with changed emphasis and for different doctrinal ends, but he had written the great commentary of the times" (Williams 1948, 258). Maldonado (Maldonatus) taught philosophy and theology at the Paris Jesuit College. It was only after abandoning his career as a teacher that he wrote his famous commentaries on the four Gospels. These surpass all preceding ones in erudition, critical diligence, and exegetical perspicacity; and are still useful tools today. About dating the Gospels, he wrote: "At what time and where the Evangelists exactly wrote, is uncertain (*incertum*)." To admit such an uncertainty was in the sixteenth century a bold enterprise, but it nevertheless remains a valid statement. Maldonatus carefully noted every semitism he came across in the texts. The commentary on Matthew, whose galley proofs he was able to finish, also treats the synoptic parallels. The various interpretations and solutions to exegetical problems of the fathers, of medieval or of modern writers, are thoroughly noted. For each case, the arguments in favor and against a position have been diligently pondered in order to reach an intelligible and warranted judgment. Maldonado did not always follow the fathers, but his interpretation of textual passages also differed from their consensus. His analysis of the "poor in spirit" (Mt 5:3) rejects the fathers' interpretation of humility, instead interpreting this expression as consciously accepted material poverty. In cases of strongly diverging interpretations Maldonado tried to harmonize the authors, but he remained very sober in such attempts. In contradistinction to Perera and other commentators, he did not shy away from controversial theological questions. His discussion of Matthew 26:26 comments elaborately on metaphorical interpretations of the Eucharist among Calvinists, and addresses the associated philological questions with diligence and exegetical competency. His commentary was reprinted several times. The last and best edition dates from 1874. Despite the availability of his works, the prejudice that an Enlightener could not learn anything valuable from a Jesuit prevented the reception of Maldonado in the eighteenth century. Most of the difficulties Hermann Samuel Reimarus (1694–1768) found in the Gospel resurrection narratives already had been identified by Maldonado one hundred fifty years earlier. Maldonado's arguments in response to these difficulties are still remarkable (e.g., the commentary on Mt 28:3). Yet Reimarus never read this commentary and neither did G. E. Lessing (1729–81). Alcázar taught in Seville and Córdoba. His commentary on the Revelation of John was a milestone in exegesis, since he interpreted this biblical book for the first time and consistently from the background of first- and second-century history. He identified in it the struggle of the church with Judaism and paganism at the time of the biblical author. In the apocalyptic woman of Revelation 12 he saw a symbol for the church. Protestant exegetes like Hugo Grotius (1583–1645), Catholics like Jacques-Bénigne Bossuet (1627–1704), enlightened exegetes, and contemporary scholars have followed his interpretation. Consequently, one could no longer understand the "whore of Babylon" in Revelation 17 or the Antichrist as symbols for the Roman papacy. It was especially Grotius who was ferociously attacked by his Protestant peers for having given up this important piece of confessional polemic. Of particular value are the insufficiently researched commentaries and sermons on the New Testament of Alfonso Salmerón (1515–85). Salmerón belonged to the earliest companions of Ignatius of Loyola. As papal theologian he participated in all three sessions of the Council of Trent (1545–63). His extensive exegetical work is critical and offers also a biblical theology. It was published from 1597 to 1602 in sixteen volumes. The most famous Jesuit exegete is certainly Cornelius a Lapide (1567–1637). His monumental, often reprinted work comprises commentaries on all books of the Old and New Testament (with the exception of Job and Psalms). However, this is mostly a compilation from other authors. His commentary on Genesis is based predominantly on the exegesis of Perera. Especially in his commentary on the Gospels, he compiled an enormous amount of exegetical and spiritual information, which he mostly offered without any critical reflection. Of better quality is his commentary on the letters of Saint Paul. The short philological commentary to the entire Bible by Juan de Mariana (1536–1624) stands in the best humanist tradition. Another short commentary by the Jesuit Jacobus Tirinus (1580–1632) of 1632 had a wider circulation. It offered traditional exegesis, but failed to reach the critical niveau of the earlier Jesuits. Robert Bellarmine's 1611 commentary to the Psalms, however, was an impressive book. He treated critical questions and even discussed the Hebrew text frequently, but overall he followed the Vulgate. He aimed to extract the precise meaning of the texts for meditative reading. Among Catholic exegetes, who were not Jesuits, Wilhelm Estius (1542–1613) is most prominent. He studied in Louvain and taught at the University of Douai. His commentary on all letters of the New Testament was reprinted until the nineteenth century. He argued in a sober fashion and was only interested in the literal meaning of the text. This was also true of the Jesuit Jacques Bonfrère (Bonfrerius) (1573–1642), who also taught at Douai. He published commentaries to all historical books of the Old Testament except the book of Esther; as for the New Testament, he wrote commentaries on the Gospels, Acts, and the letters of St. Paul. He used a traditional Catholic hermeneutic, which he explained in his introduction to the Pentateuch. He stressed the point of the "obscuritas" or lack of clarity of Holy Scripture. The impreciseness of scripture was emphasized by Catholics in order to demonstrate the necessity of tradition and the magisterium for a proper explanation of the Bible, and to refute Protestant criticism that referred to the clarity and absolute authority of scripture (Gibert 2008).

# 3  A LONELY CULMINATION: RICHARD SIMON (1638–1712)

After the Thirty Years' War, the downfall of Jesuit and all Catholic exegesis began. The Catholic Church was on the defensive and its theology predominantly apologetic. This apologetic had two main targets—namely Protestantism and the beginning skepticism of the Enlightenment. Only one theologian realized that such a defense was only possible if critical research was not neglected, but increased: Richard Simon. With him Catholic exegesis reaches its lonely culmination. He "combines critical boldness with Catholic conservatism" (McKane 1989, 111). Born to a Breton craftsman in Dieppe, he was educated in an Oratory and later joined their order. He studied not only Latin, Greek, and Hebrew, but also all the important Oriental languages. His knowledge of Jewish culture and literature was unsurpassed. He warned the Jesuits already in 1670 about their negligence of biblical languages, and consequently about the decreasing quality of their biblical scholarship. Yet even his reminder of the glorious Jesuit past in exegesis was not heard. Simon was also a member of an informal network of scholars, the so-called *Respublica literaria*, and was one of the first scholars to publish his books not in Latin, but in French, in order to reach a broader public, including educated women. The titles of all of his main works begin with "*Histoire critique*," with which he made the term "critical" a commonplace in societal conversation. Perhaps his most important early work is the translation of a little book by Rabbi Leone Modena (1571–1648), *Cérémonies et coutumes qui sont aujourd'hui en usage parmi les Juifs*. To the 1681 edition of this work he added his own essay "Comparaison des Cérémonies des Juifs et de la Discipline de l'Église" (Le Brun and Stroumsa 1998). In the preface he wrote: "Since the authors of the New Testament were Jews, it is impossible to explain this book without any reference to Judaism." Simon was among the first to understand that a proper study of theology should include studies of Judaism, an idea that even today has been only partly realized. His first main work was the *Histoire critique du Vieux Testament* of 1678. The eminent French bishop and theologian Jacques-Bénigne Bossuet (1627–1704), however, suspected the book of heresy and had the entire first edition of 1,300 copies burnt and Simon banned from his order, without prior hearing or any possibility of defense. Bossuet had read in the table of contents that the entire text of the Pentateuch had not been written by Moses. Simon assumed that the text had been written partially by Moses, partially by inspired scribes who had been instructed by Moses, as well as by inspired final redactors. This theory was not new and had already been presented by André Maës (Andreas Masius) (1514–73), which Simon acknowledged. Like most of Simon's other works, this book also was later published in the Netherlands and began to stir up numerous academic controversies. The most vehement criticism came from Protestant authors, who still defended a verbal inspiration of scripture and the Masoretic Hebrew text of the Bible as authentic. The English translation of Simon's *Critical History of the Old Testament* of 1682 became the major instigation for the English poet John Dryden (1631–1700) to convert to Catholicism. Simon's reflections on hermeneutics had convinced him that the authority of Holy Scripture could only be preserved within the context of ecclesiastical tradition; and furthermore, that this tradition conceded biblical criticism sufficient liberties. Questions of criticism and theological interpretation do belong, however, to different realms and should not be intermingled. In all questions about criticism, that is in philological and historical issues, dogmatic theology cannot have a say. For a theological interpretation, dogmatic theology predefines the course of the exegete through the "rule of faith" (*regula fidei*), which is the binding faith of the church. This differentiation could be helpful even today. Simon himself hoped that a universal acknowledgement of the theological opinions of the Greek and Latin fathers of the first four centuries could bring about a reunion of the churches. There was little textual criticism of the Hebrew Bible prior to the seventeenth century. For their Hebrew text, the editors of the *Complutensian Polyglot* utilized at least seven different manuscripts, but no one attempted to imitate their work for another hundred years. What other scholar owned—like Reuchlin— a Hebrew manuscript of the entire Old Testament? Besides Protestant scholar Louis Cappel (1585–1658), only Simon owned one, and he also undertook groundbreaking, original research. Simon grasped the importance of textual criticism as the history of a living text, and anticipated insights classical philology would not reach until two or three hundred years later. In this context, it is important to note Simon's judgment about his own teacher of exegesis, Jean Morin (1591–1659). Morin was a convert from Protestantism, had also become an Oratorian, studied the Septuagint, and published the *Editio princeps* of the Samaritan Pentateuch, whose alphabet he was able to decipher (Auvray 1959). This was included in Brian Walton's (1600–61) *Polyglot*, published 1653–58 in London, and still today a useful text. Morin commented that the Samaritan text concurred at times with the Septuagint against the Hebrew Masoretic text. Such findings undermined Protestant convictions about the "Hebrew truth" (*veritas hebraica*) of the Old Testament and aroused fierce opposition. [Richard] Simon writes about his teacher: "No one has written more on biblical criticism, nor with more erudition, than Father Morin of the Oratory." His main aim was

> to undermine, as far as possible, the present Hebrew text in order to augment the value of the Septuagint version and the Hebrew Pentateuch of the Samaritans. He argued that the Hebrew text of the Jews was corrupt in most of the places where it differs from the Greek version of the Septuagint, the Hebrew copy of the Samaritans, and even the Vulgate. He thought that in so doing, he was doing the Church a great service . . . But he may not have been aware that the Church, in authorizing the old version of the Septuagint and the new translation by St. Jerome, never pretended to condemn the Hebrew text, nor did it accuse the Jews of having corrupted it. (Gibert 2008, 771)

This discovery began to prevail only slowly. He also defended the critics of Morin, which testifies to Simon's unbiased scholarship and clear judgment: "There is a necessary intermediate position between this position and that of the Protestants he is opposing, whereby justice will be meted out to Jews and Christians, to Catholic doctors and the wisest Protestants, who never pretended that the Hebrew copies of today were flawless" (Gibert 2008, 771). After working on the Old Testament, Simon began research on the New Testament. Thus he laid down the basics for all biblical research, which today fall into the category of introductory questions—for example, textual criticism; the age, origin and authors of a text; the process of textual production and redaction; as well as the problems of translation. The *Histoire critique du texte du Nouveau Testament* of 1689 is in fact the first modern introduction to the New Testament. In it Simon treats not only the abovementioned issues, but also the question of inspiration (chapters 23–25). He rejects verbal inspiration and assumes that in literary matters, the Holy Spirit relied on the abilities of the human authors. In three other chapters, Simon analyzes the idiosyncrasies of the biblical languages. New Testament Greek is for him "Synagogue Greek." This conviction has since been verified after many scholarly detours (Reiser 2005). In chapter 11, Simon also puts to rest the thesis of a Latin original of the Gospel of Mark. Moreover, he presents to his readers an astoundingly complete history of biblical exegesis, Jewish and Christian alike, from its beginnings to his own day. His *History of the Commentaries of the New Testament* of 1693 comprises over 1000 pages and remains, even now, useful and informative reading. His translation of the New Testament was published in 1702 in France, but then was immediately forbidden by Bossuet. A telling example for Simon's work and the situation of the churches is the so-called *Comma Johanneum*. It is a textual addition to 1 John 5:7, according to which "Father, Logos and Holy Spirit" are one. This verse was for all confessions the most important biblical proof for a doctrine of the Trinity in the New Testament. Simon was the only scholar of the seventeenth century who attempted to examine this verse critically, without dogmatic presuppositions. For him, the truth of the doctrine of the Trinity did not hinge on this verse, because Simon strictly differentiated between critical and theological questions. By comparing all available manuscripts and old translations, he arrived at the conclusion that the accretion has no right to be included in the biblical text. For this scholarly judgment, he was attacked from all sides. Catholics were upset because Simon defended Luther, who had rejected including *Comma Johanneum* in his translation of scripture. Only after Luther's death would it be added to the translation. During the nineteenth century, the textual addition vanished from critical editions and consequently from biblical translations. Likewise, it was omitted from the Nova Vulgata of 1979. The *Authorized Version*, as well as the Catholic translation of Ronald Knox and many orthodox editions and translations, still include this accretion. Richard Simon, whom one might call the most important scholar in the history of modern exegesis, had a tragic fate. Until his death, he remained a Catholic priest, had a pious death and was buried in the parish church of his hometown Dieppe. Just as he was attacked during his lifetime, so he was calumniated and ostracized after his death. Every evil that conservative and traditionalist circles of all confessions could imagine was projected onto him—one only has to read Jonathan Swift's *A Tale of a Tub* and *The Battle of Books*. Even today, the greatest part of his scholarly work remains unacknowledged by exegetes, or is reduced to clichés. His biblical hermeneutic remains practically unknown. Most fathers of the Second Vatican Council (1962–65) were probably unaware that they actually elevated Simon's theory of inspiration to an official church teaching (Burtchaell 1969, 44–88). He still unjustly has the reputation of a proud scholar, a cold rationalist critic, a heretic in disguise, and an incessant cause of scandal. Simon's works were rarely read diligently, but instead mostly used as pawns for different agendas. The fact that Simon was friends with a Jew and defended Jews against unjust treatment has only recently come to the attention of historians, and refutes older polemics and defamations about his stance towards Judaism (Reiser 2007, 188–98). A real reception of Simon has never occurred, but would be fruitful for the future of Catholic scholarship.

# 4 CATHOLIC EXEGESIS IN THE ENLIGHTENMENT

Richard Simon already knew what twentieth century hermeneutic would later elaborate upon: exegesis without presuppositions or background beliefs, and thereby absolutely objective exegesis, is impossible. Every exegete reads the texts with a prior understanding. Simon also knew that one can easily imagine oneself to be objective and he believed that those who prided themselves on their search for pure truth without prejudice were especially likely to fall victim to such imaginary objectivity. Simon's critique targeted the Socinians and Enlighteners who, being free from ecclesiastical presuppositions, believed themselves to be entirely free of any presuppositions and prejudices as well, and thus utterly objective. It is this fantasy of objectivity that makes it, according to Simon, impossible to convince somebody of the falsehood of one of his opinions. In this regard, Simon again has been proven right. The so-called Enlightenment did not so much produce new knowledge, but rather consisted of a mental climate change and paradigm shift in what appeared plausible. Suddenly, reason alone had become the absolute sovereign in all realms of worldly and human life, and was validated as the only authority in interpreting scripture. This rationalism was a mental filter that consequently eclipsed miracles and the supernatural as a whole. Direct divine actions in the world were declared impossible. A specific human being, Jesus of Nazareth, could not be simultaneously human and divine, it was stated. These philosophical presuppositions were combined with a general skepticism and feeling of superiority toward the scholarly and cultural achievements of the past. Skepticism and condescension expressed themselves also in a hostility toward all traditions, dogmas, and ceremonies; in particular, all ecclesiastical ones. Reverence for former grandeur was replaced by a naïve belief in progress that included a moral perfectibility of the human being. Such views took stronger hold within Protestantism than in Catholicism, but Catholic theology was slowly affected by them too. Most Catholics, however, attempted to accept these only insofar as they were compatible with ecclesiastical teaching. For Catholic exegesis the *regula fidei*, the rule of faith, remained the same as it had been for Richard Simon: the proper background for a theological understanding of scripture. However, Simon's hermeneutical differentiation between critical and theological interpretation had not been accepted, so the efforts to remain within the boundaries of the church's teaching caused much academic embarrassment and dishonesty in dealing with questions of biblical criticism. Eighteenth-century exegesis did not attempt to follow Richard Simon, nor to maintain his high level of critical research; on the contrary, he and his exegesis were suspected of heresy. Thus, Catholic exegesis during the Enlightenment period could not progress beyond Simon, nor—despite so many new findings—could it even retain the niveau of the sixteenth-century Jesuits. This intellectual mistrust indirectly supported religious skepticism and had catastrophic consequences, which reached their culmination in the so-called Modernist crisis at the beginning of the twentieth century. The most famous Catholic exegete of the eighteenth century is a good example for the abovementioned problems: Dom Augustin Calmet (1672–1757). He entered the Benedictine abbey of Toul in Lorraine, and between 1707 and 1716, together with ten confreres, published his monumental literal commentary on all books of the Old and New Testament, *Commentaire littéral sur tous les livres de l'Ancien et du Nouveau Testament*, comprising 23 volumes of roughly 20,000 pages (Martin 2008). Calmet discussed specific exegetical issues in his *Dissertationes*, which were published in four volumes. He reused this material in a multivolume biblical handbook, the *Dictionnaire historique, critique, chronologique, géographique et littéral de la Bible*. All of these works were translated into Latin by

Giovanni D. Mansi, and many of them also were translated into German and English. Until the end of the nineteenth century, Calmet's works were considered standard by Catholics and seen as exegetical masterpieces. Even among Protestants, nothing comparable to Calmet's achievement existed, only the less reader-friendly commentaries of Jean Le Clerc (1657–1736) (Schwarzbach 2001, 136). Calmet had an irenic nature and was, in many regards, naïve and gullible. He was full of contempt for the great Jewish commentaries, but was no great philologist himself. Rather, he was a compiler of all kinds of information, especially cultural history. He was a "man of the Enlightenment despite himself" (Schwarzbach 2001). He viewed the biblical narratives in a rationalist spirit, finding in them problems, contradictions, anachronisms, and errors that he tried to harmonize with the findings of historical or scientific research. However, he ceased his reflections if the facts and arguments led him to conclusions that deviated from the traditional faith of the church. Less scrupulous minds did not abhor to follow these paths. For Calmet there were no hermeneutical problems. In difficult questions of criticism, he would decide in favor of traditional explanations or would leave those questions to the reader. Simon and the great Jesuit exegetes of the past had done exegesis differently; it is unsurprising, therefore, that Calmet did not appreciate either of them. This accounts for the "ambiguous effect" of his writings (Laplanche 1994, 64). His biblical commentary has possibly done more for the rise of disbelief than did all of eighteenth-century anti-Christian literature. A few examples can buttress this claim. In order to avoid the fate that befell Simon, Calmet began his preface to the commentary on the Pentateuch with the statement: "The Pentateuch is the work of Moses." He only concedes small accretions caused by a later redaction and mistakes in the process of copying the text. A number of dissertations follow the preface: one about writing books in antiquity, one about the land of Ophir, on circumcision, on the age of money, and on ancient chronology. On the first verse of Genesis, he comments: "to create" means, first, to pull out of nothingness, and second, to give a thing its form. Tradition obliges us, he states, to embrace the first meaning. He does not even mention that Simon had refuted such an explanation decades earlier. The paradise narratives are, according to Calmet, historical reports that Moses embellished with symbolic elements. He rejected the view of Philo of Alexandria and of Thomas de Vio Cajetan (1469–1534) that these accounts were metaphorical stories and contained parables. Likewise, Calmet fails to mention Origen. Richard Simon's criticism of Luther for not having observed the symbolic content of these stories is also completely ignored. In reference to Jonah, Calmet wonders how a fish could swallow the prophet with all his clothes, how he could survive in his belly for three days, and why God brought about such a miracle. However, he vehemently rejects the interpretation of "unbelievers" that this story was a fairy tale or a parable. The problem of literary genres of such narratives, which Simon carefully termed "sacred fictions," and how they can express a theological truth, first regained importance in the twentieth century (Reiser 2007, 355–71). The Benedictine scholar had problems with the biblical image of God because it did not fit his enlightened expectations: What kind of God would exclude Moses from the promised land because of his lack of trust, or would turn Lot's wife into a pillar of salt, or punish David's curiosity with the death of

70,000 people? If God treats his friends like that, how will he treat the unbelievers? (Schwarzbach 2001, 143). In his *Dictionnaire historique*, Calmet treats the question of whether this Gospel was originally written in Latin—a hypothesis that Simon had refuted with invincible proofs decades earlier. Even the *Comma Johanneum* is analyzed in a lengthy *Dissertatio*. This time, however, Calmet mentions Simon's arguments against the veracity of the verse and also mentions other critics, but decides—without good reasons—to regard it as authentic, relying only on decisions of the North African church from the fifth century, and the Council of Trent. That the verse is absent from all early Greek manuscripts, he "explains" as an early mistake of a scribe. Calmet could not digest the amount of information and erudition he had amassed. "It is not that Calmet was incapable of a critical evaluation of sources—he was. It is just that he judged them (shrewdly, I believe) in terms of their theological authority, rather than in terms of their cogency or their consistency with other scientific information" (Schwarzbach 2001, 145). It is no surprise, therefore, that Calmet's works were like a gold mine for anti-Christian literature. Voltaire's friend, Madame du Châtelet, who had read the *Commentaire littéral*, only needed to pass over Calmet's theological conclusions in order to arrive at her own radically deist deductions. The example of Calmet demonstrates that it is insufficient to "just" be orthodox; one also has to have the better arguments. The ecclesiastical state of exegesis at the end of the eighteenth century can be illustrated with two almost simultaneous events that both occurred on German soil, where the Protestant territories had become the promised land of liberal critical exegesis and remained so until the midst of the twentieth century. In the fall of 1777, a young and talented exegete from Mainz, the Catholic priest Johann Lorenz Isenbiehl (1744–1818), had published a book on Isaiah's prophecy (Is 7:14). He attempted to show that the prophecy was not about Jesus, and that Matthew (Mt 1:23) used this quotation only as an analogy to Jesus. His monograph was conversant with the best critical scholarship of his time, because Isenbiehl had studied with Johann David Michaelis (1717–91) in Göttingen. His theory did not question any Catholic dogma but shed a questioning light on the Gospel of Matthew—a fact that Isenbiehl did not realize. The book sparked a major debate, which was mostly polemical and only seldom scholarly. Ecclesiastical authorities publicly condemned the book, as did six theology departments—among them Salzburg, Strasbourg, and the Sorbonne. Finally the pope condemned the book, and Isenbiehl was ordered to unconditionally accept the papal decision with full submission of will and intellect by Christmas 1779. The young priest bowed to the decision, which also meant the end of his academic career (Reiser 2007, 278–87; Lehner 2013). That the situation among Protestants was not much better can be seen when one considers that orthodox Protestants supported Rome's decision against Isenbiehl. No orthodox theologian was interested in weakening or questioning the important Isaiah prophecy. At the same time, however, the Protestant churches also were shaken by an exegetical scandal. This became known as the "fragment controversy" and centered on radically deist interpretations of biblical texts, especially the fragment known as *Vom Zwecke Jesu und seiner Jünger*. The texts had been authored by the Hamburg scholar Hermann Samuel Reimarus (1694–1768) and posthumously published by Gotthold Ephraim Lessing

(1729–81) (Freund 1989; English translations: Voysey 1879; Talbert 1970). The scandal ended in a similar way to the Isenbiehl affair. The publications were confiscated and Lessing's freedom from censorship was revoked; while his orthodox opponent, Melchior Goeze (1717–86), the main pastor of Hamburg, triumphed.

An extreme example of a rationalist exegete was the Norbertine Johann Jahn (1750–1816). He was a well-known and highly regarded Orientalist who published works on introductory questions to Old Testament exegesis and what has been called "biblical archaeology" (research and exposition of the social, cultural and religious institutions of Judaism). From 1789, he taught at the University of Vienna, but was forced to retire in 1806. In a posthumously published essay, he mused about what Jesus did during the forty days between the Resurrection and the Ascension. According to Jahn, the Resurrection was a physical resuscitation, because it was possible to touch Jesus' body with its wounds. When the New Testament speaks about Jesus "appearing," this is to be understood figuratively. After his resuscitation, Jesus was naked as he left his grave. He went to the gardener in order to get some clothes. He presented himself in these clothes to Mary Magdalene, who therefore mistook him for the gardener. Another reason why she did not immediately recognize him was that Jesus had not had food or drink for fifty-six hours and was still disfigured by his passion. The same can be said of the disciples who met Jesus on the road to Emmaus. Likewise, Christ did not enter through closed doors (John 20:19–26) but entered normally or opened them miraculously. Jesus, in his regained body, visited hundreds, if not thousands of his followers, and thus proved that he was again alive. He did not present himself to the Sanhedrin because the Jewish council would have killed him again. Jahn was convinced he had resolved all problems with these and other similarly erudite hypotheses. It is understandable that the ecclesiastical authorities had no tolerance for a theological teacher like Jahn; and it is curious that no further actions were taken against him. A positive light is shed on the Enlightenment in the Habsburg territories by the fact that the volume which contained the investigation leading to Jahn's forced retirement was published in 1821 in Tübingen. The editor was Jahn's friend, Ernst Gottlieb Bengel (1769–1826), grandson of the famous Johann Albrecht Bengel (1687–1752) and teacher of Ferdinand Christian Baur (1792–1860). Louis XV's personal physician, Jean Astruc (1684–1766) was yet another famous Catholic exegete who deserves mention here. As a self-taught researcher, he improved the theories about the origins of the Pentateuch and differentiated sources Moses had supposedly worked with, based upon the use of their names for God, either JHWH or Elohim. His book was published in 1753 and republished in 1999 (Gibert 2010, 299–308). His thesis became famous and was often referred to—yet today the same question is again open for discussion. Another important contributor to textual criticism of the Old Testament was the Italian Giovanni Bernardo de Rossi (1742–1831). And only on the fringes of the Catholic world could a private scholar publish substantial exegetical works, seething with Enlightenment thought, in Scotland. That was Alexander Geddes (1732–1802). He was no rationalist like Jahn, but dared to accept Richard Simon's explanation of the same first three chapters of the book of Genesis that Calmet had rejected. Geddes explained the story of the creation of the world as "a most beautiful mythos, or philosophical fiction, contrived with great wisdom, dressed in the garb of real history, adapted to the shallow intellects of a rude and barbarous nation." The narratives in the second and third chapters of Genesis he even labeled for his "religious but intelligent reader" as "poetic tales" (Fuller 1984, 45; Goldie 2014). Yet only scholars like the Protestant Johann Gottfried Eichhorn (1753–1827) in Göttingen accepted such theses with a public endorsement. Today no scholar or church authority has a problem with poetic tales in the Bible, but we still have not established what this means for their theological interpretation and the truth of their story.

## BIBLIOGRAPHY

Arias Montano, Benito. 2006. *Prefacios de Benito Arias Montano a la Biblia Regia de Felipe II: Estudio introductorio, edición, traducción y notas de María Asunción Sánchez Manzano.* Universidad de León.

Auvray, Paul. 1959. "Jean Morin (1591–1659)." *Revue Biblique* 66: 396–414.

Burtchaell, James T. 1969. *Catholic Theories of Biblical Inspiration since 1810: A Review and Critique.* Cambridge: Cambridge University Press.

Domínguez Reboiras, Fernando. 1998. *Gaspar de Grajal (1530–1575): Frühneuzeitliche Bibelwissenschaft im Streit mit Universität und Inquisition.* Münster: Aschendorffsche Verlagsbuchhandlung.

Freund, Gerhard. 1989. *Theologie im Widerspruch: die Lessing-Goeze-Kontroverse.* Stuttgart u.a: Kohlhammer, 1989.

Fuller, Reginald Cuthbert. 1984. *Alexander Geddes 1737–1802: A Pioneer of Biblical Criticism.* Bradford-on-Avon: The Almond Press.

Gibert, Pierre. 2008. "The Catholic Counterpart and Response to the Protestant Orthodoxy." In *Hebrew Bible/Old Testament: The History of Its Interpretation.* Vol. 2 of *From the Renaissance to the Enlightenment,* edited by Magne Sæbø, 758–773. Göttingen: Vandenhoeck & Ruprecht.

Gibert, Pierre. 2010. *L'invention critique de la Bible: XVe–XVIIIe siècle.* Paris: Éditions Gallimard.

Goldie, Mark. 2014. "Alexander Geddes: Biblical Criticism, Ecclesiastical Democracy, and Jacobinism." In *Enlightenment and Catholicism in Europe: A Transnational History,* edited by Ulrich L. Lehner and Jeffrey Burson. Notre Dame: University of Notre Dame Press.

Horst, Ulrich. 2008. "Robert Bellarmin und die *Vulgata*: Ein Beitrag zur Diskussion über die päpstliche Unfehlbarkeit." *Theologie und Philosophie* 83: 179–208.

Laplanche, François. 1994. *La Bible en France entre mythe et critique, XVIe–XIXe siècle.* Paris: Albin Michel S.A.

Le Brun, Jacques, and Gedaliahu Stroumsa, eds. 1998. *Les Juifs présentés aux Chrétiens. Cérémonies et coutumes qui s'observent aujourd'hui parmi les Juifs par Léon de Modène traduit par Richard Simon suivi de Comparaison des cérémonies des Juifs et de la discipline de l'Église par Richard Simon.* Paris: Les Belles Lettres.

Lehner, Ulrich L. 2013. "Against the Consensus of the Fathers? The Travail of Eighteenth-Century Catholic Exegesis and the Case of J. L. Isenbiehl of 1777/78." *Pro Ecclesia* 22: 189–221.

Martin, Philippe, and Fabienne Henryot, eds. 2008. *Dom Augustin Calmet: un itinéraire intellectuel.* Paris: Riveneuve éditions.

McKane, William. 1989. *Selected Christian Hebraists.* Cambridge: Cambridge University Press.

Pfeiffer, Rudolf. 1976. *A History of Classical Scholarship from 1300–1850*. Oxford: Oxford University Press.

Reiser, Marius. 2009. "Die Auswirkungen der Aufklärung auf die Bibelauslegung am Beispiel Johann Wolfgang Goethes." *Trierer Theologische Zeitschrift* 118: 63–77.

Reiser, Marius. 2007. *Bibelkritik und Auslegung der Heiligen Schrift. Beiträge zur Geschichte der biblischen Exegese und Hermeneutik*. Wissenschaftliche Untersuchungen zum Neuen Testament 217. Tübingen: Mohr Siebeck.

Reiser, Marius. 2005. "Die Quellen des neutestamentlichen Griechisch und die Frage des Judengriechischen in der Forschungsgeschichte von 1696–1989." *Biblische Zeitschrift* 49: 46–59.

Reventlow, Henning Graf. 1985. *The Authority of the Bible and the Rise of the Modern World*. Philadelphia: Fortress Press.

Sæbø, Magne, ed. 2008. *Hebrew Bible/Old Testament: The History of Its Interpretation*. Vol. 2 of *From the Renaissance to the Enlightenment*. Göttingen: Vandenhoeck & Ruprecht.

Schenker, Adrian. 2008a. "From the First Printed Hebrew, Greek and Latin Bibles to the First Polyglot Bible, The Complutensian Polyglot: 1477–1577." In *Hebrew Bible/Old Testament: The History of Its Interpretation*. Vol. 2 of *From the Renaissance to the Enlightenment*, edited by Magne Sæbø, 276–294. Göttingen: Vandenhoeck & Ruprecht.

Schenker, Adrian. 2008b. "The Polyglot Bibles of Antwerp, Paris, and London: 1568–1658." In *Hebrew Bible/Old Testament: The History of Its Interpretation*. Vol. 2 of *From the Renaissance to the Enlightenment*, edited by Magne Sæbø, 774–785. Göttingen: Vandenhoeck & Ruprecht.

Schwarzbach, Bertram E. 2001. "Dom Augustin Calmet: Man of the Enlightenment Despite Himself." *Archiv für Religionsgeschichte* 3: 135–148.

Schwarzbach, Bertram E. 1987. "La Fortune de Richard Simon au XVIIIe siècle." *Revue des études juives* 146: 225–239.

Schwarzbach, Bertram E, ed. 2011. *Gabrielle-Emilie Le Tonnelier de Breteuil, marquise Du Châtelet-Lomond: Examens de la Bible*. Paris: Honoré Champion.

Stummer, Friedrich. 1928. *Einführung in die lateinische Bibel*. Paderborn: Ferdinand Schöningh.

Talbert, C. H., ed. 1970. *Reimarus: Fragments*. Philadelphia: Fortress.

Voysey, C., ed. 1879. *Fragments from Reimarus consisting of Brief Critical Remarks on the Object of Jesus and His Disciples*. London: Williams and Norgate.

Wicks, Jared. 2008. "Catholic Old Testament Interpretation in the Reformation and Early Confessional Eras." In *Hebrew Bible/Old Testament: The History of Its Interpretation*. Vol. 2 of *From the Renaissance to the Enlightenment*, edited by Magne Sæbø, 617–648. Göttingen: Vandenhoeck & Ruprecht.

Williams, Arnold. 1948. *The Common Expositor: An Account of the Commentaries on Genesis, 1527–1633*. Chapel Hill: University of North Carolina Press.

# CHAPTER 6

# PROVIDENCE, PREDESTINATION, AND GRACE IN EARLY MODERN CATHOLIC THEOLOGY

## THOMAS MARSCHLER

DEBATE over providence, predestination, and grace led Catholic theologians of the early modern period to formulations at once highly controversial and ingeniously constructive. The "grace controversy" between the Jesuit Molinists and the Dominican Báñezians was, according to Friedrich Stegmüller, "the most exciting and portentous event in the modern history of Catholic theology and at the same time the grandiose conclusion to a century churned up with religious ideas" (Stegmüller 1935, VII). The scene was set for these debates by the papal condemnations of the teachings of Michel Baius (1513–89) in 1567 and Cornelius Jansen the Younger (1585–1638) in 1653: the debates played out between the poles of a neo-Pelagian concentration on the claims of integral human nature before God, and the Augustinian concept of its utter dependence since the Fall on the operation of salvific grace.

## 1 THE THEOLOGICAL CONNECTION BETWEEN PROVIDENCE, PREDESTINATION AND GRACE IN FRANCISCO SUÁREZ, SJ

Since the beginning of the sixteenth century, Catholic dogmatics has generally followed the order of Thomas Aquinas's (1225–74) *Summa Theologiae*. In his teaching on God in the *Prima Pars*, Thomas devotes one question each to providence and predestination (I, q. 22–23). The doctrine of grace is treated at length in the *Prima Secundae* (I–II, q. 109–14). The theologians of the early modern period retained these separate contexts for the discussion of the three topics while, however, emphasizing the connectedness of their subject matter and accentuating new aspects. This is exemplified in the disputations of the Jesuit Francisco Suárez (1548–1617). Suárez's teaching on God (1st ed. 1606), retains the close link between providence and predestination, but clearly shifts the emphasis in favor of the latter. While he offers only a brief section on providence at the end of the teaching on divine attributes (Suárez 1856–78, De deo uno 3.10 [I:231–35], he develops the topic of predestination in a separate treatise (Suárez 1856–78, De deo uno 3.10 [I:236–532]) which, set between the treatment of God's being and attributes and the treatise on the Trinity, constitutes one of the three main foci of his *De deo uno et trino*. In Suárez's view, after the Holy Trinity only predestination can be adjudged a strictly supernatural subject of scholarly reflection on God (Suárez 1856–78, De deo uno, Prooemium [I, XXIII]), the divine attributes and providence having been addressed in the metaphysical teaching on God (Suárez 1856–78, Disputationes metaphysicae 30.14-17 [XXVI:165–224]). Suárez's fundamental determinations of providence and foreordination initially operate within an area of consensus determined by the fathers, above all Augustine. By "providence" he understands God's plan for the entire universe, which unfolds as God guides the whole as well as every particular toward the goals he intends for them (Marschler 2013, 32–40). He ascribes great importance to the distinction between "natural" and "moral" providence: the former applies to all creatures and includes the conservation of being granted by God and the divine *concursus* in all creaturely activity; the latter concerns only angels and human beings to the extent that they are beings who pursue the goal of their existence in freedom. It finds expression in "commandments, words of advice, promises, threats, rewards and punishments" (Suárez 1856–78, De deo uno 3.10.7 [I:232b]), thus pointing beyond philosophical deliberation to the sphere of free divine acts of revelation. Providence is an expression of God's sovereign and just dominion but also of his goodness and wisdom. Knowing and willing conjoin in its constitution (Suárez 1856–78, De deo uno 3.10.10 [I:233b]).

In his freedom, God decided to open up a goal to rational creatures, transcending the capacity of their nature as established in creation and orienting them towards eternal life (Suárez 1856–78, De praedestinatione 1.1.6 [I:237b]; 1.4.5 [I:243b]). In God this goal is presupposed from all eternity as a certain determination, whereas according to the doctrine of the Council of Trent (Denzinger and Hünermann 2010, 1540.1565–66), it normally remains hidden from the creature (Suárez 1856–78, De praedestinatione 1.3.5 [I:240a]). Since in predestination the path, the necessary means by which the goal can be reached, and the goal itself are fixed (Suárez 1856–78, De praed. 15.5.15 [I:248b]), predestination can be regarded as part of providence (on the more exact definition of the relationship, see Suárez 1856–78, De praed. 1.15 [I:305a–309b]). This points to the supernatural dimension of providence, thus enabling a (theological) solution to many difficult problems (for example, the suffering of many of the just on earth) (Suárez 1856–78, De deo uno 3.10.14 [I:234b]). Predestination, however, takes into consideration the aspect of the choice of goal, whereas providence is oriented more towards obtaining the right means of reaching it (Suárez 1856–78, De praed. 15.5.17 [I:249a]).

Alongside the question of how, on God's part, intellect and will work together in the act of predestination, the theological schools asked how this certain goal of human existence can be reconciled with the unimpaired reality of creaturely freedom. This topic links the treatises on predestination and grace. If grace (understood as *gratia creata*) is the means through which God makes possible the orientation and election of created beings to eternal life during their earthly existence, the relationship of grace to predestination is like that of created, temporal effects to their uncreated, eternal cause (Suárez 1856–78, De praed. 1.19 [I:309b–313b]). Accordingly, the independent treatise *de gratia* deals with God in his activity of sanctification and illustrates central attributes of God from the perspective of their manifestation in salvation history (Suárez 1856–78, De gratia, Prooem. [VII, p. IX–X]). Suárez's teaching on grace has also been considerably developed beyond Aquinas's text. Originally filling three folio volumes, this is the most elaborate of Suárez's theological works (Scorraille 1917, 2:377).

Suárez begins with six detailed prolegomena in which he treats systematic and historical presuppositions of his topic. The first two parts, on free will as the "foundation of grace" (Suárez 1856–78, De gratia, no. 7 [VII, p. XI–XII]) and on divine foreknowledge, point toward controversial questions of the times. The subsequent division of the treatise according to actual and habitual grace (Suárez 1856–78, De gratia, lib. I–V/VI–XI), the roots of which lie in the fourteenth century but are now theologically differentiated and consolidated, continued to shape the Catholic treatise on grace until well into the twentieth century. Whereas the major questions *de auxiliis* are discussed in the first part (the need for divine grace in the natural and supernatural spheres, the distinction between sufficient and efficacious grace in the interplay with human freedom), the second section contains the thorny debates about justification, the nature of salvific grace and merit, and the final perseverance of the recipient of grace, classifying them as problems already present in the texts of the Council of Trent.

The publication history of Suárez's *De gratia* illustrates the explosive nature of debates on the theology of grace at the beginning of the seventeenth century. In the last years of his life, the Jesuit had sought permission in Rome to be allowed to publish his work *De auxiliis*. In April 1617, a few months before his death, a letter reached him written by Cardinal Scipione Borghese in the name of the pope, forbidding the publication (Scorraille 1917, 2:234f.). Whereas the first and third volumes of Suárez's teaching on grace were published soon after his death in 1619, it was over three decades before the third part, *De auxiliis*, also became publicly available in Lyons in 1654 as a result of a private initiative and without the consent of the Jesuit Order (Scorraille 1917, 2:398ff). Thus even Suárez was not able to escape the strict ruling of the decree of August 28, 1607, a dilatory decision by Paul V (1552–1621) that put an end to inconclusive disputations concerning the compatibility of God's grace with human freedom. It was not until the Jansenist debates of the mid-seventeenth century that this decision, supported by a "decree of the Inquisition of 1 December 1611 forbidding all further writings on the doctrine of grace unless they were expressly authorized by the Holy Office" (Pastor 1927, 180), was gradually relativized.

# 2   The Central Positions in the "Grace Controversy"

The "grace controversy" which unfolded following the publication of the Dominican Domingo Báñez's (1528–1604) commentaries on the *Prima* and *Prima Secundae* (Salamanca 1584) and the Jesuit Luis de Molina's (1535–1600) "Concordia liberi arbitrii cum gratiæ donis, divina præscientia, providentia, prædestinatione et reprobatione" (Lisbon 1588) went on for two decades (see the overview in Stegmüller 1960). We examine the theological alternatives that were debated in the *Disputationes de auxiliis*.

## 2.1   The common theological foundation

The competing theses of the theological schools in the field of providence, predestination, and grace can only be correctly classified if one bears in mind the shared framework of theological premises within which they were expressed. The theology of Augustine served as an undisputed basis which was never questioned, not even in the arguments with the Reformers. The debates *de auxiliis* were in large part a struggle for interpretational hegemony in the exegesis of Augustine's texts. Thus the terms of reference for all the schemes included the doctrines of original sin; infallible predestination; the necessity, gratuity and priority of grace; and the conviction that God does not move man merely "extrinsically" with his grace but also (and predominantly) "intrinsically." Taken over from medieval Scholasticism and deepened were both the metaphysical analysis of *gratia (interna) creata* and the thesis of the essentially supranatural character of grace and of the theological virtues. From the sixteenth century onward, theology had to face up to a new challenge from the reformers' theology of grace, above all from Luther's concept of freedom, his theses on the preparation and nature of justification or on the assurance of salvation, and also from Calvin's doctrine of predestination. The answers given in the Council of Trent's 1547 Decree on Justification constituted for all Catholic authors the authoritative template for the tracts on grace. Against Luther, the conviction was defended that original sin did not completely destroy man's ability to produce morally good acts even without divine grace. Since, however, the Council of Trent had taught that even those justified by God required the help of a "special grace" in order to persevere in the good (Denzinger and Hünermann 2010, 1541.1572), doubt was raised concerning the sinner's ability to perform good deeds on a permanent and unqualified basis. Subtle debates were conducted on the exact extent of the remaining freedom for good (for example, in fulfilling the requirements of natural law) and its dependence on divine assistance. This already touches on the central issue of the early modern theology of grace: how is the relationship between divine grace and human freedom to be determined? In the following we shall try to shed light on the two most important attempts at an answer.

## 2.2  Báñezian Thomism

There is one fundamental theological-metaphysical conviction at the heart of the theology of grace put forward in the seventeenth century Thomist school since Domingo Báñez: God is the cause of every motion and change in the universe, not only because he is the "unmoved mover" at the beginning of creation, but also because he subsequently enables and supports every action of his creatures. The human will is no exception. When it transitions from potency to act, it requires a cause for the determination that is thereby accomplished (Alvarez 1611, 64f; Garrigou-Lagrange 1936, 51 et passim). The will's dependency on God for being and motion exemplifies the *esse ab alio* as the fundamental determination of every created being (as distinct from the divine *actus purus*) (Alvarez 1611, I.9, disp. 96 [763]). This causal premotion, which is more than a mere *moral* stimulus on God's part, is called by the Thomists *praemotio/praedeterminatio physica*. Initially controversial, these terms were accepted in the course of the debate, even as being synonymous (Hübener 1989). God's eternally established sovereignty, which manifests itself in the causal *prae* of his willing and acting towards creation, is particularly visible in the supernatural sphere. Creaturely freedom can only orient itself to its eternal goal if it is antecedently elevated; that is, made capable of such acts by God himself. The distinction between efficacious and (merely) sufficient grace cannot, according to the Thomist model, be determined "extrinsically" through the decision of the creature, but must come *ab intrinseco*, from God's grace itself. God is in no way dependent on the creature—not even on the level of his own foreknowledge of the creature's free decisions. This makes it clear how man's free collaboration with the divine impulse of grace is to be understood. It cannot possibly be a matter of combining two "competing" partial causes. Rather, God and free will are each to be regarded as total causes, albeit on two levels which must be strictly separated from one another: God is the primal cause, human freedom the secondary (and thus at the same time immediate) cause of all the acts it performs: as *itself* human freedom effects that which God has in advance made it capable of (Alvarez 1611, I.9, disp. 98 [779f]): "to 'predetermine' . . . means nothing other than to cause the will to determine itself; as physically premoving the free will means nothing other than bringing about truly effectively, through an inwardly approaching motion, that this will moves itself" (Alvarez 1611, I.9, disp. 91 [731]). As Aquinas taught, God moves all things in accordance with their nature: natural things in a natural manner, free ones in keeping with their freedom (Alvarez 1611, I.3, disp. 18–23 [138–233]). Thus God's moving the free will towards himself as the highest good does not inflict any coercion on the human being, even as it defines the doctrine of predetermination: God alone can be the inner motive principle of the human will; even the angels and demons, as the highest created powers, can only ever influence man's will from outside.

This basic metaphysical-theological principle resulted in a particular understanding of human freedom (Alvarez 1611, I.12, disp. 115 [914–22]). It rejects the Molinist definition that regards free will as presupposing all the factors necessary for acting; namely, the capacity to act or not to act or to do either one thing or another. For the Thomists, the combination of the determining factors of "presence of all the necessary prerequisites for acting" with "indeterminateness" is an unacceptable contradiction. In their opinion, the *praerequisita ad operandum* include the causal predetermination of the will to concrete action (in the context of the theology of grace, through God's efficacious grace). The capacity of willing does not "simultaneously" (*in sensu composito*) possess the indifference also to do the opposite. This indeterminateness can only be admitted *in sensu diviso*: the will could, in a differently determined act, also do the opposite of what it has now decided to do. The Thomists see this as satisfying the insistence of the Council of Trent that the human being receiving the call to God's grace can also resist it (Alvarez 1611, I.9, disp. 92 [743f]). Behind this lies a highly intellectualized definition of freedom that sees its innermost ground as lying in the indifference of practical reason toward all finite goods, which as such are incapable of unequivocally determining a will that is orientated towards the good in general.

> Freedom is the capacity of the will and of reason to realize in action one of two possibilities or to refrain from acting. Although freedom subsists formally in the will as its proximate and immediate subject, with respect to its roots and foundations it nevertheless lies in the intellect. For it is founded and rooted in the indifference of the judgement through which the intellect judges that an object, which the will imagines must be loved, does not possess a necessary or natural connection with the universal good to which the will is naturally orientated, that is, as regards its specification. (Alvarez 1611, I. 9, disp. 92, no. 7 [918])

The directly determined will remains free in its roots to the extent that this indifference in judging is preserved, even when the will has committed itself with an action. And when God as the highest good fixes the will in himself, the unique case arises that the human being is relieved through grace of the otherwise insurmountable tension between the infinite reaching of the will and the finite choice of goods that cannot satisfy it. God binds the will to himself as the infinite good, which means that human striving can come to rest even though for the creature the certainty of this rest is not the result of seeing it directly but only the perception in faith shaped by love. "Not being able to resist this, indeed not even being able to desire to, is no impairment of freedom but rather its fulfilment" (Ramelow 1997, 49). Thus in one crucial point those given grace on earth already resemble those given bliss in heaven, whose freedom is not decreased, but rather perfected, by no longer being able to turn away deliberately from God. For the Thomists, the doctrine of the physical predetermination of the will is the crucial argument for God's being able in his decree to foresee with certainty from all eternity man's free decisions and, on the basis of this knowledge, to direct the world according to his plan. If God's grace enables human beings to act (as he intends), it becomes superfluous to ask whether these plans can be thwarted by the creature's resistance.

Although the Thomist approach is convincing in its systematic coherence, it is burdened with three closely related problems. One is formulated in the question of why God, in view of his role as universal mover, cannot also be regarded as the direct originator of human sin. Is the withholding of efficacious grace not responsible for a human being not repenting, in other words sinning? The problem seems to be exacerbated by the fact that leading Thomists equate this refusal of grace with a "blinding" or "hardening" of the sinner by God. Admittedly, they do add by way of explanation that the unwillingness of the human being himself remains the true cause of his failure to repent. God is in no way obliged to put an end to this state of affairs through his gift of grace. This refusal can be explained with the doctrine of original sin; but then at the very least the sin of the first human being still remains in need of an explanation.

The second query points to the possibility of distinguishing between sufficient and efficacious grace, a distinction that seems to be canceled in the Thomist system. Alongside a grace that is of itself infallibly successful, one that is conditionally efficacious is in danger of becoming a meaningless concept—since apart from God there is not supposed to be any cause that could actualize the mere possibility of sufficiency (Alvarez 1611, I.9, disp. 102 [808–13]). The Thomists' sufficient grace does from a human perspective contain an objectively real but subjectively unattainable potential; it lies within the power of the sinner only to deny himself this, thus making it ineffective. From God's perspective it belongs on the plane of a willing that has never really been realized (the *voluntas antecedens* as opposed to the *voluntas consequens*), the relevance of which can be doubted.

Third and finally, it remains unclear whether the Thomist approach is able to do adequate justice to the biblical teaching of God's universal salvific will. If divine predestination points to an absolute decree, the enforcement of which takes place by means of an infallibly efficacious gift of grace, the rejection of certain people seems likewise to have to be ascribed to a positive act of will on God's part from all eternity (Alvarez 1611, I.11, disp. 109 [856]). This, too, is not performed conditionally by God (referring to a person's foreseen demerit or refusal), but absolutely (Alvarez 1611, I.11, disp. 110, no. 9 [866]). For the rejected, the lack of grace is thus to be considered the formal effect of divine reprobation for which no cause is to be discerned beyond the divine will (on the background, see Stiglmayr 1964). Critics have always seen there to be a great danger of this view leading to the concept of double predestination. The Thomists themselves point to the insoluble mystery of the co-existence of divine mercy and justice:

The fact that of two people who are preveniently moved by the same movement of grace one consents and cooperates with the grace, decides on a pious act and is converted, whereas the other persists in sin, cannot be ascribed to the pure, naturally indwelling, specific and interior freedom common to both the good and the bad, the reprobate and the elect; instead, the fact that one is converted must be ascribed to the absolute and efficacious decree of God, who wanted in his mercy to convert him and meet his needs with the effective help of his preveniently efficacious grace, whereas he [God] justly left the other in the mass of perdition with the help of merely sufficient grace. (Alvarez 1611, I.9, disp. 97 [774])

Whether the "strict Thomists" of the seventeenth century actually renewed or falsified the pure teaching of the *Doctor angelicus* with their system of grace was a matter of contentious dispute for centuries. Since the end of neo-Thomism as the ideal in Catholic theology shortly after Vatican II (1962–65), it has become easier to acknowledge the newness of the emphases introduced by Báñezianism:

> In a strange interpenetration of the Thomist idea of order (the *ordo universalis* must be realized in the display of God's mercy and justice; paradoxically even the permitting of evil serves this *ordo*), Scotist Voluntarism (determining goals or aims before means; explaining predestination through the "ab aeterno" of the divine, absolutely efficacious willing; according to the Báñezians election and reprobation are indeed acts of the intellect, but presuppose an act of will) and the thinking of St Augustine, which still takes its bearings from Holy Scripture (Jacob and Esau in their grace or reprobation represent a type of all election or rejection), an election is taught that precedes any decision on the part of the creature (*praedestinatio ante praevisa merita*). (Stiglmayr 1964, 159f)

The Thomists after Vincent Contenson (1641–74) themselves clearly moderated the teaching on the restriction of sufficient grace, as is already apparent in the theology courses of the Salmanticenses and then in Billuart (1658–1757) (Flynn 1938). Alongside a recognition of the objective problems of the thesis, this probably came about as a result of the Jansenist controversy and the doctrinal concessions of the congruist Molinists (Stiglmayr 1964, 162–67).

## 2.3  Molinism

"Molinism" is, as research over the past hundred years has shown, undoubtedly even more of a problematic catch-all term than "Báñezianism". "If a Molinist is understood to be someone who agreed with all of Molina's theses, then there were no Molinists except Molina," is Klaus Reinhardt's hyperbolic comment (Reinhardt 1965, 241). Thus the concept remains usable only as a vague general term that brackets together certain majority theses within Jesuit theology since the end of the sixteenth century on how to determine the relationship between divine grace and creaturely freedom. It has long since been established that the historical origins of these theses are not to be associated exclusively with Molina's name and that the teachings of his *Concordia* were considerably modified by the Jesuits in subsequent decades (see already Lurz 1932, 36.218).

The undisputed fundamental conviction of the seventeenth-century Jesuit school is the rejection of a physical predetermination of human freedom by a God issuing universally effective decrees in both the natural and supernatural spheres. In their definition of freedom, Molinists claim what was rejected by the Thomists: "That agent is called 'free' who, with all the prerequisites for acting having been posited, is able to act and is able not to act, or is able to do one thing in such a way that he is also able to do some contrary thing" (Molina 1953, p. 1, disp. 2, n. 3 [14, I:8ff]). If creaturely freedom has to be defined as an underivable and spontaneous capacity for self-determination that is incompatible not merely with coercion but also with necessity, then it cannot—either in its actual enactment or in the determination therein fulfilled—be traceable completely to a causal impulse from God. This option has been seen as the translation of the decision-centered practice of Ignatian spirituality into theology (Reinhardt 1965, 219), but even more as an attempt to effectively defend the Catholic dogma against the Lutheran concept of *servum arbitrium*. Philosophically, Molina builds on Scotus (Molina 1953, p. 1, disp. 24, n. 8 [157]). Like him, Molina denies neither the necessity of the *concursus Dei generalis* nor the need for divine grace in order for supernatural acts to come about. He confirms the antecedence of God's gracious action, taken in the Augustinian sense of the *interna vocatio Dei* (God's internal calling) directed to man's intellect and will, and also affirms man's inability to bestow a supernatural quality on his acts by his own freedom. But at the same time Molina is convinced that God never wants to bypass human freedom with his gracious action. As a rule, God does not give someone an inner vocation if that person has not previously been reached by the Church's proclamation of the faith (Molina 1953, p. 1, disp. 9, n. 4–6 [45]); and the prevenient grace only becomes effective as a *moral* impulse when the assent of the human will is present. If, therefore, of two people to whom the Gospel has been preached one repents and the other does not, this must not be attributed to the inefficacy of the grace as such, because grace is not "the sole and complete cause of assent to faith" (Molina 1953, p. 1, disp. 12, n. 1 [56, I:17]). Rather, the prevenient grace approaching the human being from outside and our free decision to collaborate with it work together as two parts of a universal cause in the one indivisible supernatural act; it is only our analytical minds that make a distinction between them. This is where Molina's famous metaphor belongs of the "two pulling a ship" (Molina 1953, p. 2, disp. 26, n. 15 [170, I:30]): our free consent or cooperation is the reason for the difference between efficacious as opposed to sufficient grace (Molina 1953, p. 3, disp. 40, n. 11–12 [249f]); conversely, it is the creature's refusal that prevents the supernatural act from coming about.

Molinism attempts to explain how, given these premises, one can speak of a predestination by God that is one from all eternity with the foreknown efficacy of his grace. Molina developed this over the two decades preceding the publication of the *Concordia*, at about the same time as his confrère Pedro de Fonseca (1528–99). The crucial element is that he approaches it from God's foreknowledge. Alongside the "natural-necessary" knowledge that applies to everything in God's power (irrespective of its realization) and the "free" knowledge that refers to what is actually existing and arises from God's decrees, Molina here distinguishes a third form, namely "middle knowledge": "With this, God, with his supreme and inscrutable knowledge of the essential being of every free will, has seen what this [i.e., free will] would do according to its inherent freedom if it were to find itself in this or that order or even in an infinite number of orders of things even though it could, on the other hand, if it so wished, actually do the opposite" (Molina 1953, p. 4, disp. 52, n. 9 [540]). God knows in advance certainly and infallibly, together with the free decrees of his will, all the possible contingent circumstances determined by free actions of creatures (free secondary causes)—including those that are never in fact realized. This implies a prior vision of the free decisions of creatures that takes place in these circumstances.

Among the preconditions of creaturely acts are the external or internal impulses of grace received from God. But although God foreknows under what conditions certain human beings will cooperate with grace and obtain merits, he does not declare the merits to be the cause of God's infallible predestination. "The foreseen merits are not the *medium propter quod* but the *medium per quod et sine quo non*. The infallibility of predestination lies not in the nature of the graces but rather in God's foreknowledge" (Reinhardt 1965, 188f). On the basis of his antecedent knowledge of the possible worlds and the actions of the creatures in them, God freely decides by a universal decree in favor of a single real world, whose course he can survey and in which his gifts of grace are so attuned to the conditionally foreseen free decisions of the creatures that his goals will be achieved. "The concept of 'possible worlds' undoubtedly expanded the specu- lative scope of the possible. However, in its actual function, it served to speculatively reduce the scope of the practical possibilities that human freedom opens up and to make them readily comprehensible—for God and for the philosopher who wants to understand the conditions pertaining to the possibility of divine freedom in knowl- edge and action" (Ramelow 1997, 47). The further discussion of Molina's solution inside and outside the Jesuit school highlights some of the difficulties that confronted his theses. Thomists saw the *scientia media* hypothesis as doomed to failure in its attempt to safeguard God's certain knowledge of the free acts of human beings without physi- cal predetermination, since in view of the contingency of the causes, the truth value of statements about something conditionally future remains uncertain. What can- not be called true "with certainty" could, with Aristotle, be qualified as not knowable (even by God) (Alvarez 1611, I.2, disp. 7, n. 17 [80f]). While Molina expressed himself clearly in favor of an indeterminateness of the future contingents because he saw this as being the only way of guaranteeing human freedom, after him a growing majority of Jesuits affirmed "the fixed truth value of singular propositions about future contin- gents" (Knebel 1991, 270), employing more strongly nominalist explanations side by side with realistically oriented ones (Reinhardt 1965, 104–27; Ramelow 1997, 93–123). What proved even more complicated was the question of the medium of God's cogni- tion in the case of his "middle knowledge." Basically, the theologians were faced with the possibility of contemplating an either extra-divine or inner-divine *medium quo* (Lurz 1932, 84–116; Reinhardt 1965, 132–44). If an eternal existence of things "beside" God is excluded, the contingent future events themselves can be considered a possible medium of knowledge. In taking this path, which was pioneered by some Nominalists, one is again confronted with the uncertain truth value of propositions concerning it and its possible dependence on divine knowledge itself. If, on the other hand, one attempts to ground the *scientia media* in God's knowledge of the creaturely secondary causes that bring it about, it can be objected that either it would have to be possible to deduce their free decisions with certainty from the circumstances of their acts (which would amount to a deterministic reduction of freedom; Garrigou-Lagrange 1936, 68), or that they enable God to make a (perhaps very good, but never certain) prognosis only of the probability of their future acts. Gregory of Valencia (1549–1603) tried to solve the problem with the novel thesis of a preparatory and virtual independent decision on the part of the human will, which God could know in advance as regards the concrete decision (Hentrich 1928). Speculations as to God's insight into the "moral necessity" to which decisions of the human will may be subject remained popular among other Jesuits of the time (Knebel 2000, 190ff, 223f and passim). In the second major paradigm for a solution that points to a medium of knowledge within God in order to illustrate his apprehension of the *futura conditionata*, the recourse to the will of God is excluded for the opponents of strong predefinition models. Consequently, only God's essence can be assumed to be the medium to the extent that it causes the reality of the creature or (merely) makes it knowable for God as in a mirror. Molina had been thinking along these lines when he pointed to the "divine intellect's unlimited power of representation vis-à-vis its object," to God's *supercomprehensio*, through which "the knowledge of a contingent object [becomes] *ex parte subjecti* necessary knowledge" (Ramelow 1997, 228). Many later Jesuits continued with this approach and modified it; Antonio Pérez (1599–1649) and Martin Esparza (1606–89), for example, speak of an "intentional pre-existence" of the conditional truths in the divine eternity (Ramelow 1997, 202f, 222f). But does this path lead out of the circular argument that arises when a creature's assent to divine grace is meant to provide the ground for conditional knowledge of this assent and thus also for the actual gift of grace, whereas at the same time it is divine grace in the first place that makes the real existence of the creature's assent possible, and this in turn is ontologically identical with the conditional assent on which the *scientia media* depends (Knebel 1991, 279, n. 100)? In the end, all that is left is to speak of (with Bernaldo de Quiros and Aldrete) is a *mutua causalitas* (Ramelow 1997, 262), which sets out rather than resolves the problem. This, too, proved incapable of refuting the charge that a predestination constructed with the help of *scientia media* calculations radically neutralizes what is proper to creaturely freedom because it makes the biographies of free creatures look in God's eternal knowledge like abstractly definable ideas. When, shortly before the middle of the seventeenth century, the Suárez school campaigned for the existence—repudiated by Molina himself—of a *scientia media reflexa*, in which God also knows prospectively how he will possibly act given conditional future events, theological discourse turned more and more into planning a strategy, conceived on God's behalf, with the aim of immunizing his providential plans as skillfully as possible against all "disruptions" on the part of creaturely freedom (Ramelow 1997, 263–69). It did not escape the notice of the opponents of this expansion of the theory that assuming God's knowledge of his own decrees before he issued them threatened to stifle not only creaturely but also divine freedom in calculations of necessity (Ramelow 1997, 266f).

A second main objection from the Thomists had accused Molina's approach of bringing God into a problematic dependency relationship vis-à-vis his creatures, in that his predestination was seen as a reaction to (albeit hypothetical) free decisions on the part of these creatures (Alvarez, I.12, disp. 121, n. 2 [960]). In fact, the Jesuit had taken into account the "overall balance" of God's middle knowledge with respect to his decision in favor of one of the countless possible worlds, and had thus made the predestination of the individual, which occurs together with the choice of a certain order, logically coordinate or subordinate to God's foreseeing of his merits. This line of argument was pursued explicitly by the Jesuit Leonardus Lessius (1554–1623) in his treatise on grace, first published in 1610. This book provoked major controversies within the Society of Jesus, the course of which has been documented in detail by Xavier-Marie Le Bachelet (Le Bachelet 1931). Lessius's most important critics within his own order were Robert Bellarmine (1542–1621) and Francisco Suárez with their own model of grace, which was later called "Congruism". Aquaviva (1543–1615), the general of the order, soon also joined in the argument over Lessius's book, as did several leading Dominican theologians. In 1611 it spread as far as Pope Paul V, who feared a rekindling of the recently concluded debates *De auxiliis*. Despite all the hostility, Lessius scarcely departed from his core theses. On December 14, 1613, Aquaviva put an end to the controversy with his practical, not speculatively oriented decree that obliged all Jesuits to adhere to the Congruist thesis (Le Bachelet 2:236–45). His influence is to be seen among leading Jesuits such as Arriaga (1592–1667), Tanner (1572–1632), or Ruiz de Montoya (1562–1632). Through the republication of his book on grace (1626), Lessius himself also maintained a presence in the ongoing debate up to and beyond his death in 1623. Aquaviva's decree was never formally revised, but in practice decreased in relevance as the contexts of the discussion changed (Le Bachelet 2:382–85).

The crucial difference between strict Molinism and Congruism lies in the fact that the latter speaks of a distinction between sufficient and efficacious grace *in actu primo* by giving strictly intrinsic, not extrinsic reasons for the efficacy of grace. God distributes his graces in a targeted manner and does not "scatter them around" (Ramelow 1997, 275), because he knows for whom the power of these gifts, which is sufficient for everyone, will in fact actually become effective. He brings into reality the world that he has foreseen as possible qua *scientia media* and in which precisely those achieve salvation whom he determined for this, prior to their merits (*ante praevisa merita*). This distinction took account of the criticism of the Dominicans, who, in Augustinian tradition, strictly rejected a reason for predestination in man, as well as the reference from within their own order to General Borja's 1565 *Ratio Studiorum* (Reinhardt 1965, 219ff). For the Congruists, God's original *praedilectio* thus achieves the same effect on a human being through a moral influence as the physically efficacious grace of Thomism. As Knebel has pointed out, in the Congruist calculation human decisions made under the influence of grace, as God apprehends them in advance in his *scientia media*, are treated in a fairly standardized, atomized, and serial manner, being seen mechanistically almost like the output of "supernatural mass production" (Knebel 2000, 172; Knebel 2007, 15f). From this there evolved a praxis model with a "completely means-end rationality" (Knebel 1991, 290). Although the pluralization of the Congruist *scientia media* calculation led in some authors to a renewed desire for a synthesizing meta-reflection—as documented, for example, in Antonio Pérez's concept of a *scientia media universalissima* (Ramelow 1997, 90–93)—the concentration on the individual case nevertheless remains evident. The formal unconditionality of individual freedom remains constant throughout the course of every action and is, according to God's providential plan, guided through a finite sequence of concrete decision-making situations in such a way that in the end the goal intended by God is reached. Only the idea of a *creatura rebellis* that rejects every divine grace in all possible worlds remains a problem that even the subtlest Congruist scheme finds hard to eliminate. It is here that we get the clearest confirmation of the thesis boldly formulated by individual Jesuits that God has given his omnipotence into the hand of our free will (Knebel 2000, 186, n. 262, pointing to passages in Izquierdo and Mauro).

Over the course of time there have been clear changes in the verdicts on whether the continuity rather than the difference between Molina and Suárez should be emphasized, and whether the road from one to the other is to be regarded as one of progress or decline from the original *scientia media*. The older Jesuits pursued a noticeable interest in playing down the differences between Molinism and Congruism (see, e.g., Schneemann 1881), and the increasing convergence between the Society of Jesus and the Thomist tradition was even accounted by some interpreters to be "the greatest progress in the history of Molinism" (Lurz 1932, 223). In more recent times, however, the "moral-external" determination of man in Congruism and the "physical-intrinsic" in Thomism have quite frequently been categorized as equally problematic attacks on human freedom—combined with the call for consideration to be given to fundamentally new ways of explaining the relationship between nature and grace (Greiner 2011).

## 3  A BRIEF RETROSPECTIVE

The early modern struggle over grace and predestination has—like the Scholasticism of the period as a whole—received largely negative, at times almost pitying assessments in later times. It has been seen as the sad squandering of great intellectual potential, a getting bogged down in frightful subtleties and proof of an inability to be innovative in crossing the narrow boundaries of a paradigm that offered nothing more to discuss. The neo-Thomism of the early twentieth century attempted to unveil Molina as nothing less than the forefather of the "anthropological turn" that reached its zenith in Kant; whereas the Jesuits tried in a similarly one-sided manner to emphasize Molina's fidelity to Aquinas. With the rise in twentieth-century Catholic theology of a subject- and freedom-oriented way of thinking, the Molinist heritage was generally rated considerably more highly, whereas Báñezian Thomism has found hardly any defenders. Down to the most recent debate on the analytical philosophy of religion, Molinism has remained present as an option to be taken seriously, albeit leaving out the theological dimension of grace (Perszyk 2012).

Undeniably, Molinism aims at a separation between a natural structure in which God can intervene at any time and a sphere of creaturely freedom that is inviolable even for God, and to which he only has access through the back door of his prior knowledge. The unique nature of the *esse morale* is discovered and celebrated here, but at the same time the groundwork is laid for the modern diastasis between nature and freedom, which manifests itself definitively in Kant. In his important research, Knebel has pointed to further connections that have crossed over, often unrecognized, from the Jesuit school into modern philosophy. In the treatise on grace, for example, the beginnings are to be found of the optimism debate so central for Leibniz, as well as the development of highly complex discourses on a "statistical paradigm of moral necessity" (Knebel 2000, 275–486; Ramelow 1997, 123–30), with which the essentially unfathomable factual truth that grace-filled people do sin is made rationally comprehensible. Linked with the concept of moral necessity is a pointer "to the fact that the world also works reliably in the realm of events that are dependent on the free will" (Knebel 2000, 557); that is, it is rationally predictable. The *scientia media* hypothesis attempts in this way to resolve the problem, which had been virulent since Scotus and unavoidable for Aristotelian-type epistemology, of how to reconcile creaturely contingency with the theological discourse on necessity (Knebel 2007, 17f). Even though it would hardly be likely to make any sense to present the whole of modern philosophical thinking as a reception history of the Báñezian-Molinist disagreements (against Ocaña García 2000), the above-mentioned points of contact with the early modern doctrine of grace have ensured the continued interest in it by philosophical interpreters right down to the present day, whereas scarcely any notice is taken of it in contemporary theology.

## BIBLIOGRAPHY

Álvarez, Diego, OP. 1611. *De auxiliis divinae gratiae et humani arbitrii viribus et libertate.* Lyon.

Báñez, Domingo, OP. 1614. *Scholastica commentaria in primam partem Doctoris Angelici D. Thomae usque ad sexagesimam quartam quaestionem complectentia.* Douai.

Denzinger, Heinrich, and Peter Hünermann, eds. 2010. *Kompendium der Glaubensbekenntnisse und kirchlichen Lehrentscheidungen/Enchiridion symbolorum definitionum et declarationum de rebus fidei et morum.* 43rd ed. Freiburg: Herder.

Garrigou-Lagrange, Réginald. 1936. "Prémotion physique." In *Dictionnaire de Théologie Catholique,* vol. XIII/1, 31–77. Paris: Letouzey.

Greiner, Michael. 2011. "Gottes wirksame Gnade und menschliche Freiheit. Wiederaufnahme eines verdrängten Schlüsselproblems." In *Theologische Anthropologie,* edited by Thomas Pröpper, vol. 2, 1351–1436. Freiburg: Herder.

Flynn, Leo. 1938. *Billuart and his Summa Sancti Thomae.* London.

Hentrich, Wilhelm. 1928. *Gregor von Valencia und der Molinismus.* Innsbruck: Rauch.

Hübener, Wolfgang. 1989. "Praedeterminatio physica." In *Historisches Wörterbuch der Philosophie,* vol. 7, 1216–1225. Basel: Schwabe.

Knebel, Sven K. 2007. "Einleitung zu: Diego del Mármol S. J., Tractatus de auxilio efficaci divinae gratiae, ec eius cum libero arbitrio creato concordia." In *Die scholastische Theologie im Zeitalter der Gnadenstreitigkeiten*, edited by Ulrich L. Lehner, vol. 1, 9–54. Nordhausen: Bautz.

Knebel, Sven K. 1991. "Scientia media: Ein diskursarchäologischer Leitfaden durch das 17. Jahrhundert." *Archiv für Begriffsgeschichte* 34: 262–294.

Knebel, Sven K. 2011. *Suarezismus. Erkenntnistheoretisches aus dem Nachlass des Jesuitengenerals Tirso González de Santalla, 1624–1705: Abhandlung und Edition.* Amsterdam: B. R. Grüner.

Knebel, Sven K. 2000. *Wille, Würfel und Wahrscheinlichkeit. Das System der moralischen Notwendigkeit in der Jesuitenscholastik, 1550–1700.* Paradeigmata 21. Hamburg: Meiner.

Le Bachelet, Xavier-Marie. 1931. *Prédestination et grâce efficace. Controverses dans la Compagnie de Jesus au temps d'Aquaviva, 1610–1613.* 2 vols. Louvain: Museum Lessianum.

Lurz, Wilhelm. 1932. *Adam Tanner SJ († 1632) und die Gnadenstreitigkeiten des 17. Jahrhunderts.* Breslau: Müller & Seiffert.

Marschler, Thomas. 2013. "Verbindungen zwischen Gesetzestraktat und Gotteslehre bei Francisco Suárez im Begriff der lex aeterna." In *Auctoritas omnium legume: Francisco Suárez' "De Legibus" zwischen Theologie, Philosophie und Jurisprudenz*, edited by Oliver Bach, Norbert Brieskorn, and Gideon Stiening, 27–51. Stuttgart and Bad Cannstatt: Frommann-Holzboog.

Molina, Luis de, SJ. 1953. *Concordia liberi arbitrii cum gratiae donis, divina praescientia, providentia, praedestinatione et reprobatione, ad nonnullos primae partis D. Thomae articulos*, edited by Johannes Rabeneck. Oniae: Collegium Maximum.

Ocaña García, Marcelino. 2000. *Molinismo y libertad.* Córdoba: Publ. Obra Social y Cultural Cajasur.

Pastor, Ludwig von. 1927. *Geschichte der Päpste im Zeitalter der katholischen Restauration und des Dreißigjährigen Krieges: Leo XI und Paul V (1605–1621).* Freiburg: Herder.

Perszyk, Ken, ed. 2012. *Molinism: The Contemporary Debate.* Oxford: Oxford University Press.

Ramelow, Tilman. 1997. *Gott, Freiheit, Weltenwahl: Die Metaphysik der Willensfreiheit zwischen A. Perez SJ (1599–1649) und G. W. Leibniz (1646–1716).* Brill's Studies in Intellectual History 72. Leiden, New York and Köln: Brill.

Reinhardt, Klaus. 1965. *Pedro Luis SJ (1538–1602) und sein Verständnis der Kontingenz, Praescienz und Praedestination.* Portugiesische Forschungen der Görres-Gesellschaft, Zweite Reihe, Bd. 2. Münster: Aschendorff.

Schneemann, Gerhard. 1881. *Controversiarum de divinae gratiae liberique arbitrii concordia initia et progressus.* Freiburg: Herder.

Scorraille, Raoul deSJ. 1917. *El P. Francisco Suárez de la Compañia de Jesús.* 2 vols. Barcelona: Subirana.

Stegmüller, Friedrich. 1935. *Geschichte des Molinismus I: Neue Molinaschriften.* Münster: Aschendorff.

Stegmüller, Friedrich. 1960. "Gnadenstreit." In *Lexikon für Theologie und Kirche.* 2nd ed., vol. 4, 1002–1007. Freiburg: Herder.

Stiglmayr, Emmerich. 1964. *Verstoßung und Gnade. Die Universalität der hinreichenden Gnade und die strengen Thomisten des 16. und 17. Jahrhunderts.* Roma: Herder.

Suárez, Francisco, SJ. (1856–1878). *Opera omnia.* 28 vols. Paris: Vivès.

# CHAPTER 7

# BAROQUE CATHOLIC THEOLOGIES OF CHRIST AND MARY

## TRENT POMPLUN

## 1 INTRODUCTION

IT is a mundane but curious fact that the Vatican did not intervene in a single Christological debate between the years 1500 and 1800. It is not that the early modern age was without its Christological debates; still less that there were no competing conceptions of Christ implied in other highly controverted debates about grace, sin, soteriology, or the sacraments. After all, theologians engaged in disputations about Christology with the same vigor as they did more famous debates like the *de auxiliis* controversy. In fact, it could be argued that no controversy was so celebrated as the age-old debate between Thomists and Scotists about the so-called "motive" of the Incarnation. Although not everyone professed himself a Thomist or a Scotist in these debates—the Servites, for example, adopted Henry of Ghent as their common doctor, and some Carmelites favored the thought of John Baconthorpe—everyone addressed the controversy and few, if any, escaped the ambit of Duns Scotus's arguments. If the Vatican did not intervene on the venerable question of whether the Word would have become incarnate if Adam had not sinned—despite the heated rhetoric which often accompanied it—it did feel compelled to muzzle preachers and theologians who dared to enter the Mariological debates of the day, and this with some frequency. A full investigation of these debates and interventions—much less the vast array of baroque writings about Christ and Mary—requires a work of many volumes. Still, a brief survey of the debates will allow us to introduce the principal historical events that shaped early modern debates, the most important theologians who participated in them, and the major themes they addressed. A loosely chronological survey of these debates, first in Mariology and then in Christology, will allow us to see that the general drift of the age is not (as is usually reported) toward a greater Thomistic synthesis, but rather Scotus-ward. Charting this Scotistic drift, moreover, will allow us to understand some of the tensions that developed in nineteenth-century theology leading up to the definition of the dogma of the Immaculate Conception in 1854.

## 2 MARIOLOGY FROM THE COUNCIL OF BASEL TO THE LATE BAROQUE

The speculations of Thomas Aquinas (1225–74) and John Duns Scotus (ca. 1266–1308) provide the remote background for the Christologies and Mariologies of the baroque age. I say "remote," because the debates of the baroque age far exceeded the rather modest speculations of the Angelic and Marian Doctors. Although it is true that Scotus offered fairly elaborate arguments for Christ's absolute predestination and Mary's immaculate conception, these two points, which did not have any special prominence in the Middle Ages, become something of a *cause célèbre* in the early modern church. The more immediate background can be found in the preparations for the Council of Basel by the Franciscan Juan de Segovia (n.d.–ca. 1458) and the Dominican Juan de Torquemada (1388–1468) (Ameri 1954). Segovia, in outlining his argument for the Immaculate Conception, argued that in order to contract original sin, three conditions must be met: Adam must sin; the person must descend from Adam by seminal generation; and the person must be "included" in Adam by a specific divine law. Torquemada felt that only two conditions must be met: Adam must sin, and a person must descend from him via seminal generation. No moral or juridical necessity, the Dominican argued, connects the former to the latter. For Segovia, then, Mary could not be bound by any purported moral necessity to Adam, and so was entirely free from original sin. For Torquemada, no such necessity existed, and so Mary must have contracted the sin of Adam. Although I have greatly oversimplified the arguments of Segovia and Torquemada, for our purposes all we need to note is that their way of framing the debate about the Immaculate Conception would soon give rise to the distinctly "modern" controversy over Mary's exact relationship to Adam in the divine plan, a controversy which scholars generally call the *debitum peccati* (Carol 1978, 22–23).

At any rate, the arguments of Segovia and Torquemada were shelved as the council fragmented. The fathers who remained for the thirty-sixth session of the Council of Basel (September 17, 1439) defined—or attempted to define—the doctrine that "Mary, the glorious Virgin and Mother of God, by the working of the divine will and by the power of a singular and prevenient grace, was never subject to original sin but always immune, holy and immaculate, from any blame, actual or original, is to be accepted by all Catholics as pious and consonant with the worship of the Church, the Catholic faith, and right reason, and Sacred Scripture." The council fathers also forbade anyone to teach or preach the contrary, but the prohibition was largely stillborn, as the council had been

moved from Basel to Ferrara and on to Florence, where another group of fathers pronounced a decree against the now-demoted "synod" of Basel. As a result, Thomists continued to advance Torquemada's arguments against the Immaculate Conception with
some vehemence, even going so far as to declare it (and Scotists generally) as heretical. In
this respect, the *Libellus recollectorius auctoritatum de veritate conceptione B. V. Mariae*
of Vincenzo Bandello (or Bandelli, ca. 1435–ca. 1506) provoked a theological controversy
that soon engulfed theologians of many orders beyond the Dominicans and Franciscans
(Hurter 1906, 1001–6, 1114–18). Eventually, Pope Sixtus IV intervened with the constitutions *Cum praeexcelsa* (February 27, 1477) and *Grave nimis* (September 4, 1483), which
approved the Mass and Office *Sicut lilium* and attached an indulgence to it. Strictly
speaking, however, the pope's constitution only spoke of the "astonishing conception of
the immaculate Virgin" (*immaculatae Virginis mira conceptione*—that *mira*, of course,
admits a rather wide range of interpretation). Not to be deterred, in 1481 Bandello fired
off the anonymous *Tractatus de singulari puritate et praerogativa conceptionis Salvatoris
nostri Jesu Christi*, and the controversy dragged on. In the first version of the second
constitution of 1482, the pope explicitly forbade the Dominicans of Lombardy from
preaching against Scotists who supported the Immaculate Conception. In the second
version, Sixtus IV targeted any preachers who were "not ashamed . . . to affirm publi-
cally in their sermons to people of diverse cities and lands, nor cease to preach daily
that all who maintain or assert that the very immaculate and glorious Mother Virgin
was conceived without the stain of original sin are heretics or sin mortally." In all likelihood, he was especially piqued about the Dominicans' defiance of *Cum praeexcelsa*,
as he reproved their "rash attempt" (*temerarius ausus*) to claim that Franciscans and
others "sin grievously if they celebrate the office of the Immaculate Conception or lis-
ten to the sermons of those who affirm that Mary was conceived without this stain."
Here, too, it is important to note that Pope Sixtus IV did not censure Dominicans for
denying the Immaculate Conception, but merely for claiming that those who held the
doctrine or celebrated the feast sinned mortally; or worse, were heretical. In any event,
the Dominicans were neither prompt nor joyous in their obedience to the Holy See in
this regard: Chrysostomus Javellus (ca. 1471–1538), Isidore of Isolanis (1477–1528), and
Bartholomé Spina (ca. 1475–1546) impugned the Immaculate Conception in the following decades.

Still, to be fair, it is to the Dominicans that we owe the first shift in the larger
Mariological debate. For Cajetan (1468–1534), Mary's "total" preservation from original sin remained heretical. According to the great Dominican, any "total" preservation
would necessarily entail that Mary was conceived (1) without the *caro infecta*; (2) without a *debitum personale*; and (3) without concupiscence. Indeed, for Cajetan, to be
"redeemed" by Christ, one must be subject to all three of these conditions. Like earlier
Dominican theologians such as Torquemada, Cajetan argued that the fathers made no
distinction between original sin and any *debitum*, and so it followed that Mary, even
were she preserved from personal sin, was conceived with an infected flesh, a *debitum proximum*, and indeed the concupiscence that, while not sinful in itself, is yet the

"beginning" of sin. Mary could be sanctified neither in *instante infusionis*, much less *ante infusionem animae*. In this respect, Cajetan's theology of the *debitum* stands midway between medieval debates about the sanctification of Mary's soul and the modern debate about the *debitum peccati*. Cajetan apparently intended his own formulation of the *debitum personale* to safeguard the Augustinian notion of the *caro infecta*, even as he argued that Mary's soul was sanctified in the womb. It almost goes without saying that in such a view, Mary's body must remain subject to the penalties of sin, if for no other reason than that God preserved her soul alone.

Another Dominican, Ambrosius Catharinus (ca. 1483–1556), provided the chief arguments against Cajetan's position in the early sixteenth century (Bosco 1950). Catharinus affirmed that Mary *should* have incurred the stain of sin, but denied that she was conceived with infected flesh as a penalty for sin. How, he argued, can Cajetan claim that God penalizes Mary's body for sins that her soul never committed? For Catharinus, the only *debitum peccati* that Mary may be said to have is due solely to the fact that she is a human being who descends from Adam. In the technical terminology of the day, her *debitum peccati* is "remote" as opposed to the "proximate" debt by which Cajetan tried to establish her maculate conception. (Catharinus seems to have stumbled a bit in his argumentation, since personal sin has nothing to do with this issue. His rhetoric, too, seemed motivated by personal animus, since Cajetan himself had acknowledged that the *debitum remotum* was undeserving of censure.) Still, Cajetan and Catharinus served as touchstones for the debate for the next two hundred years, as can be seen in the discussion of their respective positions by the Scotist Girolamo de Montefortino (ca. 1662–1738) (Montefortino [1737] 1903, 318–22).

Despite the heated debate—or perhaps because of it—the Council of Trent avoided defining the Immaculate Conception, although Cardinal Pedro Pacheco (1488–1560) had proposed the definition during deliberations for the fifth session on original sin. The Council fathers contented themselves with remarking that the council did not intend "to include in [its] decree on original sin the Blessed and Immaculate Virgin Mary, Mother of God." In fact, the Council merely noted that all were to observe the constitutions of Pope Sixtus IV under the previously mentioned penalties (Olazarán 1946). Still, after the council concluded, Pope Pius V, in the Bull *Ex omnibus afflictionibus* (October 1, 1567) against Michael Baius, condemned the proposition "No one is free of original sin except Christ; thus the Virgin Mary died on account of the sin she contracted from Adam, and all of her afflictions, just as those of other just people, were punishments for sin, original or actual" (no. 73). The next year the pope declared the Feast of the Immaculate Conception a holy day of obligation for the entire church. As a result, the debate about Mary's Immaculate Conception shifted decisively from a debate between maculists and immaculists to a debate between those who felt a *debitum proximum* was necessary to secure the Blessed Virgin's redemption, those who felt a *debitum remotum* was sufficient, and those who argued that Mary was wholly free of any *debitum peccati* whatsoever. The Jesuits, always eclectic, proposed theories of the *debitum proximum*, *debitum remotum*, and *nullum debitum* across "party" lines. Francisco

Suárez (1548–1617), Bellarmine (1542–1621), Gregory of Valencia (ca. 1550–1603), and Gabriel Vásquez (1549–1604) argued against the *debitum remotum* in favor of a *debitum proximum* on the grounds that a *debitum remotum* was not sufficient to secure Mary's redemption *sensu proprio*. Gregory of Valencia, like the Dominican Bartholomé Medina (1527–80), believed that the *nullum debitum* position was "rash," if not heretical. Still, as a harbinger of things to come, no less a figure than Domingo Bañez (1528–1604) argued for a *debitum remotum*, and the Dominican Juan Viguerius (n.d.–1550), following the example of the Jesuits Alfonso Salmerón (1515–75) and Diego Laínez (1512–65), argued that Mary was entirely free from any *debitum peccati* whatsoever. Some Dominicans, such as Serafino Porrecta (1536–1614), simply refused to specify the nature of Mary's debt to Christ, causing later theologians to assume that they supported the Immaculate Conception. In all likelihood, they simply wanted to avoid getting embroiled in a hundred-year-old controversy.

Arguably, however, the true beginning of "modern" Mariology—and certainly the production of vast treatises on Mariology—is the celebrated "Toledo Affair" that was sparked when a now-nameless Dominican preached against the Immaculate Conception in Seville on September 8, 1613. The Franciscans took umbrage, and eventually these somewhat arcane professional controversies spread across Spain, then to be taken up by the Inquisition at Toledo. The Toledo Affair led to the popularization of the *nullum debitum* position beyond Franciscans and Mercedarians, and inspired theologians, such as the Carmelite Juan Bautista de Lezana (1586–1659), the Jesuit Ferdinand Chirinos de Salazar (1576–1646), and the Augustinian Gil da Presentação (1539–1626), to write the first "modern" treatises on Mary's *debitum peccati*. At the same time, Pope Paul V, annoyed that Dominicans were largely ignoring *Grave nimis*, forbade opposition to the Immaculate Conception in public teaching and preaching with his Constitution *Regis pacifici* (July 6, 1616), although still allowing the Dominicans to teach the Angelic Doctor's position privately. In the immediate aftermath of the Toledo Affair, Pope Gregory XV extended Paul V's censure to private discussions in 1622.

Here we enter the golden age of Mariological speculation, and the conversation begins to drift Scotus-ward. Jesuits such as Juan Perlín (1569–1638), Ambrosio de Peñalosa (1588–1656), and Juan Eusebio Nieremberg (1595–1648) argued that the *debitum remotum* was a harmful fiction, and maintained the "exemptionist" position favored by Scotists. Almost every Jesuit at Louvain supported the *nullum debitum* during the seventeenth century, arguably to avoid association with Baius (Carol 1978, 95–101). Still other Jesuits, such as Diego Granado (1571–1632) and Juan de Lugo (1583–1660), divided the *debitum* into more exotic forms in order to resist the broader confines of the debate. In this generation, too, Franciscan and Mercedarian theologians consolidated the exemptionist position in their orders. Scotists such as Angelo Volpe (ca. 1590–1647) and Tomás Francés Urrutigoyti (n.d.–1682) applied the maximalism of Scotus's teaching on the predestination of Christ to the predestination and conception of the Blessed Virgin. Since these Scotists felt no obligation to present their insights in Thomistic terms, they were free to extend the already expansive frontiers of the exemptionist tradition. Not only did they reject any *debitum peccati*, proximate or remote; these Scotists advanced what we might now call "Sophiological" arguments about the Blessed Virgin. Volpe, for example, explicitly places Mary in the unique "hypostatic" order. Juan de Rada (ca. 1545–1608), Filippo Fabri (1564–1630), and Bartolomeo Mastri (1602–73) each argued that the grace of Mary's predestination depends not on Christ's Passion, but rather upon his glorification. Urrutigoyti developed this argument in a particularly spectacular fashion. Other Scotists, such as Francisco del Castillo Velasco (n.d.–1641), rather deliberately turned discussions of Mary's *debitum* on their heads by rethinking the *debitum peccati* as a *debitum gratiae*. For their part, Mercedarians such as Sylvester de Saavedra (n.d.–1643) and Juan de Prudencio (n.d.–1657) tried to do much the same with God's *scientia simplicis intelligentiae*, and so might be seen to anticipate several modern ways of framing the question in terms of possible worlds. Dominicans denounced Saavedra to the Inquisition, to no avail.

Here the Vatican intervened. Pope Alexander VII, in the Brief *Sollicitudo omnium ecclesiarum* (December 8, 1661) declared, "The devotion of Christ's faithful toward the Virgin Mary, His most blessed mother, is ancient, according to which they believe that by a special grace and privilege of God her soul was preserved immune from the stain of original sin from the first instant of its creation and infusion into the body in view of the merits of her son Jesus Christ, the Redeemer of the human race, and in this sense honor and celebrate the feast of her conception." More explicitly than his predecessors, Pope Alexander VII bemoaned the "scandals" (*scandala*), "quarrels" (*iurgia*) and "disagreements" (*dissensiones*) that had arisen in theology "with great offense to God" (*cum magna Dei offensa*). Note that *Sollicitudo omnium ecclesiarum*, despite the fact that it was later echoed in *Ineffabilis Deus*, does not establish the Immaculate Conception as a dogma, but only as a feast; and its wording, while defining Mary's soul as immaculate, does not include her body. As it stands, all that it excludes is the peculiar way that Cajetan and his followers attempted to deny the purity of Mary's soul from the *caro infecta*. Still, if the church left room for a particular interpretation of the Angelic Doctor's position on Mary's sanctification, it did not tolerate public teaching against the Immaculate Conception. The force of Alexander VII's decree can be seen in the immediate questioning of the Carmelite Thomist Dominic of St. Teresa (n.d.–1660), who was accused of arguing against the Immaculate Conception in the *Cursus Salmanticensis*. The *disputatio* was referred to the Inquisition; although Fr. Dominic wrote a thorough defense, the tribunal asked that the offending *disputatio* be removed from subsequent editions.

By the end of the seventeenth century, Franciscans had moved well beyond Scotus's general remarks about the Immaculate Conception to advance a series of novel and rather ingenious arguments in favor of more radical "exemptionist" positions. The most detailed presentation of this position, and indeed arguably the most extensive and profound work of Mariology ever produced, is the three-volume *Opus theologicum* of the Capuchin Salvator Montalbanus (n.d.–1722) de Sambuca, who argued against the *debitum remotum* by pointing out that a hypothetical debt cannot be contracted at all, and against the *debitum proximum* by maintaining its utter incompatibility with divine grace. Such arguments became canonical for Franciscans after Montalbanus, after whom Carlos del Moral (n.d.–1731) takes pride of place. Del Moral divided Mary's preservative redemption into a *praeservatio radicalis, praeservatio formalis,* and *praeservatio perfectissime consummata* in light of Christ's predestination and passion. Montalbanus and Carlos del Moral laid the foundation for almost every modern Scotist treatment of Mary.

# 3  THE VARIOUS BAROQUE CHRISTOLOGICAL SYNTHESES

The modern Mariology of the *debitum peccati* depended upon one very specific Christological doctrine for its progress—namely, Duns Scotus's famous argument for the absolute primacy and predestination of Christ. Here, I think it no exaggeration to say that we may discern the dominance of the Franciscan school during the baroque period—in Christology as in Mariology—by charting its effects on the theologians who tried valiantly to resist it. Consider, for example, the three theological geniuses of the Dominican order—Capreolus (ca. 1380–1444), Cajetan, and Francis Silvester of Ferrara (ca. 1474–1528)—each of whom might be seen as making important concessions to the Scotist tradition. Capreolus, the *princeps Thomistarum,* marched directly into Scotus's camp, but we might do well to note that he has also adopted the Subtle Doctor's cherished method for addressing the question: namely, the application of the *signa rationis* to God's eternal decree. In this, Capreolus laid the groundwork for much of the modern Thomist approach to the topic of Christ's predestination. In this respect, at least, even the "strict" Thomists of the early modern age adopt a Scotistic approach. It is with Cajetan, however, that we see the most significant additions to the larger Thomist repertoire. In the first place, Cajetan conceded to the Scotists that God truly predestines Christ first among creatures when considered from the perspective of final causality (*in genere causae finalis*). When the problem is considered, however, from the perspective of material causality (*in genere causae materialis*), God first foresees humankind's fall. Second, Cajetan argued that all divine works *ad extra* conform to a threefold order: the order of nature, the order of grace, and the hypostatic order. In this schema, the hypostatic order presupposes both grace and nature, and grace presupposes nature. In other words, the hypostatic union perfects and builds upon God's gracious works, just as grace perfects and builds upon nature. Consequently, sin cannot be the final cause of the Incarnation, but only the occasion for the execution of the divine plan. Yet despite this novel way of approaching the problem, Cajetan can maintain the more general position of Thomas that if humankind had not fallen, God would not have become incarnate. Silvester adopted the general parameters of Cajetan's solution, but then added the further distinction between the *finis qui,* the end sought by the agent, and the *finis cui,* the person to whom the action is directed. Silvester was happy to concede to Scotus that in the genus of final causality, the glory of Christ's soul was prior to the glory and salvation of other men, but he denied that the Incarnation was prior to the salvation of humanity. For this reason, both Cajetan and Silvester are sometimes referred to as "mitigated" Thomists in the academic literature.

Much that followed in Dominican Christology negotiated the tensions between Capreolus, Cajetan, and Silvester. Some Dominicans even opted out of the Thomist tradition entirely. Ambrosius Catharinus adopted the Scotist position, even going so far as to accuse Cajetan of being a "monster." Rhetoric aside, I do not find Catharinus's arguments particularly noteworthy. Beyond his biblical arguments, which are little more than Scotistic commonplaces, Catharinus deploys sophisms that exploit temporal paradoxes: Peter, he argues, must be in a state of grace before he sins; if sin belongs to the order of nature, how can the order of nature precede the order of grace? To what order does the sin of the Antichrist belong? If it precedes the hypostatic order, to which Christ belongs, how can he be anti-Christ? These type of questions have a long history in the literature. One need not waste too much time with them, since they fail to take into account that Cajetan's orders are metaphysical, not historical stages. Giacomo Nacchianti (1502–69), fared better in his argumentation, for he rejected such arguments in favor of a purely Biblical approach. Basing himself largely on the exegesis of Col 1:15–20, Nacchianti was, like Catharinus, one of the only Dominicans to adopt the Scotist position *tout court*. Almost three hundred years later, Pietro Maria Gazzaniga (1722–99) could remark how much it pained him to see two of his Dominican brothers accept the Scotist position.

Be that as it may, the Dominicans that followed in the footsteps of Cajetan were numerous. I would count Bartholomé Medina, Domingo Bañez, Diego Alvarez (ca. 1550–1635), Jean-Baptiste Gonet (1615–81), and Charles-René Billuart (1685–1757) as mitigated Thomists after the example of Cajetan. Other Dominicans, such as John of Jean Poinsot (1589–1644) and Domenico Marini (1599–1669), followed the lineaments of Silvester more closely. Gregorius Cippullus (n.d.–1647) adopted Silvester's distinction between the *finis qui* and the *finis cui*, but explicitly rejected Cajetan's use of the genuses of final causality and material causality. Although they might also be considered mitigated Thomists, the extensive treatments by Juan Vicente Asturiensis (n.d.–1595) and Giovanni Paulo Nazario (ca. 1556–1645) are difficult to pigeonhole, and are treated as unique views in most sources. Pedro de Godoy (n.d.–1667), arguably the Dominican that drew most from new approaches pioneered by the Society of Jesus, also resists easy classification. In sum, the trend among Dominican theologians in Christology, as in Mariology, was to various Thomistic positions mitigated by Scotism. Godoy, in adopting a position suggested, but refuted, by Suárez—namely, that Christ was absolutely predestined to be a passible redeemer—might better be considered as a Scotist mitigated by Thomism. Catharinus, Nacchianti, and Viguerius were simply Scotists.

Theologians of the Society of Jesus also display an incredible diversity of views. Salmerón gave a particularly clever defense of the Scotist position in his *Disputationes in Epistolas D. Pauli,* taking special care to reply to Cajetan's arguments; whereas Gregory de Valencia followed the lead of Cajetan. Francisco Toledo (1534–96) and Vásquez, who subjected Cajetan and Silvester to withering criticism, are perhaps the two most brilliant examples of the strict Thomist position among the Jesuits. On the other hand, Luis Molina (1536–1600), Suárez, Francesco Albertini (1552–1619), and Giuseppe Ragusa (n.d.–1624) took rather independent approaches to the topic of Christ's predestination. Albertini listed six different theories, rejecting each one in turn. He based his own solution on a detailed analysis of final causality considered in light of God's *scientia media*. Ragusa, who wrote a similarly diffuse treatment, refuted almost everyone of note who had written before him, including Cajetan, Suárez, and Molina. Still, Ragusa and Agustín Bernal de Avila (1589–1642) argued a strict Thomist line against Suárez and Molina; while Albertini, Francesco Amico (or Franz Amicus) (1578–1651), Juan de Lugo, and Rodrigo Arriaga (1592–1667) expanded the mitigated Thomism of Cajetan and Silvester. In this generation we also find Scotists, such as Jean Martinon (1586–1662) and many of the Louvain Jesuits; Molinists, such as Diego Ruiz de Montoya (1562–1632), and a number of figures who resist classification, including Diego Granado, Pedro Hurtado de Mendoza (1578–1641), and Bernardo Aldrete (1596–1657). Denis Petau (1583–1652) listed a number of ends for the Incarnation apart from redemption and implied, much like Suárez before him, that they may be integrated into one total cause. His list of patristic authorities was mined for many years to come, although the Jesuit maintained a noble silence on the scholastic debate. By the late seventeenth century, however, the dominant Jesuit theologians were all Scotists: here we count Martín de Esparza y Artieda (1606–89), Felipe Aranda (1642–95), Tomás Muniessa (1627–96), Tirso González (1624–1701), and Domenico Viva (1684–1726). When Didacus Quadros (n.d.–1746) discussed the state of the art in 1734, he mentioned three Jesuit theologians—Juan de Ulloa (1639–1723), Juan Marín (1654–1725), and Juan Campoverde (1658–1737)—among *recentiores* who could not be categorized according to the usual ways of treating the issue, although all of them should be considered as providing unique approaches to arguing the Scotist position. Thus among Jesuits we find strict Thomists (Toledo, Vásquez, Ragusa, and Bernal); mitigated Thomists (Albertini, Amico, de Lugo, and Arriaga); mitigated Scotists (Aranda, Muniessa, Quadros, and Campoverde); strict Scotists (Martinon, González, and Marín); strict Molinists (Ruiz de Montoya), who assert the simplicity of the divine decree precisely to bypass the Thomist-Scotist divide; and mitigated Scoto-Molinists (Esparza, Viva, and de Ulloa), who considered themselves "single decree" Scotists. Chronologically, the trend again moves from Thomism to Scotism, with mitigated forms of both in the transition, as well as various forms of Molinism. By the eighteenth century, however, there were no major defenders of Thomism (strict or mitigated), strict Molinism, or Suárezianism in the Society of Jesus. Again, the conversation shifted Scotus-ward, with the debate concerning the validity of pure Scotism versus forms mitigated either by Molinism or post-Suárezian debates about Christ's predestination as a possible redeemer.

Scotism follows a similar pattern, although the debate shifts gradually from one between pure Scotism and forms mitigated by the same post-Suárezian debates, to debates between pure Scotism and what can only be called "hyper-Scotism." In this sense, the Scotistic drift of the early modern period affects even Scotist theologians. John Punch (1599 or 1603–1661) and Bartolomeo Mastri led the charge by building upon and developing the thought of previous Scotists such as Juan de Rada, Filippo Fabri, Maurizio Centini (n.d.–1640), Girolamo Galli (fl. 1640s), Angelo Volpe, and Bonaventura Bellut (1600–76), each of whom can be credited with original contributions to the development of Scotism. Unlike the Dominicans or Jesuits, the disciples of the Subtle Doctor comprised a unified front and advanced a steady stream of novel arguments for the absolute predestination of Christ, often incorporating the "cosmic" Christologies of the Eastern fathers as new editions of their works appeared. Most of the intra-Scotistic debates concerned the speculative question of Christ's incarnation in impassible flesh. Many Scotists (quite against the claims of twentieth-century theologians such as Emile Mersch) also developed strikingly original accounts of Christ's grace of headship and the mystical body. Volpe is perhaps the most significant in this respect. What is most important for our purposes, however, is that the early modern Scotists provide adventurous Christologies and Mariologies that were tightly integrated with one another and other speculative topics, such as predestination, possible worlds, original sin, and eschatology. As a result, some of the most fascinating Christological speculations can be found in Mariological works, such as the immense *Opus theologicum* of Salvator Montalbanus, mentioned above.

These trends are mirrored in the theologians of other religious orders who adopted various aspects of the existing Thomistic or Scotist syntheses. Diego de Tapia (n.d.–1591) made one of the more interesting attempts to harmonize Thomas and Scotus. Like Aquinas, he pleads ignorance of what God might have done if Adam did not sin. Still, the Augustinian hermit rejected the intermediate distinction between God's *scientia simplicis intelligentiae* and his *scientia visionis* by including the *scientia media* in God's *scientia simplicis intelligentiae*. In doing so, he is most likely the first to offer a solution to the problem through an analysis of possible worlds, an approach that became much more popular in the twentieth century. Pedro de Lorca (ca. 1561–1612), a Cistercian scholastic theologian, argued that in the order of intention God predestined Christ *ante praevisum lapsum*, but that in the order of execution, he decreed the redemption as the means necessary to achieve that end. Here, too, although de Lorca made several concessions of a general sort to Scotus, he still argued that if Adam had not sinned, the Word would not have become flesh, since God's chosen means would be absent. Francisco Zumel (ca. 1540–1607) adopted the Scotistic "triple causality," making Christ's glory the efficient, exemplary, and final cause of our own predestination, but still denied that God predestined Christ independently of sin. Zumel shied away from the typical Cajetanian distinctions, but did refer to our redemption as a *principalis finis cuius gratia*, a use which appears to anticipate the more common distinction used by later theologians such as Jean Poinsot. The great Mercedarians of the next generation, Sylvester de Saavedra and Juan Prudencio, adopted more explicitly Scotistic stances.

The Carmelites and Oratorians might well be the exceptions that prove the rule. For their part, Carmelites consistently offered positions that fell outside the Thomistic and Scotistic mainstream. Gabriel of St. Vincent (n.d.–1671) rejected the ordering of the *signa rationis* found in Scotus, Cajetan, and Medina (among others). On the other hand, Philip of the Most Holy Trinity (1603–71), who is perhaps better known as a mystical theologian, rejected the typical distinctions found in mitigated Thomists such as Cajetan and Silvester, and argued that God predestined Christ first *in omni genere causae*. Even so, the Carmelite father maintained that God's decree was not absolute, but required some "means" to be executed. Even if God predestined Christ before all, he would not have become incarnate had Adam not sinned. John of the Annunciation (1633–1701), the author of the treatise on Christology in the *cursus* of the Salmanticenses, might be seen as an inheritor of the tradition of Silvester of Ferrara and Jean Poinsot, to the extent that the theologian at Salamanca argued that God willed Christ as the end of all creation *in genere causae finalis cuius gratia*, but that God permitted the Fall prior to the Incarnation *in genere causae finalis cui*. Be that as it may, the Carmelite theologian provided a lengthier argument by far. Giuseppe Zagaglia (n.d.–1711), a Carmelite who followed the system of John Baconthorpe rather than Thomas Aquinas, proposed a complex solution that involved no fewer than eleven *signa rationis*. Despite its truly baroque complexity, Zagaglia's approach had more in common with the strict Thomist approach to the problem, in that he asserted unequivocally that the Incarnation was logically dependent on the Fall. Instead of applying distinctions between the Incarnation and the glorification of Christ, Zagaglia treated the redemption as a means *in ordine naturae reparatae post lapsum*, but believed that God willed it as an end *in ordine naturae reparabilis*. On the other hand, French writers who fall outside the ambit of scholasticism, such as Oratorians and members of the French School, took a variety of positions on these issues. Pierre de Bérulle (1575–1629), for example, resists classification. While he appears to embrace the Thomist position, he often uses rather Scotistic language and argumentation. Saint Francis de Sales (1567–1622) and Blessed Jean Eudes (1601–80) favor the Scotist position—Francis explicitly, Jean Eudes less so. On the other hand, the Oratorian Louis Thomassin (1619–95) was one of the fiercest critics of the Scotist position. Another Oratorian, Nicolas Malebranche (1638–1715) adopted many Scotist positions, but colored them with his own distinct genius.

# 4 EPILOGUE

Two curious facts emerge when one compares trends in Mariology and Christology in early modern Catholicism. First, the positions held by any given theologian on Mary's *debitum peccati* tend to find their correlates in the theologians' positions on the motive for the Incarnation. This is not always the case, of course. The Jesuit Bernal, for example, was a strict Thomist in Christology while being an exemptionist in Mariology. Still, after the Council of Trent, theologians who held one of the four views about the *debitum peccati* were increasingly likely to hold a corresponding view on the predestination and primacy of Christ. In other words, theologians who were strict Thomists in their Christologies tended to be strict Thomists in their Mariologies, and so tended to argue against the Immaculate Conception. As maculism ceased to be a viable option in Catholic theology, however, theologians who argued that Mary had some debt to Adam, proximate or remote, often adhered to some form of mitigated Thomism or mitigated Scotism; while those who argued against any *debitum peccati* tended overwhelmingly to support a purer form of Scotism. Second, these correlations follow a very specific historical pattern. In the generation after the Council of Trent, we see a wide diversity of Christological and Mariological views, with an almost even distribution between them. At the same time, there was hardly any unanimity in any given school: Dominicans were strict or mitigated Thomists, with a very small number of theologians sympathetic to Scotus being odd men out. Franciscans were strict or mitigated in the Christologies, and some continued to argue that Mary must have some debt to Adam. Jesuits, Carmelites, Augustinians, and other religious orders showed a similar diversity. In this generation, there were still theologians, such as Medina, Gregory of Valencia, or even the Franciscan Antonio de Córdoba (n.d.–1578), who argued that the exemptionist position was heretical. After the controversies over the *debitum* at Seville and Toledo secured the ascendency of the modern form of the Mariological debate, the middle of the seventeenth century saw a remarkable increase in the number of non-Franciscan theologians who supported either a remote debt for Mary and a mitigated form of Scotism, or no debt and a strict form of Scotism. At the same time, Scotists supported both an exemptionist Mariology and a robust, often creative form of the older arguments for Christ's predestination. The great Mercedarian theologians now supported Scotistic positions, and the Carmelites, with the notable exception of the Salmanticenses, began the drift into rather eccentric attempts to refute both Thomism and Scotism. By the eighteenth century, this Scotistic drift was almost complete. Scotists developed hyper-baroque theologies of Christ and Mary that surpassed even the most fervent Franciscan theologies of the seventeenth century. Almost all Jesuits supported a strict Scotism, with the few figures that were left of center arguing not for a Scotism with Thomist elements, but rather a Scotism merged with Molinism. Dominicans like Godoy and his heirs followed a mitigated form of Scotism, and Billuart began to look like a conservative for following Cajetan rather than Thomas on the question of Christ's predestination. By this point, even the majority of Carmelite theologians were Scotists, as were the newer forms of systematic theology based upon the writings of Saint Anselm or Henry of Ghent. At the same time, however, a new generation of Dominicans such as Bonifazio Maria Grandi (n.d.–1692), Vincenzo Ludovico Gotti (1664–1742), and Pietro Gazzaniga began to call for a return to the genuine teaching of the Angelic Doctor. The resulting tensions between a dominant Scotism and the first stirrings of neo-Thomism gave rise to many of the major trends in nineteenth-century theology. Of course, such tensions, while deserving of serious historical study, are beyond the scope of this essay.

## Suggested Reading

Astute readers will notice my immense debt to Juniper Carol's bibliographic research (Carol 1978; Carol 1986). Other valuable surveys include Bonnefoy 1954a, Bonnefoy 1954b, Catena 1955, Casado 1957, and Bonnefoy 1959.

## Bibliography

Ameri, Giancito. 1954. *Doctrina theologorum de Immaculata B. V. Mariae Conceptione tempore Concilii Basileënsis.* Rome: Academia Mariana Internationalis.

Belluti, Bonaventura. 1645. *Disputationes de Incarnatione Dominica ad mentem Doctoris Subtilis.* Catana.

Billuart, Charles-René. 1747. *Cursus Theologiae.* Vols. 12–13. Würzburg.

Bonnefoy, Jean-François. 1954a. "La negación del 'debitum peccati' en María." *Verdad y Vida* 12: 102–171.

Bonnefoy, Jean-François. 1954b. "Quelques théories modernes du 'debitum peccati.'" *Ephemerides Mariologicae* 4: 269–331.

Bonnefoy, Jean-François. 1959. *La primaute du Christ.* Rome: Casa Editrice Herder.

Bosco, Giovanni. 1950. *L'Immacolata Concezione nel pensiero del Gaetano e del Caterino.* Florence: Edizioni Il Rosario.

Cajetan. 1903. *Commentarium in Tertiam Partem Summae Theologiae in Sancti Thomae Aquinatis Doctoris Angelici Opera Omnia.* Vols. 11–12. Rome: Ex Typogaphia Polyglotta S. C. de Propaganda Fide.

Cajetan. 1588. *De Conceptione B. Mariae Virginis ad Leonem Decimum Pontificem Maximum in Opuscula omnia.* Vol. 2. Venice.

Campoverde, Juan. 1712. *Tractatus de Incarnatione Verbi Divini.* Alcalá.

Carol, Juniper. 1978. *A History of the Controversy over the "Debitum Peccati."* St. Bonaventure, NY: The Franciscan Institute.

Carol, Juniper. 1986. *Why Jesus Christ?* Manassas, VA: Trinity Communications.

Casado, Ovido. 1957. *Mariología clásica española.* Madrid: Ephemerides Mariologicae.

Castillo Velasco, Francisco. 1641. *Subtilissimi Scoti Doctorum super III Sententiarum librum.* Vol. 1. Antwerp: Apud Petrum Bellarum.

Catena, Claudio. 1955. "La dottrina immacolista negli autori carmelitani." *Carmelus* 2: 132–215.

Catharinus, Ambrosius. 1542. *Annotationes in commentaria Cajetani.* Lyons.

Catharinus, Ambrosius. 1551. *Disputatio pro veritate Immaculatae Conceptionis beatissimae Virginis Mariae.* Rome.

Catharinus, Ambrosius. (1555) 1937. *Pro eximia praedestinatione Christi.* Bastia.

Contenson, Vincent. 1687. *Theologia mentis et cordis, seu Speculationes universae doctrinae sacrae.* Cologne.

Corazón, Enrique del Sdo. 1959. "Una cuestión preliminar a la edición crítica del 'Curso Teólogico Salmanticense.'" *Salmanticensis* 6 (2): 273–321.

Dominic of St. Teresa. 1678. *Collegii Salmanticensis FF. Discalceatorum Cursus Theologicus.* Venice.

Giles of the Presentation. 1617. *De Immaculata B. Virginis Conceptione.* Coimbra.

Gonet, Jean-Baptiste. 1671. *Clypeus theologiae Thomisticae contra novos eius impugnatorus*, vol. 5. Cologne.

Gotti, Vincenzo Lodovico. 1750. *Theologia scholastico-dogmatica juxta mentem divi Thomae Aquinatis*. Vol. 3. Venice.

Granado, Diego. 1617. *De Immaculata B. V. Dei Genetricis Mariae Conceptione*. Seville.

Gregory of Valencia. 1603. *Commentariorum theologicorum tomi quatuor*. Lyons.

Hurter, Hugo. 1906. *Nomenclator literarius theologiae catholicae 2/2*. Würzburg: Wagner.

John of the Annunciation. (1687) 1879. *Collegii Salmanticensis FF. Discalceatorum Cursus Theologicus*. Vol. 9. Paris: Victor Palmé.

Lezana, Juan de. 1616. *Liber apologeticus pro Immaculata Deiparae Virginis Mariae Conceptione*. Madrid.

Lugo, Juan de. 1653. *Disputationes Scholasticae de Incarnatione Dominica*. Lyons.

Marín, Juan. 1720. *Theologiae speculativae et moralis*. Vol. 2. Venice.

Mastrius, Batholomaeo. 1661. *Disputationes Theologicae in Tertium Librum Sententiarum*. Venice.

Medina, Bartholomé. 1580. *Expositio in Tertiam Partem D. Thomae*. Salamanca.

Montalbanus, Salvator. 1723. *Opus theologicum tribus disinctum tomis in quibus efficacissime ostenditur Immaculatam Dei Genitricem utpote praeservative redemptam, fuisse prorsus immune ab omni debito tum contrahendi originale peccatum, tum ipsius fomitem incurrendi*. Palermo.

Montefortino, Hieronymus. (1737) 1903. "Dissertatio Theologica fueritne beatissima semper Virgo Maria immunis a debito contrahendi peccatum originale?" In *Ioannis Duns Scoti Summa theologica*. Vol. 5. Rome.

Moral, Carolus del. 1730. *Fons Illimis theologiae Scoticae Marianae*. Madrid.

Nieremberg, Eusebio. 1659. *Opera parthenica de supereximia et omnimoda puritate Matris Dei*. Lyons.

Olazarán, Jesús. 1946. "El dogma de la Inmaculada Concepción en el Concilio de Trento." *Estudios Eclesiásticos* 20: 105–154.

Peñalosa, Ambrosio de. 1650. *Vindicae Deiparae Virginis de peccato originali et debito illius contrahendi rigore theologico praestructae et a nemine hactenus ex professo discussae*. Antwerp.

Perlín, Juan. 1630. *Apologia scholastica sive controversia theologica, pro Magnae Matris ab originali debito immunitate*. Lyons.

Punch, John. 1661. *Commentarii theologici quibus Ioannis Duns Scoti quaestiones in libros Sententiarum*. Paris.

Quadros, Didachus de. 1734. *Tractatus Theologicus de Incarnatione Verbi Divini*. Madrid.

Rada, Juan de. 1618. *Controversiarum theologicarum inter S. Thomam et Scotum super Tertium Sententiarum Librum*. Venice.

Salazar, Chirinus de. 1618. *Pro Immaculata Deiparae Virginis Conceptione defensio*. Alcalá.

Salmerón, Alfonso. 1615. "Disputationes in Epistolas D. Pauli." In *Opera Omnia*. Vol. 15. Cologne.

Sylvestri, Francesco [Francis Silvester]. 1930. "Commentaria in Summam D. Thomae contra gentiles." In *Sancti Thomae Aquinatis Opera Omnia*. Vol. 15. Rome: Ex Typographia Polyglotta S. C. de Propaganda Fide.

Suárez, Francisco. 1856. "In Tertiam Partem D. Thomae." In *Opera omnia*. Vol. 19. Paris: Apud Ludovicum Vivès.

Ulloa, Juan de. 1719. *Theologiae Scholasticae*. Vol. 5. Augsburg.

Urrutigoyti, Tomás. 1660. *Certamen scholasticum expositivum argumentum pro Deipara ejusque Immaculata Conceptione*. Lyons.

Vásquez, Gabriel. 1612. *Commentariorum ac disputationum in Tertiam Partem S. Thomae*. Vol. 1. Ingolstadt.

Viva, Domenico. 1712. *Cursus Theologicus ad usum Tyronum elucubratus*. Padua.

Volpe, Angelo. 1642. *Sacrae Theologiae Summa Ioannis Duns Scoti Doctoris Subtilissimi*. Naples.

CHAPTER 8

..............................................................................................

# CATHOLIC MORAL THEOLOGY, 1550–1800

JEAN-LOUIS QUANTIN

## 1 WRITING THE HISTORY OF MORAL THEOLOGY

..............................................................................................

IN the seventeenth and eighteenth centuries, writing the history of religious controversies was a part and continuation of controversy. Of no field was this more true than that of Roman Catholic moral theology. The influence of such polemical accounts was enduring. The massive *History of Moral Disputes in the Roman Catholic Church*, published in 1889 by the "Old Catholics" Döllinger and Reusch—which can still be useful if read with caution—is steeped in early modern anti-Jesuitism. Polemics between Dominicans and Jesuits about the respective responsibilities of their orders in the moral system of "probabilism" continued well into the twentieth century. Anti-probabilists constructed a grand narrative. In his hugely influential *Storia del Probabilismo e del Rigorismo* (1743), the Dominican Daniele Concina (1687–1756) used biological metaphors: probabilism was born in 1577; it became adult in 1620 and kept making progress until 1656; it then entered its decay, which became irreversible after 1690. This scheme still provided the framework for the entry by the Dominican Thomas Deman in the *Dictionnaire de théologie catholique* (a huge, very well-researched piece that many historians up to the present day have mined for quotations, while overlooking its bias), with an additional part on Alphonsus Maria de' Liguori and his aftermath (Deman 1936).

This grand narrative testifies to the centrality of the issue of probabilism and to the sense among its adversaries of a heroic fight to rescue pristine Christian morality. One should be wary, however, of a simple, linear view, especially when it conflates the history of ideas and the history of practices. The impact that shifts in moral theology may have had on "ordinary" lay people is extremely difficult to ascertain: it might well be argued, albeit with some qualifications, that these debates should primarily be seen "as expressions of the inner conflicts of the clergy and their class" (Briggs 1989, 336).

# 2 CASUISTRY

In the early modern age, theology became subdivided into specialized disciplines, each with its distinctive methodology and language. The increasing autonomy of moral theology went hand-in-hand with the development of casuistry, which became its most characteristic genre—to the extent that, for many contemporaries as well as for posterity, they became virtually synonymous (Vereecke 1990). Casuistry in itself was no novelty. "Reasoning in cases" has been characterized as a "style of reasoning," the roots of which go back to classical antiquity. After "casuistry" had long been a derogatory term, it has undergone a rehabilitation in the last thirty years. Several philosophers have called for a "new casuistry" as the best possible approach to contemporary debates in medical ethics (Jonsen and Toulmin 1988; Forrester 1996). It is commonly accepted, however, that fully fledged casuistry (under the name of "cases of conscience") did not appear until the High Middle Ages. Its enormous expansion in the post-Tridentine Church was a direct effect of the new individualistic understanding of penance, at least among the clergy itself and urban elites, and of the correlative emphasis on frequent, devotional confession (Bossy 1975). The Council of Trent stipulated that penitents should confess all their mortal sins with "the circumstances that change the species of the sin"—and which it was therefore incumbent upon confessors to know. Jesuits played an essential role in the following decades, when they developed a two-tiered teaching system, which was codified in their 1599 *Ratio studiorum*. While all students of theology had to study cases of conscience, these became the core of an abridged curriculum, the *cursus minor*, devised both for spiritual coadjutors (as opposed to professed Jesuits) and for the secular clergy taught by the Society in diocesan seminaries. According to the *Ratio*, "the professor of cases of conscience" should "prescind from theological matters that have hardly any necessary connection with cases," and merely "touch in a very delimited way upon certain theological matters on which the teaching of cases depends," such as the definition of mortal and venial sin (Angelozzi 1981).

New textbooks were badly needed. In the second half of the sixteenth century, the most important one was probably the *Enchiridion confessariorum* of Martín de Azpilcueta, "the Doctor of Navarre" (1492–1586), first published in Portuguese in 1552 and then in Latin in 1573. Significantly, Navarrus was not a theologian but a canon lawyer (Lavenia 2003). The new generation of textbooks really began with the Jesuit Juan Azor (1536–1603), who published in 1600 the first volume of his *Institutiones morales*, based on his teaching at the Roman College. This was followed by several hundred titles. Nearly 1300 published works of casuistry have been identified from 1550 to 1800, more than half of which appeared in the seventeenth century; as the most successful ones were reprinted dozens of times, a plausible estimate runs to five or six million copies (Hurtubise 2005). They were typically organized according to the order of the Decalogue, which had definitely supplanted the medieval "seven deadly sins" as the structure of moral teaching (Bossy 1988), with a preliminary part on "general principles." These were given considerable space in Azor's *Institutiones*, with many biblical and patristic references. Azor professed to cover the same ground as the *prima secundae* of Thomas Aquinas' *Summa theologiae*, but he left aside both its inaugural questions, on beatitude as the final end of man, and its concluding ones on grace. These omissions have been severely criticized, from a modern Roman Catholic perspective, as testifying to a fateful shift to "a morality of obligation" (Pinckaers 1995). Theoretical preliminaries became much sketchier in subsequent authors. In his *Resolutiones morales*, published in twelve parts from 1629 to 1656, the Theatine Antonino Diana (1585–1663) got rid of them altogether. Each part was subdivided into treatises and then into "resolutions" (the basic unit): some treatises were thematic (on contracts, on fasting), but others (called "miscellaneous") were purely accumulative. There were 6595 resolutions in which, according to Diana's eighteenth-century editor, more than twenty-eight thousand questions were handled. At that stage, it seems fair to say that moral theology had been thoroughly subsumed into casuistry.

It is often said that many cases were imaginary. The objection already had been made by contemporaries, since Diana deemed it necessary to forestall it (when discussing the question "whether one who commits sodomitical fornication with an infidel man, or fornication with a Jewish or heretical woman, should explain the circumstances of persons"). He insisted that he had personally met the case in Palermo, while acting as theologian for the Confraternity of Mercy (for the redemption of Christians captured and held as slaves by the Turks). It is clear that casuists had a predilection for "test-cases," which allowed them to discuss general principles relating to the classification of sins: thus, in the case of a person who had sex with a non-Catholic, they debated whether "this circumstance changes the species of the sin," adding sacrilege to unchastity. Some cases were also clearly obsolete. It would definitely be wrong, however, to assume that "the overwhelming majority" had "no correspondence whatever with daily reality" and should be understood within "the Baroque category of astonishment" (as maintained by Sabaino in Caramuel Lobkowitz 2010, 79; against Quantin 2001, 54–55). The proliferation of cases reflected the moralists' determination to map as fully as possible a world that was becoming increasingly complex. Collections drawn up for the training of English seminary priests in the 1580s considered all the difficult situations likely to be met both by missionaries and by lay recusants (Holmes 1981).

As a subject of study, it would appear that casuistry enjoyed little intellectual prestige. Concina claimed that those often specialized in moral theology who were not qualified for higher studies. Such "pure moralists" were therefore in awe of "scholastic divines," from whom they took over the system of probabilism unexamined. It is at least undeniable that probabilism, which became the theoretical underpinning of seventeenth-century casuistry, was not evolved by casuists themselves.

# 3 PROBABILISM

The moral notion of probability ultimately derived from Aristotle's warning, in the introduction to the *Nicomachean Ethics*, that moral matters "involve much difference of opinion and uncertainty." Developments of this idea in medieval theology have been explored in a valuable Master's thesis from the University of Helsinki, which was plundered over several years by a now disgraced Leuven professor (Dougherty, Harsting, and Friedman 2009). The problem of moral uncertainty became critical under the impact of voluntarism, which stressed that the will was not predetermined by the intellect but free to make its own choices, either to act or to defer action. Whereas Aquinas' position might be characterized as "tutioristic," always advocating the safer course—that is, the course least open to the risk of sinning—fifteenth-century moralists adopted "a combination of subjective probabiliorism and extrinsic probabilism." When one is in doubt, one must examine what are the opinions approved by qualified authorities and thus "probable"; in the event of conflicting authorities, one should then choose the opinion that appears to oneself to be more probable (Kantola 1994).

Probabilism was first propounded in 1577 by the Spanish Dominican Bartolomé de Medina (1527/8–80), in his commentary on the *prima secundae* of Aquinas' *Summa theologiae* (question 19, article 6: "Whether the will is good when it abides by erring reason?"). Medina considers a situation when two opposite opinions are "probable" (i.e., "confirmed by strong arguments and by the authority of the wise"), but one more probable than the other. "The great question is whether we are obliged to follow the more probable opinion, disregarding the probable one, or it is sufficient to follow the probable one." Medina was well aware that, according to earlier theologians, one should follow the more probable opinion. His own answer was nonetheless that "if an opinion is probable, it is permitted to follow it, even though the opposite opinion is more probable." The more probable opinion is safer but "the probable opinion is safe," and one who follows it is in "no danger of sinning": one may perform a materially but not a morally evil action, as one will have an excuse.

Once formulated by Medina, probabilism quickly spread. It was further refined by the Jesuits Gabriel Vázquez (1551–1604) and Francisco Suárez (1548–1617). In his own commentary on the *prima secundae*, first published in 1599, Vázquez stressed that one could simultaneously assent to an opinion "through proper (or intrinsic) principles" (because of the reasons for it) and to the opposite opinion "through extrinsic principles," on account of the authority of those who followed it: in that case, one did not assent directly to the opinion but to its probability. Therefore, one was permitted to act according to the opinion of others, against one's own opinion, which one regarded as more probable. Suárez's work on the *prima secundae* originated from his teaching at the Jesuit College in Rome in the early 1580s, but was only published posthumously in 1628. His most important contribution was to introduce juridical axioms. *In dubiis melior est conditio possidentis* ("in case of doubt, the cause of the party in possession is better"): when it is uncertain whether a course of action is sinful or not, with probable opinions on both sides, human liberty is "in possession" and should be favored. *Lex non promulgata non obligat* ("an unpromulgated law is of no force"), and as long as there is a "reasonable doubt" as to either the existence or sense of the law, "it is not sufficiently promulgated." In the following decades, the theoretical preliminaries of works of casuistry were chiefly devoted to expounding the axioms of probabilism. There was general agreement that probabilism allowed the subject to pass from speculative doubt to the practical certainty required for action "here and now": if I follow a probable opinion, I am sure not to sin.

It has recently been argued that the success of probabilism among Jesuits, who had hitherto adhered to a standard Thomistic tutiorism, was due to the influence of ancient rhetoric—especially of Cicero's works—which became central to Jesuit culture after the Society turned itself into a teaching order. The causality thus suggested is unconvincing (Maryks 2008; Gay 2011b; Gay 2011c). A previous claim according to which casuistry "ultimately derived from the classical discipline of rhetoric" also appears exaggerated (O'Malley 1993, 145; Höpfl 2004, 15). The same should be said of links with the Molinist doctrine of grace and its optimistic view of human nature after the Fall (Mahoney 1987, 229). These developments reinforced each other and created together what might be called a Jesuit model, or style, of Catholicism. They contributed more specifically to forging a corporate identity (Visceglia 2007), which is one of the reasons why Jesuits clung obstinately to probabilism when it came under attack. At the turn of the seventeenth century, however, the success of probabilism was by no means proper to the Society of Jesus. It was adopted by theologians of all religious orders because it appeared to satisfy pressing needs of the times, within the wider context of Roman Catholic "confessionalization."

Faced with the jurisdictional claims of the modern State, the post-Tridentine Church concentrated its efforts on "the inner realm," "the forum of conscience" (Turrini 1991; Prodi 2000). Moral theology was developed as a juridical discourse and moral theologians appeared as "jurists specialized in the inner forum" (Legendre 1980). Conscience was represented as a court, which had to adjudicate the rival claims of liberty and law, using probable opinions ("in favor of the law" on the one hand, "in favor of liberty" on the other hand), which were often variations on the principle *In dubiis melior est conditio possidentis*. The casuistry of fasting, as explained, for example, by Juan Sánchez (n.d.–1624), is a good illustration. If this is Thursday and someone is unsure whether midnight has rung, he may eat flesh, "because the right and possession are for the liberty of eating"; the reverse applies on the night of Friday to Saturday, "because the possession is for the precept" of abstinence. Moralists were anxious not to impose any unwarranted restriction on human liberty. A question that played a considerable role in the development of probabilism was what the confessor should do with a penitent who relied on a probable opinion. The consensus was that the confessor, even if he adhered himself to the opposite opinion, not only might, but ought to, grant absolution: otherwise, the penitent would have to repeat his confession and thus undergo again the shame of avowal.

However, since the emphasis was on extrinsic rather than intrinsic probability (a probable opinion was in effect an opinion said to be probable by moral theologians), probabilism remained anchored in a morality of authority. The responsibility for moral choice was delegated to experts. Recognizing this extrinsicist character obviously does not mean adopting the polemical Protestant line, which culminated in the late nineteenth century in the work of Henry Charles Lea, and according to which auricular confession in general was an instrument of power over consciences too weak "to bear their burdens" (Lea 1896, 2:456). But some modern authors have mistakenly hailed seventeenth-century probabilism as embodying "the autonomy of conscience, making a solitary option for a 'less probable' solution" (Delumeau 1990, 143). In fact, the option was for the less probable opinion of others against one's own opinion, which one judged more probable—and kept regarding so even while one acted against it. The Theatine Zaccaria Pasqualigo (1600–64) even argued that one could follow "an opinion which one does not regard as probable but which one knows to be regarded as probable by others." When probabilists such as Diana permitted subjects to disobey the king's commands or to avoid taxation on the basis of a probable opinion, they meant to enable them to find an opinion contrary to the king and to use it "as an extrinsic instrument of political fight" (Burgio 1998, 142–43; Quantin 2002).

A logical consequence of this extrinsicism was to allow people to borrow and abandon opinions at will. This was developed by Juan Caramuel Lobkowitz (1606–82), a Cistercian abbot and later a bishop, an extraordinary polymath, who for a long time was only known through the caricatures of his critics and who has attracted much interest in recent years. He was much more theory oriented than casuists such as Diana. In his 1640 commentary on the Rule of St. Benedict and then in his 1652 *Theologia moralis fundamentalis*, he considers the complicated case—a clear instance of an imaginary test-case—of "Paul," an ecclesiastic who has gone to sea and who first adopts the opinion of the Jesuit Tomás Sánchez (1550–1610) about the reading of the breviary, and then the contrary opinion of Juan Sánchez, with the result that he does not say his office at all. According to Caramuel, Paul commits no sin: "a man is no slave of his opinions; when he changes a probable opinion, he uses the liberty that he has received from heaven, and he does well." Caramuel even concluded, after a subtle discussion on the nature of human will, that Paul did not sin although he had intended from the start to change his opinion.

The tendency of moralists during the first half of the seventeenth century was to extend constantly the scope of probabilism. While for early probabilists like Vázquez, priests, as a duty of charity to others, were obliged to follow the safer opinion when administering sacraments, later authors allowed them—at least in some cases—to follow both a less probable and a less safe opinion. Considerable subtlety was used to expand the limits of "probable." Some divines, such as Pasqualigo and the Sicilian Jesuit Tomaso Tamburini (1591–1675), argued that it was permitted to follow even "an opinion with the smallest degree of probability," and that it was not necessary for it to be evidently probable, but only "probably probable." The most important development was the abolition of the distinction between "speculative" and "practical" probability. At the beginning of the seventeenth century, it was quite common for moralists to warn that some opinions were speculatively probable but not safe to follow in practice.

Juan Sánchez protested that any opinion speculatively probable was safe in practice: to have a speculative opinion and to be afraid to put it into practice was tantamount to the punishment of Tantalus.

The conjunction of an ever-expanding probabilism and of an ever more detailed casuistry produced what was shortly to be denounced, first of all in French, as "lax morality," *la morale relâchée* ("laxism" is quite a late coinage that first appeared in Italian and Latin in the eighteenth century, and which it seems better to avoid). As a supposed body of divinity, this "lax morality" was a polemical construction fabricated by putting together, out of context and quite often with some rewriting, all the shocking propositions that had been declared probable by some casuists—preferably Jesuit ones. But laxity was real enough as a trend. Moral theologians had a structural tendency to favor the most "lenient" solution (*benigna* was the Latin word used), partly out of their sincere concern not to impose any undue burden on consciences, and partly because, in the very repetitive field of casuistry, this was the best way of making one's mark. Diana prided himself, according to the subtitle of his *Resolutiones morales*, in explaining "cases of conscience briefly, clearly, and in most cases leniently." His friend Caramuel provocatively congratulated him for having "made probable many opinions that were not so before." As a result, "those who follow them do not sin anymore, although they sinned before." It is essential here to avoid anachronistic value judgements. Jean Delumeau compounded his error about the nature of probabilism by distinguishing, among the "propositions" of casuists subsequently condemned by the church, those "indefensible in our eyes," and those "in advance of the times" (Delumeau 1990, 116–18). In fact, the casuists' rationale was identical: the same concern for "the honour of the world," with an explicit class bias, made them permit the killing of a slanderer (one of Delumeau's instances of "bad" casuistry) and procuring an abortion (a piece of his "good" casuistry).

# 4  THE RIGORIST REACTION

A reaction was bound to occur. As it happened, it was concomitant with and strongly colored by the major theological dispute that rocked the Roman Catholic Church from 1640 onwards, concerning the doctrine of Cornelius Jansen (1585–1638), which its opponents (in order to stress its heretical character) called Jansenism. For obvious polemical purposes, advocates of "lenient morality" often denounced their adversaries as "Jansenists" or "moral Jansenists," while also giving them, from the 1670s onwards, the nickname "Rigorists." The two movements cannot be historically separated from one another, but they should be distinguished. All Jansenists were Rigorists, but not all Rigorists were Jansenists (Quantin 2006).

Jansen studied theology at the University of Louvain in the Spanish Low Countries (present-day Belgium), where he took his doctorate in 1617; he stayed there as professor of Holy Scripture, until being appointed to the bishopric of Ypres in 1636. Since the sixteenth century, the Louvain school had specialized in "positive theology," based on the study of scripture and the church fathers. On the question of grace and predestination, it held to a strict interpretation of Augustine's late anti-Pelagian writings, and opposed Jesuit attempts to give a greater role to human freedom. Jansen devoted himself over two decades to a systematic study of Augustine, the results of which he synthesized in his life work, the *Augustinus*, which he just had time to complete before his death. It was published posthumously in 1640 and immediately attacked by Belgian Jesuits and denounced at Rome. In 1643 Pope Urban VIII condemned the work. There ensued a complex politico-religious controversy. The archbishop of Malines, Jacques Boonen, who wanted to defend Jansen's memory, fought for nearly a decade—eventually to no avail—to prevent the official publication of Urban's bull in the Low Countries. Meanwhile, he embarked on a campaign against "lax morality" in which he had better success. According to the usual mode of doctrinal regulation at the time, he had thirty-five propositions extracted from works of casuistry, and denounced them to the Faculty of Divinity of Louvain, which condemned them in 1648. This decision was not made public but the faculty subsequently condemned, in 1653 and 1657, a list of forty-three propositions that largely overlapped with the list of 1648 (Ceyssens 1958). No author was mentioned but everyone knew who was targeted. In a letter of 1654 to the Congregation of the Council (the body entrusted with the interpretation of the Council of Trent at Rome), which was printed and much circulated, Boonen claimed to have "learned through indisputable experience that Jesuits were more than others bent upon inventing lax doctrines and putting them into practice."

Only two of the condemned propositions concerned probabilism, or rather developments of it (that "a judge may not condemn someone who has been following a probable opinion," and that "the authority of a single pious and learned doctor makes an opinion probable"). Jansen himself had little to say on moral theology, although he incidentally criticized the abuse of probabilism in order to illustrate the danger of undue reliance on human reasoning. It took his disciples at Louvain until 1660 to recognize that probabilism as such was logically incompatible with their doctrine: since according to them, "ignorance of natural law does not excuse," then neither does probability. John Sinnich (1603–66), an Irish exile who had helped prepare the *Augustinus* for publication, inserted in his 1662 commentary on the First Book of Samuel (*Saul Exrex*) a huge digression against probabilism, which became an essential resource for later Louvain divines, especially in academic theses. A notable feature of this Flemish Rigorism was its strong interest in sexual questions. Louvain divines expounded an Augustinian, or ultra-Augustinian, doctrine according to which the use of marriage as a "remedy for concupiscence" was tantamount to having intercourse for pleasure only, and therefore a venial sin—whereas theologians normally considered "avoidance of fornication" a legitimate end of marriage, and some casuists even permitted intercourse for pleasure (Klomps 1964).

The focus of the Jansenist crisis soon shifted from the Low Countries to neighboring France, where a friend of Jansen's, Jean Duvergier de Hauranne, abbot of Saint-Cyran, had gained great influence as a spiritual director, especially over an abbey of Cistercian nuns in Paris, Port-Royal. Saint-Cyran encouraged his young disciple Antoine Arnaud (1612–94), a Sorbonne doctor in divinity, who was also brother to the abbess of

Port-Royal, to write in defense of Jansen. At about the same time, in 1643, Arnauld published a treatise *On Frequent Communion* in which he denounced the mechanical use of sacraments (a "perpetual cycle of confessions and crimes" instead of "firm and stable conversions"), recommended a penitential withdrawal from Communion, and stressed that priests should not absolve all who came to them in confession, "as if they were servants rather than judges." Disputes over pastoral practice thus became mixed up with debates on grace. In 1653, the new Pope, Innocent X, condemned as heretical five propositions on grace and predestination that were supposed to encapsulate Jansen's errors. Arnauld then evolved the distinction between right and fact (*le droit et le fait*): the five propositions had indeed an heretical sense that had been justly condemned—this was the question of right—but they did not appear in the *Augustinus*, or, if they did, only in the orthodox sense of Augustine—this was a matter of fact, on which the Church was not infallible. In January 1656, Arnauld and his adherents were expelled from the Paris faculty of theology.

Blaise Pascal (1623–62) jumped to their defense in a series of eighteen anonymous letters "written to a provincial by one of his friends," which were published to enormous success from January 1656 to May 1657. The first ones dealt with the dispute on grace but Pascal soon shifted to moral theology, using materials prepared for him by Arnauld and his companion Pierre Nicole (1625–95). The *Provincial Letters* not only ridiculed the practical solutions of casuists, but rejected the very principle of probabilism and the casuistic approach to morality. The only rule was "Scripture and the tradition of the Church." Casuistry and probabilism appeared specifically Jesuit—members of other religious orders, such as Diana and Caramuel, were occasionally mentioned, but presented as "defenders" or "friends" of the Society, who echoed and quoted Jesuit authors. These were tools, Pascal accused, used by Jesuits to "govern the consciences of all." The chief result was to achieve a process of "literarization" of theology: moral questions, which had been deemed the preserve of experts, were now exposed to the "public" (a new notion at the time), including lay men and women. The Jesuits' initial line of defense consisted of accusing Pascal of inaccurate quotations: this was partly true but missed the point.

At the end of 1657, the controversy appeared to peter out, but it was rekindled by the Jesuit Georges Pirot (1599–1659) in his *Apology for the Casuists*. Pirot was the casuist of the Jesuit house in Paris, and is said to have been "outraged by the manner in which Pascal, whom he regarded as an ignorant" had treated his profession. He therefore undertook to defend *en bloc* the casuistical tradition, as it had evolved in the first half of the century, denying any pertinence to Pascal's accusations of laxity. He aimed at the same nonspecialist audience that had made the success of the *Provincial Letters*, and tried to explain how casuists arrived at their conclusions. The effect was disastrous, as this appeared to confirm Pascal's accusations. The *Apology* was condemned by the Sorbonne and about twenty French bishops (Gay 2011a, 210–51).

Meanwhile, at the express request of Pope Alexander VII, the general chapter of the Dominicans, held in Rome in June 1656, had ordered all friars to "give the utmost care to avoid lax, new, and unsafe opinions" on moral questions. This started a powerful backlash against probabilism, especially in the French and Italian provinces—Concina's dating of the decline of probabilism to 1656 referred to the Dominican chapter. Most Dominican divines henceforth defended probabiliorism, the system according to which one should always follow the more probable opinion. Other orders followed suit. The chronology and geography of this rigorist swing cannot be presented in detail here, but it eventually affected the whole of Catholic Europe, including Spain and the German regions (Quantin 2003). French rigorist textbooks, which were much reprinted in the eighteenth century, especially in Italy (not until the 1770s and 1780s in Spain), proved a powerful vehicle. Alfonso Maria de' Liguori (1696–1787) later recalled how, when he entered the seminary in Naples in 1723, the first book that his professors "put in his hands was Genet, the head of probabiliorists"—a Latin translation of the so-called *Theology of Grenoble* by François Genet (1640–1702), a multi-volume work that had first been published in French from 1676 to 1684, and which had been reread by Antoine Arnauld (Pollock 1984). The only religious order that collectively refused to give up probabilism, and even forbade its members to write against it, was the Society of Jesus: hence a major internal crisis occurred when the Superior General Tirso González (1624–1705), who had gone over to probabiliorism, attempted to publish his *Fundamentum theologiae moralis* despite the opposition of Jesuit censors—the book eventually came out in 1694 (Gay 2012).

The transition from "lenient" to "severe" morality had many of the characteristics of a "scientific revolution" in the sense of T. S. Kuhn; that is, a change of paradigm. "Reasoning in cases" was replaced by the textual approach of positive theology, and accommodation to contemporary mores by the primitivist nostalgia for the early church, as scripture and the church fathers were extolled over and against "new-fangled casuists." Genet's *Moral Theology* purported to "resolve cases of conscience according to Holy Scripture, canons, and the Fathers." In his *Treatise of Monastic Studies* (1691), a manifesto that was extremely influential all over Europe, the great Benedictine scholar Jean Mabillon (1632–1707) explained that Christian morality was simple, and that the multiplication of casuists had merely perplexed it. And he quoted approvingly the preface of Antoine Godeau (1605–72)—a French bishop who had been a prominent adversary of "lax morality," as well as a friend and protector of Port-Royal—to his 1668 translation of the New Testament. According to the bishop, the New Testament was "an admirable casuist": Christians "for several centuries did not have any other," and "their life was then as holy as their creed." Nowadays, alas, "cases of conscience have been treated with exactness, everything has been examined, everything has been decided, and conscience has been lost." For theologians who had been instructed in probabilism, repudiating it and adopting the new rigorist paradigm was a conversion experience, which they described in religious terms as a work of "divine mercy."

# 5 ROMAN PRONOUNCEMENTS

An essential development—arguably the most enduring result of early modern moral controversies—was the growth of what later ages were to call the moral magisterium of the Church. Since "lenient" and "severe" moralists no longer shared any common language, official pronouncements by Church authorities, above all the papacy, appeared the only way to end polemics. Indeed, Roman interventions were to a very large extent solicited by theologians themselves. The "magisterium" of universities was in decline. Even in Gallican France, condemnations by individual bishops had only a limited impact and, for most of the seventeenth century, the *Assemblées du Clergé*, which had become the only collective instance of the episcopate, were reluctant to intervene in moral debates—many bishops were afraid that a condemnation of lax casuistry would favor Jansenism.

Up to the 1650s, Rome had seemed but little worried by trends in moral theology. A number of books, such as the *Aphorismi confessariorum*, an influential alphabetical treatise by the Portuguese Jesuit Manuel de Sá (1528–96), had been put on the *Index of Forbidden Books*, mostly *donec corrigantur*. Some of the passages objected to by Roman censors were lax (e.g., Sá's claim, which later became a staple of anti-Jesuit polemics, that it was permitted to fabricate a new title deed if one had lost the original). Many others concerned questions of ecclesiastical jurisdiction. Pascal's *Provincial Letters*, on the other hand, were condemned by a decree of the Holy Office on September 6, 1657, but exclusively as a Jansenist pamphlet: moral questions were not considered at all (Quantin 2014).

A shift is clearly visible after the publication of Pirot's ill-fated *Apologie*. The assessor of the Holy Office represented to Alexander VII that it would be "opportune for the Apostolic See, to which alone it belongs to show the faithful what to think in matters of faith and moral," to condemn the book and "to set bounds to opinions on these matters." The *Apology* was entrusted for examination to several consultors of the Holy Office, including the Franciscan Lorenzo Brancati di Lauria (1612–93), later a cardinal, a key figure in the Roman move towards rigorism. In his *votum*, Lauria indignantly denied that the adversaries of the casuists were all Jansenists: "those doctors who do not follow lax opinions on moral questions" are "eminently Catholic, since they are more faithful to the Gospel, which teaches that the road that leads on to life is narrow, and the gate is small." The *Apology* was duly condemned by a decree of the Holy Office in August 1659. According to a contemporary testimony, Alexander VII intended at one point to publish a bull on the very principle of probabilism. He eventually contented himself with censoring as "at least scandalous" forty-five lax propositions through two decrees of the Holy Office, in September 1665 and March 1666 (the archives are still to be explored to reconstruct the history of this condemnation).

A more wide-ranging condemnation took place under Innocent XI, a personally austere pope, whose advisers were sympathetic to some aspects of the historicized theological culture typical of France and the Low Countries, and rather hostile to the Society of Jesus (Innocent XI was engaged in a protracted conflict with Louis XIV, and French Jesuits were siding with the king against the pope). In 1677, the Theology Faculty of Louvain sent a deputation to the pope to entreat him to condemn 115 lax propositions: after a complex procedure, sixty-five were condemned by a decree of the Holy Office dated March 2, 1679 as "at least scandalous and pernicious in practice." The very principle of probabilism had been about to be included, after a majority in the theological commission had declared against it: Lauria denounced it as a frequent source of "unjust wars, usurary and simoniacal contracts, and the fickleness of libertines." It was spared after a vigorous defense by the Master of the Sacred Palace, the Dominican and future cardinal Raimondo Capizucchi (1616–91), who explained to the pope the basics of the system: a genuinely probable opinion remained probable even when opposed to an opinion notably more probable, and was therefore licit; acting against one's opinion was not the same thing as acting against one's conscience. Rome also declined to censure the claim that a confessor is obliged to absolve a penitent who follows a probable opinion. But limits were imposed: the use of a less probable and less safe opinion was not permitted in the administration of sacraments, nor to a judge; any probability "however slight" was not sufficient for action. Several propositions (e.g., on killing of a slanderer and on abortion) echoed the Louvain censures of the 1650s. The opinion that there was no venial sin in "the act of marriage exercised for pleasure only" was condemned (Quantin 2002). Gallican "liberties" prevented the decree from being officially received in France but most of its contents was adopted by the "assembly of the clergy" of 1700, when it issued at last, under the impulsion of Jacques-Bénigne Bossuet (1627–1704), bishop of Meaux, its own condemnation of lax morality, with an additional declaration against probabilism itself: the French clergy thus went further than Rome.

Anti-Jansenists counter-attacked and also made denunciations. Innocent's successor, Alexander VIII, condemned several propositions, including one which was later taken as the theological definition of rigorism, or "absolute tutiorism": "it is not permitted to follow even the most probable of probable opinions." It had been extracted, with great unfaithfulness, from Sinnich's *Saul Exrex*: in this extreme form, it had never been defended by any theologian (Pera 1960; Ceyssens 1965). Later, in 1713, Pope Clement XI's bull *Unigenitus*—which was meant to deal the last blow to French Jansenism and which resulted in reinvigorating it under a new, more overtly politicized form—condemned no less than 101 propositions extracted from a devotional bestseller by Arnauld's successor as leader of the Jansenists, Father Pasquier Quesnel (1634–1719). A few of these aimed at the principles of sacramental rigorism (e.g., that the sinner should "begin at least to satisfy the justice of God" before receiving absolution).

Lists of propositions condemned by Rome were very often reprinted in the eighteenth century and their study became part of the training of confessors. Not only were they constantly referred to by moralists, but in the absence of any official explanation—the Holy Office consistently declined to give any—they spawned "an entirely new genre of theological literature" devoted to their exegesis. One of the most influential of such works was published in 1708 by the Jesuit Domenico Viva under the title *Damnatae Theses . . . ad Theologicam trutinam reuocatae juxta pondus Sanctuarii* ("Condemned theses, measured by the theological balance according to the weight of the sanctuary"). It might be going too far to say that "some of these commentators made the condemnation of lax propositions illusory," but they often propounded a minimizing interpretation, which left latitude for various positions. Thus Viva and others understood the clause "for pleasure alone" in the 1679 decree as excluding the other purposes of marriage: otherwise, "intercourse 'for pleasure' was still theologically defensible" (Döllinger and Reusch 1889, 1:39–42; Noonan 1966, 327). Such "liberal" readings were never condemned. It would seem that the papacy had meant to trace limits and arrest developments that threatened to go out of bounds, not to impose theological uniformity. A more cynical interpretation might be that it was happy for its decrees to be circumvented, provided formal respect was paid to them. The same caution is discernible in the new form of magisterial teaching, the encyclical, favored by Pope Benedict XIV in the mid-eighteenth century. After disputes had raged in Italy between rigorists and "liberals" on money lending, Benedict's 1745 encyclical *Vix pervenit* repeated the traditional definition and condemnation of usury, but accepted that there were new types of commercial contracts, in which it was permitted to make a profit. The pope deliberately avoided going into details in order to preserve theological pluralism: "he does not disclaim rigorism but does not encourage it" (Vismara 2004, 327–69).

Even though probabilism as such was never condemned by Rome, its exponents felt bound to rephrase it so as to make it less liable to Rigorist criticisms. Caramuel himself, in his later writings, moved away from his most provocative statements and replaced probability with "noncertitude" as the basis of a secure conscience: the "noncertitude" of an obligation means that my liberty remains in possession (Fleming 2006). The most successful attempt was that of Liguori, who, building on the work of the Jesuits Antony Terrill (1621–76) and Johann Christoph Rassler (1654–1723), evolved the system of "equiprobabilism," which he fully expounded in his 1762 short treatise *Dell'uso moderato dell'opinione probabile* (subsequently included in his *Theologia moralis*). According to Liguori, when the opinion in favor of the law seems more probable, it should be followed. When the opinion in favor of the law and the opinion in favor of liberty are equally probable, one is permitted to follow the latter, not on the basis of probability as such, but because in such a case the law is not sufficiently promulgated—Suárez, as has been seen, had already made the point but had not made it the basis of his system (Deman 1936, 580–86).

A powerful hagiographical tradition has extolled Liguori's moral theology as a *via media*, which was somehow bound to triumph over the rival excesses of rigorism and "laxism." Paolo Prodi has offered a much more interesting suggestion: that Liguori made complete the depoliticization of morality, the separation between "the forum of conscience" and that of human law, with the result that his system, as opposed to that of the Jesuits, was not perceived as a threat to the civil power (Prodi 2000, 381). However, this is essentially a retrospective view. Liguori was strongly attacked during his lifetime. In 1775–76, under strong political pressure in Naples, at a time when probabilism was identified with the recently suppressed Society of Jesus, he even had to profess himself a probabiliorist (although without changing his doctrine). What has been called the "Liguorization" of Roman Catholic moral theology was a nineteenth-century development which, especially in France, accompanied the advance of ultramontanism (*Recezione* 1997). At the end of the European ancien régime, more or less mitigated versions of rigorism appeared dominant everywhere, at least in theological discourse.

## BIBLIOGRAPHY

Angelozzi, Giancarlo. 1981. "L'insegnamento dei casi di coscienza nella pratica educativa della Compagnia di Gesù." In La "Ratio studiorum": Modelli culturali e pratiche educative dei Gesuiti in Italia tra Cinque e Seicento, edited by Gian Paolo Brizzi, 121–162. Rome: Bulzoni.

Bossy, John. 1988. "Moral Arithmetic: Seven Sins into Ten Commandments." In Conscience and Casuistry in Early Modern Europe, edited by Edmund Leites, 214–234. Cambridge: Cambridge University Press.

Bossy, John. 1975. "The Social History of Confession in the Age of the Reformation." Transactions of the Royal Historical Society 25: 21–38.

Briggs, Robin. 1989. Communities of Belief: Cultural and Social Tensions in Early Modern France. Oxford: Oxford University Press.

Burgio, Santo. 1998. Teologia barocca: Il probabilismo in Sicilia nell'epoca di Filippo IV. Catania: Società di Storia Patria per la Sicilia Orientale.

Caramuel Lobkowitz, Juan. 2010. Il Tractatus Expendens Propositiones Damnatas Ab Alexandro VII Di Juan Caramuel Lobkowitz, edited by Daniele Sabaino. Lewiston, NY: Edwin Mellen Press.

Ceyssens, Lucien. 1958. "Jacques Boonen face au laxisme pénitentiel." Bulletin de la Société des Amis de Port-Royal 9: 9–61. Reprinted in Jansenistica minora, vol. 5, no. 46. Malines: Imprimerie St François, 1959.

Ceyssens, Lucien. 1965. "Les Ire, IIe, IIIe et XIXe des trente et une propositions condamnées en 1690," Revue d'Histoire Ecclésiastique 60: 33–63 and 389–428. Reprinted in Jansenistica minora, vol. 9, no. 70. Malines: Imprimerie St François, 1966.

Delumeau, Jean. 1990. L'aveu et le pardon. Les difficultés de la confession XIIIe-XVIIIe siècle. Paris: Fayard.

Deman, Thomas. 1936. "Probabilisme." In Dictionnaire de Théologie catholique. Vol. 13, no. 1, 417–619. Paris: Letouzey et Ané.

Döllinger, Ignaz von, and Fr. Heinrich Reusch. 1889. Geschichte der Moralstreitigkeiten in der römisch-katholischen Kirche seit dem sechszehnten Jahrhundert. 2 vols. Nördlingen: Beck.

Dougherty, Michael V., Pernille Harsting, and Russell L. Friedman. 2009. "40 Cases of Plagiarism." Bulletin de Philosophie Médiévale 51: 350–391.

Fleming, Julia A. 2006. Defending Probabilism. The Moral Theology of Juan Caramuel. Washington, DC: Georgetown University Press.

Forrester, John. 1996. "If p, Then What? Thinking in Cases." History of the Human Sciences 9 (3): 1–25.

Gay, Jean-Pascal. 2012. Jesuit Civil Wars: Theology, Politics and Government under Tirso González (1687-1705). Farnham: Ashgate.

Gay, Jean-Pascal. 2011a. Morales en conflit. Théologie et polémique au Grand Siècle (1640-1700). Paris: Éditions du Cerf.

Gay, Jean-Pascal. 2011b. "Review of R. A. Maryks, Saint Cicero and the Jesuits." Revue d'Histoire Ecclésiastique 106: 319–322.

Gay, Jean-Pascal. 2011c. "Doctrina Societatis? Le rapport entre probabilisme et discernement des esprits dans la culture jésuite (XVIe-XVIIe siècles)." In Le discernement spirituel au dix-septième siècle, edited by Simon Icard, 23–46. Paris: Nolin.

Holmes, Peter. 1981. *Elizabethan Casuistry*. London: Catholic Record Society.

Höpfl, Harro. 2004. *Jesuit Political Thought: The Society of Jesus and the State, c. 1540–1630*. Cambridge: Cambridge University Press.

Hurtubise, Pierre. 2005. *La casuistique dans tous ses états: De Martin Azpilcueta à Alphonse de Liguori*. Ottawa: Novalis.

Jonsen, Albert R., and Stephen Toulmin. 1988. *The Abuse of Casuistry. A History of Moral Reasoning*. Berkeley: University of California Press.

Kantola, Ilkka. 1994. *Probability and Moral Uncertainty in Late Medieval and Early Modern Times*. Helsinki: Luther-Agricola-Society.

Klomps, Heinrich. 1964. *Ehemoral und Jansenismus: Ein Beitrag zur Überwindung des sexualethischen Rigorismus*. Cologne: J. P. Bachem.

Lavenia, Vincenzo. 2003. "Martín de Azpilcueta (1492–1586): Un profilo." *Archivio Italiano per la Storia della Pietà* 16: 15–148.

Lea, Henry Charles. 1896. *A History of Auricular Confession and Indulgences in the Latin Church*. 3 vols. London: S. Sonnenschein.

Legendre, Pierre. 1980. "L'inscription du droit canon dans la théologie: Remarques sur la Seconde Scolastique." In *Proceedings of the Fifth International Congress of Medieval Canon Law, Salamanca, 21-25 September 1976*, edited by S. Kuttner and K. Pennington, 443–454. Vatican City: Biblioteca Apostolica Vaticana.

Mahoney, John. 1987. *The Making of Moral Theology: A Study of the Roman Catholic Tradition*. Oxford: Oxford University Press.

Maryks, Robert A. 2008. *Saint Cicero and the Jesuits: The Influence of the Liberal Arts on the Adoption of Moral Probabilism*. Aldershot, UK: Ashgate.

Noonan, John T. 1966. *Contraception. A History of Its Treatment by the Catholic Theologians and Canonists*. Cambridge, MA: Harvard University Press.

O'Malley, John W. 1993. *The First Jesuits*. Cambridge, MA: Harvard University Press.

Pera, Sylvano. 1960. *Historical Notes Concerning Ten of the Thirty-One Rigoristic Propositions Condemned by Alexander VIII (1690)*. Rome: Ateneo Antoniano.

Pinckaers, Servais. 1995 (1985). *The Sources of Christian Ethics*. Edinburgh: T&T Clark.

Pollock, James R. 1984. *François Genet: The Man and his Methodology*. Rome: Università Gregoriana Editrice.

Prodi, Paolo. 2000. *Una storia della giustizia: dal pluralismo dei fori al moderno dualismo tra coscienza e diritto*. Bologna: Il Mulino.

Quantin, Jean-Louis. 2014. "'Si mes *Lettres* sont condamnées à Rome . . .'. Les *Provinciales* devant le Saint-Office." *XVIIe siècle* 265: 587–617.

Quantin, Jean-Louis. 2001. *Le rigorisme chrétien*. Paris: Éditions du Cerf.

Quantin, Jean-Louis. 2003. "Le rigorisme: sur le basculement de la théologie morale catholique au XVIIe siècle." *Revue d'Histoire de l'Église de France* 89: 23–43.

Quantin, Jean-Louis. 2006. "De la rigueur au rigorisme: Les *Avvertenze ai Confessori* de Charles Borromée dans la France du XVIIe siècle." *Studia Borromaica* 20: 195–251.

Quantin, Jean-Louis. 2002. "Le Saint-Office et le probabilisme (1677–1679): contribution à l'histoire de la théologie morale à l'époque moderne." *Mélanges de l'École française de Rome: Italie et Méditerranée* 114: 875–960.

Recezione. 1997. *La recezione del pensiero alfonsiano nella Chiesa: Atti del congresso in occasione del terzo centenario della nascita di S. Alfonso Maria de Liguori (Roma 5–7 marzo 1997)*. Spicilegium Historicum Congregationis SSmi Redemptoris 45.

Turrini, Miriam. 1991. *La coscienza e le leggi: Morale e diritto nei testi per la confessione della prima Età moderna*. Bologna: Il Mulino.

Vereecke, Louis. 1990. *Da Guglielmo d'Ockham a sant'Alfonso de Liguori: Saggi di storia della teologia morale moderna, 1300–1787*. Milan: Edizioni Paoline.

Visceglia, Maria Antonietta. 2007. "Un convegno e un progetto. Riflessioni in margine." In *I Gesuiti ai tempi di Claudio Acquaviva. Strategie politiche, religiose e culturali tra Cinque e Seicento*, 287–305. Brescia: Morcelliana.

Vismara, Paola. 2004. *Oltre l'usura. La Chiesa moderna e il prestito a interesse*. Soveria Mannelli: Rubbettino.

CHAPTER 9

# CATHOLIC SACRAMENTAL THEOLOGY IN THE BAROQUE AGE

TRENT POMPLUN

## 1 INTRODUCTION

IT is impossible to describe the voluminous literature touching upon the sacraments between 1500 and 1800. In contrast to the scholastic debates about the so-called motive of the Incarnation, which, while they had Protestant analogues, remained largely intra-Catholic controversies, debates about the sacraments could fairly be said to define the entire age. Although there were several talented scholastic theologians toward the end of the fifteenth century—one thinks immediately of Stephenus Brulefer (1469–1502), Antonio Trombetta (1436–1517), Petrus Tartaretus (n.d.–1522), and Cajetan (1458–1534)—it must be admitted that the Protestant Reformers Luther (1483–1546), Huldrych Zwingli (1484–1531), Johannes Oecolampadius (1482–1531), Philipp Melanchthon (1497–1560), and John Calvin (1509–64) gave Catholic sacramental theology its dominant impetus in the sixteenth and early seventeenth centuries. Although the Council of Trent responded to each of these Reformers in turn, Catholic theology in the wake of the council was not—and cannot be—reduced to a defensive posture during the later seventeenth and eighteenth centuries, but rather developed its own scholastic controversies, a greater historical awareness of non-Catholic liturgies and sacramental theologies, and no small number of innovations brought on by the expansion of Catholicism in the missions. For the present purposes of this essay, I will merely attempt to outline some of these developments in three sections: (1) a brief bibliographic survey of the sources for early modern Roman Catholic sacramental theology; (2) an outline of some of its main scholastic controversies; and (3) a corresponding outline of the various attempts of the Holy Office to answer questions that arose in sacramental theology between the years 1500 and 1800.

# 2  THE SOURCES OF CATHOLIC SACRAMENTAL THEOLOGY

The chief source for Catholic sacramental theology during this age is the Council of Trent and (by extension) the controversies leading to it. As Luther and other Reformers set themselves against the sacramental "system" of Catholicism, the Catholic Church answered their charges with a series of talking points, lists, clarifications, and—when push came to shove—condemnations that set the tone for much of the theology to follow. *Exsurge Domine* (June 15, 1520), the bull of Pope Leo X, listed several claims about sacramental theology under the "errors of Martin Luther," including the charge that the three parts of penance (contrition, confession, and satisfaction) are found neither in scripture nor in the church fathers (no. 5); that confession of venial sins is presumptuous (no. 7); that a pope or bishop has no more ability to remits sins than the lowliest priest (no. 13); and that those who approach the sacrament of the Eucharist having relied on confession and preparatory prayers eat and drink judgment to themselves (no. 15). Many of these questions were addressed again during the Council of Trent, which published the decree on the sacraments (with canons on the sacraments *in genere*, baptism, and confirmation) after its seventh session (March 3, 1547), the decree on the sacrament of the Eucharist after its thirteenth session (October 11, 1551), and the decree on the sacraments of penance and extreme unction after its fourteenth session (November 25, 1551). It is widely acknowledged that canons issued by the council that censured various positions in sacramental theology in general were directed against Luther's *De captivitate Babylonica ecclesiae praeludium*, the Augsburg Confession, and the second edition of Melanchthon's *Apologia Confessionis Augustanae*. Oecolampadius's *De genuina verborum Domini 'Hoc est corpus meum'* and Zwingli's *De vera et falsa religione* took on special significance in the thirteenth session on the Eucharist, and the council fathers began to take notice of Calvin's *Institutes* in the fourteenth session. After the council resumed under Pope Pius IV, it promulgated doctrines and canons on communion under both species and children's communion (July 16, 1562), the sacrifice of the Mass (September 17, 1562), the sacrament of orders (July 15, 1563), and the sacrament of matrimony (November 11, 1563). For good measure, the pope also issued a Tridentine profession of faith in the bull *Iniunctum nobis* (November 13, 1564), which included the basic tenets of Catholic sacramental theology—seven sacraments of the new law instituted by Jesus Christ, and so forth—as well as a profession of the aptness of the term "transubstantiation" and the "true, proper, and propitiatory sacrifice" of the Mass for the living and the dead. As a result, post-Tridentine sacramental theology developed along strongly systematic lines.

It would be a mistake, however, to think that Catholic sacramental theology in the early modern era was restricted to the great works of the so-called silver age of scholasticism. Indeed, there is hardly a genre of early modern Catholic theology that did not celebrate the Eucharist or controvert—implicitly or explicitly—the chief theses of sacramental theology. The best known of these sources, in fact, are probably the chief works of polemical, or "controversial" theology, such as *Disputationes de Controversiis Christianae Fidei* of Robert Bellarmine (1542–1621), the *Defensio catholicae fidei contra anglicanae sectae errores* of Francisco Suárez (1548–1617), or the *Summa doctrinae christianae* of Peter Canisius (1521–97). To these, we could add the *Principiorum fidei doctrinalium demonstratio* of Thomas Stapleton (1535–98), the *Systema fidei* of Christopher Davenport (1598–1680), or the *Histoire des variations des eglises protestantes* of Bossuet (1627–1704). Controversial works were bolstered by a rapidly increasing knowledge of patristic authors and liturgies, both Eastern and Western. We see, on the one hand, humanists such as Denis Petau (1583–1652) or Louis Thomassin (1619–95) attempting to broaden the ambit of scholasticism with a greater number of patristic sources than had previously been used. But we also see, on the other hand, a dramatic interest not just in Greek, but in "Oriental" theology and liturgy, whose sources had been avidly collected since the Council of Basel. Claude de Sainctes (1525–91), Melchior Hittorp (1525–84), Jacobus Pamelius (1536–87), Jean Mabillon (1632–1707), Eusèbe Renaudot (1646–1720), Giuseppe Maria Tomasi (1649–1713), and Ludovico Muratori (1672–1750) all made important contributions to the understanding of ancient liturgies. Some works, such as the *De Concordia ecclesiae occidentalis et orientis in septem Sacramentorum administratione* of Petrus Arcudius (1570–1633), argued for the unity of Catholic and Orthodox notions of the sacraments against perceived Protestant denials of the sacraments. Other theologians, such as Francisco Macedo (1596–1681), engaged themselves with the fine points of such controversies, as witnessed by his *Disquisitio theologica de ritu azymi et fermentati*. Theologians also wrote histories of given controversies, such as those by Giuseppe Visconti (n.d.–1618) on baptism, François Hallier (1659–n.d.) on ordination, and Jean Morin (1591–1659) on penance—or the infamous work of Jacques Boileau (1635–1716) on auricular confession. The broad liturgical interests of the age also went hand-in-hand with its mysticism. The reflections of the French school with their combined fascination with Christology, Mariology, the priesthood, and the Eucharist, take center stage here, but we might also take note of lesser-known trends, such as the "mystical" readings of Old Testament texts that were common in seventeenth-century biblical commentaries in Spain. The majority of such commentaries, of course, found deep mystical allusions to the Blessed Virgin Mary, but many, such as the *De augustissino eucharistiae mysterio* of Juan Antonio Velázquez (n.d.–1669), found allusions to the Eucharist hidden beneath the literal sense of the Hebrew scriptures as well.

Such genres and works give evidence of the broader context in which early modern Catholic scholasticism itself developed. While these works are little studied—and often maligned—by Catholic and Protestant theologians today, it is difficult for an unbiased reader not to admit their systematic grandeur. Every school was represented in the baroque age. Although it is common to think of it as an age dominated by Thomism, this impression seems to be given less by reading the primary sources of the early modern era and more by reading the secondary literature of the twentieth century. Thomists were numerous, to be sure, with both Dominicans and Jesuits writing ample commentaries on their chosen doctor. But Scotists were equally well represented, with important contributions by Filippo Fabri (1564–1630), Anthony Hickey (1586–1641), and John Punch (ca. 1599–1661) to sacramental theology. We also find disciples of Anselm (ca. 1033–1109), such as José Sáenz de Aguirre (1630–99) and Juan Bautista Lardito (n.d.–1700); disciples of John Baconthorpe (ca. 1290–1347), such as Giuseppe Zagaglia (n.d.–1717); disciples of Henry of Ghent (ca. 1217–93), such as Benedetto Canali (n.d.–1745) and Markus Maria Struggl (n.d.–1760); and, of course, the well-known disciples of Augustine, Enrico Noris (1631–1704) and Gianlorenzo Berti (1696–1766), making important contributions. The great majority of these scholastic writings on the sacraments were commentaries on either the *Sentences* of Peter Lombard (as understood by an order's chosen doctor or doctors) or the *Summa theologiae* of Thomas Aquinas (1225–74). But it was also an age of the great theological monograph; whereas one usually thinks of Jansen's *Augustinus* or Molina's *Concordia* when considering early modern monographs, we see several on sacramental themes, such as the *Deus Absconditus* of Juan Álvaro Cienfuegos (1657–1739), the *De sacrificio novae legis* of Zacharia Pasqualigo (n.d.–1664), or the controversial *Disputationes de sancti matrimonii sacramento* of Tomás Sánchez (1550–1610).

# 3  SOME SCHOLASTIC CONTROVERSIES OF THE BAROQUE AGE

Catholic theologians in the early modern period usually introduced their treatises *De Sacramentis* by discussing the sacraments *in genere* before they explained individual sacraments as such. In other words, theologians began their treatises by treating the definition, division, and number of the sacraments, their manner of operation, the conditions of valid and worthy administration, and the requisites of valid and worthy reception. Questions about the definition, division, and number of the sacraments were generally aimed at refuting various Protestant denials of this or that particular sacrament, but even here, at the very beginning of treatises on the sacraments, Catholic theologians manifested a rather robust diversity of views. Theologians disagreed, for example, whether there were sacraments in Eden, with Augustinians *pro* and Thomists *contra*. Catholic theologians likewise agreed that God granted humankind some "natural" sacrament from the time of Adam's fall to Moses, while they disagreed mightily as to the precise character of such a *sacramentum naturae*. Most agreed that the *sacramentum naturae* would, by definition, be some visible sign of faith in the future Messiah, although Bonaventureans departed from this general consensus, as did Gabriel Vásquez (1549–1604). Thomists such as Jean-Baptiste Gonet (1615–81) thought it fitting that there be a number of adult sacraments in the state of nature, while Vásquez, Francisco Suárez, and Juan Cardinal de Lugo (1583–1660) did not. Debates about the sacraments of the Old Law were also quite vigorous. Not all theologians, for example, agreed that circumcision was a sacrament. Whereas the general consensus of Thomists, Scotists, and

Augustinians was positive, theologians as talented as Vásquez and Robert Bellarmine believed circumcision to be merely an external sign that distinguished the chosen people from the gentiles. Within the general consensus, Thomists and Scotists argued about whether the sacrament of circumcision conferred grace *ex opere operato*. It almost goes without saying that no serious treatise on the sacraments failed to deploy the whole range of early modern theories of signs and signification in its explanation of the nature of the sacraments in general.

As we have already seen, Catholic theologians broadly felt that Jesus Christ instituted the seven sacraments of the New Law *immediate ac per se ipsum*. Catholic theologians also agreed that the sacraments of the New Law consisted of two elements—the sensible element and the word (*res et verbum*)—and they generally interpreted *res* and *verbum* as matter and form, respectively. That said, Vásquez and many Scotists made an exception for the Eucharist, which they regarded as a "permanent sacrament." Indeed, because of this exception, Scotists generally preferred to say that sacraments proceeded from the *res et verbum*. Cardinal de Lugo, on the other hand, argued that the essence of the sacrament must include the intention of the minister, although other Catholic theologians did not generally accept this theory. Similarly, whereas all Catholic theologians agreed that the sacraments confer special sacramental graces in addition to sanctifying grace, they disagreed here too about the exact nature of such graces. There are similar debates about whether God might lavish some with greater graces than others in the sacraments and whether a sacrament of the living, which can only be worthily received when the recipient is in a state of grace, might still confer the *iustificatio prima* and so produce the same effects as sacraments of the dead, such as baptism and penance.

At times, we see "classic" philosophical debates, such as the debate between Thomists and Scotists on the relative merits of the intellect and will, influence debates in sacramental theology. When the Council of Trent anathematized anyone who denied that baptism, confirmation, and holy orders imprinted upon the soul an indelible spiritual "character," Thomists and Scotists immediately set about arguing whether the sacramental character was to be found in the intellect or the will. Just as debates about the physical premotion, the *scientia media*, and congruism dominated treatises on grace, debates about whether sacraments were physical or moral causes of grace fairly abounded in Catholic theology of this era as well. Of course, theologians who conceived of sacramental efficacy as physical did not necessarily deny their moral efficacy. At the same time, theologians who favored a "moral" efficacy generally did so because they did not want to subject God's mysteries to magical or mechanical laws. That said, Thomists agreed that God, as the principal cause (*causa principalis*), physically produced sanctifying grace in the soul through the sacraments, which functioned as instrumental causes whose efficacy was inherent in the sacramental rite itself. Scotists expressed some reservations about instrumental causality in general, but more often simply denied that a material element could produce supernatural effects physically. (So, too, when Scotists and Vásquez denied that Christ could have imparted his power to mere men to institute the sacraments, it is important to note that they were merely insisting on the properly *supernatural* character of their institution.) Augustinians were divided on the issue of sacramental causality. Some, like Gianlorenzo Berti, argued that the Holy Spirit exerted a physical causality upon the soul of the recipient in the presence of an external sign. Other Augustinians favored a "moral" efficacy. Of course, several theories attempted to mediate between these two positions.

The time at which Christ instituted baptism was a hotly contested debate. Melchior Cano (ca. 1509–60), basing himself on the great injunction of Matthew 28:19, argued that Christ instituted the sacrament at his ascension. Willem Hessels van Est (1542–1613) believed the sacrament to begin with Christ's discourse with Nicodemus (Jn 3:1–15). Aquinas believed that the sacrament received the power to produce its effect at Christ's own baptism, although most modern theologians, whether Thomist or Scotist, generally felt that the sacrament required some positive injunction to be instituted, and thus placed its beginning shortly after the baptism of Jesus himself, especially since the disciples appear to have baptized people before Christ's Passion (Jn 3:26; 4:2). After the Council of Trent, theologians also wondered whether the disciples, when they baptized "in the name of Jesus" (Acts 2:38; 8:12; 10:48; Gal 3:27), did so by an extraordinary privilege or whether the phrase simply referred to Christ's baptism as opposed to John's. Nor was the sacrament of confirmation entirely free of controversy. Denis Petau, following the older canonists, believed the imposition of hands (*impositio manuum*) to be the sole matter of the sacrament. Others, such as Bellarmine and van Est, following St. Thomas Aquinas, argued the anointing with the chrism oil (*chrismatio*) to be the only matter. Most other theologians believed both to constitute the matter of the sacrament, although Ruardus Tapper (1458–1559) offered the somewhat exotic position that, by an analogy with communion under both species, either the *impositio manuum* or the *chrismatio* sufficed. Thomists and the majority of early modern theologians also felt that the chrism oil must contain balsam, although Scotists and most modern theologians believed balsam to be necessary for a licit but not a valid administration of the sacrament. So, too, Thomists and the majority of theologians, early modern and modern, felt that the oil needed to be consecrated by a bishop, although Cajetan believed that the pope could grant this privilege to a priest. Of course, these technical debates also had practical ramifications. In the instruction *Presbyteri Graeci* (August 30, 1595), Pope Clement VIII prohibited Catholics who celebrated according to the Greek Rite from administering confirmation via chrism immediately following baptism, although he recognized the possible validity of such confirmations, instructing Latin priests to confirm such chrismated infants conditionally. In many respects, this question concerned the minister of the sacrament, since confirmations were administered by Greek Catholic priests without receiving chrism oil that had been consecrated by Latin bishops. Presumably, one could still maintain that a Greek Catholic priest who received the oil of chrism from a Roman Catholic bishop could still administer a valid confirmation if he anointed an infant on the forehead immediately after baptism. In fact, the validity of such confirmations remained a disputed point until Benedict XIV denied them in the constitution *Etsi pastoralis* (May 26, 1742).

With the Eucharist, we come to the sacrament that generated the greatest amount of theological reflection among modern Catholic theologians. All Catholic theologians held that the body, blood, soul, and divinity of Jesus Christ were really, truly, and substantially present in the Eucharist. Of course, the theological controversies between Thomists and Scotists over whether the body and blood of Christ entered into the accidents of the bread and the wine *per productionem* or *per adductionem* grew quite voluminous during this time, often with novel formulations of the old positions. The sacramental mode of existence, in which Christ's body is present under the Eucharistic species, generated similarly exotic speculations. Almost every Catholic theologian of note addressed the sacramental mode of Christ's bodily presence at great length, and such discussions of internal and external quality, circumscriptive and definitive presence, impassibility and aptitudinal extension, must be counted among the most technically bewildering discussions of the baroque age. Sometimes, speculations about the effects of the glorified Christ upon our own bodies in communion took rather adventurous forms, as in the claim of Vincent Contenson (1641–74) that the Eucharist gives us a claim upon resurrection by communicating a certain "physical quality" to the body itself. Of course, much ink has been spilled over the disputed point of whether the transformation of the *res oblata* must involve the destruction of the victim, although no unanimity existed on this topic during the baroque age. Vásquez, for example, rejected the so-called "destruction" theory altogether, maintaining that the Mass, being a relative sacrifice, need not involve a slaying of Christ at all, but only that His death be represented visibly by the separation of the body and blood on the altar. In Vásquez's view, Christ, being impassible, undergoes no transformation in the double consecration beyond being made present under the Eucharistic species. Suárez, on the other hand, hoping to safeguard the Tridentine definition of the Mass as a true and proper sacrifice, argued for a real transformation of the sacrificial victim, but opted to defend the transformation not as a change for the worse (*immutatio deterius sive destructio*), but rather for the better (*immutatio melius*), as when incense becomes a sweet fragrance before the Lord. Leonard Lessius (1554–1623), arguing a tad too forcefully against Suárez, advanced the somewhat extreme position that the sacramental slaying enacted in the consecration would indeed spill Christ's blood on the altar, were Christ's own impassibility not to render it impossible. Cardinal de Lugo, accepting the notion that Christ's glorious impassibility makes a genuine physical slaying impossible, argued that the merely "moral" slaying effected by the double consecration consists in Christ's voluntary self-abasement to the condition of food and drink. Indeed, the holy cardinal notes that this abasement, by which the Incarnate Word divests himself of the powers connatural to his glorified body, is akin to the very *kenosis* by which he divested himself of his divine power during the Incarnation. Cardinal de Lugo's theory, although hardly favored in his lifetime, underwent something of a revival in the late nineteenth century. Its principal defenders in the early modern period were Juan de Ulloa (1639–1723), Domenico Viva (1684–1726), and the Scotist Franz Henno (n.d.–1713). A more exotic view was held by Cardinal Juan Álvaro Cienfuegos, who taught that the "destruction" of the sacrificial victim consisted in the suspension of Christ's senses from the consecration to the mixture of the species. Theologians of the French school tended to interpret "destruction" as "abasement," but in such a way that the Mass, as a relative sacrifice, finds its orientation not merely from the cross, but rather from Christ's "heavenly sacrifice."

Much ink, too, was spilled over the problem of the relationship of the one, bloody sacrifice of Christ on the Cross to the many "unbloody" sacrifices on our altars. All Catholic theologians agreed that the sacrifice of the Mass was in no way independent of the single sacrifice on Calvary. They all likewise agreed that the Mass could neither complement nor consummate Christ's one sacrifice. Theological explanations for how in fact the Mass was the participation, representation, and/or application of the single sacrifice on Calvary varied widely, from strict observance of Aquinas's minimalistic account to the theologies of the "heavenly sacrifice" of the Mass favored by theologians of the French school. The church made no definite decision on the debate about frequent communion that stretched over two centuries. On February 12, 1679, the decree of the Sacred Congregation of the Council *Cum ad aures* declared that, "while the holy fathers of the Church have always approved the frequent and indeed daily use of the most Holy Eucharist, they have never appointed special days for receiving it more often, nor days (or weeks) in which one abstained from it." As a result, the question of frequent communion was "left to the judgment of confessors who explore the heart's secrets."

Theologians of the early modern period also debated the exact matter of the sacrament of penance, with all Thomists, many Jesuits, and some Scotists arguing that the matter consisted in the three penitential acts of contrition, confession, and satisfaction, whereas other modern theologians, such as Andreas Vega (n.d.–1560) and Juan Maldonado (1533–83), following the examples of Bonaventure (1221–74) and Scotus (1265–1308), interpreted these acts to be necessary dispositions in the recipient, and found both the matter and form of the sacrament in priestly absolution. Although most theologians, following the example of Aquinas and the Council of Trent, maintained that the indicative form of the absolution is necessary for the valid administration of the sacrament, historians as early as Jean Morin argued that the Greek fathers had always used a purely deprecatory formula for the sacrament and that the indicative formula, while prescribed as a matter of practice, is not part of the essence of the sacrament. When debating the effects of the sacrament, theologians also disagreed whether the sacrament had the power to revive past merits, with Domingo Báñez (1528–1604) and Contenson arguing that the full measure of grace and glory can never be restored to merits lost by mortal sin. Other Thomists contended that any merits lost might be restored in proportion to the zeal and contrition of the penitent. Scotists generally argued that the sacrament of penance completely restores the sinner's lost merits, but that God sometimes withholds the grace and attendant glory due to those merits until the moment of death. Of course, the most hotly contested debate about the sacrament of penance during the early modern period was the controversy between "attritionists" and "contritionists," a debate whose technicalities can quickly boggle the mind of the most seasoned scholastic theologian. That said, all theologians agreed that "perfect" contrition is had when we love God in supernatural charity for his own sake and above all else. Some theologians, such as Cardinal de Lugo, admitted degrees in the state of perfect charity when they attempted to claim the mantle of strict contritionists, without appearing to countenance the rigorist view that perfect charity must also be wholly disinterested—a view later condemned by Pope Innocent XII in 1699. Bartholomeo Mastri (1602–73) and many other Scotists argued that contrition need not be perfect to effect justification. In fact, they even argued that justification could be effected by acts other than perfect charity and contrition. Such "imperfect" contrition, or "attrition," they argued, might very well effect justification through justice, obedience, or gratitude, so long as these virtues are directed towards God and not the reward itself. Vásquez castigated this view, although other Jesuits, such as Suárez and de Lugo, while denying it, recognized its intrinsic reasonableness.

Here, though, it is important to note that the primary debate about "contrition" and "attrition" concerns the justification that is effected *without* the sacrament of penance, because some older scholastic masters had argued that no priest could absolve a man unless God had already done so. After the Council of Trent, however, Catholic theologians unanimously taught that sacramental absolution does not require perfect contrition for its valid administration, as is shown by the condemnation of such suggestions in Michel Baius (1513–89), Cornelius Jansen (1585–1638), and the Jansenist Synod of Pistoia. Catholic theologians broadly defined proper attrition as an imperfect *amor concupiscentiae*, which might be expressed as the theological virtue of hope, or even the *timor simpliciter servilis*, which, while a fear of unhappiness, was still generated from the thought of losing God considered as the greatest good. At the very least, they agreed that any genuine attrition, inasmuch as it is based on hope, must contain at least the "beginning of charity" (*amor initialis*), since hope itself was an *amor concupiscientiae*. On the other hand, orthodox "contritionists" argued that while attrition is truly salutary, it is insufficient for the valid reception of the sacrament. On this point, it is difficult to see how they differ from attritionists in anything but name, especially since such orthodox contritionists admit that the *amor initialis* cannot be equated with the perfect charity that would effect justification even without the sacrament. And indeed the distinctions became so hydra-headed in this controversy that on May 5, 1667, Pope Alexander VII censured the harshness of the debates for causing "scandal" to the faithful. Later theologians, such as Charles-René Billuart (1685–1757), for example, continued to be orthodox "contritionists" and censure others accordingly.

Debates about extreme unction, holy orders, and matrimony were less fierce during this time period, at least in sacramental theology proper. (Controversial theologians, of course, devoted no small amount of energy to their defense.) With these sacraments, too, most of the speculative debate concerned the proper understanding of their matter and form. Sometimes, however, the debates of controversial and speculative theology overlapped, especially when Catholic theologians attempted to justify the Council of Trent's claim that Christ instituted all seven sacraments. For example, Catholic theologians did not agree whether extreme unction, which they considered the "completion of penance," could be justified by appeal to Mark 6:13. Aquinas, Bonaventure, and Scotus had each thought so, and more modern theologians such as Maldonado and Gianlorenzo Berti followed their example. Other theologians, such as Bellarmine and Suárez, did not find their arguments convincing. Much as with penance, theologians disagreed about the matter and form of extreme unction; with some writers, such as Morin, arguing that the indicative form of the prayer spoken over the recipient is sufficient for valid administration of the sacrament, while the broad majority of Thomists and Scotists maintained the form must contain a prayer for God's mercy. The general tendency of early modern theologians, quite against the grain of the earlier tradition, was to interpret extreme unction as a supernatural strengthening to prepare the dying soul for purgatory, should God not intend to heal the sick man or woman. In the early twentieth century, Joseph Kern criticized this tendency, maintaining that the sacrament aims not merely to strengthen the soul, but to perfect it (Kern 1907). Such perfect healing of the soul (*perfecta sanitas animae*), he argued, in fact remits temporal punishments and preserves the soul from the pains of purgatory.

There were similar debates about the matter and form of the sacrament of holy orders. Many modern theologians, following the lead of Bonaventure, felt the imposition of hands to be the sole matter of the sacrament, while others held out the delivery of the instruments as the primary matter of the sacrament. Not surprisingly, still others argued for both. Cardinal de Lugo held the interesting position that, while both the *impositio manuum* and the delivery of the instruments constituted the matter of the sacrament, the former did so for the Eastern church and the latter did so for the Western church. Catholic theologians also argued about whether one could be ordained a bishop without being first ordained a priest, and whether episcopal consecration imprinted the soul with a special sacramental character. The older scholastic tradition generally denied such a sacramental character, while modern theologians such as Cajetan and Bellarmine, following the examples of Durandus (ca. 1275–ca. 1332) and Gabriel Biel (ca. 1420–95), argued rather aggressively for the affirmative. Catholic theologians also argued about the general sacramental status of the minor orders. Cajetan, again following Durandus, was among the only modern theologians to deny that ordination to the diaconate was a true sacrament. Although Peter Lombard (1100–60) and Durandus had denied the sacramental nature of the subdiaconate, Thomas Aquinas, Bonaventure, and Duns Scotus had all maintained the sacramentality of the minor orders, and Bellarmine, van Est, and Billuart continued this tradition. Vásquez held out for the sacramentality of the subdiaconate, but denied the sacramental nature of the other minor orders. Most modern Catholic theologians, however, following the example of Cajetan, denied the sacramentality of the minor orders altogether. It might be interesting to note that historians such as Morin, when he treated the medieval controversy about the blessing of deaconesses, judged those blessings to be true ordinations, albeit to a minor order.

Catholic theologians of the time usually thought the sacraments of holy orders and matrimony to have been instituted more for the edification and preservation of society than for whatever personal holiness might accrue to bearers of those sacraments. This is not to say, of course, that there was not a robust theology of the priesthood in, for example, the writers of the French school. That said, debates about the matter and form of the sacrament were typical, and Catholic theologians argued about whether the form of the sacrament consisted in the blessing of the priest, the mutual consent of husband and wife, or some combination of the blessing and the marriage contract, as early modern theologians conceived it. Melchior, Bellarmine, and Suárez judged the matrimonial pact, spoken by both husband and wife, to provide both the matter and the form of the sacrament. Although most Catholic theologians believed the sacrament of marriage to be a transient act, Bellarmine and Tomás Sánchez might be thought to anticipate more modern notions of "nuptial" mysticism when they argued that the bond of marriage was a "permanent sacrament." Catholic theologians also debated many of the more practical aspects of marriage, such as whether the marriage of a husband and wife who were both unbaptized might become a sacrament if one or both of them converted and was baptized, or whether the pope could dissolve an unconsummated marriage, or indeed whether the dissolution of an unconsummated marriage caused by one's solemn religious profession could be justified according to the natural, ecclesiastical, or divine law.

# 4  The Holy Office and Catholic Sacramental Theology

The diversity of early modern sacramental theology is nowhere more evident than in the various attempts of the Tridentine church to corral it. Although it is well known that Jansenists, who severely criticized the moral "laxity" of theologians of the Society of Jesus, were themselves subject to several ecclesiastical censures, it is perhaps less known that the Holy Office also censured several propositions attributed to many so-called "laxists." More than a few of these propositions concerned abuses in the administration of the sacraments, especially the sacraments of the Eucharist and penance. Among the twenty-eight propositions censured by the Holy Office on September 24, 1665, for example, we find propositions about what constitutes solicitation in the confessional (nos. 6, 7), about Mass stipends (nos. 8–10), and about the sacrament of penance in general (nos. 11–15). On March 18, 1666, the Holy Office censured sixteen more propositions, including two concerning the proper interpretation of Trent's provisions for priests who carry out the Eucharistic sacrifice in a state of sin (nos. 38–39). It is also worth noting that the question of how the sacrament of penance is administered looms behind many of the (equally voluminous) debates about moral theology. When on March 2, 1679, the Holy Office condemned, among sixty-five "laxist" propositions, the statement that "the conjugal act exercised solely for pleasure is entirely free of venial defect and blame" (no. 9), the censure concerned the practice of confessors as much as the theological argument. Of course, the Holy Office also censured several propositions that directly concerned sacramental practice and prohibited these propositions precisely as "scandalous" (*scandalosa*) and "pernicious in practice" (*in praxi perniciosa*) (nos. 55–61). And yet, the church did not fail to censure the "rigorism" on the other side of these debates, and these censures similarly concerned sacramental practice: Among the "errors of the Jansenists" condemned by the Holy Office on December 7, 1690, we find criticisms of attritionism (no. 15), the practice of absolution (nos. 16–18), and the practice of frequent communion (nos. 22–23). Indeed, as late as the constitution *Auctorem fidei* (August 28, 1794), which condemned several propositions of the Jansenist Synod of Pistoia, we find censures about the role of servile fear in faith, and by implication, as preparation for the sacrament of penance (no. 25); the importance of conditional baptisms (no. 27); the legitimacy of private Masses (no. 28); the omission of the term "transubstantiation" in the synod's statement of the Eucharist (no. 29); the ability of priests to apply the fruits of the sacrifice of the Mass to particular individuals (no. 30); and a series of statements on the sacrament of penance (nos. 34–39), holy orders (nos. 51–56), and matrimony (nos. 58–60).

Such concerns also extended beyond the solely theological into the realm of practice. On May 26, 1593, Pope Clement VIII issued a decree to the superiors of religious orders that affirmed the seal of the confessional, especially in light of fairly widespread abuses in which superiors made use of knowledge obtained in confessions in the government of their orders. The Holy Office under Pope Innocent XI returned to this issue in its decree of November 18, 1682, which further specified that confessors could not use information obtained in the confessional if it resulted in any injury to the penitent whatsoever, even if the superior were to use the information to prevent some evil. Clement also intervened in a dispute on sacramental theology by putting an end to the widespread practice of priests pronouncing sacramental absolution of an absent person after receiving a written confession. No less an authority than Robert Bellarmine, following a general trend among the Society of Jesus, supported this practice. On June 20, 1602, the Holy Office declared the practice "false, rash, and scandalous" (*falsus, temerarius, et scandalosus*) to claim that one may confess sins to an absent confessor "and to receive absolution from the same absent confessor" (*et ab eodem ansente absolutionem obtinere*). Suárez interpreted the *et* of this last phrase to mean that the pope's decree prohibited the administration of the sacrament only in cases where both the confession *and* the absolution occurred *ex distanti*, citing the letter *Sollicitudinis quidem tuae* of Pope Leo I to Theodore of Fréjus. On June 7, 1603, the Holy Office rejected Suárez's argument.

One also sees several practical discussions concerning the sacrament of matrimony brought on by the changing circumstances of the missions and indeed Europe itself. Pope Paul III, in his constitution *Altitudo divini consilii* (June 1, 1537), echoing the Franciscan theologians who convened the Primera Junta de México in 1524, directed missionaries to allow Indian converts who could not remember which of several wives they had first married to choose one and be married "after the normal fashion" (*ut mores est*). Pope Pius V, however, clarified the issue further in his constitution *Romani Pontificis* (August 2, 1571), by noting that converts who were baptized or soon to be baptized could choose from among their wives one who also planned to be baptized. Pope Gregory XIII, considering the question of whether recent converts among indigenous peoples, if they were separated from their previous spouses, could contract a new marriage to another convert, affirmed the "Pauline privilege" in the constitution *Populus ac nationibus* (January 25, 1585). Indeed, the Holy Office, in a response to the bishops of Cochin (India) on August 1, 1759, answered a series of further questions about the "Pauline privilege." By this time, too, the church had also taken an official interest in the previous marriages of converts, on the one hand, and marriages between Catholics and Protestants, on the other. In *Matrimonia quae in locis* (November 4, 1741), Pope Benedict XIV declared that such marriages were valid even when they had not been contracted according to canons laid out in the decree *Tametsi* during the twenty-fourth session of the Council of Trent (November 11, 1563). After strongly condemning marriages between Catholics and Protestants "shamefully deranged by a mad love" (*qui insano amore turpiter dememtati*), the pope conceded that, here, too, provided no other impediment exists, the marriage must be considered valid; even if, again, it had not been contracted according to the Tridentine form. The issue of mixed marriages, especially when they were condoned by the state, led Pope Pius VI in his letter *Exsequendo nunc* to the bishops of Belgium (July 13, 1782), to allow Catholic priests to assist at a mixed marriage (after a warning had been sent to the Catholic party) as long as the priest did not assist in any sacred place, did not wear vestments, did not recite any Catholic prayers, and refused to bless them. The pope required any priest who assisted at such a marriage to extract a declaration from the Catholic party, signed in front of two witnesses, that he or she would never apostatize from the Catholic religion and would agree to educate his or her children in it. The assisting priest was also required to acquire a similar declaration from the non-Catholic party to the effect that he or she would not prohibit the Catholic spouse from the free exercise of the Catholic religion (*usum liberum religionis catholicae*), nor the education of his or her children. Of course, this was just one of the many conflicts between Pius VI and Emperor Joseph II that led to the condemnation of Joseph Valentin Eybel's "Febronianism" in *Super solidate petrae* (November 28, 1786). It was also a general sign of things to come, as Pius VI had to respond in a similar fashion to the Neapolitan bishop of Mottola, who had attempted to limit the juridical competence of the church in marriage. In essence, the bishop had attempted to argue that the twenty-fourth session of the Council of Trent, because it failed to use expressions such as "only by ecclesiastic judges" or "in all marriages," had implicitly allowed the possibility that civil judges had the power to contract at least some marriages. In *Deessemus nobis* (September 16, 1788), the pope declared this quibbling to be "without any foundation" (*omni fundamento destitui*). Of course, the next question that had to be addressed in state-sanctioned marriages was whether a Catholic might marry a divorced Protestant. The civil legislation of the Electorate of the Palatinate had declared these marriages valid, and a general recognition of the state's ability to adjudicate in such matters was beginning to spread through Europe. As a result, Karl Theodor Anton Maria von Dalberg (1744–1817), the Archbishop of Mainz, renewed the question of whether Catholic priests could assist at such marriages in a circular letter of May 20, 1803, and inquired whether a priest might be able to administer the sacraments to a Catholic spouse who had been married by a Protestant minister. In his brief to the bishop, *Etsi fraternitatis* (October 8, 1803), Pope Pius VII denied "tribunals of laypeople" (*laicorum tribunalia*) the power to dissolve marriages, as well as the pastors who would implicitly approve the marriages by their presence. Of course, the question of whether civil marriages were true marriages was one of the most hotly contested debates of the era. Although one can trace the controversy to the writings of Marc'Antonio de Dominis (1560–1624), one usually associates the argument that the church derives its power over matrimony from civil society to a variety of late eighteenth- and early nineteenth-century theologians. Pope Pius VI condemned this view in his censure of the Jansenist Synod of Pistoia, and the Holy Office under Pope Leo XIII censured it again on March 13, 1879. I suppose it fitting to end on this controversy, as the Catholic Church finds itself at the center of a very similar controversy today, yet largely ignorant of the fact that these debates are now centuries old.

## Suggested Readings

De la Taille 1921; Lepin 1926; Clark 1960; Kilmartin 1998. Readers will find many of these scholastic controversies outlined in works of dogmatic theology, such as Pohle 1915, upon which I have depended heavily.

## Bibliography

Bellarmine, Robert. 1873. *Opera Omnia*. Vol. 4. Paris.

Berti, Gianlorenzo. 1776. *Opus de Theologicis Disciplinis*. Vol. 3. Venice.

Biel, Gabriel. [1488] 1963–1976. *Expositio sacri canonis missae*. Wiesbaden: F. Steiner.

Billuart, Charles-René. 1747. *Cursus Theologiae*. Vols. 14–17. Würzburg.

Cajetan. 1903. "Commentarium in Tertiam Partem Summae Theologiae." In *Sancti Thomae Aquinatis Doctoris Angelici Opera Omnia*. Vols. 11–12. Rome: Ex Typogaphia Polyglotta S. C. de Propaganda Fide.

Cano, Melchior. 1577. *Relectio de sacramentis in genere*. Ingolstadt.

Cienfuegos, Juan Álvaro. 1728. *Vita abscondita, seu speciebus eucharisticis velata, per potissimas sensuum operationes de facto à Christo domino ibidem indesinenter exercita circa objecta altari*.

Clark, Francis. 1960. *Eucharistic Sacrifice and the Reformation*. Westminster, MD: Newman Press.

Condren, Charles de. 1677. *L'idée du sacerdoce et du sacrifice de Jésus-Christ*. Paris.

Contenson, Vincent. 1687. *Theologia mentis et cordis, seu Speculationes universae doctrinae sacrae*. Cologne.

Estius, Guilielmus. 1616. *In quatuor libros sententiarum commentaria*. Douai.

Galtier, Paul. 1956. *De poenitentia tractatus dogmatico-historicus*. Rome: Universitatis Gregorianae.

Henno, Franciscus. 1719. *Theologia dogmatica, moralis, et scholastica: de Sacramentis*. Vol. 2. Venice.

Kern, Joseph. 1907. *De sacramento extremae unctionis tractatus dogmaticus*. Regensburg: Friedrich Pustet.

Kilmartin, Edward. 1998. *The Eucharist in the West*. Collegeville, MN: The Liturgical Press.

Lepin, Maurice. 1926. *L'idée du sacrifice de la messe, d'après les théologiens depuis l'origine jusqu'à nos jours*. Paris: Gabriel Beauchesne.

Lessius, Leonardus. 1620. *Opuscula in quibus pleraque theologiae mysteria explicantur*. Antwerp.

Liguori, Alphonsus. 1779. *Theologia moralis*. Vol. 2. Venice.

Lugo, Juan de. 1644. *Disputationes Scholasticae et Morales: de Sacramento Eucharistiae*. Lyons.

Mastri, Bartolomeo. 1661. *Disputationes Theologicae in Quartum Librum Sententiarum*. Venice.

Morinus, Joannes. 1651. *Commentarius historicus de disciplina in administratione sacramenti poenitentiae*. Paris.

Morinus, Joannes. 1655. *Commentarius de sacris ecclesiæ ordinationibus, secvndum antiquos et recentiores Latinos, Græcos, Syros et Babylonios*. Paris.

Olier, Jean-Jacques. 1661. *Explication des cérémonies de la grande messe de paroisse selon l'usage romain*. Paris.

Pasqualigo, Zacharias. 1707. *De sacrificio novae legis*. Venice.

Pohle, Joseph. 1915. *The Sacraments: A Dogmatic Treatise*. 4 vols. St. Louis, MO: Herder.

Sánchez, Juan. 1624. *Selectae et practicae disputationes*. Madrid.

Sánchez, Tomás. 1619. *Disputationes de sancti matrimonii sacramento*. Venice.

Suárez, Francisco. 1860–1861. *Opera Omnia*. Vols. 20–22. Paris.

Taille, Maurice de la. 1921. *Mysterium Fidei: de augustissimo corporis et sanguinis Christi sacrificio atque sacramento*. Paris: Beauchesne.

Ulloa, J. de. 1719. *Theologiae Scholasticae*. Vol. 4. Augsburg.

Vásquez, Gabriel. 1612. *Commentariorum ac disputationum in Tertiam Partem S. Thomae*. Vol. 2. Ingolstadt.

Viva, Domenico. 1712. *Cursus Theologicus ad usum Tyronum elucubratus*. Padua.

# CHAPTER 10

····················································································

# ECCLESIOLOGY/CHURCH–STATE RELATIONSHIP IN EARLY MODERN CATHOLICISM

····················································································

## STEFANIA TUTINO

## 1 THE CHURCH: *COMMUNIO* AND *RESPUBLICA*

····················································································

IF we want to understand the ecclesiological and political developments of post-Reformation Catholicism, we should start by recalling the dualism between *communio* and *respublica*, which is at the core of the Catholic Church's self-understanding. The view of the church as *communio* or *congregatio fidelium* finds its theological roots in Augustine and in the early church fathers and conceives of the church as a sacramental and spiritual community. The notion of the church as *respublica*, which has its theoretical backbone in Aquinas (1225–74) and scholastic theology, emphasizes the political aspect of the church as a government. Even though these two notions can be considered, to a certain extent, as theological ideal-types, they did have important repercussions in the institutional organization of the Christian church. Historically speaking, the notion of the church as *communio* was especially evident in the ecclesiological shape of the early church, which was loosely organized around the local authority of the bishops and lacked a politically and theologically structured centralized authority. The view of the church as *respublica*, by contrast, was mostly articulated after the fifth century, when Christians were no longer a persecuted minority but had become a political, as well as a spiritual, center of gravity in Western Europe.

Starting with Nicholas I (n.d.–867) in the context of the Photian Schism, and then more systematically with the papacy of Gregory VII (n.d.–1085), the popes began to vigorously assert their own juridical, and not simply spiritual, authority over the *respublica Christiana*, by reaffirming and reframing Pope Gelasius's (n.d.–496) political theory. By the end of the thirteenth century, the political understanding of the church as *respublica Christiana* developed in full, especially around two sets of issues. The first concerned the nature of the church as a political commonwealth; the second concerned the forms in which the church as a political commonwealth should be governed. As for the first, Aquinas's language of natural law on the one hand, and the canonists' effort to revive Roman law and apply it to the church on the other hand, provided a systematic understanding of the church's juridical structure. This structure was based on the distinction between *potestas ordinis* (i.e., the special sacramental power that clergymen hold as a consequence of having received holy orders) and *potestas iurisdictionis* (i.e., the authority that clergymen have to govern their flock). The *potestas iurisdictionis*, in turn, was composed of two elements. The first was the *potestas iurisdictionis in foro interiori*, which was the power to regulate the consciences of the Christian faithful and which was mainly exercised in the sacrament of confession. The second was the *potestas iurisdictionis in foro exteriori*, which was the coercive and public power that ecclesiastical authority had to regulate the external forum for the sake of the faithful. This intellectual systematization essentially set up the church as a proper government and entrusted to its leaders a political and juridical power to govern itself with respect to other public bodies.

As for the second set of issues—that is, the question of which form of government was especially suited to the ecclesiastical commonwealth—the so-called papalist theologians and canonists believed that such ecclesiastical commonwealth was to be ruled by the centralized authority of the bishop of Rome, who held the *plenitudo potestatis* over the church and thus governed it as a sort of absolute monarch who did not share with the council his legislative power. Other theologians, the so-called conciliarists, recovered some aspects of the notion of the church as *communio* and argued that the pope's authority to impose laws over the church was not absolute but limited by the council as the representative of the local bishops and priests (for some important historical and theoretical specifications on this point, see Fasolt 1991).

Generally speaking, by the end of the fourteenth century, the papalist view prevailed, even though certain aspects of the episcopal and conciliarist ecclesiology of *communio* remained significant (Oakley 2003; Fasolt 1991). The tension between these two ecclesiological notions resumed in somewhat dramatic terms in the fifteenth century. At the councils of Pisa (1409) and Constance (1414–18), the conciliarists, led by the French theologian and chancellor of the University of Paris, Jean Gerson (1363–1429), seemed to gain ground over the papalist faction in consequence of the Great Schism. However, the conciliarists failed to capitalize on their strength and lost much of their political capital at the councils of Basel (1431–37) and Florence-Ferrara (1438–45), when the popes managed to assert their own authority as superior to that of the council. Even though the supreme authority of the popes was not recognized in the Eastern church, nevertheless it is undeniable that after Florence-Ferrara the popes succeeded in consolidating their ecclesiological supremacy in the

West. It was not until the very beginning of the sixteenth century, at the dawn of the Reformation, that the so-called "silver-age Conciliarists" put a distinctive version of conciliarist ecclesiology once again on the theological and ecclesiological map of the Western church (Oakley 1965; Oakley 2003). Especially important in this context was the early sixteenth-century debate between the French conciliarist Jacques Almain (ca. 1480–1515) and the Dominican theologian Tommaso de Vio, Cardinal Cajetan (1469–1534). Cajetan started from the scholastic and canonistic distinction between *potestas iurisdictionis* and *potestas ordinis* and argued that while Christ gave the latter to all priests, he gave the former directly to Peter, who then passed it to his successor popes. Almain replied by using Cajetan's same scholastic framework. He argued that if it was true that the church was to be understood as a *respublica*, in some sense akin to any other secular commonwealth, then it followed that the ultimate authority to govern, or *potestas iurisdictionis*, resided in the community of the faithful represented by the council, which then elected the pope for the sake of a better government, just as in a secular government the ultimate authority resided in the community, which then could transfer it to the sovereign (Almain 1512 [English translation in Burns and Izbicki 1997, 134–200]; Cajetan 1936 [English translation in Burns and Izbicki 1997, 1–133]; Izbicki 1999; Oakley 1965; Elliot van Liere 1997; Burns 1997; Burns 2004).

Thus, simplifying what was a much more complex set of different ecclesiological, theological, and juridical notions, at the dawn of the Reformation the church's ecclesiology was characterized by an unstable equilibrium. The fifteenth- and early sixteenth-century conciliarists seemed to have absorbed the view of the church as *respublica* but had infiltrated, as it were, into this general scholastic framework some elements of the old ecclesiology of the church as *communio*. They did so less in order to challenge the fact that the church was a proper political body than to argue that such an ecclesiastical body should not be governed by the pope as an absolute monarch. The papalists, in turn, responded by refining the notion of the church as *respublica*: the fact that the church was indeed a proper government did not mean that it was like any other secular government. While in secular governments the *potestas iurisdictionis* resided in the whole body of the commonwealth by natural law, in the ecclesiastical government the *potestas iurisdictionis* resided directly in the pope by divine law.

The Reformation put a tremendous amount of theological pressure on this already unstable equilibrium and forced Catholic theologians to rethink their positions both on the nature of the church as *respublica* and on the relationship between the Christian commonwealth and secular commonwealths. Moreover, the Reformation forced a reconsideration of the ways in which the Roman, as opposed to the Greek, church understood the political role of its leaders (on the implications of the clash between Western and Eastern ecclesiology, see Roeber 2010). Last, but definitely not least, the debates between conciliarists and papalists, and indeed the fight between Catholics and Protestants, had important repercussions in the development of new theories of political sovereignty (Skinner 1978; Giacon 1944–50; Höpfl 2004; Oakley 2003).

# 2   THE CHURCH AS *RESPUBLICA*: PAPALISM
## AND CONCILIARISM AFTER
## THE REFORMATION

In general terms, the theoretical background that dominated post-Reformation debates over the ecclesiological nature of the Catholic Church was provided by the so-called school of Salamanca or second scholastics, whose papalist arguments represented an important reference point for all Catholic theologians. The theologians of the school of Salamanca clearly saw the immense benefit, from the point of view of post-Reformation Catholicism, of reproposing Aquinas's reflections on the nature of civil society and on the nature of authority in general and adapting them to the new context, characterized by a dramatic fracture within Catholic Christendom.

When the Dominican Francisco de Vitoria (ca. 1483–1546), one of the founders and main figures of the school of Salamanca, elaborated on the nature of both the ecclesiastical and political commonwealths, he understood that stressing the difference between them was necessary not only in order to oppose the conciliarist position but also, and more importantly from Vitoria's perspective, to oppose the Protestant insistence on the priesthood of all believers and the foundation of the legitimacy of secular government by God's grace. As a result, Vitoria argued that Aquinas had sharply distinguished between the respective origin of political and ecclesiastical authority: the former is founded on natural law, the latter on divine law. In Vitoria's argument, the status of the pope as the supreme authority within the Christian commonwealth was a necessary consequence of this difference: political authority was given by God to the entire community of men and women by natural law; the power of the keys was entrusted by Christ only to Peter and his apostles, not to the entire Christian community, thus preventing laymen from exercising the *potestas ordinis* (Vitoria 1992; Giacon 1944–50; Skinner 1978; Elliot van Liere 1997).

Robert Bellarmine (1542–1621), one of the greatest theorists of post-Reformation Catholic theology, took Vitoria's arguments a step further, both theologically and ecclesiologically. He started from the assumption that the nature of the authority of the pope and clergy was substantially spiritual in nature. The distinctive spiritual character of such authority made the ecclesiastical commonwealth an ontologically different entity with respect to the human commonwealth. One of the many differences was precisely the form of government that the ecclesiastical commonwealth was supposed to assume. Whereas political commonwealths, whose source of authority resided by natural law in the community, had a choice of forms of governments (the community could in fact choose to transfer its authority to a sovereign or to a larger group of leaders such as a senate), ecclesiastical authority had its origin in the divine law. Since Christ explicitly named Peter as the rock on which his church should be built, it was clear that the form of government that Christ himself had picked for his church was the monarchical one.

In this respect then, the pope, as the only legitimate successor of Peter, was the supreme and absolute sovereign of the church, and as such he was, by divine law, the ultimate source of authority within the ecclesiastical commonwealth (Dietrich 1999; Höpfl 2004; Tutino 2010).

When post-Reformation conciliarists wanted to oppose the papalists' arguments, they needed to address the Bellarminian and, more generally, neo-Thomist position. As they did that, however, they had to also take into account the specificity of the political and historical contexts in which they lived. Post-Reformation Catholicism was not a monolithic institution, but instead it assumed very different characteristics according to the specific political and historical circumstances that affected the various national contexts. There are many examples of how the debate between conciliarists and papalists played out in post-Reformation Europe, but perhaps the most interesting example in this context is that of France, where post-Reformation conciliarism assumed remarkably complex and fascinating aspects. Post-Reformation French Gallicanism, heir to the silver-age conciliarism of Almain and John Major (ca. 1469–1550), is a perfect example of both the complexity of the ecclesiological questions faced by the post-Reformation church and the complexity of the links between post-Reformation Catholicism, Protestantism, and politics (Oakley 1995; Oakley 1996; Oakley 2003; Parsons 2004; Salmon 2004).

Edmond Richer (1559–1631) and other leaders of the Gallican faction had two objectives. The first, properly ecclesiological, was to diminish the supranational authority of the pope over the church, in order to assert the liberties and prerogatives of the local (in this case French) church. The second, more properly political, was to defend the sacred and absolute authority of the French sovereign, which, especially following the assassination of Henri IV (1553–1610) by the Catholic zealot François Ravaillac (1578–1610), was crucial for every French Catholic theologian to do. The ecclesiological and political aims of French Gallicanism were influenced by, and in turn contributed to influence, a European-wide debate. Among the participants in this debate were Paolo Sarpi (1552–1623) and the defenders of the ecclesiastical and political liberties of Venice; and the king of England James I (1566–1625), who presented his 1606 oath of allegiance as an exemplary act for any sovereign, Catholic or Protestant, worried that the supranational and supernatural theological and ecclesiological authority of the pope might jeopardize not only the true tenets of the Christian faith, but indeed the very source of political authority (Oakley 1996; Salmon 1987; Salmon 2004; Puyol 1876; Parsons 2004; Gres-Gayer 2002; de Franceschi 2007).

In this context, then, French Gallicans faced a number of challenges. They had to defend their ecclesiological stance while safeguarding their political loyalty to the king of France and without flattening their own position too much compared to that of the Protestants, and especially the kind of position expressed by James. In order to see how they met those challenges, we should examine briefly Richer's *Libellus de ecclesiastica et politica potestate* (Richer 1611), considered by many scholars a model text for understanding the complexity of the ecclesiological and political aspects of French Gallicanism and post-Reformation conciliarism in general.

Richer's text starts with a vigorous endorsement of the conciliarist principle that "all Ecclesiasticall power belongs properly, essentially and first to the Church, but to the Pope, and other Bishops, instrumentally, and ministerially" (Richer 1612, Section I). Thus the pope depends on the whole church and on its representative, that is, the council, through which he derives his authority from Christ. Once Richer set up his idea of the relationship between the pope and the council, however, he needed to address more specifically the question of the nature of the church as *respublica* or *communio*: Was the church to be considered as a sort of self-contained spiritual commonwealth—that is, a community composed of the faithful, governed by the clergy in its entirety, whose aim was purely spiritual—or was the church the juridical half of one Christian commonwealth, of which the temporal government was the other half? In the context of French Gallicanism, however, those questions were tied to the question of the definition of ecclesiastical jurisdiction, which highlighted a growing contrast between the ecclesiological aspects of the Gersonian conciliarist tradition and the political agenda that a more properly political tradition of Gallicanism had assumed in post-Reformation France. In this respect, Richer's treatment of the issue of jurisdiction is an attempt to bring together those traditions and a demonstration of how difficult it was.

Early on in his work, Richer set up secular and religious commonwealths as two different commonwealths: the church was governed by both superior and inferior magistrates (i.e., higher and lower clergy) who derived their authority directly from God; the state was governed by both superior and inferior magistrates (i.e., the "inferiour Iudges" and "Parlement"), who derived their authority directly from the king. In this manner, the political commonwealth is independent from the church and possesses its own chain of superior and inferior authorities, all properly ordered up to the highest one—that is, the king—just as the church possesses its own chain of superior and inferior authorities, up to Christ (Richer 1612, Section II).

Later in his treatise, Richer changed his position and described the Catholic Church and the state no longer as two separate commonwealths, but rather as two authorities within the same Christian commonwealth: "the Church taken either for the whole companie of the faithfull, or for the Christian Common-wealth, is contented with her sole only head, and essentiall foundation our Lord Iesus Christ. Nevertelesse in the matter of exercise and execution of government in this Christian Common-weath, shee is differently ruled by two divers persons, that is by the Pope, and the Civill Prince" (Richer 1612, Section X). Thus Richer saw the church not just as a community of faithful independent from the political community but also as a proper commonwealth, ruled by two separate authorities, the pope (through the council) and the sovereign (through the parliament).

As for questions of jurisdiction, for Richer the difference between the authority of the church and the authority of the state concerned not so much the kind of matters that each had to regulate but rather the manner in which each authority ruled. In other words, Richer separated jurisdiction and coercive power, granting to the church only the former in a distinctively nonterritorial sense. The area of jurisdiction of the church was "the inward motions of the conscience," thus "the Church by divine right hath neither territorie, right of sword, nor contentious Court" (Richer 1612, Section XI). The area of jurisdiction of the state was not limited to political matters, but it also extended to the protection of the church itself: "since the civill Prince is the Lord of the Common-wealth and Countrie, protector and defender of the divine, naturall and canonicall law, and to that end doth beare the sword; it is he alone that hath power of constraining and restraining. . . . wherefore, for the good of the Church and execution of Ecclesiasticall Canons he may make lawes" (Richer 1612, Section XII). This means, among other things, that the political sovereign was the ultimate judge of *appels comme d'abus*. Indeed, precisely because the jurisdiction of the church, as Richer had argued before, was not territorial, it was the secular state that, in some sense, granted to the French Catholic Church its territorial jurisdiction: this is the core of the *Ecclesia in Republica* theme (Parsons 2004).

Thus by the end of his text, Richer ended up endorsing more and more openly political Gallicanism at the expense of ecclesiastical Gallicanism and the coherence of his position. In fact, Richer's entire discussion of ecclesiastical jurisdiction is itself a reflection of the tensions between the two Gallican traditions. On the one hand, Richer's statements regarding the divine right of the bishops and also of the lower clergy implied an "extremist" view of the independence and authority of priests (the so-called Richerism). On the other hand, by attributing to the king not only the supreme authority in political matters but also some authority in ecclesiastical matters, Richer subordinated, to an extent, the clergy to the civil authority. This tension in Richer's book was, in a sense, the result of Richer's attempt to grapple with the theological and political aspects of the kind of papalism defended by Vitoria and Bellarmine, which was anchored to the notion of the spiritual nature of the pope's supremacy. Thus, if the French Gallicans wanted to move against the authority of the pope, they had to attack both its theo-ecclesiological premises and its political consequences. However, addressing the theological premises brought to light the fundamental differences, strategic but also theoretical, between political and ecclesiastical Gallicanism. Because Richer wanted to strengthen the political Gallicans in their fight against Roman papalism, he needed to mount an extreme criticism of the spiritual and ecclesiological supremacy of the pope. But how much could one reinforce the role of the French political authority in sorting out ecclesiastical matters against the usurped supranational and imperial authority of the pope without ending up submitting the French episcopate, whose liberties and authorities ecclesiastical Gallicanism sought to defend, to the ecclesiastical authority of the sovereign as opposed to the ecclesiastical authority of the pope?

The example of Richer's text shows clearly not only the complex interplay between politics, theology, and ecclesiology that characterized the post-Reformation debate between conciliarists and papalists, but also some of its most important implications in terms of political theory. As is evident in the case of Richer, in fact, the debate between conciliarists and papalists contributed to reframing the debate on the origin and nature of political sovereignty. Thus, taking into account this aspect of post-Reformation Catholic ecclesiology is very important if we want to understand the roots of early modern absolutism and constitutionalism (Skinner 1978; Fasolt 1991; Burgess 1992; Oakley 2003; Salmon 2004; Sommerville 1986; Sommerville 2005; Tutino 2010).

# 3  The Church as *Respublica Perfecta*: Post-Reformation Papacy and Early Modern Sovereigns

After the Reformation, both papalists and conciliarists agreed on the basic notion of the church as *respublica* and disagreed on the proper form of government that such special commonwealth was supposed to assume. The notion of the church as *respublica*, however, had important repercussions not only on the ecclesiological debates but also on the more properly political debates: once we grant that the church was a distinctive commonwealth, in which terms should the relationship between the *respublica Christiana* and the other temporal commonwealth be posed?

Even in discussing this topic we should start from the neo-Thomist solution, and especially the version given by Bellarmine in his theory of the *indirecta potestas*, or indirect power of the pope in temporal affairs, because Bellarmine's theory dominated the political and theological debates in post-Reformation Europe. Two key theoretical assumptions underpin Bellarmine's defense of the indirect papal authority. The first, which represents a re-elaboration of Vitoria's and the neo-scholastics' reflections on the nature of sovereignty, was that temporal governments had a distinctive and autonomous space with respect to the Christian church. Since, as Bellarmine wrote, "*dominium* is not founded in grace or faith, but in free will and reason, and it does not spring from the *ius divinum*, but from the *ius gentium*," then the political government is legitimate even if it is ruled by non-Christian governors. The pope, then, does not have any kind of authority over non-Christians, and therefore we cannot say, Bellarmine concluded, that he is the head of the whole world. That does not mean that his empire does not extend throughout the whole world, for the jurisdiction of his spiritual empire covers all Christians spread throughout the world. Yet if the whole world converted to Christianity, Bellarmine specified, this would not make the pope's authority in temporal matters any greater, but it would increase the number of souls subject to his spiritual authority (Bellarmine 1870–75, 2:146–47; Arnold 1934; Höpfl 2004; Tutino 2010).

The second key theoretical argument for Bellarmine's *potestas indirecta* was the fact that Christ, while he was a man on earth, had no temporal kingdom. He was indeed a king but of an "eternal and divine kingdom," and as such he did not remove any authority from the temporal sovereigns of his time. That does not mean that he could have not received any kingly authority had he wanted to. He did not want any because such authority was not necessary but rather "*supervacanea et inutlis*," for Christ's aim while he dwelled on earth was to achieve the redemption of mankind, and for this task spiritual authority was the only authority needed (Bellarmine 1870–74, 2:148–51). The argument that Christ's kingdom, because it was eternal, was also spiritual, was fundamental to Bellarmine's entire theoretical construction, because it served as a means to tie the authority of the head of the church on earth with that of the head of the church in heaven. Precisely because the pope is the head of the church on earth, it is both necessary and sufficient for him to claim the same power that Christ had while he lived as a man among men, which means that the temporal dimension of the sovereignty of the pope separates this sovereignty from the sovereignty that Christ has over the "a-temporal" church in heaven, but at the same time establishes an important link between the pope and Christ insofar as the pope received directly from Christ the authority that he himself had as a man.

Therefore, for Bellarmine (as well as for many like-minded post-Reformation Catholic theorists, such as Francisco Suárez [1548–1617] and Juan de Mariana [1536–1624]) the church was a *respublica*, indeed a *respublica perfecta*, and as such it needed to be endowed with the authority necessary to achieve its goal, which was the salvation of the souls of the faithful. By the same token, the state also was a "perfect commonwealth," and as such it was endowed with the authority and power necessary to achieve its goal, which was the temporal welfare of its subjects. The authority needed by the church to preserve itself was the supreme spiritual authority of the pope, which allowed him to intervene in temporal matters whenever the secular commonwealth obstructed the way to pursuit of the higher spiritual goal (Höpf 2004; Tutino 2010; Skinner 1978).

Bellarmine's theory of the authority of the pope as an emperor of souls, whose spiritual authority was both radically different from, and superior to, the authority of temporal sovereigns, represented an attempt to reframe radically the ecclesiological, political, and theological identity of post-Reformation Catholicism, and as such it was very controversial. Among the enemies of Bellarmine's theory were those temporal sovereigns—Protestant ones like James Stuart but also Catholic ones like the senate of Venice or, at times, the king of France—who feared that the supernatural and supranational authority of the church could put in jeopardy their own increasingly sacralized temporal supremacy and who thus supported a conciliarist ecclesiology against the political implications of papalism (Cozzi 1979; Bouswma 1968; Frajese 1984; Frajese 1988; Oakley 1996; Sommerville 1981; Sommerville 1986; Motta 2005; Tutino 2010; Wootton 1983). The enemies of Bellarmine, however, included also those Catholic papalists who believed that the authority of the pope was both spiritual and temporal (i.e., that the pope was the supreme sovereign of both a spiritual and a temporal commonwealth). These were not only canonists such as Francisco Peña (ca. 1540–1612) and theologians such as Tommaso Bozio (1548–1610), but also popes such as Sixtus V (1521–90), who thought that Bellarmine had not defended strongly enough the papal monarchy, and as such deserved to see his work included in the index of prohibited books (Frajese 1988; Tutino 2010; Prodi 1987; Jaitner 1979).

In sum, early modern Catholic ecclesiological debates were characterized by a complex interplay between theological and political concerns. It is precisely through these ecclesiological debates that the Catholic Church sought to affirm its theological and political identity as a universal, supernatural, and supranational institution in a historical context that was changing rapidly and profoundly, given the consolidation of the Protestant churches on the one hand and the increasing power of the centralized authority of territorial sovereigns on the other. Both Richer's conciliarism and Bellarmine's papalism were attempts to reframe the ecclesiology of the Catholic Church in order to adapt it to this new context; and both attempts, in a sense, failed. Richer's position, which was supposed to represent a coherent picture of the political and the ecclesiological aspects of Gallicanism, ended up showing just how divergent the aims of these two traditions of Gallicanism could be, and as such it showed the complexity of the relationship between the territorial sovereignty of the king and the supernatural authority of the church. Bellarmine's solution is also a testament to the profound identity crisis faced by post-Reformation Catholicism. The opposition mounted against Bellarmine's theory by Protestant and Catholic political leaders and by both the Catholic conciliarists and the more papalist sectors of the Roman Curia demonstrates how difficult it was to reframe the supreme spiritual and supranational authority of the pope in the face of the consolidation of the territorial churches and the increasingly absolutist nature of the sovereignty of temporal princes.

# 4 Looking Ahead: Catholic Ecclesiology and Politics on the Threshold of Modernity

Late seventeenth- and eighteenth-century Catholic ecclesiology is a valuable lens through which we can see the complex interaction between theology and politics in a context of growing absolutism and emerging nationalism. These historical developments, in fact, added novel and important dimensions to the Catholic debates on both the relationship between the pope and the council and the relationship between ecclesiastical and secular authority.

A clear example of the multidimensional and complex nature of eighteenth-century ecclesiology is the case of Johann Nikolaus von Hontheim, better known by his pseudonym of Justinus Febronius (1701–90). Febronius was the author of an important treatise titled *De statu ecclesiae*, published in 1763. Drawing from a vast array of historical scholarship and textual criticism, Febronius demonstrated that episcopalism was the pure and original way in which the *Ecclesia primitiva* was governed. Thus, Febronius reframed the ecclesiological notion of *communio* and adapted it to a tradition of episcopalism that, as Oakley argued, was essentially "pragmatic" and historical, as opposed to canonistic and theological (Oakley 2003, 186). On this basis, Febronius's treatise defended episcopal autonomy as both a suitable and historically appropriate form of government for the German imperial church and a fruitful way to meet the challenge of a confessionally divided territory, since all German Christians, according to Febronius, might be reunited around the ecclesiological principle of episcopalism.

Febronius's views were very influential in Germany and gave origin to what is called today "Febronianism"—that is, a movement that used Febronius's ecclesiological views to argue for a unified German church, which was supposed to embrace a German, enlightened, and episcopal view of the church against the papalist, Romanist, and Jesuitical baroque excesses. In so doing, as Michael Printy has argued, Febronius's ecclesiology in the context of the German Catholic Enlightenment contributed to enabling "the transition from the 'Holy Roman Empire of the two churches' to the modern dilemma of "competing Protestant and Catholic ideas of what it meant to be a German" (Printy 2009, 4).

If we move from imperial Germany to France, we will find the same complex link between ecclesiology and politics, albeit in a different religio-political context. Much like the case of Febronianism, in fact, ecclesiological debates in eighteenth-century France were a reflection of, and in turn contributed to, influencing the political debates. Between the middle of the seventeenth and the beginning of the eighteenth centuries, French Jansenists embraced certain elements of late sixteenth- and early seventeenth-century Gallican ecclesiology and gave them a new political and religious significance. The Jansenists in fact included Gallican episcopalism into a wider religious movement aimed at contrasting the Jesuits' model of Catholicism, which the Jansenists perceived as ecclesiologically papalist as opposed to episcopal, politically "Romanist" as opposed to "French," and morally laxist. The Jansenists' attempt to recover and reframe the more properly ecclesiological aspects of early Gallicanism caused an important shift in the significance of later political Gallicanism. In the late sixteenth and early seventeenth centuries, the French monarchy had supported Richer and the other Gallican theologians because their anti-papalism greatly strengthened the king's authority. In contrast, by the second half of the seventeenth century, political Gallicanism had become unpalatable for an increasingly absolutist monarchy. Indeed, the French crown found in papalist Catholicism a better ally to foster and defend its own absolutistic tendencies: The publication of the papal bull *Unigenitus* in 1713, which condemned Jansenist spirituality and episcopalism, was in fact solicited by Louis XIV.

Despite this condemnation, however, French Jansenists did not disappear. Rather, they embedded their episcopalism into a distinctive and distinctively political opposition to the absolute nature of the king's rule. In this respect, the Jansenists' combination of ecclesiology, politics, and piety contributed to polarize eighteenth-century religious and political debates: on the one side there were the supporters of the absolute monarchy, who were also the supporters of the Jesuits, who in turn were the main defenders of papalism and of the absolute nature of the pope's ecclesiological authority over the clergy. On the other side, there were those who embraced Jansenist piety and spirituality and Richerist ecclesiology against the common front constituted by all the supporters of political and ecclesiological absolutism. It is in this polarized context, Van Kley argues, that we can find the roots of the French Revolution (Van Kley 1975; Van Kley 1996).

As we saw in both the German and French cases, eighteenth-century Catholic ecclesiological debates remained an important venue for articulating political and theological questions that are at the core of the political and religious history of early modern times. Indeed, following the developments of early modern debates on ecclesiology from the sixteenth to the eighteenth centuries allows us to appreciate from a distinctive angle some of the most important political and religious features of Western history. Nevertheless, as the early modern world came to an end, the vitality of the Catholic ecclesiological debates also came to an end. It is undeniable, in fact, that starting with the French Revolution (which in this case represents both a historical catalyst and a convenient historiographical signpost), religion in general, and Catholicism more specifically, progressively lost their hegemonic power over the consciences of European men and women, who instead were governed more and more firmly by an increasingly sacralized political authority. Relegated to a marginal role in the political and social fabric of European society, the Catholic Church was deprived of much of its institutional and public authority. As a consequence, not only the ecclesiological, but also the political and theological structure of the Catholic Church progressively hardened, and Catholic ecclesiological debates lost most of the intellectual force and impact they previously had. As an example, one needs to recall that Pius IX (1792–1878) issued *Pastor Aeternus* in July 1870, barely two months before the newly formed Italian national army conquered Rome and effectively put an end to the papacy as a political force. As the Catholic Church today faces the novel and unique challenges of the modern, postmodern, and globalized world, it might need to recover some of the intellectual energy that characterized its early modern ecclesiological discussions.

## BIBLIOGRAPHY

Almain, Jacques. 1512. *Libellus de auctoritate ecclesiae*. Paris.

Arnold, Franz Xaver. 1934. *Die Staatslehre des Kardinals Bellarmin: Ein Beitrag zur Rechts—und Staatsphilosophie des konfessionellen Zeitalters*. Munich: M. Heuber.

Barbuto, Gennaro Maria. 1994. *Il principe e l'Anticristo: Gesuiti e ideologie politiche*. Naples: Guida.

Bellarmine, Robert. 1870–1874. *Ven. Cardinalis Roberti Bellarmini politiani S.J. Opera Omnia*. Edited by J. Fèvre. 12 vols. Paris: L. Vivès.

Bergin, Joseph. 1996. *The Making of the French Episcopate, 1589–1661*. New Haven, CT: Yale University Press.

Blet, Pierre. 1955. "Jésuites et libertés gallicanes en 1611." *AHSI* 24: 165–188.

Bouswma, William J. 1971. "Gallicanism and the Nature of Christendom." In *Renaissance Studies in Honor of Hans Baron*, edited by A. Molho and J. A. Tedeschi, 811–830. Dekalb: Northern Illinois University Press.

Bouswma, William J. 1968. *Venice and the Defense of Republican Liberty: Renaissance Values in the Age of the Counter-Reformation*. Berkeley: University of California Press.

Brodrick, James. 1992. "The Divine Right of Kings Reconsidered." *The English Historical Review* 107: 837–861.

Brodrick, James. 1928. *The Life and Work of Blessed Robert Francis Cardinal Bellarmine, S.J., 1542–1621*. 2 vols. London: Burns Oates and Washbourne.

Burgess, Glenn. 1993. *The Politics of Ancient Constitution: An Introduction to English Political Thought, 1603–1642*. University Park: Pennsylvania State University Press.

Burns, James H. 1981. "Politia regalis et optima: The Political Ideas of John Mair." *History of Political Thought* 2: 31–61.

Burns, James H. 2004. "Scholasticism: Survival and Revival." In *The Cambridge History of Political Thought, 1450–1700*, edited by James H. Burns and M. Goldie, 132–155. Cambridge: Cambridge University Press.

Burns, James H., ed. 1991. *The Cambridge History of Medieval Political Thought, ca. 350–ca. 1450*. Cambridge: Cambridge University Press.

Burns, James H., and M. Goldie, eds. 2004. *The Cambridge History of Political Thought, 1450–1700*. Cambridge: Cambridge University Press.

Burns, James H., and T. Izbicki, eds. 1997. *Conciliarism and Papalism*. Cambridge: Cambridge University Press.

Cajetan [Tommaso de Vio]. 1936. *De comparatione auctoritatis: Papae et Concilii*. Edited by V. M. Pollet. Rome: Institutum Angelicum.

Cozzi, Gaetano. 1956. "Fra Paolo Sarpi, l'anglicanesimo e la Historia del Concilio tridentino." *Rivista Storica Italiana* 63: 559–619.

Cozzi, Gaetano. 1963. "Gesuiti e politica sul finire del '500." *Rivista Storica Italiana* 17: 477–573.

Cozzi, Gaetano. 1979. *Paolo Sarpi tra Venezia e l'Europa*. Torino: Einaudi.

de Franceschi, Sylvio H. 2009. *La crise théologico-politique du premier âge baroque: Antiromanisme doctrinal, pouvoir pastoral et raison du prince: Le Saint-Siège face au prisme français (1607–1627)*. Rome: École française de Rome.

de Franceschi, Sylvio H. 2007. "Gallicanisme, antirichérisme et reconnaissance de la romanité ecclésiale: La dispute entre le cardinal Bellarmin et le théologien parisien André Duval (1614)." In *Papes, princes et savants dans l'Europe modern: Mélanges à la mémoire de Bruno Neveu*, edited by Jean-Louis Quantin and Jean-Claude Waquet, 97–121. Geneva: Droz.

Dietrich, Thomas. 1999. *Die theologie der kirche bei Robert Bellarmin (1542–1621)*. Paderborn: Bonifatius Druck-Buch-Verlag.

Elliot van Liere, Katherine. 1997. "Vitoria, Cajetan, and the Conciliarists." *Journal of the History of Ideas* 58: 597–616.

Fasolt, Constantin. 1991. *Council and Hierarchy: The Political Thought of William Durant the Younger*. Cambridge: Cambridge University Press.

Frajese, Vittorio. 1988. "Regno ecclesiastico e Stato moderno: La polemica fra Francisco Peña e Roberto Bellarmino sull'esenzione dei clerici." *Annali dell'Istituto Storico Italo-Germanico in Trento* 14: 273–339.

Frajese, Vittorio. 1984. "Una teoria della censura: Bellarmino e il potere indiretto dei papi." *Studi Storici* 25: 139–152.

Giacon, Carlo. 1944–1950. *La seconda scolastica*. 3 vols. Milan: Fratelli Bocca.

Gres-Gayer, Jacques M. 2002. *Le gallicanisme de Sorbonne*. Paris: Champion.

Höpfl, Harro. 2004. *Jesuit Political Thought: The Society of Jesus and the State, c.1540–1630*. Cambridge: Cambridge University Press.

Izbicki, Thomas M. 1999. "Cajetan's Attack on Parallels between Church and State." *Cristianesimo nella Storia* 20: 80–89.

Jaitner, Klaus. 1979. "De Officio Primario Summi Pontificis: Eine Denkschrift Kardinal Bellarmins für Papst Clemens VIII (Sept./Okt. 1600)." In *Römische Kurie. Kirchliche Finanzen: Vatikanisches Archiv. Studien zu Ehren von Hermann Hoberg*. Vol. I, edited by E. Gatz, 377–403. Rome: Editrice Pontificia Università Gregoriana.

Kingdon, Robert M. 2004. "Calvinism and Resistance Theory, 1550–1580." In *The Cambridge History of Political Thought, 1450–1700*, edited by James H. Burns and M. Goldie, 194–218. Cambridge: Cambridge University Press.

Martin, Victor. 1929. *Le Gallicanisme politique et le clergé de France*. Paris: Picard.

Martin, Victor. 1919. *Le Gallicanisme et la Reforme catolique: Essai historique sur l'introduction en France des decrets du Concile de Trente (1563–1616)*. Paris: Picard.

Motta, Franco. 2005. *Bellarmino: Una teologia politica della Controriforma*. Brescia: Morcelliana.

Oakley, Francis. 1965. "Almain and Major: Conciliar Theory on the Eve of the Reformation." *American Historical Review*. 70: 673–690.

Oakley, Francis. 1999. "Bronze-Age Conciliarism: Edmond Richer's Encounters with Cajetan and Bellarmine." *History of Political Thought* 20: 65–86.

Oakley, Francis. 1996. "Complexities of Context: Gerson, Bellarmine, Sarpi, Richer, and the Venetian Interdict of 1606–7." *The Catholic Historical Review* 82: 369–369.

Oakley, Francis. 2003. *The Conciliarist Tradition: Constitutionalism in the Catholic Church 1300–1870*. Oxford: Oxford University Press.

Oakley, Francis. 1962. "On the Road from Constance to 1688: The Political Thought of John Major and George Buchanan." *The Journal of British Studies* 1: 1–31.

Parsons, Jotham. 2004. *The Church in the Republic: Gallicanism and Political Ideology in France*. Washington, DC: Catholic University of America Press.

Patterson, W. B. 1997. *King James VI and I and the Reunion of Christendom*. Cambridge: Cambridge University Press.

Powis, Jonathan. 1983. "Gallican Liberties and the Politics of Later Sixteenth-Century France." *The Historical Journal* 26: 515–530.

Printy, Michael. 2009. *Enlightenment and the Creation of German Catholicism*. Cambridge: Cambridge University Press.

Prodi, Paolo. 1959–1967. *Il Cardinale Gabriele Paleotti (1522–1567)*. 2 vols. Rome: Edizioni di Storia e Letteratura.

Prodi, Paolo. 1987. *The Papal Prince, One Body and Two Souls: The Papal Monarchy in Early Modern Europe*. Cambridge: Cambridge University Press.

Puyol, Pierre Edouard. 1876. *Edmond Richer: Étude historique et critique sur la renovation du gallicanisme au commencement du XVIIIe siècle*. 2 vols. Paris: Olmer.

Richer, Edmond. 1611. *Libellus de ecclesiastica et politica potestate*. Paris.

Richer, Edmond. 1612. *A Treatise of Ecclesiasticall and Politike Power*. London.

Roeber, A. G. 2010. "The Waters of Rebirth: The Eighteenth Century and Transoceanic Protestant Christianity." *Church History* 79 (1): 40–76.

Salmon, John H. M. 2004. "Catholic Resistance Theory, Ultramontanism, and the Royalist Response, 1580–1620." In *The Cambridge History of Political Thought, 1450–1700*, edited by James H. Burns and M. Goldie, 219–253. Cambridge: Cambridge University Press.

Salmon, John H. M. 1959. *The French Religious Wars in English Political Thought*. Oxford: Clarendon Press.

Salmon, John H. M. 1987. *Renaissance and Revolt: Essays in the Intellectual and Social History of Early Modern France*. Cambridge: Cambridge University Press.

Skinner, Quentin. 1978. *Foundations of Modern Political Thought*. 2 vols. Cambridge: Cambridge University Press.

Sommerville, Johann P. 1996. "English and European Political Ideas in the Early Seventeenth Century: Revisionism and the Case of Absolutism." *The Journal of British Studies* 35: 68–194.

Sommerville, Johann P. 1982. "From Suarez to Filmer: A Reappraisal." *The Historical Journal* 25: 525–540.

Sommerville, Johann P. 1981. "Jacobean Political Thought and the Controversy over the Oath of Allegiance." Ph.D. thesis, University of Cambridge.

Sommerville, Johann P. 2005. "Papalist Political Thought." In *Catholics and the "Protestant Nation": Religious Politics and Identity in Early Modern England*, edited by E. H. Shagan. Manchester: Manchester University Press.

Sommerville, Johann P. 1986. *Politics and Ideology in England, 1603–1640*. New York: Longman.

Sutto, Claude. 1993. "Tradition et innovation, réalisme et utopie: L'idée gallicane à la fin du XVIe et au début du XVIIe siècles." *Renaissance et Réforme* 8: 278–297.

Tuck, Richard. 1979. *Natural Right Theories: Their Origin and Development*. Cambridge: Cambridge University Press.

Tuck, Richard. 1993. *Philosophy and Government, 1573–1651*. Cambridge: Cambridge University Press.

Tutino, Stefania. 2010. *Empire of Souls: Robert Bellarmine and the Christian Commonwealth*. Oxford: Oxford University Press.

Ullman, Walter. 1965. *The Growth of Papal Government in the Middle Ages*. London: Methuen.

Ullman, Walter. 1949. *Medieval Papalism: The Political Theories of Medieval Canonists*. London: Methuen.

Van Kley, Dale H. 1975. *The Jansenists and the Expulsion of the Jesuits from France, 1756–1765*. New Haven, CT: Yale University Press.

Van Kley, Dale H. 1996. *The Religious Origins of the French Revolution: From Calvin to the Civil Constitution, 1560–1791*. New Haven, CT: Yale University Press.

Vitoria, Francisco de. 1992. *Political Writings*. Edited by A. Pagden and J. Lawrance. Cambridge: Cambridge University Press.

Vivanti, Corrado. 1963. *Lotta politica e pace religiosa in Francia fra Cinque e Seicento*. Turin: Einaudi.

Wilks, Michael. 1963. *The Problem of Sovereignty in the Later Middle Ages*. Cambridge: Cambridge University Press.

Wootton, David. 1983. *Paolo Sarpi: Between Renaissance and Enlightenment*. Cambridge: Cambridge University Press.

# Reformed Theologies

# CHAPTER 11

# REFORMED THEOLOGY BETWEEN 1600 AND 1800

RICHARD A. MULLER

In the two centuries between the end of the sixteenth century and the beginning of the nineteenth, the theology of the Reformed churches saw the rise and decline of confessional orthodoxy. The theology, or more precisely, the theologies that arose in Reformed circles during that time were diverse and variegated, with differences arising out of local issues and controversies, church-political concerns in various states and principalities, varied receptions of the older theological and philosophical traditions, differing appropriations and rejections of the newer philosophical approaches of the era, and specific curricular concerns in the academies and universities. Simply making this point sets aside the older dogmatic narratives that interpreted the development of Reformed orthodoxy as a monolithic movement toward a scholastic predestinarianism; or alternatively, toward a form of dogmatic legalism—and in either case, at odds with the evangelical message of the Reformers.

The scholarship of the last several decades has convincingly set aside these older dogmatic models, not only by examining the work of individual thinkers in the diverse contexts just noted, but also by identifying patterns of Reformed appropriation of the earlier intellectual traditions, whether patristic or medieval, in particular by examining more closely the late medieval roots of the Reformation. Indeed, although the focus of the present volume is on the theological developments of the seventeenth and eighteenth centuries, the new approaches to theological development and change represent a conscious reflection of and building upon the somewhat earlier reassessments of the continuities and discontinuities between the Middle Ages and the Reformation, and of the complexities of theological interaction among the Reformers of the first two or three generations of Protestantism in the sixteenth century—as well as the many ways in which these complex interactions played out in the varied contexts of the seventeenth and eighteenth centuries. Perhaps most simply stated, reassessment of Reformed thought of the era is marked by the recognition that "Calvinism," if the term is retained, can no longer be identified as a movement founded almost solely on the thought of a single theologian or focused on Geneva as its primary intellectual center. The Reformed theologies of the seventeenth and eighteenth centuries were rooted in the thought of a group of first- and second-generation Reformers, defined in relation to a series of fairly diverse confessional documents, developed in debate with other confessionalities and over a series of intraconfessional issues, and framed in relations both positive and negative to the philosophical currents of the era, both ancient and modern.

# 1 Reformation-Era Roots and Confessional Identity: Breadth and Boundaries

The identity of the early modern Reformed theological tradition can be linked both to the positive confessional formulation that had been finalized relatively shortly after the middle of the sixteenth century, and to the controversies of the same era over predestination, free choice, and in particular, the Lord's Supper, which resulted in a clearer distinction between the Reformed and Lutheran branches of the magisterial Reformation than had been evident earlier in the century. The character and content of these confessions, ranging from the East Frisian Confession (1528), Zwingli's *Fidei Ratio* (1530), and the First Confession of Basel (1534), to the Belgic Confession (1561), the Thirty-Nine Articles of the Church of England (1563), and Second Helvetic Confession (1566) serve to explain, if only in part, the early rise of a confessional orthodoxy, the relative diversity within an identifiable confessional movement, the absence among the Reformed of early internecine strife such as plagued Lutheranism after 1546, and the rapid if acrimonious dismissal of Arminianism at the Synod of Dort (documents in Müller 1903; Schaff 1931). Over twenty Reformed confessional documents were produced between 1528 and 1566—considerably more, if catechisms are included. Unlike Lutheranism, as the Reformed movement took shape and identity in the early sixteenth century, it was multiconfessional from its beginnings. In addition, almost from the outset, its confessional documents, unlike the Augsburg Confession, went beyond the issues and articles in dispute to outline fairly broadly the basic articles of positive Christian belief, from the doctrine of God to the last things. Arguably, this broader scope and detail forestalled major internal controversy. It also provided a basis for identifying the heterodoxy of Arminius's thought from the beginning of the debate, prior to the Synod of Dort (Muller 2008). Among the Reformers involved in the creation of these documents were Georgius Aportanus (1495–1530), Hinne Rode (ca. 1468–1537), Oswald Myconius (1488–1552), Johannes Oecolampadius (1482–1531), Huldrych Zwingli (1484–1531), Martin Bucer (1491–1551), Wolfgang Capito (1478–1541), Leo Jud (1482–1542), Guillaume Farel (1489–1565), John Calvin (1509–64), John Knox (ca. 1514–72), Thomas Cranmer (1489–1556), Matthew Parker (1504–75), John Jewel (1522–71), Guido de Bres (1522–67), Jan Laski (1499–1560), and Heinrich Bullinger (1504–75).

Simply listing the names of some of the thinkers involved in the writing and editing of the Reformed confessions indicates the breadth of the movement, both geographical and theological, as well as the wisdom of identifying the movement as "Reformed" rather than as "Calvinist": the authors and the documents represent such diverse Reformation-era locations as Basel, Strasbourg, Zurich, the Low Countries, England, and Scotland. A "strict" Calvinistic reading of Reformed doctrine would exclude both earlier confessional documents written by Calvin's predecessors, and documents such as the Edwardian Articles or the Thirty-Nine Articles of the Church of England, which represent broader aspects of the Reformation and ought not to be described as Calvinistic. It is noteworthy that Reformed writers of the sixteenth and seventeenth centuries almost invariably contested the suitability of the term "Calvinist" and consistently identified their confessionality and their own more elaborate doctrinal formulations as "Reformed" (Muller 2011). This diversity of Reformed thought and confessionality, evident already in the origins of the movement, is also quite apparent in the exportation of Protestantism to the New World, where the British settlements were represented by varieties of English Puritanism in New England, a more Presbyterian approach in the Middle Colonies, and a Dutch Reformed confessionality in the original settlements of New Amsterdam. (The Baptist churches, whether in England or in America, are certainly to be regarded as branches of the Reformed movement, originating in the seventeenth century, largely in the era of the Puritan Revolution, with some branches not only differing over infant baptism, but also developing an Arminian soteriology.)

From a doctrinal perspective, these confessional documents identify a developing sense of both the breadth and the limits of Reformed Protestantism. Reformed theology, both in the late sixteenth and the seventeenth centuries, was framed largely within these boundaries and many of its internal debates concerned the nature of the boundaries in relation to particular elaborations of doctrinal points. From the earliest documents onward, although considerably varied in detail, the confessions offer a consistent reading of the issues of scripture as the Word of God and "human traditions," together with a series of emphases concerning the church. The priority of word over church was consistently asserted, together with the assumption that it belongs to the duties of the church to uphold scripture as the norm for doctrine and practice. Varied emphases are present in the identification of the church: in some of the documents catholicity is emphasized, at the same time that the church is defined not in terms of its clergy but as the gathering of believers. The visible marks of the church, preaching of the Word of God and right administration of the two sacraments (baptism and the Lord's Supper) are emphasized both as manifesting the true church and, by their absence, as indicators of false churches. The confessional polemic against traditions typically identified them as "human" and specifically as ecclesial practices: in other words, the denial of traditions was not directed against the general tradition of doctrinal meditation reaching back to the church fathers.

Affirmation of the ecumenical doctrines concerning the Trinity and Christ are present, often with a pointed statement concerning the integrity of the natures of Christ. This latter point carried with it the Eucharistic application of ruling out the ubiquitarian teachings found among Lutherans, albeit not countering a Melanchthonian approach to the hypostatic union and the presence of Christ in the Supper. On the issue of Christ's presence in the Lord's Supper, the confessions consistently rule out a physical, bodily, or local presence, uniformly condemning the Mass and transubstantiation, sometimes disputing Lutheran teaching. A spiritual relationship with Christ is affirmed, in some cases indicating that Christ is offered or presented in the sacrament, in others indicating that the sacrament itself is a remembrance accompanied by a spiritual receiving of Christ. The death of Christ is defined by the confessions as a full satisfaction for sin, and as such is consistently posed against other means of reconciliation or satisfaction, such as penance, as well as against the sacrifice of the Mass. Christ is confessed to be the one and only high priest who alone intercedes with the Father.

The confessions also offer a consistent doctrine of salvation by grace alone, accomplished through faith, not through works. Depending on the length and elaboration of the statement, the denial of meritorious works is either made explicit or strongly implied. There is a consistent denial of free will in matters of salvation. Similarly, by way of elaboration of the doctrinal point, some of the confessions indicate that faith itself is an unmerited gift of grace and many of them add discussion of divine decrees and predestination. Confessions of the mid-sixteenth century, such as the Belgic and Second Helvetic, draw out these doctrines in greater detail, specifically indicating that faith is an instrument of grace and that predestination implies both the election of some to salvation, leaving the remainder in the fallen mass of humanity or identifying the remainder as the objects of divine reprobation. Synergistic theologies are therefore ruled out, while the monergistic formulations are somewhat varied, specifically with regard to predestination.

Major national confessions of the seventeenth century, like the Irish Articles (1615), the Canons of Dort, and the Westminster Confession of Faith (1647) (documents in Schaff 1931), although more detailed than most of the sixteenth-century documents, nonetheless maintain the model of establishing boundaries while at the same time allowing for considerable diversity within a confessional orthodoxy (Pederson 2014). Both documents take the form of synopses of theology, touching on all of the more fundamental topics and identifying Reformed understandings of particular issues, such as predestination and sacraments, but also presenting the full series of largely uncontroverted doctrines, such as the Trinity, creation, and providence. With the Irish Articles and the Westminster Confession, moreover, the theme of covenant—namely of a covenant of works and a covenant of grace—entered Reformed confessionality at a time when varied understandings of the federal theme had become a major concern in Reformed theology.

## 2 PROTESTANTISM AND PHILOSOPHY

The Protestant theologies of the first half of the sixteenth century, albeit grounded in fairly traditional patterns of philosophy, most obviously versions of Christian

Peripateticism and representing a spectrum ranging from nominalist to realist approaches, are not noted for their philosophical content. By contrast, the theologies of the later sixteenth, seventeenth, and eighteenth centuries are more overtly philosophical, whether because of the increasingly detailed appropriation of patristic and medieval materials for the sake of establishing, clarifying, or defending their doctrinal formulations as both cogent and catholic, or in view of the rapidly changing philosophical environment.

The alteration of the philosophical environment of theology in the era cannot be underestimated. The philosophical crisis of the seventeenth and eighteenth centuries was also a theological crisis. It must be recognized, moreover, that the crisis cannot be reduced to the conflict between a waning Peripateticism and the forward march of rationalism from Bacon (1561–1626) and Descartes (1596–1650) to Spinoza (1632–77), Locke (1632–1704), and Leibniz (1646–1714)—as implied by many standard histories of philosophy and accepted by most of the older narratives of the history of Reformed theology. Recent scholarship, particularly in the field of early modern science, has revived a far more complex paradigm, such as originally found in the massive eighteenth-century history of philosophy by Johann Jacob Brucker (1696–1770). The crisis must be measured, as Brucker recognized, as brought on in at least two stages—the first, a humanistic reception and reappropriation of non-Aristotelian ancient philosophies; and second by the rise of what Brucker called new "eclectic" philosophies arising out of these receptions (Brucker 1756). Thus there was not only a revival of Platonist, Stoic, Epicurean, and somewhat later, Skeptical philosophy, based on the humanistic retrieval of classical texts, there was also (particularly in the seventeenth century) a rise of various, in Brucker's terms, "eclectic" philosophical alternatives to the regnant Peripateticism— among them the pantheism of Giordano Bruno, various "Mosaic" philosophies claiming in one way or another to ground physics, and in some cases metaphysics, on a reading of the first chapter of Genesis (Blair 2000); varied forms of rationalist philosophy and natural philosophy, ranging from the Baconian to the Cartesian, to the modified Democritanism of Sennert (1572–1637) and the Epicureanism of Gassendi (1592–1655), to the vitalist philosophy of the van Helmonts (Jan Baptist, 1580–1644; Franciscus Mercurius, 1614–ca. 1698).

From a theological perspective, the philosophical debates were complicated by the absence of a clear relationship between confessional orthodoxies and particular philosophies, except on very specific points of contention such as the omniscience and omnipotence of God, creation *ex nihilo*, an overarching divine providence, and the freedom and responsibility of human beings. To make the point in a slightly different way, whereas there were confessionally defined theologies, there were no confessionally defined philosophies. There was little difference, for example, between formulations and developments in metaphysics among the Reformed and among Roman Catholics—and what differences there were among Reformed metaphysicians had distinct parallels among Roman Catholics.

The theological ramifications of this massive philosophical shift are specifically identified here in the essays on scripture (Trueman), philosophy (Goudriaan), and natural law (Friedeburg). The most important developments in Reformed circles were certainly the rise of the atomistic or mechanical philosophies in the wake of Francis Bacon's *Novum Organum* and the work of the Royal Society, and particularly on the contingent among the Dutch, French, and Swiss Reformed, the rise of Cartesian metaphysics and physics as a distinct alternative to Peripatetic philosophy, as evidenced in the thought of Johann Clauberg (1622–55), Christoph Wittich (1625–87), Ruard Andala (1665–1727), and Jean-Alphonse Turretin (1623–87), among others. In the eighteenth century, given the overwhelmingly negative reaction against Spinoza's philosophy, Reformed writers sought philosophical rootage in the philosophies of John Locke, Isaac Newton (1643–1727), G. W. Leibniz, and Christian Wolff (1679–1754).

# 3  Phases of Reformed Orthodoxy

The passage of Reformed thought from the mid-sixteenth to the late eighteenth century saw an initial phase of rapid formulation; subsequently, an era of development leading both to the deployment by the close of the seventeenth century of massive and detailed theological systems, coordinated with a significant outpouring of exegetical works, and at the same time to the loss of the philosophical and hermeneutical underpinnings of orthodoxy, even as its political and institutional connections dissipated; and a final phase of marginalization and decline under the impact of altered exegetical and hermeneutical understandings and the finalization of the philosophical shift from modified Aristotelianism to forms of Cartesian, Netwonian, Lockian, and Leibniz-Wolffian philosophies. With some allowance for the vagaries of periodization, early modern Reformed thought can be distinguished into three phases: early orthodoxy extending from circa 1565 to circa 1640, high orthodoxy from circa 1640 to 1725, and late orthodoxy from 1725 to circa 1780.

Early orthodoxy corresponds with the rise and relatively full development of confessional theology in the academies and universities of Reformed lands, grounded theologically in the confessions and catechisms of the mid-sixteenth century and in the exegetical and doctrinal efforts of second- and third-generation Reformers—and facilitated politically and socially by the confessionalization of the states and principalities of Europe. The development of early orthodoxy presupposes the national and regional confessions of the mid-sixteenth century, the ensuing process of confessionalization in Reformed principalities, and the corresponding institutionalization of theological education in Reformed universities and academies. By the mid-sixteenth century, Geneva was already being eclipsed by Reformed universities in Basel and Heidelberg. In the last quarter of the sixteenth century, Cambridge had also become highly significant, and perhaps most important of all, Leiden had risen as a center of international Reformed theological education. The early seventeenth century also saw significant development in the French Reformed academies, most notably Sedan and Saumur. Other important academies arose in such cities as Herborn and Danzig. Petrus Ramus's (1515–72) method of logical bifurcation provided a significant approach to the organization of curricula and treatises that fostered the development of revised and adapted forms of scholastic argumentation. In Leiden, Franciscus Junius (1545–1602) was instrumental in defining and stabilizing theology as a discipline, both by producing the first major Protestant essay on theological prolegomena and for fostering cycles of topical disputations for degrees that represented the theological vision of the presiding faculty. Amandus Polanus von Polansdorf (1561–1610) in Basel, and Abraham Scultetus (1566–1625) in Heidelberg, offered approaches to the doctrinal reception of the church fathers, while Bartholomaus Keckermann (ca. 1571–1608) in Danzig, and Johann Heinrich Alsted (1588–1638) in Herborn, developed full academic curricula including the philosophical as well as theological disciplines. Perhaps because the traditional ties of Scotland to France carried over from largely Roman Catholic connections into Protestant affiliations, a significant number of Scottish theologians and philosophers were called upon to staff the rising French Reformed academies in the wake of the Edict of Nantes.

The method of education in these academies and universities can be broadly identified as scholastic—specifically as a method of the schools having roots in the scholasticism of the Middle Ages, as well as in some aspects of the rhetorical tradition. Materials of study and discourse were often organized as a series of questions, objections, resolutions, and responses, or as a set of theses or aphorisms for disputation. In the latter case, in disputations for a degree, the thesis to be defended would be published for the occasion, whereas the questions, resolutions, and responses typically would not. Some distinction must also be made between the initial forms of early orthodox scholasticism among the Reformed and the more developed forms found among the high orthodox theologians. Whereas Beza (1519–1605), Zanchi (1516–90), Polanus, and other writers of the early orthodox era can be legitimately identified as including elements of scholastic method in their expositions, their appropriation of the method was less detailed and their recourse to the complex of distinctions that came with it less intense than what would occur after the second decade of the seventeenth century. To be specific, Theodore Beza's scholasticsm amounts to the appropriation of a few distinctions and perhaps a more frequent recourse to causal argumentation; Girolamo Zanchi's goes a bit further, looking both to distinctions and to forms of the *quaestio*, but in neither case does appropriation of the method approach the detail and density of argumentation found either in the later Middle Ages or in the dawning second scholasticism of Roman Catholic thinkers like Suarez.

Among the significant theological developments of the era are the formulation of theological prolegomena, the establishment of a significant body of biblical commentaries of various genres as the basis for a broadly understood body of Reformed doctrine, the rise of a more detailed approach to covenant as a unifying theme of biblical history and as a set of major theological *loci*, the distinction and debate between supralapsarian and infralapsarian formulations of the doctrine of predestination, and the controversy over understandings of predestination and related doctrines brought on by Arminius and finalized confessionally at the Synod of Dort. The rise of theological prolegomena coincided with the establishment of curricula in the universities and academies of Reformed states, supported the identification of theology as a discipline, and defined it in relation to the other academic disciplines. Instrumental here was the work of Franciscus Junius, who produced the first major prolegomenon to theology written in Reformed circles, his *De vera theologia*.

Given the continued exegetical efforts of Reformed theologians following the Reformation, the seventeenth century saw the creation of a vast body of commentaries in a variety of genres and illustrative of the relative diversity of Reformed thought. The commentators continued to write in genres already established in the era of the Reformation, ranging from extensive theological and philological commentaries, to sets of briefer annotations both theological and philological, to homiletical commentaries. One can speak of an early modern Reformed exegetical tradition that both presumed considerable mastery of the biblical languages and stood in direct relation to the formulation of doctrine according to the *locus* method.

The foundations for later Reformed covenantal thought were laid by Reformers like Zwingli, Bullinger, Musculus (1497–1563), and Calvin, who identified covenant as the key to establishing both the unity and the distinction of the Old and New Testaments, and as a foundational doctrine for understanding salvation both historically and individually. This approach to covenant was initially important not only to the general interpretation of scripture but also to sacramental theology, providing a biblical foundation for justifying infant baptism against Anabaptist argumentation, and to an understanding of the stability of the law in the context of a doctrine of salvation by grace alone (Woolsey 2012; Muller 2003a, 175–89). The early orthodox development of covenantal thought, in such diverse writers as Robert Rollock (1555–99) and David Dickson (1583–62) in Scotland, John Cameron (ca. 1579–1625) in Scotland and France, Dudley Fenner (ca. 1558–87) and John Ball (1585–1640) in England, Peter Bulkeley (1583–1659) in New England, and Johannes Cloppenburg (1592–1652) in the Netherlands, brought an emphasis on covenant as the fundamental mode of divine relationship with human beings, whether before the fall in a covenant of works or nature, or after the fall in the covenant of grace or reconciliation. Beyond this basic two-covenant structure, the Reformed also developed the doctrine of an eternal covenant of redemption between God the Father and God the Son.

Contrary to various lines of argumentation in an older theologized scholarship, this development of covenantal thought should not be interpreted either as an alternative to predestinarian theology or as the result of a legalistic turn in Reformed thought. It is simply not the case that early modern theologies adumbrate the nineteenth-century tendency to use particular doctrines as central dogmas or *principia* from which other doctrinal points can be deduced. Thus, covenantal language does not serve to modify the doctrine of predestination, nor does the concept of divine decrees force a reconception of covenant: both doctrines were presented as theological *loci* grounded in exegesis and framed by traditionary and contemporary debates. Each doctrine serves a particular function in the older Reformed theology; of course, as far as possible, not creating moments of contradiction or tension in the system as a whole. Covenant is a doctrine that primarily explicates the personal and corporate dimensions of salvation in the historical economy of salvation—predestination is a doctrine that defines the purpose from a different perspective, being primarily concerned with divine intentions and ends and with the issues of eternity and time, decree and execution (Van Asselt 2001; Woolsey 2012). Covenantal thought, with its historical emphasis, can also be linked to the major exegetical development of eschatology in the face of the wars, tumults, and dislocations of the seventeenth century (see the chapter by Gribben on Reformed eschatology).

It needs to be emphasized here that neither the supra- nor the infralapsarian understandings of predestination posit more than one divine decree: their structures of "degrees" or "gradations" within the one decree serve to indicate a nontemporal logical sequence. This way of thinking is grounded in the traditional distinction between an eternal divine knowledge of all possibility and an eternal divine knowledge of willed actuality, and in the premise that God's own knowing and willing, albeit nondiscursive, can nonetheless be described in terms of a sequence of nontemporal "instants of nature." This conceptual background is clear in Franciscus Junius's responses to Arminius, written in the 1590s. Arguably, given these traditionary roots, neither of these patterns of explanation is highly speculative in the modern sense of the word, particularly not the supralapsarian pattern. There was in fact a strong connection between the supralapsarian perspective and piety: it was typical of supralapsarian writers to identify theology as a fundamentally practical discipline. They also tended to be associated either, in England, with Puritan piety or, in the Netherlands, with the *Nadere Reformatie* or "Further Reformation" piety—notable examples being William Perkins (1558–1602) and Gisbertus Voetius (1589–1676).

Although there is no neat chronological demarcation between early and high orthodoxy, there is certainly an alteration of style and issues in debates that occurred around and shortly after 1640. In the wake of the Synod of Dort, the confessional shape of international Reformed theology was largely settled, particularly given the breadth of the canons on the issue of Christ's satisfaction and the limitation of its efficacy to the elect. The next major controversy, the debate over universal grace and the theology of the Saumur theologians, notably Moise Amyraut (1596–1664), arguably took place within the boundaries established by Dort and in view of the scholastic methods and distinctions that had been put in place by the framers of early orthodoxy (Muller 2003b, 75, 79–80; Van Stam 1988; Laplanche 1965). Other controversies of the era, such as the debates between antinomian and more nomistic writers, as well as over the question of preparation for grace, saw episodes of controversy in Old and New England and later, in the early eighteenth century in Scotland as well. This was also the era of the rising influence of Cartesian thought in Reformed circles and of increasing debate over the usefulness of traditional Peripatetic approaches in philosophy (Goudriaan 2006). Further, following 1648 and the Peace of Westphalia, it was also the era of the solidification of European nation states after the end of the wars of religion.

Reformed theology in the high orthodox era took on more of the characteristics and detail of scholastic method, having developed both negatively and positively in debate with Roman Catholic theology of the so-called second scholasticism. Representative writers are Francis Turretin or Turrettini (1623–87) and Petrus van Mastricht

(1630–1706). Characteristic of the large-scale treatises and systems of this era are their detail and density of argument and more consistent recourse to the technical vocabulary and distinctions belonging to scholastic argumentation—perhaps ironically so, given the increasing loss of relevance of the Peripatetic philosophical approaches in connection with which this vocabulary had been developed. The impact of this problem is clearly seen in the last decades of the seventeenth and in the early eighteenth centuries, when the scholastic vocabulary was increasingly jettisoned by Reformed theologians, creating nearly as much difficulty for theological orthodoxy as the philosophical shifts themselves and the debates over the doctrine and interpretation of scripture and the Trinity.

The mid-seventeenth century also was the era of the massive development of covenantal thought, both exegetically and dogmatically. Although the term "federal theology" applies in its strictest sense to those writers—notably Johannes Cocceius (1603–69), Francis Roberts (1580–1651), and Herman Witsius (1636–1708)—who produced large-scale works on the doctrine in its theological connections, a majority of Reformed theologians of the era deployed a model of three covenants: works, grace, and an intra-Trinitarian covenant or *pactum*, in their theologies. The covenant of works established the ultimate standard for human righteousness; the covenant of redemption of *pactum salutis* served to define the intra-Trinitarian foundation for the work of redemption; the covenant of grace both described the historical dispensations of salvation and defined the nature of salvation by grace, grounded in Christ, and conveyed through the preaching of the gospel (Van Asselt 2001).

The decline of Reformed orthodoxy and the transition to the more rationalistic and less confessional theologies of the eighteenth century pose a series of difficult questions both concerning the periodization and causes of the transition. The tide of orthodoxy began to ebb in the last three decades of the seventeenth century, reaching what can be identified as the endpoint of clearly defined confessionality and a largely accepted, relatively traditional synthesis of theological and philosophical understandings by the third decade of the eighteenth century (Pitassi 1992; Klauber 1994). The theological and philosophical developments between circa 1660 and 1725 defy an easy categorization: what can be described at the close of high orthodoxy can also be identified as an era of transitional theology, latitudinarianism, deconfessionalization, the rise of theological rationalism in response to and appropriation of alternative philosophical foundations, whether Cartesian (Heyd 1982), Newtonian, Lockian, or Leibnizian.

In England, the pressure against dissent had begun shortly after the Restoration in 1660, leading to the mass ejection of clergy not subscribing to the Book of Common Prayer in 1662. In France, Protestants were placed under extreme pressure, and ultimately with the Revocation of the Edict of Nantes (1685), leading to the closure of the academies and emigration of large numbers of laity, clergy, and teachers. In neither case did these disruptions lead to a total loss of Reformed or Calvinist identity. In England, fairly traditional Reformed theology continued to be taught in the Church of England (Hampton, 2007) as well as among the Dissenters, while among the French Reformed there was a diaspora that brought congregations, pastors, and theologians to refuges in England, the Netherlands, and Prussia. Both the Netherlands and Protestant Switzerland saw major debates over Cartesian philosophy and the displacement of the older Aristotelianism. At the same time the rise of Spinozism, together with the critical study of scripture, beginning with Richard Simon's *Histoire critique du Vieux Testament* (1680), and the ongoing development of the mechanical philosophies, further undermined the traditional alliance of precritical exegesis with Christian Aristotelianism and traditional cosmology.

Taking the failure of dissent in England to arrive at any confessional agreement (1719), of the Scottish Secession (1722), and the end of the Helvetic Consensus Formula in Switzerland (1725) as the conclusion of high orthodoxy and the beginning of late orthodoxy, is to identify deconfessionalization and the splintering of confessional groups as the end point of a broadly defined confessional orthodoxy and the beginning of a rather different phenomenon of multiple orthodoxies within what were once fairly unified confessionalities and their academic centers. Understood in this way, late orthodoxy is the product of significant shifts in understanding both in philosophy and biblical interpretation, as well as long-term changes both in church-state relations and in the character of confessionality, which reach back into the seventeenth century. Reformed theology in the eighteenth century largely lost its institutional place in the universities and functioned in the context of secularized states uninterested in pressing the issue of confessionality either among the laity, clergy, or academicians.

The plethora of methods and styles found in the Reformed theologies of the eighteenth century bears witness to the problem of attempting to define an orthodoxy after circa 1725. One index that registers significant change both in the philosophical underpinnings of Reformed thought and the approach to interpreting scripture for theological formulation is the nearly total loss of the older prolegomena to theology and the relative disintegration of the *loci* concerning the *principia*. Whereas in the earlier Reformed orthodox approach, the prolegomena had typically identified two *principia* or foundations for theology—scripture and God—the eighteenth-century theologies tended to drop the notion of *principia* and to begin apologetically with arguments for the existence of God and discussions of the limitation of natural knowledge. In many cases also, the doctrine of the Trinity disappeared from the chapters on the doctrine of God and reentered the exposition, if only by implication, in the argumentation for the divinity of Christ. Their approach to scripture tended to be apologetic, not only arguing the need for a special revelation but also posing arguments for the legitimacy and historical value of the biblical books as the basis for acceptance of the biblical revelation. In some cases, the apologetically framed doctrine of scripture would be postponed in the structure of the theology and presented as a prologue to the exposition of the doctrine of Christ. Increasingly characteristic of a large number of theologies of the eighteenth century is an unwillingness to engage in the more narrowly defined doctrinal battles of the preceding era; the loss of scholastic vocabulary and distinctions; and either an attempt to integrate one of the newer philosophies into the language of theology, or a movement away from philosophical usages entirely, coupled with a broadly latitudinarian approach to doctrine and definition.

## BIBLIOGRAPHY

Asselt, Willem J. van. 2001. *The Federal Theology of Johannes Cocceius (1603–1669)*. Translated by R. A. Blacketer. Leiden: Brill.

Blair, A. 2000. "Mosaic Physics and the Search for a Pious Natural Philosophy in the Late Renaissance." *Isis* 91: 32–58.

Brucker, J. J. 1756. *Institutiones historiae philosophiae usui academicae iuventutis adornatae.* 2nd ed. Leipzig: Bernhard Breitkopf.

Goudriaan, A. 2006. *Reformed Orthodoxy and Philosophy, 1625–1750: Gisbertus Voetius, Petrus van Mastricht, and Anthonius Driessen.* Leiden: Brill.

Hampton, S. 2007. *Anti-Arminians: The Anglican Reformed Tradition from Charles II to George I.* Oxford: Oxford University Press.

Heyd, M. 1982. *Between Orthodoxy and the Enlightenment: Jean-Robert Chouet and the Introduction of Cartesian Science in the Academy of Geneva.* Den Haag: De Graff.

Klauber, M. I. 1994. *Between Reformed Scholasticism and Pan-Protestantism: Jean-Alphonse Turretin (1671–1737) and Enlightened Orthodoxy at the Academy of Geneva.* Selinsgrove, PA: Susquehanna University Press.

Laplanche, F. 1965. *Orthodoxie et prédication: l'oeuvre d'Amyraut et la querelle de la grâce universelle.* Paris: Presses Universitaires de France.

Müller, E. F. Karl. 1903. *Die Bekenntnisschriften der reformierten Kirche. In authentischen Texten mit geschichtlicher Einleitung und Register.* Leipzig: Deichert.

Muller, R. A. 2003a. *After Calvin: Studies in the Development of a Theological Tradition.* New York: Oxford University Press.

Muller, R. A. 2008. "Arminius and the Reformed Tradition." *Westminster Theological Journal* 70: 19–48.

Muller, R. A. 2012. *Calvin and the Reformed Tradition: On the Work of Christ and the Order of Salvation.* Grand Rapids, MI: Baker.

Muller, R. A. 2003b. *Prolegomena to Theology.* Vol. 1 of *Post-Reformation Reformed Dogmatics: The Rise and Development of Reformed Orthodoxy, ca. 1520 to ca. 1725.* Grand Rapids, MI: Baker.

Muller, R. A. 2011. "Reception and Response: Referencing and Understanding Calvin in Post-Reformation Calvinism." In *Calvin and His Influence, 1509–2009,* edited by Irena Backus and Philip Benedict, 182–201. Proceedings of the Calvin Congress, Geneva, May, 2009. New York: Oxford University Press.

Pederson, R. 2014. *Unity and Diversity: English Puritans and the Puritan Reformation, 1603–1689.* Leiden: Brill.

Pitassi, M. C. 1992. *De l'Orthodoxie aux Lumières: Genève 1670–1737.* Geneva: Labor et Fides.

Schaff, P. 1931. *The Creeds of Christendom: With a History and Critical Notes.* 3 vols. 6th ed. New York: Harper & Brothers.

Stam, F. P. van. 1988. *The Controversy over the Theology of Saumur, 1635–1650.* Amsterdam: APA-Holland University Press.

Trueman, C. R. 2007. *John Owen: Reformed Catholic, Renaissance Man.* Aldershot, UK: Ashgate Publishing.

Trueman, C. R., and R. S. Clark, eds. 1999. *Protestant Scholasticism: Essays in Reassessment.* Carlisle: Paternoster Press.

Woolsey, A. A. 2012. *Unity and Continuity in Covenantal Thought: A Study in the Reformed Tradition to the Westminster Assembly.* Grand Rapids, MI: Reformation Heritage.

CHAPTER 12

# SCRIPTURE AND EXEGESIS IN EARLY MODERN REFORMED THEOLOGY

CARL R. TRUEMAN

## 1 INTRODUCTION

UNTIL recently, Reformed orthodoxy from the period circa 1580 to 1700 has been neglected by scholars interested in the development of biblical studies or treated as an era of increasingly rigid dogmatism that slowly but surely stifled careful biblical exegesis (Reid 1962; Rogers and McKim 1979; Rolston 1972). This was in large part due to the belief that the era represented a certain dogmatic ossification of the original biblical and kerygmatic impulse of the Reformation, which led to rather wooden approaches both to the phenomenon of scripture and its interpretation (Bizer 1963). More recent scholarship, however, has placed the biblical work of seventeenth-century Reformed theologians within a wider intellectual context and has highlighted the sophistication of numerous aspects of their approach to the biblical text and its exegesis (Muller 2003a; Knapp 2002).

The basic impulse behind early modern Protestant thinking about scripture was the importance of the Word, particularly the Word read and the Word preached, within the Protestant churches. The doctrine of justification by grace through faith, and the concomitant shift away from the sacraments to the Word as the primary means of the mediation of God's presence to the congregation was of fundamental importance to Protestant pedagogy and academic priorities.

Reformed Protestantism was thus marked by a basic commitment to the authority, sufficiency, and perspicuity of scripture not only as a central part of its polemic against the Roman Catholic Church but also as essential to its understanding of the nature of the pastoral task and the Christian life.

In the early phases of the Reformation, these principles were to a large extent assumed rather than explicitly stated, or developed within the specific context of polemical challenges from Rome. By the beginning of the seventeenth century, however, the Reformed churches were moving toward a more formal development of a doctrine of scripture, in part driven by the retrenchment of the Roman Catholic Church at Trent and the significant anti-Protestant polemical work of Robert Bellarmine (1542–1621) (Bellarmine 1581–93), but more importantly by the need for positive doctrinal statements in the context of the establishment and consolidation of Reformed Protestantism.

Nevertheless, during the seventeenth century a series of intellectual developments and theological challenges continued to press the Reformed toward greater refinement, both of their doctrine of scripture and understanding of exegesis, while also calling into question whether a commitment to traditional theological formulations regarding the unity of scripture and possibility of connecting traditional doctrine to scripture, was possible. Ultimately, the tension between theological formulation, biblical exegesis, and textual criticism proved to be an unstable mix that led to the rapid decline of the classic Reformed doctrine of scripture in mainstream intellectual life in subsequent generations. While the early Reformers had had an easily identifiable polemical target and set of challenges in the Roman Catholic Church, by the end of the seventeenth century, text critics, Arminians, Socinians, and others had joined the polemical fray to place the traditional formulations of Reformed orthodoxy under intense pressure.

## 2  The Importance of Scripture in Reformed Orthodoxy

Magisterial Protestantism established the centrality of the Word early on in its development. The Word, written and then preached, was the primary means by which God revealed himself to the church, and thus the Word occupied a central place in Protestant practice. For the Reformed, this manifests itself in the central importance given to preaching in the tradition, as evidenced by the prophesyings in Zurich and London, the development of academies such as those at Geneva, which were focused on the training of men to handle the Word of God in the pulpit, and the production of handbooks and pastoral manuals that placed Word-based ministry, primarily preaching but also catechizing, at the center of the minister's tasks (Collinson 1967; Maag 1995; Manetsch 2013).

In addition, the Reformed regarded scripture as having supreme normative authority for both faith and practice, a point evident from early on in the Zurich Reformation (Stephens 1985). This was perhaps most clearly evident in the nature of their worship, which was typically very simple in terms of aesthetics when compared to that of Lutherans or Anglicans. The origins of this lie in the radical simplification of worship in Zurich at the hands of Zwingli (1484–1531) and then, perhaps more significantly, in the controversies over vestments and kneeling at Communion that were triggered by John Hooper (ca. 1495–1555) and John Knox (ca. 1514–1572) in the English Reformation, and which continued to characterize debates about the Book of Common Prayer in England under Elizabeth, and then in England and Scotland under the House of Stuart (Trueman 1994; Collinson 1967; Coffey 1997). Articulations of the role of scripture in regulating worship became increasingly sophisticated in the seventeenth century, culminating in the works of George Gillespie (1613–1648) and John Owen (1616–1683) (Gillespie 1637; Owen 1662).

Additionally, the Reformed in the seventeenth century came to regard scripture as normative for ecclesiology; therefore, in the debates that took place at the Westminster Assembly, the nature of church organization and of congregational discipline, particularly the location of the power of the keys, became important matters of debate. Furthermore, in England and Scotland, the claim of the Crown to authority within the courts of the church provoked violent reactions, both literary and ultimately military, within the ranks of the Reformed (Gillespie 1637; Paul 1985; Van Dixhoorn 2012).

# 3 THE DOCTRINE OF SCRIPTURE IN REFORMED ORTHODOXY

The radical scripture principle which developed in Reformed practice was, of course, rooted in a developing Reformed theology. By the seventeenth century, the majority of Reformed theologians identified scripture as the principle of knowing in the task of theology (Muller 2003a). This is exemplified in the placement of scripture as the locus of chapter 1 of the Westminster Confession of Faith (1647). While the argument has been made that this represents a hardening of an earlier Reformation position and the transformation of scripture into a logical axiom from which doctrine can simply be deduced, the location of the doctrine was actually determined by attention to the order of knowing. In the Westminster Catechisms, for example by way of contrast, the ordering of topics is shaped more by pastoral and pedagogical concerns.

Given the epistemological function of scripture in Protestantism from its earliest stages, the development of scripture as the principle of knowing was to be expected, especially as Roman Catholic controversialists, from John Eck (1486–1543) and Thomas More (1478–1535) onward, applied polemical pressure at precisely this point. This identification of scripture as the cognitive foundation of theology itself also pressed the Reformed toward increasing elaboration of the relationship between the doctrine of scripture and the doctrine of God, given that God was identified as the principle of being, or the ultimate ontic source, of scripture as revelation. This is significant in a number of ways—both because it led to an increasingly theological understanding of the nature of inscripturation, and also because it made explicit the connection between the text of scripture and the divine attributes.

It should be noted, however, that the development of the doctrine of scripture and the various refinements that came with it did not displace the importance in Reformed practice of the spoken word as the basis for faith. The Westminster Larger Catechism, Question 155, for example, notes that it is "especially the preaching of the Word" that is a means of grace. Thus an increased reflection upon the text of scripture should not be seen as necessarily eclipsing the original concerns of the Reformation, but rather as providing those concerns with an appropriately scholarly basis in the developing pedagogical and polemical climate of the seventeenth century.

## 3.1 Scripture: Inspiration, perspicuity, sufficiency

While the Reformers (along with earlier theologians) tended to assume the inspiration of scripture, the seventeenth century witnessed increasing reflection upon the manner of inspiration. The Reformed orthodox regarded inspiration to extend to both the content and the form of scripture, thus involving a concept of verbal inspiration (Muller 2003a, 243–44). The causal means by which this inspiration took place was the work of the Holy Spirit, who inspired the minds of the biblical authors and also kept the texts pure throughout the ages by his providential protection (Westminster Confession 1:8; Turretin 1679–85, II.x). Given the Reformed orthodox commitment to a strong notion of God's providence, the inscripturation of the Word at the hands of ordinary human beings was not necessarily a mechanical exercise, but could be regarded as something conducted according to the secondary causality that characterized human action in the eyes of the Reformed (Trueman 1998, 71–73).

As to belief in the divine origin and nature of the scriptures, the Reformed orthodox did give a place to external proofs of their inspiration—such as the exalted nature of the subject matter, the absence of errors, the overall effect of the scriptures on the reader. Such proofs could be helpful, but ultimately it was the internal testimony of the Spirit that convinced the individual of scripture's truth and inspiration (Turretin 1679–85, II.vi.11).

While the inspiration of scripture was a point of contact between the Reformed orthodox and the broader Catholic tradition, their views of scripture as sufficient and perspicuous were developed in large part in the context of polemics against the Roman church. The most famous early exposition of perspicuity was that offered by Martin Luther (1483–1546) in his response to Erasmus (1466–1536), *De Servo Arbitrio* (1525). Luther distinguished two kinds of perspicuity: external and internal. External perspicuity referred to the public aspects of interpretation: the idea that anyone with a knowledge of the vocabulary, grammar, and syntax used could find the meaning of the biblical text. Internal perspicuity referred to the faith aspect: this was not so much the meaning of the text, as the reception of the text by the individual in faith. Therefore, by external perspicuity everyone could know that Christ died; only by the action of the Spirit could they know (believe) that Christ died for them.

Seventeenth-century Reformed orthodoxy continued to emphasize both the external perspicuity of scripture and the need for the Spirit's action in true understanding and belief. Indeed, as Calvin (1509–64) had stressed the internal testimony of the Holy Spirit as necessary to recognize scripture as God's Word, so this note continued into the era of later orthodoxy (Turretin 1679–85, II.vi.13; Muller 2003a, 128). Of course, the Reformed orthodox did not regard every single passage of scripture as perspicuous, nor did they see it as precluding the need for translation of the Hebrew and Greek into the vernacular. They saw it rather as indicating that the fundamental teachings of scripture were in themselves clear. This was a somewhat tricky position to maintain, especially given the diversity of views that different groups saw the Bible as teaching, and led to the development of formal lists of "fundamental articles"—lists of doctrines that were clearly taught in scripture and had to be believed for salvation (Turretin 1679–85, I.xiv).

The doctrine of scripture's sufficiency also connected directly to the polemical context because of the way in which it opposed the notion of the necessity and authority of extra-scriptural traditions. Like perspicuity, the doctrine needs to be understood in a nuanced way and not as meaning that nothing but the biblical text was necessary in any general sense. The Reformed orthodox used the commentary tradition, both Christian and Jewish, and played a significant part in the development of linguistic and lexicographical tools. The doctrine related specifically to the regulative, normative authority of scripture as being unique in the formulation of theological statements and the regulation of the church's life.

Perspicuity and sufficiency were closely connected: there was an underlying assumption that scripture was sufficiently clear in its basic teachings that a canon of agreed interpretation was both possible and indeed readily accessible; a canon by which the notion of scripture interpreting scripture (as opposed to the magisterium of the Church interpreting scripture) was straightforward.

## 3.2 Perspicuity and sufficiency under polemical pressure

The retrenchment of Catholicism in the latter half of the sixteenth century and the rise of the Jesuits as the intellectual force of the Catholic Reformation both raised the level of sophistication of Catholic–Protestant polemics and also led to significant engagement on the doctrine and role of scripture. Whitaker's (1548–95) response to Catholic attacks on the doctrine were just the start of an ongoing polemical war (Whitaker 1594). Key to Roman Catholic claims were, of course, denials of perspicuity and sufficiency since such denials opened space for the role of the church's magisterium in interpretation.

The challenges to the Protestant doctrinal notion of scripture were not simply external. There is a certain irony in the fact that the doctrine of inspiration arose directly out of a passionate commitment to an identification of the scriptural text as the Word of God, and the authority of this Word in matters of faith and practice. Such a conviction inevitably fueled textual studies, as Protestants sought to grapple with the biblical text in the original languages. The problem then became that these textual studies themselves raised significant challenges for the Reformed orthodox doctrine that had helped to motivate them.

Perhaps most significant among these were the great polyglot Bibles. Brian Walton (1600–61) produced one such in 1657 and it rapidly aroused the ire of the Reformed orthodox. The polyglot Bibles were controversial because they highlighted the textual variants that existed, and thus raised in an acute form the thorny issue of determining what the exact form of the divinely inspired text might actually be. They also offered attempts at textual history, which in turn put further pressure on notions of sufficiency and perspicuity.

In response to this, the Reformed developed the argument that the original texts had been perfect, while minor imperfections had entered into the manuscripts as they were copied and transmitted down through the ages. For example, Owen argued that autographs were indeed perfect but these had been lost; and the subsequent scribes and copyists were not infallible, hence leading them to make minor errors in transcription (Owen 1850–55, 16:353–55).

The differences between the original autographs and the existent *apographa* did not cause significant distress to the minds of the Reformed orthodox. They did not regard the existence of variant readings within the manuscript tradition as fatal to the authority of scripture. Such errors as were there did not affect the content of the teaching of scripture, and therefore there was a sense in which the Reformed orthodox were quite happy to ascribe infallibility to the later manuscripts, subject to minor flaws as they were (Turretin 1679–85, II.x).

Where polyglot Bibles and the linguistic and textual studies they represented posed a more significant challenge to the traditional Protestant understanding of scripture was in the matter of its sufficiency and perspicuity. In engaging with Brian Walton, John Owen was particularly perturbed by the argument that the Masoretic vowel points of the Hebrew text were not part of the original but were a later innovation. This matter was also of concern to others, such as Francis Turretin (1623–87), and formed part of the polemics of the Helvetic Formula Consensus (Owen 1850–55, 16:345–421; Turretin 1679–85, II.xi.11–13; Muller 2003a, 92–94).

It is important to grasp that the debate over the vowel points was not simply driven by a desire to maintain full verbal inspiration. In earlier Reformed theology, the matter of the antiquity of the vowel points was an issue of comparative indifference (Muller 2003a, 406–7). By mid-seventeenth century, however, the cost of conceding the comparative novelty of the vowel points had implications for scriptural perspicuity (was scripture clear without the points?) and hence also for scriptural sufficiency (did the scriptural text need editorial additions in order to be comprehensible?). Thus it became increasingly clear that the matter struck at the heart of the Protestant scripture principle and explains the shift in thinking on the matter.

The issue of the vowel points also indicates that the seventeenth century witnessed a rise in the understanding both of the historical nature of the scriptures and the languages in which they were written. A key figure in this regard is Louis Cappel (1585–1658) of the school of Saumur. Cappel's own work had in fact triggered the contentious redating of the Masoretic vowel points and further research on the Old Testament had led him to conclude that the final text had undergone significant editing over time (Cappel 1624,

1650). Cappel's work had its Catholic counterparts in those of Jean Morin (1591–1659) and Richard Simon (1638–1712) and represents a more general trend of seventeenth-century biblical scholarship (Morin 1660; Simon 1678). Its significance for Reformed orthodoxy is that Cappel was working within the tradition and yet doing so in a manner that ultimately undermined confidence in sufficiency and perspicuity.

It was not, however, simply text critical issues that placed pressure on the Reformed orthodox doctrine of scripture. If the questions of the vowel points and the rising knowledge of textual variants posed challenges to perspicuity, the problem of Protestant diversity, which had always raised obvious questions relative to how straightforward scriptural authority really was, intensified in the seventeenth century.

Protestant diversity and institutional fragmentation had been a problem for Protestants trying to maintain scriptural perspicuity from early in the Reformation, as epitomized in the debate between the Lutherans and the Reformed over the meaning of "This is my body." With the rise of Anabaptist and then Baptist groups in the late sixteenth and early seventeenth centuries, the problem merely intensified. Nevertheless, the development in the late sixteenth century of Arminianism and then Socinianism brought the problem to a head. Unlike earlier radical groups that often eschewed the authority of scripture for a more loosely understood leading of the Spirit, these groups adhered to the Protestant understanding of scripture. And of these two groups, the Socinians proved in the long run to be the more radical and lethal foe.

While the Reformers had generally been prepared to operate with a hermeneutic of trust regarding the basic parameters of the Catholic creedal tradition, the advent of Socinianism represented a much more critical approach to the tradition, and one that was rooted in a radical scripture principle. Socinianism was itself a diverse movement. Some of its advocates might be regarded as representing early adumbrations of rational-ism, who read scripture through the bounds of possibility dictated by human reason. Others, such as the Englishman John Biddle (1615–62), are better characterized as bib-licists, eschewing metaphysics and speculative theology for a simple, plain reading of the scriptural text. Thus Biddle's catechetical productions involved questions and then simple, blunt biblical quotations by way of answer. In addition, at the dogmatic heart of Socinianism lay its repudiation of the doctrines of the Trinity and Incarnation and its rejection of the notion of any form of penal substitutionary atonement (McLachlan 1951; Lim 2012; Mortimer 2010).

The problems Socinianism generated for Reformed orthodoxy were manifold, but on the subject of scripture, the issues can be reduced basically to one: the challenge of a radical biblicism allied to a repudiation of traditional metaphysical categories, which thereby used the scripture principle to support a theology that was so hereti-cal, and thereby the increased pressure on the ideas of perspicuity and sufficiency. It was one thing to debate with Lutherans about the meaning of "This is my body" when large portions of the faith remained a matter of Protestant consensus; it was quite another when the scripture principle was used to demolish the Trinity and the Incarnation (Trueman 1998; Lim 2012).

Responses to Socinianism tended not to focus on the scripture principle in and of itself, but on matters of exegesis. Thus, in his massive refutation of Socinian theology, *Vindiciae Evangelicae*, John Owen found little to disagree with in the bare scripture principle underlying the Racovian Catechism and the work of John Biddle, though he did insinuate that they honored the Protestant principle only insofar as to provide cover for their perverted interpretations. Ultimately, however, the debate with Socinianism highlighted the role of certain basic commitments in approaching the biblical text. The Reformed orthodox assumed the legitimacy of basic metaphysical principles, and this was positively connected to their understanding of the "good and necessary consequences" of the biblical text. Hence, Owen attacked Biddle through a combination of biblical exegesis connected to the use of a standard theological and metaphysical vocabulary and framework, which Biddle himself would have repudiated as an alien imposition upon the biblical text. The repudiation of such metaphysics by the Socinians, and the various reconstructions of metaphysics at the hands of early Enlightenment philosophers such as Descartes (1596–1650), Hobbes (1588–1679), Locke (1632–1704), Leibniz (1646–1716), and Spinoza (1632–77) was to prove a serious and in many cases devastating challenge to the established conclusions of Reformed orthodox exegesis.

This last comment points towards another aspect of the development of theology and exegesis in the seventeenth century, which was to place Reformed orthodoxy under strain and indeed become formalized in subsequent years in a way that cemented a fundamental breach between biblical studies and theology. As text criticism developed, this produced textual challenges. These challenges led not only to gradual separation of biblical studies from dogmatics, as the interests and purposes of the two disciplines parted ways, but also, ironically, to the development of higher criticism. So much of doctrinal formulation needs to be understood historically as a speculative engagement of the received tradition of doctrinal teaching to the biblical text. Once the legitimacy of that engagement is denied, as in Socinianism, or the tools of that engagement are denied, as in the various Enlightenment philosophies that displaced their premodern counterparts, then the demands of the biblical text and the demands of the confessional theologian tended to move in independent directions. Ironically, this did not so much originate historically in a conscious determination to overthrow orthodoxy as in the context of tensions generated by the dual textual and doctrinal concerns of orthodoxy.

# 4  The Interpretation of Scripture

## 4.1  Scripture and devotion

Despite the fact that the Reformed orthodox developed their understanding of scripture in an increasingly sophisticated and complicated environment often shaped by the exigencies of polemical engagement, the primary function of scripture for the Reformed remained that of regulating Christian life and practice. In this context, it is not surprising that they regarded devotion as fundamental to scriptural interpretation. This connected to the notion that the perspicuity of scripture was not reducible simply to its external textual properties. To understand scripture truly, one needed not simply to understand its objective meaning, one also needed to believe it in a saving sense for oneself. In addition, the status of human beings as fallen and thus having minds darkened by sin, required that the Holy Spirit was necessary for true interpretation in the fullest sense of the word; hence the Reformed also emphasized the need for prayer and devotion as prerequisites for correct exegesis, both in terms of private Bible study, and preaching and indeed listening to preaching. Therefore for John Owen, prayer was a key element in approaching the biblical text (Trueman 1997). The same point is also made in handbooks instructing pastors on how to prepare for preaching (Perkins 1607).

## 4.2  Sources of exegesis

Beyond the matter of personal devotion, the Reformed orthodox also understood that scripture required interpretation and that some things necessary were not evident merely from the direct teaching of scripture, but could be derived hence only by careful and learned study. Thus the training of ministers in technical matters, such as linguistics, was important. In addition, such study also involved a careful interaction with the broader exegetical tradition.

Scholarly mythology once assumed that seventeenth century theology was built on a rather crude system of proof-texting, whereby texts were seized in isolation and used to prove doctrinal positions that had already been assumed. More recent scholarship, however, has highlighted that the seventeenth century saw a dramatic rise in the technical sophistication of the tools underlying biblical exegesis. In fact, the manner in which proof texts functioned in the seventeenth century is evidence of precisely this kind of connection with the exegetical tradition. Many confessional statements included proof texts as a means of supporting their doctrinal claims, and on the surface this phenomenon might appear to reflect a fragmentary approach to scripture and a dogmatically driven approach to doctrinal formulation.

It is very clear, for example, that the Westminster Assembly did not see the inclusion of such texts in confessional documents as essential, given the fact that it was parliament, not the divines, who required their insertion. Further, they were not actually intended to function as isolated, unanswerable proofs for doctrinal positions. Rather, they were intended to guide the thoughtful reader to consider the exegetical tradition of the passage. This, in turn, would make clear the connection between the biblical verse being cited and the doctrinal claim being made. Thus the minister preparing a sermon might note the proof texts provided in the Confession for a specific doctrinal point and then take from his shelves the most significant commentaries on the passage cited. Through reading these, he would come to an appreciation of how the Westminster divines connected scripture to doctrinal formulation with reference to exegetical traditions (Muller 2003a, 437–38, 512–13).

Indeed, far from a high view of the supreme authority of scripture leading to an isolation of scripture from tradition, this approach of providing proof texts actually served to connect the two. In fact, the Reformed orthodox approach to scripture was careful to combine both the commentary tradition and the new linguistic and textual developments.

A significant part of the background to the technical underpinnings of this is the wider context of university education. One point of obvious importance is the continuity of specific material factors. Library holdings in medieval universities continued into the early modern period and thus provided a natural core of available resources. Further, continuities in university pedagogy, such as the scholastic disputation, ensured that the Reformed were well versed in the deployment of traditional authorities, including exegetical authorities (Fraenkel 1961; Muller 2003b). Thus the Reformed were trained to approach the biblical text in a manner that involved the use of traditional sources and was also connected to prior traditions of exegesis. Certainly, Protestantism in general assumed that preachers would engage extensively with the commentary tradition on given passages as they prepared sermons (Kneidel 2011). This is reflected in many of the standard manuals on theology. In his 1662 *A Systeme or Body of Divinity*, lay theologian Edward Leigh (1602–71) provides an extensive list of historical commentaries on each of the canonical books, as does Thomas Barlow (ca. 1608–91) in his posthumously published theological syllabus (Barlow 1699).

From the late fifteenth century onward, many patristic and medieval commentaries were republished and readily available. Bernard of Clairvaux (1090–1153) was popular, as was John Chrysostom (ca. 349–407), particularly because of the latter's attention to the literal sense of scripture. The commentaries of Thomas Aquinas (1225–74) also enjoyed something of a renaissance. Thomas had been somewhat eclipsed in the later Middle Ages by the intellectual influence of the Franciscans, but his commentaries proved popular during the early modern period. In large part, this was the result of the fact that he was a significant figure in the increasing emphasis placed upon the foundational normativity of the literal sense from the twelfth century onward. His sober exegetical judgments thus resonated with a later generation of Reformed Protestants who wished to avoid the speculative excesses of allegory (Stump 1993; Muller 2003a).

The importance of the wider exegetical tradition to the Reformed is also evident in the popularity of published compendia of exegetical authorities. A. N. S Lane has demonstrated that John Calvin was in part dependent upon a number of these, and this became an established part of the Reformed approach to scriptural exegesis (Lane 1999). For example, Matthew Poole (1624–79) produced a popular compendium that covered the entire canon (Poole 1669–76), and Matthew Henry (1662–1714) also produced a commentary on the whole Bible, which was replete with such references. In addition, the Reformed also consulted widely among contemporary commentators. Thus we find Reformed authors citing Jesuits such as Cornelius a Lapide (1567–1637) and even Conrad Vorstius (1569–1622) as worth consulting on particular exegetical issues (Trueman 2011).

If the commentary tradition was important to early modern Reformed exegesis, the Reformed also benefited from the increasing technical sophistication of the linguistic tools available. As noted above, the doctrine of perspicuity increasingly became a focus for Catholic polemics in the late sixteenth and seventeenth centuries, as in the work of Robert Bellarmine and the response of William Whitaker (Bellarmine 1581–93; Whitaker 1588). This further fueled the already established interest in the original biblical languages, and also in the traditions of Jewish commentary on the books of the Old Testament.

The importance of linguistic studies is evident in the careers of the great Hebraists of the early modern period. The converted Jew, Immanuel Tremellius (1510–80), held the chair of Hebrew at Cambridge under Edward VI, and helped to establish the fundamental importance of linguistics to the university's curriculum (Austin, 2007). In the seventeenth century, this tradition reach its peak with men such as Johannes Buxtorf (1564–1629) in the Netherlands and John Lightfoot (1602–75) and Brian Walton in England (Burnett 1996; Muller 2003a, 131). It is interesting to note in this context that the main rationale for developing Hebrew as a university subject was the access it gave to the Bible in the original. While Greek was seen to have an intrinsic beauty, the consensus was that Hebrew was not a language that possessed rhetorical beauty (Feingold 1997, 449).

The study of Hebrew appears to have permeated the educated culture of Protestant church circles. John Donne (1572–1631), for example, was well-versed in the language (Goodblatt 2003). Among Reformed leaders, extensive competence in the language, as a basis for competence in handling scripture, was assumed. Even a comparatively minor member of the Westminster Assembly, Lazarus Seaman (n.d.–1675), did his daily devotions from an unpointed Hebrew Bible. To this can be added the production of extensive linguistic annotations to the Bible, such as those by Diodati (1576–1649), the Westminster Annotations, and those on the text of the Dutch *Statenvertaling*. These demonstrate the linguistic sensitivity of the authors and the desire of Reformed Biblical scholars to bring out the subtle nuances of the original texts. To these general works, we can add also more specialist monographs from the era, such as those by the controversial member of the Westminster Assembly, Thomas Gataker (1574–1654): *De nomine tetragrammato dissertatio* (1645); *De diphthongis* (1646); and *De novi instrumenti stylo dissertatio* (1648).

## 4.3  Basic themes in exegeting scripture

The Reformed orthodox built on the increasing focus on the literal meaning of the text, which was a trend in the West from the twelfth century onward. Fearing the kind of interpretative plasticity that allegorization, formalized in the medieval *quadriga*, seemed to bring in its wake, the Reformers and their successors had emphasized that scripture had one literal sense. The problem with this as baldly stated, of course, is that the Reformed were aware that scripture often seems to have more than one sense: prophecy, for example, may have an immediate reference to events close in time to the utterance and yet also, in the context of the canon as a whole, refer to events much later, such as the coming of Christ. For this reason, the Reformed often understood the single sense of scripture as having a composite sense that allows not only for strict grammatical exegesis but also for the discernment of types and figures within the text (Muller 2003a, 472–77).

Foundational to Reformed exegesis was the belief that the biblical canon pointed in a fundamental way toward the Lord Jesus Christ. Christ was both the foundation of the church, the one with whom Christians were united, and also the culmination of the revelation of God toward humanity. For the Reformed, however, Christology could not be considered in the abstract: the person and work of Christ were determined by location within a broader biblical and doctrinal structure, and this pointed to the notion of covenant, a key element of much Reformed orthodoxy.

Covenant as a significant organizing principle for scripture emerged first of all in the Reformation at the hands of Ulrich Zwingli, as he developed a rationale for infant baptism in the face of Anabaptist challenges. Other significant sixteenth-century contributions also were made by William Tyndale (ca, 1495–1536), Heinrich Bullinger (1504–75), and Robert Rollock (ca. 1555–99). By the end of the sixteenth century, Reformed theology had identified two principle covenants as shaping the history of salvation: that of works, and that of grace.

During the seventeenth century, covenant theology underwent significant development, partly in a manner that impacted the understanding of the nature of biblical history. Covenant became not simply a principle for theological organization, but also a key to understanding the development of theology within the biblical canon itself. Important in this context is the work of Johannes Cocceius (1603–69), who argued that the Bible presented the story of the people of God in terms of a series of successive historic covenants. While Cocceius' approach was opposed by Gisbertus Voetius (1589–1676), in large part because of its ethical implications regarding the Sabbath, his basic insight became influential in Reformed approaches to understanding the overall shape of the Bible, and in the work of men such as Herman Witsius (1636–1708) and John Owen, helped to form an exegetical-doctrinal synthesis. What the notion did was to provide both a doctrinal context for understanding Christ as mediator and also a historical structure for understanding the flow of biblical history relative to God's salvific purposes. It was thus crucial to the connection between exegesis and doctrinal formulation (Cocceius 1648; Owen 1661; Witsius 1694; Van Asselt 2001).

## 5 Exegesis and Systematic Formulation

While exegesis was foundational to Reformed theology, that theology itself was often finely tooled and expressed in language and categories that seem somewhat distant from the biblical text. The path from exegesis to doctrinal formulation was often a subtle and complex one, but it was also one in which the biblical text and underlying linguistic studies played a significant and normative role. In addition, prior traditional doctrinal formulations created the theological context within which the move from exegesis to doctrinal formulation took place. Further, it was assumed—to borrow a phrase from the Westminster Confession—that doctrinal conclusions could be drawn based on good and necessary consequences drawn from the text. Thus, collation and comparison of biblical texts, linguistic studies, attention to the commentary tradition, dialogue with prior doctrinal conclusions, and the use of logic within the context provided by such, were all part of the move from biblical text to doctrinal statement.

Historically, doctrinal formulation has always been vulnerable to criticism for imposing an alien grid upon scripture and for the intrusion of inappropriate philosophical categories. While there is always a danger of these things, this need not necessarily be the case. One good example is the covenant of redemption (Latin: *pactum salutis*), a doctrinal term that emerged in the mid-1640s to describe the relationship between the Father and Son in eternity, relative to the appointment of the Son as mediator of the covenant of grace. The basic concept of an arrangement between Father and Son had been part of Reformed theology since the Reformation; only in the mid-seventeenth century did the concept become formalized under the terminology of the covenant of redemption.

The dogmatic concern that underlay the development was the polemical assault by Roman Catholic theologians on the Reformed insistence that Christ was mediator according to both natures. This required reflection upon the eternal foundation of the historical economy of the Incarnation. Theologically, Reformed were required to tease out the implications of connecting dogmatic lines established by Nicene Trinitarianism and Chalcedonian Christology with their Augustinian soteriology. Exegetically, they used the biblical concept of covenant to articulate the Father–Son relationship in a way that avoided subordinationism by emphasizing the voluntary nature of Christ's humiliation.

On the surface, the covenant of redemption looks like a speculative theological construct. Nevertheless, it received significant exegetical justification at the hands of the Reformed; most notably, Patrick Gillespie (1617–75). The word-concept distinction is important here: theologians such as Gillespie developed a highly nuanced understanding of the way in which covenant terminology was used both in scripture and in the ancient world, and then they used the term as a means of referring to a concept that they found in scripture as a result of exegesis (Trueman 2010).

# 6  THE END OF REFORMED ORTHODOXY

The collapse of Reformed orthodoxy in the late seventeenth and eighteenth centuries took various forms. In England, its fate was intimately connected to national politics. So closely identified were the major architects of English Reformed orthodoxy to the Puritan cause (Owen, Baxter, Goodwin, Charnock, Watson; among others) that the Restoration of 1660 was inevitably going to involve the eclipse of their influence. The Clarendon Code, culminating in the Act of Uniformity of 1662, forced them out of both the established church and also the universities. Thus, their immediate ecclesiastical successors, without access to the kind of library holdings and education upon which Reformed orthodoxy depended, rapidly descended into Unitarianism. This transition is even evident in the later work of a man such as Richard Baxter (1615–91), whose eclectic thought seems to have moved in a direction that undergirded a basic irenicism with assumptions having certain affinities with the anti-metaphysical stance of a man like Hobbes.

At Oxford and Cambridge, the study of doctrinal theology was eclipsed both by the way in which the empiricist philosophies of Hobbes and Locke demolished the traditional metaphysical assumptions of Christian orthodoxy, and by the rise of biblical studies that were effectively divorced from the concerns of traditional Reformed dogmatics. Thomas Barlow, Owen's tutor, whose convictions involved both Reformed orthodoxy and militant conformism, was a theological anachronism at his own institution even before his death. In fact, only among the Baptists do we find traditional Reformed orthodox exegesis of any significant note, in the work of the brilliant but somewhat anachronistic figure of John Gill (1697–1771) (who received his D.D. from Aberdeen because neither Oxford nor Cambridge could grant a degree to a nonconformist).

On the Continent, the thought of Descartes, Spinoza, and Leibniz played a parallel role to that of the tradition of Hobbes and Locke in England, in destroying the standard philosophical assumptions that helped shape the move from exegesis to doctrinal formulation in Reformed orthodoxy (Israel 2001). The Genevan Academy is a case in point: there the transition from Francis Turretin to his son, Jean-Alphonse Turretin (1671–1737), also involved the transition to a more concessionary and accommodating approach to scripture. If the Helvetic Formula Consensus marked the high point of public stridency against Amyraldianism and the rejection of the antiquity of the Masoretic vowel points, it was followed by a rapid change of temper within Geneva (Klauber 1994).

Thus, by the start of the eighteenth century, with the exception of men like Gill, Reformed orthodoxy, as epitomized in its approach to scripture, was effectively finished as a mainstream academic interest. The metaphysical underpinnings of its approach, indebted as they were to pre-Enlightenment paradigms, had been demolished. Its defense of the theological and textual integrity of the Bible had been rejected, partly as a result of the linguistic and historical studies it had itself done so much to promote. Lastly, its internal stresses had taken a heavy toll, as the demands of biblical studies had moved decisively away from those of doctrinal and confessional formulation.

## Bibliography

Asselt, Willem J. van. 2001. *The Federal Theology of Johannes Cocceius*. Translated by Raymond A. Blacketer. Leiden: Brill.

Austin, Kenneth. 2007. *From Judaism to Calvinism: The Life and Writings of Immanuel Tremellius, ca. 1510–1580*. Aldershot, UK: Ashgate.

Barlow, Thomas. 1699. *Autoschediasmata, de studio theologiae: or, Directions for the Choice of Books in the Study of Divinity*. Oxford.

Bellarmine, Robert. 1581–1593. *Disputationes de controversiis christianae fidei adversus sui temporis haereticos.* 4 vols. Rome.

Bizer, Ernst. 1963. *Frühorthodoxie und Rationalismus.* Zurich: EVZ.

Burnett, Stephen G. 1996. *From Christian Hebraism to Jewish Studies: Johannes Buxtorf (1564–1629) and Hebrew Learning in the Seventeenth Century.* Leiden: Brill.

Cappel, Louis. 1624. *Arcanum punctuationis revelatum, sive de punctorum vocalium et accentum apud Hebraeos vera et germanae antiquitate, libri duo.* Leiden.

Cappel, Louis. 1650. *Critica sacra, sive de variis quae in sacris veteri Testamenti libris occurrunt lectionibus, libri sex.* Paris.

Cocceius, Johannes. 1648. *Summa doctrinae de foedere et testamento.* Amsterdam.

Coffey, John. 1997. *Politics, Religion and the British Revolutions: The Mind of Samuel Rutherford.* Cambridge: Cambridge University Press.

Collinson, Patrick. 1967. *The Elizabethan Puritan Movement.* Berkeley: University of California Press.

Feingold, Mordechai. 1997. "Oriental Studies." In *The History of the University of Oxford IV: The Seventeenth Century,* edited by Nicholas Tyacke, 449–503. Oxford: Oxford University Press.

Fraenkel, Peter. 1961. *Testimonia Patrum: The Function of the Patristic Argument in the Theology of Philip Melanchthon.* Geneva: Droz.

Gillespie, George. 1637. *A Dispute Against the English-Popish Ceremonies, Obtruded upon the Church of Scotland.* Leiden.

Goodblatt, Chanita. 2003. "From 'Tav' to the Cross: John Donne's Protestant Exegesis and Polemics." In *John Donne and the Protestant Reformation: New Perspectives,* edited by Mary A. Papazian, 221–246. Detroit: Wayne State University Press.

Israel, Jonathan I. 2001. *Radical Enlightenment: Philosophy and the Making of Modernity, 1650–1750.* Oxford: Oxford University Press.

Klauber, Martin I. 1994. *Between Reformed Scholasticism and Pan-Protestantism: Jean-Alphonse Turretin (1671–1737) and Enlightened Orthodoxy at the Academy of Geneva.* Selinsgrove: Susquehanna University Press.

Knapp, Henry M. 2002. "Understanding the Mind of God: John Owen and Seventeenth-Century Exegetical Methodology." Ph.D. dissertation. Calvin Theological Seminary.

Kneidel, Greg. 2011. "*Ars Praedicandi*: Theories and Practice." In *The Oxford Handbook of the Early Modern Sermon,* edited by Peter McCullough, Hugh Adlington, and Emma Rhatigan, 3–20. Oxford: Oxford University Press.

Lane, A. N. S. 1999. *John Calvin: Student of the Church Fathers.* Edinburgh: T&T Clark.

Lim, Paul C-H. 2012. *Mystery Unveiled: The Crisis of the Trinity in Early Modern England.* New York: Oxford University Press.

Maag, Karin. 1995. *Seminary or University? The Genevan Academy and Reformed Higher Education, 1560–1620.* Aldershot, UK: Scholar Press.

McLachlan, H. J. 1951. *Socinianism in Seventeenth Century England.* Oxford: Oxford University Press.

Manetsch, Scott. 2013. *Calvin's Company of Pastors: Pastoral Care and the Emerging Reformed Church, 1536–1609.* New York: Oxford University Press.

Morin, Jean. 1660. *Exercitationes biblicae de hebraeici graecique textus sinceritate.* Paris.

Mortimer, Sarah. 2010. *Reason and Religion in the English Revolution: The Challenge of Socinianism.* Cambridge: Cambridge University Press.

Muller, Richard A. 2003a. *Post-Reformation Reformed Dogmatics: Holy Scripture, the Cognitive Ground of Theology.* Grand Rapids, MI: Baker.

Muller, Richard A. 2003b. *Post-Reformation Reformed Dogmatics: Prolegomena to Theology.* Grand Rapids, MI: Baker.

Owen, John. 1662. *A Discourse Concerning Liturgies, and Their Imposition.* London.

Owen, John. 1661. *Theologoumena Pantodapa.* Oxford.

Owen, John. 1850–1855. *The Works of John Owen.* 24 vols. London: Johnstone and Hunter.

Paul, Robert S. 1985. *The Assembly of the Lord: Politics and Religion in the Westminster Assembly and the "Grand Debate."* Edinburgh: T&T Clark.

Perkins, William. 1607. *The Arte of Prophecying.* London.

Poole, Matthew. 1669–1676. *Synopsis criticorum aliorumque S. Scripturae interpretum.* 5 vols. London.

Reid, J. K. S. 1962. *The Authority of Scripture: A Study of Reformation and Post-Reformation Understanding of the Bible.* London: Methuen.

Roger, Jack B., and McKim, Donald B. 1979. *The Authority and Interpretation of the Bible: An Historical Approach.* San Francisco: Harper and Row.

Rolston, Holmes III. 1972. *John Calvin versus the Westminster Confession.* Richmond, VA: John Knox.

Simon, Richard. 1678. *Histoire critique du Vieux Testament.* Paris.

Stephens, W. P. 1985. *The Theology of Huldrych Zwingli.* Oxford: Clarendon Press.

Stump, Eleonore. 1993. "Biblical Commentary and Philosophy." In *The Cambridge Companion to Aquinas,* edited by Norman Kretzmann and Eleonore Stump, 252–268. Cambridge: Cambridge University Press.

Trueman, Carl R. 1998. *The Claims of Truth: John Owen's Trinitarian Theology.* Carlisle, UK: Paternoster.

Trueman, Carl R. 1997. "Faith Seeking Understanding: Some Neglected Aspects of John Owen's Understanding of Scriptural Interpretation." In *Interpreting the Bible,* edited by A. N. S. Lane, 147–162. Leicester, UK: Apollos.

Trueman, Carl R. 2010. "The Harvest of Reformation Mythology? Patrick Gillespie and the Covenant of Redemption." In *Scholasticism Reformed: Essays in Honour of Willem J. van Asselt,* edited by Maarten Wisse, Marcel Sarot and Willemien Otten, 196–214. Leiden: Brill.

Trueman, Carl R. 1994. *Luther's Legacy: Salvation and English Reformers, 1525–1556.* Oxford: Clarendon Press.

Trueman, Carl R. 2011. "Preachers and Medieval and Renaissance Commentary." In *The Oxford Handbook of the Early Modern Sermon,* edited by Peter McCullough, Hugh Adlington, and Emma Rhatigan, 54–71. Oxford: Oxford University Press.

Turretin, Francis. 1679–1685. *Institutio theologiae elencticae.* Geneva.

Van Dixhoorn, Chad B. 2012. *The Minutes and Papers of the Westminster Assembly, 1643–1652.* 3 vols. Oxford: Oxford University Press.

Whitaker, William. 1594. *Aduersus Thomae Stapletoni Anglopapistae in Academia Louaniensi Theologiae Professoris Regij Defensionem Ecclesiasticae authoritatis, quam ipse luculentam & accuratam inscripsit, tribusque libris digessit, duplicatio, pro authoritate atque autopistia S. Scripturae.* Cambridge.

Whitaker, William. 1588. *Disputatio de sacra scriptura.* Cambridge.

Witsius, Herman. 1694. *De oeconomia foederum Dei cum hominibus libri quattuor.* Utrecht.

## CHAPTER 13

...............................................................................................

# GOD, CREATION, AND PROVIDENCE IN POST-REFORMATION REFORMED THEOLOGY

...............................................................................................

### ANDREAS J. BECK

## 1 DIVERSITY AND STRUCTURE

...............................................................................................

THE doctrines of God, creation, and providence are important and fascinating *loci* in early modern Reformed theology. These *loci* reflect a rich tradition of patristic and medieval thought and also express interesting developments in the wake of the European Reformations. However, they have received comparably little attention in scholarship yet. Research that is based on an historically informed analysis of primary sources is the result of a renewed interest in Reformed orthodoxy since the end of the twentieth century. Groundbreaking is the work of Muller (2003b, vols. 3–4; see also Muller 2010), who has written the most detailed overview on the doctrine of God in early modern Reformed theology; other instructive overviews have been provided by Rehnman (2013) and Te Velde (2013; see also Te Velde 2012). Important insights into seventeenth-century debates concerning both the doctrines of God and providence can be found in monographs written by Goudriaan (2006) and Bac (2010). Noteworthy in this regard are also the studies on Jacob Arminius (1556–1609) by Muller (1991), Dekker (1993, 1996), Den Boer (2010), and Stanglin and McCall (2012). Moreover, work has been done specifically on Lucas Trelcatius, Jr. (1573–1607) by Muller (2008); on Gisbertus Voetius (1589–1676) by Beck (2001; 2007; 2010b); on Johannes Cocceius (1603–69) by Van Asselt (2001); on Richard Baxter (1615–91) by Burton (2012); on John Owen (1616–83) by Trueman (1998); on Francis Turretin (1623–87) by Meijering (1991), Vos (1999), and Rehnman (2002); on Petrus van Mastricht (1630–1706) by Neele (2009); on Melchior Leydecker (1642–1721) by Hoek (2013); and on Johann Friedrich Stapfer (1708–75) by Lehner (2007). Finally, the annotated edition and translation of the Leiden *Synopsis Purioris Theologiae* (1625) by Te Velde et al. (2014) facilitates further research on the doctrines of God, providence, and creation.

These investigations have unveiled a considerable diversity of detail that underlies the apparent uniformity resulting from the common use of the scholastic method. Although the Reformed orthodox systems were meant to fit within confessional borders—borders that in themselves showed some variety of different regions and times—they did not form a monolithic bloc. This insight, combined with the insight that important Reformers such as Martin Bucer (1491–1551), Wolfgang Musculus (1497–1563), Peter Martin Vermigli (1499–1562), and John Calvin (1509–64) themselves differed in many respects, renders the so-called "Calvin against the Calvinists" debate largely obsolete (Muller 2011). This diversity of the Reformed tradition does not, of course, exclude a great deal of common ground, much of which is rooted in patristic and medieval traditions. Indeed, the doctrines of God, creation, and providence in early modern Reformed theology can be looked at as interesting and highly developed expressions of classical theology at the dawn of the Enlightenment.

These three doctrines are interrelated. The doctrine of God is about the triune God and his eternal, *immanent* acts or works, which can be directed both to God himself (*ad intra*) or to what is outside of Him (*ad extra*). The doctrines of creation and providence concern *external* acts or works of the triune God that are directed *ad extra* (Wollebius 1935, 14–15; Voetius 1648, 403). The divine works *ad extra*, and thus creation and providence are free and contingent, whereas those immanent acts that are directed *ad intra*, such as "knowing himself," are necessary. Moreover, not only creation and providence are contingent, but also immanent acts like "knowing creatures." Following a medieval tradition, Reformed theologians such as Voetius distinguished between two dimensions in the doctrine of God: a necessary *ad intra* dimension and a free and contingent *ad extra* dimension (Beck 2001, 220–22; Muller 2010; cf. Vos et al. 1994; Ingham and Dreyer 2004, 93–99).

In this structure of theology, the doctrine of God is of vital importance, as God is seen as the ontic or essential foundation of theology, the *principium essendi*. The noetic or cognitive foundation, the *principium cognoscendi*, is scripture, not reason (Muller 2003b, 3:431–45). Indeed, the theological epistemology of the Reformed scholastics stood in line with the medieval tradition of *fides quaerens intellectum*. They neither attempted to build a rationalistic system (*pace* Weber 1937–51; Bizer 1963) nor did they single out the decree of eternal predestination as the central dogma from which such a system could be deduced (*pace* Schweizer 1854–56). Moreover, they arguably understood the doctrine of God as being Christian and Trinitarian as a whole, rather than basing a specific Trinitarian part on a general philosophical part (Muller 2003b, 3:152–59); a somewhat similar case can be made for Aquinas's doctrine of God (Emery 2007, 39–50).

The basic structure of the doctrine of God usually followed the classical rhetorical scheme "whether" (*an sit*), "what" (*quid sit*), and "who" God is (*quis sit Deus*), although some authors preferred the interrogative "*qualis*" (what sort) for the third question. Following this scheme, they typically discussed first the existence of God, moving second to his names, essence, and attributes, and third to the Trinitarian persons. Finally, they would conclude the doctrine of God with a discussion of the divine decrees, being immanent acts *ad extra*. Some authors modified this pattern, though. Thus Trelcatius, Jr. related the discussion of the divine nature, especially the names and the doctrine of the Trinity, to the question *quid sit* and reserved the question *quis sit* for the essential attributes of God. However, it is true for most if not all Reformed orthodox theologians that the triune God is envisaged from the very beginning, even if they discussed the attributes or properties common to the three persons before the specific properties of these persons. Moreover, the doctrine of the divine decrees presupposed the doctrine of the Trinity (Muller 2003b, 3:152–59; Muller 2010, 322–27; Te Velde 2013, 744–47; Beck 2001, 211–14). We follow this pattern in our discussion of the Reformed doctrine of God before we move to the doctrines of creation and providence. Since the Dutch Republic of the seventeenth century was the major center of Reformed theology, we will pay special attention to Dutch theologians such as the authors of the Leiden *Synopsis*: Voetius, Leydecker, and Mastricht.

## 2 The Triune God: Existence, Names, and Attributes

In answering the question "whether God is," the Reformed orthodox theologians discussed arguments for the existence of God. Philipp Melanchthon (1497–1560) and his pupil Zacharias Ursinus (1534–83) have been especially influential in this regard (Platt 1982, 10–33, 49–60). These arguments or "proofs" primarily functioned as an apologetic device against skepticism and "atheism" rather than pretending to build a philosophical foundation of the doctrine of God. This function only slowly changed in the mid-eighteenth century, especially for followers of Christian Wolff (1679–1754), like Daniel Wyttenbach (1706–79) and Stapfer (Muller 2003b, 3:193–95). Until then, the Reformed typically emphasized that the believer does not need any proof of God and that such proofs have no soteriological relevance (Voetius 1648, 167; Turretin 1679, 175–76). Moreover, Voetius even claimed that there were no "direct speculative atheists" who could convince themselves permanently of God's nonexistence without suppressing their conscience. He supported this claim by distinguishing an innate or implanted natural theology or knowledge of God (*theologia naturalis innata seu insita*) from an acquired natural theology (*theologia naturalis acquisita*). By virtue of the innate knowledge, the human mind can understand that the proposition "God exists" is self-evidently true, given that God is an infinitely perfect being. In that sense, the human mind as such is not neutral or a *tabula rasa*. This concept of innate knowledge has been indirectly inherited from Melanchthon and is akin to Calvin's *sensus divinitatis* or *semen religionis* (Beck 2010a; Baum, Cunitz, and Reuss 1864, 36, 38–39). To be sure, this innate knowledge should not be confused with Cartesian innate ideas, which Voetius heavily disputed. Neither could the finite human mind conceive an adequate idea of God; nor was, according to Voetius, Descartes's ontological argument in the fifth mediation any more than a case of *petitio principii*. It was precisely over against Descartes as well as the Remonstrants, Socinians, and northern-Italian Renaissance Aristotelians that Voetius maintained the innate knowledge. The acquired knowledge, though, was largely without controversy according to Voetius (1648, 140–66; 1669, 455–62; Beck 2007, 159–74). Acquired natural theology was based on the sense experience of God's creation and typically related to theistic arguments such as the five ways of Aquinas, although the Reformed orthodox referred even more often to rhetorical arguments in the sense of a posteriori testimonies. As Turretin emphasized, the orthodox "uniformly teach" that there is both an innate and acquired natural theology (1679, 6–7).

When moving to the question "what God" is, the Reformed scholastics typically dealt with the problem of predication and the difficulty of human discourse about God (see Muller 2003b, 3:195–216; Beck 2007, 209–23; Rehnman 2013, 354–66). This problem of language concerning God was extensively debated during the Middle Ages, especially after the Fourth Lateran Council (1215) had decreed that "between Creator and creature no similitude can be expressed without implying an even greater dissimilitude" (Denzinger and Hünermann, no. 806). The Reformed used to refer to the principle *finitum non capax infiniti* and insisted that no proper definition of "God" can be given. To quote Leydecker, who referred to Voetius: "God cannot be properly defined, inasmuch as He is infinite; meanwhile we describe him, according to our little measure, as a Being living by himself and subsisting in Three Persons, Father, Son and Holy Spirit" (Leydecker 1689, 48; Voetius 1648, 473–74). We see again that the Reformed had the Trinitarian God in mind throughout the *locus de Deo*. The problem of predication also entailed that "no concept of a finite mind can adequately represent God" (Voetius 1669, 27). But how then is any meaningful discourse about God possible? First, the Reformed orthodox emphasized that only God has full and original theological knowledge, that is, archetypal knowledge; whereas creatures can have merely derived, ectypal knowledge, which is based on divine revelation (Van Asselt 2002). Second, most Reformed defined this ectypal knowledge as analogical knowledge. Terms have neither a totally different nor equivocal meaning when applied to both God and creatures; nor do they have precisely the same or univocal meaning, at least not in the sense of a generic term implying a common reality. Instead, they have an analogous meaning: they denote both a difference, due to the absence of proportion between the infinite and finite, and a similarity that still renders divine discourse meaningful (Zanchi 1577, 19–21; Muller 2003b, vol. 3; Rehnman 2013, 361–65). With some caution, this solution could be called "Thomistic," although the Reformed orthodox were not interested in identifying themselves with one of the medieval schools. Moreover, some Reformed allowed only for an equivocal predication of the term "being" to God and creatures (Maresius 1649, 21). Others, such as Voetius and Baxter, arguably did not altogether deny a "univocal core" in analogical predication, albeit in a limited sense (Beck 2007, 218–23; Burton 2012, 211–13, but cf. Muller 2012, 141–43). Interestingly, this limited sense might resemble Duns Scotus's reduced concept of univocity, referring to that unity of signification that suffices to exclude contradiction. This unity only concerned an incomplete concept that posits no reality as such, and never can constitute a common genus that would include both the infinite God and finite creatures (Dumont 1998, 299–322; Vos 2006, 285–88).

While coming to the core of the question "what God" is, the Reformed orthodox usually did not start with the doctrine of the divine attributes, but first discussed the biblical names of God in detail. This emphasis on the divine names, with attention to their etymological derivation and meaning in the original languages, has often been overlooked (e.g., by Heppe 1935), although it shows a clear continuity with the Reformation (Muller 2003b, 3:246–70; Te Velde 2013, 114–24). Special attention was given to the tetragrammaton YHWH. Thus the influential Leiden *Synopsis* was aware of the problems of the traditional notation as "Jehovah." After discussing Exodus 3:14 ("God said to Moses: 'I am who I am'"), both in the Hebrew Bible and the Septuagint, and with attention to Revelation 1:4, the *Synopsis* gave this definition: "For the meaning of the name is that He exists truly and in eternity (so that it is a name for his very essence), and that He grants to every thing its essence. And in particular, its meaning is that He makes his promises to come about, and He reveals Himself as faithful and true by fulfilling them" (Te Velde et al. 2014, 159). This interpretation of the primary divine name largely resembles that of Calvin (Baum et al. 1882, 43–44). Moreover, the foundation of the concept of divine essence in Exodus 3:14 follows an important patristic and medieval tradition. The Reformed orthodox were divided on the question of whether the plural form, *Elohim*, indicated the plurality of persons in God. Voetius reported that Zanchi, Amandus Polanus von Polansdorf (1561–1610), and Heinrich Alting (1583–1644) had answered affirmatively, whereas Johannes Drusius (1550–1616) and Franciscus Gomarus (1563–1641) gave a negative answer. Voetius himself thought that the plural form as such referred to a *pluralis majestatis*, but that the context of Genesis 1:26 could be understood in terms of a plurality of persons (1669, 57).

In their discussions of the divine attributes, also called essential properties or perfections, the Reformed scholastics agreed that it made sense to classify them. They disagreed, however, on the preferred patterns of classification, although they did not necessarily consider them as being mutually exclusive. The well-known division into communicable and incommunicable attributes only became dominant in the course of the seventeenth century—a division that the Lutherans could not accept due to their doctrine of the presence of Christ according to his human nature in the Lord's Supper by virtue of a *communicatio idiomatum*. Polanus and Alting preferred to distinguish, along with many Lutherans, between negative and positive attributes (Polanus 1610, 880; Alting 1656, 14–16). Voetius added, as a third category, relative attributes, corresponding to the three Pseudo-Dionysian "ways"—the *via negationis, eminentiae* and *causalitatis* (1669, 60–61; Beck 2007, 246–47). Perhaps the most popular division among the Reformed scholastics was that between a first- and second-class genus or order of attributes. Especially in the Netherlands, the first class was often associated with nonoperative attributes of the divine essence, and the second class with operative attributes related to the divine life, including intellect and will; sometimes also power (Te Velde et al. 2014, 168–71; Voetius 1648, 584; Leydecker 1689, 62). Despite the different classifications, most of them roughly boil down to a division between attributes that are primarily related to God in himself, without respect to the creation, and those that are primarily related to his creation.

Not all Reformed orthodox dealt with the same number of divine attributes, using the same labels, but most of them included at least simplicity, infinity, immutability, and perfection in their discussion of the attributes belonging to the first class. Simplicity indicated, in the words of the Leiden *Synopsis*, "that the divine essence is altogether without any composition, whether that composition be from material and integral parts, or from the essential parts of matter and form, from genus and difference, subject and accident, act and potency, and finally, essence and existence" (Te Velde et al. 2014, 165). This also implies God's unity, singularity, and incorporeality, which in turn entails his spirituality (Polanus 1610, 141–42; Voetius 1648, 172). Referring to John 4:24, Mastricht argued that God is properly designated as "Spirit" rather than "thought," the latter of which was preferred by Cartesianizing theologians (1699, 99–100; Te Velde, 2013, 147).

While the Reformed doctrine of simplicity excluded all composition from the divine essence, it did not exclude all distinctions. Thus, they understood simplicity to be compatible with the patristic doctrine of the Trinity, albeit not with tritheism (Muller 2003b, 3:276, 279–84). When it came to the divine attributes, all Reformed orthodox argued that they were distinguished both from the divine essence and from each other "according to our conception." They differed, however, about the nature and basis of these conceptual distinctions. Following terminology of Thomists and Jesuits, most authors argued that these distinctions were not purely logical or based on human reason (*ratio ratiocinans*), but rather by reason of analysis (*ratio ratiocinata*) with a foundation in extramental reality (*fundamentum in re*). This foundation could be either related to the intrinsic form of the attributes in God (*formaliter*), to their ground for effects (*eminenter*), or to their power (*virtualiter*). All authors rejected a "real" distinction (*realiter*) that would have implied a separability of one thing from another, which had been advocated by the Socinians in order to deny the divinity of Christ (Muller 2003b, 3:284–98; Te Velde 2013, 131–34). Many of them also excluded the Scotistic *distinctio formalis*, but Voetius argued that the *distinctio rationis ratiocinatae* should be understood in such a way that it "almost coincides with Scotus's so-called formal *ex natura rei* distinction." Indeed, Voetius emphasized, as Turretin did later, that the attributes can be predicated of each other "in an identical sense," but not "in a formal sense," since they are distinguished according to their formal characteristics (1669, 59–60; Turretin 1679, 169; Beck 2007, 236–48).

Related to divine simplicity is infinity, meaning that "the divine essence is altogether free from any ending or boundary" and that "nothing is equal to or on a par with God" (Te Velde et al. 2014, 167). God's essence and perfections are without limitations. Infinity with respect to time entails eternity, and with respect to space immensity or omnipresence. Voetius and some of his pupils related God's immensity and eternity not only to actual spaces and times, but also to imaginary ones, accounting for the possibility for God to have created other worlds, which implies his presence in alternative spaces and times (Beck 2007, 255–60; Bac 2010, 398–99; Te Velde 2013, 164–65). Concerning omnipresence, the Reformed orthodox maintained, on the one hand, against Conradus Vorstius (1569–1622) and the Socinians, that God was *essentialiter* omnipresent and not just through his power; and on the other hand, against the Lutherans, that divine omnipresence could not be shared by the body of Christ (Muller 2003b, 3:338–42). The next negative attribute is immutability, which "entirely excludes alteration and change" and "indicates that the essence of God stays the same" (Te Velde et al. 2014, 167). The Reformed orthodox did not understand this divine constancy to imply unrelatedness or necessitarianism; although God is not dependent on his creation, he relates to it in a genuine sense and contingently acts in time and space (Muller 2003b, 3:308–20). All these attributes pointed to the perfection of God as the best possible Being (*summum bonum*).

The attributes of the first class are not in conflict with those of the second class, but rather are regulative for them. The life of God (*vita Dei*) signifies that his essence is "full of activity in itself, that is, living—and that in the most simple or essential way." As such, God is "the author and source of all life in created beings, and life-giving" (Te Velde et al. 2014, 171). Taking into account the *imago Dei* character of humans, and drawing on scholastic faculty psychology, the Reformed understood the life of God to comprise intellect, will, power, and affections or virtues such as righteousness, love, grace, and mercy. Concerning the intellectual attributes, most debates focused on divine knowledge rather than wisdom or prudence. In his detailed and influential disputations on divine knowledge, Voetius described it as being simple, archetypal, eternal, immutable, perfect and nondiscursive, infallible, pure act, and infinite (Voetius 1648, 249). He also affirmed and explained several important scholastic distinctions, including those between necessary and free knowledge (*scientia necessaria et libera*), knowledge of simple understanding and of vision (*scientia simplicis intelligentiae et visionis*), definite and indefinite knowledge (*scientia definita et indefinita*), and speculative and practical knowledge (*scientia speculative et practica*) (246–51). Although these distinctions reflect different terminology and perspectives, the distribution of the objects *ad extra* among both members is always largely the same: the first members of these distinctions refer to all possible states of affairs, and the second members to all factual states of affairs, whether past, present, or future. In case of the distinction between necessary and free knowledge, the first member also includes God's knowledge of himself. In all distinctions, the divine will forms the pivotal point: God's knowledge of possibilities is situated structurally (*ordine naturae*) *before* the divine act of will or decree, and his knowledge of actual reality *follows* the decree. This sequence is not one of time, to be sure, but of structural analysis, reminiscent of Scotus's moments of nature. The objects of knowledge structurally before the divine will are necessary—possibilities are necessarily possible—and those objects following the divine will are contingent and could be otherwise, since the necessary divine will is contingently related to contingent objects (Beck 2007, 265–77).[1]

These distinctions served not only to express the full range of God's knowledge, including that of possibilities which exceed his knowledge of factual reality; they also showed that God can have certain (fore)knowledge of future contingents; that is, nonnecessary events (*futura contingentia*). Indeed, this was the *Sitz im Leben* of these distinctions in medieval scholasticism. According to Voetius, the Reformed orthodox commonly argued that God's knowledge of *futura contingentia* was based solely on the free determination of the eternal divine will, which "lets them transfer from the condition of mere possibilities to the condition of future events" (1669, 587; quoting Twisse 1639, 394). This knowledge is certain by virtue of a necessary relation of consequence (*necessitas consequentiae*) between God's knowledge, the antecedent; and the contingent events, the consequent. However, the necessity of the consequent (*necessitas consequentis*) does not, as such, follow from this necessary relation of consequence. Only if the antecedent were necessary itself, would the consequent be necessary as well, by virtue of the necessary relation between the antecedent and consequent. Yet this is not the case, given the contingency of God's knowledge, based on the contingency of the divine act of will (Voetius 1636, 101–8; Turretin 1679, 221–22; Beck 2007, 338–39, 354–55; Bac 2010, 195–205).

The Reformed orthodox maintained this solution to the problem of God's (fore) knowledge of *futura contingentia* not only against the Socinians, who denied such divine knowledge altogether, but also against the Jesuit concept of middle knowledge (*scientia media*), which was introduced by Luis de Molina (1535–1600) and Petro da Fonseca (1528–99) and adopted, not only by François Suárez (1548–1617) and most other Jesuits, but also by Arminius and the Remonstrants (Molina 1988; Muller 1991, 143–66; Dekker 1996). Perhaps the most detailed Reformed responses to this new concept were written by William Twisse (ca. 1577–1646) and Voetius. The Jesuits taught that God had a third kind of knowledge next to necessary or natural knowledge of all possibilities, and free knowledge of factual reality. By this middle knowledge God knows *before* his act of will what free possible creatures would do if they were placed in specific circumstances. Based on middle knowledge and the knowledge of which circumstances God decides to create, God knows with certainty what free creatures will do. Virtually all Reformed orthodox theologians rejected this solution because it made God dependent on his finite creatures. Moreover, they considered middle knowledge to be superfluous because necessary and free knowledge already covered all knowable objects. According to Voetius, God indeed knows what free creatures would do in certain circumstances, but this knowledge presupposes the divine decree and thus in the end amounts to a variation of free knowledge. Otherwise, this knowledge would be necessary, evoking Stoic fate that eliminates divine and human freedom alike. For the Reformed orthodox, contingent reality was rooted in the divine will rather than in knowledge. In this they followed the Augustinian-Franciscan tradition, together with most Dominicans and Franciscans of their age (Voetius 1648, 264–339; Twisse 1639; Beck 2007, 264–322, 435–39; Bac 2010, 71–210).

In the interplay between God's knowledge and will, the divine will, which wills freely and contingently, plays the pivotal role. To be sure, the Reformed orthodox insisted that in itself the divine will is necessary, and also in relation to God himself, who necessarily affirms himself (*voluntas necessaria*). It is also necessary *that* God decrees something in relation to each possible state of affairs (i.e., he does or does not actualize it).

But in its relation *ad extra* to all states of affairs, the divine will is free and nonnecessary (*voluntas libera*). Thus Voetius explains that a sentence such as "God can will what
he does not-will" can be read in two ways. It is false if read "in the composite sense"
(*in sensu composito*): "God *can* (both will an object and not-will it)." Read that way, the
modal operator "can" governs the composition of the two conjunctive phrases between
parentheses, implying the blunt contradiction that God has both an act of will and the
opposite act. When read "in the divided sense" (*in sensu diviso*), however, the sentence
is true: "God wills an object, and he *can* not-will it." The actual act of will does not rule
out the *possibility* of the opposite act. In other words, God's act of will could be otherwise and thus is contingent in the sense of being nonnecessary (Voetius 1669, 115; Beck
2001, 215–16; Muller 2003b, 3:447–51). Turretin made roughly the same point when he
ascribed the "liberty of indifference" to the divine will (1679, 230–31).

Most Reformed orthodox carefully distinguished the divine will or decree from God's
revealed perceptive will, since it functions as the pivotal point between necessary and
free knowledge. Using traditional terminology, they called the former, the ontic one,
"the will of good pleasure" (*voluntas beneplaciti*), and the latter, the deontic one, "the
will of the sign" (*voluntas signi*). This basic distinction, going back to Hugh of St. Victor
and Peter Lombard, reflected different usages of the term "will" in the Bible when
applied to God (Muller 2003b, 3:457–59). Another important distinction is that between
the effective will (*voluntas efficax*), concerning the good, and the permissive will (*voluntas permissive*), concerning evil. In order to establish that God is not the author of
sin, the Reformed orthodox typically adopted the medieval doctrine of divine permission, according to which God suspended an impediment to sin rather than causing it
(Maccovius 1650, 205–12; Muller 2003b, 3:471–72; Bac 2010, 461–67; Beck 2011, 126–28).
Related to God's will is his righteousness. The Reformed differed in their answer to the
Euthyphro dilemma: "Is something right because God wills it, or does God will something because it is right?" Voetius gave an influential answer by distinguishing between
God's necessary and free right (*ius*). God's right is necessary in the sense that he cannot command anything that conflicts with his nature; in that sense he is bound by the
essential righteousness. Still, God is free to command this or that thing as long as it is
not in conflict with his necessary right. Thus God wills whatever corresponds with his
necessary right (which is structurally prior to his will) because it is right, while whatever
corresponds with his free right (which structurally follows God's will) is right because
he wills it. Voetius clearly attempted to balance his view between necessitarianism and
extreme voluntarism (Voetius 1669, 94–98; Beck 2007, 360–74).

Whereas the divine intellect and will are immanent faculties, whether directed *ad
intra* (necessary knowledge and will) or *ad extra* (free knowledge and will), the divine
potency or power (*potentia*) is an emanating faculty. It is "the attribute whereby the living, knowing, and willing God through his strength and potency has the power to perform deeds that are external to Him" (Te Velde et al. 2014, 174–77). In contrast to Calvin,
most Reformed orthodox endorsed the medieval distinction between an absolute and
ordinate potency (*potentia absoluta et ordinata*). The absolute potency is God's potency
"when treated simply by itself and separate from the will" (176–77); or, in the words of

Leydecker, it is "about all those things that can be seen as possibles in the thesaurus of God, the best possible and most beautiful Being." Against nominalistic speculations, and referring to Calvin's rejection of these speculations, Leydecker maintained that the *potentia absoluta* did not refer to that which could contradict the divine perfections. The ordinate or actual potency of God "is about those things that God has decreed to be future," meaning all factual states of affairs (Leydecker 1689, 74–75; Beck 2001, 128–32). Thus again, the first member of the distinction, absolute power, precedes the divine decree; while the second member, ordinate power, follows it in a way that is analogous to the distinctions between necessary and free knowledge and rightness. Consequently, Mastricht and others explicitly rejected the Cartesian thesis that possibilities are dependent on the divine will (Mastricht 1699, 149–50). What is possible for God to know, will, and actualize, is situated structurally before his free decree. What he knows as being factual and what he actualizes is contingent since it structurally follows his free decree.

# 3 THE TRIUNE GOD: PERSONS

When approaching the question "who" (*quis*) or "what sort" (*qualis*) God is, most Reformed orthodox shifted their focus from the essential attributes common to the three hypostases or persons, to the notional or personal attributes that belong specifically to one hypostasis, and furthermore to the three persons as such. Yet their discussions of the essential attributes were repeatedly reminiscent of the divine persons. They made efforts, for instance, to show that the doctrine of simplicity is compatible with the doctrine of the Trinity by allowing for a strong conceptual or modal distinction of the persons from the divine essence, and for a modal or even (minor) real distinction between the persons (Voetius 1648, 242–44; Turretin 1679, 200, 394–98). They basically adopted the patristic doctrine of the Trinity of the Cappadocian Fathers and the Ecumenical Councils, which was contested in the early modern period by the increasingly influential Socinians or anti-Trinitarians (Muller 2003b, vol. 4; Mulsow and Rohls, 2005). In contrast with the Remonstrants, whom they suspected to have sympathies with the Socinians, the Reformed orthodox considered the doctrine of the Trinity to be a fundamental article of faith, the use of which was essential for all Christians (Voetius 1648, 466–87; Mastricht 1699, 242, 244; Turretin 1679, 277–80). Voetius summarized the core of this doctrine in three main points. First, the Father, Son, and Holy Spirit are three truly (*revera*) distinct hypostases in their names and operations as well as in their mutual relationships. Second, these three hypostases are each true God—creator, preserver, and savior—and thus worthy of equal veneration. Third, there is an order of subsistence and operations among them: the Father is of none, the Son is only from the Father by generation, while the Holy Spirit goes out from the Father and the Son by procession (Voetius 1648, 467–68; Beck 2007, 227–32).

There are three issues that are especially characteristic of the Reformed orthodox discussions of the doctrine of the Trinity. First, many orthodox echoed in the seventeenth century Calvin's strong emphasis on the aseity of the Son. Thus Trelcatius Jr. argued against Arminius that the Son does not have his essence by generation. Maccovius (1588–1644) made the same point while further refining Calvin's teaching: the Son is *autotheos* with respect to his essence (*ratione essentiae*), but not with respect to his mode of subsisting as a hypostatic person (*ratione modi subsistendi*). Voetius edited and annotated some interesting lectures of Gomarus on this question (Muller 2003b, 4:324–32; Maccovius 1656, 52; 1650, 249–52; Bell 2011; Voetius 1648, 442–66). The second issue concerns the remarkable openness of some Reformed to the Eastern Orthodox position on the *filioque* clause. While maintaining the Western position that the Spirit proceeds from both the Father and the Son, the Leiden *Synopsis* and Cocceius showed clear sympathy for the Eastern argumentation and tried to mediate between the Western and Eastern concerns (Te Velde et al. 2014, 236–39; Cocceius 1665, 178–86; Van Asselt 2001, 180–84). In the third place, most Reformed scholastics were reluctant to speculate about the "mystery of the Trinity." With some notable exceptions, such as Polanus and Barthlomäus Keckermann (ca. 1571–1608), they rather decided to pursue "learned ignorance" when it came to the medieval teachings on the processions of the Son through the intellect and of the Holy Spirit through the will. This is also true for Voetius, although he defended the position of Duns Scotus against its condemnation by other scholastics (Muller 2003b, 4:376–78; Voetius 1669, 140–47; Beck 2007, 321–32).

The Reformed orthodox did not only deal with the internal distinguishing marks of the Trinitarian persons, but also with their outward marks, the "oecumenical offices of the three persons," as Mastricht labeled them (Mastricht 1699, 238–40; Neele 2009, 245–78). These outward marks concern works that are appropriated to specific persons, like creation preeminently to the Father, redemption to the incarnate Son, and sanctification to the Holy Spirit (Te Velde et al. 2014, 192–93). This was not meant to deny that ultimately all Trinitarian persons participate in these works, in accordance with the rule that the externally directed works of the Trinity are undivided (*opera trinitatis ad extra indivisa sunt*) (Mastricht 1699, 239). To be sure, this rule applies to immanent acts that are directed *ad extra*, like the divine decrees or decisions, just as to the external divine works *ad extra*, like creation and providence.

# 4 CREATION

For the Reformed orthodox, creation and providence were free and contingent divine works, in accordance with God's free and contingent decree. Hence God did not create "by necessity of his nature" (*necessitate naturae*); he could have created no world, a different world, or more worlds, as Voetius maintained against Aristotle (1669, 151; 1648, 566, quoting *De Caelo* I.9, 278a 26–28). The Leiden *Synopsis* defined creation as "an external action of the almighty God that cannot be shared with human creatures, whereby through himself and by his own most free will (and influenced by no one else), He founded the heavens and the earth out of nothing, at the beginning of the time" (Te

Velde et al. 2014, 247–48). In this creation "from nothing" (*ex nihilo*), the "nothing" was understood negatively as the "negation of all entity," and not privatively as the denial of something that ought to be there (254–55). The triune God is the efficient cause of creation, his highest goodness the impelling cause, his wisdom the directive cause and his infinite power the executive cause (248–53). However, there is no material cause, due to the production *ex nihilo,* which was also called "first creation" (*creatio prima*), referring to the creation of the heavens, elements, and light on the first day. From the resulting "indisposed plain matter" (*indisposita plane materia*), essential or accidental forms were produced, the process of which led to the works of the five other days, and was called "second creation" (Voetius 1648, 554). Most Reformed orthodox thus understood creation as a work of six days, following the *Physica Mosaica* and the Hexaemeron tradition, but they did not deny that God could have created the world in one single moment, as Augustine taught (Daneau 1576; Turretin 1679, 478–84; Goudriaan 2006, 105–13). The goal of creation, finally, was seen in "the revelation of the goodness, wisdom, and power of God; and the everlasting praise of these virtues through all creatures, especially those endowed with reason" (Te Velde et al. 2014, 257).

The Reformed rejected not only Aristotelian necessitarianism, but also Aristotle's claim for the eternity of the world. These rejections echoed the Paris condemnation of 219 errors in 1277 (Denifle and Chatelain 1889, 543–58). Thus Keckermann denied the eternity of the world not only as theological doctrine but also as philosophical possibility, ruling out so-called double truths in his debate with the Lutheran Daniel Hoffmann (Keckermann 1607, 43; Muller 2003a, 122–36; cf. Turretin 1679, 467–72). Another issue concerned substantial forms. Here, Voetius and others defended a neo-Aristotelian concept because they found it to be more compatible with the *Physica Mosaica* than early modern alternatives. The substantial forms could not only explain the classification of "kinds" in the biblical creation account, but also constituted the internal principles of activity in secondary causes. In contrast, the Cartesian mechanistic worldview with its rejection of substantial form seemed to create more difficulties than it might solve. In particular, it implied a denial of genuine secondary causality, leading either to occasionalism or Spinozistic pantheism, as Voetius noted with remarkable foresight (Van Ruler 1995; Goudriaan 2006, 113–33; Beck 2007, 65–69). The third issue concerned Copernican heliocentrism. In the Netherlands, Cartesian theologians tended to adopt Copernicanism while Voetius and his pupils were opposed to it. The dividing line was marked by different assessments of Cartesianism, rather than by astronomical research as such. According to Voetius, the alternative theory of Tycho Brahe (1546–1601) had at least as much demonstrative and explanatory force as Copernicanism, without compromising any statements of the Bible. There are no indications that the Reformed were worried about a downgrading of humanity by the removal of the earth from the center of the universe (Vermij 2002; Goudriaan 2006, 125–33; Jorink 2010, 89–91). Finally, I will only mention in passing the pre-Adamite speculations of Issac La Peyrère (1596–1676), which were opposed by virtually all Reformed orthodox theologians (Van Asselt 2010).

Of all creatures, human beings possessed the highest dignity since they were created according to the image of God (*imago Dei*). The Leiden *Synopsis* preferred a dichotomous anthropology but acknowledged that some Scriptures pointed in the direction of a trichotomous anthropology. Body and soul were related to each other like matter to form. The faculties of the soul were divided into the intellect and the will (Te Velde et al. 2014, 314–37). The Reformed orthodox maintained that free choice (*liberum arbitrium*) was an essential property of human beings, although they had different views on the precise relation between intellect and will in free choice. Human freedom, though, was not absolute since it fell under divine providence (Van Asselt et al. 2010). Arminius was ambivalent in that regard when he claimed that the divine act of creation, being based on the egress of God's goodness, entailed a self-limitation in relation to creatures and left them in relative independence from God (Muller 1994; 1991, 227–34).

# 5 PROVIDENCE

Like creation, divine providence was for the Reformed orthodox a free and contingent divine work. God not only creates, but also cares or "provides" for his creation (*providet*). Some Reformed distinguished an eternal, immanent providence from an actual providence in time (Leydecker 1689, 139). Combining both aspects, the Leiden *Synopsis* defined divine providence as "the actual and temporal preservation, direction, and guidance that God has achieved very wisely and justly, according to his eternal unchangeable and entirely free decree, of all individual things which exist and come into being, to the end that He has determined for them, and to the praise of his glory" (Te Velde et al. 2014, 263). More common than this division of actual providence into preservation, direction, and guidance was the slightly different division into conservation (*conservatio*) or *creatio continua*, concurrence (*concursus*), and government (*gubernatio*) (Leydecker 1689, 142). The most debated issue of this doctrine was the relation of divine providence to free human agency, for which the aspect of concurrence was especially important. The Leiden *Synopsis* emphasized that divine providence does not destroy but rather establishes human freedom. When concurring with his creatures, God through his working "directly influences the action of the created being, so that one and the same action is said to proceed from the first and the second cause, inasmuch as one work, or the completed work, results from this source" (Te Velde et al. 2014, 271). Evil and sins fall indirectly under divine providence in the sense that God willingly does not prevent them from happening, without thereby approving of them, in accordance with the doctrine of divine permission (*providentia permittens*). Every good is ascribed to God, and every evil to created causes (276–81).

Voetius went into some detail to explain the concurrence of first and second causes. In one of his disputations, he defined human freedom as "the faculty that can out of itself and according to a mode of acting that fits its nature, choose and not choose this or that, by virtue of the power of its internal, elective and vital command" (Beck 2010b, 149, 157). Thus, humans have *freedom of contradiction* to choose or not choose an object and *freedom of contrariety* to choose this or that object. According to Voetius, this twofold freedom requires a twofold indifference: indifference towards the object and "vital, internal and choosing indifference." Given this twofold indifference, the will has "ownership" over its own acts, which not even God can overturn (149). Moreover, it is free from coercion and "from intrinsic, absolute and natural necessity" (148). Still, the human will is governed by the divine decree and the divine "physical premotion to act," as Voetius maintained against the Jesuits and Remonstrants, who instead defended middle knowledge and an indifferent concurrence (150, 154–57). More precisely, the human will is governed by the divine decree in the sense that God determines the indifferent will to the same volition to which it determines itself. Given this determination, the indifference is removed, but only in the compounded or composite sense. Thus, it is not possible that the will wills object A and simultaneously wills object B (composite sense), but it retains its potency by which it can will object A and equally could will object B (divided sense). The involved necessity arising from the decree is only hypothetical or a necessity of the consequence, just as the necessity arising from the will's self-determination, and thus not imposing any coercion on the will or removing contingency and freedom from it (150, 160–65; Voetius 1636, 109–16).

Like the divine decree, the divine governing of the human will by physical or real premotion is compatible with human freedom as well. Voetius defined this premotion as "the applied power of God that awakens the creature that has the potency to the second act" (Beck 2010b, 151). The "second act" meant the concrete act of the will, in contrast to the structurally primary "first act," referring to the will in its own being. Against the Jesuits and Remonstrants he maintained that the applied power not only accompanies the act of the human will in the second structural moment, but also awakens the human will in the first structural moment. Hence it is not only called *concursus*, but also *precursus*. This divine premotion or predetermination is moderated wisely in accordance with the nature of a free cause and thus with its contingency. Moreover, the will is not forced, since "the predetermination turns the will sweetly and nevertheless strongly to the very end, to which it—certainly being moved and premoved by God—would have turned itself" (151, 165–67).

In sum, we can see that the careful application of the scholastic toolkit to the doctrine of God, thereby distinguishing between a necessary *ad intra* dimension and a free and contingent *ad extra* dimension, while maintaining divine simplicity, allowed the Reformed to subordinate in their systems finite creatures to the infinite Creator, and at the same time avoid a metaphysical or necessitarian version of determinism, which would rule out contingency and freedom from created reality. Voetius and other Reformed orthodox theologians alike clearly attempted to combine a surprisingly strong version of human freedom with a strong doctrine of divine providence, in which free creatures are not autonomous in relation to their Creator (Goudriaan 2006, 144–96; Beck 2007, 403–25; Bac 2010, 419–57). This was still true for Stapfer around 1750, although he resorted to the philosophy of Christian Wolff (Lehner 2007, 183–216).

## NOTE

1. This is a simplified account of contingent created reality, a reality that can be otherwise than it is, and which is subdivided by several Reformed orthodox into "necessary" states of affairs resulting from natural causes (e.g., the burning of fire) and "contingent" states of affairs resulting from contingent causes (notably decisions of human will); cf. Beck 2007, 418–19.

## BIBLIOGRAPHY

Alting, Henricus. 1656. *Methodus theologiae didacticae, perpetuis sanctae Scipturae testimoniis explicata et confirmata; addita est ejusdem methodus theologiae catecheticae.* Amsterdam.

Asselt, Willem J. van. 2010. "Adam and Eve as Latecomers: The Pre-Adamite Speculations of Isaac La Peyrère (1596–1676)." In *Out of Paradise,* 90–107. Sheffield, UK: Sheffield Phoenix Press.

Asselt, Willem J. van. 2001. *The Federal Theology of Johannes Cocceius (1603–1669).* Studies in the History of Christian Thought 100. Leiden: Brill.

Asselt, Willem J. van. 2002. "The Fundamental Meaning of Theology: Archetypal and Ectypal Theology in Seventeenth-Century Reformed Thought." *Westminster Theological Journal* 64: 319–335.

Asselt, Willem J. van, J. Martin Bac, and Roelf T. te Velde, eds. 2010. *Reformed Thought on Freedom: The Concept of Free Choice in the History of Early-Modern Reformed Theology.* Texts and Studies in Reformation & Post-Reformation Thought. Grand Rapids: Baker Academic.

Bac, J. Martin. 2010. *Perfect Will Theology: Divine Agency in Reformed Scholasticism as against Suárez, Episcopius, Descartes, and Spinoza.* Brill's Series in Church History 42. Leiden: Brill.

Baum, Guilielmus, Eduardus Cunitz, and Eduardus Reuss, eds. 1864. *Ioannis Calvini opera quae supersunt omnia.* Vol. 2. Corpus Reformatorum 30. Braunschweig: Schwetschke.

Baum, Guilielmus, Eduardus Cunitz, and Eduardus Reuss, eds. 1882. *Ioannis Calvini opera quae supersunt omnia.* Vol. 24. Corpus Reformatorum 52. Braunschweig: Schwetschke.

Beck, Andreas J. 2011. "'Expositio Reverentialis': Gisbertus Voetius's (1589–1676) Relationship with John Calvin." *Church History and Religious Culture* 91 (1/2): 121–133.

Beck, Andreas J. 2001. "Gisbertus Voetius (1589–1676): Basic Features of His Doctrine of God." In *Reformation and Scholasticism. An Ecumenical Enterprise,* edited by Willem J. van Asselt and Eef Dekker, 205–226. Texts and Studies in Reformation and Post-Reformation Thought. Grand Rapids: Baker Academic.

Beck, Andreas J. 2007. *Gisbertus Voetius (1589–1676): Sein Theologieverständnis und seine Gotteslehre.* Forschungen zur Kirchen- und Dogmengeschichte 92. Göttingen: Vandenhoeck & Ruprecht.

Beck, Andreas J. 2010a. "Melanchthonian Thought in Gisbertus Voetius' Scholastic Doctrine of God." In *Scholasticism Reformed: Essays in Honour of Willem J. van Asselt,* edited by Maarten Wisse, Marcel Sarot, and Willemien Otten, 107–126. Studies in Theology and Religion 14. Leiden: Brill.

Beck, Andreas J. 2010b. "The Will as Master of Its Own Act: A Disputation Rediscovered of Gisbertus Voetius (1589–1676) on Freedom of Will." In *Reformed Thought on Freedom: The Concept of Free Choice in the History of Early-Modern Reformed Theology,* edited by Willem

J. van Asselt, J. Martin Bac, and Roelf T. te Velde, 145–170. Texts and Studies in Reformation and Post-Reformation Thought. Grand Rapids: Baker Academic.

Bell, Michael D. 2011. "Maccovius (1588–1644) on the Son of God as Αυτοθεος." *Church History and Religious Culture* 91 (1–2): 105–119.

Bizer, Ernst. 1963. *Frühorthodoxie und Rationalismus*. Theologische Studien 71. Zürich: EVZ-Verlag.

Boer, William den. 2010. *God's Twofold Love: The Theology of Jacob Arminius (1559–1609)*. Translated by Albert Gootjes. Reformed Historical Theology 14. Göttingen: Vandenhoeck & Ruprecht.

Burton, Simon J. G. 2012. *The Hallowing of Logic: The Trinitarian Method of Richard Baxter's Methodus Theologiae*. Brill's Series in Church History 57. Leiden: Brill.

Cocceius, Johannes. 1665. *Summa theologiae ex scripturis repetita*. 2nd ed. Geneva.

Daneau, Lambert. 1576. *Physica christiana, sive, de rerum creaturum cognitione et usu*. Geneva.

Dekker, Eef. 1993. *Rijker dan Midas: Vrijheid, genade en predestinatie in de theologie van Jacobus Arminius (1559–1609)*. Zoetermeer: Boekencentrum.

Dekker, Eef. 1996. "Was Arminius a Molinist?" *Sixteenth Century Journal* 27: 337–352.

Denifle, Heinrich Seuse, and Aemilio Chatelain, eds. 1889. *Chartularium Universitatis Parisiensis*. Vol. 1. Paris: ex typis fratrum Delalain.

Denzinger, Heinrich, and Peter Hünermann. 2007. *Enchiridion symbolorum definitionum et declarationum de rebus fidei et morum = Kompendium der Glaubensbekenntnisse und kirchlichen Lehrentscheidungen: Lateinisch-Deutsch*. 41st ed. Freiburg im Breisgau: Herder.

Dumont, Stephen D. 1998. "Henry of Ghent and Duns Scotus." In *Medieval Philosophy*, edited by John Marenbon, 291–328. Routledge History of Philosophy 3. London: Routledge.

Emery, Gilles. 2007. *The Trinitarian Theology of St. Thomas Aquinas*. Translated by Francesca Aran Murphy. Oxford: Oxford University Press.

Goudriaan, Aza. 2006. *Reformed Orthodoxy and Philosophy, 1625–1750: Gisbertus Voetius, Petrus van Mastricht, and Anthonius Driessen*. Brill's Series in Church History 26. Leiden: Brill.

Heppe, Heinrich. 1935. *Die Dogmatik der evangelisch-reformierten Kirche dargestellt und aus den Quellen belegt*. Neu durchgesehen und herausgegeben von Ernst Bizer. Neukirchen: Buchandlung des Erziehungsvereins Neukirchen.

Hoek, Peter C. 2013. *Melchior Leydecker (1642–1721): Een onderzoek naar de structuur van de theologie van een gereformeerd scholasticus in het licht van zijn bronnen*. Amsterdam: VU University Press.

Ingham, Mary Beth, and Mechthild Dreyer. 2004. *The Philosophical Vision of John Duns Scotus: An Introduction*. Washington, DC: Catholic University of America Press.

Jorink, Eric. 2010. *Reading the Book of Nature in the Dutch Golden Age, 1575–1715*. Brill's Studies in Intellectual History 191. Leiden: Brill.

Keckermann, Bartholomäus. 1607. *Praecognitorum philosophicorum libri duo naturam philosophiae explicantes, et rationem eius tum docendae, tum discendae monstrantes*. Hanau.

Lehner, Ulrich L. 2007. *Kants Vorsehungskonzept auf dem Hintergrund der Deutschen Schulphilosophie und -theologie*. Brill's Studies in Intellectual History 149. Leiden: Brill.

Leydecker, Melchior. 1689. *Synopsis theologiae christianae, Libris VII: comprehensa, qua Fides Reformata accurata Synthesi exponitur, et demonstratur, Errores refutantur, solitaque Theologorum Methodus exornatur*. Utrecht.

Maccovius, Johannes. 1656. *Distinctiones et regulae theologicae ac philosophicae: Editae opera ac studio Nicolai Arnoldi*. Oxford.

Maccovius, Johannes. 1650. *Loci communes theologici, ex omnibus eius, quae extant . . . collecti, digesti, aucti.* Edited by Nicolaus Arnoldus. Franeker.

Maresius, Samuel. 1649. *Collegium theologicum, sive systema breve universae theologiae.* Groningen.

Mastricht, Petrus van. 1699. *Theoretico-practica theologia, qua, per singula capita theologica, pars exegetica, dogmatica, elenchtica & practica, perpetua successione conjugantur.* Utrecht.

Meijering, Eginhard P. 1991. *Reformierte Scholastik und patristische Theologie: Die Bedeutung des Väterbeweises in der Institutio Theologiae elencticae F. Turrettins unter besonderer Berücksichtigung der Gotteslehre und Christologie.* Bibliotheca humanistica & reformatorica 50. Nieuwkoop: De Graaf Publishers.

Molina, Luis de. 1988. *On Divine Foreknowledge (Part IV of the Concordia).* Translated with an Introduction and Notes by A. J. Freddoso. Ithaca/London: Cornell.

Muller, Richard A. 2003a. *After Calvin: Studies in the Development of a Theological Tradition.* Oxford Studies in Historical Theology. New York: Oxford University Press.

Muller, Richard A. 2003b. *Post-Reformation Reformed Dogmatics: The Rise and Development of Reformed Orthodoxy, Ca. 1520 to Ca. 1725.* 2nd ed. 4 vols. Grand Rapids: Baker Academics.

Muller, Richard A. 2010. "God as Absolute and Relative, Necessary, Free, and Contingent: The *Ad Intra-Ad Extra* Movement of Seventeenth-Century Reformed Language about God." In *Always Reformed: Essays in Honor of W. Robert Godfrey,* edited by R. Scott Clark and Joel E. Kim, 56–73. Escondido, CA: Westminster Seminary California.

Muller, Richard A. 1991. *God, Creation, and Providence in the Thought of Jacob Arminius: Sources and Directions of Scholastic Protestantism in the Era of Early Orthodoxy.* Grand Rapids: Baker.

Muller, Richard A. 1994. "God, Predestination, and the Integrity of the Created Order: A Note on Patterns in Arminius' Theology." In *Later Calvinism: International Perspectives,* edited by W. Fred Graham, 431–446. Sixteenth Century Essays and Studies. Kirksville, MO: Sixteenth Century Journal Publishers.

Muller, Richard A. 2012. "Not Scotist: Understandings of Being, Univocity, and Analogy in Early-Modern Reformed Thought." *Reformation & Renaissance Review* 14 (2): 127–150.

Muller, Richard A. 2011. "The 'Reception of Calvin' in Later Reformed Theology: Concluding Thoughts." *Church History and Religious Culture* 91 (1/2): 255–274.

Muller, Richard A. 2008. "Unity and Distinction: The Nature of God in the Theology of Lucas Trelcatius, Jr." *Reformation & Renaissance Review* 10 (3): 315–341.

Mulsow, Martin, and Jan Rohls, eds. 2005. *Socinianism and Arminianism: Antitrinitarians, Calvinists and Cultural Exchange in Seventeenth-Century Europe.* Brill's Studies in Intellectual History 134. Leiden: Brill.

Neele, Adriaan Cornelis. 2009. *Petrus van Mastricht (1630–1706): Reformed Orthodoxy, Method and Piety.* Brill's Series in Church History 35. Leiden: Brill.

Platt, John E. 1982. *Reformed Thought and Scholasticism: The Arguments for the Existence of God in Dutch Theology, 1575–1650.* Studies in the History of Christian Thought 29. Leiden: Brill.

Polanus von Polansdorf, Amandus. 1610. *Syntagma theologiae christianae, iuxta leges ordinis methodici conformatum atque in libros decem tributum.* Vol. 1. Hanau.

Rehnman, Sebastian. 2013. "The Doctrine of God in Reformed Orthodoxy." In *A Companion to Reformed Orthodoxy,* edited by Herman J. Selderhuis, 353–401. Brill's Companions to the Christian Tradition 40. Leiden: Brill.

Rehnman, Sebastian. 2002. "Theistic Metaphysics and Biblical Exegesis: Francis Turretin on the Concept of God." *Religious Studies* 38: 167–186.

Ruler, Han van. 1995. *The Crisis of Causality: Voetius and Descartes on God, Nature and Change.* Brill's Studies in Intellectual History 66. Leiden: Brill.

Schweizer, Alexander. 1854–56. *Die protestantischen Centraldogmen in ihrer Entwicklung innerhalb der reformierten Kirche.* 2 vols. Zürich: Orell, Fuessli und Comp.

Stanglin, Keith D., and Thomas H. McCall. 2012. *Jacob Arminius: Theologian of Grace.* Oxford: Oxford University Press.

Trueman, Carl R. 1998. *The Claims of Truth: John Owen's Trinitarian Theology.* Carlisle, Cumbria: Paternoster Press.

Turretin, Francis. 1679. *Institutio theologiae elencticae, in qua status controversiae perspicue exponitur, praecipua orthodoxorum argumenta proponuntur et vindicantur, et fontes solutionum aperiuntur.* Vol. 1. Geneva.

Twisse, William. 1639. *Dissertatio de scientia media tribus libris absoluta.* Arnhem.

Te Velde, Dolf. 2013. *The Doctrine of God in Reformed Orthodoxy, Karl Barth, and the Utrecht School: A Study in Method and Content.* Studies in Reformed Theology 25. Leiden: Brill.

Te Velde, Dolf. 2012. "Eloquent Silence: The Doctrine of God in the Synopsis of Purer Theology." *Church History and Religious Culture* 92 (4): 581–608.

Te Velde, Dolf, Willem J. van Asselt, Rein Ferwerda, William den Boer, and Riemer A. Faber, eds. 2014. *Synopsis purioris theologiae = Synopsis of a purer theology. Latin Text and English Translation: Volume 1, Disputations 1–23.* Translated by Riemer A. Faber. Studies in Medieval and Reformation Traditions 187. Leiden: Brill.

Vermij, Rienk. 2002. *The Calvinist Copernicans: The Reception of the New Astronomy in the Dutch Republic, 1575–1750.* History of Science and Scholarship in the Netherlands 1. Amsterdam: Koninklijke Nederlandse Akademie van Wetenschappen.

Voetius, Gisbertus. 1636. *Dissertatio epistolica de termino vitae.* Reprinted with own pagination in 1669. *Selectae disputationes.* Vol. 5. Utrecht.

Voetius, Gisbertus. 1648. *Selectae disputationes theologicae.* Vol. 1. Utrecht.

Voetius, Gisbertus. 1669. *Selectae disputationes theologicae.* Vol. 5. Utrecht.

Vos, Antonie. 1999. "Ab Uno Disce Omnes." *Bijdragen* 60: 173–204.

Vos, Antonie. 2006. *The Philosophy of John Duns Scotus.* Edinburgh: Edinburgh University Press.

Vos, Antonie, Henri Veldhuis, A. H. Looman-Graaskamp, Eef Dekker, and Nico W. den Bok, eds. 1994. *John Duns Scotus: Contingency and Freedom: Lectura I 39.* The New Synthese Historical Library 42. Dordrecht: Kluwer.

Weber, Hans Emil. 1937–1951. *Reformation, Orthodoxie und Rationalismus.* 2 parts in 3 vols. Beiträge zur Förderung christlicher Theologie. 2. Reihe 35, 45, 51. Gütersloh: Mohn.

Wollebius, Johannes. 1935. *Johannis Wollebii Christianae Theologiae Compendium.* Edited by Ernst Bizer. Neukirchen, Kreis Moers: Buchhandlung des Erziehungsvereins Neukirchen.

Zanchi, Girolamo. 1577. *De natura Dei seu De divinis attributis, libri V.* Heidelberg.

# CHAPTER 14

# CHRIST, PREDESTINATION, AND COVENANT IN POST-REFORMATION REFORMED THEOLOGY

## WILLEM J. VAN ASSELT

## 1 CHRIST: PERSON AND WORK

EARLY modern Reformed Christology rested on fundamental distinctions between the *ad intra* and *ad extra* operations of God and between archetypal and ectypal theology (as indicated in the introductory chapter), and was formulated within the boundaries set by the great ecumenical creeds. It also was framed by at least two significant contextual issues: one positive, the other polemical.

First, the underlying structure of Reformed Christology was determined by an understanding of the incarnation as *opus oeconomicum*, a free and contingent work *ad extra* of the triune God pertaining to the divine economy of salvation. Following Calvin, it was focused on Christ as the God-man or *theanthropos*, implying a specific view of the relationship between the person and the work of Christ. Johann Heinrich Heidegger (1633–98) summarized the basic Reformed position: "Christ undertook and executed this mediatorial office according to both natures; for, just as after the incarnation there are two natures in the Son of God, and two principles of action in one hypostasis; so the operations of both natures concur in the work of mediation, and the results produced by those operations are attributed to both natures" (Heidegger 1700, locus xix, 15). He specifically repudiates the views of the medieval doctors and Bellarmine. They had argued that Christ performed all his acts of mediation only as man, given that God cannot mediate with himself. The Reformed countered that the person of the mediator who is to be understood (1) as he is God, (2) as he is man, and (3) as he is the mediator or *theanthropos* or God-man, who fulfills the conditions requisite to the reconciliation of God and sinful mankind. Neither the divine nor the human nature by itself could mediate between God and man; both natures together perform the *opus theandricum*, or divine-human work. Second, the development of Reformed Christology rested on interconfessional controversies between the Lutheran and Reformed churches and on external controversies with Socinianism and Arminianism. The Reformed and Lutherans agreed on the basic Chalcedonian definition of the *unio personalis*, arguing that the eternal Son of God draws the human nature into the oneness of his person without division or separation, change or confusion of natures; the human nature being enhypostatic, having no independent subsistence apart from the *unio personalis* (Maccovius 1656, 107). The Reformed and Lutherans disagreed, however, over the *communicatio idiomatum*, namely, over how the properties, or *idiomata*, of each nature are communicated in the unity of the Person. The Reformed understood the interchange of attributes to take place *in concreto*; that is, at level of the person and not between the two natures. The Lutherans were of the opinion that the interchange took place *in abstracto*; that is, an interchange of divine and human attributes at the level of the abstract relation of the two (Muller 1985, 72–74). The exchange of the properties at the abstract level implied a communication of the divine properties to the human nature (e.g., omnipotence, ubiquity).

This debate over the *communicatio idiomatum* in Christology was reflected in the fundamental distinction between archetypal and ectypal theology. Whereas archetypal theology was explained as identical with the divine self-knowledge—the mutual knowledge of Father, Son and Holy Spirit (Heidegger 1700, locus i, 3)—ectypal theology refers, first of all, to the whole body of knowledge of God in the mind of God that can be communicated to creatures (*theologia ectypa simpliciter dicta*), and secondly, to the relational form of knowledge that is graciously communicated to creatures by God (*theologia ectypa secundum quid*) which consists in three forms: the theology of union of the Person of Jesus Christ, the theology of vision by angels and the saints in heaven, and the theology for human beings during their pilgrimage on earth (*theologia viatorum*). Both Reformed and Lutherans agreed that the theology of union in Christ is the principle of the two other forms of ectypal theology—the theology of vision, and that of revelation (Van Asselt 2002, 327–33; Preus 1970, 112–14).

They differed, however, over the theology of union (*theologia unionis*), as a consequence of their divergent interpretations of the *communicatio idiomatum*. Orthodox Lutheran theologians like Abraham Calov (1612–86) asserted that, by virtue of the exchange of properties between the two natures, the archetypal theology was in Christ and that Christ was therefore in possession of the infinite knowledge of God (*scientia visionis*) communicated to his human nature (Preus 1970, 170–72). The Reformed denied this emphatically by, first of all, arguing that the finitude of the human nature cannot grasp the infinity of God (*finitum non capax infiniti*). Christ's humanity did not get lost in his divinity. Christ was like us in all things, also in matters of knowledge, and because his human nature has certain limitations there was room for development in Christ's human nature (cf. Luke 2:52). The theology of union did not involve the communication of archetypal theology to Christ's human nature. Second, against the Lutheran doctrine of the *genus majestaticum* that indicates that the human nature of

Christ participates in the divine glory and majesty, the Reformed argued that this would imply a change in God's essence (Van Asselt 2002, 331–32).

Moreover, they argued that the logic of predication forbids the use of abstractions (divinity and humanity) as predicates of each other. As Theodore Beza (1519–1605) wrote: "By communication of attributes we do not mean the personal union or the form of this union, but the predication, as the logicians say, which is made because of the personal union of the two natures, in which an essential attribute or operation appropriate to one nature is assigned to the person, in the concrete, not in the abstract" (Beza 1577, 19–20). According to the logic of predication, a communication of properties of the two natures in and for themselves is impossible: "Concrete vocables belong to the person [God, man], abstract ones [deity, humanity] to either of the two natures. Thus I am right in saying that God is man and man is God, but not that deity is humanity or humanity is deity" (Wollebius 1626, 66).

Although the Reformed agreed that attributes such as omnipotence, eternity, infinity, ubiquity, and omniscience are properties of the divine nature, they denied that they can become the properties of the human nature. Only in this way, Leonard van Rijssen (ca. 1636–1700) argued, one was able to avoid "two basic heresies of the Early Church: the error of Nestorius, the patriarch of Constantinople, who divided the person by fashioning out of the two natures two persons; and the error of Eutyches, archimandrite of Constantinople who quite heatedly opposed Nestorius' splitting of Christ's person into two, but who himself confounded both natures into one." (Rijssen 1695, 11:13–14). Both views were condemned at the Council of Ephesus and the Council of Chalcedon, respectively.

Finally, the Lutheran doctrine of the omnipresence of the humanity of Christ was rejected by the Reformed, by making an important distinction between *tota res* and *totum rei*. According to Johannes Maccovius (1588–1644), applying this distinction to Christology, *totus Christus* or "the whole Christ" is omnipresent, but not "all of Christ" or *totum Christi* is omnipresent, for "the whole thing" denotes the person, "all of a thing" denotes one of both natures (Maccovius 1656, 191). In order to safeguard both the transcendence of Christ's divinity and the integrity of his humanity, the Reformed denied that the *Logos*, although fully united to the human nature, was totally contained within the human nature. Even in the incarnation the Logos also exists in an infinite way outside or beyond (*extra*) the assumed human nature. Called *extra-calvinisticum*, by Lutheran polemicists, this was not an invention of Calvin or later Calvinists but a Christological concept that had been argued by the church fathers, including Athanasius and Augustine (Muller 1985, 111).

When it comes to the work of Christ or his mediatorial office, Heidegger and his contemporaries laid great stress throughout on the fact that it is the God-man in both his natures who is the subject of this mediatorial office. Opposing the medieval, Socinian, and Arminian ideas of Christ's work, he asserted that the office of Christ is theanthropic. He emphatically repudiated the Socinian attack on the doctrines of the Trinity, their denial of the godhead of Christ and his satisfaction for sin, and what he viewed as a moralistic Christianity with an adoptionist Christology. Against the

Remonstrants, Heidegger argued that they too abolished the satisfaction of Christ in asserting that Christ died, in order that God the Father might have the right to contract with us anew: they separate the merits of Christ's work from its efficacy, "so that they as regards the actual reconciliation and salvation of men, leave little or nothing to Christ the Mediator": such views work "like a gangrene in the Christian religion and make Christ as Mediator a pauper, and crucify him afresh" (Heidegger 1700, locus xix, 2424). Grotius's theory that the punishment suffered by Christ was not an exact punishment according to God's law (*solutio eiusdem*) but simply an equivalent punishment (*solutio tantidem*), allowed *per acceptitationem* a hypothetical satisfaction, was also emphatically rejected by the Reformed, who argued both a formal and material identification between the punishment of the law and the punishment suffered by Christ: "He took our place in bearing punishment, not being separated or divided from us, but most closely joined with us, as brother appearing on behalf of his brother . . . Whatever he did and suffered for the sake of our salvation, we, as if one with Him, are held to have done and suffered" (Heidegger 1700, locus xix, 81).

Following Calvin, Heidegger also used the division of the office of Christ in a *triplex munus* referring to the prophetic, priestly, and kingly offices of Christ. In each case, he emphasized that the three offices are to be understood of the God-man in both natures. The subject of this office is not only the whole Christ (*totus Christus*) but also the whole of Christ (*totum Christi*). According to Heidegger, "Christ's office of mediator is common to every state of the church after the entry of sin. Christ Jesus is the same yesterday and today, Hebr. 13:8" (Heidegger 1700, locus xix, 26).

Because Christ was a Mediator already before the incarnation, a distinction must be made between the divine intention and the historical execution of the three offices. The order of execution regards Christ in his earthly ministry—first his prophetic office, then his priestly office, and finally his kingship now in heaven. But the order in divine intention is different: "here the kingly office comes first, as the goal of the mediation. Before all things God gave to the Son as king many brethren to be filled with eternal glory; he receives the priesthood as the means to this end . . . and prophecy follows because to him as prophet it was given to proclaim righteousness, salvation and glory unto the obedience of faith" (Heidegger 1700, locus xix, 27). This schema of the threefold office, also present in later Lutheran orthodoxy, presents a synthesis of the work of Christ that is not explicitly found in patristic and medieval theology. It applies to the Christological doctrine as a whole and gives it its balance and coherence; it shows the interconnectedness of all its parts—law and gospel, Spirit and faith, satisfaction, justification, and sanctification.

Although there was a general agreement between the two confessions that the work of satisfaction consists in both active and passive obedience of Christ, the Lutherans regarded Christ's active as well his passive obedience as being purely vicarious, whereby the passive obedience included the active. As Quenstedt indicated: "Because the human nature of the person making satisfaction was made partaker of the divine and infinite majesty, Christ's passion and death was valued and reckoned of the same worth and price as if it belonged to the divine nature" (Quenstedt 1685, theses. 39–40). For the

Reformed, however, Christ's active obedience had to be maintained in a different way. His individual fulfilment of the law pertains to his satisfaction and merit just as much as does his suffering and death or passive obedience. As the Son of God Christ was not subject to the law, but his subjection under the law of the love of God and of his neighbor is the work of his humanity. This point was elaborated by a distinction between a natural and federal subjection to the law (Heidegger 1700, locus xi, 2–5). The last is the obedience to the law, which the first Adam owed to God through the covenant of works. Both Lutherans and Reformed rejected the position of Johannes Piscator (1546–1625), who opposed the inclusion of Christ's active obedience and argued that only Christ's sufferings and death in obedience to a special mandate of the Father, or his passive obedience, could count as the meritorious cause of justification. The obedience for the sake of which God justifies men was Christ's passive obedience only; his active obedience was in this view superfluous.

Christ's descent into Hell (*descensus ad inferos*, 1 Peter 3:19) was also a matter of controversy between the two confessions which was indirectly related to the doctrine of *communicatio idiomatum*. The Formula of Concord (1580) followed Luther in taking it literally, while later Lutheran theology renewed the patristic view that Christ's descent into hell was an announcement of his victory over the devil included in Christ's state of exaltation. The Reformed, however, attributed it to the state of humiliation. They interpreted it partly of the separating of Christ's soul from his body in death, partly of his burial or descent into the grave, partly of his desolation on the cross (*Synopsis Purioris Theologiae* 1625, 27:25–32).

## 2  PREDESTINATION: NECESSITY AND CONTINGENCY

Much secondary literature argues that seventeenth-century Reformed theology is an example of a deterministic system of theology. The origin of this complaint can be traced back to Arminius and later Remonstrant theologians, who held that the Reformed doctrine of predestination, especially that of the famed Polish Reformed theologian Franeker Johannes Maccovius, introduced a necessitarian model into Reformed theology and made God the author of sin (Van Asselt 2011, 217–41). Inasmuch as "determinism" in its modern sense is a late eighteenth-century term, strictly speaking, the problem addressed by the Reformed was Stoic fatalism (Van Asselt, Bac, and Te Velde 2010, 15–18). Moreover, contrary to the complaint, Maccovius provides a significant example of early modern Reformed use of aspects of late medieval modal logic, drawing on the thought of Duns Scotus and others, to repudiate fatalism and develop an ontology of contingency as the metaphysical backdrop to the Reformed doctrine of the divine decrees (Vos 2006, 598–606; Beck 2007, 344–58; Van Asselt, Bac, and Te Velde 2010, 27–29, 41–43). Whereas the effects of natural causes were necessary, the effects of free causes were contingent and free. A natural cause is determined by its nature to the act but a free cause is able to act variously, not only at different times, but also structurally or at one and the same moment (Maccovius 1641b, 252; Van Asselt, Bac, and Te Velde 2010, 30–32). In the relationship between God and human beings, both were held to be free causes. Things are contingent, if it is possible for them to exist or not exist (*posse fieri et non posse fieri*); things are necessary if it is impossible for them not to exist (*non posse non fieri*) (Maccovius 1641a, 99; Maccovius 1641b, 252–53). The Reformed used this modal language in order to articulate distinctive *Christian* assumptions concerning created reality and its relationship to God: the philosophical component of the language serves theological concerns (Goudriaan 2006, 329).

The terms "necessity" and "contingency" were also applied to the doctrine of God. Like their medieval predecessors, the Reformed made a fundamental distinction regarding the divine acts, between the acts of God *ad intra*, directed to God himself (like "knowing himself") and acts *ad extra*, directed to his creation (like "knowing creatures"). The distinction between *ad intra* and *ad extra* dimensions in God's agency coincides with the distinction between necessity and contingency, thus enabling differentiation between God's essential and necessary knowledge, will and power *ad intra*, and God's free and contingent knowledge, and will and power *ad extra* (Van Asselt and Dekker 2001, 220–22; Van Asselt 2002, 319–35; Muller 2010). The *ad intra* acts are *essential* or necessary, the *ad extra* are free or *contingent*: "The communication *ad extra* according to which God communicates himself to the creatures is a communication which could have not happened; for it would have been possible that God did not do the things He did. So there might have been no communication to the creatures. The scholastics call the communication *ad intra* an essential communication, the communication *ad extra* an effective communication" (Maccovius 1656, 54; Van Asselt 2011, 230–34).

Following this pattern, the Reformed doctrine of divine attributes distinguished between a natural or necessary knowledge (*scientia naturalis, necessaria*) by which God knows Himself and all possibilities as things He is able to realize, and a free knowledge (*scientia libera*) by which He knows all factual states of affairs in history. The decision of the divine will divides both forms of divine knowledge; the former structurally preceding and the second following it (Maccovius 1641b, 104–5). God's essential will is absolutely necessary, but directed to contingent objects, his will is contingent. God contingently wills all that is contingent. Created reality is the contingent manifestation of divine freedom and does not emanate necessarily from God's essence. If this were not the case, all things would fundamentally coincide with God's essence and the actual world would be an eternal world and the only one possible world (Maccovius 1641a, 133).

In the Reformed view, both Catholic Counter-Reformation (L. Molina) and Remonstrant theology (Arminius) had modified this "will-based-theology" by their adaptation of middle knowledge (*scientia media*), resulting in a "knowledge-based-theology" in which there is no room for real contingency (Maccovius 1641b, 103–4; Bac 2010). For Maccovius and most of seventeenth-century Reformed theologians, the main problem of the concept of middle knowledge is that it undermines the fundamental distinction between Creator and creature. Middle knowledge, used to describe a category of divine knowledge structurally or logically antecedent to God's will, implies a necessity of the objects of divine knowledge (Maccovius 1641a, 25–26). Because middle knowledge postulates objects *extra Deum* that precede his will, a logical contradiction is involved: objects outside God always presuppose the divine will. Finally, if God's middle knowledge also contains his decree, then this would imply that it is impossible for God to choose an alternative (Maccovius 1641a, 25). Middle knowledge, then, approximates Stoic fate (*fatum Stoicum*), a natural or absolute necessity so inherent in the essential nature of things that even God is made dependent, like Homer's Jupiter (Maccovius 1641b, 253).

It is in this context that Maccovius addressed the doctrine of predestination. The question to be answered was to which dimension—the essential and absolute or the "accidental" and contingent—the divine decree in general and the decree of (double) predestination in particular belong. According to Maccovius, the decree in general and that of predestination in particular must be classified as nonessential acts, insofar as they regard the termination and extension to a certain object (*terminatio et extensio* ad hoc *vel illud objectum*). In his *Loci Communes* he pointed out that the act of decreeing itself (*actus decernens*) is an essential attribute of God, but in respect to its extension to an object (*res decreta*) it is not an essential divine attribute: "Here a distinction must be made: according to the perfection that is in God, the decrees are essential without which God cannot be, but according to the termination and extension to this or that object, in so far as they are not referring to divine perfection but only to a relation, the decrees are not essential attributes of God" (Maccovius 1641b, 84–85; Van Asselt 2011, 234–37). Not only is the *ad extra* dimension of the decree of predestination (*res decreta*) contingent, but also its *ad intra* dimension: God's decree is eternal, but related to certain objects it does not belong to the essential, absolutely necessary dimension of God's being: *sine iis Deus esse potuit*. Maccovius therefore did not accept the claim of the Arminians that the divine decree made God the author of sin and destroyed the contingency of created reality. Neglect of this distinction between necessity and contingency would entail either a necessitarian worldview or an unstable, arbitrary ontology of mere contingency (Maccovius 1656, 80, 86).

The issue of making God the author of sin was also at stake in the debates, both before and after the Synod of Dordrecht (1618–19), over "infralapsarianism" and "supralapsarianism," at the heart of which was a dispute over the order of the divine decrees and the proper object of predestination in the mind of God. The supralapsarian position derived its name from *supra lapsum*, which means "above or prior to the Fall." It understood the object of predestination to be creatable and fallible man (*homo creabilis et labilis*) and placed the divine decree of double predestination, election, and reprobation "before" the decrees to create the world and permit the Fall. Infralapsarianism derived its name from *infra lapsum*, which means "below or subsequent to the Fall." It favored created and fallen man (*homo creatus and homo lapsus*) as the object of divine predestination, and placed the decrees of predestination "after" the decrees of creation and the decree to permit the Fall (Muller 1985, 292; Van Asselt 2011, 237–38). During the period before the synod of Dordt, the two different positions were fully developed. The confessional standards of the Reformed church, such as the Canons of Dordt (1619), appear to embody the infralapsarian position but did not condemn supralapsarianism. The Westminster Confession (1647) is indeterminate on this issue. Protagonists of the supralapsarian position in the sixteenth and seventeenth centuries were mainly individual theologians such as Theodore Beza, Franciscus Gomarus (1563–1641), Peter Martyr Vermigli (1499–1562), Zacharias Ursinus (1534–83), William Perkins (1558–1602), William Twisse (1578–1646), Johannes Maccovius, Gisbertus Voetius (1589–1676), Herman Witsius (1636–1708), Johannes Hoornbeek (1617–66), and Franciscus Burman (1628–79) (Dijk 1912, 36–37; Van Asselt 2011, 144–45).

Although the terms *supra* and *infra* seem to suggest a temporal order in the divine mind, one should keep in mind that they are meant as structural or logical moments, for according to the Reformed scholastics of this period, divine simplicity does not allow any composition in God. Nor do they suggest that the decrees were God's reactions to what happened in time, before or after the Fall. The discussion about the order of divine decrees (*ordo rerum decretarum*), therefore, concerned the logical priorities within the eternal purpose of God. Discussing the differences between the *supra* and *infra* positions, Maccovius argued that it would be incorrect to view both positions as absolutely antithetical. Both positions seem to consider the order of decrees (*ordo decretorum*) from a different point of view; the *supra* position fixing more its attention to the "teleological" order of decrees, the *infra* to the "historical" order. Supralapsarians held that in every divine decree the elect stood in a special relationship with God, while the infralapsarians maintained that this personal element did not appear in the divine decrees until after the decree to create and to permit the Fall. Against Arminian opponents, Maccovius underscored the fact that both the *supra* and *infra* positions only deal with contingent conditions of man: not yet created, created, or fallen. But predestination as divine act per se, or considered absolutely, does not depend on these human conditions, but only on God's will. This will, however, does not imply absolute necessity, but a necessity *ex hypothesi* by which God contingently wills all that is contingent (Maccovius 1656, 72).

Therefore, Maccovius argued, one should distinguish several forms of necessity. The most important distinction was that between the necessity of the consequent (*necessitas consequentis*) and the necessity of the consequence (*necessitas consequentiae*), borrowed from Aristotle and medieval doctors. The necessity of the consequent is the necessity of a proposition behind "then" in a statement such as: "if and only if . . ., then . . ."; the necessity of the consequence is the consequence itself, that is, the implicative necessity. In implicative necessity neither the antecedent nor the consequent needs to be necessary—indeed, both can be contingent. The necessity of the consequent corresponds with absolute necessity and the necessity of the consequence with hypothetical necessity. By distinguishing between these different forms of necessity, the Reformed and particularly Maccovius argued that the divine decree (including predestination) did not make God the author of sin nor did it destroy the contingent nature of the created order (Maccovius 1658, 75–76). It could have been possible for sin not to happen: God does not permit sin per se but *per accidens* (Maccovius 1641b, 104, 127). Although this implicative connection between God's permission and sin is necessary, this does not mean that God is the author of sin. As sun does not cause darkness, God does not cause sin itself. Even so, if God did not move the sinning creature, it would not be moved, and therefore, it would not sin; just as a limping horse would not run and limp unless somebody would set it into motion. But the person that moves the horse is not the cause of the limping itself: the cause of limping is the foot of the horse and not the one who sets the horse in motion (Maccovius 1641a, 19, 120; Maccovius 1656, 83).

In confrontation with the highly developed terminological apparatus of their Roman Catholic, Socinian, and Arminian opponents, Maccovius and the Reformed orthodox theologians put into practice medieval modal logic by drawing it into Christian doctrine in such a way as to render it distinct from the "necessitarianism" of ancient philosophy and of all its forms that made God the cause of sin. It was not a form of needless theological speculation, but a "tool kit" for emphasizing the fundamental soteriological impetus of the entire Reformed theological enterprise.

Finally, from the fundamental discussions on archetypal and ectypal theology as an overarching paradigm, it also appears that the Reformed orthodox never used the term "Deus" (as the *principium essendi* of theology) in a neutral or unqualified sense. They provided a Trinitarian description of God's archetypal self-knowledge, and it was the triune God or *Deus foederatus in Christo* who was envisaged in their discourse about the divine decrees. The unremitting opposition of the Reformed to Socinianism gives evidence that the Trinitarian God was presupposed by all doctrines discussed in the Reformed systems; for example, the doctrine of the divine attributes, the doctrine of the divine decrees (including predestination), and the doctrines of creation and providence (Beck 2001, 205–26). No wonder then, that Francis Turretin argued extensively that Christian theology never deals with God "considered exclusively under the relation of deity . . ., but as he is our God, i.e. covenanted in Christ as he has revealed himself to us in his word not only in order to know him but also in order to worship him" (Turretin 1688, I.v.4).

# 3 COVENANT

Covenant and covenant theology also remain debated topics in the scholarship on Reformed orthodoxy. One line of scholarship has claimed that the coexistence of predestination and covenant in Reformed theology creates an unsolvable dilemma. In this view, covenant theology was originally developed in order to temper the "harshness" of double predestination and to reconcile God's sovereignty and human moral responsibility (Miller 1939, 365–431, 501–5; Weir 1990, 153–59), but was ultimately unable to solve the "tensions" between the two polar positions of covenant theology and "decretal" theology (Graafland 1996, 402). In the course of time the notion of covenant was obscured by the increasing dominance of a "predestinarian system," which as "central dogma" determined the hermeneutic of Reformed orthodoxy (Schweizer 1854–56; Graafland 1987, 593–97).

Debate in secondary literature has also been over the question of whether biblical truth can be organized under a *duplex* covenant principle in salvation history; namely, a prelapsarian covenant of works and a postlapsarian covenant of grace. There are two patterns of criticism. One pattern conceives of the *duplex foedus* scheme as compromising and corrupting the doctrine of God's sovereign grace by embodying a confusion between "covenant" and "contract," between the sphere of nature and the sphere of grace, making nature or law prior to grace (Torrance 1970, 51–76). A second criticism views covenant theology as an aberration that perverted an originally correct conception of covenant with a mechanistic, formalized, and "humanistic" Melanchthonian federalism introduced into Reformed theology through the notion of a covenant of works (Diemer 1935; Graafland 1996, 294–95). A third critique argues that there were two different traditions in Reformed covenant theology: a Genevan unilateral or unconditional covenant tradition (Calvin and Beza) and a Rhineland bilateral or conditional tradition (Heinrich Bullinger). This view also claims that the predominance of absolute double predestination led to a "paralysis" of the covenant idea (Baker 1980). Against these dogmatic readings, one must distinguish several approaches to covenant theology.

First, "covenant theology" can indicate a rather pietistic version of the *ordo salutis*, referencing the *via salutis* or stages of personal faith embedded in the community of believers. Second, it can denote a theology in which the continuity and discontinuity of salvation history in the Old and New Testaments (*ordo temporum*) is emphasized and the focus is on salvation history (Van Asselt 2001, 291–310). In the second view the diverse *foedera* are developed according to the Melanchthonian concept of the *historica series*. In this respect, the notion of a progressive history of the divine covenants presented an elaboration of the biblical narrative of redemptive history. These two components seem to be the two characteristic features of a fully developed and mature covenant theology: the *ordo temporum* or salvation history scheme, and the *ordo salutis* scheme or the methodical description of the work of God the Holy Spirit in the believers within the community of the Church (Van Asselt 1997, 95–96; Van Asselt 2001, 297–300).

The Leiden theologian Johannes Cocceius (1603–69) was the great codifier of this federal movement within Reformed theology, who drew together the various elements of earlier covenantal thought. By means of the inherited concept of covenant (*foedus*)— Cocceius himself mentions Heinrich Bullinger (1504–75), Matthias Martinius (1572–1630), and Caspar Olevianus (1536–87)—Cocceius sought to do justice to the historical nature of the biblical narrative in a coherent, biblically based dogmatics (Van Asselt 2001, 268–70). Most Reformed theologians distinguished two fundamental forms of God's covenant (*duplex foedus*) in salvation history: the covenant of works *ante lapsum*, and the covenant of grace *post lapsum*. The former was a description of the situation of man in paradise before the Fall, the second was promulgated immediately after the Fall, when the covenant of works was violated by the disobedience of Adam. The covenant of grace was held to be effective in two successive periods: *ante Christum natum*, and *post Christum natum*. The Reformed also developed the notion of a "third" covenant: an *eternal* covenant between God the Father, God the Son, and God the Holy Spirit, the so-called "covenant of redemption" or *pactum salutis*.

Some writers have argued that the introduction of a covenant of works was primarily the result of systematic, dogmatic thinking, and was an illegitimate and unbiblical addition to Reformed theology that disturbed the priority of grace over works in Reformed theology (Diemer 1935; Barth 1936–69, 4/1:59–65; Weir 1990, 158). On the contrary, for Cocceius and most of his Reformed contemporaries, the central issue addressed in the doctrine of the covenant of works was a soteriological one (Van Asselt 2001, 265–68). It did not, as has been claimed, point to a legalistic view of salvation but it articulated the soteriological aspects of the prelapsarian situation, and what is more, related creation and grace. The covenant of works underlined Paul's teaching on sin in Romans 5, and via the parallels between the first and second Adam, affirmed essential points of Christology, pointing to the doctrines of Christ's satisfaction and justification by faith— namely, to the totally unmerited character of salvation. The basis for this soteriological interpretation of the doctrine of the covenant of works and its ultimate relationship with the covenant of grace relates directly to the eternal *pactum salutis* between God the Father and God the Son. Cocceius' formulation points to the priority of the gracious divine will and intention of fellowship (*amicitia Dei*) with his creatures, and not to a purported legalistic system. Rather, the *pactum salutis* and the *duplex foedus* scheme (the covenants of works and grace) articulate the permanence of God's original and gracious intention to establish a continuous relationship of fellowship or friendship with human beings, in church and society, in family and in future generations (Van Asselt 2010, 1–15).

While all federal theologians agreed on the twofold administration of the covenant of grace—*ante et post Christum natum*—they disagreed about the place and character of the covenant at Sinai within the dispensation of grace. The question was whether there are two, three, or four periods of time, and whether the period of the Sinaitic covenant marks a distinct period (Rehnman 2000, 296–308). Still, despite differences in periodization of the Old Testament, most federal theologians had in common the view that revelation develops by stages and that each stage is to be examined in its place. They described the biblical narrative in terms of the divine covenants in such a manner that it could do justice to the historical dimension of Christian faith; namely, the confession that God became involved with human history. Consequently, the notion of a progressive history of the divine covenants presents a consequent elaboration of the basic fact that the Bible presents itself as an ongoing narrative of redemptive history.

Another question posed by the critics of seventeenth-century federal theology was whether the federalists undermined their historical and relational enterprise by introducing the notion of an eternal decree or pact, thereby inserting a dualism into the Godhead (Schrenk 1923, 140; Barth 1936–69, 4/1:65). This criticism is set aside by examining the development of the doctrine. The *pactum salutis* was not an attempt to discuss the doctrine of the divine decrees in a Trinitarian framework, initiated by Cocceius (Gass 1857, 270). A significant antecedent formulation was developed by Olevianus (Schrenk 1923, 59–62; Bierma 1996, 107–12). Nor was the doctrine a product of speculation, but the result of a long trajectory of exegetical interpretation, Theodore Beza being one of the major exegetical movers of covenant terminology in general and of the *pactum salutis* language in particular (Muller 2007, 11–65; Lee 2009, 44–49). Cocceius in his *Summa doctrinae* (1648) and the Scottish presbyterian theologian David Dickson in his *Therapeutica Sacra* (1648) consolidated the doctrine (Williams 2005). The notion of a *pactum salutis*, moreover, was developed in the *locus de foedere* and not primarily discussed in the context of the doctrine of the divine decrees or the doctrine of predestination (Van Asselt 2001, 197–287).

The central notion in the eternal pact is that of the sponsorship of Christ: as the *Logos incarnandus* Christ wills to be the sponsor and mediator of salvation: in union with his human nature and having accepted to be a sponsor or "surety," the Son has voluntarily submitted himself to the Father (Van Asselt 2001, 239–41). The concept of the *Logos incarnandus* presupposes the antecedent election of God the Father: the Father chooses the elect and gives them to the Son as their head and sponsor. According to Cocceius, this sponsorship of Christ does not precede election; election precedes sponsorship (Van Asselt 2001, 243–44). The eternal pact therefore involves an interaction between the *ad intra* and *ad extra* dimensions of divine agency. As the second person of the Trinity, the Son acts *voluntarily* as the *logos incarnandus*, thus relating the eternal or *ad intra* dimension of the eternal pact to the temporal or *ad extra* dimension of the covenant in salvation history. The doctrine thus demonstrates that the covenantal relationship between God and human beings is founded in a covenantal relationship in God Himself (G. Vos 1980, 247).

Furthermore, this *sponsio* language indicating that the eternal Son is willing to accept the role of a "surety" in the economy of salvation, enabled Cocceius to link time and eternity by referring to the will of the Son to complete the pact and testament in various dispensations of salvation history. The identification of the eternal Son as *sponsor* marked the intersection of the *pactum* and the subsequent federal relations in time by relating the eternal and temporal aspects of Christology.

Finally, Cocceius affirmed a Trinitarian economy of redemption wherein all three persons are involved. Although few of the seventeenth-century theologians speak explicitly about the role of the Holy Spirit's role in the eternal pact, Cocceius made a number of comments on the role of the Spirit in the intra-Trinitarian activity. Thus it was through the eternal Spirit that Christ "offered himself up without a spot to God." The Holy Spirit is the power of God who implements, safeguards, and administers the testament through the course of history (Van Asselt 2001, 233–36). The proper work of the Spirit in the economy of salvation is to justify and sanctify the believers through faith in the sponsor. But if righteousness and sanctification are found only in the sponsor, it is only in communion with this sponsor that such righteousness and sanctification can be obtained. Fellowship with the sponsor, in turn, is only possible through the spirit of the sponsor. Not only the *sponsor* language used in Christology but also the emphasis on the role of the Holy Spirit enabled Cocceius to forge a link between the eternal and temporal dimensions of his federal theology. This pneumatological dimension underscores the relational character of all the central notions in his federal design comprehending eternity and time: *pactum, testamentum* and *foedus* (Van Asselt 2001, 233–36).

In sum, covenant theology with its redemptive-historical outlook was not an alternative to the doctrine of the divine decrees, nor was it in "tension" with the doctrine of predestination. Rather, there was a convergence of Christology, predestination, and covenant accomplished by a comprehensive representation of God's plan of salvation coordinating the *ad intra* and *ad extra* aspects of salvation history (Van Asselt 2001, 227–47). The development of federal theology during the sixteenth and seventeenth centuries illustrates the interconnection or confluence of Christological and Trinitarian motifs in Reformed theology, and refutes the older thesis that soteriological and covenantal motifs in Reformed theology were overshadowed by a rational and metaphysical system of divine decrees.

## BIBLIOGRAPHY

Asselt, Willem J. van. 2010. "Covenant Theology: An Invitation to Friendship." *Nederlands Theologisch Tijdschrift* 64 (1): 1–15.

Asselt, Willem J. van. 2001. *The Federal Theology of Johannes Cocceius (1603–1669)*. Translated by Raymond A. Blacketer. Leiden: Brill.

Asselt, Willem J. van. 2002. "The Fundamental Meaning of Theology: Archetypal and Ectypal Theology in Seventeenth-Century Reformed Thought." *Westminster Theological Journal* 64: 319–335.

Asselt, Willem J. van. 1997. *Johannes Coccejus: Portret van een zeventiende-eeuws theoloog op oude en nieuwe wegen*. Heerenveen: Groen en Zoon.

Asselt, Willem J. van. 2011. "On the Maccovius Affair." In *Revisiting the Synod of Dordt*, edited by Aza Goudriaan and Fred van Lieburg, 217–241. Leiden: Brill.

Asselt, Willem J. van, and Eef Dekker, eds. 2001. *Reformation and Scholasticism: An Ecumenical Enterprise*. Grand Rapids, MI: Baker.

Asselt, Willem J. van, J. Martin Bac, and Roelf T. Te Velde, eds. 2010. *Reformed Thought on Freedom: The Concept of Free Choice in Early Modern Reformed Theology*. Grand Rapids, MI: Baker.

Bac, J. Martin. 2010. *Perfect Will Theology: Divine Agency in Reformed Scholasticism as against Suárez, Episcopius, Descartes, and Spinoza*. Leiden: Brill.

Baker, J. Wayne. 1980. *Heinrich Bullinger and the Covenant: The Other Reformed Tradition*. Athens: Ohio University Press.

Barth, Karl. *Church Dogmatics*. 1936–1969. 13 vols. Edited by G. W. Bromiley and T. F. Torrance. Edinburgh: T&T Clark.

Beck, Andreas J. 2001. "Gisbertus Voetius (1589–1676): Basic Features of his Doctrine of God." In *Reformation and Scholasticism: An Ecumenical Enterprise*, edited by Willem J. van Asselt and Eef Dekker, 205–226. Grand Rapids, MI: Baker.

Beck, Andreas J. 2007. *Gisbertus Voetius (1589–1676), Sein Theologieverständnis und seine Gotteslehre*. Göttingen: Vandenhoeck & Ruprecht.

Beza, Theodore. 1577. *Quaestionum et responsionum christianarum libellus, in quo praecipua christianae religionis capita kat' epitom.n proponuntur*. Editio quinta. Geneva.

Bierma, Lyle D. 1996. *German Calvinism in the Confessional Age: The Covenant Theology of Caspar Olevianus*. Grand Rapids, MI: Baker.

Diemer, Nicolaas. 1935. *Het Scheppingsverbond met Adam (het verbond der werken) bij de theologen der 16e, 17e en 18e eeuw in Zwitserland, Duitschland, Nederland en Engeland.* Kampen: Kok.

Dijk, Klaas. 1912. *De strijd over Infra- en Supralaparisme in de Gerefrormeerde Kerken van Nederland.* Kampen: Kok.

Gass, Wilhelm. 1857. *Geschichte der protestantischen Dogmatik in ihren Zusammenhange mit der Theologie.* Vol. 2. Berlin: Reimer.

Goudriaan, Aza. 2006. *Reformed Orthodoxy and Philosophy, 1625–1750: Gisbertus Voetius, Petrus van Mastricht and Antonius Driessen.* Leiden: Brill.

Graafland, Cornelis. 1987. *Van Calvijn tot Barth: Oorsprong en ontwikkeling van de leer der verkiezing in het Gereformeerd Protestantisme.* 's-Gravenhage: Boekencentrum.

Graafland, Cornelis. 1996. *Van Calvijn tot Comrie: Oorsprong en ontwikkeling van de leer van het verbond in het Gereformeerd Protestantisme.* 3 vols. Zoetermeer: Boekencentrum.

Heidegger, Johann Heinrich. 1700. *Corpus theologiae Christianae . . . adeoque sit plenissimum theologiae didacticae, elencticae, moralis et historicae systema.* 2 vols. Zürich.

Lee, Brian J. 2009. *Johannes Cocceius and the Exegetical Roots of Federal Theology: Reformation Developments in the Interpretation of Hebrews 7–10.* Göttingen: Vandenhoeck & Ruprecht.

Maccovius, Johannes. 1641a. *Collegia Theologica, quae extant omnia. Tertio ab auctore recognita, emendata, & plurimis locis aucta, in partes duas distributa.* Franeker.

Maccovius, Johannes. 1641b. *Thesium theologicarum per locos communes in Academia Franequerana disputatarum pars altera.* Franeker.

Maccovius, Johannes. 1656. *Distinctiones et regulae theologicae ac philosophicae: Editae opera ac studio Nicolai Arnoldi.* Oxford.

Maccovius, Johannes. 1658. *Metaphysica, ad usum quaestionum in philosophia ac theologia adornata et applicata, Tertium edita, explicata, vindicata, refutata per Adrianum Heereboord.* Leiden.

Miller, Perry. 1939. *The New England Mind. The Seventeenth Century.* Cambridge, MA: Harvard University Press.

Muller, Richard A. 1985. *Dictionary of Latin and Greek Theological Terms, Drawn Principally from Protestant Scholastic Theology.* Grand Rapids, MI: Baker.

Muller, Richard A. 2010. "God as Absolute and Relative, Necessary, Free, and Contingent: The *Ad Intra-Ad Extra* Movement of Seventeenth-Century Reformed Language about God." In *Always Reforming: Essays in Honor of W. Robert Godfrey,* edited by R. Scott Clark and Joel E. Kim, 56–73. Escondido: Westminster Seminary California.

Muller, Richard A. 2007. "Toward the *Pactum Salutis*: Locating the Origins of a Concept," *Mid-America Journal of Theology* 18: 11–65.

Preus, Robert D. 1970. *The Theology of Post-Reformation Lutheranism. A Study of Theological Prolegomena.* St. Louis, MO: Concordia.

Rehnman, Sebastian. 2000. "Is the Narrative of Redemptive History Trichotomous or Dichotomous? A Problem for Federal Theology." *Nederlands Archief voor kerkgeschiedenis/ Dutch Review of Church History* 80 (3): 296–308.

Rijssen, Leonard. 1695. *Francisci Turrettini ss. Theologiae doctoris et professoris Compendium theologiae didactico-elenctica, ex theologorum nostrorum institutionibus theologicis auctum et illustratum.* Amsterdam.

Schrenk, Gottlob. (1923) 1967. *Gottesreich und Bund im älteren Protestantismus, vornehmlich bei Johannes Coccejus.* Darmstadt: Wissenschaftliche Buchgesellschaft.

*Synopsis purioris theologiae.* (1625) 1881. *Disputationibus quinquaginta duabus comprehensa ac conscripta per Johannem Polyandrum, Andream Rivetum, Antonium Walaeum, Antonium Thysium, ss. Theologiae Doctores et Professores in Academia Leidensi.* Editio sexta. Curavit et praefatus est Dr. H. Bavinck. Leiden: apud Didericum Donner.

Torrance, James B. 1970. "Covenant or Contract? A Study of the Theological Background of Worship in Seventeenth Century Scotland." *Scottish Journal of Theology* 23: 51–76.

Turretin, Francis. 1688. *Institutio theologiae elenchticae in tres partes distributa.* Geneva.

Vos, Geerhardus. 1980. "The Doctrine of the Covenant in Reformed Theology." In *Redemptive History and Biblical Interpretation,* edited by Richard B. Gaffin Jr., 234–267. Phillipsburg, NJ: Presbyterian and Reformed Publishing Company.

Vos, Antonie. 2006. *The Philosophy of John Duns Scotus.* Edinburgh: Edinburgh University Press.

Weir, David A. 1990. *The Origins of the Federal Theology in Sixteenth-Century Reformation Thought.* Oxford: Clarendon Press.

Williams, Carol. 2005. "The Decree of Redemption is in Effect a Covenant: David Dickson and the Covenant of Redemption." PhD diss., Calvin Theological Seminary, Grand Rapids.

Wollebius, Johannes. 1626. *Christianae Theologiae Compendium accurata methodo sic adornatum ut ad SS. Scripturas legendas, ad locos digerendos, ad controversias intelligendas sit manuductio.* Basel.

# CHAPTER 15

..................................................................................................

# SIN, GRACE,
# AND FREE CHOICE IN
# POST-REFORMATION
# REFORMED THEOLOGY

..................................................................................................

## STEPHEN HAMPTON

THE Reformed theologians of the early modern period sought to balance their emphasis on the sovereignty of God and the primacy of grace in salvation with an equal emphasis on human dignity and responsibility. Their opponents, whether Roman Catholic, Lutheran, or Arminian, frequently suggested that the Reformed so magnified God's role in creation and redemption that human beings were reduced to utter passivity and God was made the author of sin (Van Asselt, Bac, and Te Velde, 2010, 15). Reformed theologies of sin, grace, and free will, and Reformed ethics, were therefore elaborated to rebut this charge.

To the Reformed mind, there is a logic that connects all the theological topics dealt with in this chapter. The Reformed insist that human beings are endowed with free choice—*liberum arbitrium*—whether before the Fall, or after it; whether under grace, or in glory. Human free choice entails moral responsibility, and makes it meaningful to talk about sin, which is the misuse of that elective power. The deleterious effects of sin are so grave that they can only be healed through divine grace, and it is grace alone that restores to fallen human beings the capacity for acting well in the fullest sense. This logic therefore suggests an order for the discussion: free will, sin, grace, and then ethics.

As in other areas of doctrine, much ground is shared by numerous Reformed theologians. In the interests of clarity, this chapter will examine a small number of theologians closely, rather than attempting to synthesize a wider selection. The authors have been selected, not because they were the most authoritative writers on a given topic (the irreducible diversity of the Reformed tradition means that such a claim could be made for no writer of the early modern period), but because they were all prominent teachers, who dealt with the given topic in detail, and whose writing is representative of the wider tradition. Other theologians will be brought in, as necessary, to illustrate contrasting views.

# 1 Free Choice

The *Theologiae Elenchticae Nova Synopsis*, by Samuel Maresius (1599–1673), although prompted by the work of a Belgian Jesuit, James Tirinus (1580–1636), was a comprehensive defense of Reformed theology. Maresius opens his discussion of free choice by noting that many false accusations have been leveled at the Reformed on the matter: "They clamour that we despoil men of humanity, and deny the very existence of free choice" (Maresius 1646–48, 2:2). Quite the contrary, he insists, the Reformed believe that the power of free choice is intrinsic to humanity. Nonetheless, the Reformed reject the conception of free choice proposed by many Roman Catholic and Arminian writers, including Tirinus. Free choice does not require the "liberty of indifference"—the inalienable power to do or refrain from doing something, when all the prerequisites for action, including grace and the concourse of divine providence, are present (Maresius 1646–48, 2:23–24).

It is true that unlike irrational creatures, human beings are not naturally determined to just one course of action. They are free, in other words, from "physical necessity." As a result, when human beings choose to do something under the influence of grace, they nonetheless retain a faculty within them which, were that grace withdrawn, would enable them to pursue another course of action. So if one considers free choice simply as a faculty, in isolation from all the natural and supernatural prerequisites for acting (the "divided sense"), it does indeed have both the inherent potential to select from a range of alternatives ("freedom of contrariety"), and the inherent potential to accept or reject a given course of action ("freedom of contradiction").

However, when the faculty of free choice is considered in conjunction with the natural and supernatural prerequisites from acting (the "compounded sense"), it no longer has the potential to choose another course of action or to refrain from acting; so it does not have the liberty of indifference. If it did, Maresius notes, it would be possible for human beings to frustrate the divine providence, which is absurd. Furthermore, one key prerequisite for human action is the "ultimate judgement of practical reason"—the discernment, by the intellect, of what course of action seems best in all the circumstances. If free choice involved the potential to reject this judgment, then human beings would not be rational agents (Maresius 1646–48, 2:4).

For this reason, Maresius underlines that free choice cannot be identified solely with the will. Choosing a course of action involves making an intellectual judgment about what should be done, which the will then follows as a matter of intrinsic necessity (Maresius 1646–48, 2:12). That is why Maresius calls intellectual judgment the "prime mover" of the human microcosm, "by which the will is determined to willing" (Maresius 1646–48, 2:12). It follows from this that free choice is incompatible with coercion;

because if one is forced to act contrary to one's intellectual judgment, then one's choice is not free as Maresius understands it. Free choice requires "freedom of spontaneity" (Maresius 1646–48, 2:20); and that involves the freedom to act with deliberation—ἐκ προαιρεσεώς—(Maresius 1646–48, 2:11), the freedom to act as one thinks best.

So for Maresius, free choice is incompatible with both physical necessity and the necessity of coercion: but it is compatible with other kinds of necessity. It is compatible, for example, with the necessity of dependence on God (Maresius 1646–48, 2:12). It is also compatible with "moral necessity." That is the necessity which results from a human being's moral character. Jesus's moral character is such that he cannot sin; yet his goodness is still freely chosen. The moral character of the unregenerate is such that their acts are always sinful; yet their sin is still freely chosen (Maresius 1646–48, 2:14).

Free choice is equally compatible with the necessity brought about by the divine decree. Maresius calls this kind of necessity "hypothetical necessity" or the "necessity of consequence" (Maresius 1646–48, 2:15). He is alluding here to a key distinction in Reformed reflection on free choice, between "necessity of consequence" and "necessity of the consequent" (Van Asselt, Bac, and Te Velde 2010, 35–37). And by indicating that the necessity entailed by the divine decree is a necessity of consequence, Maresius is seeking to preserve the fundamental contingency of human action. A human being may choose to act in a certain way, as a result of the divine decree—but that choice is only necessary, given the divine decree—it is not inherently or absolutely necessary. Had the divine decree been other, free choice could have been exercised differently; for as Maresius underlines, "such is the faculty of the human will that, by its intrinsic constitution and nature, it is equally apt to choose an act plainly contrary to the one it actually chooses" (Maresius 1646–48, 2:15).

In Maresius's conception of free choice, the will is invariably determined by the last judgment of practical reason; that, indeed, is what makes it a rational faculty. But this view was not universal amongst the Reformed. In his *Theoretico-Practica Theologia*, Petrus van Mastricht (1630–1706) notes Maresius's position, but disagrees with it. If Maresius were right, he argues, grace would only need to illuminate the human intellect for conversion to happen. However, scripture makes clear that conversion requires not only a new mind but also a new heart (Ez 36:26), and that saving grace directly affects the will (Phil 2:13). Van Mastricht suggests, therefore, that the will only follows the judgment of practical reason when that judgment is congruous with its habitual disposition. As a result, a sinful will may not automatically follow what the intellect judges to be the best course of action. So conversion requires not just the illumination of the intellect, but also the infusion of a new disposition in the will, inclining it toward God and spiritual good (Van Mastricht 1699, 383–84).

Maresius's wish to preserve the contingency of human actions was echoed by most other Reformed writers, well into the eighteenth century. In his *Institutiones Theologiae Polemicae*, Johann Friedrich Stapfer (1708–75) echoed Maresius's insistence that the divine decree does not eliminate the contingency of human actions, but preserves it; for God decrees that certain things should take place contingently and freely (Stapfer 1743–47, 1:108). And George Hill (1739–1810) underlines, in his *Lectures in Divinity*, that "two opposite determinations of the mind are equally possible, both being contingent . . . and the certainty that one of them shall be, is only what is called moral necessity" (Hill 1821, 3:106).

However, it has been argued that Jonathan Edwards (1703–58) abandons this Reformed commitment to the contingency of human actions (Muller 2011, 11–15). Edwards writes: "nothing can ever come to pass without a cause, or reason why it exists in this manner rather than another . . . Now if this be so, it will demonstrably follow, that the acts of the will are never contingent, or without necessity, in the sense spoken of; inasmuch as those things which have a cause, or reason of their existence, must be connected with their cause" (Edwards 1957–2008, 1:213). Edwards's reasoning is shaped by his assumption that events are only called "contingent" if they are uncaused (Edwards 1957–2008, 1:155), an assumption which other Reformed writers did not share. Edwards's work therefore represents a departure from the traditional Reformed language about free choice. That said, Edwards underlines that the necessity which applies to human actions is not a "metaphysical or philosophical necessity" brought about by logical connection, but only a "moral necessity." He also identifies this as a "necessity of consequence," which entails that the action is "not necessary in itself" (Edwards 1957–2008, 1:153). So, despite the change in language, Edwards's position is ultimately not that far from Maresius's.

# 2 SIN

The Reformed discussion of sin takes Adam's sin as the cause and archetype of all subsequent sins. Van Mastricht underlines that the primary cause of Adam's sin was not God, but the abuse of free choice. "The Reformed," he writes, "state that man committed this first sin entirely freely, since, notwithstanding the eternal decree of God, the predetermining influx of providence, and whatever else, he committed it εκ προαιρεσις, by counsel and rational consent, in which alone our free choice properly consists" (Van Mastricht 1699, 334). The divine decree may have caused the futurity of the sin; but it did not produce the sin itself. The divine providence may have provided the material substrate of the sin; but it did not generate the lawlessness—ανομιαν—that was its form. Nor did God push Adam toward the sin by withdrawing the necessary help of grace. Adam enjoyed sufficient grace to resist the sin, had he chosen to do so—even if God, in the pursuit of a wise and just purpose, did not give to Adam the confirming grace that would have prevented the sin and guaranteed obedience. In other words, Adam acted not just with the liberty of spontaneity, which his descendants retain, but with the liberty of indifference, which they do not; because nothing inherent in his nature predisposed him to sin (Van Mastricht 1699, 331).

Since the form of sin is lawlessness, it is a privative, rather than a positive thing: sin is the absence of the good moral quality which should be present in the actions of rational creatures. And sin brings to the sinner moral pollution, guilt, and liability to punishment

(Van Mastricht 1699, 343–44). Sin can be distinguished into original sin and actual sin, although both are the consequence of Adam's transgression. Van Mastricht admits that "original sin" is not a phrase found in scripture; but, on the basis of Genesis 8:21, Psalm 51:5; Romans 7:17 and elsewhere, he argues that it is a biblical idea. Van Mastricht believes that original sin must be understood as both imputed and inherent: Adam's sin has corrupted the nature which he passed on to his posterity; Adam's guilt is also actual and shared by all his natural descendants.

Adam's sin is justly imputed to his descendants, Van Mastricht argues, because he broke God's law as a public person, and was the representative of his posterity under the Covenant of Works. Furthermore, he suggests, human beings have all sinned in Adam, in the same way that they may be justified in Christ, namely by imputation. It is on account of this imputed sin, Van Mastricht believes, that God punishes human beings by not conferring on them the original righteousness of his image; otherwise, it would be unjust to impose such a severe punishment on innocent people (Van Mastricht 1699, 345).

Van Mastricht defines inherent original sin as "the deviation of the entirety of our nature from the rectitude of the divine law." It is the absence of the original righteousness in which Adam was created, and which his descendants should still possess. Every part and faculty of humanity has been corrupted: the intellect; the will; the conscience; the affections; the body. This corruption involves an aversion to goodness, particularly to all good that is spiritual and saving, and a corresponding inclination to evil (Van Mastricht 1699, 346). This corruption is propagated to all Adam's descendants, and is not merely a matter of imitation. That said, it is a depravation of the human nature and therefore an accident (Van Mastricht 1699, 353); it does not transform human nature into a different substance.

Pelagians and Socinians, Van Mastricht notes, insist that sin must be voluntary, and so reject the suggestion that anyone might be guilty of a sin which they did not choose to commit. Van Mastricht agrees that acts which are truly involuntary, in that they are committed against the inclination, and without any collusion of the will, cannot be sins. He argues, however, that the consent of the will does not have to be antecedent to the act: consent can also be concomitant with the act, as it is where the will applauds a sin already in existence. He suggests that the will does consent, in this way, to the evil inclinations which arise as a result of original sin. It follows that even the first stirring of sin in the human heart—concupiscence—involves the will, and is therefore properly sinful (Van Mastricht 1699, 347).

For Van Mastricht, original sin subjects human beings to a triple death. As sinners, they are subject to natural death, which is the promised penalty for sin. But they are also subject to the spiritual death which results from the loss of original righteousness; namely, the inability to do anything which is spiritually good, and the slavery to sin, the world, and the Devil, which that impotence brings. As a consequence of this second and spiritual death, human beings can no longer aspire to final union with God. In the absence of that union, they are condemned to suffer a third and eternal death (Van Mastricht 1699, 374). Van Mastricht insists that all human beings, with the exception of

Christ, are infected by inherent original sin. Even infants, who have not committed any actual sins, are nonetheless guilty on account of their inherited corruption, and are consequently liable to death and damnation (Van Mastricht 1699, 351). The atoning death of Christ is therefore necessary for all people—because it is only through Christ's death that sin of any sort can be forgiven. Even the regenerate are still afflicted by inherent original sin, which is why St. Paul speaks, in Romans 7, of the ongoing struggle within believers between the flesh and the Spirit (Van Mastricht 1699, 352).

Van Mastricht is clear, in other words, that original sin has devastating consequences for humanity. Even so, he does not want its consequences to be exaggerated. Original sin has corrupted human faculties, but it has not destroyed them. Human beings retain their natural capacity to will, to understand, and to act freely; so the impotence brought by original sin is "a spiritual impotence, not to any good whatever, whether natural, civil or moral, but to spiritual and saving good" (Van Mastricht 1699, 375). Even before they are regenerate, in other words, human beings are free to engage in naturally good actions such as eating and drinking. They are also free to pursue civilly good actions, such as being thoughtful to their neighbors. They are even free to pursue ecclesiastically or morally good actions, such as attending church, praying, and abstaining from crime. The only kind of activities which the unregenerate are incapable of performing, or even willing, are saving activities such as believing and hoping in Christ. Van Mastricht underlines that God has tempered the spiritual death which human beings suffer, leaving human beings endowed with some natural principles of truth that can guide their lives, such as the knowledge that God exists and that one should do as one would be done by. Human beings even retain some propensity to goodness, and although this inclination is transitory and listless, it produces some likeness of true virtue, which can be approved. God also frequently intervenes in the lives of the unregenerate with refraining grace, so that original sin does not break forth in the worst forms of wickedness (Van Mastricht 1699, 375).

This refraining grace is essential, Van Mastricht argues, because actual sin is the offspring of original sin, born "like a daughter from a mother" (Van Mastricht 1699, 360), so human beings cannot avoid actual sin in this life (Van Mastricht 1699, 365). In the absence of original righteousness, human inclinations are naturally evil: the corrupted mind easily admits error, and the corrupted will, now averse to the things of God, burns with godless desires instead. Van Mastricht notes that actual sins are not called "actual" because original sin is merely a potential sin; they are called "actual" because they are acts which deviate from the law of God, as opposed to original sin, which is a habitual deviation from that law. So an actual sin is a corrupt deed, whereas original sin is a corrupt disposition. Actual sins require a reasoned decision on the part of the sinner, which is why infants, although affected by original sin, are incapable of committing actual sin (Van Mastricht 1699, 360). Van Mastricht holds that all actual sins are in their own nature mortal, since every sin, however slight, represents a breach of God's law and impinges upon God's infinite majesty. That is why the Reformed reject the Roman Catholic suggestion that some sins are inherently mortal, and others merely venial.

Maresius also addresses the question of venial and mortal sin. He underlines that the denial that some sins are intrinsically venial, does not mean that the Reformed hold all sins to be equal: the fact that all sins are punishable by death does not mean that some sins are not worse than others. Furthermore, Maresius is prepared to admit that sins can be either mortal or venial "in the event"; in which sense, all sins committed by the elect are venial, and all sins committed by the reprobate are mortal. Maresius is even prepared to grant, albeit with some misgivings, that certain sins might properly be called mortal, because they are so serious that they may wound the conscience and reduce habitual grace, even though they cannot extinguish it completely. Such sins would therefore exclude the sinner from the degree of divine favor that was previously enjoyed, although only in terms of the execution of that favor in the gift of grace, not in terms of God's saving intention for the sinner (Maresius 1646–48, 1:553).

As we have seen, Van Mastricht believed that the sin of Adam was directly imputed to his descendants, but this view was not shared by all Reformed writers. In one of the *Theses Theologicae*, the French theologian, Josue de la Place (1596–1665), argued that there is no scriptural warrant for this view. He argued that the phrase in Romans 5:12, which was often used to support it, "εφ'ώ παντες ήμαρτον"—"in whom all have sinned"—is better translated "because of whom all have sinned." La Place also suggests the imputation of Adam's sin to his descendants is contrary to reason. For if Adam's sin is imputed to his descendants, why is not his death also imputed to them, thus liberating them from the liability to mortality? And how can his descendants' wills be deemed to have consented to Adam's sin, when he died long before those wills began to exist? Equally, if Adam was punished as God had promised, how is it compatible with the divine justice that others are also punished for his sin? Given the difficulties with imputed sin, La Place argues that the Christian religion should be liberated from this unnecessary imposition. Original sin is best conceived as arising only from the inherent corruption which has been transmitted from Adam (Cappel, Amyraut, and La Place 1641–51, 1:202).

La Place's view of original sin was immediately disputed; and at the Third Synod of Charenton (1644–45), the representatives of the French Reformed Church agreed to the following statement: "There was a report made in the Synod of a certain writing . . . holding forth this doctrine, that the whole nature of original sin consisted only in that corruption, which is hereditary to all men, and denieth the imputation of his first sin. This Synod condemneth the said doctrine as far as it restraineth the nature of original sin to the sole hereditary corruption of Adam's posterity, to the excluding of the imputation of that first sin by which he fell" (Quick 1692, 2:473). Taking advantage of the synod's failure to name him personally, La Place responded by arguing that the synod had not actually condemned his views at all. The synod, he noted, condemns only those who deny the imputation of Adam's sin. But imputation can be understood in two ways. Imputation is "immediate and antecedent," if Adam's sin is imputed to his descendants, prior to the transmission of hereditary corruption. Taken this way, imputation is understood—as indeed Van Mastricht understands it—as the cause, not the consequence, of hereditary corruption. Imputation is "mediate and consequent," if Adam's sin is imputed to his descendants only subsequent to the transmission of hereditary corruption. Taken this way, imputation is understood as the consequence, not the cause, of hereditary corruption. La Place contends that, since he was entirely happy with mediate and consequent imputation, the synod's decree was not directed at him (La Place 1655, 18).

In his *Institutes of Elenctic Theology*, Francis Turretin (1623–87) gave this argument short shrift. "If we look at the matter more closely," he wrote, "it will plainly appear that this distinction was devised to raise a smoke; retaining the name of imputation, in fact it takes away the sin itself. For if on this account only, the sin of Adam is said to be imputed to us mediately (because we are constituted guilty with God and become liable to punishment on account of the hereditary corruption which we draw from Adam), there will be properly no imputation of Adam's sin, but only of inherent corruption" (Turretin 1992, 1:615). It is no surprise, therefore, that Turretin was involved in preparing the *Helvetic Consensus* (1675), whose Canon XII explicitly condemns those who deny the immediate imputation of Adam's sin. The *Helvetic Consensus* was not, however, enforced for very long, even in Switzerland; and in 1722, the governments of Prussia and Great Britain requested that it be abolished, for the sake of Protestant unity. Daniel Wyttenbach (1706–79), may have been prepared to defend the *Consensus* a couple of decades later (Wyttenbach 1741–47, 2:609), but other Reformed writers did not feel compelled to do so. Hermann Venema (1697–1787) certainly taught mediate rather than immediate imputation (Venema 1850, 518). And Johann Stapfer (1708–75) complained that "it is more subtly than usefully disputed in the schools, whether guilt is derived from Adam's sin mediately, or immediately, since the same thing is held on both sides, and asserted against the Pelagianisers" (Stapfer 1743–47, 4:564).

# 3  GRACE

Maresius argues that grace may be understood in two ways: "affective grace" denotes the love and favor that God has for the elect in eternity; "effective grace" denotes both the actual power that God exerts in the conversion, regeneration, and sanctification of the elect, and the spiritual benefits conferred by that power, whether for the edification of the whole church, or for the salvation of an individual. Affective grace therefore concerns human beings, but effective grace works inside them (Maresius 1646–48, 2:137). Within effective grace, Maresius makes the further distinction between "grace freely given" and "grace which makes acceptable." The former describes gifts such as those mentioned in I Corinthians 12, which promote the salvation of others, but do not guarantee the salvation of the recipient. The latter are the "liberating, medicinal and salvific" gifts, which inhere in the recipients habitually and subjectively. Through these gifts, God's favor is made manifest, and they are guided towards Heaven.

Maresius underlines that human beings do not become acceptable to God on account of medicinal grace. Rather they are acceptable by virtue of God's favor and the Christ's merits. So "justifying grace"—the gracious divine decision to justify an elect person on account of the merits of Christ—should further be distinguished from "habitual grace"—the infused supernatural habits of the theological and moral virtues. The latter flow from justifying grace, and are poured into the elect by an actual motion of God. Justifying grace therefore precedes habitual grace. And among the theological and moral virtues that are conferred as a result of justifying grace, faith is the only one by which the elect are formally and effectively justified; though the other virtues may be said to justify declaratively and consequently (Maresius 1646–48, 2:141).

Maresius underlines that these supernatural habits are unlike natural habits. Natural habits are at the disposal of the human will: a person who can walk may exercise that ability whenever he chooses. Supernatural habits, by contrast, are stirred into action by the Holy Spirit, who dwells in the recipients of habitual grace (Maresius 1646–48, 2:143). Maresius disagrees with some Roman Catholic theologians, who suggest that people imbued with habitual grace require an additional gift of "actual grace" before habitual grace bears fruit. For Maresius, the Spirit's powerful presence is quite sufficient. As a result, Maresius is suspicious of the distinction between habitual and actual grace—a distinction, he notes, which is not found in Aquinas. That said, if by "actual grace" is meant simply the Spirit's activity in exciting supernatural habits into action, Maresius does not object, although he prefers the term "moving grace" (Maresius 1646–48, 2:144). And since the Holy Spirit dwells with believers permanently, he argues that moving grace is also permanently present as to the principle of its motion, even if it is not permanently active.

A further distinction which Maresius explores is that between "prevenient grace" and "cooperating grace." Through prevenient grace, God prepares a person's will to embrace God's saving work in them. Prevenient grace does not merely stand at the door and knock, leaving it up to the recipient's free choice whether to accept the grace or reject it; prevenient grace actually breaks open the door, moving and determining the recipient's free choice to work with God in the process of salvation. So prevenient grace does not work by moral suasion, nor is it simply an invitation on God's part; rather, it efficaciously convinces and powerfully draws the recipient (Maresius 1646–48, 2:147–48).

Prevenient grace is followed by cooperating grace. Cooperating grace completes the work of prevenient grace, by strengthening and confirming the pious motions that prevenient grace has inspired. Maresius is clear, however, that cooperating grace is no more dependent upon human free choice than prevenient grace. Cooperating grace is not a response to something which a human being chooses to do, independently, after receiving prevenient grace. It is the complement of prevenient grace, ensuring that the inclinations that prevenient grace inspires in the elect bear practical fruit (Maresius 1646–48, 2:150). This work of grace, Maresius insists, is without coercion. Grace illuminates the intellect with an accurate grasp of the good, and once the intellect has been illuminated, the will necessarily embraces that good. So the will infallibly follows the movement of grace, but without any reluctance; which is why the Reformed are happy to describe grace as "irresistible" (Maresius 1646–48, 2:153–54).

Turretin's discussion of grace begins with another distinction, namely that between "sufficient grace" and "efficacious grace." This was a distinction made by a number of Roman Catholic writers. "Sufficient grace" is help sufficient to enable conversion, if the recipient chooses to be converted; "efficacious grace" actually brings about conversion. Turretin concedes that one might talk about grace which is sufficient, relatively speaking, in that God provides many people who are not destined for salvation with sufficient external means and internal illumination for some knowledge of the truth, for temporary faith, as well as for conviction of sin and therefore inexcusability. "But, for conversion," he underlines, "we recognise no sufficient grace which is not also efficacious" (Turretin 1992, 2:511). In the workings of efficacious grace, the Spirit acts in a manner suitable to rational creatures: "the Spirit does not force the will and carry it on unwillingly to conversion, but glides most sweetly into the soul . . . and operates by an infusion of supernatural habits, by which it is freed little by little from its innate depravity, so as to become willing from unwilling, and living from dead" (Turretin 1992, 2:524). As a consequence, "liberty in this affair conspires in a friendly way with necessity" (Turretin 1992, 2:525).

In the work of conversion, the Spirit does not act without the Word. However, the Spirit does not only work mediately, through the Word, but also works immediately within the recipient of grace. "Such and so great is the corruption into the soul by sin," he writes, "that although there always remains in it a natural power of understanding and willing, still the moral habit or disposition of judging and willing properly has so failed that it can no longer be moved by the presentation of the object . . . unless the faculty itself is first renovated." That is why the objective and extrinsic grace of the Word must be accompanied by the subjective and intrinsic operation of the Spirit (Turretin 1992, 2:526–27). Turretin underlines, however, that the insistence that grace works immediately within its recipients should not be confused with Enthusiasm; because, unlike the Reformed, Enthusiasts claim that the Spirit works separately from the Word and without regard to the mind's own reasoning processes, impressing on the mind knowledge that is not drawn from the Word (Turretin 1992, 2:541).

Turretin is more reluctant than Maresius to describe grace as "irresistible." The term, he argues, is barbarous and ill-adapted to the way grace works. Such is the effect of original sin, that human beings are not only able to resist the work of grace, but invariably do so. However, this resistance is inchoate and incomplete in the elect, and is overcome by efficacious grace. Turretin underlines, though, that "the divine action does not injure but strengthens the liberty of the will, and nothing hinders the same action from being performed freely (i.e. of his own accord by man) and yet being done by the invincible grace of God" (Turretin 1992, 2:553). So although grace inclines the will, it does so without coercion: it works not extrinsically but intrinsically; and it works in congruity with human nature, not undermining it, but perfecting it (Turretin 1992, 2:558).

# 4 Ethics

For Pierre Du Moulin (1568–1658), ethics begins with the human will. The will is the faculty of the soul which moves a human being to action. The will is naturally drawn to the good and no one chooses what is evil for its own sake, but only because it appears to be good. The will can be considered as ordered toward two things: either the end of human life, or the means to that end; and ethics is consequently concerned with those two areas of inquiry (Du Moulin 1645, 17). The end of human life is the untroubled possession of the highest good; namely, union with God. The intellect was made to know God, and the will to love God, and both are perfected in that union. When human beings fell into sin, they lost this union, and they cannot be happy unless it is restored. The whole business of religion is therefore to restore it (Du Moulin 1645, 23). Du Moulin therefore disagrees with the Stoic philosophers, who argued that virtue itself is the highest good. Instead, he argues that "without true knowledge of God and piety, all virtue vanishes, and is a name without the thing" (Du Moulin 1645, 41).

Du Moulin believed that moral virtues are the means to humanity's end. His views therefore present a challenge to those who suggest that the magisterial Protestant traditions lost touch with virtue ethics (e.g., Gregory 2012, 206–9). Through virtue, Du Moulin argues, human beings are acceptable to God, as well as useful to their nation, their neighbors, and themselves (Du Moulin 1645, 43). Du Moulin defines virtue as "the habit of a good will, holding the mean which is prescribed by right reason" (Du Moulin 1645, 47). He therefore follows Aristotle and Aquinas in holding that all virtues occupy the middle ground between two vices, one of defect and one of excess. The virtue of temperance is the mean between self-indulgence and self-destructive austerity; the virtue of liberality is the mean between excessive profusion and avarice; etc. (Du Moulin 1645, 55). Since they are habits, virtues are properties that inhere in the will, and predispose the will to choose actions that are just, and to avoid the contrary. They therefore regulate the natural appetite, and enable the will to avoid sin. Like all habits, virtues are the result of repeated actions, and in the case of virtues, of morally good actions. For Du Moulin, an action is morally good only if it meets a number of stringent conditions. The agent must know that the action is good in its own nature, and consonant with God's law. The action must be undertaken for a good end and must employ good means to that end. The action must be undertaken without reluctance or procrastination, but promptly and with relish. The agent must contemplate the action with gladness, and must bring it to completion through constancy and perseverance (Du Moulin 1645, 60).

Human virtues are a reflection of God's nature, for God possesses all virtue in the divine essence (Du Moulin 1645, 44). The virtues are therefore one aspect of the image of God, in which human beings were created (Du Moulin 1645, 75). Before the Fall, human beings were abundantly adorned with virtue, enjoying a rectitude of will that reflected the divine justice (Du Moulin 1645, 76). After the Fall, however, just as human knowledge of God was reduced to a few glimmers of understanding, so the original virtues were reduced to limited remnants—such as shame, modesty, conscience, generosity, and tolerance, which can be found amongst all peoples (Du Moulin 1645, 77). These natural endowments are not real virtues, but only "semi-virtues"; although they do may make it easier for a person to acquire the moral virtues, and so may be considered as the seeds of true virtue (Du Moulin 1645, 79).

As has been observed, for Du Moulin an action is only morally good if it is consonant with God's law. He believes that God's laws are both naturally impressed upon human minds, and also subsequently revealed. Since they are impressed upon the human mind, these natural laws bind all of humanity and are, of their nature, immutable (Du Moulin 1645, 122). The better laws of gentile legislators are all drawn from this natural law, without which human society would be impossible. Such is the depravity of human beings, however, that many human laws have also been enacted that are wicked and plainly contrary to natural law (Du Moulin 1645, 120); but where human laws do reflect aspects of natural law, they can be described as divine (Du Moulin 1645, 123). Du Moulin's striking emphasis on natural law supports the recent scholarship that challenges inherited assumptions that natural law reasoning does not sit comfortably within a Reformed theological worldview (e.g., Grabill 2006, 13–17).

Du Moulin's ethical work was conceived as part of his philosophical, rather than his theological, oeuvre. So it demonstrates that the Reformed were quite prepared to discuss ethical questions, outside an explicitly theological framework, even if that discussion was undoubtedly shaped by their theological views, and particularly their understanding of the Fall. More commonly, however, the Reformed discussed ethics on the basis of the Ten Commandments. Chapter XIX of the Westminster Confession underlines the Decalogue's centrality to the Reformed ethical reflection; noting that, after Adam's Fall, God's law "continued to be a perfect rule of righteousness; and, as such, was delivered by God upon Mount Sinai, in ten commandments, and written in two tables: the first four commandments containing our duty towards God; and the other six, our duty to man." Even so, when Reformed writers approach the Ten Commandments, the natural moral capacity of humanity remains a key motif. For John Edwards (1637–1716), the Decalogue illustrates "that righteousness and holiness, which have respect to natural religion, and which flow from the law of nature and right reason" (Edwards 1713–26, 2:278). The quintessence of the Decalogue, he suggests, is love; for love is "the ground of all the other virtuous endowments and graces. They are all but various modifications and different applications of love" (Edwards 1713–26, 2:289). In their fallen state, human beings are incapable of loving, except in a carnal and sensual way; so they must receive a "diviner flame of celestial love" in regeneration, as a grace of the Holy Spirit (Edwards 1713–26, 3:31). This new love embraces God for himself, and others for God's sake (Edwards 1713–26, 2:294); indeed, it is "the act of the soul whereby it is united to him" (Edwards 1713–26, 2:290). And although this love is a supernatural gift, it is nonetheless entirely consonant with reason: "for his innate wisdom, mercy, justice, faithfulness, his unspotted holiness and purity, with all the other excellencies and perfections belonging to his glorious essence, are the adequate object of our love. If we act but like men and rational creatures, we cannot but admire and love these . . . ." (Edwards 1713–26, 2:294).

# 5 CONCLUSION

The freedom and moral capacity of human beings lies at the heart of the Reformed theological vision. As rational creatures, human beings have the ability to choose whatever their intellect presents to them as good. This ability is the basis of moral responsibility and is an inalienable aspect of human nature. By distinguishing between different kinds of necessity, the Reformed seek to explain how free choice, and the fundamental contingency of human action, are not impaired by the divine decree. For the Reformed, all sin is mortal in nature, and all sinners would be destined to condemnation, were it not for the death of Christ. The Reformed distinguish original sin from the actual sins that flow from it. They conceive of original sin as both inherent—infecting all the human faculties—and imputed, although there is debate as to how that imputation is best understood. But despite the damage done by sin, the Reformed argue that human beings retain some knowledge of God and some semblance of virtue. They are also capable of actions which, whilst not saving, are good in a civic or moral sense. For the Reformed, grace is the only medicine which can repair the damage done by sin. Grace springs from the divine favor, and manifests itself in human beings in the form of supernatural virtues, which are brought to life by the indwelling Spirit. Grace is sovereign in the work of redemption, but does no damage to free choice. The Reformed conceive union with God to be the highest end of human existence, an end that is properly sought through the pursuit of virtue. Virtues are habits that incline a person to good actions, and God's law is the proper norm of those actions. This law is not only revealed in the Decalogue, but also written into human nature. The twofold love of God and of neighbor, which fulfils this law, is impossible for fallen human beings. It is instead received as a gift from the Holy Spirit.

## BIBLIOGRAPHY

Asselt, Willem J. van, J. Martin Bac, and Roelf T. Te Velde. 2010. *Reformed Thought on Freedom: The Concept of Free Choice in Early Modern Reformed Theology.* Grand Rapids, MI: Baker.

Cappel, Louis, Moïse Amyraut, and Josué de la Place. 1641–51. *Theses theologicae in Academia Salmuriensi . . . disputatae.* Saumur.

de la Place, Josué. 1655. *De imputation primi peccati . . . disputatio.* Saumur.

Du Moulin, Pierre. 1645. *Opera philosophica: logica, physica, ethica.* Amsterdam.

Edwards, John. 1713–1726. 3 vols. *Theologia reformata.* London.

Edwards, Jonathan. 1957–2008. 26 vols. *Works.* New Haven: Yale University Press.

Grabill, Stephen J. 2006. *Rediscovering the Natural Law in Reformed Theological Ethics.* Grand Rapids: Eerdmans.

Gregory, Brad S. 2012. *The Unintended Reformation: How a Religious Revolution Secularized Society.* Cambridge: Harvard University Press.

Hill, George. 3 vols. *Lectures in Divinity.* Edited by Alexander Hill. Edinburgh.

Maresius, Samuel. 1646–1648. 2 vols. *Theologiae elenchticae nova synopsis.* Groningen.

Muller, Richard A. 2011. "Jonathan Edwards and the Absence of Free Choice: A Parting of Ways in the Reformed Tradition." *Jonathan Edwards Studies* 1 (1): 3–22.

Quick, John. 1691–1692. 2 vols. *Synodicon in Gallia reformata.* London.

Stapfer, Johann Friedrich. 1743–1747. 5 vols. *Institutiones theologiæ polemicæ universæ, ordine scientifico dispositæ.* Zurich.

Turretin, Francis. 1992. 3 vols. *Institutes of Elenctic Theology*. Translated by George Musgrave Giger. Edited by James T. Dennison, Jr. Phillipsburg, NJ: P & R Publishing.

Van Mastricht, Peter. 1699. *Theoretico-practica theologia*. Utrecht.

Venema, Hermann. *Institutes of Theology*. Edited and translated by Alex W. Brown. Edinburgh.

Wyttenbach, Daniel. 1741–1747. 3 vols. *Tentamen theologiae dogmaticae methodo scientifica pertractatae*. Bern.

CHAPTER 16

# CHURCH AND CHURCH/ STATE RELATIONS IN THE POST-REFORMATION REFORMED TRADITION

IAN HAZLETT

## 1 INTRODUCTION

THE "Leiden Synopsis," a Reformed digest, wanted to "make clear to all and sundry that there is total unanimity in what we believe and think, and that we share a consensus in all the heads of theology" (Leiden Synopsis 1625, *4). The Synopsis included the church and sacraments. On both there was a working consensus in Reformed circles, but no complete homogeneity, especially on ecclesiology. Post-1600 sacramental thought was stable and consistent. Historic differences between "Zwinglian" and "Calvinist" angles faded, although discord with Lutherans remained. Ecclesiology was potentially controversial, especially when one includes episcopalian and congregationalist churches in Britain as Reformed. If they rejected the Reformed brand of ecclesiology, they still shared large swathes of Reformed doctrine. Initially, such diversity (including church-state relations and liturgy) was not a breaker of fellowship. However, later statements according confessional (and so divine) status to particular concepts of ministerial order, church polity, and discipline, strained fraternal links. Serious disruptions were confined mostly to Britain from circa 1580 to 1660. General solidarity was explicable by the need for survival and identity protection in a world where the fortification of Reformed institutions was paramount. It was helped by the Reformed attitude that assumed unity of faith, while accepting at least verbal flexibility on some doctrines and adaptation to regional circumstances. In any event, the Reformed could not insist on Procrustean uniformity, there being no mandate and machinery with which to impose it. There was, then, a slight tension between the Leiden Synopsis's "total unanimity" and "shared consensus," since even within Reformed orthodoxy there were areas of less zip-fastened thought.

After 1600, most Reformed theology textbooks tended to minimize internal and ecclesiological and sacramental differences. It was in the mid-seventeenth-century British Isles, especially England, that mayhem occurred over ecclesiology with total discord and disruption prevailing for a generation (Dorner 1871, 49–65).

As for the sacraments, from about 1600 the previously high temperature surrounding the issue cooled. Respective positions became embedded. Most authors wrote with relative restraint, if robustly and in a doctrinaire fashion. The Lutheran-Reformed divide on the Lord's Supper, Christology, and predestination remained, but a peaceable modus vivendi set in, along with intermittent concord impulses mostly from the Reformed. Among them an increasingly common understanding prevailed on the sacraments, combining perspectives that had originated in Zurich, Strasbourg, Geneva, and Heidelberg; even if from about 1600 onwards the mature Zurich theology appeared to be more influential. From about 1700, thinking on the church and sacraments experienced stasis, as was the case in general (Muller 1987, 96–97). This resulted in little creative thinking on those topics. Up until then, Reformed orthodoxy had been shaped with the contours of predestinarian and covenant of grace motifs; the confessional debut of the latter was in the 1643 Westminster Confession (7). The development bore on ecclesiology and the sacraments.

## 2 Ecclesiology

### 2.1 Context and basic perspectives

The chief premise determining the Protestant view of the church was that repentant believers are saved solely by God's mercy and the merit of Christ, the only mediator, thus excluding human contribution. This was reiterated in Reformed confessions of faith. Conceptions of church, ministry, and sacraments followed logically, reinforced by predestinarian and covenant theology to ring-fence redemption as unilaterally divine and its particularist application. This determined the continuing rejection of the Roman view of the infallible church. In Reformation thought, the visible church being not a divine institution does not dispense salvation—it only proclaims it. Excluded are all human and institutional inputs or guarantees. As the Irish Articles (1615) stated: "We must renounce the merit of all our said virtues, of faith, hope, charity . . . we must trust only in God's mercy and the merits of . . . our only redeemer, saviour and justifier, Jesus Christ" (36). Church and sacraments are considered in this light.

The Genevan Francis Turretin (1623–87) remarked that the fiercest controversy of the age was over church (Turretin 1685, 18.1.1). For the Reformed, belief in the true and invisible church of Christ was a credal article. This ruled out trust and faith in the visible church, a fallible body. Therefore, Roman criteria for an authentic church were dismissed. The Zurich theologian, Johannes Heidegger (1633–98), dismissed Robert Bellarmine's (1542–1621) fifteen notes of true Catholic identity (Heidegger 1732, 26.76–91). For Protestant thinkers those marks can harbor error, corruption, and impurity; they cannot validate a true church, especially when their operation seems to derogate from the exclusiveness of Christ's redemptive work. Turretin noted: "One cannot prove the Church of Rome to be the true church, because it clashes with the fundamentals" (Turretin 1685, 18.14.6).

## 2.2 Defining the church

Reformed vocabulary is traditional. The true church is invisible, one, holy, the body or bride of Christ, catholic or universal, the communion of saints, militant, triumphant, eternal, and infallible. The Reformed vision adapted this to decretal predestination and the covenant of grace (Hauschild 1999, 446–91), the double divine framework, operated by the Trinity, sustaining the true church. This church exists partly in the visible church—but elusively, and it can even exist on earth without a visible church. The true, invisible church is not so much a community of the elect as the spiritual convocation of elect individuals—past, present, and future. They have the saving faith gifted by God, have responded to the call of the Word and the Spirit, and enjoy communion with Christ and each other. They have, therefore, "effectual calling"; that is, are living in a state of grace, regenerated and exercising righteousness. For them, the visible church is a cradle in the process of salvation—comparable to the "chain of salvation" whereby "salvation is ordained by God in Heaven, promised by the Word in Scripture, merited by Christ in man's nature, sealed by the sacraments in the church, received by faith in the heart" (Wollebius 1660, frontispiece).

In Reformed thinking, the word "church" always needs clarification, since identifying its proper membership requires discrimination. Heidegger envisaged a threefold category of individuals—the uncalled elect, the elect called externally, and the effectually called. This means that "All citizens of the Church are elect, but not all elect are citizens of the Church" (Heidegger 1732, 26.6). Such thinking is traceable to the 1530 *Reckoning of Faith* (6) by Zwingli (1484–1531). Accordingly, the invisible and visible churches were not identical; the former an object of faith, the latter a societal body in which there can be faked faith. Nonetheless, the true church could still be within the visible church, but only partially. This provoked the Roman rebuke that this meant two churches, reducing the true church, unsignposted, to a Platonist utopia. Reformed writers denied this, for profession of faith and institutional church membership do not necessarily imply communion with Christ. Yet the two churches may still coincide. When they do overlap, they are indeed one, but not empirically. It is outside the true church that there is no salvation, not the visible church whose holiness is unsteady and to which uncalled elect might not even belong.

However, there were blurring tendencies. The Westminster Confession affirmed that "outside [the visible church] there is no *ordinary* possibility of salvation" (25.2). Seeing that this seemed to bar any elect outside the visible church not yet called by the Word, or those not yet effectually called, it looks like a constriction, but only prima facie. Moreover, extraordinary salvation was conceivable in the Zurich theology. Following Zwingli's idea that one may also wish for the eternal life of virtuous pagans and that God had some allies among Gentiles, the Second Helvetic Confession observed that while "there is no *certain* salvation outside [the Church] ... we know that God had some friends in the world outside the commonwealth of Israel" (17.13–14).

Within Reformed theology, there was no unanimity on the relationship between the parish congregation and the visible church Catholic. The predominant thinking was that the local church was a particular embodiment of the wider church. The latter is the ecclesial starting point and has precedence, for to the "catholic visible church Christ has given the ministry, oracles, and ordinance of God, for the gathering and perfecting of saints" (Westminster Confession, 25.3), delegated locally. All parochial gatherings of Christians are subordinate to that. An alternative ecclesiology was advanced by English Puritans, including John Owen (1616–83), William Ames (1576–1633), and Thomas Goodwin (1600–80) (Trueman 2013, 285–88). This was that the local congregation is sovereign. It has precedence and is independent of any higher ecclesiastical authority, since in the local congregation Christ's authority is not mediate, but direct through the Spirit (via pastors). It is, then, the true visible church. Their key text was Ephesians 4:4. The local church is part of the one mystical body of Christ, united with the Spirit, and a union of faith and love to be manifested on the last days. Such a pneumatology determined this alternative ecclesiology (Wisse and Meijer 2013, 505–9). It repudiates the notion that church unity in Christ can only operate via a corporate, superior institution. This explains why congregationalists accepted most of the Westminster Confession, except its ecclesiology and church-state relations. They defined the church as the visible, local, empirical congregation of saints or believers separated from the world. Their Savoy Declaration (1658) rejected the authority of any higher ecclesiastical body by affirming that "the visible catholic church of Christ [does not] have any officers to rule or govern in, or over, the whole body" (26.2). The local congregation is autonomous. This is far removed from Reformed orthodoxy, but it does emanate from within the Reformed theological family.

## 2.3  Identifying the visible true church

The formal marks of a proper church were usually seen as threefold: preaching, two sacraments, and church discipline, and was the standard view (Leiden Synopsis 1625, 40.45). The context was demarcation from the Roman Church, seen as "untrue" or at least "impure." Puritans also applied the last epithet to the reformed Church of England. However, in respect of the stated marks, the numerical figure was not always fixed at three. The third, discipline, was not always formally cited as a mark in the pre-1600 era, even if discipline was common to all Reformed churches—"an absolute necessity in the church," as the Second Helvetic Confession stated (18.20). The role of discipline and its complementary value in the Christian life was always affirmed.

Discipline as a third mark originated with Johannes Oecolampadius (1482–1531) and Martin Bucer (1491–1551), but the sole two marks of preaching and the sacraments as in the Augsburg Confession were adhered to by John Calvin (1509–64) and some confessions, while others specified three marks. Preaching and the sacraments, conductors of the Word, constitute the Church; without them there can be no church, whereas hypothetically there could be an exemplary church without discipline. However, it is notable that later, the two or three marks were expressed in more hierarchical terms, so that the sacraments and preaching were not co-equal. The transition from the idea of several necessary marks to an actual emphasis on ultimately only one "necessary and perpetual mark" of the church, the Word and orthodox doctrine, was made by Theodore Beza (1519–1605) (Maruyama 1978, 159–73). A century later, Benedict Pictet (1655–1724) echoed this: "Above all is the pure preaching of the divine Word," for the sacraments and discipline can be out of service (Pictet 1696, 13.6.2). This helps explain why within Reformed churches massive predominance was accorded to preaching and teaching (orthodox doctrine), especially since Communion was infrequent. The primacy of preaching also pervades the Westminster *Directory for Public Worship* (1645).

On the interaction between the marks, there is variety of vocabulary, formulation, and presentation among post-Reformation writers. Definition in terms of two or three, or even of "marks," is not decisive. Some said that the only marks are doctrine and discipline, where doctrine includes preaching, and "discipline" the sacraments. And while the Westminster Confession, avoiding "marks," cites the church as having "the ministry, oracles, and ordinances of God" (25), it is elsewhere that discipline is mentioned in terms of the power of the keys—delegated by Christ to the "officers of the church" (30).

## 2.4 Church authority

Identifying an authentic church also mutated into terms of a threefold "church authority": ministry, order, and discipline. The first is preaching and administering the sacraments. Both transmit the divine promise of forgiveness of sins for the repentant, so that the minister has no personal authority.

The second authority, order, safeguards right faith and practice based on scripture which preceded the outward church; it explains and protects them from error, as by a confession of faith. A confession is a testimony of faith, not a norm of it and not conscience-binding. A confession is useful and provisional, but the church does not stand or fall by it. As Turretin put it: scripture is divine and infallible, but confessions are "human documents" that cannot bind the conscience "except so far as they are found to be in agreement with the Word" (Turretin 1685, 18.30.9–10). The church also regulates worship while permitting degrees of liberty. In contrast, episcopalian Reformed churches were less permissive, as they adhered to prescriptive liturgies, seen as a better way of habituating the people into the divine plan of salvation.

The third power is discipline, seen as pastoral and pedagogical, not punitive. Sins causing public offence, moral or doctrinal, trigger discipline and could entail minor or major excommunication. The latter, reversible on repentance, usually meant social exclusion and isolation; but only denunciation was in order, not fulminating damnation. While discipline's rationale was to keep Christ's church pure, it was also intended to help save sinners, and to stay God's wrath in the face of profanity (Westminster Confession, 30.3). High-profile excommunication could also involve the civil authority.

## 2.5 The ministry

The sole head of the church is Christ, but his rule in the external church operates through human agency—the ministry. This offers salvation mediately and instrumentally as "God's co-workers." Such ministry is upheld against Anabaptist and spiritualist notions, which envisaged direct rule by Christ through the Spirit. It also opposes the traditional Roman concept of priesthood, seen as a spiritual caste lording it over Christian consciences and appeasing the deity rather than performing "service." Essential is vocation along with inward and outward calling, the latter corporately, followed by ordination. Rigorous testing established authenticity and secured accreditation, as ministry is holy, and ministers are sent by Christ. This is an ordinary call. An extraordinary call involving no ecclesiastical vetting and so "immediate" was possible. God initiates it "either to set up a new regime in the Church or to restore one that has collapsed" (Wollebius 1634, 1.26.3). Examples of this are rare. It was a hypothetical idea inspired by examples in scripture. In Reformed thought, clarified earlier by Beza, the extraordinary ministry was foundational, once and for all only, while its legacy continued in the ordinary ministry (Maruyama 1978, 233–235). Consequently, apostolic succession is not of persons but of doctrine. This is why some (like Beza) cite apostolic, that is, orthodox doctrine as the cardinal mark of the church linked to preaching and the sacraments. Turretin concurred: "the true church of Christ is wherever apostolic doctrine is presented along with the legitimate use of the sacraments and preaching" (Turretin 1685, 18.12.11).

Normative in the Calvinian Reformed theory of ministry is that the right of calling a minister is exercised by the wider representative church, like a district presbytery or synod—an assembly of ministers and elders exercising the *presbyterium*, and thereby conciliar and collegial authority. A civil figure of authority could attend an installation in an acknowledging or confirming role, but ultimately, church autonomy was crucial, especially for the Genevan tradition. By the 1600s such a view was being challenged. English independents or congregationalists ascribed the right of electing a minister to the local congregation only. Or, local patrons could claim the right of appointing ministers. Or, episcopal Reformed churches in the British Isles reserved rights to a bishop.

The fourfold ministry was implanted in core Reformed tradition, despite de facto contraction to three. The first two were pastors (or ministers) and doctors (teachers).

They were teaching presbyters, and reflect the Reformation concern with the cognitive appropriation of the faith and its articulation. There was no unanimity about the office of a church doctor in practice, so that it never materialized. The lack of scriptural precision helps explain this, as the Dutch theologian, Petrus van Mastricht (1632–1706) pointed out (Mastricht 1724, 7.2.20). The third and fourth offices in the fourfold model were adjunctive elders and deacons. The (ruling) presbyters or elders saw to governance and discipline, and met with the pastor in committee (session). Deacons dealt with money and alms. The actual threefold ministry, "ordinary and perpetual" (Maruyama 1978, 233), became the norm. It was epitomized in the Westminster Assembly's *The Form of Presbyterial Church Government* (1645).

## 2.6 Church government

Within broad Reformed Protestantism three ecclesiological concepts collided: episcopal, presbyterial, and congregational, all claiming biblical sanction. The first was monarchical, the second aristocratic, and the third democratic—this last was often characterized as "fanatic," "anabaptist," "independent," "Brownist," "separatist," or "libertine." In England there was an intense struggle between these concepts, but the major clash was between episcopal and presbyterial notions. (All agreed, however, that spiritually, Christ was the head of the church.)

Irreconcilable polarization ensued. The presbyterial position was grounded on autonomous spiritual jurisdiction, ministerial parity, and hierarchical conciliar government. What came to be nonnegotiable was that it claimed to be scriptural and valid by divine right. It developed as another mark of a true church, a matter of belief, not just preference. It was incompatible with Reformed churches in the British Isles that retained the historic episcopate, a hierarchical ministry of bishop, priest or minister, and deacon. For in the end, episcopal apologists also appealed to a divine right theory, based on scripture and tradition. Thereby, episcopacy was not just a matter of usefulness and well-being in the church; it belonged to the church's essence.

For the early reformers, episcopal polity was not a dogmatic issue, even if they set it aside. Bucer, Heinrich Bullinger (1504–75), Calvin, and Peter Martyr (1499–1562) had a pragmatic attitude, at least provisionally: hierarchical episcopacy could be expedient in times of need for reform. In Britain, however, a sharp theological divide fueled standoffs. The result was a Pyrrhic victory for presbyterianism at the Westminster Assembly of Divines. Its plan was to implement presbyterian polity, but this succeeded only in Scotland (1690).

Presbyterian advocates in Britain were Andrew Melville (1545–1642), Walter Travers (1548–1635) and Thomas Cartwright (1535–1603). Formative interventions came from Beza and Hadrian Saravia (1532–1612) (Maruyama 1978, 174–96). In 1575, Beza sent a private memorandum to Scotland: "On the Threefold Episcopacy." He rejected two forms of episcopacy—that of the papacy (tyranny), and that of human convenience and papacy-free tradition (Anglican). The only legitimate episcopacy was God's apostolic order grounded in ministerial equality—the presbyterian principle. Novel here was that the divine order and the presbyterian system were considered identical. This challenged episcopacy by divine right, leading to an exchange of publications between Beza and Saravia from 1590 to 1610 (Maruyama 1978, 174–195). Saravia considered ministers (bishops, pastors, deacons, elders) as unequal in principle, not only in their functions but also in status. After all, he argued, apostles were superior to evangelists and prophets, evangelists superior to bishops, and bishops superior to presbyters (priests) or elders. Further, while there is equality in ministry of Word and sacraments, there is inequality in church government. Repudiating this, Beza held that the biblical episcopal office, being collective, corresponds to the fourfold *presbyterium* sitting in presbytery or synod as the true "divine episcopacy." All moderators are *primus inter pares* with no eminence or superior authority. These were the best safeguards against abuse.

Subsequently, the benchmarks were ultimately Beza and Saravia. It is notable that some of the defenders of episcopacy (if not by divine right) were otherwise firmly Reformed in theology, like Archbishop Whitgift (1530–1604), William Whitaker (1548–95) and King James VI & I (1566–1625) whose maxim, "no bishop, no king," increased the stakes. Reformed theologians who argued for a "reduced" or semi-episcopacy to accommodate presbyterianism (as trialed in Scotland 1610–38) included John Reynolds (1549–1607) and the Irish primate, James Ussher (1581–1656). The gap was insurmountable. Thereafter, Bezan doctrinaire presbyterianism became the badge of Reformed church structure. Van Mastricht formulated a classical description of "a threefold joint session of the church ministry: presbyterial, diocesan or classical, and synodal or provincial or national or oecumenical" (Mastricht 1724, 7.2.25).

# 3   CHURCH-STATE RELATIONS

## 3.1  Spheres of competence

In the Pauline and Augustinian traditions, the reformers evaluated temporal power positively. Their zeal for good relations with the civil authorities was also a reaction to initial Catholic opinion that they were subversive and fomenting anarchy. Zwinglian magisterialism was so strong that distinctive ecclesiastical jurisdiction evaporated. A methodological innovation in theology was that most confessions and textbooks itemized the "magistrate." This elevated the topic to a credal level, involving not just duty and obedience, but also Christian conscience. Subsequent Reformed writers continued this line, but also with discreet consideration of questions of dissent and resistance.

The reformers had also affirmed divine authority for secular government along with its religious responsibility. The two spheres were subject to God, so that Christians straddled both worlds. However, following the Reformation's elimination of the medieval distinction between the spiritual and lay estates, and its denial that the earthly church embodies necessarily the true and invisible church (the kingdom of Christ), considering church-state relations in the usual binary manner is an oversimplification. For in Reformation theology, the picture was tri-dimensional: the temporal sphere (state), the spiritual sphere (invisible kingdom of Christ), the visible church (a fallible image of the former). That was the theology. The relative downgrading of the visible church may have encouraged Christian rulers to interfere more in the Reformation open church.

All secular rulers had been characterized as "lieutenants of God" (Scots Confession, 24). They had the second table of the Mosaic law observed as natural law, coercively if necessary, and so for the common good. Moreover, a Christian government ought also to ensure the application of the first table of the divine law dealing with religion—*cura religionis*. This role of watchman referred to securing the "true faith" and "pure worship," free of idolatry and heresy, as Old Testament reforming monarchs (godly princes) had done. Accordingly, there is a link between the political and religious obligations of Christian rulers. As Pictet expressed it, in religion the rulers are "nurses, shepherds, and fathers" (Pictet 1696, 13.13.3). When listing some of the model kings of Israel, Pictet added Emperor Constantine (AD 272–337). All Reformed theologians welcomed the Constantinian model, whereby the state religion embodied in the church enjoys the protection and patronage of the secular authority.

Pictet added a Calvinist note of caution by asserting that this role implies no governmental competence in the church's spiritual jurisdiction (*in sacra*); he cites the lines of demarcation as doctrine, preaching, the sacraments, conscience, church discipline, and the ministerial office (Pictet 1696, 13.13.4). The same point had been made previously by not only the Thirty-Nine Articles and the Irish Articles on the "supreme governor of the church," but also by the Westminster Confession. The two jurisdictions are parallel. Yet the civil supportive role is stressed: while excluded from ministry and discipline, the rulers must maintain church unity and peace, help keep God's truth pure and whole, suppress heresy and abuses, guarantee church ordinances, convoke synods and attend to ensure transactions conform to the mind of God (23.3). This still grants considerable authority to the government. Moreover, the English parliament vetoed the chapter on distinct spiritual jurisdiction (30.1). This was a typical problem in Calvinist contexts— religio-political reality usually prevailed over church theory.

There was alternative Reformed thinking. The 1658 congregationalist Savoy Declaration endorsed most of the Westminster Confession, but it not only rejected the latter's views on church government and discipline, it also sought to curtail some of the prerogatives of the magistrate in general religious affairs (*circa sacra*). While the state religion is Christian and rulers should protect it as a duty to the first table of the law, they need not enforce uniformity in everything. Freedom and toleration should be broadened (although not to Roman Catholics), so that the government should not meddle in doctrinal differences where there is the same "foundation" (Savoy Declaration, 24.3).

Various positions in the Reformed spectrum were irreconcilable. The first, rooted in Zurich, conceded to the civil authority so much that it led to a unitary entity composed of a *corpus Christianorum* in which the magistrates governed everything. This was not just a state religion, but a state church. Magistrates supervised most aspects of church life and doctrine. Such a fusion ("single sphere") can be variously designated: radically "Constantinian-Theodosian," "caesaro-papist," or "Erastian." It also appealed to architects of the Church of England. The second was the Genevan tradition, stressing not separation between church and state but their distinctiveness, so that autonomous spiritual jurisdiction of the church must be kept intact to avoid a mixing of secular and spiritual interests. Here the task was to seek the golden mean between the two spheres, especially when they intersected. While collaboration was desirable, a special role of the Calvinist church was that of "watchman" to signal encroachment by the rulers, but it was seldom exercised formally. However, the risk of conflict, especially low-level, in this general understanding was very high. The third, the London Savoy concept, kept the magistrate at an even greater arm's length to the extent that the ancient concept of "one state, one church, one theology, one worship" was threatened.

By way of illustration, certain specific areas of church-state interface in the Calvinist tradition were often contentious. One was the calling and installation of ministers. Debates exposed ecclesiological fissures within general Reformed Christianity. "Erastian" magistrates argued for the civil power's prerogative to appoint ministers—a view articulated by people of Reformed backgrounds like Thomas Erastus (1524–83), Hugo Grotius (1583–1645), Thomas Coleman (1598–1647) and John Selden (1584–1654), the last two being Westminster divines. Such an issue, which also involved "patronage," disturbed the Scottish church for centuries to come.

The other issue, church discipline, was double: is the church or the magistrate in charge?—and is the civil power itself subject to discipline? Heidegger in Zurich was sufficiently Calvinist to object to increasing state intrusion on spiritual matters. Complaining about Erastus and Coleman, and appealing to Matthew 18:15–18, he deplored the ideas of confining church authority to preaching and the sacraments, and about rulers' immunity from church censure (Heidegger 1732, 27.35).

In the 1560s in Heidelberg, Erastus had criticized linking discipline and excommunication to a ban from Communion (Gunnoe 2011, 163–210). Further, he objected to the consistorial courts involving both civil and church officials and the underlying conception of church-state relations. From the Old Testament he concluded that there should only be one government in a Christian state, the civil one, with the exclusive right to penalize offenders. Admiring the Zurich model, he denied separate ecclesiastical jurisdiction. A private controversy ensued between Erastus and Beza, who held that disciplinary competence belongs to the presbytery, not the magistrate, thus insisting on double jurisdiction. The dispute, with Bullinger's collusion, was hushed up until 1589 when the various manuscripts exchanged were published (Maruyama 1978, 112–129). Erastus was lauded in anti-Calvinist Protestant circles, such as by the Church of England apologist, Richard Hooker (1554–1600), who cited Erastus in his *Laws of Ecclesiastical Polity*. At the Westminster Assembly of Divines, opponents of Erastian speakers were the Scots, George Gillespie (1613–48) and Samuel Rutherford (1600–62). Their books (1646) on the subject were important contributions to presbyterian theory; namely, Gillespie *Aaron's Rod Blossoming*, and Rutherford's *The Divine Right of Church Government and*

*Excommunication.* In short, there was no uniform Reformed position on not only discipline, but also church-state relations.

## 3.2 Obedience and resistance

Following Romans 13, the Reformers had taught that the divinely constituted state is owed loyalty and prayerful support, be the rulers Protestant, Catholic, or non-Christian. As the Westminster Confession (23.4) later put it: "Infidelity, or difference in religion, doth not make void the magistrates' just and legal authority." This would seem to rule out disobedience if the sovereign power failed to implement the first table of the divine law, an exception being John Knox (ca. 1514–72). The Reformation's attitude on civil obedience was conservative. They did routinely specify the medieval limitation applying when rulers require anything contrary to the second table of God's law. Already in 1523, Zwingli's Sixty-Seven Articles (42–43) considered disregarding the "rule of Christ" and arbitrary rule as justifying deposition. This was rooted in medieval political theory. It was not very prominent in Reformed doctrinal textbooks, although Calvin discussed it tentatively, Peter Martyr Vermigli (1499–1562) and Beza more expansively. General discussions on how far resistance was permissible or mandatory, should be passive or active, a right and a duty, and popular or by lesser magistrates, were subdued or absent.

Post-1600 Reformed theologians continued in the same vein. Pictet offered a modest "something" on the magistrate (Pictet 1696, 13.13), but no allusion to questions of disobedience or resistance. It was more from individuals faced with religious persecution or arbitrary rule that resistance-theory writings appeared. These spoke of limitation of powers, sociopolitical contracts or covenants, popular sovereignty, armed or constitutional resistance, the rule of law, etc. Catalytic were the St. Bartholomew's Day massacre, the Dutch Revolt, the French wars of religion, the Stewart theory of the divine right of kings, the revocation of the Edict of Nantes, and the British "Glorious Revolution" (Hauschild 1999, 206–40).

To cite some representative writers, these include the reputed lead author of the Huguenot monarchomachian tract, *Defence of Liberty against Tyranny* (1579), Philippe Duplessis-Mornay (1549–1623); Johannes Althusius (1563–1638); and Samuel Rutherford. The first argued that the monarch is subject to the rule of law. This involves a covenant between God, monarch, and people—the two tables of the divine law. Government is conditional on honoring this covenant; when seriously infringed by the ruler, then popular resistance, even by force, is permissible, but by lesser magistrates. Persecution in the name of the first table causing disorder allows "seditious" action against a "tyrant" (Johnson and Leith 1993, 356–58). The tract was published in the same year as George Buchanan's (1506–82) *De jure regni* in Edinburgh; Buchanan had similar ideas, but justified tyrannicide more explicitly. His covenantal schema helped usher in the nemesis of the house of Stewart in Britain.

The Emden jurist, Althusius, reflected on the Dutch Revolt and new republic. Informing his thought were writings by Calvin, Beza, and Buchanan. In his *Politica*

(1603), Althusius equated natural law with the Decalogue and developed a Christian social contract theory. He envisaged popular sovereignty as an image of divine sovereignty, humans being bearers of the image of God. Violations of the tripartite covenant threatening the "rule of law" and the "rule of rights," and thereby natural and divine law, constitute tyranny meriting constitutional resistance (Witte 2013, 602–5). Similar constitutionalist ideas, but open to violent revolution, are expressed by the Calvinist theologian and political theorist, Pierre Jurieu (1637–1713). Like Hugo Grotius (1583–1645), he held that the "laws of war" can be invoked to depose tyrants (Dodge 1947, 61–67).

A book by the Scottish Westminster divine, Samuel Rutherford, added to the arsenal of Reformed jurisprudence and resistance theory. This was *Lex, Rex: The Law is King* (1644). In the train of Buchanan, Knox, and the Catholic John Major (1467–1550), Rutherford used the covenant motif as well as the two-kingdom concept of church and state. He denied monarchical absolute sovereignty; popular consent is conditional, and resistance to tyranny including regicide is legitimate. However, among contemporaries like John Milton (1608–74), Rutherford was denounced for his doctrinaire presbyterianism and opposition to both freedom of conscience and relative religious toleration.

# 4 The Sacraments

## 4.1 Generalities

Post-1600 Reformed sacramental thought reflected continuity with the Zurich Consensus (1549) of Bullinger and Calvin in 1549 (Pelikan and Hotchkiss 2003, 812–17). That represented accommodation between two poles, on the Eucharist particularly. The Zurich theology stressed profession of faith, remembrance, symbolism, inwardness, and contemplation by those of faith; Christ is only present to the mind. Genevan thinking originated in an amalgam of Luther (1483–1546), Calvin, and Bucer. (On pre-1600 sacramental history and Reformed perspectives, see Wandel 2014, 15–191; Rohls 1997, 177–237; Johnson and Leith 1993, 307–24; McKim 1998, 217–58; Andresen 1988, 46–63, 212–18, 272–84; and Hauschild 1999, 429–33. On post-1600 thought, see Heppe 1950, 590–656; and Wisse and Meijer 2013, 509–14). This could speak of the sacraments as channels and means of grace—at least in a manner of speaking—so that in the Lord's Supper there was a parallel offering or exhibition of the sign and the reality (Christ) signified, merged by a sacramental union. This gift enabled elect believers (especially dispirited ones) to have, through the Holy Spirit, communion with the true body of Christ in heaven, as fortifying sacramental nourishment.

Bucer had held that inner-Protestant Eucharistic controversies were pointless, since fundamental belief, as he saw it, was the same. The Genevan position derived in part from this Strasbourg theology of a via media with the Lutherans, as embodied in the Wittenberg Concord of 1536; it was viewed with suspicion in German Switzerland (except Basel). For such a concord still seemed both to ascribe too much status to the sacraments as automatic vehicles or instruments of grace, and to associate too much the presence of Christ and his body (located in heaven) with the sacramental elements; hence it was regarded as still not sufficiently detached from traditional doctrines of the real presence. Any notion that the sacraments might offer and mediate grace somehow inherent in or tied to the sacramental signs was firmly repudiated in later Reformed orthodox thinking.

This apparent Zurich preponderance was arguably coincidental, ensuing rather from the impact of decretal predestination and the covenant of grace. Since the saving faith of the elect in the covenant had been determined eternally and irrevocably by God before-hand, the sacraments were secondary to this. They could not actually impart, offer or mediate what was already acquired through Christ's broken body, although they might help, through the Spirit, apply the benefits of it. This could be by boosting the falter-ing faith of those effectually called, or helping induce the effectual calling of the unwit-ting elect. It was possible, then, to consider the sacraments as dispensable, but usually more as not being absolutely necessary for salvation (Leiden Synopsis 1626, 43, cor. 2). However, since sacraments were divine institutions, the church could not abandon them. Yet, reflecting more the Genevan theology, there was still a "hypothetical necessity" for the sacraments, in order to "assist infirmity and weakness" and "strengthen faith" (Pictet 1696, 14.1.12). Accordingly, Reformed theology strove to reconcile the prior fact of the salvation of the elect by predestination and covenantal privilege with its ritual offer in the sacraments. The balance between the spoken Word and the visible Word was unequal. The former had primacy, since Reformed writers (recalling Augustine) referred to the sacramental sign as an "appendix," "appendage," an accessory not ultimately compulsory; but their use was still mandatory due to their dominical basis. There was another para-dox: Reformed theology accepted that the Word was offered to all, but not the visible Word—intended for the worthy elect only. This was a point of conflict with the Lutherans.

Also shaping Reformed sacramental thinking was a spiritualizing thrust and an aversion to a materialist concept of grace—a sort of unconscious, inherited Neoplatonism. It derived from Humanism, especially Erasmian. It was metaphysical dualism, whereby matter and spirit are antithetical and incompatible, with apparent corroboration in John 6:63: *The Spirit gives life, the flesh is of no avail.* The invisibility and inwardness of grace is an *idée fixe.* A real presence could not possibly be corporal, tangible or substantial. These dualist notions were early Zwinglian leitmotifs, and while advanced Reformed doctrine made no appeal to them, their effect remained. The sacramental signs, then, were simply illustrative and instrumental, finite things utterly incapable of bearing anything infinite or divine.

In Reformed sacramental thought the priority was to generate assurance among dif-fident believers of their election and justification. (In infant baptism the grasp of this assurance was obviously deferred.) Certitude of faith was paramount, abandoning the uncertainty that might provoke recourse to self-help. Further, since adoption into the covenant of grace had responsibilities, beneficiaries were reminded of duties to God and neighbor; thereby sanctification accompanying justification is not passive, but a righteous way of life. The sacrament was not something holy per se, rather something that makes holy. God conveys the Word of assurance and promise of grace graphically—like an authentically sealed letter. Reformed terminology, then, became dominated by the defining sacraments as "signs and seals of the covenant of grace" (Westminster Confession, 27.1).

Lastly, before 1600 Reformed writings dismissed the sacramental teachings of the Roman Church, Lutheranism, and Anabaptists (no infant baptism). After 1600, other heterodoxies were added—first, Arminianism, with its element of choice in faith and its less pessimistic anthropology. It diluted original sin and depleted both baptismal cleansing from sin and regeneration. Second, Socinianism, with its anti-Trinitarianism. Since the sacraments were Trinitarian institutions in constitution, operation, and effect, Socinian reduction of them to moral rite of passage was condemned. Post-1700 Reformed statements fended off other alternatives—not only Baptist, Catholic, Lutheran, Arminian, and Socinian, but also Quaker (no sacraments), and the repristination of original Zwinglianism in Church of England Latitudinarians like Bishop Benjamin Hoadly (1676–1761). The *Lectures in Divinity* (1821) of the Calvinist St. Andrews professor, George Hill (1750–1819), exemplify how the gamut of sacramental heterodoxy was dealt with in theology faculties (Hill 1834, 497–517).

## 4.2 Baptism

Baptism was envisaged as a ritual acknowledgement of adoption into the divine covenant, ingrafting into Christ, and initiation into the earthly church. If not explicitly stated, this applied only to the elect. While adult baptism was conceivable, it normally involved babies, analogous with Old Testament circumcision. This appeal was grounded in the fundamental unity of the two testaments. Reformed manuals routinely focused on the issue due to infant unawareness, so that a proleptic dimension governs the ritual, much being left to future nurture. Baptism proclaims the promise of the forgiveness of sins as in washing from sin; the water signifies the blood of Christ's redemptive sacrifice—"our Red Sea," as the Belgic Confession (34) had elegantly expressed it. Spiritual rebirth (regeneration) follows, so that a baptized believer is dead to the world of self-destruction.

A selection of representative authors in Spinks's study reflects consistency in the Reformed approach to baptism (Spinks 2006, 50–56). William Ames held that the sacrament has three functions—informing, reminding, and sealing of the covenant of grace to the elect, whose role in this as infants is obviously passive. This suggests that being in the covenant and being of the elect are not necessarily the same thing—but this issue was generally treated ambiguously. Ames held that covenantal membership precedes baptism, so that the redemptive significance of the ceremony is relative. Wollebius exemplifies the Reformed tendency to substitute the word "seal" for "sacrament." He also used the patristic "mystery," because of the suprasensory reality conveyed. The "efficient cause" of baptism is the Trinity, and its administrators are solely human agents, the "instrumental cause." Wollebius added that baptism is not absolutely necessary for the salvation of individuals illegitimately baptized or who died before baptism. Turretin made the same point. Remarking that the reality signified by the sign is Christ and his benefits, he adds that this boosts faith and eventual public witness not only of thanks to God, but love of neighbor, so that the sacramental gifts of baptism are not just personal. The Westminster Confession (28) highlights that grace is not bound to the sacrament, and that its efficacy is not a necessary consequence. With such thinking, the Reformed tradition avoided sacramentalist false confidence. The Westminster *Directory for Public Worship* reiterates that caveat. Moreover, in justifying infant baptism—the children of believers are part of the covenant of grace before baptism—it affirms that they are already "federally holy." Later, Thomas Ridgely (1667–1734), had a strongly Trinitarian understanding of baptism. Its virtue does not lie in the ordinance per se, but in the operation of the Holy Spirit who conveys the will and blessing of Christ, the sole initiator. Nor is the ritual perfunctory; it is the beginning of holy living and progressive righteousness.

Lastly, the erosion of Reformed soteriology by the eighteenth century is reflected in the modified Genevan baptismal rite introduced in 1724. Still alluding to the Fall and corruption, the force of the previous statement on original sin, going back to Calvin, is attenuated. This reflects an ingress of Arminian ideas. Furthermore, in the new Eucharistic liturgy adopted, the same softening of Augustinian pessimistic anthropology is discernible; it is not longer, as it were, "Christ alone," rather "Christ and I together" as a moral impetus (Grosse 2008, 627–28).

## 4.3 The Lord's Supper

Apart from covenantal and tacit predestinarian orientation, there was little innovation in Reformed Eucharistic thought post-1560. New were formalist methodologies. These were not all imitations of each other, as there were varieties of definition, terminology, and even priorities. The starting point was the Last Supper; just as baptism had been anticipated by circumcision, so the Eucharist originated in the Passover. In contrast with the Roman Catholic point of view, the Reformed saw the Last Supper as the first Eucharist, eliminating notions of a sacrifice, an altar, transubstantiation, communion in one kind, etc.

As with baptism, the Reformed view of the Eucharist was bifocal. There were parallel realities—visible and invisible, physical and spiritual, letter and spirit, external and internal, sign and reality, celebrant and originator, instrument and divine institution, finite and infinite, tangible and intangible, earthly and heavenly, human and divine, food for the body and for the soul, and so on. Heidegger articulated it neatly: "The food and the drink of the eucharistic feast are twofold, one being symbolical, corporal and visible—bread and wine, the other real, spiritual and invisible—the body of Christ broken for us and his blood shed for us for remission of sins" (Heidegger 1732, 25.104). This perception aligned with the early Reformed perceptions, particularly of Bucer and Calvin; it was also compatible with Zurich concerns that between the sign and reality signified there was no mixture, mutual co-inherence, (con)fusion, conjunction, local inclusion, and organic merging, since Christ's body is in heaven. There were still rhetorical analyses of the meaning of "*This is my body*," since a literal meaning was excluded (repudiating transubstantiation and Lutheran notions of the ubiquity of Christ's body). Yet the truth of the sacramental body of Christ was upheld in view of inner-Reformed agreement that the sacrament was more than a commemorative occasion and that the signs were not bare and empty, "no bark without core" (Heidegger 1732, 25.111). A concept originating in Luther—the "sacramental union"—was availed of. The Reformed used this to affirm that for true believers only (and so not objectively, a sticking point with the Lutherans) the bread is Christ's body sacramentally, mystically, and spiritually, under the sole aegis of the Holy Spirit. The Spirit enables the sacramental and spiritual, but not oral, eating and enjoyment of the substance of Christ's body in heaven—the food of salvation and earnest of resurrection. This communion is sharing in the merit and benefits of "Christ crucified" (Westminster Confession, 29.7), whose body is both *represented* and substantially *presented* in the sacrament (Irish Articles, 94). Accordingly, the sacramental encounter with Christ, human and divine, related to the entire ceremonial and Trinitarian actions, is not to be minimized by focusing narrowly on the elements that do not cause communion.

This suggested that with many provisos, Reformed thought regarded the sacrament of the Lord's Supper as a channel of grace, but it also held back from making it an absolute necessity. The Word saved, not the sacrament. The beneficiaries were the true believers, whose faith was strengthened by feeding on the body of Christ in this nutritional sacrament, as Calvin had believed; but the elect were already saved. The Supper was intended for them above all—a "feast of the fellowship of the covenant of grace" (Heppe 1950, 629, 635). Sacramental grace was endorsing, not constitutive. As the Irish Articles (92) framed it: it is a sacrament of "preservation in the church, sealing unto us our spiritual nourishment and continual growth in Christ."

Finally, it was characteristic of the Reformed churches in general to press for sacramental concord with the Lutherans in the interest of Protestant unity. While the impetus was often religio-political, initiated by British and Prussian rulers and Huguenot leaders—emboldened in part by the Polish Sendomir Consensus (1570)—theological argumentation in this cause came now also from Zurich. This was new, for previously Zurich had been the chief obstacle. Two examples were, first, Theodor Zwinger (1597–1654), whose *Erklärung* pleaded (optimistically) for concord with the Lutherans on the basis of the 1534 First Confession of Basel (Zwinger 1655, 78–79). The second, more extensive, was Heidegger's *Manuductio*. He affirmed, citing Bucer, that "there is nothing to be found in [the Augsburg Confession] that differs from the thinking of our confessions" (Heidegger 1687, 22, 220–23). A breakthrough remained indefinitely elusive.

## BIBLIOGRAPHY

Andresen, Carl, ed. 1988. *Handbuch der Dogmen- und Theologiegeschichte. Band 2: Die Lehrentwicklung im Rahmen der Konfessionalität.* Göttingen: Vandenhoeck & Ruprecht.

Dodge, Guy Howard. 1947. *The Political Theory of the Huguenots of the Dispersion with Special Reference to the Thought and Influence of Pierre Jurieu.* New York: Columbia University Press.

Dorner, J. A. 1871. *History of Protestant Theology.* Vol. 2. Translated by George Thomson and Sophia Taylor. Edinburgh: T&T Clark.

Grosse, Christian. 2008. *Les rituels de la cène: Le culte eucharistique réformé à Genève (XVIe-XVIIe siècles).* Geneva: Librairie Droz.

Gunnoe, Charles D., Jr. 2011. *Thomas Erastus and the Palatinate: A Renaissance Physician in the Second Reformation.* Leiden: Brill.

Hauschild, Wolf-Dieter. 1999. *Lehrbuch der Kirchen- und Dogmengeschichte. Band 2: Reformation und Neuzeit.* Gütersloh: Chr. Kaiser and Güterloher Verlagaus.

Heidegger, Johannes H. 1732. *Corpus theologiae christianae.* Zurich.

Heidegger, Johannes H. 1687. *In viam concordiae protestantium ecclesiasticae manuductio.* Zurich.

Heppe, Heinrich. 1950. *Reformed Dogmatics Set Out and Illustrated from the Sources.* Translated by G. T. Thomson. Revised and edited by Ernst Bizer. London: George Allen & Unwin.

Hill, George. 1834. *Lectures in Divinity.* 6th ed. Edinburgh & London.

Johnson, William Stacy, and John H. Leith, eds. 1993. *Reformed Reader: A Sourcebook in Christian Theology. Vol. 1, Classical Beginnings, 1519–1799.* Louisville, KY: Westminster/John Knox Press.

Leiden Synopsis. 1625. *Synopsis purioris theologiae.* Leiden.

Maruyama, Tadataka. 1978. *The Ecclesiology of Theodore Beza: The Reform of the True Church.* Geneva: Librairie Droz.

Mastricht, Petrus van. 1724. *Theoretico-practica theologiae.* Reprint. Utrecht.

McKim, Donald K., ed. 1998. *Major Themes in the Reformed Tradition.* Eugene, OR: Wipf & Stock.

Muller, Richard. 1987. *Post-Reformation Dogmatics. Vol. 1, Prolegomena to Theology.* Grand Rapids, MI: Baker Book House.

Pelikan, Jaroslav, and Valerie Hotchkiss. 2003. *Creeds & Confessions of Faith in the Christian Tradition.* Vol. 2–3. New Haven, CT: Yale University Press.

Pictet, Bénédict. 1696. *Theologia christiana.* Geneva.

Rohls, Jan. 1997. *Reformed Confessions: Theology from Zurich to Barmen.* Translated by John Hoffmeyer. Louisville, KY: Westminster John Knox Press.

Spinks, Bryan D. 2006. *Reformation and Modern Rituals and Theologies of Baptism: From Luther to Contemporary Baptism.* Burlington, VT: Ashgate.

Trueman, Carl. 2013. "Reformed Orthodoxy in Britain." In *A Conpanion to Reformed Orthodoxy,* edited by Herman J. Selderhuis, 261–291. Leiden: Brill.

Turrettino, Francisco [Francis Turretin]. 1685. *Institutio theologiae elencticae.* Geneva.

Wandel, Lee Palmer, ed. 2014. *A Companion to the Eucharist in the Reformation.* Leiden: Brill.

*The [Westminster] Confession of Faith, the Larger Catechism, the Shorter Catechism, the Directory for Publick Worship, the Form of Presbyterial Church Government, with Reference to the Proofs from the Scripture.* 1913. Edinburgh: Blackwood.

Wisse, Maarten, and Hugo Meijer. 2013. "Pneumatology: Tradition and Renewal." In *A Conpanion to Reformed Orthodoxy,* edited by Herman J. Selderhuis, 465–518. Leiden: Brill.

Witte, John, Jr. 2013. "Law, Authority and Liberty in Early Calvinism." In *A Conpanion to Reformed Orthodoxy,* edited by Herman J. Selderhuis, 591–612. Leiden: Brill.

Wollebius, Johannes. 1660. *The Abridgment of Christian Divinitie.* Translated by Alexander Ross. 3rd ed. London.

Wollebius, Johannes. 1634. *Theologiae christianae compendium.* Basel.

Zwinger, Theodor. 1655. *Erklärung und Rettung der reinen Lehr von dem Abendmal unsers Herren Jesu Christi.* Basel.

# CHAPTER 17

# EARLY MODERN REFORMED ESCHATOLOGY

## CRAWFORD GRIBBEN

IT is in the area of eschatology, perhaps, that Reformed scholastic theologians seem least likely to meet the expectations of their modern readers. These audiences have rescued early modern Protestant theologians from the condescension of posterity by recognizing their disciplinarily holistic and methodologically self-reflexive theological interventions, and by noting their concern for developing the exegesis of Scripture by engaging with valuable theological interventions from across the history of the church. Drawing on works by Heinrich Heppe, Karl Barth, and Richard A. Muller, a new wave of scholarship has launched a series of critical enquiries into the genres, sources, thematic emphases, and ecclesial obligations of Reformed scholasticism (Heppe 1935; Muller 2003; Trueman and Clark, 1999; van Asselt 2001b). A great deal of this work has focused on loci within theology proper and soteriology, with particular care often being given to the development of covenant theology in Continental contexts, and the development of piety in Scottish, English, and North American contexts, for example. But very little of this work has focused on Reformed eschatology. In his extensive survey of this body of literature, Heppe discussed the locus of eschatology within a single short chapter on glorification, overlooking a number of important elements within the evolution of Reformed eschatology, including the idea of a future millennium, which he brushed aside in a single sentence, despite the fact that the revival of interest in this doctrine was one of the elements that most seriously challenged the emergence and consolidation of a confessional consensus across Reformed Europe in the period of high orthodoxy: of all of the post-Reformation eschatological innovations, as we will see, millennial theory was unique in making an impact upon the Reformed confessions (Heppe 1935, 557–70). Heppe's elision is a useful reminder that every survey, including the present chapter, is necessarily selective and will unavoidably reflect its author's interests and biases. A number of scholars have sought to correct his imbalance, including Willem J. van Asselt, whose magisterial corpus of work on Cocceius (1603–69) included an important treatment of his development of a sevenfold structure for redemptive history, which drove toward his discussion of apocalyptic theories (van Asselt 1999; van Asselt 2001b). But this general neglect of early modern Reformed eschatology may also be explained by the fact that its exponents, in many of their more speculative suggestions, were so often and so obviously mistaken, as in their frequent attempts to predict dates for end-times events. On the whole, readers of early modern Reformed writers, especially English writers, have found the eschatological reflections of Protestant scholastics less than helpful, for it was in their attempt to describe the individual and cosmic movement into eternity that these writers seemed most bound by and reflective of their own historical moment. This scholarly neglect of Reformed eschatology reflects the difficulty of combining its exegetical poverty and socio-cultural myopia within a contemporary narrative that argues for the recovery and utility of early modern Protestant theological texts. But eschatology, for all that it demonstrates the limits of Reformed scholastic thinking, was nevertheless a part of this world; and however problematically, constituent of its intellectual formation. In eschatology, as in other loci, we continue to require a "fuller picture of the development of Reformed orthodoxy" (Muller 2003, 4:420).

This chapter will document some of the principal debates about eschatology among Reformed theologians in and beyond early modern Europe. It will pay attention to thematic variation across time and space. While we can easily identify a conversation about millennialism throughout early modern Europe, for example, we must also remember that this conversation facilitated the exchange of ideas between writers and readers in very different contexts and across the entire period. Consequently, we should not assume that millennial ideas gained traction in different places at the same time, for similar reasons, or even among the similar communities in different contexts. Millennial theory was popular in England at least one century before it made any similar kind of headway in Scotland, for example, and that despite the fact that for much of this period the dominant religious communities in both nations shared a common Calvinism; and in England, millennial theory was more common among Independents and Baptists in the middle period of the seventeenth century and Anglicans in the latter period of the seventeenth century than it ever was among Presbyterians. At the same time, millennial ideas were central to the communal imagination in British North America in a way that was never true of their use in England: millennial theory was much closer to the mainstream in some of the North American colonies than in any of the nations of the Old World. These instances of regional and chronological variation raise the question of whether it is ever possible to speak of a national millennial position. While this chapter will pay particular attention to the debate about millennialism—here reflecting my own scholarly bias, albeit with the excuse that millennial theory did most to challenge the development of a common eschatological confession—it will not assume that other sometimes related unorthodox ideas necessarily developed in parallel with it. In other words, the proclivity of an individual, region, or church community toward millennial theory does not imply the existence of an equal sympathy for the doctrine of psychopannychia, for example. Neither should we be tempted to adopt the perspective of many early modern critics of millennial theory, including Thomas Edwards, in *Gangreana* (1646), who argued that "heresies" tended to cluster or develop together—for often they did not. Of course, this reference to heresy assumes that there existed a confessional mainstream that delineated the borders of orthodoxy, and against which theological novelties could be measured. This chapter will locate the evolution of Reformed eschatology in parallel with the formation of a European Reformed confessional mainstream, demonstrating how the eschatological positions of the Reformed confessions emerged, developed, and in some instances, overturned elements of the earlier confessional consensus.

This chapter will also pay attention to the variety of genres in which eschatological thinking was developed. While a great many Reformed scholastic theologians developed specific interest in eschatological themes, a great deal more eschatological thinking took place within popular culture. European Calvinism is only beginning to be considered as a movement of popular culture, but it is in such non-elite texts as ballads, conversion accounts, congregational records, and life writing that we can find the clearest evidences of those ideas, which could be considered without being published.

As in other areas of intellectual history, this survey will also pay attention to similarities and differences in the language within which Reformed eschatology was elaborated. One of the key challenges in writing the history of ideas is to distinguish between ideas that are expressed in similar terms, and to understand that similar sets of ideas can be given multiple descriptors. The modern debate about pre-, post- and amillennialism is a case in point. The *Oxford English Dictionary* describes "premillennialism" and "postmillennialism" as emerging with their modern meaning only in the nineteenth century; it provides no discussion of the emergence of "amillennialism" (Gribben 2011a, 12). These terms may not be the most useful in describing early modern eschatological theories, therefore, and their exegetical presuppositions may in fact hinder our appreciation of the nuances and complexities of early modern millennial thinking—some of which, after all, could not agree with the basic assumption of each of these positions that Revelation 20 describes only one period of 1000 years. It is too easy to mistake differences in language for differences in ideas, and similarities of language for an identity of ideas. For the study of early modern Reformed eschatology is a study of the uses of language as much as a study of the development and dissemination of ideas.

# 1  REFORMED ESCHATOLOGY, CATHOLICS, AND ANABAPTISTS

The Protestant Reformation was, in certain respects, a revolution in eschatological thinking: responding to the claims of Catholics, Reformed theologians argued against the doctrines of purgatory and limbo; against the assumptions of many Anabaptists, Reformed theologians argued that the doctrine of the millennium had no biblical support (Froom 1948; Tuveson 1949; Cohn 1993; Wilks 1994; Weber 1999; Rowland and Barton 2002; Rowland 2002; Landes 2003). Writers of the Protestant Reformation offered a radical simplification of traditional Christian eschatology alongside stout resistance to the apocalyptic immediacy being proffered by Anabaptists (Torrance 1953; Quistorp 1955; Ball 1975).

The challenge of the Calvinist Reformation to the doctrines of purgatory and limbo was perhaps the most significant eschatological claim of the first generation of Protestant reformers, striking as it did at a conviction that had shaped a great deal of late medieval piety. Just as the introduction of Protestant reform had shattered the confessional unity of Europe, so too its ideological development worked to break established links between the living and the dead. The doctrine of purgatory, which was more popular in northern than in southern Europe, had provided pastoral assistance to the grieving by offering them the reassurance that they could work to ameliorate the suffering in the intermediate state of those whom they had lost (MacCulloch 2003, 13–14). This act of kindness toward the dead was often made possible by financial contributions to the church—and there is evidence even in the early Reformation that wealthy individuals were continuing to make provision for their posthumous welfare by establishing chantries, within which their soul would be the subject of regular prayer (Scarisbrick 1984, 12–14; Haigh 1993, 34–35). This combination of economics and individual eschatology was subject to abuse, of course, and these abuses helped to make the doctrine of purgatory a central platform of the Protestant critique of late medieval Christianity. The energy of this Protestant hostility to the fiscal-ecclesiastical complex was given focus in Luther's (1483–1546) famous response to the selling of indulgences (Swanson 2007).

But the Protestant rejection of the doctrines of purgatory and limbo was neither total nor final. There is evidence that many early Protestants found it difficult to abandon their loved ones to their posthumous fate. William Shakespeare's *Hamlet* (ca. 1599) offers a telling moment in the popular history of the doctrine: the Prince of Denmark returns from university in Wittenberg, of all places, to encounter the ghost of his father returned from purgatory, in a plot twist that resonates with the ontological uncertainties of the Protestant experience of being suddenly unable to assist the familial dead. Literary critics and cultural historians have used *Hamlet* and other early modern dramas about ghosts to argue that the stage replaced the church as the sacred site within which the living could communicate with the dead (Greenblatt 2001). But even as traveling players toured these plays around the country, the arguments against prayers for the dead found some theological traction, as the "Aberdeen doctors," a group of eminent theologians within the early seventeenth-century Church of Scotland, suggested that there could be occasions in which it would be appropriate to pray for the dead. The theme was taken up at the end of the seventeenth and early eighteenth centuries by large numbers of "nonjuring" Episcopalians, those clergy of the Church of England who could not be reconciled to the establishment of the so-called "Glorious Revolution" (Gribben 2006). In theology and in popular culture, the ghosts of purgatory haunted the Reformed imagination: the Reformation's revolution in eschatology was never complete.

While Reformed theologians also worked hard to differentiate their eschatological perspective from that of the radical Reformation, their rejection of millennial theory was much less striking. Hostility toward millennial theory had an established pedigree in the medieval church. And in the early Reformation, Anabaptist ideas about a future golden age on earth had become notorious after a series of traveling preachers gained influence in Münster in 1532–33 (Cohn 1957; Howard 1993; Flanagan 1995; Baumgartner 1999). The town had recently been converted to Lutheranism, and in the religious ferment that accompanied this change, Melchior Hoffmann (1495–1543), a recent convert to the Anabaptists, began to preach that the world would end exactly 1500 years after the crucifixion—in 1533. This preaching was persuasive—so much so that the local leader of the Lutheran party was persuaded to throw in his lot with the radicals. He added to Hoffman's preaching a number of communistic principles he developed from the recently printed and unreliably attributed Fifth Epistle of Clement. The city's leaders were unable to contain the rising excitement, nor to prevent the city being overwhelmed with poor refugees eager to share in the millennial plenty that the preachers promised. As Hoffman was imprisoned, Jan Matthys (1500–34) took his place, and argued that believers should actively prepare for the coming millennium. The Anabaptist leaders proclaimed that the world would end in 1534—and invited anyone who wished to be saved to join their community in Münster. Now in power, the Anabaptists ordered the expulsion of any remaining Lutherans and Catholics, and established an eschatological regime, burning books, abolishing private property, and imposing polygamy. The town was besieged, and its promise of plenty failed. Famine set in by April 1535, and the millennial regime collapsed in a bloodbath. But not before Catholic, Lutheran, and Reformed Europe had learned its lesson—the link between millennial theory and social upheaval would prove to be enduring across the Continent and for more than two centuries.

Throughout the period, therefore, Reformed theologians defined their eschatology by denying the claims of Catholics and Anabaptists. Their arguments became unfortunately negative—so much so that a number of Catholic theologians believed that this revolution in eschatology was more radical than its proponents intended. Far from being worried about their obsession by eschatology, some Catholic apologists feared Protestants had become curiously neglectful of the last things. Irena Backus has demonstrated the existence of a large number of Catholic apologists who drew on certain kinds of Protestant hesitance about eschatology to argue that a rejection of the canonicity of Revelation had become a foundational element of reform (Backus 1998; Backus 2000). These Catholic theologians were certainly identifying a key weakness in the Protestant arsenal of ideas—a weakness that they, as well as later generations of Reformed Protestants, would seek to exploit.

# 2 The Reformed Confessional Tradition and the Emergence of Eschatological Optimism

The communities from which these writers came were concerned to police any tendency to eschatological speculation. The earliest confessions of faith produced by Protestant national churches emphatically repudiated both the fear of purgatory and the expectation of a future millennium. Like the doctrine of purgatory, the expectation of a future millennium had a long, if unofficial, intellectual lineage. Drawing on the Hebrew Bible's descriptions of an apparently future period of human flourishing, and developing structures of history and an apocalyptic timetable from the New Testament and other early Christian writings, a number of antique and medieval religious communities had narrated specific sets of claims about the individual and cosmic movement into eternity. Few of these groups adopted the incipient universalism of, for example, Origen. But many of them did appropriate, from a wide range of canonical, noncanonical, and sometimes contradictory sources, expectations that the world would pass through several ages—those of the Father, the Son, and the Spirit—and that these ages would last for six thousand years. These six millennia, corresponding to the six days of activity in creation, would be followed by a seventh millennium, and this would correspond to creation's day of rest (Gribben 2000, 26–28).

These positions had found only marginal support within the medieval church. The theological mainstream of Christendom, eastern and western, had largely followed the reading of eschatology and providence outlined by Augustine in *City of God* (425). As Augustine understood it, Revelation 20 offered not a blueprint for a future golden age—a position that he had once defended—but a structure of history between the advents that could explain the fate of the true church, if not the fate of its multiple social and political contexts. The condemnation of millennial theory was not emphatic—the frequently made assertion that millennialism was condemned by the Council of Ephesus (431) has recently been challenged (Svigel 2003). If millennial theory was never made respectable, neither was it ever quite eradicated. The rejection of millennial theory, which had become a standard element of medieval theology, was reiterated at the Reformation, as popular Bible reading unleashed another and more dangerous round of eschatological speculation.

This hostility toward millennial theory was written into some of the earliest confessional documents to emerge from the movement of reform. The Augsburg Confession (1530), which was composed by Philip Melanchthon (1497–1560) and published with Luther's support, condemned "Anabaptists" both for denying the eternal punishment of the wicked and for disseminating "Jewish opinions, that, before the resurrection of the dead, the godly shall get the sovereignty in the world, and the wicked shall be brought under in every place" (Hall [1842] 1992, 106). It is telling that this condemnation of Anabaptist millennial theory was issued before the incident at Münster that would most make it notorious. Two decades later, the Church of England's Forty-Two Articles of Religion (1553) reiterated this rejection of millennial theory, claiming that "they that go about to renew the fable of heretics called Millenarii be repugnant to Holy Scripture, and cast themselves headlong into a Jewish dotage" (Bray 1995, 309–10). The fact that this error was dropped from later editions of the Anglican articles was more indicative of the fact that English theologians had been following European trends without any local need than that they were moving to tolerate millennial speculation. Similarly, the Second Helvetic Confession (1566) condemned those "Jewish dreams, that before the day of judgement there shall be a golden world in the earth; and that the godly shall possess the kingdoms of the world, their wicked enemies being trodden under foot" (Hall 1842, 88). The Second Helvetic Confession, which represented the opinions of the Reformed churches of Scotland, Geneva, Poland and Hungary, finally established the European Protestant consensus, to which would be appended the identification in the Irish Articles (1615) of the Antichrist as the papacy.

By the early seventeenth century, however, the Reformed churches were finding it more difficult to rein in their adherents' millennial fervor. The Geneva Bible, the wildly popular translation prepared by Reformed exiles and which in subsequent English editions grew to feature some 300,000 words of marginal annotation, advanced perspectives on prophetic passages of Scripture that seemed to challenge the confessional rejection of "Jewish fables." For the future of the Jews loomed large in the annotations of Romans 9–11, for example, and the tens of thousands of copies of the Geneva Bible that circulated in and across the French- and English-speaking world popularized an optimism about the future conversion of the Jews and the glittering prospects of the Gentile church, which seemed to exist in tension with the nonmillennial emphases of the confessional tradition. The Geneva Bible gained the sanction of at least one Reformed community when the Scottish parliament required that all substantial householders should purchase a copy of the text. This Bible—known locally as the Bassandyne Bible—was the only translation to be published in Scotland before 1610 (Gribben 2000, 70). By the end of the sixteenth century, a translation that had been produced without ecclesiastical sanction, and which offered interpretations of the sacred text that did not always conform to the expectations of the confessional tradition, was beginning to demonstrate the eschatological latitude that would come to typify important communities of English-speaking Reformed Protestants. It was a popular cultural artifact—the most compendious and scholarly edition of scripture to date—that began to erode the confessional tradition.

## 3 THE CHALLENGE TO REFORMED CONFESSIONS IN PERSONAL AND COSMIC ESCHATOLOGY

The Reformed confessions of faith did not successfully impede the development of eschatological speculation. Some of this speculation concerned personal eschatology. The traditional loci of the last things had been challenged in the earlier period of the Reformation as Protestants divested themselves of what they dismissed as the superstitious accretions of medieval piety. Four last things were identified—death, judgment, heaven, and hell. But some thoughtful Protestants also pushed to reconsider the possibility of an intermediate state. John Wycliffe (1320–84) and William Tyndale (1494–1536) had responded to the doctrine of purgatory by contending that souls "slept" between the individual's death and resurrection. Martin Luther made similar arguments for

Christian mortalism, which he circulated in his tracts and commentaries. But there did not seem to be any connection between the contexts in which this new doctrine was being developed. And when John Calvin (1509–64) made this psychopannychia the subject of his first substantive work, which was written in 1534, published in Latin in 1542, and translated into English as *An excellent treatise of the Immortalytie of the Soule* (1581), he did not reference Wycliffe, Tyndale, or Luther. Within the world of the Reformed, varieties of the doctrine of psychopannychia were taken up by otherwise politically and theologically conservative Puritans such as George Wither (1588–1667), as well as religious and political radicals such as Richard Overton (1640–63) and John Milton (1608–74). Emerging from this radical context, early Baptists developed a vigorous culture of eschatological debate, typified by Samuel Richardson's *A discourse of the torments of hell: The foundation and pillars thereof discovered, searched, shaken and removed* (1658). But the doctrine of psychopannychia failed to convince the writers of the baptistic confessions, and the emerging discourse of mortalism, despite its finding support among the first generation of reformers, struggled to find momentum in later generations within the Reformed communities.

Seventeenth-century theologians found it easier to offer revisions of cosmic eschatology. Among the Reformed, and across Western Europe, but particularly in England, their speculative bent re-energized millennial theory (Christianson 1978; Bauckham 1978; Firth 1979; Patires and Wittreich 1984; Peterson 1993; Backus 2000; Gribben 2000; Hotson 2000a; Hotson 2000b; Laursen and Popkin 2001; Jue 2006; Crome 2014). As we noted above, seeds of eschatological optimism had been sown in the annotations of successive editions of the Geneva Bible: the comments on the latter-day conversion of the Jews, which dated from the 1560 edition, were buttressed by revised annotations on Revelation toward the end of the sixteenth century (Gribben 2000, 67–79). By the early seventeenth century, prominent theologians and churchmen in England and Ireland were working—apparently independently of each other—to challenge the established reading of Revelation 20:1–11. Both Thomas Brightman (1562–1607), an English clergyman, and James Ussher (1581–1656), professor of theology at Trinity College Dublin and future archbishop of Armagh, began to contend that these verses referred to two periods of one thousand years within the structure of Christian history—an opinion later confirmed by the Dutch theologian Johannes Cocceius (Gribben 2000, 88; van Asselt 2001a, 24). Suddenly, Reformed churchmen with otherwise impeccable credentials were admitting that the *locus classicus* of millennial theory was referring to a period in the future. European theologians—who, again, appear to have been working independently—developed similar arguments. Johannes Piscator (1546–1625) and Johann Heinrich Alsted (1588–1638), working on the confessional borderlands of central Europe, made similar suggestions for the possibility of a future millennium (Gribben 2011a, 41–42). Of course, during this period, these mid-European intellectuals would have been hard-pressed not to have turned their thoughts to the last book of the Bible. The Thirty Years' War had unleashed a spectacular frenzy of violence, which was widely reported in the run-up to the outbreak of civil war in Britain and Ireland. Reeling from the unprecedented impact of "wars, and rumors of wars," Reformed Protestants returned to biblical prophecy as they sought to establish a viable rhetoric in the European wars of religion—and millennial theory, in England, became almost creedal.

# 4  Eschatology, Religious Radicalism, and Popular Culture

These innovations in eschatology continued to grow in popularity, especially in English contexts, through the middle of the seventeenth century. At a popular level, radical groups with no acute feeling for confessional limitations of discussion were able to organize around new prophetic leaders and to disseminate ideas by taking advantage of the new freedom of the press. In the early 1640s, titles in this emerging culture of popular print gained market share by reporting stories of monster births, portents, and apocalyptic battles in the sky (Potter 2009). There is evidence that this new popular prophetic frenzy was beginning to influence some Reformed scholastics. For in London, in the mid-1640s, members of the Westminster Assembly identified their project in eschatological terms, with George Gillespie (1613–48) suggesting that the assembly had been convened as part of an apocalyptic timetable. But the confessional text that was produced by the assembly did not reflect these enthusiastic claims. Instead, its discussion of eschatology tended to reflect the more cautious and moderate claims of the Reformation tradition. Those English Independent and Scottish Presbyterian delegates who formed the committee to prepare the Directory for Public Worship included within its text their more advanced eschatological views (Gribben 2000, 108–18). The Westminster Confession did not contain the eschatological hopes of some of the divines, and neither did it fulfill the need for a national confession of faith. The London Parliament never adopted the confession *in toto*, and in the 1650s the governments of the British republic continued to pursue the possibility of a national religious settlement. The conclusion to these protracted discussions was the Savoy Declaration (1658), a statement of faith drawn up by leaders of Congregationalism, which now seems to have been intended to fashion an official state orthodoxy (Powell 2011). Reflecting the confidence of its authors, this confession's expectations of latter-day glory were robust. But it was spectacularly mistimed, being published in the immediate aftermath of the death of Oliver Cromwell, and though it did not seem obvious at the time, in the death throes of the republic itself. Twenty years later, after years of persecution, English Baptists entirely played down this optimism in their revision of the Savoy Declaration (1677). But that did not stop some Baptists from hailing the Glorious Revolution (1689) in millennial terms (Newport 2000). Throughout the period, and across Europe, confessions of faith could not contain the impulse toward optimism that remained instinctive in many parts of the Reformed world.

Neither could these confessions of faith always command the loyalty of their adherents—and especially as the locus of prophetic authority moved from an inspired text to an inspired prophet. Whether following George Fox (1624–91) into the Quakers, or John Pordage (1607–81) and Jane Leade (1624–1704) into the Philadelphian Society, believers could leave Reformed churches to make the *eschaton* entirely immanent, or to argue for theories of universal salvation. But insofar as this movement into new prophetic communities encouraged the development of heretical doctrines, it took adherents outside the communities of the Reformed.

# 5 Eschatology, "Late Orthodoxy," and De-confessionalization

There is no doubt that eschatological feeling was dampened in the latter part of the seventeenth century. Across Europe, the end of the Thirty Years' War had facilitated a cooling of eschatological hopes. Apocalyptic thinking appears to have grown less popular in this post-apocalyptic landscape. Some pockets of eschatological speculation did continue. In England, after the Restoration, as Warren Johnston has illustrated, clergy of the established church continued to develop strikingly new readings of the relevant biblical texts (Johnston 2011). Some of these clergy, now working in an environment in which definite theological commitments had become somewhat unfashionable, went on to develop links with groups that would have been regarded as unorthodox even in the mid-century period—such as the Philadelphians, who took part in a European community of reading and experimental spirituality (Hirst 2005).

But this cooling of eschatological aspirations did not long continue. In the mid-eighteenth century, a series of "revivals" of popular piety drove another round of theological revision and experimentation within the Reformed Atlantic. In New England, the preaching of George Whitefield (1714–70) and Jonathan Edwards (1703–58) encouraged dramatic accounts of conversion and the renewal of a large number of communities. This "Great Awakening" became an Atlantic phenomenon when Independents in London and Presbyterians in Scotland began to circulate Edwards's narratives of "surprising conversions." As excitement grew, there were similar scenes in a number of areas in the western central belt of Scotland. In and around Cambuslang, correspondents of Edwards preached rousing sermons and promoted the necessity of evangelical conversion. Their efforts were successful, as the published accounts of spiritual experience suggest (Beebe 2013). But the Scottish revival was in many ways more limited than that of New England—both in terms of space, in that it failed to impact the broader religious environment of Great Britain, and in conceptions of time, in that it failed to encourage the same kinds of millennial expectation that had been both a cause and consequence of the awakening in the colonies. Meanwhile, across Europe, as W. R. Ward has demonstrated, a vital eschatological piety became part of the sensibility of early evangelicals (Ward 2006).

By the late seventeenth and early eighteenth centuries, the legacy of Reformed scholastic theology was more obvious in dissenting groups than in many of the established churches (van Asselt 2011, 167–93). It was during this period that the Church of Scotland, for example, oscillated away from and again toward the Westminster Confession as its subordinate standard. But whatever the claims of the Kirk's constitution, its memory of seventeenth-century orthodoxy was growing vague. It was telling that Thomas Boston's (1676–1732) republication of *The Marrow of Modern Divinity* (1645) should prove so controversial—for the book that was condemned by the General Assembly as antinomian had been approved for publication by members of the Westminster Assembly, which had provided the Scottish church with its confession of faith (Caughey 2013). Of course, the process of de-confessionalism was even more evident in England, where the Particular Baptist minister John Gill had a closer relationship to the early modern scholasticism than did many of his peers in the established church. This messiness of ecclesial relationships and the parallel breakdown in theological commitment challenges our discussion of "late orthodoxy," even as it allowed for the continuation of the theological experimentation that had so characterized earlier periods of Reformed theological tradition. It may have been Gill's intellectual proximity to the earlier writers of "high orthodoxy" that explains his ability to combine a robust and emphatic high Calvinism with an extraordinarily speculative, aspirational, and entirely idiosyncratic millennial hope (van Asselt 2011, 132–65).

# 6 CONCLUSION

The first generation of Reformed Protestants offered a radically simplified but ultimately conservative reading of medieval Christian eschatology. Unlike Luther and some of his followers, they did not tend to advance varieties of psychopannychia, nor did they consider excluding Revelation from the canon of scripture. Instead, their confessions of faith outlined individual eschatology in terms of the four last things, and outlined cosmic eschatology by insisting on the otherworldliness of the conditions of the new heavens and earth. But Reformed Protestants could not avoid eschatological innovations, particularly in the context of the Thirty Years' War and associated wars of religion, during which many believers imagined themselves to be living through the end of the world. Consequently, those confessions of faith that were negotiated in the seventeenth century offered more adventurous readings of biblical prophecy. Innovations in personal eschatology were left to marginal communities of religious radicals, as innovations in cosmic eschatology were developed within the Reformed mainstream. The confessional and ecclesiastical documents produced in the period of high orthodoxy were, ironically, often reflective of expectations for latter-day glory or even of the millennium itself. These confessions offered an unstable foundation for future theological development, but were often, in practical terms, eclipsed in the political turmoil of the later seventeenth century. And all the while, Reformed Protestants were continuing to read and reflect upon the biblical passages that their peers used variously to support or negate their eschatological claims. The confessional tradition continues today, as modern Reformed Protestants develop their eschatological claims in line with their foundational documents. But it is striking to notice how often they do so on the basis of entirely different exegetical claims.

## BIBLIOGRAPHY

Asselt, Willem J. van. 2001a. "Chiliasm and Reformed Eschatology in the Seventeenth and Eighteenth Centuries." In *Christian Hope in Context*, edited by A. van Egmond and D. van Keulen, 11–29. Studies in Reformed Theology 4. Zoetermeer: Meinema.

Asselt, Willem J. van. 2001b. *The Federal Theology of Johannes Cocceius (1603–1669)*. Leiden: Brill.

Asselt, Willem J. van. 2011. *Introduction to Reformed Scholasticism*. Grand Rapids, MI: Reformation Heritage Books.

Asselt, Willem J. van. 1999. "Structural Elements in the Eschatology of Johannes Cocceius." *Calvin Theological Journal* 34: 76–104.

Backus, Irena. 1998. "The Church Fathers and the Canonicity of the Apocalypse in the Sixteenth Century: Erasmus, Frans Titelmans, and Theodore Beza." *Sixteenth Century Journal* 29: 651–665.

Backus, Irena. 2000. *Reformation Readings of the Apocalypse: Geneva, Zurich, and Wittenberg: Geneva, Zurich and Wittenberg*. Oxford: Oxford University Press.

Ball, B. W. 1975. *A Great Expectation: Eschatological Thought in English Protestantism to 1660*. Leiden: Brill.

Beebe, Keith Edward, ed. 2013. *The McCulloch Examinations of the Cambuslang Revival (1742)*. 2 vols. Woodbridge, UK: Boydell.

Bauckham, Richard. 1978. *Tudor Apocalypse: Sixteenth-Century Apocalypticism, Millenarianism and the English Reformation: From John Bale to John Foxe and Thomas Brightman*. Appleford, UK: Sutton Courtenay Press.

Baumgartner, Frederic. 1999. *Longing for the End: A History of Millennialism in Western Civilization*. New York: Palgrave.

Bray, Gerald, 1995. *Documents of the English Reformation*. Cambridge: James Clarke.

Capp, B. S. 1972. *The Fifth Monarchy Men*. London: Faber and Faber.

Caughey, Christopher E. 2013. "Puritan Responses to Antinomianism in the Context of Reformed Covenant Theology, 1630–1696." Unpublished PhD thesis. Trinity College Dublin.

Christianson, Paul. 1978. *Reformers and Babylon: English Apocalyptic Visions from the Reformation to the Eve of the Civil War*. Toronto: University of Toronto Press.

Cohn, Norman. 1993. *Cosmos, Chaos and the World to Come: The Ancient Roots of Apocalyptic Faith*. New Haven, CT: Yale University Press.

Cohn, Norman. 1957. *The Pursuit of the Millennium*. London: Mercury Books.

Crome, Andrew. 2014. *The Restoration of the Jews: Early Modern Hermeneutics, Eschatology, and National Identity in the Works of Thomas Brightman*. Dordrecht: Springer.

Crouzet, Denis. 1990. *Les Guerriers de Dieu: La violence au temps des troubles de religion*. Champ Vallon: Seyssel.

Fix, Andrew. 1999. *Fallen Angels: Balthasar Bekker, Spirit Belief, and Confessionalism in the Seventeenth-Century Dutch Republic*. Dordrecht: Kluwer Academic Publishers.

Firth, Katherine. 1979. *The Apocalyptic Tradition in Reformation Britain, 1530–1645*. Oxford: Oxford University Press.

Flanagan, Thomas. 1995. "The Politics of the Millennium." *Terrorism and Political Violence* 7 (3): 164–175.

Froom, L. E. 1948. *The Prophetic Faith of Our Fathers: The Historical Development of Prophetic Interpretation*. 4 vols. Washington, DC: Review and Herald.

Greenblatt, Stephen. 2001. *Hamlet in Purgatory*. Princeton, NJ: Princeton University Press.

Gribben, Crawford. 2011a. *Evangelical Millennialism in the Trans-Atlantic World*. New York: Palgrave Macmillan.

Gribben, Crawford. 2011b. "Millennialism." In *"Drawn into Controversie": Reformed Theological Diversity and Debates within Seventeenth-Century British Puritanism*, edited by Michael A. G. Haykin and Mark Jones, 83–98. Reformed Historical Studies. Göttingen: Vandenhoeck & Ruprecht.

Gribben, Crawford. 2000. *The Puritan Millennium: Literature and Theology, 1550–1682*. Dublin: Four Courts.

Gribben, Crawford. 2006. "Theological Literature, 1560–1707." In *Edinburgh History of Scottish Literature*, edited by Ian Brown, 231–237. Vol. 1 of 3. Edinburgh: Edinburgh University Press.

Haigh, Christopher. 1993. *English Reformations: Religion, Politics and Society under the Tudors*. Oxford: Clarendon Press.

Hall, Peter, ed. [1842] 1992. *Harmony of the Protestant Confessions*. Edmonton: Still Waters Revival Books.

Heppe, Heinrich. 1935. *Reformierte Dogmatík*. Neukirchen.

Hirst, Julie. 2005. *Jane Leade: Biography of a Seventeenth-Century Mystic*. Aldershot, UK: Ashgate.

Hotson, Howard. 2000a. *Paradise Postponed: Johann Heinrich Alsted and the Birth of Calvinist Millenarianism*. Dordrecht: Kluwer Academic Publishers.

Hotson, Howard. 2000b. *Johann Heinrich Alsted, 1588–1638: Between Renaissance, Reformation, and Universal Reform*. Oxford: Clarendon Press.

Howard, Tal. 1993. "Charisma and History: The Case of Münster, Westphalia, 1534–1535." *Essays in History* 35: 48–64.

Jue, Jeffrey K. 2006. *Heaven upon Earth: Joseph Mede (1586–1638) and the Legacy of Millenarianism*. Dordrecht: Springer.

Johnston, Warren. 2011. *Revelation Restored: The Apocalypse in Later Seventeenth-Century England*. Woodbridge, UK: Boydell.

Landes, Richard, Andrew Gow, and David C. Van Meter, eds. 2003. *The Apocalyptic Year 1000: Religious Expectation and Social Change, 950–1050*. Oxford: Oxford University Press.

Laursen, John Christian, and Richard H. Popkin, eds. 2001. *Continental Millenarians: Protestants, Catholics, Heretics*. Dordrecht: Kluwer Academic Publishers.

MacCulloch, Diarmaid. 2003. *Reformation: Europe's House Divided, 1490–1700*. London: Penguin.

Muller, Richard A. 2003. *Post-Reformation Reformed Dogmatics*. 4 vols. Grand Rapids, MI: Baker.

Murdock, Graeme. *Calvinism on the Frontier, 1600–1660: International Calvinism and the Reformed Church in Hungary and Transylvania*. Oxford: Clarendon Press.

Newport, Kenneth G. C. 2000. *Apocalypse and Millennium: Studies in Biblical Eisegesis*. Cambridge: Cambridge University Press.

Patrides, C. A., and Joseph Wittreich, eds. 1984. *The Apocalypse in English Renaissance Thought and Literature: Patterns, Antecedents and Repercussions*. Manchester: Manchester University Press.

Peterson, Rodney L. 1993. *Preaching in the Last Days: The Theme of "Two Witnesses" in the Sixteenth and Seventeenth Centuries*. Oxford: Oxford University Press.

Potter, Lois. 2009. *Secret Rites and Secret Writings: Royalist Literature, 1641–1660.* Cambridge: Cambridge University Press.

Powell, Hunter. 2011. "The Dissenting Brethren and the Power of the Keys, 1640–1644." Unpublished PhD thesis, University of Cambridge.

Quistorp, H. 1955. *Calvin's Doctrine of the Last Things.* London: Lutterworth Press.

Rowland, Christopher, and John Barton, eds. 2002. *Apocalyptic in History and Tradition.* Sheffield: Sheffield Academic Press.

Rowland, Christopher. 2002. "Afterword." *Journal for the Study of the New Testament* 25: 2.

Scarisbrick, J. J. 1984. *The Reformation and the English People.* Oxford: Blackwell.

Svigel, Michael J. 2003. "The Phantom Heresy: Did the Council of Ephesus (431) Condemn Chiliasm?" *Trinity Journal* 24 (1): 105–112.

Swanson, Robert N. 2007. *Indulgences in Late Medieval England: Passports to Paradise.* Cambridge: Cambridge University Press.

Torrance, T. F. 1953. "The Eschatology of the Reformation." *Eschatology: Scottish Journal of Theology Occasional Papers* 2: 36–62.

Trueman, Carl R., and R. S. Clark, eds. 1999. *Protestant Scholasticism: Essays in Reassessment.* Carlisle, UK: Paternoster.

Tuveson, Ernest Lee. 1949. *Millennium and Utopia: A Study in the Background of the Idea of Progress.* Berkeley: University of California Press.

Ward, W. R. 2006. *Early Evangelicalism: A Global Intellectual History, 1670–1789.* Cambridge: Cambridge University Press.

Weber, Eugene. 1999. *Apocalypses: Prophecies, Cults, and Millennial Beliefs through the Ages.* Cambridge, MA: Harvard University Press.

Wilks, Michael, ed. 1994. *Prophecy and Eschatology: Studies in Church History, Subsidia 10.* Oxford: Blackwell.

# Lutheran Theologies

# CHAPTER 18

# EARLY MODERN LUTHERANISM

## A. G. ROEBER

THIS section of the *Handbook* examines the Christian tradition most commonly associated with the onset of the Protestant Reformation. Self-identified as "Evangelicals," a term still used among European adherents, proponents were controversially either members of a theological movement, or by necessity and conviction, founders of a perhaps visible, perhaps known only to God, separate church. Whether staunch defenders of an ecclesial self-concept or champions of the sovereignty of individual conscience, "Lutherans," as they are more commonly known today in Africa, Asia, and the Americas, emerged as the central figures in the sixteenth-century religious conflicts that exploded within and expanded quickly beyond the bounds of the Holy Roman Empire.

Precisely because those who identify themselves as "Evangelical-Lutheran" do not agree on the nature of what "Lutheranism" was, or is, the individual chapters of this section of the *Handbook* must perforce attempt to explain the root causes of such disagreements and their consequences. Thus, in the chapters that follow, scholars take up the central and complex topics of the Lutheran understanding of God and creation; scripture and exegesis; the Lutheran understanding of what is meant by "the church"; Lutheran sacramental theology; the key theological concept of forensic justification; and the late seventeenth-century attempt to renew the Lutheran churches of the empire devastated by the impact of the Thirty Years' War and the "Little Ice Age" via a movement that has come to be known as Pietism.

## 1 THE PROBLEM OF THE REFORMER

At the very heart of the dilemma that surrounds the subject matter of this chapter stands the figure of the reformer, Martin Luther (1483–1546). The very fact that, contrary to his own wishes, those convinced by his theological insights began even during his lifetime to use his name as an identifying marker of their theology, stands as an inescapable reminder of the difficulties that confront scholars who have undertaken the task of explicating the early modern theology of "Lutheranism." A key question that challenges both authors and readers alike is simply how much attention should be paid and what consequences should be attributed to the writings and statements of the man himself? How much instead should be focused on the public, confessional documents most of which he did not author but clearly influenced, statements that attempted to resolve internal disagreements among Evangelicals that had become obvious even before the Reformer's death in 1546? Because of the later, tortured political history of Central Europe, Luther was reborn as the heroic Germanic national symbol, and in this reincarnated persona, overshadowed and in some cases completely misrepresented Luther the theologian. The quest for recovering an authentic Lutheran theological voice began only, in the judgment of many scholars, in the post-World War I years of the so-called "Luther Renaissance." But even then, although some participants would eventually be recruited from other European and North American universities and seminaries, the predominant parsings of Luther have remained solidly in the hands of German theologians until very recently. As a result, specifically German-national concerns about Luther the theologian are not always easily reconciled with the perspectives of those from other national-theological traditions.

## 2  The Problem of Lutheranism and Political History

The difficulty of interpreting Lutheranism properly cannot be divorced from the manner in which the history of this theological tradition itself came to be shaped by world events. Most readers will already be familiar with that general story, one that has always interwoven the theological with the sociopolitical, economic, and international issues of the sixteenth century. The initial impact of Lutheran theology expressed itself in the spoken, written, and published language of the then-Empire. By that language we mean both Latin treatises and debates; but more importantly, the mastery and dissemination of a somewhat standardized German vernacular written form, in the shaping and utilization of which Luther played a central and deservedly honored role that extended far beyond the confessional bounds of Lutheranism (Weber 2008). The profound impact of Lutheran hymnody in this vernacular for conveying the official theology and giving expression to unofficial endorsement of at least some of the movement's insights, and how that dissemination was supported by political leaders, can hardly be overstated. More than one of the authors in this section and recent scholarship in general recognize this central aspect of early modern Lutheran theology (Brown 2005; Roeber 2013b). Even when Lutheran theology spilled over the borders of the empire into Scandinavia, the Balkans, and the eastern Baltic, the German language and hymnody provided a baseline of reference because of the importance the entire theological movement placed upon the use of the vernacular in both public and private devotion. Nonetheless, at no time in the history of Europe have all German speakers been subjects of one political ruler; much less, since the sixteenth century, boasted a settled confessional agreement and identity.

# 3  THE PROBLEM OF THE STANDING OF CONFESSIONAL STATEMENTS

Some historians of the Reformation would argue that the splintering of theological positions was inevitable given Luther's own nonsystematic theological writing, and the polemical atmosphere that almost immediately surrounded his early invitations to theological debate regarding abuses in the church of which he was a priest and Augustinian monastic. Scholars continue to disagree fiercely on how to reconcile the position of a man who declared on the one hand that his 1529 *Small Catechism*—a masterful, concise, indispensable hermeneutical lens for the unlearned—represented the most important of his voluminous writings as the "layman's Bible." On the other hand, the tradition he shaped continued to have recourse to his early individualistic, nearly antinomian position on subjective conscience, the transparency of scripture and his apparent willingness to reject the authority of ancient tradition, church fathers, and decrees and canons of councils and popes alike. Whether there was a "young" versus an "old" Luther is not a central topic of concern for the scholars whose chapters comprise this section of the *Handbook*. But the continued arguments that swirled around Luther's own oft-times ambiguous position on just such matters could not help but shape the debates over the confessional statements that issued first in the Augsburg Confession of 1530 and were not effectively silenced even a half century later in the final version of the wistfully entitled *Book of Concord*.

Granting the influence on Luther of his closest associate Philip Melanchthon, the latter especially in helping to form future pastors via the locus method of instruction, it is instructive to ask if the somewhat unstable nature of the Lutheran theological enterprise could not have been avoided. A genuine ambiguity flowed from the felt need to critique the existing Roman Church while simultaneously refusing to acknowledge the accuracy of both the Reformed, and especially the radical, free-church Protestant movements that sprang up within a few years of Luther's published writings. It is especially important to note that in sharp contrast to Lutheranism, which consolidated its confessional identity around a fairly narrow range of theological questions, the Reformed tradition developed some twenty-plus confessional statements (Muller, "Reformed Theology" in this volume), and in so doing may have avoided the excessive and bitter internal debates that continued to plague Lutheranism well beyond the founding generation of Lutheran theologians.

# 4  THE PROBLEM OF THE MEDIEVAL LEGACY

Among the many manifestations of this unresolved tension, few have the capacity a half millennium later of eliciting such fierce disagreement as does the topic of Luther's indebtedness to, or renunciation of, medieval Catholic mysticism. That topic, among many others, could not be investigated in full, but it remains central to Saarinen's essay on justification and is one of the more engaging aspects of the challenge facing those who seek to understand where to position "Lutheranism" in the larger context of western Christianity's history (Meyer and Sträter 2002; Hann and Leppin 2007). Given the ongoing debates over the questions of secularity, secularism, and "postsecular" worldviews in which Lutheranism's real or supposed role continues to receive attention, this dimension of Lutheran theology's impact far beyond an early modern era—however conceived and defined—will undoubtedly continue to elicit further commentary (von Braun, Gräk, and Zachhuber 2007; Gregory 2012).

A closely related topic that also could not be given its own separate treatment is the significance of Trinitarian theology in Lutheran dogmatics. This theme Kolb investigates with the important observation that for the most part, post-Luther theologians remained reluctant to engage in speculative theology, remaining content with discussion of God's attributes. In so doing, however, they demonstrated little connection between the importance of Lutheran Trinitarian thought with its heavy Christological emphasis, and the broader question of how that theology might hold implications for the Lutheran understanding of the church itself. To pursue such questions further, students must investigate the details of the so-called Kenosis-Christology debates of the seventeenth century. The reverberations of that struggle to reconcile Chalcedonian teaching on the two natures and one person of Christ with the famous Philippians 2:7 passage remained unresolved, but returned forcefully in the theology of the Danish theologian and philosopher Søren Kierkegaard (1813–55). Limitations of space and the need to preserve a degree of uniformity across the confessional groups of essays also left unexamined the reception of Aristotle by Luther and among Lutheran theologians in general. The standard narrative persists of a seventeenth-century reversal of Luther by scholastic theologians who lamented his lack of attention to systematics. This interpretive framework continues to inform a narrative of declension from Luther who, influenced by the rise of nominalism, supposedly rejected the moderate realism of Aristotle. At the level of rhetoric and preaching, and surely in part reflective of the former Augustinian monk's indebtedness to that strain of medieval Catholicism, some scholars have noted, this may have been true. But Luther's understanding of the way things work in God's creation does not reflect such a trajectory (Dieter 2001). For example, as one witness to this fascinating problem there exists Luther's lecture to his students on dialectic given in 1540, which remains recognizably Aristotelian (Luther WA 60, 140–57). Of necessity then, such *conundra* will demand deeper reflection on Luther's cosmology, and whether his insights and convictions that may well have remained deeply conflicted were faithfully conveyed, or lost, in the welter of controversies the Formula of Concord was meant to quiet. Those who struggle to present Lutheran dogmatics in a twenty-first century context necessarily reencounter Luther's struggles with his Augustinian heritage, as well as the related question of his indebtedness to scholasticism (Hinlicky 2015).

If we bear in mind the importance Lutheranism has placed on pastoral education, then the long history of Melanchthon's influence helps to explain the impact of didactic developments on subsequent creators of what generally has been described as Lutheran "orthodoxy," among them Martin Chemnitz (1522–86) and Johann Gerhard (1582–1637). But too narrow a focus on the impressive works of these theological giants can also obscure the existence within the tradition of pastoral training that focused on difficult ethical questions. Not surprisingly, then, a literature emerged on issues of conscience that to some degree found parallels in Catholic and other Protestant traditions, which developed their own responses to dilemmas at the parish level that demanded attention. The very existence of these works needs to be acknowledged, lest the unjustified criticism be perpetuated that because of its theological profile, Lutheranism failed to develop a concern for ethics, and hence was ill-equipped to confront individual, social, and political challenges. Whatever the supposed weaknesses of Lutheranism's ability to "speak truth to power," no serious student of the tradition can afford to overlook the effort invested in addressing questions of conscience (Mayes 2011).

With the exception of a brief mention by Stephenson regarding the uncertain status of marriage as blessed but nonsacramental, the entire topic of human sexuality, gender, and marriage also could not be given the attention it deserves. In part, this oversight reflects the unfinished nature of ongoing research, which has tended to remain overly focused on sixteenth-century patterns and questions of medieval legacy, and only rarely integrates the issues raised by a specifically Lutheran law of marriage with seventeenth- and eighteenth-century developments. This is especially the case in the context of Pietism and the polemics that erupted around marriage and its quasi-sacramental and theological standing among Lutherans as opposed to other Protestant confessions and groups (Witte 1997; Breul and Soboth 2012; Roeber 2013a; Luebke and Lindemann 2014).

# 5 The Problem of Eurocentrism and Lived Religion

Some readers will also undoubtedly wonder if a more global approach to Lutheran theology might have been desirable, even if the extension of explicitly Lutheran theology at the level of lived religion remained largely confined to very small communities of emigrated Scandinavians and German speakers in Swedish, Dutch, and later

English North America, the Danish Caribbean, South India, and Russia. No theological treatises emerged from those transplanted communities until the latter part of the eighteenth century. But the manner in which Lutheran theology may have been transformed in the process of adjusting to non-European contexts has not gone entirely unnoticed. In this volume, Lehmann and Strom most explicitly raise this issue in their interpretation of the Pietist renewal movement. It is worth asking, therefore, whether the changes in Lutheran theology from the sixteenth to the late eighteenth centuries emanated exclusively from European concerns and developments, or whether the experience of these Evangelicals beyond the original heartlands of Lutheranism also shaped the later theological contours of the tradition (Roeber 2001 and 2013b; Wellenreuther 2013).

Perhaps most provocative of all, the very question of how one defines and defends a supposed "epoch" of history cannot be divorced from the European sources of such periodizations. Bernd Hamm has pointedly reminded everyone that "theologians have long pled for the abandonment of the fiction that history has any inherent sense," and insists that the only proper interpretive framework for understanding the thirteenth to the eighteenth centuries remains the Reformers' own—namely, "the inconclusive open-endedness of the Reformation scenario" (Hamm 2014, 238, 236). Hamm's challenge should be read in tandem with Paul Shore's analysis of confessionalization (in this volume). But even a deepened awareness of the difficulties that surround the struggle to appreciate official and nonofficial understandings of a particular confessional tradition between the sixteenth and the late eighteenth centuries does not resolve disagreements that surrounded the vexed question of where the prince's responsibilities for a Protestant confession left off, and where the official theologians' began. It would be anachronistic in a handbook on the early modern period to speak of a developed "Two Kingdoms" theology, since that very term was itself a creation of a twentieth-century German theologian. Even so, readers who wish to pursue the general questions of what was meant over time by "the state" and differing understandings of what "church" meant among Evangelical Lutherans, will need to probe further the question of just how much changed in the legal-constitutional definitions of the sovereignty prince and state properly exercised as protectors, or de facto bishops in overseeing and guarding the "true" faith of their subjects.

The closely related question of whether Lutheran or Reformed theology more successfully carved out an independent voice for theologians to critique political power also deserves further inquiry, since all of the participants in these debates admitted that all authority was granted by God. Agreement stopped there, precisely because the ultimate authority that scripture itself was deemed to possess left open—in unsettling and potentially dangerous political and social ways—the question of whether implementation of what scripture taught could ever be safely entrusted to princes and whether a "natural law" underlay a rightly ordered Christian family, worshipping community, and worldly authority. With the modification of confessional states, doubts about the authority of scripture, and the transformation of older schemes of what had been thought of as "natural law," Lutheranism by the late early-modern decades confronted a range of questions its sixteenth-century theologians could hardly have imagined (see von Friedeburg in this volume; Roeber 2006). Perhaps in no other area of Lutheran contributions to early modern theology do such questions, now posed in a global, post-Christian context, remain a matter of greater contemporary and urgent concern.

## BIBLIOGRAPHY

Breul, Wolfgang, and Christian Soboth, eds. 2012. *Der Herr wird seine Herrlichkeit an uns offenbahren: Liebe, Ehe und Sexualität im Pietismus*. Halle: Harrassowitz.

Brown, Christopher Boyd. 2005. *Singing the Gospel: Lutheran Hymns and the Success of the Reformation*. Cambridge, MA: Harvard University Press.

Dieter, Theodor. 2001. *Der junge Luther und Aristoteles: Eine Historisch-systematische Untersuchung zum Verhätnis von Theologie und Philosophie*. Berlin: De Gruyter.

Gregory, Brad S. 2012. *The Unintended Reformation: How a Religious Revolution Secularized Society*. Cambridge, MA: Harvard University Press.

Hamm, Bernd. 2014. "Farewell to Epochs in Reformation History: A Plea." *Reformation & Renaissance Review* 16 (3): 211–245.

Hamm, Bernd, and Volkerr Leppin, eds. 2007. *Gottes Nähe unmittelbar erfahren: Mystik im Mittelalter und bei Martin Luther*. Tübingen: Mohr Siebeck.

Hinlicky, Paul R. 2015. *Beloved Community: Critical Dogmatics after Christendom*. Grand Rapids, MI: Eerdmans.

Law, David R. 2013. *Kierkegaard's Kenotic Christology*. Oxford: Oxford University Press.

Luebke, David M, and Lindemann, Mary, eds. 2014. *Mixed Matches: Transgressive Unions in Germany from the Reformation to the Enlightenment*. New York, Oxford: Berghahn Books.

Luther, Martin. 1883–2009. *D. Martin Luthers Werke: Kritische Gesamtausgabe (Weimarer Ausgabe)*. 120 vols. Weimar: H. Böhlaus Nachfolger.

Mayes, Benjamin T. G. 2011. *Counsel and Conscience: Lutheran Casuistry and Moral Reasoning after the Reformation*. Göttingen: Vandenhoeck & Ruprecht.

Meyer, Dietrich, and Udo Sträter, eds. 2002. *Zur Rezeption mystischer Traditionen im Protestantismus des 16. Bis 19. Jahrhunderts: Beiträge eines Symposiums zum Tersteegen-Jubiläum 1997*. Cologne: Rheinland-Verlag.

Roeber, A. G. 2013a. *Hopes for Better Spouses: Protestant Marriage and Church Renewal in Early Modern Europe, India, and North America*. Grand Rapids, MI: Eerdmans.

Roeber, A. G. 2006. "The Law, Religion, and State Making in the Early Modern World: Protestant Revolutions in the Works of Berman, Gorski, and Witte." *Law & Social Inquiry: Journal of the American Bar Foundation* 31 (1): 199–227.

Roeber, A. G. 2013b. "Lutheranism in the Atlantic World in the Age of Revolutions." In *The Transatlantic World of Heinrich Melchior Mühlenberg in the Eighteenth Century*, edited by Hermann Wellenreuther, Thomas Müller-Bahlke, and A. Gregg Roeber, 295–317. Halle: Verlag der Franckeschen Stiftungen.

Roeber, A. G. 2001. "What the Law Requires Is Written on Their Hearts: Noachic and Natural Law among German-Speakers in Early Modern North America." *William & Mary Quarterly* 3rd Ser. LVIII (4): 883–912.

Von Braun, Christian, Wilhelm Gräk, and Zachhuber, eds. 2007. *Säkluarisierung: Bilanz und Perspektiven einer umstrittenen These*. Berlin: LIT Verlag.

Weber, Julie Tomberlin. 2008. "Translation as a Prism: Broadening the Spectrum of Eighteenth-Century Identity." In *Ethnographies and Exchanges: Native Americans, Moravians, and Catholics in Early North America*, edited by A. G. Roeber, 195–207. University Park, PA: The Pennsylvania State University Press.

Wellenreuther, Hermann. 2013. *Heinrich Melchior Mühlenberg und die deutschen Lutheraner in Nordamerika, 1742–1787: Wissenstransfer und Wandel eines atlantischen zu einem amerikanischen Netzwerk*. Berlin: LIT Verlag.

Witte, John Jr. 1997. *From Sacrament to Contract: Marriage, Religion, and Law in the Western Tradition*. Louisville, KY: Westminster John Knox.

# CHAPTER 19

# SCRIPTURE AND EXEGESIS IN EARLY MODERN LUTHERANISM

### BENJAMIN T. G. MAYES

## 1 MORE THAN POLEMICS: THE RICHNESS OF SCRIPTURE IN ORTHODOX LUTHERAN THEOLOGY AND USE

LUTHERAN exegesis in the orthodox period (1580–1750) (Kolb 2006; Koch 2000, 211–59; Matthias 1995; Wallmann 1992) took place in a wide variety of contexts and forms. In both Latin and German, Lutherans in Germany wrote cursory explanations of biblical books; preached through books of the Bible and Apocrypha at midweek worship services; published postils and sermon studies for the liturgical year; published polyglot Bibles; wrote rhymed paraphrases of biblical books; and published pedagogical, philological, and exegetical Bible commentaries (Koch 1990; Burnett 2012, 93–137; Walch 1765, 4:400–1050). Yet most research on Lutheran theology in the eighteenth and especially the seventeenth centuries has focused just on their dogmatics and the use of philosophy in theology. While the orthodox doctrine of scripture and the rise of textual and historical criticism of the Bible has been studied by many, other areas have been neglected—in particular the biblical commentaries of the orthodox period—resulting in the opinion that the Lutheran orthodox neglected scriptural exegesis, or approached the Bible merely in the search for proof texts to buttress their preconceived, traditional dogmas. Hand-in-hand with this approach goes the view of Lutheran orthodoxy as "dead" and sterile, this view still finding its proponents in encyclopedias and textbooks (Steiger 2008).

This view of "dead orthodoxy" can in large part be corrected by an awareness of the churchly and academic practices that led to so much of the theological literature of the time. Cursory Bible reading was uncommon among Lutheran laypeople in the seventeenth century; a Bible came into each literate home with Pietism in the eighteenth century, as the cost of Bible printing came down and Bible societies and governments gave financial support. Disputations were a regular feature of university education and the source of most dogmatic and systematic writings, as well as of many scriptural commentaries. Sermons for the historic church year made for popular devotional reading and communication of the Christian message throughout the seventeenth and eighteenth centuries. Sermon series on books of the Bible (usually held on weekdays) were common among Lutherans, and led to a large number of other scriptural commentaries. Latin continued as the international language of learning, as it had for centuries before the Reformation. Finally, a desire to put scripture to use and apply its teachings to individual problems and situations led to the development of a casuistry literature among Lutherans. The Lutheran approach to the Bible and exegesis in the early modern period presents a richness to researchers that has, for the most part, been unexplored for centuries (Appold 2004; Frymire 2010; Mayes 2011; Steiger 2008; Muller 1998; Sheppard 1998; Reventlow 2009; Appold 2010).

## 2 Johann Gerhard and the Inspiration of Scripture

Johann Gerhard (1582–1637) is perhaps the best known and most influential Lutheran theologian of the seventeenth century, remembered especially for his monumental *Theological Commonplaces* and his short devotional works (Steiger 2003; Fischer 2000; Gerhard 2009). His main exegetical works are his completion of the *Harmony of the Gospels*, begun by Martin Chemnitz and Polycarp Leyser; the notes on several books in the glossed Bible commissioned by Duke Ernst the Pious (on which see section 4 below); and his early treatise on hermeneutics, which was incorporated into the *Theological Commonplaces* (Gerhard 1622; Glassius and Gerhard 1641; Gerhard 2007b).

The Lutheran approach to Holy Scripture can be seen clearly in a controversy that arose from 1621 to 1630, involving Gerhard and Hermann Rahtmann (1585–1628), a pastor in Danzig who emphasized the difference between Holy Scripture and the Word of God, claiming that God's Word cannot be put into writing. When hearing preaching or reading the Bible, God's will and the Gospel cannot be known, Rahtmann claimed, unless the Holy Spirit assists the reader or hearer in a supplementary action; that is, apart from the means of the scriptural word, even if the scriptural word provided the kindling for the Spirit's work of engendering understanding and faith. According to Rahtmann, scripture as writing cannot convert or save anyone.

Rahtmann's view of scripture was opposed by most other Lutherans. The orthodox Lutherans instead emphasized that God is free to bind Himself to a covenant, and also to scripture. Just as in Christ the divine and human natures can be distinguished but not separated, so also the external letter of scripture and the Spirit working internally can be distinguished but by no means separated. The orthodox also said that the Spirit is inherent in scripture even apart from its use, a claim motivated in part by Christological, anti-Nestorian concerns. After consideration, Gerhard opposed Rahtmann's doctrine and put his views into writing in 1628, stating that the Holy Spirit is inseparable from scripture (Steiger 2008, 710–15; Wallmann 1995, 51; Grübel 1671, 201–74).

The Lutheran orthodox response to Rahtmann centered on the doctrine of the inspiration of scripture. This doctrine, more than perhaps any other, has provoked controversy. Researchers cannot yet agree whether the response to Rahtmann and the orthodox Lutheran view of scripture as being God's Word in written form represents a change of theology in the direction of bibliolatry—where an extra kind of faith is required, toward the Bible and not just toward the Gospel (Michel 1985, 10–12, 23; Reventlow 2009, 17; Pelikan 1983, 343–45)—or whether the Lutheran position was a clarification of earlier Lutheran and ancient Christian teaching, motivated by the soteriological function of the Bible (Koch 2000, 237–38; Preus 2003; Muller 1998). The Lutheran orthodox view of inspiration has been reproached for denying the literary uniqueness of the biblical authors (Michel 1985); yet this view cannot hold up when one considers the extensive attention given by all the Lutheran orthodox to the genres of scriptural writings and the characteristics of the human writers of scripture (Jung 1999; Preus 2003; Preus 1970; Steiger 2008; Keller 1984). Again, it has been criticized for not being "historical" in the sense that the Lutheran orthodox claimed that the content of revelation did not change through history (Reventlow 2009; Kraus 1982). Yet such criticisms must be tested against the fact that the Lutheran orthodox give much attention to the historical situation of the biblical text, including the micro- and macro-contexts of a passage—the people being addressed, the speakers, the time; and the history, culture, practices, geography, and ethics of the people speaking and being addressed (Steiger 2008).

Regarding the canon of the New Testament, Lutherans before Gerhard, such as Martin Chemnitz, doubted the authorship and authority of the antilegomena books of the New Testament: Hebrews, James, 2 Peter, 2 and 3 John, Jude, and Revelation. After Gerhard the authorship of these books could still be doubted, but not their inspiration and authority. Regardless of the human author, Gerhard and later Lutherans claimed divine authorship for them all (Preus 1970; Gerhard 2009, 249–78, §§ 274–300; Keller 1984, 150–51). As for the Old Testament, only the Hebrew Bible was considered canonical, not the apocryphal (or "deuterocanonical") books. On the other hand, the apocryphal books remained important. For example, Ecclesiasticus served as the basis of countless sermons and school texts aimed at moral formation (Gerhard 2009, 80–113, §§ 67–107; Steiger 2008; Koch 1990).

Although the early church's historic testimony to the canon of scripture was of great importance for Lutherans, this testimony does not give the present church any authority over scripture. Besides the church's testimony, other criteria of the canon and authority of scripture must be considered, both external and internal—chiefly the internal testimony of the Holy Spirit. Scripture is αὐτόπιστος (i.e., it authenticates itself), which means that in the course of exegetical work, the interpreter will be acted upon by the Holy Spirit through scripture and be brought to the understanding of scripture and faith in its message (Gerhard 2009, 68–84, 410–33, §§ 36–51, 453–80; Steiger 2008; Kirste 1976; Appold 2010).

## 3  FRIEDRICH BALDUIN AND DOGMATIC EXEGESIS

Much orthodox Lutheran exegesis was dogmatic and polemical. While this dogmatic exegesis has been criticized as the theologian's search for proof-texts to buttress his previously conceived, traditional dogmatic theses (Reventlow 2009; Quack 1975), others have noticed that, with some exceptions, Lutherans approached scripture as a whole and only then derived doctrine from it. Moreover, Lutherans used many other genres of commentary and uses of scripture besides just dogmatic exegesis. In this Lutheran dogmatic exegesis, exegetes were interested in presenting the doctrines of the Christian faith as resting on certain, clear passages of scripture (*loci classici* or *sedes doctrinae*) (Jung 1999; Hägglund 2007; Steiger 2008; Appold 2010; Preus 2003; Muller 1998; Koch 1990).

This approach to exegesis, which gathered dogmatic points of teaching as a result of exegetical work, can be seen in Johann Gerhard's *Method of Theological Study*. From the very beginning of theological study, Gerhard leads his students to read scripture in two ways: cursorily and accurately. In the cursory reading, the student reads through the Bible every year in the vernacular or Latin, reading didactic books of scripture in the morning and historical books in the evening. The accurate reading of scripture requires students to study the Bible in Greek and Hebrew every day, reading a trusted commentary alongside, and writing observations and excerpts in large blank books that would serve future ministers as a portable library. In disputations, students were instructed to take the foundations of their position first from scripture, including necessary conclusions drawn from it, and only thereafter to bring forth testimonies of the early church fathers and decrees of councils as witnesses, followed by an argumentative use of the adversaries' assent and philosophy. Doctrinal and exegetical tradition was cultivated and revered, but not seen as above criticism (Gerhard 1620; Mayes 2013).

The exegesis of Wittenberg theology professor Friedrich Balduin (1575–1627) sets forth this same approach to dogmatic exegesis. Besides writing a significant Lutheran casuistry (Mayes 2011), Balduin's work centered on exegesis and dogmatics. In his *Idea Dispositionum Biblicarum* (1622), Balduin directs the reader of scripture first of all to pray, and then to explain and analyze the text regarding its structure. After a biblical pericope has been explained and partitioned, the next step is to gather doctrines from the text. This is because knowledge without application (*usus*) "puffs up," and God teaches us useful things. All that has been written was written for our teaching (*doctrina*); scripture is divinely inspired and useful for teaching, etc. (1 Cor. 8:1; Isa. 48:17; Rom. 15:4; 2 Tim. 3:16). Gathering of doctrines is not left to the whim of the interpreter; Balduin provides nine rules, which draw mainly on scripture (but also on early church fathers) for their support. Finally not just the text, but also the doctrines, are to be applied both to the "well" and the "sick" (Balduin 1622; Appold 2005).

In his commentaries on the Pauline Epistles, Balduin put this method into practice. For each chapter of Paul's epistles, Balduin provides a summary and general outline, the biblical text in Greek and Latin, analysis and explanation of the text, a paraphrase, questions that arise from the text with their answers (usually resolving apparent contradictions, sometimes polemical), and finally theological aphorisms—a plethora of doctrinal statements resting on each section of Pauline text (Balduin 1654).

Balduin's dogmatic exegesis shows that the search for dogmas in the text of scripture came especially from the desire to make salutary application (*usus*) of the text to the lives of Christians. Yet dogmatic, doctrinal exegesis was only a part of Lutheran exegetical activity. There were other *usûs*.

# 4 SALOMON GLASSIUS, SCRIPTURE'S INTERPRETATION, AND ITS USE

Since Lutherans required clear statements of doctrine, and all doctrine had to be drawn from scripture, the proper rules of scriptural interpretation were highly important. Biblical hermeneutics was born out of dealing with Holy Scripture, not conceived in the abstract and applied to scripture later. In this way, the Holy Spirit, working through one's reading of scripture, was viewed as the only authentic interpreter of His own inspired text.

Following the famous texts on biblical hermeneutics by Matthias Flacius Illyricus (1520–75) and others, Salomon Glassius (1593–1656) made a significant hermeneutical contribution that was cherished by Lutherans for well over a century and a half (Steiger 2008; Flacius 1580; Franz 1619; Gerhard 2007b; Keller 1984; Hägglund 1951; Kolb 1998; Jung 1999; Walch 1765, 4:207–306). Glassius, Johann Gerhard's favorite student, spent most of his career in the service of the church and of Duke Ernst "the Pious" of Sachsen-Gotha as ecclesiastical superintendent. Besides exegetical works, homilies, and devotional works, Glassius should be remembered for his *Philologia Sacra* (1623–36), a large work of hermeneutics; as well as his general editorship of the large glossed German Bible commissioned by Duke Ernst (*Biblia* 1641).

Originally the *Philologia Sacra* included five books, covering the style and writing of Holy Scripture (including the integrity and purity of the Old Testament and New Testament books), the sense of Holy Scripture (including not only the literal but also the mystical sense), sacred grammar, and sacred rhetoric (Glassius 1705; Steiger 1995;

Hägglund 2006). His work was reprinted several times into the eighteenth century, indicating its enduring popularity. Glassius's work is very much in line with the Lutheran hermeneutics works that came before his. On at least one point, however, Glassius seems to have gone in his own direction: the mystical sense of scripture.

Johann Gerhard had made clear in his *Tractatus de Interpretatione* that the scope of scripture is Christ. The Holy Spirit intended one literal sense of each passage in scripture; allegories and the like—the mystical sense of scripture—are not various senses, but various inferences or applications from the one literal sense. Thus the mystical sense when discovered by interpreters proves nothing, but when the apostles interpret something allegorically (or mystically), solid proof can be taken from their allegories (Gerhard 2007b, §§ 133, 136, 210). This does not mean that Gerhard avoided using the mystical sense, however. In his sermons for the church year, each sermon begins with a type of Christ from the Old Testament before explaining the Gospel pericope and applying it to the heart (repentance, faith, and virtues) (Gerhard 1870, ix–x). Gerhard uses the mystical sense frequently throughout his writings, but avoids it when engaging in disputes about doctrine.

Glassius took this approach to the mystical sense and developed hermeneutical rules for it: The mystical sense is inherent to the biblical text in many places, and is distinct from the various allegories and applications that the interpreter may bring to the text. Tropes and metaphors belong not to the mystical sense but to the literal. The mystical sense is subdivided into three categories: allegory, type, and parable. Glassius distinguishes between innate and "illate" types. The latter are types that the interpreter "brings to" scripture, rather than being intrinsic to the text and intended by the Holy Spirit. Illate types are not illegitimate, however, since Christ commands people to "search the Scriptures" (John 5:39). Glassius also gave rules for determining where types are present and for avoiding abuses (Johansson 2010; Diestel 1869, 376–77).

Glassius' approach reveals a degree of disagreement in how Lutherans viewed the mystical sense of scripture. One way was to see the mystical sense as an alternative to the grammatical meaning of the words. If the words seem to say something against common reason, the analogy of faith, or good morals, then the literal reading is rejected and a figure is introduced. Glassius, however, regarded the mystical sense not as an alternative to the literal sense, but as an addition to it. The literal sense is one, and sometimes in addition there is a mystical meaning. All the Lutheran orthodox agreed that where the apostles identify a type in the Old Testament, there a type was truly intended by the Holy Spirit. But should the New Testament's identification of types and allegories be seen as exhaustive (such that no other types are to be sought), or as instructive (such that the apostles' finding of types in the Old Testament should be illustrative for the exegete's work)? Here there was no complete agreement (Stroh 1977, 49–50; Walch 1765, 4:225–39). After Glassius, Lutherans continued to discuss and debate the mystical sense of scripture. Although some eighteenth-century historians considered it only a dispute about terminology, Abraham Calov (1612–86) explicitly disagreed with Glassius' hermeneutics on this teaching of the mystical sense, while Johann Jacob Rambach (1693–1735) was one of the mystical sense's chief Lutheran proponents (Mayes 2008; Jung 1999, 127–28).

The Lutheran orthodox required both piety and learning of exegetes in order to carry out their task rightly. In order to help them do this, both pious and learned writings from the era abound (Walch 1765, 4:331–68). The learning required for biblical exegesis includes the biblical languages, rhetoric, and logic; as well as metaphysics, physics, ethics, politics, geography, chronology, and history.

While the church year did not usually include Old Testament readings for Sundays and festivals, Lutheran liturgies continued to use Introit Psalms, and Old Testament passages were used at the outset of many sermons (e.g., Gerhard 2003). Moreover, Lutherans often used a *lectio continua* to preach through entire Old Testament books at midweek services (e.g., Herberger 2010). Of the biblical languages, Gerhard and Flacius claimed that Hebrew was the most important (Steiger 2008). In order to understand the Hebrew Bible better, Gerhard recommended that students also learn Aramaic and Syriac, in order to engage the rabbinic exegetical tradition and to show where the rabbis interpreted a passage as prophetic of the Messiah (Gerhard 1620, 59–71). While interest in kabbalah, the mystical-esoteric Jewish spiritualism, continued among Lutherans, Christian publishing of kabbalistic texts waned after 1560 (Koch 2000, 315; Burnett 2012, 126–27; e.g., Gerhard 2007a, 25–27, E2 § 27). Yet the market for Hebrew books in Lutheran lands did not wane, due to the Reformation's focus on *sola Scriptura* in the original languages as authority in matters of faith. From 1561 to 1660, Lutherans published more books dealing with Hebrew than any other confession—mostly grammars, dictionaries, concordances, Bibles, commentaries, and Christian liturgical works in the Hebrew language (e.g., Glassius 1622). Up to 1660, Christian Hebraism focused on the text of the Bible and linguistic analysis of it. Afterwards, the field became focused on historical criticism of the Hebrew Bible. In this period, too, most of the Christian manuals for advanced study of Hebrew, including Hebrew composition, were written by Lutherans (Burnett 2012, 3–135).

Glossed Bibles were the early modern equivalent of what are now called "study Bibles." Lutherans produced these in both German and Latin. German glossed Bibles include those by Lucas Osiander (Stuttgart, 1626), Johann Olearius (Leipzig, 1678–81), and Abraham Calov, who cites Luther heavily (Wittenberg, 1681–82). Pietistic glossed Bibles include the Ebersdorfer Bible (by von Rothe and Zinzendorf, 1726), and the Bibles edited by Christoph Matthaeus Pfaff (Tübingen, 1729) and Joachim Lang (Leipzig, 1743). Latin glossed Bibles by Lucas Osiander (Tübingen, 1578) and Andreas Osiander the Younger (Tübingen, 1600) emended and commented on the Vulgate text. Lutherans continued to use and revere the Vulgate while regarding it merely as a translation, not as authentic (as was claimed by the Council of Trent, session 4, decree 2). In some passages, such as James 2, the wholly new Latin Bible translation by Sebastian Schmidt of Strasbourg (1617–96) resembles a glossed Bible, though its main importance is that this literal, word-for-word translation was the only full Latin Bible translation produced by a Lutheran (Walch 1765, 4:73–76, 185–88; Jacob 1986).

The most popular of the Lutheran glossed Bibles was a remarkable work commissioned in 1635 by Duke Ernst "the Pious" of Sachsen-Gotha and published in 1641. This Bible—variously named *Kurfürstenbibel, Nürnberger Bibelwerk, Weimarisches*

*Bibelwerk*, and Ernestinian Bible—had Johann Gerhard as its general editor until his death in 1637, and thereafter, Salomon Glassius. Despite its enormous size, the "Ernestinian Bible" was reprinted repeatedly until the early twentieth century in both Germany and the United States. Glassius' preface, starting from 2 Tim. 3:14–17, gives a full orthodox Lutheran doctrine of Holy Scripture. The rebirth and renewal of the human creature is set forth as the goal of the Bible. In contrast to Luther's Bible prefaces, "Law and Gospel" is not a theme; it is mentioned only once in passing. Instead, Glassius focuses on the uses or benefits (*Nutzbarkeiten*) of scripture, which include: teaching, comforting consciences, rebuking, correcting, and training in righteousness. This Ernestinian Bible strives to explain the literal sense of scripture; not all of the "uses" mentioned by St. Paul in 2 Tim. 3:14–17 could be indicated (Glassius 2011; Glassius and Gerhard 1641; Glassius and Gerhard 1902; Quack 1975, 182–97). Until his death, Glassius edited and revised new editions of the Ernestinian Bible and composed new practical applications (uses) for each chapter, which were then included in this Bible beginning with the 1686 edition (Glassius 1651; Walther 1902).

The Ernestinian Bible is illustrative of the Lutheran exegesis of the entire period. From Flacius to Abraham Calov, the "salutary use of Holy Scripture"—especially in teaching, rebuking, warning, and consoling—was a standard feature of Lutheran exegesis. The distinction of Law and Gospel, however, is understated in the post-Reformation era. Glassius in his *Philologia Sacra* does not deal with it at any length. Apparently the fourfold *usus* of scripture was more significant for exegesis (Preus 1977, 93–94).

## 5  PIETISM AND THE ENLIGHTENMENT

Lutheran theology of the seventeenth and eighteenth centuries is notable for its defense of scripture's authority against attacks from many quarters. The controversy with Hermann Rahtmann has been mentioned above (see section 2). Another intra-Lutheran controversy was sparked by Georg Calixt (1586–1656), a professor in Helmstedt, who sought to overcome the divisions between Lutheran, Roman Catholic, and Reformed churches by basing theology not just on scripture, but also on the confession of faith of the first five Christian centuries. An orthodox Lutheran response was stated in the *Consensus Repetitus Fidei Verae Lutheranae* ("Repeated Consensus of the Truly Lutheran Faith," 1655), of which the Wittenberg professor Abraham Calov was a chief author. It defended scripture's plenary inspiration (not limited just to matters of redemption), and the full authority of scripture alone over all ecclesiastical tradition (Mayes 2004; Staemmler 2005).

Lutherans faced an even more significant opponent of scriptural authority in the Socinians. Named after Fausto Sozzini (1539–1604), the Socinians were Unitarians who criticized not just individual tenets of traditional Christian doctrine, but most of all, its presuppositions. Even after their schools and publishing headquarters in Rakow (Racovia), Poland, were destroyed by the Jesuits in 1638, their questions and thinking lived on and became the root of the Enlightenment's criticism of the Bible and orthodox doctrine. The heart of Socinianism was really the denial that Christ had made satisfaction for sins and reconciliation with God. In place of this Christian doctrine came a moral religion in which Jesus is a model of God's will and a guarantor of His promises. This viewpoint facilitated rational criticism of Christianity and the Bible. Early seventeenth-century Socinianism stressed the sufficiency of the New Testament, but later in the century the role of reason in determining truth became more pronounced. With it came critical exegetical principles, among which was the rule that nothing may be asserted that contradicts sound reason or is contradictory in itself. At first, Socinians did not believe miracles were against reason, whereas to them the doctrine of the Trinity most certainly was. This system of reason, scripture, and revelation was in place before the great movements in philosophy and science of the seventeenth century. Later, the Enlightenment would take the same approach to reason, revelation, and scripture, and would deny or explain away the scriptural miracles, too (Scholder 1990).

As the intensive study of scripture continued, controversies on the text of scripture arose. In the late seventeenth and early eighteenth centuries one such controversy centered on the style of Greek in the New Testament, as to whether it should be judged on the basis of secular Greek classics. If so, it was feared that Hebraisms and other features of Koine Greek might be viewed as errors (Walch 1765, 4:276–85, 321–31). More famous than this, though perhaps not as significant at the time, was the controversy on the vowel pointing of the Old Testament. Similar to their Reformed counterparts, most Lutheran orthodox theologians held that the vowel pointing of the Hebrew Old Testament was inspired and original to the text and was necessary to make the text unambiguous—a position not held by Martin Luther. A significant Lutheran defense of vowel pointing is Abraham Calov's *Criticus sacer biblicus* (1646), which set forth a vindication of the integrity of the Hebrew Old Testament and vowel points against Robert Bellarmine (1542–1621) and Jean Morin (1591–1691).

Calov's work makes clear that a precursor to the popular dethronement of the Bible as the highest authority was a form of Roman Catholic polemic that sought to undermine the clarity of scripture and thereby necessitate the church's magisterium in order to obtain the authentic meaning of scripture. Against Catholic polemicists such as Jean Morin and Richard Simon (1638–93), Lutherans such as Johann Benedikt Carpzov (1639–99) and Salomon Deyling (1677–1755) stressed scripture's sole authority and clarity without the need for the magisterium; yet not without study, academic skills, and the enlightening work of the Holy Spirit (Scholder 1990, 19–25; Burnett 2012, 122–23; Steiger 2008, 747–49; Reventlow 2009, 3:225–27; 4:73–83; Flacius 1580, 2:364–65; Gerhard 2009, 295–311, §§ 334–53).

A similar criticism of scripture's clarity, at least with regard to Old Testament prophecies fulfilled in Christ and the New Testament church, was mounted by the Dutch jurist and exegete Hugo Grotius (1583–1645). Grotius explained scripture philologically and followed Jewish interpretation where Christians traditionally had seen prophecies of Christ, such as Isaiah 7 and 53. Grotius' chief Lutheran opponent was, again, Abraham Calov. Against Grotius and others, Calov stressed the unity of scripture and in his *Biblia Illustrata* (1672–76) strove to show that Old Testament prophecies of Christ were included in the literal sense; they were not allegories added by the interpreter. Calov was looking at the wide context of the entire Christian canon and thus was able to find Christian meaning in a whole range of passages in which Grotius found none (Reventlow 2009, 3:209–23; Jung 1999, 129–226; Elliott 2012).

Through the course of the seventeenth and eighteenth centuries, new scientific discoveries and philosophies challenged the way Lutherans and others had traditionally understood the scriptures and spurred on a variety of reactions. Copernicus' and Kepler's astronomical discoveries were generally rejected by orthodox Lutherans as incompatible with scripture, forcing Kepler, for instance, to find a way to reconcile his new views with Joshua 10. This same basic pattern was repeated with each new discovery in the fields of biblical studies (such as in biblical geography and chronology) and of philosophy. It was especially the philosophy of René Descartes that moved the thinkers of Europe to approach religion from a standpoint of doubt toward authority and acceptance only of rationally demonstrable facts (Scholder 1990, 46–132; Elert 1962, 414–31).

The Enlightenment reached Germany late, after taking hold in France, England, and the Netherlands. As the Lutheran orthodox faced rational-historical arguments, they too began to respond increasingly with arguments intended to stand up to rational scrutiny. For example, Valentin Ernst Löscher (1674–1749), who vigorously defended the canonicity and authority of Holy Scripture, elevated the role of the natural knowledge of God in order to help refute English skepticism and empiricism. His argumentation often lists rational arguments in the first place, followed by biblical passages. This argumentative strategy was far more pronounced in Siegmund Jakob Baumgarten (1706–57). While holding to the main points of orthodox doctrine, Baumgarten strove to prove all the doctrines of faith rationally and demonstrably; miracles and Old Testament prophecies became proof of the faith rather than things that must be believed (Steiger 2008; Michel 1985, 23; Scholder 1990, 110–14; Greschat 1971; Schloemann 1988).

Baumgarten's student, Johann Salomo Semler (1725–91), continued with his mentor's approach to reason, but jettisoned the orthodox view of scripture. While he defended the resurrection of Jesus, his interest was only in a religion of human moral development. His approach to the Bible is representative of the Enlightenment, in which exegesis separated the Bible from the foregoing dogmatic exegesis to find its supposed historical meaning behind and apart from the canonical form of the text. The theory of accommodation (that all of scripture was adapted to the worldview and superstitions of its first audience) was applied throughout and allowed the reinterpretation of parts of scripture that were viewed as unworthy or impossible (such as miracles). Rather than being submissive to the text of Holy Scripture, the Enlightenment exegete was a critic of the biblical text. By the end of the eighteenth century, this had become the prevalent approach to scripture. While Lutheran orthodoxy with its regard for Holy Scripture as the Word of God survived, it was no longer dominant in Germany (Reventlow 2009, 4:175–90; Scholder 1990; Sheppard 1998; Legaspi 2010; Kleinig 1996).

German Pietism brought about several changes in Lutheran exegesis and devotion. German Bibles began to be printed economically, on a large scale, especially by the Cansteinische Bibelanstalt in Halle, founded in 1710, enabling widespread lay Bible reading. For Pietists, the Bible was at the center of all reforms and was the norm for judging the present form of the church. Pietist exegesis usually sought spiritual edification more than intellectual knowledge.

Among Pietist exegetes, Johann Albrecht Bengel's (1687–1752) fame is due not just to his role as a Pietist Lutheran pastor and Bible commentator (*Gnomon Novi Testamenti*, 1742), but also for his interest in establishing the authentic text of the Greek New Testament. By the early eighteenth century, the criticisms of the received texts of the Hebrew Old Testament and Greek New Testament had made clear that some errors had crept into the texts as they were copied and passed down through the centuries. Recognizing this, Bengel claimed not the full inerrancy of a particular manuscript tradition of the New Testament, but the full infallibility and truthfulness of all canonical scriptures in their autographs. The copies that came down through the ages had minor errors, and had to be freed from copyists' errors on the basis of manuscript evidence. Noting the great confusion then reigning on how to evaluate the many Greek manuscripts of the New Testament, he charted a course between always condemning the received readings of the *Textus Receptus* and always defending them. His investigations of the genuine readings of the New Testament were presented in the four parts of his *Apparatus criticus* (1734). Part two is the main section; here Bengel examines the chief variant passages individually. On the "Johannine comma" (1 John 5:7–8), Bengel argues that it is original and authentic, but was omitted not by Arians in the early church, but by churchmen, due to the "arcane discipline" of keeping the Trinitarian baptismal formula secret, or to avoid Sabellianism. In part three, Bengel shows that divine wisdom and power can be observed in the variant readings. With his New Testament textual studies and his annotations in the *Gnomon*, Bengel thus charted a path for a faithful Christian understanding of the Bible in an age of skepticism (Bertsch 2002; Ludwig 1952; Pelikan 1952; Thompson 2004; Bristol 1950; Fritsch 1951; Bengel 1763).

## BIBLIOGRAPHY

Appold, Kenneth G. 2004. *Orthodoxie als Konsensbildung*. Tübingen: Mohr Siebeck.

Appold, Kenneth G. 2005. "Scriptural Authority in the Age of Lutheran Orthodoxy." In *The Bible in the History of the Lutheran Church*, edited by John A. Maxfield, 19–33. St. Louis, MO: Concordia Historical Institute.

Appold, Kenneth G. 2010. "Abraham Calov on the 'Usefulness' of Doctrine." In *Hermeneutica Sacra: Studies of the Interpretation of Holy Scripture in the Sixteenth and Seventeenth Centuries*, edited by Torbjörn Johansson, Robert Kolb, and Johann Anselm Steiger, 295–312. Berlin: De Gruyter.

Balduin, Friedrich. 1654. *Commentarius In Omnes Epistolas Beati Apostoli Pauli*. Frankfurt.

Balduin, Friedrich. 1622. *Idea Dispositionum Biblicarum*. Wittenberg.

Bengel, Johann Albrecht. 1763. *Apparatus criticus ad Novum Testamentum: criseos sacrae compendium, liman, supplementum ac fructum exhibens.* 2nd ed. Tübingen.

Bertsch, Lothar. 2002. *Johann Albrecht Bengel: Seine Lebensgeschichte.* Holzgerlingen: Hänsler.

Bristol, Lyle O. 1950. "New Testament Textual Criticism in the Eighteenth Century." *Journal of Biblical Literature* 69 (2): 101–112.

Burnett, Stephen G. 2012. *Christian Hebraism in the Reformation Era (1500–1660).* Leiden: Brill.

Diestel, Ludwig. 1869. *Geschichte des Alten Testamentes in der christlichen Kirche.* Jena: Mauke.

Elert, Werner. 1962. *The Structure of Lutheranism: The Theology and Philosophy of Life of Lutheranism Especially in the Sixteenth and Seventeenth Centuries.* Translated by Walter A. Hansen. St. Louis, MO: Concordia.

Elliott, Mark W. 2012. "Looking Backwards: The Protestant Latin Bible in the Eyes of Johannes Piscator and Abraham Calov." In *Shaping the Bible in the Reformation: Books, Scholars and Their Readers in the Sixteenth Century,* edited by Bruce Gordon and Matthew McLean, 291–302. Library of the Written Word 20. Leiden: Brill.

Fischer, Erdmann Rudolph. 2000. *The Life of John Gerhard.* Translated by Richard J. Dinda and Elmer M. Hohle. Malone, TX: Repristination Press.

Flacius, Matthias. 1580. *Clavis Scriptvrae S. seu de Sermone Sacrarum literarum.* 2 vols. Basel.

Franz, Wolfgang. 1619. *Tractatus Theologicus . . . de Interpretatione Sacrarum Scripturarum.* Wittenberg: Matthaei Seelfisch.

Fritsch, Charles T. 1951. "Bengel: Student of Scripture." *Interpretation* 5 (2): 203–215.

Frymire, John M. 2010. *The Primacy of the Postils.* Leiden: Brill.

Gerhard, Johann. 1622. *In Harmoniam Historiae Evangelicae De Passione, Crucifixione, Morte Et Sepultura Christi Salvatoris Nostri, Ex Quatuor Evangelistis contextam, Commentarius.* Frankfurt am Main: Johannes Jakob Porß.

Gerhard, Johann. 1620. *Methodus Studii Theologici.* Jena.

Gerhard, Johann. 2007a. *On the Nature of God and on the Most Holy Mystery of the Trinity.* Edited by Benjamin T. G. Mayes. Translated by Richard J. Dinda. Theological Commonplaces Exegesis II-III. St. Louis, MO: Concordia.

Gerhard, Johann. 2009. *On the Nature of Theology and on Scripture.* Edited by Benjamin T. G. Mayes. Translated by Richard J. Dinda. Rev. ed. Theological Commonplaces Exegesis I. St. Louis, MO: Concordia.

Gerhard, Johann. 1870. *Postille: Das ist Auslegung und Erklärung der sonntäglichen und vornehmsten Fest-Evangelien.* Berlin: Gustav Schlawitz.

Gerhard, Johann. 2003. *Postilla: An Explanation of the Sunday and Most Important Festival Gospels of the Whole Year.* Malone, TX: Center for the Study of Lutheran Orthodoxy.

Gerhard, Johann. 2007b *Tractatus de legitima scripturae sacrae interpretatione (1610): Lateinisch—Deutsch.* Edited by Johann Anselm Steiger and Vanessa von der Lieth. Stuttgart-Bad Cannstatt: Frommann-Holzboog.

Glassius, Salomon. 1651. *Enchiridion S. Scripturae Practicum.* Gotha.

Glassius, Salomon. 1622. *Institutiones Grammatices Hebraeae.* Erfordiae.

Glassius, Salomon. 1705. *Philologia sacra qua . . . scripturae, tum stylus et literatura, tum sensus et genuinae interpretationis ratio et doctrina . . . expenditur.* Leipzig.

Glassius, Salomon. 2011. "Salomon Glassius' Vorrede zum Nürnberger Bibelwerk (1640). Kommentierte Edition." In *Philologia Sacra: Zur Exegese der Heiligen Schrift im Protestantismus des 16. bis 18. Jahrhunderts,* edited by Johann Anselm Steiger, 155–226. Neukirchen-Vluyn: Neukirchener Verlagsgesellschaft.

Glassius, Salomon, and Johann Gerhard, eds. 1641. *Biblia, Das ist: Die gantze H. Schrifft, Altes und Newes Testaments Teutsch/ D. Martin Luthers: / Auff gnädige Verordnung deß . . . Herrn Ernsts/ Hertzogen zu Sachsen . . . Von etlichen reinen Theologen . . . erkläret.* Nürnberg.

Glassius, Salomon, and Johann Gerhard, eds. 1902. *Das Weimarische Bibelwerk: Biblia das ist die ganze Heilige Schrift Alten und Neuen Testaments verdeutscht von Doctor Martin Luther, and auf Herzog Ernst's Verordnung von etlichen reinen Theologen dem eigentlichen Wortverstand nach erklärt.* Neue Ausgabe, dritte Auflage. St. Louis, MO: Fr. Dette.

Greschat, Martin. 1971. *Zwischen Tradition und neuem Anfang: Valentin Ernst Löscher und der Ausgang der Lutherischen Orthodoxie.* Witten: Luther-Verlag.

Grübel, Christian, ed. 1671. "Thesauri Conciliorum Et Decisionum Appendix Nova." In *Thesauri Conciliorum Et Decisionum,* 2nd ed. Vol. 4. Jena.

Hägglund, Bengt. 1951. *Die Heilige Schrift und ihre Deutung in der Theologie Johann Gerhards: Eine Untersuchung über das altlutherische Schriftverständnis.* Lund: CWK Gleerup.

Hägglund, Bengt. 2007. *History of Theology.* Translated by Gene J. Lund. 4th English ed. St. Louis, MO: Concordia.

Hägglund, Bengt. 2006. "Pre-Kantian Hermeneutics in Lutheran Orthodoxy." Translated by Robert Kolb. *Lutheran Quarterly* 20 (3): 318–336.

Herberger, Valerius. 2010. *The Great Works of God, or, Jesus, the Heart and Center of Scripture.* Translated by Matthew Carver. St. Louis, MO: Concordia.

Jacob, Edmond. 1986. "L'oeuvre exégétique d'un théologien strasbourgeois du 17 siècle: Sébastien Schmidt." *Revue d'histoire et de philosophie religieuses* 66 (1): 71–78.

Johansson, Torbjörn. 2010. "Das Leiden Christi vom Alten Testament her gedeutet: Beobachtungen zur frühen evangelisch-lutherischen Passionsauslegung." In *Hermeneutica sacra: Studies of the Interpretation of Holy Scripture in the Sixteenth and Seventeeth Centuries,* edited by Torbjörn Johansson, Robert Kolb, and Johann Anselm Steiger, 261–293. Berlin: De Gruyter.

Jung, Volker. 1999. *Das Ganze der Heiligen Schrift: Hermeneutik und Schriftauslegung bei Abraham Calov.* Stuttgart: Calwer Verlag.

Keller, Rudolf. 1984. *Der Schlüssel zur Schrift: die Lehre vom Wort Gottes bei Matthias Flacius Illyricus.* Hannover: Lutherisches Verlagshaus.

Kirste, Reinhard. 1976. *Das Zeugnis des Geistes und das Zeugnis der Schrift.* Göttingen: Vandenhoeck und Ruprecht.

Kleinig, Vernon P. 1996. "Confessional Lutheranism in Eighteenth-Century Germany." *Concordia Theological Quarterly* 60 (1–2): 97–125.

Koch, Ernst. 1990. "Die 'Himlische Philosophia des heiligen Geistes': Zur Bedeutung alttestamentlicher Spruchweisheit im Luthertum des 16. und 17. Jahrhunderts." *Theologische Literaturzeitung* 115:706–720.

Koch, Ernst. 2000. *Das konfessionelle Zeitalter: Katholizismus, Luthertum, Calvinismus (1563–1675).* Leipzig: Evangelische Verlagsanstalt.

Kolb, Robert. 1998. "Flacius Illyricus, Matthias (1520–1575)." In *Historical Handbook of Major Biblical Interpreters,* edited by Donald K. McKim, 190–195. Downers Grove, IL: InterVarsity Press.

Kolb, Robert. 2006. "Lutheran Theology in Seventeenth-Century Germany." *Lutheran Quarterly* 20 (4): 429–456.

Kraus, Hans-Joachim. 1982. *Geschichte der historisch-kritischen Erforschung des AltenTestaments.* 3rd ed. Neukirchen-Vluyn: Neukirchener Verlag.

Legaspi, Michael C. 2010. *The Death of Scripture and the Rise of Biblical Studies.* Oxford: Oxford University Press.

Ludwig, Ernst. 1952. *Schriftverständnis und Schriftauslegung bei Johann Albrecht Bengel*. Stuttgart: Chr. Scheufele.

Matthias, Markus. 1995. "Orthodoxie: I. Lutherische Orthodoxie." *Theologische Realenzyklopädie*. Berlin: de Gruyter.

Mayes, Benjamin T. G. 2011. *Counsel and Conscience: Lutheran Casuistry and Moral Reasoning after the Reformation*. Göttingen: Vandenhoeck & Ruprecht.

Mayes, Benjamin T. G. 2013. "Lumina, Non Numina: Patristic Authority According to Lutheran Arch-Theologian Johann Gerhard." In *Church and School in Early Modern Protestantism: Studies in Honor of Richard A. Muller on the Maturation of a Theological Tradition*, edited by Jordan Ballor, David Sytsma, and Jason Zuidema, 457–470. Leiden: Brill.

Mayes, Benjamin T. G. 2008. "The Mystical Sense of Scripture According to Johann Jacob Rambach." *Concordia Theological Quarterly* 72 (1): 45–70.

Mayes, Benjamin T. G. 2004. "Syncretism in the Theology of Georg Calixt, Abraham Calov, and Johannes Musäus." *Concordia Theological Quarterly* 68 (3–4): 291–317.

Michel, Karl-Heinz. 1985. *Anfänge der Bibelkritik: Quellentexte aus Orthodoxie und Aufklärung*. Monographien und Studienbücher. Wuppertal: R. Brockhaus.

Muller, Richard A. 1998. "Biblical Interpretation in the 16th & 17th Centuries." In *Historical Handbook of Major Biblical Interpreters*, edited by Donald K. McKim, 123–152. Downers Grove, IL: InterVarsity Press.

Pelikan, Jaroslav. 1952. "In Memoriam: Johann Albrecht Bengel." *Concordia Theological Monthly* 23 (11): 785–796.

Pelikan, Jaroslav. 1983. *Reformation of Church and Dogma (1300–1700)*. Chicago: University of Chicago Press.

Preus, Robert D. 1977. "The Influence of the Formula of Concord on the Later Lutheran Orthodoxy." In *Discord, Dialogue, and Concord: Studies in the Lutheran Reformation's Formula of Concord*, edited by Lewis William Spitz and Wenzel Lohff, 86–101. Philadelphia: Fortress Press.

Preus, Robert D. 2003. *The Inspiration of Scripture: A Study of the Theology of the Seventeenth-Century Lutheran Dogmaticians*. 2nd ed. St. Louis, MO: Concordia.

Preus, Robert D. 1970. *The Theology of Post-Reformation Lutheranism*. Vol. 1. St. Louis, MO: Concordia.

Quack, Jürgen. 1975. *Evangelische Bibelvorreden von der Reformation bis zur Aufklärung*. Gütersloh: Gütersloher Verlagshaus G. Mohn.

Reventlow, Henning. 2009. *History of Biblical Interpretation*. Translated by Leo G. Perdue. Atlanta: Society of Biblical Literature.

Schloemann, M. 1988. "Wegbereiter wider Willen. Siegmund Jacob Baumgarten und die historisch-kritische Bibelforschung." In *Historische Kritik und biblischer Kanon in der deutschen Aufklärung*, edited by Reventlow Wolfenbütteler Symposion, 149–155. Wiesbaden: Harrassowitz.

Scholder, Klaus. 1990. *The Birth of Modern Critical Theology: Origins and Problems of Biblical Criticism in the Seventeenth Century*. Translated by John Bowden. London: SCM Press, and Philadelphia: Trinity Press International.

Sheppard, Gerald T. 1998. "Biblical Interpretation in the 18th & 19th Centuries." In *Historical Handbook of Major Biblical Interpreters*, edited by Donald K. McKim, 257–280. Downers Grove, IL: InterVarsity Press.

Staemmler, Heinz. 2005. *Der Kampf der kursächsischen Theologen gegen Helmstedter Synkretismus: unter besonderer Berücksichtigung ihrer Schrift "Consensus Repetitus fidei vere Lutheranae" von 1655.* Waltrop: Hartmut Spenner.

Steiger, Johann Anselm. 2008. "The Development of the Reformation Legacy: Hermeneutics and Interpretation of the Sacred Scripture in the Age of Orthodoxy." In *Hebrew Bible/ Old Testament: The History of Its Interpretation,* edited by Magne Sæbø, 2:691–757. Göttingen: Vandenhoeck & Ruprecht.

Steiger, Johann Anselm. 2003. "Johann Gerhard: Ein Kirchenvater der lutherischen Orthodoxie." In *Theologen des 17. und 18. Jahrhunderts: konfessionelles Zeitalter—Pietismus— Aufklärung,* edited by Peter Walter and Martin Jung, 54–69. Darmstadt: Wissenschaftliche Buchgesellschaft.

Steiger, Johann Anselm. 1995. "Rhetorica sacra seu biblica: Johann Matthäus Meyfart (1590– 1642) und die Defizite der heutigen rhetorischen Homiletik." *Zeitschrift für Theologie und Kirche* 92 (4): 517–558.

Stroh, Hans. 1977. "Hermeneutik im Pietismus." *Zeitschrift für Theologie und Kirche* 74:38–57.

Thompson, Alan J. 2004. "The Pietist Critique of Inerrancy? J. A. Bengel's Gnomon as a Test Case." *Journal of the Evangelical Theological Society* 47 (1): 71–88.

Walch, Johann Georg. 1765. *Bibliotheca Theologica Selecta Litterariis Adnotationibus Instructa.* Vol. 4. Jena: sumtu viduae Croeckeriane.

Wallmann, Johannes. 1992. "Lutherische Konfessionalisierung—Ein Überblick." In *Die Lutherische Konfessionalisierung in Deutschland,* 33–53. Gütersloh: Gerd Mohn.

Wallmann, Johannes. 1995. "Die Rolle der Bekenntnisschriften im älteren Luthertum." In *Theologie und Frömmigkeit im Zeitalter des Barock: gesammelte Aufsätze,* 46–60. Tübingen: Mohr Siebeck.

Walther, C. F. W. 1902. "Neue Vorrede." In *Das Weimarische Bibelwerk,* Neue Ausgabe, dritte Auflage, iii–vii. St. Louis, MO: Fr. Dette.

# CHAPTER 20

# GOD, CREATION, AND PROVIDENCE IN EARLY MODERN LUTHERANISM

## ROBERT KOLB

To obtain an accurate picture of seventeenth-century Lutheran theology, students of the period dare not restrict their view to the classic dogmatic works that have largely determined the understanding of "Lutheran orthodoxy" and movements that grew out of it. They must also recognize that this system of thought took form in several genres, each with its own unique modes of expression. Even Johann Gerhard (1582–1637), the master teacher of Lutheran orthodoxy, made as great an impact with his devotional and homiletic works as with his great *Loci communes theologici*. Abraham Calov (1612–86) not only produced his twelve-volume *Systema locorum theologorum* (1655–77), but also his *Biblia illustrata* (1672–76), which guided pastors and laity in their reading of scripture. Reading more broadly in this era's rich literary productions gives a more precise impression of how Lutheran theology functioned. In their dogmatic tomes the Lutheran university professors usually turned within each locus to the topic's "practical application" [*usus practicus*]. "Lutheran theologians at the end of the sixteenth and beginning of the seventeenth centuries recognized the communication of their insights in sermons, devotional literature and treatises of consolation as a central, integral, genuine part of their theological work," and research into such works demonstrates how closely they reproduced the teachings of the university theologians (Bitzel 2002, 19–21 and passim; Wallmann 1992, 45). Access to the doctrines of God, creation, and providence in early modern Lutheranism comes through a range of literary forms.

All theology unfolds in conversation. The university theologians, who largely taught exegesis but are labeled dogmaticians because of their massive systematic works, conversed with students heading for pastoral ministry or teaching, but also with ecumenical conversation partners, sometimes polemically, sometimes more irenically, often appreciative of opponents' insights. Preachers and poets conversed with the pious, their parishioners. They conversed with the biblical writers—their dogmatic arguments are drenched in Bible passages—with the ancient church fathers, with classical authors, and medieval and contemporary thinkers across the spectrum of Western European thought. All confessed their faith in these conversations, faith in the Triune God.

Following Augustine, John of Damascus, and Peter Lombard, Philip Melanchthon began his *Loci communes* of 1535 on with the topic "God," since God is the goal or purpose of theology (Ratschow 1966, 2:15–17). Beginning in the 1550s, Lutherans highlighted the importance of Luther's concept of the *Deus revelatus* by placing before "God" the topic "Word of God," at first generally defined as the second person of the Trinity, the message of scripture, and the scripture itself (Kolb 1997). Without the proper epistemological approach to the person of God, he is not understood properly. Succeeding generations also treated God's Word at the beginning of their dogmatic texts, in "prolegomena," which demonstrated that the foundations of what they taught lay solidly upon God's inspired scripture. Then they turned to "God" and his primal activity, creating and upholding his creation. Although Luther's distinction between *Deus absconditus* and *Deus revelatus* had faded in the dogmatic discussions of the period, remnants of it remained. Gerhard himself found Christ "the focal point" of scripture (Gerhard 1609, 25.)

# 1 GOD

Luther's presentation of God presumed the ancient creedal confession of God as Trinity—Father, Son, and Holy Spirit. His brief summary of his confession of the faith in 1528 used a Trinitarian structure to organize the chief points of his teaching (WA 26:499, 1–569, 29; LW 26:360–72); his catechisms discarded the twelvefold division of the Apostles Creed, replacing it with a Trinitarian structure (BSLK 510–12; 646–62, BC 354–56, 431–40; cf. his Smalcald Articles, BSLK 414–15, BC 300, and his 1538 commentary on the Apostles and Athanasian Creeds and the *Te Deum Laudamus*, which employed the traditional language of the begottenness of the Son and the procession of the Holy Spirit, WA 50:262, 1–283, 14; LW 34:201–29). Luther's proclamation of God in lecture and sermon conveyed the divine Person always in conversation and community with his human creatures; a God of strong emotions, both wrath and love, a God who is *absconditus* and must remain beyond human grasping—unpreached—but simultaneously a God who is *revelatus*, graciously coming into conversation through the oral, written, and sacramental forms of his Word—God preached (Paulson 2014). Luther proclaimed no doctrine of God apart from his relationship with humanity, and no explanation of what it means to be human that did not find its center in the person's fearing, loving, and trusting in God above all things. Seventeenth-century Lutheran theologians did not lose the core elements of Luther's proclamation of God: his warning against exploring the inscrutable Hidden God; his affirmation that God acts through his creative, re-creative

Word in its various forms; his personal confrontation and conversation with the God who is there "for you," both as provider and savior.

## 1.1  God's inscrutability

Luther's successors argued that by definition God lies beyond examination by human logic or metaphysical principles. What he is, defining him *quidditative*, lies outside the ken of human beings, not only as sinners but also as creatures, who can only observe his attributes and his works (Sparn 1976, 139–53). In Luther's train, these Lutheran "ortho-dox" dogmaticians remained quite modest in attempts to plumb the depths of God's being. They acknowledged the problem of using human language to speak of God in his essence, and so they argued that description of that essence or what it means that he is Spirit can be predicated of God only analogically, not univocally or equivocally (Preus 1972, 39). Johann Konrad Dannhauer (1603–66) viewed the attempt to define God as an assault on his transcendence, an examination of the mystery of his being doomed to failure (Dannhauer 1695, 92). Gerhard had noted the difficulty of teaching the gospel itself because of the sublimity of the mystery of God and the weakness of the human mind (Gerhard 1863, 1:241–42). Similarly, Calov distinguished between God's hidden and revealed will, observing that the hidden God defies human scrutiny, while God's Word reveals him infallibly (Calov 1655, 442).

## 1.2  God revealed in his works, attributes, and names

Gerhard explained that the teaching "about God" was necessary to clarify for what pur-pose human beings exist, to demonstrate why God has revealed himself, and to address the misery of not knowing God because of the blindness of the human mind. Thus, this locus "about" is useful for bringing human beings to that knowledge of God that bestows life and salvation (Gerhard 1863, 1:242). Johann Andreas Quenstedt (1617–88) began his presentation on God by positing that the purpose of both the human creature and all theology (including, presumably, the topic "God") is to know, praise, and enjoy God (Quenstedt 1696, 250).

Some seventeenth-century theologians portrayed God by rehearsing his works (Ratschow 1966, 2:155–62), but most treated his actions under other topics such as sote-riology or ecclesiology. Gerhard was the first to lead Lutheran teachers away from the Trinitarian focus of ancient creeds and the Augsburg Confession as their framework for this locus, the method that had been developed by Melanchthon and his immediate successors. Gerhard participated in the ecumenical discussion of God by way of elabo-rations on his names, which brought his personhood to the fore (Gerhard 1863, 1:243–66; cf. Calov 1690, 53–56, where he distinguished positive and negative, substantive and adjectival, proper and metaphorical, and grammatical-rhetorical names of God) and discussions of the standard Melanchthonian questions: *whether* God exists and who he is. After affirming that there is only one God (Gerhard 1863, 1:266–95), Gerhard discussed God's attributes in detail (Gerhard 1863, 1:295–370). The distinct attributes were attributed to the one divine essence, thus preserving the unity of the Godhead and his immutability (Preus 1972, 53–55).

Although the list of divine attributes noted by seventeenth-century Lutheran dogmaticians may have owed much to Greek philosophical imagination of what the divine must be, these theologians always demonstrated these attributes with copious scriptural references, often offering readers a careful exegetical explanation of Hebrew and Greek terms. Gerhard's definition is typical: God is "the best of goodness, the greatest in power, the one, ultimate, principle of existence." God is the "highest being" (*summum ens*), "pure action" (*actus purus*) "a spiritual being ... absolutely without composition, infinite, of immeasurable goodness, wisdom, and power ... righteous and faithful," Father, Son, and Holy Spirit, so described that Preus can comment, "Gerhard is describing the acting, speaking, saving God who has made Himself known in His acts of redemption and who is even now acting and speaking in the church" (Gerhard 1863, 1:285; Preus 1972, 48). Gerhard insisted that "God is not to be sought under the category of substance but under the category of relationship" (*Deum quaerendum esse non in praedicamento substantiae sed relationis*) (Gerhard 1863, 28; cf. Sparn 1976, 180–81). His omnipotence and his love, as exhibited in creation, redemption, and sanctification, continued to claim high place in their lists of divine characteristics.

No standard list of divine attributes emerged among the seventeenth-century dogmaticians. Gerhard's original list contained nineteen; Calov listed a modest ten in one work, twenty-two in another; Quenstedt thirty-one, and after him Johann Wilhelm Baier (1647–95), fifteen; and David Hollaz (1648–1713), twenty-four (Preus 1972, 59–60; cf. Ratschow 1966, 2:76–81). The lists differed little in fact, since combinations of attributes often reduced the number.

Gerhard's Genesis commentary points readers of Genesis 1 to God's goodness, wisdom, and power. Recognition of his goodness cultivates love for God and his wisdom, trust in God, and fear of God, echoing Luther's explanation of the first commandment (Gerhard 1637, 13). Similarly, Calov treated God's goodness and his holiness together; God's holiness expresses his essence, which is found centered in his goodness, grace, and mercy. The "use" of this doctrine is that believers love and celebrate God as the highest good and holiness, strive after holiness, avoid and flee evil, and find sustenance in every adversity in God's goodness. This meant, clearly, that God could not be the cause of sin and evil (Calov 1655, 331–44).

The seventeenth-century Lutheran professors mixed nouns and adjectives in presenting God as unity; Spirit; "simplex" in the sense of the purity, indivisibility, and independence of his being; majestic in his transcendence, glory, holiness and sovereignty; immutable (whereby they employed the Greek philosophical term but often interpreted it as the biblical concept of faithfulness, which also found expression under their describing God as true or truthful). He is infinite, eternal, immeasurable or without limit of any kind, incomprehensible. God's omnipotence, omnipresence, omniscience, and omnisapience, along with his goodness and all the attributes, such as mercy and grace, which belong to it, gained special treatment by these Lutheran dogmaticians, an indication that they took very seriously the personal relationship between God and his human creatures. Discussions of God's omnipotence also took place under other topics, including "creation" and "providence," rather than under "God." The medieval distinction between *potentia absoluta* and *potentia ordinata* proved useful for some dogmaticians to distinguish God's working apart from the order he built into creation, in miracles, and his regular preservation and governance of his creation. This distinction was understood, of course, without any hint of a terrible arbitrariness in God (Preus 1972, 105–7). With the advance of metaphysics into Lutheran discussions, theologians such as Balthasar Meisner (1587–1626) reflected something of Luther's Ockhamistic orientation in insisting that "everything that does not imply contradiction is possible for God" (Sparn 1976, 38–39). Luther's recapture of ancient Christianity's understanding of God's righteousness as his goodness and mercy reverted in his seventeenth-century successors to a medieval understanding of his righteousness as his rewarding the good and punishing evil (Calov 1655, 565–69).

With accents inherent in the continuing controversy with Reformed theologians over Christ's presence in the Lord's Supper, God's omnipresence attracted detailed attention. Following Nikolaus Selnecker (1530–92), seventeenth-century Lutheran dogmaticians treated four modes of divine presence: a universal presence in his preservation and guidance of all creatures; a gracious presence through his Word in his church; a glorious, eschatological presence in heaven; and the presence of Christ as God and man. This last mode of presence in later seventeenth-century authors moved to the locus on Christology (Preus 1972, 86–90). His omnipresence consisted not in substantial propinquity, argued Calov, but in the efficacious execution of his benevolent will for his creatures. This presence is a mystery which moves believers to adore him, walk in his grace, expect and desire his glory, and find comfort in the midst of evil in his presence (Calov 1655, 612–22). Later writers emphasized under Selnecker's second mode (Christ's gracious presence with believers) the mystical union, which brought God and believer together in the most intimate of relationships, preserving the distinct character of Creator and creature in each but binding them closely together. Developed from the works of Johann Arndt (1555–1621), who in turn built on the thinking of Wittenberg professor Friedrich Balduin (1575–1627), this concept provided the comfort of God's delivering and supporting presence with the believer (Mahlmann 1996; Preus 1972, 90–94).

The dogmaticians treated God's will in discussions of his attributes and there struggled with the mystery of the continuation of sin and evil in the lives of the baptized. Wary of actually proposing ultimate solutions of the theodical problem but insistent on asserting that God is in no way the cause of evil, they distinguished God's absolute will and his conditional will. They did not propose explanations of why or how Satan and Adam and Eve could introduce sin into God's good creation, but they asserted the distinction between God's active, effecting will (*voluntas efficiens*) and his permissive will (*voluntas permittens*), affirming God's absolute freedom and his unconditional love for his chosen people (Preus 1972, 96–100).

## 1.3 God is Trinity

In contrast to their approach to teaching about God's attributes, seventeenth-century Lutheran thinkers maintained the earlier Wittenberg focus on the Trinitarian foundation of the faith, both in the locus "on God" and in discussing Christology and the person of the Holy Spirit. Issues related to the person of Christ and the relationship of his two natures contributed also to Lutheran Trinitarian formulations (Sparn 1976, 101–63; Haga 2012, 218–69). During the course of the seventeenth-century, the rise of Socinianism and other systems of thought hostile to the doctrine of the Trinity compelled Lutherans to sharpen their critique of anti-Trinitarian thinking. They often labeled it "atheistic," a category into which they fitted ancients and contemporaries who taught the eternity of the world and denied the immortality of the soul and resurrection of the body. Gerhard initiated Lutheran discussion of such atheists, following Roman Catholic and Reformed leads (Barth 1971, 2–23).

Trust in Father, Son, and Holy Spirit delivers sinners from God's wrath, and only trust in the Trinity can save, according to these dogmaticians. At the heart of their doctrine of the Trinity was their belief that the second person took on a truly and completely human nature. Gerhard placed his Christological locus immediately after his locus on the Trinity, before "On Creation" (Gerhard 1863, 1:447–60), following the example of Leonhart Hütter (1563–1616) (Brunners 2006, 64–107). Seventeenth-century Lutherans insisted that this biblical teaching lies completely beyond the capabilities of human reason. Without any imaginative adaptations they affirmed that God is of one essence and exists in three persons with "the most intimate, intrinsic communication or interpenetration (περιχώρησις) between the Persons" (Preus 1972, 123, cf. 113–31; Ratschow 1966, 2:82–154). This perichoresis also found expression in the Christological application of the communication of attributes to the sharing of the divine nature's characteristic of being able to be present in more than one place in whatever form God wishes it to be present. This became part of their argument for insisting on the true presence of Christ's body and blood in the Lord's Supper.

The question whether the doctrine of the Trinity was taught in the Old Testament became a matter of controversy when Georg Calixt (1586–1656) of Helmstedt and his adherents challenged that standard element (Gerhard 1863, 1:418–44) of contemporaries' teaching (e.g., Calov 1690, 93–102; cf. Staemmler 2005, 64–70).

## 1.4 The natural knowledge of God

Each seventeenth-century Lutheran dogmatician felt compelled to discuss the natural knowledge of God, though curiously, largely on the basis of scripture passages (Preus 1972, 21). They thought biblically but recognized that some in their world did not, and needed to hear rational arguments. Gerhard introduced a posteriori proofs for God's existence into Lutheran dogmatics. They included the orderly succession of moving objects leading the First Mover; the chain of efficient *causae* that lead to the First

Cause; the sufficient reason of God's necessity per se; the existence of reason, wisdom, and teleology; and the natural human inclination toward prayer (Gerhard 1863, 1:267–69; Ratschow 1966, 2:18–44; Preus 1972, 35–36). The revelation found in "the book of nature" also played a significant role in devotional literature; for example, Arndt's *True Christianity*, the fourth book of which presents the witness of creation and the human heart, albeit anchored in the biblical confession regarding creation (Col 1:15–19; Ps 19, 104, 139; Rom 8:20–21; 1 Cor 15:40–45) (Arndt 2007, 4:3–7, 208–15).

As challenges arose from John Locke and other empiricists to the concept of natural knowledge of God, Calov could argue that "there is no notion in many by nature concerning God before the exercise of reason, no particular thought about God which man has actually known since birth, but there is a definite capacity, or disposition, for such thought." He concluded that this natural knowledge was partly inborn, partly acquired. But he, like all other dogmaticians in his milieu, conceded no more than a general knowledge of God and providence apart from God's revealing himself in Christ and scripture (Calov 1655, 25–40; Calov 1690, 46–51; Preus 1972, 24, 27). Valentin Ernst Löscher (1673–1749) continued this critical engagement with the likes of Hobbes, Spinoza, Bayle, and Locke into the eighteenth century (Greschat 1971, 220–62). Preus regrets that many "Orthodox" presentations "on God" "do not come through with the clarity and impact" typical of their work in other loci, that "On God" is "the least Biblical and most scholastic *locus* in Lutheran dogmatics," that the attributes do not arise out of God's works, but out of philosophical formulations regarding his essence, and that the comfort which the dogmaticians tried to highlight under each topic does not come through here as strongly as it might (Preus 1972, 109–11), although Gerhard and others also found "practical use" (*usus practicus*) for the doctrine of God.

# 2 CREATION

Preus labels the dogmaticians' treatments of the doctrine of creation "one of the most impressive contributions of post-Reformation Lutheran theology" because the dogmaticians "attempt to relate it to all Christian theology and apply it to life," particularly emphasizing *creatio ex nihilo* and *creatio per verbum. Creatio ex nihilo* laid the foundation for Gerhard's exegesis of Genesis 1 as well (Gerhard 1637; cf. Gerhard 1863, 2:3–4). The ultimate purpose (*finis*) of creation, according to Matthias Hafenreffer (1561–1619), Calov and others, is the glory of God; its secondary purpose the benefit of humanity (Haffenreffer 2010, 56; Calov 1690, 180; cf. Ratschow 1966, 2:163–84). Preus perhaps overestimates how slight the attention paid to the *creatio prima* really was in their works, although it is true that their focus falls on *creatio continua*, initially within the topic of "creation" and then developing into a distinct locus from the early seventeenth century on (Preus 1972, 167). In fact, Gerhard, Calov, and others develop something of a biblical cosmology in rehearsing the development of creation on each of the six days of the creation week (Preus 1972, 180–90). Arndt also developed such a cosmology within the framework of the Hexaemeron in his fourth book "on True Christianity" (Arndt 2007, 4:1–207).

Their doctrine of creation reaffirmed seventeenth-century Lutheran theologians' placing God at the beginning, center, and end of human life. Almighty God created by his power and thus is responsible for all things which exist. Copenhagen professor Cort Aslakssøn (1584–1624) rejected Aristotle's view that the world is eternal; the doctrine that the world came into being by accident; that it was formed by another divine force or being, not the Trinity; and that two creative forces, good and evil, exist. In his wisdom God gave his creatures "individuality, suitability, harmony, and specificity. He adorned them with functions, beauty, and charm, revealing his goodness" (Preus 1972, 169). Aslakssøn and his colleagues accentuated God's using his Word to create, as had Luther; they sometimes defined that Word according to John 1:3 as the second person of the Trinity, who became enfleshed as Jesus Christ (λόγος), and sometimes as a speaking akin to human words (ῥῆμα) (Preus 1972, 170–72). God is sovereign creator and created all that exists out of nothing, echoing Luther's assertion that all things are nothing more than the nouns that God speaks (WA 42:17, 15–32, LW 1:21–22). He who brought order and form to what he had fashioned from nothing remains totally engaged with his creatures, sustaining them. These theologians sharply opposed ancient Stoics and contemporary Deists who posited that God lets his creation run on its own.

God exercised total freedom in creating: he bestows existence and life on his creatures out of pure, unconditioned grace, demonstrates his goodness and his unqualified, unrestricted love for his creatures, especially human creatures (Hütter 2006, 112–15). His creation gives reason for them to live lives of praise and obedience to him, for even under sin they experience God's goodness in his material blessings and created gifts, as is clear in commentaries of the period, particularly on Genesis and Psalms. His original creative act foreshadows and presents the pattern of his re-creative work through his word of forgiveness, life, and salvation in Christ (Preus 1972, 175–80; cf. Hütter 2006, 108–9; Gerhard 1637, 8). In his devotional *Sacred Meditations*, Gerhard concentrated on the believer's life of repentance and trust but drew the parallel between creation and re-creation in baptism: "just as at creation, so also in our regeneration the Spirit broods upon the waters and bestows on them his life-giving power; the Holy Spirit is present in the water of baptism and makes it a saving instrument of our regeneration" (Gerhard 2000, 1:100).

Paul Gerhardt (1607–76) and others expressed this understanding of creation in the hymns that implanted faith in and appreciation of the Creator deep in the hearts of the faithful. Accentuating the order and beauty of the creation in hymns such as "Geh' aus, mein Herz, und suche Freud," Gerhardt saw creation as God's "personal expression of love" for human beings: "God is for Gerhardt not an abstract Supremacy—through the important stable factors of the cosmos, sun, moon, stars, as well as the necessary things of daily life, water and grain, wine and bread, wind and weather, forest, and meadow, the world often appears in Gerhardt's hymns as manageable, fitting into central German, middle class life" (Brunners 2006, 129, 165). Gerhardt's "Nun ruhen alle Wälder" and "Auf der Nebel folgt die Sonn'" (Lund 2011, 335–36, 329–31) cultivated a sense of God's friendly presence in the created order, which early modern Germans often experienced as a capricious, harsh, and cruel adversary.

# 3 PROVIDENCE

Bengt Hägglund calls trust in God's providence "particularly characteristic of early Lutheran piety" (Hägglund 2003, 93), and, indeed, dogmatic theology. Gerhard added it to the Melanchthonian list of topics. He captured Luther's understanding that any God worthy of the name must be involved with his creation in an ongoing fashion. Gerhard echoed Luther's grouping God's daily care and governance of his world conceptually together with his gracious election of his chosen under the term *praedestinatio* (Kolb 2005, 38–40) by placing his locus "on election and reprobation" immediately after "providence," a unique positioning in Lutheran theology (Gerhard 1863, 2:48–106). He distinguished three aspects of God's governance of his creation: his foreknowledge, his setting of the course of human history through his decrees that planned both salvation in Christ and the preservation of all creation, and his active sustaining and governing of that creation, a threefold definition employed by others as well (Gerhard 1863, 2:18–27; Hütter 2006, 140–43; Calov 1690, 198; Ratschow 1966, 2:208–47, Preus 1972, 197–99). God's providence grows out of his attributes of goodness, wisdom, power, righteousness, and immeasurability (Calov 1690, 193–94). The goal of this locus is to cultivate the knowledge and praise of God and to benefit human beings, especially the pious (König 2006, 102–3).

As Preus notes (Preus 1972, 204–8), Gerhard and his successors on Lutheran theological faculties connected God's providential care for all his creatures closely with his presence; for God, whose nature it is to love what he created, is personally and emotionally engaged with his creatures. Quenstedt equates God's omnipresence with his activities in providing for and governing the universe, occasionally directly but generally through secondary causes, which he continues to steer and employ according to his gracious will (Quenstedt 1691, 1:531–32). Quenstedt and others ascribe the upholding of the order of creation to all three persons of the Trinity, with special focus on Christ's kingdom of power, effecting his will through his creative Word, just as in his kingdom of grace he works through his absolving, redemptive Word (Is 9:5; Mi 5:1; Rev 16:14; Acts 10:36; Ps 8; 1 Cor 15:27–28) (Quenstedt 1691, 3:262–63, 265–67).

In their loci on providence, the Lutherans took care to distance themselves from every form of determinism; their polemic against what they perceived as a Reformed tendency to diminish human responsibility emerged, for instance in Haffenreffer's *Loci*, who between 1601 and 1603 greatly expanded his treatment of this topic to counter Reformed views, insisting that God controls all things while adamantly affirming that he has so created human beings with total responsibility to obey his law (Hafenreffer 2010, 58–70; cf. Ohlemacher 2010, 363–64). Gerhard used the distinction between God's πρόγνωσις and his προορισμός or προθέσις to maintain God's omniscience on the one hand, while protecting him from charges of causing evil (Gerhard 1863, 2:19–26). Gerhard developed an extensive analysis of such arguments. That God is not the cause of evil is axiomatic; his wrath against sin poured on Christ on the cross demonstrates that. Gerhard employs the concept of God's permissive will, which only shifts the problem but does not solve it. God abandons evildoers and delivers them over to Satan; he restricts their evil actions and sees that all works for good, despite their rebellious designs. Gerhard dealt with eighteen problematic Bible passages at length, where God seems to promote evil and ignore his own law (e.g., Gen. 22:1–10; Gen. 37:12–36; Ex. 4:21) and demonstrated in each case how these instances fit into God's plan and governance (Gerhard 1863, 2:34–42). He continued by meeting objections to the existence of providence with a confession of God's presence and goodness that did not logically provide a theodicy, but affirmed the power and love of the Creator.

Seventeenth-century Lutherans expressed their confidence in God's providence in their preaching, devotional literature, and hymns, although that confidence was often expressed despite the crosses allowed by God or inflicted by Satan upon believers. The diary of a farmer near Ulm, Hans Heberle, recorded the course of daily life during the Thirty Years' War, reflecting his trust in God's providence. In his impotence before natural and military forces beyond his control, Heberle took refuge in prayer, believing firmly that God is the governor and lord of history (Haag 1992, 61–75, 347–58). He undoubtedly received encouragement from local preaching in this faith. For example, Bonifatius Stöltzin (1603–77), pastor in Kuchen near Ulm, published sermons on the pericopes (1667), emphasizing God's control over history, in which human beings experience his wrath and his mercy. Blame for evils in daily life lay squarely on Satan and sinners, for God is faithful in taking care of his people, and present with them in the midst of evils he permits to take place (Haag 1992, 17–19). In his Latvian postil (1654), Georg Mancelius (1593–1654) strongly emphasized both God's providential assistance and personal responsibility in the conflict with Satan to maintain God's will and order in both faith and life (Krēsliņš 1992, 171–76, 188–96). God's providence could be questioned, naturally, in the face of evils—such as natural catastrophes like storms, fires, or floods—and seventeenth-century Lutheran pastors confronted these catastrophes with words of warning, interpreting them as God's judgment and call to repentance, and with consoling words that reminded their people of God's unwavering concern for their welfare (Kurihara 2014; Holtz 1993, 51–70).

Devotional literature also emphasized God's providential care, imparting comfort and support for believers in both their battles with Satan, spiritual afflictions and doubts, and their physical suffering from illness, war, and other causes (see, e.g., Arndt 2007, 2:516–718). A beleaguered Lutheran pastor in Prague during the Thirty Years' War, Sigismund Scherertz (1584–1639), reflected the strong emphasis on God's providential presence in believers' lives in the midst of persecution and war as, well as other afflictions, including the death of children (Bitzel 2002).

Lutheran hymnody also cultivated this confident faith. Elke Axmacher has shown that the contention that seventeenth-century Lutheran hymnody ignored the works of contemporary theological professors is false. The parallels between their wording and Paul Gerhardt's, for instance in "Befiehl du deine Wege" (Lund 2011, 322–25), demonstrate how closely the hymnist harvested the works of Hütter, Gerhard, Balthasar Mentzer (1565–1627), and others, as he commended God's providential faithfulness and individual care to those who used his hymns in combat with Satan and in facing every kind of need in daily life (Axmacher 2001, 107–42). Particularly for those confronting trials or death, hymns by Gerhardt ("Jesu, allerliebster Bruder") (Lund 2011, 326–29), Georg Neumark (1621–81) ("Wer nun der lieben Gott last walten") (Lund 2011, 337–38), Johann Franck (1618–77) ("Du o schönes Weltgebäude") (Lund 2011, 340–42), and others, sang the good news of God's providence to troubled hearts.

The assertion that God governs and directs all that happens in his creation inevitably raises the question of contingency. Both Wittenberg reformers taught that God the almighty Creator is responsible for all things and that he has created his human creatures with full responsibility for their actions. Part of Melanchthon's solution, his view of contingency, led him to oppose Luther's use of the terminology of "absolute necessity," terminology the senior colleague abandoned after writing *De servo arbitrio* (Kolb 2005, 32–60, 70–95). Hütter was typical in following Melanchthon, distinguishing three kinds of necessity: that of things divinely predicted, that of things arising from immutable causes, and that of things that are true but also contingent. Preus notes the lack of clarity in this third category and explains it by identifying it as an instance of the Lutheran attempt to hold God's providential lordship in tension with human responsibility (Preus 1972, 212; Hütter 1619, 228). In general, seventeenth-century Lutherans vacillated between ignoring the challenges to faith in God's providence posed by experiences of evils, and dealing in detail with contentions that God causes evil or that his providential care is not total and complete.

# 4 CONCLUSION

The views of God, creation, and providence represented in the "orthodox" theologians, devotional writers, and preachers of the seventeenth century elicited challenges of various kinds from various sides by century's end. The disciples of the last strong "orthodox" voice, Löscher, continued his emphasis on faith, but the faith took on an ever more "reasonable" character (Greschat 1971, 319). Efforts to defend the Lutheran confession against others, particularly Reformed views of providence and election deemed deterministic by Lutherans, led to emphases on human responsibility that inevitably weakened Luther's understanding of the biblical teaching on God and his providing care (Dingel 1998).

It is much easier to observe that the later "orthodox" theologians insufficiently engaged the new "enlightened" approach to explanations of reality to maintain a strong position for their ideas than it is to identify precisely why this turned out to be the case. (see Sparn 1976, 203–14). Such interpretations that have been advanced largely reflect the ideals of modern observers more precisely than the perceptions and objectives of early eighteenth-century Lutheran thinking. Certainly, a part of the answer lies in the continuing struggle to define the relationship of culturally dominant and culturally determined metaphysical formulations regarding reality to the biblical witness. Much of this "orthodox" view, conveyed in the piety of the people, in part in the movements labeled "pietistic," survived in hymns, devotional and some liturgical practices that gave birth to a revival of confessional theology in the nineteenth century.

## BIBLIOGRAPHY

Arndt, Johann. 2007. *Vier Bücher Von wahren Christentumb/Die erste Gesamtausgabe (1610)*. Edited by Johann Anselm Steiger. Hildesheim: Olms.

Axmacher, Elke. 2001. *Johann Arndt und Paul Gerhardt: Studien zur Theologie, Frömmigkeit und geistlichen Dichtung des 17. Jahrhunderts*. Tübingen: Francke.

Barth, Hans-Martin. 1971. *Atheismus und Orthodoxie: Analysen und Modelle christlicher Apologetik im 17. Jahrhundert*. Göttingen: Vandenhoeck & Ruprecht.

*Die Bekenntnisschriften der evangelisch-lutherischen Kirche (BSLK)*. 1992. 11th ed. Göttingen: Vandenhoeck & Ruprecht.

Bitzel, Alexander. 2002. *Anfechtung und Trost bei Sigismund Scherertz*. Göttingen: Vandenhoeck & Ruprecht.

*The Book of Concord (BC)*. 2000. Edited by Robert Kolb and Timothy J. Wengert. Minneapolis, MN: Fortress.

Brunners, Christian. 2006. *Paul Gerhardt: Weg—Werk—Wirkung*. Göttingen: Vandenhoeck & Ruprecht.

Calov, Abraham. 1655. *Systema Locorum theologicorvm e sacra potissimvm Scriptvra et antiqvitate*. Wittenberg: Hartmann.

Calov, Abraham. 1690. *Theologia postiva. Per definitiones, causas, affectiones et distinctiones, locos theologicos . . . propens*. Frankfurt/M and Wittenberg: Quenstedt.

Dannhauer, Johann Konrad. 1695. *Hodosophia Christiana, seu Theologia positiva*. Leipzig.

Dingel, Irene. 1998. "Recht und Konfession bei Samuel von Pufendorf." In *Recht—Macht—Gerechtigkeit*, edited by Joachim Mehlhausen, 516–540. Gütersloh: Gütersloher Verlagshaus.

Gerhard, Johann. 1637. *Commentarius Super Genesin*. Jena.

Gerhard, Johann. 1863. *Loci theologici*. Edited by Eduard Preuss. Berlin: Schlawitz.

Gerhard, Johann. 2000. *Meditationes Sacrae (1606/7): Lateinisch-deutsch*. Edited by Johann Anselm Steiger. Stuttgart-Bad Canstatt: Fromman-Holzboog.

Gerhard, Johann. 1609. *De vita Jesu Christi, Homiliis viginiquinque, illustrata*. Darmstadt.

Greschat, Martin. 1971. *Zwischen Tradition und Neuem Anfang: Valentin Ernst Löscher und der Ausgang der Lutherischen Orthodoxie*. Witten: Luther-Verlag.

Haag, Norbert. 1992. *Predigt und Gesellschaft: Die Lutherische Orthodoxie in Ulm 1640–1740*. Mainz: Zabern.

Hafenreffer, Matthias. 2010. *Compendium doctrinae coelestis*. Edited by Bengt Hägglund and Cajsa Sjöberg. Skara: Skara Stifsthistoriska Sällskap.

Haga, Joar. 2012. *Was There a Lutheran Metaphysics? The Interpretation of the Communicatio Idiomatum in Early Modern Lutheranism*. Göttingen: Vandenhoeck & Ruprecht.

Hägglund, Bengt. 2003. "De providentia. Zur Gotteslehre im frühen Luthertum." In Bengt Hägglund, *Chemnitz—Gerhard—Arndt—Rudbeckius*, edited by Alexander Bitzel and Johann Anselm Steiger. Waltrop: Spenner.

Holtz, Sabine. 1993. *Theologie und Alltag: Lehre und Leben in den Predigten der Tübinger Theologen, 1550–1750.* Tübingen: Mohr/Siebeck.

Hütter, Leonhart. 2006. *Compendium locorum theologicorum ex Scripturis sacris et libro concordiae, Lateinisch—deutsch—englisch.* Edited by Johann Anselm Steiger. 3 vols. Stuttgart-Bad Cannstatt: Fromman-Holzboog.

Hütter, Leonhart. 1619. *Loci communes theologici.* Wittenberg.

Kolb, Robert. 2005. *Bound Choice, Election, and Wittenberg Theological Method From Martin Luther to the Formula of Concord.* Grand Rapids: Eerdmans.

Kolb, Robert. 1997. "The Ordering of the *Loci Communes Theologici*: The Structuring of the Melanchthonian Dogmatic Tradition." *Concordia Journal* 23: 317–337.

König, Johann Friedrich. 2006. *Theologia positiva acroamatica (Rostock 1664).* Edited and translated by Andreas Stegmann. Tübingen: Mohr/Siebeck.

Krēsliņš, Jānis. 1992. *Dominus narrabit in scriptura populorum. A Study of Early Seventeenth-Century Lutheran Teaching and Preaching and the Lettische lang-gewünschte Postilla of Georg Mancelius.* Wiesbaden: Harrasowitz.

Kurihara, Ken. 2014. "Whether We Live or Die, We Are the Lord's: Lutheran *Wetter* Discourses and Spiritual Interpretation of Natural Disasters." In *The Science of the Supernatural in Early Modern Europe*, edited by Kathryn A. Edwards. Basingstoke: Palmgrave Macmillan.

Lund, Erik, ed. 2011. *Seventeenth-Century Lutheran Meditations and Hymns.* New York: Paulist.

*Luther's Works (LW)*, 1958–86. St. Louis, MO/Philadelphia, PA: Concordia/Fortress.

*Martin Luthers Werke (WA)*, 1883–1993. Weimar: Böhlau.

Mahlmann, Theodor. 1996. "Die Stellung der *unio cum Christo* in der lutherischen Theologie des 17. Jahrhunderts." In *Unio: God und Mensch in der nachreformatorischen Theologie*, edited by Matti Repo and Rainer Vinke, 72–199. Helsinki: Luther-Agricola-Gesellschaft.

Ohlemacher, Andreas, 2010. *Lateinische Katechetik der frühen lutherischen Orthodoxie.* Göttingen: Vandenhoeck & Ruprecht.

Paulson, Steven. 2014. "Luther's Doctrine of God." In *The Oxford Handbook to Martin Luther's Theology*, edited by Robert Kolb, Irene Dingel, and Lubomir Batka, 187–200. Oxford: Oxford University Press.

Preus, Robert D. 1972. *The Theology of Post-Reformation Lutheranism, Volume II: God and His Creation.* St. Louis, MO: Concordia.

Quenstedt, Johann Andreas. 1691. *Theologia didactico-polemica: Sive systema theologicum.* Wittenberg: Quenstedt.

Ratschow, Carl Heinz. 1966. *Lutherische Dogmatik zwischen Reformation und Aufklärung, Teil II.* Gütersloh: Mohn.

Sparn, Walter. 1976. *Wiederkehr der Metaphysik. Die ontologische Frage in der lutherischen Theologie des frühen 17. Jahrhunderts.* Stuttgart: Calwer Verlag.

Staemmler, Heinz. 2005. *Die Auseinandersetzung der kursächsischen Theologen mit dem Helmstedter Synkretismus: Eine Studie zum "Consensus Repetitus fidei vere Lutheranae" (1655) und den Diskussionen um ihn.* Waltrop: Hartmut Spenner.

Wallmann, Johannes. 1992. "Lutherische Konfessionalisierung—ein Überblick." In: *Die lutherische Konfessionalisierung in Deutschland, Wissenschaftliches Symposion des Vereins für Reformationsgeschichte*, edited by Hans-Christoph Rublack, 33–53. Gütersloh: Mohn.

# CHAPTER 21

# FORENSIC JUSTIFICATION AND MYSTICISM IN EARLY MODERN LUTHERANISM

## RISTO SAARINEN

THE doctrine of justification defined the identity of Lutheran theology, distinguishing it from Roman Catholicism. The view of justification by faith alone (*sola fide*) was generally considered as Martin Luther's main contribution to the Reformation. Because of its symbolic and identity-creating significance, the so-called "doctrine of justification" has often been understood to embrace God's entire salvific and reconciling action toward the human race (McGrath 1986; Wright 2009, 65). In this article, "justification" is understood in a narrower sense, meaning the concept employed by the apostle Paul in the New Testament and its predominantly Latin equivalents in early modern Lutheran theology. The concept of mysticism refers primarily to the phrases *unio mystica, unio spiritualis* and *unio cum Christo* employed in the context of justification. Broader issues of spirituality are only mentioned in passing. Special attention is paid to the issue of subjectivity.

In Western theology, the Latin concept *iustificatio* connotes the idea of *iustum facere*, making a person righteous. I call this connotation "effective justification." The Greek term *dikaiosis* does not express this connotation; moreover, the Greek phrases employed by Paul—for example, *dikaiosyne theou, dikaioo, dikaios*—allude to the setting of the law court. As Paul in some central passages, in particular Romans 3:21–4:25, refers to the Jewish Bible, it is plausible to interpret the relevant phrases as depicting God's action as a judge in a cosmic law court, making pronouncements about humans. I call this idea "forensic justification."

# 1 Catholics and Lutherans
# in the Reformation

Thomas Aquinas expresses the Catholic teaching when he says that the justification of the sinner is the forgiveness of sins (*Summa theologiae*, II/1:q113 a1; cf. Romans 4:5–8). This justification entails a personal renewal. The Council of Trent condemns Lutherans for neglecting this personal renewal or effective justification. The council holds, for instance, that justification "consists not only in the forgiveness of sins but also in the sanctification and renewal of the inward being" (*Decrees* 1990, 673). It condemns a position that holds "that people are justified either solely by the attribution of Christ's justice, or by the forgiveness of sins alone, to the exclusion of the grace and charity which is poured forth in their hearts by the Holy Spirit and abides in them; or even that the grace by which we are justified is only by the good-will of God" (*Decrees* 1990, 679). Thus Catholicism teaches that justification is both forensic and effective; it condemns such versions of merely forensic justification in which forgiveness is distributed arbitrarily.

The normative Lutheran position on justification is expressed in the Latin text of the *Augsburg Confession* (CA) IV as follows: "Human beings . . . are justified as a gift (*gratis*) on account of Christ through faith when they believe that they are received into grace and that their sins are forgiven on account of Christ . . . God reckons (*imputat*) this faith as righteousness (Romans 3-4)" (*Book of Concord* 2000, 39–41).

The crucial divine act in this event is that of "reckoning." The Pauline verb behind this word is *logizomai*, which became translated into Latin as *reputare* (Romans 4:3, 5:9 Vulgata) and *imputare* (Romans 4:4, 4:8, 5:13 Vulgata). The Pauline verb can mean reading, counting, or simply "considering as." A strictly forensic view of justification interprets this word as the declaration or pronouncement of the judge. At the same time, the Latin concept of "imputation" can also be interpreted to mean gift giving, or some other concrete transfer that is not merely forensic but rather economic or even effective.

While the normative Lutheran vocabulary of justification can be claimed to bypass the effective dimension, it strongly affirms the Latin concept of imputation. Rolf (2008) shows that this concept has many dimensions for Luther: in addition to its forensic aspects, the concept contains economic, processual, and effective elements. For Luther, the event of imputation communicates Christ to the believer, thus establishing a strong connection between forensic justification and the presence of Christ in faith (Rolf 2008, 180–206). The theological elaboration of this connection is typical of early Lutheranism.

While Luther receives the idea of "reckoning" from Paul and Augustine, he differs from the latter in emphasizing the deeply interpersonal nature of imputation (Rolf 2008, 33–40). When God reckons believers as righteous, they are personally involved in this event. In some sense this fits well with the law court imagery, but one can also remark that a legal process need not assume any lasting interpersonal involvement between the judge and the accused person.

Protestant theology has traditionally distinguished between three aspects of imputation (Rolf 2008, 27; Fesko 2012):

  (i)   the non-imputation of sins;
  (ii)  the imputation of faith (as righteousness, Romans 4:3–5);
  (iii) the imputation of the righteousness of Christ (to/for the believer).

While (i) and (ii) clearly appear in Luther, (iii) becomes integrated into the Lutheran view of justification only by Matthias Flacius Illyricus (Rolf 2008, 180). CA IV (quoted above) formulates (ii) as a doctrinal norm. Since Luther teaches a strong connection between justification and the presence of Christ in faith, some elements of (iii) are already present in his theology. Later Lutheranism struggles with different interpretative options: if (iii) is seen in terms of calculative, measurable justice, the doctrine of justification becomes forensic and economic, approaching the Western theology of atonement. If (iii) is understood in terms of sacramental gift, justification becomes effective, approaching the ideas of renovation and healing.

## 2  FROM FLACIUS TO GERHARDT

Matthias Flacius develops formulations which came to be regarded as genuine expressions of Lutheran orthodoxy. Writing against Andreas Osiander, another Lutheran who developed a strong doctrine of effective justification, Flacius considers that "imputation seems to mean a transfer of something [*translatio*], not, however, essential, but only rational transfer" (Vainio 2008, 110, quoting Flacius 1563, 126). With the help of this consideration, he can define justification in forensic terms: "The justification of the sinner is the act of God in which he transfers or transcribes, all the time, like a Judge on his seat, the righteousness of His Son to believers, i.e. those who come to the throne of grace ... in a certain rational or imputative application, which however is powerful, real and effective" (Vainio 2008, 110, quoting Flacius 1563, 135). This description of imputation in terms of (iii) means complications with the view of CA IV, which speaks of the imputation of faith (ii). As Flacius finds both the Catholic view of effective justification and Osiander's emphasis on the real indwelling of divinity unacceptable, he can only approve of such "rational" transfer that does not entail any essential righteousness. In order to avoid unacceptable views while approving CA IV, Flacius distinguishes between "personal" and "real" imputation. The imputation of Christ's righteousness (iii) is personal: it occurs in God's mind in a rational but not real or habitual manner. In a sense, this matches well with the Pauline act of *logizomai*.

The imputation of faith (ii), on the other hand, is imputed to be real by God. God reckons the faith as righteousness, although human faith as such does not have real virtue or power to bring about righteousness. Against the Council of Trent, Flacius thus holds that this imputation is no mere illusion; it is real because God makes it happen. In this manner Flacius maintains that both (ii) and (iii) can take place within a fairly forensic setting. He needs to admit, as shown above, that the imputation is in some sense "powerful, real and effective." These realities take place in God's mind, as rational changes which do not entail any change in the believer (Vainio 2008, 111–12, quoting Flacius 1563, 126–27).

Martin Chemnitz likewise considers that "the righteousness which is imputed to, or on account of which we are accepted to eternal life, is not something inhering in us . . . but it is firmly rooted in the obedience of Christ alone" (Vainio 2008, 153; Chemnitz 1989, 554). He considers that "Paul everywhere described the article of justification as a judicial process wherein the conscience of the sinner . . . is restored, absolved, and freed from the sentence of condemnation and received to eternal life for the sake of the obedience and intercession of the Son of God, our Mediator, which is laid hold of and made one's own through faith" (Vainio 2008, 151; Chemnitz 1989, 480). Unlike Flacius, however, Chemnitz has no hesitation in teaching that faith means an indwelling of Christ: "He dwells in our hearts in a divine and incomprehensible manner which is believed alone by faith in the promise, not by our reason or by some perceptible or visible or local condition of intellect and reason; so that even though we do not feel or understand that Christ is in us or how he is in us, yet by faith, according to his promise we understand with certainty that he truly dwells in our hearts" (Vainio 2008, 149; Chemnitz 1971, 451). Chemnitz thus advocates Luther's strong connection between justification and Christ's presence in faith; obviously, this does not mean that such presence is "something inhering in us" in the sense of human merit or habit. Thus Chemnitz can avoid a merely illusory view of justification, as well as an overwhelmingly rationalist interpretation of imputation. At the same time, his view of justification preserves the forensic frame of justification by faith.

The *Formula of Concord* formulates many intentions of Flacius and Chemnitz in a consensual manner that became normative for Lutherans: "The only essential and necessary elements of justification are the grace of God, the merit of Christ, and the faith that receives this grace and merit in the gospel's promise, through which Christ's righteousness is reckoned to us. From this we obtain the forgiveness of sins, reconciliation with God, our adoption as children, and the inheritance to eternal life" (*Book of Concord* 2000, 566).

At the same time the *Formula of Concord* leans on a strongly anti-Catholic, forensic justification in stating that:

—renewal and sanctification do not belong to justification,
—the righteousness of faith before God consists only in the . . . forgiveness of sins,
—in this life believers . . . have first of all the righteousness of faith that is reckoned to them and then thereafter the righteousness of new obedience. (*Book of Concord* 2000, 566–67)

The need to create distance from Osiander and the Council of Trent is visible in these statements. At the same time, they leave room for subsequent discussion on the strong connection between forensic justification, on the one hand, and the indwelling of Christ, on the other. Obviously, these two poles are not creations of the sixteenth century, but are both prominent in Paul's theology of salvation.

Mahlmann (1996) and Nüssel (2000) have shown in great detail how the view of a mystical indwelling of Christ became a significant Lutheran doctrine during the seventeenth century. Given the forensic leanings of the *Book of Concord*, this was not self-evident. Mahlmann points out that the spiritualist teachings of Valentin Weigel, as well as the Christological debates of those years, contributed to this development. In addition, the idea of the indwelling of Christ in faith was already present in the writings of Luther and Chemnitz in a fully orthodox fashion.

Johann Arndt's treatise *De unione credentium cum Christo Jesu* (1620) describes how Christ unites with the soul of the believer through the work of the Holy Spirit. This union takes place in faith. The medium of this event is the Word of God: God is present in the world in and with his Word. Mahlmann (1996, 98) considers that Arndt's emphasis of the indwelling through the word (*per verbum*) is his own contribution to the broader discussion regarding sound spirituality.

Arndt already makes some use of mystical traditions when he explains the Lutheran idea of Christ present in faith. However, it is only his famous pupil Johann Gerhard who undertakes an extensive discussion of mysticism in the context of the Lutheran view of justification. Gerhard aims at defending justification by faith alone with the help of mystical traditions. Though he prefers to speak of *unio spiritualis*, he sometimes also uses the phrase *unio mystica* to depict the union of the believer with Christ (Steiger 1997; Nüssel 2000, 260).

Gerhard makes use of the two natures of Christ to illustrate the union of the believer with Christ. However, particularly signification for our theme is that justification constitutes the framework in which this union takes place. The "transfer" of the righteousness of Christ ([iii] above) is a mystical gift and an extremely real imputation: "With this mystical *antidosis* [return gift] Christ takes into him our sins and gives us in faith his righteousness . . . this is no merely verbal predication, but most effective, and, so to say, most real imputation" (Nüssel 2000, 262, quoting Gerhard 1885, 536). In this manner the figure of imputation is also employed to depict the mystical union with Christ.

While Steiger (1997, 116) considers that the mystical union is for Gerhard as primary as forensic justification, Nüssel (2000, 266) holds that forensic justification nevertheless retains a logical (though not temporal or ontological) priority over the mystical union. This is because the divine act of "reckoning" or "considering as" remains the primary ground of justification; the spiritual union and the exchange of gifts express this ground. One instance of visualizing this logical order is the slight difference between the concepts of *unio* and *inhabitatio* in Gerhard: while *unio* refers to the initial connection with Christ that actualizes the imputation, *inhabitatio Dei* means the broader outcome of this process (Vaahtoranta 1998, 249). In sum, Gerhard manages to integrate mystical traditions into the Lutheran view of justification without compromising the basic idea that Christians are saved by faith alone.

# 3  Johann Friedrich
## König: Justification by Faith

Three simultaneous layers are operative in the early modern Lutheran discussions concerning forensic justification and mysticism. Within an identity-building layer, attempts are made to distinguish genuine Lutheranism from other Christian confessions. Within an exegetical layer, the relationship between justification and being in Christ in Pauline soteriology is scrutinized. In addition to these, the emergence of a philosophical layer, attempting an intellectual sophistication of the theological issues, becomes visible during the seventeenth century.

A powerful tool in this philosophical sophistication is the so-called analytical method, introduced by Jacobo Zabarella and developed in Protestant theology by Bartholomäus Keckermann, Georg Calixt, and Abraham Calov (Appold 1998, 16–29; Nüssel 2000, 300–12). The analytical method claims to proceed from effects to causes and from particulars to universals. It claims to pay attention to the practical nature of religion and theology, reconstructing the task, goal, and subject of theology from available particular facts (Muller 2006, 184–87).

The analytical method enables a considerable sophistication in discussing doctrinal matters. As the method claims to be practical and relate to tasks and goals, its theological applications often focus on the salvation of human beings and on eternal life as the task and goal of theology. The method paves a way to the modern ideas of the central dogma and order of salvation. I will restrict my treatment to the portrayal of forensic justification and mysticism in the hugely popular Lutheran textbook of Johann Friedrich König, *Theologia positiva acroamatica* (König 2006, originally published 1664; Stegmann 2006). The word *acroamatica* in this context means "sophisticated" in contrast to rudimentary or catechetical. König represents ideas that can also be found in the larger Lutheran dogmatics of, for example, Gerhard and Calov.

König's textbook consists of three parts: (I) God (the goal of theology), (II) the restitution of the sinful human being (the subject of theology) and (III) the principles and means of salvation (as relating to both the goal and the subject). In Part III, the principles of salvation are organized in a Trinitarian fashion: they regard the will of the Father, the redemption achieved by Jesus Christ, and the grace of the Holy Spirit. Justification and the mystical union appear in the middle of the chapter on the Spirit; they are preceded by vocation, regeneration, conversion, and penitence, and followed by renovation. This sequence is not, however, temporal but logical. After renovation, König's next major chapter on the means of salvation concerns the relationship of word, sacraments, and faith. While the Word of God and the sacraments constitute the "given" (*dotika*) means, faith expresses the reception (*leptikon*) of salvation (König 2006, 280–324).

The treatment of justification begins with an extensive collection of relevant biblical passages. Against Catholics, König (2006, 306) stresses that nowhere in the Bible do the relevant concepts denote an infusion of new quality; instead, they can mean a knowledge of divine righteousness, a procedure in which justice is pronounced between litigating parties, or a liberation from sin. When the Bible speaks of the justification of the sinner, the concept denotes "a forensic act through which one is constituted as righteous in the law court" (*actum forensem, quo quis justus constituitur judicialiter*). While König thus employs a strictly forensic concept of justification, the entire pneumatological chapter entails the treatment of regeneration, mystical union, and renovation.

The forensic act of justification is elaborated through an analysis of all relevant causalities. König (2006, 306–8) assumes that justification is an effect which comes about through several causes. The effective causes (*c. efficiens, impellens*) are the Triune God, the free grace of God, and the merit of the obedience of Christ. Among the transmitting causes (*c. media*) one needs to distinguish between divine giving (*dotike*) and human reception (*leptike*). Word and sacraments belong to divine giving, whereas faith transmits justification in human reception. The *media* causes are the means of salvation; they connect the central topics of Part III intimately with forensic justification.

König thus constructs a theology of giving and the gift as a framework for his doctrine of justification. Although justification does not mean any infusion of quality and remains a purely forensic act, this act is transmitted in terms of gift giving. Moreover, although justification occupies a relatively small place in Part II, the means of salvation (Part III) are embedded into the chapter on justification in Part II. Given this, in which sense does the forensic justification really remain forensic when the analysis of causality is performed? König (2006, 308) formulates this as follows: "The 'given' (*dotike*) from the side of God are the word and sacraments. They offer and apply to the believer the justifying and saving obedience of Christ, to be apprehended in faith donated in regeneration."

Depending on how this formulation is read, the event of justification can be understood in more or less forensic terms. If sacraments are understood to transmit justification, the position approaches the condemned Roman Catholic view of infusion. However, if God's "giving" primarily refers to offering necessary information about salvation so that the believer comprehends the event, it remains more clearly forensic. Vainio (2008, 21) notes that the concept of "apprehending faith" comprises both cognitive and effective dimensions in the Lutheran Reformation. In addition, the idea of personal appropriation is here relevant; we return to it below.

König is very well aware of different interpretive options and gives his own understanding (2006, 308): "In the event of justification, faith has its own kind of causality, which is nothing else than organic [*organica*], insofar as it justifies through apprehending the merit of Christ. The reason of this cause [*ratio causandi*] is that justifying power which is ascribed to faith . . . only from the apprehended justifying object."

König distances himself here (2006, 308–10) from several views in which justifying faith appears as human work, dignity, or quality. For instance, the view that faith would be simply "our" apprehensive act (*quatenus est apprehensio et actus noster*) is criticized. König thus refutes both a full-fledged epistemic interpretation that makes apprehension a human cognitive act, and a quasi-Catholic effective view in which the apprehensive capacity becomes a quality. He manages to do this through weakening the instrumental causality of faith. In transmitting justification, faith is an instrument which can apprehend something; however, this apprehension is neither a human cognitive act nor a new quality exercising a power. In faith, something is apprehended but the believer is not the final subject of this apprehension.

This view of the "organic" causality of faith is a fascinating sophistication that calls for adequate illustrations. For instance, a violin is a musical instrument although it is not the violin but the musician who is the subject of music. There may, however, be a transfer of quality from the musician to the violin. Can the violin be said to "apprehend" something from the musician? Probably not. König, in any case, is careful not to give mechanistic illustrations. Instead, he illustrates his point as follows (2006, 310): "Neither faith alone nor the merit of Christ alone is imputed, but the faith that apprehends the merit of Christ, or, synonymously, the merit of Christ apprehended by faith. These two can be distinguished, but, as they are constantly related to one another, they cannot be separated in this event."

In this sense, faith as the organ of justification cannot be compared to a violin as a musical instrument. Although the "apprehension" is neither human knowledge nor human work, it is nevertheless something that cannot be reduced to its object. While the justifying power of faith can be fully ascribed to the object of faith, faith is nevertheless necessary in the sense that it cannot be bypassed in the event of justification. This means, among other things, that the organic causality of faith is its "own kind," as König states above.

In sum, König's view of faith comes close to Rolf's (2008, see above) conclusion that Lutherans teach an interpersonal view of imputation. Although the framework of justification can be called forensic in early Lutheran theology, the emphasis on faith brings about something that does not completely fit with the law court imagery. We may call this provisionally the organic involvement of the believer. In this involvement, faith is not a means of salvation, but it is nevertheless needed as an organ. Such an involvement differs from full-fledged subjectivity, but the postulate of "faith alone" nevertheless entails the view that the person of the believer cannot be eradicated from the event of justification.

Given that faith shapes the subject in this "organic" manner, we may ask whether a new kind of subjectivity emerges in the early Lutheran theology of justification. We return to this issue after looking at König's view of *unio mystica*.

## 4  KÖNIG AND *UNIO MYSTICA*

When a person is justified, the mystical union with God emerges. This sequence is logical or conceptual rather than temporal. For König (2006, 316), the order of the different aspects of salvation relates to human concept formation: "The temporal moment of this union is the same as the moment of regeneration, justification and renovation. All these events take place in the same instance of time. One of them is prior to the other according to our mode of understanding connoted by the different concepts. Thus regeneration and justification are prior to the union, as it only exists from faith and after the faith." König receives the Lutheran discussion taking place from the *Formula of Concord* to Johann Gerhard. The union can also be called *unio spiritualis*. Properly speaking, it means a union of substances (*substantiarum*) rather than a substantial (*substantialis*) union, as neither of the two parties fully disappears in the other. At the same time the "unification" (*unitio*) is highly intimate or mystical, as it comprises the divine substance, on the one hand, and the true substance of the faithful, their soul and body, on the other. König (2006, 314–18) attempts to speak first of *unitio* as a process, then of *unio* as its outcome, but the two meanings come very close to each other.

Like *unitio*, the final union can best be described in terms of relationship: "Since union belongs to the class of relations, it can be pedagogically well described according to the aspects required in a relation. The parts of this relation are the subjects which enter a union . . . its foundational reason is the gracious work of the Holy Spirit, exercising unification, or concisely: the very act of unification. The relationship following from this is the union, expressing formally the most intimate presence of the unified to each other" (König 2006, 318).

König does not attempt to rationalize the details of the mystical union, but employs biblical descriptions regarding the exchange of divine properties and communication with God. In mystical communication, God equips us with all divine riches; these riches include different kinds of righteousness (e.g., *justitiam suam, jus filiale, jus regni*; König 2006, 318). König speaks of the indwelling of the Holy Trinity in the faithful, the indwelling of Christ in our hearts, and mystical marriage (314). He does not mention deification but quotes 2 Peter 1:4 twice in this context (316).

For a modern reader the distinction between the strictly restricted forensic justification and the rich overflow of good gifts in the mystical union is striking, especially since they both occur in the same instance of time. If the distinction between the two only regards human concept formation, why is it so important to condemn all Catholic views that speak about effective justification? Doesn't the Lutheran view of the mystical union rather express the same Catholic spiritual tradition that the Council of Trent affirms?

Gerhard and König may see this problem in a different light. When they manage to sharpen the distinctive Lutheran theology of forensic imputation, they can also afford to speak positively of the mystical tradition. In its right doctrinal place, the mystical tradition no longer expresses any problematic self-righteousness, but can be understood as compatible with normative Lutheranism. When the forensic justification proceeds from the apprehended theological object, the sacramental and mystical traditions provide a sufficiently objective spiritual counterpoint with regard to which the believer remains merely passive.

# 5 THE SUBJECTIVIZATION THESIS

These findings shed new light on a long-debated problem of subjectivism in early Lutheran theology. Especially in the older scholarship, a line from Luther to Pietism, Kierkegaard, and even existential philosophy has been drawn, emphasizing the first-person view of a Christian in Luther's thought (Pinomaa 1940; Pelikan 1950). This feature was turned against Lutherans by Hacker (1970), a conservative Catholic who claims that Luther's theology is seriously hampered by a strong subjectivism that makes the Reformer a forerunner of Cartesianism and an adversary of theologians who embrace a strong sense of Christian community. Hacker's ideas have recently attracted attention since they have been recommended by Joseph Cardinal Ratzinger, later pope Benedict XVI (Hacker 1970; 2009). Moreover, some of Benedict's own judgments of Martin Luther (e.g., in *Spe salvi* 7) show an influence of Hacker's ideas. Let us call the view of Hacker and Ratzinger the subjectivization thesis, meaning the claim that the early Lutheran theology was a forerunner of Cartesianism and later subjectivist and anthropocentric religious views.

The first problem that the subjectivization thesis encounters is that the condemnations of the Council of Trent do not support it. On the contrary, the condemnation of a merely forensic view of justification assumes that Lutherans do not affirm enough personal involvement. When Lutherans allegedly teach that justification occurs "only by the goodwill of God," they are condemned because they do not observe what should happen "in their hearts." Moreover, the canon regarding justification "by faith alone" condemns a position according to which the justified person does not need "to make preparation and be disposed by a movement of his own will" (*Decrees* 1990, 679). The Council of Trent thus requires more subjective involvement from the believer.

When we read what Luther's contemporary Ignatius de Loyola writes in the opening pages of his *Spiritual Exercises* (originally published 1522–24), we also see a strong first-person perspective. Ignatius thus affirms a spiritual subjectivity that may find its Lutheran counterpart in Johann Gerhard's *Meditationes sacrae* ([1606] 1707). This subjective tradition has its origins in the medieval mysticism of Bernard of Clairvaux.

To discuss the subjectivization thesis properly, it needs to be set into the context of various ideas that derive from antiquity. The concept of self has always been a concern of philosophy (Sorabji 2006). Among various philosophical developments, the Stoic view of personal appropriation (*oikeiosis*) is a classical view that can be found in seventeenth-century Lutheranism. During this period, Neo-Stoicism was popular and authors like Cicero and Seneca were an integral part of education. For the Stoics, *oikeiosis* means the instinct of self-preservation, as well as the attachment of self to self and others. The two Latin concepts employed for this purpose in König's textbook are *applicatio* and *appropriatio*. While *applicatio* looks at the process of attachment from the perspective of the external giver (German: *Zueignung*), *appropriatio* concerns the recipient (German: *Aneignung*). However, in Lutheran Orthodoxy and Pietism, *applicatio* often comprises both dimensions (Kramer 1971; Franz 2000; Horn 2004).

In König's textbook, salvation is organized in a Trinitarian manner: the Father delivers the principle of saving will, the Son that of redemption and the Holy Spirit that of "an applicative [appropriating] grace of the Holy Spirit" (*gratia Spiritus Sancti applicatrix*, König 2006, 174). The grace of the Spirit concerns primarily vocation, rebirth, conversion, mystical union and renovation (278). For the relationship between forensic justification and mysticism, it is significant that justification is ascribed to the external and forensic work of the entire Trinity (312), whereas the mystical union concerns the applicative grace of the Holy Spirit (318). The mystical union thus manifests a more appropriate reality than forensic justification alone. While forensic justification imputes righteousness to a generic "sinful human being," sanctification applies or appropriates grace to personal believers and children of God.

However, forensic justification also involves personal subjectivity in its concept of faith. As stated above, König considers that the organic causality of faith entails a sort of interpersonal involvement between God and the believer. This involvement is specified in König's discussion of faith as a "receiving" (*dotike*) means of grace. Here (König 2006, 386), the justifying faith (*fiducia*) is thematicized as the appropriating reception of an individual (*receptio seu apprehensio ... appropriativa ad me et te in individuo*). When such reception is called the justifying faith, it does not concern the theoretical dimension of apprehension, but that practical apprehension "which involves the whole heart and will in leaning on the merit of Christ" (*quae totius cordis et voluntatis in merito Christi recumbentiam involvit*).

These formulations show, on the one hand, that justification by faith concerns the individual appropriation, or personal involvement. On the other hand, faith is by no means a free-floating subject that makes salvation anthropomorphic. Rather, the vocabulary employed by König is that of classical *oikeiosis*: the applicative work of the Holy Spirit and the individual appropriation of the believer constitute the attachment that makes the individual a member of the Christian community. König (2006, 388) describes the form of justifying faith as "the individual application and appropriation of the known and approved object." In this manner individuality and a certain shape of subjectivity are affirmed. Philosophically, it is rather a Neo-Stoic *oikeiosis* than any Cartesian subjectivity that is at stake here. Theologically, König shows against the Council of Trent that it is not the goodwill of God alone, but also the personal involvement of the heart that characterizes the Lutheran doctrine of justification by faith.

From this perspective one can properly understand König's final definition (2006, 910) of justifying faith: "The justifying and saving faith is solely the work of the pure grace of God who brings about regeneration. This work is performed in humans ... through the administration of Word and Sacraments. Through these, the promise of grace ... and the merit of God-man is applied and appropriated to individual persons, mediated by the inner movement of their hearts, for salvation and the glory of merciful God."

Through the vocabulary of *applicatio* and *appropriatio*, König can present an involvement of "organic" subjectivity that does not compromise forensic justification by faith, but shows in which sense the hearts of the believers are attached to this event.

Given that this structure exemplifies a Christian adaptation of *oikeiosis*, we can say that the dimension of sanctification, or *unio mystica*, belongs to this adaptation as its second part. If justification by faith means the birth of a Christian subject with an individual attachment, sanctification relates this individual to a spiritual community. The personal relationship to Christ in the mystical union is the root of community building, bringing about neighborly love. The so-called renovation as the logical step following justification and mystical union is described by König (2006, 322) with words that resemble the emergence of the Stoic sage: "The form of renovation consists in the correction of intellectual errors, the eradication of affects inclining towards evil and the mastery of the bodily members as instruments of justice." The relationship of forensic justification and spiritual renovation in König can thus be compared to the relationship between adequate self-care and cosmopolitan friendship in the Stoic conception of *oikeiosis*. While this comparison may sound strange from a modern perspective, the idea of *oikeiosis* was since Philo of Alexandria understood in terms of religious mysticism, belonging in this sense to classical Christianity (Horn 2004, 1405).

Obviously, the doctrine of justification is not, as such, fundamentally related to Stoicism. I have employed the Stoic doctrine of *oikeiosis* to highlight the nature of subjectivity available in early Lutheranism. To defend the Lutheran view, König explains in great detail in which precise sense the individual attachment of the believer is important in justification by faith. This explanation is not Cartesian or subjectivist. It employs the classical vocabulary of self-attachment in the sense of *oikeiosis*. Its philosophical roots are, therefore, closer to Cicero and Seneca than to early modern philosophy.

# 6 EIGHTEENTH-CENTURY PIETISM

Although the Hacker-Ratzinger thesis is false, the general issue of subjectivization is important for the history of Lutheranism. Already Martin Luther employs an interpersonal notion of imputation, and eighteenth-century Pietism has a strong notion of individual subjectivity. The line from Luther to Pietism does not, however, grow from Luther's inherent subjectivism or his pre-Cartesian notion of faith. The emergence of "organic subjectivity" in early Lutheranism rather employs a complex dialectic: after Luther, the Council of Trent demands more personal involvement from the Protestants. In responding to this challenge, Lutheran orthodoxy refines the notion of justifying faith so that the quasi-Stoic vocabulary of *applicatio* and *appropriatio* is employed to explain in which sense the justifying faith is "my" faith.

In the history of philosophy, the modern idea of "appropriation" is normally considered to be the invention of Pietist hermeneutics, followed by the Enlightenment concepts of private property and subjectivity (Kramer 1971; Franz 2000). As shown above, these ideas are already present in the theology of justification developed in Lutheran orthodoxy. This finding makes our topic relevant beyond the immediate concerns of theologians.

After Philipp Jakob Spener's *Pia desideria* ([1675] 1964), Pietist hermeneutics develops the vocabulary of application and appropriation, demanding a variety of practical and personal religious applications that are distinct from a merely theoretical understanding (Kramer 1971; Franz 2000). August Hermann Francke, for instance, considers that while everybody can understand the importance of Christ in the Bible, only very few true believers can apply this understanding to the growth of one's own inner humanity (Francke 1702, 104, as quoted in Franz 2000, 158). Although such demand of subjective appropriation entails a criticism of Lutheran orthodoxy, it also borrows from it the vocabulary of individual application.

The awakening of the so-called organic subjectivity in Lutheran orthodoxy is followed by the full-fledged subjectivity of the Enlightenment. In Lutheranism, the emergence of subjectivity is particularly visible in eighteenth-century German Pietism. We can only highlight this development insofar as it concerns our main theme. For this reason, I will focus on a representative and influential Pietist text; namely, Nikolaus Ludwig von Zindendorf's exposition of the Second Article of Faith in Luther's *Catechism*.

As the founder and leader of the Herrnhut community, Zinzendorf was a Lutheran cosmopolitan whose theology played a significant role in various evangelical and missionary movements around the world. His exposition, often known as *Berlinische Reden* (Berlin Speeches), shows how the traditional Lutheran doctrine was employed to meet the new missionary situation of the Enlightenment. Instead of sophisticated theological definitions, Zinzendorf aims at rhetorical clarity and sincerity. This does not imply, however, a general neglect of doctrine. On the contrary, Zinzendorf aims at adhering to the Lutheran ground from which new evangelizing attempts can be undertaken.

Justification and sanctification are treated thematically in Speech 14. Its thematic basis is Luther's phrase "in eternal righteousness, innocence and blessedness" (*Book of Concord* 2000, 355). Zinzendorf (1758, 165) calls justification "a method" or "a means": justification is the means to come to eternal righteousness; sanctification brings us eternal innocence; and redemption brings eternal beatitude. He thus understands the three concepts of Luther's *Catechism* in terms of successive salvation order, typical of eighteenth-century Lutheran Pietism.

The treatment of justification opens with a statement that God has a method for all humanity, as well as for each particular soul. The saving work of Christ concerns all humanity; in this manner "the blood of Jesus Christ is the cause of our righteousness" (Zinzendorf 1758, 173–74). Regarding the first-person perspective of the individual soul, Zinzendorf (1758, 174) emphasizes a simple faith:

> If we do not want to believe in a simple manner, the law exercises its power on us, and we remain under pain and trouble until the Holy Spirit has sympathy for us and shows the Saviour in our heart. When we see this (troubled and exhausted, in conflict with the world), then the justification of the individual soul takes place . . . . Then the soul has the eternal privilege, so that, through the blood of Jesus Christ, it can proceed through the world, through sin and trouble, yes, through hell, and is never stopped, proceeding to the eternal blessedness.

This description employs the first-person perspective, highlights emotions, and avoids intellectual detachment. At the same time, it contains features that connect Zinzendorf with Lutheran orthodoxy: the applicative work of the Spirit, the personal role of the human heart and, most importantly, the context of justification by faith.

After this short description of justification, Zinzendorf (1758, 175) describes sanctification. It proceeds through the entire life of a Christian, developing gradually: "Goodness has its degrees. The human person becomes more chaste, more humble, more generous, more industrious, or, to put it more clearly, the schoolchild becomes an adult, and little by little a schoolmaster. One learns to grasp the secret of holiness in a deeper and deeper manner."

The final union with Christ belongs to the blessedness that follows sanctification. Zinzendorf's description of blessedness (1758, 175) is not mystical or contemplative, but practical: "when the peace of the Saviour rules in our hearts, all our daily work is being with the Saviour."

As Zinzendorf proclaims the gospel rather than presents a theoretical treatise, the relationship between justification and sanctification is outlined in very practical terms. The difference in style and genre should not, however, conceal the underlying continuity from Lutheran orthodoxy to eighteenth-century Pietism: Zinzendorf aims at laying out the same doctrine of justification as König. The Pietist emphasis on practical application highlights the first-person perspective: the proclamation concerns our faith and lifestyle. While this emphasis employs the Enlightenment concept of personal subject, it also continues what has been labeled as the organic subjectivity of the early Lutheran theology of justification by faith.

## BIBLIOGRAPHY

Appold, Kenneth. 1998. *Abraham Calov's Doctrine of Vocatio in Its Systematic Context.* Tübingen: Mohr Siebeck.

Arndt, Johann. 1620. *De unione credentium cum Christo Jesu.*

BenedictXVI. 2007. *Spe salvi: Encyclical Letter.* www.vatican.va.

*Book of Concord.* 2000. *The Book of Concord: The Confessions of the Evangelical Lutheran Church*, edited by R. Kolb and T. J. Wengert. Minneapolis: Fortress Press.

Chemnitz, Martin. 1989. *Loci Theologici I-II.* St. Louis, MO: Concordia.

Chemnitz, Martin. 1971. *Two Natures in Christ.* St. Louis, MO: Concordia.

*Decrees.* 1990. *Decrees of the Ecumenical Councils I-II*, edited by N. P. Tanner. London: Sheed & Ward.

Fesko, J. V. 2012. *Beyond Calvin: Union with Christ and Justification in Early Modern Reformed Theology (1517–1700).* Göttingen: Vandenhoeck & Ruprecht.

Flacius, Matthias Illyricus. 1563. *De voce et re fidei.* Basel.

Francke, August Hermann. 1702. *Oeffentliches Zeugnis vom Werck, Wort und Dienst Gottes.* Vol. 2. Leipzig.

Franz, Michael. 2000. "Aneignung." In *Ästhetische Grundbegriffe.* Vol. 1, 153–193. Stuttgart: Metzler.

Gerhard, Johann. 1885. *Loci Theologi.* 9 vols. Edited by F. Frank. Leipzig.

Gerhard, Johann. (1606) 1707. *Meditationes sacrae.* Leipzig.

Hacker, Paul. 2009. *Das Ich im Glauben bei Martin Luther.* Mit Vorwort von Papst Benedikt XVI. Bonn: Nova et vetera.

Hacker, Paul. 1970. *The Ego in Faith: Martin Luther and the Origin of Anthropocentric Religion*. Chicago: Franciscan Herald Press.

Horn, C. 2004. "Zueignung (Oikeiosis)." In *Historisches Wörterbuch der Philosophie*. Vol. 12, 1403–1408.

König, Johann Friedrich. 2006. *Theologia positiva acroamatica*, edited by A. Stegmann. Tübingen: Mohr Siebeck.

Kramer, W. 1971. "Applikation." In *Historisches Wörterbuch der Philosophie*. Vol. 1, 457–458.

Loyola, Ignatius de. 1992. *The Spiritual Exercises*. Chicago: Loyola Press.

Mahlmann, Theodor. 1996. "Die Stellung der unio cum Christo in der lutherischen Theologie des 17. Jahrhunderts." In *Unio: Gott und Mensch in der nachreformatorischen Theologie*, edited by M. Repo and R. Vinke, 72–199. Helsinki: Luther-Agricola Society.

McGrath, Alister E. 1986. *Iustitia Dei: A History of the Christian Doctrine of Justification*. Cambridge: Cambridge University Press.

Muller, Richard A. 2006. *Prolegomena to Theology*. Vol. 1 of *Post-Reformation Reformed Dogmatics: The Rise and Development of Reformed Orthodoxy* ca. *1520–ca. 1725*. 2nd ed. Grand Rapids, MI: Baker.

Nüssel, Friederike. 2000. *Allein aus Glauben: Zur Entwicklung der Rechtfertigungslehre in der konkordistischen und frühen nachkonkordistischen Theologie*. Göttingen: Vandenhoeck & Ruprecht.

Pelikan, Jaroslav. 1950. *From Luther to Kierkegaard*. Saint Louis, MO: Concordia.

Pinomaa, Lennart. 1940. *Der existentielle Charakter der Theologie Luthers*. Helsinki: AASF.

Rolf, Sibylle. 2008. *Zum Herzen sprechen: Eine Studie zum imputativen Aspekt in Martin Luthers Rechtfertigungslehre und zu seinen Konsequenzen für die Predigt des Evangeliums*. Berlin: Ev. Verlag.

Spener, Philipp Jakob. (1675) 1964. *Pia desideria*. Minneapolis: Fortress.

Stegmann, Andreas. 2006. *Johann Friedrich König. Seine Theologia positiva acroamatica im Rahmen des frühneuzeitlichen Theologiestudiums*. Tübingen: Mohr Siebeck.

Steiger, Johann Anselm. 1997. *Johann Gerhard (1582–1637): Studien zu Theologie und Frömmigkeit des Kirchenvaters der lutherischen Orthodoxie*. Stuttgart: Frommann-Holzboog.

*Summa theologiae*. 1888–1906. Thomas Aquinas. Vatican: Polyglot Press.

Vaahtoranta, Martti. 1998. *Restauratio imaginis divinae: Die Vereinigung von Gott und Mensch, ihre Voraussetzungen und Implikationen bei Johann Gerhard*. Helsinki: Luther-Agricola Society.

Vainio, Olli-Pekka. 2008. *Justification and Participation in Christ: The Development of the Lutheran Doctrine of Justification from Luther to the Formula of Concord (1580)*. Leiden: Brill.

Wright, Tom. 2009. *Justification: God's Plan and Paul's Vision*. London: SPCK.

Zinzendorf, Nikolaus Ludwig von. 1758. *Berlinische Reden*, edited by G. Clemens. London.

..............................................................................................................

# CHAPTER 22

# EARLY MODERN LUTHERAN ECCLESIOLOGY

..............................................................................................................

## OLA TJØRHOM

THE outbreak of the Thirty Years' War in 1618 and the beginning of the French Revolution in 1789 are vital markers of the early modern era. Theologically and ecclesially, however, it makes sense to start with developments in the Reformation during the latter decades of the sixteenth century and end roughly two hundred years later, when Friedrich Schleiermacher and neo-Protestantism entered the stage. In this period, the Lutheran tradition was dominated by three deviating currents: orthodoxy—more precisely high and late orthodoxy, classical Pietism, and Enlightenment theology. Despite the simultaneous emergence and consolidation of several national churches, ecclesiological reflection was a secondary concern within these currents. Orthodox ecclesiology became an exercise in controversy with Roman Catholicism as a central adversary, while its sacramental theology chiefly was directed against Reformed or Calvinist positions. Both Pietists and rationalists ranked individualizing approaches above corporate and embodied manifestations of Christian life.

Still, significant developments can be traced in this era: first, even if neither orthodoxy nor Pietism and Enlightenment theology saw ecclesiological issues as a key task, they had vital implications in this field. Some of these implications were problematic, others helpful in renewing the doctrine on the church. Second, ecclesiology was conducted within a distinctively changed ecclesial setting. After the peace treaties of Augsburg in 1555 and Westphalia in 1648, not only the existence of separate churches, but also their coexistence within the same nations became a reality on the European continent. Third, novel paradigms in philosophy, culture and political life provided the wider framework of ecclesiological contributions. On this basis, theologians were prompted, or forced, to depart from narrow ecclesiocentrism and to reflect on the church in the context of the larger society.

This chapter aims at providing a brief overview of ecclesiologically relevant trends within early modern Lutheranism, emphasizing broader perspectives rather than specific details. While concentrating on the span from 1600 to 1800, some references to previous and subsequent developments are included. Even if there were geographical variations, the German situation is most relevant here. More specifically, I shall deal with the topic's context, the major currents of the period, and the resulting ecclesiological picture. The primary focus will be on the church, with reflections on the sacraments as a supplementary perspective. Studies of Pietism and Enlightenment theology—partly also of orthodoxy—pay limited attention to ecclesiology. Thus, the ecclesiological gaps of these currents are affirmed. I refer readers to further information in the chapter by Lehmann and Strom in the present volume.

# 1 THE CONTEXT

The ecclesiology of the Lutheran reformers exposes a diverse picture. The Augsburg Confession of 1530 (AC), and its author Philipp Melanchthon, applied a dialogic and irenic approach—posing the Reformation as a renewal movement within the one church. The basic "catholicity" of the AC appears more clearly perhaps in hindsight than was the case in the sixteenth century. In its basic tenets, this movement claimed to teach nothing that deviates from the universal (catholic) church. Existing controversies pertain to a limited number of practical "abuses"—most notably Eucharistic celebration under one species, so-called private masses, and the exclusion of priests' right to marry. Martin Luther was informed about and accepted, if with some reluctance, Melanchthon's "pussyfooting" (*Leisetreten*). Yet, his ecclesiology was already at an early stage strongly marked by the controversy with the papacy and became increasingly polemical. Luther also preferred a more elementary, focused, and gospel-centered vision of the church. Concerning the sacraments, the early reformers on the Lutheran wing remained basically "catholic"—not least in their insistence on the real presence. But fairly soon, proclivities towards a theology with Calvinist features challenged this position. Thus, the double front of the Lutheran Reformation was actualized. Denouncing "Papists" and "Enthusiasts" became a central component of post-Reformation ecclesiology.

When the Lutheran tradition was organized as a separate church after the peace at Augsburg (1555), three tasks surfaced as essential for the leading orthodox theologians: first, they had to settle emerging internal disputes in soteriology and ecclesiology. Second, they had to identify a position that could serve as an identity-shaping foundation—or an institutional theory—for the new body. And third, they had to formulate a juridically viable church polity, which could be adopted and practiced in Lutheran states. The *Formula of Concord* (FC) of 1577 and the subsequent publication of *The Book of Concord* in 1580 aimed at responding to these needs. FC contains no article on the church, but some deliberations on ecclesial rites (Article X). Here, ordinances which are neither commanded nor forbidden in Scripture are considered: can demands to implement such rites under any circumstances be obeyed? The answer is that this can be granted if the required practices are not in conflict with God's word and not enforced as obligatory. Accordingly, FC partly sides with Mathias Flacius's assertion that "nothing in the area of confession and scandal can be regarded as an indifferent matter." In view of the Lord's Supper, more detailed deliberations are included (Article VII). Here both the Zwinglian and the Roman positions are rejected. Mainly mere symbolism, but also transubstantiation and the sacrifice of the mass fail in expressing the proper meaning of the real presence—namely that "the body and blood of Christ are truly and essentially present [in the Holy Supper], and are truly distributed and received with the bread and wine."

In spite of these assertions, differences on adiaphora and Christ's mode of presence in the Eucharist continued. And the attempts to outline an adequate ecclesiological platform by locating a *via media* between "Papism" and "Enthusiasm" were challenged. Additionally, another discrepancy came to play an ever more important role. Already the early reformers stressed the dialectics between the *ecclesia large dicta* and the *ecclesia proprie dicta*, as well as the church's existence as a *corpus permixtum* which embraced saints and sinners. But they primarily spoke of the church as "hidden" (*verborgen*), in the sense that only God could identify its true members, and not as "invisible" in its essence. Within post-Reformation thought, this was developed into a double or dual concept of church, where the visible and invisible aspects were seen as deviating, or in some cases as mutually excluding concerns. Similarly, the dichotomy between true and false church was underscored. Thus, Lutheran ecclesiology entered the early modern era with an ambiguous understanding of the church's nature and structures. In Pietism and later currents, this ambiguity became acute.

During the initial phases of early modernity, the general ecclesial setting was marked by divisions, the birth of new churches and battles against "heretics." Most of the "heretics" were schismatics, but some broke with the fundamentals of faith—as in the non-Trinitarian position of sixteenth-century Socinianism and its followers. Wars were in large part caused by religion. After the peace of Augsburg, Lutheranism went through a process of massive confessionalization. The theology of Lutheran orthodoxy exposed a strong proclivity towards controversy and polemics, perpetuating the double front of the reformers. Within the Catholic Church, a similar development took place. The Council of Trent's bid for renewal (1545–63) was to a notable degree attached to the launching of doctrines contrary to the legacy of the Reformation. Thus, even Catholicity became confessionalized. At first, such attitudes were actively promoted by national sovereigns, regarding them as a consolidating impulse. But after the peace of Westphalia (1648), which implied that different churches had to live side-by-side within the same territories, confessionalism was increasingly felt as a political problem. In the wake of Pietism, a less confessionalist approach to faith was favored. This trend was vigorously supported by Enlightenment philosophy and theology. While Catholicism retained its confessionalized profile, a Protestantism that was *Evangelisch* rather than Reformed and Lutheran grew forth. This pointed towards the ecclesial unionism which entered the stage, especially in German nations, during the latter part of the eighteenth and nineteenth centuries. All these factors had a decisive influence on ecclesiology.

The broader philosophical, cultural, and political context had significant ecclesiological implications, too. This was the case regarding a series of revolutions in the comprehension of knowledge and its acquirement. The process started with Cartesian skeptical rationalism. Gradually, this position was contested and eventually surpassed by Lockean empiricism. Then, at the end of the epoch, Kantian criticism introduced a synthesis that became highly influential within Protestantism. Consequentially, non-ontological and antimetaphysical attitudes became dominant. This development was based on a new worldview, as explored by Galileo and Bruno, Kepler and Newton. In art, the baroque provided vital impulses in church life throughout the seventeenth century. Aiming at celebrating the glory of God and regaining the church's hegemony, it gradually assumed pompous and almost suffocating forms—especially in church architecture and visual arts, and primarily on the Catholic side. Among Lutherans, the baroque contributed strongly to renewal of church music and worship life—with J. S. Bach, Schütz and Buxtehude as key figures. During the next century, there were sequels of rococo style, neo-classicism, and finally romanticism. The last also inspired theological reflection. Within the political realm, central powers like the Holy Roman Empire and the papacy were challenged by surging nationalism. Furthermore, feudal absolutism was defied by a new awareness of the individual person. The Thirty Years' War was the most important event during the early modern era in Europe. It was largely fought on Imperial soil, with disastrous consequences. In addition to desperate need and misery, it brought about a decline in moral consciousness. After the war, religion and the churches came to play less central roles in the continental European public sphere. All these factors had a bearing on church life, and thus on ecclesiology. In this field, there was a shift from ontologically grounded doctrines to a more practice-oriented and "contextual" approach. Enlightenment theology, in particular, realized that this shift could not be reversed.

## 2 The Currents

As already pointed out, the three dominant currents of early modern Lutheranism were orthodoxy, Pietism, and theology anchored in the ideals of the Enlightenment. Basically, these trends are clearly diverging: orthodoxy was objectivizing through its emphasis on a divinely inspired Bible and formalized doctrine; classical Pietism was personalizing through its consistent focus on the individual faithful and her/his pious life; Enlightenment theology was rationalizing by its appeal to reason and nature. Yet, the present currents were also to some extent overlapping—not only chronologically, but also in content. While a majority of Pietists came from an orthodox theological background and often stuck to this position, both Enlightenment proponents and Pietists exposed strong individualizing proclivities.

Within Lutheran orthodoxy, one normally distinguishes between early orthodoxy (approx. 1550 to 1600), high orthodoxy (1600 to 1685), and late or reform orthodoxy

(1685 to approx. 1730). Ecclesiologically speaking, this distinction is of less relevance. Due to the stress on doctrine, academic theologians had enormous influence on church life throughout this period. Among these were Martin Chemnitz (1522–86), Johann Gerhard (1582–1637), Abraham Calov (1612–86), Johannes Andreas Quenstedt (1617–88), and David Hollaz (1648–1713). Wittenberg University played a key role in fighting internal and external heresies.

In view of the location and framework of ecclesiology, Quenstedt's differentiation between "principles" and "means" must be taken into account. The church and its sacraments were placed among the means. Thus, the doctrine on the church was to a notable degree instrumentalized. Hollaz' distinction between *ecclesia repraesentiva seu coetus doctorum*, in practice the church leadership, and *ecclesia synthetica*, the church as a whole, contributed to defining the scope of ecclesiological deliberations. Within the *ecclesia synthetica*, visible and invisible aspects were kept together. Yet, orthodox ecclesiology was primarily concerned with the visible manifestations and structures of the church. This was underpinned by a transferal of Luther's teaching on the three "estates" or "hierarchies" of human existence—the state and temporal government, family and married life, and the church with its *Amt*—to the ecclesiological realm. However, just as the concept of the three estates had static and hierarchical implications within social ethics, it provided space for an equally static approach to the church. Additionally, the confession of faith and church polity, as well as public judicial systems, were closely connected in orthodox theology—articles of faith (*Glaubenssätze*) functioned as statutes (*Rechtssätze*). The ensuing "politicized" ecclesiology aimed at maintaining the territorial unity of the Lutheran congregations and states. Under this system, the newly founded church was ruled by nobility and princes, who exercised wide-ranging episcopal powers, assisted by theologians in doctrinal matters. Thus, bonds between church and state strengthened.

In orthodox ecclesiology, the church is mainly understood as a teaching body or as the guardian of true doctrine. This charge was accomplished through a meticulous system of theological *loci* and lengthy sermons that the faithful were expected to conform to. Yet, the church's teaching obligation was not anchored in a dynamic concept of tradition, but solely in the word of God. And this word was in practice identified with the Bible, which was understood as divinely inspired in all details through dictation by the Holy Spirit. Both the word and the Bible were treated as complete and ever valid as such; the church played no active role here. Its task in securing correct interpretation was based on and bound to norms taken from Scripture itself. In this connection, it served solely as a passive instrument or a channel in mediating the word. Accordingly, the orthodox reception of Luther's insistence that the church is *creatura verbi*, an entity which is created and caused by God's word, was of a rather static kind. The resulting ecclesiological model was shaped in the mold of the double front of the reformers. It was directed chiefly against the "Papists," who according to the orthodox view put themselves above God's word, as well as Trent's insistence on the "insufficiency" of the Bible. But it also implied a critical distance over against the "Enthusiasts" and their "spiritual" or immediate reading of Scripture.

Johann Gerhard was a firm advocate of this position, stressing the church's uncondi-tional submission to the word. In his instructions to future pastors in *Loci Theologici*, he affirmed that

> We believe the canonical Scriptures because they are the canonical Scriptures, that is, because they have been brought about by God and written by direct inspiration of the Holy Spirit. And we do not believe them because the church testifies concerning them ... The canonical books are the source of faith. From this source the church itself and all its authority must be proved. One believes in a principium because of itself, not because of something else.... We must choose one of two alterna-tives: either the church or Scripture is the source of our faith and religion. We believe the church insofar as it agrees with Scripture ...; we do not believe in Scripture because of the church, that is, the testimony of men, but because of itself, because it is the voice of God. (Preus 1970, 305)

In practice, however, the constantly expanding orthodox dogmatics went far beyond the scriptural foundation. And academic theologians assumed the role of sovereign bishops.

The emphasis on confessional controversy in the ecclesiology of orthodox Lutheranism led to a largely "negative" approach to and understanding of the church. One might suggest that quite a few orthodox theologians had a better grip on what the church is *not* than what it is and has to offer in a positive sense. However, Georg Calixt (1586–1656) chose an entirely different path. He served as professor at the University of Helmstedt, where impulses from irenic Melanchthonian humanism were intact. His chief concern was to join the mutually combative ecclesial tradi-tions. For this purpose, he identified a set of "fundamental articles" which could serve as foundation of church unity. Such unity could be realized along two lines— a synchronous *consensus universalis* and a *consensus antiquitatis* that was anchored in the Old Church. Since Calixt declined to recognize the Formula of Concord, he was passionately attacked by orthodox theologians for his "syncretism"—not least by the Wittenberger Abraham Calov (Wallmann 1961). Yet his plan for church reunion, though unfulfilled, gained sympathy among political rulers. Calixt became one of the first precursors of the Protestant Prussian union of the early nineteenth century, and similar proposals. His focus on "fundamental articles" has played an important role in modern ecumenism.

In the sacramental theology of orthodox Lutheranism, two concerns remained cen-tral: first, deliberations on Christ's mode of presence in the Lord's Supper were contin-ued. Here the Christologically based *communicatio idiomatum*, an exchange between Christ's divine and human attributes, was elaborated in great detail—and in stark contrast to Zwinglian and Calvinist positions. Moreover, the polemics against the Roman Catholic insistence on transubstantiation were kept up and intensified. Second, Lutherans insisted in their confessional documents that baptism was permanent, the doorway to God's grace and the initiation into the Church. These teachings were directed against Anabaptist practices. Apart from this, it may seem as if the sacraments were more or less taken for granted and not in need of further theological explication. The ordained ministry was charged with the correct preaching of the Gospel and the proper administration of the sacraments. The pastor was depicted as a protector of established doctrine and a civil servant rather than a caring shepherd. Personal piety was measured by doctrinal purity. Such purity was in many cases bolstered through coercion by temporal authorities. Toward the end of the period, the need for renewal was evident.

Orthodox Lutheran ecclesiology did not bring much that took it beyond the Formula of Concord. It reflects a heavy stress on the church as a confessing and teaching entity. This is an important aspect of ecclesial life; however, an awareness of what the church is and gives in a positive sense, as outlined in Luther's writings and Augustana, was lacking here.

Responding to the requirement of renewal, not least with a view to the situation of the laity, was the main goal of the Pietist movement. This movement flourished within the Lutheran Church from approximately 1670 onward. While classical Pietism faded around the beginning of the nineteenth century, several of its tenets were continued by the Evangelical awakenings and their neo-Pietism. The mysticism of Johann Arndt (1555–1621) and his six books on "true Christianity" was an important source of inspiration. Among the most significant theologians of Lutheran Pietism, we find Philipp Jakob Spener (1635–1705), August Herrmann Francke (1663–1727) and Johann Albrecht Bengel (1687–1752). Halle, where the newly founded university adopted a Pietist profile, and Württemberg became its main centers. Nicolaus Zinzendorf (1700–60) was also influential among Lutherans. Contrary to late orthodoxy, Pietism appealed strongly to the faithful. It was more ecumenically open and had a "radical" wing where elements from the radical Reformation lived on (Wallmann 1987; Obst 2002; Breul, Meyer, and Vogel 2010; Schneider 2010, 15–36).

Traditional ecclesiology was a marginal topic among Pietists; their concern for structured institutions and outward means of grace was limited. This depended partly on orthodox excesses, but chiefly on the core of pietistic theology. Here everything that was crucial to the appropriation of salvation was located on the personal level. This process occurred within a meeting between God and the individual faithful, and there was neither space nor need for intermediating bodies. Thus, the institutionalized church was at best regarded as a practical framework, at worst as an impediment in attaining authentic faith. This view was substantiated through a stressing of personal regeneration, a detailed and obligatory *ordo salutis*, and early experience theology. Factors like these developed into an anthropologized substitute for ecclesial life. Instead of the visible body, Pietism emphasized the *ecclesiola in ecclesia*—the little church within the church, or the community of genuine believers. It took shape in a number of independent *collegiae pietatis* that were grounded in a common sensation of salvation and a shared devotional life. The *ecclesiola* was perceptible as fellowship, but invisible in terms of formal structures. Visible manifestations of the church were treated as secondary to the largely invisible nature of the "little" church. Francke placed the "merely baptized" in the outward church, and the truly faithful in the inner "spiritual" church.

As a consequence of this, the foundation of the first Lutheran state or folk churches was severely shaken. Furthermore, Pietists saw God's word as an effective means of grace. But it had to be received through a personal faith that was accompanied by true Christian life. It was also ranked above the discernible sacraments. Even if a central role was attributed to baptism, rebirth was often detached from it. And any suggestion that the Lord's Supper had an "automatic" impact on man's relationship to God was denounced.

Some of the most explicit pietistic contributions to ecclesiology can be found in its church criticism. Such critical utterances were central in the theology of Spener and his influential book *Pia desideria* (1675), in which a broadly conceived ecclesial renewal was argued. Spener's criticism was aimed at the idea of church, as well as the factually existing Lutheran institution. These were the main points of his reform scheme: (i) encouragement of Bible study within the "pious societies"; (ii) space for the laity in church leadership; (iii) the need to combine knowledge of doctrine with practical Christian life; (iv) a moderation of confessional polemics; (v) renewal of theological training with a focus on *praxis pietatis*; and (vi) a new preaching style that centered on the edification of the soul. Despite its tempered form and the fact that it called for few concrete changes, Spener's program was met with fierce orthodox opposition—partly for doctrinal reasons, and partly since the pietistic conventicles threatened the existing church's order. However, it was received with excitement by the laity and gained increasing support among temporal rulers—not only in German lands like Saxony and Württemberg, but also in Denmark and Norway. Fairly soon, Pietism was established as the prevailing current in major parts of Lutheranism.

While elaborate ecclesiological doctrine was of secondary interest to Pietists, their stressing of Christian life and devotional practices had significant implications in the field of ecclesiology. This stress was gradually broadened. Spener's implementation of the so-called common priesthood—or, more precisely, the priesthood of baptized believers—gave the laity a new status. Francke's impressive engagement in diaconal work and missionary enterprises linked personal piety to the wider society and the world. Mission was conceived as a means of transforming the world through transforming humanity. The famous Halle orphanage became a model in responding to the needs of deprived people. The successful pedagogical and catechetical efforts of Francke and other Pietists also had a huge impact in civil society. The culturally open "educated Pietism" of the nobility and the ever more influential bourgeoisie pointed in a similar direction. Moreover, Zinzendorf placed personal faith within the context of communal life in the Herrnhut colony—in accordance with the principle "no Christianity apart from community" and by encouraging *Philadelphia* instead of sectarianism. This entailed a strengthening of the ecumenical commitment and scope of Pietism. All these factors contributed to an expanded and renewed approach to the church, which deviated from a more ontologically anchored preoccupation with its "nature" among Lutheran orthodox and Roman Catholic theologians. This suggests that at least some strains of classical Pietism were more ecclesiologically relevant and fruitful than often assumed.

However, the strong underscoring of personal piety resulted in a certain amount of zealotry among the devout. There were also cases of hypocrisy and subsequent public scandals. Some parts of the movement exposed a propensity toward apocalyptic speculations and chiliasm. Such speculations even occurred in the otherwise sober theology and exegesis of Bengel. And ecstatic groups came forth. Thus, one might argue that Pietists paved the way for theological rationalism along two lines: positively by their emphasis on the individual human being, and negatively by an inclination towards irrational fanaticism.

The ecclesiological implications of Pietism prompted a new attentiveness to personal faith and Christian life. In this way, a formalized and overobjectivized ecclesiology was adjusted. Yet, pietistic ecclesiology emerges as pragmatic to the point of pure functionalism. Accordingly, an awareness of the significance of the church in itself, beyond the level of pure means and beyond serving solely as a practical framework of personal faith, vanished.

Enlightenment theology grew in the wake of the European *Aufklärung*, parallel to the new biblical scholarship and historical-critical exegesis. It culminated between 1750 and 1800, coinciding with the early phase of modernity. Its proponents appealed to critical human reason, but also to the order of nature—thus anticipating the Kantian combination of rationalism and empiricism. They considered ethics to be far more important than dogma. Their rationality could be speculative, but also practical— aiming at helping believers to understand what they believed in. Enlightenment theologians often joined personal piety with "radical" tenets—Christ was depicted as a moral teacher, God as an impersonal source of love and reason. The current comprised moderate strands like suprarationalism, theological Wolffianism (anchored in Christian Wolff's philosophy), and neology, together with pure deism and extreme rationalism. It was broadly Protestant and never specifically Lutheran. Its influence within the Lutheran Church was limited, and it was passionately denounced by the "old Lutheranism." Some of its adherents started out as Lutherans—for example, Johann Christoph Edelmann (1698–1767), Siegmund Jakob Baumgarten (1706–57), and Johann Salomo Semler (1725–91). Yet their Reformation identity tended to vanish. In Semler's case, Lutheranism was a part of his "private religion," but not of his public service as a doctor of theology. Several of the philosophers who contributed substantially to the Enlightenment—such as Gottfried Wilhelm Leibniz (1646–1716), Christian Wolff (1679–1754), Immanuel Kant (1724–1804), and Johann Gottfried Herder (1744–1803)—came from a Lutheran background. Not least thanks to Leibniz and Wolff, the German Enlightenment ended up as far more open to religion than its militant counterpart in France.

Chiefly due to fierce opposition from conservative Christian groups and romanticism, Enlightenment theology has often been caricatured beyond recognition. These caricatures still linger and should be adjusted. As part of the broader European *Aufklärung*, rational theology contributed in providing a basis for essential values like care for the individual person, tolerance, and freedom of thought. It helped to cleanse religion from superstition. It was a source of inspiration to academic theologians and scholarship. And it promoted a sense of unity in Protestant circles. Admittedly, there is an ambiguity—or *Dialektik*—to the Enlightenment, which suggests that it was not always capable of transforming its ideals into realities. Theodor Adorno and Max Horkheimer saw its "myth" as a premonition of attitudes that unfolded in the totalitarian movements of the twentieth century and in popular "culture industry" (Adorno and Horkheimer 1997). But this current did bring about significant improvements in peoples' lives. Moreover, the mentioned "dialectics" does not apply so much to the theology of the period. Generally, Enlightenment impulses prepared the involved churches for an open encounter with emerging modernity, in stark contrast to the Catholic "anti-modernism" of the nineteenth and early twentieth centuries.

However, ecclesiology was an even more marginal topic within Enlightenment theology than in Pietism. While its contributions in the field of creation and the first article of faith are numerous, its ecclesiological implications were at best of a more indirect kind—or in quite a few cases factually nonexistent. The reasons are similar to the pietistic neglect, though of a less "pious" and more "secular" nature: (i) a personalized understanding of man's relationship with God; (ii) limited sense for the communal or collective dimension of religious life; (iii) a preference for the invisible church, the visible institution was regarded as superfluous or directly counterproductive to sensible religiosity; (iv) disregard of outward means of grace together with a perception of the sacraments that came close to mere symbolism; and (v) a concept of religion that was more abstract and intangible than the current approach to religious life. These factors were often fused with harsh church criticism, in which common creeds and organized Christian life were seen as inferior or outdated. When confessional neo-Lutheranism grew in the wake of the Reformation anniversary of 1817, the most important argument against theological rationalism and surging neo-Protestantism was their deficiency in ecclesiology and sacramental theology.

Semler started out as a pietistically inclined Lutheran. Via impulses from Reformation humanism, he changed his position and ended up as a leading figure in neology. This shift was partly caused by familiarity with the ferocious campaign against Wolff, which was orchestrated at the University of Halle at an earlier stage. Even if Semler's scholarship was impressively wide, his contributions to biblical research are most vital. Here he distinguished between legalistic Judaic Christianity and the liberating sentiments of the Pauline school. Thus the New Testament exemplified doctrinal pluralism and not unity. The later differentiation between the Kingdom of God, being at the core of Jesus' preaching, and the church, was also hinted at in his writings. Semler's study of the canon process led to the conclusion that it was historically conditioned rather than governed by the church. His position provoked intense debates far beyond the confines of theology. Even Goethe alluded to the controversies in *Die Leiden des jungen Werther* (1774)—ironically distancing himself from the fashionable moral-critical new reformation of Christianity. Later on, however, the great romantic ended up supporting an historical-critical reading of Scripture.

In his systematic work, Semler drew a sharp line between "religion" and "theology." This was accompanied by a focus on "private religion" and the freedom it grants. He opposed enforced adherence to a doctrinal standard prescribed by the church, as in orthodoxy, and an equally standardized devotional pattern, as in Pietism. This did not mean that all forms of institutionalized Christian life were rejected. But he insisted that the liberating potential of true religion was incompatible with ecclesial authoritarianism. Moreover, he was critical of the Catholic Church and argued that Catholicism and Protestantism could not be reconciled. Generally, Semler claimed that the principal task of the church was to secure space for personal religion and protect it against irrational deadlocks. Apart from this, he saw little need for visible ecclesial institutions. His strong emphasis on the historical and moral aspects of the Christian religion was accompanied by a disregard of its ecclesial and sacramental forms. Seen in retrospect, some suggest that Semler—in his failure to realize that Christian life is attached to an actual worshipping community—contributed to a marginalization of ecclesiology and sacramental theology (Kantzenbach 1965, 225f).

Despite modest interest among theologians, two of the most eminent Enlightenment philosophers reflected on the church. In *Demonstrationes Catholicae* from the late 1660s and early 1670s, Leibniz sketched his grand project of church reunification. The united church would include Roman Catholics, Protestants, and Eastern Orthodox. It would be governed through papal primacy and had the Augsburg Confession as its doctrinal foundation. Leibniz developed detailed plans for the realization of the project. And he placed it within the larger framework of humanity, predicting that a unified church would contribute to a common culture, widely shared values, and prevention of wars. These ideas had a certain similarity with Calixt's proposal and became an inspiration to later unification initiatives.

Due to his experiences of pietistic pressure, Kant adopted a critical distance to the institutionalized church, binding dogmas, and predefined piety patterns. This attitude was also based on his perception of religion: an historical faith (*historischer Glaube*) grounded in revelation is accidental; a doctrinally-juridically based church faith (*statuarischer Kirchenglaube*) is insufficient; true faith is morally and not dogmatically anchored. The ecclesiological implications of these tenets are unfolded in *Die Religion innerhalb der Grenzen der blossen Vernunft* (1793). According to Kant, the church has—or should have—a moral focus. He described it as "an ethical communal entity" (*ein ethisches gemeines Wesen*) and "a people of God under ethical laws," which aims at establishing the moral reign of God on earth. The church must be grounded in rational religion, because only such an approach—as opposed to an historical faith—can be communicated to everybody, and thus grants its universality: "*Der reine Religionsglaube ist zwar der, welcher allein eine allgemeine Kirche gründen kann; weil er ein blosser Vernunftglaube ist, der sich jedermann zur Überzeugung mitteilen lässt . . .* " (*Die Religion innerhalb der Grenzen der blossen Vernunft*, 5:762). Even if these ideals partly can be accomplished within visible institutions, Kant opts for a chiefly invisible and individualized church—or "a voluntary union of the heart" (*eine freiwillige Herzensvereinigung*) that is free of compulsory doctrine. While parts of Enlightenment theology rationalized the Christian faith, it can be argued that Kant replaced faith by a common rationalized religion. His deliberations on the church were controversial, but they had a huge influence on neo-Protestantism. (Anderson and Bell 2010, Wood 2009, and ch. 38 in this volume.)

In terms of material ecclesiology, Enlightenment theology is of limited relevance. And the sacraments play a minimal role here. However, this theology was produced in a situation where churches and Christian faith had become far less influential. Many of its adherents realized that the new situation in philosophy, culture, and politics demanded new ways of doing theology. This insight was also valid and partly applied in their ecclesiological reflections. Most importantly, an awareness grew that all attempts to offer sustainable visions of the church had to take the wider society and world into account. Accordingly, metaphysically based ecclesiologies and ecclesiocentric positions were abandoned. Even if the contributions of Enlightenment theologians in this field may appear as outdated in their specific contents, the principle remains: no ecclesiology without contextuality.

# 3 OUTCOME AND OUTLOOK

In regard to the further consequences and results of the ecclesiological reflections that surfaced within early modern Lutheranism, I shall limit myself to five brief observations:

1. After Kant, a new space or *Sitz im Leben* for faith was sought. Here Friedrich Schleiermacher (1768–1834), with his romantically inspired synthesis of Pietism and Enlightenment impulses, became the prominent figure. According to Schleiermacher, religion was an end in itself and not a pure means. He described faith as *Gefühl*, more precisely as an intuitive consciousness of the self and a feeling of absolute dependence which is universally present in humanity. The church grows out of this concept of faith, emerging as a *creatura fidei*. It comes into being when Christ draws the faithful into his perfectly realized awareness of God. In uniting the regenerated in a common life, it is primarily invisible; as a fellowship of all who have been subjected to preliminary effects of grace, it adopts a visible form. Schleiermacher was also concerned with the social and public role of the church, and its task as an instrument in permeating human culture with the spirit of Christ. Such ideas were essential in Prussian church unionism—where he exercised huge influence, the idealistic-Hegelian "cultural Protestantism" and the wider flow of neo-Protestantism. However, "Old Lutherans" as well as nineteenth-century neo-Lutheranism, with leading figures like Kliefoth, Stahl, and Vilmar, denounced the Prussian union and Friedrich Schleiermacher's theology—not least due to alleged ecclesiological deficits.
2. During the early modern era, a gradual movement away from original or authentic Reformation ecclesiology as expressed in the Augsburg Confession and Luther's writings can be discerned. Both Pietism and Enlightenment theology became broadly Protestant or *Evangelisch*. But also the otherwise staunchly

Lutheran orthodoxy, with its stress on the teaching church, reflects a deviation in its ecclesiological approach. The tension between these currents continues in post-Reformation ecclesiologies. Some of them adhere to a sort of "liberal-Pietism"; others are doctrinally and denominationally focused. It can be questioned, however, if any of these currents have succeeded in revitalizing the ecclesiology of the AC and the Lutheran reformers.

3. All the central currents of early modern Lutheranism have something to offer in an ecclesiological perspective. Orthodox theologians underscored the crucial role of Scripture, creeds, and confessional identity. Pietism fostered alertness to the centrality of Christian life and practical devotion. Enlightenment theology and philosophy assisted the church in its response to new paradigms in thought and ethics, culture and ideology. Especially the latter current was conscious of the requirements of a drastically changing situation in which the churches had become increasingly marginalized. Since the breakthrough of modernity, there has been a growing acknowledgement that viable ecclesiologies must be nonontological, contextual, and directed at the realities of factually existing churches.

4. Yet the dual concept of church was a notable problem in early modern Lutheran ecclesiology. While the relationship between visibility and invisibility was understood in terms of a dialectical interchange by the reformers, the subsequent currents developed a bias here—orthodoxy in favor of aspects of the outward institution, Pietism and Enlightenment theology prioritizing a spiritual or inner community of individuals. Obviously, the church exists on both these levels. But they must be kept together through a mutual perspective that prevents ecclesiological dualism. Such a perspective was largely lacking in early modernity, and is often absent today as well.

5. The church is a *complexio oppositorum*, in the sense that it embraces and unifies factors that are frequently understood as conflicting. This is a key point in the ecclesiology of *communio*, in its past and present versions. Here the visible and invisible aspects of the church are kept together. As a vertical communion which encompasses our participation in Trinitarian life, it predominantly exists beyond empirical perception. Yet, it becomes visibly shaped on the horizontal level as an inclusive human community—a community that is called to serve as the priest of all creation. And these two dimensions of the church belong indissolubly together. Thus seen, the *communio* model teaches us something that is essential to ecclesiology—that is, to abstain from tearing apart things joined by God. This is a challenge to previous and contemporary visions of the church (Tjørhom 2010).

Early modern ecclesiologies mirror a shift from doctrinal and institutional consolidation to individually and rationally motivated innovation. Surely, the growing commitment to reflect ecclesiologically in line with changing contexts and in dialogue with new paradigms in philosophy and theology must be welcomed. Enlightenment theologians realized that substantial developments in these areas could not be reversed. However, a proclivity toward abstraction emerged here. This also had damaging repercussions in sacramental theology. Since the latter stages of early modernity, there has been a need to leave falsely spiritualized concepts behind and regain an awareness of the church's existence as an entity that is constituted by outwardly visible marks, in keeping with Article VII of the Augsburg Confession. This body can in some respects be "hidden," but not entirely invisible. Without such an awareness, there is a danger that the church will degenerate into a mere idea.

## BIBLIOGRAPHY

Adorno, Theodor W., and Max Horkheimer. 1997. *Dialectic of Enlightenment.* London: Verso Books.

Anderson, Pamela S., and Bell, Jordan. 2010. *Kant and Theology.* London: T&T Clark Continuum.

Anselm, Reiner. 2000. *Ekklesiologie als kontextuelle Dogmatik: das lutherische Kirchenverständnis im Zeitalter des Konfessionalismus und seine Rezeption im 19. und 20. Jahrhundert.* Göttingen: Vandenhoeck & Ruprecht.

Beutel, Albrecht. 2009. *Kirchengeschichte im Zeitalter der Aufklärung: ein Kompendium.* Göttingen: Vandenhoeck & Ruprecht.

Breul, Wolfgang, Marcus Meier, and Lothar Vogel, eds. 2010. *Der Radikale Pietismus: Zwischenbilanz und Perspektiven der Forschung.* Göttingen: Vandenhoeck & Ruprecht.

Byrne, James M. 1997. *Religion and the Enlightenment: From Descartes to Kant.* Louisville, KY: Westminster John Knox Press.

Diestelmann, Jürgen. 1996. *Actio Sacramentalis: die Verwaltung des heiligen Abendmahles nach den Prinzipien Martin Luthers in der Zeit zur Konkordienformel.* Gross Oesingen: Verlagshaus Harms.

Gericke, Wolfgang. 1989. *Theologie und Kirche im Zeitalter der Aufklärung: Kirchengeschichte in Einzeldarstellungen,* Bd. III/2. Berlin: Evangelische Verlagsanstalt.

Greschat, Martin, ed. 1982. *Orthodoxie und Pietismus: Gestalten der Kirchengeschichte,* Bd. 7. Stuttgart: Kohlhammer.

Greschat, Martin, ed. 1983. *Die Aufklärung: Gestalten der Kirchengeschichte,* Bd. 8. Stuttgart: Kohlhammer.

Heckel, Martin. 2001. *Deutschland im konfessionellen Zeitalter: Deutsche Geschichte.* Vol. 5. Göttingen: Vandenhoeck & Ruprecht, neue Taschenbuchauflage.

Kantzenbach, Friedrich W. 1966. *Orthodoxie und Pietismus.* Gütersloh: Gerd Mohn.

Kantzenbach, Friedrich W. 1965. *Protestantisches Christentum im Zeitalter der Aufklährung.* Gütersloh: Gerd Mohn.

Obst, Helmut. 2002. *August Hermann Francke und die Frannckeschen Stiftungen in Halle.* Göttingen: Vandenhoeck & Ruprecht.

Preus, Robert D. 1970. *The Theology of Post-Reformation Lutheranism.* Vol. 1. St. Louis, MO: Concordia.

Scheible, Heinz. 1997. *Melanchthon: eine Biographie.* München: C. H. Beck.

Schneider, Hans. 2010. "Understanding the Church: Issues of Pietist Ecclesiology." In *Pietism and Community in Europe and North America, 1650–1750,* edited by Jonathan Strom. Leiden: Brill.

Schorn-Schütte, Luise. 2009. *Geschichte Europas in der frühen Neuzeit: Studienhandbuch 1500–1789.* Stuttgart: Schönigh.

Tjørhom, Ola. 2010. "The Ecclesiology of Communion: On the Church as a Vertically Organized, Socially Directed and Ecumenically Committed Fellowship." *The Heythrop Journal* 51 (5): 893ff.

Wallmann, Johannes. 1987. "Geistliche Erneuerung der Kirche nach Philipp Jakob Spener." In *Pietismus und Neuzeit: ein Jahrbuch zur Geschichte des neueren Protestantismus*. Vol. 12. Göttingen: Vandenhoeck & Ruprecht.

Wallmann, Johannes. 2012. *Kirchengeschichte Deutschlands seit der Reformation*. Tübingen: Mohr Siebeck.

Wallmann, Johannes. 2005. *Der Pietismus: ein Handbuch*. Göttingen: Vandenhoeck & Ruprecht.

Wallmann, Johannes. 1961. *Der Theologiebegriff bei Johann Gerhard und Georg Calixt*. Tübingen: Mohr Siebeck.

Wiesner-Hanks, Merry E. 2006. *Early Modern Europe: 1450–1789*. Cambridge: Cambridge University Press.

Wood, Allan W. 2009. *Kant's Moral Religion*. Ithaca, NY: Cornell University Press.

# CHAPTER 23

# SACRAMENTS IN LUTHERANISM, 1600–1800

## JOHN R. STEPHENSON

WITH respect to the doctrine and practice of the "sacraments," historic Lutheranism's middle way between Rome and Geneva may appear to the outside observer as a crooked path rather than a straight road. While rejecting Trent's listing of no fewer than seven sacraments, many erudite Lutheran theologians of our period would give only qualified approval to the Reformed reduction of the number of sacraments to no more than two. Though it did not perfectly fit the conventional Lutheran definition of sacrament, confession and absolution remained a major feature of Lutheran teaching and observance until the closing decades of the eighteenth century, and was acknowledged to share common features with baptism and Eucharist. We must therefore begin by justifying its inclusion in this account.

## 1 DEFINITIONAL DISSONANCE

Luther himself saw to it that "sacrament" is a curve ball when thrown at those who think in the way of the Book of Concord of 1580. As with other technical terms, he tweaked historic churchly vocabulary here too, suggesting in 1520 that one consider Christ the one sacrament (1 Tim 3:16); with baptism, Eucharist, and penance as the three corresponding sacramental signs (AE 36:18). Yet by the end of the same treatise, he doubted penance's inclusion in the list, since the Lord attached no external sign to the administration of absolution (AE 36:124). But absolution resurfaced in the Large Catechism as the "third sacrament" (LC V, 74), and the elderly Reformer's last word on the matter was that, "We gladly confess penance to be a sacrament with the power of the keys to absolve, for on account of Christ it has the promise and faith of the remission of sins" (AE 34:356).

In fact, "Concordia" Lutherans were free to include between two and four ceremonies under one conceptual umbrella. If "sacrament" means a rite instituted by Christ that conveys grace (specifically the forgiveness of sins), Melanchthon's Apology defines not only baptism and Holy Communion but also "penance" (i.e., absolution) as sacraments in the strict sense (AP XIII, 4), and the same article finds a rationale for labeling ordination a sacrament also (AP XIII, 11). Although Luther did not speak of ordination this way, he insisted that "the imposition of hands is not a tradition of men, but God makes and ordains ministers" (AE 5:249). But if a sacrament requires a physical element along the lines of baptismal water and Eucharistic bread and wine, absolution is not a sacrament. Moreover, if explicit dominical institution is a necessary component of a sacrament, ordination does not belong in this category; besides, it does not convey the forgiveness of sins.

Tellingly, the Lutheran confessions contain no separate article on the sacraments, considered generically. Instead, they focus on particular rites instituted by Christ that may or may not be subsumed under the rubric of "sacrament." When the Orthodox dogmaticians of the seventeenth century wrote under this precise heading, they restricted the term to baptism and Eucharist in the strict sense, while admitting that this nomenclature may be applied more widely to embrace other rites also. As David Hollaz's (1646–1713) definition largely overlapped with that of John Gerhard (1582–1637), both zeroed in on the concurrence of divine institution, outward element, and promise of grace (Hollaz 1741, 1041; Schmid 1961, 523). At the 1586 colloquy of Montbéliard between the Reformed Theodore Beza (1519–1605) and the Lutherans Jacob Andreae (1528–90) and Lukas Osiander (1534–1604), the latter highlighted the common features of baptism and Eucharist by arguing that these two sacraments contained both an earthly and a heavenly material (Schmid 1961, 526f; Raitt 1993; Hollaz 1741, 1041). In the case of Holy Communion the *materia coelestis* united with the consecrated bread and wine was obviously Christ's body and blood, but it proved more difficult to specify the "heavenly matter" connected with baptismal water. John Andrew Quenstedt (1617–88) was typical of the later dogmaticians in seeing no contradiction in asserting that the whole Blessed Trinity, the Holy Spirit, and the blood of Christ respectively could rightfully be considered the *materia coelestis* of baptism (Schmid 1961, 540). No corresponding *materia coelestis* lurked within the confines of absolution.

A visitor to St. Thomas, Leipzig, around 1680 would have heard second pastor and soon-to-be Hebrew professor August Pfeiffer (1640–98) insisting, on the basis of John 20:23, that Jesus established pastoral absolution in the upper room on the evening of the first Easter day (Pfeiffer 1685, 613). Pfeiffer's sermon series on the Augsburg Confession is valuable in offering a folksy vernacular overview of the whole range of late Lutheran orthodox dogmatics. Serving in a different capacity in the same location a couple of generations later, cantor J. S. Bach (1685–1750) professed Pfeiffer's doctrine as he sought out successive pastors to hear his confession and impart the Lord's forgiveness to him (Stiller 1984, 203f). Whether or not absolution fell into the formal category of sacrament, its practice enjoyed the status of a sacrament until Pietism began to change Lutheranism from the inside. In his homily on AC XIII, Pfeiffer explicitly acknowledged absolution's sacramental status, and he was prepared to label the laying on of hands a sacrament also, on condition that one understood the ministry evangelically, not in terms of the Roman sacrificing priesthood (Pfeiffer 1685, 741, 742). Gerhard, too, admitted the legitimacy of this nomenclature with respect to ordination, in which "the gifts of the Holy Ghost, necessary for the discharge of the duties of the ministry of the Church, are conferred and increased" (Schmid 1961, 610f).

"How many sacraments are there?" is thus an awkward question when posed from the angle of the Lutheran confessions. Change the terminology to "means of salvation" (*media salutis*), a term favored throughout the orthodox epoch, or "means of grace" (*Gnadenmittel*), an expression that came into vogue sometime in the seventeenth century (Pfeiffer 1685, 617 et passim) and dominated thereafter, and one will get a crisper reply. The orthodox Lutherans built on Luther's disputes with Andrew Karlstadt (AE 40:147, 213f) and Ulrich Zwingli (AE 37:192), as compounding Latin with Greek to forge technical terms, they held forth on the *media dotika* or means through which Christ's gifts of salvation are bestowed and on faith as the *medium leeptikon*, or means by which they are received. The notion of *media dotika* governed the concept of sacrament, and not vice versa. And the faith that received the gifts encompassed the three components of knowledge (*notitia*), assent (*assensus*), and trust (*fiducia*; Schmid 1961, 410f, 414; Pfeiffer 1685, 747–808) with *fiducia* as the clinching factor that made it possible for children to appropriate salvation before reaching the age of reason.

## 2  Sources

The chief resource for ascertaining formal Lutheran sacramental doctrine during these two centuries is in the first place the scholastic-style treatises of the orthodox dogmaticians that continued to appear beyond the turn of the eighteenth century, even as their ecclesial constituency dwindled drastically in size. Indispensable as the sometimes arid and forbidding volumes of the orthodox Lutherans are to the researcher, if contemplated in isolation they could give a false impression. For one thing, actual teaching and practice in the decades of Pietist and rationalist dominance departed dramatically from the textbooks that still stood on the bookshelves (see the essay on Pietism by Lehmann and Strom in this volume). For another, the much-caricatured "dead" orthodoxy was mainly the invention of its opponents. In order to acquire an accurate picture of Concordia Lutheranism in this whole epoch, we need to supplement highly cerebral Latin disquisitions with such monuments of living piety as liturgies, hymns, sermons, accounts of worship and its attendant ceremonies, and devotional writings. Preaching to a town and gown parish, Pfeiffer quoted Hebrew, Greek, and Latin with abandon and fashionably sprinkled his discourses with French loan words, but his sermons evince a lively piety and he was clearly connecting with his listeners, with whom he waxed familiar at times.

Moreover, Leipzig's two main parishes would not have needed to feature (from 1694 and throughout most of the eighteenth century) an extra weekday Mass that could last for several hours if the clergy had bored their people rigid (Stiller 1984, 40). The *lex orandi lex credendi* principle applies with full force to Lutheranism also. In this context the striking difference between how Lutheran pastors were clad at the altar and what they did there in 1600 and 1800, respectively, illustrates the pronounced mutations in sacramental doctrine across this stretch of time.

# 3  DIVERSITY FROM THE OUTSET

To state that between the start and end of our time frame Lutheranism went through the successive but also interlocking stages of orthodoxy, Pietism, and rationalism is to tell less than the whole story.

Across much of northern Germany, in all of Scandinavia, and in other parts of Europe, Lutheranism at the beginning of the seventeenth century gave the impression of being a vigorously sacramental religion, not least with respect to the frequent and devout celebration of the Eucharist. In those glory days of Lutheran orthodoxy, some French visitors were so impressed by the "sober liturgical splendor" of a Lutheran parish in Siebenbürgen that they believed themselves to have stumbled into a Roman Catholic service until persuaded otherwise by "abuse of the pope afterward" (Macculloch 2003, 308). Since the altar retained crucifix and candles and the celebrant mostly continued to wear a chasuble and to practice traditional ceremonies, the telltale sign of the pictorial depiction of a Lutheran as opposed to Catholic Eucharist was the administration of the chalice (Schatz 2004, 30, 32, 34, 40, 56, 66, 95, 96, 99, 110, 112). These outward indications of determined sacramentalism correspond to the taunt of pastor and hymn-writer Philipp Nicolai (1556–1608) that "the Calvinistic dragon is pregnant with all the horns of Mohammedanism" (Janssen 1966, 360).

And yet there were significant external differences between the various regions of German Lutheranism even from the start of the Reformation. Württemberg in the south-west corner of the Empire immediately succumbed to Reformed style, and hence inevitably before long to Reformed substance also; its order of divine service differed little from what Zwingli established in Zurich as he followed the pattern of the non-sacramental medieval preaching service (Graff 1937, 151). Thus the Apology's assertion of the normative quality of the celebration of the Eucharist on every Sunday and festival (AP XXIV, 1) should not cause us to view our whole period through rose-colored spectacles. Although Oxford's Daniel Waterland (1683–1740) could claim in 1737 that "the Lutherans do excel other Protestants: for they have a communion every Sunday and holy day throughout the year" (Stephenson 2003, 144), even in northern Germany provision was made in the late 1520s already for the celebration of a shortened "dry" Mass when no communicants registered for the sacrament (Graff 1937, 14). In the absence of a central authority, wide diversity of practice was inevitable.

# 4  A Significant Shift Within the Orthodox Period

Lutheran orthodoxy, which stretched from the promulgation of the Book of Concord to dominate the seventeenth century and squeak into the eighteenth, was not monochrome but passed through the three distinct phases of its "golden," "high," and "silver" epochs (Preus 1970, 45f), in the third of which Pietist influence was discernible here and there. If medieval scholasticism went from the spring of the twelfth-century Renaissance through the high summer of Aquinas and Bonaventure to the fall and winter of the next two centuries, a similar process seems to have happened with Lutheran scholasticism also. "In the silver age of orthodoxy dogmatics becomes more chopped up, more rigidly arranged than formerly. An unparalleled clarity of expression is achieved but at a cost: the later 'systems' make more demanding reading" (Preus 1970, 46). As with other theological movements, development entailed decay as well as fruition. As we shall see, a fateful change in Lutheran perception of the real presence came about not long after Martin Chemnitz (1522–89) dominated the beginning of the "golden" age.

# 5  Tsunamis from Within and Without: Second Reformation, Syncretism, and Pietism

Notwithstanding its heroic struggle, Lutheran Orthodoxy proved in the long run unable to maintain the Concordia Lutheranism of 1580 that it was determined to preserve.

## 5.1  The Calvinist insurgency

The "Second Reformation" (Nischan 1994; Macculloch 2003, 343–48) that began in the second half of the sixteenth century saw leading princes convert from the unaltered Augsburg Confession to the Reformed faith, either bringing their subjects with them (e.g., in the Rhineland Palatinate and other territories) or waging a remorseless war of attrition against Lutheranism that led to its blending into a Reformed-dominated compound (e.g., most famously, in Brandenburg-Prussia). Historians routinely portray Frederick William I, the Great Elector of Brandenburg (1620–88, reigned 1640–88), as a paragon of tolerance and upholder of religious freedom (Nichols 1956, 43; Ogg 1963, 443), but David Ogg's encomium of a ruler who "did not persecute dissentients" and under whose scepter "freedom of thought was permitted" would have greatly surprised the bard of Lutheranism, Paul Gerhardt (1607–76). For the Great Elector's tolerance of

Jews and Catholics did not extend to the overwhelming Lutheran majority of his subjects, whom he forced to bend to his own religion. In 1656 he prohibited the inclusion of the Formula of Concord in the ordination vow of Lutheran pastors, and in 1662 he both forbade his subjects to attend the orthodox university of Wittenberg and held a "friendly [!] colloquy" (*amicabile colloquium*) between Lutheran and Reformed clergy in Berlin, the upshot of which resulted in a silencing of Lutheran criticism of Reformed dogma. For refusal to obey the edict of this contemporary Nebuchadnezzar, Gerhardt was ejected from the third pastorate at Saint Nicholas, Berlin, and thrust into misery at a time of multiple family bereavements. The hymn he subsequently composed confessing the real presence has only recently been rendered into English (Stephenson 2003, 1f).

## 5.2  Dilution from within

By the time the Great Elector's campaign against Concordia Lutheranism was in full swing, the Orthodox had coined the term "syncretism" to describe attempts to entice or force Lutherans into ending their separation from the Reformed; the syncretists, officially Lutheran in their confession, understandably thought of themselves as peacemakers (Walch 1730, 283), as they emphasized common ground based on the shared heritage of the three major Western confessions from the early Christian centuries, seeking especially to soften the points of difference between Lutherans and Reformed. The "syncretist controversy" pitted the theological faculties of the universities of Helmstedt and Wittenberg in general, and their principal spokesmen Georg Calixt (1586–1656) and Abraham Calov (1612–86) in particular, against each other. In the course of his extended description of this long-running battle, Jena historian Johann Georg Walch (1693–1775) focused briefly on the Landgrave of Hesse's forcing the Lutheran theologians and clergy of the university city of Rinteln into the "Cassel colloquy" of 1661, at which they were pressured into professing maximum consensus with the Reformed ministers of Marburg. Predictably, the Lutherans were obliged to accept the legitimacy of Reformed ceremonies intended to deny the real presence (i.e., the breaking of the sacramental bread) and to admit that the Reformed celebrated Holy Communion aright (Walch 1730, 287). A vigorous literary campaign spearheaded by Calov could not prevent the loss of yet another territory to Concordia Lutheranism. Although the University of Jena supported Wittenberg in its opposition to the results of the Cassel colloquy, its theologians withheld support from Calov's *Consensus repetitus* of 1655, in which Leipzig joined Wittenberg in proposing a draconian statement of the orthodox line for which they sought confessional status. There was no clear winner in the syncretistic dispute, with most sister institutions following the lead of Jena by sitting on the fence. But the trends of the times favored the so-called syncretists; the stricter Lutheranism was slowly passing from the scene, and Calov's polemical overkill may have hastened this process.

## 5.3  An internal change of direction

A good half of Walch's lengthy but racy narrative is taken up with the "Pietist controversies" (Walch 1730, 532–1024.). Philip Jacob Spener (1635–1705), the father of Pietism, was a product of orthodoxy's third phase. He early fell under significant Reformed influence through both his origins in Alsace (where Martin Bucer had left his mark) and his travels in Switzerland and France; moreover, he was influenced by the literature of English Puritanism in German translation (Schmid 2007, 29, 31; Spener 1964, 9, 11; Aland 1986, 237). In formal terms, Spener still verbally confessed the bottom line of the orthodox understanding of the means of grace in general and of the sacraments in particular (Tappert 1964, 63, 67), although his spiritual center of gravity subtly moved from the Sunday and festival divine service of word and sacrament to the extra gatherings of the pious for mutual edification (*collegia pietatis*). The major changes he set in motion arose from his shift of emphasis from the unmerited divine gifts on which Lutherans had been schooled to rely to the tendency of building assurance on the Christian's keeping of the law in its third use. As he bequeathed the view that believers should be able to pinpoint the date of a conversion experience, August Hermann Francke (1666–1727), Spener's most famous disciple and an organizational genius, drew attention away from baptism as the constituting event of Christian existence.

# 6  INDIAN SUMMER OF ORTHODOXY

Once the Second Reformation, syncretism, and Pietism had done their work and rationalism was in full swing, worship, the means of grace in general, and sacraments in particular, were understood and experienced much differently than had been the case in the heyday of Lutheran orthodoxy. Against this background, Bach's Leipzig and the contemporary Dresden of the theologian and general superintendent Valentine Ernst Loescher (1673–1749) were the homes of a localized Indian summer of Concordia Lutheranism. Karl Barth's admiring account of Löscher's controversy with the Pietists, which revolved mainly around the sacraments and means of grace, offers further grounds for questioning the notion of "dead" orthodoxy. "Löscher's standing in the Church and theology [was] that of a lost position. But in the history of theology it is not success, but the superiority of a viewpoint, that is decisive. And one certainly cannot deny that to Löscher" (Barth 1972, 141).

# 7  SPECIFIC RITES

An account of the doctrine and practice of baptism, the sacrament of the altar, absolution, and ordination summarizes the orthodox position and points out changes that occurred in the centuries under review, especially under the influence of Pietism, which did so much to mold the Lutheranism that entered the nineteenth and subsequent centuries. Although ordination was only conferred on baptized men who had enjoyed years of reception of absolution and Holy Communion, we deal with it first, since the ordained were the ordinary ministers of baptism and absolution and the sole ministers of the Eucharist.

## 7.1  Ordination and the role of clergy within the "ecclesiastical order"

A main concern of the Augsburg Confession focused on refuting John Eck's (1486–1543) claim that the Lutherans allowed laymen to function in a clerical capacity. Accordingly, the orthodox followed AC V and XIV by distinguishing sharply between the royal priesthood of the baptized and the ordained ministry. The boundaries between the two only began to blur significantly a couple of decades after Spener launched the Pietist movement with his *Pia Desideria* of 1675. Following Luther (AE 37:364), the orthodox dogmaticians distinguished three "orders" or "estates" in the church, describing holders of the office of the ministry as the "ecclesiastical order," ruling princes as the "political order," and the family-based laity as the "domestic order" (Schmid 1961, 605–16). There was agreement with Chemnitz that God called men into the *Predigtamt* (preaching office) through the united action of the three estates (Chemnitz 1981, 35). Public conferral of the office happened through ordination, which Hollaz described as "ordinately" but not "absolutely" necessary. By this he meant that a called man might commence his ministry if plague or siege prevented access to the services of the already ordained. "Apart from this case it [ordination] must not be omitted" (Hollaz 1741, 1339). Gerhard conceded that bishops, or superintendents, should rightfully administer ordination, but followed the Book of Concord in arguing the legitimacy of presbyteral ordination (Schmid 1961, 610). After Spener queried the fruitfulness of the ministry of clergymen of questionable piety (Tappert 1964, 47), anti-Donatist concern prompted Löscher to inaugurate emphasis on the "grace of office" (*Amtsgnade*) that undergirded God's sure use of deficient laborers in his vineyard (Schmid 2007, 280–83). In cooperation with Francke, the Prussian Carl Hildebrand von Canstein (1667–1719) began in 1711 the mass printing of inexpensive Bibles. Prior to that, most Lutherans accessed scripture through the preaching, catechesis, and pastoral care of the clergy. Since Luke 10:16 was the word of Christ most frequently quoted by the Book of Concord in connection with the office of the ministry, the orthodox Lutherans were especially attuned to hear the voice of their Lord himself when ministers spoke in the discharge of their office.

Orthodox acceptance of lay emergency baptism represented unbroken continuity with medieval Catholicism, not departure from it; and admission that even absolution might in cases of dire need be administered by a layman involved less of a rupture with earlier tradition than may appear at first sight. As he justified the latter practice,

Melanchthon (Tr 67) quoted a statement attributed to Saint Augustine from Gratian's *Decretum*, the foundational medieval textbook of canon law. Since baptism is ordinarily necessary for salvation, a layman (oftentimes a midwife) might, in case of emergency, administer this first and foundational sacrament. August Pfeiffer spoke for all when (quoting Tr 67) he allowed for emergency lay administration of absolution also (Pfeiffer 1685, 613). But these (traditional) concessions did nothing to modify the fact that ordained men were the ordinary ministers of the *media dotika* sacraments. Expounding John 20:23 from his pulpit, Pfeiffer declaimed, "Ordinarily, however, God has conferred this office on certain persons. In our text, with the word *apheete* [receive] Christ immediately means his apostles, with whom he was talking at that time, yet by implication and deduction he understands thereby all assistants and successors of the apostles in the preaching office. . . . It follows that all legitimate successors of the apostles are ministers of absolution" (Pfeiffer 1685, 613). While the congregation should rightly join in prayer and hymn-singing, "Preaching, baptizing, marrying, giving the blessing, and consecrating are ministerial acts, duties laid on the preacher alone, and people should leave him unperturbed therein and remain silent" (Pfeiffer 1685, 563). "Christ does not want the special consecration that occurs through the words of institution to be performed by the whole congregation, but by his minister, who is a steward of his mysteries" (Pfeiffer 1685, 564).

## 7.2 Baptism

Until late seventeenth-century rationalist philosophers started to call the supernatural order into question, unanimity reigned among Lutherans of all stripes concerning the essence of baptism, administered by pouring with (or immersion into) water in the name of the Trinity. For infants, this rite wrought regeneration and incorporation into Christ, and Lutherans followed the Reformer in supposing baptism to produce the phenomenon of infant faith (*fides infantium*). Should an adult already have come to saving faith through proclamation of the gospel, baptism confirmed and sealed the gifts just named (Schmid 1961, 537).

Lutheran variation across space and time concerning baptism involved ritual enactment, not dogma as such. Most of the older church orders reproduced Luther's baptismal rite of 1526, with only superficial variations. Included in the first edition of the Book of Concord and hence enjoying confessional status, this rite was remarkable for its retention of a major and minor exorcism, its uniquely Lutheran quality shining forth in the officiant asking the child directly whether it wanted to be baptized and calling upon it to renounce the devil and profess the Creed. Although the godparents responded on the child's behalf, the rite was deliberately worded to express Luther's conviction of the faith of infants. The Württemberg family of rites omitted the signing with the cross and the exorcism, and Reformed influence made itself felt in the Strasbourg area, where the questions were posed to the godparents (Graff 1937, 286f), not to the infant.

Aegidius Hunnius (1550–1603) became the first representative of orthodoxy to favor abolition of the baptismal exorcism, and a goodly number of mainline dogmaticians (including Gerhard and Hollaz) only tepidly defended this component of the baptismal rite, showing openness to its replacement with prayer (Graff 1937, 296). Under pressure at the Cassel colloquy, the Lutherans of Rinteln agreed to this (Walch 1730, 293). Spener favored the omission of exorcism (Graff 1937, 297), and even the strict Wittenberg theological faculty admitted in 1634 that the practice qualified as an adiaphoron and was accordingly dispensable (Graff 1937, 297). Pfeiffer, conversely, mounted a spirited defense of exorcism (Pfeiffer 1685, 523–525). A series of prohibitions set in during the course of the eighteenth century, with the result that the practice became rare by century's end (Graff 1937, 298).

## 7.3  Sacrament of the altar

Well after the onset of Pietism, Lutherans continued to confess the objective presence of Christ's body and blood in Holy Communion, insisting that even nonbelievers partaking of the consecrated elements received the holy things with their mouths (*manducatio impiorum, manducatio oralis*). While all communicants received the Lord's body and blood supernaturally united with bread and wine, only those who did so in repentant faith received the benefits of a renewal of forgiveness, strengthening along their earthly pilgrimage, and a hidden bestowal of the glory of the life to come in body and soul. A rich treasury of hymnody proclaimed these beliefs, with the sixth stanza of "Soul, adorn thyself with gladness" paraphrasing a significant section of Aquinas' *Lauda Sion*. At the same time, evidence suggests a certain weakening of commitment to sixteenth-century doctrine and practice even before the rise and spread of the Pietist movement.

Most orthodox dogmaticians in the seventeenth century veered sharply from the Formula of Concord and from Lutheranism's two chief teachers on a crucial ingredient of Eucharistic doctrine that was fraught with major implications for liturgical practice. The Formula had quoted Luther to the effect that the consecration (recitation of the words of institution) effects the real presence of Christ's body and blood in the Eucharistic elements (SD VII, 78). Chemnitz had even described the consecration as productive of a "great, miraculous, and truly divine change" (Chemnitz 1978, 258), and in the *History of the Sacramental Controversy* that he co-authored with Timothy Kirchner and Nicholas Selnecker, he spoke of a "sacramental transformation" (Chemnitz 1591, 185) of the bread and wine. Already in 1590, Aegidius Hunnius professed the "Philippist" view that the union of the Lord's body and blood with bread and wine does not take place until the actual reception of the elements (Teigen 1986, 90–92). Although he could reproduce Aquinas' *Adoro te devote* as a testimony to the real presence (Gerhard 1867, 5:22), John Gerhard likewise denied the effective consecration (Gerhard 2000, 224f). While he confessed that the consecrated elements imparted Christ's body and blood to communicants and appealed "that you, devout Christian, treat the blest bread and wine with fitting reverence and veneration," Pfeiffer nevertheless insisted that the real presence occurred "not indeed when the priest has the bread and wine in and under his hands, but in the moment when they are eaten and drunk by the communicants" (Pfeiffer 1685, 580). A decisive shift in the Reformed direction took place here, prompting Tom G. A. Hardt (1934–98) to observe the loss of Luther's "concrete sacramental faith" and its transposition from henceforth into the realm of "popular piety" (Hardt 1971, 289). Yet even as Luther's doctrine metamorphosed into an understanding en route to Calvin's conception of the Lord's presence in the sacrament, bells continued to be rung in the Leipzig churches at the consecration, and cloths were reverently held under communicants' mouths at the distribution to prevent accidents to the holy things (Stiller 1984, 160, 138); popular piety was slow in catching up to the doctrine actually being taught in universities and parish churches.

Outright rejection of *manducatio impiorum* and *manducatio oralis* came slowly, however. Spener's ongoing rootedness in the third phase of orthodoxy shines through his acknowledgement of "the glorious power in the sacramental, oral, and not merely spiritual eating and drinking of the body and blood of the Lord in the Holy Supper. On this account I heartily reject the position of the Reformed when they deny that we receive such a pledge of salvation in, with, and under the bread and wine, when they weaken its power, and when they see in it no more than exists outside the holy sacrament in spiritual eating and drinking" (Tappert 1964, 63). These words contradict Tappert's claim, in the introduction to his translation of the *Pia Desideria*, that Spener was little troubled by Reformed Eucharistic doctrine (Spener 1964, 26). Elector Frederick III of Brandeburg (1657–1713, reigned 1688–1713, king in Prussia from 1701) had ulterior motives in calling Spener to the Lutheran consistory in Berlin in 1691, but whatever friendliness the latter felt toward the Reformed did not extend to inviting them to partake of the Lutheran Holy Communion (Wittenberg 1985, 14–16).

## 7.4 Absolution

Whether they placed it in the category of word or sacrament, the orthodox understood absolution as a means of salvation instituted by the risen Christ to be administered to penitent Christians by the apostles and their ministerial successors. As it answered the question, "What is confession?" the Small Catechism encapsulated the heart of the Lutheran Reformation by defining absolution as not the mere assurance but the actual bestowal of divine forgiveness: "Confession has two parts. First, that we confess our sins, and second, that we receive absolution, that is, forgiveness, from the pastor as from God himself, not doubting, but firmly believing that by it our sins are forgiven before God in heaven" (SC Office of the Keys). Absolution was usually imparted with the sign of the cross and the laying on of hands (Graff 1937, 375); if the Lord had failed to institute an external sign, pastoral practice supplied one. Wittenberg's Leonhard Hutter (1563–1616) noted that the third reason why absolution may be considered a sacrament in the broad sense is "Because in many places the outward ceremony of laying on of hands is customary and in use at absolution" (Hutter 1693, 321).

During the seventeenth and well into the eighteenth century, confession and absolution were practiced both privately and corporately, with the latter coming into increasing vogue with the passage of time. The "confessional chair" (*Beichtstuhl*) situated at the east end of the church was a familiar item of Lutheran ecclesiastical appointments, and there were concerns that conducting such a sensitive means of grace in public view endangered confidentiality for both pastor and penitent (Krispin 2012). While penitents were not obliged to list all major infractions of divine law, they were encouraged to unburden themselves in this private setting to which the seal of confession strictly applied: "before the pastor we should confess only those sins which we know and feel in our hearts" (SC Office of the Keys).

An eight-stanza composition by cantor Nikolaus Herman (ca. 1500–61) put Lutheran conviction concerning this means of grace in a nutshell:

> All those whose sins you thus remit,
> I truly pardon and acquit,
> And those whose sins you will retain
> Condemned and guilty shall remain.
> The words which absolution give
> Are his who died that we might live;
> The minister whom Christ has sent
> Is but his humble instrument.
> When ministers lay on their hands,
> Absolved by Christ the sinner stands;
> He who by grace the Word believes
> The purchase of his blood receives.

(LSB 614, sts. 5 & 6)

Philip Jacob Spener helped to inaugurate a sea change in the Lutheran doctrine and practice concerning absolution, and as a result, the orthodox position fell under increasing attack, though Gotha's Ernst Salomo Cyprian (1673–1749) still stoutly argued the divine institution of private confession in a work published shortly after his death (Graff 1937, 379). On the surface, Spener made the received heritage his own, but he fenced his agreement that confession and absolution "are an effective means of evangelical comfort and the forgiveness of sins" (Tappert 1964, 67) with a hedge of qualifications. Spener feared lest the impenitent or imperfectly penitent would disregard the need for true contrition and amendment of life by placing their trust foursquare in the word of absolution. Accordingly, Spener opted for the impartation of conditional absolution (Graff 1937, 376), taking the view that the pastor's word was true only when spoken to the reborn Christian whose contrition and amendment of life were in order. Moreover, he mistakenly claimed that Luther valued private confession "so that a preacher might be able to deal with each penitent individually as was needed: to evaluate the state of his soul, to encourage, explore, instruct, chastise, exhort, give counsel, and the like" (Krispin 2012, 26). Thus for him, absolution was no longer a creative word of God that changed the condition of the guilty sinner. Ironically, while desiring a maximum of

contrition, confession, and amendment of life on the penitent's part, Luther's inner torment over the impossibility of knowing when sufficient had been done in these areas
was only relieved by his placing full trust in absolution; as far as he was concerned, the
Reformation brought about enhanced appreciation of the "power of absolution" (SA III.
iii.20). Spener unwittingly reversed the process of Luther's breakthrough, canonizing
Gabriel Biel's mantra that "To him who does what in him lies God will not deny his
grace" (*facienti quod in se est, Deus non denegat gratiam*). "In this, Spener came full circle and made central the very bane that Luther sought to eschew from confession and
absolution" (Krispin 2012, 26).

Spener's move away from the earlier understanding of confession and absolution
was sandwiched between two outright attacks on this means of salvation, each of them
significantly located on the soil of Brandenburg-Prussia. Sharing Spener's concern that
people were being deluded into supposing that mechanically walking through a rite
guaranteed forgiveness, Theophilus Grossgebauer (1627–61) and Caspar Schade (1666–
98) attacked the continuance of private confession itself (Schmid 2007, 177–87). Schade's
pamphlet *Beichtstuhl, Satansstuhl, Höllenpfull* ("confessional stool, Satan's stool, pit of
hell") provoked immediate outrage among the faithful but led many Pietists beyond
Lutheran confessional boundaries.

For the orthodox Lutherans faithful to the Concordia of 1580, Christ was no remote
figure trapped in the irrecoverable past or separated from his earthly flock by immense
spatial distance. Luther's teaching, taken into the Formula of Concord (SD VII, 100,
101) on the omnipresence of Jesus's manhood in the "repletive" mode and of the special
sacramental presence of his body and blood in the "definitive" mode went hand in hand
with strong emphasis on the indwelling of the divine-human Lord and of the Trinity,
in the church in general and in each believer in particular. The "noble life of Christ in
the soul" was a major theme of the devotional writer John Arndt (1555–1621), who was
especially beloved of the Pietists. In 1640, Johannes Hülsemann (1602–61) incorporated
this biblically founded teaching, which resounded through Lutheran liturgy and hymnody, into the presentation of dogma under the title of the "mystical union" (*unio mystica*). The syncretist Georg Calixt contradicted the Formula of Concord by reducing the
indwelling from that of the Holy Spirit himself to that of his (created) gift, spurring his
orthodox opponents to even warmer embrace of this article of faith (Koch 2000, 240).
Hollaz's clear articulation of the mystical union, which he understood as a "substantial" union of the Lord with his own (Hollaz 1741, 927–42), invites comparison with the
patristic motif of deification. Once the various forces at work in the eighteenth century
combined to snuff out the old Christology, Concordia Lutheranism's understanding of
the sacraments and the mystical union fell by the wayside.

## 7.5  On the margins—confirmation and marriage

Despite Luther's disparaging remarks about confirmation (AE 36:91), a minor strand in
the church orders attested the bestowal of the Holy Spirit himself through this rite (Graff

1937, 315f). As is shown elsewhere in this volume, even where a different understanding of confirmation (as the culmination of the catechetical process or as acceptance of the discipline of the church) prevailed, the rite was oftentimes experienced as a "sacramental" force. Notwithstanding the denial of marriage's sacramental status by Luther (AE 36:92), in the sense in which he and the orthodox dogmaticians used the term—after all, Christ did not institute it as a means of grace bestowing forgiveness of sins—entrance into matrimony might be viewed and apprehended on a similar scale. Luther may have been guilty of a certain inconsistency here, as he began his Marriage Booklet (the liturgical rite of matrimony included in the Book of Concord) with the observation that marriage is a "secular matter," but ended it with a prayer confessing how the estate of matrimony "pictures the sacrament" of the relationship of Christ with his bride, the church (AE 53: 111, 115). Commenting on Genesis 24 in 1527, Luther picked up the third of marriage's purposes listed by Augustine (progeny, faithfulness, "sacrament"): "For the marital estate is a sacrament and parable of Christ and Christendom" (WA 24. 422, 21–22). The materials lay to hand for a "sacramental" understanding of marriage (Roeber 2013, 26), even if the Lutheran theologians made little use of them. In order to do so, they would have had to emphasize a component of the concept of "sacrament" that they downplayed rather than denied outright; namely, Augustine's definition that "a sacrament is a sign of a sacred thing."

# 8 Collapse of Classical Lutheranism

The last and most devastating of the tsunami-force movements to undermine Concordia Lutheranism came from the Enlightenment rationalism that arrived in Germany somewhat later than in England and the Netherlands. The historian Walch is himself usually classed as a "moderate" representative of the final phase of orthodoxy; as he recounted his narrative, he was part of the first person plural of orthodoxy, but Pietism left its mark on him, nor was he unaffected by the Enlightenment. In place of an abrupt transition from old to new, "mediating" schools of theology cushioned the transition from orthodoxy through Pietism to rationalism. Karl Barth told how neology and the neologians paralleled the English moderate deists, not denying revelation outright, but deriving their core beliefs from natural religion and theology and calling on revelation to provide an increasingly superfluous supplement. Barth entertained his hearers with quotations from Saxon country pastor Traugott Günther Roller's (1744–94) sermons on the customary lections for the church year, in which he sidelined the mysteries and miracles of Christmas, Easter, and Pentecost in favor of imparting common-sense counsel for good living (Barth 1972, 96). While Leipzig orthodoxy long held the Enlightenment at bay, it ultimately proved as powerless against the great movement of the century as King Canute against the oncoming tide. Rationalism's advance gained speed with the onset of Johann Georg Rosenmüller's (1736–1815) twenty-year tenure as superintendent. Rosenmüller introduced public, corporate confession, heaping scorn on the private administration of absolution; he started the process of detaching celebration of the sacrament of the altar from the main Sunday service; and he saw to it that the bells at the consecration fell silent in 1787 and that the wearing of the chasuble was discontinued in 1795. It comes as no surprise that exorcism at baptism became optional at Saint Thomas' church, scene of the earlier activity of Pfeiffer and Bach, from 1788 onwards, or that this precedent was followed by the other city churches within a decade (Stiller 1984, 159f). For Rosenmüller, pastors did not pronounce performative utterance in the Lord's name or serve as instruments in the achievement of supernatural acts; the core of the service was now the sermon, defined as ethical instruction. Rosenmüller derided the Lutheran conception of sacramental presence as it had been taught by Pfeiffer as bondage to the medieval notion of transubstantiation (Stiller 1984, 163).

As the eighteenth century drew to its close, the old belief in biblical inspiration rapidly evaporated as the skepticism of Hermann Samuel Reimarus (1694–1768), who began the "quest of the historical Jesus," and of his publicist Gotthold Ephraim Lessing (1725–81) gained ground and a new, critical approach to scripture and the Christian tradition was ushered in by Halle's Johann Salomo Semler (1725–91). The Christ proclaimed from Germany's Lutheran pulpits was in the main no longer the divine-human savior of Philip Nicolai's famous chorales, whose divine attributes suffused his manhood, making possible his atoning work and his ongoing activity in baptism and Eucharist, along with his abiding presence in his church and people through the mystical union.

## ABBREVIATIONS

AE      American Edition of Luther's Works.

LSB     Lutheran Service Book Prepared by The Commission on Worship of The Lutheran Church—Missouri Synod St Louis: Concordia Publishing House, 2006 Documents in Book of Concord

AC      Augsburg Confession

AP      Apology of the Augsburg Confession

LC      Large Catechism

SC      Small Catechism

SA      Smalcald Articles

Tr      Treatise on the Power and Primacy of the Pope

SD      Solid Declaration (of Formula of Concord)

## BIBLIOGRAPHY

Aland, Kurt. 1986. *A History of Christianity II: From the Reformation to the Present.* Philadelphia: Fortress Press.

Barth, Karl. 1972. *Protestant Theology in the Nineteenth Century*. London: SCM Press.

Chemnitz, Martin. 1978. *Examination of the Council of Trent, Part II*. St. Louis, MO: Concordia Publishing House.

Chemnitz, Martin. 1981. *Ministry, Word, and Sacraments: An Enchiridion*. St. Louis, MO: Concordia Publishing House.

Chemnitz, Martin, Timotheus Kirchner, and Nicolas Selnecker. 1591. *Historia deß Sacramentstreits.*

Gerhard, Johann. 1867. *Ioannis Gerhardi Loci Theologici: Cum Pro Adstruenda Veritate Tum Pro Destruenda Quarumvis Contradicentium Falsitate Per Theses Nervose Solide Et Copiose Explicati; Opus Praeclarissimum Novem Tomis Comprehensum ....* 3 Vols. Edited by Eduward Preuss. Berlin: Gustav Schlawitz.

Gerhard, Johann. 2000. *A Comprehensive Explanation of Holy Baptism and the Lord's Supper.* Malone, TX: Repristination Press.

Graff, Paul. 1937. *Geschichte der Auflösung der alten gottesdienstlichen Formen in der evangelischen Kirche Deutschlands.* Göttingen: Vandenhoeck & Rupprecht.

Hardt, Tom G. A. 1971. *Venerabilis & Adorabilis Eucharistia: en Studie I den Lutherska Nattvardsläran under 1500–Talet.* University of Uppsala: Studia Doctrinae Christianae Upsaliensa 9.

Hollaz, David. 1741. *Examen Theologicum Acroamaticum.* Leipzig.

Hutter, Leonhard. 1693. *Compendium Locorum Theologicorum.* Wittenberg.

Janssen, Johannes. 1966. *History of the German People at the Close of the Middle Ages IV.* New York: AMS Press.

Koch, Ernst. 2000. *Das kongessionelle Zeitalter: Katholizismus, Luthertum, Calvinismus (1563–1675).* Leipzig: Evangelische Verlagsanstalt.

Krispin, Gerald S. 2012. "Philip Jacob Spener and the Demise of Holy Absolution in the Lutheran Church." *Logia* XXI (Holy Trinity 2012), 1: 19–27.

*Luther's Works. 1955–1986.* American Edition. 55 vols. Edited by Jaroslav Pelikan and Helmut T. Lehmann. St Louis, MO: Concordia Publishing House; Philadelphia, PA: Fortress Press.

Macculloch, Diarmaid. 2003. *The Reformation.* New York: Viking.

Nichols, James H. 1956. *History of Christianity 1650–1950: Secularization of the West.* New York: Ronald Press Company.

Nischan, Bodo. 1994. *Prince, People, and Confession: The Second Reformation in Brandenburg.* Philadelphia: University of Pennsylvania Press.

Ogg, David. 1963. *Europe in the Seventeenth Century.* 8th revised ed. London: Adam & Charles Black.

Pfeiffer, August. 1685. *Der wolbewährte Evangelische Aug-Apfel Oder Schrifftsmässige Erklärung aller Articul Der Augspurgischen CONFESSION.* Leipzig.

Preus, Robert D. 1970. *The Theology of Post-Reformation Lutheranism I: A Study of Theological Prolegomena.* St. Louis, MO: Concordia Publishing House.

Raitt, Jill. 1993. *The Colloquy of Montbéliard: Religion and Politics in the Sixteenth Century.* New York: Oxford University Press.

Roeber, A. G. *Hopes for Better Spouses: Protestant Marriage and Church Renewal in Early Modern Europe, India, and North America.* Grand Rapids, MI: Eerdmans, 2013.

Schatz, Helmut. 2004. *Historische Bilder zum Evangelisch-Lutherischen Gottesdienst.* Ansbach.

Schmid, Heinrich. 1961. *The Doctrinal Theology of the Evangelical Lutheran Church.* Minneapolis, MN: Augsburg Publishing House.

Schmid, Heinrich. 2007. *The History of Pietism*. Milwaukee, WI: Northwestern Publishing House.

Spener, Philip Jacob. 1964. *Pia Desideria*, edited and translated by Theodore G. Tappert. Philadelphia, PA: Fortress Press.

Stephenson, John R. 2003. *The Lord's Supper*. Northville, SD: Luther Academy.

Stiller, Günther. 1984. *Johann Sebastian Bach and Liturgical Life in Leipzig*. St. Louis, MO: Concordia Publishing House.

Teigen, Bjarne W. 1986. *The Lord's Supper in the Theology of Martin Chemnitz*. Brewster, MA: Trinity Lutheran Press.

Walch, Johann Georg. 1730. *Historische und theologische Einleitung in die Religionsstreitigkeiten Der Evangelisch-Lutherischen Kirche, Von der Reformation an bis auf ietzige Zeiten*. Jena: Johann Meyers Witwe.

Wittenberg, Martin. 1985. *Kirchengemeinschaft und Abendmahlgemeinschaft, kirchengeschichtlich gesehen*. Fürth: Flacius Verlag.

# Other Christian Theologies and
Awakening Movements

# CHAPTER 24

# EARLY MODERN SOCINIANISM AND UNITARIANISM

## SARAH MORTIMER

SOCINIANISM was perhaps the most notorious heresy in early modern Europe. Theologians from across the major confessions denounced it as a monstrous body of errors and blasphemies, claiming that it would lead to the destruction of both church and state. Such a strident response to Socinian ideas was understandable, for their denial of the central orthodox doctrines of the Trinity, the divinity of Christ, and the atonement led them to rewrite Christianity in new and controversial ways. Faced with opposition across Europe, the Socinians never managed to gain more than a small number of adherents, and as a community they remained on the fringes of European religion, both geographically and intellectually. But their importance was far greater than this might suggest. Their ideas gained ground during this period, and not least because they were able to capitalize on the problems of more mainstream theological traditions, especially the Reformed.

Early modern theologians and politicians were fascinated by the specter of Socinianism, and of the Unitarianism which developed later in the period, but interest in both movements declined in the nineteenth and twentieth centuries. During the twentieth century, scholarship on both movements tended to be produced by Unitarian historians keen to provide their movement with a respectable, even inspiring, history which showed the courage of their forebears in the face of persecution and their commitment to reason in an age of superstition (Wilbur 1946 and 1952; McLachlan 1951). More recently, scholars have begun to reassess the two movements and to study them within the broader context of the early modern period (e.g., Mortimer 2010; Lim 2012). This chapter will set out the key themes of Socinian and Unitarian theology, and suggest the challenge it posed to mainstream Western Christianity.

# 1 Socinus

The Socinian movement took its name from the Italian theologian Faustus Socinus (1539–1604); by the time of his death there was a recognizable community with a shared commitment to the main outlines of his theology. That community was in Rakow, in central Poland, a historic center of Anabaptism and radical religion thanks to the influence of tolerant local aristocrats. Socinus himself was not native to the area; it was only in the late 1570s that he moved to Poland, having spent the earlier part of his life in Florence. His initial views were formed in Italy, for he came from a family with a strong interest in the currents of reform within the Italian church and with a tradition of legal scholarship. The Italian influences on him remained strong, and he brought to Rakow his own engagement with humanist and philological study. In particular, Socinus admired Desiderius Erasmus (1466–1536) for his critical edition of the New Testament, of which the Italian made much use, and for his strong emphasis on the ethical duties of the Christian. With this scholarly background, Socinus was well placed to set out the doctrines which he shared with the Racovians in a clear and systematic way. He penned a number of tracts and pamphlets which were printed on the community's press and in 1605, a year after his death, the Racovians printed their own catechism. The first edition was in Polish, but it was swiftly translated into Latin and German in order that it might reach an international audience (Rees 1818; Wilbur 1945, 387–407).

The version of Christianity found in the Racovian Catechism had several striking features. Most crucially, Socinus and his co-religionists argued that Christ had revealed to human beings a new way of salvation, of which they had had no knowledge before. Indeed, it was central to Socinus's theology that human beings had no natural knowledge of God, a theory which he proved by pointing to societies in Brazil which, he claimed, performed no religious worship. Moreover, he denied the doctrines of original sin and the natural immortality of the soul, denying the central Christian story of man's Fall and redemption. What Christians had, therefore, was not any innate sense of the divine or of their own sinfulness, but instead the message of Christ as recorded in the gospels. Socinus saw the scriptures as an historical text relating important events in the past, relevant to Christians because they provided examples (in the form of Christ's actions), laws given by Christ, and promises of reward and punishment. In particular, the account of the resurrection proved that those who obeyed God would be rewarded with eternal life. In other words, then, although men did not have natural knowledge of God, what they had instead was a credible, textual account of what God had revealed through Christ. As this suggests, what was unusual about Socinus was his willingness to take seriously the idea that Christianity was based upon a specific set of events in the past. This method stood in sharp contrast to his contemporaries, who viewed Christianity as a set of eternal truths about man's fall and redemption applicable to all peoples and all times and places (Rees 1818; Socinus 1668, 1:264–81, 1:534–40; Mortimer 2010).

Christ revealed God's will to men, but that did not make him a divine figure co-essential with God the Father, nor part of any eternal Trinity. For Socinus, it was important that Christ was a human being who lived and died in first-century Palestine, whose example of obedience to the divine will could be followed by all people. In making this case, Socinus followed other Italian and Polish anti-Trinitarians, all of whom insisted that the doctrine of the Trinity was not in the Bible but was instead an invention of the clerics. The influence of the Protestant principle of "sola scriptura" on Socinus's argument is clear, and the Italian theologian was insistent that men must interpret the message revealed in the scriptures in exactly the same way as any other human text. Precisely because religion was alien to human nature, men and women had to make sense of it using human ideas and human principles, and to Socinus it was quite impossible that there could be three persons in one essence. Socinus did not doubt the importance of Christ, however, and he argued that God had raised him from the dead and given him divine power and authority (Socinus 1668, 1:281–86, 2:423–39).

The anti-Trinitarian character of Socinian Christianity entailed a new explanation of how human beings could relate to God, and what salvation might mean. The doctrine of the Trinity provides Christians with a way of understanding the activity of God within the world and within human time; it describes a God who is in an active and dynamic relationship with himself and with human beings. By rejecting the Trinity and the pre-existence of Christ, Socinus could maintain that the revelation brought by Christ was new, and he could draw a sharp line between that revelation and the norms of the human world. For Socinus, Christianity was unlike any code of ethics or rules which men could come up with on their own, for it encouraged men to renounce their own earthly self-interest for the sake of reward in the afterlife. Only when Christ had revealed the possibility of eternal life could humans be expected to sacrifice themselves for others. At the most fundamental level, Socinus's theology was a rejection of any concept of participation by human beings in divine activity or essence. The only way that God interacted with humans, at least in this present time, was through the traces of his revelation, and these are not found in the human heart or in natural reason, but only in the gospel texts themselves (Socinus 1668, 2:455–58).

God's values were not entirely alien to humans, however. When discussing the meaning of the death of Christ, Socinus was keen to insist that God and men shared a common framework of justice and right. Within that framework it was perfectly legitimate to forgive sin without demanding satisfaction and God, just like any absolute ruler, could pardon offences as he saw fit. The analogy between God and a human prince was important to Socinus, providing him with ammunition for an assault upon the doctrine of substitutionary atonement. For him, God's justice was not retributive and it did not entail the punishment of sin. Arguing from Roman law and appealing to an ethic of mercy and of human responsibility, Socinus claimed that God would forgive the sins of all those who truly repented. The innocent Christ had not been punished in our place, for that would contravene all notions of justice, both human and divine. His death and resurrection had instead shown the fate of those who sought to put God's laws into practice, and should inspire us all (Socinus 1668, 2:115–247).

The Socinian reading of Christianity was of political as well as theological importance for the community at Rakow. Like many Anabaptist communities, the Racovians sought to put a pure version of Christianity into practice, even when this conflicted with earthly laws and norms. Pacifism was central to this pure Christianity, and the Racovians rejected war and capital punishment even when Turkish invasions threatened their homeland. Their reluctance to take up arms dismayed their neighbors, but they found in Socinus an eloquent champion for a position very similar to their own. It was he who explained to a Polish and then a European audience how committed the Racovians were to an interpretation of Christianity that did not comply with earthly political practices (Kot 1957). Socinus also developed further their insistence on individual free will, and on Christianity as an active choice, showing that these ideas could be defended from the Bible. But a Christian must, he insisted, approach that text as a historical document, relating the life and ministry of a man in first-century Palestine who gave to the world the new message of God for human beings.

## 2 THE DEVELOPMENT OF SOCINIANISM

The ideas of Socinus were circulated widely after his death, and they found a sympathetic audience among some of those who were disappointed with recent trends in theology. The early seventeenth century saw a return to a scholastic style of theological argument and to Aristotelian concepts, but this was not welcomed by all. One of the attractions of Socinus's theology was that it offered a way of making sense of Christianity without recourse to these intellectual tools. Furthermore, his strong insistence on ethics and on the agency of individuals went down well among Christians disappointed with what they saw as the antinomian tendencies in Lutheranism and Calvinism, but who were keen to live out what they saw as the message of Christ. But Socinus's ideas were not read in a vacuum, of course, and as new readers took up some of his ideas, they also began to change them. As a result, the seventeenth century saw a process of adaptation and development within Socinian thinking.

Two institutions proved particularly fertile ground for Socinus's ideas: the Academy of Altdorf near Nuremburg in Germany, and the University of Leiden. In the 1610s, the latter institution was rocked by a number of interrelated controversies, especially that over the legacy of Jacob Arminius (1560–1609). Like Socinus, Arminius was keen to show that human beings must take some responsibility for their own salvation, but they took a rather different view of the relationship between God and human beings. For Arminius, all human beings were offered grace and were able to accept it if they chose to do so; and Christians were bound by the ethics of the natural law laid down at creation. This theology, recognizably Thomist in its outlines, was very different from Socinus's thought, but several of Arminius's friends and allies, including Hugo Grotius (1583–1645), sought to combine his approach with the stronger emphasis on human freedom and choice that they found in the Italian scholar. The Arminians sought to reconcile the tension between a theology based on a particular, Christian revelation and one anchored more firmly in human reason. They also wanted to explain and defend human freedom and responsibility, and here they found Socinian theology helpful (Muller 1991; Mortimer 2009).

At Altdorf, a group of students began to read the writings of Socinians and Arminians, and to do so in a sympathetic but not uncritical way. Of these, the Franconian Johan Crell (1590–1633) was the most important, and his writings came to define "second generation" Socinianism. Unlike Socinus, Crell argued that human beings could use their reason to gain knowledge of God; they could see that the world must have been created and that it must be governed by a supreme ruler. For Crell, this ruler must be a single person, and he went on to show at great length that both scripture and reason supported a Unitarian concept of God. From around this time, Socinianism began to be more strongly associated with this insistence that neither scripture nor reason could be used to defend the Trinity, but that the evidence of both showed one God. Jesus Christ was the human being to whom God revealed his will, and whose perfect obedience led to his resurrection and exaltation; but Jesus did not share in the divine substance as those who followed the Athanasian Creed maintained (Crell 1631; Zeltner 1729).

Crell's arguments soon became notorious, not only because of their own intrinsic merits but also because they tapped into wider problems with contemporary explanations of the Trinity. The doctrine of the Trinity relies upon a complex metaphysical structure, and in particular upon a specific notion of substance; it is crucial to the Trinitarian case that the divine substance can be distinguished into persons without thereby being divided. By the mid-seventeenth century, however, when the new natural philosophies of Rene Descartes (1596–1650) and Thomas Hobbes (1588–1679) were gaining ground, the concept of substance was undergoing a redefinition. Hobbes and Descartes tended to identify substances with individual things or bodies, and this in itself made it much harder to sustain the Athanasian understanding of the Trinity. Even those who were wary of the kind of nominalist metaphysics associated with Hobbes struggled to formulate an acceptable alternative. The most obvious was, perhaps, a renewed engagement with Platonic metaphysics, but when the Platonic concept of emanation was applied to the Trinity this tended to produce either a subordinationist account, or one which implied that there were three gods rather than one (Muller 2003, 99–103).

The Socinians were able to take advantage of the problems created by contemporary historical research, as well as philosophical discussions. By the middle of the seventeenth century the diversity of opinion among the church fathers was becoming clear, and the Jesuit scholar Denis Petau was especially concerned to show this. In the second volume of his *Dogmata Theologica* (1644–50), he described the diversity of opinion among church fathers on the doctrine of the Trinity; for him it was clear that that most of the Greek fathers had held to a subordinationist Christology in which the Father was greater than the Son. For Petau this was evidence of the work of the Holy Spirit in guiding the Catholic Church to the (Trinitarian) truth, but his work could also, of course, be used for a very different purpose: to undermine the Trinity. As this suggests, by the second half of the seventeenth century a range of ideas about the Trinity had developed, many of them critical. Although some were indebted to Socinian arguments, it is important to remember that not all anti-Trinitarianism was Socinian (Petau 1644–50; Galter 1931).

As well as challenging the doctrine of the Trinity, the Socinians also took issue with substitutionary atonement, and here their ideas were no less important for European intellectual life. Socinus, as we have seen, had denounced the idea that Christ had died to satisfy the wrath of God. His alternative—that his death showed his obedience to God and provided an example to human beings—found some sympathizers, especially among the Arminian community, which was quickly charged with Socinianizing. To distance himself and his friends from any trace of heresy, Hugo Grotius wrote a tract against Socinus's views on the atonement. Grotius's alternative was, however, a governmental theory of the atonement that itself de-emphasized the punitive or vindicatory aspect of Christ's death and stressed instead its connection to divine order within the world. Grotius's work provoked a response from Johan Crell, which defended Socinus by examining further the concepts of justice and punishment. In this debate, all parties were led to consider the basis for authority and jurisdiction in civil societies as well as in Christian theology, and Crell and Grotius both came to develop theories of individual natural rights. They both came to argue, albeit in different ways, that societies were formed through the transfer of rights from individuals to the state, an argument which would soon come to characterize the "modern" school of natural law. Just as the changing ideas about the Trinity have to be understood against the background of new philosophies, it is clear that theories of the atonement are also related to contemporary notions of justice, punishment, and individual rights (Mortimer 2012).

Although there was a growing chorus of discomfort with the doctrine of the Trinity and with substitutionary atonement, this did not necessarily translate into support for the Socinian community, and certainly not in the short term. Indeed, after the death of Crell the fortunes of the Racovians were on the wane. Their position in Poland became extremely precarious once the Counter-Reformation gained momentum, and in 1658 they were expelled from Rakow and the surrounding area. Many of the brethren went to the United Provinces; there they continued to move further away from the original tenets of Socinus. The common ground between Grotius and the Socinians had already been revealed through the controversy over the atonement, and during the later seventeenth century the Racovian community moved closer to Grotius and indeed to Arminian ideas. The pacifism of the earlier Racovians, and their unwillingness to engage in civic life, no longer seemed appropriate to later generations who were anxious to play a full role in the life of their new countries. They also began to join in with the Arminian and Remonstrant campaign for toleration and liberty of conscience (Jobert 1974; Kot 1957; Simonutti 2005).

The role of reason in Socinian theology also began to change. Even in the 1620s, several of the Racovians, including Joachim Stegman and Samuel Przypkowski, had written works which insisted upon the role of reason in religious matters, and upon the need to read scripture in accordance with the principles instilled in us through reason. In the *Brevis Disquisitio*, written by Joachim Stegmann sometime before his death in 1633 and published posthumously, it was argued that right reason must be the only judge of scripture. By right reason, Stegmann meant the principles which all human beings use in their everyday lives. Moreover, he argued that scripture on its own was not the only, or perhaps even the most important source of knowledge about God—there were, he thought, principles of truth and of religion which are known from nature or simply from our consideration of the world around us, which we must use to judge and to make sense of any revelation. This was a different understanding of reason from that to be found in Socinus's writing, and it has the potential to de-emphasize the role of the scriptures and the person of Christ. Stegmann in this work used his notion of reason to maintain the unity of God against the Trinitarians; he also saw himself as part of the Racovian community. What unites him with Socinus is a shared anti-Trinitarian doctrine rather than a particular ethos, spirit, or approach to religion. It was from around this time that the association between Socinianism and reason started to become entrenched (Stegmann 1635).

The works of Socinus were not forgotten, however. In the 1660s an edition of these, along with the works of Crell and other luminaries of the Socinian movement, was prepared and would be issued as the *Bibliotheca Fratrum Polonorum*. This publishing venture made the works of the Socinians accessible to the Latinate public, and helped to ensure their longevity. During the eighteenth century, however, the doctrine of the Trinity tended to move to the background of theological debate, at least in continental Europe, and so the challenge posed by Socinianism was not felt so strongly. Only in the nineteenth century would Trinitarian theology come back into prominence, revivified in Germany by the philosophers of idealism (Powell 2001).

# 3 SOCINIANISM AND UNITARIANISM IN ENGLAND

The leaders of the Racovian community fled to the United Provinces, as we have seen, but it was in England that their ideas had the most impact. There had been interest in Socinian writing among English scholars and clerics from the reign of James I (r. 1603–25), and increasingly vocal support for the ideas of the Racovian community began to be heard from the mid-seventeenth century. Although interest in Socinianism died down after the Restoration of Charles II, there was a noisy and public debate over the Trinity in England in the 1690s. Eventually, an English Unitarian movement emerged and this movement would help to shape the modern Unitarian Church as it developed in British North America.

Initially, it seems to have been the Socinians' critique of the Roman Catholic Church and their ethical interpretation of Christianity that attracted English readers to their works. Certainly it was these aspects of Socinian writing that appealed to William Chillingworth (1602–44) and Lucius Cary, Lord Falkland (1610–43), when they discussed religious matters at Great Tew, Falkland's country house, in the 1630s. Both Chillingworth and Falkland wanted to see a church which granted reason and criticism an important role. They applauded the Socinians' efforts to limit the authority of the clergy and promote virtuous conduct. Neither openly expressed doubts about the Trinity or the atonement, but they helped to bolster the critical and ethical strand within English religious thinking in the years before the civil war (MacLachlan 1951; Trevor-Roper 1987; Mortimer 2010).

Socinian ideas circulated more widely in the 1650s, after the execution of the king and during the Commonwealth regime. An English translation of the Racovian catechism was published in 1652, but even the Rump Parliament refused to allow the circulation of such works and the Latin version was burnt by order of Parliament. The translator was almost certainly John Biddle (1615–62), a schoolteacher and convinced Unitarian who managed to assemble a small congregation during the Cromwellian Protectorate. Biddle's ministry to his flock was interrupted by long spells in prison, but his friends helped to spread his objections to Trinitarian doctrine. Soon the continental Socinians' views became intertwined with homegrown anti- and non-Trinitarian interpretations of Christianity. When, in the 1690s, the lapsing of the Licensing Act allowed a greater freedom of religious expression, there was a vigorous and scholarly discussion of the relationship between God the Father, Christ, and the Holy Spirit. The most prolific pamphleteer at this time was Stephen Nye (1648–1719), who drew on Socinian resources to promote a Unitarian view of God and to denounce "Athanasian" Christianity (MacLachlan 1951; Lim 2012, 38–67).

Although few English people agreed with Nye, the late seventeenth century did see the development of alternatives to Athanasian Trinitarianism, and especially of Arianism. Arius, perhaps the most notorious heretic of the fourth century AD, had insisted that Christ was not equal to God the Father but was created by him before the creation of the world. Arianism, therefore, was a theology of subordination, but one which (unlike Socinianism) emphasized the pre-existence of Christ. The most famous adherents of Arian Christianity were men associated with natural philosophy and mathematics, like William Whiston (1667–1752) and Isaac Newton (1642–1727)—although Newton in particular was keen to keep his theological views quiet. As this suggests, at least some scholars found the Trinity hard to accept because the intellectual framework in which it had been developed no longer had much purchase upon them. Whiston and Newton were keen to understand the world around them by using mathematics and new, non-Aristotelian philosophies. They found it impossible to reconcile the Trinity with this scientific approach. Moreover, Newton spent much time and energy wrestling with the scriptural text, and the view of God which he found there was an Arian one (Wiles 2001, 62–110).

It was not only the Socinians' ideas about the Trinity which caught the attention of an English audience, however. The Socinians and Arminians had offered a set of new ideas about human moral agency and the need for ethical action, and they had offered a way of understanding these without recourse to concepts of original sin or substitutionary atonement. As the clergymen of the Restored Anglican Church sought to explain justification and human actions, they increasingly found Socinian and Arminian ideas helpful. Naturally they denied that they were moving in a heterodox direction, but concern about the moral implications of solifidianism led some theologians, including George Bull (1634–1710), to lean heavily on a Socinian account of justification (Hampton 2008).

In the seventeenth century, Socinian ideas were most often examined in private, but by the eighteenth century some theologians were willing to reveal their Arian theology in public. When Samuel Clarke (1675–1729) published his *Scripture Doctrine of the Trinity* in 1712, the scholarly controversy over the Trinity kicked off again in earnest. Clarke was already famous for the Boyle Lectures he had given on the nature of God, and was well established as an eloquent and learned royal chaplain. To explain the doctrine of the Trinity, he took all the relevant passages from the New Testament (by his reckoning, 1251 in number) and examined them one by one. His conclusion was an Arian one, in which Christ was firmly subordinated to God the father. After some fierce criticism from his fellow clergymen, Clarke was dismissed from his office as royal chaplain, and the preferment that had been expected for him never came. He remained within the Church of England, however, and many of those who shared his doubts about the more orthodox doctrine of the Trinity remained quietly within the Anglican fold, hopeful that one day the church might allow a wider range of views upon this question. Only in 1772, with the rejection of the "Feathers Tavern Petition" calling for a relaxation of the terms of subscription, did those hopes for reform subside. At this point a small number of convinced anti-Trinitarians left the church, while the Church of England became increasingly dominated by high church and evangelical clergy (Wiles 2001, 110–32).

For most of the eighteenth century, therefore, Socinian and Unitarian voices were rarely heard in England. But it is clear that under the surface, there was both considerable discontent with the Trinitarian doctrine of the Church of England and intense commitment to preserving it. This commitment was related to the strong sense within the Anglican Church that the church itself was the mystical body of Christ, and that to deny the divine nature of Christ was also to question the value and role of the church. Socinianism and Unitarianism could be, and were, seen as part of an attack upon the English confessional state and upon the principles of divine order and hierarchy that underpinned it. And this connection between radical religion and politics came to the fore in the last quarter of the century, when Unitarians outside the established church mounted a strident challenge to Anglican, Trinitarian values (Waterman 1996).

The central figure for the Unitarian movement from the 1770s and 1780s was Joseph Priestley (1733–1804). Priestley was a scientist and an educator; his work on gases was especially influential, not least for his claim to have discovered oxygen. As a natural philosopher, and tutor at the Warrington Academy, Priestley was keen to root out what he saw as irrational belief and superstition wherever he found it, and was convinced that the Church of England was in need of extensive reform. By the late 1780s his studies were primarily historical, devoted to showing that the doctrine of the Trinity was absent from primitive Christianity. By this time he saw himself as a full-blown Unitarian, and hoped that religion in England could be transformed into the rational worship free of mystery and superstition that he believed had once obtained among the earliest Christians. For him, as for the earlier Socinians, true religion entailed a sincere effort by individuals to live moral and ethical lives, an effort which was only undermined by Western Christianity's predominantly Augustinian understanding of man's Fall and redemption through Christ. But Priestley went much further in his rejection of anything that suggested that the church or its ministers had the power to assist people in this endeavor. For him, human beings really were on their own before God.

The prospects for establishing such a religion in England were not good, but there was one Unitarian chapel at Essex Street in London, set up by Theophilus Lindsey (1723–1808) in 1774. This chapel used a version of the English Prayer Book, but one stripped of all phrases that suggested the Trinity; the doxologies, for example, were addressed to God the Father alone. Priestley was supportive of this endeavor, but his understanding of religion was even more radical than Lindsey's, and he came to deny that the church or its ministers could play any part in mediating between God and the individual. His brand of Unitarianism came to reject all references to absolution, consecration, or even baptism. Naturally he rejected the doctrine of the atonement, but he did believe in a universal restitution of all things at the end of time. The doctrine of the Trinity enabled the more orthodox Christians to understand how God might participate in human affairs in the present, but for Priestley at least it was only in the future that God would intervene and ensure human salvation (Schofield 2004).

Before Unitarian worship had a chance to establish itself, political events in Europe polarized English opinion and led to a temporary collapse in support for Priestley and his friends. The French Revolution of 1789 and the violence that followed inspired a strong English reaction in favor of church and king. Priestley's impolitic support for the French did not help him, and in 1792 his house in Birmingham was burnt down. Realizing that the future was bleak in England, he immigrated to America, where he soon found support among the dissenting congregations there. Many of the liberal churches were, however, keen to distance themselves from Priestley's brand of Unitarianism and to emphasize their independent roots. His influence on the development of the American Unitarian movement has only recently been rediscovered (Bowers, 2007).

The early Unitarian churches in North America preached a version of Christianity that was very different from Socinus's. Their ministers insisted on the capacity of all men to discern the divine through their reason and intellect, and they believed that Christian ethics would lead to happiness and fulfilment in this life, as well as the world to come. But these differences should not mask a fundamental similarity, however; for what was most remarkable about all the Socinian and Unitarian Christians was their renunciation of a theology centered on man's Fall in Adam and his redemption through Christ. That theology had, since at least the fourth century, particularly in the Latin West, entailed the divinity of Christ on the grounds that only a divine redeemer could save humans from their sin. Not only did these theological principles govern the way that Christians read the scriptures, they also provided the core narrative that sustained religious worship. When Socinus challenged these ideas, he found himself rewriting Christian theology and he claimed to do so on the basis of the Bible alone. Like all interpreters, however, he brought his own views to the text, with the result that his version of Christianity was one which owed much to the traditions of humanism and jurisprudence with which he was familiar. Later readers followed suit, shaping their theology in accordance with their own philosophies of nature and of the law. In the seventeenth and eighteenth centuries, when optimistic attitudes to human nature and human effort were increasingly widespread, a theology which privileged reason and morality seemed attractive to some, even though it proved hard to create and sustain a worshiping community. After the French Revolution, attitudes began to change, especially in Europe, and Unitarianism would retreat to the margins. Only in northeastern America, where the human capacity for divine truth continued to be proclaimed, did a Unitarian version of Christianity live on, albeit one rather different from Faustus Socinus's theology.

## BIBLIOGRAPHY

Bowers, Jerome. 2007. *Joseph Priestley and English Unitarianism in America*. University Park, PA: Penn State University Press.

Crell, Johan. 1631. *De Uno Deo Patre Libri duo libri duo, in quibus multa etiam de Filii Dei & Spiritus Sancti disseruntur*. Rakow.

Galter, Pierre. 1931. "Petau et la preface de son 'de trinitate.'" *Recherches de science religieuse* 21: 462–476.

Hampton, Stephen. 2008. *Anti-Arminians: The Anglican Reformed Tradition from Charles II to George I*. Oxford: Oxford University Press.

Jobert, Ambroise. 1974. *De Luther à Mohila: la Pologne dans la crise de la chrétienté, 1517–1648*. Paris: Institute d'études slaves.

Kot, Stanisław. 1957. *Socinianism in Poland: The Social and Political Ideas of the Polish Antitrinitarians in the Sixteenth and Seventeenth Centuries*. Translated by Earl Morse Wilbur. Boston: Starr King Press.

Lim, Paul. 2012. *Mystery Unveiled: The Crisis of the Trinity in Early Modern England*. Oxford: Oxford University Press.

McLachlan, Herbert John. 1951. *Socinianism in Seventeenth-Century England*. London: Oxford University Press.

Mortimer, Sarah. 2012. "Human and Divine Justice in the Works of Grotius and the Socinians." In *The Intellectual Consequences of Religious Heterodoxy, 1600–1750*, edited by S. Mortimer and J. Robertson, 75–94. Leiden: Brill.

Mortimer, Sarah. 2009. "Human Liberty and Human Nature in the Works of Faustus Socinus and His Readers." *Journal of the History of Ideas* 70: 191–211.

Mortimer, Sarah. 2010. *Reason and Religion in the English Revolution: The Challenge of Socinianism*. Cambridge: Cambridge University Press.

Muller, Richard. 1991. *God, Creation, and Providence in the Thought of Jacob Arminius: Sources and Directions of Scholastic Protestantism in the Era of Early Orthodoxy*. Grand Rapids, MI: Baker.

Muller, Richard. 2003. *The Triunity of God*. Vol. 4 of *Post-Reformation Reformed Dogmatics: The Rise and Development of Reformed Orthodoxy, ca. 1520 to ca. 1725*. Grand Rapids, MI: Baker.

Powell, Samuel. 2001. *The Trinity in German Thought*. Cambridge: Cambridge University Press.

Schofield, Robert. 2004. *The Enlightened Joseph Priestley: A Study of His Life and Work from 1773 to 1804*. University Park, PA: Penn State University Press.

Simonutti, Luisa. 2005. "Resistance, Obedience and Toleration: Przypkowski and Limborch." In: *Socinianism and Arminianism: Antitrinitarians, Calvinists, and Cultural Exchange in Seventeenth-Century Europe*, edited by M. Mulsow and J. Rohls, 187–206. Leiden: Brill.

Socinus, F. 1668. *Fausti Socini Senensis Opera omnia in duos tomos distincta*. 2 vols. Irenopoli [Amsterdam].

Stegmann, Joachim. 1635. *Brevis Disquisitio*. Eleutheropolis [Amsterdam].

Rees, Thomas, ed. 1818. *The Racovian Catechism, with Notes and Illustrations; Translated from the Latin*. London: Longman, Hurst, Rees, Orme, and Brown.

Trevor-Roper, Hugh. 1987. "The Great Tew Circle." In *Catholics, Anglicans and Puritans: Seventeenth Century Essays*, 166–230. London: Secker & Warburg.

Waterman, A. M. C. 1996. "The Nexus between Theology and Political Doctrine in Church and Dissent." In *Enlightenment and Religion: Rational Dissent in Eighteenth-Century Britain*, edited by Knud Haakonssen. Cambridge: Cambridge University Press.

Wilbur, Earl Morse. 1945. *A History of Unitarianism: Socinianism and its Antecedents*. Cambridge, MA: Harvard University Press.

Wilbur, Earl Morse. 1952. *A History of Unitarianism in Transylvania, England, and America*. Cambridge, MA: Harvard University Press.

Wiles, Maurice. 2001. *Archetypal Heresy: Arianism through the Centuries*. Oxford: Oxford University Press.

Zeltner, Gustav Georg. 1729. *Historia crypto-Socinismi Altorfinæ*. Leipzig.

# CHAPTER 25

# EARLY MODERN ANABAPTIST THEOLOGIES

JEFF BACH

## 1 MODERN THEOLOGIES

THE Anabaptist movement refers to a reform movement that emerged in the sixteenth century, deriving its name from the practice of adult baptism administered upon confession of faith that was practiced by all of the groups within the movement. The Anabaptist movement appeared in multiple centers with multiple leaders. Not all of their communities of faith survived to the end of the sixteenth century. Anabaptism thus cannot be portrayed as a unified, systematic theology developed by one theologian (Stayer, Packull, and Deppermann 1975, 85). In addition, many Anabaptist leaders did not live long enough to write fully developed theologies. Because the Anabaptist movement tended to emphasize the role and participation of its members, the role of one formative thinker or teaching office had much less status for most Anabaptists than was the case for Protestantism and the Roman Catholic Church during the Reformation era. Due to these factors, Anabaptist theology cannot fit one unified or normative description. However, in spite of multiple origins and diverse writers, Anabaptist theologies reveal some overlapping tendencies, as C. Arnold Snyder has noted (Snyder 1997, 5–9).

## 2 ORIGINS

The Anabaptist movement emerged in several centers in central Europe between 1525 and 1540. The first group formed among associates of Ulrich Zwingli (1484–1531) in Zürich, Switzerland from 1522 to 1525. As Zwingli advocated reform in theology and church practice, some of his friends such as Conrad Grebel (ca. 1498–1526), Felix Mantz (ca. 1498–1527), and George Blaurock (1492–1529) became convinced that reform should proceed without waiting for approval from the city council. After two public disputations in Zürich in 1523, Zwingli declared that the city council should decide the pace of reform, including abolishing the Mass (Williams 1992, 185–87). Grebel and his friends became convinced that a biblical reform of the Mass ultimately led to the reform of baptism, which they believed should be administered only to adults who confess their faith (Stayer, Packull, and Depperman 1975, 94–95). On January 21, 1525, the first Anabaptist baptism took place when Conrad Grebel baptized the others who shared this view in the house of Felix Mantz in Zürich (Williams 1992, 214–16). The break from Zwingli provoked immediate efforts to suppress the movement, which suffered severe persecution. Michael Sattler, the former prior of the Benedictine monastery of Saint Peter near Freiburg im Breisgau in the Black Forest, became involved with the Swiss Anabaptists. Because of his leadership at a meeting of Anabaptists at Schleitheim in February 1527 and in drafting the seven articles of faith known as the Brotherly Union, or Schleitheim Confession, Sattler played an important leadership role among Swiss Anabaptists (Snyder 1984, 97–100). Sattler and his wife, Margaretha, a former Beguine, were arrested and tried in the spring of 1527. Sattler was burned at the stake and Margaretha was drowned two days later.

In the social upheaval of the peasants' uprisings of 1525, another circle of Anabaptists emerged in southern Germany. Hans Hut (ca. 1490–1527), a one-time follower of Thomas Müntzer (before 1491–1525), abandoned the militant uprisings and in 1526 was baptized by Hans Denck (ca. 1500–27). He preached adult baptism as a sign of an inward suffering of purification in order to be joined to Christ. Baptism was also an eschatological preparation for the impending judgment of Christ (Packull 1977, 79–83). Hut died during an attempt to break out of jail in 1528 after a very brief ministry. Hut left some influences on some Anabaptists, but no lasting group (Seebass 1982, 56–60).

A leader influenced by both the grievances of the peasants and the Zürich Anabaptists was a doctor of theology, Balthasar Hubmaier (1480 or 1485–1528). He had studied at Freiburg and Ingolstadt, and was a prominent preacher in Regensburg before moving to Waldshut on the border of Swiss and imperial lands. He participated in the second Zürich disputation in 1523, the year of his transition toward Anabaptism. He was baptized in Waldshut in 1525. He supported the grievances of the peasants in 1525, fled to Moravia and was arrested in 1527 (Bergsten 1978, 84–87, 216–24, 361–78). He was burned at the stake in 1528 in Vienna. He left numerous Anabaptist writings, including a catechism, a personal confession of faith, and Anabaptist liturgies for baptism and the Lord's Supper. Unlike most Anabaptists, Hubmaier dreamed of establishing an Anabaptist territorial church that would allow for armed force by the government to defend the church.

In the region where Hut was active, another person helped to define the Anabaptism of southern Germany. Hans Denck (ca. 1500–27) contributed to a much more spiritual-ized Anabaptism. Denck baptized Hut, and the two reflect an interiorized, spiritualized dimension to Anabaptism (Packull 1977, 48–57). Denck studied at Ingolstadt and knew biblical languages. After time in Basel, he taught in Nuremberg (1523–25), then lived briefly in Augsburg, Strasbourg, and Worms. He died of plague in Basel in 1527. Denck's path led to an increasingly interior, spiritualized view of faith, to the point that he questioned the value of any outward practice, including baptism and the Lord's Supper (Denck 1956, 108–10). Denck stressed the inward encounter with Christ in the soul.

The ministries of Hut and Hubmaier influenced several emerging groups of Anabaptists in the Tirol Valley in Austria, who had been evangelized by George Blaurock. One group, led by Jacob Widemann (or Wiedemann, d. 1535/1536), adopted community of goods in 1528 and maintained pacifism. Jacob Hutter (ca. 1500–27) joined them soon after this, and in 1529 became their leader. His wife, Katherina, helped to spread the faith (Snyder and Hecht 1996, 178–81). Jacob Hutter directed the communitarian group closer to a biblicist and pacifist Anabaptism (Zieglschmid, Friedrich, Braitmichel, and Zapf 1943, 87, 89–91). Hutter's name became attached to the group, known as Hutterites, before his execution in Innsbrück in 1536.

A different group of Anabaptists developed in northern Germany and the Low Countries in the wake of the apocalyptic preaching of Melchior Hoffman (1495–1543), who joined an Anabaptist circle in Strasbourg in 1530 (Deppermann 1987, 204–6; 217–19). Predicting the return of Christ in judgment for 1533, Hoffman preached in the Netherlands and northern Germany. He administered baptism as a sign of repentance and an eschatological seal in preparation for Christ's impending judgment on the godless (Deppermann 1987, 328–31). He suspended baptizing in 1531 upon the execution of some of his followers in Amsterdam. After Hoffman was imprisoned in Strasbourg in 1533, some of his Dutch followers further radicalized his apocalyptic preaching and resumed baptizing. Jan Matthijs (n.d.–1534) and Jan van Leyden (1509–36) took the lead of Hoffman's movement, known as Melchiorites, and called them move to Münster, where they believed that Christ would return. A pastor in Münster, Bernd Rothmann (1495–1535), was sympathetic to Anabaptist views. When Jan Matthijs and Jan van Leyden came to the city, the Anabaptists gained a majority on the city council and the lead in religious reform. Up to this time, the Münster Anabaptists were peaceful (Deppermann 1987, 333–38). When the exiled bishop of Münster launched a counterassault on the city, the Anabaptists became increasingly militant. Jan Matthijs died in an attack on the besieging troops. Jan van Leyden was crowned king in the manner of David in 1534. He introduced polygamy and community of goods, and ruled despotically within the city (Stayer 1991, 135–38). Weary of the siege, a few Anabaptist citizens betrayed the city to the armed forces against them in 1535. Troops of the bishop and Protestant princes slaughtered the inhabitants. The three main leaders were captured and finally tortured to death in early 1536 (Williams 1992, 580–82).

The Anabaptist movement in the Dutch provinces and northern Germany faced a profound crisis with the collapse of Münster. The claims of visions and the call to hasten the Kingdom of God with violence had led to disaster. The majority of the movement now came under the leadership of a priest from Friesland, Menno Simons (1496–1561), who joined an Anabaptist circle led by Obbe Philips (ca. 1500–68), an early convert to the Melchiorites. Menno was baptized in 1536. He upheld the pacifism and biblicism of Obbe's group, along with the necessity of an organized church. Menno died a natural death in 1561, leaving a large body of writings. His ministry and writings steered the Dutch and northern German Anabaptists away from Hoffman's apocalyptic hermeneutics, creating instead the peaceful Mennonites (Williams 1992, 582–98).

A minority of the remaining Dutch Anabaptists followed David Joris (ca. 1501–56), who spiritualized the apocalyptic teachings of Hoffman to pursue an inward purification to receive Christ and His spiritual kingdom. Joris allowed his followers to conform outwardly to the established traditions. He moved to Basel in 1543 under an alias and met secretly with followers until his death in 1556.

An additional tiny remnant of northern Anabaptists remained a militant, marauding gang led by Jan van Batenburg (1495–1538), who was baptized in 1535. He considered himself the "new David" to lead a militant remnant to punish the "godless." (Williams 1992, 582–83). He continued the polygamy practiced within Münster and a form of community of goods, but discontinued baptism and the Lord's Supper after 1536. The group attacked churches, monasteries and the estates of wealthy citizens. He was arrested and executed in early 1538. A few marauders persisted in his ways, but disappeared by the 1580s. Overall, the Mennonites were the most numerous and successful of the Dutch and northern German Anabaptist movement.

One additional significant Anabaptist leader came from the Tirol Valley in Austria and adopted Anabaptist views in light of the preaching and suffering of the Anabaptists there. Pilgram Marpeck (ca. 1495–1556) was an engineer of mines from a prominent family. After marriage and baptism in Krumau in early 1528, he moved on to Strasbourg in 1528 (Klassen and Klaassen 2008, 109, 115–27, 149–63, 231–43, 315–24). He debated with Protestant reformers and the spiritualist, Caspar von Schwenkfeld (1489–1561), and directed the city's forestry service. He was expelled from Strasbourg in 1532, eventually settling in Augsburg in 1544 where he lived until his death in 1556, overseeing the city's forestry office. His professional skills and expertise made authorities reluctant to persecute him. Marpeck tried to bring Anabaptists from disparate origins together in his travels, ministry and writing. He advocated engagement with civic life as long as it did not conflict with biblical principles. He left no lasting group of followers.

The Anabaptist movement as a whole was constituted primarily by these main groups whose theologies emerged from a variety of leaders with sometimes divergent emphases. By the end of the sixteenth century, the Swiss Brethren (descendants of Grebel's movement), the Dutch Mennonites, and the Hutterites were the primary surviving Anabaptist groups—all pacifists and all finding in scripture and the witness of the ancient church in Acts their primary grounding for faith and practice.

# 3 Theological Characteristics

## 3.1 Baptism

The defining characteristic that all Anabaptist groups shared was adult baptism of those who confessed their sins and confessed faith in Christ's gracious forgiveness. Their adult baptism must be interpreted in light of one of the overarching theological controversies in the early modern era; namely, the forgiveness of sins based on justification by faith and the status of the forgiven before God. Protestant theologies (Lutheran, Zwinglian, Calvinist) drew their views of justification by faith alone from their readings of Augustine's understandings of original sin, the damage to the human will from sin, and divine omnipotence in God's electing who would be saved from sin and who would not. Anabaptists were aware of debates around these concepts, even if many of them were not trained or prepared to enter such debates on the same rhetorical footing as professional theologians. For Anabaptists, the forgiveness of sins was a gift of divine grace through faith, not an achievement accomplished by requesting and receiving baptism. The Schleitheim Confession (1527) stated that baptism is given to those who "believe truly that their sins are taken away in Christ" (Yoder 1973, 36). In *A Christian Catechism*, Hubmaier described baptism as "an outward and public testimony of the inner baptism in the Spirit, which a person gives by receiving water, with which one confesses one's sins before all people." The believer "testifies thereby that one believes in the forgiveness of his sins through the death and resurrection of our Lord Jesus Christ" (Hubmaier 1989, 349). Menno Simons wrote in *Christian Baptism* (1546) that "faith precedes baptism," and from faith "baptism issues as a sign and token of obedience" (Menno 1956, 239). In his confession of faith for the Hutterites, Peter Rideman (or Riedemann, 1506–56) wrote that "those who have heard the Word, believed the same and have recognized God should be baptized" (Rideman 1970, 77). The baptized must be born in a spiritual manner, which comes "through the Word, faith and the Holy Spirit." Adult baptism tied faith to the believer who repents in faith, rather than to a parent or sponsor making promises on behalf of an infant who could not confess sin or faith. Anabaptists typically saw faith as a gift from God, the result of the working of the Holy Spirit, who was also the source of repentance prior to baptism. Most Anabaptist writers emphasized spiritual rebirth as accompanying faith and baptism. Spiritual rebirth was the result of the continuing work of the Holy Spirit before and after baptism to regenerate human character, transforming the human will and desire toward the will of Christ. In *The New Birth* (1556) Menno wrote that those who repent, believe, and are baptized are regenerated and "lead a penitent and new life, for they are renewed in Christ and have received a new heart and spirit" (Menno 1956, 93).

With the transfer of baptism to adulthood and confession of faith, Anabaptists had to answer regarding the destiny of infants who would not be baptized. Typically, Anabaptists answered that infants were covered by the merits of Christ's suffering and did not need baptism until they reached an ability to discern good from evil, as Conrad Grebel wrote in a letter to Thomas Müntzer in 1524, rejecting Müntzer's practice of infant baptism (Grebel 1985, 290). Menno Simons wrote in *Christian Baptism* (1539) that if children do not live long enough to hear the gospel, believe it, and confess faith as well as bring forth fruits of repentance, then they "die under the promise of God, and that by no other means than the generous promise of grace given through Jesus Christ" (Menno 1956, 241). Peter Rideman, the Hutterite writer, included the doctrine of original sin in his confession of faith, but redefined it somewhat, stating that original sin is an inherited inclination to sin, and with it a pleasure in sin. However, he believed that children could not fully know the difference between good and evil, and also could not confess faith.

Thus "Christ is also their reconciler" until they can hear the gospel, believe, repent, and confess faith and be accepted into the church (Rideman 1970, 58). All of the Anabaptists adopted a view of the freedom of human will (Snyder 1997, 153), thus reflecting a moderated inheritance from medieval theology and rejecting the Augustinian views of Protestants.

Some Anabaptists, such as Hut and Hoffman, held an urgent eschatological dimension in their understandings of justification and baptism. After the disaster of Münster, leaders such as Menno Simons, Pilgram Marpeck, and the Hutterites softened this element in Anabaptist theologies of baptism.

Adult baptism upon repentance from sin and confession of faith in salvation through the grace of Christ was an overarching common characteristic of most of the Anabaptist movement. Their theology and practice of baptism, and the view of church and ethics derived from it, set the Anabaptists apart from other branches of Christianity in the early modern period.

## 3.2 Community and discipline

Most Anabaptists saw baptism as an outward sign of faith in Christ's redemption from sin. Equally important for most Anabaptists, baptism also marked entry into a disciplined church of mutual accountability among believers. They held a strong confidence in the power of the Holy Spirit to continue the ongoing renewal of the human condition after baptism, so that members could live according to the teachings of Jesus with the Spirit's help. Baptism upon confession of faith led to a concept of the church as a visible, gathered body of committed believers. With perhaps only a few exceptions, Anabaptists did not believe that humans attain sinless perfection, so the gathered church was not flawless. Rather, it is a body of believers who were being transformed by faith that the church should be without spot or wrinkle. Hubmaier wrote in *A Christian Catechism* (1527) that the church includes "all the people who are gathered and united in one God, one Lord, one faith and one baptism, and have confessed this with their mouths" (Hubmaier 1989, 351). He believed that the local congregation might err, but the wider confessing church would be "without spot, without wrinkle, is controlled by the Holy Spirit and Christ" (Hubmaier 1989, 352). In *Christian Baptism* (1539) Menno described the church as consisting of those who "hear and believe the Word of God," who are "baptized into the body of Christ on their own faith" and are "regenerated of the Word of God," and who will live obediently according to the will of Jesus Christ (Menno 1956, 274).

An important corollary to the importance of the gathered community of believers was the practice of mutual correction and church discipline. Nearly all significant theological writings of early Anabaptism held a significant place for discipline and the ban. In *A Christian Catechism* (1527) Hubmaier described how the newly baptized should live according to the divine Word, and promise to the church to "dutifully accept brotherly discipline from it and its members" (Hubmaier 1989, 351). The second article of the

Schleitheim Confession grounds the practice of the ban on Matthew 18 (Yoder 1973, 36). Rideman's confession of faith calls for the church to exclude those who will not receive from the church admonition to correct their errors (Rideman 1970, 132). Mutual accountability and discipline superseded the Roman Catholic sacrament of penance, transferring it from responsibility of the priest to the shared expectation and practice of all the members of the congregation (Snyder 1997, 349–56).

Church discipline among the Hutterites and the Dutch and northern German Anabaptists sometimes included the practice of shunning, or cutting off social interaction with members who transgressed the teachings of the faith until they repented and asked forgiveness. Menno Simons eventually accepted the harsher practice of shunning held by his assistant, Leenaert Bouwens (1515–82) (Williams 1992, 743). After Menno's death, disagreements among Dutch Mennonite leaders over the severity of social avoidance fractured the Mennonites into more subgroups. During the seventeenth century, Dutch Anabaptists softened their use of the ban and experienced some reunion (Snyder 1997, 228–30).

In the late seventeenth century, a separation developed among Swiss Anabaptists living in Alsace and southwestern Germany. In 1693, Jacob Ammann (fl. ca. 1690–1708) in Alsace insisted on strict discipline and introduced the practice of shunning (J. Ammann 1993, 34–35, 40–42). His followers were known as the Amish, and congregational discipline is still a characteristic of their group today. A later group of Anabaptist-influenced separatists, the Schwarzenau Brethren (founded in 1708 in Schwarzenau, Germany, also known as the Brethren), also adopted the ban and a limited practice of shunning in their appropriation of Anabaptist beliefs (Mack 1991, 66–67, 92–93). For most Anabaptists, mutual correction expressed a desire for the ongoing work of the Holy Spirit to constitute the gathered, visible church of believers who would be accountable for following the teachings of Jesus.

## 3.3 Discipleship

In light of the high view of the Holy Spirit's power to renovate human will, many Anabaptists advocated obedience to the teachings of Jesus. The ethical impulse in Anabaptist theology was neither an effort to earn God's salvation nor the consequence of mere human will or resolve. Rather, a godly life of discipleship was the consequence of repentance, faith, rebirth, and baptism. In his *Confession of the Distressed Christians* (1552), Menno wrote that his movement did not "boast of being perfect and without sin" (Menno 1956, 505–6). The quest to live obediently was a gift from the Holy Spirit by grace. Some ethical teachings that were commonly affirmed among many Anabaptist writers included avoiding the swearing of oaths, living humbly and simply, and sharing material resources (Snyder 1997, 307–16). Another distinctive teaching characteristic of most Anabaptists was peace and the love of enemy. These ethical teachings were grounded in teachings of Jesus in the New Testament. Additionally, the concern for sharing of material resources and the egalitarian status of being sisters and brothers echoed some of the social concerns from the grievances of the peasants' uprisings in the 1520s, according to James Stayer (Stayer 1991, 89–92).

Several Anabaptist writers commented on the refusal to swear oaths (based on Matthew 5:33–37). The Schleitheim Confession prohibited oaths (Yoder 1973, 37), as did Peter Rideman's Hutterite account of faith (Rideman 1970, 114–19). Menno Simons rejected the swearing of oaths in his *Confession of the Distressed Christians* (1552) (Menno 1956, 517–21). The refusal of oaths was an additional mark of how some Anabaptists saw the church refusing to conform to coercive powers of the government. Avoiding oaths demonstrated a higher allegiance to God and a desire to live in honesty and integrity (Snyder 1997, 257–305). In a letter to Swiss Anabaptists in 1543, Pilgram Marpeck advocated a less strict position on oaths, perhaps because of his own involvement in civil government (Marpeck 1978, 368).

In the earliest years of the Anabaptist movement, some diverse attitudes toward marriage appeared. Cases where one spouse converted to Anabaptist views and the other did not, created the danger that the non-Anabaptist spouse might report the other to authorities, which could lead to arrest and perhaps persecution (Snyder 1997, 325–35). Swiss Anabaptists seem to have allowed for members to separate from non-Anabaptist spouses, but not divorce them (Yoder 1973, 104). The Hutterites allowed for new converts to leave a marriage with a nonmember, since members were expected to live in a communal economy, but did not support remarriage (Rideman 1970, 97–102). Among some of Melchior Hoffman's followers, separation and taking a new spouse in a "spiritual marriage" (but not legal marriage) was seen as an extension of freedom in the new life in Christ. These trends led ultimately to polygamy among the Münsterites and the Batenburgers (Williams 1992, 568–70, 583). David Joris likewise endorsed the possibility of believers leaving their spouses and forming new spiritual marriages (Joris 1994, 275–76). Patriarchal hierarchy prevailed in all of these relationships.

After the middle of the sixteenth century, Anabaptists encouraged members to choose only fellow Anabaptists as spouses and to raise children in such families to accept the Anabaptist faith. Overall, attitudes toward marriage among the Anabaptist groups that persisted after the middle of the sixteenth century reflected the patriarchal patterns of marriage in European society in general, with a growing preference for marriage only within the group in a union that would last a lifetime.

## 3.4 Peace, love of enemies, and suffering

One of the broadly shared marks of discipleship among Anabaptists was a commitment to love for enemies and refusal to use violence. In the sixteenth century, Anabaptists referred to themselves as "defenseless" (*wehrlos* in German, *weerloos* in Dutch). Writing to Thomas Müntzer in 1524, Conrad Grebel stated that Christians should "use neither worldly sword nor war." Grebel denounced violence and counseled a readiness to suffer (Grebel 1985, 290). By the time Hans Hut was baptized, he had abandoned the revolutionary militancy of Thomas Müntzer (Williams 1992, 268).

The Schleitheim Confession specifically prohibited the use of the sword (Yoder 1973, 39). Peter Rideman's Hutterite confession faith forbade fighting and killing (Rideman 1970, 108).

By emphasizing the New Testament teachings of Jesus to love enemies and reject the use of violence, Menno Simons steered northern Anabaptism away from the apocalyptic violence of Münster. He wrote already in 1535 against the Münsterites, asserting that Jesus Christ is the only true king and true "David" for Christians. As Christ was defenseless and loved his enemies, so the sheep in Christ's flock must love enemies, renounce violence, and be ready to suffer (Menno 1956, 42, 44–45). In his *Foundation of Christian Doctrine* (1539), Menno refuted the persistent charges from Protestant and Roman Catholic leaders that all Anabaptists were Münsterites, declaring that the remaining Anabaptists used no weapons other than the "sword" of the word of God (Menno 1956, 198). Instead, they were subjects of Christ's spiritual kingdom, not an earthly kingdom. In a *Reply to False Accusations* (1552), Menno wrote that "the Prince of peace is Jesus Christ" and "His body is the body of peace; His children are the seed of peace," who are commanded "to love their enemies" (Menno 1956, 554).

Unlike Protestant definitions of the church, many Anabaptists believed, as Menno wrote in his *Reply to False Accusations* (1552), that suffering is a mark of true Christians and the church (Menno 1956, 555). Dirk Philips (1504–68) wrote in his *Enchiridion* that suffering is one of the characteristics of the church (Philips 1992, 373).

The legacy of suffering continued with Anabaptists after the sixteenth century in various ways. During the seventeenth century, the Hutterites in Moravia were fiercely persecuted. In Switzerland, the last execution of an Anabaptist (Hans Landis) took place in 1614, but repressive measures and imprisonments continued throughout the seventeenth century. In the Netherlands, political leaders made efforts to tolerate the Mennonites as early as 1579. These efforts generally prevailed by the end of the century. The Mennonites in the Netherlands also benefited from the rapid rise in wealth in Dutch society during the seventeenth century. Dutch Mennonites assimilated to the prevailing culture and relaxed some of their distinctive traits. In 1660, a Dutch Mennonite merchant, Thieleman Jansz van Braght (1625–64), published a massive anthology of martyr stories, primarily of Anabaptists, known in English as *Martyrs Mirror* (van Braght 1660). Building on smaller collections of Anabaptist martyr stories that began with *Het Offer des Heeren* ("The Sacrifice of the Lord") in 1562, the greatly expanded *Martyrs Mirror* traced the suffering of Christians through the centuries back to Christ and the apostles. The bulk of the work was devoted to Anabaptist martyrs in the sixteenth and early seventeenth centuries. The martyr stories are one of the most important sources for learning the activity and words of Anabaptist women's actions and words. At the time when the Dutch Mennonites were accommodating rapidly to the comforts of Dutch culture and toleration, van Braght sought to remind them of the radical sacrifices and faith made just a century earlier (Luthy 2013, 9–12). The *Martyrs Mirror* was translated into German for the first time in 1748 in Ephrata, Pennsylvania, and became very meaningful to German speaking Mennonites and Amish in North America. Through the *Martyrs Mirror*, and through martyr hymns in the *Ausbund*, first published in 1564 and still used in Amish worship today, the legacy of Anabaptist suffering is still remembered among the Amish and some plain Mennonite groups in America.

## 3.5 Ordinances

Anabaptists did not frequently use the term "sacrament" for the rituals of the church, although the term does appear. Often Anabaptists preferred the term "ordinances" for the rituals of baptism and the Lord's Supper, connoting that the practices were ordained and instituted by Christ and maintained by the apostles. Anabaptists did not define the term "ordinance" precisely. In his *Enchiridion*, Dirk Philips described "the true scriptural use of the sacraments," namely "baptism and the Supper" as one of seven ordinances ordained by Christ for the church (Philips 1992, 363, 365). Anabaptists accepted only baptism and the Lord's Supper as the two sacraments or ordinances of the church.

Anabaptist views on the Lord's Supper were primarily influenced by the symbolic interpretation of the elements, typical of both Ulrich Zwingli and Dutch sacramentarians, a movement that denied the literal presence of the flesh and blood of Christ in the Eucharist (Williams 1992, 181–196). Most Anabaptists insisted that only believing members could partake of the Lord's Supper. This view is a corollary to their theology of the church, which is constituted only of confessing believers. The role of accountability and correction within the church reinforced the importance of admitting only believers to the Lord's Supper.

Balthasar Hubmaier created the only formal Eucharisic liturgy among the Anabaptists, "A Form for Christ's Supper" (Hubmaier 1989, 393–408). No Anabaptist group adopted this liturgy as a lasting practice. Hubmaier's liturgy required members to recommit their willingness to receive and give correction in the church, and pledge their willingness to suffer for each other prior to reception of the elements (Hubmaier 1989, 403). Gradually, somewhat standardized formularies for how the ordinances should be conducted took shape, but no other writers created theologically formal liturgies.

In addition to baptism and the Lord's Supper, some of the Dutch Mennonites practiced footwashing in conjunction with the Lord's Supper, in imitation of Jesus's washing of the disciples' feet at the last supper (John 13). Dirk Philips named footwashing as the third ordinance established by Christ for the true church (Philips 1992, 367). Footwashing represented renewed inward spiritual cleansing and a model of humility. Additionally, a comment from Menno in his *Admonition on Church Discipline* (1541) implies that the Dutch Mennonites might have practiced footwashing as an occasional act of hospitality, but not associated with the Lord's Supper (Menno 1956, 417). In the seventeenth century, footwashing disappeared from the Dutch Mennonites, and the Swiss Brethren never practiced it. However, during the Amish division in 1693, Ulli Ammann (1661–after 1733) noted that a distinctive point for his group was the insistence on practicing footwashing at the Lord's Supper, which is still observed by the Amish today (U. Ammann 1993, 98). Many of Jacob Ammann's detractors among the Swiss Anabaptists considered him an innovator for introducing this practice. The Schwarzenau Brethren, founded in

1708 and influenced by Anabaptist writings, also adopted footwashing with their communion observance and still practice it (Mack 1991, 62). During the nineteenth and twentieth centuries, some Mennonite congregations began to readopt footwashing.

## 3.6 Christology

Anabaptists tended to affirm traditional Christian doctrinal views on Jesus Christ and the union of divine and human natures in Christ. Because he shared fully in human and divine nature, he alone could forgive sins, and serve as an ethical model for how the forgiven should live. Melchior Hoffman developed a divergent Christology that affected nearly all of those in his stream of Anabaptism. Hoffman believed that Jesus Christ's flesh came entirely from heaven and received nothing of the humanity of Mary. The biblical basis for this view was Hoffman's interpretation of John 1:14 ("the word became flesh"). Sometimes called a celestial flesh Christology, Hoffman's view affirmed that Christ had a real human body, but that Christ became flesh, rather than took on flesh from Mary. Hoffman wrote in 1530, "He [Jesus] did not take flesh upon himself, but became himself flesh and corporal, in order that he might himself give salvation" (Hoffman 1957, 198). Hoffman believed that only if Jesus had no flesh from a human source could he atone for the sins of humanity in his death and resurrection (Snyder 1997, 379–90). Menno Simons, like most Dutch and northern German Anabaptists, held Hoffman's Christology. In a *Brief Confession on the Incarnation* (1544) Menno wrote that Jesus was "conceived not of her [Mary's] womb, but in her womb, wrought by the Holy Spirit through faith, of God the omnipotent Father, from high heaven" (Menno 1956, 436).

A brief and very limited Christological controversy arose in Dutch Anabaptism in the 1540s. Adam Pastor (n.d.–1560/1570), one of the ministers, denied completely the divine nature of Christ (Williams 1992, 739–40). Pastor was expelled from fellowship in 1547 and had little influence on the Anabaptist movement. The other branches of the Anabaptist movement did not accept Hoffman's Christology. Menno's Christology persisted in Dutch Anabaptism into the seventeenth century but was gradually abandoned.

## 3.7 Eschatology

Views on the end times were the most controversial and divergent among Anabaptists, and yet catalyzed theological development. Hans Hut, Melchior Hoffman, and the Münsterites believed that Christ's return and judgment upon the godless were imminent (Williams 1992, 266–67, 390–92, 576–81). The Münsterites believed that they should use violence against the forces of the godless to hasten Christ's return.

Because of the crisis at Münster, eschatology propelled further development of Anabaptist theologies. David Joris promoted a spiritualizing turn for eschatology, internalizing the coming kingdom as an inward, spiritual kingdom of Christ's rule (Joris

1994, 276–78). Menno Simons developed a more thorough biblical grounding for northern Anabaptist theology, illustrated by his *Reply to False Accusations* (1552). He transferred the urgency of the coming kingdom to an urgency of preparation for it through repentance, while using Christ's teaching of love for enemies to close off the possibility of bringing in the kingdom by force (Menno 1956, 547–54). By the seventeenth century, eschatological views among Anabaptists had quieted significantly.

# 4  CONCLUSION

By the seventeenth century, only the Mennonites in the North, the Swiss Brethren in Switzerland, Alsace, and southern Germany (later also called Mennonites in America), and the Hutterites primarily in Moravia survived. All three of these Anabaptist groups were biblicist and Christocentric in the ways in which they grounded their theologies. They were all pacifists. The Hutterites and the Swiss Brethren came to a posture of distance from the broader culture and from the governing order due to persecution. The Dutch Mennonites more willingly engaged in the life of Dutch society, and in the eighteenth century began to hold public office. The Dutch Mennonites struggled through a series of divisions in the seventeenth century, but also worked toward reunion, not always successfully. The extensive writings of Menno Simons and Dirk Philipps constituted the theological legacy of the Dutch Mennonites. However, by the eighteenth century, Rationalism and Socinianism also influenced them considerably.

The Hutterites relied on Peter Rideman's *Account of Our Religion* and their massive internal history, the *Geschichtbuch* ("The History Book," or "The Chronicle"), as their theological touchstones. The Hutterite chronicles combined accounts of the preaching of the earliest Swiss Anabaptists along with stories of suffering and faith to create a written source for their theological grounding. The two-volume chronicle remains important among the Hutterites today.

The Swiss Anabaptists had far fewer written sources for their theology than did the Mennonites or the Hutterites. However, collections of some sermons, letters and other writings circulated. The *Ausbund* and their preaching tradition carried on the Swiss Anabaptist theological legacy. In the eighteenth century, interactions with Pietism influenced some small changes.

At the end of the seventeenth century and throughout the eighteenth century, Mennonites migrated to North America and later Ukraine. In the eighteenth century, Hutterites migrated to Russia (and in 1874 to North America). Their theologies that had taken shape in the early modern period went with them, even as they interacted with new influences. Historical scholarship in the twentieth century did much to rediscover some significant Anabaptist writings from the sixteenth century, and led to new assessments of the theological legacy of a movement that charted the path to gathered churches of believers that are independent from prevailing governments and voluntary in membership.

# Bibliography

Ammann, Jacob. 1993. "Summary and Defense (November 22, 1693)." In *Letters of the Amish Division: A Sourcebook*, translated and edited by John D. Roth with Joe Springer, 29–48. Goshen, IN: Mennonite Historical Society.

Ammann, Ulli. 1993. "Summary and Defense (1698)." In *Letters of the Amish Division: A Sourcebook*, translated and edited by John D. Roth with Joe Springer, 83–104. Goshen, IN: Mennonite Historical Society.

Bergsten, Torsten. 1978. *Balthasar Hubmaier: Anabaptist Theologian and Martyr*. Valley Forge, PA: Judson Press.

Denck, Hans. 1956. "Wiederruf." In *Religiöse Schriften. Vol. 2 of Schriften*, edited by Walter Fellmann, 104–110. Gütersloh: C. Bertelsmann Verlag.

Deppermann, Klaus. 1987. *Melchior Hoffman: Social Unrest and Apocalyptic Visions in the Age of Reformation*. Translated by Malcolm Wren. Edinburgh: T&T Clark.

Dirk Philips. 1992. "Enchiridion or Handbook of Christian Doctrine and Religion." In *The Writings of Dirk Philips 1504–1568*, translated and edited by Cornelius J. Dyck, William E. Keeney, and Alvin J. Beachy, 59–440. Scottdale, PA: Herald Press.

Grebel, Conrad. 1985. "Grebel to Müntzer." In *The Sources of Swiss Anabaptism: The Grebel Letters and Related Documents*, translated and edited by Leland Harder, 284–292. Scottdale, PA: Herald Press.

Hoffman, Melchior. 1957. "The Ordinance of God." In *Spiritualist and Anabaptist Writers: Documents Illustrative of the Radical Reformation*, translated and edited by George Huntston Williams and Angel M. Mergal, 184–203. Philadelphia: Westminster Press.

Hubmaier, Balthasar. 1989. "Christian Catechism." In *Balthasar Hubmaier: Theologian of Anabaptism*, translated and edited by H. Wayne Pipkin and John H. Yoder, 340–365. Scottdale, PA: Herald Press.

Hubmaier, Balthasar. 1989. "A Form for Christ's Supper." In *Balthasar Hubmaier: Theologian of Anabaptism*, translated and edited by H. Wayne Pipkin and John H. Yoder, 393–408. Scottdale, PA: Herald Press.

Joris, David. 1994. "The Apology to Countess Anna of Oldenburg 1540–1543." In *The Anabaptist Writings of David Joris*, translated and edited Gary K. Waite, 270–286. Waterloo, ON: Herald Press.

Klaassen, Walter, and William Klassen. 2008. *Marpeck: A Life of Dissent and Conformity*. Scottdale, PA: Herald Press.

Luthy, David. 2013. *A History of the Printings of the Martyrs' Mirror: Dutch, German, English, 1660–2012*. Aylmer, ON: Pathway.

Mack, Alexander Sr. 1991. "A Brief and Simple Exposition of the Outward but yet Sacred Rights and Ordinances of the House of God." In *The Complete Writings of Alexander Mack*, translated by Donald F. Durnbaugh and edited by William R. Eberly, 43–105. Winona Lake, IN: BMH Books.

Marpeck, Pilgram. 1978. "Another Letter to the Swiss Brethren (1543)." In *The Writings of Pilgram Marpeck*, translated and edited by William Klassen and Walter Klaassen, 362–368. Scottdale, PA: Herald Press.

Menno Simons. 1956. "The Blasphemy of Jan van Leyden." In *The Complete Writings of Menno Simons c. 1496–1561*, translated by Leonard Verduin and edited by J. C. Wenger, 33–50. Scottdale, PA: Herald Press.

Menno Simons. 1956. "A Brief Confession on the Incarnation." In *The Complete Writings of Menno Simons c. 1496–1561*, translated by Leonard Verduin and edited by J. C. Wenger, 229–287. Scottdale, PA: Herald Press.

Menno Simons. 1956. "Christian Baptism." In *The Complete Writings of Menno Simons c. 1496–1561*, translated by Leonard Verduin and edited by J. C. Wenger, 229–287. Scottdale, PA: Herald Press.

Menno Simons. 1956. "Confession of the Distressed Christians." In *The Complete Writings of Menno Simons c. 1496–1561*, translated by Leonard Verduin and edited by J. C. Wenger, 422–454. Scottdale, PA: Herald Press.

Menno Simons. 1956. "Foundation of Christian Doctrine." In *The Complete Writings of Menno Simons c. 1496–1561*, translated by Leonard Verduin and edited by J. C. Wenger, 105–226. Scottdale, PA: Herald Press.

Menno Simons. 1956. "A Kind Admonition on Church Discipline." In *The Complete Writings of Menno Simons c. 1496–1561*, translated by Leonard Verduin and edited by J. C. Wenger, 409–418. Scottdale, PA: Herald Press.

Menno Simons. 1956. "The New Birth." In *The Complete Writings of Menno Simons c. 1496–1561*, translated by Leonard Verduin and edited by J. C. Wenger, 89–102. Scottdale, PA: Herald Press.

Menno Simons. 1956. "Reply to False Accusations." In *The Complete Writings of Menno Simons c. 1496–1561*, translated by Leonard Verduin and edited by J. C. Wenger, 543–577. Scottdale, PA: Herald Press.

Packull, Werner O. 1977. *Mysticism and the Early South German-Austrian Anabaptist Movement 1525–1531*. Scottdale, PA: Herald Press.

Rideman, Peter. 1970. *Account of Our Religion, Doctrine and Faith*. Translated by the Hutterian Society of Brothers. Rifton, NY: Plough Publishing House.

Seebass, Gottfried. 1982. "Hans Hut: The Suffering Avenger." In *Profiles of Radical Reformers: Biographical Sketches from Thomas Müntzer to Paracelsus*, edited by Hans-Jürgen Goertz, 54–71. Scottdale, PA: Herald Press.

Snyder, C. Arnold. 1997. *Anabaptist History and Theology: Revised Student Edition*. Kitchener, ON: Pandora Press.

Snyder, C. Arnold. 1984. *The Life and Thought of Michael Sattler*. Scottdale, PA: Herald Press.

Snyder, C. Arnold, and Linda A. Huebert Hecth, eds. 1996. *Profiles of Anabaptist Women: Sixteenth-Century Reforming Pioneers*. Waterloo, ON: Wilfrid Laurier University Press.

Stayer, James M., Werner O. Packull, and Klaus Depperman. 1975. "From Monogenesis to Polygenesis: The Historical Discussion of Anabaptist Origins." *Mennonite Quarterly Review* 49 (2): 83–121.

Stayer, James M. 1991. *The German Peasants' War and Anabaptist Community of Goods*. Montreal: McGill-Queen's University Press.

van Braght, Tieleman Jansz. 1660. *Het Bloedigh Tonel der Doops-Gesinde En Wereloose Christenen*. Dordrecht: Jacoob Braat.

Waite, Gary K. 1990. *David Joris and Dutch Anabaptism, 1524–1543*. Waterloo, ON: Wilfrid Laurier University Press.

Williams, George Hunston. 1992. *The Radical Reformation*. 3rd ed. Sixteenth-Century Essays & Studies 15. Kirksville, MO: Sixteenth Century Journal Publishers.

Yoder, John H. 1973. *The Legacy of Michael Sattler*. Scottdale, PA: Herald Press.

Zieglschmid, Andreas Johannes Friedrich, Kaspar Braitmichel, and Hauptrecht Zapf. 1943. *Die älteste Chronik der Hutterischen Brüder: ein Sprachdenkmal aus frühneuhochdeutscher Zeit*. Ithaca, NY: Cayuga Press.

# CHAPTER 26

# ARMINIAN, REMONSTRANT, AND EARLY METHODIST THEOLOGIES

### KEITH D. STANGLIN

## 1 JACOB ARMINIUS

### 1.1 Life and works of Arminius

Jacob Harmenszoon (Arminius) (1559–1609) was born and raised in the small Dutch town of Oudewater. Since his father died before 1559, Arminius must have been born before the traditional date given for his birth (October 10, 1560) (C. Bangs 1985, 25–26). He received his early education in Utrecht and Marburg. While he was away in Marburg, his mother, older siblings, and much of his extended family perished in the Spanish massacre in his hometown in 1575. Arminius later took his theological training in Leiden, Basel, and Geneva.

After his studies were complete in Geneva, Arminius was ordained as a preaching minister in the Oude Kerk (Old Church) in Amsterdam, where he labored from 1588 until 1603. As Arminius preached through the Epistle to the Romans, he came under fire for his comparatively optimistic view of the life of Christian holiness (expressed in Romans 7) and his opinions about predestination (expressed in Romans 9). A story has circulated since his death, and is sometimes perpetuated today, that Arminius once held the supralapsarian opinion of his teacher in Geneva, Theodore Beza (1519–1605), and came to affirm conditional predestination early in his Amsterdam ministry. Arminius, so the story goes, was invited to write a treatise defending supralapsariansim, but never wrote it because he became convinced of the doctrine's error. Bangs (C. Bangs 1958, 1–12; 1985, 138–41) has called this story into question, pointing out that Arminius never hinted at this alleged shift and probably never held to the supralapsarianism of Beza. It is just as likely that Arminius, as an heir to the earlier stages of the Dutch Reformation that favored latitude on the question of predestination, probably always held to conditional predestination, which brought him into controversy in Amsterdam in the 1590s.

When two of the three members of the theological faculty in Leiden died, Arminius was called in 1603 to be a professor of theology in Leiden. After being awarded the doctoral degree, he began his duties of lecturing and presiding over disputations in the Staten (Theological) College of Leiden University. During his tenure as a professor in Leiden, Arminius became an increasingly controversial figure, primarily because of his stance against the doctrine of absolute predestination. His most proximate opponent in Leiden was his faculty colleague, Franciscus Gomarus (1563–1641). His strongest ally during these tumultuous years was his longtime friend, Johannes Uytenbogaert (1557–1644), the court preacher in The Hague. In addition to the disputes over the doctrine of predestination, which began in Leiden in 1604, from 1605 to 1606 Arminius was also involved in a Christological debate with his other faculty colleague, Lucas Trelcatius, Jr. The question concerned the propriety of describing the second person of the Trinity as *autotheos* (God [from] himself), which Arminius thought could be done only in a qualified manner, a belief which has implications about the Son's aseity according to his divine nature (Muller 1988; Stanglin and McCall 2012).

Arminius is most well known for the controversies surrounding predestination and the doctrines closely connected to it—namely, human free will, divine grace, and salvation. Because of his distinct beliefs, Arminius was constantly under the scrutiny of Reformed theologians and ministers who suspected him of teaching contrary to the Belgic Confession and Heidelberg Catechism. Besides the theological disagreements, there was also political suspicion about anyone who would advocate the idea of human cooperation in salvation, for the Reformed establishment saw this as a step toward what were then identified polemically as the Pelagianizing tendencies of Roman Catholicism, and the Dutch at this point had been in a state of ongoing war with Roman Catholic Spain for about four decades. By 1608, the magistrates of Holland could not ignore the fact that the debates were no longer contained in the academy but had spilled over into the churches and even the streets. Arminius was invited and appeared before the States of Holland on October 30, 1608, to present his views regarding the contested doctrines, published later as *Verclaringhe*, or *Declaratio sententiae*. A subsequent conference in August 1609 held between representatives of the two positions failed to resolve the disputes. A few weeks later, on October 19, 1609, Arminius died from complications of what was probably tuberculosis.

Arminius wrote a number of treatises during both his Amsterdam ministry and his time as a professor in Leiden. In addition to the *Declaration of Sentiments* (1608), his most lengthy and detailed works are the *Dissertation on Romans 7* (1591–93/1600), *Conference with Franciscus Junius on Predestination* (ca. 1596–98), *Examination of Perkins' Pamphlet on Predestination* (ca. 1602), *Examination of the Theses of Franciscus Gomarus on Predestination* (1604), and *Apology against Certain Theological Articles* (1608). Along with these and other polemical-apologetic works are five orations delivered at Leiden

University that are more constructively arranged. All these writings appeared in print only posthumously. In the absence of a systematic theology, the best key to the broad range of Arminius's theology is the collection of extant public and private disputations from Leiden, each one consisting of propositions on a given theological topic to be defended by his students. The final (incomplete) set of private disputations, as well as twenty-five public disputations, were also collected and published posthumously. These Latin works that had been printed first separately in small collections were gathered and published in Leiden as *Opera theologica* in 1629 (Frankfurt, 2nd ed., 1631; 3rd ed., 1635), which became the basis for the nineteenth-century English translation (*Works*).

A few other works that were not gathered into the *Opera*, and therefore not translated into English and seldom used, have been published in later collections. Most of Arminius's extant letters were printed with those of contemporaries and later Arminians in 1660 (Van Limborch, 2nd ed., 1684; 3rd ed., 1704). A small collection of poems from his student days was published in 1925. Most recently, the remaining thirty-six public disputations were published in a critical edition in 2010 (Stanglin 2010). Nevertheless, other letters, fragments, and a student's notes on his lectures on the Epistle to the Galatians all remain unpublished (Stanglin and Muller 2009).

## 1.2 Theology of Arminius

Arminius's theology has much in common with Reformed theology at this stage of its development. He was, after all, a student of Beza, then a minister in the Reformed church, and later a professor at a Reformed seminary. Arminius's teachings on scripture, the essence and attributes of God, the Trinity, incarnation and atonement, pneumatology, and ecclesiology, for the most part, all track closely alongside the lines characteristic of this phase of early orthodox Reformed theology. Even when the outcomes are different, his use of concepts such as the order of decrees and covenant theology betray his Reformed presuppositions. At the same time, however, Arminius charted his own course, especially in matters of soteriology and doctrines directly related to them.

Before identifying those distinctive outcomes, it is appropriate to observe that Arminius's soteriology was driven by concerns central to the Reformed and more generally Augustinian tradition. First, like scores of theologians before him, Arminius sought to reconcile divine grace and human freedom. Another motivation for Arminius was the problem of evil or, as it relates to God, theodicy. Third, Arminius was concerned about the believer's assurance of salvation, particularly with the opposite poles of despair and carnal security, and this motivated him to search for a better solution between the two extremes. These three motivating factors are points of departure, issues that demanded solutions, not central dogmas to his system of theology. Arminius considered the solutions of the developing Reformed orthodoxy to fall short on each of the three issues (Stanglin 2007).

The main theological differences can be fairly summarized in three points, all of which hang together in Arminius's thought, just as their contraries cohere in Reformed theology (Stanglin and McCall 2012, 200). The first is Arminius's theology of creation, which claims that creation is God's first act of grace, an act in which he freely obliges himself to creation (Muller 1991). God, as holy love and goodness itself, wills only the good for creation and thus created in order to share his eternally good communion with creation. For Arminius, God's desire for all to be saved means that each individual human being is loved for this purpose, something that Arminius's Reformed opponents could not express except with great qualification. For the Reformed, the reprobate are simply passed over with no divine intention to save. For Arminius, the divine self-limitation is expressed in his claims that God cannot reprobate the creature for anything other than sin, and that ultimately not everyone that God wants to be saved will be saved. God's love is directed primarily toward his own essence as the good of his own essential righteousness, and secondarily toward the fallen human creature and its blessedness, ensuring that God will never condemn anyone except for impenitent unbelief and sin (Stanglin 2007, 219–31; Den Boer 2010, 154–66).

Second, predestination—that is, individual election to salvation and reprobation to condemnation—is conditional. In his *Declaration of Sentiments*, Arminius proposes four divine decrees. In sum, God wills antecedently to save all through the mediator Jesus Christ, but by his consequent will God elects to salvation those who accept his gracious gift of faith and condemns those who do not. The difference can be summed up with these questions: do people believe because they are elect (Reformed), or are they elect because they believe (Arminius)? Each individual's willingness to receive faith is known by way of God's middle knowledge, a concept Arminius borrowed from the Jesuit Luis de Molina. God has predestined to save those who are in Christ by penitent faith and to condemn impenitent unbelievers, and God knows whether or not a specific person would accept the gift of saving faith and become a believer (Muller 1991; Stanglin and McCall 2012; Gunter 2012; Dekker 1993).

The third point, already implied in the second, is that divine grace, whose initial action all parties agreed is necessary for salvation, can be resisted and refused. For Arminius, grace does everything that the Reformed claim, except it does not work by an irresistible force. God gives further saving grace to those who accept (or refuse to resist) the initial, prevenient grace.

These distinctive emphases point to the solutions to the three concerns noted above. First, with respect to the relationship between divine grace and human freedom, divine grace initiates the salvation of the fallen individual; in this regard, Arminius was no Pelagian. But grace perfects human nature; it does not supplant human nature by irresistibly coercing the will. Second, concerning the problem of evil, God is sovereign over all creation and he does concur even with the evil choices of free moral agents (Hicks 2012). But God, who created to communicate goodness, did not create any human being for the end of eternal destruction. He did not ordain the Fall or make sin inevitable. Otherwise, Arminius argues, God would be the author of sin and the only true sinner. Third, with regard to assurance of salvation, Arminius insisted that the Reformed doctrines of unconditional election and irresistible grace can lead to carnal security and antinomianism, just as unconditional reprobation and the concept of temporary faith can lead present believers to doubt and despair. Instead, arrogant security is defeated because God requires the acceptance of and continuance in faith as the condition of election, and despair over possible reprobation is defeated because God created and loves each individual for the purpose of salvation.

# 2 Dutch Remonstrantism

## 2.1 Emergence of Remonstrants

Less than three months after Arminius's death, on January 14, 1610, forty-three Dutch Reformed ministers sympathetic to Arminius's positions signed the *Remonstrance*, which documented in five articles the teachings that they felt should be allowed within the church. They may be summarized as follows:

1. God chose to save through Jesus Christ all those who through grace would believe in him and persevere to the end.
2. Jesus Christ obtained forgiveness of sins sufficient for all.
3. Fallen humanity can think or do nothing that is truly good by free will.
4. God's grace, which is not irresistible, is necessary for thinking or doing any good.
5. True believers are enabled by grace to persevere to the end, and it may be possible for them to forfeit this grace. (Uytenbogaert 1646, 524–29; Schaff 1931, 545–49)

Those who signed and supported these positions were known thereafter as Remonstrants.

At a conference in The Hague in 1611, the opponents of the Remonstrants, known as Contra-Remonstrants, rebutted these Arminian teachings with five articles of their own. As the decade of the 1610s wore on, the debate between these two parties intensified, as it was conducted not only in churches and on the streets, but also through a caustic "pamphlet war," whose increasing output only sharpened the divisions (Hakkenberg 1989; Israel 1995, 439). The United Provinces, now under the strong leadership of the Contra-Remonstrant Prince Maurits, convened the Synod of Dordt (or Dordrecht, 1618–19) in order to clarify Reformed doctrine on predestination and related matters against the Remonstrants. The result of the Reformed council was the promulgation of its own five theological articles and the official rejection of the distinctively Remonstrant opinions from the Reformed Church. In its wake, the Dutch statesman Johan van Oldenbarnevelt (1547–1619) was executed on trumped up charges of treason, about two hundred Remonstrant ministers who refused to subscribe to the Canons of Dordt were deprived of their livings, and more than eighty were expelled from the country (Israel 1995, 462–63). Several of these banished ministers were sentenced to permanent imprisonment when they were discovered back in their country teaching Remonstrant doctrine.

After the death of Prince Maurits in 1625, the Remonstrants enjoyed increasing toleration as the government was gradually unwilling to enforce the laws against them. The Remonstrant Brotherhood (*Remonstrantse Broederschap*) even set up its own seminary in Amsterdam in 1634. From this center, Remonstrant theology spread its influence throughout the Low Countries during the seventeenth and eighteenth centuries. Their churches were not influential outside Dutch borders, but their intellectual contributions were noted throughout Europe.

The most famous Remonstrant, Hugo Grotius (1583–1645), is known today less for his theological talents than his contributions to the development of international law and diplomacy. Yet he is credited with the so-called governmental theory of the atonement, which influenced later Remonstrants and went beyond the penal substitution theory held by Arminius. Grotius wrote dozens of theological and biblical treatises, including the celebrated apologetic work *De veritate religionis Christianae* (revised in 1640) and annotations on the whole Bible and Apocrypha. In 1621 Grotius escaped his imprisonment in the Loevestein Castle (just east of Dordrecht), where several Remonstrant ministers were also incarcerated through the 1620s, and he fled to Paris. He spent much of the remainder of his life outside his homeland.

Ecclesiastically within the Netherlands, the key leader of the first generation of Remonstrant theologians after Arminius was Arminius's friend Uytenbogaert. But the theologians of the Remonstrant Seminary would become the most influential voices of Remonstrant theology. Simon Episcopius (1583–1643), former student of Arminius and his successor in the Leiden faculty, was the leader of the Remonstrant party at the Synod of Dordt and first theology professor in the seminary (1634–43). He was succeeded in this position by Étienne de Courcelles (1586–1659), and later by Philip van Limborch (1633–1712). Jean LeClerc (1657–1735) taught at the seminary with Van Limborch and is best known for his critical biblical scholarship.

## 2.2 Remonstrant theology

Post-Arminian Remonstrant theology began in 1610 with the composition of the Remonstrance. However, the confessionalization of post-Dordt Remonstrant theology was first articulated in the Confession of 1621, a summary of Remonstrant beliefs written by Episcopius (Episcopius 1622). Throughout the seventeenth century, the three great theologians of the early Remonstrant movement (Episcopius, De Courcelles, and Van Limborch) each produced widely read theological treatises and textbooks that helped to codify Remonstrant theology and to secure its place among the great systems of Protestant Christianity. In many of the major topics of theology, the Remonstrants held positions that resembled a broadly Reformed Protestantism. The important differences that did obtain between Remonstrant theology and Reformed orthodoxy were in some ways extensions of the issues that distinguished Arminius from his Reformed colleagues; though in other respects, the Remonstrants went well beyond Arminius.

The same elements emphasized in Arminius's theology (integrity of creation, conditional predestination, and resistible grace) were carried forward by the Remonstrants. Other distinctive features of Remonstrant theology became prominent; these features may be illustrated, albeit not exhaustively described, in four key points. First, beginning with Episcopius, the Remonstrant theologians were criticized by their Reformed opponents for giving undue credit to the role of reason in theology. Whereas other confessional groups tended to resist the emerging Enlightenment epistemologies, by contrast, Remonstrant theologians seemed particularly open to Cartesian rationalism as well as British empiricism. Indeed, not only was De Courcelles a friend of René Descartes and the translator of his *Discourse on Method*, but Van Limborch was a direct and notable influence on John Locke. This increasing reliance on human reason is noticeable, for example, with respect to the interpretation of scripture. Episcopius, De Courcelles, and Van Limborch claimed that scripture is perspicuous to such a degree that anyone using common sense, apart from the guidance of the Holy Spirit, can interpret its central doctrines correctly (Daugirdas 2009; Stanglin 2014).

A second distinctive element concerns the doctrine of God. The Remonstrant theologians explicitly taught subordinationism within the Trinity. Although Arminius was accused of undermining the deity of Christ, his account could be traced to various writings of the Church Fathers, and arguably was not outside the bounds of Reformed confessionality. The Remonstrants, on the other hand, advocated the subordination of the second person of the Trinity not only in order, but also in dignity and in power. Their doctrine was not Socinian at first, but later Remonstrant Christology exhibits the direct influence of Socinianism (Hampton 2008).

Third, the Remonstrants articulated a distinct anthropology and soteriology. In contrast with Reformed theologians and Arminius, Remonstrant theology was gradually characterized by a more optimistic view of fallen humanity and a rejection of the Augustinian account of original sin. This more positive view of human ability resulted in an attenuated view of the operation of grace and the efficacy of the atonement (Hicks 1991; Ellis 2006).

Fourth, in the area of ecclesiology, the Remonstrants were tireless in their promotion of religious toleration. Arminius and Grotius had already called for a fairly broad toleration of Protestant denominations before the Synod of Dordt. As would be expected from a persecuted group, this call for tolerance became more prominent leading up to and following Dordt (J. Bangs 2010).

## 2.3 Discontinuity with Arminius

One of the striking features of Remonstrant theology is its rapid development beyond the thought of Arminius, particularly in its interaction with and eclectic use of the philosophies of the early Enlightenment. As noted above, by the end of the seventeenth century, Remonstrant theologians had drawn on the Cartesian and Lockean philosophies and had developed markedly different concepts of the nature of scripture and its interpretation, Trinity, Christology, atonement, anthropology, sin, and the operation of grace. It should not be surprising that a theological trajectory would develop alongside the shifts in early modern thought and culture.

A more significant question is why Remonstrant theology exhibited this high degree of theological discontinuity with Arminius so quickly. Two points are worth considering. The first point is what might be called the loss of Arminius in the debates leading up to the Synod of Dordt. The debate regarding predestination triggered by Gomarus and Arminius at Leiden University, beginning in 1604, gradually became more widespread and public. Arminius's death in 1609 came comparatively early in the life of this iteration of the controversy. Although he remained an inspiring figure in the Remonstrant movement, which increasingly became known as "Arminian," nevertheless Arminius himself was not present during the fiercest period of the struggle. The Remonstrants carried on the debate without him. From the Contra-Remonstrant perspective, the selection of Conrad Vorstius (1569–1622) to fill Arminius's chair at Leiden raised the stakes even higher, for Vorstius's recent book on the attributes of God (1606; 2nd ed. 1610) was seen as a denial of divine immutability, impassibility, and infallible foreknowledge. Vorstius was also suspected of close connections with Socinians. Because of the vehement international opposition to his appointment, Vorstius never taught at Leiden. But in the eyes of their opponents, the Remonstrants could not shake the air of suspicion that accompanied their initial support of Vorstius.

In the decade-long debate and pamphlet war that lasted from the Remonstrance of 1610 to the Synod of Dordt, the Contra-Remonstrants engaged Remonstrant thought and the slippery slope embodied by the threat of Vorstius, but Arminius was increasingly absent from the "Arminian" controversy. When Arminius was posthumously consulted, by his detractors and sympathizers alike, it was most often for his doctrine of predestination. But the fuller exposition and implications of Arminius's theology, much of it hidden in disputations that were never collected and published, were not useful for the polemics of the time. In the development of Remonstrant theology, Arminius's name was often invoked, but the broad scope of his thought was frequently absent.

A second reason for the noticeable discontinuity between Arminius and later Remonstrants is their different situation with respect to the privileged church of the Dutch state. As a prominent theologian within the Dutch Reformed Church, Arminius's primary theological context was that of emerging Reformed orthodoxy. His colleagues and students, his primary interlocutors, subscribed to the Belgic Confession, as did he. He was certainly marginalized, but he was still an insider whose conversations took place on the inside. The context of the Remonstrants, especially after the Synod of Dordt, was quite different. As outsiders driven from the established church, the Remonstrants shared a common identity with other dissenting but tolerated groups suspected of heterodoxy, especially Socinians and Mennonites, perhaps opening Remonstrant thought to influences that the movement would not have so readily embraced had it remained within the Reformed Church.

# 3 English Arminianism
# and Wesleyanism

## 3.1 Backgrounds of Methodism

In order to understand the rise of Methodism, it is helpful to recognize two prominent characteristics of the early modern Protestant Church of England. The first feature is the native and ongoing debate about Reformed soteriology. What became known
in England as Arminianism began as a sort of anti-Calvinism within the Church of
England. The *Thirty-Nine Articles* of the Church are famously moderate in tone and, on
the topic of predestination (Article 17), ambiguous enough to permit both a Reformed
and an Arminian interpretation. As long as there had been influence from Continental
Reformed theology in England, there had also been a reaction to those distinctive elements of Protestant Reformed theology (Tyacke 1987). By the 1590s, for example,
Cambridge had become a bastion of Reformed thought, and one of the long-time divinity professors, Peter Baro (1534–99), came into controversy for opposing unconditional
predestination (Stanglin 2005). Such Anglican resistance to Reformed soteriology can
only improperly be called Arminianism, for the movement was vibrant before and independent of Arminius. Nevertheless, as a result of ongoing contact between England
and its Dutch neighbors, the epithet of Arminianism came to stand not only for the
indigenous anti-Calvinism within the Church of England, but also for high church
Anglicanism over against the those forms of Puritanism that remained committed to
Reformed theology.

These two threads of Reformed and Arminian theology continued to coexist
throughout seventeenth- and eighteenth-century Anglicanism. Archbishop William
Laud (1573–1645) promoted Anglican Arminianism, but the advocates of Reformed theology came to power in England during the Commonwealth. After the Restoration of
the monarchy, widespread dissatisfaction with "wars of religion" signaled the beginning
of the decline of Reformed orthodoxy, but it was not without its influential advocates
throughout the eighteenth century (Hampton 2008). At the same time, Arminianism
was increasingly favored (Nuttall 1962; Rack 2002, 26–27). Even among Presbyterians
there were many who, essentially Arminian in their outlook, refused to subscribe to the
Westminster Confession of Faith (Steers 2009).

Another significant feature within the Church of England was the impact of Pietism.
Like Arminianism, Pietism was both indigenous to the Church and reinforced from the
European Continent. By the end of the seventeenth century, the moralistic emphasis
on "holy living" had become a dominant influence in the Church of England (Allison
2003). The Puritan emphasis on good works and moral casuistry, often reflective of
the Pietism of the Dutch *Nadere Reformatie* (Further Reformation), was modified by
Moravian and Lutheran influences. Sparks of evangelical revival were reflected in the
establishing of para-church organizations such as the Society for Promoting Christian

Knowledge and the Society for the Propagation of the Gospel, founded in 1698 and 1701, respectively (Rack 2002, 14).

## 3.2 John Wesley and the Methodists

As these seeds were being sown in the Church of England, John Wesley (1703–91) was born in Epworth to Samuel and Susanna Wesley. Samuel was an Anglican cleric, but Susanna arguably had a deeper impact on the theology and piety of John. In 1709, at the age of five, the Wesley home burned down, and young John was rescued at the last moment from the fire. This experience of the "brand plucked from the fire" made a lasting impression on him and became a metaphor for salvation wrought by God. John Wesley later attended Oxford and was elected a fellow of Lincoln College in 1726. He was ordained as a deacon in the Church of England and, in 1728, a priest. By 1729, John Wesley and his brother Charles (1707–88) were heavily involved in a group that became known as the "Holy Club," which was one of many such groups throughout the university whose members were fervent in the spiritual disciplines of prayer, fasting, and Bible study, as well as works of mercy such as visiting prisoners and giving alms to the poor. As early as 1732, the participants in these groups were derisively called "Methodists" for their strict adherence to pietistic methods and regulations.

In 1735, John and Charles Wesley departed England for the American colony of Georgia in order to minister to the immigrant community and the native American Indians. During the journey, John was deeply impressed by the piety and faith of the Moravians on board the same ship, and he could not help feeling that such assurance of salvation was missing in his spiritual life. For various reasons, his mission in Georgia was not well received and his presence became a disruption to the peace of the community in Savannah. He fled Georgia and was back in England by February 1738, rejoining his brother Charles who had already returned from Georgia in 1736.

While John Wesley had been away, societies promoting revival had continued to spread throughout England. Upon his return, Wesley continued his interaction with the pietistic Moravians as he sought a measure of personal assurance of salvation. On May 24, 1738, while attending a prayer meeting on Aldersgate Street in London, Wesley's heart was, as he put it, "strangely warmed." He testified to those present of the feeling of trust and assurance that he now possessed. He proved his new energy for the work in England by organizing the grassroots revival movements into a "connexion" for mutual faith and support. The connexion was consolidated by an annual conference of preachers led by Wesley. Circuits, or itinerant preaching "rounds," were eventually assigned to ensure that the Methodist message spread to new places (Heitzenrater 2013; Rack 2002; Tomkins 2003).

Along with the revivalist George Whitefield (1714–70), John and Charles Wesley transformed formal preaching in England into a popular means of teaching (Davies 1996, 143–83). Their written works also reflect their overriding concern to communicate the gospel to the average person. Charles produced a vast number of poems and hymns that helped to spread Anglican orthodoxy in a Methodist key. John's reputation was that of a folk theologian, a man of the people. He did not produce technical theological treatises, but as an indefatigable writer who lived to a ripe old age, he left a voluminous body of accessible works, including abridgments of the writings of others, as well as his own theological tracts, journals, and sermons, the last of which have been the most influential.

During his whole life Wesley insisted that he was "a Church of England man" and that the goal was never to separate from the Church of England. Rather, these Methodist societies, which by 1750 were associated primarily with the Wesleys, were intended to encourage revival and the pursuit of personal holiness within the Church. Steps taken along the way, however, led to *de facto* separation from the established church in England. Once Francis Asbury (1745–1816), Thomas Coke (1747–1814), and others were sent as Methodist missionaries to North America, the separation proceeded more rapidly. Coke had already been ordained in England, but he then ordained Asbury in Baltimore. A conference of American Methodists met in Baltimore on Christmas Eve 1784 to approve Coke and Asbury as their superintendents (or bishops), in effect establishing the Methodist Episcopal Church in America. In 1775, there were 3,418 Methodists in the American colonies. Already by 1791, the year of Wesley's death, the number of Methodists in the United States exceeded 80,000, surpassing their entire number in England (Heitzenrater 2013; Rack 2002, 283; Salter 2003).

From its beginning, the Wesleyan movement was motivated by "vital piety," and most interpreters agree that sanctification is the one concept that dominates John Wesley's thought (Heitzenrater 2013, 337; Lindström 1996, 217–18; Oden 2012, 2:238; Outler 1964, 30). Indeed, the most distinctive elements of Wesleyanism flow from this emphasis on holiness and the concomitant concern over antinomianism. For Wesley, holiness is not an instantaneous blessing that God pours out monergistically (Maddox 1998, 54). Instead, the believer is expected to make gradual progress in holiness toward the goal of perfection, and believers can experience this goal of entire sanctification in this life. As Wesley makes clear in his sermon on "Christian Perfection," the perfected believer neither possesses perfect knowledge nor is free from infirmities (Wesley 1984–, 2:99–121). Rather, it is a certainty of perfect love for God and neighbor, and it comes generally when one is facing death, for it is then that a person casts aside all earthly desires that impede one's relationship with God (Outler 1964, 31–32). Wesley's perspective on Christian perfection developed over his long life of teaching on the subject, and his strong language became more qualified over time, which probably contributed to the increasing claims of perfection among Methodists after 1760 (Lindström 1996; Maddox 1994, 180–87; Maddox 1998; Wood 1999; Maddox 1999; Heitzenrater 2013, 234; Collins 2009).

Not all individuals or movements associated with the evangelical revivals, or even with Methodism, were Arminian in sentiment. In the early years of the Methodist movement, Reformed and Arminian perspectives coexisted in relative peace. This coexistence was threatened when the Methodist movement became more organized and increasingly identified with Wesley's leadership. Wesley's emphasis on sanctification was directly connected with the concern that the Reformed doctrines of predestination and grace, which were prevalent especially among the revival movements, lead to anti-nomianism. Wesley had always held to conditional predestination and resistible grace, and he advocated them in his teaching. It is not the idea or even terminology of "pre-venient" grace that became controversial, but that the operation of this grace was per-suasive rather than efficacious. When fellow Methodist George Whitefield insisted on unconditional predestination, both parties became more vocal in the debate. In 1741, there was a written controversy over the doctrine, and tracts were published from both sides (Heitzenrater 2013; Maddox 1994; Oden 2012, 2:176–81).

These publications did not settle the controversy, which continued to ebb and flow and cause division within the evangelical revivals. The flashpoint came in the Methodist Conference Minutes of 1770, which emphasized a greater need to encourage good works as a condition of salvation. As a result, a new written debate was sparked. On Wesley's side were Walter Sellon, Thomas Olivers, and most important, John Fletcher (1729–85), whose *Checks to Antinomianism* defended the Wesleyan movement against charges of Pelagianism and became as influential as Wesley's writings in subsequent Methodism. On the other side of the debate were Richard Hill and Augustus Toplady (1740–78). Toplady's publications, especially *Historic Proof of the Doctrinal Calvinism of the Church of England*, attempted to document the rise of Arminianism in the Church of England and equate it with Pelagianism, portraying Wesley as an innovative and dangerous sec-tarian (Toplady 1774). The title of Wesley's journal that began its circulation in 1778, *The Arminian Magazine*, is a reflection of the firm stand he took in the debate against the Calvinist Methodists. The strong language regarding good works that appeared in the 1770 Minutes, and the ongoing defense of the sentiments behind that language, ostra-cized any remaining Methodists who were inclined toward Reformed soteriology (Rack 2002, 454–61; Heitzenrater 2013, 267–76; Gunter 2007).

Another influential feature of Methodism stems from Wesley's emphasis on expe-rience. Although it is almost certainly connected to Wesley's attraction to the British empiricism so popular in eighteenth-century England, this appeal to experience has ramifications beyond philosophical epistemology, and is exhibited in at least two dis-tinguishing features of Methodism. The first aspect, related to the epistemology of salva-tion, is the emphasis on the subjective experience of conversion and assurance. To be sure, such a conversion experience was common in Pietist and revivalist circles; it is not unique to Methodism. But the stress on Wesley's sudden "heart-warming" experience on Aldersgate Street—an account that took on a life of its own and was given more sig-nificance than Wesley himself gave it—became paradigmatic in subsequent Methodist revivals and evangelical awakenings.

The second aspect of the emphasis on experience is related more generally to reli-gious epistemology and the proper criteria for theological formulations. It was typi-cally Anglican to appeal to scripture, tradition, and reason in theology; to these criteria Wesley added experience, which, together with the other three, Outler famously called the "Wesleyan quadrilateral" (Outler 1985). Within the quadrilateral, as practiced dynamically by Wesley, scripture holds the primary place, and experience does not function to reveal new truths but only to confirm scripture (Outler 1985; Maddox 1994,

40–47; Oden 2012, 1:83–116). Yet the very fact that scholars have rightly recognized this additional testimony to the typical Anglican formula indicates the new experiential emphasis that Wesley brought to the question of discerning Christian theological truth.

# 4 ARMINIAN LEGACIES

Whether they are seen in their Remonstrant or in their Wesleyan manifestations, there are several emphases common to these traditions that can be traced back to Arminius himself. One concern common to both of these Arminian trajectories is the stress on good works and the warning against the danger of antinomianism. Like Arminius, both Remonstrants and Wesleyans have been accused of moralism or even Pelagianism, and depending on the figure in question, these charges may be justified in some instances, though in Arminius's case they are not. At any rate, Arminianism is known for its expectation of progress in the life of sanctification. The Wesleys and later Wesleyans in particular have been well known for works of mercy and compassion for the poor and marginalized of society. A second common legacy is the emphasis on toleration of other Christian groups who disagree on certain points of theology. Just as Arminius urged greater latitude within the Reformed Church and expressed deep concern over dissensions, the Remonstrants were among the most outspoken advocates of toleration in the early modern period, and Wesley himself was known for his "catholic spirit" of cooperation and fellowship with all Christians. Finally, Arminianism in its various forms is built on the foundation of a holy God who loves all creation for the goal of eternal fellowship and is not willing that any should perish. The creature is a willing participant in redemption, persuasively brought into communion with God.

## BIBLIOGRAPHY

Allison, Christopher FitzSimons. 2003. *The Rise of Moralism: The Proclamation of the Gospel from Hooker to Baxter*. Reprint. Vancouver: Regent College Publishing.

Arminius, Jacobus. 1629. *Opera theologica*. Leiden. (English translation in *The Works of James Arminius*, translated by James Nichols and William Nichols. 3 vols. Reprint. Grand Rapids: Baker, 1986.)

Bangs, Carl. 1958. "Arminius and Reformed Theology." PhD Diss., University of Chicago.

Bangs, Carl. 1985. *Arminius: A Study in the Dutch Reformation*. 2nd ed. Grand Rapids: Zondervan.

Bangs, Jeremy. 2010. "Dutch Contributions to Religious Toleration." *Church History* 79 (3): 585–613.

Boer, William A. den. 2010. *God's Twofold Love: The Theology of Jacob Arminius (1559–1609)*. Translated by Albert Gootjes. Göttingen: Vandenhoeck & Ruprecht.

Collins, Kenneth J. 2009. "The State of Wesley Studies in North America: A Theological Journey." *Wesleyan Theological Journal* 44 (2): 7–38.

Daugirdas, Kestutis. 2009. "The Biblical Hermeneutics of Socinians and Remonstrants in the Seventeenth Century." In *Arminius, Arminianism, and Europe: Jacobus Arminius (1559/60–1609)*, edited by Th. Marius van Leeuwen, Keith D. Stanglin, and Marijke Tolsma, 89–113. Leiden: Brill.

Davies, Horton. 1996. *Worship and Theology in England: From Watts and Wesley to Martineau, 1690–1900*. Reprint. Grand Rapids: Eerdmans.

Dekker, Evert. 1993. *Rijker dan Midas: Vrijheid, genade en predestinatie in de theologie van Jacobus Arminius, 1559–1609*. Zoetermeer: Boekencentrum.

Ellis, Mark A. 2006. *Simon Episcopius' Doctrine of Original Sin*. New York: Peter Lang.

Episcopius, Simon. 1622. *Confessio, sive declaratio, sententiae pastorum, qui in foederato Belgio Remonstrantes vocantur*. Harderwijk.

Fletcher, John. 1835. *Checks to Antinomianism*. In *The Works of the Reverend John Fletcher*. Vol. 1. New York: B. Waugh and T. Mason for the Methodist Episcopal Church.

Gunter, W. Stephen. 2012. *Arminius and His Declaration of Sentiments: An Annotated Translation with Introduction and Theological Commentary*. Waco: Baylor University Press.

Gunter, W. Stephen. 2007. "John Wesley, a Faithful Representative of Jacobus Arminius." *Wesleyan Theological Journal* 42 (2): 65–82.

Hakkenberg, Michael Abram. 1989. "The Predestinarian Controversy in the Netherlands, 1600–1620." PhD diss., University of California at Berkeley.

Hampton, Stephen. 2008. *Anti-Arminians: The Anglican Reformed Tradition from Charles II to George I*. Oxford: Oxford University Press.

Heitzenrater, Richard P. 2013. *Wesley and the People Called Methodists*. 2nd ed. Nashville: Abingdon Press.

Hicks, John Mark. 2012. "Classic Arminianism and Open Theism: A Substantial Difference in Their Theologies of Providence." *Trinity Journal* 33: 3–18.

Hicks, John Mark. 1991. "The Righteousness of Saving Faith: Arminian versus Remonstrant Grace." *Evangelical Journal* 9: 27–39.

Israel, Jonathan. 1995. *The Dutch Republic: Its Rise, Greatness, and Fall, 1477–1806*. Oxford: Clarendon Press.

Limborch, Philip van, ed. 1684. *Praestantium ac eruditorum virorum epistolae ecclesiasticae et theologicae*. Amsterdam.

Lindström, Harald. 1996. *Wesley and Sanctification: A Study in the Doctrine of Salvation*. Reprint. Nappanee, IN: Francis Asbury Press.

Maddox, Randy. 1998. "Reconnecting the Means to the End: A Wesleyan Prescription for the Holiness Movement." *Wesleyan Theological Journal* 33 (2): 29–66.

Maddox, Randy. 1994. *Responsible Grace: John Wesley's Practical Theology*. Nashville: Kingswood Books.

Maddox, Randy. 1999. "Wesley's Understanding of Christian Perfection: In What Sense Pentecostal?" *Wesleyan Theological Journal* 34 (2): 78–110.

Muller, Richard A. 1988. "The Christological Problem in the Thought of Jacobus Arminius." *Nederlands archief voor kerkgeschiedenis* 68: 145–163.

Muller, Richard A. 1991. *God, Creation, and Providence in the Thought of Jacob Arminius: Sources and Directions of Scholastic Protestantism in the Era of Early Orthodoxy*. Grand Rapids, MI: Baker.

Nuttall, Geoffrey F. 1962. "The Influence of Arminianism in England." In *Man's Faith and Freedom: The Theological Influence of Jacobus Arminius*, edited by Gerald O. McCulloh, 46–63. New York: Abingdon Press.

Oden, Thomas C. 2012. *John Wesley's Teachings*. 3 vols. Grand Rapids: Zondervan.

Outler, Albert C. 1964. "Introduction." In *John Wesley*, edited by Albert C. Outler, 3–33. New York: Oxford University Press.

Outler, Albert C. 1985. "The Wesleyan Quadrilateral in John Wesley." *Wesleyan Theological Journal* 20 (1): 7–18.

Rack, Henry D. 2002. *Reasonable Enthusiast: John Wesley and the Rise of Methodism*. 3rd ed. London: Epworth Press.

Salter, Darius L. 2003. *America's Bishop: The Life of Francis Asbury*. Nappanee, IN: Francis Asbury Press.

Schaff, Philip, ed. 1931. *The Creeds of Christendom, with a History and Critical Notes*, 6th ed. Vol. 3. Reprint. Grand Rapids: Baker, 1998.

Stanglin, Keith D. 2007. *Arminius on the Assurance of Salvation: The Context, Roots, and Shape of the Leiden Debate, 1603–1609*. Leiden: Brill.

Stanglin, Keith D. 2005. "'Arminius *avant la lettre*': Peter Baro, Jacob Arminius, and the Bond of Predestinarian Polemic." *Westminster Theological Journal* 67: 51–74.

Stanglin, Keith D. 2010. *The Missing Public Disputations of Jacobus Arminius: Introduction, Text, and Notes*. Leiden: Brill.

Stanglin, Keith D. 2014. "The Rise and Fall of Biblical Perspicuity: Remonstrants and the Transition toward Modern Exegesis." *Church History* 83 (1): 38–59.

Stanglin, Keith D., and Thomas H. McCall. 2012. *Jacob Arminius: Theologian of Grace*. New York: Oxford University Press.

Stanglin, Keith D., and Richard A. Muller. 2009. "*Bibliographia Arminiana*: A Comprehensive, Annotated Bibliography of the Works of Arminius." In *Arminius, Arminianism, and Europe: Jacobus Arminius (1559/60–1609)*, edited by Th. Marius van Leeuwen, Keith D. Stanglin, and Marijke Tolsma, 263–290. Leiden: Brill.

Steers, David. 2009. "Arminianism amongst Protestant Dissenters in England and Ireland in the Eighteenth Century." In *Arminius, Arminianism, and Europe: Jacobus Arminius (1559/60–1609)*, edited by Th. Marius van Leeuwen, Keith D. Stanglin, and Marijke Tolsma, 159–200. Leiden: Brill.

Tomkins, Stephen. 2003. *John Wesley: A Biography*. Grand Rapids: Eerdmans.

Toplady, Augustus. 1774. *Historic Proof of the Doctrinal Calvinism of the Church of England*. 2 vols. London.

Tyacke, Nicholas R. N. 1987. *Anti-Calvinists: The Rise of English Arminianism c. 1590–1640*. Oxford: Clarendon Press.

[Uytenbogaert, Johannes.] 1646. *Kerckelicke historie, vervatende verscheyden gedenckwaerdige saecken*. S. l.

Wesley, John. 1984–. *The Bicentennial Edition of the Works of John Wesley*. Edited by Richard P. Heitzenrater and Frank Baker. Nashville: Abingdon Press.

Wood, Laurence W. 1999. "Pentecostal Sanctification: In Wesley and Early Methodism." *Wesleyan Theological Journal* 34 (1): 24–63.

CHAPTER 27

......................................................................................................

# EARLY MODERN PIETISM

......................................................................................................

## JONATHAN STROM AND HARTMUT LEHMANN

# 1 INTRODUCTION

THE Pietist movement emerged in the seventeenth century to become one of the most dynamic reform movements in Protestantism after the Reformation. Centered in Germany, this heterogeneous movement reached across Protestant Europe to North America, even extending as far as South India. Pietism was not first and foremost a doctrinal reform movement but an attempt to renew the Christian life and bring profession of faith and lived experience into greater correspondence. Nonetheless, a series of factors shaped the theology of its leading figures and had implications for theological developments of the seventeenth and eighteenth centuries. The crises of the seventeenth century challenged many assumptions of confessional Protestantism, opening the way for new theological interpretations and directions. The Reformation era left a number of issues unresolved or ambivalent with regard to prophecy, scripture, and the Christian life. Further, these challenges allowed some Pietists to adopt radical ideas, particularly those of the Spiritualists, even as they often domesticated them for an ecclesial context. The precise definitions and contours of Pietism remain in dispute among historians, but the following will focus on the German context. Even so, we should not overlook that many scholars draw parallels between aspects of Pietism and renewal movements in Protestantism and in Roman Catholicism that share similar goals (Lehmann 2007; Lehmann 2012; Strom 2002).

# 2 SPENER'S INITIATIVE AND THE BEGINNINGS OF PIETISM

The roots of Pietism reach back to the piety and spiritualist movements of the early seventeenth century. Johann Arndt (1555–1621), for instance, represented a new emphasis on the Christian life and religious experience. Recent scholarship has identified the range of mystical and heterodox sources throughout Arndt's work, but above all Arndt sought to harmonize his practical theological works with the doctrine of the confessional church. Controversy attended Arndt's legacy, but his devotional works, including *True Christianity*, became some of the bestselling works of the seventeenth century and found wide acceptance among Lutheran orthodox theologians, as well as the more radical critics of established Christianity (Illg 2011; Schneider 2006; Wallmann 2005a).

Older views of a sclerotic scholasticism in German Protestantism, especially Lutheranism, have given way to a more dynamic picture of confessional Protestantism, in which reform remained a powerful motif throughout the confessional theology of the seventeenth century as it struggled to respond to the challenges of the day. Pietism would build on reform currents and the emphasis on experiential piety of the Arndtian tradition, but also would depart from it in some important aspects (Kolb 2006; Strom 1999).

Philipp Jakob Spener's (1635–1705) 1675 reform tract, *Pia Desideria*, often stands as the founding document of the Pietist movement. In these "pious wishes," Spener criticized defects in the three estates of the Lutheran church—the rulers, clergy, and laity. His critique echoed many other contemporary criticisms and would not have been out of place among most reform-minded theologians of the era. The truly distinctive elements of Spener's *Pia Desideria* emerged in his optimistic prognosis for the church in the future and in his prescriptive proposals for reform (Spener 1988).

Spener's "hope for better times" represented a form of millenarian thinking that was largely foreign to earlier Lutheran eschatology. Though Spener rejected the crude chiliastic views of the *Clavis Apocalyptica*, his more moderate position—sometimes known as *chiliasmus subtilis*—foresaw a future in which Christ promised an imminent better state for the church on earth, including the conversion of the Jews and the fall of papal Rome. Spener's attenuated post-millennialism postponed the expectation of a last judgment, creating the possibilities for new, more optimistic views of the future as part of the understanding of the development of Christian history (Sparn 1992; Wallmann 1981; Wallmann 1982).

In the *Pia Desideria* and his reforms in Frankfurt-am-Main, Spener departed from traditional Reformation theology in other respects as well. For example, he called for the establishment of conventicles, *collegia pietatis*, in order that the Word may "dwell more richly" among Christians (Col. 3:16). The impetus for these small groups came from two laymen in Frankfurt, but they became a central part of the early Pietist movement in which leaders such as Spener adduced that regular preaching from the pulpit was not sufficient to inculcate scriptural piety among the laity. These conventicles went beyond small instructional groups, and especially as the idea of an *ecclesiola in ecclesia* developed in the 1670s, they became a gathering of the pious within the church through which reform would emanate. This contrasted distinctly with most previous reform proposals of the seventeenth century, which had sought to reform the church through territorial regulations and church ordinances. Pietists found justification for conventicles in the early writings of Luther, but their practice had been foreign to almost all of the subsequent Lutheran tradition and posed a challenge to clerical authority and ecclesiology in the confessional age (Bellardi 1994; Matthias 1993a).

In part, Spener's understanding of the *collegia pietatis* was based on his revived understanding of the early Reformation notion of the common priesthood, or as he generally rendered it, the "spiritual priesthood." The common priesthood or the priesthood of all believers, to use its modern formulation, had a very uneven history in the Reformation and post-Reformation history. It disappeared almost entirely from Lutheran discourse in the later sixteenth century. A few radicals and reformers earlier in the seventeenth century suggested its revival, but Spener was the first major theologian to give it such renewed prominence. By no means did Spener see the common priesthood as usurping the authority of the ministry. Instead, he viewed it as an important adjunct, necessary for the revitalization of lay piety and the reform of the church. He made the ministry and laity interdependent, and even granted in some cases to the pious laity the right to judge doctrine. Spener's preferred formulation of the spiritual priesthood, *das geistliche Priestertum*, had not only pneumatological import as the English implies, but also an implicit sociological critique of the ministry; that is, "die Geistlichen" in German Protestantism identified the ordained clergy (Strom 2011).

With a renewed emphasis on the common or spiritual priesthood, Spener also emphasized a greater role for scriptural reading and devotion for the laity that would become characteristic of Pietism. With the aid of the Holy Spirit, the laity could, according to Spener, grasp almost all of scripture. Johannes Wallmann has argued that Pietism represents a shift from catechetical Christianity characteristic of the Reformation to a biblical Christianity. Pietism hewed closely to the increasing emphasis on verbal inspiration in seventeenth-century orthodoxy. But Pietism also made reading of the entire Bible central to school instruction and lay devotion. Wallmann characterizes this as a shift from the Reformation principle of *sola scriptura* to *tota scriptura* (Wallmann 1994, 47–50). The renewed emphasis on the entirety of the biblical text had other implications as well. It led some Pietists to emphasize unfulfilled prophetic passages, whereas others focused on textual criticism of the Luther Bible and the recovery of the original texts themselves (Aland 1970; Wallmann 1994).

Spener's emphasis on the conversion of the Jews marked a departure from the anti-Judaism of Luther. His concern was not unique in seventeenth-century Lutheranism, but Spener linked the Jews' conversion to his reform agenda and placed it within the context of his "hopes for better times," making it part of his salvation history. The emphasis on the conversion of the Jews as instantiating a new era would become an important part of millennial expectations and missionary endeavors among Pietists, in contrast to many Evangelicals in Britain and North America who did not share this vision. In actual fact, Pietist conversions of Jews remained modest (Clark 2009).

Spener also urged a more practical theological education in the *Pia Desideria*. In this he followed many of the educational reforms proposed in the seventeenth century. Although he sought to improve the piety of candidates for the ministry, Spener did not emphasize that only true and presumably converted Christians could be effective ministers of the Gospel as some later Pietists did, including August Hermann Francke (1663–1727) or Joachim Lange (1670–1744) (Strom 2009).

The public response to the *Pia Desideria* was initially positive in most cases, although some, like Balthasar Mentzer (1614–79), raised doubts privately about the *collegia pietatis*. The first public theological controversy in Pietism concerned the nature of theology and the role of the Holy Spirit. Influenced by Georg Calixt (1586–1656), Georg Konrad Dilfeld (ca. 1630–84) argued that professing correct theology and doctrine was an intellectual enterprise, independent from faith or the illumination of the Holy Spirit, and he charged Spener with enthusiasm for his emphasis on piety and the necessity of the Spirit's work on theological students. In some respects Spener welcomed Dilfeld's attack, for it allowed him to demonstrate his orthodoxy. In this 1680 tract, *Die allgemeine Gottesgelehrtheit aller Gläubigen Christen und rechtschaffen Theologen*, he was able to cite Luther and the Lutheran orthodox tradition extensively to show that correct theology presupposes the gift of the Holy Spirit (Wallmann 1968).

# 3  The Genesis of Pietism in the Context of the Crises of the Seventeenth Century

The reform agenda of Pietism, as well as Pietist theology, should be seen in relation to the religious convictions of the generations of Protestants that preceded Spener and his cohort of followers. It is important, therefore, to take a closer look at the various religious reactions to the serious social, political, and cultural crises from the 1570s to the 1670s that formed the context for Pietism.

Beginning in the eighteenth century, historians assumed that the terrible losses of human lives in the preceding century were mainly caused by the Thirty Years' War. In the 1970s and 1980s, however, some historians became aware that the story was more complicated. Specialists in the field of climate history discovered that average temperatures in Europe had declined considerably since the 1570s, and they coined the term "Little Ice Age" for this era of more frigid climatic conditions. Demographers who took up this view were now able to explain that the rapidly rising mortality rates of the age were the result of a triple attack: falling temperatures brought long and cold winters and shorter, wet summers that caused frequent crop failures; bad harvests in turn caused shortages of food supplies and even famines; malnourishment, in turn, made people more susceptible to illness and diseases of all kinds. Still, no one doubts that the horrors of the Thirty Years' War added much hardship to this deadly scenario, as the soldiers of all sides involved in the most merciless controversy between Protestants and Catholics, between Sweden and the emperor, took whatever they could get. Pillaging was part of warfare—villages were burnt to the ground, and crops in the fields were destroyed to hurt the opposing parties. Moreover, cruelties of all kinds were committed, including frequent massacres of civilians. Spener, born in 1635, had witnessed the last phase of the Thirty Years' War. But as we now know, this war was only the last chapter of a story that had begun in the 1570s (Lehmann 1980; Lehmann 1999).

From the beginning of the Little Ice Age, all over Central Europe many devout Christians worried a great deal. As they became victims of the sequence of military engagements—in retrospect called the Thirty Years' War—their worries turned into despair. Pastors and parishioners wondered why God would demand such suffering and impose such unimaginable hardship on them. Had they sinned more than former generations? Had the devil initiated an all-out attack against God's regiment and God's creation? Or did the terrible events that they witnessed possess yet another meaning? Did God want to tell his children that the end of times was near? (Behringer et al. 2005; Lehmann 1980; Lehmann 1986).

In recent historiography there is agreement that some of the specific religious attitudes of the age can be understood as reactions to the experience of an historic climatic deterioration and widespread war: first, the rapid rise of the persecution of witches; second, renewed hope for the Second Coming, and renewed interest in eschatology; third, the production and consumption of devotional literature. As people wanted to save their souls, they attacked those whom they considered agents of the devil, they longed for resurrection and eternal salvation, and in order to learn how to live a truly Christian life they turned to edifying books and tracts (Jakubowski-Tiessen and Lehmann 2003; Lehmann 1999; Lehmann and Trepp 1999).

## 3.1 Witch hunting as a way of defeating the influence of the devil

A burgeoning new literature now exists on the witch craze of the late sixteenth and the seventeenth century. Not only were old women accused of practicing witchcraft, but also men and even children. Those arrested and accused of being witches were tortured to confess that they had concluded a secret contract with the devil. Those who did confess not only admitted that they had been enlisted by the devil as his agents, but when interrogated under torture, also gave the names of other people who supposedly had done the same. As a result of the widespread application of torture, the number of people accused of practicing witchcraft grew rapidly, as did the numbers of those who were executed and burned at the stake. Although estimates differ, one can assume that more than ten thousand people were killed in Central Europe in the decades between 1570 and 1630 because their contemporaries believed them to be witches, and several thousand more victims can be counted in the subsequent decades. Protestants were involved in this no less than Catholics. For both, as they set out to hunt down, arrest, torture, and kill witches, one argument counted more than any other: the belief that these people had entered into a close relationship with God's potent adversary, the devil, by signing a contract that obliged them to injure as best they could their fellow humans and their means of making a livelihood; that is, their crops and animals (Behringer 2004; Lehmann and Ulbricht, 1992; Robisheaux 2013).

Not all Christians were convinced of the blessings, and the effectiveness, of witch hunting. In the late 1620s, as the witch craze reached its climax, Johann Matthäus Meyfart (1590–1642), a Protestant preacher, and Friedrich von Spee (1591–1635), a Jesuit priest, openly argued that it was a sin to kill people because they had admitted that they were witches. Torture would never reveal the whole truth. Only God knew the truth; therefore one should leave this matter to God on the day of the Last Judgment. Two generations later, Philipp Jakob Spener, the founder of Pietism, went a step further as he expressed the view that witches were sinners like others sinners. Provided that they repented of their sins, they could and should be brought back into the community of all Christians. In the course of the eighteenth century, enlightened thinkers criticized witch hunting even more severely. For them, the practice was a remnant of medieval superstition (Lehmann 1992; Behringer 2004).

In theological terms, witch hunting was founded upon a Manichean world view. Two opposing camps were at battle: God and his faithful children were confronted by a fallen angel, the devil, who did his utmost to do harm. The devil would not hesitate to destroy as much of God's creation as possible. Failing harvests, dying cattle, illness and disease—all of these were understood as the work of the devil. By eliminating witches, the agents of the devil, God's good creation could be protected and in due course restored.

## 3.2 Renewed interest in eschatology and the Second Coming

In the late sixteenth century, some of the most learned Protestant theologians were convinced that the hardships that they and their generation were experiencing—in the form of famine, premature and unexpected death of children and adults, warfare and diseases—were signs sent by God. Through all of this, they believed that God wanted to warn humankind and tell his loyal children to be prepared for the end of times and the Second Coming. As a result, watching, describing, and interpreting the "signs of the times" became a widespread occupation. Some contemporaries concluded that salvation history had progressed to a critical point and that the Second Coming could occur any day. Others began to speculate and calculate so that they would fix upon a definite date. They took all the hints and all the figures that they could find in the Revelation of St. John and compared them to the events of their own time. Some were convinced that the thousand years of Christ's reign had begun somewhere in the early Middle Ages and were ending in their own time, while others believed that the millennium was yet to begin (Gäbler 2004).

Mainly Protestant Christians talked and speculated about the "signs of the times." They believed that the rediscovery of the true gospel by Martin Luther had initiated the last chapter of salvation history before the Second Coming. Some of them expected that God would carry out the Last Judgment immediately after Christ had returned. Others argued that the returning Christ would begin a glorious reign of a thousand years, a position traditionally called chiliasm. Some even believed that Christ would reign together with his most loyal children for two subsequent millennia.

Philipp Jakob Spener's version of eschatology had far-reaching implications. God, according to Spener, had granted to his children an extended period of hope during which they could work towards building God's future kingdom. With this claim, Spener created a new understanding of his own time as well as providing a new vision of the future. The key to this kind of theology was the belief in the Kingdom of God and the lesson for all true children of God was clear: if they wanted to attain eternal salvation, they had to engage themselves in building this kingdom (Krauter-Dierolf 2005; Lehmann 1980).

## 3.3 Production and consumption of devotional literature

Beginning in the late sixteenth century, the number of books and tracts that can be classified as devotional or edifying, grew in an unexpected, impressive way. These tracts and books served mainly one purpose: they were meant to console those in spiritual need, to show them how to live a better life as a Christian, and to find the right means for ridding themselves of sinful thoughts and behavior; in short, to make progress towards sanctification. To provide certainty in spiritual matters was the aim of these guides; thus their readers should have a better chance to gain eternal life.

A large variety of tracts and books aimed at these ends. Funeral sermons did so as they characterized those who had died as exemplary Christians, and indeed, with rising mortality, this genre became extremely important; small tracts with so-called "Last Words" did the same, as they came from people who were already on the way to Christ and had thus received a glimpse of what followed after death. But also large volumes with hundreds, in some cases even several thousand pages were published; mostly books with a meditative character such as the "Four" and later "Six Books of True Christianity" written by Arndt. Spener's "Pia Desideria" was first published as the foreword to one of the devotional books written by Arndt.

Devotional books and tracts far outnumbered all other publications in the course of the seventeenth century. Special features of this wave of edifying literature were their inter-confessional and international character. Protestant authors freely borrowed from Catholic sources, and vice versa. Moreover, German-speaking authors took themes and ideas from Dutch Reformed, English Puritan, and in some cases even from French Jansenist, Spanish mystical, and late medieval Italian sources. As holdings in libraries tell us, even long after the Little Ice Age was over, this kind of literature continued to be influential. It was a remarkably rich treasure that the Pietists inherited, and which they used well into the eighteenth century; and in the case of Johann Arndt, far beyond (Sträter 1987; Schrader 2004; Serkova 2013).

Within Central European Protestantism, it seems that Pietists learned a great deal from the lessons taught by the severity of seventeenth-century living conditions. In a number of respects, Spener and his followers can be seen as a third generation in a sequence of reform movements. The Reformed Puritans were the first who attempted to reform not only Christian doctrine, but also the way Christians lived. In a different setting, the Catholic Jansenists were the second to try the same. The moderate Lutheran Pietists, in turn, learned from both, but with the help of their vision of God's future kingdom, they carried the task of reforming Christian life much further (Lehmann et al. 2002).

# 4 Disillusionment of the Pious and Beginnings of Radical Pietism

## 4.1  Radical Pietists in Frankfurt

A number of Spener's early followers took his criticisms of the church and proposed reforms in a more radical direction. Johann Jakob Schütz (1640–90), a co-founder of the *collegia pietatis* in Frankfurt, became disillusioned with moderate reforms by the late 1670s and sought a more radical break with the established Lutheran church. Schütz and others in his circle removed themselves from regular attendance at church services and especially participation in the Lord's Supper with the "unworthy" and began meeting in conventicles beyond the control of the Frankfurt ministry. The incipient separatism signaled an ongoing tension in Pietism between those who sought to reform the church from within (church Pietism) and those for whom the established churches had lost their validity (radical Pietism). Radical Pietists came to see the established church as "Babylon," and in turn became more open to heterodox sources, from theosophists like Jakob Böhme to hermetic and alchemical lines of thought. Many challenged traditional Protestant doctrines, and some would eventually seek to establish their own distinct religious communities, and immigrate to the New World (Deppermann 2002; Schneider 2007; Ward 2006).

Spener responded to this first radical challenge with his 1684 tract, *Der Klagen über das verdorbene Christenthum mißbrauch und rechter gebrauch*. Spener acknowledged many of the criticisms of the church, but he sought to constrain such complaints to those issues that constructively challenged rather than undermined the church. Nevertheless, radical currents within Pietism would continue to press against the limits of Protestant orthodoxy in Frankfurt and elsewhere—particularly on questions of prophecy, ecclesiology, and the sacraments—and often went beyond them. Initially, Spener succeeded in restraining, though not eliminating, the most radical trends in the new movement. However, by the end of the 1680s, a new wave of Pietist controversies would emerge.

New theological directions would more clearly define both radical and church Pietists (Wallmann 2005b).

## 4.2  Pietist disturbances and new challenges

The second wave of Pietism, as some historians designate it, began in Leipzig in the late 1680s when the young scholar August Hermann Francke, influenced by Spener, adopted elements of Pietism in his *collegium philobiblicum*. At first praised by the professors of the theology faculty for their biblical devotion, Francke and his allies soon drew the ire of the university and city authorities as the convening of conventicles spread beyond the university to include ordinary townspeople. The idea that everyone from washer-women to shoemakers had the ability to interpret scripture in unsupervised groups challenged clerical authority and self-identity, and clergy and the civil authorities saw this as an inducement to enthusiasm and sectarianism. As students and other adherents were pushed out of Leipzig, the Pietist movement spread quickly across middle and north Germany. The ensuing appearance of radical conventicles and dramatic reports of prophecy and visions, especially among young women, disrupted religious and social life and provoked strong opposition among ecclesiastical and civil authorities. Social disruption contributed much to the controversies surrounding Pietism and should not be underestimated as part of the opposition, but several theological issues also became explicit topics of dispute (Mori 2004; Albrecht-Birkner and Sträter 2010).

Most prominently, perhaps, was the question of enthusiasm and new prophecies that went beyond scripture. There had been a long debate in seventeenth century Lutheranism on the nature of prophecy, but the frequency of prophecies and ecstatic experiences claimed by these men and women revived older controversies and elicited new condemnations. The so-called "inspired maids" of Erfurt, Gotha, Halberstadt, Quedlinburg and Halle reported visions, locutions, and ecstatic experiences, some with somatic manifestations of stigmata or illness. The anti-Pietist clergy and theologians took a hard line against these, and reveled in publishing the more outlandish claims. One of the most prominent of these visionaries, Rosamunde Juliana von der Asseburg (1672–1712), a young noblewoman, became famed throughout Germany for her visions and locutions of Christ—drawing even the interest of Leibniz. Johann Wilhelm Petersen (1649–1727), an early supporter of Spener, championed von Asseburg and even published a collection of her revelations. When a series of her specific predictions proved false, it discredited her and embarrassed her leading proponents. Moderate Pietists, such as Spener, never denied the possibility of extra-biblical revelations; but he, like most other church Pietists, increasingly expressed his distance from prophecy, though it continued to play a central role among many radical Pietists (Mori 2004; Cook 1998; Matthias 1993b).

One of the most controversial theological issues to appear in the Pietist controversies of the late 1680s and early 1690s concerned chiliasm, or millenarian ideas. Spener's famous "hopes for better times" suggested a moderate, postmillennial position, but both radical prophets and some Pietist clergy espoused much more explicit millennial schemes that brought them into conflict with the Augsburg Confession's condemnation of Anabaptist millenarianism. Through their mutual study of the book of Revelation, Johann Wilhelm Petersen and his wife, Johanna Eleonora Petersen (1644–1724), a prominent Pietist in her own right, argued vigorously for the coming thousand-year kingdom. Johann Wilhelm Petersen's public advocacy for "chiliasm" and his support for the divine nature of von Asseburg's revelations led to his removal from office as superintendent in Lüneburg in 1692. Supported with a pension from the Elector of Brandenburg and freed from any ecclesial duties, Petersen and his wife became tireless advocates of radical Pietist positions, including the doctrine of the *apokatastasis panton*. Millennial conceptions remained controversial, but they continued to have a hold on both radical as well some church Pietists, especially Johann Albrecht Bengel (1687–1752). Attenuated forms of millenarianism expressed themselves throughout Pietism as expectations for the establishment of the Kingdom of God (Ehmer 2005; Jung 2005; Schneider 2007).

The practice of conventicles raised questions of ecclesiology for their opponents and supporters. Opponents saw them as promoting heresy and sectarianism, and at the same undermining the established office of ministry. Anti-Pietist edicts routinely condemned the divisive nature of conventicles. Supporters, in contrast, saw in conventicles the possibility of an intense form of Christian fellowship and devotion that the established church could not provide, as well as a mechanism for erecting accountability for those dedicated to a true Christian life. The open-ended nature of many conventicles did allow for the diffusion of heterodox ideas, but the harsh and often indiscriminate criticism of conventicles by ecclesial and civil authorities only reinforced Pietists in their conviction of the corrupt nature of the established church, putting in motion a radicalizing dynamic of persecution and intensified critique (Mori 2004; Schneider 2007; Strom 2003).

One of the most controversial issues of the late 1680s and 1690s concerned the question of regeneration and perfectionism. Striving to show the qualitative distinction between the regenerate and the mass of nominal Christians, some Pietists came to emphasize the lack of sinfulness among truly reborn Christians. Church Pietists, such as Spener, had modified traditional Lutheran doctrine to make regeneration something that could be lost and regained repeatedly, allowing them to affirm baptismal regeneration but also to account for the apparent lack of regeneration among many Christians. Scholars disagree on the importance of regeneration to all Pietists, but ideas of a thoroughgoing renewal of the regenerate that tended toward perfectionism were present throughout many strands of Pietism in this period, including the young Francke. Later, Francke and other church Pietists sought to emphasize the distinctive life of the regenerate in upholding the commandments; without, however, making any claims to perfection (Mori 2004; Schneider 2007; Yoder 2011; Wallmann 1986).

Early Pietists tended to emphasize the common priesthood, which they traced back to Luther, in Spener's rephrasing, the "spiritual priesthood" as noted above. But church Pietists increasingly emphasized the need for true or converted Christians in the pastoral office. This made pious training for the ministry at places like Halle all the more critical. Though mindful to avoid outright Donatism, Francke and his later colleague Joachim Lange emphasized the necessity for regenerate Christians to lead the church. Implicitly, then, the true church for Pietists would be led by a converted ministry. Against this increasingly subjective understanding of ministerial authority, orthodox Lutherans came to emphasize the objective authority of the office of ministry. Valentin Ernst Löscher (1673–1749), one of the leading theological antagonists of the Pietists, came to emphasize a specific *Amtsgnade* or "grace of the office" that endowed all ordained ministers with the grace necessary to carry out their office (Strom 2009; Strom 2011).

## 4.3  Radical Pietism and church Pietism

The lines between radical and church Pietists remained fluid, but after the disruptive events of the late 1680s and early 1690s, a divergence occurred. Church Pietists sought to remake the established church according to their new vision, whereas radical Pietists moved in other directions. Influenced by Jane Leade (1623–1704) and John Pordage (1607–81), some radical Pietists such as the Petersens moved in a Philadelphian direction, which emphasized communities of brotherly love that transcended national and confessional boundaries. Characteristic of the Philadelphians was their emphasis on the imminent millennial kingdom, the doctrine of the *apokatastasis panton*, and the role of the divine Sophia who connected the humanity of Christ with an androgynous humanity. Philadelphian ideas leavened almost all varieties of radical Pietism in the eighteenth century (Schneider 2007).

Many Philadelphians never moved toward clear separation from established churches, but some radical Pietists did explicitly found exclusive communities of faith. The Schwarzenau Brethren, for instance, criticized the established churches, but rather than spiritualizing the sacraments as many radicals did, they interpreted the biblical command to baptize literally and instituted believer's baptism. Though these "New Baptists" could find some level of toleration in Germany, especially in Wittgenstein and Krefeld, they encountered repeated persecution and eventually fled to North America (Bach 2003; Meier 2008; Schneider 2007).

New Baptists struck out from church Pietists in a direction that paralleled and was influenced by earlier Anabaptist communities. Others developed even more radical forms of community. The Mother Eva Society (a.k.a. the Buttlar gang) emerged out of a Philadelphian, millenarian context of the early 1700s and became notorious throughout Germany for its bizarre sexual practices, which though distorted in the extreme, nonetheless reflected the deep uneasiness of some radical Pietists about original sin, sexuality, and embodiment. Still others who recognized the "outpourings of the spirit" of their time created innovative forms of community. The Community of True Inspiration that emerged after 1714, in part influenced by the French prophets, institutionalized the practice of ecstatic prophecy within their community, becoming one of radical Pietism's most enduring societies (Meier 2008; Schneider 2007; Temme 1998).

Other radical Pietists moved more freely across the boundaries between radical and church Pietism. Gottfried Arnold (1666–1714), the author of the groundbreaking historical work *Unparteyische Kirchen- und Ketzter Historie* (1699, 1700), vehemently rejected the established church in the 1690s and embraced celibacy and a mystical understanding of the divine Sophia. Shocking some of his supporters, he nevertheless married in the early 1700s and took a clerical position in the Lutheran church. Though moderating his criticisms of the church, he never abandoned his mystical emphasis even as he construed it in a more Trinitarian context (Erb 2005, 186). Likewise, Heinrich Horch (1652–1729) and Conrad Bröske (1660–1713) regularly crossed the boundaries between radical and church Pietism (Erb 2005; Schneider 2007; Shantz 2013).

# 5 Theological Developments amid the Establishment of Pietism

In the 1690s, church Pietists developed distinctive reforms that took their most concrete form in Halle. With the support of the Elector of Brandenburg, Frederick III (1657–1713), Pietists dominated the theology faculty of the newly formed university and just outside Halle's city walls, August Hermann Francke established the famous orphanage, whose extensive schools and enterprises made it one of the most innovative institutions of its kind in Europe. Education was central to Francke's conception of a universal reform in the church that would emanate from such institutions. Together, the university and Francke's institutes would form the most dynamic center of Pietism of the time, and in many ways Halle became synonymous with Pietist theology in the first half of the eighteenth century (Breul 2013).

As church Pietists turned away from prophetic visions and ecstatic experiences as signs of the truly regenerate, they sought other ways of charting spiritual development. Some especially emphasized individual conversion as one avenue to discern the regenerate from the mass of nominal Christians. Pietists could draw on a long tradition in the Lutheran tradition of *Busse und Bekehrung*, repentance and conversion, to elaborate their understanding of conversion. But unlike earlier Lutherans who construed ongoing conversion as a part of the continuing life of faith, many Pietists such as Francke came to see conversion as a discrete process or event that separated fundamental unbelief from true, saving faith. Indeed, Francke's own conversion account, which described his wrestling with "atheism" and nearly instantaneous breakthrough to true faith, symbolizes the Pietist ideal of a definitive turning point. Conversion experiences proved deeply problematic for many Pietists, and Francke's own account, despite its nearly canonical status in the historiography, never enjoyed the exemplary position in the eighteenth century that is often ascribed to it. Nevertheless, the emphasis on conversion signaled the desire of many Pietists to distinguish believers from nonbelievers, and a tendency to construe doubt as constitutive of unbelief (Althaus 1959; Wallmann 2005b; Strom 2014).

For polemical purposes, opponents regularly portrayed Pietists as Arminians in order to attack them as lax on the central Reformation doctrine of justification. In truth, the distinctions between the orthodox and Pietists on justification and conversion are not as clear. Just as the orthodox did, Pietists argued that power to convert lay in God's hands alone. And just as many orthodox theologians did, Pietists allowed that one might resist God's saving work in some capacity. In fact, during the explicit debates on the question of the timing of conversion, orthodox opponents accused Pietists, for example, of embracing Calvinist views of predestination for seeking to restrict chronologically the time in which one must repent and limiting the universality of grace. Orthodox theologians also took a more latitudinarian position on grace und repentance in the 1710s, when they traded charges with one of the leading Pietist theologians and author of the first Pietist systematic theology, Justus Joachim Breithaupt (1658–1732), of embracing Calvinist predestination; Breithaupt, in turn, accused his opponents of semi-Pelagianism (Brecht 1993; Breithaupt 2011).

Polemics aside, both church Pietists and the orthodox claimed to uphold the confessions of the church and stand as the true heirs of Luther. Unlike the radical Pietists, who spiritualized or in some cases instituted believer's baptism, church Pietists did not challenge the confessional expressions of the sacraments, but their criticisms of nominal Christians and lax church discipline surrounding the sacraments led to significant changes in ritual practice. Pietists attacked what they saw as the perfunctory nature of private confession, and their criticisms contributed to its decline in the eighteenth century. The exorcism in the liturgical ritual of baptism also drew Pietist critics, who saw it as outmoded and magical. Many of these criticisms would find support among rationalists in the eighteenth century, though for very different reasons. The Pietist critique of sacramental practices reflected an increasingly individualistic and subjective turn in Pietist theology (Jacobi 1997; Yoder 2011).

Pietist theologians, such as Breithaupt, followed the tradition of Lutheran dogmatics in many respects but increasingly emphasized the identity of true theology and saving faith in contrast to the later Wittenberg theologians, such as Calov (1612–86) and Quenstedt (1612–88), who construed theology as a *scientia practica*, emphasizing its objective nature. For the Pietists, proper theological knowledge flowed from the illumination of the Spirit, and thus was not solely governed by reason and the external words of Holy Scripture. Only through the illumination of faith could a theologian come through the Word and reason to recognition of spiritual truths (Koch 2011).

The importance of faith and illumination (*Erleuchtung*) to the task of theology should not obscure, however, that the basis of theological authority for Pietists remained the Bible. On a devotional level, they extended Spener's call for engagement with scripture in all estates and promoted the printing and distribution of Bibles with new fervor. At Halle, Francke and his allies established the first Bible society in Protestantism and developed high-speed presses dedicated to the production of inexpensive Bibles. Francke's short introduction to reading scripture, *Einfältige Unterricht*, was reprinted widely and prefaced millions of Bibles in the eighteenth and nineteenth centuries, and he put reading scripture in the larger context of

Luther's triad of *oratio, meditatio,* and *tentatio* (Bayer 2011; Francke 2011; Gawthrop and Strauss 1984).

The concern with scripture also led to new scholarly investigations of the biblical texts. Francke's early critical inquiries into the received biblical texts and Luther's German translation in the *Observationes Biblicae* (1695) provoked a strong reaction from orthodox opponents as well as from some Pietist allies; and while he abandoned this approach quite early, other Pietists, especially Johann Albrecht Bengel; would continue the Pietist tradition of critical source work. Francke's ongoing hermeneutical work showed clear Pietist characteristics. He developed a distinction between the husk and kernel of scripture, the latter closely identified with Christ. He further came to distinguish between the *sensus literae* and *sensus literalis*, arguing that the true meaning of scripture intended by the Holy Spirit went beyond the lexical meaning of the text. He further developed a third plane of meaning, the *sensus mysticus*, which was only accessible to the illumined or regenerate. Just as with devotional reading, a proper scholarly approach depended on the practices of *oratio, meditatio*, and *tentatio*, but with a stronger emphasis on *meditatio* (Bayer 2011; Matthias 2005; Reventlow 2010).

One of the major contributions of Pietism to modern Protestantism was a new understanding of mission activity. Well into the seventeenth century, Protestants had interpreted the Great Commission as a task of the early church, but over the course of the seventeenth century Pietists and other evangelicals came to understand Matthew 26 as an obligation for contemporary Christians. A more optimistic eschatology, which promised better conditions for the earthly church in the future, contributed to the Pietist drive to spread the Gospel beyond Europe. This took concrete form with the foundation of the Danish-Halle mission to South India, which stands as the first sustained Protestant mission to the non-Western world. Halle Pietists and Zinzendorf's Moravians would be in the vanguard of Protestant missions throughout the eighteenth century; an impulse traceable to their understanding of the expansion of the Kingdom of God (*Reich Gottes*) (Robert 2009; Wellenreuther 2004).

Pietist reforms also extended to marriage and the household, but these could take very different directions. Drawing on Luther, Spener sought to recover aspects of a sacramental understanding of marriage, and he emphasized a companionate model of marriage that influenced many Pietists who remained within the established church. But where for Spener a more mystical understanding led to the elevation of Christian marriage and friendship, other more radical Pietists saw earthly marriage and sexuality as a hindrance to spiritual progress. Some, especially those in the Böhmist tradition such as Johann Georg Gichtel (1638–1710), rejected "fleshly marriage" altogether and embraced celibacy. Others, such as Ernst Hochmann von Hochenau (1670–1721), saw marriage among the unregenerate as purely civil, whereas marriage for true Christians had several levels—including a procreative marriage of the regenerate, a chaste marriage without sexual union, and at its pinnacle, a form of marriage in which the soul becomes engaged as bride to Christ. Influenced in part by Hochmann, Zinzendorf (1700–60) took a different tack and emphasized true Christian marriage but sought to remove lust from conjugality, not by advocating chastity but diverting sexuality within marriage towards devotion and contemplation of Christ. Ambivalence about marriage and sexuality was characteristic of many Pietists; even central figures like August Hermann Francke held up the ideal of celibacy for missionaries (Breul 2010; Breul and Salvadori 2014; Roeber 2013; Schneider 2007; Peucker 2015).

# 6 Regional Centers and Varieties of Pietism

The expansion of Pietism was remarkable in the first decades of the eighteenth century. By the 1730s and 1740s, groups that adhered to the religious principles of Spener could be found in small as well as in large territories; in the northern parts of Central Europe as well as in the south; in towns and villages, among common folk and at some of the courts. Furthermore, groups of devout believers that can be labeled Pietist existed in Scandinavia, the Baltic States, parts of Hungary, and of course also in the British colonies in North America. It is important to note, however, that not all of these groups were the same; in fact, they did not even hold the same kind of religious belief even though they considered themselves to be part of the religious renewal initiated by Spener. In retrospect, we should distinguish mainly four different types.

## 6.1 The Francke foundations at Halle and their followers

When August Hermann Francke died in 1727, his son and successor August Gotthilf Francke (1696–1769) inherited the responsibility for a large institution with an international reputation. A number of schools existed at Halle; schools for children of different abilities and social classes. The teachers for these students were trained in a special college. In addition, the Francke foundations had founded a pharmacy that produced medicine that was sold nationally but also shipped overseas. Thousands of Bibles were printed at the Cansteinsche Bibelanstalt, closely connected with the foundations. Many of these Bibles were for export, often together with pharmaceutical products. Halle alumni worked as chaplains in the Prussian army; others devoted their life to missionary work. From the first decade of the eighteenth century, the Halle mission at Tranquebar in South India played a special role. At home in Halle, the elder and younger Francke were surrounded by a devoted circle of teachers, administrators, physicians, and artisans. They prided themselves on having a large library that held most of the publications by Pietists. Over the years, they also built a museum with artifacts of foreign cultures and natural specimens, sent to them by their missionaries. With the help of letters and newspapers, Halle had become the center of a network of Christians actively involved in reform and believing in the coming Kingdom of God. In short, when Frederick the Great (1712–86) came to power in Berlin in 1740, the Halle foundations were a kind of empire within his realm (Gawthrop 1993; Hinrichs 1971; Marschke 2014).

Key to understanding this empire is the concept of the Kingdom of God. The schools served this purpose, as did the pharmacy, the printing-shop, and all the other activities. As the Kingdom of God was universal, it was self-evident to everybody working in or connected with Halle that they should also work on an international level, as best as they could. From the start, the Prussian authorities had given material support and legal protection to the Francke foundations. This led to a number of conflicts. On the one hand, neither of the two Franckes had any scruples about a close relationship between their undertaking and the absolutist Prussian state. On the other hand, they rejected the political demand that they should restrict their activities to the Prussian state. In the years after 1740, when Frederick the Great ridiculed the Pietist way of life and openly supported a secular understanding of enlightenment, the climate in which the Francke foundations had prospered began to change. Decline set in (Brecht 1995).

One reflection of this decline was the inability of Halle Pietists to provide intellectual leadership into succeeding generations. The heirs of the Pietist tradition in Halle, Gotthilf August Francke and Johann Anastasius Freylinghausen (1670–1739), were not theological thinkers of stature. The promising young Pietist theologian, Johann Jacob Rambach (1693–1735), left Halle for Giessen in 1731. He was among the most creative, particularly in extending Francke's hermeneutics, but his early death meant that his full theological project would not be realized. The best-known Halle theologian after Rambach was Siegmund Jacob Baumgarten (1706–57), who was fully a product of the Pietist milieu, including Francke's schools. But Baumgarten came to differ from the older Pietist tradition in that he incorporated elements of Wolffian rationalism into his theology. He could be critical of Lutheran orthodoxy, rejecting its scholasticism and views of scriptural inerrancy, but Baumgarten also distanced himself from Pietist subjectivism. By the mid-1730s, Pietists in Halle, including G. A. Francke, attacked Baumgarten for his "Wolffian" pedagogy. Though his work remained within the bounds of confessional Lutheranism, Baumgarten's measured adoption of rationalist methods, application of history to biblical texts, and views on toleration, place his theology closer to the Enlightenment than to Pietism. Pietism's failure to cultivate a viable alternative meant that Baumgarten, and especially his student Johann Salomo Semler (1725–91), could remake Halle into the leading Enlightenment faculty of theology in eighteenth-century Germany (Sorkin 2008).

## 6.2 Württemberg Pietists on an exclusive road toward salvation

While Halle Pietists were convinced that they were governed by a Christian sovereign, Württemberg Pietists never trusted the ducal authority whom they were expected to obey. Following the example of Louis XIV (1638–1715), the reigning dukes in Stuttgart built large and expensive castles, and they indulged in hunting and festivities of all kinds. In short, they loved the splendor and luxury of Baroque culture. Pietists in this southwestern territory of the Old Empire were shocked when a Catholic member of the ruling family ascended to the throne in 1733. Pietists in Württemberg had a much closer relationship with the estates, the traditional political body of local representatives. When one of the dukes, Karl Alexander, suddenly died in 1737, the estates formed an interim government until the new duke, Karl Eugen, came of age in 1744. The estates used this period in order to formulate a decree in which they spelled out the duties and rights, as well as the limits, of Pietist conventicles, the famous *Pietistenreskript* of 1743 (Lehmann 1969).

No one had more influence in Pietist circles in Württemberg than Johann Albrecht Bengel. Like many Pietists, Bengel had a radical background; but like many others, he moved more to the center as he took on a position of authority and became the headmaster of a school near Stuttgart. Bengel was remarkable in that, on the one hand, he scrupulously studied the biblical text to identify the original text (that is, what he considered the true word of God); yet on the other hand, Bengel drew on the figures he found in the Revelation of St. John to calculate the exact date of the Second Coming. After years of studies and intensive speculative calculations, he concluded that Christ would return in 1836. It was not social action that was important, Bengel taught, but an ascetic way of life was the prerequisite for attaining eternal salvation. In the following decades, Württemberg Pietists therefore excelled in a combination of eschatology and strict ethics. Eschatology taught them the progress of salvation history, while devotional books helped them to lead a truly Christian life (Ehmer 2005; Mälzer 1970).

Friedrich Christoph Oetinger (1702–82) and Philipp Matthäus Hahn (1739–90) were the two most important students of Bengel. While Oetinger published widely on theological topics, Hahn made himself a name as an inventor of clocks that showed both worldly or secular time as well as the progress of salvation history. After Bengel's death in 1752, Württemberg Pietists adopted a life of nearly complete seclusion. They abhorred politics, but tried to support the circles of their friends and families. By the 1780s, the social background of Württemberg Pietism had changed and the official church was confronted by a new generation of Pietists: simple folk, farmers, and weavers. They preached that salvation history had progressed considerably and that true Christians had to assemble separately from the church congregation. Johann Georg Rapp (1757–1847) was the most famous within the cohort, and certainly the most obstinate; Johann Michael Hahn (1758–1819) perhaps the most influential. After years of persecution by ducal authorities, Rapp decided to immigrate to the United States. Hahn also experienced persecution. But he chose to stay in Württemberg as he was given a place of refuge on a noble estate (Lehmann 1969; Lehmann 1995).

## 6.3  Nikolaus Ludwig von Zinzendorf and the Herrnhut community, the Moravians

In the late 1720s, Count Nikolaus Ludwig von Zinzendorf assembled a remarkable group of people on his noble estate at Herrnhut, which included local people with a deep interest in religion, as well as refugees from Bohemia and Moravia who were distant descendants of fifteenth-century Hussites. Under the leadership of Zinzendorf, this community experienced a spiritual awakening, which led in turn to the formation of a very special community, the *Herrnhuter Brüdergemeine*. In the following years, hundreds upon hundreds of people, from near and far, wanted to join the *Brüdergemeine*. Soon Herrnhut was overflowing. Zinzendorf solved this problem by establishing additional communities in other locations; not only in Germany, but also in other countries. By the time of his death in 1760, the *Herrnhuter*, or *Moravians* as they were called in English, had become an international society with local communities in many European countries, as well as in North America, the Caribbean, and India (Vogt 2005).

In the early 1730s, Zinzendorf formulated an innovative mission for his followers: they should go out into the world and bring the gospel to the people who had not had a chance to hear and learn the true word of God. Zinzendorf also believed in the Second Coming, but was convinced that Christ would not return until everyone on the planet had had a chance to become a Christian. Moravian missionaries were special in more than one way. Wherever they went, they lived among the common people. While, for example, Halle Pietists were active at the court in Copenhagen, Moravian missionaries preached to the simple folk on the outskirts of the Danish realm. Moreover, they attempted to learn the language of the common people, whether in the Baltic among Estonians and Lithuanians, or in the Caribbean among black slaves. Local authorities, therefore, often mistrusted them. All Moravian missionaries were expected to write letters to the center regularly. These letters were copied and then sent to the other outposts. As a result, the Moravians developed a strong sense of community in spite of the huge distances that separated many of them (Mettele 2009; Mettele 2010; Sensbach 2009; Wellenreuther 2004).

Zinzendorf was a university-educated scholar and deeply knowledgeable about the Christian tradition, but he was not a typical academic theologian. He wrote in German for a lay audience. Despite his roots in Halle's famous *Pädagogium*, Zinzendorf diverged from Francke's Pietism and its emphasis on personal conversion. He turned to Luther's theology of the cross, developing distinctive themes of the blood and wounds of Christ and mystical "encounter with the Savior." Influenced by the Philadelphian movement, Zinzendorf conceived of several *tropoi paideias* in which God used the different confessions or denominations to bring all to Christ. He believed in a synthesis of the best elements of the various religious movements of his time, including Judaism (Atwood 2004; Vogt 2005).

What Moravian missionaries taught was much more simple. They placed primary emphasis on conversion and the experience of rebirth. As best they could, they also tried to teach basic ethics—without, however, completely separating new converts from their cultural background. Within Europe, Moravian missionaries often served as messengers between Pietist conventicles which had lost contact with other members of the movement. This proved most important during the time of the French Revolution and Napoleonic Wars. Moravians, therefore, formed a link between eighteenth- and nineteenth-century Pietism (Meyer 1995; Weigelt 2000).

## 6.4  Pietists living at the court of noble families

Not all noble families within the Holy Roman Empire had the means to lead a life in baroque splendor. Some courts simply lacked the size, others the means. Not all dynasties possessed the power to rule in an absolutist manner. It is interesting to note that Pietists gained some influence in some of these smaller courts in the course of the eighteenth century. In Halle's case, this proved to be the small county of Wernigerode, a number of kilometers to the west in the Harz Mountains. In some cases, the whole noble family formed a kind of conventicle, including the ruling head; in others, and more often, the conventicle at the court consisted of the mother of the ruling head, his wife, and some of the other females at the court; and of course the court preacher. These were the people who did not participate in hunting pleasures, games of power and war, affairs with female companions, and the like. These conventicles formed a kind of cultural and moral antithesis to the court, a kind of constant reproach. As one can imagine, the court preachers were in a most dangerous position. In cases when the ruling head and his company of friends felt threatened by what they heard about the activities of the court preacher, or even a rumor coming from the conventicle, the court preacher was fired and replaced by someone who was more cautious, if not closer to the baroque way of life. In other places, however, Pietist influence at a noble court lasted well into the nineteenth century.

# 7  PIETIST CURRENTS IN NORTH AMERICA

Immigration to North America allowed some Pietists to realize their vision of Christianity outside of the legal constraints of the old Empire. Almost all forms of Pietism would eventually find expression in the New World, but especially radical Pietists and Moravians would take particular advantage of its opportunities. In contrast, without an established church structure church Pietists in North America faced major challenges in adapting, but they also expanded and profoundly shaped the development of early Lutheranism in North America.

## 7.1  Radical Pietist immigration

At a very early point, more radical Pietists developed a keen interest in North America, and the New World played a key role in the formation of the Frankfurter *Landkompagnie* that sought to encourage German immigration to Pennsylvania in the 1680s. The first substantial Pietist immigration to North America occurred in 1694. Johann Jakob Zimmerman (1644–93), a former Lutheran minister from Württemberg with strong Spiritualist convictions, gathered a group of radical Pietists intent on leaving for Pennsylvania. He died before they could embark, but a young theologian, Johannes

Kelpius (1667–1708), assumed leadership for the group traveling to Pennsylvania. Kelpius' spiritualism drew on Jacob Böhme and combined millennialism, cabbalistic speculations, and astrology. He developed a distinctive view of North America's place within the coming millennium. For Kelpius, the woman in the wilderness of Revelation 12:6 was to be sought in Pennsylvania's undeveloped countryside. In Wissahickon, near Germantown, he and his like-minded "monks" practiced celibacy and withdrew from society. The community disbanded after Kelpius' death in 1708, but it signaled the longlasting presence that radical streams of communal Pietism would have in North America during the eighteenth century (Lashlee 1967; Roeber 1995).

Conrad Beissel (1691–1768), a journeyman baker from the Palatinate, established a much more durable community of radical Pietists in Ephrata, Pennylvania. Beissel had imbibed esoteric and radical Pietist currents in Germany from Phildelphians, Böhmists, and Inspirationists before he immigrated in 1720. In Pennsylvania he came into close association with the New Baptists or Dunker Brethren, and was rebaptized in 1724. Beissel became a minister of a small congregation in Conestoga, but his emphasis on the seventh-day Sabbath and celibacy brought him into conflict with the Dunkers. By the 1730s, he had established a new community of celibates and householders in Ephrata that would become one of most distinctive communal societies in early America. Beissel's theology drew on Jacob Böhme and his later disciple Johann Georg Gichtel, and included a gendered understanding of the Fall and an emphasis on the divine Sophia. As did many Philadelphians, he also advocated for an eventual restoration of all things. But Beissel also developed unique emphases on spiritual rebirth through a twofold conversion and spiritual death, accompanied by a mystical impregnation that signaled union with the divine. Though controversial, Ephrata flourished and became especially well known for its music, arts, and printing. The community continued after Beissel's death in 1768 but was also riven by disagreement over his legacy (Bach 2003).

The New Baptists, or Dunker Brethren, constituted the most successful radical Pietist expression in the New World. The Dunkers first immigrated in 1719. In part influenced by Swiss Anabaptism, they pursued believer's baptism, the ban, and a gathered church. Their ecclesiology represented a thorough rejection of the magisterial Protestant notion of *corpus mixtum* in favor of the visible expression of the true church. Like Anabaptists, they embraced pacifism, but they also had distinctive practices and beliefs derived from their radical Pietist heritage. For example, Alexander Mack (1679–1735), the leader of the Dunker Brethren, embraced the Philadelphian restoration of all things, as did many other Brethren. Influenced by Gottfried Arnold (1666–1714), the Brethren also reinstituted the ancient practice of the love feast, and their eschatology shows radical Pietist influences; though in contrast to the Philadelphians and the Inspirationists, they rejected direct extrabiblical revelation and emphasized instead a rigorous biblicism. More than any other group, the Dunker Brethren show the influence of Anabaptism on radical Pietists. Taking advantage of the lack of church structures among the German immigrants in Pennsylvania, they became the most successful Pietist community in the New World (Meier 2008).

## 7.2 Zinzendorf and the Moravian ecumenical vision

Straddling the world of radical and church Pietism in North America were the *Herrnhuter* or Moravians, followers of Nikolaus Ludwig von Zinzendorf, who advocated an ecumenical vision of the church. In contrast to the sectarian impulse of the Dunker, Zinzendorf drew heavily on Philadelphian ideas and sought to unite Christians across confessions within an ecumenical society. Zinzendorf saw North America as a particularly promising field in which to implement his vision among German immigrants of various confessions. Despite some initial success in America, Zinzendorf failed to realize his ecumenical goals against the determined opposition of church Pietists, especially the Halle-trained Heinrich Melchior Mühlenberg (1711–87). Instead, Moravians became best known in North America for their communal experiment in Bethlehem and missions to the Native Americans. On St. Thomas in the Caribbean, Moravians enjoyed extraordinary success among the African populace, forming what Sensbach has described as the origins of "Afro-Atlantic" Evangelicalism (Atwood 2004; Sensbach 2005; Sensbach 2009; Vogt 2005).

## 7.3 Mühlenberg and the expansion of Halle Pietism

The church Pietists were slower to make a mark in North America. The resettlement of Salzburg refugees to Georgia in 1733, which Halle Pietists facilitated, became the first sustained extension of church Pietism to North America. Ebenezer, as it became known, was to be a model community, complete with orphanage in the Halle tradition. Ebenezer's direct influence beyond Georgia was limited, however, and it was only with the arrival of Heinrich Melchior Mühlenberg in 1742, whom Halle dispatched to North America to organize Lutherans, that church Pietism gained a wider influence among German immigrants. Mühlenberg sought to forestall the ecumenical designs of Zinzendorf and the Moravians, and he organized the loosely associated Lutheran clergy into the Ministerium of Pennsylvania. Mühlenberg represented the moderate Pietism of Spener and Francke, adhering to the confessions but also emphasizing the simplicity of biblical truth and "a complete change of heart and a living faith." He adapted the traditional Lutheran liturgy to the American context (Roeber 1995; Wellenreuther 2013).

# 8 The Complicated Relationship of Pietism and the Enlightenment

Historians had long explained that Pietism and the Enlightenment formed two separate and distinct periods of cultural, religious, and intellectual European history that followed one another. Pietism had grown out of orthodoxy, and the Enlightenment, in turn, had replaced Pietism. In the past few decades, however, almost everyone working on the cultural and religious history of the seventeenth and eighteenth centuries has become convinced that orthodoxy, Pietism, and the Enlightenment existed side by side for several decades, in particular with Pietism and Enlightenment fighting with one another on some issues, and cooperating in others. The discussion to clarify these areas continues, but at the moment no simple solution seems in sight (Gierl 1997).

## 8.1 The coexistence of Pietism and the Enlightenment

Periodization helps to bring some light into this complex mixture of arguments and counter arguments. At the beginning of the eighteenth century, in most parts of Central Europe Pietism was vibrant and growing. Pietists were full of optimism; new projects were launched almost every year, and most of them were achieved within a relatively short period of time. Spener's shadow loomed large over religious life, and devotional tracts were published by the hundreds. By contrast, in continental Europe adherents of Enlightenment were still in a minority in the early eighteenth century. They tried to identify the issues that they wanted to advance, and more often than not they failed. There were also some fields of cooperation between Pietists and enlightened thinkers, as both were opposed to Lutheran orthodoxy. At the newly founded university of Halle, for example, a Pietist like August Hermann Francke and the enlightened philosopher Christian Thomasius successfully cooperated in university politics and agreed on many issues. Education was high on their agenda, as were some matters like the fight against superstition, including belief in witchcraft. Some scholars still believe that this cooperation could have led to a happy, productive, and lasting marriage. Yet, they fail to recognize the growing competition between the two parties also at a place like Halle, a competition that resulted in an open controversy less than two decades later. In the early 1720s August Hermann Francke successfully conspired with Berlin authorities, with the result that the enlightened philosopher Christian Wolff (1679–1754) was removed from his chair at Halle. Pietists considered this as a victory over unbelief, not just over dangerous competition. Pietists perhaps arrived at the apex of their influence in Prussian politics during the 1720s (Geyer-Kordesch 2000; Marschke 2014).

## 8.2 From cooperation to competition and conflict

The tide turned when Frederick the Great came to power in 1740. This well-educated king with a strong interest in philosophy disliked Pietists. He opened his court for artists and scholars from all over Europe, in particular from France. A controversial celebrity like Voltaire (1694–1778) was a guest of honor at the Berlin court. It was more than a symbolic gesture when Frederick the Great ordered that Christian Wolff should be allowed to return to his former position at Halle, while Pietists grudgingly observed Wolff's triumphant return. Not surprisingly, in the following decades the influence of proponents of Enlightenment grew continuously in Central Europe while the number of Pietists dwindled, and the remaining Pietists withdrew into their conventicles (Marschke 2014).

By the 1770s, French rationalism had conquered not only the minds of the Berlin elite, but also of professors of philosophy and the sciences in many German universities. As Zinzendorf had left the *Herrnhuter* with a pile of debt at the time of his death, this most enterprising group within Pietism now was forced to restrict their activities more and more. As noted above, even at the university at Halle, supporters of Enlightenment such as Johann Salomo Semler now occupied the main chairs. Only in remote areas of the Holy Roman Empire—for example, in some villages in Württemberg—Pietists continued to meet in their traditional assemblies, the conventicles. In 1780, some of the remaining Pietists, led by Johann August Urlsperger (1728–1806) from Augsburg, formed the so-called *Christentumsgesellschaft*, a society for the propagation of the true word of Christ, at Basel. In the beginning, this society had only one purpose: namely, the publication of works that criticized enlightened thinkers, and in particular rationalism. Within a few years, however, the Basel center managed to create a network of local chapters all across Protestant Central Europe. Letters were the main means of communication between the center and the local chapters. Often, messengers from *Herrnhut* served as persons who established contacts and kept them alive. After the outbreak of the French Revolution, when concepts of rationalism seemed to triumph over traditional values openly, the determination of the leaders of the *Christentumsgesellschaft* to become more active grew stronger. Basel, together with London, became a counterrevolutionary force. With financial and logistical help from London, the Basel society formed new daughter societies that had specific tasks: first, a society for the publication and dissemination of Bibles (*Bibelanstalt*); then, no less important, a society devoted to foreign missionary work (*Missionsanstalt*); finally, several institutions to support orphans and children in need (*Rettungsanstalten*). Within just a few years, these models were copied in other parts of Germany (Lehmann and Lohmeier 1983; Weigelt 1995).

## 8.3  Differing visions of the future of humankind

Both Pietism and the Enlightenment claimed to have the right ideas for finding a pathway toward a better future for humankind. They both advanced the education of children, and the better training of teachers. They both wanted to help the poorer segments of society, and advocated a system of ideas that combined theoretical concepts with practical measures. But the differences between the two were far stronger than their common notions. For Pietists, all practical measures, in education as well as in social work, were essential and meaningful only as parts of their efforts in building the Kingdom of God. The Kingdom of God was the vision that inspired them, the hope that supported them, even when times were hard. The reward that they expected was eternal salvation. On the day of the Last Judgment God would, as they hoped, give credit to their labor in the vineyard of the Lord. Even those who did not publicly proclaim that they were expecting the Second Coming, were convinced that the more time, energy, and compassion they invested in the building of God's kingdom, the sooner Christ would return. This belief united all of them—Zinzendorf's *Herrnhuter* settlements, the Halle descendants of Francke, and even the Pietists in Württemberg who had withdrawn into their conventicles (Gäbler 2004; Neumann and Sträter 2000; Ohlemacher 1986).

By contrast, the Enlightenment had a different vision of the future. Enlightened thinkers proclaimed that the future life of humankind could be improved, step by step, if people used the rational capacities that God had endowed them with during creation. Measures they advocated concerned the field of medicine: for example, vaccination against smallpox, reforms in legal matters (like the abolition of the death penalty); new techniques in agriculture (like the introduction of better ploughs, crop rotation, and more effective fertilizers); better methods of breeding cattle, and better facilities for storing grains. Enlightened pastors hoped to raise the standard of public education. They did not shy away from preaching about agricultural reform. Furthermore, political thinkers and philosophers discussed in their journals how the political system could best be improved—by social contracts, as some argued; by the division of legislative, executive, and judicial power, as others explained. Within Germany, however, all enlightened reformers knew well that the sovereigns' belief in absolutism, also in the form of enlightened despotism, would stop any experiments that would threaten the prerogative of the crown. Even an enlightened ruler like Frederick the Great was adamant in that respect. To be sure, the German Enlightenment, unlike French rationalism, always rested on a sound Christian basis, and neologists like Semler criticized radical Deists. But late eighteenth-century Pietists lived in a completely different intellectual and scholarly world than Enlightenment thinkers in Germany. Biblical criticism was perhaps the one issue that separated them most. While rationalist theologians dissected biblical texts historically and philologically, as best as they could, Pietists tended to approach the traditional text of the Bible as the true word of God that every believer could understand with faith and prayer and without any scholarly help (Sheehan 2005).

If we compare enlightened programs with the Pietist view of the future, it is important to note that according to enlightened thinkers the future was an open playing field, with no limit in sight as long as humankind remained faithful to the laws of reason. This is exactly the proposition to which no Pietist would agree. Pietists were convinced that they knew the power of the devil and omnipresence of sin. They were aware how much they depended on God's grace and forgiveness. Personal rebirth was their aim, and once they were reborn, a life on the road to an ever more perfect sanctification. They obeyed God's commands in a most scrupulous manner as they knew that God's judgment would be harsh. In short, what separated Pietism from enlightenment was a completely different view of the role of humankind within the course of salvation history—one could also say, a completely different Christian anthropology. Once the French Revolution had begun, these differences became crystal clear to everyone who wanted to know. For many Pietists, the upheaval in France was a sign sent by God indicating that the Second Coming was approaching rapidly. Through this, the stage was set for a completely different development of both parties in the course of the coming centuries (Gäbler 2004).

# 9  THE LEGACY OF PIETISM IN THE NINETEENTH AND TWENTIETH CENTURIES

After the middle of the nineteenth century, works on Pietism described it as a religious reform movement within Central European Protestantism, which originated in the last decades of the seventeenth century and lasted, with minor exceptions, until the middle of the eighteenth century. Albrecht Ritschl's magisterial three-volume study of Pietism is perhaps the best example of this, even though Ritschl was provoked to deal with his topic by Pietists of his own time. However, as time passed this view appeared less and less convincing. Some church historians argued that within nineteenth- and twentieth-century Protestantism there were a number of religious groups that called themselves "Pietists" and tried to follow the example and traditions of earlier Pietists. Clearly, there were also traits and elements typical of Pietism within some of the religious movements of later periods, even though these groups did not call themselves Pietists. Therefore, when the Historical Commission for the Study of Pietism planned a new comprehensive history of Pietism that was supposed to replace Ritschl's work in the 1980s, it was decided not only to include what some historians call "classical Pietism," but also a volume on Pietism in the nineteenth and twentieth centuries. Through this, a completely new view of Pietism emerged. New questions had to be answered. What is the relationship between Pietism and nineteenth-century evangelical biblicism? What kind of relationship exists between Pietism and twentieth-century fundamentalism? To what extent did the reform movements within nineteenth- and twentieth-century Protestantism borrow theological concepts and social ideas from Pietism? At present, there are no conclusive answers to these questions. While some church historians argue that it is confusing to extend the history of Pietism into the era after the French Revolution, others insist that exactly this extension opens up new avenues for a better understanding of the relationship of Pietism and the processes of modernization (Lehmann 2000; Lehmann 2005).

## 9.1  The tradition of biblicism

What were the theological themes characteristic for Pietism that had an influence in nineteenth- and twentieth-century Protestant reform movements? With few exceptions, late seventeenth- and eighteenth-century Pietists practiced what they understood as a straightforward interpretation of the Bible. This led many Pietist scholars to focus on recovering the authentic texts of the original scripture, and a new emphasis on proper translation. They believed that God would help them to understand the true meaning of biblical texts, and if the text did not disclose its meaning immediately, then through prayer God would reveal it. Some historians argue that Pietist philology and zeal for new translations contributed, if inadvertently, to the rise of rationalist approaches to the "Enlightenment" Bible (Frei 1974, 34–40; Sheehan 2005, 95). As rationalist scholars employed refined historical, philological, and comparative methods to scrutinize and in some cases criticize biblical texts in the course of the eighteenth century, Pietists recurred to traditional interpretations that their Enlightenment contemporaries criticized as simplistic. The same pattern continued in the nineteenth and twentieth centuries. As biblical studies became a highly specialized field of research within theological faculties across the Western world and subjected the biblical texts to increasing scrutiny, a substantial number of Protestants (mostly ordinary churchgoers, but also some pastors), saw no reason to use the insights of these scholars. Quite the contrary, forms of biblical literalism became a hallmark of these Protestants, and a practice that distinguished them from all of those whom they considered only lukewarm Christians (Frei 1974; Sheehan 2005; Shantz 2013).

Biblicism became then relatively widespread both among members of state churches or former state churches, as well as in free churches, including Pentecostal congregations. From the early nineteenth century, this biblicist impulse was part and parcel of attempts to print, publish, and distribute Bibles to as many people as possible, and nineteenth-century Pietists and Evangelicals continued the early Pietist practice of disseminating Bibles at home and abroad, pioneered by the Canstein Bible Society in the eighteenth century. These later Pietists invested much effort in translating the biblical texts into other languages and making them available to missionaries. This continued up through the Cold War, when Bibles were smuggled into communist countries, most notably Communist China.

## 9.2  The theology of the Kingdom of God

Another trait that had characterized late seventeenth- and eighteenth-century Pietists was their belief in the coming Kingdom of God. Everything that they planned and achieved, they understood as work toward the building of God's kingdom, or as labor in God's vineyard. Missions abroad qualified for such labor, as did efforts on the domestic mission front. In the course of the nineteenth century, foreign missions played an ever more important role for those who considered themselves as children of God's coming kingdom. Missionary societies were founded in England and Scotland, the Netherlands and Switzerland, Germany, the United States, and other countries, many of which had explicit Pietist connections and affiliations, including those in Basel, Berlin, and Leipzig. Foreign missions fascinated contemporaries. Nineteenth- and even twentieth-century heirs of Pietism were convinced that it was the duty of true Christians to bring the light of civilization to the uncivilized nations of the world. They held as an exclusive treasure that once all parts of humankind had heard God's word, Christ would return. Typically, missionaries reduced the biblical message to a few elementary beliefs, and their biblical literalism often became an essential part of the Christian doctrine taught beyond Europe. In this way, biblicism became part of the religious identity of many of the new Christian churches that were founded and began to flourish in the era after decolonization and the end of European-American imperialism (Ohlemacher 1986).

## 9.3 The belief in spiritual rebirth

Throughout the late seventeenth and eighteenth centuries, Pietists regularly reported how important religious rebirth and religious awakening had been for them. August Hermann Francke's famous conversion narrative became one of the best-known literary examples of spiritual rebirth. To be reborn distinguished God's children from the children of the world, and religious rebirth and conversion was considered as a distinctive religious experience of chosen individuals; the regenerate would assemble with others and form new communities in which God's children would help one another on the road to sanctification. For some, rebirth was a unique act; for others, it was a recurring task that they had to master again and again. This continued into the nineteenth century, but a decisive change also occurred as nationalism gripped the minds of many people in the Western world. Now a new theological concept appeared: namely, the notion that not only individuals could be reborn but also whole nations. Just as God had concluded a covenant with the people of Israel, he could also choose nations to become people of a new covenant. Striking examples of this can be found among several nations with a strong Protestant tradition; among them the United States of America, Great Britain, and Germany (Hutchison and Lehmann 1994).

## 9.4 Renewed hopes for the Second Coming

Pietists of the seventeenth and eighteenth centuries propagated conceptions of eschatology that would have been foreign to classical Protestantism of the Reformation era. Pietists did not espouse a single view, but all shared a powerful interest in eschatology. Some, especially radical Pietists, were premillennialist and apocalyptic, while others such as Spener held moderate postmillennial views, in which the return of Christ was postponed until his children began building his kingdom. Some hoped that they would live until the very moment of Christ's return and become part of his rule of a thousand years; others, like Johann Albrecht Bengel, placed this historic final moment of salvation history beyond their own lifetime into the future. Pietist preoccupation with the Second Coming gave millennial expectations and theories, even as they remained controversial, a place within the established churches of the eighteenth and nineteenth centuries. This distinguished Pietism from some other Evangelical movements of the eighteenth century, especially Methodism, which largely lacked the millenarian emphases characteristic of many Pietists. Pietist eschatology generally became more pessimistic after the French Revolution, but one legacy of Pietism may be seen in the flourishing of millenarian ideas among many Evangelicals in the nineteenth and twentieth centuries in Europe and North America (Ward 1992; Moltmann 2004).

## 9.5  Changing conditions for fulfilling a traditional task

During the nineteenth and twentieth centuries, within many countries of the Western world the ethical heritage of the Pietists was equally important. Pietists had taught to care for orphans and widows, the weak and disadvantaged. This message retained its meaning and attraction even after the French Revolution, which had promised inner-worldly progress. As industrialization progressed in the course of the nineteenth century, and as a new class of socially disadvantaged people emerged, Christians were challenged to act. Help for the poor now gained a new dimension. Many of those who remembered the *praxis pietatis* Spener and Francke had taught, also created asylums and hostels for mentally and physically handicapped people. These institutions formed the very center of nineteenth-century domestic mission work. Differences between societies are significant, however. In the United States, for example, the campaign against slavery was accompanied by campaigns against prostitution and alcoholism. In Central Europe, by contrast, the mentally and physically handicapped were the focus of those who labored for God's kingdom.

Over a hundred years ago, Ernst Troeltsch noted that Pietism flourished at a pivotal point between the classic Protestantism of the Reformation era and the new Protestantism characteristic of the modern age. Pietism provided a decisive impetus for many characteristics that are now associated with modern Protestantism, especially its Evangelical expressions. David Bebbington has described four central qualities of Evangelicalism—including conversionism, activism, biblicism, and crucicentrism—that correspond closely with central emphases of Pietists. In addition, Pietism transmitted distinctive themes of mission and millenarianism to Protestantism of the nineteenth and twentieth centuries. Elements of Pietism influenced denominations in North America as diverse as Mennonites and Methodists, and in Germany and Scandinavia many pious Protestants continued to ally themselves self-consciously with the Pietist movement of previous centuries. The legacy of Pietism is not without innovative and progressive aspects, but particularly in the nineteenth and twentieth centuries, it tended to associate itself with conservative forces in church and government. The long-term influence of Pietism on modern Christianity remains an open question still awaiting answers from further research (Troeltsch 1986; Bebbington 1989; Gäbler 2000).

### Bibliography

Aland, Kurt. 1970. "Bibel und Bibeltext bei August Hermann Francke und Johann Albrecht Bengel." In *Pietismus und Bibel*, 89–147. Witten: Luther-Verlag.

Albrecht-Birkner, Veronica, and Udo Sträter. 2010. "Der radikale Phase des frühen August Hermann Francke." In *Der radikale Pietismus: Perspektiven der Forschung*, edited by Wolfgang Breul et al. Göttingen: Vandenhoeck & Ruprecht.

Althaus, Paul. 1959. "Die Bekehrung in reformatorischer und pietistischer Sicht." *Neue Zeitschrift für Systematische Theologie* 1: 3–25.

Atwood, Craig D. 2004. *Community of the Cross: Moravian Piety in Colonial Bethlehem.* University Park, PA: Penn State University Press.

Bach, Jeff. 2003. *Voices of the Turtledoves: The Sacred World of Ephrata.* University Park, PA: Penn State University Press.

Bayer, Oswald. 2011. "Lutheran Pietism, or Oratio, Meditatio, Tentatio in August Hermann Francke." *Lutheran Quarterly* 25 (4): 383–397.

Bebbington, D. W. 1989. *Evangelicalism in Modern Britain: A History from the 1730s to the 1980s.* London: Unwin Hyman.

Behringer, Wolfgang, Hartmut Lehmann, and Christian Pfister. 2005. *Kulturelle Konsequenzen der "Kleinen Eiszeit"/Cultural Consequences of the "Little Ice Age."* Göttingen: Vandenhoeck & Ruprecht.

Behringer, Wolfgang. 2004. *Witches and Witchhunts: A Global History.* Cambridge: Polity Press.

Bellardi, Werner. 1994. *Die Vorstufen der collegia pietatis bei Philipp Jakob.* Giessen: Brunnen.

Brecht, Martin. 1995. "Der Hallische Pietismus in der Mitte des 18. Jahrhunderts—seine Ausstrahlung und sein Niedergang." In *Der Pietismus im 18. Jahrhundert,* edited by Martin Brecht and Klaus Deppermann, 319–357. Göttingen: Vandenhoeck & Ruprecht.

Brecht, Martin. 1993. "Philipp Jakob Spener, sein Programm und dessen Auswirkungen." In *Pietismus vom siebzehnten bis zum frühen achtzehnten Jahrhundert,* 279–389. Göttingen: Vandenhoeck & Ruprecht.

Breithaupt, Joachim Justus. 2011. "Des Seligen Herrn Abt Breithaupts eigenhändig aufgesetzter Lebens-Lauf . . . ." In *Joachim Justus Breithaupt (1658–1732): Aspekte von Leben, Wirken und Werk im Kontext,* edited by Reimar Lindauer-Huber and Andreas Lindner, 23–53. Stuttgart: Steiner.

Breul, Wolfgang. 2013. "August Hermann Franckes Konzept einer Generalreform." In *Geschichtsbewusstsein und Zukunftserwartung in Pietismus und Erweckungsbewegung,* edited by Wolfgang Breul and Jan Carsten Schnurr, 69–83. Göttingen: Vandenhoeck & Ruprecht.

Breul, Wolfgang. 2010. "Ehe und Sexualität im radikalen Pietismus." In *Der radikale Pietismus: Perspektiven der Forschung,* edited by Wolfgang Breul, Lothar Vogel, and Macus Meier, 403–418. Göttingen: Vandenhoeck & Ruprecht.

Breul, Wolfgang, and Stefania Salvadori. 2014. *Geschlechtlichkeit und Ehe im Pietismus.* Leipzig: Evangelische Verlagsanstalt.

Clark, Christopher. 2009. "'The hope of better times': Pietism and the Jews." In *Pietism in Germany and North America 1680–1820,* edited by Jonathan Strom, Hartmut Lehmann, and James Van Horn Melton, 251–270. Farnham, UK: Ashgate.

Cook, Daniel J. 1998. "Leibniz on Enthusiasm." In *Leibniz, Mysticism and Religion,* edited by Allison P. Coudert, Richard H. Popkin, and Gordon M. Weiner, 107–135. Dordrecht: Springer Netherlands.

Deppermann, Andreas. 2002. *Johann Jakob Schütz und die Anfänge des Pietismus.* Tübingen: Mohr Siebeck.

Ehmer, Hermann. 2005. "Johann Albrecht Bengel (1687–1752)." In *The Pietist Theologians: An Introduction to Theology in the Seventeenth and Eighteenth Centuries,* edited by Carter Lindberg, 224–238. Malden, MA: Blackwell.

Erb, Peter C. 2005. "Gottfried Arnold (1666–1714)." In *The Pietist Theologians: An Introduction to Theology in the Seventeenth and Eighteenth Centuries,* edited by Carter Lindberg, 175–189. Malden, MA: Blackwell.

Francke, August Hermann. 2011. "Simple Instruction, or How One Should Read Holy Scripture for One's True Edification." *Lutheran Quarterly* 25 (4): 373–382.

Frei, Hans W. 1974. *The Eclipse of Biblical Narrative: A Study in Eighteenth and Nineteenth Century Hermeneutics*. New Haven: Yale University Press.

Gäbler, Ulrich. 2004. "Geschichte, Gegenwart, Zukunft." In *Glaubenswelt und Lebenswelten*, edited by Hartmut Lehmann and Martin Brecht, 19–48. Göttingen: Vandenhoeck & Ruprecht.

Gäbler, Ulrich et al. 2000. *Der Pietismus im neunzehnten und zwanzigsten Jahrhundert*. Göttingen: Vandenhoeck & Ruprecht.

Gawthrop, Richard L. and Strauss, Gerald. 1984. "Protestantism and Literacy in Early Modern Germany." *Past & Present* 104 (1): 31–55.

Gawthrop, Richard L. 1993. *Pietism and the Making of Eighteenth-Century Prussia*. Cambridge: Cambridge University Press.

Geyer-Kordesch, Johanna. 2000. *Pietismus, Medizin und Aufklärung in Preussen im 18. Jahrhundert: Das Leben und Werk Georg Ernst Stahls*. Tübingen: Niemeyer.

Gierl, Martin. 1997. *Pietismus und Aufklärung: Theologische Polemik und die Kommunikationsreform der Wissenschaft am Ende des 17. Jahrhunderts*. Göttingen: Vandenhoeck & Ruprecht.

Hinrichs, Carl. 1971. *Preussentum und Pietismus: Der Pietismus in Brandenburg-Preussen als religiös-soziale Reformbewegung*. Göttingen: Vandenhoeck & Ruprecht.

Hutchison, William R., and Hartmut Lehmann. 1994. *Many are Chosen: Divine Election and Western Nationalism*. Minneapolis: Fortress Press.

Illg, Thomas. 2011. *Ein anderer Mensch werden: Johann Arndts Verständnis Der Imitatio Christi als Anleitung zu einem wahren Christentum*. Göttingen: Vandenhoeck & Ruprecht.

Jacobi, Juliane. 1997. "Das Bild vom Kind in der Pädagogik August Hermann Franckes: Kinderbilder und Kindheit." In *Schulen machen Geschichte. 300 Jahre Erziehung in den Franckeschen Stiftungen zu Halle*, edited by Carmela Keller, 29–40. Halle/Saale: Verl. der Franckeschen Stiftungen.

Jakubowski-Tiessen, Manfred, and Hartmut Lehmann. 2003. *Um Himmels Willen: Religion in Katastrophenzeiten*. Göttingen: Vandenhoeck & Ruprecht.

Jung, Martin H. 2005. "Johanna Eleonora Petersen (1644–1724)." In *The Pietist Theologians: An Introduction to Theology in the Seventeenth and Eighteenth Centuries*, edited by Carter Lindberg, 147–160. Malden, MA: Blackwell.

Koch, Ernst. 2011. "Orthodoxes und pietistisches Theologieverständnis. Im Blick auf Joachim Justus Breithaupt." In *Joachim Justus Breithaupt (1658–1732): Aspekte von Leben, Wirken und Werk im Kontext*, edited by Reimar Lindauer-Huber and Andreas Lindner, 141–154. Stuttgart: Steiner.

Kolb, Robert. 2006. "Lutheran Theology in Seventeenth-Century Germany." *Lutheran Quarterly* 20 (4): 428–456.

Krauter-Dierolf, Heike. 2005. *Die Eschatologie Philipp Jakob Speners: Der Streit mit der lutherischen Orthodoxie um die Hoffnung besserer Zeiten*. Tübingen: Mohr Siebeck.

Lashlee, Ernest L. 1967. "Johannes Kelpius and his Woman in the Wilderness: A Chapter in the History of Colonial Pennsylvania Religious Thought." In *Glaube, Geist, Geschichte: Festschrift für Ernst Benz zum 60 Geburtstag*, 327–338. Leiden: Brill.

Lehmann, Hartmut. 1995. "Endzeiterwartung und Auswanderung: Der württembergische Pietist Johann Michael Hahn und Amerika." In *Alte und Neue Welt in wechselseitiger Sicht*, 185–204. Göttingen: Vandenhoeck & Ruprecht.

Lehmann, Hartmut. 2005. "Erledigte und nicht erledigte Aufgaben der Pietismusforschung: eine nochmalige Antwort an Johannes Wallmann." *Pietismus und Neuzeit* 31: 13–20.

Lehmann, Hartmut. 1986. "Frömmigkeitsgeschichtliche Auswirkungen der 'Kleinen Eiszeit.'" In *Volksreligion in der modernen Sozialgeschichte*, edited by Wolfgang Schieder, 31–50. Göttingen: Vandenhoeck & Ruprecht.

Lehmann, Hartmut. 1992. "Johann Matthäus Meyfart warnt hexenverfolgende Obrigkeiten vor dem Jüngsten Gericht." In *Vom Unfug des Hexen-Processes: Gegner der Hexenverfolgung von Johann Weyer bis Friedrich Spee*, edited by Hartmut Lehmann and Otto Ulbricht, 223–229. Wiesbaden: Harrassowitz.

Lehmann, Hartmut. 1999. "Die Krisen des 17. Jahrhunderts als Problem der Forschung." In *Krisen des 17. Jahrhunderts: Interdisziplinäre Perspektiven*, edited by Manfred Jakubowski-Tiessen, 13–24. Göttingen: Vandenhoeck & Ruprecht.

Lehmann, Hartmut. 2000. "Die neue Lage." In *Der Pietismus im neunzehnten und zwanzigsten Jahrhundert*, edited by Ulrich Gäbler and Martin Sallmann, 2–26. Göttingen: Vandenhoeck & Ruprecht.

Lehmann, Hartmut. 2012. "Perspektiven für die Pietismusforschung." *Theologische Rundschau* 77: 2, 226–240.

Lehmann, Hartmut. 1969. *Pietismus und weltliche Ordnung in Württemberg vom 17. bis zum 20. Jahrhundert* (Habilitationsschrift Cologne, 1967). Stuttgart: W. Kohlhammer.

Lehmann, Hartmut. 2007. "Probleme und Perspektiven der Pietismusforschung." In *Transformationen der Religion in der Neuzeit: Beispiele aus der Geschichte des Protestantismus*, edited by Hartmut Lehmann, 103–204. Göttingen: Vandenhoeck & Ruprecht.

Lehmann, Hartmut. 1980. *Das Zeitalter des Absolutismus: Gottesgnadentum und Kriegsnot*. Stuttgart: W. Kohlhammer.

Lehmann, Hartmut, and Dieter Lohmeier. 1983. *Aufklärung und Pietismus im dänischen Gesamtstaat 1770–1820*. Neumünster: Wachholtz.

Lehmann, Hartmut, and Anne-Charlott Trepp. 1999. *Im Zeichen der Krise: Religiosität im Europa des 17. Jahrhunderts*. Göttingen: Vandenhoeck & Ruprecht.

Lehmann, Hartmut, and Otto Ulbricht. 1992. *Vom Unfug des Hexen-Processes: Gegner der Hexenverfolgung von Johann Weyer bis Friedrich Spee*. Wiesbaden: Harrassowitz.

Lehmann, Hartmut, Hans-Jürgen Schrader, and Heinz Schilling. 2002. *Jansenismus, Quietismus, Pietismus*. Göttingen: Vandenhoeck & Ruprecht.

Mälzer, Gottfried. 1970. *Johann Albrecht Bengel: Leben und Werk*. Stuttgart: Calwer Verlag.

Marschke, Benjamin. 2014. "Halle Pietism and Politics in Prussia." In *A Companion to German Pietism (1600–1800)*, edited by Douglas H. Shantz, 472–526. Leiden: Brill.

Matthias, Markus. 2005. "August Hermann Francke (1663–1727)." In *The Pietist Theologians: An Introduction to Theology in the Seventeenth and Eighteenth Centuries*, edited by Carter Lindberg, 100–114. Malden, MA: Blackwell.

Matthias, Markus. 1993a. "Collegium pietatis und ecclesiola: Philipp Jakob Speners Reformprogramm zwischen Wirklichkeit und Anspruch." *Pietismus und Neuzeit* 19: 46–59.

Matthias, Markus. 1993b. *Johann Wilhelm und Johanna Eleonora Petersen: Eine Biographie bis zur Amtsenthebung Petersens im Jahre 1692*. Göttingen: Vandenhoeck & Ruprecht.

Meier, Marcus. 2008. *The Origin of the Schwarzenau Brethren*. Translated by Dennis Slabaugh. Philadelphia: Brethren Encyclopedia.

Meyer, Dietrich. 1995. "Zinzendorf und Herrnhut." In *Der Pietismus im achtzehnten Jahrhundert*, edited by Martin Brecht and Klaus Deppermann, 3–106. Göttingen: Vandenhoeck & Ruprecht.

Mettele, Gisela. 2009. *Weltbürgertum oder Gottesreich: Die Herrnhuter Brüdergemeine als globale Gemeinschaft, 1727–1857*. Göttingen: Vandenhoeck & Ruprecht.

Mettele, Gisela. 2010. "Identities across Borders: The Moravian Brethren as a Global Community." In *Pietism and Community in Europe and North America*, edited by Jonathan Strom, 155–177. Leiden: Brill.

Moltmann, Jürgen. 2004. *The Coming of God: Christian Eschatology*, edited by Margaret Kohl. Minneapolis: Fortress Press.

Mori, Ryoko. 2004. *Begeisterung und Ernüchterung in christlicher Vollkommenheit: Pietistische Selbst- und Weltwahrnehmungen im ausgehenden 17. Jahrhundert*. Halle: Verlag der Franckeschen Stiftungen.

Neumann, Josef N., and Udo Sträter. 2000. *Das Kind in Pietismus und Aufklärung*. Tübingen: Verlag der Franckeschen Stiftungen Halle.

Ohlemacher, Jörg. 1986. *Das Reich Gottes in Deutschland Bauen: Ein Beitrag zur Vorgeschichte und Theologie der deutschen Gemeinschaftsbewegung*. Gottingen: Vandenhoeck & Ruprecht.

Peucker, Paul. 2015. *A Time of Sifting: Mystical Marriage and the Crisis of Moravian Piety*. University Park, PA: Penn State University Press.

Reventlow, Henning Graf. 2010. *From the Enlightenment to the Twentieth Century*. Vol. 4 of *History of Biblical Interpretation*. Translated by Leo G. Perdue. Society of Biblical Literature Resources for Biblical Study. Atlanta: Society of Biblical Literature.

Robert, Dana Lee. 2009. *Christian Mission: How Christianity Became a World Religion*. Malden, MA: Wiley-Blackwell.

Robisheaux, Thomas. 2013. "The German Witch Trials." In *The Oxford Handbook of Witchcraft in Early Modern Europe and Colonial America*, edited by Brian P. Levack, 180–198. Oxford: Oxford University Press.

Roeber, Anthony Gregg. 2013. *Hopes for Better Spouses: Protestant Marriage and Church Renewal in Early Modern Europe, India, and North America*. Grand Rapids: Eerdmans.

Roeber, Anthony Gregg. 1995. "Der Pietismus in Nordamerika im 18. Jahrhundert." In *Der Pietismus im achtzehnten Jahrhundert*, edited by Martin Brecht and Klaus Deppermann, 666–699. Göttingen: Vandenhoeck & Ruprecht.

Schneider, Hans. 2006. *Der fremde Arndt: Studien zu Leben, Werk und Wirkung Johann Arndts (1555–1621)*. Göttingen: Vandenhoeck & Ruprecht.

Schneider, Hans. 2007. *German Radical Pietism*. Lanham, MD: Scarecrow Press.

Schrader, Hans-Jürgen. 2004. "Die Literatur des Pietismus—Pietistische Impulse zur Literaturgeschichte. Ein Überblick." In *Glaubenswelt und Lebenswelten*, edited by Hartmut Lehmann, 386–403. Göttingen: Vandenhoeck & Ruprecht.

Sensbach, Jon F. 2009. "'Don't Teach My Negroes to Be Pietists': Pietism and the Roots of the Black Protestant Church." In *Pietism in Germany and North America 1680–1820*, edited by Jonathan Strom, Hartmut Lehmann, and James Van Horn Melton, 183–198. Farnham, UK: Ashgate.

Sensbach, Jon F. 2005. *Rebecca's Revival: Creating Black Christianity in the Atlantic World*. Cambridge, MA: Harvard University Press.

Serkova, Polina. 2013. *Spielräume der Subjektivität: Studien zur Erbauungsliteratur von Heinrich Müller und Christian Scriver*. Universitätsverlag Rhein-Ruhr.

Shantz, Douglas H. 2013. *An Introduction to German Pietism: Protestant Renewal at the Dawn of Modern Europe*. Baltimore: Johns Hopkins University Press.

Sheehan, Jonathan. 2005. *The Enlightenment Bible: Translation, Scholarship, Culture*. Princeton, NJ: Princeton University Press.

Sorkin, David. 2008. *The Religious Enlightenment. Protestants, Jews, and Catholics from London to Vienna*. Princeton, NJ: Princeton University Press.

Sparn, Walter. 1992. "'Chiliasmus crassus' und 'Chiliasmus subtilis' im Jahrhundert Comenius: Eine mentalitätsgeschichtliche Skizze." In *Johannes Amos Comenius und die Genese des modernen Europa*, edited by Norbert and Jan. B. Lasek Kotowski, 122–129. Fürth: Flacius-Verlag.

Spener, Philipp Jakob. 1988. *Pia desideria*, edited by Theodore G. Tappert. Philadelphia: Fortress Press.

Sträter, Udo. 1987. *Sonthom, Bayly, Dyke und Hall: Studien zur Rezeption der englischen Erbauungsliteratur in Deutschland im 17. Jahrhundert*. Tübingen: Mohr Siebeck.

Strom, Jonathan. 2011. "The Common Priesthood and the Pietist Challenge for Ministry and Laity." In *The Pietist Impulse in Christianity*, edited by Christian T. Collins Winn, Christopher Gehrz, Gordon William Carlson, and Eric Holst, 42–58. Eugene, OR: Pickwick.

Strom, Jonathan. 1999. *Orthodoxy and Reform: The Clergy in Seventeenth-Century Rostock*. Tübingen: Mohr Siebeck.

Strom, Jonathan. 2009. "Pietism and Revival." In *Preaching, Sermon and Cultural Change in the Long Eighteenth Century*, edited by Joris van Eijnatten, 173–218. Leiden: Brill.

Strom, Jonathan. 2014. "Pietist Experiences and Narratives of Conversion." In *A Companion to German Pietism (1600–1800)*, edited by Douglas H. Shantz, 293–318. Leiden: Brill.

Strom, Jonathan. 2003. "The Problem of Conventicles in Early German Pietism." *Covenant Quarterly* 61 (4): 3–16.

Strom, Jonathan. 2002. "Problems and Promises of Pietism Research." *Church History* 71: 536–554.

Temme, Willi. 1998. *Krise der Leiblichkeit: Die Sozietät der Mutter Eva (Buttlarsche Rotte) und der radikale Pietismus um 1700*. Göttingen: Vandenhoeck & Ruprecht.

Troeltsch, Ernst. 1986. *Protestantism and Progress: The Significance of Protestantism for the Rise of the Modern World*. Philadelphia: Fortress Press.

Vogt, Peter. 2005. "Nicholas Ludwig von Zinzendorf (1700–1760)." In *The Pietist Theologians: An Introduction to Theology in the Seventeenth and Eighteenth Centuries*, edited by Carter Lindberg, 207–223. Malden, MA: Blackwell.

Wallmann, Johannes. 1994. "Vom Katechismuschristentum zum Bibelchristentum: Zum Bibelverständnis im Pietismus." In *Die Zukunft des Schriftprinzips*, edited by Richard Ziegert, 30–56. Stuttgart: Deutsche Bibelgesellschaft.

Wallmann, Johannes. 1986. *Philipp Jakob Spener und die Anfänge des Pietismus*. 2nd ed. Tübingen: J. C. B. Mohr.

Wallmann, Johannes. 2005a. "Johann Arndt (1555–1621)." In *The Pietist Theologians: An Introduction to Theology in the Seventeenth and Eighteenth Centuries*, edited by Carter Lindberg, 21–37. Malden, MA: Blackwell.

Wallmann, Johannes. 2005b. *Der Pietismus*. Göttingen: Vandenhoeck & Ruprecht.

Wallmann, Johannes. 1981. "Pietismus und Chiliasmus: zur Kontroverse um Philipp Jakob Speners 'Hoffnung besserer Zeiten.'" *Zeitschrift für Theologie und Kirche* 78 (2): 235–266.

Wallmann, Johannes. 1968. "Spener und Dilfeld: Der Hintergrund des ersten pietistischen Streites." In *Theologie in Geschichte und Kunst: Walter Elliger zum 65. Geburtstag*, edited by S. Herrmann and O. Söhngen, 214–235. Witten: Luther Verlag.

Wallmann, Johannes. 1982. "Zwischen Reformation und Pietismus: Reich Gottes und Chiliasmus in der lutherischen Orthodoxie." In *Verifikationen*, edited by Eberhard Jüngel et al., 187–205. Tübingen: Mohr.

Ward, W. Reginald. 2006. *Early Evangelicalism: A Global Intellectual History, 1670–1789*. Cambridge: Cambridge University Press.

Ward, W. Reginald. 1992. *The Protestant Evangelical Awakening*. Cambridge: Cambridge University Press.

Weigelt, Horst. 1995. "Der Pietismus im Übergang vom 18. zum 19. Jahrhundert." In *Der Pietismus im achtzehnten Jahrhundert*, 700–754. Göttingen: Vandenhoeck & Ruprecht.

Weigelt, Horst. 2000. "Die Diasporaarbeit der Herrnhuter Brüdergemeine." In *Der Pietismus im neunzehnten und zwanzigsten Jahrhundert*, edited by Ulrich Gäbler and Martin Sallmann, 113–149. Göttingen: Vandenhoeck & Ruprecht.

Wellenreuther, Hermann. 2013. *Heinrich Melchior Mühlenberg und die deutschen Lutheraner in Nordamerika, 1742–1787: Wissenstransfer und Wandel eines atlantischen zu einem amerikanischen Netzwerk*. Berlin: Lit.

Wellenreuther, Hermann. 2004. "Pietismus und Mission: Vom 17. Jahrhundert bis zum Beginn des 20. Jahrhunderts." In *Glaubenswelt und Lebenswelten*, edited by Hartmut Lehmann, 168–194. Göttingen: Vandenhoeck & Ruprecht.

Yoder, Peter. 2011. *Blood, Spit, and Tears: August Hermann Francke's Theology of the Sacraments*. Ph.D. Diss., University of Iowa.

# CHAPTER 28

## EARLY MODERN JANSENISM

### EPHRAIM RADNER

JANSENISM was a backward- and forward-looking phenomenon. As such, it was no different from much of the Counter-Reformation culture of the late sixteenth and early seventeenth centuries, in which the movement arose (Hsia 2005). Jansenism's concern was the renewal of the Catholic Church, and thus included criteria that were inevitably from the past, but also self-consciously repositioned applications that were potentially transformative of that bequest.

The main Counter-Reformational commitment of the founders of Jansenism, Cornelius Jansen (1585–1638) and Jean Duvergier de Hauranne, the abbé of Saint-Cyran (1581–1643), was a return to the church's primitive purity. They shaped this purpose with a strong Augustinian theology of grace. In early seventeenth-century France, however, this was bound to hopes for political support, given the traditionally strong hand of the French monarchy over the church. And it gave an opening to Gallican ideas, as well as establishing from the start the decidedly public character of Jansenism. So while the post-Tridentine reform movement of France provides the real religious context for Jansenism, the peculiarities of French politics altered the very notion of "Tridentine" Catholicism, and wrenched it, as it were, from its sixteenth-century contours into developing modernity (Blet 1964). In this sense, Jansenism embodied a field of contestation between old and new in a unique way. Its final political, and even more so its theological fate, was sealed by the triumph of the new (Kolakowski 1995).

Jansenism's outworkings were complex and have given rise to diverse interpretations. Strowski's judgment that there is no such thing as "Jansenism," but only individual "jansenists," is too extreme, but nonetheless suggestive, given the heterogeneity of Jansenist commitments and their uneven embrace (Strowski 1910). As a historical movement, Jansenism was shaped by two key political-ecclesiastical demands that have often been used to identify different "periods" in its development (Hildesheimer 1992). The first defining episode was the papal condemnation of "Five Propositions" drawn from the posthumous volume of Cornelius Jansen on Augustine. The detailed list came in the bull *Cum occasione* of 1653, but was already set in motion by an earlier, more general condemnation of Jansen, *In eminenti*, of 1642. This was eventually linked to a demand that

French clergy and religious sign a "formulary" accepting the bulls' contents. Opposition to the formulary became an initial "Jansenist" identity marker, though rationales for signing it were adopted by some. Most dramatic, in the public's eye, was the witness of the Port-Royal community of reformed Cistercian nuns and their supporters, whose life, in various ways, was interwoven with followers of Jansen (Weaver 1978). A measure of stability returned in 1669, and a period of varied and fruitful activity by Jansenist theologians ensued. Unresolved matters from the past erupted again in 1701, however, with both the Vatican and the French court moving against Jansenist sympathizers. Meanwhile, the convent of Port-Royal-des-Champs outside Paris, the center of earlier refusal to sign the formulary, was closed and then destroyed by royal order in 1708–10. Now came the second defining moment for the movement: the sweeping rejection, in the papal bull *Unigenitus* (1713), of the Oratorian Augustinian theologian Pasquier Quesnel (1634–1719), whose popular commentaries on the New Testament were deemed too close to Jansen. The attempt to impose this bull on the French clergy led to widespread resistance, and in 1717 a group of bishops instigated the call for a general council to deal with the dispute. Those supporting this call were known as *appellants*, and they became the core of eighteenth-century Jansenism. The appellant movement is largely connected with later eighteenth-century French, and then Italian, interest in constitutional and conciliar reform of church and state. The movement generally disappears after the French Revolution, although individual sympathizers appear in the nineteenth century.

Besides Jansen and Saint-Cyran, these two political struggles—around the bulls *Cum occasione* and *Unigenitus*—swept up prominent families, like the Arnaulds (Sedgwick 1998), the Pascals (Pouzet 2001), and their friends; as well as the entire Sorbonne and its lines of influence and power, the court and Richelieu initially; and finally the Vatican itself, and its relations to the French monarch, its French bishops, and then other European jurisdictions (Blet 1964; Thuau 1968; Gres-Gayer 1991, 1996, 2007; Dieudonné 2003; Forrestal 2004). Discipline, banishment, and imprisonment not only etched a profile of confessional courage upon the movement, but led to the geographical migration of some if its ideas, especially in the Lowlands, where in 1724 the Diocese of Utrecht, led by the independently consecrated bishop Cornelius van Steenhoven, separated from Rome, becoming the basis for the Old Catholic Church (Palmer 2004). By the eighteenth century, self-conscious supporters of the earlier Jansenist writers and some of their projects had diversified into a range of interests and activities, whose common features retained certain theological commitments and habits, but whose public personae now took the form of political anti-Jesuitism and finally, in the eyes of many, constitutional Gallicanism and even republicanism. It was in this form that it touched events in late eighteenth-century Italy. The causal lines of this development, if even discernable, are much debated.

I will take the position that there were continuities of underlying logic in *theological* emphasis, which gave rise to various practical commitments, but that individual Jansenists took these up in often inconsistent ways. These finally crumbled into a more inchoate jumble of anti-establishment impulses. In what follows I will try to outline several areas of Jansenist activity that had a larger ecclesial influence and in which these continuities can be seen.

# 1 GENERAL THEOLOGY

What is called "Jansenism" can be historically traced back, rather precisely, to the ecclesial reform plans of two friends, Jansen and Duvergier de Hauranne (Orcibal 1947/8, 1989; *Dictionnaire* 2004). The two had been students at Louvain in the early seventeenth century, then worked together in France. After 1617, Jansen was back in Louvain, as a professor of exegesis. Saint-Cyran, for his part, was working as canon theologian in Poitiers, and then as a spiritual director in Paris. The two friends seemed to have agreed to press forward with a concrete plan to restore the teaching of Augustine, for the sake of the church's renewal. Jansen worked indefatigably to present what he hoped would be a transformative work on Augustine's theology, which finally appeared in 1640, after his death: the enormous *Augustinus*.

It has been said that if Jansenism can be reduced to any common theological concept, it is "efficacious grace," and only that (Strowski 1910). It was a movement motivated by a relentless desire to reappropriate the theology of grace drawn from the late anti-Pelagian Augustine. Why this orientation? The seventeenth century experienced a broad Augustinian revival (*Siècle* 1982; Neveu 1994; Flasch 1998; Harrison 2007). But Jansenism marked a peculiar return: the *late* Augustine with his almost savage focus on divine sovereignty. This was Jansen's work. In his case, he was formed within a university context already embroiled in the ongoing bitter debates around what had become the *De Auxiliis* controversy, a series of public disputations before the Pope between 1598 and 1607 (Stone 2005). The basic issue, which had pitted Jesuits against Dominicans, was the ground upon which God elected individuals to salvation. The Spanish Jesuit Luis de Molina (1535–1600) became the focus of the discussion for many, given the provocative nature of his 1588 book *De liberi arbitrii cum gratiae donis . . . concordia*. His popularized views later became a cultural scapegoat in the stinging ironies directed against the Jesuits by Pascal's *Lettres Provinciales* (1656–57). Early seventeenth-century opponents of Molina attacked his notion of a "sufficient" grace upholding the free exercise of the will. God could omnisciently calculate the universal use of this grace by each individual for every possible world, and then predestine accordingly in line with his purposes. The universe, that is, was God's orchestration of individually free actions. To Molina's detractors, this was to imagine a world that was practically speaking godless, because in fact its texture was formed solely out of undifferentiated grace deployed by autonomous individuals. Jansen called the argument "pagan," and in his *Augustinus* explicitly outlined at length the parallels between the Molinists like his colleague Lessius and the "semi-Pelagians."

Saint-Cyran, spiritually renewed by his encounter with Bérulle, had defended the rigorous prayer life of the nuns of Port-Royal convent. He was imprisoned by Richelieu in 1638, dying shortly after his release in 1643. In a famous letter from jail, of February 1, 1643, he not only provides a kind of activist manifesto, but offers a succinct indicator of what was at stake. The task of defending Jansen's Augustinian vision, he writes, is "the best cause there has ever been and for which one might lose one's life"; for "grace is the effect and image of the incarnation, and who defends one defends the other." (Hermant 1905).

The letter marks a kind of symbolic official start to Jansenism as a "movement." It sets the young Antoine Arnauld (1612–94) on his life's work—ordering, in a sense, much of his prodigious polemical output for decades to come. But Saint-Cyran here also, in the quote above, discloses the core concern: the Incarnation as the singular and particular reality of God's life in relation to individuals. This links the theological question to wider concerns shared with influential French theologians and reformers like Pierre de Bérulle (1575–1629): the press for a historical center to the Christian faith's claims and witness that could be demarcated and enacted in temporal and concrete terms. Jansenism will take this up in its practical and pastoral dimensions with an energy that Bérulle, with his more platonic and contemplative concerns, did not (Dagens 1952).

The logic of the actual debates over "grace" that ensued has proven confusing, and given rise to contradictory analyses (Laporte 1923; Abercrombie 1936; de Lubac 1965; Kolakowski 1995). Hume understandably called them "unintelligible" and "not worth of a man of sense" (Hume 1741). Despite claims like de Lubac's that Jansenism's focus on efficacious and "extrinsicist" forms of grace had the consequence of conceptualizing a state of "pure nature" and thus positing realms of life autonomous from God, certainly its goal was just the opposite: to make every detail of historical existence utterly God-dependent because drawn *ex nihilo*, and intrinsically disclosive of the particular character and will of God (Gerberon 1676). This was certainly Augustinian; however, its application to developing notions of "history" itself proved novel.

The reforming focus of the movement, for one thing, sought *change* within the practices and attitudes of the church. Saint-Cyran takes this up in terms of ordering one's life towards a complete overtaking by the Spirit, building on the notion of victorious "love" or "delectation" that he took from Augustine (Saint-Cyran 1647). The kind of totalizing aspect of possession or divine impulsion here moves concern in what will become the notorious "rigorist" direction of Jansenist spirituality: it is always, it seems, "all or nothing" with respect to faithfulness or infidelity. But this pneumatic orientation of late Augustine also grounds what became a Jansenist conviction in the divinely disclosive aspect of all creation, including historical existence.

The question of divine grace and the extent of its reach found its initial practical focus, one that proved an ongoing thorn well into the eighteenth century, in the character of penance. Here, the debate with the Jesuits took concrete form: what is demanded of the penitent's heart for absolution to be given (and hence, for the reception of communion)? Jansenists insisted on full "contrition" (versus the less-consuming sentiment of "attrition")—that is, in conformity with earlier tradition, a full sorrow for sin and commitment to sin no more (Quantin 2001; Gay 2011). Anything less would contradict the full reach of God's grace by which human beings live or die. This led to Arnauld's controversial argument for abstention from the Eucharist (Arnauld 1643). More fundamentally, the question was: does God save the *sinner*? Since the latter is a given in Jansenism's embrace of late Augustinian notions of Original Sin, the depth of human lostness could only be met by the greater reach of divine grace. Over and against the Molinist tendency to make the theology of grace depend on theodicy—how could God condemn those to whom he had not given grace that could be freely embraced or rejected?—Jansenists always reversed the order.

It is likely that this ordering set up an impossible standard, one that was both fertile in its creative impulse but also finally subversive of the movement's own perdurance, especially on the political front. If, as Christian Jouhaud argues, Richelieu set in motion the sacralization of the state for the sake of temporal peace—"salvation in the present"—Jansenism's exclusivist commitments could not countenance the compromises the state demanded (Jouhaud 2006). A policy of "dirty hands" was off the table. Thus, Jansenius' 1635 "Mars Gallicus," an attack on the French king for alliances with Protestants, quickly undercut any trust the movement would have in the court. But it also set the tone for the paradoxical witness of Jansenists: the search for "purity" could never lead to the abandonment of the Catholic Church, precisely because the fullness of divine grace must permit the complete suffering for the truth in the midst of a church chosen by God. Jansenists were always among those most hostile to Reformed theology, and their attacks were based on the "other" Augustine, who also defended the historical forms of the church's life as themselves predestined (Nicole 1684). The nineteenth- and twentieth-century notions of *laicisation* in France suggested an opening up of "salvation" to the nonreligious. Jansenism's "democratizing" impulses, however, were pursued in a more Puritan sense, and aimed at opening up the church's life for the spread of an exclusivist Christianity to all spheres of society (Hamon 1983). Within the debates over grace, the purported moral "laxism" of Jesuit casuistry became the enemy out of concern that its accommodations fueled cultural disengagement from God. Jansenists' failure to achieve their goal was marked by their final dissolution at the hands of anti-Christian Republicanism.

Here, Kolakowski's (1995) evaluations are surely right: the Jansenist vision of a completely subjective historical sphere bound up with the particularities of God's truth in Christ could not sustain the realities of a culturally expanding world. As the so-called "Chinese Rites" controversy took form (Mungello 1994), Jansenists like Sébastien Joseph du Cambout de Ponchateau (1634–90) and Arnauld took the side of Franciscans and Dominicans against the Jesuits, in demanding that evangelism give no quarter to local cultural frameworks of understanding: the whole Cross, and nothing but the Cross! This was not, at root, a cultural chauvinism. Arnauld often stressed the sins of the *missionaries*, rather than the idolatries of the Chinese in making his arguments (Arnauld 1662). To argue *for* the "virtues of the pagans" as real, as did François de la Mothe le Vayer and later Bayle, was simply a way of encouraging Christian self-deception (Shelford 2000). *No one* is virtuous; and this insistence constituted a reverse theodicy of European—and especially ecclesial—sinfulness.

But the reality of "pagan virtues" was something that the Catholic Church, for all her nominal commitment to Augustine, eventually embraced, also in part because of her conflict with Reformed Christianity, with which Jansenism became associated. The Augustinian doctrine itself came under increasing pressure from the demands of European society, beset by its ongoing, often religiously oriented divisions. Jansenist Augustinianism seemed increasingly out of step with the needs of civil society (Bayle 1715).

Not that Jansenists had no interest in the issues of universal reason and explication. The Cartesian connections of several Jansenists fueled this, as in the famous *Grammaire* of Arnauld and Claude Lancelot, which, through a careful theory of signs, sought to ground grammar in a universal framework of signification (Arnauld 1660; Schmaltz 1999). But too much has been made of this. More important was the clear divorce Jansenists made between the sciences of logic and faith, and where exactly faith was placed. They ultimately insisted that it be located within the realm of history, and hence of testimony. Pascal most famously describes the disjuncture (see the preface to his treatise on the vacuum), but it is more influentially laid out in the *Logique*, one of the few Jansenist works, other than those of Pascal, still in print (Arnauld 1662; Pascal 1663). Arnauld himself had applied the distinction's presuppositions furiously in his attack on the bull *In Eminenti* (1642) that had condemned Jansen's *Augustinus*, by raising numerous factual questions regarding the bull's authenticity (Arnauld 1778). It also founded the more specific distinction between *droit* and *fait* that many Jansenists, including Pascal and the nuns of Port-Royal, used to approach the condemnation of Jansen's teaching on grace in 1664: while the church's authority extended to doctrine—in this case the abstract *droit* of dogma— it could not cover issues of determining historical "fact" (*fait*)—that is, whether Jansen actually said such things. These last could only be approached through the probabilistic examination of evidence (Dieudonné 2003; Jouslin 2007). Of course, the Christian religion is founded on historical *faits* in the first place, and thus the distinction moves against the power of universal abstractions and finally undermines it. History becomes the arena of religious contest as well as of revelation; that is, the space in which divine grace does its work. And just in this historical arena lay Jansenism's most lasting contributions. I shall list these briefly, although each deserves its own full treatment.

## 2 BIBLE READING AND INTERPRETATION

The Bible is the one authority that crosses the boundary of reason and faith, in Jansenist terms: a word given in the midst of uncertainty, it becomes the center of Jansenist discussion in most cases and forms the basis for all authoritative claims, Augustine's included. Jansenists thus stressed, along with Protestants, the need for vernacular reading, as well as rightly ordered spiritual receipt of its contents. A collegial effort led by Isaac-Louis Le Maistre de Sacy (1613–84) produced a French New Testament (1667) and finally an entire Bible, complete with patristic commentary (1693). While not the only French translation of the period, it dominated the scene for over 200 years, and formed the basis of a renewal in devotional reading. In addition, a lay-oriented illustrated presentation of the Bible, ordered around key scriptural personages, known as the *Bible de Royaumont* (1670) proved popular among Christians of all confessions. Finally, the moral spiritual commentary on the New Testament by Pasquier Quesnel, known as the *Réflexions Morales*, likewise crossed ecclesial boundaries, as well as becoming the focus of theological controversy. Jansen himself had left several extensive commentaries that were published posthumously, and later Jansenists like Jacques-Joseph Duguet (1649–1733) become popular lecturers on Scripture whose works were widely circulated (Chédozeau 2007; Cheely 2013; Weaver 1985). In a related area, catechesis founded on scriptural formation especially flourished under Jansenist bishops (Bonnot 1984) and marked the peculiar fulfilment, in France, of the Tridentine vision.

## 3  POSITIVE THEOLOGY

In their struggles to uphold a renewed primitive Christianity of grace, Jansenists embarked on a task that paradoxically combined the commendation of faith with the detailed retrieval of its historical buttressing. This involved digging through the fathers especially, and among church councils. It also pressed Jansenists to offer documentary proofs for their references, including issues of manuscript evidence. In this, the Jansenists participated in a more general, if contested, movement of linking theological argument to an increasingly sophisticated historical apparatus, some of which spilled over to the later testimonial arguments for Jansenist miracles (Neveu 1993). But the logic of their emphasis upon history itself as divine demonstration drove them to preeminent achievements in this area. Louis-Sébastien Le Nain de Tillemont (1637–98), Adrien Baillet (1649–1706), and others provided foundational work in the areas of ecclesiastical history, hagiography, and liturgical studies. The Jansenist-inspired educator Charles Rollin (1661–1741) wrote his influential book that became known as *Traité des études* (1726–31) in this light (Rollin 1736). Rollin's vision is sometimes viewed as an example of the secularizing tendency inherent in Jansenist historical consciousness (Orain 2014). And it is true that his outline of studies had become a precarious mixture of antique liberal education and Augustinian focus on the scriptures as a divine revelation necessary to combat the corrupted reason of original sin. "Profane" historical studies, which now predominate, stand in the middle as a kind of arena in which to gauge providential wisdom amidst its Arnauldian "incertitudes," sifting "causes" for the right moral. But the moral is nonetheless preeminent, which leads to the next element.

## 4  HISTORICAL FIGURALISM

This becomes the novel Jansenist theological contribution in particular, and derives from the search to combine the Bible and church history under the aegis of divine grace and spiritual receipt. Pascal, in his *Pensées* (posthumously published in 1670), had famously read the world according to scriptural figuration, and the Jansenist reappropriation of patristic spiritual exegesis, beginning with Jansen, emphasized allegory and typology with a new energy. With the world discernably apprehended according to the divine ordering of biblical truth, the church herself came to be read according to the forms of scripture: Israel, various personal figures, and Jesus. This ecclesial figuration proved useful to Jansenist reforming goals, offering a way to measure the church's life in time, as well as to account for the failure of the goals themselves. Duguet offered a succinct outline of the method of *figuriste* exegesis, and by the eighteenth century, *figurisme* was a widespread hermeneutic orientation among Jansenists (Duguet 1716). It proved one of the single most important, if contested, intellectual props to their movement's resilience (Savon 1989; Maire 1998; Radner 2002).

## 5 Somatic Theology

Historical figuralism reoriented theological interest towards concrete temporal phenomena. This aspect of Jansenism links the movement to other forms of eighteenth-century piety, including Protestant evangelicalism (Knox 1950; Maire 1985; Vidal 1987; T. Campbell 1991). Focus on healing miracles had already emerged in the seventeenth century at Port-Royal, and in the early eighteenth century it exploded around the tomb of a Jansenist saint at the Parisian church of Saint-Médard. Under various civil and ecclesiastical pressures, the miracles both spread and then transmuted into convulsionary displays, often depicting prophetic scenes in a figuralist fashion (Kreiser 1978; Maire 1998; Radner 2002; Strayer 2008). It proved a complex phenomenon, engaging the interest of all Europe; but theologically, the miracles and convulsions remained bound to the historical/figural resolution of the central Jansenist problem of faith's relation to reason (Kahan 2010): bodies become the place where grace is unveiled.

## 6 Moral Theology

Jansenist Augustinianism posed an ethical paradox: if divine grace is a historical phenomenon, then the regulative aspect of its somatic expression is logically demanded. Thus, Jansenist writing through the eighteenth century focused relentlessly on the question of contrition and the behaviors reflective of it. Later, it would take on questions of almsgiving, usury, education, social intercourse, and more. Writing on these matters took place within a culturally given tradition that was easily assumed by the movement (Levi 1964), and it included the early spiritual letters of Saint-Cyran and moved through the celebrated *Essais de morale* of Pierre Nicole (1671–87) and later works by Duguet. In each case, the focus of reflection most often involved human passions and bodies as the site of human destiny and the (subjective) struggle for salvation. It was in its literary moralism that Jansenism became domesticated into a genre, one that continued into the twentieth century in French religious literature. But it also engaged, just in its interest in the ordering of human life, a new focus on what one might call the sociology of ethics. Montesquieu and Tocqueville were, in this area, heirs (Jaume 2013). The putative rigorism of Jansenism in fact tended to a ramified psychology that finally saw the need for compromised civil arrangements of the passions: *honneteté*, for instance, as the directed and restrained *amour-propre*. This could give rise to a range of realistic political and economic attitudes, expressed most famously, again, in the work of Nicole and Duguet, and aimed at benefiting the poor and workers, and at constraining needless luxury (Taveneaux 1965; Keohane 1980).

# 7  CONTESTED OUTLOOKS

Scholars and theologians continue to debate these and other areas of Jansenist reflection and influence. In the matter of prayer, for instance, Jansenists have been accused of undermining the potential fertility of the developing "French School" of contemplation, and so eviscerating the modern church of a potential gift. It is true that, for all their seeming Catholic sensibilities, they were set against the mystical and illuminist tendencies of many in the seventeenth century (even of some Jansenists). Nicole is often viewed as the epitome of this larger orientation: "intellectualist," "moralizing," fearful of all "affection" and "sensible" aspects of prayer, and along with Bossuet, the enemy of the mistreated Fénelon (Bremond 1967; Gorday 2012). Yet not only is this evaluation too geared to certain individuals like Nicole, whom other Jansenists criticized on this score; it does not get to the heart of the matter. As with Bossuet, the issue lay less in rigorism, anti-mysticism or Cartesian prejudices, but in scriptural concreteness: Nicole, like Bossuet, argued for the central appropriateness of petitionary prayer, and for the ordinary means of grace, of which scripturally described redemption consists. Thus, while Nicole could be deeply suspicious of miracles, other Jansenists, including Arnauld and Pascal, were not; and in the eighteenth century, for all the debates among them, Jansenists moved in this direction with notorious energy. The connection lies in the historical figures of scripture. Duguet is a good example: he commends public and "common" prayer bound to scriptural meditation, psalmic figural orderings of the mind's attention and interior passions, all aimed at the figure of Jesus in prayer (Duguet 1707). This was in part the purpose behind the broad local efforts at liturgical reform in various dioceses. And it also drove the more radical aspects of such reform; for example, in vernacularizing and laicizing the rites, which took place in some dioceses, including the Netherlands.

It is in the area of political reform and revolution, however, that today's scholars take up Jansenism. Was its focus on resistance and conscience an expression of and even a prod to developing individualism? Did this feed the growing movements of political and democratic rebellion in France and then elsewhere in Europe, as in Italy (Préclin

1929; Cottret 1984; Tackett, 1986; Hudson 1989; Van Kley 1996, 2001, 2008; Doyle 2000)? The Port-Royal convent has garnered study as a place of specifically *feminine* resistance, as it were (Weaver 1998; Conley 2009; Choudhury 2009; Kostroun 2011). But also the convulsionaries provided a sphere of prominent leadership for women, and this was negatively noted by contemporary critics of the movement. The movement later took on a feminine profile, especially in Protestant circles: in England and the United States, interest in Port-Royal in the nineteenth century in particular was part of a renaissance in private forms of feminine romantic religion (Clark 1932).

More concretely, however, we see a real change in Jansenism's political character around 1730, as Jansenist lawyers successfully sought to manipulate the "corporate" loyalties of the larger legal profession in the *Parlement* for their own ends. Although not strong in numbers, their efforts to oppose *Unigenitus* becoming "state law" moved things onto a new plane, taking hold of the (non-Jansenist) Gallican passions of their colleagues in a new way. At this point Jansenism truly becomes synonymous with a political "movement," and "appellancy" becomes a new form of politics, not theology, whose actual core is ambiguous apart from its notable destabilizing character (P. Campbell 1996). Allied now with Gallicans and the various constitutionalist programs now multiplying, Jansenists saw their religious commitments, apart perhaps from their original primitivist vision, swallowed by other concerns (Cottret 1984; Palmer 2004). As a specifically theological vision Jansenism was finished.

There was some initial religious ferment in Holland and Flanders earlier (see, e.g., Joannes van Neercassel, 1625–86), where both the University of Louvain had ongoing influence and French Jansenists in exile worked. Likewise, Italy had a strong Augustinian tradition of its own (see, e.g., Enrico Noris, 1631–1704, and Giovanni Lorenzo Berti, 1696–1766). Nonetheless, it is only in its final political phase that the nominal movement's international influence had its real purchase. This was in the form of an amalgam of anti-papalism, anti-Jesuitism, conciliarism, republicanism, and nationalism. Whether we should link this with theological Augustinianism (Stone 2006; Van Kley 2008), however, is debatable. So-called "Jansenist" epigones in the Low Countries, Italy, Austria, and Spain all strove for a variety of politically liberalizing changes, in some cases bound to a primitivist reforming vision, including ecclesial decentralization vis-à-vis Rome (Palmer 2004). The explosive Synod of Pistoia in 1786 marked its zenith and end (Bradley and Van Kley 2001). Although Jansenism could be seen as politically reactionary, for example in Ireland (O'Connor 2008), these important European events cemented the early nineteenth-century view of Jansenism as a political movement of anti-authoritarian revolution. Henri Grégoire (1750–1831), the Republican Constitutional bishop of Blois, became its epitome, with his connections to Italy, and later French figures of liberalism (Sepinwall 2005). But it is probable that Jansenist *theology*, properly speaking, had been far overtaken here, for Grégoire as for others of his generation, and it is questionable whether "Jansenism" means anything substantive at this point, except as a place keeper in a genealogical tree.

By the nineteenth century, in any case, the few remaining self-identified Jansenists could be republicans, monarchists, or quietists on the political front, convulsionaries or anti-convulsionaries (Chantin 1998). And the movement's character, despite popular attacks like de Maistre's (de Maistre 1821), ascribing to it the ills of revolution, secularization, and atheism had shrunk to a small summarizing body of literature: Pascal and Nicole mostly. These nineteenth-century judgments have tended to define contemporary evaluations as well. Only Kolakowski (1995) has ventured a truly theological (if limited) appraisal, dealing substantively with the arguments of the period about grace and raising the perennial issue about ways of conceptualizing divine sovereignty in history. On his reading, Jansenists were the "old guard" of a now lost Christian vision of divine creative power towering over human frailty and sin through Christ's grace; the Jesuit de Lubac, in his way, marked the new and modern adaptation to a more humanized universe.

## Bibliography

Abercrombie, Nigel. 1936. *The Origins of Jansenism*. Oxford: The Clarendon Press.

Armogathe, Jean-Robert. 1974. "Jansénisme: Historiographie." In *Dictionnaire de Spiritualité Ascétique et Mystique*. Vol. 8. Paris: Beauchesne.

Arnauld, Antoine. 1778. "Difficultés sur la Bulle *In Eminenti* (1644)." In *Oeuvres de messire Antoine Arnauld*. Vol. 16. Paris.

Arnauld, Antoine. 1643. *De la frequente communion*. Paris.

Arnauld, Antoine. 1660. With Claude Lancelot. *Grammaire générale et raisonnée*. Paris.

Arnauld, Antoine. 1662. With Pierre Nicole. *Logique, ou l'Art de penser*. Paris.

Arnauld, Antoine. 1662–1716. *Morale Pratique des Jésuites*. Cologne.

Arnauld, Antoine. 1778. "Premieres et Secondes Observations sur la Bulle *In Eminenti* (1643)." In *Oeuvres de messire Antoine Arnauld*. Vol. 16. Paris.

Baustert, R. 2010. *Le jansénisme et l'Europe*, actes du colloque de Luxembourg (8-10 novembre 2007), textes réunis par R. Baustert. Tübingen: Gunter Narr.

Bayle, Pierre. 1715. *Dictionnaire historique et critique*. 3rd ed. Vol. 3. Rotterdam.

Blet, Pierre. 1964. "Le condordat de Bologne et la réforme tridentine," dans Gregorianum, 45: 241–279.

Bonnot, Isabelle, 1984. "Le courant janséniste à travers les catechisms des VIIe et XVIIIe siècles." In *Actes du 109e Congrès National des Sociétés Savantes, Dijon, 1984, Section d'histoire modern et conemporaine I. Transmettre la foi: XVIe-XXe siècles, I. Pastorale et predication en France*, 59–79. Paris: C.T.H.S.

Bremond, Henri. 1967. *Histoire Littéraire du sentiment religieux en France depuis la fin des Guerres de Religion jusqu'à nos jours. Tome IV: La Conquête mystique. L'École de Port-Royal*. Paris: Armand Colin.

Bradley, James E., and Dale K. Van Kley, eds. 2001. *Religion and Politics in Enlightenment Europe*. Notre Dame, IN: Notre Dame University Press.

Campbell, Peter, 1996. *Power and Politics in Old Regime France, 1720-1745*. London: Routledge.

Campbell, Ted A. 1991. *The Religion of the Heart: A Study of European Religious Life in the Seventeenth and Eighteenth Centuries*. Columbia, SC: University of South Carolina Press.

Chadwick, Owen. 1981. *The Popes and European Revolution*. Oxford: The Clarendon Press.

Chantin, Jean-Pierre. 1998. *Les Amis de l'Oeuvre de la Vérité: Jansénisme, miracles et fin du monde au XIXe siècle*. Lyon: Presses Universitaires de Lyon.

Chédozeau, Bernard. 2007. *Port-Royal et la Bible. Un siècle d'or de la bible en France, 1650–1708.* Paris: Nolin, 2007.

Cheely, Daniel. 2013. "Legitimating Other People's Scriptures: Pasquier Quesnel's *Nouveau Testament* across Post-Reformation Europe." *Church History* 82 (3): 576–616.

Choudhury, Mita. 2009. "Gendered Models of Resistance: Jansenist Nuns and *Unigenitus.*" *Historical Reflections* 35 (1): 28–51.

Clark, Ruth. 1932. *Strangers & Sojourners at Port Royal: Being an Account of the Connections between the British Isles and the Jansenists of France and Holland.* Cambridge: Cambridge University Press.

Conley, John J. 2009. *Adoration and Annihilation: The Convent Philosophy of Port-Royal.* Notre Dame, IN: University of Notre Dame Press.

Cottret, Monique. 1984. "Aux origines du républicanisme janséniste: le mythe de l'Église primitive et le primitivisme des Lumières." *Revue d'histoire moderne et contemporaine* 31 (1): 99–115.

Dagens, Jean. 1952. *Bérulle et les origines de la Restauration Catholique (1575–1611).* Bruges: Desclée De Brouwer.

*Dictionnaire de Port-Royal.* 2004. Edited by Jean Lesaulnier and Antony McKenna. Paris: Champion.

Dieudonné, Philippe. 2003. *La Paix Clémentine: Défaite et victoire du premier jansénisme français sous le pontificat de Clément IX (1667–1669).* Bibliotheca Ephemeridum theologicarum lovaniensium, 167. Leuven: Leuven University Press-Uitgeverij Peeters.

Doyle, William. 2000. *Jansenism: Catholic Resistance to Authority from the Reformation to the French Revolution.* Houndmills, UK: Macmillan.

Duguet, Jacques-Joseph. 1716. *Règles pour l'intelligence des Saintes-Écritures.* Paris: Jacques Estienne.

Duguet, Jacques-Joseph. 1707. *Traittez sur la priere publique, et sur les dispositions pour offrir les SS. Mysteres et y participer avec fruit.* Paris: Jacques Estienne.

Flasch, K., and D. de Courquelles, eds. 1998. *Augustinus in der Neuzeit: colloque de la Herzog August Bibliotheck de Wolfenbüttel, 14017 octobre 1996.* Turnhout: Brepols.

Forrestal, Alison. 2004. *Fathers, Pastors and Kings: Visions of Episcopacy in Seventeenth-Century France.* Manchester: Manchester University Press.

Gay, Jean-Pascal. 2011. *Morales en conflit: Théologie et polémique au Grand Siècle (1640–1700).* Paris: Les Éditions du Cerf.

Gerberon, Gabriel. 1676. *Le miroir de la piété chrétienne.* Liege: Pierre Bonard.

Gorday, Peter J. 2012. *François Fénelon: A Biography. The Apostle of Pure Love.* Brewster, MA: Paraclete Press.

Gres-Gayer, Jacques M. 2007. *D'un janénisme à l'autre: chroniques de Sorbonne (1696–1713).* Paris: Nolin.

Gres-Gayer, Jacques M. 1996. *Le Jansénisme en Sorbonne: 1643-1656,* Paris: Klinksieck.

Gres-Gayer, Jacques M. 1991. *Théologie et pouvoir en Sorbonne: la Faculté de théologie de Paris et la bulle Unigenitus, 1714–1721.* Paris: Klinseick.

Hamon, Léo. 1983. Editor. *Du jansénisme à la laïcité: Le jansénisme et les origines de la déchristianisation.* Paris: Éditions de la maison des sciences de l'homme.

Harrison, Peter. 2007. *The Fall of Man and the Foundations of Science.* Cambridge: Cambridge University Press.

Hermant, Godefroi. 1905. *Mémoires de Godefroi Hermant sur l'histoire ecclésiastique du XVIIe siècle (1630–1663).* Edited by A. Gazier. Paris: Plon.

Hersche, Peter. 1977. "Der Spätjansenismus in Österreich." In *Veröffentlichungen der Kommission für Geschichte Österreichs*. Vol. 7. Vienna: Österreichische Akademie der Wissenschaften.

Hildesheimer, Françoise. 1992. *Le jansénisme. L'histoire et l'héritage*. Paris: Desclée de Brouwer.

Hsia, R. P-Chia. 2005. *The World of Catholic Renewal, 1540–1770*. Cambridge: Cambridge University Press.

Hudson, David. 1989. "The *Nouvelles Ecclésiastiques* and the French Revolution, 1789–1793." *Journal of European Ideas* 10 (4): 405–415.

Hume, David. 1741. "Of Superstition and Enthusiasm." Essay XII in *Essays Moral and Political*, 141–151. Edinburgh: R. Fleming and A. Alison.

Jaume, Lucien. 2013. *Tocqueville: The Aristocratic Sources of Liberty*. Translated by Arthur Goldhammer. Princeton: Princeton University Press.

Jouhaud, Christian. 2006. "Catholic Conciliar Reform in an Age of Anti-Catholic Revolution." In *Religious Differences in France: Past and Present*, edited by Kathleen Perry Long, 73–90. Kirksville, MO: Truman State University Press.

Jouslin, Olivier. 2007. *La campagne des Provinciales de Pascal: Étude d'un dialogue polémique*. 2 vols. Clermont-Ferrand: Presses Universitaires Blaise Pascal.

Kahan, Michèle Bokobza. 2010. "The Case of Carré de Montgeron, a Jansenist and a Convulsionary in the Century of Enlightenment." *Eighteenth-Century Studies* 43 (4): 419–433.

Keohane, Nannerl O. 1980. *Philosophy of the State of France: The Renaissance to the Enlightenment*. Princeton, NJ: Princeton University Press.

Knox, Ronald. 1950. *Enthusiasm: A Chapter in the History of Religion, with Special Reference to the XVII and XVIII Centuries*. Oxford: Clarendon Press.

Kolakowski, Leszek. 1995. *God Owes Us Nothing: A Brief Remark on Pascal's Religion and on the Spirit of Jansenism*. Chicago: University of Chicago Press.

Kostroun, Daniella. 2011. *Feminism, Absolutism, and Jansenism: Louis XIV and the Port-Royal Nuns*. Cambridge: Cambridge University Press.

Kreiser, B. Robert. 1978. *Miracles, Convulsions, and Ecclesiastical Politics in Early Eighteenth-Century Paris*. Princeton, NJ: Princeton University Press.

Laporte, Jean. 1923–53. *La doctrine de Port-Royal*. 2 vols in five. Paris: Presses Universitaires de France/Vrin.

Levi, Anthony. 1964. *French Moralists: The Theory of the Passions, 1585–1649*. Oxford: Clarendon Press, 1964.

Lubac, Henri de. 1965. *Augustinisme et théologie modern*. Paris: Aubier.

Maire, Catherine. 1998. *De la Cause de Dieu à la cause de la Nation. Le Jansénisme au XVIIe siècle*. Paris: NRF, Gallimard.

Maire, Catherine. 1985. *Les convulsionnaires de Saint-Médard: Miracles, convulsion et prophéties à Paris au XVIIIe siècle*. Paris: Gallimard/Julliard.

Maistre, Joseph de. 1821. *De l'Église gallicane dans son rapport avec le Souverain Pontife pour servir de suite à l'ouvrage intitulé Du Pape*. Lyon/Paris: Rusand & Beaucé-Rusand.

Meerbeeck, Michel van. 2006. *Ernest Ruth d'Ans, patriarche des jansénistes (1653–1728): Une biographie*. Louvain-la-Neuve: Éditions Nauwelaerts.

Mungello, D. E., ed. 1994. *The Chinese Rites Controversy: Its History and Meaning*. Monumenta Serica Institute. Nettetal: Steyler Verlag.

Neveu, Bruno. 1993. *L'Erreur et son juge: remarques sur les censures doctrinales à l'époque moderne*. Naples: Bibliopolis.

Neveu, Bruno. 1994. *Erudition et religion au XVIe et XVIIIe siecles*. Paris: Albin Michel.

Nicole, Pierre. 1684. *Les pretendus reformez convaincus de schism*. Paris.

O'Connor, Thomas. 2008. *Irish Jansenists, 1600–1670: Religion and Politics in Flanders, France, Ireland, and Rome*. Dublin: Four Courts Press.

Orain, Arnaud. 2014. "The Second Jansenism and the Rise of French Eighteenth-Century Political Economy." *History of Political Economy* 46 (3): 463–490.

Orcibal, Jean. 1989. *Jansénius d'Ypres (1585–1638)*. Paris: Études augustiniennes.

Orcibal, Jean. 1947–48. *Jean Duvergier de Hauranne: abbé de Saint-Cyran et son temps, 1581–1638*. Gembloux: J. Duculot.

Palmer, Douglas. 2004. "The Republic of Grace: International Jansenism in the Age of Enlightenment and Revolution." Unpublished doctoral dissertation. Ohio State University.

Pascal, Blaise. 1963. *Oeuvres Complètes*. Edited by Louis Lafuma. Paris: Seuil.

Pouzet, Régine. 2001. *Chronique des Pascal: 'les affaires du monde' d'Étienne Pascal à Marguerite Périer (1588–1713)*. Paris: Champion.

Préclin, Edmond. 1929. *Les jansénistes du xviiie siècle et la Constitution civile du clergé*. Paris: Librairie Universitaire J. Gamber.

Radner, Ephraim. 2002. *Spirit and Nature: The Saint-Médard Miracles in Eighteenth-Century Jansenism*. New York: Crossroads.

Rollin, Charles. 1736. *De la manière d'enseigner et d'étudier les belles lettres, par raport à l'esprit & au coeur*. Paris: Veuve Estienne, 1736.

Rosa, Mario. 1999. *Settecento religioso. Politica della Ragione e religione del cuore*. Venice: Marsilio.

Quantin, Jean-Louis. 2001. *Le Rigorisme chrétien*. Histoire du Christianisme. Paris: Les Éditions du Cerf.

Saint-Cyran, Jean Duvergier de Hauranne Abbé de. 1647. *Lettres Chrestiennes et Spirituelles*. 2 vols. Paris: Jean le Mire.

Saugnieux, Joël. 1975. *Le jansénisme espagnol du XVIIIe siècle: ses composantes et ses source*. Oviedo: Universidad de Oviedo.

Savon, Hervé. 1989. "Le figurisme et la 'Tradition des Pères'." In *Le Grand Siècle et la Bible*, edited by Jean-Robert Armogathe, 757–785. Paris: Beauchesne.

Schmaltz, Tad M. 1999. "What Has Cartesianism To Do with Jansenism?" *Journal of the History of Ideas* 60 (1): 37–56.

Sedgwick, Alexander. 1998. *The Travails of Conscience: The Arnauld Family and the Ancien Régime*. Cambridge, MA: Harvard University Press.

Sepinwall, Alyssa Goldstein. 2005. *The Abbé Gregoire and the French Revolution: The Making of Modern Universalism*. Berkeley: University of California Press.

Shelford, April G. 2000. "François de La Mothe Le Vayer and the Defence of Pagan Virtue." *The Seventeenth Century* 15 (1): 67–89.

*Le Siècle de Saint Augustin*. 1982. Collective issue of *XVIIe Siècle*. 135.

Stella, Pietro. 2006. *Il giansenismo in Italia*. 2 vols. Rome: Edizioni di Storia e Letteratura.

Stone, Martin W. F. 2006. "The Antiquarian and the Moderniser: Giovanni Lorenzo Berti (1696–1766), Pietro Tamburini (1737–1827), and Contrasting Defenses of the Augustinian Teaching on Unbaptised Infants in Eighteenth-Century Italy." *Quaestio* 6: 335–372.

Stone, Martin W. F. 2005. "Michael Baius (1513–1589) and the Debate on 'Pure Nature': Grace and Moral Agency in Sixteenth-Century Scholasticism." In *Moral Philosophy on the Threshold of Modernity*, edited by Jill Krave and Risto Saarinen, 51–90. Dordrecht: Kluwer Academic.

Strayer, Brian, E. 2008. *Suffering Saints: Jansenists and Convulsionnaires in France, 1640–1799*. Eastbourne, UK: Sussex Academic Press.

Strowski, F. 1910. "Sur Port-Royal et le jansénisme." *Revue des questions historiques*. 43 (87): 483–491.

Tackett, Timothy. 1986. *Religion, Revolution, and Regional Culture in Eighteenth-Century France: The Ecclesiastical Oath of 1791*. Princeton, NJ: Princeton University Press.

Tans, J. A. G. 2007. *Pasquier Quesnel et le jansénisme en Hollande*. Paris: Nolin.

Taveneaux, René. 1965. *Jansénisme et politique*. Paris: Colin.

Thuau, Étienne. 1968. *Raison d'État et pensée politique à l'époque de Richelieu*. Paris: Colin.

Van Kley, Dale K. 2001. "Catholic Conciliar Reform in an Age of Anti-Catholic Revolution: France, Italy and the Netherlands, 1758–1801." In *Religion and Politics in Enlightenment Europe*, edited by James E. Bradley and Dale K. Van Kley, 46–118. Notre Dame, IN: Notre Dame University Press.

Van Kley, Dale K. 2008. "Religion and the Age of 'Patriot' Reform." *Journal of Modern History* 80 (2): 252–295.

Van Kley, Dale K. 1996. *The Religious Origins of the French Revolution: From Calvin to the Civil Constitution, 1560–1791*. New Haven, CT: Yale University Press.

Vidal, Daniel. 1987. *Miracles et convulsions jansénistes au XVIIIe siècle: le mal et sa connaissance*. Paris: Presses Universitaires de France.

Weaver, F. Ellen. 1978. *The Evolution of the Reform of Port-Royal: From the Rule of Citeaux to Jansenism*. Paris: Beauchesne.

Weaver, F. Ellen. 1998. *Madame de Fontpertuis: une devote janséniste, amie et gérante d'Antoine Arnauld et de Port-Royal*. Paris: Klincksieck.

Weaver, F. Ellen. 1985. "Scripture and Liturgy for the Laity: The Jansenist Case for Translation." *Worship* 59 (6): 510–521.

## CHAPTER 29

..........................................................................................................

# EARLY MODERN
# MORAVIANISM

..........................................................................................................

CRAIG D. ATWOOD

## 1 INTRODUCTION

..........................................................................................................

THE history of the Moravian Church or Unitas Fratrum falls into three distinct periods.
The first lasted from 1457 to the destruction of the Church following the defeat of the Czech
Protestants at the beginning of the Thirty Years' War in 1620. The second covers the period
from the revival of the Church under Count Nikolaus von Zinzendorf in the 1720s to 1818,
when the Church dropped some of its most distinctive practices and doctrines. The third
period is not included in this essay. In broad terms, we can identify at least nine consistent
themes of Moravianism from its beginning in the mid-fifteenth to the end of the eighteenth century: (1) the priority of the New Testament over the Old Testament in terms of
revelation and authority over the life of the church; (2) the separation of church and state
with an insistence that faith can never be coerced; (3) a rejection of violence, with a possible exception for self-defense; (4) a belief that biblical interpretation, doctrines, rituals,
and hymns should be judged by how well they lead people in faith, love, and hope; (5) an
existential rather than a rationalistic approach to theology; (6) the conviction that true
Christianity must be expressed within a community of faith that fully includes women and
children; (7) Christocentrism in devotion, theology, and ethics; (8) a millennial hope that
provides a model for what the church should strive to be; and (9) a suspicion of metaphysics and systemic theology separated from the lived experience of Christ.

## 2 ORIGINS IN THE CZECH REFORMATION

..........................................................................................................

The origins of Moravianism are found in the Czech Reformation of the fifteenth century, which began as a protest against perceived abuses and corruption in the medieval

Catholic Church. Jan Hus (n.d.–1415) was the most outspoken and theologically sophisticated advocate of reform until he was executed by the command of the Council of
Constance for claiming that the church had erred at times. When word reached Prague
that Hus had been burned at the stake, his followers rebelled against Emperor Sigismund,
who had consented to his execution. Five unsuccessful crusades were launched against
the Hussites beginning in 1419 (Kaminsky 1967). The Czechs established a national
church that was governed by a consistory dominated by professors at the university. The
most distinctive feature of this Bohemian church was that the laity, including women
and children, was allowed to drink from the chalice during communion. Since they
served communion "in both kinds," these Christians were often called the Utraquists.
For many years the archbishop of Venice ordained priests for the Utraquists against the
orders of the papacy. In 1575 the Utraquists and Lutherans in Bohemia signed a joint
confession of faith called the Confessio Bohemica. The Utraquist Church was destroyed
with the forced re-catholicization of Bohemia and Moravia under the Habsburgs in the
seventeenth and eighteenth century.

Some Hussites pushed for more radical reform of practice and doctrine than was
acceptable to the Utraquist consistory. Influenced by the Waldensians, radical Hussites
rejected many elements of medieval Catholicism in an attempt to restore the church
to what they held it to have been before the conversion of Emperor Constantine in the
fourth century. The radicals abolished the doctrine of purgatory, prayers for the dead,
invocation of the saints, the feast of Corpus Christi, and the veneration of the host.
They also simplified the mass and used only Czech in worship. Priests wore simple
robes, and the exposition of Scripture emerged as the focal point of worship. Inspired
by the hope that Christ would soon establish his thousand-year reign on earth, thousands of Hussites established a commune in 1420 in a fortified town they named Tabor
(Kaminsky 1967). They elected a priest named Nicholas Pelhřimov to be their bishop.
This is the first instance in the early modern period of a church establishing a new episcopacy on its own authority. Nicholas wrote a confession of faith and catechism that
are remarkably similar to later Reformed confessions and catechisms. The most notable innovation of the Taborites lay in their redefining confirmation as a rite of personal
affirmation of one's faith following a period of Christian instruction. The Inquisition
complained that even Taborite women could read and discuss the Bible. Combined
Utraquist and Catholic forces defeated the Taborites at the Battle of Lipany in 1434, but it
was another twenty years before the city of Tabor capitulated.

# 3 CHELČICKÝ

One figure stands out as an independent and theologically creative voice during the
Hussite Reformation. Peter Chelčický (n.d.–1456?) was an educated landowner in
southern Bohemia who was convinced that Hus did not go far enough in his critique
of the church (Wagner 1983). He came to Prague during the early days of the rebellion

in 1419 and debated theology and Scripture with the university masters. Like most of his generation, Peter was unaware that the Donation of Constantine, which purported to grant temporal authority in the western part of the Roman Empire to the bishop of Rome, was a forgery. This document figured prominently in conflicts between church and state throughout the Middle Ages, but Peter asserted that the Catholic Church had ceased to be a Christian church when it assumed secular authority. For a while Chelčický was allied with the Taborites, but he left Tabor when their priests endorsed violence in the name of the gospel. Chelčický did not organize a separate church or become a priest, but like-minded believers circulated his theological works throughout Bohemia and Moravia. Chelčický appears to have been the first European writer to fundamentally challenge the notion of Christendom, particularly the idea that the body and Christ and the body politic are the same. He argued that the medieval notion of society being comprised of three estates (nobility, clergy, and commoners) was a pagan rather than a Christian idea. The true body of Christ, he argued, is nonhierarchical and is characterized by love and mercy rather than violence and fear (Brock 1957). Since the church is defined as a community of love, violence and coercion are excluded from it. For Chelčický, true apostolic succession came not through the laying on of hands at the consecration of bishops; rather, it can be demonstrated only by those who follow the example of the apostles who were willing to be martyrs rather than engage in either violence or deception.

Chelčický laid the foundation for what would later become the doctrine of the Unitas Fratrum, also known as the Moravian Church. Unlike the other Hussites, Chelčický did not view the Old Testament as equally authoritative as the New Testament, arguing that if God had wanted the old law with its punitive measures to remain in force, he would not have established a new covenant through Christ. He defined the true church in terms of obedience to Christ's teachings and questioned the idea that the sacraments can confer grace without faith and willing participation on the part of the believer. Infant baptism is a pledge and promise made by parents to raise a child according to the law of Christ, and the child must take on this commitment by personal confirmation of faith as an adult. Holy Communion is a participation in Christ and an assurance of pardon for sins, but it is also a pledge to model one's life on the example of Christ. Interestingly, he retained the doctrine of transubstantiation.

# 4  UNITY OF THE BRETHREN

The capitulation of Tabor and the death of Chelčický in the 1450s marked the end of the first generation of the Czech Reformation and the beginning of Moravianism. In the 1450s a man named Gregory, later called the Patriarch (n.d.–1474), and a group of friends attended worship in the Týn Church where Jan Rokycana, the head of the Utraquist Church, was preacher. Rokycana shared with Gregory the writings of Chelčický, and Gregory and his circle decided to put Chelčický's ideas into practice. Near the village of Kunwald they formed a strict covenant community based on the Sermon on the Mount (Brock 1957). They called it the Jednota Bratrsky, variously known today as the Unitas Fratrum, Unity of the Brethren, the Bohemian Brethren, or the Moravian Church. Gregory became a type of itinerant preacher gathering the remnants of the radical Hussite brotherhoods, Waldensians, and other dissenters into his Unity. Like the later Anabaptists, members of the Unity were pacifist and refused to swear oaths, which meant that they could not participate in secular government.

After several of the Brethren were arrested and tortured by the crown in the 1460s, Gregory decided to break completely with the Utraquist Church. In 1467 they held a synod of the Brethren and elected Matthew of Kunwald to be their bishop (Crews 2008). Although the Brethren rejected the episcopacy of the Catholic Church, they wanted to maintain a sense of continuity with the ancient church. To symbolize this, they asked a Waldensian elder to lay hands on Matthew. Unlike most Protestant churches, the Unity of the Brethren maintained three orders of ministry. Deacons were young men who assisted the priests in administering the sacraments and preaching. Bishops presided over the inner council that governed the church. Except for a brief period from 1609 to 1621, theirs was an illegal organization throughout the Holy Roman Empire, but powerful nobles protected the Brethren on their estates in Bohemia, Moravia, and Poland.

One of the most important innovations of the Brethren was that Christians should distinguish between what is essential for salvation, what ministers to salvation, and what is incidental to salvation (Atwood 2009). The Brethren argued that there are two types of essential activities: God's action and the human response to God. It is essential that the Father creates, that the Son redeems humans from sin and death, and that the Holy Spirit blesses believers and makes them holy. These are forms of grace that do not depend on human works or even human faith. It is also essential that humans respond to God's grace through faith, love, and hope. Those who would be saved must believe in God as creator, redeemer, and sanctifier. But faith without love is not truly faith; it is mere belief. The Brethren taught that love for neighbor is one of the essential marks of the church, and this formed the basis of their strict church discipline and pacifism. The third essential was less well defined than faith and love but was another mark of true Christianity. Hope was primarily directed toward the afterlife, but it also included hope for the coming kingdom of Christ on earth. Nonessential matters or adiaphora included things like what language should be used in worship, whether priests wore robes or ordinary clothing, whether or not to use candles and special vessels for communion, what hymns to sing, and even the structure of the institutional church. The Brethren believed that the state should play no role in the life of the church, but they particularly objected to the state imposing a common liturgy.

The distinction between essentials and nonessentials goes back at least to the time of Augustine, but the Brethren added a middle term they called ministrative things. These were means that God has provided to the church to guide people toward the essentials of faith, love, and hope. They are sacred only because they point to the essential work of God. If they are used for any purpose other than leading people to faith, love, and hope, they cease to be sacred. Included in this category are Scripture, the priesthood,

sacraments, the ancient creeds, preaching, and doctrine. The Brethren justified the ordination of their first bishop on the basis of this distinction between essentials and ministerials. They argued that the priesthood and episcopacy of the Utraquist and Catholic
Churches had become so corrupt that a new priesthood was needed that was rooted in
the priesthood of Christ. Unlike most churches in the early modern period, the Brethren
were willing to rewrite their confessional statements and catechism every generation
or so. Initially the Brethren retained the traditional seven sacraments, but after contact
with Luther in the 1520s they adopted the position that there are two sacraments and
five major rites of the church. They viewed baptism like circumcision; it was a sign of the
covenant that obligated parents and the congregation to raise a child according to the
law of Christ. The Brethren taught that baptism needed to be completed through confirmation, which was a public profession of faith that included the promise to live according to the ethical standards of the Brethren.

True to the Hussite heritage, the Brethren insisted on the importance of communion
and the lay chalice but rejected the doctrine of transubstantiation as a type of idolatry.
They argued that Christ is truly spiritually present in communion but that the bread
remains bread (Atwood 2009). John Calvin and Martin Bucer adopted a very similar
view of the real presence in the sixteenth century. During the sixteenth century there
was conflict among the Brethren's priests over the meaning of the spiritual presence
of Christ, with some leaning toward a Zwinglian perspective. The Brethren placed
high value on confession and absolution. Like the early Church, public sins had to be
confessed before the whole congregation before they could be absolved. Priests were
assisted by male and female elders, called Judges, who helped maintain discipline in
the community, provided pastoral care and counseling, and even heard confessions.
Some women were ordained as deaconesses who assisted priests in their pastoral care
of women. This was a rare example of women having leadership roles in congregations
prior to the twentieth century.

Although they insisted on maintaining their separate ecclesiastical existence, the
Brethren were willing to work with other Protestants. The Unity established close relationships with many of the Protestant reformers, especially Philip Melanchthon and
Martin Bucer. The Brethren played a significant role in two of the landmarks of ecumenism in the early modern period: the Consensus of Sandomier in Poland and the signing
of the Confessio Bohemica. These agreements were much like modern "full communion" agreements between different churches that allow for pulpit exchanges and sharing in Holy Communion (Crews 2008). It appears that the Protestant understanding of
catechism and confirmation originated with the Brethren, and they may have influenced
Calvin's approach to church discipline and the Eucharist. Their greatest contribution to
the development of Protestantism was in the area of hymnody. Many Protestant reformers were impressed by the Brethren's practice of congregational singing, and German
translations of the Brethren's hymns were included in many Protestant hymnals.

The Brethren openly criticized the establishment of Protestant state churches and
insisted that true Christianity must be voluntary. This did not mean a complete withdrawal from society or social responsibility, however, since they believed that the

command to love one's neighbor meant that Christians should alleviate the suffering of the poor and infirm (Atwood 2009). They eventually dropped their original prohibition against swearing oaths, arguing that it can be helpful for Christians to serve on juries so they could try to ameliorate the cruelty of justice. Over time, the Brethren moderated their original pacifism and allowed members of the church to serve in the military if conscripted, but they still urged members to avoid taking life except in self-defense or to protect the weak from the violence of the powerful.

# 5  JOHN AMOS COMENIUS

The famous pedagogical reformer John Amos Comenius (1592–1670) was the leading advocate of Moravianism in the seventeenth century. He was educated at the Reformed Academy Herborn and Heidelberg University. Comenius returned to Moravia where he served as a pastor in the Unity of the Brethren and a teacher in their school at Fulnek. In 1618 Czech Protestants rebelled against their Habsburg rulers and offered the crown to Frederick V, the Elector of the Palatinate. After his coronation, the emperor sent troops into Bohemia and crushed the rebellion at the Battle of White Mountain in 1620. Protestantism was outlawed in Bohemia and Moravia, and Comenius was forced into exile in Poland along with thousands of Brethren. While in Poland, Comenius continued writing and published a number of works on pedagogy and school reform. He also tried to keep the legacy of Moravianism alive by publishing works in Latin and German on the history, doctrine, and ethical teachings of the Unity.

Comenius called his program of reform "Pansophy," which meant universal wisdom because it encompassed pedagogical, political, and religious reform. Comenius argued that the Bible predicts that there will be a millennial age of peace and justice. Rather than passively waiting for the return of the Messiah, Christians should do all they can to prepare the world to welcome Christ as king. Comenius objected to the tendency of many theologians in the seventeenth century to focus on human depravity rather than the reality of redemption. Salvation, for Comenius, was not simply about reaching heaven; it was also a matter of bringing health and healing to individuals, families, the social order, and ultimately the globe. This would be a process of gradual improvement and continual reform marked by an increase in faith, love, and hope (Comenius 1993).

This "reformation of human affairs" was part of God's work in the world, but God works through human agency (Comenius 1995). Comenius proposed numerous concrete steps that Christians could take to ameliorate suffering, promote justice, and increase knowledge and wisdom. Comenius also proposed that nations establish an international council to settle disputes without recourse to war and that churches unite in an ecumenical council. Schools should use the natural gifts and inclinations of students rather than relying on fear and punishment to force students to learn (Murphy 1995). God, he argued, has instilled in humans a desire to learn and given men and women reason so they can learn. Teachers need to work with what God has given rather than employing violent methods. Likewise, he argued that coercion is contrary to the gospel. Inquisitions, crusades, and compulsory baptism add to the misery of the world without leading people to faith.

Drawing on the theology of the Brethren, Comenius asserted that most of the conflict between Christians could be overcome if churches clearly distinguished between the essentials, ministerials, and incidentals. Dogma should be simple, and churches should be judged by how well they lead people to faith, love, and hope. He contrasted the "church of Cain" that was governed by pride and violence to the "church of Abel" that was characterized by simplicity and joyful obedience to God (Comenius 1993). Rather than wounding one other through words and tearing the church apart through dogma, theologians should be tolerant of divergent viewpoints, especially on doctrines that cannot be clearly proved by Scripture.

# 6 Herrnhut

It is not clear what role Moravianism played in the Pietist movement that conventionally is dated from the 1670s, but the similarities between the Unity of the Brethren and the Pietist program are striking. Pietists tended to focus on Christian experience and personal morality rather than metaphysics and in many ways echoed the Brethren's insistence that faith must be completed in love. Like the Brethren, Philipp Jakob Spener and other Pietists were millenarians whose social reform efforts were motivated by a "hope for a better day." Pietists tended to promote Philadelphianism rather than confessionalism (Vogt 2005). It is thus not surprising that when dozens of Czech Protestants decided to flee Moravia they were drawn to the estate of one of the most prominent representatives of German Pietism, Count Nikolaus Ludwig von Zinzendorf (1700–1760). Moravians began settling on his estate in 1722 and founded a town named Herrnhut in the parish of Berthelsdorf. From the beginning, Herrnhut was a source of concern to Saxon authorities since the Unity of the Brethren was not one of the three confessions recognized in the Holy Roman Empire and the Moravians were subjects of the Habsburg emperor. Eventually Zinzendorf was forbidden to accept any more Czech refugees.

Under Zinzendorf's influence, the residents of Herrnhut signed a Brotherly Agreement in 1727 that established the village as a unique form of voluntary Christian community to be governed by the ethical norms of the New Testament. Herrnhut was also allowed to hold worship services separate from the Lutheran parish, and the residents experimented with a number of early Christian practices such as Agape meals, footwashings, and the kiss of peace. They also called each other Brother and Sister. Since there were only three recognized confessions in the Holy Roman Empire, Zinzendorf argued that the Herrnhuters were somehow both the resurrection of the Unity of the Brethren and a part of the Lutheran Landeskirche. In 1735, David Nitschmann was consecrated as a bishop by the last two living bishops of the Unitas

Fratrum. Moravian Church historians generally refer to the organization created by Zinzendorf in Herrnhut as the "Renewed Moravian Church" in contrast to the "Ancient Unity" (Hamilton 1967). The Herrnhuters adopted the name "Brüdergemeine," or community of Brethren, but in English-speaking lands they were commonly called the Moravians.

# 7  RELATIONSHIP OF ZINZENDORF'S BRÜDERGEMEINE TO THE UNITY OF THE BRETHREN

There are some clear lines of continuity between the doctrine and practice of the Brüdergemeine and the Unity of the Brethren, which can be identified as central to Moravianism. Until the 1800s, the Herrnhuters were pacifists and avoided swearing oaths or serving in government. This was often a point of tension with secular authorities, particularly in America during the revolution. Herrnhuters used the German word *saal* (hall) for their worship spaces rather than *kirche* (church). *Saal* is the rough equivalent of the Czech word *sbor*. In communion the Herrnhuters adopted the practice of standing for the consecration of the elements rather than kneeling, and their attitude toward baptism of infants and the meaning of confirmation was consistent with that of the Unity of the Brethren. It is also probably not accidental that the Herrnhuters established offices for women that were roughly equivalent to the offices of "sister judge" and deaconess in the Unity of the Brethren. Many of the hymns of the Brethren were incorporated into the Herrnhut Gesangbuch, and July 6 was set aside as a memorial day for Jan Hus.

The differences between the Herrnhuters and the Unity of the Brethren are also striking. The Herrnhut community used the Augsburg Confession and Luther's Smaller Catechism rather than the Brethren's confession of faith and catechism. The Herrnhuters drew much more heavily on Catholic and Lutheran mystical literature than the Brethren would have been comfortable with. Whereas the Brethren focused on the ethical demands of Jesus, the Herrnhuters encouraged people to view Jesus as a lover or husband (Vogt 2005). The Herrnhuters were much less austere than the Brethren and were particularly famous for their music and art. Perhaps the most important difference between the two groups was that the Herrnhuters' millennialism included a dramatic mission effort to non-Christian peoples around the globe. Zinzendorf also hoped that his Brüdergemeine would be a leaven that would ignite the zeal of all Christian churches, even the Eastern Orthodox churches, by helping them to recognize their essential unity in Christ. As part of this effort he briefly established relationships with the Patriarch of Constantinople, the Coptic Patriarch in Cairo (Manukyan 2011), and included Anglicans, Lutherans, and Reformed representatives in his "Order of the Grain of the Mustard Seed."

# 8 Theology of the Heart

Although the Moravian refugees contributed to the creation of the Brüdergemeine, Zinzendorf was the leading theologian, liturgist, guiding spirit, and patron of the community. His followers generally called him the Ordinary or the Disciple. The terms "Moravianism" and "Zinzendorfianism" were virtually synonymous in the eighteenth century. Zinzendorf believed that rationalism, whether Deist or Orthodox, posed a great threat to Christianity in his day, and he offered Jesus mysticism as a way to revive spirituality (Freeman 1998). Zinzendorf is often identified as one of the early German romantics because of the importance he placed on emotion and spontaneity, but he saw himself as an heir of the paradoxical theology of the Luther, who challenged the role of metaphysics in Christian doctrine. Zinzendorf's "religion of the heart" was not simply sentimentality. He used the heart as a metaphor for the center of one's being rather than passing emotional states. He argued that theology should be grounded in human experience rather than logical systems. It is easy to trace the Moravian influence on Friedrich Schleiermacher, who redefined religion in terms of subjectivity and feeling. Zinzendorf and the Moravians also had a profound impact on John Wesley early in his career (Podmore 1998).

Zinzendorf was in some ways a forerunner of the existentialist theology. Like Kierkegaard, who participated in Moravian worship as a child, Zinzendorf was critical of theologians for failing to recognize the limits of rationalism. Zinzendorf rejected the idea that faith is grounded in intellectual assent to dogmas. He was one of the few theologians to claim that the mentally handicapped and infants can have saving faith if their hearts are united with Christ. In his exegesis of Luke 1 when John the Baptist leaps in his mother's womb as Mary approaches, Zinzendorf argued that faith can begin in utero. Faith is existential; it is the orientation of the believers toward God and a trust in God. The abstract language of dogmatics distanced people from the biblical narrative rather than leading them into childlike faith. Thus, he urged preachers to use concrete evocative language that could break through abstractions and connect the heart of the listener to the revelation of God in Scripture.

# 9 Theological Innovations

Zinzendorf challenged the prevalent Western Christian Trinitarian theology that taught the Father as creator, the Son as redeemer, and the Holy Spirit as sanctifier. He pointed out that the New Testament identifies the Son as the creator, or at least that creation was through the Son/Logos (Jn 1; Col 3). In his exegesis of Jesus' claim that no one comes to the Father except through him, Zinzendorf insisted that no one knows the Father without the revelation of Christ (Freeman 1998). In other words, philosophy cannot reveal the Father. However, he accepted the claim that all people have an innate awareness that there is a creator. Obviously, the ancient Hebrews knew there was a creator God prior to the appearance of the Son in flesh. Zinzendorf came to the conclusion that the Son is the creator, not the Father. He drew support for this view from some of the writings of the early church. More provocatively, he argued that YHWH/Elohim in the Old Testament was the Son who became incarnate as Jesus the Christ. The idea that the Son is the creator meant for Zinzendorf is that all people have a relationship with Christ and know something of Christ before the gospel is ever preached. It also meant that redemption was closely tied to creation. Zinzendorf objected to theologians who spoke of the atonement in terms of the Father/creator killing the Son as a substitutionary sacrifice. Instead, it was the creator who willingly gave himself for his creatures and in doing so conquered death and sin. Zinzendorf drew support for this view from the church fathers, especially Irenaeus and Athanasius. Although the Moravians did not use the controversial title "Theotokos" for Mary, they did not object to the term since God was incarnate in the Virgin's womb. Moravian hymns and litanies celebrated the paradox of the creator becoming a creature and God dying on the cross in order to vanquish death. The Jesus mysticism of the Moravians was simultaneously Christocentric and theocentric since Christ was fully God. After Zinzendorf's death, the Moravians gradually pulled back from this Christus Victor model of the atonement and adopted more traditional Trinitarian language (Spangenberg 1959).

Like Irenaeus and Athanasius, Zinzendorf insisted that the atoning work of the Savior began with the incarnation. The full humanity of Jesus was as important to Zinzendorf as the full divinity. Labor and rest, eating and sleeping, singing and praying were all interpreted through the life of Jesus, who did all these things. Daily life should be experienced as a form of worship, a continual liturgy. Moravian communities did not recognize a dichotomy between the sacred and the secular. Any meal could become a love feast. Hymns were sung through the workday. Carpenters and potters could be missionaries. Birth and death were especially sacred moments. The doctrine of the incarnation was the theological basis for the "choir system" of the Moravians in the eighteenth century (Atwood 2004). This was an extension of the Pietist idea of the ecclesiola or the bands. There were separate corps or choirs for small children, boys, girls, single men, single women, married men, married women, widows, and widowers. Each choir had devotions and pastoral care that focused on the particular needs and concerns of people in that station in life. Children heard about Jesus being obedient to his parents and learning how to read and write. Mothers used Mary as their model for how to treat their children. Single men heard about how Jesus was able to control his sexual desires and remain a virgin. Choir leaders were taught how to help young people through puberty, how to prepare people for marriage, how to deal with depression and anxiety, and how to help people grieve the loss of a spouse (Smaby 1989).

The Moravians of the eighteenth century were one of the very few groups in Christian history that taught that redemption in Christ included the redemption of sexuality. The circumcision proved that Jesus was biologically male, and Moravians celebrated the feast of the circumcision as a day special for boys. The fact that Jesus was conceived in

Mary's womb meant that women's bodies are also blessed, and the festival days of Mary were important for the girls. Moravian hymns also promoted a bridal mysticism that celebrated the paradox of the creator being united in marriage with his own creation. Religious experience was expressed in frankly erotic terms, especially in the married choirs. Women and men were encouraged to view Jesus as their spouse and lover and to consider earthly marriage as a symbol of the true spiritual marriage to the Savior. Ideally, children could be conceived in prayer rather than lust so that they would not be tainted with sin (Atwood 2004).

Zinzendorf brought together many aspects of his religion of the heart in a single provocative symbol: the pierced side of Jesus. Zinzendorf believed that the centerpiece of the revelation of God in Scripture was the moment when the centurion thrust his spear into Jesus' chest as narrated in the Gospel of John. In Moravian iconography, that wound is always on the left side, indicating that the heart of Jesus was pierced. Since Jesus was the incarnation of the Creator, this meant that the heart of God was opened on the cross, providing a point of entry into God's own compassion for his creation. Zinzendorf also argued that the cross was part of the recapitulation and redemption of creation. God once opened the side of Adam to create Eve in Eden; on the cross the side of Jesus was opened to give birth to the church. Thus Christians are doubly united to Jesus as flesh of his flesh, just as Eve was the spouse of Adam and flesh of his flesh. The side wound was thus a multivalent symbol of regeneration, incorporation into the mystical body of Christ, mystical marriage, and atonement through the death of the Savior (Atwood 2004).

Zinzendorf revised Trinitarian doctrine in other ways as well. He insisted that the most appropriate term for the third person of the Trinity is "Mother." This is a word that children and adults in every society can understand without need for explanation. It is concrete and evocates an emotional as well as intellectual response in the hearer, unlike terms like "Spirit," "Fire," or "Advocate." Zinzendorf claimed that the Holy Spirit performs functions in the church similar to those of earthly mothers: giving life, nurturing, guiding, and correcting believers. For more than twenty years the Moravians regularly worshiped the Holy Spirit as the Mother of the Church and even had an annual church festival called the Mutterfest (Atwood 2004). One of the reasons Moravians were successful missionaries to non-European traditional cultures was because they presented a God with a maternal aspect. This created increased criticism of the Moravian Church, and after Zinzendorf's death the church gradually repressed this type of devotion. After the death of Zinzendorf, the Moravians gradually evolved into a fairly typical Protestant evangelical church with an active global mission, but throughout the early modern period Moravianism represented a creative and often radical attempt to live according to the teachings and example of the New Testament church.

## BIBLIOGRAPHY

Atwood, Craig D. 2004. *Community of the Cross: Moravian Piety in Colonial Bethlehem.* University Park: Pennsylvania State University Press.

Atwood, Craig D. 2009. *Theology of the Czech Brethren from Hus to Comenius.* University Park: Pennsylvania State University Press.

Brock, Peter. 1957. *The Political and Social Doctrines of the Unity of the Czech Brethren in the Fifteenth and Early Sixteenth Centuries.* The Hague: Mouton

Comenius, John Amos. 1969. *Johannes Amos Comenini Opera Omnia.* 18 vols. Prague: Academia scientiarum Bohemoslovakia.

Comenius, John Amos. 1998. *The Labyrinth of the World and Paradise of the Heart.* Translated by Andrea Sterk and Howard Louthan. New York: Paulist Press.

Comenius, John Amos. 1993. *Panorthosia or Universal Reform: Chapters 19–26.* Translated by A. M. O. Dobbie. Sheffield: Sheffield Academic Press.

Comenius, John Amos. 1995. *Panorthosia or Universal Reform: Chapters 1–18 and 27.* Translated by A. M. O. Dobbie. Sheffield: Sheffield Academic Press.

Crews, Daniel C. 2008. *Faith, Hope, and Love: A History of the Unitas Fratrum.* Winston-Salem, NC: Moravian Archives.

Engel, Katherine Carté. 2009. *Religion and Profit: Moravians in Early America.* Philadelphia: University of Pennsylvania Press.

Freeman, Arthur J. 1998. *An Ecumenical Theology of the Heart: The Theology of Count Nicholas Ludwig von Zinzendorf.* Bethlehem, PA: Moravian.

Hamilton, J. Taylor, and Kenneth G. Hamilton. 1967. *History of the Moravian Church: The Renewed Unitas Fratrum 1722–1957.* Bethlehem, PA: Interprovincial Board of Christian Education of the Moravian Church in America.

*Journal of Moravian History.* Published twice yearly by Pennsylvania State University Press.

Kaminsky, Howard. 1967. *A History of the Hussite Revolution.* Berkeley: University of California Press.

Manukyan, Arthur. 2011. *Konstaninopel und Kairo: Die Herrnhuter Brüdergemeine im Kontakt zum Ökumenischen Patriarchat und zur Koptischen Kirche. Interkonfessionelle und interkulturelle Begegnungen im 18. Jahrhundert.* Orthodoxie, Orient und Europa 3. Würzburg: Ergon Verlag,

Murphy, Daniel. 1995. *Comenius: A Critical Assessment of His Life and Work.* Dublin: Irish Academic Press.

Podmore, Colin. 1998. *The Moravian Church in England, 1728–1760.* Oxford: Clarendon Press.

Sensbach, Jon F. 2005. *Rebecca's Revival: Creating Black Christianity in the Atlantic World.* Cambridge, MA: Harvard University Press.

Smaby, Beverly Prior. 1989. *The Transformation of Moravian Bethlehem from Communal Mission to Family Economy.* Philadelphia: University of Pennsylvania Press.

Spangenberg, August Gottlieb. 1959. *Idea Fidei Fratrum, or An Exposition of Christian Doctrine as Taught in the Protestant Church of the United Brethren or Unitas Fratrum.* Translated by Benjamin LaTrobe. Winston-Salem, NC: Board of Christian Education of the Southern Province of the Moravian Church.

Spangenberg, August Gottlieb. 1971. *Leben des Herrn Nikolaus Ludwig Grafen und Herrn von Zinzendorf und Pottendorf.* Hildesheim: Georg Olms.

Wagner, Murray. 1983. *Peter Chelčicky: A Radical Separatist in Hussite Bohemia.* Scottdale, PA: Herald Press.

Wheeler, Rachel M. 2008. *To Live Upon Hope: Mohicans and Missionaries in the Eighteenth-Century Northeast.* Ithaca, NY: Cornell University Press.

Vogt, Peter. 2005. "Nicholas Ludwig von Zinzendorf (1700–1760)." In *The Pietist Theologians. An Introduction to Theology in the Seventeenth and Eighteenth Centuries*. Edited by Carter Lindberg, 207–223. Oxford: Blackwell.

Zinzendorf, Nikolaus Ludwig. 1962. *Hauptschriften in Sechs Bänden*. Edited by Erich Beyreuther and Gerhard Meyer. Hildesheim: Georg Olms.

Zinzendorf, Nikolaus Ludwig. 2001. *A Collection of Sermons from Zinzendorf's Pennsylvania Journey*. Translated by Julie Weber. Edited by Craig D. Atwood. Bethlehem, PA: Moravian Church Publications Office.

# PART III

## THEOLOGY AND THE OTHERS

# Western Christian Theologies and
# Other Religions or Churches

# CHAPTER 30

...........................................................................

# WESTERN THEOLOGIES AND JUDAISM IN THE EARLY MODERN WORLD

...........................................................................

## STEPHEN G. BURNETT

## 1 INTRODUCTION

...........................................................................

A casual reading of seventeenth- and eighteenth-century theological works that discuss Jews and Judaism might leave readers wondering whether Christian theology concerning them had changed at all since the Middle Ages. Catholic, Lutheran, and Reformed theologians continued to characterize Jews as being blind, stubborn, unbelieving, and wicked. Christians held not only the Jewish leaders who arranged Jesus' execution responsible for deicide, but all Jews since that time. Theologians of all confessions applied the verse "Let his blood be upon us and upon our children" (Mt 27:25) to the Jews of their own day. Jews lived under God's curse of "hardened hearts" so that they resisted conversion to Christianity, and they continued to hate Christ, the Christian faith, and Christians. Because Jews were so often and prominently associated with moneylending, they were characterized as greedy. They were also associated with magic and magical practices (Karant-Nunn 2010, 133–57). Theologians of all confessions believed that Judaism was a religion that was invented by the rabbis to alienate Jews further from the only true faith. Eighteenth-century Protestant theologians who were influenced by the Enlightenment thought much the same as their predecessors. Johann David Michaelis (1717–91) believed the Jews were "blinded" and "hardened" against Christianity. Johann Solomon Semler (1725–91) called them "the most wicked, rejected people on earth" (Löwenbrück 1995, 103–4).

Post-Tridentine Catholicism promoted certain kinds of anti-Jewish prejudice. Catholic writers such as Matthaeus Rader (1561–1634) kept alive the memory of past ritual murder accusations (Hsia 1988, 218–22). Pilgrimages to the memorial chapels such as the Saint Salvator Chapel in Passau, the site of a synagogue where a desecration of the

Eucharist allegedly took place in 1477, served to remind Christians about both a Jewish "crime" and the Eucharistic miracle that took place there (Hsia 1988, 222).

Apart from diction and characterization, the arguments that Christians used to demonstrate the falsity of Judaism and the truth of Christianity were quite similar to those used during the Middle Ages. In 1651, Johannes Buxtorf the Younger (1599–1664) advised Johannes Cocceius (1603–69) about books he would need for his new position at the University of Leiden, when writing against the Jews: "You must yourself acquire, to use alongside Raymundus [*Pugio fidei*]: Porschetus [*Victoria ... adversos impios Hebraeos*], the *Fortalitium Fidei* [Alphonso de Espina], *Stella Messiae* [Petrus Nigri], Hieronymus de Sancta Fide, the book that is called *Zelus Christi* [Pedro de la Cavalleria], published at Venice, Paulus de St. Maria ...." (van Rooden 1989, 179). These medieval *Adversus judaeos* works, readily available in reprint, continued to inform Christian anti-Jewish polemical arguments throughout this period.

Despite these striking similarities between medieval and early modern portrayals of Jews and Judaism, theologians of the seventeenth and eighteenth centuries did think somewhat differently about Jews and Judaism than their predecessors. These changes in portrayal can be traced above all to Christian Hebraism and to a greater awareness of Judaism as it was practiced in their own day. Both of these developments had their roots in the sixteenth century.

# 2 Christian Hebraism and the Portrayal of Judaism

Christian Hebraism in early modern Europe was an intellectual movement that borrowed and adapted ideas, information and scholarly practices from post-biblical Hebrew literature to meet Christian religious and cultural needs. It grew out of both the quest for ancient wisdom through kabbalistic learning, and biblical humanism, which stressed a return to the sources of the Christian faith. The Protestant Reformation and the Catholic response to it provided motives and means for larger numbers of Christians to learn Hebrew. Protestants believed that the Bible was the final authority for resolving controversies involving doctrine and church practice (sola scriptura), and that the received texts of the Old and New Testaments in their original languages were authoritative texts. Consequently, Greek and Hebrew instruction would become a regular feature of Protestant theological education during the early modern period. Some Catholic theologians were also motivated by a desire to return to the sources and read the biblical texts in their original languages, but the need to counter Protestant Hebrew expertise was decisive in spurring Catholic rulers and the Jesuit order to make Hebrew an important part of Catholic theological education as well (Burnett 2012, 16–39).

By 1600, a degree of Hebrew literacy was becoming increasingly common among Christian theologians. Many were able to read the Hebrew Bible with some degree of understanding; a much smaller number were capable of reading post-biblical Jewish literature. Scholars such as the Buxtorfs, Constantin L'Empereur (1591–1648), John Selden (1584–1654), and Christian Knorr von Rosenroth (1631–89), translated, adapted, and summarized these texts for Christian use. Christians still wrestled with the perennial problem of how far they could *trust* Jewish authors as authorities on the Hebrew language, the preservation of the Hebrew Bible text, and their own history. Using Jewish authors as authorities to defend Christian doctrines, above all the integrity of the Hebrew Bible text, created tension within Protestant theology.

Christian translations of Jewish texts into western European languages, above all into Latin, made them more accessible to a broader reading public. During the seventeenth and eighteenth centuries, Christian Hebraists translated a wide variety of Jewish texts, including the entire Mishnah (van Rooden 2005, 97–110), the Zohar (Coudert 1999, 110–18), Maimonides' *Guide to the Perplexed* (1629), and Judah ha-Levi's *Kuzari* (1660). The translation of these important texts meant that they could be readily included in theological discourse. The Roman and Spanish indices of prohibited books declared both the Talmud and kabbalistic books off-limits to Catholic scholars, and the Congregation of the Index routinely banned translations of Jewish books, which deterred Catholic scholars in southern Europe from publishing Judaica translations during the seventeenth century (Burnett 2012, 230, 240–41).

Christian theologians of the seventeenth and eighteenth centuries also had a far better understanding of living Judaism than their predecessors. Anthonius Margaritha (ca. 1500–42) first provided Christians with a cradle-to-grave account of Jewish faith and life in his book *Der Gantz Jüdisch Glaub* (1530). He sought to prove that Jews were not true followers of the Old Testament law, but followed laws and customs of their own making. In addition to his discussion of Jewish life, Margaritha also translated part of the prayer book into German, including prayers such as the *Alenu* that Christians found offensive (Walton 2012, 63–66). Only in the seventeenth century did Christian Hebraist scholars begin to study Judaism as a living religion, incorporating it within the scope of Christian scholarly endeavor. Growing Christian interest in Judaism, a degree of mastery of Hebrew, the increasing availability of Jewish texts for them to study, and the assistance of Jews, including converts, meant that Christian theologians of the seventeenth and eighteenth centuries had a far better understanding of Judaism than even their sixteenth-century predecessors. Not surprisingly, this new awareness was expressed most commonly in anti-Jewish polemics.

Ernst Benz characterized Christian Kabbalah as a "step-child" of theology, but its relationship to Jewish Kabbalah is even more problematic (Benz 1958). Giovanni Pico della Mirandola (1463–94) and Johann Reuchlin (1455–1522), the founders of Renaissance Christian Kabbalah, understood kabbalistic literature and learning to be a pathway back to the *prisca theologia*, ancient learning that predated Greek philosophy. They were fascinated by its obvious similarities to Neoplatonic and Hermetic thought, and to the mystical thought of Pseudo-Dionysius the Areopagite (5th century AD–6th century AD). Christian Kabbalah represents a mediation of some Jewish kabbalistic concepts into a Christian religious and especially philosophical context, rather than a wholesale adoption of Jewish Kabbalah (Dan 2006, 63–64). Wilhelm Schmidt-Biggeman identified several common elements of early modern Christian Kabbalah: interest in the opening words of the Bible (In the beginning . . . ), the role of the Word of God in the process of Creation, divine names together with their meaning and their predicates, the symbolic nature of the Hebrew alphabet, and the techniques of kabbalistic biblical interpretation (Schmidt-Biggeman 2013, 2:192). By the end of the sixteenth century, the works printed in Johannes Pistorius' *Artis cabalisticae tomus* (1587) and Francesco Zorzi's two books *De harmonia mundi* (1525) and *In scripturam sacram problemata* (1536), constituted a "canon" of kabbalistic texts. Much of later Christian kabbalistic thinking was inspired and informed by these Latin texts rather than through direct study of Jewish kabbalistic works.

Christian kabbalistic study was energized by Christian Knorr von Rosenroth's *Kabbala Denudata* (1677–78). The *Kabbala Denudata* not only contained a Latin translation of the Zohar, but a good deal of explanatory material, including Latin translations of Lurianic kabbalistic texts (Schmidt-Biggeman 2013, 3:63–148). Knorr von Rosenroth and his associate Francis Mercury von Helmont (1614–99) believed the Zohar to be a religious key to breaking down the barrier that separated Christians from Jews, since they thought that the book contained veiled references to both the triune nature of God and to Jesus the Messiah. A common understanding of the nature of God and agreement that the Messiah had already come would facilitate the conversion of the Jews. Their understanding of both doctrines, however, departed from received Christian orthodoxy in important ways, making it unacceptable to many Christians (Coudert 1999, 125–29). Knorr von Rosenroth's work did provoke a good deal of theological discussion, especially among English thinkers such as Henry More (1614–87), Lady Anne Conway (1631–79) and George Keith (1638/9–1716) (Coudert 1999, 177–240). Nontheologians, including John Locke (1632–1704) and Gottfried Wilhelm Leibniz (1646–1715), also studied Knorr von Rosenroth's Zohar translation (Coudert 1999, 271–329). Christian Kabbalah was inspired by Jewish scholarship and it involved biblical interpretation, but Kabbalists of the seventeenth and eighteenth centuries, like their sixteenth-century predecessors, were rarely theologians themselves. Their work most influenced Christians on the margins of the major confessions rather than more orthodox theological thinkers.

# 3 DOCTRINE OF SCRIPTURE

Western theologies of the seventeenth and eighteenth centuries contained frequent references to Jews under three topics: the doctrine of scripture, controversial theology (including theological books written for missionary outreach to Jews), and eschatology. The problem of religious authority was central to the self-definition of all early modern churches. By identifying the Bible—Hebrew Old Testament and Greek New Testament in their received textual versions—as the only source of religious authority, faith and practice, and the final arbiter of religious controversies, Protestants became theologically beholden to Jewish scholarship in a way that left them vulnerable to attack by Catholic polemicists. Protestants assumed that the received texts of the individual books of the Hebrew Bible had been accurately copied by a succession of Jewish scribes, and that where early translations of the Bible such as the Septuagint and the Vulgate differed from the Hebrew text, it was the translations that erred, not the Hebrew Bible. The majority of Protestant Hebraists through the early to mid-seventeenth century also believed that the Hebrew vowel points were written by the biblical authors themselves and were therefore part of the canonical Hebrew Bible text.

Johannes Buxtorf the Elder's (1564–1629) works relating to the biblical text itself were fundamental contributions to biblical scholarship. His book *Tiberias* (1620) was the first Latin language introduction to the vocalization of the biblical text, its paratextual elements, and the Masoretic apparatus. Buxtorf provided the generally accepted argument for the position that the vowel points dated from the biblical age, no later than the "Great Synagogue" of Ezra, Nehemiah, and their fellow contemporary prophets. Buxtorf based his position largely upon evidence drawn from Jewish tradition, including arguments advanced by Jacob ben Hayyim (ca. 1470–ca. 1538) in his introduction to the Rabbinic Bible (1524–25) and by Azariah de Rossi (ca. 1511–ca. 1578) in *Light of the Eyes*. *Tiberias* appears to be a philological work addressing a rather abstruse subject, but it addressed theological questions that Robert Bellarmine (1542–1621) raised concerning the Hebrew Bible text (Burnett 1996, 216–27). Francis Turretin's (1623–87) discussion of the integrity of the Hebrew Bible text provides a robust example of how Buxtorf's findings could be used in systematic theology (Turretin 1992, 106–13).

Louis Cappel (1585–1658), a Reformed professor of Hebrew at the Saumur Academy, responded to Buxtorf's *Tiberias* with two works of his own. He wrote *Arcanum* (which he published anonymously in 1624) as a direct refutation of Buxtorf's position on the age of the vowel points. His principal arguments against the antiquity of the vowel points were philological, not based upon Jewish tradition. He believed that many passages in the Septuagint could only be explained if the translators had used an unvocalized Hebrew text as their *Vorlage*. Cappel argued that the textual evidence of the early biblical translations, the church fathers, and even the Targums could not be left out of consideration when studying the history of the biblical text. Yet Cappel did not believe that the Hebrew Bible text had become less perspicuous as a result of his findings.

Jean Morin (1591–1659) was the first Catholic Hebraist to make sustained use of Hebrew philology in an effort to undermine Protestant confidence in the received Hebrew Bible text. In his introduction to a new edition of the Septuagint in 1628, Morin argued that the Greek translation was superior to the Masoretic text, which the Jews had altered in places. His most important contribution to the debate was his edition of the Samaritan Pentateuch, which appeared in the Paris Polyglot Bible (1632). A received Hebrew Bible text that agreed in many places with the Septuagint rather than the received Hebrew text cast doubt upon the reliability of the Old Testament text and therefore could be cited in anti-Protestant polemics. Morin's willingness to denigrate the received Hebrew text provoked not only Protestants to dispute his claims, but also some fellow Catholic scholars.

Cappel's re-entry into the debate over the reliability of the consonantal Hebrew text stirred controversy even further. After publishing *Arcanum punctationis revelatum*, Cappel devoted himself to a detailed study of the Masoretic text of the Hebrew Bible, comparing it with the Septuagint and also with New Testament quotations of the Septuagint. In making these comparisons, he identified an array of different kinds of textual corruption, including the possibility of differences in word division, haplography and dittography, and misreadings or metathesis of individual consonants. In light of his findings, he felt free to offer conjectural emendations to the received Hebrew text when he thought it was warranted. He compiled these findings into his magnum opus *Critica sacra* (1650). Cappel's revolutionary conclusions provoked a number of polemical responses, most notably by the younger Johannes Buxtorf in his *Anticritica* (1653). Whether we understand them within the theological context of their times or the history of biblical scholarship, the debates over the integrity of the Hebrew Bible text and the text-critical value of early translations such as the Septuagint and the Vulgate were among the most important scholarly discussions involving Hebrew that took place during the Reformation era (Burnett 2012, 122–24).

The theological debate over the integrity of the Hebrew Bible text and the age of the vowel points continued through the seventeenth and eighteenth centuries, and scholars within all four major theological traditions disagreed on these questions. Lutheran theologians tended to follow Buxtorf's line of reasoning until the early eighteenth century, although some such as Johann Conrad Dannhauer (1603–66) believed that the age and authority of the vowel points was an open question (Preus 1957, 134–46). The Reformed and Anglican scholars were thoroughly divided, with some (such as the younger Johannes Buxtorf, André Rivet [1572–1651], and Francis Turretin) defending Buxtorf's position, and others (including Louis Cappel, and Brian Walton [1600–61]) rejecting it. Catholic scholars also disagreed among themselves, with Jean Morin and James Gordon (1541–1621) arguing that the Masoretic text was corrupt, while others such as Simeon de Muis (1587–1644) vehemently disagreed (Burnett 2008, 791). Discussions of the reliability of Jewish scribes in transmitting the received Hebrew Bible text and the origins and authority of the Hebrew vowel points figured prominently in both theological treatises and polemics of the seventeenth and eighteenth centuries.

# 4 CONTROVERSIAL THEOLOGY

Theologians of the seventeenth and eighteenth centuries faced a different set of challenges than their medieval predecessors where writing anti-Jewish polemics was concerned.

Their works were shaped by the need to establish clear theological boundaries between themselves and other confessional churches, schismatics, anti-Trinitarians, and atheists, as well as with Judaism. Their primary tasks were to draw clear boundaries for orthodoxy and to demonstrate the theological illegitimacy of their opponents. They were less concerned with missionary persuasion than with demonstrating the truth as they understood it. Friedrich noted that for seventeenth-century Lutheran theologians, a careful exposition of the principal Old Testament texts related to the coming of the Messiah served both to prove the truth of Christianity and as a tool for missionary outreach. Protection of Christians from "Jewish wickedness" was a higher priority for them than persuading Jews to convert (Friedrich 1988, 51). This task became particularly urgent as Christians became more aware of Judaism as a religion, began to study Jewish anti-Christian polemical literature, mostly circulated in manuscript, and had increased contact with Sephardic Jews who had been educated as Christians and were willing to argue with Christians about the truth of their faith.

Johannes Buxtorf the Elder's *Juden Schul* (1603) was a principal source for Christians to learn about Judaism as a faith and a way of life. Buxtorf drew upon a number of earlier portrayals of Judaism written by converts such as Anthonius Margaritha, but he also consulted Hebrew and Yiddish language books written by Jews for Jews about the practice of Judaism. His aim was to prove that Judaism was a false faith invented by the rabbis, rather than an authentic religion based upon the scriptures. Buxtorf's characterization of living Judaism in the rest of *Juden Schul*, over 500 pages of exposition, was intended to discredit it as a biblical religion. In the core of the book, chapters 3 to 25 (pp. 159–550) he explained Jewish customs and practices performed daily, weekly, or during the liturgical year. Apart from obvious editorial remarks at the beginning and end of chapters, glossing code words, and using biblical quotations as foils to Jewish practice, Buxtorf most often indicated his disagreement through short, snide comments rather than conscious distortion or parody.

Buxtorf's *Juden Schul* would directly or indirectly affect Christian opinion about Judaism for centuries after its composition. Later Christian authors, whether Christian Hebraists or Jewish converts, often quoted from Buxtorf's descriptions with or without attribution in their own books (Burnett 1996, 85–86). The book also elicited responses from Jewish readers, most importantly from Leon Modena (1571–1648) in his *Historia de' riti hebraici* (1637). Thanks to Buxtorf and a host of later imitators, Christian scholars had ready access to basic information about Jewish beliefs, practices, and prayers (especially those that covertly insulted Christ and Christianity). This "new knowledge" of Judaism, presented in a polemical form, further complicated Jewish-Christian relations, as did the discovery and popularization of anti-Christian texts written by Jews.

Christian theologians had long been aware that Jews had written books attacking their faith. Bishop Agobard of Lyons (n.d.–840) complained about a version of *Toledot Yeshu* (the Life of Jesus) (Krauss 1995, 68). By the seventeenth and eighteenth centuries, Christian Hebraists had better access to Jewish polemical books, whether through library collections or Jewish acquaintances who owned them. The often biting, bitter passages in these books, when quoted by Christians, added to the angry tone of their own anti-Jewish polemical books. Three Christian polemical authors in particular stand out among their peers: Johannes Müller (1598–1672), Johann Christoph Wagenseil (1633–1705), and Johann Eisenmenger (1654–1704). Müller's *Judaismus* (1644) reflects his acquaintance with Jewish literature, quoting from twenty-six Jewish imprints and three polemical manuscripts, including Isaac Troki's *Hizzuk Emunah*. Müller's goal in writing this massive work was both apologetic, to arm Christians to respond to Jewish arguments against their faith, and also conversionary, though Friedrich notes that the latter motive played only a minor role (Friedrich 1988, 80–81).

Johann Christoph Wagenseil edited a notorious two-volume compendium of Jewish polemics against Christianity entitled *Tela Ignea Satanae* (1681). The book contains the Hebrew text and Latin translation of six Jewish anti-Christian polemical books: the *Carmen memorial* (mnemonic poem) of Yom Tov Lippman Muhlhausen's *Nizzahon*, *Nizzahon Vetus*; the *Disputations* of R. Yehiel (Paris 1240) and Nahmanides (Barcelona 1263); Isaac Troki's *Hizzuk Emunah*; and *Toledot Jeshu* (Kraus 1995, 143). Wagenseil added a lengthy introduction (104 pages) and rebuttals of the *Carmen memorial* and *Toledot Jeshu*. Wagenseil asserted that to refute Jewish arguments against Christianity and convert the Jews, scholars had to know what they thought about Christianity. The publication of these texts, Wagenseil believed, would expose their secrets to the public and deter them from writing such books in the future. Armed with this new knowledge of Judaism, Christian theologians would be better equipped to dispute with Jews (Schreckenberg 1994, 684). Unlike the younger Buxtorf and Constantin L'Empereur, Wagenseil did not fear that these books might be used by non-Jews to attack Christianity (van Rooden 1989, 172–73). He could not have known that later Enlightenment figures would use his scholarship to attack the Christian faith. Voltaire (1694–1778) and the French Encyclopedists found Isaac Troki's (ca. 1533–ca. 1594) arguments especially useful (Schreiner 2004, 420).

Johann Andreas Eisenmenger wrote the most venomous polemical work of the early modern period: *Entdecktes Judentum* (1711). He devoted nineteen years to studying both Jewish texts and contemporary Judaism to prepare himself. In the book he made public, as the title page of volume 1 explains:

> The manner in which the hardened Jews dreadfully blaspheme and speak irreverently of the most holy Trinity, speak contemptuously of the holy mother of Christ, condemn and curse to the utmost the New Testament, the Christian religion . . . and all Christendom. . . . All this taken from their own books, very many in number and perused . . . with great pains, with citation of the Hebrew texts and accurate translation . . . prepared as an honest report for the information of all Christians. (Eisenmenger 1711)

The work was so controversial that the first printing was partially suppressed because of its dangerous character (Krauss 1995, 144). Even among Christians its contribution was hotly debated, with some such as Johann David Michaelis (1717–91) branding it as a "Lästerschrift," a blasphemous work (Rohrbacher 2005, 183).

In the context of early modern academic theology, this new knowledge of Judaism was used to differentiate more precisely the differences between Christianity generally and individual confessional traditions more specifically from Judaism, to the detriment of the latter. Greater knowledge of Jewish polemics against Christianity had the effect of increasing the suspicions of theologians rather than easing tensions. When Johann Christoph Wolf (1683–1739) published a Latin translation of Mordecai ben Nissan's *Dod Mordecai* (1724), he gave the book a polemical edge lacking in the original by adding material from another Karaite book, Isaac Troki's *Hizzuq Emunah*.

# 5 Eschatology and the Jews

The "eschatological Jew" had played an important role in the Christian understanding of the End of Days since the patristic period (Cohen 2005, 280). Most confessional theologies of the seventeenth and eighteenth centuries understood that the conversion of the Jews would be a sign of the approaching end of the age, following St. Augustine.

> And so in that [last] judgment, or in connection with that judgment, we have learnt that those events are to come about: Elijah the Tishbite will come; Jews will accept the faith; Antichrist will persecute; Christ will judge; the dead will rise again; the good and evil will be separated; the earth will be destroyed in the flames, and then will be renewed. All those events, we must believe, will come about; but in what way, and in what order they will come, actual experience will then teach us with a finality surpassing anything our human understanding is now capable of attaining. However, I consider that these events are destined to come about in the order I have given. (Augustine 1972, 963 [Bk XX, chap. 30])

Augustine provided a sequence of events associated with the approach of Judgment Day that included the mass conversion of the Jews, and he proposed the order in which they would occur. By so doing, he also made Jewish conversion into an article of faith, like the Last Judgment itself, but one that had little or no impact upon the present.

Catholic theologians of the seventeenth and eighteenth centuries discussed the question of Jewish conversion in connection with the appearance of the Antichrist, whether he had already come or would come in the future. They asserted that he had not yet come, especially in response to Luther who condemned the pope as Antichrist as early as 1520, in his *Address to the Nobility of the German Nation* (McGinn 1994, 203). Jesuit exegetes at the end of the sixteenth century argued on the basis of their study of the New Testament and the fathers that the Antichrist was a "future figure without ties to current events." This view had the effect of pruning back the "medieval legendary accretions to Antichrist by returning to a rather strict Augustinian teaching on the Last Enemy" (McGinn 1994, 226). Robert Bellarmine argued in *De Summo Pontifice* that there were six signs of the coming of the Antichrist, including the preaching of Enoch and Elias that would convert the Jews. None of the signs had yet taken place (Bellarmine 1856, 434 [Bk 3, chap 6]). Francesco Suárez (1548–1617) argued similarly in his work *De Antichristo* (McGinn 1994, 227). The revelation of the Antichrist and the conversion of the Jews were both signs that had not yet come to pass. Pope Paul IV (1555–59) placed special emphasis on missionary outreach to the Jews, and he founded institutions such as the Convert House (Domus catechumenorum) in Rome to support it, because he believed that the End of Days was approaching. Jewish missionary efforts were sustained during the seventeenth and eighteenth centuries through the church's general support for missions rather than from a sense of eschatological urgency (Stow 1977, 200–21, 263–77).

Lutheran theologians were divided among themselves over the place of Jews within their eschatology, not least because Luther himself held two different views of the matter at different points in his career. In his early and frequently reprinted *Kirchenpostille*, Luther taught that Paul's assertion that "all Israel would be saved" (Rom 11:26) referred to Jews (Luther 2013, 75:340–41). By 1543, Luther denied that the passage had anything to do with a mass conversion of the Jews (Wallmann 2004, 147). High orthodox Lutheran theologians, such as Johann Conrad Dannhauer, taught the conversion of the Jews to which Paul referred was the conversion of individual Jews over the course of church history, and that "all Israel" in Romans 11 referred to the single church consisting of Jewish and Gentile Christians. Earlier Lutheran theologians, particularly those who lived before the Thirty Years' War, believed that there would be a mass conversion of the Jews before the End of Days. The first generation of Pietists, including Philip Jacob Spener (1635–1705), agreed. Spener believed that the church had to reform itself to be successful in its mission to the Jews, since in its unreformed state it provoked the Jews to blaspheme the Christian faith. Spener's ideas on how to implement a mission to the Jews differed little from his orthodox Lutheran contemporaries. While he served as a pastor in Frankfurt am Main, he argued that the city's magistrate should require Jews living there to attend regular conversionary sermons (Wallmann 2004, 158). The most successful Lutheran missionary to the Jews in early modern Germany was Esdras Edzard (1629–1708), a wealthy Hamburg clergyman who was involved in the baptism of 148 Jews from 1657 to 1708 (Friedrich 1988, 110). Some of his most important fiscal and moral supporters were the town's high orthodox ministers (Wallmann 2004, 144). The famous *Institutum Judaicum* in Halle was only founded in 1728, after the death of August Hermann Francke (1663–1727), and it reflected the higher priority that later Pietists placed on Jewish missions (Wallmann 2004, 159–61). Lutherans were divided on the question of whether a mass conversion of the Jews would be a sign of the End of Days. Following the later Luther, many theologians denied that such a conversion would take place (eliminating its value as a sign), while others, following the early Luther, continued to do so.

The Reformed and Anglican traditions, together with their Arminian offshoots in England and the Dutch Republic, were far more concerned with eschatology than either Catholicism or Lutheranism. Most Dutch theologians of the seventeenth century expected a mass conversion of the Jews before the End of Days (van den Berg 1970, 140). Reformed orthodox theologians also understood that the church had a responsibility to preach the Gospel to Jews, but they justified this on the basis of their broader theology. Gisbertus Voetius (1589–1676) called for Christians to remove obstacles to the conversion of the Jews by living pious lives, praying, showing sympathy and good will toward them, having a sound understanding of the Scriptures, learning oriental languages, and disputing with Jews to show them the error of their ways. He also warned Christians against the twin dangers of doubting that a future conversion of the Jews would occur and expecting their imminent conversion (van den Berg 1970, 142).

Among some Reformed and Arminian theologians in the Dutch Republic and England, however, millenarianism found a theological home during the seventeenth century. (By the mid-sixteenth century most Protestant theologians rejected millenarianism in response to the Münster Anabaptist uprising. Millenarianism was condemned in the Augsburg Confession [1530], the Forty-Two Articles of Religion [1552], the Second Helvetic Confession [1566], and the Formula of Concord [1577] [Hotson 2000, 3].) The first major academic theological studies that espoused millenarianism were published in 1627: Johann Heinrich Alsted's *Diatribe de mille annis apocalypticis* and Joseph Mede's *Clavis apocalyptica*. The works of these two men, together with Thomas Brightman (1562–1607), formed the intellectual foundation of a respectable form of millenarianism (Katz 1982, 93–94; Hotson 2000, 4). The combination of catastrophic events, which readily inspired these thinkers to look for signs of the End of Days, with the intensive study of chronological passages such as Daniel 9, led some Reformed and Arminian theologians to believe that the End of Days was upon them, and therefore that the conversion of the Jews would happen soon. Some of them felt that it was their obligation to see that this came to pass (van der Wall 1988, 73). Petrus Serrarius (1600–69) and his circle of Dutch and English colleagues and correspondents were very active in promoting projects that would facilitate the conversion of the Jews. Serrarius himself made personal contacts with Menasseh ben Israel (1604–57), Nathan Shipira (fl. 1655–57), Baruch Spinoza (1632–77), and other Jews. He sought to find Hebrew scholars who would translate the Mishnah into Latin and the New Testament into Hebrew. He gave charitably to poor Jews in Palestine, as did his friends Henry Jessey (1603–63), John Durie (1596–1680) and Samuel Hartlib (1600–62). Serrarius supported Durie's ecumenical efforts to unite all Protestant churches, in part to remove a stumbling block to Jewish belief. On the basis of these signs of the times, they and other millenarians sought to fix the date of the great Jewish conversion, identifying variously 1650, 1655, and 1660 (van der Wall 1988, 78). In England, Jessey placed Jewish conversion before 1658, while others put the year variously at 1654, 1656, and before 1658 (Katz, 99). Speculation concerning the year of the Jewish conversion continued well into the eighteenth century. John Locke, for example, identified 1732 as the correct year, with the millennium beginning in 1777 (Coudert 1999, 279).

# 6 CONCLUSION

Theologians of this time had a somewhat different relationship to Judaism than their predecessors because they knew more about it, and because of the permanent division of Christendom into mutually hostile Christian confessions, together with a number of smaller dissenter groups. Protestant theologians found Jewish scholarship useful when defending the authenticity of the Masoretic text, but they also had to consider how "trustworthy" Jews were in interpreting that same biblical text. Controversial theologians devoted considerable effort to marking and patrolling the boundaries of true religion, as well as attacking and undermining their theological foes. They continued to criticize Jews for their blindness and unbelief, and they branded Judaism an illegitimate faith. But Jews were now part of a host of other foes of Christian truth whose teachings they felt obliged to refute. Most confessional theologians continued to believe that a mass conversion of the Jews in the future would be one of the signs of the impending Last Judgment.

## BIBLIOGRAPHY

Augustine. 1972. *Concerning the City of God against the Pagans*. Translated by H. Bettenson. Edited by D. Knowles. Baltimore, MD: Penguin.

Bellarmine, R. 1856. *Disputationum Roberti Bellarmini Politiani S. J. De Controversiis Christianae Fidei Adversus Hujus Temporis Haereticos*. Vol. 1. Naples: Joseph Giuliano.

Benz, E. 1958. *Die christliche Kabbalah; Ein Stiefkind der Theologie*. Zürich: Rhein Verlag.

Burnett, S. 2012. *Christian Hebraism in the Reformation Era (1500–1660): Authors, Books, and the Transmission of Jewish Learning*. Leiden: Brill.

Burnett, S. 1996. *From Christian Hebraism to Jewish Studies: Johannes Buxtorf (1564–1629) and Hebrew Learning in the Seventeenth Century*. Leiden: Brill.

Burnett, S. 2008. "Later Christian Hebraists." In *Hebrew Bible/Old Testament: The History of its Interpretation. Vol. 2 of From the Renaissance to the Enlightenment*, edited by Magne Saebø and Michael Fishbane, 785–801. Göttingen: Vandenhoeck & Ruprecht.

Cohen, J. 2005. "The Mystery of Israel's Salvation: Romans 11: 25–26 in Patristic and Medieval Exegesis." *Harvard Theological Review* 98 (3): 247–281.

Coudert, A. 1999. *The Impact of Kabbalah in the Seventeenth Century: The Life and Thought of Francis Mercury van Helmont (1614–1698)*. Leiden: Brill.

Dan, J. 2006. *Kabbalah: A Very Short Introduction*. Oxford: Oxford University Press.

Eisenmenger, J. A. 1711. *Entdecktes Judenthum, Oder Gründlicher und Wahrhaffter Bericht, Welchergestalt Die verstockte Juden die Hochheilige Drey-Einigkeit . . . lästern und verunehren*. 2 Vols. Königsberg, Prussia: n.p.

Friedrich, M. 1988. *Zwischen Abwehr und Bekehrung. Die Stellung der deutschen evangelischen Theologie zum Judentum im 17. Jahrhundert*. Tübingen: Mohr Siebeck.

Hotson, H. 2000. *Paradise Postponed: Johann Heinrich Alsted and the Birth of Calvinist Millenarianism*. Dordrecht: Kluwer.

Hsia, R. 1988. *The Myth of Ritual Murder: Jews and Magic in Reformation Germany*. New Haven, CT: Yale University Press.

Karant-Nunn, S. 2010. *The Reformation of Feeling: Shaping the Religious Emotions in Early Modern Germany*. Oxford: Oxford University Press.

Katz, D. 1982. *Philosemitism and the Readmission of the Jews to England, 1603–1655*. Oxford: Clarendon.

Krauss, S. 1995. *The Jewish-Christian Controversy from Earliest Times to 1789. Vol. 1: History*. Edited by William Horbury. Tübingen: Mohr-Siebeck.

Löwenbrück, A.-R. 1995. *Judenfeindschaft im Zeitalter der Aufklärung*. Frankfurt: Peter Lang.

Luther, Martin. 2013. "Luther's Works, Vol. 75: Church Postil I." edited by Benjamin T. G. Mayes and James L. Langebartels. St. Louis, MO: Concordia Publishing House.

McGinn, B. 1994. *Antichrist: Two Thousand Years of the Human Fascination with Evil*. San Francisco: HarperSanFrancisco.

Preus, R. 1957. *The Inspiration of Scripture. A Study of the Theology of the Seventeenth Century Lutheran Dogmaticians*. Edinburgh: Oliver and Boyd.

Rohrbacher, S. 2005. "'Gründlicher und Wahrhaffter Bericht': Des Orientalisten Johann Andreas Eisenmenbers Entdecktes Judenthum (1700) als Klassiker des 'wissenschaftlichen' Antisemitismus." In *Reuchlin und Seine Erben: Forscher, Denker, Ideologen und Spinner*, edited by Peter Schäfer and Irina Wandrey, 171–188. Ostfildern: Jan Thorbecke.

Schmidt-Biggeman, W. 2012–2013. *Geschichte der christlichen Kabbala*. 3 vols. Stuttgart-Bad-Cannstatt.

Schreckenberg, H. 1994. *Die christlichen Adversus-Judaeos-Texte und ihr literarisches und historisches Umfeld (13.-20. Jh)*. Frankfurt: Peter Lang.

Schreiner, S. 2004. "Isaiah 53 in the Sefer Hizzuk Emunah ('Faith Strengthened') of Rabbi Isaac ben Abraham of Troki." In *The Suffering Servant: Isaiah 53 in Jewish and Christian Sources*, edited by Bernd Janowski and Peter Stuhlmacher, 418–461. Grand Rapids, MI: Eerdmans.

Stow, K. 1977. *Catholic Thought and Papal Jewish Policy, 1555–1593*. New York: Jewish Theological Seminary.

Turretin, F. 1992. *Institutes of Elenctic Theology*. Translated by G. Giger. Edited by J. Dennison. Vol. 1: *First through Tenth Topics*. Philipsburg, NJ: P & R Publishing.

Van den Berg, J. 1970. "The Eschatological Expectation of Seventeenth-Century Dutch Protestantism with Regard to the Jewish People." In *Puritans, The Millennium and the Future of Israel: Puritan Eschatology 1600 to 1660*, edited by P. Toon, 137–153. Cambridge: James Clarke.

Van der Wall, E. 1988. "The Amsterdam Millenarian Petrus Serrarius (1600–1669) and the Anglo-Dutch Circle of Philo-Judaists." In *Jewish-Christian Relations in the Seventeenth Century*, edited by J. van den Berg and E. van der Wall, 73–94. Dordrecht: Kluwer.

Van Rooden, P. 1989. *Theology, Biblical Scholarship and Rabbinical Studies in the Seventeenth Century: Constantijn L'Empereur (1591–1648), Professor of Hebrew and Theology at Leiden*. Leiden: Brill.

Van Rooden. 2005. "Willem Surenhuys' Translation of the Mishna and the Strange Death of Christian Hebraism." In *Reuchlin und Seine Erben: Forscher, Denker, Ideologen und Spinner*, edited by P. Schäfer and I. Wandrey, 97–110. Ostfildern: Jan Thorbecke.

Wallmann, J. 2004. "Der alte und neue Bund: Zur Haltung des Pietismus gegenüber den Juden." In *Glaubenswelt und Lebenswelten*. Vol. 4 of *Geschichte des Pietismus*, edited by H. Lehmann, 143–165. Göttingen: Vandenhoeck & Ruprecht.

Walton, M. 2012. *Anthonius Margaritha and the Jewish Faith: Jewish Life and Conversion in Sixteenth-Century Germany*. Detroit, MI: Wayne State University Press.

CHAPTER 31

# WESTERN THEOLOGIES AND ISLAM IN THE EARLY MODERN WORLD

EMANUELE COLOMBO

## 1 INTRODUCTION

WESTERN theologies on Islam in the early modern period have been influenced by different historical events that at times supported continuities and at other times introduced fractures with previous periods.[1]

A first crucial event was the growth of the Ottoman Empire and its expansion into Europe. By the mid-fifteenth century, the growing Ottoman threat played a crucial role in shaping Western images of Islam; during the sixteenth century the Ottomans reached the apex of their expansion in the West and were perceived as powerful rivals to Christian Europe, strengthening the idea that the "Turks"—an expression that labeled Muslims in general—were the enemy par excellence of Christianity (Dupront 1997; Poumarède 2004).

A second significant aspect was the fluctuating definition of Muslims in Western theologies. While Muslims were traditionally considered distinct from Jews, in the course of the later Middle Ages Western canon law introduced the maxim that all that was said of the Jews applied to the Muslims, and both groups became "the interchangeable constituent parts of the broader category 'infidelity'" (Stantchev 2014, 96; Freidenreich 2011). In the early modern period, the religious fragmentation of Christendom begun by the Lutheran Reformation introduced a new perception of Islam. The "Mohammedan sect" started to be used in theological literature as a rhetorical weapon for internal religious debates between Catholics and Protestants.

Third, since the thirteenth century the ideas of crusade and mission developed in the West, representing two concurrent and contemporary European approaches toward Islam (Kedar 1984). During the fifteenth century, when many Orthodox Christians fled to Western Europe after the fall of Constantinople (1453), the project of freeing the Holy Land and converting Muslims was associated with the desire for unification of the Eastern churches with Rome. Additionally, contacts with Eastern Christians, who perceived Muslims as "one amongst several non-Christian peoples or simply as paradigmatic of these gentiles" (Freidenreich 2012, 56), contributed to the development of a new idea of mission that flourished in the post-Tridentine era and required revised approaches to Islam, different from the well-established Western doctrinal view.

Finally, since the Middle Ages, European attitudes toward Islam have been multifaceted. In contrast to the rhetorical emphasis on hostility between Christianity and Islam, there were also peaceful encounters and economic and cultural exchanges, and "in many cases mutual interest and pragmatism dictated the relationship between Muslim rulers and European powers, especially on the local level" (Teule 2012, 10; König 2012). Curiosity about Muslims grew in Europe during the Renaissance, originating in an ambivalent feeling of attraction and repulsion. The same attitude continued during the early modern period, when European travelers and merchants contributed to the increased fascination with Islam. Christians, primarily in southern Catholic Europe, but also in northern Protestant Europe, developed scholarship in Arabic studies, springing from the desire to better understand the Muslim world and to connect with Eastern Christians; the printing press was a key instrument for the spread of this knowledge.

# 2 The "Mohammedan Heresy": Heritage of the Middle Ages

When early modern Christians sought to comprehend Islam and engage in polemics against it, they turned naturally to translations and texts produced between the twelfth and early fourteenth centuries (Tolan 2002, 275).

An emblematic example of this attitude is the work by the Zurich theologian Theodor Bibliander (1509–64), the *Machumetis saracenorum principis* (1543, 2nd ed. 1550), which is considered one of the most important early modern texts on Islam published in the Latin West. This work reproduced for the first time in print the *Corpus Cluniacensis*, the authoritative medieval source collection on Islam that included the Latin translation of the Qur'an by Robert of Ketton (ca. 1110–60), accomplished through the initiative of Peter the Venerable of Cluny (ca. 1092–1156), along with a set of medieval polemical works. In this sixteenth-century "encyclopedia of Islam," Bibliander wanted to provide Christian scholars with the instruments to oppose the Islamic threat and evangelize Muslims (Miller 2013; Lamarque 2007). The introduction and comments highlight the polemic nature of his work, an approach consistent with the medieval literature published in the second volume. Bibliander's compendium shaped the early modern view of Islam in the sixteenth and seventeenth centuries, and contributed to the spread of some erroneous and tendentious information about Islam and misinterpreted quotations from the Qur'an (Bobzin 1995; Malcolm 2007).

Despite the fact that the Catholic Church officially prohibited Bibliander's work, it circulated even in Catholic environments. Additionally, a similar approach to Islam can be found in one of the most influential Catholic bibliographic encyclopedias, Antonio Possevino's (1533–1611) *Bibliotheca selecta* (1593, 1603, 1607). In Book 7, devoted to heresies and enemies of the Church, Possevino offers a particularly harsh image of Mohammed and Islam, and reiterates the legend that Mohammed had been instructed by a heretical Christian monk named Sergius (or Nestorius). When suggesting a list of readings about Islam, Possevino quotes standard medieval authors. In Spain, the *Confusión o confutación de la secta Mahomética* (1515) by Juan Andrés (active 1487–1515), a *faquih* (scholar of Islamic law) who converted to Catholicism and was ordained a priest, became one of the models of a number of *antialcoranes*, works devoted to confuting the Qur'an. The book became popular well beyond the Iberian Peninsula and in the following decades had seven editions in Italian, French, German, Latin, and English. Andrés reiterated popular beliefs, mistakes, and legends about Islam; as Norman Daniel wrote, "he might easily have written two centuries earlier" (Daniel 1960, 278). However, the use of Arabic sources, the choice of vernacular instead of Latin, and the lively and simple style of the prose allowed the work of Juan Andrés—and other contemporary Spanish authors, such as Bernardo Pérez de Chinchón (ca. 1488–1556)—to circulate beyond the circles of theologians and intellectuals.

Legends about Islam were also shared by serious scholars and Arabists who, although able to give new contributions to the knowledge of Islam, did not avoid polemical approaches. Filippo Guadagnoli (1596–1656), one of the most prominent seventeenth-century Catholic Arabists, used Juan Andrés as a source for his work and described the life of Mohammed according to a traditional stereotype. The English Anglican Orientalist William Bedwell (1563–1632) published in 1615 his *Mohammedis Imposturae* (or *Mohammed Unmasked* in the second edition); a translation of an Arabic dialogue originally printed in Rome in the 1570s, it "contains those objections to the Qur'an which had turned into commonplaces in the late Middle Ages" (Hamilton 1985, 68). The French scholar Guillaume Postel (1510–81), who knew Arabic and had a direct knowledge of the Muslim world, fluctuated between a universalistic approach that minimized differences of belief between Christianity and Islam, and the acceptance of conventional negative views. Postel corrected some of the mistakes of his predecessors and in his *De orbis terrae concordia* (1544) emphasized the qualities of the Turks, who performed a great service for the world in defeating paganism (Bouwsma 1957; Bobzin 1995, 202ff). However, he also repeated some of the traditional anti-Muslim arguments, such as the conviction that Mohammed falsely attributed miracles to himself (Moubarac 1977). In the mid-seventeenth century, Blaise Pascal (1623–62) used the same argument that since Mohammed did not perform real miracles, he had to be considered a false prophet. Pascal was probably inspired by Raimon Martí's *Pugio fidei*, a twelfth-century anti-Muslim and anti-Jewish work published in Paris in 1651 (Hossain 1991, 182–83). On the

Protestant side, we consistently find the same clichés. The Moravian writer John Amos Comenius (1592–1670), for example, reiterated the idea that Islam "was an artificial and purely human construct, a mish-mash of Judaism, Christianity, and some other elements, deliberately put together by Mohammad" whose goal was "to gain worldly kingdoms by trickery" (Malcolm 2007, 487–88).

Catholics and Protestants, relying on the same medieval sources, agreed in identifying Muslims as dangerous enemies. Sometimes they labeled them as pagans or infidels; at other times, they supported the idea that Islam was a false religion and Mohammed a false prophet; more often, they described the "Mohammedan law" as a sect, a heresy of Christianity. Both Catholics and Protestants shared a polemical approach toward Islam; however, they often used the very same arguments to fight against each other.

# 3  Islam in a Divided West: Contrasting Christian Views

Catholics and Protestants shared the fear of the expansion of Islam, which they often interpreted as a punishment of God and the accomplishment of the prophecies of the Book of Revelation. On both sides, there were calls for a united effort against the Turks, but more often the anti-Muslim literature was embedded in the religious polemics of the divided Christendom.

The translation of the Qur'an published by Bibliander was introduced by a *praefatio* written by Martin Luther (1483–1546); while refuting "the pernicious belief of Mohammed," he harshly criticized the Catholic Church, comparing the "idolatrous Mohammedans" to the "Papists" (Francisco 2007). Luther was reluctant to completely transfer the notion of the Antichrist from the pope to the Turks: Muslims were an external enemy, and the Antichrist should have been a sneaky internal adversary; the pope fit better with this description. Melanchthon, however, reinforced the idea of the "double Antichrist," attacking Christianity from the East (the Turks) and from the West (the pope). This image was used as a model for Protestant–Catholic controversies until the end of the seventeenth century: "The Turks were often seen by the Protestants as God's scourge for papal pride, and some expressed a hope that the rival powers of Pope and Sultan would annihilate each other, leaving a power vacuum that might be filled by an expansion of the Protestant Reformation" (Vitkus 1999, 211; Malcolm 2007; Crousaz 2014).

On the other side, Catholics represented Lutherans as "other Turks," using the hottest topics in Catholic–Protestant polemics. For example, in his *Alcorani seu legis Mahometi* (1543), Guillaume Postel listed twenty-eight errors shared by Muslims and Protestants and claimed that the way used by Mohammed in falsifying the Christian doctrine was far more acceptable than the one used by Protestants. In order to strengthen this point, in *De la République des Turcs* (1560) Postel showed that unlike Luther, Mohammed did not abolish the Eucharist; the distortion of Islam in support of the anti-Lutheran polemic is evident and was not unusual at that time (Malvezzi 1956, 243–46).

Two popular books, both written in Latin by English authors, directly addressed the Catholic–Protestant debate. William Rainolds (ca. 1544–94), professor of theology at the English College of Reims and a convert to Catholicism, authored the *Calvino-Turcismus* (published posthumously in 1597, 2nd ed. 1603). Two years later, the strongly anti-Catholic Dean of Exeter, Matthew Sutcliffe (ca. 1550–1629), responded with the publication of *De Turcopapismo* (1599, 2nd ed. 1604), in which he presented a mirror of the same arguments pairing Catholics with Muslims. This rhetoric, with endless variations and nuances, was widespread in early modern Europe (Mout 1978; Mout 1988). The comparison with Islam was also used against anti-Trinitarian religious groups who, according to both Catholic and Protestants, could be compared to Muslims in their denial of the Trinitarian dogma. Socinians were one of the favorite targets of these polemics, according to the common argument that schismatic divisions of Eastern Christian churches were one of the causes of the rise of Islam (Mulsow 2010; Loop 2013).

While using the interpretations of the Qur'an as rhetorical weapons against internal enemies, Catholics and Protestants also emphasized some positive aspects of Islam in order to demonstrate that their Christian adversaries were worse than Muslims. They valued, for instance, Muslims' fidelity to their religious prescriptions, their reverent behavior in mosques, welcoming attitude toward visitors, and constancy in prayer. In Anabaptist and Mennonite circles, pro-Turkish sentiments often arose from the sense of grievance against Christian persecutors, whose intolerant policies were compared to the Turks' more sympathetic attitude (Waite 2010). In an indirect way, Catholic–Protestant debates that involved Islam contributed to spreading a more positive view of some aspects of Muslim habits and beliefs. The same appreciation can be found in the early modern missionary literature.

# 4 Christian Missions and Islam: Between Theory and Experience

Since the thirteenth century, the mendicant orders counted among their tasks the resumption of the apostolate with Muslims; their attempts were occasionally successful in countries subject to Catholic rule, but resulted in an overall failure in Muslim lands. At the same time, while some Dominicans and Franciscans attempted to preach Christianity to the Muslims, other members of their orders preached crusades against them, considering both activities indispensable and complementary (Kedar 1984).

During the early modern period, a new missionary impulse toward Muslims developed among Christians as part of a more general movement of spreading the Gospel in the world. Capuchins, Jesuits, and Discalced Carmelites strengthened their presence in the Middle East and the Friars Minor developed a missionary attitude in the Holy

Land, where they had been present since the thirteenth century. Additionally, members of religious orders were dedicated to the apostolate to Muslims in the West. In Spain, after the forced expulsion of the *moriscos* (1609–14), missionaries worked for the conversion of Muslim slaves and servants; the same happened in Italian port cities, Malta, and Eastern Europe. As a consequence of this enthusiasm, a rich missionary literature such as descriptions of the Holy Land, catechisms for Muslims, and collections of sermons circulated throughout Europe (Colombo 2009; Heyberger 2009).

One of the recurring arguments in those books was the attempt to contrast the idea, common even among Christian authorities, that converting Muslims was an impossible task and it was useless even to try. This approach was supported by the idea that "each one can be saved in one's own law," a claim usually attributed to Islam and confuted in anti-Muslim polemics, but sometimes shared by many Christians who lived amongst Muslims (García-Arenal 2009). It was an expression of a sort of "toleration" not uncommon in early modern Europe and supported by famous works such as the *Colloquium heptaplomeres* (1588), attributed to Jean Bodin (Leaders Kunz 2008; Kaplan 2007; Schwartz 2008).

A feature of missionary literature on Islam was an apparent disconnection between "theory" and "experience": it reiterated arguments of the medieval Latin polemical literature, but was also open to understanding and appreciating some aspects of Muslim culture. In Catholic environments, the missionary literature generally reflected the debates that took place in the theological school of Salamanca during the second half of the sixteenth century on the conversion of the "Indians" and the possible methods of integrating the *moriscos* (Poutrin 2012). The failure of forced conversions, the need for a serious religious education before imparting baptism, and the necessity of using forms of communication understandable by the interlocutors dominated those books. Despite the theological definition of Islam as heresy, Muslims were in fact considered "pagans," "infidels," or "idolaters"; definitions that gave them the benefit of ignorance and suggested using with them the same missionary strategies experimented with other extra-European peoples (Colombo 2014). Some well-known cases include the French Jesuit Michel Nau (1633–83), a missionary for almost twenty years in Syria; and Tirso González de Santalla (1624–1705), who before becoming the thirteenth superior of the Society of Jesus was a missionary in Spain and published a popular *Manuductio ad conversionem Mahumetanorum* (Heyberger 2008; Colombo 2012). These authors made timid attempts to build bridges, trying to understand what was acceptable in Muslim culture and accommodating their approach accordingly. On the mission ground, it was more important to highlight commonalities rather than emphasize differences; for example, while in their religious polemics Catholics condemned the Muslim misinterpretation of the role of the Virgin Mary, in missionary literature the respect granted to Mary by Muslims was considered a possible bridge with Islam. Additionally, missionaries insisted on the importance of the shared belief in monotheism, an approach systematically developed by Christians only in the twentieth century, but already present in Catholic and Protestant literature in the 1600s (Heyberger 2012a; Malcolm 2007).

Seventeenth-century published dialogues between Christians and Muslims provide remarkable examples of this missionary approach. Since the Middle Ages, fictional dialogues were a traditional literary genre used to demonstrate the superiority of Christianity over Islam. In the late seventeenth century, there was a revival of dialogues mainly written by Catholic missionaries and intended for apostolic work, but also aimed at a more general audience not directly connected with proselytism. The theological arguments were based on the same assumptions of the traditional polemical literature. However, the overall attitude of Latin religious appeared more open and benevolent, and the missionaries' experiences that often emerged in the dialogues led to forms of accommodation in human relations (Heyberger 2012a).

The attempts at accommodation often led to misunderstandings and condemnations. In the 1640s, while working in Rome for the Congregation de Propaganda Fide—created in 1622 by Gregory XV—the Arabist Filippo Guadagnoli completed a second version of a polemical treatise in Latin and Arabic against the Qur'an (*Considerationes ad Mahomettanos*, 1649). Guadagnoli was not a missionary: he was a member of the Clerics Regular Minor, a religious order devoted to the study of Oriental languages, and served as the first Italian professor of Arabic and Syrian at Sapienza University in Rome. However, he clearly conceived his *Considerationes* to facilitate the dialogue with and apostolate to Muslims. In the second Arabic version of the book, Guadagnoli highlighted the passages in which the Qur'an did not contradict scripture in a chapter entitled, "The Qur'an does not contradict the Gospel in the passages where it says the truth." In this way, he wanted to promote the circulation of his book in Muslim environments, avoiding its immediate destruction. After a long process of revision of the book, Propaganda Fide stated that it was not acceptable and should be destroyed (Pizzorusso 2010; Trentini 2010). Similar episodes happened frequently; in 1694, when the Venetians occupied the Aegean island of Chios, they found three hundred Muslim women who claimed to be Catholic but still lived according to the Muslim tradition. The Jesuit missionaries on the island were accused of having supported their deception in simultaneously belonging to two religions; an anonymous pamphlet accused the Jesuits of "tolerating" Islam, showing how delicate was the boundary of accommodation and originating a theological debate similar to the ones that developed in the same period in China and Malabar (Colombo 2009).

# 5 Knowing Islam: The Rise of Arabic Studies

In dealing with Islam, it was no easy matter to abandon the controversialist tradition. However, during the seventeenth century, the number of genuine specialists was increasing; instrumental to this approach also were the increasing number of contacts with Eastern Christians, who had lived with Muslims for centuries (Griffith 2008; Girard 2011).

On the Protestant side, the Dutch scholar Joseph Justus Scaliger (1540–1609) should be mentioned, whose main interest was history and chronology. He highlighted the idea that the knowledge of Islam should not be connected to attempts to convert Muslims, and supported a scholarly study of the Qur'an (Hamilton 1985, 83–85; Grafton 1994). Scaliger's work made possible significant contributions by his students, the famous Arabists Thomas van Erpe (1584–1624) and Jacob van Gool, or Golius (1569–1667) (Vrolijk 2011; Van Leeuwen and Vrolijk 2013). Van Erpe worked on a survey on the rise of Islam, which he developed from his reading of the thirteenth-century Coptic historian al-Makîn; his work was refreshingly impartial and shattered some myths about Islam. Published by Golius in 1625, shortly after van Erpe's death, with the title *Historia saracenica*, it was "the first break in the west with the Byzantine tradition of historiography" (Hamilton 2001, 175). Golius also completed an Arabic-Latin dictionary and contributed to the creation of a collection of Oriental manuscripts in Leiden, the largest in the Protestant world. This tradition of research was later pursued by the Swiss philologist and theologian Johan Heinrich Hottinger (1620–67), who had an exceptionally wide knowledge of Arabic sources and published an influential *Historia orientalis* (1651, 2nd ed. 1660). In some respects, Hottinger's approach reflected the religious agendas of his time: through his scholarship on Islam, he wanted to defend the Reformation and attack the Catholic Church, provoking harsh disputes with Catholic scholars (Heyberger 2012b). At the same time, he often displayed impressive insights into different aspects of Islamic religion and culture (Loop 2013). The most prominent Protestant Arabist of the seventeenth century was certainly the Englishman Edward Pococke (1604–91). His work flourished within a long tradition of Arabic studies in early modern England (Feingold 1996; Toomer 1996). Chaplain to the English merchants in Aleppo and supporter of the Anglican church, Pococke was persuaded of the importance of spreading Christianity in the Muslim world; for this purpose, he translated the Anglican catechism into Arabic in 1671. At the same time, he showed a more sympathetic approach to Islam than many of his predecessors in his *Specimen historiae arabum* (1650), a scholarly edition of a thirteenth-century Islamic history written by a Persian Christian scholar (Gregory Bar Hebraeus [1226–86]) for both Muslim and Christian audiences. In his work, Pococke succeeded in his goal of using a large range of Arabic sources for a better, more objective understanding of the history of Islam (Toomer 1996).

During the same period in Catholic Europe, there was an even greater development of Arabic studies with a stronger emphasis on missionary purposes. The need for language proficiency had been officially sanctioned at the Council of Vienne in 1311. Behind the proposal of the council stood the famous Majorcan philosopher Ramon Lull (1232–1315), who "after witnessing the failure of the crusaders to convert Islam with the sword, became convinced that reason would succeed where crusades had not" (Hamilton 1985, 70). Christian works, according to the council, were to be translated into Arabic and missionaries were to master Arabic in order to read and confute Muslim propaganda. However, proposals for the teaching of Arabic at the universities of Bologna, Paris,

Oxford, and Salamanca remained a dead letter, and similar arguments were repeated later; for example, by the Valencian humanist Juan Luis Vives (1492–1540) and the Flemish traveler and humanist Nicolas Clénard (1492–1542).

In seventeenth-century France, the call to the apostolate in the Islamic world was supported by Cardinal Richelieu (1585–1642); and his advisor, the Capuchin Père Joseph (1577–1618), contributed to the development of Arabic studies (Dew 2009). Among the most prominent French scholars, André du Ryer (ca. 1580–1660) authored one of the first published Turkish grammars in the West and the first French translation of the Qur'an (1647). Probably to justify his interest in the Qur'an, du Ryer perpetuated some anti-Islamic polemics and myths, but he also showed "a genuine knowledge of, if not sympathy with, the Qur'an" (Hamilton and Richard 2004, 18).

During the seventeenth century, a group of scholars active in Spain studied Arabic and produced translations, grammars, and dictionaries. Additionally, Arabic erudition in Spain was key for writing Spanish history and reflecting on its Arabic past (Harris 2007; García-Arenal and Mediano 2013).

Rome became an important center for the teaching of Arabic in order to prepare missionaries destined for the Levant. Experiencing the growth of missionary activity, in 1610 Paul V urged the religious orders to create language schools. Jesuits, Carmelites, and Clerics Regular Minor opened schools of Arabic in Rome, although it was not always easy to find students. The Congregation de Propaganda Fide supported courses of theological controversies in Arabic in order to strengthen the basic theological education and linguistic preparation of missionaries (Pizzorusso 2009), and several schools in Rome continued to operate during the eighteenth century (Girard 2010a). One of the major shortcomings was that the missionaries were often trained in classical Arabic, which allowed them to read or write texts but not to have conversations and actual encounters. However, recent scholarship has shown the circulation of handbooks and grammars of "vernacular Arabic"—that is, the spoken language—written by Franciscan missionaries (Girard 2013).

Arabic manuscripts were considered a privileged source of information and as instruments for conversion. Since its foundation, the Vatican Library in Rome preserved a collection of Arabic books that increased and became particularly rich in the sixteenth and seventeenth centuries (Levi della Vida 1939; Proverbio 2010; Girard 2011, 287–313). During the seventeenth century, other important collections were created in Venice, Florence, and Milan. Catholic institutions also created important Arabic printing presses. After a pioneering experiment involving an Arabic press in the Jesuit Roman College (1564), Cardinal Ferdinando de' Medici founded the Medici Oriental Press in Florence (1584); the quality of its Arabic script surpassed all previous attempts in Europe and would remain unparalleled long after the press had closed in 1614 (Tinto 1987; Jones 1994). A few years later, the Polyglot Press of Propaganda Fide in Rome begun to publish grammars, lexicons, dictionaries, translations of the Gospels, and works of confutation of the Qur'an.

The most important publishing achievement of Propaganda Fide was the Arabic translation of the Bible (*Biblia Sacra Arabica*, 1671), conceived as an instrument for

Eastern Christians but also for Muslims. It was a long-term project that started in the 1620s and raised endless doubts and discussions: scholars and theologians supported either fidelity to the Vulgate, or the inevitable flexibility required by Arabic (Girard 2011, 435–54). The translation involved, among others, the prominent Arabists Filippo Guadagnoli and Abraham Ecchellensis.

In his work, Guadagnoli used classic polemical arguments against Islam and presented the standard biography of Mohammed, well known in the Western tradition. Later, as we have seen, he tried to accommodate his arguments to a missionary perspective, an attitude that provoked the censorship of his book but never obscured his celebrity as a scholar. One of the critiques against Guadagnoli's attempt to accommodate Islam came from the Maronite Abraham Ecchellensis (1605–64), probably the most prominent and brilliant representative of a large group of Eastern Arabic-speaking Christians (Copts, Jacobites, and Maronites) who lived in Rome during the seventeenth century and greatly contributed to the growth of Arabic studies. Ecchellensis translated several Christian and Muslim Arabic manuscripts into Latin, and in his scholarship he mixed a rigorous scientific approach in the publication of unknown Arabic sources, and an apologetic approach in defense of the Catholic Church. When he highlighted some positive aspects of Arabic culture, for instance, he immediately separated them from Islam, which could not be seen from a positive perspective (Heyberger 2010b).

The Arabic studies that developed in Europe during the seventeenth century combined a serious philological approach to a confessional commitment—anti-Islamic, anti-Catholic, or anti-Protestant. Interest in the translation of Arabic sources and commitment to the study of the language contributed to a better knowledge of Arabic culture, but the prism through which these sources were interpreted limited a sympathetic approach toward Islam.

# 6  Toward the Eighteenth Century: Ludovico Marracci and George Sale

One of the most important Catholic scholars of Arabic studies in the late seventeenth century was certainly Ludovico Marracci (1612–1700), a member of the Clerics Regular of the Mother of God and professor of Arabic at Sapienza University in Rome. He worked on many projects connected to Oriental studies, such as the Roman edition of the Arabic Bible and the translation, at the request of the Holy Office, of the Lead Books of Sacromonte, a fraudulent collection of lead tables discovered near Granada in 1595 and allegedly bearing a Christian Gospel in Arabic (Barrios Aguilera and García-Arenal 2006). An impressive work by Marracci was his *Prodromus in refutatione Alcorani* (1691), a broad and erudite refutation of the Qur'an later inserted in his *Alcorani textus universus*

(1698), which included also a complete Arabic version of the Qur'an, a scholarly Latin translation, and a description of the life of Mohammed. In his confutation of the Qur'an, Marracci used polemical language not radically different from the medieval anti-Muslim Christian approach. Mohammed was described as a false prophet and Islam showed its falsity in comparison with Christianity (Elmarsafy 2009). At the same time, the harsh confutation did not affect the reliability of the translation of the Qur'an and the quality of the scholarly work in its interpretation. There was a sincere desire to understand Islam without distortions, which Marracci achieved through the use of Arabic sources (Nallino 1940). Marracci's *Alcorani textus universus* was translated into German in 1703, republished in 1721, and considered one of the reference books on the topic in eighteenth-century Europe. Later, it was almost completely forgotten until the twentieth century, when the English Islamologist Edward Denison Ross, and then the Italian Orientalists Giuseppe Gabrieli and Giorgio Levi della Vida, rediscovered his work and praised Marracci's critical approach to the sources (Pedani 2000).

At the beginning of the eighteenth century, the Anglican Orientalist George Sale (1697–1736) had great success with his English translation of the Qur'an. Sale used Pococke and especially Marracci's work, but took a different approach from the latter. Introducing his translation with a "Preliminary Discourse," Sale showed himself more sympathetic toward Islam and Mohammed. While he did not consider Islam at the same level as Christianity, Sale acknowledged the importance of Mohammed as a legislator who brought monotheism to the pagans: Christians could follow Muslims in many aspects of their tradition. The polemical target of Sale was not Islam but Catholics, who were accused, following a well-known stereotype, of misrepresenting Islam.

Marracci and Sale made the Qur'an accessible to European readers, with translations more literal and closer to the Arabic than their predecessors, and incarnated two different and complementary approaches to Islam (Bevilacqua 2013). They both preserved some typical early modern features: Marracci used the classic approach of the confutation, while Sale reiterated Protestant anti-Catholic propaganda. But they also introduced something new: Marracci offered a massive, detailed, and erudite study of the Qur'an and Islamic Arabic sources; while Sale, less learned and less innovative in terms of scholarship, was open to the consideration of Islam as another religion, whose differences with Christianity could raise questions, rather than just supporting a polemical approach. These two aspects—superb scholarship and a less apologetic approach—were combined together only later in the history of Christianity.

# 7 Conclusion

During the late eighteenth century, there were no exceptional developments in Christian theology on Islam. Theoretical approaches were based on the seventeenth-century literature and on Marracci's and Sale's scholarship, and the circulation of missionary literature decreased. The influence of the early modern approach became very important in the following decades and was discussed again in the nineteenth and twentieth centuries.

In his essential study, Norman Daniel wrote that early modern Christian engagement with Islam largely imitated the medieval image; the same position has been echoed by other scholars (Goddard 2000; Wheatcroft 2004; Fletcher 2004). An extensive overview of the early modern period has not yet been written; however, recent studies have shown that early modern engagements with Islam were not univocal, but gave rise to important changes from the past. The divisions within Christianity introduced the use of Islam as a pretext for the fight among Catholics, Protestants, and other Christian groups. At the same time, the development of extra-European missions supported attempts to find a common ground between Christianity and Islam. Finally, the growth of Arabic and Islamic studies and the invention of the printing press facilitated the circulation of more precise information and substantial progress in the knowledge of Islam in Europe. Without completely detaching from the Christian medieval tradition, these new approaches, which culminated in the works by Marracci and Sale, opened the door to the possibility for a reconsideration of Islam, a process that was actually accomplished in Western theologies only during the twentieth century.

## Note

1. I am grateful to Aurélien Girard and Davide Scotto for their valuable suggestions.

## Bibliography

Armour, Rollin. 2002. *Christianity and the West: A Troubled History*. Maryknoll, NY: Orbis Books.

Balagna Coustou, Josée. 1984. *L'imprimerie arabe en Occident (XVI^e, XVII^e, XVIII^e siècles)*. Paris: Maisonneuve et Larose.

Barrios Aguilera, Manuel, and García-Arenal, Mercedes. 2006. *Los plomos del Sacromonte. Invención y Tesoro*. Valencia: Universitat de València.

Bennassar, Bartolomé, and Sauzet Robert, eds. 1998. *Chrétiens et musulmans à la Renaissance. Actes du 37^e colloque international du CESR (1994)*. Paris: Honoré Champion.

Bevilacqua, Alexander. 2013. "The Qur'an Translations of Marracci and Sale." *Journal of the Warburg and Courtauld Institutes* 76: 93–130.

Birchwood, Matthew. 2007. *Staging Islam in England: Drama and Culture 1640–1685*. Woodbridge, UK: D. S. Brewer.

Bobzin, Hartmut. 1995. *Der Koran im Zeitalter der Reformation: Studien zur Frühgeschichte der Arabistik und Islamkunde in Europa*. Berlin: Orient-Institut der Deutschen Morgenländischen Gesellschaft.

Bobzin, Hartmut. 1996. "'A Treasury of Heresies': Christian Polemics Against the Koran." In *The Qur'an as Text*, edited by S. Wild, 157–175. Leiden: Brill.

Bouwsma, William J. 1957. *Concordia Mundi: The Career and Thought of Guillaume Postel (1510–1581)*. Cambridge, MA: Harvard University Press.

Bunes Ibarra, Miguel Ángel. 1989. *El enfrentamiento con el Islam en el Siglo de Oro: Los antial-coranes*. Madrid: CSIC.

Burman, Thomas. 2007. *Reading the Qur'ān in Latin Christendom, 1140–1560*. Philadelphia: University of Pennsylvania Press.

Christ-von Wedel, Christine. 2005. *Theodor Bibliander (1505–1564): Ein Thurgauer im Gelehrten Zürich der Reformationszeit*. Zürich: Verlag Neue Zürcher Zeitung.

Colding Smith, Charlotte. 2014. *Images of Islam, 1453–1600. Turks in Germany and Central Europe*. London: Pickering & Chatto.

Colombo, Emmanuele. 2012. "Even among Turks: Tirso González de Santalla (1624–1705) and Islam." *Studies on Jesuit Spirituality* 44: 1–41.

Colombo, Emmanuele. 2014. "'Infidels' at Home: Jesuits and Muslim Slaves in Seventeenth-Century Naples and Spain." *Journal of Jesuit Studies* 1: 192–211.

Colombo, Emmanuele. 2009. "Jesuits and Islam in Seventeenth-Century Europe: War, Preaching and Conversions." In *L'islam visto da occidente: Cultura e religione del Seicento europeo di fronte all'Islam*, edited by B. Heyberger, M. García-Arenal, E. Colombo, and P. Vismara, 315–340. Milan: Marietti.

Crousaz, Karine. 2014. "Pierre Viret et l'Islam." In *Pierre Viret et la diffusion de la réforme: pensée, action, contextes religieux*, edited by K. Crousaz and D. Solfaroli Camillocci. Lausanne: Antipodes.

D'Errico, Gian Luca, ed. 2015. *Il Corano e il pontefice. Ludovico Marracci fra cultura islamica e Curia papale*. Rome: Carocci.

Daniel, Norman. 1960. *Islam and the West: The Making of an Image*. Edinburgh: Edinburgh University Press.

Dew, Nicholas. 2009. *Orientalism in Louis XVI's France*. Oxford: Oxford University Press.

Dimmock, Matthew. 2005. *New Turkes: Dramatizing Islam and the Ottomans in Early Modern England*. Aldershot, UK: Ashgate.

Dupront, Alphonse. 1997. *Le mythe de croisade*. Paris: Gallimard.

Echevarria, Ana. 1999. *The Fortress of Faith: The Attitude towards Muslims in Fifteenth-Century Spain*. Leiden: Brill.

Elmarsafy, Ziad. 2009. *The Enlightenment Qur'an: The Politics of Translation and the Construction of Islam*. Oxford: Oneworld.

Feingold, Mordechai. 1996. "Decline and Fall: Arabic Science in Seventeenth-Century England." In *Tradition, Transmission, Transformation: Proceedings of Two Conferences on Pre-Modern Science Held at the University of Oklahoma*, edited by F. Jamil Ragep and Sally P. Ragep, 441–469. Leiden: Brill.

Felici, Lucia. 2007. "L'Islam in Europa: L'edizione del Corano di Theodor Bibliander (1543)." *Cromohs* 12: 1–13.

Fletcher, Richard. 2004. *The Cross and the Crescent: Christianity and Islam from Muhammad to the Reformation*. New York: Viking.

Francisco, Adam. 2007. *Martin Luther and Islam: A Study in Sixteenth-Century Polemics and Apologetics*. Leiden: Brill.

Freidenreich, David. 2011. "Muslims in Western Canon Law, 1000–1500." In *Christian-Muslim Relations: A Bibliographical History*. Vol. 3 (1050–1200), edited by D. Thomas and A. Mallett, 41–68. Leiden: Brill.

Freidenreich, David. 2012. "Muslims in Eastern Canon Law, 1000–1500." In *Christian–Muslim Relations: A Bibliographical History*. Vol. 4 (1200–1350), edited by D. Thomas and A. Mallett, 45–57. Leiden: Brill.

García-Arenal, Mercedes. 2009. "Religious Dissent and Minorities: The Morisco Age." *The Journal of Modern History* 81: 888–920.

García-Arenal, Mercedes and Rodriguez Mediano, Fernando. 2013. *The Orient in Spain: Converted Muslims, the Forged Lead Books of Granada, and the Rise of Orientalism*. Leiden: Brill.

Girard, Aurélien. 2011. *Le christianisme oriental (XVII^e–XVIII^e siècles): Essor de l'orientalisme catholique en Europe et construction des identités confessionnelles au Proche–Orient*. Thèse dirigée par: M. Bernard Heyberger. Paris: École Pratique des Hautes Études.

Girard, Aurélien. 2010a. "L'enseignement de l'arabe à Rome au XVIII^e siècle." In *Maghreb–Italie: des passeurs médiévaux à l'orientalisme moderne (XIII^e–milieu XX^e siècle)*, edited by B. Grevin, 209–234. Rome: École française de Rome.

Girard, Aurélien. 2010b. "Des manuels de langue entre mission et érudition orientaliste au XVII^e siècle: les grammaires de l'arabe des caracciolini." *Studi medievali e moderni* 14: 279–296.

Girard, Aurélien. 2013. "Les manuels d'arabe en usage en France à la fin de l'Ancien Régime." In *Manuels d'arabe d'hier et d'aujourd'hui (France–Maghreb, XIX^e–XXI^e siècle)*, edited by S. Larzul and A. Messaoudi, 12–26. Paris: Bibliothèque nationale de France.

Goddard, Hugh. 2000. *A History of Christian–Muslim Relations*. Chicago: New Amsterdam Books.

Grafton, Anthony. 1994. *Joseph Scaliger. A Study in the History of Classical Scholarship*. Oxford: Oxford University Press.

Griffith, Sidney H. 2008. *The Church in the Shadow of the Mosque: Christians and Muslims in the World of Islam*. Princeton, NJ: Princeton University Press.

Hamilton, Alastair. 2001. "The Study of Islam in Early Modern Europe." *Archiv für Religionsgeschichte* 3: 169–182.

Hamilton, Alastair. 1985. *William Bedwell the Arabist*. Leiden: Brill-Leiden University Press.

Hamilton, Alastair, and Francis Richard. 2004. *André du Ryer and Oriental Studies in Seventeenth-Century France*. London: Oxford University Press.

Harper, James, ed. 2011. *The Turk and Islam in the Western Eye, 1450–1750: Visual Imagery before Orientalism*. Farnham: Ashgate.

Harris, Katie. A. 2007. *From Muslim to Christian Granada. Inventing a City's Past in Early Modern Spain*. Baltimore: The Johns Hopkins University Press.

Heyberger, Bernard. 2009. "L'islam dei missionari cattolici (Medio Oriente, Seicento)." In *L'islam visto da occidente: Cultura e religione del Seicento europeo di fronte all'Islam*, edited by B. Heyberger, M. García-Arenal, E. Colombo, and P. Vismara, 289–314. Milan: Marietti.

Heyberger, Bernard. 2008. "Nau, Michel." In *Dictionnaire des orientalistes de langue française*, edited by F. Poullion, 717–718. Paris: Karthala.

Heyberger, Bernard. 2010a. "L'islam et les Arabes chez un érudit maronite au service de l'Église catholique (Abraham Ecchellensis)." *Al-Qantara* 31: 481–512.

Heyberger, Bernard, ed. 2010b. *Orientalisme, science et controverse: Abraham Ecchellensis (1605–1664)*. Turnhout: Brepols.

Heyberger, Bernard. 2012a. "Polemic Dialogues between Christians and Muslims in the Seventeenth Century." *Journal of the Economic and Social History of the Orient* 55: 495–516.

Heyberger, Bernard. 2012b. "L'islam dans la controverse entre catholiques et protestants: la *De origine nomini papae* d'Abraham Ecchellensis (1661) réponse à l'*Historia Orientalis* de Johan Heinrich Hottinger (1651 et 1660)." In *Énoncer/Dénoncer l'autre: discours et représentations du différend confessionnel à l'époque moderne*, edited by C. Berant and H. Bost, 389–400. Turnhout: Brepols.

Hossain, Mary. 1991. "Pascal and Islam," *Journal of Islamic Studies* 2: 180–194.

Housley, Norman. 2012. *Crusading and the Ottoman Threat, 1453–1505*. Oxford: Oxford University Press.

Jones, Robert. 1994. "The Medici Oriental Press (Rome 1584–1614) and the Impact of Its Arabic Publications on Northern Europe." In *The "Arabick" Interest of the Natural Philosophers in Seventeenth-Century England*, edited by G. A. Russell, 88–108. Leiden: Brill.

Kaplan, Benjamin. 2007. *Divided by Faith: Religious Conflict and the Practice of Toleration in Early Modern Europe*. Cambridge, MA: Harvard University Press.

Ķedar, Benjamin Z. 1984. *Crusade and Mission: European Approaches toward the Muslims*. Princeton, NJ: Princeton University Press.

König, Daniel G. 2012. "Medieval Western European Perceptions of the Islamic World: From 'Active Othering' to the 'Voices in Between.'" In *Christian–Muslim Relations. A Bibliographical History*. Vol. 4 (1200–1350), edited by D. Thomas and A. Mallett, 17–28. Leiden: Brill.

Lamarque, Henri, ed. 2007. *Le Coran à la Renaissance. Plaidoyer pour une traduction*. Toulouse: Presses universitaires du Mirail.

Leaders Kunz, Marion. 2008. "The Concept of Toleration in the *Colloquium Heptaplomeres* of Jean Bodin." In *Beyond the Persecuting Society: Religious Toleration before the Enlightenment*, edited by J. Ch. Laursen and C. J. Nederman, 125–144. Philadelphia: University of Pennsylvania Press.

Levi della Vida, Giorgio. 1939. *Ricerche sulla formazione del più antico fondo die manoscritti orientali della Biblioteca Vaticana*. Città del Vaticano: Biblioteca Apostolica Vaticana.

Loop, Jan. 2008. "Johann Heinrich Hottinger (1620–1667) and the 'Historia Orientalis.'" *Church History and Religious Culture* 88: 169–203.

Loop, Jan. 2013. *Johan Heinrich Hottinger: Arabic and Islamic Studies in the Seventeenth Century*. Oxford: Oxford University Press.

MacLean, Gerald. 2007. *Looking East: English Writing and the Ottoman Empire before 1800*. Basingstoke, UK: Palgrave Macmillan.

Malcolm, Noel. 2007. "Comenius, the Conversion of the Turks, and the Muslim–Christian Debate on the Corruption of Scripture." *Church History and Religious Culture* 87: 477–508.

Malvezzi, Aldobrandino. 1956. *L'Islamismo e la cultura europea*. Firenze: Sansoni.

Meserve, Margaret. 2008. *Empires of Islam in Renaissance Historical Thought*. Cambridge, MA: Harvard University Press.

Miller, Gregory. 2013. "Theodor Bibliander's *Machumetis saracenorum principis eiusque successorum vitae, doctrina ac ipse Alcoran (1543)* as the Sixteenth-Century 'Encyclopedia' of Islam." *Islam and Christian–Muslim Relations* 24: 241–254.

Moser, Christian. 2009. *Theodor Bibliander, annotierte Bibliographie der gedruckten Werke*. Zurich: Theologischer Verlag Zürich.

Moubarac, Youakim. 1977. *Recherches sur la pensée chrétienne et l'Islam dans les temps modernes et à l'époque contemporaine*. Beirut: Université libanaise.

Mout, Nicolette. 1978. "Calvinoturcisme in de zeventiende eeuw: Comenius, Leidse oriëntalisten en de Turkse bijbel." *Tijdschrift voor Geschiedenis* 91: 576–607.

Mout, Nicolette. 1988. "Calvinoturcismus und Chiliasmus im 17. Jahrhundert." *Pietismus und Neuzeit* 14: 72–84.

Mulsow, Martin. 2010. "Socinianism, Islam and the Radical Uses of Arabic Scholarship." *Al-Qantara: Revista de Estudios Árabes* 31: 549–586.

Nallino, Carlo Alfonso. 1940. "Le fonti arabe manoscritte dell'opera di Ludovico Marracci sul Corano." In *Raccolta di scritti editi ed inediti*. Vol. 2, edited by C. A. Nallino, 90–134. Rome: Istituto per l'Oriente.

Pedani, Maria Pia. 2004. "Ludovico Marracci e la conoscenza dell'Islam in Italia." *Campus Maior: Rivista di Studi Camaioresi* 6–23.

Pedani, Maria Pia. 2000. "Ludovico Marracci: la vita e l'opera." In *Il Corano: Traduzioni, traduttori, e lettori in Italia*, edited by G. Zatti, 9–30. Milan: IPL.

Pizzorusso, Giovanni. 2010. "Filippo Guadagnoli, i caracciolini e lo studio delle lingue orientali e della controversia con l'Islam nel XVII secolo." *Studi Medievali e Moderni* 27: 245–278.

Pizzorusso, Giovanni. 2009. "La preparazione linguistica e controversistica dei missionari per l'Oriente islamico: scuole, testi e insegnanti a Roma e in Italia." In *L'islam visto da occidente: Cultura e religione del Seicento europeo di fronte all'Islam*, edited by B. Heyberger, M. García-Arenal, E. Colombo, and P. Vismara, 253–288. Milan: Marietti.

Poumarède, Géraud. 2004. *Pour en finir avec la croisade: Mythes et réalités de la lutte contre les Turcs aux XVIᵉ et XVIIᵉ siècles*. Paris: Presses universitaires de France.

Poutrin, Isabelle. 2012. *Convertir les musulmans: Espagne 1491–1609*. Paris: Presses universitaires de France.

Proverbio, Delio V. 2010. "Alle origini delle collezioni librarie orientali." In *Le origini della Biblioteca Vaticana tra Umanesimo e Rinascimento (1447–1534)*, edited by A. Manfredi, 467–485. Vatican City: Biblioteca Apostolica Vaticana.

Quinn, Frederick. 2008. *The Sum of All Heresies. The Image of Islam in Western Thought*. Oxford: Oxford University Press.

Saïd, Edward. 1978. *Orientalism*. New York: Routledge.

Schwartz, Stuart. 2008. *All Can Be Saved: Religious Tolerance and Salvation in the Iberian Atlantic World*. New Haven, CT: Yale University Press.

Scotto, Davide. 2011. "Cultura latina e Islam tra 'esperienza' e 'proiezione'. A proposito di un libro recente." *Rivista di Storia e Letteratura Religiosa* 47: 173–190.

Secret, Francois. 1998. *Postel revisité: nouvelles recherches sur Guillaume Postel et son milieu*. Paris: S.E.H.A.

Segesvary, Victor. 1973. *L'Islam et la Réforme: étude sur l'attitude des réformateurs zurichois envers l'Islam (1510–1550)*. Lausanne: Editions L'Age d'Homme.

Smith, Charlotte Colding. 2014. *Images of Islam 1453–1600: Turks in Germany and Central Europe*. London: Pickering & Chatto.

Southern, Richard. 1962. *Western Views of Islam in the Middle Ages*. Cambridge, MA: Harvard University Press.

Stantchev, Stefan K. 2014. "'Apply to Muslims What Was Said of the Jews': Popes and Canonists Between a Taxonomy of Otherness and Infidelitas." *Law and History Review* 32 (1): 65–96.

Teule, Herman G. B. 2012. "Christian–Muslim Religious Interaction 1200–1350. A Historical and Contextual Introduction." In *Christian–Muslim Relations. A Bibliographical History*. Vol. 4 (1200–1350), edited by D. Thomas and A. Mallett, 1–16. Leiden: Brill.

Tinto, Alberto. 1987. *La tipografia medicea orientale*. Lucca: Fazzi.

Tolan, John. 2002. *Saracens: Islam in the Medieval European Imagination*. New York: Columbia University Press.

Tommasino, Pier Mattia. 2013. *L'Alcorano di Macometto. Storia di un libro del Cinquecento europeo*. Bologna: Il Mulino.

Toomer, Gerald. 1996. *Eastern Wisdom and Learning: The Study of Arabic in Seventeenth-Century England*. Oxford: Oxford University Press.

Trentini, Andrea. 2010. "Il caracciolino Filippo Guadagnoli controversista e islamologo. Un'analisi dei suoi scritti apologetici contro l'islam." *Studi Medievali e Moderni* 27: 297–314.

Van Leeuwen, Richard, and Arnoud Vrolijk. 2013. *Arabic Studies in the Netherlands: A Short History in Portraits, 1580–1950.* Leiden: Brill.

Vitkus, Daniel. 1999. "Early Modern Orientalism: Representation of Islam in 16th and 17th Century Europe." In *Western Views of Islam in Medieval and Early Modern Europe: Perception of Other,* edited by D. Blanks and M. Frassetto, 207–230. New York: St. Martin's Press.

Vitkus, Daniel. 2003. *Turning Turk: English Theater and the Multicultural Mediterranean, 1570–1630.* New York: Palgrave Macmillan.

Vrolijk, Arnoud. 2011. "The Prince of Arabists and His Many Errors: Thomas Erpenius's Image of Joseph Scaliger and the Edition of the Proverbia Arabica (1614)." *Journal of the Warburg and Courtauld Institutes* 73: 297–325.

Waite, Gary. 2010. "Menno and Muhammad: Anabaptists and Mennonites Reconsider Islam, 1525–1657." *The Sixteenth Century Journal* 41 (4): 995–1016.

Wheatcroft, Andrew. 2004. *Infidels: A History of the Conflict between Christendom and Islam.* New York: Random House.

## CHAPTER 32

···········································································································

# THE CHURCHES OF
# THE EAST AND THE
# ENLIGHTENMENT

···········································································································

## DIMITRIOS MOSCHOS

## 1 DEFINING THE PROBLEM

···········································································································

THE evaluation by church historians of the encounter of the churches of the East with modern thinking after the fifteenth century was described in a concise manner in the diverse statements of Chrysostomos Papadopoulos (1868–1938) and Georges Florovsky (1893–1979) at the Congress of the Orthodox Theological Faculties in Athens in 1936. Papadopoulos saw the church as miraculously untouched by the temptations of secularized Western Christianity and Islamization. Florovsky, on the contrary, was more critical, citing the alienation of theological method from the life of the Eastern church in the past. The former, as elaborated by the West mainly through scholasticism, failed to reflect the latter, which remained unaffected by Western influence (a problem he described as "pseudomorphosis") (Alivisatos 1939, 206, 231). This critical attitude toward the West and the Enlightenment was adopted also by some modern Greek theologians (e.g., Yannaras 2006). Historians of the early modern Greek Enlightenment dissented from this approach and against the reactionary voices within the Orthodox Church, explaining this tendency as a defense of the authority of the church and its position in the power structure of the Ottoman Empire.

This overall picture of a church enduring the intrusion of Western thought into the East (either victoriously or in a decadent course of alienation) reveals the importance that the feature of "purity" has played in the Eastern church, which rejects Western interpolation offering the possibility of "rediscovering" genuine Christianity, but also charges the West with the obligation of due repentance towards its victim. Wendebourg (1997), and earlier Podskalsky (1981) in his exhaustive study of the theological production of Greek post-Byzantine theology, both heavily criticized these attitudes. Instead, some have argued that it is more productive to understand the relations between the Eastern church and the predominant West via a "postcolonial" approach (Demacopoulos and Papanikolaou 2013).

In reality, the churches of the East interacted inevitably and constantly with their cultural environment, revealing a remarkable creativity. Therefore, it is misleading to locate the identity of the Eastern church in passivity. Instead, active interaction enabled Orthodox theologians to reassess the church's own relation with modernity and to enter into the discussion of a rearrangement with the modern secular world in the twentieth century. We first depict the complexity of the relations between East and West in transfer mechanisms, cultural products, and sociology of knowledge. Second, we examine the evolution of intellectual trends.

# 2 "Without a Kingdom": Mapping the Landscape of Intellectual Centers in the Post-Byzantine East

The late Byzantine world of the thirteenth to fifteenth centuries ambivalently regarded the West either as a threatening enemy or as a cultural transmitter, as the Byzantines themselves experienced a flow of mathematical and astronomical knowledge from India and Persia. Cities like Constantinople, Thessaloniki, and Nicaea developed an intellectual activity that predated the philosophical achievements of the Italian Renaissance; notably the use of Plato in order to create a philosophical paradigm that could support the quantitative approach to the physical world through mathematics (Moschos 1992). On the other hand, after the beginning of the fourteenth century, important works of Western theologians, such as Augustine (354–430) and Thomas Aquinas (1225–74), were translated from Latin into Greek, and those translations promoted intellectual encounter with Western thought (Plested 2012, 63–136).

In the fifty years of the late Byzantine empire's agony that ended in 1453, the catastrophe foreseen among educated Greeks drove many into a massive flight to the West, marking a long and devastating "brain drain" that was noted by those theologians who chose to stay, including Georgios Scholarios (1405–72), who became the first patriarch after 1453 under the name Gennadios II. After the fall of Constantinople, manuscripts and artworks, if not destroyed, followed the Greeks who had fled into the West. This heavy loss and the radical discontinuity with late Byzantium is key to understanding the long process of the Byzantine encounter with the West. An emerging Orthodox Christian self-consciousness was shaped through its long defense against Islam, and gradually by the rise of secular thought in the West. Yet the fact that Western theologians and philosophers used basic elements of Byzantine culture and the Eastern church in order to investigate the West's own sense of its identity reveals the continued interactive relations between East and West.

Greek thinkers harbored no illusions about the consequences of 1453: "You have the kingship, therefore you have wisdom. The former needs the latter like body the soul . . . We have lost the kingship and so we are deprived of wisdom" wrote Theodosius Zygomalas (1544–1607) to Martinus Crusius (1526–1607) (Crusius 1584, 437; Podskalsky 1981, 47). This conclusion, which depicted the decline of culture and its political pre-requisites in the East, meant that the Greek East saw itself amid a complex network of mutually interacting centers of peripheral political power, but without their his-toric visible figure of a Greco-Roman Christian emperor. These lesser interacting centers created and/or promoted literary production and education, which in turn shaped the broader picture of the encounter with Western thinking, and especially the Enlightenment. Among the various centers, however, a basic difference prevailed between the Ottoman-occupied versus the Venetian-dominated Greek East. In the Ottoman territories, a renewed administrative and spiritual center in the person of the Patriarch of Constantinople extended to lesser centers of spiritual guidance—most famously, the monastic community of Mount Athos. Venice, on the other hand, adopted a very specific policy with regard to its Greek subjects (in the Aegean Sea, Crete, and the Ionian Islands), forbidding the presence of Orthodox bishops but allowing a limited ecclesiastical organization. Above all, the Venetians enabled positive contact with the intellectual and artistic currents of the Italian Renaissance and tolerated a flourishing Greek community within the bounds of its own capital. Outside the radius of the eastern Mediterranean, other centers played similar roles; especially in the politics that emerged from the papal see, as well as those of the princes of later Romania and Moscow. The last two tried hard in the following centuries to restore a "Byzance après Byzance," especially after 1589, when the metropolitan see of Moscow obtained belated recognition of its self-proclaimed elevation to a patriarchate independent from Constantinople. Another important part of the Orthodox Slavic world encountered the West within the borders of the Polish-Lithuanian Commonwealth (Roudometof 2013, 59–78).

At a lower, interregional level, numerous communities of Greeks in Ottoman and Venetian territories and European cities acquired financial independence, which they turned to political influence. Between the second half of the seventeenth century to roughly 1750, the Greeks took into their hands a great part of the trade of the Ottoman Empire with the West. These thriving communities inside and outside the Ottoman Empire competed with each other in founding and supporting schools, paying for churches and their priests, and printing books. In Constantinople, influential Greeks paid the huge debts of the patriarchate and became increasingly involved in church politics. After 1669, they took over important positions within the Ottoman imperial institutions. Many members of this influential group resided near the patriarchate in the quarter called Phanar ("Lantern," Turkish *Fener*), and therefore became known as Phanariots (Runciman 2003, 360–84). Communities of Orthodox Ruthenians and Ukrainians played a similar role within the Polish-Lithuanian Commonwealth. This network of power centers, whose leaders attempted to impose their aims upon and rein-force their positions against rivals, explains the complex landscape of competing cen-ters of intellectual activity and education. Efforts to found printing houses, the growing number of printed books in Greek that actually emerged in Venice and later in Austria and Germany, the establishment of a patriarchal academy, the competition between the church and the rich Greek merchants to found lower or higher schools—all were signs reflecting the change in Eastern Christian society, which (despite the attempts of the Russian czars) had to find and reassert its own identity without the existence of an Orthodox emperor. It is against this background that one should place the story of the Orthodox encounter with the West and the Enlightenment.

## 3 EARLY MODERN THINKING IN THE EAST AS A BYPRODUCT OF EUROPEAN RELIGIOUS WARS

### 3.1 Toward institutional changes

The churches of the East were never completely cut off from the broader trends in European intellectual movements. Nevertheless, ecclesial relations with the West became much more difficult and complicated after the last decades of the sixteenth century, as the struggle between the Roman Catholic Church and the Protestant Reformation reached the East. Rome had tried to extend its spiritual dominion over the East with a series of measures that included the foundation of the College of St. Athanasius in Rome for Greek students (1571), and the intense missionary activity of Jesuits in the Ottoman Empire and Polish-Lithuanian Commonwealth. Attempts to realize a union based on the decree of the Council of Ferrara-Florence of 1438–39, which failed to gain acceptance among the Orthodox after the imperial delegation returned to Constantinople, nonetheless resulted in the 1596 Council of Brest, where many Orthodox bishops agreed to accept papal primacy and doctrine but were allowed the continued use of Byzantine liturgical rites. Among Protestants, a small group of German theologians from Tübingen sent a Greek translation of the Augsburg Confession to Constantinople and began a correspondence with Patriarch Jeremiah I (1536–95), in an attempt to gain the Eastern church's approval of Lutheran doctrines and practices. This correspondence of 1574 to 1581 did not produce a spectacular outcome (Wendebourg 1986), but forced the Eastern church to refurbish the quality of its own theological argumentation. This attention to theological argument produced visible results in the next century, with the series of learned churchmen who came from Venetian-occupied Crete. The most important of these was Cyril Loukaris (1572–1638), who experienced the events of union in Poland. When elected Patriarch of Constantinople in 1620, he tried to reform the Greek Eastern church, inviting in 1624 his fellow student in Padua, Theophilos Corydaleus (ca. 1570–1646), a disciple of Cesare Cremonini (1550–1631), to teach in the patriarchal school in the capital and in 1627 to found a printing house in the city.

Similarly, in the Slavic-speaking Eastern church, the activity of Jesuits and the glamor of their scholastic method motivated the brilliant bishop of Romanian origin, Peter Mohyla (1596–1646), to create in Kiev an academy of higher education in 1631, which included the achievements of scholasticism in its curriculum and Latin as the language of instruction in order to systematize, further, and support the teaching of Orthodox theology (Hauptmann 1981). The impact on the Orthodox Church of the early modern Enlightenment in the eighteenth century under Catherine the Great and Metropolitan Platon cannot be appreciated apart from these earlier seventeenth-century developments (Wirtschafter 2013).

## 3.2  The quest for a method

These institutional and cultural developments in the Eastern church, caused by the confessional divisions in the West and their rivalry for the East's approval, had their parallels in theological method. Naturally, the disruption of the late Byzantine period prohibited the Eastern church from conceiving and elaborating intellectual challenges it now faced, as it had once done during the Byzantine Empire's periods of strength. The most obvious symptom of the disruption took the form of the abandonment of the centuries-long tradition of Platonic or neo-Platonic study (Anghelou 1985), which especially in the fourteenth century had supported the turn to the mathematical sciences. The response of Patriarch Jeremias to the agenda of the Tübingen Lutherans consisted of a quotation of passages from the church fathers and council decisions about the issues of justification, or veneration of the saints, but offered no reflection on the actual contemporary discussion of such issues by Orthodox theologians (Wendebourg 1997). It seemed at that time that the most advanced method of theological argumentation was the scholastic approach cultivated at the College of St. Athanasius in Rome. Numerous Greek students studied there, despite the visible danger of conversion to Roman Catholicism (Tsirpanlis 1980). The only real alternative for those intent upon remaining current with discussions about knowledge and science was the study of Aristotle in Venetian Padua, which had the advantage of being beyond suspicion as a source of papal propaganda. As a result, a succession of intellectuals and theologians emerged there, who (mainly through Corydaleus) pursued a totally secular study of Aristotelian teachings about nature and knowledge derived from the teacher of Corydaleus, Cesare Cremonini. This approach was not consonant with a traditional Orthodox understanding of Aristotle, but it was up to date and regarded by some, at least, as somehow neutral for theology (Tsourkas 1967; Kitromilides 2013, 28–29). Therefore, although the Aristotelian Theophilos Corydaleus was initially criticized as too modern and liberal by Orthodox theologians, in the next decades his method became sacrosanct, to such an extent that those like Anthrakitis (1660–1736) who rejected it fell under condemnation. Corydaleus's commentaries were copied and used as the main teaching material, while another important philosopher who tried to combine Aristotle with church teachings in a more traditional fashion, Nicolaos Kursulas (1602–52), was simply ignored (Podskalsky 1981, 242–44).

The quest for a proper method of knowledge resulted in a deeply unbalanced approach to theological controversies. The protector of Corydaleus, Patriarch Cyril I Loukaris, pursued the goal of effective defense by the new European Protestant powers—Holland, and to a lesser extent England (Hering 1968). Not only from political calculation, but also from his sincere belief in an innovative turn to the genuine tradition of the ancient church, Loukaris wrote a confession which is at its core a Calvinist version of Eastern Orthodox dogma. The unprecedented example of a Calvinist Orthodoxy reflected a premature encounter with an updated European discussion about salvation, ethics, ecclesiology, the sacraments, and veneration of the saints and prayers for the deceased. This text was condemned immediately after Loukaris's tragic death (executed by the Ottomans after Roman Catholic political intrigues) in 1638. Yet his views inaugurated a period of intense discussion within Orthodox circles about the articulation of faith statements, or the proper and improper use of Aristotelian categories in theological questions. Corydaleus's pupil, the scholar and Phanariot Ioannis Karyofyllis (1600–93), for example, rejected the doctrine of transubstantiation, regarding it as a scholastic intrusion into the mystery of the Eucharist in the church. The dispute about transubstantiation, however, was at base a methodological one about the possible use of Aristotle in doing Orthodox theology (Tzirakis 1977). Opponents of transubstantiation, such as Karyofyllis, were accused unjustly of being crypto-Protestants, while supporters of the term were characterized as pro-Romans.

After the condemnation of Loukaris's confession, his admirers turned to a more modest formulation of the Orthodox teaching, using scholasticism in a more measured fashion. Peter Mohyla wrote a confession that used the scholastic *disputationes* and was framed by a classic set of questions and answers. His confession was sanctioned at the Council of Iasi in 1672 and remained a standard text for the exposition of the core faith of the Eastern church as a "middle course" between Catholicism and Protestantism. The work belongs, therefore, to the genre of basic confessional texts of the Reformation and Roman churches.

## 4 Theological Issues and the Eclectic Use of Enlightenment in the East in the Eighteenth Century

During the last decades of the seventeenth century, significant changes took place in the East. In 1669 Crete fell under the Ottomans and a base of a mixed Greco-Venetian culture was lost. The advance of the Habsburgs was marked by the treaty of Karlowitz in 1699, which brought Balkan Orthodox populations under Austrian rule and forced the sultan to pay attention to his Christian subjects. The dexterous Phanariot Greeks, who served as negotiators for the Ottomans, were rewarded with promotion to high positions, such as minister of foreign affairs or heads of the Romanian principalities.

Numerous rich Greeks settled in Vienna and other cities of Central Europe, as well as in France. Many of these influential figures financed schools in their new homes in addition to their Ottoman-occupied hometowns. In Moldavian and Walachian principalities, Phanariot dynasties such as the Mavrokordatos family (Henderson 1970, 20–27) acted as patrons of culture and promoters of Greek educational institutions, which in their turn served as transmitters of European cultural trends in the East (Camariano-Cioran, 1974). In Russia, the new Czar Peter I introduced a series of reforms immediately after his enthronement in 1689. This late seventeenth-century development provided the setting for a more powerful intrusion of Western European intellectual currents, and especially various forms of the European Enlightenment. The impact of the Enlightenment in the East is usually studied under the criterion of its contribution to philosophy (Kondylis 1988), or its influence on political activity and education (Kitromilides 2013). Its impact on theology, however, must extend beyond the assessment of disputed doctrinal questions with Western Christendom. Instead, we will try to explore the influence of the Enlightenment upon the way in which theological thought and the actual operation of Church life developed in the new landscape by examining three areas.

# 5  Human Knowledge and Knowledge of God

## 5.1  Toward an Eastern Orthodox Enlightenment

The most prominent feature of the movement of Enlightenment (i.e., the emergence of reason over established traditions, prejudices, and ignorance) raised inevitably the question of whether this "dare to know" (*sapere aude*) was compatible with or even necessary for the knowledge of God, or access to the way in which he allows himself to be known—that is, revelation. The old question about the relation between faith and reason had re-ignited within the Western church; notoriously in the dispute between the Jansenists and the Jesuits, debates over fideism and reason, and in the disputes about the critical approach to the textual sources of the Christian faith, from scripture to the writings of theologians. In the East, in sharp contrast, one notes a different mode of expressing these questions, even though the process turned out to be an analogous one.

The use of secular learning in the form of a classical cultural heritage within the Orthodox Church already had emerged as a primary issue of contention in Byzantine times. The use of Greek philosophy for "training only" by the church provided the necessary basis for the theoretical and practical support of education in Greek, primarily for the purpose of staffing of church-related positions. The decree of the patriarchal synod of 1593 ordered every see to organize and finance its own schools (Sathas 1870, 91). In the seventeenth century, patriarchal letters were issued forbidding the ordination of illiterate priests (ca. 1664), while in 1749 an academy was founded at Mount Athos itself, with an innovative curriculum under the direction of Eugenios Voulgaris (1716–1806) (Kitromilides 1996). These examples point to a clear recognition by the Eastern Christian authorities within the Ottoman Empire of the theological importance of an educated clergy.

Attempting to convey to nonscholars a basic understanding of the literal sense of God's Word lay behind the effort of theologians and church leaders to make the language of the Bible accessible to as broad a sector of believing Christians as possible, and to enable the reworking of its message for application in everyday life. This manifested itself in the attempt made by Cyril Loukaris and his assistant Maximos Kallioupolitis (Maximos of Gallipoli, n.d.–1633) (Manousakas 1986) to provide translations of the Koine scriptures into modern Greek, as well as in the commentaries and homilies of Elias Miniatis (1669–1714), Vikentios Damodos (1700–52), or Eugenios Voulgaris; the last of whom was the author of a biblical commentary titled *Adoleschia Philotheos*. Damodos and Voulgaris in particular contributed in a major fashion to the emergence of what we can justifiably call an "Orthodox Christian Enlightenment."

These translation efforts emerged in the Greek-speaking Orthodox world at a time when the intense use of Aristotelian logic, very often in the form of the scholastic method, became the lingua franca in the theological conversations and curriculum of the respected Kievan Academy. The conviction that human intellectual facilities are pivotal for accessing God's Revelation was thus inevitably implied in the pastoral work and intellectual activity (polemically or apologetically) of the Eastern church. The impact of an even more revolutionary scholasticism, in the form of Cartesianism, eventually emerged in the work of a series of theologians, teachers of logic and natural sciences, and translators and plagiarists of Western texts. Vikentios Damodos, who had taken a law degree at the University of Padua, founded a school in Kefallinia (1721) and published his *Concise Ethics* as part of a larger *Concise Philosophy* for didactic reasons (Henderson 1970, 28–33). Damodos's *Ethics* is actually a slightly amended translation of that part on ethics taken from the *Institutiones Philosophicae* written by the Cartesianist Edmond Pourchot (1651–1734). The other parts of Damodos's work are also largely translations (Demetracopoulos 2010). Through Pourchot's translation, a sizable portion of Aquinas's thought about free will and the pursuit of happiness came into use in Greek theological and philosophical teaching materials. The brilliant philosopher, translator, and later bishop of Cherson of the Russian Church, Eugenios Voulgaris, exhibited the same pattern as he translated the *Metaphysics* of Pourchot (Henderson 1970, 41–75). In these cases, Aquinas was tagged under "Aristotelian logic" generally, while the Dominican theologian's name was mentioned only polemically because of his contribution to unacceptable dogmatic teachings such as the filioque, the notion of created and infused grace, and his Trinitarian theology. Through Pourchot, Cartesianism intruded upon the methodology of these works in the East. Nevertheless, Voulgaris remained rather ambivalent towards Cartesianism, precisely because of its theological implications—that is, the relations between an infinite Creator and an equally infinite creation (Kondylis 1988, 183). On the contrary, the teacher of natural sciences and successor to Voulgaris, Bishop

Nikephoros Theotokis (1731–1800), rejected Cartesianism, basing his arguments completely upon Newtonian grounds and adopting a position that insisted upon a complete distinction between the theological realm and the natural sciences.

## 5.2 The time of collision

In the latter half of the eighteenth century, the tension between the passionate missionaries of Western Enlightenment, secular scholars, teachers and activists (notably Adamantios Korais, 1748–1833, who lived in Paris) who used the classical Greek literature as a tool on behalf of free thinking, and those who sought to represent the official teaching of the institutional church, and who also acted within the frame of Ottoman absolutism, became immense. Indeed, the conflict became so intense that it undermined the project of an "Orthodox version" of Enlightenment. A bitter fight over the assessment of education and knowledge generally broke out. In 1793 the teacher of the Greek community in Vienna, Christodoulos Pamplekis (1733–93), was posthumously excommunicated because of his deist and anti-clerical writings (Pamplekis 2013). It was the first official ecclesiastical condemnation of a writer who openly criticized Orthodox teachings (such as the veneration of saints or angels) from a deist position. Churchmen like Athanasios Parios (1721–1813) defended only the preparatory role of the "wonderful grammar" ("*τά καλά γραμματικά*") and condemned fiercely the rest of scientific knowledge imported from the West as leading to conceit and impiety, as he argued especially in his 1802 essay *Response to the Irrational Zeal of the Philosophers Coming from Europe*. Patriarch Gregory V (1797–98, 1806–8, and 1818–21) created a committee in 1798 to censor dangerous books (a relatively novel practice in the East, though common enough in various absolutist states of Europe) and founded a printing house in Constantinople, the better to control the editions of classical Greek texts according to his theological standards. His encyclical of 1819 was of the same tenor, denouncing mathematics and natural sciences as destructive of church life (Gedeon 1976, 210–211, 136, 123). Voltaire in particular came in for condemnation by nearly every Orthodox commentator. The ethos that had surrounded the 1766 translation of *Memnon* by Voulgaris now seemed very distant. All these developments contributed to a general mistrust of secular knowledge, an attitude that characterized traditional Orthodox theological circles in the years after 1821 and discouraged a systematic approach to theological education; an attitude reflected in the critique against the professors who taught at the new theological faculty at the newly founded University of Athens in 1837.

Nevertheless, it would be mistaken to blame Eastern "mysticism" or hesychastic theology for this general pattern of the rejection of secular "Western" knowledge. The use of hesychastic theology had emerged as a point of contention with the West in the late medieval centuries. During the sixteenth and seventeenth centuries, the disagreement over whether the "energies" of God could be seen by the created eye of humans already in this life was mainly used as a polemical defense aimed at notions of created grace and Latin Trinitarian dogmatics. Yet the hesychast tradition inevitably raised the crucial question of just how knowledge of God was possible and what could be said regarding the experience of his presence. It is significant that between 1696 and 1699, a controversy between the schoolmaster of the Giouma school at Ioannina in northwestern Greece, Georgios Sougdouris (n.d.–1725), with the local bishop Clemens (1680–1715) and his teacher Bissarion Makris (1635–99), highlighted the distinction between essence and energy in God that had been accepted in Orthodox circles since the vindication of Gregory Palamas (1296–1357). Sougdouris now presented a neat Aristotelian thesis that such distinctions could only be discerned in theory—a thesis adopted now by the Synod of Constantinople. Nevertheless, a young pupil of the Ioannina school, Methodios Anthrakitis, after further studies in Padua and his return to Ioannina, was accused of having abandoned the accepted traditional method of Corydalistic Aristotelianism and of propagating the teachings of the Jesuit Miguel de Molinos (1628–96). This somewhat bizarre accusation was probably based more on hearsay information than upon an analysis of Anthrakitis's actual writings. Anthrakitis had actually tried to combine the intellectualist notion of knowledge taken from Descartes and Malebranche with the idea of union with God through the divine energies; the latter as they had been exposited in the hesychastic theology of Gregory Palamas. Anthrakitis had been exposed to Palamas's theology in Ioannina twenty years earlier and accepted it (Chrestou 1969). The fact that he was the only intellectual condemned by the church for his philosophical and not theological teachings seventy years before the peak of the fight against Enlightenment with the case of Christodoulos Pamplekis, makes clear that daring speculations in theological matters such as the knowledge of God were taking place quite apart from the classical dispute about the use of scholasticism. Such experiments combined contemporary Western thinking with Byzantine theology.

The most prominent example of the hesychastic view on knowledge of God is the revival of the discourse about deification (theosis) through prayer and asceticism by the so-called Philokalia movement. In the second half of the eighteenth century, two important men worked independently to assess critically and produce a single edition of Byzantine ascetic writers and Church Fathers about prayer, spiritual life, and ascetical practices. Appearing under the name of *Philokalia* (Love of Beauty), the work actually represented the labors of two men from very different backgrounds. The Ukrainian Paisij Velitčkovskij (1722–94), worked on Mount Athos between 1746 and 1764 in order to collect these disparate works and translate them into Church Slavonic. His efforts produced a major return to the ascetic spirituality taken from Greek Byzantine sources both in Romanian monasteries (where he settled) and later in Russia. The other scholar-monastic, Nikodemos Kallivourtzis (1749–1809), better known as the Hagiorite (i.e., "of the Holy Mountain" [*Hagion Oros*], Mount Athos), continued these labors after 1775 and published them with the cooperation of his senior companion and mentor Macarios Notaras (1731–1805) in 1782 in Venice. The fact that these persons (who were later canonized as saints), together with the aforementioned Athanasios Parios and Neophytos Cafsocalyvitis (1713–84), were engaged in a dispute about the proper way of celebrating memorial services for the dead in Mount Athos gave them the nickname "Kollyvades" (derived from Kollyva—the boiled wheat eaten at these memorial services). The Philokalic movement or Kollyvades has been described as one of "res-sourcement," a return to the original sources of Orthodox spirituality (Kallistos [Ware] 1991). Yet the efforts of the Kollyvades were by no means merely a conservative turn; or even less so, a condemnation of the proper use of human reason. In the foreword of his *Synaxaristes* (collection of saints' lives), for example, Nikodemos notes that he undertook a critical purging of his material "which appear[s] to be opposed to the Scriptures and to be improbable to sound reason and critics" (Nikodemos (the Hagiorite) 2005, xv). At the same time, Nikodemos used edifying Roman Catholic works to support his battle against Western secularization. That was especially apparent in his work *The Unseen Warfare*, which is an adapted version of the *Combattimento Spirituale* by Lorenzo Scupoli (Fragkiskos 1993). Roman Catholic theological efforts had by the late eighteenth century been selectively and carefully chosen as occasional allies in a battle against Western secularism.

# 6 ON GOD AND CREATION

The vital question for Christian thinking of how God relates to the world was answered by Orthodox theologians from their reading of the scriptures. Christian theologians, they insisted, saw in those writings the creation of the world ex nihilo and the radical difference between the infinite and eternal God and a finite world created in time. Yet the core of this teaching continued to be transferred through the archaic view of a closed universe with earth at its center and the celestial dome above it, a picture substantiated intellectually later by Aristotle and used by the church fathers. A mathematical model of this geocentric world calculated by Ptolemy defined astronomy for centuries. All of this structure collapsed with the gradual acceptance of the heliocentric hypothesis advanced by Copernicus. The heliocentric universe—after a bitter fight over its theological implications in the West—came to the East only after a considerable delay, at the end of the eighteenth century. The unrelenting opponents of this theory among theologians, such as Sergios Makraios (1734/40–1819) and Dorotheos Voulismas (1737/41–1818), began their polemics from an insistence upon the literal interpretation of scripture, which they insisted taught clearly the geocentric understanding of the universe (Makrides 1995). The real challenge, though, lay elsewhere: in the possibility that the universe might consist of multiple worlds. This disturbing possibility opened new alternatives for thinking about the relation between God and created nature, since if multiple worlds existed, perhaps one had to be prepared to confront an inherent possibility of the universe's infinity as well. Various Orthodox scholars, such as Nikiphoros Theotokis, had already accepted the reality of a heliocentric universe. A natural scientist by profession, in his work *Elements of Physics*, Theotokis took for granted the validity of heliocentrism and managed to do so without facing serious questions about his Christian identity. Others, like Eugenios Voulgaris, tried to make a compromise between the geocentric and heliocentric models by adopting the theory of Tycho Brahe in order to avoid having to reconcile the two cosmologies (Kondylis 1988, 109–28). The escalation of this debate at the turn of the century showed clearly that the real problem lay in the emerging political context of the French Revolution. As a result, anyone identified as an adherent of modern theories of any sort fell under suspicion as a partisan of political radicalism.

# 7 TOWARD A CHRISTIAN MODEL OF PRACTICAL ETHICS

The most striking feature of the encounter of the Eastern church with the Enlightenment in the second half of the seventeenth century and the whole eighteenth century was the turn to a cohesive theoretical founding of practical ethics. This turn did not belong to the strictly theological questions such as grace, scripture, the sacraments, or ecclesiological issues, and therefore is usually not considered as a theological issue per se. Nevertheless, one should definitely interpret this turn as a response to the emerging anthropology and sociology of the Enlightenment and therefore, eventually and inevitably, related to the church and its theology. In the West, those who chose to reject what they derided as mythical or superstitious belief and equally disdainful of the moral authority of the church and its tradition, held out the possibility of the enlightened man who could now aspire to a personal as well as common welfare, and make a conscientious contribution to a free and progressive society. In some respects, elements of this notion of civic virtue also played an important role in the transfer of Enlightenment ideas to the East. A series of guides for good manners, one of the markers of a socially conscious and polite, enlightened participant in modernity, were published during the second half of the eighteenth century in the West, and many of these were translated into Greek.

Faced with these developments, many theologians and churchmen reacted in various ways. Some began to compose their own theoretical manuals on ethics. Most of these works consisted of slightly revised translations of Western Christian writers, including the denunciation of and calls for state repression of the excesses of morally lax lifestyles of freethinkers. Vikentios Damodos's work exemplified this genre. In a sense, these efforts built upon an earlier series of penitential manuals that had been printed during the seventeenth and early eighteenth centuries. Many of them were adaptations of relevant Roman Catholic manuals, but they were no less warmly received and copied (Tsakiris 2009). These earlier efforts marked the first obvious turn to a concern for the practical regulation of Christian life, which in its turn inaugurated a more sustained focus among those concerned with pastoral care in the East on everyday life; in part as a reaction to the turn to the practical, but now increasingly secularized emphasis of ethics in parts of Europe most deeply touched by the Enlightenment.

On another level, the popular missionary Kosmas Aetolos (of Aetolia, 1714–79) who visited large areas in the Greek mainland, attempted to turn his audiences to a more conscientious observance of the Gospels' ethical teachings, insisting on help for the poor and the fair treatment of women by men. He combined this objective with efforts to found schools in order to reach ordinary Christian subjects of the Ottoman Empire to attain a better education in Greek language and culture. This twofold objective of Kosmas has been described with some justification as socially and politically revolutionary (Podskalsky 1981, 343–44), and therefore can serve as a creative example of Orthodox Christian Enlightenment. Here too, the question of daily Christian practical behavior (focusing on love and mutual forgiveness) emerged as the major concern and strove to apply practically the monastic recovery of ascetic discipline and the resultant ethics advocated by the *Philokalia* movement.

The foreword to the *Philokalia*, a small compendium on Christian anthropology, stresses the freedom of the human will, which serves as a basis for the importance of spiritual life. This defense of free will provides the background for a call to progress in the spiritual life with the purpose of deification (theosis) focusing on the "inner self." Such progress comes, therefore, as a consequence of an exercise of free will and not upon a demonstration of having performed or exhibited merely external virtues (Nikodemos (the Hagiorite) 1782, 1–3). One can plausibly see this return to the inner self—on the one hand, a clear recovery of an ancient theme in Orthodox theology—as also a positive reaction to the importance of "virtue" (albeit understood in a correct, Orthodox manner) in the positive anthropological view of human dignity endorsed by the Enlightenment. Similarly, Nikodemos the Hagiorite in 1804 published his *Chrêstoêtheia* in which he sought to provide a practical guide for ethical everyday living for all Orthodox Christians (an Orthodox "savoir-vivre") by using teachings and admonitions from early church fathers, notably John Chrysostom. Although the actual impact of Nikodemos's effort appears to have been minimal, the work was conceived as an antidote to books like the 1558 work *Galateo* by Giovanni della Casa, which was known to Nikodemos. In his *Chrêstoêtheia*, Nikodemos condemned certain allegedly Christian, but in reality "folk religion" practices, as mere superstitions. In the same context, the Kollyvades' encouragement of regular reception of the Eucharist by the laity should be understood as part of their concern for encouraging devotion; that the development of the inner person would enhance the struggle to acquire Christian virtue. Taken together with the attempt to eradicate village superstition, the Kollyvades contributed in their own fashion to a kind of Orthodox Christian Enlightenment. The condemnation of superstition by Nikodemos was typical of most Greek pro-Enlightenment scholars, such as Adamantios Korais (1748–1833), who living in Paris as a writer and philologist was the most prominent agent of the transfer of the principles of political Enlightenment to Greeks through his brilliant editions of ancient Greek authors (Kitromilides 2010).

In the realm of social and political theory, the Eastern church had to confront a growing insistence emanating from Enlightenment Europe on the importance of law as a social contract between rulers and ruled, and the consequent endorsement of a more egalitarian and democratic basis for an enlightened, progressive society. The hierarchical church reacted sharply against appeals for democratic or contractual thinking, exemplified perhaps best by the denunciations of figures like Rhigas Velestinlis (1757–98). Others targeted the Phanariots in particular, by charging them with being self-interested and compliant servants of Ottoman absolutism and corruption, collaborators with unenlightened tyranny. Such charges could only appear in anonymous pamphlets, such as the *Hellenike Nomarchia* (1806), and they characterized a growing trend of anticlericalism that emerged in the last decades of the eighteenth century (Clogg 1976). The Orthodox Church hardened its position in concert with monarchies and both Catholic and Protestant established churches, especially after the French revolutionary regicide of 1793. Both Russian and Greek Orthodox Churches increasingly condemned Voltaire, the Freemasons, and all revolutionary ideas. Pamphlets emerged, such as *Paternal Instruction*, which called for obedience to the Ottoman sultan who ruled "by the Divine Providence," an assertion that produced the fierce denunciatory reaction of Adamantios Korais's (1748–1833) *Fraternal Instruction*.

Nevertheless, the nervous, defensive attitude struck by Orthodox hierarchs cannot be taken as emblematic of the whole of the social and political teachings of the Orthodox Church. In the less turbulent years before 1789, Damodos stressed that the basis upon which the head of a household or a church leader exercised authority had to be "politic" and not despotic (Dimaras 1975, 109); in other words, grounded in the concept of justice. A scholar and philosopher of the stature of Eugenios Voulgaris introduced the Greek term for religious tolerance in his work *Treatise on Religious Toleration* (1767). There he maintained that religious minorities in any regime should enjoy religious freedom.

Voulgaris's lesser-known contemporary, Bishop Theophilos of Veroia in western Macedonia (Papaphilis, 1715–93), writing his *Procheiron Nomikon* (*Handbook of Ecclesiastical Law*) published after 1750, had stressed in his foreword the importance of the rule of law, which must characterize every form of public authority, in contrast to a mere tyranny. He drew his examples from classical Greek and Roman antiquity (Theophilos 1887, 12–14).

Some thirty years later (1800), the traditionalist Nikodemos the Hagiorite, often represented as a classic "anti-Western" Orthodox writer, who respected Voulgaris, edited his famous canonical collection, the *Pedalion* ("Rudder"). In some of his commentaries on specific ecclesiastical canons he appeared to confirm his reputation as anti-Western and anti-Enlightenment, defending intervention by political and ecclesiastical authority in order to purge blasphemy through criminalization of heresy and idolatry. Basing his arguments on the Roman law tradition of the Byzantine Empire, he could find ample grounds for appealing to pious emperors to undertake such measures. He referred explicitly to the works of Voltaire as worthy of such repressive measures. Yet, at other points in his commentaries, Nikodemos explicitly forbade clerics the use of physical force or violence in punishing impiety. Instead, he stressed that Christian profession of faith can only be a result of a free choice, never of coercion (Nikodemos (the Hagiorite) and Agapios Hieromonk 1982, 520; Papathanasiou 2010). Nikodemos's ambivalent position on freedom and repression can be variously interpreted, but the political and social reality in which he lived—the Ottoman Empire—combined with the reliance upon canons drawn from the ancient and medieval Byzantine Empire, suggest some considerable tension between those inherited norms and his anthropological teaching on human freedom reflected in his foreword to the *Philokalia*.

# 8  CONCLUSION

The relationship between the Eastern church and the European Enlightenment, there-fore, must be understood as having constituted more than intellectual subjugation by the West, or alienation of the East; or equally misleadingly, as an Orthodox triumphal mainte-nance of a supposed doctrinal and intellectual "purity" immune from baneful "Western" influence. To reduce the relationship to a conflict between progressive and conservative, scholasticism and Cartesianism, also oversimplifies the story. The entire catalogue of issues associated with the Enlightenment—the emphasis on inductive reasoning, the final triumph of a heliocentric universe, the importance of law, the insistence upon rational bases of knowledge, rejection of superstition and ignorance, the insistence upon human free will—and many other characteristics of Enlightenment thinking were translated, discussed, reshaped or rejected in the East on different ecclesiastical and political occa-sions and in widely varying contexts in periodic encounters with Catholic and Protestant Christendom, or the experience of the French Revolution. In that process, and faced with the pressing need for increased educational opportunity for Christian populations in the East, alleged conservatives like Kollyvades affirmed selectively important perspectives and values of the Enlightenment. Celebrities of an "Orthodox Christian Enlightenment," like Voulgaris, paradoxically hesitated to accept the proofs for a heliocentric universe. Still, his own case and the long-term process of the East's engagement with the Enlightenment produced new currents in political, ecclesiastical, and theological reflection among the Orthodox. It was no accident that the archimandrite Theoklitos Pharmakidis (1784–1860), a churchman and scholar who emerged from the circle of Adamantios Korais and his publicizing tool, the review *Logios Hermês*, played a leading role in the Church of Greece's proclamation of independence from the Patriarchate of Constantinople in 1833, transfer-ring the principle of self-governance from an ethnic-national, to an ecclesiastical level (Pharmakidis 1840, 14). The monk and priest Theophilos Kairis (1784–1853), living in the modern Greek state as a teacher, could even proclaim a "religion of Reason" of his own invention (Kitromilides 2013, 291–335). Not only the national Greek revolution and the ongoing struggle over the shape of the ecclesiastical institutions there, but also the involve-ment of the Orthodox Church in the ecumenical movement after 1920, and the explosion of Russian theological and religious thinking after 1917, are all in a way the belated fruits of that long encounter with the Enlightenment.

# ACKNOWLEDGEMENTS

My deepest thanks to Professor P. Kitromilides, V. Makrides, Assistant Professor J. Demetracopoulos and Dr. P. Kalaitzidis, for their insights and practical aid during the preparation of this text.

## BIBLIOGRAPHY

Alivisatos, Hamilkas, ed. 1939. *Procès-Verbaux du Premier Congrés de Théologie Orthodoxe à Athènes 29 Novémbre–6 Décembre 1936*. Athens: Pyrsos.

Anghelou, Alkis. 1985. *Πλάτωνος τύχαι. Ή λόγια παράδοση στήν Τουρκοκρατία* [The fate of Plato: The scholarly tradition during the Ottoman occupation]. Athens: Hermes.

Camariano-Cioran, Ariadna. 1974. *Les académies princières de Bucarest et de Jassy et leurs professeurs*. Thessaloniki: Institute for Balkan Studies.

Chrestou, Panayiotis. 1969. "Ήσυχαστικαί ἀναζητήσεις εἰς τά Ἰωάννινα περί τό 1700" [Hesychastic debates in Ioannina around 1700]; includes a summary in English. *Klêronomia* 1 (2): 337–354.

Clogg, Richard. 1976. "Anticlericalism in pre-Independence Greece, c. 1750–1821." In *The Orthodox Churches and the West*, edited by Derek Baker, 257–276. Oxford: Basil Blackwell.

Crusius, Martinus. 1584. "Turcograeciae Libri Octo: Quibus Graecorum Status Sub Imperio Turcico." In *Politia et Ecclesia, Oeconomia et Scholis*. Basel.

Demacopoulos, George E., and Aristotle Papanikolaou. 2013. "Orthodox Naming of the Other: A Postcolonial Approach." In *Orthodox Constructions of the West*, edited by G. E. Demacopoulos and A. Papanikolaou, 1–22. New York: Fordham University Press.

Demetracopoulos, John. 2010. "Purchotius Graecus I, Vikentius Damodos' Concise Ethics." *Verbum Analecta Neolatina* 12 (1): 41–67.

Dimaras, Konstantinos. 1975. *Ἱστορία τῆς Νεοελληνικῆς Λογοτεχνίας* [History of modern Greek literature]. Athens: Ikaros.

Fragkiskos, Emmanouil M. 1993. "'Ἀόρατος Πόλεμος' (1796), 'Γυμνάσματα Πνευματικά' (1800), πατρότητα τῶν 'μεταφράσεων' τοῦ Νικόδημου Αγιορείτη" [The "Unseen Warfare" (1796), the "Spiritual Exercises" (1800), and the authorship of the "translations" of Nikodemos Hagiorite]. *Ho Eranistês* 19: 102–135.

Gedeon, Manuel. 1976. *Ή πνευματική κίνησις τοῦ γένους κατά τόν IH΄ καί IΘ΄ αἰώνα* [The intellectual currents of the nation during the 18th and 19th centuries]. Athens: Hermês.

Hauptmann, Peter. 1981. "Petrus Mogilas (1596–1646)." In *Klassiker der Theologie*, edited by H. Fries and G. Kretschmar, 378–391. Vol. 1. Munich: C. H. Beck.

Henderson, G. P. 1970. *The Revival of Greek Thought, 1620–1830*. Albany: State University of New York Press.

Hering, Günnar. 1968. *Ökumenisches Patriarchat und europäische Politik, 1620–1638*. Wiesbaden: Franz Steiner Verlag.

Kallistos of Diokleia (Ware). 1991. "The Spirituality of the Philokalia." *Sobornost* 13 (1): 6–24.

Kitromilides, Paschalis M. 1996. "Athos and the Enlightenment." In *Mt. Athos and Byzantine Monasticism*, edited by A. A. M. Bryer and Mary Cunningham, 257–272. Aldershot: Variorum.

Kitromilides, Paschalis M. 2013. *Enlightenment and Revolution. The Making of Modern Greece*. Cambridge, MA: Harvard University Press.

Kitromilides, Paschalis M. 2010. "Introduction." In *Adamantios Korais and the European Enlightenment*, edited by Paschalis M. Kitromilides, 37–90. Oxford: Voltaire Foundation.

Kondylis, Panagiotis. 1988. *Ὁ Νεοελληνικός Διαφωτισμός. Οἱ φιλοσοφικές ἰδέες* [The modern Greek Enlightenment: The philosophical ideas]. Athens: Themelio.

Makrides, Vasileios. 1995. *Die religiöse Kritik am Kopernikanischen Weltbild in Griechenland zwischen 1794 und 1821*. Frankfurt: Peter Lang.

Manousakas, M. I. 1986. "Νέα στοιχεῖα γιά τήν πρώτη μετάφραση τῆς Καινῆς Διαθήκης στή δημοτική γλῶσσα ἀπό τόν Μάξιμο Καλλιουπολίτη" [New evidence for the first translation of the New Testament in modern Greek by Maximos Kallioupolitis]. *Mesaionika kai Nea Hellênika* 2: 7–70.

Moschos, Dimitrios. 1992. "Der Streit um die Methode der Naturbeobachtung im späten Byzanz—geistesgeschichtliche und theologische Konsequenzen." *Orthodoxes Forum* 6 (2): 209–220.

Nikodemos (the Hagiorite). 1782. Φιλοκαλία τῶν ἱερῶν νηπτικῶν [Philokalia of the Niptic Fathers]. Venice.

Nikodemos (the Hagiorite). 2005. Συναξαριστής τῶν Δώδεκα μηνῶν τοῦ ἐνιαυτοῦ [Synaxaristes of the twelve months of the year]. Athens: Domos.

Nikodemos (the Hagiorite), and Agapios Hieromonk. 1982. Πηδάλιον τῆς νοητῆς νηός [Rudder of the Orthodox Catholic Church, containing all the sacred and divine canons]. Athens: Astir.

Pamplekis (Christodoulos from Akarnania). 2013. Ἀπάντησις ἀνωνύμου . . . ἐπονομασθεῖσα περί Θεοκρατίας [Anonymous answer . . . under the title on theocracy]. Athens: Koultoura.

Papathanasiou, Athanasios. 2010. "Ζητήματα ἀνεξιθρησκίας στόν Ἅγιο Νικόδημο τόν Ἁγιορείτη" [Issues of tolerance by St. Nikodemos Hagiorite]. *Epistêmonikê Epitheorisê tou metaptychiakou programmatos "Spoudes stên Orthodoxê Theologia"* 1: 227–247.

Pharmakidis, Theoklitos. 1840. Ἀπολογία [Apology]. Athens: Aggelos Aggelidis.

Plested, Marcus. 2012. *Orthodox Readings of Aquinas Changing Paradigms in Historical and Systematic Theology.* Oxford: Oxford University Press.

Podskalsky, Gerhard. 1981. *Griechische Theologie in der Zeit der Türkenherrschaft 1453–1821.* Munich: C. H. Beck.

Theophilos of Campania (Procheiron). 1887. Πρόχειρον Νομικόν [Handbook of laws], edited by K. Vasileiadis. Istanbul: Antonios Maxouris.

Roudometof, Viktor. 2013. *Globalization and Orthodox Christianity. The Transformations of a Religious Tradition.* New York: Routledge.

Runciman, Steven. 2003. *The Great Church in Captivity: A Study of the Patriarchate of Constantinople from the Eve of the Turkish Conquest to the Greek War of Independence.* Cambridge: Cambridge University Press.

Sathas, Konstantinos. 1870. Βιογραφικόν Σχεδίασμα περί τοῦ Πατριάρχου Ἱερεμία Β΄ (1572– 1594) [Biographical outline of the Patriarch Jeremia II (1572–1594)]. Athens: A. Ktenas-S. Oikonomos.

Tsakiris, Vasilios. 2009. *Die gedruckten griechischen Beichtbücher zur Zeit der Türkenherrschaft.* Berlin: Walter de Gruyter.

Tsirpanlis, Zacharias. 1980. Τὸ Ἑλληνικό Κολλέγιο τῆς Ρώμης καί οἱ μαθητές του (1576– 1700): Συμβολή στή μελέτη τῆς μορφωτικῆς πολιτικῆς τοῦ Βατικανοῦ [The Greek College of Rome and its students (1576–1700): A contribution to the study of educational policy of the Vatican]. Analecta Vlatadon 32. Thessaloniki: Patriarchikon Idrima Paterikon Meleton.

Tsourkas, Cléobule. 1967. *Les débuts de l'enseignement philosophique et de la libre pensée dans les Balkans, La vie et l'oeuvre de Théophile Corydalée (1570–1646).* Thessaloniki: Institute for Balkan Studies.

Tzirakis, N.E. 1977. Ἡ περί μετουσιώσεως (transsubstantiatio) εὐχαριστιακή ἔρις. Συμβολή εἰς τήν ὀρθόδοξον περί μεταβολῆς διδασκαλίαν τοῦ ΙΖ΄ αἰῶνος [The debate about transubstantiation in the Eucharist: A contribution to the Orthodox teaching about the transformation of the elements in the Eucharist in the 17th century]. Athens.

Wendebourg, Dorothea. 1997. "'Pseudomorphosis': A Theological Judgment as an Axiom for Research in the History of Church and Theology." *Greek Orthodox Theological Review* 42 (3/4): 321–342.

Wendebourg, Dorothea. 1986. *Reformation und Orthodoxie. Der theologische Briefwechsel zwischen der Leitung der württembergischen Kirche und dem Ökumenischen Patriarchen Jeremias II in den Jahren 1574–1581.* Göttingen: Vandenhoeck & Ruprecht.

Wirtschafter, Elise. 2013. *Religion and Enlightenment in Catherinian Russia: The Teachings of Metropolitan Platon.* DeKalb, IL: Northern Illinois University Press.

Yannaras, Christos. 2006. *Orthodoxy and the West.* Translated by P. Chamberas and N. Russell. Brookline, MA: Holy Cross Orthodox Press.

# CHAPTER 33

# ORTHODOX INFLUENCES ON EARLY MODERN WESTERN THEOLOGIES

## A. G. ROEBER

By "Orthodox" one designates the form of Christianity that emerged in the first Roman imperially called councils of the fourth century. The "correct" or "upright" universality or catholicity of both worship and teaching received expression in the use of the Greek word that only later came to distinguish communities that separated from the empire (hence "Oriental Orthodox") and even later, from the Roman (or Latin) West. Early modern Orthodox influences on Western theologies occurred as an exchange that by that era came from profoundly unequal partners. By comparison with Roman Catholics or Protestants, the Orthodox—regardless of whether they lived inside or beyond the bounds of the Ottoman Empire, and equally regardless of "Eastern" versus "Oriental"— lacked monetary, educational, and mobility resources. That reality put them at a distinct disadvantage vis-à-vis their Western counterparts. Orthodox theology was most often used as a pawn in Catholic–Protestant polemics; concrete Orthodox theological influences upon Catholic or Protestant theology were fleeting, sporadic, and inconclusive. The suggestion of one Jesuit that John of Damascus's (ca. 675–749) work *On the Orthodox Faith* was superior to Aquinas's (1225–74) *Summa* fell into a void created by the confessionalist atmosphere of the sixteenth and seventeenth centuries (see Leinsle, this volume.) The polemical atmosphere of the sixteenth and seventeenth centuries dominated all aspects of "influence" and "exchange" before dwindling, in the second half of the eighteenth century, into both hardened positions and insubstantial contact. Instead of theological influences that shaped the West, the Orthodox adopted alternatively "compensatory" strategies defending or exaggerating their peculiar theological tradition vis-à-vis "the West" (Makrides 2006).

Nonetheless, in the areas of ecclesiology, liturgical and nonliturgical piety, and in the fascination in the West for the importance of contemplative prayer and mysticism,

Orthodox Christianity never completely disappeared from the consciousness of Western early modern theology.

Ecclesiological influence continued in the conciliarist understanding of the church in the debates in the fifteenth century at the Pisa and Basel councils. That ecclesiology continued to intrigue Luther (1483–1546) and Protestants a century later, as they sought evidence from antiquity and their present age for a non-Roman understanding of the church. The disagreement over whether the late medieval attempts to heal the schism between East and West had been accomplished but then broken by the East (Rome's position), or that the nonacceptance of signed documents by the majority of clergy, laity, and monastics in the East meant that no union had taken place at all (the Orthodox position), illustrated both the appeal and the uncertainties that continued to swirl about the role of conciliarism (Halecki 1968; Gill 1959). It also explains the term "Uniate" as a concept and negative identification of those bishops and their followers who chose in the late sixteenth century areas of east-central Europe to accept papal authority and doctrine, while retaining much of the liturgical and cultural hallmarks of the Orthodox. Luther's own admiration for "the Greeks," however, no less so than was the case for the "Uniates," did not extend to Orthodox ecclesiology. That would have required acknowledging that the ultimate authority regarding doctrine, worship, and discipline is located in the consensus and acceptance of the ecumenical councils and canons rather than in the office of a universal bishop. Protestants were happy to do without Rome, but generally accepted only the first four councils, none of the canons, and proclaimed a written scripture as the authority over and above any declarations of any councils. Hence, for Protestants there was no clear distinction between bishops and presbyters—a point on which Rome itself was not entirely clear; and the continued authority of the disciplinary canonical tradition as well as that of the church fathers never elicited very favorable remarks from Protestant observers. These dimensions of Orthodoxy were only selectively used, or rejected altogether (Backus 1997). Protestant rejection of Orthodox ecclesiology manifested itself in the exchange between Patriarch Jeremias (ca. 1530–95) and the Tübingen theologians in the 1570s (Mastrantonis 1982). The stalemate that ensued did not end Protestant fascination. This reemerged in the seventeenth century with the arrival of scholars such as Metrophanes Kritopoulos (ca. 1589–1639) in England and at Helmstedt (Davey 1987), and the forlorn discussions at Oxford University concerning the founding of a Greek college, presumably with some interest in fostering an actual ecclesial tie between the Church of England and the Chalcedonian Orthodox (Doll 2006). The spike in interest for a serious union demonstrated by the English and Scots nonjurors in late seventeenth-century England quickly revealed the profound theological disagreement with the Orthodox about the nature of the church. These Anglicans insisted on the primacy of Jerusalem as the first church, despite the Orthodox sense of the nonnegotiable reordering of the commemorative diptychs in the absence of the equivalent authority that had established them in the first place; namely, an ecumenical council. Nor could the nonjurors be persuaded of Orthodox Eucharistic theology, the role of the Theotokos, and the importance of prayer to the saints and on behalf of the departed (Shukman 2006). The Bohemian theologian Nicholas Comenius (1592–1670) had been aware of the Orthodox understanding of the church, and one segment of those who had followed the lead of Jan Hus (ca. 1369–1415) in contesting Rome's authority claims did attempt to make contact with the East before Luther and Melanchthon (1497–1560) followed their example. The very existence of ancient churches that did not accept Rome's views on papal authority over the entire church continued to attract Protestant interest (Atwood 2009). This pattern persisted into the early eighteenth century's "Renewed Unitas Fratrum" leadership whose central figure, Nikolaus Ludwig, Graf von Zinzendorf (1700–60) again sought the endorsement of Constantinople for the "Moravians" as a true, ancient and apostolic church (Manukyan 2010; Roeber 2010). By the second half of the eighteenth century, however, Protestants increasingly showed little interest in continuing to study or to shape their ecclesial concerns with reference to Orthodox theology. In part, this trend can be traced to the emergence of Peter the Great's (1672–1725) re-imagined Russia, a vision that first left the Moscow patriarchate vacant, then abolished in favor of the Holy Synod in promoting an aggressively Erastian notion of the church wholly subordinated to the throne (Shukman 2006). Theologians at Halle and Jena had first greeted Peter as a reformer who would bring a superstitious Orthodoxy into line with a renewed Protestantism against Roman corruption; those illusions, encouraged perhaps by the abolition of the patriarchate and creation of the synod, vanished with Peter's death. The Russian ecclesial development disrupted Russia's own historic attempt to copy—with considerably enhanced Tsarist eminence—the Byzantine relationship between throne and altar (Cracraft 1971; Dagron 2003). The Russian experiment, coming at a time when Central European, Greek, and Arabic Orthodox remained under the sway of the Ottoman Empire, meant that the ecumenical patriarch's role in Constantinople as the sole legitimate link between the Grand Porte and the Christian *millet* offered little that was attractive for study or emulation to a burgeoning evangelical Protestantism. Orthodox ecclesial theologies were even less impressive to a Roman church that was now firmly committed to the Tridentine teachings on the papacy and attendant ecclesial theology and discipline (see Tutino's essay in this volume).

No discussion of the impact of Orthodoxy on the West can be separated from the phenomenon of Orthodox who converted to the Roman church, and the resulting polemics that characterized the entire seventeenth century (Hering 1968). Orthodox condemnation of perceived Roman Catholic prosyletizing, and Orthodox theologians who demonstrated interest in both Reformed theology and Lutheran Pietism, alerted Western theologians to the continued presence and perspectives within the Orthodox tradition that merited their attention, as well as their criticism. These influences converged from two distinct Orthodox geographic areas: first, the Greek-speaking Mediterranean, where the Venetian possessions had guaranteed a longer liturgical and theological exposure of Orthodox and Latin Christians to one another; and second, the controverted area of east-central Europe, the Polish-Lithuanian Commonwealth, Transylvania, and Russia.

Among the most famous Greek Orthodox who converted to Catholicism, Leo Allatios (ca. 1586–1669) exercised considerable influence, not the least because of his polemical attacks on his Orthodox contemporaries, especially the Patriarch Cyril Loukaris (1572–1638). Born on the island of Chios in 1586, Allatios, even after his conversion "never forgot the Orthodox church . . . and his most famous work . . . of 1648 . . . emphasizes the historical connection between the two oldest branches of Christianity" (Hartnup 2004, 1). His magisterial work, however, revealed a fierce polemical edge and illustrated the degree to which Allatios had become convinced of the universal claims of papal authority, the Western tradition of penance, and the papacy's stewardship of grace (Allatios 1970). For their part, a number of Greek clergy, partly in response, sought alliances with Protestant centers of learning, an effort that fed into the late seventeenth-century attempts to found and sustain a Greek college at Oxford. These efforts had become attenuated in various degrees and in various locales by the early eighteenth century. Observers in the twenty-first century rightly find puzzling the fact that although Orthodox theologians such as Gennadios Scholarios (ca. 1400–ca. 1473) had known and admired the work of Thomas Aquinas, the deep differences between Orthodox theological anthropology and that of the West were either not recognized or purposefully ignored in the fifteenth century. These had begun to surface in the context of the magisterial Reformation's debates with Rome. It was, in the opinion of one scholar, "a serious mistake of fifteenth-century theologians, Catholic and Orthodox alike, to overlook their differing anthropologies" (Livanos 2006, 2; Barbour 1993). Orthodox teaching on the nature of what it means to be human and how God relates to his creation had the potential to sharpen, rather than diminish, the Catholic–Orthodox divide as awareness of the distinctions broadened in the context of Protestant–Catholic polemics. One cannot overlook, either, that the post-Tridentine Roman church's emphasis upon an exclusive soteriology that increasingly treated the Orthodox as heretical contributed to the sense of provocation. The Orthodox response erupted into an actual identification of Rome as an heretical church in 1756, as the Patriarch of Constantinople Cyril V (n.d.–1775), after failing to persuade his own synod the year before, issued a letter with the endorsement of the patriarchs of Alexandria and Jerusalem insisting upon baptism according to the Orthodox rite as universally obligatory for converts. The decision reversed centuries of theological teaching articulated at Constantinople in 1484, reiterated at Moscow in 1655, reconfirmed in 1667, and again in 1718 (Pagodin 1996–97). Effective Jesuit prosyletizing among the Antiochian Arab Christians had divided the Orthodox in the Syrian context by the 1720s between those accepting and rejecting papal claims to authority. The resulting alteration in Greek Orthodox teaching regarding reception into the church was never accepted in Russia, resulting in different relationships to the West in divergent disciplines within Orthodoxy itself. The recovery of Byzantine theological roots in Neo-Platonism and the rejection of the neo-Aristotelian influence of the Padua-trained Theophilos Korydalleus (1570–1646) by Eugenios Voulgaris (1716–1806) now sharpened the anti-Roman polemics that issued from Voulgaris's pamphlets. First exchanging a long correspondence with the French Jansenist Pierre Leclerc (1706–81), Voulgaris encouraged the neo-conciliarism advanced by the French opponents of the Jesuits. By 1763, however, Voulgaris had intentionally sought out contacts in Leipzig, Halle, and Berlin, where the struggle to articulate how theological tradition and new understandings of what counted as "rational" Voulgaris found more congenial than continued contact with the Jansenists. Voulgaris was even less impressed by Voltaire (1694–1778), whom he met during his stay in the German cities and with whom he disagreed on nearly all matters theological and philosophical (Batalden 1982).

In matters of ecclesial discipline and the importance of clerical example, the different canonical teachings regarding clerical marriage that had surfaced as one of the sources of controversy at the Trullan Council of 692 now re-emerged in Orthodox–Catholic conflicts in tradition, but also because of the uncertainty that surrounded the whole topic of ecclesiology. Not until after the Council of Trent did Catholics or Protestants actually have at their disposal any systematic treatises on ecclesiology. Beginning with the canonical opinions of Peter Lombard (ca. 1096–1164), the Catholic tradition had for centuries not identified bishops as part of the "sacramental orders" of the church, suggesting instead that the episcopacy was an office of dignity only. Priests and deacons constituted the apostolic foundational orders. The Orthodox teaching on the bishop, as well as the defense of marriage for deacons and priests, received reaffirmation by early modern polemicists such as Voulgaris, but at the level of lived experience also manifested itself in the Calabrian area of Italy where Robert Bellarmine's (1542–1621) sixteenth-century attempts to actualize the Tridentine disciplinary canons on clerical celibacy met with noncompliance. The region, although officially Roman Catholic, remained rooted in the culturally Orthodox expectation that local clergy would be responsible husbands and fathers, a pattern that persisted in Siena as well before the area succumbed to Tridentine conformity. The call for a restoration of a diaconate that surfaced at Trent in 1563 also did not envision permanent married deacons but the reaffirmation of the celibate tradition of the West. No surviving documents or commentary suggest an appeal to, or commentary upon Orthodox understandings of the orders of bishop, presbyter, and deacon (Gentilcore 1992; Ott 1969; Osborne 2007).

Russian Orthodox suspicion of Roman ecclesiology had emerged with striking clarity by 1440. But the roots of the explosive conflict between Rome and Moscow that culminated in the controversial 1596 Council of Brest-Litovsk and the rise of the "Uniates" lay in the Mongol destruction of Kiev in 1240. The move of the Metropolitan of Kiev to the grand principality of Vladimir (1299) and to Moscow (1325) provided a critical component of Moscow's bid for legitimacy as its ruler consolidated dominion from the 1240s to 1478 over neighboring principalities and cities, including Novgorod. Unhappy southwestern leaders of the Rus suffered a major reversal of fortune when Jagiello of Lithuania (ca. 1356/62–1434) married the queen of Poland and became Roman Catholic in 1386. With the death of Metropolitan Cyprian (ca. 1336–1406) in 1406, the possibility of a council that would realize unification of Eastern and Western churches (in a commonwealth of Orthodox realms, Muscovy, Poland, and Lithuania) also perished. The decisive geopolitical shift north and east predisposed Kiev toward renewed efforts for union with the West. Thus, even before the Greek-born student of Gemisthos Plethon (ca. 1355–1452), Isidore (1385–1463), the Russian participant in the ill-fated Council of Florence-Ferrara, could reach Moscow to proclaim the successful ending of the schism, he faced the improbable task of convincing not only Muscovy and Kiev but the Orthodox in the Polish-Lithuanian Commonwealth of the Union. That Vasili of Moscow (1371–1425) cultivated and promoted theological disagreement about the authority of councils and the papacy for political ends, no one doubts (Gill 1959). By 1448, Moscow had unilaterally replaced the rejected Isidore with Jonas of Ryazan (n.d.–1461). Rome, for its part, condemned Jonas, recognized instead the consecration of Gregory, Isidore's former deacon as Metropolitan of "Lower Russia" and regarded Kiev as lying unquestionably under papal jurisdiction (Papadakis 1994; Halecki 1968). The decision taken in 1596 at Brest-Litovsk that from Rome's perspective restored the broken union of Florence-Ferrara on a local scale had the effect of solidifying the theological disagreements that had proliferated in the face of the impending collapse of Constantinople and the provincializing of various centers of east-central European Orthodoxy.

Nor were the possibilities of achieving an Orthodox-Catholic union confined to the meeting in Brest. The Catholic prince of Transylvania cultivated his Orthodox counterpart in Wallachia in a concerted effort to root out Reformed theological inroads, a campaign that was only interrupted by increasing Orthodox suspicions and Protestant resistance within the Transylvanian Diet (Keul 2009). In Galicia, the collapse of the old Galicia-Volhynia Kingdom in 1340 had triggered a multi-confessional migration of peoples, with the predominant power shaped by Latin Catholicism. Although Orthodox parishes and clergy regained some measure of protection in the 1430s, the stage was set in the Ruthenian area for the bitter polemics that surrounded the 1596 Union (Himka 2005). By the eighteenth century, Orthodox ecclesiology had run its course as a topic of Protestant interest in the Hungarian and Slavic cultural areas of Europe. Although some Orthodox clerics and scholars would continue to find personal union with Rome, the controversies of the preceding two centuries gave rise to theological academies (in Russia, especially) that showed no interest in pursuing unification with Rome, a posture the Greek Orthodox had already adopted in their decision to impose a novel discipline that no longer recognized Roman Catholic baptism "by economy."

Contact with "Oriental Orthodox" among Protestants beyond Europe remained equally sporadic, inconclusive, and theologically insignificant. The first Protestant mission to the Danish colony of Tranquebar in 1706 brought Halle-trained Lutherans into contact with both Armenian Orthodox, Syrian Apostolic Orthodox of the East, and the St. Thomas Christians. Fascinated by the antiquity of their traditions, Lutheran pastors wrote reports back to Europe that initially envisioned an anti-Roman alliance with these groups. Closer examination of questionable liturgical piety, unacceptable veneration of the Mother of God, and ignorance of the scriptures characterized all three groups in the opinion of the disappointed Lutherans. For their part, irritated Catholic missionaries who had been in the South Indian field much longer attacked the proselytizing of their flocks by Protestant heretics. At no point did the theological legacy of the Orthodox groups have any lasting impact upon their Catholic or Protestant counterparts (Tamcke 2006; Roeber 2013).

# 1 Liturgy and Piety

Orthodox influence upon Western theology, if modest or polemically provocative in the realm of ecclesiology, played an equally limited role in shaping liturgical and non-liturgical piety in the West. It too could not escape from polemics and interconfessional tensions. Early seventeenth-century Protestants pardonably believed briefly that the Orthodox had endorsed their understanding not only of papal authority, but also and perhaps more importantly, Reformed doctrines of grace and the rejection of Roman notions of the church and the sacraments. The exposure to Roman Catholic liturgical life, as well as formal philosophical and theological study at Padua, had hardened the attitude of the Cretan-born Meletius Pigas (1549–1601), by 1593 Patriarch of Alexandria. His younger relative Cyril Loukaris also studied in Padua and knew Venice as well. Loukaris, first replacing his aged relative Pigas as Patriarch of Alexandria, by 1621 Patriarch of Constantinople (Davey 2000), at some point in the mid-1620s authored an "Orthodox Confession of Faith" that reaffirmed the Orthodox condemnations of both Rome and the Protestant Reformation. The teachings of Loukaris represented by his later Reformed-influenced work of 1629 fell under condemnation at the 1672 Synod of Jerusalem. The resulting Confession of Dositheos represented the high point of con-vergence between Roman Catholic teachings on the numbering of the sacraments, the objective transmutation of the elements of the Eucharist, the absolute necessity of the invocation of the Theotokos and the saints, the number of inspired books of scripture included in the Greek Septuagint, and the insistence upon intercessory prayers for the departed. Unwittingly, the closer identification of Orthodox theological teachings with the categories developed by scholastic Catholic theologians laid the groundwork for convincing arguments (presented especially to the Arab Orthodox in the Levant) by 1724 that union with Rome would guarantee a correct piety against the threat of Protestant error (Gedeon 1890, 626–28; Noble and Treiger 2014, 36–39). The cultivation of a disciplined attempt to live out the implications of accepted interpretations of bibli-cal piety that defined the Christian life meant that Greek Orthodox expertise was much sought after among the German-speaking Pietists. An effort emerged at Halle to secure the most accurate translation of the Greek New Testament. Greek Orthodox theolo-gians who arrived to undertake the task, however, quickly left since their Lutheran hosts declined to allow the Orthodox celebration of the liturgy (Moennig 1998). Nonetheless, the influence of the Orthodox teaching on the damaged but reparable image and like-ness of God caught the attention of some within this Protestant Pietist movement (Lehmann and Strom, in this volume). Tentative moves toward the notion of a pro-cess of "sanctification" among the "justified" echoed also in Charles Wesley's (1707–88) hymnody within the Church of England's Methodist movement, if not demonstrably in ecclesiology (Kimbrough 2005, 2007). The Orthodox liturgical emphasis upon the *epiklesis* in the Eucharistic anaphora met with considerably more interest and copying as it entered conservative Anglicanism via the Scottish nonjurors' rite in the eighteenth century (Woolfenden 2006). The general "mystical" critique of rationalist theology in Great Britain that emerged among the majority of British Protestants, however, did not spring from any deep awareness of the Orthodox liturgical or para-liturgical tradition (Young 1998). Nor did Protestants or Catholics adjust their respective theological practices to emulate Orthodox devotions to the saints, the Theotokos, or intercessory prayer for the departed.

The role of confession and absolution also emerged both as a point of potential Orthodox influence and interconfessional dispute. The obscure Nikephoros Paschaleus (1570–1650) (possibly from Corfu) issued a number of liturgical publications into the 1620s through the publisher Antonio Pinelli in Venice, where Paschaleus was also pastor of the Orthodox Saint George Church. Besides unpublished works on the Orthodox fasting cycles, his most famous influential work was his 1622 *Encheiridion methodikon*, a book of pastoral theology that appeared under the guise of a "how-to" manual for poorly trained Orthodox priests authorized to hear confessions and pronounce absolution. The escalating tensions between Rome and Constantinople during Loukaris' initial service as ecumenical patriarch may have led to an initial Wittenberg-Lutheran subvention of Paschaleus's work, as Loukaris himself supported the spread of Zacharios Gerganos's (fl. 1631) catechetical writing as an antidote to Roman prosyletizing (Tsakiris 2009). But Paschaleus's own political leanings toward the union of East and West reflected the longstanding harmonious Catholic–Orthodox relations on Corfu and did not fit within Loukaris's need for anti-Roman arguments. The actual content of the manual was Catholic, introducing the threefold understanding of repentance, confession, and performance of "satisfaction" into the understanding of the mystery. The source for Paschaleus's manual was almost certainly the Jesuit Luca Pinelli's (1542–1607) *Del sacramento della penitenza* of 1616 (Tsakiris 2009, 36, 38). Not surprisingly, Loukaris reacted sharply against this theology, one made even more dangerous with the 1629 appearance of the manual by the pro-union Orthodox writer Neophytos Rodinos (ca. 1579–1669). These seventeenth-century publications also provided both Catholic and Protestant critics ample opportunity to bemoan the corruption of Orthodox penitential practice, illustrated by the repeated insistence of Orthodox bishops that money, even if in the most modest amounts, needed to be collected voluntarily, not by force or demand, from the laity who had come to confession. Those funds were critical to the support of the beleaguered patriarchs of Constantinople, Jerusalem, and Alexandria, as well as the Athos and Sinai monasteries in their struggle for survival under Islamic rule. The penitential collections were defended as well as indispensable for blocking the influence of pro-union priests and Roman prosyletizing, especially by Jesuits. Loukaris' major ally in the war of confessional manuals emerged when Metrophanes Kritopoulos published a theological treatise from Memphis, Egypt. Connecting true sorrow and confession to final absolution in the reception of the Eucharist, Kritopoulos simplified the confessional process by omitting any discussion of "satisfaction" or a listing of sins or specific penances that typified both Catholic manuals and that of the pro-union enemies of Loukaris. But the full version of Kritopoulos's confessional manual was never published, and after his death in Wallachia one year after the murder of Loukaris, the

pro-Roman influence of Rodinos's manual was guaranteed. That influence was confirmed by the repudiation of Loukaris at the Jerusalem Council and the subsequent
publication of the confession of Dositheos. The latter, although a formidable polemi-
cist and critic of the Roman church, and especially of Greeks like the convert Allatios,
was motivated primarily by a theological rather than a political agenda. His combat in
Jerusalem with Franciscan friars and equally unpleasant encounters with Jesuits in east-
central Europe, whom he regarded as opponents his own theologians could not best in
debate, rested from first to last on his desire to promote a revitalized Orthodox ecclesial life (Russell 2013). The subsequent eighteenth-century confessional manuals, unlike
their predecessors, arguably shaped Orthodox theological discussions internally, but
no influence or even awareness of these manuals among Catholic or Protestant theologians matched the intensity of the seventeenth century polemical exchanges. Thus,
the manuals of Methodios Anthrakites (1660–1736), Theodoretos Saloufas (n.d–1746),
Chrysanthos Notaras (ca. 1663–1731), Patriarch Kallinikos II (fl. 1688–1702), and most
famously, the 1794 *Exomologetarion* by Nikodemos the Hagiorite (1749–1809) reflected
the inward turn of Orthodox theologians both to the study of patristic understandings
of the church's mysteries, and to a much stricter following of the church's canonical and
ascetic tradition, neither of which exercised any appreciable influence upon Western
theologians or liturgists (Tsakiris 2009, 303; Chamberas 1989; Dokos 2006). The bruis-
ing seventeenth-century polemics and shifting political fortunes of the Orthodox
increasingly revealed to them how little they could expect to gain from attempting
long-standing theological alliances with any Western counterparts. Their conclusion
matched a declining interest in Orthodox theology on the part of Western Christians—
Catholic or Protestant.

Orthodox influence upon the West emanating from the Slavic tradition remained at
once more traditional than that which emanated from the aggrieved Greeks, but at the
same time, much more limited. In part, geographic distance of the new Russian ecclesiastical center that claimed for itself the status of the old Kievan Metropolitanate in 1589
accounted for this pattern. But Russian monastic renewal owed much to St. Maximus
the Greek (ca. 1475–1556), who though born in the Ottoman Empire, studied in Florence
and Venice and became a Dominican friar before abandoning the West to become a
monastic on the Holy Mountain of Athos. Beyond his profound influence in translating
Greek liturgical texts into Slavonic, Maximus exemplified the hesychast movement he
had learned during his thirteen-year sojourn on Athos. It was in this area of contemplative prayer and renewal that Orthodoxy continued to fascinate those in the West, who
from time to time came into contact with its existence. That fascination remained at a
distance, however. Nicholas of Cusa (1401–64) had provided what was perhaps the closest Western theological approximation of the Orthodox convictions about theosis, in
part because of the later cardinal's involvement both with conciliarism and diplomatic
efforts to bring about a reconciliation between the Byzantines and Rome (Hudson 2007).
Cusa's mystical theology, however, remained under suspicion in the Roman church that
had, since the thirteenth century, progressively driven mysticism to the margins of the
church's official life (McGinn 1998). Cusa's synthesis of Dionysian, Eckhartian, and

Eriugenian insights transcended the "dialectical Neoplatonic mysticism" of his predecessors. Recovery of a mystical tradition in the West, however, remained deeply controversial. Despite his well-known repudiation of Dionysius, Martin Luther remained
deeply indebted to Johann Tauler (ca. 1300–61) and the "theology of the ground"
(Leppin 2007), in which the older theology of the desert fathers, Bernard of Clairvaux
(1090–1153), and Meister Eckhart (ca. 1260–ca. 1328) continued to testify to the image
and likeness of God in the human soul that was to be fed continually in sacramental,
especially Eucharistic, piety (McGinn 2005). For their part, the Byzantine critics of the
late medieval West did not base their unhappy reaction upon a supposed rejection of the
rational by Western theologians in favor of some "irrational" mysticism. Instead, from
Scholarios's generation and through the eighteenth century, the "basis for critiquing the
West was not that the West was rationalistic . . . but that it was imperialistic and innovative" (Livanos 2006, 126; Williams 1999).

The most potentially fruitful area of Orthodox theological impact upon the West
might have been expected to be felt in the monastic circles of the Catholic Church.
The renewed Benedictine tradition of the early modern Catholic reform especially,
had enjoyed the longest connection to the Orthodox. A monastic house of St. Mary,
founded by monks from the Italian Republic of Amalfi on Mount Athos had continued as part of the Athonite community until at least the eleventh century, if not later
(Bonsell 1969). Greek monastics from Santa Maria di Grottaferrata had penetrated the
British Isles before their community gradually abandoned the Greek rites by the 1100s
(Knowles 1963). The most significant interruption of what might have proven the influence of Orthodox theology upon the West occurred when Nicholas of Cusa's mystical insights on theosis and filiation fell into obscurity with the cardinal's own death in
1464. Although clearly indebted to Augustine and Anselm in his commitment to "faith
seeking understanding," Cusa explicitly drew upon Dionysius, John of Damascus, and
a tradition of "non-seeing seeing" and "learned ignorance" that was decisively nonintel-
lectual and more akin to the apophatic insights of the Orthodox (McGinn 2005, 432–83).
Cusa's contemporary and sometime-companion, Denys the Carthusian (1402–71), also
knew and used John of the Ladder (ca. 579–649) in his writings. But these late fifteenth-
century reflections may represent the high point of a Western monastic and ecclesiastical apprehension of at least some dimensions of the Orthodox mystical traditions,
which appear to have had little or no impact upon the reform efforts of the Catholic
Tridentine era, with perhaps one important exception. Filippo Neri (1515–95) founder of
the Oratorians, born in Florence, admired the spiritual fervor of Savonarola, but spent
his adult life in Rome. His spiritual formation emerged from a deep study of Augustine
(354–430), John Cassian (ca. 360–435), the desert fathers, and John of the Ladder. His
pursuit of spiritual perfection centered upon the acquisition of humility, and the conviction that the love of God cannot be separated from constant charity expressed in
practical acts of compassion toward all of humanity. Never interested in producing a
systematic theology of his own, Neri's spiritual profile emerges from his poetry and
letters. But during his long life he gained the reputation as the "Reformer of Rome"
because of his joyous affirmation of the goodness of God and his love for his creation, a

cheerful demeanor that flowed from a rigorous ascetic discipline accompanied by regular confession of sin and frequent reception of the Eucharist. Unmistakably Roman in the expression and understanding he gave to the pursuit of perfection, he nonetheless stands as a singular example of the impact Orthodox theology continued to work upon a sixteenth-century Latin. At the same time, the very uniqueness of his own personal sanctity appears not to have altered, permanently or significantly, the predominance of polemics in the exchanges between the East and the Catholic and Protestant West (Cistellini 1982).

More typical in the succeeding centuries was the debate within Catholic circles over the proper balance between study and the prayer cycle of the monastery. This erupted in the epic battle between the Benedictine reformer and intellectual Jean Mabillon (1632–1707) and his fierce critic, the Trappist leader Armand-Jean Le Bouthie de Rance (1626–1700) (see Leinsle in this volume). This early eighteenth-century exchange took place, however, entirely within a Western, Catholic context that never referenced Eastern monastics or authorities. That trajectory had already been signaled in the brilliant work of the Jesuit Denis Petau (1583–1652). Requested by members of his order in Constantinople to write a major piece "against the errors of the Greeks," Petau was never able to respond. In various brief observations, however, he recapitulated the Latin position in the *filioque*; reaffirmed the Latin Manuel Kalekas's (n.d.–1410) defense of the use of dialectic in theological exposition against Nikephorus Gregoras (ca. 1295–1360), and concluded that Gregory Palamas (1296–1359) had fundamentally misunderstood the meaning of the Pseudo-Dionysus's teachings by subjecting them to a distinction between God's "essence" and "energies" Petau maintained was not that obvious in the Dionysian corpus (Hofmann 1976, 27–28, 111, 131–32). Similarly, the most strictly meditative and eremitic movements within the Benedictine tradition, beginning with the Carthusians in 1084 and the Carmelites, most famously Teresa of Avila (1515–82), developed a tradition of "mental imagery" that, when discovered by Orthodox observers, generally fell under condemnation. The rejection of the hesychast tradition by the West that had found expression in the confrontation between Gregory Palamas and Barlaam of Calabria (ca. 1290–1348) in the fourteenth century meant that only rarely by the early modern era can Orthodox spiritual fathers and mothers be found who expressed at least some guarded endorsement of the use of such images in meditation. Thus, both Theophan the Recluse (1815–94) and even earlier, Nicodemos the Hagiorite in his *Unseen Warfare* gave a cautious blessing to those who sought to ward off demonic imaginary suggestions by use of positive imagination, but still condemned reliance upon visions or ecstatic revelations (Sveshnikov 2009, 38).

These developments too, taken in tandem with parallel developments in the areas of ecclesiology and liturgical/para-liturgical piety illustrated how little influence Orthodox monastic-ascetic practices and the East's mystical insights and teachings now exercised upon the Western monastic, ascetic, and spiritual traditions. Instead, the engagement of the Orthodox with the consequences of various manifestations of "Enlightenment" would intensify both the compensatory as well as the aggressive responses to the theological issues already raised in the early modern era (see Moschos's essay in this volume).

# BIBLIOGRAPHY

Allatios, Leo. 1970. *De ecclesiae occidentalis atque orientalis perpetua consensione libri tres.* Farnborough, UK: Gregg.

Atwood, Craig D. 2009. *The Theology of the Czech Brethren from Hus to Comenius.* University Park: Pennsylvania State University Press.

Backus, Irena Dorota. 1997. *The Reception of the Church Fathers in the West: From the Carolingians to the Maurists.* Leiden: Brill.

Barbour, Hugh Christopher. 1993. *The Byzantine Thomism of Gennadios Scholarious and his Translation of the Commentary of Armandus de Bellovisu on the De ente et essentia of Thomas Aquinas.* Vatican City: Libreria editrice vaticana.

Batalden, Stephen K. 1982. *Catherine II's Greek Prelate: Eugenios Voulgaris in Russia, 1771–1806.* New York: Columbia University Press.

Bonsell, Dom Leo. 1969. "Benedictine Hagiorites." *Eastern Churches Review* 2 (3): 262–267.

Cistellini, Antonio. 1982. "Oratoire Philippin." In *Dictionnaire de Spiritualité Ascétique et Mystique Doctrine et Histoire; Fascicules LCCIV-LXXV,* edited by M. Viller et al., 853–876. Paris: Beauchesne.

Cracraft, Joel. 1971. *The Church Reforms of Peter the Great.* Stanford, CA: Stanford University Press.

Dagron, Gilbert. 2003. *Emperor and Priest: The Imperial Office in Byzantium.* Translated by Jean Birrell. Cambridge: Cambridge University Press.

Davey, Colin. 1987. *Pioneer for Unity: Metrophanes Kritopoulos (1589–1639) and Relations between the Orthodox, Roman Catholic and Reformed Churches.* Warrington, UK: Hutson Print.

Davey, Colin. 2000. "The Gospels of Jakov of Serres, the Family Brankovic and the Monastery of St. Paul on Mount Athos." In *Through the Looking Glass: Byzantium through British Eyes,* edited by Robin Cormack. Burlington, VT: Ashgate, 135–144.

Doll, Peter M. 2006. *Anglicanism and Orthodoxy: 300 Years after the "Greek College" in Oxford.* New York: Peter Lang.

Gedeon, Manouel Joannou. 1890. *Patriarchikoi Pinakes: Eideseis istroikai viographikai peri ton Patriarchon Konstantinoupoleos (36–1884 AD).* Constantinople: Lorenz & Keil.

Gentilcore, David. 1992. *From Bishop to Witch: The System of the Sacred in Early Modern Terra d'Otranto.* Manchester, UK: Manchester University Press.

Gill, Joseph. 1959. *The Council of Florence.* Cambridge: Cambridge University Press.

Halecki, Oscar. 1968. *From Florence to Brest (1439–1596).* Hamden, CT: Archon Books.

Hartnup, Karen. 2004. *"On the Beliefs of the Greeks": Leo Allatios and Popular Orthodoxy.* Leiden: Brill.

Hering, Gunnar. 1968. *Oekumenisches Patriarchat und europäische Politik, 1620–1638.* Wiesbaden: Franz Steiner Verlag.

Himka, John-Paul. 2005. "Confessional Relations in Galicia." In *Galicia: A Multicultured Land,* edited by Chris Hann and Paul Robert Magocsi, 22–35. Toronto: University of Toronto Press.

Hofmann, Michael. 1976. *Theologie, Dogma und Dogmenentwicklung im theologischen Werk Denis Petaus Mit einem biographischen und einem bibliographischen Anhang.* Bern, Frankfurt, and Munich: Herbert Lang, Peter Lang.

Hudson, Nancy J. 2007. *Becoming God: The Doctrine of Theosis in Nicolas of Cusa.* Washington, DC: Catholic University of America Press.

Keul, István. 2009. *Early Modern Religious Communities in East-Central Europe: Ethnic Diversity, Denominational Plurality, and Corporative Politics in the Principality of Transylvania, 1526–1691.* Leiden: Brill.

Kimbrough, S.T. 2005. *Orthodox and Wesleyan Scriptural Understanding and Practice.* Crestwood, NY: St. Vladimir's Seminary Press.

Kimbrough, S.T. 2007. *Orthodox and Western Ecclesiology.* Crestwood, NY: St. Vladimir's Seminary Press.

Knowles, Dom David. 1963. *The Monastic Order in England: A History of Its Development from the Times of St. Dunstan to the Fourth Lateran Council, 940–1216.* Cambridge: Cambridge University Press.

Leppin, Hartmut, and Hauke Ziemssen. 2007. *Maxentius: der Letzte Kaiser in Rom.* Mainz: Von Zabern.

Livanos, Christopher. 2006. *Greek Tradition and Latin Influence in the Work of George Scholarios.* Piscataway, NJ: Gorgias Press.

Makrides, Vasilios N. 2006. "Greek Orthodox Compensatory Strategies towards Anglicans and the West at the Beginning of the Eighteenth Century." In *Anglicanism and Orthodoxy 300 Years after the "Greek College" in Oxford,* edited by Peter M. Doll, 249–287. Oxford: Peter Lang.

Manukyan, Arthur. 2010. *Konstantinopel und Kairo: die Herrnhuter Brüdergemeine im Kontakt zum Ökumenischen Patriarchat und zur Koptischen Kirche. Interkonfessionelle und interkulturelle Begegnungen.* Würzburg: Ergon-Verlag.

Mastrantonis, George. 1982. *Augsburg and Constantinople: The Correspondence between the Tübingen Theologians and Patriarch Jeremiah II of Constantinople on the Augsburg Confession.* Brookline, MA: Holy Cross Orthodoxy Press.

McGinn, Bernard. 1998. *The Flowering of Mysticism: Men and Women in the New Mysticism (1200–1350).* New York: Crossroad.

McGinn, Bernard. 2005. *The Harvest of Mysticism in Medieval Germany (1300–1500).* New York: Herder and Herder.

Moennig, Ulrich. 1998. "Die griechischen Studenten am Hallenser Collegium orientale theologicum." In *Halle und Osteuropa: Zur europäischen Ausstrahlung des hallischen Pietismus,* 299–329. Hallesche Forschungen 1. Halle: Verlag der Franckeschen Stiftungen Halle im Max Niemeyer Verlag Tübingen.

Nikodemos the Hagiorite. 2006. *Exomologetarion: A Manual of Confession.* Edited and translated by George Dokos. Riverside, CA: Uncut Mountain Press.

Nikodemos the Hagiorite. 1989. *A Handbook of Spiritual Counsel.* Edited and translated by Peter A. Chamberas. New York: Paulist Press.

Noble, Samuel, and Alexander Treiger, eds. 2014. *The Orthodox Church in the Arab World 700–1700: An Anthology of Sources.* Foreword by Metropolitan Ephrem (Kyriakos). DeKalb: Northern Illinois University Press.

Osborne, Kenan B. 2007. *The Permanent Diaconate: Its History and Place in the Sacrament of Orders.* New York: Paulist Press.

Ott, Ludwig. 1969. *Das Weihesakrament.* Freiburg: Herder.

Pagodin, Ambrosius. 1996–1997. "On the Reception into the Orthodox Church" In *Vestnik Russkogo Khristianskogo Dvizheniya, Paris, New York, Moscow* I (173); II (174). Reprinted and edited by Alexander Mileant. La Canada, CA: Holy Trinity Orthodox Mission.

Papadakis, Aristeides. 1994. *The Christian East and the Rise of the Papacy. The Church 1071–1453 A.D.* Crestwood, NY: St. Vladimir's Seminary Press.

Roeber, A. Gregg. 2013. *Hopes for Better Spouses: Protestant Marriage and Church Renewal in Early Modern Europe, India, and North America.* Grand Rapids, MI: Eerdmans.

Roeber, A. Gregg. 2010. "The Waters of Rebirth: The Eighteenth Century and Transoceanic Protestant Christianity." *Church History* 79 (1): 40–76.

Russell, Norman. 2013. "From the 'Shield of Orthodoxy' to the 'Tome of Joy': The Anti-Western Stance of Dositheos II of Jerusalem (1641–1707)." In *Orthodox Constructions of the West*, edited by George Demacopoulos and Aristotle Papanikolaou, 71–82. New York: Fordham University Press.

Shukman, Ann. 2006. "The Non-Jurors, Peter the Great, and the Eastern Patriarchs." In *Anglicanisn and Orthodoxy: 300 Years after the "Greek College" in Oxford*, edited by Peter M. Doll, 174–191. Oxford: Peter Lang.

Sveshnikov, Sergei. 2009. *Imagine That: Mental Imagery in Eastern Orthodox and Roman Catholic Private Devotion*. Charleston, S.C.: BookSurge Publishing.

Tamcke, Martin. 2006. "Lutheran Contacts with the Syrian Orthodox Church of the St. Thomas Christians and with the Syrian Apostolic Church of the East in India (Nestorians)." In *Halle and the Beginning of Protestant Christianity in India. Vol. 2 of Christian Mission in the Indian Context*, edited by Andreas Gross et al., 831–878. Halle: Franckesche Stiftungen.

Tsakiris, Vasileios. 2009. *Die gedruckten griechischen Beichtbücher zur Zeit der Türkenherrschaft: Ihr kirchenpolitischer Entstehungszusammenhang und ihre Quellen*. Berlin: Walter de Gruyter.

Ware, Timothy. 1964. *Eustratios Argenti: A Study of the Greek Church under Turkish Rule*. Oxford: Clarendon Press.

Ware, Timothy. 1963. *The Orthodox Church*. London: Penguin.

Williams, Stephen, and Frell, J. G. P. 1999. *The Rome That Did Not Fall: The Survival of the East in the Fifth Century*. London: Routledge.

Woolfenden, Gregory. 2006. "Orthodox Influences on Anglican Liturgy." In *Anglicanism and Orthodoxy 300 Years after the "Greek College" in Oxford*, edited by Peter M. Doll, 225–247. Oxford: Peter Lang.

Young, B. W. 1998. *Religion and Enlightenment in Eighteenth-Century England: Theological Debate from Locke to Burke*. Oxford: Oxford University Press.

*Western Christian Theologies*
*and Philosophies*

CHAPTER 34

....................................................................................................

# DESCARTES, CARTESIANISM, AND EARLY MODERN THEOLOGY

....................................................................................................

AZA GOUDRIAAN

## 1 DESCARTES AND THEOLOGY

....................................................................................................

ON more than one occasion, René Descartes (1596–1650) expressed his desire to do philosophy and stay out of theological debates (Bardout and Marion 2010). He wanted to separate theology and philosophy from each other—a strategy for which Paul Dibon used the shorthand of *séparatisme cartésien* (Dibon 1990, 704, 724). The recent history of research may seem to have honored Descartes's intention by frequently reading the often so-called "father of modernity" (Robertson et al. 2008) in such a decidedly nontheological way that a well-known specialist of Descartes saw reason to plea for a "desecularization of Descartes," declaring that "Descartes's theism pervades his entire philosophical outlook" (Cottingham 2012, 16). Indeed, in Cartesian metaphysics, from the *Discours de la méthode* (1637) via the *Meditationes de prima philosophia* (1641) until the *Principia philosophiae* (1644), God has a very significant place. There is, therefore, good reason for the sustained scholarly attention that Descartes's theory of God has received in recent years (Arbib 2013).

A total separation between philosophy and theology was, of course, impossible, and Descartes himself acknowledged a certain thematic overlap between faith and philosophy (Gouhier 1972, 213; Bardout and Marion 2010, 208). Moreover, in the reception history of the seventeenth and eighteenth centuries the new philosophy of Descartes was quite often read and evaluated in theological terms. Both supporters and opponents incorporated theological standards when they explained why Descartes's philosophy was either helpful or dangerous (Israel 2001, 23–58). In Lutheran Uppsala, for example, the mathematician and theologian Johan Bilberg (1646–1717) noted in 1685 that Cartesian dualism was a very helpful incentive for the human soul to seek God and abandon any preoccupation with material things (Knuuttila 2001, 1244). On the other hand, Roman Catholic theologians at the University of Caen asserted in 1677 that "Descartes' principles of philosophy seem to us contrary to sounder theological doctrine" (McClaughlin 1979, 567).

Opposition against and agreement with the philosophy of Descartes did not coincide with the confessional divisions of the early modern period. For the most part, positive reception and negative rejection transcended confessional boundaries, disapproval being the majority view in initial reactions from Roman Catholic, Reformed, and Lutheran writers. In any case, the question may be asked what the significance was of the confessional viewpoint, both in Descartes himself and in early modern receptions of his philosophy. This chapter focuses on Descartes's philosophy from the perspective of the confessional theologies that responded to him. What were the main theological issues in the debates on the philosophy of Descartes? Descartes's religion and theology have been studied by different authors (including Gouhier 1972; Marion 1986; and Devillairs 2004), and the reception history of Cartesanism has been the subject of numerous investigations (including Ariew 2011; De Raymond 2003; Dibon 1990; Israel 2001; Lindborg 1965; Schmaltz 1999; Schmaltz 2002; Schmaltz 2004; Schmaltz 2008; Trevisani 2011; and Verbeek 1991; Verkbeek 1992; Verbeek 1993). The question to what extent the reception of Cartesianism was shaped by differences between confessions, however, is not frequently answered. With respect to the German reception it has even been noted that the "confessional motives that triggered or profoundly influenced the school conflicts about Cartesian rationalism have entered into oblivion" (Marti 2011, 425). It may be helpful, therefore, to ask the question how debates about the philosophy of Descartes were related to confessional boundaries and intraconfessional distinctions.

## 2 DESCARTES, THEOLOGY, AND CONFESSIONAL BOUNDARIES

Descartes himself was clear about his Roman Catholic convictions. The Calvinist Jacobus Revius (1586–1658) reports that Descartes told him once that "our whole theology is in St. Thomas" (Revius 2002, 9). If historically accurate, this statement would reflect the Jesuit *ratio studiorum* that guided educational institutions such as the College of La Flèche (De Raymond 2003, 22–23, 68–70). Descartes spoke in an inclusive way about "our theologians" (AT 1996, 3:267), meaning the Roman Catholic confreres of his addressee Marin Mersenne (1588–1648), a group that was clearly distinct from the "ministers of this country," the Netherlands. Descartes could refer to the consensus of the "universal Catholic Church," as expressed at the Lateran Council, in one breath with the consensus of "all philosophers" (AT 1996, 7:425). Having been educated at the Jesuit College of La Flèche, Descartes in later years remained interested in knowing how Jesuits assessed his philosophy (Gouhier 1972, 127–30; Ariew 2011). Yet, as Descartes wrote to Constantijn Huygens (1596–1687), he wanted to stay away from "religious controversies" and be left alone by Jesuits and Reformed ministers alike (AT 1996, 3:784). In 1642, "both the ministers and the Jesuits" seemed as yet unwilling to accept Descartes's new philosophy (AT 1996, 3:782).

Descartes's contemporaries and subsequent generations knew him as a Roman Catholic who received his education from the Jesuits, and they occasionally also described his ideas in confessional terms. Thus, Johannes Heine (1610–86), a Reformed theologian of Herborn, paraphrasing a letter in which Descartes wrote that "his philosophy is very much in line with theology (of the Papists, that is) and in no part against it," expressed his fear that students would be enticed, *duce Cartesio*, to embrace the errors of papism (Menk 1985, 148). Similarly, in the 1670s, some in England regarded Cartesian philosophy as an enterprise supported mainly by Jesuits and intended to advance Catholicism and undermine Protestant religion (Henry 2013, 134). On the other hand, however, the Jesuit Louis Le Valois (1639–1700) asserted that Descartes's view of matter was "in line with the errors of Calvin" (Scheib 2008, 107; Schmaltz 2002, 41, 68; Sortais 1929, 54). Le Valois accused "Descartes and his most famous followers" of "being in accord with Calvin and the Calvinists on principles of philosophy that are against the doctrine of the church" (Bouillier 1970, 1:579–82). Similar views were maintained by other Roman Catholics as well, such as the Jesuit Antoine Boschet (1642–99) (De Raymond 2003, 91). This critique was mainly motivated by the Cartesian view of the Eucharist, which was one of seemingly only few controversies on Cartesianism that were fought more strictly along confessional lines. The Cambridge Platonist Ralph Cudworth (1617–88), too, associated Descartes with Calvinism, but for a totally different reason: he criticized Descartes for teaching, in Danton Sailor's words, "both of the complementary errors to be found in Atheistic Fatalism and Divine Fatalism, i.e. Hobbesism and Calvinism" (Sailor 1962, 140; Gasparri 2007b, 135).

Among the religious or theological terms that early modern authors used to describe Cartesian philosophy, the most significant may have been atheism, enthusiasm, and Pelagianism. The most radical description, obviously, was that Descartes's philosophy entailed *atheism*. It was an observation made by scholars from different confessional backgrounds (Heyd 1995, 110). Descartes defended himself against the accusation by the Reformed professor Gisbertus Voetius (1589–1676) in Utrecht (Verbeek 1991). The charge of atheism is also found in, for example, the French Jesuit Jean Hardouin (1646–1729) (Bouillier 1970, 1:578), the Anglican Samuel Parker (1640–88) (Pacchi 1988, 305–6), and the Lutheran Conrad Samuel Schurzfleisch (1641–1708) (Borghero 2001, 399–400). Still, the charge of atheism came in different forms. In Gisbertus Voetius and Martin Schoock (1614–69), it aimed at the combination of two elements in Descartes's reasoning: his doubting denial of God and his rejection of the foundations of traditional arguments for God's existence on the one hand, and what Voetius and Schoock saw as the presentation of a totally unconvincing alternative on the other hand (Verbeek 1991; Goudriaan 1999, 183–86). Descartes's response was that presenting an unconvincing alternative revealed incompetence rather than atheism (AT 1996, 8/2:164–68). Other critics linked atheism specifically with the Cartesian doubt of everything, including God. There were those—like, for example, the Reformed scholar Jacobus Revius (Goudriaan 1999, 186–87), the anonymous author of an Oratorian text (Schmaltz 2004, 217), and the Lutheran theologian Justus Christoph Schomer (1648–93) (Schomer 1703, 3)—who argued until well into the eighteenth century that this doubt involved an atheism that was, at least, temporary (Borghero 2001, 399–400; Marti 2011, 430; AT 1996, 8/2:367). Still others argued that the method of doubt was not inherently atheist, but had atheism as its practical result (Borghero 2001, 398–99). Samuel Clark (1675–1729), Henry More (1614–87), and Isaac Newton (1642–1727) connected the charge of atheism with another part of Cartesian philosophy: they saw it as an implication of Descartes's mechanistic view of the world (Pannenberg 1996, 151–52; Pacchi 1988, 294, 305–6; Henry 2013). After the publication of Spinoza's (1632–77) works, the atheism diagnosis acquired still another connotation when the philosophy of Descartes came to be accused of "Spinozism," as was the case in late seventeenth-century and early eighteenth-century Italy (Comparato 1998b, 984–85). Reading Descartes through the lens of Spinozism was by no means a typically Roman Catholic phenomenon; it was also done by Dutch Protestants (Israel 2001, 482–84).

Another qualification of Cartesianism that had a clear theological connotation was *enthusiasm*. The originally Protestant label of enthusiasm indicated some combination of a claim to being directly inspired by God and a neglect, if not contempt, for "means of grace" such as the use of Holy Scripture (Heyd 1995). It was applied to Cartesianism by a Reformed critic such as Martin Schoock, who observed that Descartes's argument made a transition from a subjective idea to the existence of the object of this idea (Verbeek 1991, 216–18; Heyd 1995, 113; Savini 2004). The critique of Cartesian enthusiasm had different connotations. It was not the specialty of one of the major confessions at the time: as Heyd has shown, it is, in addition to Reformed circles, also found in Anglican, Lutheran, and Roman Catholic authors (Heyd 1995, 114–39; Henry 2013, 128).

Some of Descartes's contemporaries and later readers asserted that several of his ideas qualified as *Pelagianism*, the late ancient heresy that denied original sin (Scribano 1988, 15–23; Verbeek 1992, 44–45; Lennon 2013; Goudriaan 2012, 192–99). Samuel Maresius (1599–1673), for example, a Reformed theologian who initially was a supporter of Descartes, later in his life made this charge of Pelagianism (Maresius 2009, 8–9, 17–19; Frank 1865, 80). Not only Protestants, however, identified a Pelagian element in Descartes. The Jansenist Antoine Arnauld (1612–94), otherwise a defender of Cartesianism (Ariew 2011, 272–75), observed that Descartes's "letters are full of Pelagianism" (Schmaltz 2008, 144; Schmaltz 2004, 212). This assessment related to Descartes's remarks on the human will, which according to the philosopher "makes us in a certain way similar to God and seems to exempt us from being subject to Him" (AT 1996, 5:85). This high regard for free will notwithstanding, Descartes did not publicly endorse "the Arminians, who seem to be those who have the greatest deference to free will." He noted that "even" the Remonstrants denied that free will and human prayer compromised the immutability of God (AT 1996, 4:316). In his conversation with the Reformed student Frans Burman (1628–79), the philosopher reportedly distanced himself more explicitly from the Remonstrants, declaring that with respect to the divine decrees and how these relate to human prayer, he felt more affinity with the views of the Reformed theologian Franciscus Gomarus (1563–1641) than with those of the Remonstrants or the Jesuits: God, decreeing what He will give to humans, simultaneously decrees the human prayer that will precede these gifts (AT 1996, 5:166). There were certainly parallels between Descartes and the Remonstrants (Verbeek 1992, 1–6), and in 1644 Etienne de Courcelles (1586–1659), a Remonstrant theologian, translated the *Discours de la méthode* and two other texts into Latin; but it is not clear that he incorporated Cartesian philosophy in his theology to any significant extent (Thijssen-Schoute 1989, 433–35).

The use of theological labels such as atheism, enthusiasm, and Pelagianism, then, seems not clearly differentiated along confessional lines. The transconfessional character of the criticism was mirrored by a positive reception of Cartesianism that likewise transcended confessional boundaries. Initially, the number of Cartesians among Reformed Protestants was particularly notable. A Lutheran critic, writing in 1678, observed that most followers of Descartes were Calvinists—theologians such as Frans Burman, Abraham Heidanus (1597–1678), and Christopher Wittich (1625–87). He knew no Roman Catholic Cartesians, especially because of the implications of Cartesianism for the doctrine of transubstantiation. And he hoped "better things" of Lutherans (Alberti 1678, § 27). Cartesian philosophy, however, did attract adherents among Lutherans, certainly in the eighteenth century (Bohatec 1912, 51–55) and clearly also among Roman Catholics.

If positions on Cartesian philosophy, in general, crossed confessional boundaries, the further question can be asked whether it is possible to identify certain groups within the different confessions that were particularly keen to embrace Cartesian philosophy. Especially Cocceianism and Jansenism can be mentioned here. The question of their specific affinity with Cartesianism has been a subject of scholarly debate.

# 3 Cartesianism and Cocceian Theology

In 1676, university and civic authorities in Leiden censured a number of views that were connected, broadly speaking, with two intellectual traditions: Cartesianism and Cocceianism. The Reformed theologian Johannes Cocceius developed a federal theology with an exegetical, systematic, and ethical profile that differed clearly from both mainstream Reformed theology and especially from the theology of the Further Reformation movement (Van Asselt 2001). As a matter of fact, a number of influential Dutch Cartesians, especially theologians, favored the theological positions of Cocceius (Van Asselt 2001, 340). One could think of Frans Burman, Christoph Wittich, and Petrus Allinga (1658–92). Valentin Alberti (1635–97), a German Lutheran theologian, joined Cartesianism and Cocceianism together as a "twofold Kappa" by which the

Dutch Republic was troubled (Alberti 1678; on this work see De Angelis 2010, 309–17). It is hard, however, to find clear evidence of an intrinsic affinity between the theology of Cocceius and the philosophy of Descartes. Cocceius himself is known to have written in a critical way about Cartesian doubt, and as late as 1669, the year of his death, he admitted: "I have not yet been able to study the new philosophy" (Van Asselt 2001, 80). Among those who followed Cocceius in theology were several well-known writers who were also convinced Cartesians. Various explanations have been offered for this "alliance" of Cartesianism and Cocceianism (Van der Wall 1996; Van Asselt 2001). The Cartesian interests of several Cocceians should probably be explained by factors external to Cocceian theology per se (Van Asselt 2001). The conceptual overlap between the two systems is limited, which is illustrated by the fact that there were anti-Cartesian Cocceians. Still, Van der Wall's suggestion that the notion of a separation of philosophy and theology may provide an explanation seems rather plausible (Van der Wall 1996). Cocceius was not an advocate of using the Bible in philosophical matters (Van Asselt 2001, esp. 93–94). This conviction may have provided a common ground between Cocceian theology and Cartesianism, while it separated both Cocceians and Cartesians from the *philosophia sacra* approach that was a major concern of Voetius.

## 4 Cartesianism and Jansenism

Jansenism and Cartesianism have been considered allies since the late seventeenth century. "The theologians of Port-Royal," said Pierre Jurieu (1637–1713), "have as much affection for Cartesianism as they have for Christianity" (Schmaltz 2004, 212). Francisque Bouillier (1813–99), the author of a classic history of Cartesianism, argued that Jansenism and Cartesianism shared an important conviction and favored Augustinian thinking. For Cartesians, as Bouillier saw it, "God is the unique efficient cause, the sole actor who acts in us; the Jansenists attribute everything to the grace that works everything in us without us: here is the point where Jansenism and Cartesianism meet each other." In addition, Jansenism and Cartesianism had a common enemy: the Jesuits (Bouillier 1970, 1:432–33). Bouillier's view of a "natural alliance between the doctrines of Jansenius and those of Descartes" (Bouillier 1970, 1:434) has been criticized on several grounds. First, Jansenists and like-minded people included significant opponents of Descartes, such as Louis-Paul du Vaucel (1640–1715) and Isaac-Louis Le Maistre de Sacy (1613–84) (Schmaltz 2004, 212–13). Moreover, while a tendency to occasionalism and divine monocausality can be noted in French Cartesianism (Rodis-Lewis 1993)— which at first sight might seem to dovetail nicely with the Jansenist focus on grace and God's sovereignty—this was one quite specific interpretation of Descartes, whose confidence in his own philosophy and in the power of free will did not fit very well at all with the Augustinian anthropology of Pierre Nicole (1625–95), Antoine Arnauld, and others (Schmaltz 2004, 212; Janowski 2004). The Paris condemnation of 1691 was indeed concerned with both Cartesian and Jansenist tenets. Schmaltz has argued, however, that a combined attack on the two was at the time "politically convenient" rather than being founded in doctrinal affinity (Schmaltz 2004).

The fact that Cocceian, Jansenist, and other theologies were combined with Cartesian philosophy, or selected elements of it, may give a new meaning to Descartes's words in a 1641 letter, that "there will be no difficulty, it seems to me, in accommodating theology to my way of philosophizing" (AT 1996, 3:295). Theologies that embraced Descartes's "manner of philosophizing" could be very different indeed. On the other hand, theologies from opposed confessional backgrounds could reveal a striking consensus in their criticism of Cartesian philosophy.

## 5 TRANSCONFESSIONAL CRITICISMS

Major confessions—Roman Catholics, Lutherans, and Reformed Protestants—displayed a remarkable degree of consensus in their rejection of certain elements in Cartesianism. This can be seen easily by comparing Roman Catholic condemnations (at Louvain in 1662, by the Paris Oratorians in 1678, by the University of Paris in 1691, by the Jesuits in 1706; all conveniently accessible in English translation in Ariew 1994) with an official censure in a Reformed context (Leiden 1676) and in Lutheran works of controversy that discuss Cartesianism (such as Alberti 1678; Osiander 1684; Weismann 1745).

Cartesian *doubt* was a major concern to the different confessions. Descartes's metaphysics begins with doubt of all things, including the existence of God. This doubt, he indicated, was more than a suspension of judgment: the objects of doubt are rejected as being false or fictitious. Doubt was mentioned in the Leiden condemnation of 1676 (Molhuysen 1918), the Paris condemnation of 1691, the Jesuit list of 1706 (Ariew 1994), and in Lutheran texts as well (Osiander 1684; Weismann 1745). The interpretations and responses varied. Studying the debates between 1660 and 1715, Carlo Borghero (2001) has made a conceptual distinction between three different assessments of Descartes's doubt. These may be found in one and the same author: the view that Descartes was not a real skeptic, the notion that he was a skeptic by implication though not by intention, and the idea that Descartes was indeed a skeptic. These different assessments are found throughout different confessions. The majority view, reflected in the condemnations, was that Cartesian doubt was real and that it was not a good thing, neither philosophically nor theologically. God's existence as an object of Cartesian doubt is mentioned specifically in the Leiden (1676) and Paris (1691) condemnations. Cartesians however, from Johannes Clauberg (1622–65) to Antoine Le Grand (1629–99), frequently endorsed the first interpretation, insisting on the mere methodical and provisional character of Cartesian doubt (Borghero 2001).

The Cartesian *dualism* of mind (as a substance defined by thinking—*cogitatio*) and matter (as a substance defined by extension—*extensio*) was targeted, in one way or another, by many condemnations. The definition of the *mind* as essentially thinking was rejected by the Reformed in Leiden (1676), by the Oratorians in Paris (1678), and it also appears in the list of the Lutheran historian Weismann (1677–1747) (1745). An important problem with the definition of the mind as a thinking substance was that "thinking," being an action, could not define a substance; and being transitory, would cast doubt on the immortality of the soul (Goudriaan 2006, 243–50; Osiander 1684, 210–13). The definition of *matter* as, essentially, extension featured in both Roman Catholic (Louvain 1662, Paris Oratorians 1678, University of Paris 1691, Jesuits 1706) and Lutheran (Weismann 1745) lists of rejected positions. Some objected that defining matter as extension would lead to the conclusion that a plurality of worlds is impossible (Ariew 2011, 246, 314). This would impose a limit on the omnipotence of God that neither Roman Catholics nor Protestants (Van Mastricht 1677, 379–83) could accept. Moreover, the assumed impossibility of a vacuum, wrote Bishop Pierre-Daniel Huet (1630–1721), would exclude both creation from nothing (*ex nihilo*) and the possibility for God to annihilate things. The bishop thought that these consequences would also undermine the real presence of the body of Christ in the Eucharist (Huet 1689, 143–44). It was not from a Roman Catholic viewpoint alone, however, that the definition of matter as extension proved to be controversial.

Descartes's view of extension included the notion that "this world, or the totality of corporeal substance, has no limits of its extension" (*Principia philosophiae*, 2.21; AT 1996, 8-1:52). The theory that the world is indefinite or infinite met with disapproval from different confessional sides (Louvain 1662; Leiden 1676; the Jesuit censure of 1706; Weismann 1745). The theory triggered the question whether the creation of another world, beyond this assumed indefinite or infinite world, was possible. The negative response by Cartesians received broad criticism in Roman Catholic and Reformed condemnations (Louvain 1662, Leiden 1676, Paris 1678, Jesuits 1706) as well as in Lutheran authors (Osiander 1684, 171–81; Grapius 1714, 27–29). If the world is considered to be infinite or indefinite, then an attribute that belongs to God alone is being ascribed to the world. Maybe Protestants more often than Catholics added the biblical argument that scripture itself ascribes limits or boundaries to the earth (Osiander 1684, 181–88; Grapius 1714, 29–31).

Furthermore, Roman Catholic, Reformed, and Lutheran lists alike referred to the independent status of philosophy vis-à-vis theology. It seems likely that the censors of Leiden (Heidanus 1676, 89) and the University of Paris (1691; Ariew 1994, 5) targeted later Cartesians rather than Descartes himself. Petrus Van Mastricht (1630–1706), for example, at this point cited Descartes *against* the Cartesians, among whom he counted Spinoza (1677, 34–62). Nevertheless, it is clear that Descartes's strategy of separating philosophy from theology (see, e.g., AT 1996, 4:119) was not unrelated to the positions of these later Cartesians. According to Descartes, philosophy had nothing to say about articles of faith that transcend natural human reason, such as the Trinity and the divine and human natures of Christ. Descartes stated repeatedly that theology, in this respect, should not be subjected to the norms of philosophical rationality. He rather professed the submission of his understanding to the articles of faith. However, there was also an area of common ground between theology and philosophy, and the existence and attributes of God provided an important part of this shared territory. As a philosopher, Descartes wrote extensively about these. Moreover, at least in the case of the Eucharist, Descartes developed a philosophical theory that he considered to be supportive of the theological doctrine of transubstantiation. Biblical passages about the world and other secular issues might well be considered another shared area of interest of both theology and philosophy, but here Descartes warned the theologians against what he considered "abuse" of the Bible: the attempt to obtain secular knowledge from it (Bardout and Marion, 2010). This latter point went clearly against the attempt, exemplified in the *physica sacra* tradition, to coordinate the Bible and philosophical thinking. The Cartesian separation of theology and philosophy became an influential part in some sections of Cartesianism; in Dutch Cartesianism maybe more so than in French Cartesianism. In the late seventeenth century, Italian Cartesians also emphasized the philosophical freedom from theology (Comparato 1998b, 988; Comparato 1998a, 1008). As the cases of Abraham Heidanus and Christoph Wittich show, Reformed theologians, too, supported the Cartesian separation between theology and philosophy (Goudriaan 1996, 166–69; Schmidt-Biggemann 2001, 443–44).

One of the other Cartesian ideas that found opponents across confessional boundaries was the view that the will, not the intellect, makes judgments, or that it can avoid error. It was mentioned both in the Reformed (1676) and the Jesuit censures (1706), and it appeared also on Weismann's list (1745). It is important, furthermore, to realize that the official censures mentioned above do not provide an exhaustive picture of the transconfessional consensus. When one Catholic censor at Rome in 1663 (Armogathe and Carraud 2001, 117) and the University of Paris in 1691 rejected the Cartesian assumption that traditional arguments for God's existence were ineffective, those of Thomas included (Ariew 1994, 5; AT 1996, 8-2:175–76), the University took the same stance as a Reformed theologian such as Revius had done in 1647 (Revius 2002, 78, 158–61).

Descartes's theory of the creation of eternal truths has received considerable attention over the last few decades (the relevant texts of Descartes are listed in Gasparri 2007b, 249–62; Marion 1991, 270–71). In his famous letters to Mersenne of 1630, Descartes argues that God created essential truths, which could have been very different from what they currently are. Both supporters and critics of this theory were found across confessional boundaries. The relatively limited number of those who accepted the creation of eternal truths included, for example, the Franciscan thinker Antoine Le Grand, who was probably the only Cartesian to take this position in early modern England (Gasparri 2007b, 139; Gasparri 2007a, 334), and a Reformed theologian such as Frans Burman (Gasparri 2007b). If the theory was rarely mentioned on official lists of rejected Cartesian ideas—the Jesuit list of 1706 being an exception (Ariew 1994, 6)—the silence was no indication of widespread support. The Cartesian view on God's power and will had opponents on different sides of the theological spectrum. In anti-Cartesian polemics the question was frequently rephrased as "whether God could also do contradictory things?" (Grapius 1713, 92f; with reference to AT 1996, 7:431–32; and AT 1996 4:118). This latter question had obvious implications for God's truthfulness and reliability, and it was often answered negatively, by the Jesuit Antoine Rochon (fl. 1672) (Scheib 2008, 30–31, 97–99), just as well as by the Reformed professor Melchior Leydekker (1642–1721)

(Leydekker 1677, 176–89) and by the Lutheran Osiander (1622–97) (Osiander 1684, 100–114). Cartesians, too, such as Pierre Poiret (1646–1719) or Johannes Braun (1919–2004), were willing to contradict Descartes on this point (Grapius 1713, 94).

Descartes's "invention of the *causa sui*" (Marion 1996, 153; Lee 2006), the theory according to which God is the cause of Himself, was not mentioned in the official censures of 1662, 1676, 1678, 1691, and 1706. The *causa sui* was embraced by several Reformed authors—Lutheran theologian Grapius (1671–1713) (Grapius 1713, 79f) refers, among others, to Johannes Clauberg, Petrus Allinga, Henricus Groenewegen (1640–92), and Christoph Wittich. The notion found critics across the confessional spectrum—from Roman Catholics (Antoine Arnauld and Johannes Caterus [1590–1657]) to Lutherans (Osiander 1684, 84–93), and Reformed Protestants such as Revius and Leydekker (Leydekker 1677, 136–39).

# 6 CONFESSIONAL DIVERSITIES

The theological reception of Descartes was not only marked by moments of transconfessional consensus, it also revealed confessional differences. The single most important issue of confessional disagreement seems to have been the doctrine of the Eucharist. Roman Catholics and Protestants used opposite doctrinal standards when assessing whether Descartes's theory was in line with transubstantiation. Descartes himself wrote about the subject, and believed his philosophy supported this doctrine (Tilliette 2006; Scheib 2008). Several Roman Catholic scholars, such as Antoine Arnauld and Robert Desgabets (1610–78), defended Descartes's theory (Watson 1982; Scheib 2008). Others, however, were not convinced. Transubstantiation is perhaps the issue that placed Descartes's works on the Index in 1663 (Ariew 2011, 219). The Catholic censures of 1662, 1678, and 1706 convey disagreement with Descartes's view that "real accidents" could not exist. As Roger Ariew has noted, opposition to Descartes's denial of absolute accidents "was surely the most frequently repeated criticism of Cartesianism" (Ariew 2011, 245).

Roman Catholic opponents found themselves in agreement with those Protestants who, likewise, did not see how Descartes's position could indeed support transubstantiation. A Lutheran critic such as Valentin Alberti wrote that Descartes "sinned against Papism" (Alberti 1678, §18) and he quoted Plempius's (1601–1671) statement that "a Catholic man could not embrace the philosophy of Descartes" (Alberti 1678, §19). While Alberti was unaware that any Roman Catholic Cartesians existed at all, in 1713 the Lutheran controversialist Grapius was able to list a number of Roman Catholic attempts at combining Cartesian philosophy with belief in transubstantiation. He considered none of these efforts to be convincing. Transubstantiation was a *dogma antiscripturarium* and a clear and distinct perception of the accidents after the consecration should make abundantly clear to a Cartesian mind that transubstantiation did not occur (Grapius 1713, 96–98).

The Reformed tradition rejected the notion of transubstantiation, and in his book against theological Cartesianism, Samuel Maresius mentioned Descartes's philosophical position with its inherent denial of transubstantiation as one of the strong points of this philosophy (Maresius 2009, 3). In 1650, Revius concluded, after having quoted extensively from the *Responsiones*, that Descartes "derided" the doctrine of transubstantiation. He pointed out a number of different aspects of Descartes's "audacity against his theologians" (Revius 1650, 94–103). At the same time, however, Revius pointed out that the "denial of real attributes" was not only a problem for Roman Catholics, but had also implications in an area that "we and they have in common," since "if there are no real accidents, there are no theological habits, faith, hope, and love" (Revius 1650, 103). Revius, then, considered Cartesian philosophy not only as incompatible with Roman Catholic transubstantiation but also with the supraconfessional notion of theological habits as accidents of the human being.

An issue that seems to have received more attention from Protestants than from Roman Catholics is the Cartesian approach to the Bible. Descartes's own references to the Bible have been very well investigated by Vincent Carraud (1989; 1990; 1992). The Bible is not mentioned in the condemnations of Louvain (1662), the Paris Oratorians (1678), or the University of Paris (1691), but it figures in the Leiden censure of 1676 and in Weismann's list of controversial issues. This is not to say that the Bible is not mentioned in Catholic assessments at all: in a 1706 censure of the idea of divine monocausality, the Jesuits reject the view that Biblical statements about human actions need to be taken figuratively since God alone is cause of human actions. The issue of divine monocausality, however, has less to do with Descartes's own philosophy than with later Cartesian thought.

In later Protestant discussions, a much-debated issue was the use of biblical passages in the interpretation of nature. The Genesis account of creation was different from Descartes's hypothesis about a world that emerged from matter put into motion. The Cartesian hypothesis was criticized by both Lutheran and Reformed Protestants, but some Protestant scholars endeavored to interpret the book of Genesis as being in harmony with Cartesianism (De Angelis 2010, 310; Walch 1726, 2227–29, 2505). In addition, the Copernican hypothesis seems hard to reconcile with the Biblical passages on the immobility of the earth (Vermij 2002; Howell 2002; Goudriaan 2006). With respect to these and other issues, Cartesians developed a hermeneutical theory that emphasized the notion of accommodation. The Reformed Cartesian Christoph Wittich suggested (probably not being the first [Frank 1865, 87]) that on questions of nature the Bible often speaks in language that is accommodated to the false opinions of the common people. This theory was widely debated throughout northern Europe (Del Prete 2013; De Angelis 2010; Vermij 2002). Wittich's axiom was clearly in line with the Cartesian separation between theology and philosophy, but it was more radical than Descartes's understanding of divine accommodation, since the philosopher had attributed truth even to accommodated language: in his eyes, it "contained indeed some truth, but as related to humans" (*veritatem quidem aliquam, sed ut ad homines relatam*; AT 1996, 7:142). In any case, to numerous Reformed and Lutheran observers, Wittich's hermeneutic seemed to undermine the reliability of scripture (e.g., Van Mastricht 1677; Osiander 1684). To a certain extent he allowed humans to distinguish, within the biblical texts, the inaccurate from the accurate language (which is different from the metaphorical versus the nonmetaphorical).

# 7 CONCLUSION

The theological receptions of Descartes are informative not only about the different ways in which this new philosophy was received, but also about Christian theology in the early modern period. The interaction between theologians and Cartesian philosophy reveal both transconfessional consensus and confessional particularity. The consensus throughout different confessions is perhaps most noteworthy in light of the prevalence of interconfessional controversy in this the era. Early modern Europe is easily conceived of as an intellectual world fragmented by confessional antagonism. The reception of Descartes does indeed reveal variations that can be explained by confessional differences. Perhaps more significant, however, is that confessional divisions have only limited explanatory value as far as the reception history of Descartes's philosophy is concerned. Not only did Descartes find adherents throughout the main confessions, but also the anti-Cartesian theological opposition shared a wide range of identical objections—seemingly independently from the existing confessional disagreements. This is not surprising, insofar as the main subject of the reception history is philosophical theology or *theologia naturalis*, not confessional doctrines per se. Both Roman Catholic and Protestant Cartesians adopted Cartesian ideas, and anti-Cartesians from various confessional backgrounds turned out to share fundamental notions of philosophical theology in spite of—or along with—their confessional disagreements. Transconfessional agreements in early modern theology are perhaps still understudied as far as their content, motives, and significance are concerned. Detailed comparative investigations of theological Cartesianisms and anti-Cartesianisms—as well as their historical genealogies—across the major confessions would not only advance our knowledge of the variegated relations between theology and philosophy in early modern Europe; they could also shed new light on important common grounds shared by otherwise conflicting theologies.

## NOTE TO BIBLIOGRAPHY

References to Descartes's works are from Charles Adam and Paul Tannery, eds., *Œuvres de Descartes*, 11 vols., Paris: Vrin, 1996 (abbreviated as AT 1996).

## BIBLIOGRAPHY

Adams, Charles, and Paul Tannery, eds. 1996. *Œuvres de Descartes*. 11 vols. Reprint. Paris: Vrin.

Arbib, Dan. 2013. "Le Dieu cartésien: Quinze années d'études (1996–2011)." *Revue philosophique de la France et de l'étranger* 138: 71–97.

Alberti, Valentin. 1678. Διπλοῦν Κάππα, quod est Cartesianismus et Coccejanismus, Belgio hodie molesti, nobis suspecti . . . et qua errores nostraeque Ecclesiae interesse examinati. Leipzig.

Ariew, Roger. 2011. *Descartes among the Scholastics*. Leiden: Brill.

Ariew, Roger. 1994. "Quelques condamnations du cartésianisme: 1662–1706." *Bulletin Cartésien XXII, Archives de philosophie* 57: 1–6.

Armogathe, Jean-Robert, and Vincent Carraud. 2001. "La première condamnation des Œuvres de Descartes, d'après des documents inédits aux archives du Saint-Office." *Nouvelles de la République des Lettres* 2: 103–137.

Asselt, Willem J. van. 2001. *The Federal Theology of Johannes Coccejus (1603–1669)*, Leiden: Brill.

Bardout, Jean-Christophe, and Jean-Luc Marion. 2010. "Philosophie cartésienne et théologie: Distinguer pour mieux unir?" In *Philosophie et théologie à l'époque moderne, Anthologie tome III*, edited by Jean-Christophe Bardout, 199–217. Paris: Cerf.

Bizer, Ernst. 1958. "Die reformierte Orthodoxie und der Cartesianismus." *Zeitschrift für Theologie und Kirche* 55: 306–372.

Bohatec, Josef. 1912. *Die cartesianische Scholastik in der Philosophie und reformierten Dogmatik des 17. Jahrhunderts*. Leipzig: A. Deichert.

Borghero, Carlo. 2001. "Cartesius scepticus: Aspects de la querelle sur le scepticisme de Descartes dans la seconde moitié du XVIIe siècle." In *Le scepticisme au XVIe et au XVIIe siècle: Le retour des philosophies antiques à l'Âge classique*, edited by Pierre-François Moreau, 391–406. Paris: Albin Michel.

Bouillier, Francisque. 1970. *Histoire de la philosophie cartésienne*. 2 vols. Reprint of 3rd ed. (1868). Geneva: Slatkine.

Carraud, Vincent. 1989. "Descartes et la Bible." In *Le Grand Siècle et la Bible*, edited by Jean-Robert Armogathe, 277–291. Paris: Beauchesne.

Carraud, Vincent. 1992. "Descartes et l'Écriture sainte." In *L'Écriture sainte au temps de Spinoza et dans le système spinoziste*, 41–70. Paris: Presses de l'Université de Paris-Sorbonne.

Carraud, Vincent. 1990. "Les références scripturaires du corpus cartésien." *Bulletin Cartésien XVIII, Archives de Philosophie* 53: 11–21.

Chappell, Vere, ed. 1992. *Essays on Early Modern Philosophers from Descartes and Hobbes to Newton and Leibniz*. Vol. 3. Cartesian Philosophers. New York: Garland.

Cohen Rosenfield, Leonora. 1957. "Peripatetic Adversaries of Cartesianism in 17th Century France." *Review of Religion* 22: 14–40.

Comparato, Vittor Ivo. 1998a. "Anhänger und Gegner der cartesischen Philosophie." In *Allgemeine Themen, Iberische Halbinsel, Italien*. Vol. 1 of *Die Philosophie des 17. Jahrhunderts*, edited by Jean-Pierre Schobinger, 991–1009. Basel: Schwabe.

Comparato, Vittor Ivo. 1998b. "Die Rezeption der cartesischen Philosophie." In *Allgemeine Themen, Iberische Halbinsel, Italien*. Vol. 1 of *Die Philosophie des 17. Jahrhunderts*, edited by Jean-Pierre Schobinger, 973–990. Basel: Schwabe.

Cottingham, John. 2012. "The Desecularization of Descartes." In *The Persistence of the Sacred in Modern Thought*, edited by Chris L. Firestone and Nathan A. Jacobs, 15–37. Notre Dame, IN: University of Notre Dame Press.

De Angelis, Simone. 2010. *Anthropologien. Genese und Konfiguration einer 'Wissenschaft vom Menschen' in der Frühen Neuzeit*. Berlin: De Gruyter.

Del Prete, Antonella. 2013. "Y a-t-il une interprétation cartésienne de la Bible? Le cas de Christoph Wittich." In *Qu'est-ce qu'être cartésien?*, edited by Delphine Kolesnik-Antoine, 117–142. Lyon: ENS Éditions.

Del Prete, Antonella, ed. 2004. *Il Seicento e Descartes: Dibattiti cartesiani*. Florence: Le Monnier Università.

De Raymond, Jean-François. 2003. *Descartes et le nouveau monde: Le cheminement du cartésianisme au Canada XVIIe-XXe siècle*. Paris: J. Vrin.

Devillairs, Laurance. 2004. *Descartes et la connaissance de Dieu*. Paris: J. Vrin.

Dibon, Paul. 1990. *Regards sur la Hollande du siècle d'or*. Naples: Vivarium.

Frank, Gustav. 1865. *Geschichte der Protestantischen Theologie*. Vol. 2. Leipzig: Breitkopf & Härtel.

Gasparri, Giuliani. 2007a. "La creation des verites éternelles dans la postérité de Descartes." *Revue philosophique de la France et de l'étranger* 132: 323–336.

Gasparri, Giuliani. 2007b. *Le grand paradoxe de M. Descartes: La teoria cartesiana delle verità eterne nell'Europa del XVII secolo*. Florence: Leo S. Olschki.

Gellera, Giovannni. 2013. "The Philosophy of Robert Forbes: A Scottish Scholastic Response to Cartesianism." *The Journal of Scottish Philosophy* 11: 191–211.

Goudriaan, Aza. 2012. "Pelagianism and the Philosophical Orientation of Reformed Orthodoxy." In *Philosophie der Reformierten*, edited by Günter Frank & Herman Selderhuis, 183–201. Stuttgart–Bad Canstatt: Frommann-Holzboog.

Goudriaan, Aza. 1999. *Philosophische Gotteserkenntnis bei Suárez und Descartes, im Zusammenhang mit der niederländischen reformierten Theologie und Philosophie des 17. Jahrhunderts*. Leiden: Brill.

Goudriaan, Aza. 2006. *Reformed Orthodoxy and Philosophy, 1625–1750: Gisbertus Voetius, Petrus van Mastricht, and Anthonius Driessen*. Leiden: Brill.

Goudriaan, Aza. 1996. "Die Rezeption des cartesianischen Gottesgedankens bei Abraham Heidanus." *Neue Zeitschrift für systematische Theologie und Religionsphilosophie* 38: 166–197.

Gouhier, Henri. 1972. *La pensée religieuse de Descartes*. 2nd ed. Paris: Vrin.

Grapius, Zacharias. 1713. *Theologia recens controversa absoluta*. Rostock.

Grapius, Zacharias. 1714. *Theologia recens controversa continuata*. Rostock.

Heidanus, Abraham. 1676. *Consideratien over eenige saecken onlanghs voorgevallen in de Universiteyt binnen Leyden*. 3rd. ed. Amsterdam.

Henry, John. 2013. "The Reception of Cartesianism." In *The Oxford Handbook of British Philosophy in the Seventeenth Century*, edited by Peter R. Anstey, 116–143. Oxford: Oxford University Press.

Heyd, Michael. 1995. *"Be Sober and Reasonable": The Critique of Enthusiasm in the Seventeenth and Early Eighteenth Centuries*. Leiden: Brill.

Howell, Kenneth J. 2002. *God's Two Books. Copernican Cosmology and Biblical Interpretation in Early Modern Science*. Notre Dame, IN: Notre Dame University Press.

Huet, Petrus Daniel. 1689. *Censura philosophiae cartesianae*. Paris.

Israel, Jonathan I. 2001. *Radical Enlightenment. Philosophy and the Making of Modernity, 1650–1750*. Oxford: Oxford University Press.

Janowski, Zbigniew. 2004. "Jansenists, Cartesians and Anti-Cartesians. A Reply to Tad Schmaltz." In *Il Seicento e Descartes: Dibattiti cartesiani*, edited by Antonella Del Prete, 222–229. Florence: Le Monnier Università.

Knuuttila, Simo. 2001. "Schweden und Finnland." In *Das heilige Römische Reich deutscher Nation, Nord–und Ostmitteleuropa*. Vol. 4 of *Die Philosophie des 17. Jahrhunderts*, edited by Helmut Holzhey, 1227–1245. Basel: Schwabe.

Kolesnik-Antoine, Delphine. 2013. *Qu'est-ce qu'être cartésien?* Lyon: ENS Éditions.

Krop, Henri A. 2004. "Der Cartesianismus." In *Grossbritannien und Nordamerika, Niederlande*. Vol. 1 *of Die Philosophie des 18. Jahrhunderts*, edited by Helmut Holzhey and Vilem Mudroch, 1083–1093. Basel: Schwabe.

Lee, Richard A.Jr. 2006. "The Scholastic Resources of Descartes's Concept of God as Causa Sui." In *Oxford Studies in Early Modern Philosophy*, edited by Daniel Garber & Steven M. Nadler. Vol. 3. Oxford: Clarendon Press.

Leech, David. 2014. "More et la lecture athée de Descartes," *Les etudes philosophiques* 108: 81–97.

Lennon, Thomas M. 2013. "Descartes and Pelagianism." *Essays in Philosophy* 14: 194–217.

Lennon, Thomas M. 2008. *The Plain Truth: Descartes, Huet, and Skepticism*. Leiden: Brill.

Leydekker, Melchior. 1677. *Fax veritatis seu exercitationes ad nonnullas controversias quae hodie in Belgio potissimum moventur*. Leiden: Daniel van Gaesbeeck & Felix Lopez.

Lindborg, Rolf. 1965. *Descartes i Uppsala: Striderna om "nya filosofien" 1663–1689*. Stockholm: Almqvist & Wiksell.

Maresius, Samuel. 2009. *Samuel Desmarets, De abusu philosophiae cartesianae surrepente et vitando in rebus theologicis et fidei dissertatio theologica*. Reprint of the 1670 edition. Preface by Giulia Belgioioso, introduction by Igor Agostini and Massimiliano Savini. Hildesheim: Olms 2009.

Marion, Jean-Luc. 1986. *Sur le prisme métaphysique de Descartes: Constitution et limites de l'onto-théo-logie dans la pensée cartésienne*. Paris: PUF.

Marion, Jean-Luc. 1996. *Questions cartésiennes II: Sur l'ego et sur Dieu*. Paris: PUF.

Marion, Jean-Luc. 1991. *Sur la théologie blanche de Descartes: Analogie, creation des verities éternelles et fondement*. New edition. Paris: PUF.

Marti, Hanspeter. 2011. "Konfessionalität und Toleranz: Zur historiographischen Topik der Frühneuzeitforschung." In *Diskurse der Gelehrtenkultur in der Frühen Neuzeit: Ein Handbuch*, edited by Herbert Jaumann, 409–439. Berlin: De Gruyter.

Mastricht, Petrus van. 1677. *Novitatum cartesianarum gangraena*. Amsterdam.

McClaughlin, Trevor. 1979. "Censorship and Defenders of the Cartesian Faith in Mid-Seventeenth Century France." *Journal of the History of Ideas* 40: 563–581.

Menk, Gerhard. 1985. "'Omnis novitas periculosa' Der frühe Cartesianismus an der Hohen Schule Herborn (1649–1651) und die reformierte Geisteswelt nach dem Dreißigjährigen Krieg." In *Comenius: Erkennen—Glauben—Handeln*, 135–163. Sankt Augustin: Hans Richarz.

Molhuysen, P. C. 1918. *Bronnen tot de geschiedenis der Leidsche Universiteit*. Vol. 3. 's-Gravenhage: Martinus Nijhoff.

Muller, Richard A. 2003. *Post-Reformation Reformed Dogmatics: The Rise and Development of Reformed Orthodoxy, ca. 1520 to ca. 1725*. 4 vols. Grand Rapids, MI: Baker.

Osiander, Joh. Adam. 1684. *Collegium considerationum in dogmata theologica Cartesianorum*. Stuttgart.

Pacchi, Arriggo. 1988. "Der Cartesianismus". In *England*. Vol. 3 of *Die Philosophie des 17. Jahrhunderts*, edited by Jean-Pierre Schobinger, 291–309. Basel: Schwabe.

Pannenberg, Wolfhart. 1996. *Theologie und Philosophie: Ihr Verhältnis im Lichte ihrer gemeinsamen Geschichte*. Göttingen: Vandenhoeck & Ruprecht.

Revius, Jacobus. 2002. *Jacobus Revius, A Theological Examination of Cartesian Philosophy: Early Criticisms (1647)*, edited by Aza Goudriaan. Leiden: Brill.

Revius, Jacobus. 1650. *Statera philosophiae cartesianae*. Leiden.

Robertson, Neil, Gordon McOuat, and Tom Vinci, eds. 2008. *Descartes and the Modern*. Newcastle: Cambridge Scholars Publishing.

Rodis-Lewis, Geneviève. 1993. "Der Cartesianismus in Frankreich." In *Frankreich und Niederlande*. Vol. 2 of *Die Philosophie des 17. Jahrhunderts*, edited by Jean-Pierre Schobinger, 398–445. Basel: Schwabe.

Rodis-Lewis, Geneviève. 1981. "Polémiques sur la création des possibles et sur l'impossible dans l'école cartésienne." *Studia cartesiana* 2: 105–123.

Rother, Wolfgang. 2001. "Die Hochschulen in der Schweiz." In *Das heilige Römische Reich deutscher Nation, Nord- und Ostmitteleuropa*. Vol. 4 of *Die Philosophie des 17. Jahrhunderts*, edited by Helmut Holzhey, 447–474. Basel: Schwabe.

Ruler, J. A. van. 1995. *The Crisis of Causality. Voetius and Descartes on God, Nature and Change*. Leiden: Brill.

Sailor, Danton B. 1962. "Cudworth and Descartes." *Journal of the History of Ideas* 23: 133–140.

Savini, Massimiliano. 2004. "La critique des arguments cartésiens dans l'Admiranda methodus de Martin Schoock." In *Il Seicento e Descartes*, edited by Antonella Del Prete, 168–197. Florence: Le Monnier Università.

Scheib, Andreas. 2008. "Dies ist mein Leib." In *Philosophische Texte zur Eucharistie-Debatte im 17. Jahrhundert*. Darmstadt: Wissenschaftliche Buchgesellschaft.

Scheib, Andreas. 2011. "Die *Libertas Philosophandi* als Praktische Metaphysik? Ein Beispiel aus der frühen Descartes-Rezeption." In *Departure for Modern Europe: A Handbook of Early Modern Philosophy (1400–1700)*, edited by Hubertus Busche, 409–423. Hamburg: Felix Meiner.

Schmaltz, Tad M. 1999. "What Has Cartesianism To Do with Jansenism?" *Journal of the History of Ideas* 60: 37–56.

Schmaltz, Tad M. 2008. "Cartesian Freedom in Historical Perspective." In *Descartes and the Modern*, edited by Neil Robertson, Gordon McOuat, and Tom Vinci. Newcastle: Cambridge Scholars Publishing.

Schmaltz, Tad M. 2002. *Radical Cartesianism: The French Reception of Descartes*. Cambridge: Cambridge University Press.

Schmaltz, Tad M. 2004. "A Tale of Two Condemnations: Two Cartesian Condemnations in 17th-Century France." In *Il Seicento e Descartes. Dibattiti cartesiani*, edited by Antonella Del Prete, 203–221. Florence: Le Monnier Università.

Schmidt-Biggemann, Wilhelm. 2001. "Die Schulphilosophie in den reformierten Territorien." In *Das heilige Römische Reich deutscher Nation, Nord- und Ostmitteleuropa*. Vol. 4 of *Die Philosophie des 17. Jahrhunderts*, edited by Helmut Holzhey, 392–447. Basel: Schwabe.

Schomer, Justus Christoph. 1703. *Collegium novissimarum controversiarum in universam theologiam*, edited by Henricus Ascanius Engelke. Rostock.

Scribano, Maria Emanuela. 1988. *Da Descartes a Spinoza: Precorsi della teologia razionale nel Seicento*. Milan: Franco Angeli.

Sortais, Gaston. 1929. "Le Cartésianisme chez les Jésuites Français au XVIIe et au XVIIIe siècle." *Archives de philosophie* 6: 3.

Tepelius, Johannes. 1674. *Historia philosophiae Cartesianae*. Nuremberg: J. Andreae et al.

Thijssen-Schoute, C. Louise. 1989. *Nederlands cartesianisme*, edited by Th. Verbeek. Utrecht: HES.

Tilliette, Xavier. 2006. *Philosophies eucharistiques de Descartes à Blondel*. Paris: Cerf.

Trevisani, Francesco. 2011. *Descartes in Deutschland: Die Rezeption des Cartesianismus in den Hochschulen Nordwestdeutschlands*. Zürich: LIT Verlag.

Verbeek, Theo. 1992. *Descartes and the Dutch: Early Reactions to Cartesian Philosophy, 1637–1650*. Carbondale: Southern Illinois University Press.

Verbeek, Theo. 1991. "Descartes and the Problem of Atheism: The Utrecht Crisis." *Nederlands Archief voor Kerkgeschiedenis/Dutch Review of Church History* 71: 211–223.

Verbeek, Theo. 1993. "From 'Learned Ignorance' to Scepticism: Descartes and Calvinist Orthodoxy." In *Scepticism and Irreligion in the Seventeenth and Eighteenth Centuries*, edited by Richard H. Popkin and Arjo Vanderjagt, 31–45. Leiden: Brill.

Vermij, Rienk. 2002. *The Calvinist Copernicans: The Reception of the New Astronomy in the Dutch Republic, 1575–1750*. Amsterdam: KNAW.

Walch, Johann Georg. 1726. *Philosophisches Lexicon*. Leipzig.

Wall, Ernestine G. E. van der. 1996. "Cartesianism and Cocceianism: a Natural Alliance?" In *De l'Humanisme aux Lumières: Bayle et le protestantisme: Mélanges en l'honneur d'Élisabeth Labrousse*, edited by Michelle Magdelaine, 445–455. Paris: Universitas.

Watson, Richard A. 1982. "Transubstantiation among the Cartesians." In *Problems of Cartesianism*, edited by Thomas M. Lennon, et al. Montreal: McGill-Queen's University Press.

Weismann, Christian Eberhard. 1745. *Introductio in memorabilia ecclesiastica historiae sacrae Novi Testamenti*. Vol. 2. Halle.

# CHAPTER 35

# LEIBNIZ, WOLFF, AND EARLY MODERN THEOLOGY

## URSULA GOLDENBAUM

THERE has been little sustained interest in the theology of Gottfried Wilhelm Leibniz (1646–1716) and Christian Wolff (1679–1754). Philosophers tend to neglect it altogether (with the exceptions of Fouke and Goldenbaum), and we have only one systematic study of Leibniz's theological positions, written by the Catholic theologian Aloys Pichler (Pichler 1869–70). Wolff has received even less attention, although the theological influence of "Wolffianism" has been discussed (Lempp 1976; Aner 1929). It was only after the Second World War that Protestant theologians (Hirsch 1968; Ratschow 1983; Sparn 1986) showed a more serious interest in Leibniz, although this did not extend to Wolff (with the exception of Michael Albrecht's work). At first glance, this is surprising, given the close engagement of both philosophers in the much-needed reconciliation of Christian religion with modern science. There is no doubt that Leibniz's and Wolff's metaphysical systems—and even their logic and epistemology—had great influence on German theology throughout the eighteenth century, and that their ideas sparked some of the most heated public debates of that period (Goldenbaum 2004; Kröger 1979). But these debates display a strong current of theological resistance against the innovations of Leibniz and Wolff, beginning with the publication of Leibniz's *Theodicy* in 1710 (Lorenz 1997). The major theorems under theological critique were those of the best possible world, of preestablished harmony, of the human capability to obtain a priori knowledge of real things (even of God), and finally the foundation of morals—and to some extent of salvation—on the striving for greater perfection. These were the arguments that Leibniz and Wolff had to overcome.

## 1 LEIBNIZ'S TURN FROM LAW TO THEOLOGY—METAPHYSICS

The story is often told that ordinary people in Hannover skewed Leibniz's name to "Loewe-Nix," or "non-believer" (Eberhard and Eckhart 1982, 224); very likely this began with an anecdote those same people heard from their pastors! It is less generally known that Leibniz's deep concern for the Christian religion was responsible for his shift from law to metaphysics in the first place. In 1668, he was already established as a professional lawyer at the court of the Archbishop of Mainz, when he first encountered the French controversy about the possibility of Christian mysteries vis-à-vis the claims of modern science and Cartesianism. How could transubstantiation be possible if corpuscles and local motion produced what we sense? Unsurprisingly, Descartes's work had been placed on the *Index librorum prohibitorum* in 1663.

To be sure, Leibniz had become a partisan of modern mechanical philosophy as a student, and never abandoned his convictions against scholastic Aristototelianism. In 1668, though, he realized at once the enormous danger mechanical philosophy posed to the plausibility of the Christian mysteries (Goldenbaum 1999). Because nobody could believe in something impossible, Leibniz began to work intensively to demonstrate their possibility (although not their truth), and as a first step, he focused on an essential characteristic of the mysteries—that of being mysterious. Accordingly, he questioned any proposition a possible attacker might criticize on the grounds that any such proposition could itself result from an unjustified interpretation of the mystery, and thus be doubted (Leibniz 1923, VI:1:518–35). This strategy worked well against any positive attack against the mysteries (see also Antognazza 2007, 16–44).

As a second step, Leibniz worked out a new metaphysics capable of demonstrating the logical possibility of the Christian mysteries, while also upholding modern mechanical philosophy. The publication of his two metaphysical hypotheses of 1671 (Leibniz 1923, VI:2:219–76) displays already his distinction between phenomena and substances and identifies substances with the mind, thus foreshadowing his mature metaphysics. Third, Leibniz defended the mysteries against Spinoza's (1632–77) critique. The Dutch-Jewish philosopher had raised the problem of how something could be discussed that was, by definition, incomprehensible—as the mysteries (Spinoza 2001, ch. 13). Leibniz, acknowledging the problem as a *nodus durus*, developed his new concept of clear and confused ideas by arguing that we can grasp the *meaning* of these ideas, even if not conceiving them distinctly (Leibniz 1923 VI:1:550–51; Goldenbaum 1999). Leibniz's reports to the Catholic ruler Johann Friedrich (1625–79), and to the famous Jansenist cleric and Cartesian Antoine Arnauld (1612–94)—from May and November 1671, respectively—reveal his enthusiasm about this newfound solution (Leibniz 1923, II:1:174–85, 275–87).

What is remarkable about Leibniz's decision to defend the Christian mysteries (a stance he would maintain until the end of his life) is his general refusal to abandon any of the Christian mysteries, in sharp contrast to many of his contemporaries in the *Republique des lettres*. Because the mysteries had helped to define the Christian religion from its earliest times, he argued, denying them would sever the bond with Christians of the past, who held these mysteries to be true (Leibniz 1923, VI:1:530). Moreover, abandoning Christian mysteries to human will would, in effect, create a new religion grounded in human haughtiness. However, precisely because the mysteries were incomprehensible, human understanding of them remained open to some interpretation—as long as we took them to be true and in agreement with the core teachings of Jesus Christ. The core teachings of Christianity, though, were love and the promise of salvation (see Leibniz's correspondence with Pelisson, in Leibniz 1923, I:6:n.59–61, 65, 68, 75, 78).

## 2  GOD'S INTELLECT, OR EPISTEMOLOGY
## AS THE BASIS OF METAPHYSICS
## AND THEOLOGY

Just as Galileo (1564–1642) stated that geometrical demonstrations constitute a degree of certainty that equals God's knowledge (Galileo 1967, 103), a statement which became part of his accusation in his trial (Galileo 1907, 326–27), Leibniz was convinced that mathematical knowledge can produce "adequate ideas" that do not differ from those in God's intellect (Leibniz 1996, 48–50). Of course, God has nothing but adequate ideas, of all possible things, and also owns them all intuitively. In contrast, human beings have only a few adequate ideas, and usually reach them in a discursive way, by means of demonstration. However, most human ideas are inadequate; derived from the five senses or from empirical knowledge. Such inadequate ideas could not be demonstrated (i.e., analyzed into simple concepts) and were thus not *necessarily* true after the manner of adequate ideas. Notwithstanding the small number of available adequate ideas, Leibniz, like other rationalists, stressed their enormous significance. Adequate ideas were a priori knowledge. These ideas made us similar to God (*imago Dei*) and distinguished us from animals, thus confirming the special status of humans in God's creation.

Although human knowledge is finite and can never reach adequate ideas of the entire world, the certainty of our knowledge of adequate ideas can never be questioned by any of our inadequate ideas. Moreover, the conviction that this universe was created by the most perfect being, according to its absolute good intentions, provides us with the certainty that even unknown or inadequate ideas are nonetheless connected to the adequate ideas we know. Leibniz never truly succeeded in his attempts to provide a thoroughgoing a priori demonstration of an absolutely perfect being—although his hypothesis of preestablished harmony came close. But if the possibility of such absolutely perfect being could be shown, he argued, it would be its privilege to exist necessarily (Leibniz 1969, 647; cf. though Wolff 1962–, II:8:1–12). God's existence could be proven a posteriori though, from the unity and interconnectedness of the created world (its preestablished harmony), as well as from the certainty that no finite thing could have come into existence by itself. Knowing that finite things such as ourselves exist, we can conclude that some self-reliant and most perfect being must exist (Leibniz 2001, 109; Wolff 1962–, II:7.1–7.2:25–114).

Leibniz uses causal definitions to identify adequate ideas (Leibniz 1969, 293). Picking up on the traditional distinction between nominal and real definitions (going back to Aristotle), he defines them in a new way. Nominal definitions contain sufficient, distinctly recognized properties of things that serve to identify them among others. Real definitions display the reality of things. However, the only type of real definitions Leibniz provides are causal definitions, first introduced by Hobbes (1588–1679) (Hobbes 1839, 71–73, *De corpore* I:6, § 13). Such definitions include the cause of the *definiendum*, thereby displaying their possibility and thus reality of its essence. If a circle is explained by its rule of construction—by which it is brought about—we know the circle is possible and have its adequate idea. But if something is contradictory in itself (e.g., a round square), it is impossible in itself, and we cannot have an idea of it—although we can use the words. Wolff builds his logic on this approach (Wolff 1962–, II:1.2:214–15).

Since we have only a small number of causal definitions and thus adequate ideas of things, mostly in mathematics, we have to rely mainly on nominal definitions. While causal definitions allow us to deduce all possible properties of the *definiens*, a nominal definition of a thing can still give us a scope within which we can deduce consequences—until a contradiction occurs, always remaining aware of the presupposed condition that this nominal definition does not contain a hidden contradiction. This epistemological approach provided a new avenue to empirical knowledge, even to history—although historical knowledge could never reach the certainty of philosophical knowledge (Wolff 1962–, II:1.1:1–13), except if supported by divine revelation.

Theologians felt threatened in their monopoly on truth by philosophical confidence in the human capacity for a priori knowledge as certain as that of God. The certainty of scientific truth could be justified by demonstration (i.e., by experiment), while history (and therefore theology) had only subjective sense perceptions; and moreover, only the sense perceptions of people who could no longer be heard as witnesses. Thus, while *they* may well have been inspired, *we* knew about their prophecies by hearsay only. It was this fundamental revolution in epistemology that would cause the "ugly ditch," as Lessing (1729–81) called it (Lessing 1897, 5–7) and that Kierkegaard (1813–55) also complained about (Kierkegaard 2002, 92); this refers to the distinction between necessary truths and truths of fact that has shaped German Protestant theology ever since (Hirsch, 22). But Leibniz and Wolff would also provide answers to this problem that allowed a proper ground for theology.

# 3 THE CONTINGENCY OF THE CREATED WORLD DUE TO ITS DEPENDENCE ON GOD'S WILL

Given the infinity of possible worlds in God's intellect, being in themselves series of compossible things, God must have willed to create one such world through his power. If he had willed otherwise, another world had been chosen, ruled by other laws and including another series of compossible things. This world is thus contingent; even the natural laws are contingent and by no means eternal truths. The only necessary things which have thus to be the same in all possible worlds are the eternal truths of abstract things such as mathematical truths, logic, or natural law, because their opposite is impossible or contradictory. Therefore, truths of fact about contingent things of this world incline but do not necessitate, as Leibniz famously formulated (Leibniz 1969, 310). Nonetheless, there had always to be a reason for anything to happen; God's will and his creation is governed by the principle of sufficient reason. Contingency for Leibniz and Wolff is anything but chance, and rather a form of soft determinism.

However, Leibniz and Wolff distinguished between absolute necessity and a softer necessity. While absolute necessity is a given if the opposite would include a contradiction, contingency is ruled by the principle of sufficient reason, according to which the opposite would not contradict the thing and could well happen to it—although not in *this* chosen world, in which no sufficient reason for such an event had been provided to make it happen. God foresaw everything, including every sufficient reason and cause at creation. Therefore, he knows all the complete concepts of all created things, to which belongs everything that will ever happen to them. Still, things as such could happen otherwise—if another possible world had been chosen.

While this view works to serve modern science, there seems to be no space for miracles, or indeed any sudden intervention of God in his world. Overall, the incidence of miracles is on the decline in the view of Leibniz and Wolff; however, they both argue in favor of the fundamental possibility of miracles by distinguishing between the natural order and God's extraordinary order of the created world (Leibniz 1969, 306–7; Wolff 1962–, II:7.1–7.2:344–45). While the first is ruled by natural laws (*maximes subalternes*) available to human science, the higher general order is known only to God. Miracles are part of the world's general order and were foreseen by God when he created this world— they are in fact essential to this world being the best of those possible. To be sure, the incarnation of Jesus Christ is read as a sign that this world is indeed the best, and as a reason for God's choice of this world (Leibniz 2001, 168). Leibniz will address these two orders as the divine realms of nature and grace, and of efficient and final causes.

However, we find some reluctance to accept many miracles as they traditionally had been believed to happen, given that many apparent miracles had come to be understood as natural events, which could be explained by natural causes. Miracles somehow disturbed the natural course of the universe. Wolff explicitly asks for a *miraculum restitutionis*; that is, for the world to return to its common order after a divine miracle (Wolff 1962–, II:7.1:509). Both philosophers reject a view held by Spinoza and Locke, who saw miracles simply as rare or unusual events. Instead, they belong to the higher general order of this world and are brought about by supernatural divine power. Thus, they were not in conflict with reason (or order), but rather above human reason. Also, they did not happen all of a sudden, according to an arbitrary single volition of God (although it may appear so to human beings). Instead, they had been willed by God when he created this world. But creation, as well as its annihilation or the end of the world, were true miracles that could not have happened by natural power. This is also true for the Christian mysteries, including the appearance of Jesus Christ. These truths we know exclusively from the Holy Scriptures, whose divine origin can be shown (Wolff 1962–, II:7.1:19–20), and which furnish us with the knowledge needed to strive for salvation.

Leibniz's and Wolff's God was the creator of the world but with a stress on *the world*, namely the *entire* universe with everything in it, going far beyond the mere environment of human beings (Rateau 2011, 35–58). God's goal was not exclusively, as Voltaire's Pangloss seems to assume, the suiting of the world to human beings' wishes or their happiness, although such happiness or rather beatitude was also part of God's plan (Leibniz 1969, 326–28; Wolff 1962–, II:7.1:671–72). While God wanted everything to be good, and even desired beatitude for all human beings according to his antecedent will (before creation), he had to permit some unavoidable evil according to his consequential will at creation (Leibniz 2001, 137–38). Nothing God creates can be as perfect as he is himself. All created things must be finite, and thereby necessarily more or less imperfect. This unavoidable imperfection (*malum metaphysicum*) of everything created is the cause for all the evil in the world (Leibniz 2001, 135–38; Wolff 1962–, II:7.1:351–58).

Nonetheless, he chose as much good for each creature as was possible in the best possible world he resolved to create. God being the most perfect being, all-powerful, wise, and good, it is only the best possible world which can fulfill his good intention to express his own glory. To be the best world, it had to be the most diverse among all (com)possible worlds. It is here that human beings gain their central role in God's creation. Because of their rational nature they are uniquely capable of reflecting the diversity of the world, thereby multiplying it even more. This gives human beings—and in particular their adequate ideas—their essential significance, making them similar (*imago Dei*) and special to God, allowing them to keep their personality and to belong to the City of God (Leibniz 1969, 326–28, 640; Wolff 1962–, II:7.2:1052–54).

# 4 HUMAN BEINGS—FREE WILL, SIN, GRACE, AND SALVATION

God created this world by creating monads (Leibniz), respectively elements of the world (Wolff), which would bring about all things in this world via the force they had received from God, and in particular all the phenomena we sense. It is here that Wolff deviates from Leibniz: while the latter sees monads as mere mental forces bringing about all bodily phenomena (*bene fundata* however), the former retains a (Cartesian) dualism (as most scholars assume) or (Spinozistic) parallelism of minds and bodies. But in spite of this difference, both philosophers hold that the perceptions of the mind have to be explained from foregoing perceptions, just as the body's actions have to be explained by their bodily causes, according to the principle of sufficient reason as well as the principle of contradiction. This is the marvelous preestablished harmony created by God, which in itself constitutes proof of his existence.

But according to this preestablished harmony, a body cannot act on an idea, and neither can an idea act on a body. This view was in best agreement with modern science as Leibniz points out (Leibniz 1969, 651). Since Galileo, it was widely accepted that a body could not move if not moved by another body. This principle of inertia implied that no body could be moved by an idea. The new conservation law also stood in the way of the common assumption that an idea could have an impact on bodily motion. Any effect in bodies produced by an idea would change the amount of motion or force of the universe and thus disturb its natural order. The question arose how a mind could move its body at will, and further how we can will freely. That is why preestablished harmony was a challenge to theologians who understood free will as a free *choice* of the will.

Having saved God's free will and the contingency of finite beings without abandoning the causality of modern science, Leibniz and Wolff took on the defense of human free will. They dismissed as indifferentism the common understanding of free will as free choice of the will. Like God, human beings will what they consider to be best. While God chooses the best because he knows what is indeed best and thus acts in complete freedom, human beings rarely know what is truly best, and thus choose what they think it is. Not surprisingly, this often turns out to be the wrong choice. Freedom for Leibniz and Wolff is acting according to adequate ideas, leading to greater perfection. The more adequate ideas we obtain, the greater capacity we have to choose those actions which will make us more perfect. Moreover, we will make our fellows and the world more perfect. Striving for perfection according to adequate ideas will also make us more similar to God, whose choices are infallible.

In addition, the more we come to know God's creation adequately, the more we recognize that this world is the best one possible. Thereby we learn about God's wisdom and goodness which creates the deepest love for God in us, giving us the desire to become more perfect, in order to come closer to God's perfection (Leibniz 1969, 641, 652). The more we comprehend God, the more we will love him and his creation, and the more we will love our neighbor. This love had already been taught by Moses, and given more clarity by Jesus Christ, and it is the core of the Christian religion (Leibniz 1969, 50–51; Wolff 1985, 113–23). Leibniz introduces his new definition of love as bridging the gulf between egotistic self-love and the love of all—loving something makes the lover enjoy the pleasure of the beloved as her own pleasure. This concept of love is also taught by Wolff (Wolff 1962–, II:7.1:668–72).

Leibniz and Wolff distinguish three kinds of evil (Leibniz 2001, 135–38; Wolff 1962–, II:7.1:351–38). As mentioned above, the dominant concept of evil in their thought is that of metaphysical evil, the unavoidable lack of perfection in every creature. Because the lack of perfection is always a lack of power to act, things less perfect are acted upon by others. Moral evil is the lack of the good will to strive for greater perfection, which again is due to the lack of understanding vis-à-vis the bad consequences of a badly chosen action—the decrease of one's own perfection. Such moral evil is considered to be a major source for natural evil—for example, habitual lying may be the likely cause for being socially marginalized (although the cause is not always so obvious). According to the Leibniz-Wolffian concept of perfection as the morally good, sin is nothing but imperfection and is, moreover, relative; that is, less perfect than other actions. Evil is thus not absolutely opposed to goodness. In this view, sin completely loses its absolute, demonic, irrational ground, a perspective that aroused theological concerns.

But if everybody could become more perfect by striving for perfection according to adequate ideas, why would humans need grace? Moreover, if everything had been foreseen and decided at creation by God, without him adding anything in the course of the created world, what role was left for divine grace? Leibniz and Wolff understood grace as God's constant concourse with all his creatures (Leibniz 1969, 323, 652; Wolff 1962–, II:7.1:666; II:7.2:847–63). Everything active in our deeds is due to God's power, and we could not act in the least without him maintaining us and his creation. God in his infinite goodness wants to provide his grace to every creature in this world, but only to the extent that it will serve the entire plan of the best of all possible worlds. Accordingly, grace is not exclusively given to Christians. But it depends on the willingness to accept the measure of grace offered to all, which will, again, depend upon an understanding of the perfection emanating from it. The widespread human complaint about God allowing evil—like the question of why God did not create a better world—are both due to the human unwillingness to accept the measure of divine grace given to them (Leibniz 2001, 206; Wolff 1962–, II:7.1:531–32). By contrast, it is the good will to strive for perfection according to adequate ideas that allows us to recognize God's decrees as the best. Against misreadings from the Kantian tradition, it should be emphasized that Leibniz and Wolff perceive the individual's good intention (their good will) as tantamount to their moral perfection and as a precondition for God's grace (Wolff 1985, 135).

Wolff makes the human striving for perfection a natural law and bases his entire moral philosophy on it (Wolff 1962–, II:10.1:118–19). It is our moral duty to strive for perfection according to adequate ideas. Because all human beings need to live in society, it is truly the best for each of us to strive for the perfection of ourselves, of others, of our society and of the world, according to adequate ideas. This rational moral philosophy allows Wolff to find morality in other, non-Christian societies, a perception confirmed by Jesuit reports about the Chinese, who lived together in a peaceful and virtuous state, even though lacking Christian revelation. It is remarkable that both Leibniz and Wolff taught explicitly that peoples other than Christians not only possessed morality, but also had their own great lawgivers who enshrined these morals publicly. Leibniz is cautious in this respect, naming only Moses besides Jesus Christ while referring to other peoples (Leibniz 2001, 49–51), but Wolff explicitly mentions Mohammed and Confucius as great teachers of law and morals—in addition to Moses and Jesus Christ (Wolff 1985, 117–23). Interestingly, this would dramatically change with Kant (1724–1804) and the enlightened Protestant theologians, who claimed Jesus Christ to be the first teacher of public morality, thereby denying true virtue to non-Christians (Kant 2009, 71, 129–32, 113–16, 142–43).

Responding to the Lutheran *Formula of Concordia* (1577), which denied that the pagans' good works count as morally good before God because they did not originate from true faith, Wolff worked out a detailed justification for his argument that pagans could be virtuous—a position he had assumed in his notorious lecture on Chinese practical philosophy. Taking up the widespread distinction of being driven by either external or internal motives, the former leading to mere righteousness, while the latter alone could lead to true virtue, Wolff argued that pagans too could act by means of the inner conviction of moral law (Wolff 1985, 243). Therefore they could reach true philosophical, though not theological, virtue. Wolff's insistence on the pagans' capability to act virtuously became, beside preestablished harmony, the major stumbling block for conservative theologians and led to his ban. The sharp distinction between the externally good behavior of non-Christians (who nonetheless remain immoral), and the internal goodness derived from the Christian faith was of enormous influence on Lutheran philosophers from Pufendorf (1632–94) to Kant, and justified their harsh opposition to Leibnizian-Wolffian philosophy and theology.

However, both Leibniz and Wolff emphasized the difference between rational virtue and the higher piety or theological virtue that originates from the Gospels of Jesus Christ, which is the most powerful divine help available to human beings striving to overcome their weakness and sin. The message of Jesus Christ and his promise of salvation strengthen our trust in God and provide a strong incentive for us to strive for greater perfection. But even so, just as religious poetry and songs for God's glory could strengthen pious faith and love for God, so too could our rational understanding of God's goodness and wisdom fuel our love for him. This in turn reveals the significance of Jesus Christ for human beings' morality, and more broadly, for salvation.

Leibniz mentions the savior only a few times in his *Theodicy*, and Wolff does not offer much more. They clearly recognize the divinity of Jesus Christ, and see the man Jesus Christ as exemplary in terms of moral perfection. Also, both philosophers emphasized his importance as a teacher of the true religion for human beings, enabling them to reach salvation (Leibniz 1969, 327–28). In his *Theodicy*, moreover, Leibniz makes the belonging of Jesus Christ to this chosen world the major reason for God's choice of it as the best (Leibniz 2001, 167–68). In contrast to most contemporary Protestant theologians, however, there is no emphasis on the savior's suffering and sacrifice, on his blood shed for humankind, or on salvation *through* Jesus Christ as the exclusive escape from this miserable world (Sparn 1986, 162–63).

Both philosophers hold that salvation may well happen to pagans who lived a virtuous life without knowledge of Christ (Leibniz 2001, 173–77; Wolff 1985, 135–45). Moreover, according to Leibniz, even heretics may be saved, if only they live a virtuous life and strive *sincerely* for truth. Leibniz and Wolff point here to the inscrutable decrees of God, who could make the same happen by a miracle, and ask us to leave the judgment to God! By contrast, they addressed with more resolution the potential salvation of unbaptized children—a question that became increasingly urgent for theologians during the eighteenth century. Knowing God as the most perfect, wise, and good being, and knowing the concept of justice as the love of the wise who loves all—the damnation of innocent children who never had an opportunity to sin would contradict the very concept of God, and was therefore impossible (Leibniz 2001, 95–96, 236–38; Wolff 1962–, 7.2:1036–47).

# 5 How to Read the Holy Scriptures

Descartes's proofs of the existence of God as the most perfect being attracted many critics, who opined that philosophical proofs did little to confirm the existence of the

*Christian* God. Spinoza's concept of God as an impersonal substance lacking will and intellect was considered a mere consequence of Descartes's view. In contrast, Leibniz and Wolff took pains to retain the attributes of God, as described by the Holy Scriptures. They retained the Protestant principle of *sola scriptura*, and restricted figural reading to those passages where the context clearly indicates such a reading to be appropriate (Leibniz 1923, VI:1:549, 553). Leibniz therefore disagrees with Galileo, who had tried to solve the discrepancy between the Copernican system and the Book of Joshua by arguing that the prophet knew very well that the earth moves around the sun, but accommodated his speech to the people's understanding. Spinoza saw this to be in contradiction with the text. Leibniz agreed with Spinoza that Joshua meant what he said, but held with Galileo that the prophet knew the (Copernican) truth. As even strict Copernicans continued to speak about "sunset" and "sunrise" although they knew the earth would actually move around the sun, so did the prophet Joshua. Our language does not change easily with the increase of adequate ideas, but often remains bound to our sensory perceptions (Bertoloni Meli 1988).

Wolff too provides evidence for the agreement of the Holy Scriptures with his (and Leibniz's) doctrine, thereby showing his familiarity with the Hebrew text. He argues, for example, that according to the Hebrew vernacular God literally says that the created world is the best (Wolff 1962–, II:7.1:374), and that God's will is the last reason for everything to exist (Wolff 1962–, II:7.1:408–9); both statements being in perfect agreement with his and Leibniz's metaphysics. In order to be a science, natural theology had to demonstrate its propositions and therefore to start with definitions (Wolff 1962–, II:7.1:3), but Christian natural theology had to take its nominal definitions of God from the Holy Scriptures (Wolff 1962–, II:7.1: 9–10). A demonstration can begin with a nominal definition, and one can safely deduce propositions from it as long as no contradictions occur. These propositions remain hypothetical because they are considered true under the assumption that the nominal definition does not include a hidden contradiction (Wolff 1962–, II:7.1:3–8). In this way we can achieve a mixed science, using both mere deduction and demonstration, as well as nominal definitions based on sense perception (Wolff 1962–, II:1.2:703).

Leibniz had already developed a precise concept of hypothesis after his return from Paris, in order to situate empirical knowledge within his epistemology (see his letter to Fabri [Leibniz 1923, II:1:441–66]). But he developed this concept with a side glance toward the much-needed reconciliation between science and the wording of the Holy Scriptures (Bertoloni Meli 1993, 158–60). The ban of Copernicus (1473–1543) and Galileo by the Catholic Church was a major impediment, Leibniz argued, because we need hypotheses to explain phenomena wherein rational argument and empirical observation are connected, because we cannot achieve merely adequate ideas of contingent things. Due to the uncertainty of empirical knowledge, we may come up with competing hypotheses explaining the same observed phenomena. None of them is absolutely true, but we can rank them according to their capability to explain the greatest number of observed phenomena in the simplest way. The best hypothesis counts as truth. Accordingly, Leibniz considers the Copernican system to be a mere hypothesis which nonetheless has to be acknowledged as truth, because due to its simplicity it has to be ranked above that of Ptolemy (90–168). This modern epistemological approach rolled out the red carpet for the Roman Church, who had banned the Copernican system and his defender Galileo for teaching this hypothesis as truth. In this way, Leibniz urged the Roman theologians to lift the ban (Bertoloni Meli 1988).

Systematically working out this approach in his logic, Wolff uses it also in his *Natural Theology* when addressing the Holy Scriptures. If one needs to understand a book dealing with stories or doctrines instead of definitions and demonstrations, one has to connect each of its words with the concepts the author of the book had linked to them (Wolff 1962–, II:7.1:420–22, II:1.3:643). On the other hand, the author—in order to be understood—should use such words as the audience would connect with the concepts the author has in mind (Wolff 1962–, II:1.3:692–93, II:7.1:454–55). Because the author of the Holy Scriptures knows everything by adequate ideas, and also understands the manner in which human beings know by means of words and signs (Wolff 1962–, II:7.1:277–78), each word of the Holy Scriptures expresses God's intention in such a way that the addressed audience would connect it to the appropriate concept. If it were not so, the words would be empty words, without meaning. However, for one to understand the meaning of the words, it is not necessary that one conceives distinctly the concepts to which the words used refer. It suffices that we associate clear, albeit confused ideas with the words. This is theologically relevant for the mysteries that we cannot know distinctly (Wolff 1962–, II:7.1:431–34), as laid out by Leibniz.

It is this linguistic aspect of Wolff's approach to divine revelation that would inspire a new German translation of the Pentateuch, published in 1735 by the young Wolffian Johann Lorenz Schmidt (1702–49) in Wertheim (Schmidt 2011). Because the Old Testament had been revealed to the Hebrew people, one had to ask how *they* understood what they were told. Accordingly, if one wanted to discern God's message from the Old Testament, one had to study the core text without referring to its Christian understanding. Instead, one had to study the history of the Jews to learn about their then-current use of the words. As a result of this modern hermeneutics, the "Wertheimer"—as he would be called after his place of publication—lost the prophecies of Jesus Christ in his translation of the books of Moses, causing a wave of outrage among Lutheran theologians in the German territories. It ended with a ban on the book throughout the German empire and a trial against the translator (who managed to escape) (Spalding 1998). Nonetheless, this translation would cause a public debate throughout the German empire, lasting approximately four years (Goldenbaum 2004, 175–508). This controversy provoked many critical attacks on Schmidt's work, but also inspired new approaches intended to save the prophecies of Jesus Christ in the Old Testament—the turn to esthetics and poetry among them. It was now in the figurative sense of Old Testament Hebrew poetry where the prophecies of Jesus Christ were to be found. Six months after the publication of the *Wertheim Bible*, Alexander Baumgarten (1714–62), a student at Joachim Lange's (1670–1744) theology department at Halle, published his programmatic *Reflections on Poetry*, calling for a new science of esthetics to reevaluate the senses.

# 6 SUMMARY

To summarize, Leibniz and Wolff after him developed their metaphysics to address the challenge modern science posed to the theologies of all three Christian denominations. They did reshape and adapt Christian theology to modern science, but without giving up Christian dogma. It is rarely acknowledged that they achieved their goal (see though Hirsch 1968, 21; Sparn 1986). Leibniz could point proudly to authorities from all three major Christian denominations who had approved his *Theodicy* (Leibniz 1742, 53). It is remarkable that neither Leibniz nor Wolff were placed on the index of forbidden books (Palumbo 2006), as happened even to the pious Malebranche (1638–1715). In addition, both philosophers paved the way for tolerance of non-Christian religions through their explicit acknowledgment of the natural moral capability of all human beings and the moral teachings of all religions. The potential of this approach would be recognized and developed further by the Jewish philosopher Moses Mendelssohn (1729–86), when he argued for the equal citizenship rights of non-Christians—in contrast to the German intellectual heroes who refused them (except Lessing).

During the seventeenth and early eighteenth centuries, most theologians outside the intellectual centers of Europe did not yet feel the enormous intellectual pressure that modern science and philosophy would exert on theology. They enjoyed their widely accepted authority to interpret the Holy Scriptures and Christian religion in familiar ways, and according to the partiality of their own denomination. They insisted on God's free will—as well as on that of humans—as arbitrary choice. Due to the fall of man, they argued, this world is evil. The human intellect was thus corrupt, and any claim of a priori knowledge was nothing but human haughtiness. Preestablished harmony would undermine free will and make God the cause of the evil in the world. Finally, the striving for perfection, recommended by Leibniz and Wolff as the starting point for morals as well as for salvation, was perceived as selfish and insufficient to serve as a reliable foundation for duty.

The theological resentment directed toward Leibniz and Wolff throughout the eighteenth century persisted among influential theologians such as Herder and Schleiermacher who, paradoxically, would embrace Spinoza and pantheism (in Christianized form), rather than Leibnizian or Wolffian rationalism. Leibnizian-Wolffian theology continued to be rejected by theologians throughout the nineteenth and twentieth centuries—including Tholuck, Harnack, Gogarten, and Barth, who rather preferred to side with the voluntarism of the Calvinist Bayle, than with the rationalist theology of the Lutherans Leibniz and Wolff (Sparn 1986, 139–42). Looking, however, to the downfall of German Protestantism and its leading theologians with the *Deutsche*

*Kirche* (Erickson 1985), the question arises whether the overtly voluntaristic and anti-rationalist interpretation of Christian religion has not been one of the major causes. By contrast, Leibniz's and Wolff's interpretation of the Christian religion can serve as inspiration not only for the ecumenical project of our time (see Rudolph 2013), but also for a fresh approach to other religions.

## BIBLIOGRAPHY

Albrecht, Michael, ed. 2011. *Die natürliche Theologie bei Christian Wolff.* Aufklärung 23. Hamburg: Meiner.

Aner, Karl. 1929. *Die Theologie der Lessingzeit.* Halle: Niemeyer.

Antognazza, Maria Rosa. 2007. *Leibniz on the Trinity and Incarnation: Reason and Revelation in the Seventeenth Century.* Translated by Gerald Parks. New Haven, CT: Yale University Press.

Baumgarten, Alexander. 1954. *Reflections on Poetry: Alexander Baumgarten's Reflectiones philosophicae de nonnullis ad poema pertinentibus (1735).* Berkeley: University of California Press.

Bertoloni Meli, Domenico. 1993. *Equivalence and Priority: Newton versus Leibniz: Including Leibniz's Unpublished Manuscripts on the Principia.* London: Clarendon Press.

Bertoloni Meli, Domenico. 1988. "Leibniz on Censorship of the Copernican System." *Studia Leibnitiana* 20: 19–42.

Eberhard, Johann August, and Johann Georg von Eckhart. 1982. *Leibnizbiographien.* Hildesheim: Olms.

Erickson, Robert P. 1985. *Theologians under Hitler: Kittel, Althaus and Hirsch.* New Haven, CT: Yale University Press.

Fouke, Daniel. 1992. "Metaphysics and the Eucharist in the early Leibniz." *Studia Leibnitiana* 24: 145–159.

Galilei, Galileo. 1967. *Dialogue Concerning the Two Chief World Systems.* Translated by Stillman Drake. Berkeley: University of California Press.

Galilei, Galileo. 1907. "Dok. 20 (Car. 387r–393r)." In *Opere: Edizione Nazionale*, edited by Antonio Favaro. Vol. 19. Florence: Barbèra.

Goldenbaum, Ursula. 2004. *Appell an das Publikum: Die öffentliche Debatte in der deutschen Aufklärung 1697–1786.* Sieben Fallstudien. 2 Teile. Berlin: Akademie Verlag.

Goldenbaum, Ursula. 2002. "Spinoza's Parrot, Socinian Syllogisms, and Leibniz's Metaphysics: Leibniz's Three Strategies of Defending Christian Mysteries." *American Catholic Philosophical Quarterly* 76 (4) (Special Issue): 551–574.

Goldenbaum, Ursula. 1999. "Transubstantiation, Physics and Philosophy at the Time of [Leibniz's] Catholic Demonstrations." In *The Young Leibniz and his Philosophy (1646–1676)*, edited by Stuart Brown, 79–102. Dordrecht: Kluwer.

Harnack, Adolf. 1900. *Geschichte der Preußischen Akademie der Wissenschaften zu Berlin.* Vol. 1.1. Berlin.

Hirsch, Emanuel. 1968. *Geschichte der neuern evangelischen Theologie.* Vol. 2. Gütersloh: Mohn.

Hobbes, Thomas. 1839. *Opera Philosophica quae latine scripsit omnia.* Edited by Gulielmi Molesworth. Vol. 1. London: Bohn.

Kant, Immanuel. 2009. *Religion within the Boundaries of Mere Reason, and Other Writings.* Translated and edited by Allen Wood and George di Giovanni. Introduction by Robert Merrihew Adams. Cambridge: Cambridge University Press.

Kierkegaard, Søren. 2002. "Afsluttende Uvidenskabelig Efterskrift." In *Søren Kierkegaard: Skrifter*, edited by Søren Kierkegaard Forskningcenteret, 92. Vol. 7. Copenhagen: Gads Forlag.

Kröger, Wolfgang. 1979. *Das Publikum als Richter: Lessing und die "kleineren Respondenten" im Fragmentenstreit*. Wolfenbütteler Forschungen 5. Nendeln/Liechtenstein: KTO-Press.

Leibniz, Gottfried Wilhelm. 1742. *Epistolae ad diversos*, edited by Christian Kortholt. 4 vols. Leipzig.

Leibniz, Gottfried Wilhelm. 1996. *New Essays on Human Understanding*. Translated and edited by Peter Remnant and Jonathan Bennett. Cambridge: Cambridge University Press.

Leibniz, Gottfried Wilhelm. 1969. *Philosophical Papers and Letters*. Translated and edited by Leroy E. Loemker. Dordrecht: Reidel.

Leibniz, Gottfried Wilhelm. 1923. *Sämtliche Schriften und Briefe*. Edited by the Berlin-Brandenburg Academy and the Academy at Göttingen. Berlin: Akademie Verlag.

Leibniz, Gottfried Wilhelm. 2001. *Theodicy*. Translated by E. M. Huggard, edited by Austin Farrer. Eugene, OR: Wipf and Stock.

Lempp, Otto. 1976. *Das Problem der Theodicee in der Literatur und Philosophie des achzehnten Jahrhunderts bis auf Kant und Schiller*. Reprint of Leipzig 1910 edition. Hildesheim: Olms.

Lessing, Gotthold Ephraim. 1897. "Vom Beweis des Geistes und der Kraft." In *Sämtliche Schriften*, edited by Karl Lachmann and Franz Muncker. Vol. 13. Leipzig: Göschen.

Lorenz, Stefan. 1997. *De mundo optimo: Studien zu Leibniz' Theodizee und ihrer Rezeption in Deutschland (1710–1791)*. Stuttgart: Steiner.

Palumbo, Marguerita. 2006. "Die Römische Inquisition und der 'Fall' Leibniz." In *Einheit in der Vielheit: Akten des Internationalen Leibniz-Kongresses*, edited by Herbert Breger. Nachtragsband. Hannover: Gottfried-Wilhelm-Leibniz-Gesellschaft.

Pichler, Aloys. 1869–1870. *Die Theologie des Leibniz*. Munich.

Rateau, Paul. 2011. "Ce qui fait un monde. Compossibilité, perfection et harmonie." In *Lectures et Interpretations des Essais de théodicée de G. W. Leibniz*, edited by Paul Rateau, 35–58. Stuttgart: Steiner.

Ratschow, C. H. 1983. "Gottfried Wilhelm Leibniz." In *Gestalten der Kirchengeschichte*, edited by Martin Greschat, 122–153. Vol. 8. Stuttgart: Kohlhammer.

Rudolph, Hartmut, Wenchao Li, and Hans Poser, eds. 2013. "Leibniz und die Oekumene." In *Studia Leibnitiana*, Sonderheft 41. Stuttgart: Steiner.

Schmidt, Johann Lorenz. 2011. "Die göttlichen Schriften von den Zeiten des Messiä." In *Christian Wolff: Gesammelte Werke*, edited by Ursula Goldenbaum, 128–128.2. Vol. 3. Hildesheim: Olms.

Spalding, Paul S. 1998. *Seize the Book, Jail the Author: Johann Lorenz Schmidt and Censorship in Eighteenth-Century Germany*. West Lafayette, IN: Purdue University Press.

Sparn, Walter. 1986. "Das Bekenntnis des Philosophen: Gottfried Wilhelm Leibniz als Philosoph und Theologe." *Neue Zeitschrift für systematische Theologie und Religionsphilosophie* 8 (2): 139–178.

Spinoza. 2001. *Theological-Political Treatise*. Translated by Samuel Shirley. Indianapolis, IN: Hackett.

Wolff, Christian. 1962–. *Gesammelte Werke*, edited by Jean École et al. Hildesheim: Olms.

Wolff, Christian. 1985. *Oratio de Sinarum philosophica practica/Rede über die praktische Philosophie der Chinesen*. Translated and edited by Michael Albrecht. Hamburg: Meiner.

## CHAPTER 36

# THE CHALLENGES OF EMPIRICAL UNDERSTANDING IN EARLY MODERN THEOLOGY

### STEPHEN GAUKROGER

## 1 SENSATION AS THE STARTING POINT OF KNOWLEDGE

In the course of the thirteenth century, Aristotelianism was introduced into Western philosophy, replacing the Neoplatonism that had played a key role in the formulation of Christian theology by the church fathers. Whereas Neoplatonism had conceived the origins of knowledge as lying in contemplation, it was a fundamental premise of Aristotelianism that all knowledge started from sensation. Aristotelianism was introduced by theologians—there were no philosophers who were not theologians at this time—and for theological reasons. Aristotelian metaphysics, with its elaborate doctrine of substance, essence, accident, and potentiality and actuality, provided a means for dealing with complex theological questions—particularly the Incarnation and the Trinity—in what was considered to be a sufficiently compelling way to convince non-Christians of the basic truths of Christianity, and to resolve problems of heterodoxy.

There was a price to pay for this shift, however. The doctrine of personal immortality was something basic and relatively unproblematic in Neoplatonism, mainly because the notion of a disembodied existence of the soul formed part of the basic understanding of what the soul was. By contrast, personal immortality was highly problematic in the Aristotelian understanding of the soul; for conceived as the organizing principle of the body, the soul ceased to exist with the death and corruption of the body. The Christian doctrine of personal immortality was (or at least became) a theological dogma, whereas

Aristotle's account was a theory within natural philosophy. In the view of the greatest exponent of scholastic Aristotelianism, Thomas Aquinas (1225–74), the task of the philosopher-theologian was to reconcile natural-philosophical doctrines and theological ones. The former had no bearing on what religious views one held, and were common to everyone, since they rested on sense perception. Theological views, by contrast, did depend on what religious views one held, and they rested on revelation. Aquinas construed metaphysics as a neutral discipline that could adjudicate between the two, resting only on truths of reason; and reason, like sensation, was common to everyone. This procedure probably was modeled on the attempts to reconcile secular and ecclesiastical law, where contradictions were to be resolved without destroying the elements comprising them.

There were advantages and disadvantages in this, and both were of immense consequence (see Gaukroger 2006, chs. 2–4). The chief advantage was that Christian theology became part of a broad, ambitious program that was far more inclusive than earlier forms. Patristic theology had ignored natural philosophy and had made metaphysics just an appendage to theology, with no autonomy. Scholastic theology was able to engage a diverse range of questions, drawing on a wide variety of resources in an effort to present a coherent and comprehensive worldview—for example, questions about science that earlier forms of theology, and religions other than Christianity, had simply ignored.

The disadvantages lay in the relative standing of the elements that a Christianized metaphysics sought to reconcile. Because revelation was regarded as secure in a way that knowledge derived from sensation could never be, reconciliation tended to be unidirectional in favor of theology, but the crucial point is that this was not a feature of metaphysics as such; rather, it is a feature of the disciplines that metaphysics seeks to reconcile. With the revival of a form of Neoplatonism by Italian Renaissance thinkers such as Ficino and Patrizi, however, the question of the immortality of the soul was pushed to the foreground, and here the project of reconciliation began to come apart.

The situation in 1600 was that Christian theology in the West was tied inextricably to an empirical discourse about the nature of the world, in which sensation, observation, and subsequently experimentation play a leading role. This was not something imposed from outside: it was a path that potentially offered great benefits, allowing its exponents to defend the intellectual authority of Christianity over what came to be conceived as other religions, and to defend the intellectual authority of orthodoxy over heterodoxy. Crucial in this respect was the fact that there was a traditional feature of Christianity that allowed it to form a metaphysically mediated bond with natural philosophy: namely, the sense of its identity lying in doctrine.

This is a very distinctive feature of Christianity. Before the modern era, Christian theologians treated all religious differences in terms of differences in doctrine, and they construed Islam and Judaism, for example, as forms of heresy rather than different religions. In the course of the seventeenth and eighteenth centuries, this changed—the view developed that there were different religions, although these were still distinguished on a doctrinal basis. It is in the seventeenth century that we witness the first attempts to distinguish other religions from Christianity (Harrison 1990), an exercise renewed in the nineteenth century when there was a concerted move to offer comprehensive classifications of world religions (Masuzawa 2005). The point I want to stress is that different religions were distinguished exclusively on a doctrinal basis: irrespective of what these other religions believed to constitute their own religious identity, they were assimilated to sets of core Christian doctrinal beliefs. There are distinctive beliefs in other religions of course, but Christianity is quite unique in its construal of the identity of a religion as lying in its beliefs on theological questions. In Islam, Buddhism, Confucianism, Hinduism, and Judaism, very different things—such as particular daily rituals, practices (meditation and chanting), striving to attain balance and order, or a notion of return from exile—are the crucial factors. The doctrinal focus of Christianity, which had become fully established by the fourth century (MacCulloch 2009, ch. 6), is something peculiar to it.

From the point of view of our present concerns, what is distinctive about Christianity is not so much the content of the doctrines it espouses, but the fact that it defines itself in terms of doctrines. This feature of Christianity meant that building up and protecting a body of doctrine was a fundamental task and, at least from the fourth century onwards, an indispensable ingredient in defining its identity. Doctrinal consistency was at a premium, and this was achieved by means of systematic theology. From the time of the patristic thinkers onwards, at the core of Christianity and shaping its sense of authority, was its striking concern with heresy and its naturally proliferating sectarianism. What was at issue in the thirteenth-century scholastic reconciliation of Christianity and Aristotelian natural philosophy, as well as in the subsequent seventeenth-century attempts to align Christian theology and natural philosophy (for example, among mechanists), was not a question of the relation between "science and religion," but rather a question of bringing together a Christian doctrine with natural-philosophical tenets formulated in terms of a natural-philosophical doctrine.

In short, the doctrinal self-image of Christian theology—the idea that what gives Christianity its identity is not its devotional practices or moral teachings, for example, but its basic doctrines—makes possible and reinforces the model of Christian theology as the guiding element in a comprehensive package, in which the aim is to understand not just the supernatural realm, but the natural realm and our place in it. In the pursuit of this aim, revelation, empirical inquiry, hermeneutics, and other factors are able to play a role. In theory they played an equal role, for there can be no inconsistency. As Thomas Burnet was to put it in his *Sacred Theory of the Earth* (1684), "We are not to suppose that any truth concerning the natural world can be an enemy to religion: for Truth cannot be an enemy to Truth, God is not divided against himself" (Burnet 1684, a2). But in reality reconciliation proved elusive.

## 2  NATURAL THEOLOGY AS AN ANTIDOTE TO SECTARIANISM

There were immense problems, beginning with the sixteenth-century worries over the incompatibility between the doctrine of the immortality of the soul and the Aristotelian argument that the soul is the (inseparable) organizing principle of the body, which came to a head in the 1630s with the conflict between Christian teaching and Galileo's arguments for the motion of the earth. Here we have a conflict between revelation and a tradition of Christian teaching on the one hand, and an empirically based physical theory on the other. But this is not the only issue where physical inquiry impinges on questions of Christian belief; and if we focus on these problems to the exclusion of everything else, we will miss a fundamentally important development: the use of empirical inquiry to decide theological questions.

One problem with the doctrinal self-image of Christianity was an intense sectarianism, resulting in the Reformation. The precision with which doctrines were defined— by contrast with devotional practices or moral scruples, for example—was such that the slightest deviation could result in serious heterodoxy. There were what might be regarded as empirical attempts to establish criteria for an accurate and objective interpretation of scripture, effectively starting with Reuchlin and Erasmus around the beginning of the sixteenth century. These deployed principles of textual criticism—principles that established dating, authorship, and interpolations on textual grounds—but if they settled some theological issues, at the same time they problematized others. In his translation of the Gospel of John, for example, Erasmus, reflecting on the meaning of the Greek term *logos*, changed the translation of the opening words from "In principio erat verbum" to "In principio erat sermo," thereby challenging a long tradition of theological inquiry into the "Word." Consequently, while the new philological and textual resources came to be widely deployed, their role in deciding theological issues was highly contentious.

There was, however, another way in which empirical inquiry could be used to settle theological questions: through the development of natural theology, allied with a form of "experimental" natural philosophy. The alliance is not as artificial as it may at first seem. Peter Harrison has identified an "experimental" tradition in early modern theology itself, noting that "in the religious literature, experimental knowledge relies upon trials and observations, it places priority on first-hand witnessing, it is useful, it provides motivations for practical activities, it is explicitly sought after rather than passively received, and, finally, it stands in contrast to knowledge that is merely notional or speculative, or based on books and authorities" (Harrison 2011, 422).

The key figure here is Robert Boyle, for whom an empirical understanding of the natural world can be promoted as revealing God's purposes in a way that avoids sectarianism. Around 1649, and while under the influence of the Protestant reformer Samuel Hartlib, Boyle began to consider natural philosophy as the path to natural theology, and this shaped his approach to natural philosophy throughout his career (see Hunter 2002, ch. 2). In *A Disquisition about the Final Causes of Natural Things*, composed in the mid-1670s, Boyle identifies "two chief sects of modern philosophizers" who deny

that the naturalist ought at all to trouble to busy himself about final causes. For *Epicurus*, and most of his followers (for I except some late ones, especially the learned *Gassendus*) banish the considerations of the ends of things; because the world being, according to them, made by chance, no ends of any thing can be supposed to have been intended. And on the contrary, Monsieur *des Cartes*, and most of his followers, suppose all the ends of God in things corporeal to be so sublime, that it were presumption in man to think his reason can extend to discover them. (Boyle 1772, 5:393)

But for Boyle the whole point of pursuing natural philosophy in the first place is that it reveals to us the handiwork and purposes of God in a way that goes deeper than anything else we can achieve by use of natural reason:

For the works of God are not like the tricks of jugglers, or the pageants, that entertain princes, where concealment is requisite to wonder; but the knowledge of the works of God proportions our admiration of them, they participating and disclosing so much of the inexhausted perfections of their author, that the further we contemplate them, the more foot-steps and impressions we discover of the perfections of their Creator; and our utmost science can but give us a juster veneration of his omniscience. And as when some country fellow looks upon a curious watch, though he may be hugely taken with the rich enamel of the case, and perhaps with some pretty landskip that adornes the dial-plate; yet will not his ignorance permit him so advantageous a notion of the exquisite maker's skill, as that little engine will form in some curious artist, who besides that obvious workmanship, that first entertains the eye, considers the exactness, and knows the use of every wheel, takes notice of their proportion, contrivance, and adaptation all together, and of the hidden springs, that move them all: so in the world, though every peruser may read the existence of a Deity, and be in his degree affected with what he sees, yet he is utterly unable to descry there those subtler characters and flourishes of omniscience, which true philosophers are sharp-sighted enough to discern. (Boyle 1772, 2:30)

Indeed, Boyle notes, philosophers of almost all religions "have been, by the contemplation of the world, moved to consider it under the notion of a temple" (Boyle 1772, 2:31), and "if the world be a temple, man sure must be the priest, ordained (by being qualified) to celebrate divine service not only in, but for it" (Boyle 1772, 2:32). The natural philosopher has become not only religiously motivated but religiously empowered. Boyle accepts that science may be used by the libertine, who attempts to "misemploy it to impugne the grounds, or discredit the practice of, religion," but the more one studies natural philosophy the more one comes to reject the libertine hypothesis that the world is produced by "so incompetent and pitiful a cause as blind chance or the tumultuous joslings of atomical portions of senseless matter" (Boyle 1772, 5:514). Pagan philosophers had made natural philosophy the basis for their moral philosophy, and the study of nature had been traditionally regarded by many Christian philosophers as either a distraction or idolatrous. Boyle's response, accentuating a feature of the religious natural history tradition, is to transform natural inquiry into what is in effect a form of worship, the natural philosopher being singled out by the skills that enable him to search deep into the nature of things, to see what others have missed in God's creation. Against those English divines who "out of a holy jealousy (as they think) for religion, labour to deter men from addicting themselves to serious and thoughtful inquiries into nature, as from a study unsafe for a Christian, and likely to end in atheism" (Boyle 1772, 2:15), he replies that,

> Provided the information be such, as a man has just cause to believe, and perceives, that he clearly understands, it will not alter the case, whether we have it by reason, as that is taken for the faculty furnished but with its inbred notions, or by experiments purposely devised, or by testimony human or divine, which last we call revelation. For all these are but differing ways of informing the understanding, and of signifying to it the same thing. (Boyle 1772, 2:31)

Of the problems that Boyle's approach gave rise to, one especially pressing question was whether the means by which progress was achieved in the experimental sciences might not also be appropriate in theology. In the preface to his *Christianity Not Mysterious* (1696), John Toland laments that in his age, "a Man dares not openly and directly own what he thinks of Divine matters, tho it be never so true and beneficial, if but it slightly differs from what is receiv'd by any Party, or what is established by law." Yet, as he points out,

> The Pravity of most Mens Dispositions, and the Ambition of particular Persons makes this matter seem less strange in Politick and Secular Affairs; and yet a Man may not only make new Discoveries and Improvements in Law or Physick, and in the other Arts and Sciences inpunibly, but also for so doing be deservedly encourag'd and rewarded. (Toland 1696, v)

Toland's point is that in disciplines such as law and medicine, there is constant progress in understanding, effected through the critical engagement of the practitioners of these disciplines, and it is not clear why religion should be any different.

General questions of expertise are raised here. At issue is not just what the expertise of theologians is, but to what it should be extended or limited. The condemnations of heliocentrism by the Roman Catholic Church, in the early decades of the seventeenth century, were formulated in terms derived from Melchior Cano's (1509–60) *De locis theologicis* (1563), which was designed to provide the church with a set of systematic procedures establishing grounds for and degrees of authority in response to the Protestant questioning of this authority, as well as to humanist criticisms of its misuse of sources. Cano identifies both intrinsic and extrinsic sources of authority. The former include, among other things, the Gospels, pronouncements of the church whether as a whole or in council, and some opinions of the fathers and scholastics. Extrinsic sources include natural philosophy and philosophy more generally, as well as history, which now becomes a separate source of authority (see Franklin 1963, 106-15). Just what degree of authority historical arguments can have in resolving questions of religious dogma depends on our assessment of such matters as the reliability of historical authors, and this in turn depends on familiarity with the full range of historical sources. However, since such sources will yield only probable beliefs, not certain knowledge, reasonable doubt is sometimes appropriate, and to meet such doubt we need to balance a number of factors: above all, the reliability of the author and the intrinsic plausibility of what is claimed. *De locis* was to play a pivotal role in the adjudication of natural-philosophical disputes. Both sides in Galileo's trial, for example, took it as authoritative, even though they were unable to agree on which sections were relevant to the dispute (see Blackwell 1991).

# 3  THE HISTORY OF THE WORLD

The difficulties encountered in reconciling empirical accounts of the earth's motion, of the kind offered by Galileo, and traditional Christian teaching, were notorious. But parallel problems generated by a conflict between Christian teaching and empirical historical investigation were in many ways far more intractable.

A formative text here is Thomas Burnet's *The Theory of the Earth* (1684), which focused on the incompleteness of revelation as an account of the formation of the earth, and sought to render it complete by supplementing it with the Cartesian account of its geological formation. Since the latter was an explicitly hypothetical theory, a rational reconstruction of a geological process which did not make reference to datable events, Burnet set out to show how revelation could be used to supply concrete historical details. Each of the accounts was understood to be incomplete as a description of the whole process; but since Burnet considered them both true in substance, if not in every detail; and since he also considered that truths, whatever their provenance, cannot contradict one another, he reasoned that the combination of the two should yield something far more comprehensive than either taken by itself.

As far as revelation was concerned, Burnet's view was that Genesis was written to accommodate the capacities of the ignorant, and that a literal reading of Genesis could not possibly yield an understanding of how the cosmos was formed. The idea was not that the account in Genesis should be abandoned, but rather that its interpretation had to be guided by whatever understanding could be gleaned from natural philosophy. As far as natural philosophy was concerned, any attempt to offer an account of the formation of the earth had to describe a historical process, but the account Burnet considers the best—that of Descartes—offered merely a hypothetical reconstruction of events, suggesting that this was a path that God could have followed, not the one he did follow. Burnet's project was therefore to flesh out Descartes' rational reconstruction of the earth's formation as a real historical process; and for this Genesis, which provided the only available account there was of the early history of the formation of the cosmos, was crucial. Burnet's reconstruction was, as might be expected, contentious in a number of respects, with his geological reconstruction requiring that mountains were formed at the same time as the Flood, in direct con-tradiction with the Genesis account, in which they pre-existed the Flood. Moreover, his combination of the Cartesian theory of the formation of the earth with Genesis led him to the view that the world in its original state was as God designed it, but the world in its present state was not: it had degenerated through the geological pro-cesses that the Cartesian theory describes, and it was therefore wholly inappropriate to use it as a basis for devotion and understanding of God's intentions in creation. Indeed, Burnet's use of Cartesian natural philosophy was itself contentious, for there were alternative natural philosophies, not least—by the 1690s—that of Newton, which offered more scope for divine intervention in natural events; and the naturalist John Woodward, for one, argued at length that the scale of the Flood was such that it could not be explained in natural terms alone, but required a supernatural power (Woodward 1695, 58, 165).

There were those who sought to refute Burnet simply by pitting scriptural passages against his claims (e.g., Warren 1690; Croft 1685), but it should be noted that this was not an especially common response. In the main, the idea that one could combine natu-ral philosophy and Genesis was not ruled out: after all, those natural philosophers who were party to these disputes accepted the truth of Genesis at some level, and those who worried about recent natural-historical reconstructions of the formation of the earth were not opposed to natural history as such, but were concerned about its potential conflict with Genesis. That there should not be such conflict was a shared assumption. The problem was that not everyone believed that Burnet had successfully effected a reconciliation.

Burnet had been particularly concerned by the fact that the amount of water required for the Flood, if it did indeed rise to the mountaintops, would have been several times that available in the oceans (Burnet 1680, 10–15), and he was aware of writers such as La Peyrère, who had used such considerations to conclude that the Flood could not have been a universal event but was more likely to be an epi-sode in local Jewish history (Le Peyrère 1655). Clearly, Burnet concluded, if the two accounts are to be reconciled, the world must have been very different in its earlier stages than it is now, and he speculates that in the early stages of its development—corresponding to the terrestrial paradise—it would have had a perfectly smooth spherical surface, subsequently broken open by various forms of violent geologi-cal activity which resulted in mountains and ocean basins. One aspect of Burnet's approach was the apparent discrediting of the Mosaic account, a question with which Newton took issue. In a letter to Burnet of 1681, for example, Newton pointed out that to claim that Moses wrote for the ignorant, a claim that Newton does not deny, does not mean that what he wrote is false: "As to Moses I do not think his description of ye creation either Philosophical or feigned, but that he described realities in a language artificially adapted to ye sense of ye vulgar" (Newton 1959–77, 2:331). Newton makes it clear that Moses depicted the process of creation exactly as it occurred: as he put it, "the things signified by such figurative expressions are not ideall or moral, but true" (Newton 1959–77, 2:333).

In 1696, a revised Newtonian version of Burnet's thesis was offered in William Whiston's *New Theory of the Earth*. Rejecting the Cartesian natural philosophy underpinning Burnet's account of the tilting of the Earth's axis to explain the Flood, he turned to Newton's account of the comet of 1680/1, arguing that the vapors of the comet's tail would have been enough to bring on the torrential rain that caused Noah's Flood. Yet the difficulties of reconciling the Mosaic account with a natural-historical one are evident. For one thing, Whiston could not accept that the biblical account of creation was an account of the creation of the cosmos: it read much more like an account of the creation of the earth, which is quite a different matter. Moses' account, Whiston insists, was neither literal nor allegorical. It is "a historical and true representation of the formation of our single earth," but the standard literal interpretation of the Mosaic account "represents all things from first to last so disorderly, confusedly, and unphilosophically, that 'tis intirely disagreeable to the Wisdom and Perfection of God" (Whiston 1696, 64). A more consistently Newtonian approach was that of John Keill's *An Examination of Dr. Burnet's Theory of the Earth* of 1698, where a strong contrast is drawn between the Cartesian view of a nature devoid of, and in no need of, final causes, and the Newtonian stress on the need for God's intervention in and regulation of his creation. The thrust of this physico-theological approach had been brought out explicitly in Ray's *The Wisdom of God* of 1691, where the incompleteness of the mechanical philosophy was stressed, in particular its inability to deal with the phenomena examined in natural history. Ray's point, one that will be repeated in various forms over the next century and a half, is essentially that we should not seek a comprehensive view of nature in purely natural terms, for the unity of the natural realm lies in its instantiation of a divine plan, and in seeking to understand this divine plan, natural philosophy cannot proceed as if it required no resources outside its own.

What I want to draw attention to here is the way in which natural philosophy comes to be locked into an enterprise that is in crucial respects quite unprecedented. In particular, in the final analysis it does not matter whether it is natural philosophy or natural theology/revelation that is doing the work. Burnet focuses on the inadequacies of a literal understanding of Genesis and how these might be made good by interpreting it using a natural-philosophical account of the formation of the earth. Ray, in contrast to Burnet's view that nature in its present state is degenerate, insists that it is the finished product of divine wisdom, and he focuses on the incompleteness of natural philosophy as a description of natural phenomena; an incompleteness that can be made good only by incorporating it into a natural-theological understanding. But in both cases the aim of the exercise is to secure a union of natural theology/revelation and natural history/natural philosophy. The different means by which this was achieved, and the different motivations that drove the two programs, must not blind us to the fact that something very similar, and very radical, is being proposed in both cases: the incorporation of natural history/natural philosophy into a representation of the world provided by Christianity. The two are being unified into something that offers a general picture of the world and our place in it. Note, however, that it is Christianity's worldview that natural philosophy becomes party to in this conception, not the other way around. What was required of and offered by the comprehensive conception of the world at stake was shaped by considerations internal to the mythological aspirations of Christianity. In this respect, Christianity is very much the dominant player, and the move is one that will have profound repercussions for the cultural standing of natural philosophy.

# 4 ENLIGHTENMENT

The association between science and Christianity began to be threatened from the end of the seventeenth century, and the problems came from both sides of the partnership. As far as Christianity was concerned, it had generally been assumed that religion was a universal feature of all peoples and essential to morality, but Pierre Bayle—drawing on travel reports, including those of Jesuits—was able to mount a convincing case that China was a well-ordered and highly moral nation of atheists (Bayle 1696–7). Voltaire will later play on this theme, beginning in his *Essai sur les Moeurs* (Voltaire 1769), for example, with accounts of India and China, undermining the use of Christianity as a reference point that was virtually constitutive of general histories up to this point. This discussion acts to provide a counter-history designed to displace the Judeo-Christian scheme, and thereby emphasizes the contingency of using Christianity as a model for any form of general understanding.

To the extent to which one wished to connect Christian theology and morality, there were significant problems, as Locke eloquently pointed out in his *Letter on Toleration*:

> our modern English History affords us fresh Examples, in the Reigns of *Henry* the 8th, *Edward* the 6th, *Mary*, and *Elizabeth*, how easily and smoothly the Clergy changed their decrees, their Articles of Faith, their Form of Worship, every Thing according to the Inclination of those Kings and Queens. Yet were those Kings and Queens of such different Mind in Point of Religion, and enjoined thereupon such different Things, that no Man in his Wits (I had almost said none but an Atheist) will presume to say that any sincere and upright Worshipper of God could, with a safe Conscience, obey their several decrees. (Locke 1722, 2:242)

The reliability of religious edicts is not argued here on theological grounds, but rather on the grounds of historical evidence. It is Gibbon who will later press this mode of inquiry in a detailed and comprehensive way, treating Christianity as just one historical phenomenon like any other, to be subjected to the same kind of empirical scrutiny; for example, with regard to the use of primary sources at the expense of traditional Christian accounts (Gibbon 1776).

But if Christian theology was coming to be seen as contingent, what about Christian morality? There had after all always been theological disputes, but the morality espoused by Christianity seemed secure. Various attempts were made in the early decades of the eighteenth century to establish that morality was something "natural," which was not unique to Christianity, or perhaps even religion generally, but was captured particularly well by Christianity (e.g., Clarke 1738, 2:513–733). Along these lines, Richard Cumberland (1672), proposed that our moral sense comes through experience, and that what we learn from this experience is that nature is designed in such a way as to preserve its constitution through mutual cooperation. Cumberland certainly believed that the morality we would learn from this experience would be commensurate with Christian teaching, but once learning morality is made an empirical issue, this could no longer be assumed.

Locke's rejection of innate ideas is crucial here, for it had traditionally been thought that we have an innate idea of morality; but if there were no innate ideas, then morality was something that had to be learned. The radical French Lockean tradition culminates in the work of Diderot, for whom everything is learned: we must learn how to see, for example (he uses cases where someone previously blind who gains their sight will not be able to see at first), just as much as we must learn how to be moral (Diderot 1749). Diderot's answer to how we learn to be moral is a social and pedagogic one, a matter of producing balanced, socially responsible citizens—but now considered something antithetical to religious education, with its inculcation of dogma. In the second half of the eighteenth century, this became one of the chief aspirations not just of philosophers (e.g., Rousseau 1762), but also of physicians (e.g., Le Camus 1753). Questions concerning morality and what might broadly be characterized as spirituality were transferred wholesale from a religious to a secular realm (see Gaukroger 2010, chs. 11-12). The principal rationale for this was that such a transfer opens these questions up to empirical inquiry: they no longer occupy a realm of conceptual truth or religious belief, but are now open to a form of examination that secures agreement on the basis of evidence.

The relationship between Christianity and empirical understanding was weakened in another respect, and this time the problem lay in science. In the seventeenth century, the dominant form of natural inquiry—mechanism—aspired to a systematic form, offering a single unified, integrated account of the natural realm. This was something with which natural theology could interact in a productive way. But toward the end of the century the credibility of mechanism began to decline, as experimental programs that rejected the kinds of fundamental understanding claimed by mechanism began to replace it. In the eighteenth century, such discrete empirical inquiries flourished in the study of chemistry, electricity, natural history, and physiology, for example. Outside natural history, it was not possible for religious understanding to be combined with these forms of inquiry.

It was ultimately not the French Enlightenment idea of religion as a vicious conspiracy of priests that did it the most damage in the eighteenth and nineteenth centuries, but rather the historicization of Christianity. Bayle first pursued the idea that the point was not to investigate the development of religious doctrine, something Christian scholars had been doing for centuries, but rather to enable one to stand back from religion in general, and Christianity in particular, and to consider it as an object of study without any assumptions as to the validity of its claims to truth. Hume and Gibbon followed him in this, and the *medicins philosophes* of the French Enlightenment in effect treated Christian doctrines about the soul, the passions, and mental life generally as just one of a number of competing theories that could be subjected to medical and behavioral evidence and assessed accordingly.

# 5 Conclusion

Early modern Christianity was not at odds with empirical inquiry. Rather, in many ways it embraced it. But Christianity was never just a form of empirical inquiry, and in the eighteenth century, when competing accounts of the kinds of questions that it had regarded as its own domain came to the fore, the problem was that it was treated on a par with other empirical forms of inquiry. These issues were faced explicitly only at the end of the eighteenth century, in the debates among German theologians, philosophers, and others on the relative standing of reason and faith (see Beiser 1987). What emerged from this was something that ultimately distanced Christian thinking from the task of being a partner in an empirical understanding of the world, as it gradually returned to the pre-modern idea of reconciliation between relatively autonomous spiritual and physical realms.

## BIBLIOGRAPHY

Bayle, Pierre. 1696–1697. *Dictionaire Historique et Critique.* 2 vols. Rotterdam.

Beiser, Frederick C. 1987. *The Fate of Reason.* Cambridge, MA: Harvard University Press.

Blackwell, Richard J. 1991. *Galileo, Bellarmine, and the Bible.* Notre Dame, IN: University of Notre Dame Press.

Boyle, Robert. 1772. *The Works of the Honourable Robert Boyle.* Edited by Thomas Birc. 6 vols. London.

Burnet, Thomas. 1684. *Sacred Theory of the Earth.* London.

Burnet, Thomas. 1680. *Telluris theoria sacra.* London.

Cano, Melchior. 1563. *De locis theologicis.* Salamanca.

Clarke, Samuel. 1738. *The Works of Samuel Clarke.* 4 vols. London.

Croft, Herbert. 1685. *Some Animadversions Upon a Book Intituled The Theory of the Earth.* London.

Cumberland, Richard. 1672. *De legibus naturae.* London.

Diderot, Denis. 1749. *Lettre sur les aveugles.* London.

Franklin, Julian. 1963. *Jean Bodin and the Sixteenth-Century Revolution in the Methodology of Law and History.* New York: Columbia University Press.

Gaukroger, Stephen. 2010. *The Collapse of Mechanism and the Rise of Sensibility.* Oxford: Oxford University Press.

Gaukroger, Stephen. 2006. *The Emergence of a Scientific Culture.* Oxford: Oxford University Press.

Gibbon, Edward. 1776. *The Decline and Fall of the Roman Empire.* Vol. 1. Dublin.

Harrison, Peter. 2011. "Experimental Religion and Experimental Science in Early Modern England." *Intellectual History Review* 21: 413–433.

Harrison, Peter. 1990. *"Religion" and Religions in the English Enlightenment.* Cambridge: Cambridge University Press.

Hunter, Michael. 2002. *Robert Boyle (1627–91): Scrupulosity and Science.* Woodbridge, UK: Boydell Press.

Keill, John. 1698. *An Examination of Dr. Burnet's Theory of the Earth.* Oxford.

La Peyrère, Isaac de. 1655. *Prae-Adamitae, sive exercitatio super versibus duodecimo, decimotertio, & decimoquarto, capitis quinti Epistolae D. Pauli ad Romanos.* Amsterdam.

Le Camus, Antoine. 1753. *Médicine de l'esprit.* Paris.

Locke, John. 1722. *The Works of John Locke.* 2nd ed. 3 vols. London.

MacCulloch, Diarmaid. 2009. *A History of Christianity.* London: Viking Books.

Masuzawa, Tomoko. 2005. *The Invention of World Religions.* Chicago: University of Chicago Press.

Newton, Isaac. 1959–1977. *The Correspondence of Isaac Newton.* Edited by H. W. Turnbull, J. F. Scott, A. R. Hall, and Laura Tilling. 7 vols. Cambridge: Cambridge University Press.

Ray, John. 1691. *The Wisdom of God Manifested in the Works of Creation.* London.

Rousseau, Jean-Jacques. 1762. *Émile, ou du l'Education.* The Hague.

Toland, John. 1696. *Christianity Not Mysterious.* London.

Voltaire, François Marie. 1769. *Essai sur les mœurs et l'esprit des nations.* Geneva.

Warren, Erasmus. 1690. *Geologia or a Discourse Concerning the Earth before the Deluge.* London.

Whiston, William. 1696. *A New Theory of the Earth, from its Origins to the Consummation of All Things.* London.

Woodward, John 1695. *An Essay towards a Natural History of the Earth and Terrestrial Bodies.* London.

# CHAPTER 37

# SPINOZA AND EARLY MODERN THEOLOGY

## JONATHAN I. ISRAEL

In the "introduction" to the English version of his *Spinoza's Critique of Religion* (1997), Leo Strauss notes the historical importance of a critic treating the Bible as "a literary document like any other" to be "studied and interpreted like any other literary document." Denying that the Bible is divine revelation "is the true foundation of Biblical science in the modern sense. It is for this reason and only this reason that Spinoza's work is of fundamental importance." Strauss was the first to contextualize this central contention of Spinoza's *Tractatus Theologico-Politicus* (1670), viewing it as both his individual theological contribution and part of a wider phenomenon that Strauss was among the first to label the "Radical Enlightenment." The latter he conceived as an immensely long historical process commencing with Epicurus and other antitheological tendencies in Hellenistic philosophy and evolving through medieval Averroism and Maimonides' Jewish philosophy into a broad cultural challenge to Jewish and Christian theology and the wider philosophical and cultural underpinning of Judaeo-Christian-Islamic civilization, culminating in the eighteenth-century Radical Enlightenment proper, of which he considered Spinoza a major precursor.

## 1 LEO STRAUSS AND SPINOZA'S "RADICAL ENLIGHTENMENT"

The arguments of Spinoza's *Tractatus Theologico-Politicus* (1670) and *Ethics* (1678), contended Strauss, represent an intellectual revolution less in themselves than as part of a broader Western atheistic tendency culminating in Machiavelli and Hobbes, as well as Spinoza, but expressed in philosophical terms most completely by the latter. "The context to which [Spinoza's thought] belongs is the critique of Revelation as attempted by the radical Enlightenment. That critique represents only one particular stage of the critique of religion originating in Greek antiquity and was continued and renewed in the age in which belief in Revelation predominated" (Strauss 1981, 2). In characterizing the generalized challenge that the antitheology of his "radical Enlightenment" represented as opposed to the theological underlay of the Judaeo-Christian-Muslim traditions, Strauss identified three main components: first, rejection of divine revelation along with Creation and miracles, which he considered the chief foundation of the *radikale Aufklärung*; second, the notion that this critique is only one stage, if the culminating one, of his long process reaching back to Hellenistic thought; third, that there is a basic assumption underlying Spinoza's critique of religion concerning the universal validity of knowledge, or science, that Spinoza shares with the entire body of the wider tradition of "radical Enlightenment" (Strauss 1997, 15, 17).

Strauss returns to this thesis of a shared general assumption underlying Spinoza's critique of religion in his fifth chapter of *Spinoza's Critique of Religion*, where he brings it up in connection with Spinoza's reply to one of his sharpest contemporary critics, Albert Burgh (1650–1708), the son of a Dutch regent who had recently converted to Catholicism and become a Franciscan friar. Defending revelation and religious authority, Burgh vehemently rebuked Spinoza, exclaiming "each philosopher has recourse to reason, and not one of them succeeds in convincing the other. Are there not, within philosophy, just as many sects which are unable to convince each other as in revealed religion?" (Strauss 1997, 140). "Only positive science," that is, *Wissenschaft* (translated by Strauss's translator E. M. Sinclair as "scientific" but invariably employed by Strauss to mean *wissenschaftlich* [i.e., scholarly and scientific]), entitles philosophy and reason to mount their objections to revealed religion. Uncovering contradictions and discrepancies between the different prophecies within scripture, contended Spinoza, is doing something essentially different from merely pointing to disagreements among theologians and religious leaders. One knows when steps taken in philosophy reveal the "truth," he explains, "in the same way that you know that the three angles of a triangle are equal to two right angles. That this suffices no one will deny who has a sound brain and does not dream of unclean spirits who inspire us with false ideas as if they were true. For truth reveals both itself and also the false" (Spinoza 1995, 342).

Only "science," concluded Strauss—that is, learning, research, and scholarship—could provide a grounding that religious believers do not possess, which is universal and common to all men and could in principle validate such a critique of revealed religion: "only to the extent that Spinoza constructs his system under the aegis and in the spirit of positive science, and in a manner strictly scholarly, and 'subjects himself to scientific [i.e., *wissenschaftlich* or scholarly] scrutiny in consequence,'" does he proceed and operate "with greater right than his opponents who believed in revealed religion." Spinoza's opinion that his countertheology was more scientific than mainstream theology, Strauss believed, "precedes essentially the constitution of [Spinoza's] philosophy, as appears also from the fact that it is common to the whole radical Enlightenment" (Strauss 1997).

# 2  THE CONNECTION OF BIBLE CRITICISM
## AND NATURALISM

Two crucially important points about Spinoza's relationship to theology emerge from Strauss's discussion in the 1920s, and they provide a convenient starting point for this present summary: first, that there is a close relationship between Spinoza's Bible criticism and his radical naturalism, and his conception of human knowledge and science; and second, that this particular conjoining of elements underpins an entire "Radical Enlightenment," which over many centuries challenged the edifice of Judaeo-Christian-Muslim theology at every level. In explaining what he meant by a "God" who is unknowing, creates nothing, does not govern the course of history or nature, makes no miracles and authorizes no revelation, Spinoza defines God both in his main philosophical work, the *Ethics* (1678), and his main political work, the *Tractatus Theologico-Politicus*, as well as his foray into Bible criticism, as a singular and absolutely infinite substance which he equates with nature, conceived as an infinite all-inclusive immanent cause, "the immanent, not the transitive, cause of all things" as he expresses in Proposition 18 of Part One of the *Ethics* (Spinoza 1985, 428). God is the inherent creative force (*natura naturans*) as well as all that actually is (*natura naturata*) (Spinoza 1985, 409, 417, 420–21). In his reply to Burgh, Spinoza postulates "an infinite God by whose efficacy all things absolutely come into being and are preserved" (Spinoza 1995, 341).

Spinoza's God, then, is the creative power of nature, and everything that actually is, conceived as the totality of everything, with nothing lying beyond it and no such thing as supernatural agency, the miraculous, or revelation does or could exist. Since nothing can be conceived without or beyond God, according to Spinoza, "the more we learn about natural things, the greater and more perfect the knowledge of God we acquire. Further ... the more we learn about natural things, the more perfectly we come to know the essence of God (which is the cause of all things), and thus all our knowledge, that is, our highest good, not only depends on a knowledge of God but consists in it altogether" (Spinoza 2007, 59; Donagan 1996, 354). It is this insistence that all knowledge that is genuine accords with the laws of nature as identified by us and that there is no other authentic "truth," that elevates and exalts science and scholarship into the sole valid knowledge, not just rivaling but by definition negating and excluding all religious authority as conventionally understood. This stance is indeed foundational for the Radical Enlightenment. For the Radical Enlightenment there is only one source of truth—science and scientifically based scholarship in the humanities—so that "science" understood as *Wissenschaft* (or in Dutch, *wetenschap*) always and inevitably conflicts with and negates religious authority (in contrast to the moderate Enlightenment credo that science operates in harmony with religion).

The idea that the will of God and the laws of nature are identical and that all supernatural agency is precluded is, then, the core of Spinoza's theology and of the Radical Enlightenment challenge to religion, tradition, conventional thinking and mainstream

Western philosophy and science. Although the main focus in what follows here is on basic theology rather than morality or "practical theology," a fundamental consequence of Spinoza's stance follows directly: namely, that the rules of morality underpinning the legal and political order that every human society requires must consequently stem from the dictates of reason and science alone, and can have no objective or authoritative basis in religion, tradition, or what some regard as holy books or revelation. According to his philosophy, the moral teaching of the churches has no authoritative basis, and in certain respects is bogus and actually immoral. Thus, for example, Burgh, by converting to Catholicism, has become deluded by notions of the devil, "a Prince, God's enemy, who against God's will, ensnares most men (for the good are few) and deceives them, whom God therefore delivers over to this master of wickedness for everlasting torture. So divine justice permits the Devil to deceive men with impunity, but does not permit men, haplessly deceived and ensnared by the Devil, to go unpunished" (Spinoza 1995, 341).

# 3 SPINOZA AND THE ANTI-TRINITARIANS

If to Maimonides or Aquinas, as well as most later theologians and philosophers, Spinoza's definition of God would have amounted to atheism, Spinoza himself indignantly rejected this charge claiming that someone who "declares that God must be recognized as the highest good" does not lack true "religion" and is no atheist. Furthermore, while most Christian theologians in his own time and subsequently did denounce Spinoza as an "atheist," by no means all did. While the circle around Spinoza in the 1650s, 1660s, and 1670s certainly included writers who were irreligious libertines and freethinkers, it also comprised close friends and allies—like Pieter Balling (n.d.–1669), who translated much of his earlier work into Dutch, Jarig Jelles (ca. 1620–83), who composed the Preface to the *Opera Posthuma* in 1677, and Jan Rieuwertsz (ca. 1616–87), the Amsterdam publisher who published and distributed all his books, including those that could be sold only clandestinely—who were eager students of his writings, and sympathetic to and immersed in his philosophical system, while nevertheless at the same time sincere Christians of a particular stamp (Israel 2001, 164, 170–71, 342–58; Hunter 2005, 37–46). They were Socinian Collegiants belonging to an influential group of deeply pious and sincere, and also in part anti-Trinitarian believers that flourished in Amsterdam, Rotterdam, and Rijnsburg, particularly during the mid and later seventeenth and early eighteenth centuries.

Collegiants were fringe Christians, highly heterodox by definition, rejecting all forms of organized priesthood or clergy and the principle of ecclesiastical authority. But they also were divided among themselves into disparate theological streams (Fix 1991; Israel 1995, 911–25). What was probably a minority were principled anti-Trinitarians, combining anti-Trinitarianism with a broader willingness to abandon biblical literalism and interpret scripture by the light of reason alone, without recourse to tradition or ecclesiastical teaching. While all Socinians identified the light of reason as man's chief guide in matters of faith and biblical interpretation, probably only a small minority, much as with the English Unitarians in the late eighteenth century, took this rule to the point of insisting on a close symbiosis of theology and philosophy, and merging the light of reason in biblical scholarship with the philosophical-scientific reasoning of Descartes and Spinoza. Other fervently committed Collegiants who knew Spinoza personally, like Pieter Serrarius (1600–69), a Spiritualist theologian who, as we see from Spinoza's correspondence remained in regular contact with him for some years, did embrace the Trinity, Christ's divinity and other "mysteries," and concomitantly the miraculous nature of man's salvation through Christ, positions that necessarily involved rejecting Spinozism as a creed, as well as the notion that his theology could be fused or combined with a coherent nonchurch Christianity without priesthood. Only one strand among the Collegiants were dogmatic anti-Trinitarians of a strongly philosophical bent, eager to combine the reason they claimed grounds Christian belief with philosophical reason, rather than with the Holy Ghost or supernatural inspiration. But even then, as we see in Balling's case, and later in that of Jan Bredenburg (1643–91), the Rotterdam Collegiant whose theology proved a particularly divisive influence among the Dutch Collegiant congregations in the 1680s and subsequently, there remained, as Bayle noted, an element of ambiguity in their approach, a susceptibility to "double-truth" positions, and undeviating resolve to square reason with faith that clearly and significantly separated their theology from that of Spinoza (Bayle 1740, 4:259).

Collegiant anti-Trinitarian biblical fundamentalists like Frans Kuyper (1629–91), who in the 1680s took to denouncing the trend toward embracing philosophical reason among the Collegiants as a self-destructive, atheistic betrayal from within, denounced and separated themselves from figures like Balling, Jelles, and Bredenburg, who resolutely carved out a zone of compatibility with Spinozist positions. The latter alone were amenable to Spinoza's "Jesus Christ," a personage presented as an altogether exceptional human being possessing "superhuman wisdom," but otherwise a mortal human; Spinoza's "Jesus" acting as a bridge that helped to ground their theological trend in a way that had far-reaching historical implications. Entering into alliance with Spinoza, these men conceived "Spinozism" as a religious creed as well as a philosophy, and one that should properly be construed, as Jelles does in his "Vooreeden" [preface] or "Praefatio" to the *Opera Posthuma*, as a "Christian philosophy"; that is, one in full accord with scripture and the true foundations of the Christian religion when approached in a purely rational manner. The mistaken contrary impression was much more widespread, according to Jelles, only because most "Christians" follow the letter instead of the spirit of scripture (Akkerman and Hubbeling 1979, 103–09; Jelles 1979, 120–23; Hunter 2005, 56).

If Spinoza gained from collaborating with the anti-Trinitarian philosophical Collegiants friendship, support, and an urban network for propagating his publications and influence, the Dutch Socinians found allying with Spinoza useful—due to, first, a Bible criticism and theory of priestcraft of unrivaled force and sophistication with which to reinforce their efforts to discredit the orthodox churches (including the Mennonites and nearly all rival Dissenters) as corruptors of revelation and impostors;

second, a conception of morality as something that men must construct on the basis of reason and Christ's example alone, without recourse to any priesthood; and finally, a philosophy that helped buttress their pleas for comprehensive toleration.

Was then this "Spinozism" construed as a Socinian Collegiant creed, a set of beliefs distinct, and to a degree detachable from, Spinoza's philosophy? Many modern scholars wrongly assume there was no such thing as Dutch "Spinozism" in the late seventeenth century, despite frequent denunciations in the writings of orthodox Calvinist, Lutheran, and Catholic theologians; these being just a rhetorical display by opponents of heterodoxy and freethinking mounted for polemical purposes. References to *Spinozismus* are thus frequently dismissed as just empty polemics routinely invoked by academics and preachers—Remonstrant (Arminian) and Mennonite, as well as Calvinist, Catholic, Lutheran—more or less all reducible to the claim that Spinozism was just "atheism" and nothing more. But this view is scarcely compatible with the evidence.

The most highly rated and longest remembered among the early German refutations of the *Tractatus Theologico-Politicus* was that of Johann Musaeus, a ninety-six page tract published at Jena, with a preface dated April 1674 and dedicated to Duke Johann Friedrich of Braunschweig-Lüneburg. It is entitled *Tractatus Theologico-Politicus, Quo Auctor quidam Anonymus, conatu improbo, demonstratum ivit, Libertatem Philosophandi . . . Ad veritatis lancem examinatus* and denounces what Musaeus considered to be the sweepingly subversive cultural, social, and intellectual implications of Spinoza's "freedom to philosophize." A vigorous defender of church power and the princely court system prevailing in Germany at the time, he cites numerous passages from Spinoza's text to show that the anonymous author sought to overthrow Christianity, as generally understood, and replace it with a comprehensive *Naturalismus*, denying the possibility of miracles and everything supernatural. Spinoza, he argues, is also "second to none" as an advocate of a wide-ranging, pernicious toleration, like that which could be found in Amsterdam, which legitimizes all strands of opinion and would remove all barriers presently operative in Germany against Socinians and other anti-Trinitarians (Musaeus 1674).

No less basic to his alliance with Socinianism than his theory of toleration and freedom of expression (which like Bayle's extends much further than Locke's), was Spinoza's attempt to detach Christ from the orthodox churches and his comprehensive assault on the priesthood—whether Catholic, Protestant or Greek Orthodox—as "impostors." In this respect, no other philosopher could have been so useful to the Dutch and German Socinians and to what in Britain and the United States came to be known as the Unitarians. Particularly in teaching "practical theology," the rudiments of true morality, Spinoza, like Lodewijk Meyer (1629–81), viewed a Collegiant-style or type of religious teaching based on scripture freed from priestly overview as capable of playing a positive and also—since most people cannot be philosophers and must discipline their lives on the basis of religion—indispensable role in buttressing society and the moral order. Spinoza combined his skeptical-critical view of the Bible with the most devastating attack on ecclesiastical authority and the traditions of the churches yet seen; combining both, no less importantly, with a view of Christ as the supreme moral teacher whose philosophy is embedded in the Gospels. This assisted Socinians as well as naturalists in their campaign to demonstrate that "true Christianity," the genuine teaching of Christ, in no way corresponds to the allegedly corrupted doctrines of orthodox theologians and ecclesiastics who, according to Spinoza, had utterly perverted the Christian religion ever since the time of the Apostles (Israel 2007, xvii).

Christ, contends Spinoza, was not a "prophet," a term that has a somewhat pejorative resonance in his terminology, but rather someone whose mind was adapted "to the universal beliefs and doctrines held by all mankind, that is to those concepts which are universal and true." He was thus foundational, the supreme guide to humanity, but only insofar as he embodied the primacy of science and scholarship. Spinoza develops this thesis in his *Tractatus Theologico-Politicus*, doubtless in part out of tactical considerations; but in part probably also sincerely as a way of cementing his collaboration with the Collegiants and building an effective social reformism on this basis. In particular, he looked forward to the day when religion would finally be "reduced to the extremely few, very simple dogmas that Christ taught to his own," consisting quintessentially of the practice of justice and charity alone (Spinoza 2007, 161).

## 4 THE RIVAL THEOLOGIES OF DUTCH AND GERMAN SPINOZISM

Dutch and German Spinozism certainly *was* a distinct, coherent, and rival theology, and one about which theologians of almost every stripe had abundant reason to feel agitated and alarmed. Among the best and most concise summaries of Spinozist theology in later Dutch Golden Age culture was recorded by Balthasar Bekker (1634–98), the famous Frisian theologian notorious in the 1690s for denying the reality of magic, witchcraft, and satanic intervention in human minds and life. Earlier, before the publication of his *De Betoverde Weereld* (1691), which made him both famous and infamous, Bekker visited Spinoza at his lodgings in The Hague, toward the close of his life at some point during the period 1674–76. When compiling his continuation of Hornius's ecclesiastical history, published in 1683, Bekker subsequently appraised Spinoza's theological significance and impact in the following way:

> one must admit Spinoza's views have spread [in Dutch society] and become rooted all too far and too much in all parts and social orders, that they have infected many of the best minds, including among the residences of the great; and that people of very ordinary status enraptured by [his views] as if by something divine, have been brought to godlessness. Meanwhile, as a result, the number increases of those who profess religion and religious doctrine only to conform, and more from human than divine considerations. And if that continues, God help us, what a blow through the heavy fall of such a mass of people will be given to the frame of God's House. (Bekker 1685, 39)

This assessment tallies with a great deal of other commentary identifying a dramatic shift in attitudes in the 1670s and 1680s; a shift engineered by what the Rotterdam Remonstrant minister Johannes Molinaeus in 1692 called the "seductive philosophy" of Spinoza, Hobbes, and Meyer's *Philosophia*, whereby "countless intellects and minds in our Fatherland have been poisoned" and led to reject Christ not only philosophically and openly but as—or more—often in a concealed manner, such as described by Bekker; that is, pretending to be Christians (Molinaeus 1692, 24–25).

The theology of "Spinozism" Bekker summarized in six principal points:

1. That there is no substance, or being, other than God and that all creatures are but modes or aspects of God.
2. That this one substance has two essential properties (that we can discern), one being extension and the other thought, with an infinite number of others about which we know nothing.
3. That everything depends on an infinite number of causes which follow from one another in an infinite order and in infinite ways.
4. That, hence, nothing, and no action, is good or evil in itself.
5. That the Holy Scriptures are not originally from God and that their [human] authors erred in many things.
6. That miracles occur solely due to natural causes and are hence explicable [only in natural terms].

The Bekker furore of 1691–94 over the question of whether magic and demonic power actually exist, and whether the devil can exert an influence on human life, featured among the foremost public controversies agitating the Dutch reading public during the late seventeenth century. It fed the angry suspicions of both Protestant and Catholic orthodox that liberal theologians of a Cartesian or Cartesio-Cocceian bent, like Bekker or the no less famous Leiden Cartesian professor of theology, Christopher Wittichius (1625–87), divines making major concessions to philosophical reason in their theology and cutting back the scope of the supernatural, were ill-advisedly—and perhaps even with subversive intent but in any case ruinously—encouraging the growth of Socinianism and opening the door to "Spinozism." Among Collegiants, only the philosophical Socinians embraced components of Spinoza's theology more or less openly, or more clandestinely; but all Socinians faced accusations that they were replacing theology with philosophical reason. The chief objection leveled against them, explained Bayle in his *Dictionnaire*, is that in refusing to believe "that which seemed to them in opposition to the *Lumières Philosophiques* and in subscribing to the inconceivable Mysteries of the Christian religion," they were opening the way "to Pyrrhonism, Deism, and Atheism." It was an accusation Bayle claimed to consider justified, for by denying the divinity of scripture "one turns the concept of revelation on its head, without which all is merely philosophical argument" (Bayle 1740, 4:236–37).

Dutch Socinianism with a Spinozistic infusion must have extended further than the Collegiant movement, because the latter's free, open, mostly undisturbed meetings of nonchurch Christians rejecting the Trinity were permitted (and even then precariously and solely on a purely *de facto* basis), only by the city governments of Amsterdam and Rotterdam and the authorities at Rijnsburg. Their conventicles were officially forbidden elsewhere in the Dutch Republic, including many places where highly unorthodox religion with a strong rational and anti-Trinitarian bent nevertheless took root under cover of a variety of masks, often assuming a rather different character from that of the Collegiant movement proper. It is therefore safe to assume that Socinian variants of Spinozism ramified rather widely as part of the broader penetration of "seductive philosophy" along the lines described by Bekker, Molinaeus, and others. The comments of Bayle, Bekker, Molinaeus, Van Til, and other writers about the advance of "seductive philosophy" in the 1670s and 1680s also show that crypto-Spinozist sentiments allied to crypto-Socinianism penetrated not just fringe religious movements but also the world view of individuals officially belonging to the Reformed Church, including Adriaan Koerbagh's (1633–69) elder brother, Johannes Koerbagh (1634–72), a crypto-Socinian theology candidate who also in effect became a Spinozistic Reformed theologian (Wielema 2004, 87; Israel 2001, 185–91). In the United Provinces, there was also a proliferation of newly formed clandestine churches and currents operating outside the Reformed Church, whose spiritual leaders felt at least some requirement to engage with Spinoza's theology (Wielema 2004, 14–16, 87, 121).

Consequently, the world's first encyclopedia of religion and theology, the *Cérémonies et coutûmes religieuses de tous les peuples du monde*, edited by Jean-Frédéric Bernard (ca. 1683–1744) in Amsterdam, published in seven volumes and handsomely illustrated with hundreds of engravings by Bernard Picart (which were included in the 1720s and early 1730s), was far from being bizarrely eccentric or sowing confusion by including "Spinozism" as a creed and a form of religion, as well as a potent factor in the development of strands of the Christian heterodox fringe. Dutch religious heterodoxy in the late seventeenth and early eighteenth centuries could not avoid identifying Spinoza as a central factor in the Collegiant disputes and key influence in the rise of new fringe Christian movements, as well as "Deism." Bernard's massive and ambitious compendium, which has attracted considerable scholarly interest recently (Hunt, Jacob, and Mijnhardt 2010a and 2010b), also appeared in English in the 1730s in London, in a version prepared by an unknown hand referred to on the title page of the first volume simply as "a Gentleman, sometime since of St John's College in Oxford." This version follows the original Dutch in treating "Spinozism" as a creed and points "our curious readers" to where they may "find a full account of Baruch or Benedict Spinoza in Bayle's Dictionary, to which may be added his Life, published by Maximilian Lucas, one of his Disciples" (Picart and Bernard 1731–39, 225).

While it remains hotly disputed among Dutch Church historians whether Hattemism, a fringe church strong in Zeeland that was strictly forbidden by the authorities, forged by Pontiaan van Hattem (1641–1706) shortly after Spinoza's death, really had meaningful links to Spinozism, the *Ceremonies et coutûmes religieuses* claims it did. Indeed, most contemporary or near-contemporary sources classify Hattemism as a movement in which Van Hattem and his disciples "added," as the English version of the *Cérémonies* puts it, "some of their own notions to the system of Spinoza, and interrelated the whole with the mystical notions of the Pietists." Meeting furtively in private homes, the Hattemists formed a movement that pervaded southern Dutch towns and some villages in the late seventeenth century. The *Cérémonies* characterizes them as a group that met only in the strictest secrecy, taking stringent precautions to admit no one they could not trust owing to what *Cérémonies'* editors call "the grievous penalties inflicted upon them by an edict of the States of Holland" commanding that "they shall be banished or cast into prison, and severely punished as enemies to virtue, to divine worship, and disturbers of the public peace, that their books shall be suppressed, and the authors, printers and publishers proceeded against as directed in the edict [of the States, of 1678] about Spinozism" (Picart and Bernard 1731–39, 28, 225).

Bernard's text lists among other heterodox works spurring controversy in early eighteenth-century Holland the *Ingebeelde Chaos* [Imaginary Chaos] by Hendrik Wyermars (ca. 1685–after 1749), the defiant young Spinozist sentenced to fifteen years' imprisonment in Amsterdam in 1710 for violating the prohibition on publishing "Spinozistic" books (Israel 2001, 13, 132, 252, 265, 322–27). Wyermars, explains the *Cérémonies*, contended "that the Trinity is only three modifications of the Supreme Being, that Extension is essential to God, and is the second person, that Creation is from all eternity, etc. He and some others, namely one Deurhof, have had some followers, and held as they do still some small assemblies, in a very private manner, to avoid the persecutions which the magistrates might make against them" (Picart and Bernard 1731–39, 227–28; Wielema 2004, 142–46). But if the world of Dutch anti-Trinitarian heterodoxy in the late seventeenth and early eighteenth centuries, down to around 1720, was fragmented, variegated, and highly divisive (especially after the quarrel about the Spinozist proclivities of Johan Bredenburg provoked a formal rift splitting the Collegiants into Spinozistic-Socinian and anti-Spinozist "Biblicist" anti-Trinitarians in the 1680s), the Socinian Collegiants survived the eighteenth century as a coherent, organized force and Dutch Socinianism, or Unitarianism, can be said to have been part of a growing Western phenomenon rapidly assuming formidable dimensions across the trans-Atlantic world, in particular in England and New England.

## 5 SPINOZA AND UNITARIANISM

The *Cérémonies*, much like Bayle and later Diderot's disciple and d'Holbach's assistant, Jacques André Naigeon (1738–1810), author of the article "Unitaires" in the seventeenth volume of Diderot's and d'Alembert's *Encyclopédie*, first published in 1765, stresses the centrality of the philosophical tendency in eighteenth-century Unitarianism, maintaining that its dissident theology extended far beyond merely anti-Trinitarianism. Since Socinians believe "man was of his own nature mortal, even before the Fall, and was never endowed with original or primitive justice" and that consequently, for them, there is no such thing as original sin, that no redeeming power can reside in sacraments or the spiritual functions of the clergy and that God "might have forgiven the sins of mankind, and reconciled men with divine justice, and pardoned them, without the satisfaction of Christ," they effectively dismantled the entire edifice of conventional Christian theology (Picart and Bernard 1731–39, 208–9). In fact, suggested the self-declared atheist Naigeon, Socinians should not really be considered a theological stream at all, being better thought of as a sect of *philosophes* who in order not to shock received opinion and religious sensibilities too freely "did not want to openly demonstrate their purely deist sentiments, nor did they want to formally and without exception reject the whole concept of revelation; and so with regard to the Old and New Testaments, they did what the Epicureans did with regard to the gods in whom they verbally professed their belief yet in reality wiped out" (Naigeon 1765, 388).

Considered in this light, Collegiant Socinianism as transmitted, or replicated, in Britain and America in the form of organized philosophical Unitarianism, may perhaps be classified as a lastingly significant theological ally of the Spinozistic radical tradition. It was the sole intrinsically religious component of the Radical Enlightenment in the English-speaking world, as also elsewhere, and an enduring one; a trend powerfully advanced by Joseph Priestley and such lesser figures as John Jebb and William Frend, a current that can be said to have developed important ties throughout the trans-Atlantic context with the Radical Enlightenment both in general and, in particular, with Spinozism conceived as an underground creed. Priestley nowhere refers to any links with Spinoza or Spinozism; but he does explicitly acknowledge in several places in his writings his sympathies for and philosophical proximity to, contemporary materialism and democratic radicalism as it evolved in France, as indeed does John Jebb (1736–86), the Cambridge don forced out of Cambridge in 1775 on account of his heterodoxy and democratic reformism.

In particular, five key affinities may be noted. First, despite retaining a strongly biblical thrust and fervent trust in divine Providence ruling the universe, Priestleyan Unitarianism embraced a Spinozistic philosophical determinism and materialism, conflating spirit and matter into one. Thus, for example, Priestley reissued Anthony Collins' Spinozistic and atheistic tract on liberty and necessity in 1779, explicitly proclaiming himself an exponent of "philosophical necessity" in the same (Spinozistic) sense as Collins, providing an approving preface to the text by his own hand (Priestley 1790, xi). Second, Priestley and Jebb committed themselves to a corporeal conception of the mind and soul, which implies that it dies with the body even if, like the Dutch rationalist Collegiants, they nevertheless still professed to retain immortality of the soul in some residual fashion (Page 2003, 87), a difficult procedure philosophically. Here too, Spinoza acted as a bridge between materialism and Unitarianism, providing a reductive doctrine of "immortality of the soul" which, though deeply perplexing to students of Spinoza's philosophy down to today, is undeniably an inherent feature of his system (Matheron 2011; Nadler 2006, 153, 260, 265).

Third, unlike most other eighteenth-century British religious movements, Priestleyan Unitarianism embraced an extremely radical and sweepingly democratic political reform program, not unlike the *philosophisme* of Diderot and d'Holbach, more or less completely repudiating the existing British constitution, mixed monarchy, and the principle of aristocracy, and urging the adoption of representative democracy. Fourth, Priestleyan Unitarianism shared, albeit with a different religious tone, in *philosoph-isme*'s claim that practically everything was wrong with the prevailing general system of ideas, education, authority, and morality in Christendom; and that corruption was essentially the fault of priestly impostors, "superstitious" rites, mystifying theology, and false religion—or what Jebb called the "contagion of corrupted doctrine" spread "by the craft and cunning of a designing and despotic priesthood" (Jebb 1787, 161). Finally, like Spinozism, Priestleyan Unitarianism embraced a comprehensive rather than a limited Lockean toleration that sought to shield non-Christians no less than heterodox Christians, and finally free the atheists too from intolerance, persecution, and penal laws (Bradley 2006, 364–65).

Consequently, both the religious and irreligious wings of the Radical Enlightenment can perhaps be said to have shared a quasi-theological dimension in their millenarian expectation that a new dawn was coming, to be ushered in by revolution, the demolition of all existing religious, social, cultural, and educational attitudes and forms. Priestley gave eloquent expression to this particularly striking affinity in the dedication to his colleague, the Unitarian minister Theophilus Lindsey, of his *An History of the Corruptions of Christianity in Two Volumes* (1782). "The gross darkness of that night," he wrote, "which has for many centuries obscured our holy religion, we may clearly see, is past; the morning is opening upon us; and we cannot doubt but that the light will increase, and extend itself more and more, unto the perfect day. Happy are they who contribute to diffuse the pure light of this everlasting gospel" (Priestley 1782, v).

# 6 The Spinozist Challenge to Apologetic Theology

During the eighteenth and nineteenth centuries, Spinoza's philosophy remained a central challenge to Protestant, Catholic, and Jewish theology alike. While it is not the case that most French Catholic apologists and opponents of the *philosophes* during the eighteenth century postulated a close link between Spinoza and the rise of the *philosophique* challenge to revealed religion and ecclesiastical authority, a substantial minority did. These writers conceptualized the threat in terms broadly similar to those of orthodox Protestants and Jews. When each particular thread of atheistic materialism is examined, it emerges, held Catholic apologists like the Abbé Claude-François Houtteville (1688–1742), Laurent François (1698–1772), the Abbé François-André Pluquet (1716–90), Michel-Ange Marin (1697–1767), Guillaume Maleville (1699–1771), Henri Griffet (1698–1771), Daniel Le Masson des Granges (1706–66), and Dom Nicolas Jamin (1711–82), that these more or less all originate in Spinoza's thought and, in that guise, they assume "the appearance" of coherence. Despite his weak demonstrations, contends François, Spinoza says everything that can be said "against the prophets, and those persistent men of today who are nothing but their mere reflections" (François 1751, 2:42). Spinozism remained a principal philosophical target for eighteenth- and nineteenth-century theologians because there were count-less *incrédules* like Marin's fictitious "Dutch" freethinker, Van-Hesden, who were unaware that their core ideas derived from and depended on Spinozism and were urgently in need of being rescued from the path of "error." Most *esprits forts*, remarks Marin, never consciously designed to embrace Spinoza's principles and mostly failed to realize that their freethinking was chiefly grounded in the philosophies of such a universally condemned thinker (Marin 1762, 1:iv; 2:25, 2:75). Were all the vast masses of *incrédules* corrupting France, Marin's hermit assures the boat captain and passen-gers that figure in his novel, magically to be rolled up into a single universal pat-terned textile, Spinoza would be the original pattern and sample of this cloth (Marin 1762, 1:67–70).

François, Maleville, Pluquet, Le Masson, and Marin agree with Bayle that Spinoza denies divine Creation of the world and species more cogently than anyone else, and comes closest among antiscripturalists to proving that we cannot find in scripture "an understanding of natural and spiritual phenomena" (Marin 1762, 4:144), as Maleville puts it. He was also the first thinker who dared "streamline his lack of faith into a sys-tem." In his chapters on miracles, Creation and final causes, and when treating Bible criticism, Maleville's chief target is always Spinoza and those he considers "Spinozists," such as Boulainvilliers, Collins, and d'Argens. Many readers, observes Maleville, wanted to know whether it was with reason that Spinoza was everywhere daily accused of overthrowing the authority of the sacred books and if so, to know how it happens that Spinoza manages to be so incisive, cogent, and skillful in arranging his arguments. In any work seriously intending to defend religion and scripture against the *incrédules*, insisted Maleville, the champion of faith cannot honestly dispense with setting out the arguments of this famous man in all their force and subtlety.

Maleville apologizes in his *Religion naturelle* for citing Spinoza's texts more frequently than those of any other thinker. His justification for doing so is that all too often in the past, Christian apologists had failed to engage with the most systematic challenge confronting them. For if one once assumes nature's works "have no God as author," as Maleville expresses it, "Spinoza reasons admirably well." If the cosmos is not after all cre-ated by an intelligent workman, no one explains more convincingly than he how man-kind's preoccupation with final causes originally arose (Maleville 1756–58, 2:48; Vernière 1982, 427–30). There might be inconvenience in according Spinoza great prominence, but the Christian apologist's responsibility is not to hide this writer's arguments but to demolish his system (Maleville 1756–58, 4:154). Spinoza needs to be closely studied by the Catholic priesthood given the considerable effort required to identify Spinoza's weak points; effort requisite by every priest who thinks seriously about his faith, since so much clandestine literature is philosophically anchored in Spinozism (Maleville 1756–58, 1:30, 2:46–48, 2:51–52, 2:115–31, 3:323–28, 4:107–80, 4:206–14, 4:254, 5:36–38, 5:141–63, 6:127–29). Close examination in turn meant drawing the public's attention to it, and what a blow to the *incrédules* and a triumph for revelation should it transpire that Spinoza's main theses "were nothing but weak ones" after all! (Maleville 1756–58, 4:155).

Maleville was unique, though, in stressing Spinoza's general cogency. The centrality of Spinoza and Spinozism in the worldview propagated by *anti-philosophie* more typically led to odd, paradoxical formulations attempting to assert both "the appearance" of coherence and his philosophy's actual incoherence. In dedicating his book to the primate of the Catholic Low Countries, the Archbishop of Mechelen, Count Franckenberg, Griffet portrays Spinoza as someone who had won a vast name for himself "by the strength and singularity of his ideas," despite not being, properly speaking, the inventor of his system at all. Spinoza's thought is really just a rehash of Lucretius and Pliny the Naturalist, who in turn, held Griffet, derived their ideas from older Greek predecessors. Likewise, with his geometric method of presentation, Spinoza impresses only "simplistic, superficial minds" who suppose his "demonstrations" possess the rigor of mathematical explanations. Deeper minds see through his "ridiculous sophisms."

But this way of arguing created a paradox. Spinoza, for the *anti-philosophes*, was a unique specimen of impostor, self-contradictory and "sans jugement" but yet, unlike Lucretius or Hobbes, a continuing menace; being someone who Griffet conceded had "plenty of sectarians" (Griffet 1770, 7). Hence Marin, Maleville, Houtteville, François, Pluquet, and other eighteenth-century French writers broadcast Spinoza's maxims and views often at great length, affirming their impact and incisiveness while simultaneously holding him to be rife with inconsistency. His Bible criticism, with its thesis being that the Pentateuch was not written by Moses but rather by Ezra, is dismissed as worthless deception by François (François 1751, 1:452–526; Marin 1762, 4:3–156; Marin 1762, 5:1–196). But Spinoza's claim that there are no truths in scripture other than moral truths proved a seductive doctrine with undeniable revolutionary reverberations that *anti-philosophes* felt compelled to counter in an explicit, systematic fashion. For it was impossible to propagate the central tenet of the "religious Enlightenment," namely that Christian (or Jewish) theology, science, and philosophy form a harmonious whole justified by reason, without showing that this rationally based harmony is only apparently and ineffectually rejected by Spinozism.

# 7 CONCLUSION

Spinoza ends the fourteenth chapter of *Tractatus Theologico Politicus* by restating why no one can demonstrate that Bible-based theology contains any truth at all, and why all men of good will must acquiesce in this whether they like it or not, urging that it is only by separating philosophy from theology and accepting that the theology proclaimed by revealed religion cannot provide universal truths that a more compelling basis for society's moral and legal order can be found and promoted. Only by marginalizing theology can the disputes over religion, doctrine, and ecclesiastical authority, which tore European society apart during the Middle Ages, Reformation, and Wars of Religion, be transcended. Spinoza invites readers to "take the trouble repeatedly to reflect [on these observations], and understand that he had not written them simply to make novel remarks, but to correct abuses, and indeed that he hoped one day to see them corrected" (Spinoza 2007, 185).

Presenting Spinoza as the supreme voice of modern incredulity, materialism, and political subversion was, from the standpoint of French, Italian, Spanish, and German *anti-philosophie*, usual and indispensable but also a distinctly risky procedure. Spinoza's leadership of the philosophical army undermining religion, morality, and the social order is in part utilized to lend continuity, coherence, unity, and a clear profile to the seditious, atheistic philosophical tradition that the *anti-philosophes* vowed to crush. Spinoza served as the unifying thread and also as a device for denying the originality of Meslier, Fréret, Du Marsais, d'Argens, Boulanger, Diderot, Helvétius, Saint-Lambert, Deleyre, Delisle, Volney, and latterly d'Holbach and Naigeon, as well as Boulainvilliers, "le commentateur de Spinosa," as Maleville calls him. Yet equally, the *anti-philosophes* insisted on Spinoza's supposed "obscurity," unoriginality and lack of cogency. This was not an easy thesis to advance or make credible to those willing to read and think.

## BIBLIOGRAPHY

Akkerman, F., and H. G. Hubbeling. 1979. "The Preface to Spinoza's Posthumous Works 1677 and its Author Jarig Jelles (c. 1619/20–1683)." *Lias* 6: 103–173.

Bayle, Pierre. 1740. *Dictionnaire historique et critique*, 5th ed. 4 vols. Amsterdam: Brunel. First published 1697 by Leers.

Bekker, Balthasar. 1685. *Kort begryp der algemeine kerkelyke historien, zedert het jaar 1666 daar Hornius eindigt, tot den jare 1684*. Amsterdam: Baltes Boekholt.

Bradley, James E. 2006. "Toleration and Movements of Christian Reunion, 1660–1789." In *Enlightenment, Reawakening and Revolution, 1660–1815. Vol. 7 of The Cambridge History of Christianity*, edited by Stewart J. Brown and Timothy Tackett, 348–370. Cambridge: Cambridge University Press.

Donagan, Alan. 1996. "Spinoza's Theology." In *The Cambridge Companion to Spinoza*, edited by Don Garrett, 343–382. Cambridge Companions to Philosophy. Cambridge: Cambridge University Press.

Fix, Andrew C. 1991. *Prophecy and Reason: The Dutch Collegiants in the Early Enlightenment*. Princeton: Princeton University Press.

François, Laurent. 1751. *Preuves de la religion de Jesus-Christ: contre les Spinosistes et les Deistes*. 3 vols. Paris: Estienne & Herissant.

Griffet, Henri. 1770. *L'insuffisance de la religion naturelle prouvée par les vérités contenues dans les livres de l'Écriture Sainte*. Vol. 1. Liège.

Hunt, Lynn, Margaret C. Jacob, and W. W. Mijnhardt. 2010a. *Bernard Picart and the First Global Vision of Religion*. Los Angeles: Getty Research Institute.

Hunt, Lynn, Margaret C. Jacob, and W. W. Mijnhardt. 2010b. *The Book That Changed Europe: Picart & Bernard's Religious Ceremonies of the World*. Cambridge: Belknap Press of the Harvard University Press.

Hunter, Graeme. 2005. *Radical Protestantism in Spinoza's Thought*. Aldershot, UK: Ashgate.

Israel, Jonathan I. 2007. *Introduction to Theological-Political Treatise*, by Benedictus de Spinoza, viii–xxxiv. Edited by Jonathan I. Israel. Cambridge: Cambridge University Press.

Israel, Jonathan I. 2001. *Radical Enlightenment: Philosophy and the Making of Modernity, 1650–1750*. Oxford: Oxford University Press.

Jebb, John. 1787. *The Works, Theological, Medical, Political, and Miscellaneous of John Jebb*. Vol. 3. London.

Jelles, Jarig. 1979. "Voorreeden." In "The Preface to Spinoza's Posthumous Works 1677 and its Author Jarig Jelles (c. 1619/20–1683)." *Lias* 6: 110–153.

Maleville, Guillaume. 1756–1758. *La Religion naturelle et la révélée etablies sur les principes de la vraie philosophie et sur la divinité des écritures ou Dissertations philosophiques, théologiques et critiques contre les incrédules*. 6 vols. Paris: Nyon.

Marin, Michel-Ange. 1762. *Le Baron Van-Hesden, ou la République des incrédules*. 4 vols. Toulouse.

Matheron, Alexandre. 2011. "Remarks on the Immortality of the Soul in Spinoza." In *Spinoza's Ethics: A Collective Commentary*, edited by Michael Hampe, Ursula Renz, and Robert Schnepf, 295–304. Brill's Studies in Intellectual History 196. Leiden: Brill.

Molinaeus, Johannes. 1692. *De betoverde werelt van D. Balthazar Bekker: handelende van den aert en 't vermogen, van 't bewind en bedrijf der goede en quade engelen, onderzogt en weder-leydt: in twee predikaetien; d' eerste van 't gebruik en misbruyk der philosophie; de tweede van den aert en 't bedrijf der goede engelen: en laetstelik in een verhandelinge van de booze geesten, of van den duyvel en zijne engelen*. Rotterdam.

Musaeus, Johann. 1674. Preface to *Tractatus Theologico-Politicus, Quo Auctor Quidam Anonymus, conatu improbo, demonstratum ivit, Libertatem Philosophandi*. Jena.

Nadler, Steven M. 2006. *Spinoza's* Ethics: *An Introduction*. Cambridge Introductions to Key Philosophical Texts. New York: Cambridge University Press.

Naigeon, André. 1765. "Unitaires." In *Encyclopédie; ou Dictionnaire raisonné des sciences, des arts et des métiers*. Vol. 17, edited by Denis Diderot and Jean Le Rond d'Alembert, 387–404. Paris.

Page, Anthony. 2003. *John Jebb and the Enlightenment Origins of British Radicalism*. Westport, CT: Praeger.

Picart, Bernard, and Jean-Frédéric Bernard. 1731–1739. *The Religious Ceremonies and Customs of the Several Nations of the Known World*. Vol. 6. London.

Priestley, Joseph. 1782. *An History of the Corruptions of Christianity*. Vol. 1. Birmingham, UK.

Priestley, Joseph. 1790. Preface to *A Philosophical Inquiry Concerning Human Liberty*, by Anthony Collins. Birmingham. First published 1717 by R. Robinson.

Spinoza, Benedictus de. 1985. *The Collected Works of Spinoza*. Edited and translated by Edwin Curley. Vol. 1. Princeton, NJ: Princeton University Press.

Spinoza, Benedictus de. 1985. *The Letters*. Translated by Samuel Shirley. Indianapolis: Hackett Publishing.

Spinoza, Benedictus de. 2007. *Theological-Political Treatise*. Edited by Jonathan Israel. Translated by Jonathan Israel and Michael Silverthorne. Cambridge Texts in the History of Philosophy. Cambridge: Cambridge University Press.

Strauss, Leo. 1981. *Die Religionskritik Spinozas als Grundlage seiner Bibelwissenschaft: Untersu-chungen zu Spinozas theologisch-politischen Traktat*. Veröffentlichungen der Akademie fur die Wissenschaft des Judentums. Philosophische Sektion 2. Darmstadt: Wissenschaftliche Buchgesellschaft. First published 1930 by Akademie Verlag.

Strauss, Leo. *Spinoza's Critique of Religion*. 1997. Translated by E. M. Sinclair. Chicago: University of Chicago Press. First published 1965 by Schocken Books.

van Bunge, Wiep. 1990. *Johannes Bredenburg (1643–1691): een Rotterdamse collegiant in de ban van Spinoza*. PhD dissertation, Erasmus Universiteits Drukkerij.

van der Wall, Ernestine G. E. 1987. *De mystieke chiliast Petrus Serrarius (1600–1669) en zijn wereld*. PhD dissertation. Rijksuniversiteit.

Vernière, Paul. 1982. *Spinoza et la pensée française avant la Révolution*. 2nd ed. 2 vols. Paris: Presses Universitaires de France.

Wielema, M. R. 2004. *The March of the Libertines: Spinozists and the Dutch Reformed Church (1660–1750)*. Hilversum: Uitgeverij Verloren.

CHAPTER 38

...............................................................................................

# THE ANTI-THEOLOGICAL THEOLOGY OF JEAN-JACQUES ROUSSEAU

...............................................................................................

## CAROLINA ARMENTEROS

## 1  A THEOLOGY FOR AN AGE OF DOUBT

...............................................................................................

IT might seem odd to claim that Jean-Jacques Rousseau was sympathetic to theology. This was, after all, the author of the *Social Contract* (1762), a work condemned for "impiety" by various Christian confessions; the pedagogue of *Emile, or On Education* (1762), the book that scandalized Europe by denying original sin and arguing that children should not hear of God before the age of fifteen; the prizewinner of the *Discourse on the Origin of Inequality* (1754), whose narrative suggested that evil sprang not from human intentions, but from accidents and social circumstances. Nor was Rousseau's reputation among theologians improved by the fact that his philosophy inspired the French revolutionaries during the de-Christianization campaigns.

Yet it would be wrong to claim that Jean-Jacques was an enemy of theology. For his antitheological sensibilities supported one of the most solid—if not *the* most solid—argumentative defenses of Christianity that the eighteenth century produced. The Savoyard vicar, the deist character of *Emile* whose *Profession of Faith* provides the most comprehensive exposition of Rousseau's theology, voiced a message exceptionally well suited to secure the faith in an age of skepticism: "If your feelings were more stable," said this compassionate clergyman to the doubting young man, "I would hesitate to expose to you my own; but, in the state in which you are, you will gain something from thinking like me" (Rousseau 1967, 3:204).

## 2 Private and Public Religion

Rousseau's desire to establish the reality of human spirituality on foundations of doubt did not result in a refusal of theology, but in an antitheological theology suspicious of the intellect. The Savoyard vicar declines to submit reason to religious authority—the aspect of his message that has been traditionally emphasized—yet he also places little store by the intellect as a path to the divine: "Do not expect from me either learned discourses or profound reasoning, I am not a great philosopher, and I have little desire to be one" (Rousseau 1967, 3:104). Rather than call on his reason, the vicar relies on his conscience, a "divine instinct, [an] immortal and celestial voice" which "insists on following the order of nature against all the laws of men" (Rousseau 1967, 3:201). Conscience is the seat of divine sentiment and the source of the two forms of self-love—*amour de soi* and *amour-propre*. *Amour de soi* manifests as natural desire, like the vicar's admiration of Jesus and wish to know the most sacred truths, while *amour-propre*, the desire to be for others, is realized—when benign—as submission to social conventions and needs. Examples of it include the vicar's continuing to say Mass with deep reverence, and performing pastoral duties with great kindness, despite having lost his traditional faith. Yet if conscience is instinctual and sentimental, it is also in harmony with reason, for if reason cannot guide the impulses of conscience, it must certainly confirm them. Conscience thus functions as a sentimentalist equivalent of natural law that contains the principles of right action.

For Rousseau, love is sacred and the deep source of religion. *Amour de soi*, the natural love of self, emanates an intimate religion of self-expansion, while *amour-propre*, the desire to be for others that manifests as love of one's community or fatherland, produces public religion. Private and public religion should harmonize. The vicar is at once a faithless and an excellent priest not only because he can respect things he does not understand, but also because he does not wish to harm other people's piety. Rousseau himself applied this reasoning when advising an agnostic young man not to perturb priests and sadden his mother by publicizing his objections. Simultaneously, though, private and public religion are diametric opposites in Rousseau's thought. The religion of the heart—natural religion—is universal, while public religion is the aleatory product of circumstance. This distinction is reminiscent of the one posited by the German neologists. The difference is that Rousseau is fundamentally uninterested in religion as a historical phenomenon, or in history as the key to unlocking sacred mysteries. His concept of public religiosity is instead political: the civil religion of the *Social Contract* is a Machiavellian attempt to cease "[separating] the theological system from the political system" (Rousseau 1967, 2:574) and to encourage devotion to the city. This was the purpose of its five positive dogmas, which prescribed belief in an afterlife; in the happiness of the just; in the punishment of the unjust; in the sacredness of the laws and the social contract; and in an intelligent, benevolent, predictive and provident Divinity. Politics also determined the civil religion's negative dogma, which consisted in being tolerant toward all cults containing "nothing contrary to the citizen's duties," since "wherever theological intolerance is admitted, it is impossible for it not to have some civil effect; and as soon as it has it . . . the true masters are the priests, and kings are only their officers" (Rousseau 1967, 2:580). The civil religion's purpose, in short, is to ensure that the temporal power is always superior to the spiritual, and that politics can determine religion but religion not politics.

The primacy of politics over religion mirrors the priority of experience over dogma in the process of spiritual growth. Whether individually or politically, religion for Rousseau must be arrived at through experience. It must not be intellectually imposed. Emile's tutor, in fact, considers that intellectual understanding is not only unnecessary but also potentially obscuring of spirituality. That is why Emile must be introduced to the idea of God only once his emotions have matured through social relations and by interacting with the physical world. If theological education is sufficiently delayed, and if its contents are simple enough, the child will be able to deduce God from his inner experience in the same way that he is able to reason out how to position a frisbee from the casting of his own shadow. God, in short, is a matter of direct experience, not of subordination to intellectual systems. And true theology has limited uses for reason.

True theology, furthermore, is mystical, not only in a personal, intimate sense, but also in a political one. The civil religion of the *Social Contract* is transcendent in that it requires citizens to deposit themselves wholly in political society, not simply through their civic actions, but also mentally and emotionally. The general will, Rousseau makes clear, is the mystic ocean where the individual will goes to die and becomes absorbed in an entity divine and greater than itself. As for political society, insofar as it is itself a being that demands the voluntary self-offering of its members, it functions as the equivalent of a mystic God. The disparity is that Rousseau's political society lends a lesser freedom to the individual than God does to the devotee, since any individual possessing a will that fails to submit to the general will must, according to the famous dictum that Rousseau borrowed from Spinoza, be "forced to be free."

## 3 MYSTICAL SENSIBILITIES

That Rousseau's political and educational theory should be suffused with mysticism is unsurprising when considering that Rousseau himself had mystical experiences, most famously the illumination on the road to Vincennes described in the *Confessions*, when he went into a trance, lost track of time, and regained consciousness to find his shirt drenched with tears of ecstasy he had shed unconsciously. This is a classic example of a mystical event, in which extreme bliss is experienced simultaneously with the loss of perception of time and of subject-object distinctions. Rousseau seems to have had another experience of this kind, when he was run over by a dog at Ménilmontant and came to in a "delicious moment" when he was "born . . . to life" and had the sensation of filling "all the objects [he] perceived" with his "light existence" (Rousseau 1967, 1:507).

Incidents of this kind had life-directing consequences for him: in his last years, attaining higher states of consciousness became a priority for him. He spent as much time as he could in nature—most famously on the botanical walks recounted in the *Reveries of the Solitary Walker* (1776–78), during which he expanded himself boundlessly to fuse with Creation. These were years too when he made efforts to shut down his mind, selling all his books and giving up reading. Thus his antitheological theology must be seen as the anti-intellectualist product of his mystic abilities and rich inner life, and not simply as a philosophical rejection of dogmas like original sin. His strong sense of reason's insufficiency when confronting the realm of the beyond is probably best and most memorably conveyed by the vicar's famous comparison of the deaths of Jesus and Socrates: "Socrates taking the poisoned cup blesses the one who presents it to him and who cries; Jesus, in the midst of the most awful torment, prays for his furious tormentors. Yes, if the life and death of Socrates are those of a sage, the life and death of Jesus are those of a God" (Rousseau 1967, 3:213).

Rousseau's suspicion of reason also inspired his attacks on *philosophie*. Like the young Rousseau, the Savoyard vicar objected that philosophy could only "multiply . . . doubts" without providing consolation or happiness, that it doomed people to "float on the sea of human opinions, without a rudder, without a compass" (Rousseau 1967, 3:184). Life had never been "more constantly disagreeable," the vicar remembered, than during the time he spent in "disquiet and anxiety" after losing his faith (Rousseau 1967, 3:185). Only the "inner light"—the divine instinct and "love of truth" that constitutes conscience—was able to reverse this state of mind. Conscience revealed to him that every opinion contains a portion of truth, that God's existence is the most common and probable of all opinions, and that he himself existed as an active and intelligent being. Reason could not embrace the All. "I have read Nieuwentyt with surprise," wrote Rousseau, "and almost with scandal. How can that man have wanted to write a book on the marvels of nature, which show the wisdom of its author? Even if his book were as large as the world, it would not have exhausted its subject" (Rousseau 1967, 3:192). Creation, for Rousseau, can never be contained entirely within the mind, but only experienced within the soul as the "sentiment of existence" (Gauthier 2006). The cultivation of this sentiment seems to have provided Rousseau with the happiest moments of his life—moments when he extended himself ecstatically to find his true, eternal self in the midst of fleeting nature.

Self-extension, in turn, formed the core of Rousseau's ethics. "I love myself too much," he mused in the ninth *Reverie*, "to hate anybody. It would be to restrain, to compress my existence, and I would like rather to extend it over the whole universe" (Rousseau 1967, 1:527). Morally, self-expansion through love resulted in a deontology that emphasized the quality of intentions and was largely unconcerned with outcomes. As such, it complemented Rousseau's account of evil as the product of accident and circumstance. This does not mean, however, that in the political realm Jean-Jacques was oblivious to consequences: as a thinker in the Machiavellian tradition, he was committed to replacing, in his ideal city, Christian deontology with a results-oriented political morality. Thus the *Social Contract*'s civil religion may ask for willing self-offerings, but it is ultimately an obligatory institution whose dogmas can be violated only on pain of exile or death. This must be so because otherwise political life might not be secured. If compulsion were absent, if everybody adhered to the mysticism of self-expansion and the deontology of pure intentions, politics as the realm of power's exercise would be diminished or cease to exist, since everyone would meld with Creation and be emotionally self-sufficient. Importantly, too, while mandatory, public religion is also practical, in the sense that it must tolerate all religions that do not contravene its dogmas. In this it resembles the vicar's private religion, whose universality renders it compatible with whatever cult predominates.

## 4 A Controversial Reception

Rousseau's attempt to reconcile private and public religion caused much controversy in French-speaking Europe. *Emile* was condemned by the Sorbonne, by the archbishop of Paris, by the Assembly of the French Clergy, and by the Genevan City Council. It inspired the famous apologist Nicolas-Sylvestre Bergier (1718–90) to compose one of his most popular and pugnacious works, *Deism Refuted by Itself* (1765), which maintained that the Gospels had to be read holistically, not selecting from them the elements one wished to reconcile with one's idea of reason, as Rousseau did, but accepting also miracles, authority, and dogma. Rousseau was inconsistent in Bergier's view, for if religious experience could not be understood entirely through reason, then what grounds could one have for refusing dogma on the basis of reason? Joseph de Maistre (1753–1821) leveled similar charges. Rousseau, he complained, objected to revelation because it was an exception and as such unconformable to reason, and because human language lacked the clarity needed to convey divine things. Yet Rousseau sought out the very exceptions he condemned, asking God to speak to him directly and thus dispense him from the task of interpretation—a demand that Maistre thought both arrogant and self-contradictory (Maistre 1996, *Religion E* 395).

## 5 Discreet and Enthusiastic Posterities

Simultaneously, however, Maistre founded his entire system of thought on Rousseau, and more specifically on a refutation of his thought that borrowed many theological elements from it—most importantly, the idea that human communities are bound by the sacred, and that religion is indispensable to the integration of society (Maistre, *On the State of Nature* and *On the Sovereignty of the People* [both composed ca. 1794–96]). A similarly formative ambivalence to the Genevan underlay the work of Maistre's fellow counterrevolutionary Louis de Bonald. Holding that the individual cannot be anterior to society as the *Social Contract* and the *Discourse on the Origins of Inequality* suggest, the viscount developed an early form of sociology—or, as W. Jay Reedy has called it, sociolatry—that posited social relations as sacred, nontranscendable and absolutely determining of the individual (*Primitive Legislation* [1802]). Rousseau's anti-Voltairean idea of a society integrated and animated by religion thus helped to found sociology by influencing the Catholic conservatives who criticized him while borrowing from his thought.

In fact, and contrary to common opinion, Rousseau's most faithful preservers in the late eighteenth century were not the revolutionaries who celebrated his ideas—and who seem, in reality, to have known little about his work. Those who really knew and continued Rousseau's philosophy were aristocratic counterrevolutionaries (McDonald 2013). This fact has long been masked by the duty that Christian thinkers generally felt to criticize Rousseau for attacking religion. For example, Madame de Genlis (1746–1830) commented that she would feel "very afraid" if she caught her servants reading *Julie* or the second *Discourse*, an observation suggesting that she would never read them herself. But the reality is that she drew extensively on Rousseau when devising her own pedagogy, especially in her masterwork, *Adele and Theodore, or Letters on Education* (1782). Similarly, although the popular Catholic writer Madame Leprince de Beaumont (1711–80) did not advertise her debt to Jean-Jacques, her children's catechism in *The Americans, or The Proofs of the Christian Religion by Natural Lights* (1771) was taken directly from the fifth book of *Emile*, and differed from it only in being more laden with theology.

Overall, Christian apologists made "immense" use of Rousseau to defend the faith (McMahon 2002, 35). The abbé Gérard (1737–1813) filled the five volumes of apologetics that comprised *The Count of Valmont, or The Bewilderment of Reason* (1774–76) with quotes from Rousseau, the "involuntary apologist." His fellow cleric Dom Louis (dates unknown) was more enthusiastic: in *The Heavens Open to the Whole Universe* (1782), he exposed a naturalistic religion akin to the Savoyard vicar's, denouncing "fables" and denying hell (Masson 1970, 181). Jean-Jacques' legacy was evident too in the fact that historical proofs of revelation began to fall by the wayside (201), and that many of his clerical followers ceased mentioning the teaching or militant Church to speak only of the benevolent one (208). But the most important sign of Rousseau's influence was probably the anti-intellectualist and ethical-pragmatic turn taken by late eighteenth-century French clerics who emphasized cultivating a good heart over deploying reason. Such was the case of the abbé de Beauvais (dates unknown) in his *Sermon on the Immortality of the Soul* (n.d.), of the abbé Bellet (dates unknown) in *The Rights that the Christian and Catholic Religion Exercises over Man's Heart* (1764), and of the abbé Lamourette (1742–94) in *The Delights of Religion* (1788). Rousseau further inspired the spirituality of deeply felt giving that flourished among Catholic clergy on the eve of the French Revolution and that included Bergier (Manuel 1983, 23), while in Germany his influence was felt, distantly but palpably, in Schleiermacher's "religion of feeling."

As the Savoyard vicar's intimate religion thrived in the Catholic world among clergy and laymen alike, the *Social Contract's* civil religion inspired revolutionary cults. In the footsteps of Rousseau, these new sects thought religion indispensable to political integration and stability, and argued that religion should constitute the Republic in ways that were rationally comprehensible. The new faiths varied greatly in content. They ranged from the Cult of Reason, which was anathema to Rousseau's religious anti-intellectualism, to Theophilanthropy, which was deeply Rousseauian not only in preaching that civic duty is religious duty, but in adopting Jean-Jacques' religious practicality to the extent of elevating civic actions to the highest—indeed the only—form of prayer (Mathiez [1913] 1975, 62).

After the Revolution, though, civil cults waned, while the vicar's vision prospered, suffusing Chateaubriand's (1768–1848) *Genius of Christianity* (1802). The kind cleric's voice could be heard in the book's religious sentiment, in its reverence for nature, in its celebration of the beauty of belief rather than its truth, and in its portrayal of Christianity as a practical religion—rather than as the historical and factual one of late eighteenth-century apologetics. Chateaubriand's romantic, solitary souls steeped in pain and privileged by inspiration also represent the spiritual-mystical pole of Rousseau's religious thought, not the sociopolitical one of the civil religion. Indeed, as the nineteenth century commenced and Napoleon's concordat with the papacy drew near, Rousseau the decrier of Christianity and the crafter of the civil religion fell nominally into oblivion even as Romanticism absorbed—and dissolved—the Savoyard vicar's *Profession of Faith*.

## BIBLIOGRAPHY

Everdell, William. 1989. *Christian Apologetics in France, 1730–1790: The Roots of Romantic Religion*. New York: Edwin Mellen Press.

Gauthier, David. 2006. *Rousseau: The Sentiment of Existence*. Cambridge: Cambridge University Press.

Maistre, Joseph de. 1996. CD-ROM du Fonds de Maistre. *Archives de Joseph de Maistre et de sa famille*. Archives départementales de la Savoie.

Manuel, Frank. 1983. *The Changing of the Gods*. Hanover, NH: University Press of New England.

Masson, Pierre-Maurice. 1970. *La religion de Jean-Jacques Rousseau*. Geneva: Slatkine.

Mathiez, Albert. (1913) 1975. *La théophilanthropie et le culte décadaire. Essai sur l'histoire religieuse de la Révolution*. Geneva: Slatkine.

McDonald, Joan. 2013. *Rousseau and the French Revolution, 1762–1791*. London: Bloomsbury.

McMahon, Darrin. 2002. *Enemies of the Enlightenment: The French Counter-Enlightenment and the Making of Modernity*. Oxford: Oxford University Press.

Rousseau, Jean-Jacques. 1967. *Œuvres complètes [de] Rousseau*. Edited by Michel Launay. Paris: Seuil.

# CHAPTER 39

# KANT'S PHILOSOPHICAL AND THEOLOGICAL COMMITMENTS

## PETER YONG AND ERIC WATKINS

IMMANUEL Kant (1724–1804) was a major Enlightenment philosopher, whose three great *Critiques* (Kant 1902–) were published in 1781, 1788, and 1790, immediately revolutionizing theoretical and practical philosophy, and exercising a tremendous influence on the broader intellectual world, including Christian theology. Part of Kant's influence in religious matters was critical (in line with some significant strands of Enlightenment thought in eighteenth-century Germany), since he offered powerful objections to three theistic proofs that had been staples of traditional Christian apologetics. However, he also offered both a theoretical argument in support of belief in God's existence, based on the possibility of things; and a practical argument, based on moral considerations. Further, late in his career, he went on to provide influential accounts of several doctrines central to orthodox Christianity, such as the creation of humanity in the image of God, original sin, and grace, which were at least consistent with, if not derivative of, his core philosophical commitments. As a result, Kant's engagement with the theology of his day is more constructive than is often realized.

## 1 KANT ON THEISTIC PROOFS

In his *Critique of Pure Reason*, Kant embarks on an ambitious philosophical project that proposes to discredit the arguments and positions of his rationalist and empiricist predecessors alike as dogmatic, and to establish a positive epistemology that would provide the metaphysical underpinning for Newtonian science. Specifically, Kant attempts to show that traditional arguments for the existence of human freedom, the immortality of the soul, and God's existence are fallacious, and that our cognitive capacities are limited in ways that prevent us from having cognition of ultimate reality, including these objects of traditional metaphysics, even if our faculties do suffice to give us knowledge of the natural world. Of special interest in this context are Kant's objections to the three traditional theistic proofs: the cosmological argument, the argument from design, and the ontological argument.

Kant's strategy for dealing with these three theistic arguments is complex; he articulates independent objections to the first two while also arguing that they ultimately depend on the ontological argument, which is subject to a fatal flaw that undermines all three theistic proofs in one fell swoop. Kant's main objection to the cosmological argument—which assumes the existence of something contingent and infers that its ultimate cause must be God as an absolutely necessary being—is that, to infer from a contingent to a necessary existence, one must assume a causal principle that is justified only for the empirical world and that therefore cannot be used to infer a necessary being distinct from nature. However, Kant suggests that even if this inference were allowed, one would still need to appeal to the ontological argument to move from the existence of a necessary being to that necessary being existing as an *ens realissimum* (i.e., as God), a move that only the ontological argument attempts to make good on.

The argument from design, which Kant calls the "physico-theological" proof, starts with our experience of order, purposiveness, and beauty in nature and infers that God must be the cause of these specific contingent features. As with the cosmological argument, Kant contends that, even if successful, the argument from design would not be sufficient to prove the existence of God. Rather, Kant objects that such an argument could establish, at most, a highest *architect* of the world, responsible for the particular *forms* of things found in it, but not a *creator* of the world that would be responsible for its *matter*. Insofar as we are inferring a cause that we do not experience, its features ought to be proportionate to what we do experience, but a proper concept of God is too far above everything empirical for us to be able to form a determinate concept of God on the basis of what we infer from experience.

A further difficulty with both of these arguments is their failure to provide apodictic certainty. Since they begin from contingent empirical facts such as the existence and purposiveness of the universe, they can, at best, provide us with only probabilities and a form of intellectual comfort. They thus cannot lay claim to apodictic certainty that would compel our assent. To satisfy reason's demand for such certainty, Kant claims that the ontological argument is required.

The ontological argument takes different forms with different thinkers, but as Kant understands it, its most basic move is to infer that God's existence follows analytically from our concept of God, since our concept of God is that of an *ens realissimum*, or most real being, and if existence is a reality, then God must have the reality of existence. Kant raises multiple objections to this argument: (i) it slides from an analytic truth about our concepts to a synthetic truth about actual existence, and (ii) it proceeds by simply defining something into existence. However, his most famous objection is that it wrongly assumes that existence is what he calls a "real predicate." That is, the argument assumes that existence is a reality just like other realities, such as the redness of an apple or the roundness of a circle. But, according to Kant's analysis, existence does not function like other real predicates. As he points out, the concept of 100 existing thalers (dollars, Euros, pounds, etc.) does not contain anything more than that of 100 possible thalers. In both cases, we have the very same concept (i.e., 100 thalers). Yet the significant difference between them is that the first one refers to an actual object, whereas the second one does not. As a result, existence is not a real predicate, thus rendering false a central assumption of the ontological argument (though Plantinga [1966] responds to Kant's criticism). Given the dependence of the other two proofs on the ontological argument, all three theistic proofs must be rejected (Sala 1990).

Interestingly, however, Kant does not rest content with attacking the traditional theistic proofs. In his early *The Only Possible Argument in Support of a Demonstration of the Existence of God*, published in 1763, Kant not only presents many of the criticisms of the traditional theistic proofs just described, but also outlines a fourth theistic proof, which he accepts. The basic thought is that possibilities are not brute facts but require a sufficient reason just as much as actualities do, and, it turns out, only God can serve as the ground of all possibility. It is true that Kant modifies the status of the conclusion to this argument in the *Critique of Pure Reason*, such that it is a regulative principle rather than an objective cognition, but he is firmly committed to thinking of it as a requirement of reason. Moreover, in the *Critique of Practical Reason*, Kant supplements this argument with one based on moral considerations. The main line of argument here is that for us to act in accordance with the moral law, we have to presuppose that the highest good, which consists in our happiness being proportionate to our virtue, is possible; but the highest good would not be possible unless God were in a position to proportion our happiness to our virtue. As a result, we must believe that God exists (Adams 1995). In fact, Kant goes on to develop a similar argument to establish the immortality of the soul, thus establishing two doctrines important to Christianity (Winter 2000).

# 2 KANT'S POSITIVE (CHRISTIAN) THEOLOGY

Kant's interest in religion is not limited to the standard onto-theological questions of metaphysics and epistemology—questions concerning the existence and attributes of God and the justificatory status of religious belief—but also extends into the domain of constructive theology. On a traditional reading of Kant's project, one would expect him either to explicitly condemn classical doctrines outright or at least to tactfully ignore them, since they might seem to go beyond what reason can establish a priori. However, Kant was in fact concerned to provide a philosophically rigorous interpretation of certain elements of Christian theology. Here we set forth the main features of Kant's account of some of the core doctrines of a traditional Christian faith, viz. the creation of humanity in the image of God, the fall into original sin, and atonement. (For further discussion of how Kant's account relates to contemporary Christian theological ethics, see Hare [1996].)

The creation of humanity in the image of God plays a twofold role in Christian theology: the image of God sets humanity apart from the rest of creation, and it is identified with the divine logos in whom humanity was created (see, e.g., Col 1:15–17). Kant strives to maintain both aspects of this doctrine in his own philosophical theology. On the one hand, Kant claims that, as a moral being, human beings were created as "the genuine end of nature." Because of humanity's moral calling, human nature stands apart from the rest of creation. Whereas one can in general appropriately treat natural objects as mere means to an end, rational agents must be respected as ends in themselves (Kant 2007, 167). So, for example, while it might be morally permissible to take a rock and use it merely to promote one's purposes (e.g., by decorating one's lawn with it), it would be morally impermissible to use a person in such a manner. On the other hand, Kant maintains that this purpose for creation—rational being in its full moral perfection—must have existed in God from all eternity and he identifies it with God's Word "through which all other things are." (Kant 1996, 103). It is thus in Christ, the eternal Word of God as the idea of humanity in its moral perfection, that God creates the world. Kant thus seeks to affirm both aspects of the traditional doctrine of the *imago dei*.

Kant also seeks to retain and clarify other central elements of Christianity, such as the Fall and redemption. According to Kant, humanity's fall into sin can be understood in light of the fact that every empirical decision is conditioned by a "prior" purely intelligible choice regarding what maxim, or fundamental principle for action, to adopt. This fundamental choice of one's moral character consists in the degree to which one would be willing to subordinate happiness to the demands of the moral law. Kant claims that all human beings have to some extent subordinated the demands of the moral law to considerations of happiness. Accordingly, there will always be some situation where one would be willing to transgress the moral law to receive some particular benefit. In this respect, Kant can account for the Pauline claim that "there is no distinction here . . . all under sin—there is none righteous (in the spirit of the law), no, not one" (Kant 1996, 85). Kant labels this universal failing "radical evil." Such evil is radical since it involves a universal human propensity to adopt a corrupt maxim (Kant 1996, 83). Kant thus maintains that humans have fallen (since they are willing to subordinate the moral law to happiness in at least some circumstances) and live in a state of original sin. Specifically, Kant distinguishes between three ways in which humanity is beset by evil: frailty (in sometimes failing to act according to the good elements of the maxims one has adopted), impurity (in sometimes needing other incentives besides the moral law to motivate one's actions), and depravity (in adopting maxims that subordinate the moral law to nonmoral concerns on some occasions). (See Kant 1996, 77–78. For a fuller discussion of Kant's interpretation of radical evil, see Wood [1970].)

Kant also maintains the traditional view that God has not abandoned humanity in its state of sin and misery, but reaches out in grace to redeem it. To begin, Kant notes that from a practical perspective, it is necessary to believe that one can change one's fundamental moral maxim and become pleasing to God. Yet a change could not come about by a gradual reform of one's empirical character (since one's empirical character is based on one's antecedent choice of a fundamental maxim and not vice versa), but instead must "be effected through a revolution in the disposition of the human being (a transition to the maxim of holiness of disposition)." One must hope that it is possible to attain a new moral character, one which unconditionally subordinates happiness to the moral law, and in this sense, hope to be "born again" (Kant 1996, 92). But because such a change would have to occur at the level of one's fundamental moral character, it cannot be seen empirically. In the empirical world one would see progress from bad to better behavior, but that is consistent with no change at all at the level of one's fundamental choice of maxim (Kant 1996, 92; Lehner 2007).

Kant claims that to hope for the possibility of transformation is to hope for the incarnation of the Son of God. Since "the idea has . . . established itself in the human being without our comprehending how human nature could have even been receptive of it," we should say that "the prototype has come down to us from heaven, that it has taken up our humanity." This is "the abasement of the Son of God," who takes up all of the sufferings of human life in order to promote "the world's greatest good" (Kant 1996, 104). We have to trust in this incarnation to believe that we have adopted an upright moral disposition and thus have become "an object of divine pleasure" (105). Though our empirical actions can reveal no more than a limited progress from bad to better behavior, we must nonetheless believe that such progress evinces our adoption of a new moral maxim and trust that God in grace imputes to us the righteousness of our new holy character, rather than continuing to hold us guilty for our prior choice to adopt a maxim that subordinates the moral law to happiness on at least some occasions (116).

Kant admits that divine justice with respect to our previous moral person would still need to be satisfied, but he claims that this satisfaction occurs through the act of conversion itself (Kant 1996, 113). "In his new disposition . . . in the sight of a divine judge for whom the disposition takes place of the deed, he is morally another being. And this disposition which he has incorporated in all its purity . . . —this very Son of God—bears as vicarious substitute the debt of sin for him, and also for all who believe" (115). Thus, in conversion the old, morally vicious person no longer exists and a new, morally virtuous person takes his or her place. Furthermore, the trials of life that manifest the new virtuous character, can be seen as punishments of the old moral character. Given the supposition of radical evil and the subsequent need to change our fundamental moral character, it follows from Kant's ethical principles that it is practically necessary to believe in divine grace and redemption. He calls this practical faith in the Son of God.

By adopting these elements of a traditional Christian narrative of creation, fall, and redemption, Kant also confronts some of the tensions that come with that theological tradition. In particular, Kant's position has frequently been charged by theologians (such as Karl Barth) and philosophers of religion (such as Nicholas Wolterstorff) with failing to reconcile his account of grace with his account of moral responsibility. (For a good summary of the various iterations of this charge, see Mariña [1997].) The intuition is that if I am to change *my* moral character, it must be *me* (and not someone else) who brings about this change. I must choose to adopt a new maxim. But this implies that it is something I am responsible for. God could not make this change for me. And if this is the case, then my change of heart must be something I can achieve on my own. Yet this appears to contradict the concept of grace, which claims that salvation is not something one can achieve on one's own.

Interpreters offer various solutions to the problem, which mirror the solutions offered frequently within the broader theological tradition. For example, Andrew Chignell (2013) argues that Kant can claim that our ignorance of the laws of noumenal causation make it possible, for all we know, that God can work a moral miracle so as to change a person's moral character without violating that person's free will. Alternately, Jacqueline Mariña (1997) suggests that, for Kant, the change of one's moral disposition is not a condition for *earning* grace, but rather for *receiving* God's grace, which is freely given to all. These solutions resemble those offered by the wider theological tradition, which stresses either the overwhelming mystery of grace or the need to cooperate with it. Thus even the apparent difficulties of Kant's position show the extent to which he operates within a traditional theological framework.

In light of his powerful criticisms of traditional theistic apologetics and his constructive appropriation of Christian doctrine, Kant's account of religion can be seen as having a twofold relevance for theology. On the one hand, it is difficult to overstate the historical importance of Kant's philosophy for the development of liberal Protestantism; and negatively, for the formation of nineteenth-century Catholic theology (Fischer 2005). For instance, the theological programs of Hegel and Schleiermacher would have been unthinkable apart from the critical revolution that Kant initiated. On the other hand, Kant's own constructive project serves as an example of what it might mean to appropriate and explain traditional Christian theology in one's own intellectual context.

## BIBLIOGRAPHY

Adams, Robert Merrihew. 1995. "Moral Faith." *Journal of Philosophy* 92: 75–95.

Barth, Karl. 2002. *Protestant Theology in the Nineteenth Century: Its Background and History*. Grand Rapids: Eerdmans.

Chignell, Andrew. 2013. "Rational Hope, Moral Order, and the Revolution of the Will." In *The Divine Order, the Human Order, and the Order of Nature: Historical Perspectives*, edited by E. Watkins, 197–218. New York: Oxford University Press.

Fischer, Norbert, ed. 2005. *Kant und der Katholizismus: Stationen einer wechselhaften Geschichte*. Freiburg im Breisgau: Herder.

Hare, John. 1996. *The Moral Gap: Kantian Ethics, Human Limits, and God's Assistance*. New York: Oxford University Press.

Kant, Immanuel. 2007. "Conjectural Beginning of Human History." In *The Cambridge Edition of the Works of Immanuel Kant: Anthropology, History, and Education*, translated by Allen Wood, edited by G. Zöller and R. Louden, 160–175. New York: Cambridge University Press.

Kant, Immanuel. 1902–. *Gesammelte Schriften*. 29 vols. Berlin: De Gruyter.

Kant, Immanuel. 1996. "Religion within the Boundaries of Mere Reason." In *The Cambridge Edition of the Works of Immanuel Kant: Religion and Rational Theology*, translated by G. Giovanni, edited by A. Wood and G. Giovanni, 39–215. New York: Cambridge University Press.

Lehner, Ulrich L. 2007. *Kants Vorsehungskonzept auf dem Hintergrund der deutschen Schulphilsophie und -theologie.* Leiden and Boston: Brill.

Mariña, Jacqueline. 1997. "Kant on Grace: A Reply to His Critics." *Religious Studies* 33: 379–400.

Plantinga, Alvin. 1966. "Kant's Objection to the Ontological Argument." *Journal of Philosophy* 63: 537–546.

Sala, Giovanni. 1990. *Kant und die Frage nach Gott: Gottesbeweise und Gottesbeweiskritik in den Schriften Kants.* Berlin: de Gruyter.

Wolterstorff, Nicholas. 2009. "Conundrums in Kant's Rational Religion." In *Inquiring about God: Selected Essays, Vol. 1,* edited by T. Cueno, 56–67. New York: Cambridge University Press.

Winter, Aloysius. 2000. *Der andere Kant: zur philosophischen Theologie Immanuel Kants.* Hildesheim: Olms.

Wood, Allen. 1970. *Kant's Moral Religion.* Ithaca: Cornell University Press.

CHAPTER 40

....................................................................................................

# EARLY MODERN THEOLOGY AND SCIENCE

....................................................................................................

JOHN HENRY

## 1 Introduction

....................................................................................................

DURING the Middle Ages, natural philosophy—the philosophical study of the natural world and the closest analogue to what we now call science—came to be regarded as the dutiful handmaiden to the "Queen of the Sciences," theology (Lindberg 2013; Grant 1996). This arrangement worked well when effectively there was only one form of religion, Roman Catholicism, and only one form of natural philosophy, scholastic Aristotelianism. It is not entirely coincidental that the fragmentation of religious authority after the Reformation was accompanied by a proliferation of new natural philosophies. Certainly, Thomas Hobbes (1588–1679) was not the only thinker to believe that "Aristotelity" was "a handmaid to the Romane Religion" (Hobbes 1651, 370). Accordingly, it was necessary for any good Protestant to embrace a different philosophy. For example, the new breed of alchemists who followed the reforming Swiss iatrochemist, Paracelsus (1493–1541) (who was disparaged by some of his contemporaries as the Luther of medicine), were quick to embrace a chemical philosophy. As the English medical reformer Noah Biggs (fl. 1651) wrote, the new chemical philosophy is "the handmaid of Nature, that hath outstript the other Sects of Philosophy" (Biggs 1651; Mendelsohn, 1992). Examples like these make it clear that religious concerns should be acknowledged as a significant factor in the proliferation of new natural philosophies, which was a prominent aspect of the period known to historians as the Scientific Revolution. It can be seen, therefore, that the medieval "handmaiden" tradition was *not* abandoned after the Reformation, and did *not* give way to a separation of science from religion. On the contrary, the handmaiden tradition continued to flourish: church leaders of every stamp continued to regard natural philosophy as an important support for their particular confession of Christianity; while natural philosophers continued to present their new versions of natural philosophy as offering better support to religion than Aristotelianism ever did (or better than any other rival new philosophy could offer).

Due to the previous dominance of Aristotelianism, and its continuing hold over secular thought (e.g., in the curricula of university arts faculties), it was inevitable that proponents of the new philosophies should be forced into apologetic accounts of how their philosophies supported their faith. Leading figures in the promotion of new philosophies, therefore, took it upon themselves to devise and explain the theological implications of their approach to the natural world. The result was "a secular theology," developed by laymen, and oriented toward the world, God's creation, rather than to revelation. "Never before or after were science, philosophy, and theology seen as almost one and the same occupation" (Funkenstein 1986, 3).

# 2 SECULAR THEOLOGIES

The beginnings of such apologetic and secular theologies can be seen in various Renaissance attempts to displace Aristotelianism by some other recently recovered ancient system of philosophy. Justus Lipsius (1547–1606) spoke out for Stoicism, seeing it as a useful adjunct to Christianity at a time when Europe was riven with religious wars. Following the revival of Platonism by Marsilio Ficino (1433–99), there were repeated attempts to promote a Platonic theology, until in 1592 Francesco Patrizi (1529–97) was finally condemned by the Inquisition, on the grounds that his Platonism was so similar to Christianity that it was more likely to be seen as an alternative to, rather than a support for, Christianity (as, indeed, Augustine had suggested centuries before in his *Confessions* 7:20) (Firpo 1950–51). Other natural philosophers even sought to rehabilitate Epicurean atomism, defending Epicurus against charges of hedonism and atheism. This culminated in the work of Pierre Gassendi (1592–1655) (Osler 1985), but had found earlier representatives in Desiderius Erasmus (1466–1536), Michel de Montaigne (1533–92), and Francis Bacon (1561–1626) (Hadzits 1935).

These thinkers, and others, were simply trying to show that their favored philosophies would make perfectly acceptable handmaidens to theology, but a remarkable group of thinkers in the seventeenth century engaged much more significantly with theology. Arguably the most important of these was René Descartes (1596–1650), a major figure in the Scientific Revolution and one of the most influential thinkers on modern thought. He developed what was to become known as the mechanical philosophy, which constituted a completely new way of comprehending the natural world. Descartes knew that his new system of philosophy could not work without the involvement of God, and he took pains to build his system around a new purpose-built secular theology.

Descartes believed that he could explain all physical phenomena in terms of the contact actions, collisions, friction, and so forth, between invisibly small particles which were held to constitute all things (his system owed a lot to ancient atomism). The austerity of this system encouraged him to think that he could stipulate a small number of "laws of nature" which codified exactly what would happen when bodies collided. After centuries in which a "law of nature" was any regularity in nature (e.g., cows produce milk, sparks fly upwards), Descartes now reduced the laws of nature to three propositions that stipulated how bodies move, and supplemented these with seven rules stipulating what happened when bodies of different relative sizes and motions collided with one another. Finally, Descartes realized that these laws and rules were only valid on the assumption that the total amount of motion in the universe was constant, and therefore could not be lost as time went on, but only transferred from one body or set of bodies to another. Immediately, Descartes referred the constancy of the amount of motion in the universe to the immutability of God—at Creation, God set the universe moving by endowing it with a given amount of motion. Furthermore, Descartes also realized that it made no sense to consider inanimate bodies to be capable of "obeying" laws, and therefore God must be underwriting the laws, upholding them by his involvement (Henry 2004). As Robert Boyle (1627–91), the leading mechanical philosopher in England explained, "it is plain that nothing but an intellectual being can be properly capable of receiving and acting by law," because "a body devoid of understanding and sense" cannot conform "to laws that it has no knowledge or apprehension of" (Boyle [1686] 1996, 24–25).

For the most part, Descartes seems to suggest that God's involvement is, as it were, indirect. God chooses to uphold the laws as though they are principles of secondary causation (subordinate to himself as the primary cause), and so the world system, once it has been set in motion, is capable of circling on without any direct intervention from God. Here and there, however, there are what might be construed as hints towards a more direct involvement by God, and whether or not Descartes was ever committed to this view (Garber 1993), a number of his followers, most notably Nicholas Malebranche (1638–1715), developed this into a full-blown occasionalist theology (Nadler 2000). In this view, matter is completely passive and inert and therefore incapable of acting in any way, much less in accordance with a law of nature. The activity which we see going on all around us leads us to the conclusion, therefore, that God must be directly intervening to bring these things about. God is the only efficient cause at work in the world.

Descartes's system of physics, even if we assume the nonoccasionalist interpretation, was ultimately dependent on God. Accordingly, Descartes even felt the need to offer, as security, a proof of the existence of God—his famous ontological argument—which he incorporated into his preliminary announcement of his new system of physics, *The Discourse on the Method* of 1637, and defended in his *Meditations on First Philosophy* of 1641, which was intended to demonstrate the sound theological foundations of his new physics to the theologians of the Sorbonne (to whom it was dedicated).

Moreover, it was in these same two works that he also insisted that his new physics demonstrated the truth of the soul-body dualism which had recently become an official doctrine of Roman Catholicism. Although Descartes's argument about the necessarily immaterial nature of the immortal soul—which allowed him to define two categorically distinct substances: extended things, or bodies, and thinking things, which are incorporeal—has been described as "one of the most notorious non sequiturs in the history of philosophy" (Cottingham 1992, 242), and was vigorously criticized by many of Descartes's philosophical contemporaries, Descartes himself never gave up on it, but continued to defend its validity to his dying day. There can be no doubt, therefore, that he saw this as a crucially important theological concomitant of his new physics. Descartes was explicit in claiming that he had hereby fulfilled the instruction of the Fifth Lateran Council (1512–17) that philosophers should help the Church by bending their efforts to demonstrate the natural immortality of the soul.

Presumably because soul-body dualism was a new Catholic dogma, it attracted the attention of other new philosophers. The English Roman Catholic, Sir Kenelm Digby (1603–65) published *Two Treatises* in 1644. The first, *On Body*, was derived from Descartes's system and Epicurean atomism, and purported to show the full extent of what could be explained by the interactions of bodies. The second treatise, *The Nature of Mans Soule*, purported to deal with all remaining phenomena—that is to say, those phenomena which could not be explained in materialistic terms. The existence of such phenomena showed that immaterial souls must be at work. Moreover, because mortality was defined in somatic terms as the dissolution and dispersal of the parts of the body, the soul must be immortal. The immaterial soul could not be broken down into its constituent parts, as a body could, and so must be indissoluble and immortal (Henry 1982).

But this in turn divided Catholics and Protestants. The Anglican natural philosopher Robert Boyle, seeking to distance his own version of the mechanical philosophy from any links to Catholic dogma, took exception to the claim that the immortality of the soul must be *natural*—that is, simply an aspect of its nature. Disregarding Digby's definition of mortality in terms of dissolution into constituent parts, Boyle imagined souls which could simply fade away after separation from the body, but which God has chosen to maintain perpetually by an act of his will (Boyle [1674] 2000, 8:23–24). It is perhaps a sign of the nonexpert nature of such theological discussions by seventeenth-century thinkers that the Anglican physician and natural philosopher Walter Charleton (1619–1707) published in 1657 *The Immortality of the Human Soul, Demonstrated by the Light of Nature*. As the title suggests, Charleton argues here that the soul is immortal according to its intrinsic nature, seemingly unaware that the soul's *natural* immortality is a Catholic position. Presumably, Charleton's primary concern here was to combat contemporary atheism, and he either chose to disregard the confessional niceties, or was simply carried away by his own enthusiasm (believing that he could prove the existence of the soul by naturalistic arguments, he could not forbear from doing so).

By the middle of the seventeenth century, the concept of matter, or body, was inseparable from the secular theological concerns of natural philosophers. Because Descartes's law-driven system only required God's intervention at Creation, it was easy for contemporary atheists to simply omit God altogether. One way to fight this, for devout contemporaries, was to use natural philosophy to show that matter was not, as Descartes had said, completely passive and inert, but was endowed with principles of activity. The assumption here was that the Cartesian starting position was correct—matter was by its own nature inert and lifeless—and therefore, if bodies could be shown to display principles of activity, the source of that activity needed to be explained. For the religiously obsessed alchemist Isaac Newton (1642–1727), the chemical interactions of the materials he used in his alchemy were proof of the existence of what he called "active principles" in bodies. Later in his career, he added gravitational attraction, as a universal active principle in all bodies. While Newton believed that Descartes's philosophy offered "a path to Atheism" (Newton 1962, 143), his own philosophy relied upon the existence of God—because how else could active principles be endowed upon naturally inert matter?

Unfortunately for Newton and other devout thinkers, atheism was capable of bending any scientific position to suit its own purposes. Through the eighteenth century, for example, various discoveries which seemed to point to the existence of vitalistic principles in living organisms, and which therefore could be (and were) used to reject the claims of atheistic mechanical philosophers that living things were (as Descartes had said) mere automata, also failed to stop the atheists. It was an easy matter for atheists to use these discoveries (such as Albrecht von Haller's discovery of "irritability" in living tissues even where no nerves were present) to show that earlier assumptions that matter was inert were simply wrong, and that matter is by its own nature active or even vital. Writing in 1734, Voltaire (1694–1778) tried to use the vitalist discoveries to show the absurdity of the atheists' position. These materialists, he wrote, are forced to say "that the material world has thought and sentiment essential to itself, because it has no way to acquire them . . . This thought and this sentiment would have to be inherent in matter as are extension, divisibility, and capacity for motion . . ." (Voltaire 1877–85, 22:201–2).

Voltaire's point was that bodies have no way to acquire thought and sentiment except by the intervention of God, but materialists who deny God are committed to the absurd belief that thought and sentiment are as essential to matter as extension is. Voltaire's atheist contemporaries, however, simply denied the absurdity of this latter claim and insisted that matter could be essentially sentient. The notorious atheist Julien Offray de La Mettrie (1709–51), famous for his *L'homme machine* (1748), in which he denied the existence of the human soul—which for Descartes separated humans from all other animals—and insisted that humans too were mere machines, also wrote that same year, *L'homme plante*. This less well-known additional book simply argues that a machine can be made of sentient parts but still be merely a machine—nothing extra has to be added by a deity to make it live (Reill 2005; Thomson 2008).

These ideas intertwined with changing ideas about the nature of the soul. Although Descartes insisted on the dual nature of human beings—body and soul being inextricably linked—he made it clear that the passions (or emotions) were aspects of bodily physiology. The function of the immaterial soul became confined to the most abstract levels of intellection and ratiocination. When John Locke (1632–1704) denied the Cartesian notion of innate ideas, including a supposed innate ability of the soul to reason, the scene was set for replacing the soul with the mind. If the mind acquired its contents and abilities solely through experience, as Locke insisted in his influential *Essay Concerning Human Understanding* (1690), it was hard to see it as an entity with a separate existence from the body—as traditional religious belief, and Descartes, demanded. Although the story is extremely rich and complex in detail, among the educated the general historical trend throughout our period was to abandon the concept of the soul in favor of the more naturalistic, and more somatic, concept of the mind (Porter 2003; Thomson 2008).

We have been following one thread (matter and activity) through the secular theology of the early modern natural philosophers, but there were of course a number of other issues. Developing concepts of force required theological underpinning (Hatfield 1979; Garber 1992), as did the concept of space, increasingly seen as infinite in extent as a result of the spread of Copernican astronomy (Koyré 1957; Copenhaver 1980). Pascal's famous comment that "the eternal silence of these infinite spaces frightens me" (Pascal 1960, 110) pointed to the fact that the medieval notion of the empyrean heaven lying beyond the sphere of the fixed stars could no longer be held, when the stars were envisaged as so many suns, perhaps with planets of their own, scattered at different distances through an infinite cosmos.

Most remarkably of all, in seeking to establish their claims about the relationship between God and the world, some of these secular theologians found it necessary to reconsider the nature of God himself (Funkenstein 1986). The materialist mechanical philosopher and political theorist, Thomas Hobbes (1588–1679), seemed to commit himself to belief in a corporeal God (Leijenhorst 2005)—which led others to see him as an atheist (Mintz 1962). Similarly, the Cartesian mechanical philosopher, Baruch Spinoza (1632–77), regarded thought and extension to be attributes of God, and thereby seems to have brought the relationship between God and his Creation to a level of immanence that led most contemporaries (in spite of his own denials) to see him as a pantheist (Nadler 1999). Even Newton felt the need to insist that God "constitutes Duration and Space," and therefore echoed St Paul: "In him are all things contained and moved." Newton's most public announcement of the theology underlying his natural philosophy appeared in the "General Scholium" which he added to the second edition of his *Principia mathematica* in 1713 (Snobelen 2001). Bringing this to a close, he wrote: "This concludes the discussion of God, and to treat of God from phenomena is certainly part of natural philosophy" (Newton 1999, 943). Natural philosophy inevitably led to theology.

# 3 NATURAL THEOLOGY

By writing this, Newton was both acknowledging the prior development of natural theology in the preceding century, and adding his own considerable authority to its promotion through the eighteenth century and beyond. Although the use of the natural world to prove the existence and at least some of the attributes of God, can be seen much earlier (including Romans 1:20, and in at least three of Thomas's five proofs of the existence of God), and is implicit in the medieval handmaiden tradition (Lindberg 2013), the systematic attempt to use detailed natural phenomena to establish God's existence, wisdom, benevolence, and so forth, becomes a significant philosophical movement in the seventeenth century, especially in Britain (Brooke 1991, 192–225; Harrison 2005).

Among the first to appear were *The Darknes of Atheism Dispelled by the Light of Nature* (1652), by Walter Charleton; and *An Antidote against Atheism* (1653) by the Cambridge Platonist, Henry More (1614–87). Other writers in this tradition include John Ray (1627–1705), William Derham (1657–1735), and the highly influential William Paley (1743–1805). The movement was especially promoted by the annual "Boyle Lectures," founded by a bequest in the will of Robert Boyle to counter atheism. The first series of lectures was delivered in 1692 by Richard Bentley (1662–1742), a rising scholar in the Anglican Church, who chose to base his natural theology on the physics of Newton's *Principia mathematica*, which had been published only five years before. Other leading Boyle lecturers were Newton's friend, Samuel Clarke (1675–1729), and William Derham, whose lectures were published as *Physico-Theology, or a Demonstration of the Being and Attributes of God from His Works of Creation* (1713), and proved to be especially influential.

The main stratagem of natural theology was the argument from design. Such arguments seemed to be reinforced with the advent of the microscope, when it became possible to see the extraordinarily fine details of Creation. One of the greatest microscopists of the seventeenth century, the Dutch entomologist, Jan Swammerdam (1637–80), was motivated by his faith and his desire to reveal the design even in the invisible aspects of the natural world (Ruestow 1996). One of the culminating arguments from design was presented by William Paley, in his *Natural Theology* (1802). Just as we readily conclude from seeing a watch (even if we've never seen one before) that it must have been made by an intelligent artificer, so we can conclude that natural objects, especially living organisms, must have been made by an even more consummate intelligence: "every indication of contrivance, every manifestation of design, which existed in the watch, exists in the works of nature" (Paley 2006, 16).

The terms of Boyle's will made it explicit that the Boyle lectures should also combat deism (which for Boyle was as big a threat to Christianity as any other form of infidelity), but it is hard to resist the conclusion that lecturers like Bentley, Clarke, Derham, and others, weakened Christian authority by relying so much on natural theologies based only on the latest developments in the sciences. Certainly, the American statesman and Newtonian physicist Benjamin Franklin (1706–90) tells us in his *Autobiography* (1771) that when he was "scarce fifteen," he "became a thorough Deist" as a result of reading Boyle Lectures (Franklin 1993, 58).

The more natural philosophers, and philosophical theologians (such as Henry More), resorted to the phenomena of the natural world to prove the existence of God, the more they promoted deism—which is, after all, a religious position entirely based on natural theology. Increasingly, toward the end of the early modern period, thinkers like Franklin, Voltaire, and others, no doubt regarded their deism as a superior position to that based on scripture and doctrinal tradition. Such was the authority of the natural sciences, especially after Newton, that the deists could easily lay claim to basing their faith on the securest and most reliable principles of knowledge. In the earlier part of our period, however, it seems reasonable to suppose that those promoting natural theology still thought of themselves as good Christians, but they recurred to natural theology because they saw no other means of combating the atheism that they saw as such a growing threat to their times.

# 4 Natural Philosophy and Atheism

This is not the place to discuss the emergence of atheism in the early modern period, but it is necessary to consider what role if any natural philosophy—or what might be called, albeit anachronistically, scientific ways of thinking—played in that emergence. It is often supposed that the new philosophies of the Scientific Revolution were a major factor in the forging of atheism—but this seems to be based on little more than the perception that today the scientific worldview is seen as inimical to the religious worldview, and therefore it must always have been so. In fact, atheism seems to have emerged as the result of a number of factors, including perceptions of the corruption of the church and anticlericalism, growing awareness of cultural relativism (that advanced civilization was possible in non-Christian, or even irreligious societies—as in Islam or China), the rise of skepticism (partly as a result of the breakdown of traditional authorities and partly as a result of the rediscovery of ancient skepticism), and so forth. It cannot be denied, however, that atheists quickly seized upon natural philosophy and interpreted it to suit their purposes. It would be very surprising if they had not (Buckley 1987).

After all, so strong was the "handmaiden tradition" that it was taken for granted that natural philosophy supported theology. Furthermore, as we have seen, because of the proliferation of new philosophies, thinkers were more active than usual in showing just how their new philosophies conformed to, and supported, whatever theology it was they favored. Given the fact that the Scriptural designation of atheists as fools (Psalm 14:1) was often associated with their inability to understand the way the handmaiden supported theology, the atheists had no choice but to show how natural philosophy could be seen instead as a handmaiden to atheism.

The historical evidence seems to suggest, however, that atheism had already built up its own momentum *before* it turned to natural philosophy for additional support. It was certainly not the case that the leading natural philosophers themselves were led by their own investigations toward atheism; and it does not seem to have been the case that atheism as a general movement emerged as a result of developments in the natural sciences. What is undeniable, however, is the fact that it was all too easy for atheists to appropriate the latest scientific ideas to suit their purposes—and indeed to suit them very well. The mechanical philosophy was quickly embraced by contemporary atheists, and the quotation from Robert Boyle above (Boyle [1686] 1996, 24–25), in which he insisted that the concept of laws of nature only made sense if God was underwriting the laws, was written in response to contemporary atheists who simply saw laws of nature as autonomous principles of causation. Similarly, we have already considered the example of vitalistic principles in living matter. Seen as a godsend by devout natural philosophers when they were first discovered—an addition to their arsenal against atheism—the inherent vitality of organic matter simply came to be seen by the atheists as further proof that living things could spontaneously emerge without having to be specially created by God (Reill 2005).

For the faithful, part of the problem was their own inability to present a united front against atheism. The Cambridge Platonist Henry More hinged his philosophical theology on the dualistic claim that matter was completely passive and inert, and that immaterial spirit was the principle of activity in the world. If matter moves, spirit must be involved, because inert matter cannot move itself. He developed this into the notion that there must be an all-pervasive Spirit of Nature at work in the world and responsible for all change. He drew upon some of the experiments of Robert Boyle, interpreting them as demonstrations of the existence of this Spirit of Nature. Boyle took issue with this, but their disagreement was not just confined to the interpretation of experiments, but also involved fundamental disagreement in theology (Henry 1990). Boyle pointed out that his experiments showed the law-like behavior of bodies, and could be understood in broadly Cartesian terms—God is only required to make bodies act in accordance with laws of nature, or principles of secondary causation; he does not have to create a universal intermediary Spirit of Nature, and there is no warrant for supposing experiments show the existence of such a spirit. With regard to theology, Boyle's God was capable of endowing bodies with active principles, but More insisted that active matter was a contradiction in terms and that not even God could make matter active. Boyle felt that More was restricting God's omnipotence, while More felt that Boyle was undermining what he took to be an unassailable argument against materialist atheism.

There was a similar dispute later between John Locke and the Bishop of Worcester, Edward Stillingfleet (1635–99). In his influential *Essay*, Locke pointed to our lack of understanding of the processes of thought by suggesting, contrary to Cartesian dualists, that God could, if he chose, make matter think. Stillingfleet was appalled. In his dispute with Locke he made it clear why: "Either it is impossible for a material substance to think, or it must be asserted, that a power of thinking is within the essential properties of matter . . ." (Stillingfleet 1710, 3:542). For Stillingfleet, not even God could make matter think—to allow that he could is to make it possible for an atheist to deny any link between thinking and incorporeality. But Locke did not wish to restrict the bounds of God's omnipotence, even if doing so made it possible to forge an argument that linked our experience of thinking with the existence of immaterial substance (Henry 2011).

The most famous argument of this kind was that between the leading Continental philosopher, G. W. Leibniz (1646–1715), and Isaac Newton (hiding behind and speaking through his friend Samuel Clarke) (Vailati 1997). In the opening letter of his correspondence with Clarke, Leibniz not only alludes to Locke's lamentable speculation about thinking matter, but he also takes Newton and his followers to task for developing a theology in which "God Almighty wants to *wind up* his Watch from Time to Time: . . . the Machine of God's making, is so imperfect, according to these Gentlemen; that he is obliged . . . to *mend* it, as a Clockmaker mends his Work" (Alexander 1956, 11). But Leibniz's God, like Descartes's, was only required at the Creation, and Newton had already seen this leading to atheistic appropriations of Cartesianism. Accordingly,

Newton wanted to make sure his God was obliged to intervene from time to time, and was perpetually present. As Clarke explained: "Whosoever contends, that the Course of the World can go on *without* the Continual direction of *God*, the Supreme Governor; his Doctrine does in Effect tend to Exclude God out of the World" (Alexander 1956, 14).

If devout natural philosophers could not decide upon the best way to refute atheism, they also played into the atheists' hands by unintentionally providing them with support. The natural philosophers always sought to provide fully comprehensive and self-contained explanations of natural phenomena. Although they always acknowledged God as the first or primary cause, they did not at any point simply refer their readers to that cause; the aim was always to explain things in terms of natural secondary causes. Even Newton, who famously relied (to Leibniz's chagrin) on a "God of the gaps," did not explicitly refer his readers to direct intervention by God to explain any physical phenomena. If God had to "wind up his watch," he did so, according to Newton, by means of the gravitational pull of a passing comet, which would increase the speed of a decelerating planet. Just how this was supposed to ensure the continued activity of God in the World, which Newton wanted to claim, is by no means certain, and since Newton was not a theologian, he did not trouble to spell out the theology fully (Kubrin 1967; Henry 1994).

Natural philosophers, then, played into the hands of atheists by leaving God out of their detailed accounts of how the world works. Moreover, the new philosophies tended to promote deism at the expense of revelation, and therefore contributed to a weakening of the authority of the churches, and again can be seen as inadvertently supporting atheism. Although the notion of a personal Providence was never explicitly dismantled by natural philosophers, it was clearly incompatible with the law-based mechanical universe; as Alexander Pope wrote in his *Essay on Man* (1732), "the first Almighty Cause/ Acts not by partial, but by gen'ral laws" (Epistle I:5).

Indeed, Pope's *Essay on Man* has been seen as "the declaration of faith" of a new religion (Hazard 1954, 422), but if that is true, it was a religion that owed much to the new natural philosophies of the seventeenth century. Although most well known now through the satirical attack upon it in Voltaire's *Candide* (1759), Leibniz's attempt to solve the theological problem of evil by insisting this is "the best of all possible worlds," proved to be remarkably influential, and Pope's *Essay* summed up the English version of it. It was widely assumed throughout Europe by the middle of the eighteenth century that Newton had really uncovered the rational and mathematical principles which God had used in creating the world. That being the case, it was no longer possible to dismiss the problem of evil by declaring that we cannot know the workings of God's mind. Newton had shown how God's mind worked and we must therefore find a rational answer to the problem of evil. God, in accordance with his goodness—and in accordance with principles of good and evil which were co-eternal with and independent of God—was obliged to create the best world possible, and if aspects of that world seem evil, they are effectively the result of compromises God was obliged to make.

This went hand-in-hand with another influential idea which also took its cue from triumphant Newtonianism. In the closing words of his *Opticks* (1717), Newton had optimistically suggested that "if natural Philosophy in all its Parts, by pursuing this Method, shall at length be perfected, the Bounds of Moral Philosophy will be also enlarged" (Newton 1952, 405). This gave rise to a movement known to historians as moral Newtonianism, part of which pursued morality into the realms of mathematics, to develop a "moral calculus." This was summed up nicely by Francis Hutcheson (1694–1746) in his *Inquiry into the Original of Our Ideas of Beauty and Virtue* (1726): "The moral Evil, or Vice, is as the Degree of Misery and Number of Sufferers; so that, that Action is best which accomplishes the greatest Happiness for the greatest Numbers" (Hutcheson 2004, 125).

The rejection of an individual Providence in favor of a Providence which had to conform to general laws was certainly the result of the rise of science in the Enlightenment, following on from the Scientific Revolution, and is a clear indication of its impact upon contemporary theology. There were of course alternative theologies which stood outside this tradition—Calvinists rejected the view that there were absolute concepts of good and evil that restricted God's arbitrary will in Creation, and to which he had to conform. Accordingly, they continued to regard the problem of evil as an unsolvable mystery (the Fall provided an explanation for the existence of *moral* evil in God's Creation, but not for the existence of *natural* evils such as earthquakes, etc.). Even so, Newtonian-Leibnizian theology proved highly influential, but its aloof God was no longer anyone's personal God. While for Descartes, God chose to underwrite the laws of nature and to make sure that bodies acted in accordance with them, for many Enlightenment thinkers God himself had to conform to the laws of nature. Once again, it was easy for the atheist to step in and take charge of the idea of laws of nature.

## 5 PROTESTANTISM AND SCIENCE

A persistent theme in the historiography of science sees Protestantism as making greater contributions to the advance of the natural sciences than Catholicism. This "Protestantism and Science thesis" seems to have exerted itself not by clear and unassailable evidence but by numerous restatements and new explanatory theories (Cohen 1990).

One obvious reason why Catholics might have been more hampered in scientific achievement was the existence of the Congregation of the Index, and its very well-known condemnation of Galileo in 1633. Descartes was perfectly explicit in saying that he suppressed the intended publication of his system of mechanical philosophy when he heard about Galileo's condemnation (Descartes [1637] 2006, 35).

There has been a tendency, from the late nineteenth century onwards, to see Galileo's condemnation as indicative of what is claimed to be fundamental incompatibility between science and religion (Draper 1875; White 1895), but as we have seen, there was no such incompatibility. It is now known that Galileo's condemnation was the result of a unique set of circumstances and cannot stand as representative of any general enmity between science and religion. The details are complex, but essentially Galileo was condemned because he had deceived Pope Urban VIII into giving him permission to write his *Dialogue on the Two Chief World-Systems* (1632) without informing Urban that he had (allegedly) promised the previous pope, Paul V, that he would never publicly discuss the Copernican theory. As it turns out, the document in the Vatican file that suggests Galileo had made such a promise to Paul V is highly suspicious on a number of grounds, and contradicted by other documents in the file. Even so, such were the political exigencies of the case, that Galileo was condemned. It seems clear now, however, that enemies of Galileo had successfully doctored the evidence against him (Fantoli 2005; Finocchiaro 2005). Be that as it may, Descartes was presumably not the only good Catholic natural philosopher who believed that the Galileo affair indicated that he could not freely pursue his philosophy where it led him (Ashworth 1986; Dear 1991).

Approaching the Protestantism and Science thesis from the Protestant side, scholars have largely failed to provide compelling reasons why Protestant theology should have favored scientific work in a way that Catholic theology did not. This is especially true of attempts to narrow the historical focus by claiming that it was Puritanism in seventeenth-century England and Pietism in eighteenth-century Germany that particularly encouraged science (Merton 1968; Cohen 1990). English "Puritanism" has proved too protean a designation to provide a sound basis for useful historical arguments (Webster 1974; Mulligan 1980), while German Pietism has to be approached with caution.

It seems undeniable that August Hermann Francke (1663–1727), one of the leaders of the Pietist reform movement within Lutheranism, subscribed to the handmaiden tradition. Furthermore, the Pietists were adept at putting scientific, especially medical, knowledge to use in the service of their practical theology. Recent research has shown how the Pietists in Halle produced high quality pharmaceuticals which they used not only for the bodily health of their followers, but as a means of bringing in much-needed revenue through sales, and also, as a means of drawing back into their influence wavering Lutherans, especially in faraway centers of German settlement—most notably in North America (Wilson 2000). There can be no denying, however, that Francke and other theologians in the University of Halle, saw the rationalist mechanical philosophy of their colleague Christian Wolff (1679–1754), now regarded as a leading Enlightenment thinker in Germany, as inimical to religion. Francke and others accused Wolff of atheism and in 1733, he was expelled from the University and banished from all Prussian territories (Becker 1991). Clearly, it is impossible to declare Pietism in Halle to be either for or against the natural sciences in any general way. Indeed, the situation in Halle seems to have been, like the Galileo affair, the result of a unique set of circumstances and should not be used as a basis for drawing general conclusions.

But if a narrow focus makes it difficult to see clear historical trends, by pulling back to consider characteristically Protestant theological concerns, we can begin to perceive indications as to how those concerns might have influenced thinking about the natural world.

It has been suggested that the greater excitement among Protestants about impending apocalyptic or millennial fulfillment was a major stimulus toward innovation in the natural sciences. Crucial to this argument is the undeniable fact that Francis Bacon (1561–1626), a major figure in the Scientific Revolution, took as his motto a prediction of the end times from Daniel (12:4): "many shall run to and fro, and knowledge shall be increased." Bacon saw the first part of this prediction as a reference to the Renaissance voyages of discovery that had now taken place, and he saw it as his religious duty (given his position in the administration of the English state) to help to bring about the advancement of knowledge. Bacon had an international reputation as a would-be reformer of natural philosophy—he is most renowned for promoting the use of the experimental method, and for insisting that natural knowledge should be put to use for the benefit of mankind—but it has to be said that his major influence was in Protestant England. It was in England, and nowhere else, that the millennial dimension to his work was recognized and taken up by followers (Webster 1975).

Similarly, the Lutheran insistence upon a "priesthood of all believers," and the concomitant urge to read the Bible for oneself, rather than rely upon the intermediary interpretation of a Catholic priest, has been seen as a major factor leading Protestants to increased innovation in the sciences (Harrison 1998). The Protestant Reformers tried to minimize any overly creative interpretations of the Bible by encouraging literalist interpretations as much as possible, and the historical evidence suggests that this also influenced the reading of what had always been known as "God's other book"—the book of nature. Rejecting earlier emblematic or allegorical interpretations of flora and fauna, natural history became focused upon observed facts and avoided any extra levels of meaning (Ashworth 1980; Harrison 1998). This in turn affected other aspects of the study of the natural world, including a new emphasis upon observation, fact gathering, and avoiding the use of complex ratiocinations in explanations of natural phenomena. Increasingly, Protestants began to identify such complex chains of reasoning with scholastic philosophy, and the new philosophies came to be seen as more intelligible and more acceptable to the new Protestant ways of reading the world (Harrison 1998; Gaukroger 2006).

Finally, greater innovation in the sciences among Protestants has been seen as the result of a revival among Protestants of Augustinian views about the Fall and the degenerate state of postlapsarian humankind (Harrison 2007). Catholics, generally speaking, stuck to the Thomist view that Adam had only lost former supernatural attributes at the Fall, but his natural attributes, including his reason and other mental powers, remained unaffected. Protestants, especially Calvinists, by contrast reverted to the Augustinian view that the Fall resulted in a loss of natural powers, including a diminishing of the acuity of the senses, and greatly reduced mental capabilities.

This highly negative view of the postlapsarian capacities of humankind led Protestants to reject rationalist approaches to natural philosophy, on the grounds that human reason is too weak and prone to error to lead to the truth, and to insist instead upon observation and the experimental method to learn as much as is humanly possible about the nature of the world (Harrison 2007). The argument hinges, therefore, upon whether this anti-rationalist and empiricist approach can be seen to lead to greater achievements in the sciences than the more speculative and rationalist approaches still cherished by Catholic natural philosophers. We cannot survey the historical evidence here, but it is worth noting that by the middle of the eighteenth century even the leading French *philosophes* were abandoning their allegiance to rationalist Cartesianism—dismissing Descartes's rationalist philosophy as a "philosophical romance" (Voltaire [1733] 1961, 17)—and singing the praises of the English empiricist philosophers, most notably Francis Bacon, Robert Boyle, John Locke, and Isaac Newton (Voltaire [1733] 1961, 46–84; D'Alembert [1751] 1995, 74–85). For the leading natural philosophers of the French Enlightenment, the anti-rationalist and empiricist approach was indeed the most fruitful approach for the advancement of the sciences.

It should be noted that the three historiographical theories which make a link between Protestant theology and enhanced achievement in the sciences (the millennial theory, the theory based on Protestant attitudes to the Bible, and the theory based on the revival of Augustinian anthropology) all depend upon the claim that *empiricist* approaches were stimulated by the theological position in question—and that, by implication, these empiricist approaches were in the long run more fruitful. The historical development of the experimental method, and its rise to prominence as virtually a definitive way of acquiring "scientific" knowledge, is highly complex and many secular factors are involved alongside these three aspects of (predominantly) Protestant theology (Harrison 2007, 245–58). Nonetheless, when the complete history of the rise of the experimental method comes to be written, these three aspects of the theological background will have to be included.

## BIBLIOGRAPHY

Alexander, H. G., ed. 1956. *The Leibniz-Clarke Correspondence*. Manchester, UK: Manchester University Press.

Ashworth, William B. 1986. "Catholicism and Early Modern Science." In *God and Nature: Historical Essays on the Encounter between Christianity and Science*, edited by D. C. Lindberg and R. L. Numbers, 136–166. Berkeley: University of California Press.

Ashworth, William B. 1980. "Natural History and the Emblematic World-View." In *Reappraisals of the Scientific Revolution*, edited by D. C. Lindberg and R. S. Westman, 303–332. Cambridge: Cambridge University Press.

Becker, George. 1991. "Pietism's Confrontation with Enlightenment Rationalism: An Examination of the Relation between Ascetic Protestantism and Science." *Journal for the Scientific Study of Religion* 30:139–158.

Biggs, Noah. 1651. *Mataeotechnia medicinae praxeos: The Vanity of the Craft of Physick . . .* London.

Boyle, Robert. (1674) 2000. *The Excellency of Theology Compar'd with Natural Philosophy*. Vol. 8 of *Works*, edited by M. Hunter and E. B. Davis, 5–98. London: Pickering and Chatto.

Boyle, Robert. (1686) 1996. *A Free Enquiry into the Vulgarly Received Notion of Nature*. Edited by E. B. Davis and M. Hunter. Cambridge: Cambridge University Press.

Brooke, John Hedley. 1991. *Science and Religion: Some Historical Perspectives*. Cambridge: Cambridge University Press.

Buckley, Michael J., SJ. 1987. *At the Origins of Modern Atheism*. New Haven, CT: Yale University Press.

Cohen, I. Bernard, ed. 1990. *Puritanism and the Rise of Modern Science: The Merton Thesis*. New Brunswick, NJ: Rutgers University Press.

Copenhaver, Brian P. 1980. "Jewish Theologies of Space in the Scientific Revolution: Henry More, Joseph Raphson, Isaac Newton and Their Predecessors." *Annals of Science* 37: 489–548.

Cottingham, John. 1992. "Cartesian Dualism: Theology, Metaphysics and Science." In *The Cambridge Companion to Descartes*, edited by J. Cottingham, 236–257. Cambridge: Cambridge University Press.

D'Alembert, Jean Le Rond. [1751] 1995. *Preliminary Discourse to the Encyclopaedia of Diderot*, translated by Richard N. Schwab. Chicago: University of Chicago Press.

Dear, Peter. 1991. "The Church and the New Philosophy." In *Science, Culture, and Popular Belief in Renaissance Europe*, edited by S. Pumfrey, P. L. Rossi, and M. Slawinski, 119–139. Manchester, UK: Manchester University Press.

Descartes, René. (1637) 2006. *A Discourse on the Method of Correctly Conducting One's Reason and Seeking Truth in the Sciences*. Translated by Ian Maclean. Oxford: Oxford University Press.

Draper, John W. 1875. *History of the Conflict between Religion and Science*. London: Kegan, Paul, Trench & Co.

Fantoli, Annibale. 2005. "The Disputed Injunction and Its Role in Galileo's Trial." In *The Church and Galileo*, edited by E. McMullin, 117–149. Notre Dame, IN: University of Notre Dame Press.

Finocchiaro, Maurice A. 2005. *Retrying Galileo, 1633–1992*. Berkeley: University of California Press.

Firpo, L. 1950–51. "Filosofia italiana e Controriforma. II. La condanna di F. Patrizi." *Rivista di Filosofia* 41: 150–173; 42: 30–47.

Franklin, Benjamin. 1993. *Autobiography and Other Writings*. Oxford: Oxford University Press.

Funkenstein, Amos. 1986. *Theology and the Scientific Imagination from the Middle Ages to the Seventeenth Century*. Princeton, NJ: Princeton University Press.

Garber, Daniel. 1992. *Descartes' Metaphysical Physics*. Chicago: University of Chicago Press.

Garber, Daniel. 1993. "Descartes and Occasionalism." In *Causation in Early Modern Philosophy*, edited by S. Nadler, 9–26. University Park: Pennsylvania State University Press.

Gaukroger, Stephen. 2006. *The Emergence of a Scientific Culture: Science and the Shaping of Modernity, 1210–1685*. Oxford: Clarendon Press.

Grant, Edward. 1996. *The Foundations of Modern Science in the Middle Ages: Their Religious, Institutional, and Intellectual Contexts*. Cambridge: Cambridge University Press.

Hadzits, G. D. 1935. *Lucretius and His Influence*. London: Longmans, Green and Co.

Harrison, Peter. 1998. *The Bible, Protestantism and the Rise of Natural Science*. Cambridge: Cambridge University Press.

Harrison, Peter. 2007. *The Fall of Man and the Foundations of Modern Science*. Cambridge: Cambridge University Press.

Harrison, Peter. 2005. "Physico-Theology and Mixed Sciences: The Role of Theology in Early Modern Natural Theology." In *The Science of Nature in the Seventeenth Century*, edited by P. R. Anstey and J. A. Schuster, 165–183. Dordrecht: Springer.

Hatfield, Gary. 1979. "Force (God) in Descartes' Physics." *Studies in History and Philosophy of Science* 10: 113–140.

Hazard, Paul. 1954. *European Thought in the Eighteenth Century from Montesquieu to Lessing*. London: Hollis and Carter.

Henry, John. 1982. "Atomism and Eschatology: Catholicism and Natural Philosophy in the Interregnum." *British Journal for the History of Science* 15: 211–239.

Henry, John. 1990. "Henry More versus Robert Boyle: The Spirit of Nature and the Nature of Providence." In *Henry More (1614–1687): Tercentenary Studies*, edited by Sarah Hutton, 55–75. Dordrecht: Kluwer Academic Publishers.

Henry, John. 2004. "Metaphysics and the Origins of Modern Science: Descartes and the Importance of Laws of Nature." *Early Science and Medicine* 9: 73–114.

Henry, John. 2011. "Omnipotence and Thinking Matter: John Locke and the Use of Reason in Religion." In *Materia, Atti del XIII Colloquio Internazionale del Lessico Intellettuale Europeo (Roma, 7–9 gennaio 2010)*, edited by D. Giovannozzi and M. Veneziani, 357–379. Florence: Leo S. Olschki.

Henry, John. 1994. "'Pray do not ascribe that notion to me': God and Newton's Gravity." In *The Books of Nature and Scripture: Recent Essays on Natural Philosophy, Theology and Biblical Criticism in the Netherlands of Spinoza's Time and the British Isles of Newton's Time*, edited by J. E. Force and R. H. Popkin, 123–147. Dordrecht: Kluwer Academic Publishers.

Hobbes, Thomas. 1651. *Leviathan: Or the Matter, Forme, and Power of a Commonwealth Ecclesiasticall and Civil*. London.

Hutcheson, Francis. 2004. *An Inquiry into the Original of our Ideas of Beauty and Virtue in Two Treatises*. Indianapolis: Liberty Fund Inc.

Koyré, Alexandre. 1957. *From the Closed World to the Infinite Universe*. Baltimore: Johns Hopkins University Press.

Kubrin, David. 1967. "Newton and the Cyclical Cosmos." *Journal of the History of Ideas* 29: 325–346.

Leijenhorst, Cees. 2005. "Hobbes, Heresy, and Corporeal Deity." In *Heterodoxy in Early Modern Science and Religion*, edited by J. Brooke and I. Maclean, 193–222. Oxford: Oxford University Press.

Lindberg, David C. 2013. "Science and the Medieval Church." In *Medieval Science*, vol. 2 of *The Cambridge History of Science*, edited by D. C. Lindberg and M. H. Shank, 268–285. Cambridge: Cambridge University Press.

Mendelsohn, J. Andrew. 1992. "Alchemy and Politics in England, 1649–1665." *Past and Present* 135: 30–78.

Merton, Robert K. 1968. "Puritanism, Pietism and Science." In *Social Theory and Social Structure*, 628–660. New York: Free Press.

Mintz, Samuel I. 1962. *The Hunting of Leviathan: Seventeenth-Century Reactions to the Materialism and Moral Philosophy of Thomas Hobbes*. Cambridge: Cambridge University Press.

Mulligan, Lotte. 1980. "Puritans and English Science: A Critique of Webster." *Isis* 71: 457–469.

Nadler, Steven. 2000. "Malebranche on Causation." In *The Cambridge Companion to Malebranche*, edited by S. Nadler, 112–138. Cambridge: Cambridge University Press.

Nadler, Steven. 1999. *Spinoza: A Life*. Cambridge: Cambridge University Press.

Newton, Isaac. 1962. "De gravitatione et aequipondio fluidorum." In *Unpublished Scientific Papers of Isaac Newton*, edited by A. R. Hall and M. Boas Hall, 89–156. Cambridge: Cambridge University Press.

Newton, Isaac. 1952. *Opticks, or a Treatise of the Reflections, Refractions, Inflections, and Colours of Light*. New York: Dover.

Newton, Isaac. 1999. *The Principia: Mathematical Principles of Natural Philosophy*. Translated by I. B. Cohen and A. Whitman. Cambridge: Cambridge University Press.

Osler, Margaret J. 1985. "Baptizing Epicurean Atomism: Pierre Gassendi on the Immortality of the Soul." In *Religion, Science, and Worldview: Essays in Honor of Richard S. Westfall*, edited by M. J. Osler and P. L. Farber, 163–183. Cambridge: Cambridge University Press.

Paley, William. 2006. *Natural Theology: Or Evidences of the Existence and Attributes of the Deity, Collected from the Appearances of Nature*. Oxford: Oxford University Press.

Pascal, Blaise. 1960. *Pensées: Notes on Religion and Other Subjects*. Edited by Louis Lafuma. Translated by John Warrington. London: Dent.

Porter, Roy. 2003. *Flesh in the Age of Reason: The Modern Foundations of Body and Soul*. New York: W. W. Norton.

Reill, Peter Hans. 2005. *Vitalizing Nature in the Enlightenment*. Berkeley: University of California Press.

Ruestow, Edward G. 1996. *The Microscope in the Dutch Republic: The Shaping of Discovery*. Cambridge: Cambridge University Press.

Snobelen, Stephen D. 2001. "'God of Gods and Lord of Lords': The Theology of Isaac Newton's General Scholium to the *Principia*." *Osiris*, Second Series, 16: 169–208.

Stillingfleet, Edward. 1710. *Works*. 6 vols. London.

Thomson, Ann. 2008. *Bodies of Thought: Science, Religion, and the Soul in the Early Enlightenment*. Oxford: Oxford University Press.

Vailati, Ezio. 1997. *Leibniz and Clarke: A Study of Their Correspondence*. Oxford: Oxford University Press.

Voltaire. (1733) 1961. *Philosophical Letters*. Translated by Ernest Dilworth. Indianapolis: Bobbs-Merrill Company Inc.

Voltaire. 1877–1885. *Traité de métaphysique. Ouevres complètes*. Vol. 22. Edited by Louis Moland. Paris: Garnier frères.

Webster, Charles. 1975. *The Great Instauration: Science, Medicine, and Reform, 1626–1660*. 2nd ed. London: Duckworth.

Webster, Charles. 1974. *The Intellectual Revolution of the Seventeenth Century*. London: Routledge and Kegan Paul.

Westfall, Richard S. 1958. *Science and Religion in Seventeenth-Century England*. New Haven, CT: Yale University Press.

White, Andrew Dixon. 1895. *A History of the Warfare of Science with Theology in Christendom*. London: Macmillan.

Wilson, Renate. 2000. *Pious Traders in Medicine: A German Pharmaceutical Network in Eighteenth-Century North America*. University Park: Pennsylvania State University Press.

# CHAPTER 41

# THE RISE OF NATURAL LAW IN THE EARLY MODERN PERIOD

ROBERT VON FRIEDEBURG

## 1 INTRODUCTION

IN contemporary discourse, debates on how to clarify the existence and range of supra-positive norms since antiquity have been conventionally addressed as part of "natural law," although the term was seldom used by either Plato or Aristotle (Ilting 1978, 245–66). During the Middle Ages, debates on natural law were mainly stipulated by speculations regarding the knowledge created men could be assumed to have about the creator's intentions and orders. These debates were neither meant to provide a detailed catalogue of laws or rights, nor legitimacy for a specific civil authority.

Beginning with the Reformation, publications and debates about natural law began to mushroom. The rise of natural law responded to the need for finding new rationales for obligating men. From the second third of the seventeenth century, though prepared by speculations about law and the state of nature in the preceding century, the works of Hugo Grotius (1583–1645), Thomas Hobbes (1588–1679), Samuel von Pufendorf (1632–94), and John Locke (1632–1704) transformed the political philosophy and learned architecture of Latin Europe. To provide the basis for the laws and arrangements of human society, jurists and philosophers marginalized confessional revelation theology on the will of God as revealed in scripture. Instead, they argued with respect to the dictates of right (human) reason, partly by referring to an alleged (analytical) state of nature, partly by making assumptions about human nature as created by God. Along the way, civil authority assumed the role of obligating agency within each sovereign state. Natural law primarily insisted on obligations. Rights, insofar as they were formulated, mainly followed from these obligations. The exception seems to have been Hobbes, and he argued that the rights individuals had in the state of nature were in themselves of little use and definitely not securely enforceable. Despite the heterogeneity among seventeenth- and eighteenth-century proponents of natural law, they all contributed to the marginalization of insight into the will of the divine creator, as interpreted by the confessional churches, and to providing a new basis for obligating men to civil authority in this world.

Though the generalized form of granting specified rights to each human being as such remains squarely a phenomenon of the second half of the twentieth century (Eckel 2014), various formulations of the preamble to the American Declaration of Independence and the Declaration of the Rights of Man during the French Revolution (1793) have led to identifying the early modern natural law debate as an important intellectual breeding ground for these later developments. Given the perseverance of slavery in French colonies from 1802 and in the United States until 1865, and the Christian roots of the antislavery campaign in England, the intellectual origins of modern human rights are anything but clear-cut. But even so, for Latin Europe, the rise of natural law as a legal-philosophical basis for the ordering of society accordingly is not in dispute (Luig 1972). In recent decades, the beginning of this rise was backdated into the sixteenth century, in particular by taking Melanchthon (1497–1560) (Schmoeckel 2008; Schmoeckel 2014, 53–134; Strohm 2000; Strohm 2002), Spanish scholasticism, and Grotius more seriously, stirring vigorous debate (Tuck 1993; Brett 2003; Brett 2011; Zagorin 2000; Zagorin 2007). Though the large majority of natural law authors of the seventeenth and eighteenth centuries were baptized in a Protestant rite, direct necessary consequences of the specific confessional outlook of a given author on his natural law arguments remain questionable, in particular given the differences among Catholic and Protestant authors (Brett 2011). With this inclusion of many sixteenth-century authors, arguments on natural law have become, if anything, more heterogeneous. In what follows, this contribution is strongly influenced by the work of Annabel Brett (Brett 2003; Brett 2011), Knud Haakonssen (Haakonssen 1996), and Perez Zagorin (Zagorin 2000; Zagorin 2007).

Commonly, three interlocking developments have been made responsible for the rise of natural law during the early modern period. First, increasing historical scrutiny concerning the accurate meaning of Roman law in the light of legal humanism also undermined the direct applicability of the *Corpus Iuris Civilis* to the present. The demand for ethical golden rules of equity as a basis for positive law had been voiced since the fifteenth century, and joined the sixteenth- and seventeenth-century search for more secure methods to establish truth. Second, the development of mutually exclusive confessional revelation theologies eventually undermined the monopoly of confessional theology for interpreting the will of the divine creator. Finally, the expansion of Latin Europe's possessions, trade, and wars around the globe led to a shift in political imagination away from dynasties and princes bound together by Latin Christendom and toward "states" as the projected unity of spatial districts, people, specific laws, and even specific political economies and goals, from considerations of Rohan (1638) to Pufendorf's introduction to the *Historie der vornehmsten Reiche und Staaten* (1684). Within these states and among them, natural law was supposed to identify the basics of right and wrong. Moreover, the increasing use of the term natural law, and the increasing importance of debates on what that meant, were not least affected by the use of the term for mutually irreconcilable or not even fully developed arguments, all contributing to the growing importance of the term. For example, those who fought their prince occasionally resorted to an ill-defined right to self-defense by natural law during the sixteenth and seventeenth centuries (Friedeburg 2002, 216–26, 236–43).

It must be stressed that the relationship of the three points of this triangle toward each other, and the relationship of sustained philosophical argument to the spread of a lingo of natural law without such grounding, remain problematic in trajectory and periodization. Members of all the major emerging confessions participated in the increasing number of publications touching on natural law, such as the Lutheran professor of Greek, Melanchthon; the Lutheran jurist Oldendorp (ca. 1486–1567); Catholic scholastics such as Francis Suarez (1548–1617); the Calvinist Althusius (1563–1638); and the Remonstrant Grotius. The emerging Enlightenment and men like Jean Barbeyrac (1674–1744) emphasized a breach with the past that was allegedly accomplished by Grotius and tended to downplay the role of the Spanish scholastics. Recent research has highlighted the heterogeneity of natural law arguments within and between confessions. Important contributors such as Leibniz (1646–1716) still worked on a nonconfessional yet Christian natural law (Hunter 2003). But by the end of the seventeenth century, even explicit opponents of a secular natural law, such as Veit Ludwig von Seckendorff (1626–92), distinguished among laws given to the citizens and members of a state by their civil authority, divine laws obeyed by men as Christian believers, and laws obeyed by virtue of "reason and nature" (Seckendorff 1691). The surge to address the demand for a new comprehensive philosophical basis of law beyond confessional revelation theologies and Roman law proved irresistible. Despite the fact that the early modern rise of natural law was embedded in fundamental changes in function and context of what was argued, the options then considered remained rooted in arguments formulated in antiquity that were further developed during the Middle Ages. To the classic and medieval background we must thus turn first.

## 2  THE CLASSIC AND MEDIEVAL BACKGROUND

Up to the end of the Middle Ages, two major streams can be distinguished. One argument essentially developed Aristotle's assumptions about a natural teleology, an ἐντελέχεια (entelechy): the world, and in it men, just as animals and plants, had inherent goals that it was their very nature to follow. Since men had, although in varying degrees, the ability of reasoning, such reasoning had to be applied to action in order to choose rightly Accordingly, in his *Nichomachean Ethics*, book 5, justice is defined as the appropriate relationship, appropriate according to the goal, of an action or person to a situation, not as an absolute to be described as a prescription. Therefore, in book 5 chapter 6, political justice is not described in terms of the contents of certain prescriptions, but defined as being found

> among men who share their life with a view to self-sufficiency, men who are free and either proportionally or arithmetically equal . . . For justice exists only between men whose mutual relations are governed by law . . . this is why we do not allow a man to rule, but rational principle, because a man behaves thus in his own interests and becomes a tyrant. The magistrate on the other hand is the guardian of justice, and, if of justice, then of equality also. And since he is assumed to have no more than his share, if he is just (for he does not assign to himself more of what is good in itself, unless such a share is proportional to his merits . . .) The justice of a master and that of a father are not the same as the justice of citizens, though they are like it, for there can be no injustice in the unqualified sense toward things that are one's own, but a man's chattel, and his child until it reaches a certain age and set up for itself . . . Therefore the justice or injustice of citizens is not manifested in these relations; for it was as we saw according to law, and between people naturally subject to law, and these as we saw are people who have an equal share in ruling and being ruled.

In chapter 7, among "justice between citizens," "natural" and "legal" justice is further distinguished, the one "which everywhere has the same force," and the other for a particular place, a given polis and its specific positive regulations.

It follows from these assumptions that "when the whole state is wholly subject to the will of one person, namely the king, it seems to many that it is unnatural that one man should have the entire rule over his fellow-citizens, when the state consists of equals: For nature requires that the same right and the same rank should necessarily take place amongst all those who are equal by nature; . . . for this is law, for order is law; and it is more proper that law should govern than any one of the citizens" (*Politics*, book 3, chapter XVI, 1287a). The goal inherent in the nature of Aristotle's polis-members required a living together in equality and under an order adequate to that equality. By the same token, the rule of a master over his slaves and cattle was appropriate to the nature of those slaves. Natural justice was served by submitting to what nature had ultimately dictated according to the goal of each creature, a goal given by its very nature. Creatures of the same nature need be treated in the same fashion; among the members of the polis, reciprocity and equality had to be respected. His argument was a response to the dispute, recorded in Plato's *Gorgias* (ca. 380 BC), between Socrates on the one hand and the sophists Gorgias, Polos, and Kallikles on the other. According to Plato, Socrates had refuted their argument that there were no common human norms beside the plurality of individual wills and interests and that humans therefore could use any means possible to further their own advantage over others (Winkel 2016).

Besides Aristotle, Cicero became a major source for notions of natural law. He had defined natural law in his *De Legibus* I, 6 as highest immutable reason ingrained in nature ("lex est ratio summa insita in natura"). Reason itself, as part of that nature, commands rational beings to do certain things and not to do others. Issues of specific content, such as the legitimacy of self-preservation, and hence self-defense, were argued ad hoc and as political expediency demanded, as in Cicero's defense of Milo who had been indicted for his responsibility in the killing of Clodius in 52 BC. Other items, such as religion, family, or friendship mentioned in the same context rather came as conventional expectations. In *De Re Publica*, III, 11, 19, his formulation "tribuere id cuique" was mirrored by Ulpian's later "suum cuique tribuere" (D. 1, 1, 10), and animals were not explicitly excluded from natural law; whereas in *De Finibus* (3.20.67), natural law was only part of the life of rational human beings (Winkel 2016). The *Corpus Iuris Civilis* took up a number of prescriptions as orders of natural law, though for all animals, such as procreation and the raising of offspring (Inst. I, 2).

Christian theologians followed Paul's letter to the Romans 2:14–15, in turn rooted in a Jewish commentary tradition and in Greek philosophy, and identified the Decalogue with natural law, as implanted into men's hearts (Otto 2006, 74). The *Decretum Gratiani* mentioned marriage, inheritance, the right to bring up your own children, and explained them as items mentioned in the Decalogue and Gospels. Christian theologians appropriated Aristotelian teleology and integrated it with the Christian creator-god. God's intentions and greatness could thus be gauged from his creation, though his entire reason and wisdom could not be fully known or comprehended by mortal men. Natural law thus came to address that part of divine reason accessible to a limited degree to created men. Men were assumed to be equipped both with knowledge about divine commands and the ability to fulfill certain acts that followed from these commands as part of the divine order of creation, such as the commands of the Decalogue. Natural law addressed speculations about the ability of men to recognize and understand their relationship to their divine creator (Schmoeckel 2008). For example, to Aquinas (1225–74), natural law addressed the spark of divine light mirrored in us, accessible to human reason only to a degree, given the fundamental inequality between men and their creator. Thus natural law was subject to change, according to changes in human nature and man's ability to understand the will of the divine creator, and therefore also different from the unchangeable divine eternal law. Nevertheless, Aquinas did mention as the substance of natural law what had been earlier argued by Cicero and Ulpian, namely the "suum cuique tribuere" (Perkams 2008, 136). Other arguments addressed the possibility of ordering natural law and civil law chronologically, or distinguishing different levels of natural law, such as a law of nature comprising the natural instincts of men and beasts, a *ius gentium primaevum* common to all men as rational creatures, ordering obedience to God and parents, and a *ius gentium secundarium*, developing within human societies and practiced in most human polities (Ilting 1978, 264–65; Thier 2014; Brett 2003, 181–282).

Developed primarily by Duns Scotus (1265–1308) and William of Ockham (1285–1347), an alternative argument denied that divine commands could be assumed to be consistent with our created nature. Rather, the obliging will of God wills us to perform certain acts. Duns Scotus argued that the *lex naturalis* only entailed that humans love God and forbade them to hate him, but that it even remained doubtful whether the third commandment, to praise the Lord, was part of that *lex naturalis* in this strict sense (Honnefelder 2005, 123–24). The other commandments were not part of this strict *lex naturalis* but only in a wider sense, insofar as they were generally acknowledged to agree with the principles of the *lex naturalis*. Thus, voluntarism insisted on the need to oblige the will of an all-powerful God. The freedom of this God also meant that there could be no unchangeable contents of an eternal divine law, for God was not bound, but free to change his will (Ilting 1978).

# 3  REFORMATION AND EMPIRE

During the sixteenth century, two developments moved the rise of natural law to center stage. Mainly within emerging Protestantism, natural law developed into a potential catalogue of suprapositive prescriptions ordering our life in this world. Natural law was also discussed with regard to the new experiences and challenges of world-encompassing European empires.

Martin Luther (1483–1546) wrote his 1517 *Disputation against Scholastic Theology* under the influence of Ockham's nominalism, as taught by Gabriel Biel (ca. 1420–95). However, contrary to Biel, Luther denied that men were able to love God sufficiently with their own powers: "To love God above all things by nature is a fictitious term" (Dieter 2014, 33, 37). Humans cannot, *pace* Aquinas, live up to the commands of the divine creator, but they can understand God's message in the Gospels (Stöve 2002). But Luther also denied Ockham's claim that God was satisfied with the limited performance of men's natural abilities. Instead, an unbridgeable gulf separated these demands from men's limited capabilities. Created nature thus allowed humans to understand the divine command, but not to fulfill it sufficiently (against Ockham and nominalism), nor was human nature part of a natural entelechy enabling men to live up to God's commands. For the more limited purposes of living in this world and irrelevant for attaining grace, however, it remained possible to delineate a natural law, perceptible despite the limits of the human mind based on reason alone.

Philip Melanchthon had first argued that the institution of civil authority originated with the Fall (Melanchthon, *Loci* 1521, in Melanchthon 1978, 346). But from the 1530s, he understood civil order as part of creation (Melanchthon CR 16, col 442: "Talis politia est ordinatio dei") and thus of natural law (Dreitzel 1970, 140–42; Frank 2005; Strohm 2002; Melanchthon 1532; Melanchthon 1538; Melanchthon 1543). Melanchthon concluded from his reading of Aristotle that the polity could educate its citizens, and that its laws could not only be obligations, but also give direction. In this context, he developed his approach to the three uses of law: obligating even those who do not believe; to present men their sins and instill them with fear; and finally for the true believers, the ability to recognize what good works are, though their performance was not sufficient for salvation. For this third use, natural law became a catalogue of prescriptions for men living together in this world regarding their relations to each other. He thus began to transform natural law from an exercise in philosophizing about the relationship between God and creation into a catalogue of prescriptions usable for purposes of inner-worldly relations

(Schmoeckel 2008; Schmoeckel 2014), without disputing the relevance of the revealed word of God as interpreted by theology.

He developed his ideas from his comments on Aristotle's *Nichomachean Ethics* (1529–31), to his comments on Cicero's *De officiis* (1562) (Dreitzel 1970, 90–96; Strohm 2000; Deflers 2005, 175–273; Scheible 1997, 86–94). Plato and Cicero were his prime sources regarding common principles of (human) reason (Melanchthon CR 16:389). His detailing of prescriptions, however, went beyond these sources. For example, the Bruni Latin translation of Aristotle's book 5 of the *Nichomachean Ethics* had not provided any catalogue of laws (Bruni 1469, 89). But Melanchthon provided six specific natural laws, partly in accordance with various suggestions about the substance of natural law we mentioned above: (1) to honor and obey God and punish those in disobedience; (2) to not harm others without just cause; (3) procreation, the conservation of the species; (4) the order to distinguish truth and falsehood and to keep contracts; (5) to respect property, an issue Melanchthon says the philosophers understood as *ius naturae*, others as *ius gentium*; and (6) the institution of human authority (Melanchthon 1530–32, 383–87; Friedeburg 2015, 213–21). Jurists in Melanchthon's wake, like Johann Oldendorp, attempted to bring the Decalogue, natural law, the *Corpus Iuris* and current positive law into a concrete relationship of successive dependency on each other (Friedeburg and Seidler, 120–26).

From the second half of the sixteenth century, a heterogeneous group of primarily Catholic and Reformed authors began to relate natural law to notions of *civitas* or *regnum* in the sense of a "shared juridical space that transcends the natural being of its subjects" (Brett 2011). They began to make claims regarding to what extent such a *civitas* was legally able, or not able, to do: for example, to claim *dominium* over the seas, related to discussions of how *dominium* as part of natural law had developed. For this debate, civil positive law was of little help. Instead, the nature, origins and extent of civil order increasingly became the focus of debates on what natural law was. Speculations about natural law prior to the introduction of civil order and about the introduction of civil order itself entered debate, but also about rights of individuals before or against civil order. For example, Domingo de Soto (1494–1560) argued that self-preservation (*jus se conservandi*) was a basic right provided by natural law, while Aquinas had only argued a general natural inclination for self-preservation—not a right (Brett 2011, 20–21). Increasingly, writers on natural law moved away from assumptions based on a natural entelechy and toward the construction of man as free to choose among different options of action, and thus to being primarily the "subject of law." Government was consequently described as "commanding choice" by virtue of its laws, a choice necessarily made by "subjects capable of choice" (Brett 2011, 62). In effect, debates on natural law changed subtly from clarifying the place of men in a natural entelechy, or with regard to the will of God, to legal contexts of subjects vis-à-vis a civil government commanding choice by law.

In his *De legibus, ac Deo legislatore* (1617), Francis Suarez attempted to further develop Thomist natural law into a general moral-philosophical foundation of society: He remained oriented toward Aquinas's starting point that God created humans capable of fulfilling his commands by being part of a developmental entelechy. He argued that the laws specific to each community were positive and open to negotiation; that divine eternal law was only known in a very general sense and only if promulgated by God. Natural law was that part of divine law that applied to the moral nature of men—part obligation, but also part of divine creation. Men arrange according to their nature their affairs in society, while the moral natural law obliges them to act in certain directions and not in other directions. In case of a breakdown of specific artificial manmade institutions of government, men in need can refer to other people's private property: goals set by natural law could override what was instituted by human contract only (Haakonssen 1996, 16–18). Suarez tried to reconcile the tension between voluntarism and nominalism with the emphasis on the obligating will of God, and Thomist realism with its emphasis upon a created entelechy enabling humans to fulfill God's will, by distinguishing different notions of the meaning of law. Natural law was promulgated both in the Decalogue and in human reason; within the human mind, natural law existed as an "act of judgment." For God, natural law existed as his will and his reason. In this argument, according to Knud Haakonssen, "natural law is both indicative of what is in itself good and evil [intellectualist/realist], and preceptive [obligatory] in the sense that it creates an obligation in people to do the good and avoid the evil." Suarez apparently held some notion of subjective rights as the means to achieve the goals of natural law, such as *dominium* over ourselves (liberty) and over goods (property) (Haakonssen 1996, 22–23).

# 4  GROTIUS, HOBBES, AND PUFENDORF

Whatever the affinity of Protestantism to an emerging new meaning of natural law, the heterogeneous ensembles of arguments and confessions characterized as "Protestant" lacked effectively two qualities: first, they had no effective juridical hierarchy by which to find and establish the truth of a matter that the Church of Rome at least in principle had. Second, they lacked enforcement mechanisms to quell diverging developments of doctrine.

Hugo Grotius indirectly exemplifies these weaknesses. During his time as advisor to Oldenbarneveldt in the Netherlands, Grotius openly supported an attitude that the Reformed Church should not interfere in the affairs of magistrates in the Republic of Holland. Grotius simultaneously peppered his *De Iure Belli ac Pacis* with biblical references to buttress his own argument (Nellen 2015). In the Prolegomena, paragraph 5, Grotius attacked Socrates' opponents, the sophists, for denying that there was any meaningful law of nature for human beings (Grotius 1625). In paragraph 6, he insisted that from all insight gathered so far into the matter, adults and even children have knowledge that prompts them to take into account the good of others. "With an impelling desire for society," he then argued in paragraph 8, "the maintenance of social order ... is the source of law properly so called." This law of nature orders to "abstaining from that which is another's, the restoration to another of anything of his which we may have, together with any gain which we may have received from it" (Grotius 1625, Prolegomena 8, 12–13). Grotius's attack on the sophists led Richard Tuck to understand both him and Hobbes as being similarly engaged in reconstructing the legitimacy of government against the challenge of skepticism (Tuck 1993, 1154–1345). Others insist that Grotius primarily used the traditional humanist reservoir of sources, such as Cicero and Roman law, and Baldus (Zagorin 2000). To Grotius, "Ius naturale in the strict sense is, then, every action which does not injure any other person's suum, which in effect means that it is every *suum* which does not conflict with the *sua* of others." On that basis, Grotius argued that also the retrospective history of mankind showed that social interaction was effectively possible, irrespective of religious persuasion (Haakonssen 1996, 27).

The protection of the "suum" thus became a central notion for Grotius in order to organize social intercourse among men. Grotius relied for his own outline of natural law on Cicero's explorations in *De lege* and on Roman (private) law. Cicero's own arguments had been meant to refute Sophist arguments identifying the Roman military with pirates. Against this claim, Cicero had intended to justify Roman expansion with a natural law doctrine based on Stoic arguments (Straumann 2015, 89); arguments that in turn claimed a rational order of the universe. Grotius took over Cicero's natural law while neglecting the Stoic framework. Teleological considerations concerning the good life, for example, in terms of living in harmony with the rational order of the world, moved to backstage. "Justice" became primarily related to the protection of titles to property (Straumann 2015, 107). As a result, Grotius's natural law came about by the

> crucial move to gear the Aristotelian framework of justice toward a theory of justice ultimately inspired by Cicero and the Roman jurists that has nothing in common with Aristotle's eudemonistic concerns. Grotius uses the elements of Aristotelian Ethics suited to adaptation to the obligation and property law categories of Roman Private Law . . . Grotius thus foists the theory of justice developed by Aristotle for the context of the polis onto a property orientated theory of justice of Roman provenance which he then transfers to the sphere of the oceans, understood as the stage of nature, and has them develop their full legal effect there. . . . (Straumann 2015, 124)

In doing so, Grotius moved further away from an Aristotelian entelechy as well as from a Thomist rational understanding of God and his wishes. Instead, he formulated effective grounds for obligations and duties enforced on the individual by power, utility, or (individual) interest, but independent of virtue, however understood. Grotius produced his argument on obligation in *De Iure Pacis ac Belli* by claiming the intelligibility of natural law and the effectiveness of its obligating nature, in particular with respect to understanding also the claims of others resulting from natural law, and by that mutual understanding the possibility of an order based on individuals who recognized that their individual interests were best served by also recognizing the interests of others. Grotius' actors are thus individuals with *sua* and the willingness to respect the *sua* of others (Haakonssen 1996, 28).

In assuming men's ability to grasp the law of nature and act correctly upon it, Grotius proved to be "in anachronistic terms, a realist," insofar as human beings can understand the demands of natural law following from their need of sociability, though without direct recourse to divine revelation (Haakonssen 1996, 34). Instead of referring to categories of moral goodness as defined in scripture, individuals were meant to submit to natural law in the pursuit of their interest in their *sua*. To this end, Grotius developed a theory of binding promises as part of natural law based on the (human) will (*recta voluntas*) and human reason (*usus rationis*) (Hartung 2004, 295–96, on Grotius, *De Jure Belli ac Pacis*, chapter 11, De promissis), not on *relations of justice among men*. Indeed, as Annabel Brett concluded "Grotius's analysis of promising therefore posited, in a human being with the use of reason outside any civil state, a natural power of disposing of his or her actions at will that is, by implication, liberty as a natural right . . ." Brett fully acknowledges that Grotius did not explicitly address the issue in these terms, but indeed stayed away from any such conclusion (Brett 2011, 106–7). She supports Knud Haakonssen's crucial insight that "natural law theory in general was not deeply individualistic and dominated by ideas of subjective right . . . [for] few thinkers embraced the idea that moral agency, or personhood, might consist in asserting claims against the rest of the world with no other guidance than one's lights," though precisely Grotius and Hobbes as major icons of the rise of natural law theories did make "attempts at this argument" (Haakonssen 1996, 5). Such attempts can be found in Grotius's Theses LVI. Their basis proved to be Roman law *remedies*, that is, juridical *actiones*, open to a Roman citizen in order to recover what was one's *dominium*. With respect to just causes rendering a war a just war, Grotius distinguished defense, recovery, punishment, and failure to fully discharge an obligation, oriented to Roman law *actiones*, and transformed them into the four natural rights to self-defense, property, the collection of debts, and to punish (Straumann 2015, 161, 170).

From Grotius, debates on natural law began to attempt to develop a general foundation for civil order and its positive laws (Stolleis 1988, 277–278). Samuel von Pufendorf did include in his conception of the relation of men prior to the institution of a civil state bonds, such as the family, that allow individuals to work together and interact to a substantial degree. But natural law writers did not return to the identification of physical and moral entities, the "deriving of moral duties from a moral nature embedded in the person." Instead, in one way or the other, they argued that our moral duties, "arise through [artificial and this-worldly] imposition (impositionis)" (Hunter 2003, 175).

The relationship of Hobbes and Grotius has been subject to intense controversy (Tuck 1993; Zagorin 2000). Grotius attempted to legitimize Dutch commercial interests, including recovering or claiming goods from the Spanish and Portuguese (Haakonssen 1996, 30); Hobbes wrote *The Elements, De Cive* and *Leviathan* against the background of the British wars of religion. As Pufendorf remarked, a number of Hobbes's points were primarily made to undermine the legitimacy of the opponents of the king in the most fundamental sense, by attacking their arguments; in particular with respect to the intelligibility and obligating nature of God's commands as revealed in scripture, and of the ancient constitution of the kingdoms of England and Scotland. To the opponents of the king, both sources were obliged to defend, even against magistrates legitimately instituted, God's word and the law against the servants of the king. To Hobbes, a pervasive belief in these claims among gullible people had led England (and Scotland and Ireland) into the misery of civil wars (Friedeburg 2015, 544–54). Hobbes denied any obligation sufficient to keep the peace among men but that of a superior (human) agency, and resorted to the dictate of right reason among men to submit to the law of nature; that is, to seek peace, in order to avoid the terrible state of nature, in the only way that such avoidance was possible—by submitting to an effectively obligating authority, the Leviathan. For while Hobbes identified the seeking of peace as natural law, he did *not* assign obligating force to it, and thus did not conceive natural law as true law. For a true law could only come from an obligating agency. Natural law, in Hobbes's moral philosophy, therefore appears "to efface itself" (Zagorin 2007, 253).

The origins of this argument go back to Leonardo Bruni's (ca. 1370–1444) comments on Aristotle and the neo-Aristotelianism developing from there. In applying Aristotle's physics to politics, Bruni had argued that the imposition of a form, a government, on matter—the people—is the precondition for the civil state to the point of marginalizing issues of faith or virtue in favor of the functional necessity of submission (Mager 1994, 566–70). For Hobbes, in order to describe the terrible state of nature crucial for his argument, Thucydides' description of the plague in Athens, where all social relations collapsed in the face of imminent death and lack of law-enforcing agencies, became an important tool, too (Rahe 2008, 249–320). He put no trust in human language as establishing common notions consistent and strong enough to produce obligating force. Again, sections in Thucydides' description of the civil war within Corcyra hint toward the devaluation of language as a means of rational communication. Hobbes took to heart Thucydides' point about the lack of substance of political ideals. In contrast to what Grotius had argued, the experience of the state of nature suggested to the dictate of right reason the obligation to almost (Zagorin 2000, 39) abandon one's natural right. Confessional theologians attacked both Grotius and Hobbes, for both avoided the interpretation of divine orders by confessional revelation theology. But their arguments ran in different directions (Zagorin 2000, 27).

The execution of the king of Scotland and England in January 1649 was generally condemned in Europe, in particular in the Dutch Republic, and dramatically undermined arguments in favor of legitimate resistance against a lawbreaking king or his servants; an undermining that had also been the aim of Hobbes's argument. But crucially, the way Hobbes had argued his case, denying even an epistemological basis for determining right and wrong independent of civil authority (Haakonssen 1996, 32–33), was roundly condemned. "Hobbes was too useful to be ignored but at the same time too dangerous to leave unchallenged" (Parkin 2003). Subsequently, Pufendorf succeeded in "whitewashing" (David Wootton) parts of Hobbes' arguments to make aspects of them acceptable in Enlightenment Europe (Haakonssen 1996, 31).

Hobbes had noted in his list of pretexts for rebellion the claim to "have a propriety . . . distinct from the dominion of the sovereign power." Having such a "propriety" distinguished a slave, a servant, or a child from a citizen. Common belief in such claims had led, in Hobbes's view, to the disaster of the British wars of religion and the disintegration of monarchy. To Pufendorf's mind, this persuasion motivated Hobbes to argue as he did. He wanted systematically to extinguish any argument in favor of legitimate resistance. Pufendorf in turn criticized Hobbes for having collapsed the contract constructing the state ("in generatione civitatum") with the election of a ruler; a ruler who, according to Hobbes, did not become himself part of this very contract (Pufendorf 1672, lib VII, chapter II, section 9: 679: "inter regem optimatesque nullum pactum intercedere"). Pufendorf suggested that Hobbes argued in this way because of claims put forward by those who had brought "down the regal power" in England, in particular by arguing that there was "a reciprocal faith between the prince and the people" (Pufendorf 1729, 642, 879–80: "fidem inter regem et cives esse reciprocam"). Pufendorf agreed that there were reasons to worry about the dangers of rebellion and thus also about the pretenses made by rebels (Pufendorf 1672, VII, II: 880). Nonetheless, he held that logically, any submission to a ruler as part of founding a state necessarily involved a prior agreement to submit to such a "state" and a different agreement to agree with a ruler to rule that state in a certain manner. This latter agreement necessarily involved obligations on the ruler or rulers, too. For those submitting to being ruled had a right to be ruled according to the aims they pursued when generating the state for their own purposes in the first place (Pufendorf 1672, VII, II: 880). Therefore, should explicit obligations on the ruler be missing, the resulting rule was similar to a "dominium over servants" or to the rule of a military leader over mercenaries (Pufendorf 1672, VII, II: 881: "jus domini in servum, potestas patria in eum"). Pufendorf criticised the Hobbesian construction wherein the sovereign could give legal and legitimate commands beyond the realm of what the true aim of the founding of the state had been. The ruler could, for example, order subjects to kill family members (Pufendorf 1672, VII, II: 882–83). Pufendorf also insisted that certain orders concerning lawmaking or war and peace, made by rulers, had to be understood to be decisions of the state by virtue of the ruler's office. But other actions, such as eating or drinking or marrying, were not to be considered matters of state. Only that which "ad finem civitatum spectant" was to be understood as the ruler's public will (Pufendorf 1672, VII, II: 887). Thus, the monarch governed the people and his will was the will of the *civitas*, the state, only insofar as the expression of his will agreed with the specific conditions upon which the people had agreed, when uniting into a *civitas*.

These differences with Hobbes rested not least on Pufendorf's argument about the substantial ability of men in the state of nature to live together, form families, and interact. Though their interaction lacked an effective superior, and thus had only insufficient obliging force, social and economic life was still possible in a manner quite distinct to Thucydides' description of human relations during the plague in Athens, as employed by Hobbes. To Pufendorf, (created) human nature creates in turn certain features of human interaction to be addressed as natural law, such as self-preservation, a recognition that one's own abilities are insufficient for such self-preservation, sociability (i.e., the ability to successfully interact with others), and the mutual recognition by men of these abilities and the need for social life. Rights in this account derive mainly from the mutually acknowledged duty under natural law to observe and respect these rights not only as one's own rights, but as those of others, too (Haakonssen 1996, 38–39).

According to Knud Haakonssen, this feature raises the issue of a fundamental ambiguity in Pufendorf's thought in relation to the nature of the obligation of natural law. If Pufendorf understood sociability—that is, recognizing and respecting other people's rights—to rest on an acute understanding of effective self-preservation, then the obligating force of natural law is reduced to self-interest. If sociability, however, was meant to be an inherent feature of its own, then a dilemma arises. It rests on a divine being only active as a creator of beings invested with sociability. But it is then questionable whether one should talk about natural law as obligating force, or if obligation is willed by God. The issue then becomes how we have to understand our obligations to God in the first place (Haakonssen 1996, 42–45).

It is telling for the rise of natural law during the seventeenth century that seemingly nominalist/voluntarist and realist options returned, but only after they had been taken away from confessional theology and become the domain of philosophy and jurisprudence. It was ultimately this capture of the debate under the heading "natural law," no matter how fundamentally different the various natural law positions remained toward each other, that allows us to address the whole process as the "rise of natural law."

# 5  The Eighteenth Century

Once this breakthrough had been accomplished by the reception of a few authors who still today dominate the canon of political thought, the further development of natural law took quite different paths, highly dependent on the philosophical scene and political environment in each polity. In the Protestant territories of the Holy Roman Empire, Christian Thomasius (1655–1728) and Christian Wolff (1679–1754) further developed natural law as the normative framework for the territorial ruler, shielding him from claims of the established churches, and effectively supporting his "absolutism" for the course of reform (de Wall 2006; Hunter 2001; Hunter 2007).

In England, debates developed around the question whether an original deist natural religion could be identified that had been "shrouded" by a "superstitious cortex" of dominant churches (Harrison 1990, 92). The enormously influential David Hume (1711–76) sought by his writings to actively combat the twin major dangers of superstition and enthusiasm. He agreed with Grotius, Hobbes, and Pufendorf that men needed to live in society and, in order to do so, needed to be effectively obligated. Hume understood riots of his own time, for example in London, as an outcome of the dangers of insufficient obligation and the abuse of alleged rights and liberties. But he rejected theories of contract that explained existing societal institutions by the will of those entering a contract: such an individual will only worked within very close, small communities. Beyond them, humans were led by (artificial, manmade) practices into which they were born and that were upheld (or broken) by "luck, foresight and imitative behaviour"

(Haakonssen 1996, 103–6). In effect, Hume provided further philosophical foundation for the increasing importance of historical inquiry into the inner-worldly contingency of the development of societies into polities that would eventually push back the notion of a "state of nature" and a "contract" establishing the civil state. Hume therefore rejected the two notions prevalent in England's political factions—the "Tory" one that authority was ultimately divinely instituted, and the "Whig" one that it derived from a contract establishing civil society—and instead argued that allegiance to government rested on interests to be protected and justice to be served. Insofar as these interests are served, allegiance to the government then became habitual, though constantly endangered by enthusiasm and superstition. Thus, the perception and opinions among a people of what protection and justice are and how they are served constantly played an important role (Haakonssen 1996, 112–13).

In Britain's American colonies, by contrast, arguments about the need to defend the constitution of the colonies, under which its subjects and their property were protected and justice was served, against the corruption of a tyrant and government conspiracy, developed not least from English thought developed in response to the violations of law by Charles I (r. 1625–1649) and Charles II (r. 1660–1685), by such writers as Thomas Harrington and Algernon Sydney (1623–83), none of them primarily natural law writers (Bailyn 1992, 34–35). Indeed, in his *Discourses concerning Government*, a particularly influential book in the American colonies, Algernon Sydney had likened the need of the English nation to defend itself against the violations of its rights by Charles II to the right of every individual man to defend himself, citing the acquittal of a man who had killed a thief (Friedeburg 2002, 242). After Britain's victory over France in the Seven Years' War had effectively removed all plausible military threat from the colonies, and hence any need for large-scale military protection, these colonies also rejected all further financial demands. Beyond this constellation, American jurisprudence seemed to be characterized by a much stronger emphasis on natural rights. But as Knud Haakonssen argued, in order to arrive at subjective rights, the argument had to be developed that individuals were able to impose sufficient obligation on themselves, as a basis for the exercise of rights, rather than needing to be obligated by another party. In particular, the last step was at odds with the natural law paradigm, in which rights only followed to fulfill obligations. Indeed, the earliest systematic attack on this sequence in order to found an American, rights-centered counterargument, Haakonssen found only *after* the end of the War of Independence. During the beginning of the critique and the actual War of Independence, Grotius, Pufendorf, and Locke were generally quoted as authoritative texts by *both* loyalists and patriots alike (Bailyn 1992, 32–33, 77–78), for none of them had advocated a unilateral right to revolt based on alleged individual rights from a state of nature. But conspiracy theories about the corruption of government and its attempt at enforcing tyranny and slavery on British subjects, as Charles I and Charles II had attempted (Bailyn 1992, 34–51), explained to colonists the need to defend themselves against such enslavement rather than consistent arguments from natural law with its delicate balance of rights and obligations.

# BIBLIOGRAPHY

Bailyn, Bernard. 1967. *The Ideological Origins of the American Revolution*. Cambridge, MA: Harvard University Press.

Brett, Annabel. 2011. *Changes of State: Nature and the Limits of the City in Early Modern Natural Law*. Princeton: Princeton University Press.

Brett, Annabel. 2003. *Liberty, Right and Nature*. Cambridge: Cambridge University Press.

Bruni, Leonardo. 1469. *Aristoteles: Ethica ad Nicomachum*. Bayrische Staatsbibliothek.

Deflers, Isabelle. 2005. *Lex und Ordo: Eine rechtshistorische Untersuchung zur Rechtsauffassung Melanchthons*. Berlin: Duncker & Humblot.

Dieter, Theodor. 2014. "Luther as Late Medieval Theologian: His Positive and Negative Use of Nominalism and Realism." In *Oxford Handbook of Martin Luther's Theology*, edited by Irene Dingel, Volker Leppin, and L'Ubomir Batka, 31–48. Oxford: Oxford University Press.

Dreitzel, Horst. 1970. *Protestantischer Aristotelismus und absoluter Staat: Die Politica des Henning Arnisaeus, ca. 1575–1636*. Wiesbaden: Steiner.

Eckel, Jan. 2014. *Die Ambivalenz des Guten: Menschenrechte in der internationalen Politik*. Göttingen: Vandenhoeck & Ruprecht.

Frank, Günter. 2005. "The Reason of Acting: Melanchthon's Concept of Practical Philosophy and the Question of the Unity and Consistency of His Philosophy." In *Moral Philosophy on the Threshold of Modernity*, edited by J. Kraye and R. Saarinen, 217–233. Dordrecht: Springer.

Friedeburg, Robert von. 2015. *Luther's Legacy: The Thirty Years' War and the Modern Notion of "State" in the Empire, 1530s to 1790s*. Cambridge: Cambridge University Press.

Friedeburg, Robert von. 2002. *Self-Defence and Religious Strife in Early Modern Europe: England and Germany 1530–1680*. Aldershot, UK: Ashgate.

Friedeburg, Robert von, and Michael Seidler. 2007. "The Holy Roman Empire of the German Nation." In *European Political Thought 1450–1700*, edited by Howell L. Lloyd, et al., 102–175. New Haven, CT: Yale University Press.

Grotius, Hugo. *De Iure Belli ac Pacis (1625)*. 1925. Translated by Francis W. Kelsey. Oxford: Oxford University Press.

Haakonssen, Knud. 1996. *Natural Law and Moral Philosophy: From Grotius to the Scottish Enlightenment*. Cambridge: Cambridge University Press.

Harrison, Peter. 1990. *"Religion" and the Religions in the English Enlightenment*. Cambridge: Cambridge University Press.

Hartung, Gerald. 2004. "Althusius' Vertragstheorie im Kontext spätmittelalterlicher Jurisprudenz und Scholastik." In *Jurisprudenz, Politische Theorie und Politische Theologie*, edited by Frederick S. Carney, et al., 287–304. Berlin: Duncker & Humblot.

Honnefelder, Ludger. 2005. *Duns Scotus*. Munich: Beck.

Hunter, Ian. 2003. "The Love of a Sage of the Command of a Superior: The Natural Law Doctrines of Leibniz and Pufendorf." In *Early Modern Natural Law Theories*, edited by T. J. Hochstrasser and P. Schröder, 169–194. Dordrecht: Springer.

Hunter, Ian. 2001. *Rival Enlightenments: Civil and Metaphysical Philosophy in Early Modern Germany*. Cambridge: Cambridge University Press.

Hunter, Ian. 2007. *The Secularization of the Confessional State: The Political Thought of Christian Thomasius*. Cambridge: Cambridge University Press.

Ilting, Karl-Heinz. 1978. "Naturrecht." In *Geschichtliche Grundbegriffe*, edited by Otto Brunner, et al., 4: 245–313. Stuttgart: Klett-Cotta.

Luig, Klaus, 1972. "Zur Verbreitung des Naturrechts in Europa." *Tijdschrift voor Rechtsgeschiedenis* XL: 539–557. Leiden: Brill.

Mager, Wolfgang. 1994. "Republik." In: *Geschichtliche Grundbegriffe*, edited by Otto Brunner, et al., 5: 549–652. Stuttgart: Klett-Cotta.

Melanchthon, Philip. 1532. "Commentarii at Epistolam Pauli ad Romanos." In *Corpus Reformatorum* (CR), edited by Karl Gottlieb Bretschneider and Heinrich Ernst Bindseil. Vol. 21. Halle.

Melanchthon, Philip. 1538. "De dignitate legume." In *Corpus Reformatorum* (CR), edited by Karl Gottlieb Bretschneider and Heinrich Ernst Bindseil. Vol. 21. Halle.

Melanchthon, Philip. 1530-32. "Enarratio libri V Ethicorum Aristoteles." In *Corpus Reformatorum* (CR), edited by Karl Gottlieb Bretschneider and Heinrich Ernst Bindseil, vol. 16, 279–416. Halle.

Melanchthon, Philip. 1850. "Librum Politicorum Aristotelis." In *Corpus Reformatorum* (CR), edited by Karl Gottlieb Bretschneider and Heinrich Ernst Bindseil. Vol. 16. Halle.

Melanchthon, Philip. 1543. "De Magistratus Civilibus." In *Corpus Reformatorum* (CR), edited by Karl Gottlieb Bretschneider and Heinrich Ernst Bindseil. Vol. 21. Halle.

Melanchthon, Philip. 1978. *Melanchthons Werke in Auswahl*, edited by Robert Stupperich. II Band, 1. Teil, edited by Hans Engelland. Gütersloh: Evangelische Verlagsgemeinschaft.

Nellen, Henk. 2015. *Hugo Grotius: A Lifelong Struggle for Peace in Church and State, 1583–1645*. Leiden: Brill.

Otto, Eckart. 2006. *Mose*. Munich: Beck.

Parkin, Jonathan. 2003. "Taming the Leviathan—Reading Hobbes in Seventeenth-Century Europe." In *Early Modern Natural Law Theories*, edited by T. J. Hochstrasser and P. Schröder, 31–52. Dordrecht: Springer.

Perkams, Matthias. 2008. "Aquinas' Interpretation of the Aristotelian Virtue of Justice and His Doctrine of Natural Law." In *Virtue Ethics in the Middle Ages: Commentaries on Aristotle's Nichomachean Ethics, 1200–1500*, edited by Istvan P. Bejczy, 131–152. Leiden: Brill.

Pufendorf, Samuel von. 1672. *De Iure Naturae et Gentium*. Lund.

Pufendorf, Samuel von. 1729. *The Law of Nature and Nations, Done into English by Basil Kennett . . . To which are added All the large Notes of Mr Barbeyrac*. London.

Rahe, Paul A. 2008. *Against Throne and Altar: Machiavelli and Political Theory under the English Republic*. Cambridge: Cambridge University Press.

Scheible, Heinz. 1997. *Melanchthon*. Munich: Beck.

Schmoeckel, Mathias. 2008. "Erkenntnis durch ratio und conscientia: Die Begründung der modernen Wissenschaftlichkeit des Rechts durch Melanchthons Naturrechtslehre." In *Religion und Rationalität*, edited by G. K. Hasselhoff and M. Meyer-Blanck, 179–220. Würzburg: Ergon.

Schmoeckel, Mathias. 2014. *Das Recht der Reformation*. Tübingen: Mohr Siebeck.

Seckendorff, Veit Ludwig von. 2006. "Entwurff oder Versuch Von dem allgemeinen oder natürlichen Recht/nach Anleitung der Bücher Hugo Grotii." In *Seckendorff, Veit Ludwig von, Teutsche Reden und Entwuff von dem allgemeinen oder natuerlichen Recht*, 403–466. Reprint of 1691 edition. Tübingen: Max Niemeyer Verlag.

Stolleis, Michael. 1988. *Geschichte des öffentlichen Rechts*. Munich: Beck.

Stöve, E. 2002. "Natürliches Recht und Heilige Schrift. Zu einem vergessenen Aspekt in Martin Luthers Hermeneutik." In *Recht und Reformation. Festschrift für Gottfried Seebass*, 11–26. Gütersloh: Gütersloher Verlagshaus.

Straumann, Benjamin. 2015. *Roman Law in the State of Nature: The Classical Foundation of Natural Law.* Cambridge: Cambridge University Press.

Strohm, C. 2000. "Die Voraussetzungen reformatorischer Naturrechtslehre in der humanistischen Jurisprudenz." *Zeitschrift der Savigny Stiftung für Rechtsgeschichte* 117: 398–413.

Strohm, C. 2002. "Zugänge zum Naturrecht bei Melanchthon." In *Der Theologe Melanchthon*, edited by G. Frank, et al., 339–356. Stuttgart: Frommann-Holzboog.

Thier, Andreas. 2014. "Heilsgeschichte und naturrechtliche Ordnung: Naturrecht vor und nach dem Sündenfall." In *Naturrecht in Antike und früher Neuzeit*, edited by Matthias Armgardt and Tilman Repgen, 151–172. Tübingen: Mohr Siebeck.

Tuck, Richard. 1993. *Philosophy and Government 1572–1651.* Cambridge: Cambridge University Press.

Wall, Heiner de. 2006. "Staat und Staatskirche als Garanten der Toleranz." In *Christian Thomasius 1655–1728*, edited by Heiner Luck, 117–133. Hildesheim: Olms.

Winkel, Laurens. 2016. *Deux conceptions du droit naturel dans l'Antiquité.* Paris: Revue historique de droit français et étranger.

Zagorin, Perez. 2000. "Hobbes without Grotius." *History of Political Thought* 21: 16–40.

Zagorin, Perez. 2007. "Hobbes as a Theorist of Natural Law." *Intellectual History Review* 17: 239–255.

# CHAPTER 42

EIGHTEENTH-CENTURY
NEOLOGY

ERIC CARLSSON

AROUND 1770, neology (*Neologie*), a term originating in eighteenth-century literary criticism, came to be applied to a movement among German Protestants to revise Christian theology in keeping with modern, enlightened norms. By the twentieth century the label had mostly shed its initial pejorative overtones and now simply designates the post-Wolffian form of *Aufklärung* theology. The movement peaked during the reign of Frederick the Great (r. 1740–86) of Prussia, where it gained semi-official sponsorship, but it found supporters among Lutheran and Reformed clerics and scholars throughout the German states and beyond. Construing Christianity as a practical religion consonant with modern knowledge and grounded in the self-reflective experience of the pious, reasonable individual, neology spurned key parts of Protestant orthodoxy and Pietism, while defending the presumed essence of Christianity against deism and unbelief. Proponents drew on theories of natural religion and a new language of feeling and sentiment, and they seized on critical history as a particularly useful tool for their reconstructive efforts. Historical scholarship offered a means of rethinking the nature and authority of scripture, of distancing the claims of the dogmatic tradition, and of recasting theology as a progressive enterprise. In historicizing scripture and creeds and shifting focus from dogma (*fides quae creditur*) to the faith and experience of the believing subject (*fides qua creditur*), neology marks a sea change in the history of Protestant thought. While the movement has been held responsible for secularizing Christian theology from within, its central concerns and approaches were taken up most immediately by the German liberal Protestant tradition.

Spanning a loose network of individuals with overlapping concerns, neology had no single dominant voice. Its ranks included pastors, court preachers, superintendents, and government officials, notably Johann Friedrich Wilhelm Jerusalem (1709–89), who had a prolific career in the service of the Braunschweig court; as well as August Friedrich Wilhelm Sack (1703–86), Johann Joachim Spalding (1714–1804), Friedrich Germanus Lüdke (1730–92), and Wilhelm Abraham Teller (1734–1804), who all ended up in various posts in Berlin. The scholarly underpinnings of neology were supplied by members of the leading Protestant theology and philosophy faculties, including Johann August Ernesti (1707–81) at Leipzig; Johann Salomo Semler (1725–91), Johann August Nösselt (1734–1807), Johann August Eberhard (1739–1809), and August Hermann Niemeyer (1754–1828) at Halle; Johann Gottlieb Toellner (1724–74) and Gotthilf Samuel Steinbart (1738–1809) at Frankfurt/Oder; Johann David Michaelis (1717–91), Gottfried Less (1736–97), and Gottlieb Jakob Planck (1751–1833) at Göttingen; and Johann Jakob Griesbach (1745–1812), Johann Gottfried Eichhorn (1752–1827), and Johann Philipp Gabler (1753–1826) at Jena.

The theological Enlightenment reached a broad public through various media. Clergy updated liturgies, hymnals, and prayer books, and took to the pulpit, the putative lectern of the *Aufklärung*, to preach ear-catching sermons that steered clear of speculative theology and stressed practical matters and daily living. Gifted writers like Jerusalem and Spalding penned popular bestsellers commending an enlightened version of the faith to the skeptical and modern-minded. Academics generated a vast output of biblical and historical scholarship, much of which was made accessible through debates and reviews in the journal press, not least Friedrich Nicolai's *Allgemeine deutsche Bibliothek* (1765–1806), which Eichhorn in 1794 could claim had worked a "wonderful new revolution in theology" (cited in Aner [1929] 1964, 11) (K. Barth [1947] 2002; Hirsch 1964; Sparn 1985; Hornig 1998; Beutel et al. 2006; Beutel 2009).

Neology overlapped with and drew on other versions of the theological Enlightenment, especially Anglican Latitudinarianism and Arminian and Collegiant strands of Dutch and Swiss Reformed thought. From the perspective of Western theology more broadly, neology's roots stretched deeply into the Christian humanist tradition. Humanism combined philological and historical scholarship with an irenic and individualistic construal of the faith that stressed human freedom and dignity and the ethical teachings of Jesus, often at the expense of sacraments, creeds, and ecclesiastical authority. While theological humanism had been muted in Germany since the late sixteenth century, Philipp Melanchthon and Georg Calixtus were often cited, justifiably or not, as homegrown exemplars of a scholarly and nondogmatic Lutheranism. Also influential among *Aufklärung* theologians was a large body of text-critical and historical work on the Bible by scholars such as Jean Le Clerc, Richard Simon, John Mill, Richard Bentley, Jean-Alphonse Turretin, and Johann Jakob Wettstein, who not infrequently shared humanist concerns. And while neologians universally opposed naturalism and "atheism," their apologetic efforts led them to engage with and learn from radical critiques of revealed religion, including Spinozist and deist writings that raised pressing historical and philosophical questions about miracles, special revelation, and the reliability of the biblical texts (Reventlow et al. 1988; Reventlow 2010; Schubert 2002; Sheehan 2005; Sorkin 2008).

Neology's unique profile among Enlightenment theologies reflected the specific features of intellectual and ecclesio-political life in eighteenth-century Germany. Three native movements were particularly significant. First, the biographies of leading neologians testify to the pervasive legacy of Pietism. Although they rejected its stress on personal conversion and alleged enthusiasm, theological *Aufklärer* shared its practical emphasis on personal experience and moral transformation over mere creedal loyalty. Second, from Leibnizian and Wolffian philosophy neology absorbed an optimistic anthropology and confidence in an uncomplicated harmony of reason and revelation, which insisted that revealed "truths above reason" would never contradict truths ascertained by rational methods. A third crucial source was eclecticism, a movement that drew on history, natural law, and empiricist philosophy to overcome Orthodox "prejudice" and dogmatism, and yield an irenic form of Lutheranism designed to shore up the faith against naturalism and freethinking (Albrecht 1994). Johann Franz Buddeus (1667–1729), Christoph Matthäus Pfaff (1686–1760), Johann Georg Walch (1693–1775), and Johann Lorenz von Mosheim (1693–1755) developed a "pragmatic" historiography that gently historicized confessional differences and wrote church history not as a clash between the City of God and the City of Man, or between orthodoxy and heresy, but instead described through the lens of providence the contexts of human intentions and actions in time (Reill 1975; Sparn 1989; U. Barth 2004; Fleischer 2006; Beutel 2009).

Uniting central themes in Pietism, Wolffianism, and eclecticism was the prolific Siegmund Jacob Baumgarten (1706–57), who at Halle educated a cadre of future neologians. Baumgarten's chief legacy to theology sprang from his apologetic interests. Perceiving that the main front against freethinking had shifted from philosophy to history, he linked eclectic historiography with the Wolffian mathematical method and quest for "certain knowledge," thereby transforming dogmatics into an historical discipline. To counter deist attacks, Baumgarten also tweaked Orthodox approaches to scripture. Abandoning the doctrine of the Bible's verbal, plenary inspiration, he distinguished scripture's central message regarding "the union of man with God"—a key Pietist trope—from incidental matters of history and nature, which had been accommodated to ancient conceptions. The Bible thus became a vessel of revelation but could not strictly be identified with it: under Baumgarten's aegis, Lutheranism was transformed from a "Bible faith" to a "revelation faith" (Hirsch 1964, 2:378). The distinction between scripture and revelation would be a hallmark of neology, opening the door to a more thoroughly critical approach to the biblical writings (Schloemann 1974; Sparn 1989; Sorkin 2008).

In their efforts to set forth "a teaching of Christianity that meets the needs of our time" (Less 1780, viii), neologians shared the German Enlightenment's practical and anthropocentric orientation. Griesbach's dictum that "the Christian religion . . . is thoroughly practical" (Griesbach 1789, 36) voiced a bedrock principle. Jerusalem characteristically defined "our religion" as "the love of God, which makes itself active in a universal beneficence and love of mankind" (Jerusalem 1769, 358), and Spalding described religion's goal as "the restoration of the divine image" in humans (Spalding 1772, 215). While the idea that true Christianity was to be measured by love of God and neighbor was by no means unique to neology, the movement departed from tradition in placing the religious experience of the individual subject at the center of theological discourse. In his programmatic *Reflection on the Determination of Man* (1748; eleventh edition 1794), Spalding offered an apology for revealed religion, written in the first person, which began with the sensory, aesthetic, and moral experience of the self-reflective individual and concluded that Christian revelation, particularly its doctrines of personal immortality and future reward, best served the "determination of man," the happiness and ethical development of the human species (Spalding 2006). Spalding's method and aims speak to the larger neological project. While *Aufklärung* theologians affirmed the need for special revelation, the primary locus of revelatory activity shifted from scripture to the subjective apprehension of the truths it contained in the "feelings" (*Gefühle*) of the pious, enlightened individual. Indeed, insisted Spalding, it was only as theological knowledge became "enlightened feeling" that it could form the basis of a "Christianity of experience" (*Erfahrungschristentum*) that would issue in moral transformation (Spalding 2005; Printy 2013; Brinkmann 1994). It was not quite accurate to claim, as contemporary and later critics did, that neologians simply reduced religion to morality. Rather, religion and morality were together fitted into a divinely ordained scheme whereby humans might fulfill their teleological potential. While it was not a large step from there to an ethically construed "religion within the boundaries of mere reason," neology continued to operate within a framework constituted by revelation and providence.

Neology's practical principle drove its doctrinal revisions and its rethinking of dogma's claims on individual Christians. Since, as Teller put it, "religion is a matter of the heart and life and not an understanding lost in deep reflections or a head stuffed full of formulas and expressions" (Teller 1792, 110), the pedagogical task became to set forth concepts that would stir an active piety. Theological enlighteners took a dim view of metaphysical speculation and doctrinal subtlety, for they were seen to leave people confused and did nothing to foster moral growth. For a doctrine to be useful it needed to be comprehensible to reason: the mandate for a practical Christianity worked in tandem with both rationalist and empiricist assumptions to enshrine the criteria of reasonableness and simplicity at the center of *Aufklärung* theology (Scholder 1966; Sparn 1985; Hornig 1998; Beutel 2009).

In their project to simplify and rationalize the dogmatic tradition, neologians adopted various strategies. One device was to revise doctrines deemed unhelpful to practical piety and ethical development. Most characteristically, theological *Aufklärer* unanimously rejected the whole complex of dogma associated with the "black-biled Augustine" and replaced it with an optimistic anthropology, grounded in the *imago dei*, that stressed human dignity, freedom, and moral perfectibility. A frontal assault was launched on the doctrine of original sin as unjust, an insult to human autonomy, inimical to moral progress—and at any rate, a late doctrinal innovation. Sin was conceived as a disturbance in, not a destruction of, a fundamentally good human nature, and divine grace was seen to be already operative in nature, not pitted against it. The critique of original sin underscores the anthropocentric slant of *Aufklärung* theology, and it led to a modification of other doctrines, beginning with Christology. Jesus Christ was seen not primarily as the second person of the Trinity and an atoning sacrifice for sin, but as a unique, divinely inspired and enlightening teacher—the "Socrates of Galilee"—and a perfect model of a life dedicated to God. Toellner, Steinbart, and Jerusalem revived a subjective, moral-influence theory of the atonement, whereby Jesus' death served as the highest expression and ideal of self-giving love. Shifts in anthropology and Christology entailed a recasting of other central doctrines. The problem of sin and salvation came to be reframed as a pedagogical issue: how best to move towards ethical perfection in the present moral and social life. The church, no longer a sacramental body, became redefined as a religious society and a divine institution for the individual and collective ethical development of humankind (Aner [1929] 1964; K. Barth [1947] 2002; Sparn 1985; Bödeker 1989; Schubert 2002).

Another means of lessening the weight of inherited dogma was to sever the link between theology and religious experience. It was Semler who reflected most trenchantly on religious individualism and theorized the distinction (not entirely without Lutheran precedent) between *Theologie* and *Religion*. Theology referred to official church teaching and its exposition and critical engagement by theologians and scholars at a given historical moment. "Inner, personal religion," by contrast, was "subordinate not to any human form of thinking but to God and conscience alone"; it was the domain of all Christians on the basis of experience regardless of theoretical understanding (Semler 2012, 94; Semler 2009). Semler's distinction had a dual emancipatory purpose. For one thing, denying the immediate relevance of theology to Christian life created a space wherein scholars were permitted to engage critically with the tradition. The distinction thus grounded the concept of a "liberal theology" (*theologia liberalis*), a "free mode of theological teaching" (Semler 1777) unhampered by ecclesiastical authority and directly responsible for the edification of the laity. At the same time, Semler's division aimed to liberate the ordinary believer from the potential tyranny of dogma, and to leave worship and religious experience unharmed by critic and church authority alike. The theology-religion distinction resonated broadly—it found echoes in Herder, Kant, and Hegel—and reflects a situation in which piety and religious thought were increasingly separating from ecclesiastical structures and mediation. When Friedrich Schleiermacher in 1799 responded to religion's "cultured despisers" by setting religious experience over against dogmatic theology, he was thus not commencing a new line of argument but developing a well-established concept (Fleischer, "Einleitung," in Semler 2012; Hornig 1996; Bödeker 1989).

In their labors to revise the theological tradition, neologians found a most effective tool in historical scholarship. As noted, a "pragmatic," supraconfessional approach to ecclesiastical and doctrinal history entered German Protestantism via eclecticism. Beginning in the 1740s, key *Aufklärung* theologians—Baumgarten, Mosheim, Sack, Jerusalem, Semler, Nösselt, and Less, among them—turned to history for apologetic purposes, asserting the basic reliability of the New Testament witness to Jesus against deist attacks. While apologetic uses of history continued, by the 1760s the main battle lines had shifted towards Protestant orthodoxy. In the hands of the enlightened scholar, historical criticism could be wielded to expose the contextual and contingent nature of creeds and to make the case that dogmatic formulations, which reflected the church politics, debates, and *Weltanschauungen* of particular times and places, were error-prone, sometimes contradictory, and always transient "local" attempts to objectify religious understandings. As such they could never rise to the level of universal, timeless statements with binding authority on all Christians. Recognition of the relative and provisional nature of doctrinal statements could combine with faith in an undogmatic "essence of Christianity" (*Wesen des Christentums*), as the vital religious element behind Christianity's specific historical manifestations. By separating between the universal, moral truth of the gospel and particular, time-bound attempts to express that truth, historical analysis offered a means of overcoming the burden of history and preparing the way for a future expansion of religious consciousness (Fleischer 2006; Reill 1975; Hornig 1998).

Awareness of historical change melded with the Enlightenment's optimistic anthropology and faith in providence to generate a dynamic conception of Christianity as a religion capable of future development and perfection. Semler, who pioneered this line of thought in the early 1770s, depicted the early church not as a golden standard for all time, but as an age of childhood and immaturity, whose religious conceptions remained bound to a mythological outlook. In this historical scheme, the Protestant Reformation marked a giant step forward insofar as it rejected papal tyranny and advanced freedom of conscience and private religion. Semler held out hope, however, for a future when religious consciousness would expand, parochial sectarianism would be transcended, and the Christian religion would dissolve all individual historical denominations into itself, becoming a universal religion of love embracing all of humanity (Semler 1771–75; Semler 2009; Semler 2012). In the 1790s Teller, drawing on Semler as well as Gotthold Lessing's *The Education of the Human Race* (1779–80), schematized this vision into a three-stage view of history that progressed from Christianity's age of childhood, when faith depended on authority, to a stage where it was based on private insight, to a final epoch in which faith gave way to practical knowledge (Teller 1792). Neological ideas of perfectible religion would nourish the secular millenarianism of Kant and idealist philosophies of history in the nineteenth century (Hornig 1996; Fleischer 2006).

The conviction that critical history could fuel religious reform generated a large crop of innovative biblical scholarship. The text-critical, historical, and conceptual work of Ernesti, Semler, Michaelis, Griesbach, Eichhorn, and Gabler, in particular, remained programmatic far into the nineteenth century. *Aufklärung* biblical scholars insisted on a historical-contextual reading of the Bible as an extension of the Protestant *sola scriptura* principle. Tying a text's meaning to authorial intention and original context was intended to safeguard against both dogmatic eisegesis, as well as Pietist and spiritualist readings that found allegorical or hidden senses available only to the illumined. Using history, neologians could wield the *sola scriptura* principle to critique dogmatic formulations, but the Bible did not remain an uncomplicated, timeless norm. While acknowledged to *contain* God's Word, the biblical documents were not taken to be coextensive with revelation. The distinction between the Word of God and the scriptures had ample precedent, including in Luther, but the theological *Aufklärung* drove a deeper wedge between the two, severing the tight link between the Bible, revelation, and dogma forged by Orthodox inspiration theory. Semler brought this development to its culmination in his *Treatise on the Free Investigation of the Canon* (1771–75), which dissolved the unity of the biblical canon. Semler historicized its component books, detailed the different canons used by various segments of the church, and questioned the value of the early church's historical witness for determining whether a given text was in fact of divine origin. "The only proof" for divine inspiration was rather to be found in "the inner conviction brought about by the truths that confront [the reader] in Holy Scripture (but not in all parts and individual books)" (Semler 1771–75, 2:39). Semler confined the Bible's authority to its "moral teaching," which gave "guidance to inner improvement." The authority to pronounce on the Bible's true religious meaning was thereby wrested from dogmatic theologians and the spiritually illumined and ascribed to the pious, enlightened scholar equipped with moral discernment and historical methods (Hornig 1996; Reventlow 2010; Legaspi 2010; U. Barth 2004).

The demand for a moral message altered how the Bible was read. Features in the text deemed superstitious or unedifying—for example, accounts of demonic possession, belief in a personal devil, or chiliastic expectations—were rendered moot through recourse to the exegetical principle of accommodation. In its classical form, this theory held that God had couched his Word in the particular worldviews and cultural forms of the ancient Jewish and pagan worlds. *Aufklärung* theologians went a step further and added that those worldviews had often been erroneous, but that for the sake of expediency Jesus and the apostles had nevertheless made use of them to communicate their moral message. The modern interpreter's task therefore became to strip off the time-bound accretions and convey "the unchanging teaching of the gospel" in contemporary German (Teller 1773, xvii). Neology's accommodation theory abetted a theological anti-Judaism that was always a latent and often an overt structural feature of *Aufklärung* biblical hermeneutics, which pitted a nationalistic, superstitious, and legalistic Judaism against Protestant Christianity's universal, moral message. With the theological unity of the biblical canon dissolved, the meaning of scripture became detached from its narrative form and salvation-historical framework, which in assigning primacy to Israel in the divine plan had ensured Judaism's continued theological significance for Christianity. These hermeneutic shifts opened the door to a marked anti-Jewish strand that would persist in nineteenth-century liberal Protestantism (Frei 1974; Gerdmar 2009; Reventlow 2010; Legaspi 2010).

Neology occupies a pivotal place in the development of Protestant theology and of German intellectual history more broadly. From the eighteenth century on, the theological *Aufklärer*, while acknowledged to be pious and sincere, have been held responsible for relativizing and secularizing the Christian tradition from within. It is indeed possible to trace multiple historical and conceptual lines from neology's anthropocentrism, individualism, critique of dogma, and historical progressivism to secular idealist, Romantic, and even atheistic movements of the late eighteenth and nineteenth centuries. At the same time, through its historical consciousness, dialectical stance toward tradition, and valorization of religious experience, neology raised questions and set trajectories that would continue to shape the liberal Protestant tradition of the following century and beyond.

# BIBLIOGRAPHY

Albrecht, Michael. 1994. *Eklektik: Eine Begriffsgeschichte mit Hinweisen auf die Philosophie-und Wissenschaftsgeschichte.* Stuttgart-Bad Cannstatt: Frommann-Holzboog.

Aner, Karl. (1929) 1964. *Die Theologie der Lessingzeit.* Hildesheim: Georg Olms.

Barth, Karl. (1947) 2002. *Protestant Theology in the Nineteenth Century.* Translated by John Bowden. Grand Rapids: Eerdmans.

Barth, Ulrich. 2004. *Aufgeklärter Protestantismus.* Tübingen: Mohr Siebeck.

Beutel, Albrecht. 2009. *Kirchengeschichte im Zeitalter der Aufklärung.* Göttingen: Vandenhoeck & Ruprecht.

Beutel, Albrecht, Volker Leppin, and Udo Sträter, eds. 2006. *Christentum im Übergang: Neue Studien zu Kirche und Religion in der Aufklärungszeit.* Leipzig: Evangelische Verlagsanstalt.

Bödeker, Hans Erich. 1989. "Die Religiosität der Gebildeten." In *Religionskritik und Religiosität in der deutschen Aufklärung,* edited by Karlfried Gründer and Karl Heinrich Rengstorf, 145–195. Heidelberg: Lambert Schneider.

Brinkmann, Frank Thomas. 1994. *Glaubhafte Wahrheit—Erlebte Gewißheit: Zur Bedeutung der Erfahrung in der deutschen protestantischen Aufklärungstheologie.* Rheinbach- Merzbach: CMZ-Verlag.

Fleischer, Dirk. 2006. *Zwischen Tradition und Fortschritt: Der Strukturwandel der protestantischen Kirchengeschichtsschreibung im deutschsprachigen Diskurs der Aufklärung.* 2 vols. Waltrop: Hartmut Spenner.

Frei, Hans W. 1974. *The Eclipse of Biblical Narrative: A Study in Eighteenth- and Nineteenth-Century Hermeneutics.* New Haven, CT: Yale University Press.

Gerdmar, Anders. 2009. *Roots of Theological Anti-Semitism: German Biblical Interpretation and the Jews, from Herder and Semler to Kittel and Bultmann.* Leiden: Brill.

Griesbach, Johann Jacob. 1789. *Anleitung zum Studium der populären Dogmatik.* 4th ed. Jena: Cuno.

Hirsch, Emanuel. 1964. *Geschichte der neuern evangelischen Theologie.* 3rd ed. 5 vols. Gütersloh: C. Bertelsmann.

Hornig, Gottfried. 1996. *Johann Salomo Semler: Studien zu Leben und Werk der hallenser Aufklärungstheologen.* Tübingen: Max Niemeyer.

Hornig, Gottfried. 1998. "Lehre und Bekenntnis im Protestantismus, Part I: Von der Frühorthodoxie bis zur Aufklärungstheologie des 18. Jahrhunderts." In *Handbuch der Dogmen- und Theologiegeschichte,* edited by Gustav Adolf Benrath and Carl Andresen, 71–146. Göttingen: Vandenhoeck & Ruprecht.

Jerusalem, Johann Friedrich Wilhelm. 1769. *Betrachtungen über die vornehmsten Wahrheiten der Religion.* 2nd ed. Braunschweig.

Legaspi, Michael. 2010. *The Death of Scripture and the Rise of Biblical Studies.* New York: Oxford University Press.

Less, Gottfried. 1780. *Christliche Religionstheorie fürs gemeine Leben, oder Versuch einer praktischen Dogmatik.* Göttingen.

Printy, Michael. 2013. "The Determination of Man: Johann Joachim Spalding and the Protestant Enlightenment." *Journal of the History of Ideas* 74 (2): 189–212.

Reill, Peter Hanns. 1975. *The German Enlightenment and the Rise of Historicism.* Berkeley and Los Angeles: University of California Press.

Reventlow, Henning Graf. 2010. *History of Biblical Interpretation*. Vol. 4 of *From the Enlightenment to the Twentieth Century*. Translated by Leo G. Perdue. Atlanta: Society of Biblical Literature.

Reventlow, Henning Graf, Walter Sparn, and John D. Woodbridge, eds. 1988. *Historische Kritik und biblischer Kanon in der deutschen Aufklärung*. Wiesbaden: Otto Harrassowitz.

Schloemann, Martin. 1974. *Siegmund Jacob Baumgarten: System und Geschichte in der Theologie des Überganges zum Neuprotestantismus*. Göttingen: Vandenhoeck & Ruprecht.

Scholder, Klaus. 1966. "Grundzüge der theologischen Aufklärung in Deutschland." In *Geist und Geschichte der Reformation: Festgabe Hanns Rückert zum 65. Geburtstag*, edited by Heinz Liebing and Klaus Scholder, 460–486. Berlin: Walter de Gruyter.

Schubert, Anselm. 2002. *Das Ende der Sünde: Anthropologie zwischen Reformation und Aufklärung*. Göttingen: Vandenhoeck & Ruprecht.

Semler, Johann Salomo. 1771–75. *Abhandlung von freier Untersuchung des Canon*. 4 vols. Halle: Carl Hermann Hemmerde.

Semler, Johann Salomo. 2012. *Letztes Glaubensbekenntniß über natürliche und christliche Religion (1792), mit Beilagen*. Edited by Dirk Fleischer. Nordhausen: Traugott Bautz.

Semler, Johann Salomo. 2009. *Ueber historische, geselschaftliche und moralische Religion der Christen (1786), mit Beilagen*. Edited by Dirk Fleischer. Nordhausen: Traugott Bautz.

Semler, Johann Salomo. 1777. *Versuch einer freiern theologischen Lehrart*. Halle.

Sheehan, Jonathan. 2005. *The Enlightenment Bible: Translation, Scholarship, Culture*. Princeton, NJ: Princeton University Press.

Sorkin, David. 2008. *The Religious Enlightenment: Protestants, Jews, and Catholics from London to Vienna*. Princeton, NJ: Princeton University Press.

Spalding, Johann Joachim. 2006. *Die Bestimmung des Menschen*. Edited by Albrecht Beutel, Daniela Kirschkowski, and Dennis Prause. Tübingen: Mohr Siebeck.

Spalding, Johann Joachim. 2005. *Gedanken über den Werth der Gefühle in dem Christentum*. Edited by Albrecht Beutel and Tobias Jersak. Tübingen: Mohr Siebeck.

Spalding, Johann Joachim. 1772. *Ueber die Nutzbarkeit des Predigamtes und deren Beförderung*. Berlin.

Sparn, Walter. 1985. "Vernünftiges Christentum: Über die geschichtliche Aufgabe der theologischen Aufklärung im 18. Jahrhundert in Deutschland." In *Wissenschaften im Zeitalter der Aufklärung*, edited by Rudolf Vierhaus. 18–57. Göttingen: Vandenhoeck & Ruprecht.

Sparn, Walter. 1989. "Auf dem Wege zur theologischen Aufklärung in Halle: Von Johann Franz Budde zu Siegmund Jakob Baumgarten." In *Zentren der Aufklärung I. Halle: Aufklärung und Pietismus*, edited by Norbert Hinske, 71–89. Heidelberg: Lambert Schneider.

Teller, Wilhelm Abraham. 1792. *Die Religion der Vollkommnern als Beylage zu desselben Wörterbuch und Beytrag zur reinen Philosophie des Christenthums*. Berlin.

Teller, Wilhelm Abraham. 1773. *Zusätze zu seinem Wörterbuch des neuen Testaments*. 2nd ed. Berlin.

# INDEX

CPSIA information can be obtained
at www.ICGtesting.com
Printed in the USA
BVHW082135091019
560717BV00003B/3

9 780190 082864